1001 MOVIES

THAT SHOCKED THE WORLD

A CHRONOLOGY OF CULT, HORROR AND BANNED FILMS, 1895-2018

VINCENT KAPNER

New York • Paris • Uranus

Sparker Publishing Entertainment

1001 MOVIES THAT SHOCKED THE WORLD, 1895-2018
First published by Sparker Publishing in 2018
This edition copyright © 2018 Sparker Publishing
Copyright © Vincent Kapner 2018

The author asserts the moral right to
be identified as the author of this work

A catalogue record of this book is
available at the British Library

Cover & interior images courtesy of
Tarwyn Productions Inc.

CONTENTS

Author's Preface

As any fan of horror and cult cinema knows, the mapping out of the genres is no easy task: just as the budding cartographer thinks he has almost fully navigated the world of horror, new horizons suddenly appear, populated with mysterious islands of untrodden snow – areas barely explored before. These discoveries put the longitude and latitude all out of whack as the horror fan realises that the world of ghouls and goblins is actually much bigger than he had originally thought. And so the cartographer continues on his way, hoping to master the new-found lands and their strange inhabitants.

Let it be said from the outset that *1001 Movies That Shocked the World* doesn't claim to be a comprehensive guide to the world of horror, cult and banned films. It's merely an overview of the terrain. Up until a few months ago, I had no idea that there existed such films as *The Chase* (1946) and *Gayniggers From Outer Space* (1992). I have explored the movie jungle looking for weird and obscure gems for more than 20 years, and still I find myself surprised by new discoveries that had previously escaped my notice.

When I first became obsessed with cult films as a teenager, I naïvely assumed that I could walk into a large book store and find an A-Z guide to the most disturbing and controversial films ever made. I just assumed that that type of book must have already been written, considering how fascinating the topic was to a curious teen such as myself. This was back in the 90s when many intriguing films were either banned or heavily censored. I was disappointed that no such book was to be found on the shelves at Waterstones. I left the store deflated, but I remember vaguely making a promise to myself that perhaps one day I would write the damned book myself. Fast forward more than twenty years and roughly ten thousand movies later, and here it is: 1001 movies (plus a radio broadcast and a handful of TV shows) that *collectively* shocked the world.

I worked on the book in my spare time for the last few years. I sourced the films usually by word-of-mouth via online film forums or my own research. I would binge watch a bunch of movies and write about them in quick succession when the obsessive drive took hold. I

didn't rush the book, but there were times when I was a little impatient, and this has resulted in a few shorter reviews. I apologise for that, but if each film was given an equal amount of space, this book would be three or four times as big. There are omissions too: due to limited space, I didn't include *The Wicker Man* (1973) or *The Candy Snatchers* (1973) or *Neon Demon* (2016), but at the last minute I made space for the insane *Possession* (1981) and the blackly comic series, *Black Mirror* (2011 –), horror shows I have wanted to write about for years. You may notice that the 50s and the 60s are a little sparse for titles in this volume. That's because there isn't many stand-out movies from that era that are particularly challenging. Most of the risque subject-matter explored in film in the 1950s, for instance, had already been covered during the pre-code years two decades earlier.

Anyway, on with it. This book includes over a thousand film entries that explore often dark subject-matter in fictional form. If you are easily offended then I suggest you drop this book and go and find something else to read. I promised I would behave myself, and for the sake of others' sensitivities I have done so, but I have no time for what Clint Eastwood called 'the pussy generation.' This is a book for adults. Preferably open-minded adults. Please approach the book with that in mind. This is not a 'safe space.' We explore such subjects as cannibalism, rape, rape-revenge, sadism, sadomasochism, serial killers, snuff movies, stalk 'n' slash epics, mad doctors, Nazis, torture, vampires, zombies, mass murderers, misogyny, necrophilia, and just about every other unsavoury subject under the sun. What I'm trying to say is – don't shoot the messenger!

All in all, this is a celebration of the darker side of film, from the dawn of cinema in 1895 to some of the latest releases of 2018. Whether you dive in and devour the book cover to cover, or dip in occasionally to read about a particular film, is entirely up to you. However you use this guide, I hope your viewing experiences are enhanced.

Vinnie K,
Spring, 2018

Introduction

I

In March 2017, a low-budget cannibal movie entitled *Raw* was released in theatres trailing a months-long publicity campaign. According to reports, the film had caused faintings and mass walk-outs when it played at the Toronto International Film Festival, and there was even articles in the press that emphasised the shocking and grotesque elements in a leering fashion, with an array of graphic publicity stills. The way the media handled the film was in stark contrast to just a couple of decades earlier. Back in 1996, newspapers such as the *Daily Mail* were calling for David Cronenberg's *Crash* to be banned. However, a little over twenty years later, and the same newspaper carried an infomercial for *Raw*, complete with lurid stills and a 'journalist' piece that read like it was written by the film-makers themselves hoping to sell the movie. How times change.

Later on in this introduction we'll take a look at the development of controversial film from the medium's inception back in 1895, but to begin, here's a brief lightning tour of what to expect in the pages ahead:

The 1910s – Kicking off with the first feature horror film ever made, *Dante's Inferno* (1911), and continuing with the controversial *From the Manger to the Cross* (1912), *The Inside of the White Slave Traffic* (1913), *The Birth of a Nation* (1915), the banned eugenics/anti-abortion polemic, *Where Are My Children?* (1916), and D.W. Griffith's epic, *Intolerance* (1916), among many others. It was the decade that saw the establishment of the Hollywood studio system, and concluded with the highly controversial *The Cabinet of Dr. Caligari* (1919).

The 1920s – This decade saw the rise of German Expressionism and the fall-out of World War I. From the war horrors of *J'Accuse!* (1920), to the creepy Euro-horrors of *Nosferatu* (1922) and *Haxan* (1922) and Fritz Lang's sci-fi epic, *Metropolis* (1927). It was a decade of experimentation and a battle of ideas. The first of the Soviet propaganda films caught the world by surprise, such as *Strike* (1924), *Battleship Potemkin* (1925) and *Mother* (1926), among others. The best of these were truly staggering achievements, considering the medium was still very much in its infancy.

The 1930s – From *All Quiet on the Western Front* (1930) to Orson Welles' infamous *War of the Worlds* broadcast (1938), the 1930s was a decade of showmanship and innovation, with the introduction of sound, and the Hollywood studios striding ahead to dominate the medium. Art films and documentaries were competing at the box-office with Universal monster movies such as *Dracula* (1931) and *Frankenstein* (1932), during the height of the Great Depression. The pre-code movies were in full swing, with such daring and challenging titles as *Safe in Hell* (1931), *Her Man* (1930) and *Scarface* (1932), going head-to-head with the outrageous *Freaks* (1932) and *Island of Lost Souls* (1932). It was a decade that also saw exploitation films flourishing underground once the Hays Code had clamped down on the mainstream studio output.

The 1940s – The war years saw Hollywood turn dark and pessimistic with Film Noir and Jacques Tourneur's horror cycle that included *Cat People* (1942) and *I Walked With a Zombie* (1943). At turns exceptionally eerie and confrontational, the films also emphasised the grittiness and realism of the previous decade's pre-code titles, but with an underlying cynicism. Alfred Hitchcock made his Hollywood debut with the daring *Rebecca* (1940), and the controversy continued with such one-off classics as *The Lost Weekend* (1945), *Leave Her to Heaven* (1945), *The Spiral Staircase* (1946) and *Duel in the Sun* (1946). The Nazi propaganda films went out with a last hurrah in the defiant, full colour *Kolberg* (1945), in which the German public were encouraged to fight on to the death.

The 1950s – The 1950s saw a greater flexibility of form, with the socially challenging *Riot in Cell Block 11* (1953) and *Blackboard Jungle* (1954). Meanwhile, horror cinema was using alien metaphors to draw the audience's attention to the 'red scare,' in films such as Don Siegel's *Invasion of the Body Snatchers* (1955) and *Them!* (1954). In Europe, Hammer unleashed the first gruesome full-colour horror film, *The Curse of Frankenstein* (1957), while Michael Powell's career was in tatters after the release of the serial killer drama, *Peeping Tom* (1959). Also at the end of the decade, Frenchman Georges Franju made the masterpiece, *Eyes Without a Face* (1959), which caused faintings at the Edinburgh Film Festival and no end of scandal in the papers.

The 1960s – The 60s began with Hitchcock's *Psycho* (1960), a horror film that went back to basics with a blunt monochrome visual style and a dark psychological angle. It was a decade in which the Hollywood studios' dominance came under threat from the explosion of indie films. For the first time, the major studios no longer had the entire market covered, and this resulted in a torrent of quirky gems and cult classics, such as *Seconds* (1966) and *Night of the Living Dead* (1968). The Italians began unleashing their own oddities, from *Mondo Cane* (1962) to Mario Bava's highly stylised *Black Sabbath* (1963). And many of these imported exploitation efforts were just as polished and professional as anything the studios were churning out. Titles such as *Mark of the Devil* (1969), *The Honeymoon Killers* (1969), *Horrors of Malformed Men* (1969) and *The Wild Angels* (1966), broke further taboos, revelling in nudity and bloodshed. From the gore-drenched *Blood Feast* (1963) to the disturbing bluntness of *Titicut Follies* (1967) and the sexual exploration of *I Am Curious – Yellow* (1967), the 1960s was a transitional period as ambitious film-makers battled to get their voices heard.

The 1970s – The 1970s saw the floodgates open, with every taboo known to man explored and exploited on the big screen. Owing to the cheapness of celluloid at the time, and also the artist's desire to push the boundaries, everything was suddenly fair game. For every controversial hit like *The Devils* (1970), *Straw Dogs* (1971), *A Clockwork Orange* (1971) and *The Exorcist* (1973), there were dozens of variations on the underground exploitation scene, such as *The Baby* (1973), *The Mad Bomber* (1973),*Eugenie De Sade* (1970), *I Drink Your Blood* (1971) and *Love Me Deadly* (1973). One of the most prominent underground films of the time that became a hit was David Cronenberg's *Shivers* (1975), a subversive piece of work that perfectly captured the decade that had spawned it. The 1970s can be considered the 'golden age' of cutting edge cinema – nihilism, misanthropy and punk rock attitudes combined to produce some of the most contentious titles of the decade. And the conservative critics (and censors) despised them.

The 1980s – The 1980s saw the rise of home video and the 'video nasties' scare in Britain. Of course, the 80s produced a more glossy, neon-lit aesthetic in the movies, but the contentious ideas were still very much at the forefront of films such as *Videodrome* (1982), *Crimes of Passion* (1982), *Body Double* (1984), *Angst* (1983), *Angel* (1984) and *The Exterminator* (1980). Even the big-budget, glossy hits of *The Shining* (1980) and *The Keep* (1984) plunged the viewers into labyrinths of disturbing ideas, provided the viewers were willing to fully engage with the ideas explored on screen. On the opposite end of the scale, low-budget items such as *Maniac* (1980), *Henry: Portrait of a Serial Killer* (1986) and *Men Behind the Sun* (1988) were seemingly created as endurance tests whereby the viewers were challenged to either turn away or turn off.

The 1990s – The 90s saw the cinema's descent into nihilism complete. Films such as Peter Jackson's *Braindead* (aka *Dead-Alive*, 1992), Abel Ferrara's *Bad Lieutenant* (1992) and Geoffrey Wright's *Romper Stomper* (1992) had caused controversy on both the left and right sides of the political spectrum. However, Cronenberg's *Crash* (1996) marked a distinct turning point. The media outrage which greeted *Crash* was the last time the conservative critics voiced strong objections to the release of a film. After *Crash*, there was no more outrage in the press, even in the late 90s which was an abyss of misanthropy and nihilism, as seen in such films as *Freeway* (1996), *Freeway 2: Confessions of a Trickbaby* (1998), *Funny Games* (1997), *I Stand Alone* (1998), *Sex: The Annabel Chong Story* (1999) and *Romance X* (1999). Not even the anarchic mainstream hit, *Fight Club* (1999), with its excessive violence and glorification of terrorism, caused much of a reaction among the critics. The times had changed.

The 2000s – By the turn of the millennium, controversy was deliberately sought by film-makers as a way of promoting their movies. From Japan came *Audition* (2000) and *Ichi the Killer* (2001), the latter was locked in the offices of the BBFC for over a year while examiners decided on how to censor the film for the general public. Films like *Baise-Moi* (2001), *Battle Royale* (2001), *Chopper* (2000) and *Irreversible* (2002) were considered fairly controversial, but compared to *Crash*, this all seemed like faux-outrage used as a way of masking the nihilism and social apathy that had engulfed the West in the ensuing years. When *Antichrist* (2009) hit cinemas, Lars Von Trier's controversial film was discussed on breakfast television as a 'topic of the week' talking point, with no outrage whatsoever. This despite the film's blatantly misogynous theme on the 'evils' of womankind.

The 2010s – This decade saw much of the same. Tom Six's *Human Centipede* trilogy seemed to revel in its own blackly comic excesses, spreading the disgust via word of mouth to ensure a modest success at the box-office. Some of the most controversial films of the time, such as *Grotesque* (2009) and *A Serbian Film* (2010), were deliberately crafted to be as soul-crushing and as outrageous as possible. Even the mainstream was happy to take part in the same game, as witnessed with the release of *The Tortured* (2010), a film which invited its audience to revel in the extreme torture of a sadistic paedophile. The twist ending made it clear that the protagonists were brutalising the wrong man. Thus sending the viewers home in disgust for the part they had played in the horrendous violence on screen.

The first feature-length horror movie ever made, *Dante's Inferno* (1911), was met with a hostile reaction from the very same newspaper that ran the infomercial for *Raw* almost a century later. Almost every council in the country either cut or banned the film according to their own offended sensibilities, until the end result vanished from theatres with barely a trace. In Part II of this introduction I will briefly map out the history of horror and cult cinema before *L'Inferno*'s arrival in 1911, just to put things in perspective before the main attractions begin.

II

1895: *The Execution of Mary, Queen of Scots*

The earliest film on record to include elements that would later be defined as horror was a short loop entitled *The Execution of Mary, Queen of Scots*. Running for just 18-seconds, the clip is a re-enactment of the title character's death. She is forced to kneel and lean on the chopping block. The executioner steps forward and proceeds to lop off her head with an axe, before holding aloft the severed member, in full view of the camera. Released on 28 August, 1895, *The Execution* was produced by film pioneer, Thomas Edison, and is also considered one of the earliest films to utilise special effects – in this case an edit so that actress, Mrs. L. Thomas, could be replaced by a mannequin before the axe makes contact. It is not known how audiences reacted at the time, but the film was a mainstay on the kinetoscope circuit in America, as a vent for morbid curiosity. In the following year, however, a pair of French film-makers released a novelty item that ignited a legendary response from the audience – a reaction that is still remembered today...

A Train Arrives

The birth of cinema goes hand in hand with one of its longest lasting legends. In Paris in January 1896, a new Lumière exhibit had enticed a scurry of onlookers. The marquee had promised *cinematographe*, or 'Moving Pictures!' as a new sensation for the public. The cinematograph was thus born, and the patrons who had frequented the 'house of spectacle' were restless with excitement.

The lights dimmed. The spectators fell silent. In front of them a screen measuring approximately 8ft by 8ft suddenly burst into life in a glow of light. Those who had gathered for the event couldn't believe their eyes as they focused on the scene of ordinary people standing around on a platform. 'This is incredible – it must be magic,' the viewers beamed as they witnessed a black and white photograph come to life with the people in the picture turning their heads and acknowledging the camera in real time. It was as if a portal to a new world had opened up before their eyes. The spectators began laughing and gasping in amazement at the new invention.

However, to the side of the platform was a train track that reached to vanishing point. And on that vanishing point, an object was slowly enlarging into view. The object was black, and gave off wafts of steam. And as the object grew larger on screen, the laughing and cheering quickly died down. Within seconds, the onlookers realised that the object was a train, and – *worse* – it was heading right for them.

Legend has it that the spectators ran screaming from their seats and caused a violent stampede in their efforts to escape being squished to death by the oncoming locomotive. Of course, there is every reason to believe that the story may have been ever-so-slightly exaggerated over the decades since the incident occurred. But those types of urban legends don't appear out of nowhere. Even if it was just *one person* who fled the hall in fear, this little tale would still be worth telling.

That incident serves as the rightful place from which we can begin tracing the roots of cult and horror film. It was the first time in recorded history that members of the public had fled from a movie theatre in fear. And it wouldn't be the last. Though ever-obscure nowadays, *L'Arrivée d'un train en gare de La Ciotat* (*The Arrival of a Train at Ciotat Station*, 1896) will always be remembered as the first film to achieve what so many thousands of horror films have failed to do in the hundred plus years since its premier – scare the living daylights out of its audience.

Interestingly, the Lumière brothers chose to film the oncoming train as part of their studies and research into 3D film. So, perhaps the horrified reaction of the crowd wasn't entirely accidental after all. Unfortunately, the brothers seemed to drop their innovative attitude to the possibilities of film quite early on, and began resting on their laurels somewhat. However, around this time there was another Frenchman in the field making a name for himself – a man whose incredible work really *could* be seen as magic...

Méliès: The Man, the Magic, and the Misery

If the simple, innocuous arrival of a train could cause such a fuss at the dawn of film, a few years later brought the first riots to the cinema. Early trick film pioneer, Georges Méliès, had made nine short films on the arrest and trial of Alfred Dreyfus, and they were screened back-to-back throughout France. *The Dreyfus Affair* (*L'Affaire Dreyfus*, 1899) the film, turned out to be just as controversial as the real-life events that had inspired it. And the ensuing chaos that followed the film wherever it played led to an intervention by the police, who demanded that the contentious ending be removed. However, even the tempered version of *L'Affaire Dreyfus* failed to put an end to the fist-fights among audiences, who were either sympathetic or hostile to Dreyfus' plight.

Like the novelist Émile Zola, Méliès was a passionate defender of Dreyfus, whom he felt was targeted for no other reason than because he was Jewish. Dreyfus was a lieutenant-colonel in the French Army. He was arrested for treason when it was discovered that French military intelligence had been passed on to the Germans. And, despite there being around 300 Jewish generals in the French military at the time, the blame fell on Dreyfus, the Jewish 'outsider.' In January 1895, he was found guilty in a court martial, publicly stripped of rank in a humiliating manner, and banished into exile on Devil's Island. Méliès' film presents the series of events in minute-long snippets, covering his initial arrest, his meeting with his wife, and re-trial in which journalists came to blows in the middle of the courtroom.

The series' documentary-like realism was at odds with what Méliès had become known for – as a pioneer of the *cinema fantastique*, or fantasy film. He made more than 500 shorts between 1896 and 1912, many of them serving as experiments in special effects techniques. These 'trick films' were purposely aimed towards the "fairground clientele," which put him at odds with his more high-minded contemporaries, who looked down on him as a lowly showman. Heavily inspired by his own background in magic and musical theatre, Méliès made it his forte to explore the magical possibilities of film while the medium was still in its infancy.

His production company, Star Film, explored a number of genres, including horror, fantasy, comedy, science fiction, and even adult films, though *After the Ball* (*Après le bal*, 1897), is the only 'stag' film of his which survives today. Méliès' film-making career came to end in 1912, largely due to his brother Gaston's reckless business decisions and his terrible habit of damaging the film stock of new productions before they had even been processed. By 1914, Georges was bankrupt, and only spared having his home repossessed by the God-send of a government moratorium against the action. And, during World War I, the French Army confiscated hundreds of his original Star Film prints and melted them down for the silver and celluloid deposits, to make heels for shoes (perhaps in revenge for his support of Dreyfus years earlier?).

Added to his misery was the fact that Pathé – his great rival in the industry for many years – took ownership of Star Film in 1923. Méliès was so enraged that he burned all the prints he had left, along with the sets, props and costumes. Only around 200 of his films survive today, and that's only because print copies were submitted to the U.S. Library of Congress in order to protect their copyright in America (it wasn't just Pathé who gave Méliès a headache – in America, another film pioneer, Thomas Edison, resorted to practically remaking the Frenchman's films as a cynical way of trying to squeeze him out of the industry).

Georges Méliès died of cancer in relative poverty in 1938. By that time, he had attracted a cult following among film fans – including future film-makers, Marcel Carné and Georges Franju – who would visit him regularly at the nursing home to ensure that his passing was as comfortable as possible. Fellow film-maker, Walt Disney, paid tribute to Méliès – along with animator, Émile Cohl, who had died hours earlier – noting how they had 'discovered the means of placing poetry within the reach of the man in the street.' Indeed, Méliès' striking imagery is some of the most fondly remembered of cinema's early years. Films such as *The Vanishing Lady* (*Escamotage d'une dame chez Robert-Houdin*, 1896), *The Haunted Castle* (*Le Manoir du diable*, 1896), *A Nightmare* (*Le cauchemar*, 1896), and *The Astronomer's Dream* (aka *La lune à un mètre*, or *One Metre to the Moon*, 1898), showcased their creator's knack for finding surreal icons in everything from stark skeletons and levitating luggage, to fork-wielding demons and the moon invading a window to spit out dancing children.

My own personal favourite is *The Four Troublesome Heads* (*Un homme de têtes*, 1898), which stars Méliès himself as a stage magician who is compelled to remove his own 'troublesome' head and place it on a table, only to grow another in its place. This process is repeated again and again until the small collection of chattering Méliès heads disturbs his concentration. So he bashes the heads in with a banjo. This charming short was made entirely from scratch by his own devising. While nowadays cinema is thought of as a collaborative art form, some of the earliest expressions of film were pioneered by auteurs trying to make sense of the new medium, sometimes creating shorts in which they were the sole creative force on both sides of the camera. Méliès was very much a hands-on film-maker who insisted on building his own sets by hand. He even designed and constructed his own camera, which he nicknamed 'The Machine Gun,' due to the loud rattling sound it made while being operated.

His tireless tinkering with film and cameras led to him discovering many of his trademark tricks by accident. The editing trick of objects 'disappearing' was discovered when he cut out a section of damaged film from a reel and taped the remaining loose ends back together. And when he ran the repaired reel through a projector, he saw that the 'edit' had made it appear as though a woman had transformed into a man.

With more than half of his output lost to the flames, it seems unlikely that we will ever get to fully appreciate the man and his work. However, there is hope. In 2016, a long lost print of *Match de prestidigitation* (aka *A Wager Between Two Magicians*, 1904) was found in an archive in the Czech Republic. How many more lost reels could there be lying in wait under the silent dust of forgotten basements, sleeping away the decades and awaiting rediscovery? Only time will tell. And, who knows, perhaps one day a whole *treasure trove* of Méliès' lost works will be found, and alight the screen once again in the timeless magic of cinema.

The Clampdown Begins

As the 20th Century dawned, the new medium of the cinematograph was largely thought of as the harbinger of cultural and moral decay of the masses. The upper-classes, for the most part, stayed clear of the moving pictures, except for the more adventurous among them who began collecting film reels for their own private consumption. And this 'underground' culture was alluded to almost seventy years later in the British retro-inflected horror classic, *The Abominable Dr. Phibes* (1971) in a scene in which the Detective (comic actor, Terry Thomas), 'alone' at home one night, sets up his vintage projector and pours himself a glass of brandy while amusing himself with images similar to *Fatima's Coochie-Coochie Dance* (1896).

Dr. Phibes used humour to demonstrate how film was generally looked upon at the beginning of the 20th century – as something shameful and unsavoury. Only frustrated men in the dead of night would indulge in such a disagreeable act of watching motion pictures alone in the dark.

Indeed, with little to no government regulation at the time, it was inevitable that the grey market of film production would quickly begin trotting out erotic pictures. Early pioneers of the adult film were the Frenchmen, Eugene Pirou and Albert Kirchner, who, between them, produced some of the earliest surviving erotic films. Kirchner directed most of them himself, under his pseudonym, 'Léar,' including *Le Coucher de la Mariee* (1896), a seven-minute clip (of which only three-minutes of footage survives). The film features actress, Louise Willy, performing a bedroom striptease for the viewers while her husband sits behind a folding screen, unable to see what is going on. The film – and the theatre play it was based on – proved immensely popular. And the lucrative trade ensured that other French film-makers would churn out their own series' of risqué striptease films for the growing market.

According to the BFI researcher, Stephen Bottomore, Kirchner could well have been behind Léar & Co., a production company that was set up in Cairo and faced prosecution for exporting pornographic films into Europe in 1901. If that *is* the case, then we know that it was the same Kirchner who opened a basement cinema club at the Olympia Theatre in Paris. He eventually sold all of his films to the Gaumont company, and died soon after.

Only a small number of French adult films survive from that era, the most memorable of them includes the Pathé reels, such as *Le bain des dames de la cour* (*Bath of the Court Ladies*, 1904), *Venir ses cheveux* (*Coming Her Hair*, 1905), and *Le réveil de Chrysis* (*Chrysis' Awakening*, 1903), the latter is set on a balcony somewhere in African colonial territory, where a nude young beauty awakens, having slept on a lion skin rug out in the open. Her black maid gently fans her down and lights her a cigarette. Chrysis then rises to her feet and stretches as she looks out over the balcony. The maid wraps a cloth around her master's waist and tucks it in at the front so that it holds in place like a skirt. The pair then leave the balcony and head indoors, arm in arm. Lasting barely a minute in length, this short clip was typical of the tasteful and artistic erotica that was being produced by the French at the time.

The aforementioned *Coochie-Coochie Dance* upped the ante somewhat by featuring a sensual belly-dance by a mysterious performer called 'Fatima.' Released as a short nickelodeon kinetoscope film in 1896, Fatima's gyrating hips and exposed flesh was a hit with the male demographic, despite the many censored versions that showed up in various territories across the world. In fact, though this short clip barely gets a mention nowadays, *Fatima's Coochie-Coochie Dance* was one of the unspoken early titles that was instrumental in establishing American film culture.

The breaking of taboos such as these may seem tame nowadays, but one must remember that many of the acts depicted in these early clips were illegal back in those times. Take *The May Irwin Kiss* (1896), for example. This 47-second loop featured the very first kiss on film. The Kinetoscope ad promised to reveal 'the mysteries of the kiss,' only to show a short peck on the lips between a loving couple. This huckster trick of film ads promising to reveal far more to the viewers than the movie itself could ever deliver, became an art-form in itself with the explosion of exploitation movies in the 1930s and beyond. And *The May Irwin Kiss* was met with an early taste of the kind of moral hostility that later greeted the grindhouse flicks in decades to come. The peepshow film was branded 'obscene', and the Roman Catholic Church attempted to have the film-makers punished by law, as kissing in public was still an illegal act. However, the Church succeeded only in raising awareness of the film, and this led to an increase in profits and more defiant film-makers releasing their own imitations of the kiss, including *The Kiss in the Tunnel* (1899) and *The Kiss* (1900). Others went further in their expressions of love, such as film-maker Frederick S. Armitage, whose minute-long clip, *Birth of the Pearl* (1901), was designed as a filmic version of Boticelli's *The Birth of Venus*, complete with full frontal nudity, and none of the modesty that graced the original painting.

Even at this early stage of the game, hardcore pornography was available to those who had the right contacts. One-reelers boasting just about every sexual act conceivable – and leaving nothing to the imagination – were finding their way into brothels and private collections, particularly in Paris and London. Very little of this material survives today, though there are numerous collections that have never been made available to the wider public. The one thing historians agree upon, however, is that many of the adult films floating around Europe in 1904 were produced in Brazil.

In America, film-makers tended to stay away from 'stag' films and instead cater to other forbidden curiosities, such as death. Thomas Edison's company produced over eleven-hundred short films (and around 54 features) between 1894 and 1918. And amongst the mass of reels, alongside the well-known *The Great Train Robbery* (1903) and the earliest adaptation of *Frankenstein* (1910), the curious will also find such horrors as *The Execution of Czolgosz* (1901), which shows a dramatic reconstruction of Leon Czolgosz – President McKinley's' assassin – in the electric chair in a Panama prison. *Electrocuting an Elephant* (1903) documents the public spectacle of the killing of Topsy the unruly elephant who had killed a drunken spectator after having its trunk burned with a cigar. The animal tenses up and keels over in a haze of smoke.

By 1906, the Austrians had entered the film market, too. Perhaps inspired by the Pathé Brothers of France, Austrian film enthusiast, Johann Schwarzer, established his own production company called Saturn-Film, which specialised in filming local women in the nude. Schwarzer's company produced 52 such pictures between 1906 and 1911, and they were so popular that they were screened at men's only nights in cinema clubs, called *Herrenabende*, along with Pathé productions. However, local authorities were not impressed – Schwarzer was forced out of business in 1911 after a relentless campaign against his company, with his persecutors publishing propaganda that linked the company name 'Saturn-Film' with 'Satan-Film.' Police raided his offices and destroyed all of the 52 films (though copies had been made of around half of them, and they are preserved in archives across Europe).

With his company and livelihood in ruins, Schwarzer attempted to re-establish himself in the world of film by turning to more wholesome material, but his reputation as a Satanic smut-peddler ensured that any such avenues were closed off to him. He soon made his way to Africa to start a new life, only to return to Vienna just as World War I broke out. He was enlisted in the Army in June 1914, and died four months later at the Battle of Wirballen in Poland. He was just 34-years-old when he was killed.

The Saturn films are surprisingly tasteful, and Schwarzer had always maintained that his productions were 'of a purely artistic tendency, and we avoid tasteless subjects in favour of beauty.' Indeed, he would often go to the trouble of finding locations pretty enough to match his nudes, such as the quiet beach of *Das Sandbad* (1906), the summer lake of *Baden Verboten* (1907), and the makeshift modelling studio of *Beim Fotografen* (1908). *Der Traum des Bildhauers* (1907), even ups the playfulness by having its 'sculptured' nudes come to life and bless their creator while he takes a nap. It's also hard to believe how many layers women wore back then.

In contrast to the tastefulness of Schwarzer's films, *El Satario* was an Argentinian production that surfaced in Europe at the time, though no one has been able to put an accurate date on its release. The film was around in 1907 but it could be even older than that. Also known as *El Sátiro* (or, *The Satyr*), the clip shows a group of young women in the wilderness engaging in lesbianism before they are approached by Satan. One of the girls is forced into giving and receiving oral sex, and is then raped, before the girl's friends return to shoo the demon back to Hell. It's perhaps the oldest surviving porn film, and regarded as the first to include close-up

15

shots of genitalia and penetration.

In his book, *Black and White and Blue: Adult Cinema From the Victorian Age to the VCR* (pub. 2007), Dave Thompson makes the compelling case that pornography originated in the brothels of Buenos Aires and other South American cities in the first decade of the 20th century, with many films shipped over to Europe in a sort of underground clandestine network. Very few of those films have surfaced, however, and Thompson himself regards a French film entitled *A L'Ecu d'Or ou la bonne auberge* (*At the Good Hostel*, 1908) as the earliest explicit movie that can be accurately dated. The film itself shows a soldier having sex with a servant girl at a guest house.

In an eerie foretaste of the moral panic whipped up in the early 1980s regarding the 'video nasties' in Britain, a similar panic had already reared its head long before in the early 20th century. With the ever-growing popularity of film, whether in the cinema or as Kinetoscope 'peepshows,' the moral guardians were growing uncomfortable. Many had hoped that cinema was just a passing fad; a strange little curiosity that would disappear as soon as the novelty of 'moving pictures' had worn off. However, by 1908 it was clear for all to see that the new medium wasn't going anywhere – if anything, it was only *increasing* in popularity. And therefore, something needed to be done to get these movies under control.

In the letters section of a 1909 issue of *Kinematograph & Lantern Weekly*, a concerned member of the public had written to the publication to express their alarm at the spectacular violence seen in a recent film release entitled *The Black Hand* (1908): 'two ruffians enter a bedroom,' the letter states, 'where a child is sleeping in its cot while its mother is doing some sewing. These two men are seen to take this young child out of its bed, tie a rope around its neck, pass the rope over a peg behind the door, and actually pull the young innocent up by the neck until its feet are two or three feet from the floor whilst the mother is kept at bay.'

Anyone reading that who was familiar with the film would have been left scratching their heads as no such scene appears in the film. *The Black Hand* is actually an 11-minute crime film set and shot in New York City. It tells the tale of a pair of no-good criminals who send a letter to a neighbourhood butcher threatening to kidnap his young daughter. The butcher despairs as he cannot afford to pay the ransom. The kidnapping scene is the highlight of the film as it was shot in a verite fashion in the slush and snow of a busy street in the city. The men grab the girl and bundle her into an awaiting carriage by the side of the road. Viewers get to see ordinary members of the public walking around in their antiquated clothing and hats – people who weren't even involved in the making of the film, and yet, once the girl is taken, there are men who spring into action and attempt to rescue her before the camera is shut off.

Those members of the public were the unknowing participants in a movie scene, assuming that a genuine crime was being committed in their presence. It was a cheap but risky move on behalf of the film-makers – what if one of the nearby pedestrians was carrying a pistol and didn't mind using it on what he thought were kidnappers? This 'guerrilla-filming' technique could have ended very badly for the actors on that cold day.

However, for all the wonders of *The Black Hand*, there is no scene in the film that even *hints* at the hanging of a child. Presumably, those sorts of letters arriving at the office of *Kinematograph & Lantern Weekly* were being penned by moral crusaders attempting to spin a few porkies by exaggerating the lurid scenes of films, or – as was possibly the case with *The Black Hand* – inventing complete fabrications in order to pressure the authorities into taking action.

Whatever the case, it seemed to have worked as there arose around that time a need for unregulated films to be legislated against. The Home Secretary was inundated with letters and petitions from an increasingly angry public. And in the following year, the Cinematograph Act was passed in Britain. The law was brought in under the pretext that film stock was a very flammable material and needed to be regulated for health and safety purposes. However, the real reason it was passed was as a way of controlling the moral content of films. The authorities were alarmed to discover that film was becoming ever more popular among the working class, whom the guardians of society felt were unequipped to process such 'vulgar entertainment' without going off the deep end. Among the middle-class, cinema was seen as having the potential to pose a real threat to social order by promoting disruptive and immoral behaviour. And something needed to be done about it.

1909 was also the year the French began their own crackdown on illicit films. Raids were carried out by the police, and unsavoury material was seized and destroyed. The French authorities also banned newsreels which showed a group of Frenchmen being guillotined, and others, including a Missouri cattle rancher hanged in front of a large crowd, and the sword beheadings of Chinese bandits in Manchuria.

However, this frenzy of arrests and censoring activity can't have had much of an impact on the underground networks, as there was still no shortage of such material changing hands. And it was around that time in 1910 when Brazil and Argentina had the reputation for being world-leaders in the production and distribution of hardcore pornography. Even the Germans got in on the act with the release of *Am Abend* (1910), a sexually explicit film featuring an anonymous woman masturbating in a bedroom. A voyeur spies on her awhile through the keyhole before entering the room. The man undresses and they have sex – missionary, oral and doggy-style.

The summer of 1910 brought more controversy, and the first example of film censorship in Britain. On July 4, former heavyweight boxing champion, James J. Jeffries, returned to the ring after six years of retirement to challenge the new champ, Jack Johnson, in a 45-round prize fight, billed as the 'Battle of the Giants.' The open-air event was held in Reno, Nevada, in the scorching 110 degrees heat. It was the most anticipated sporting event of the year – despite Jeffries being past his prime – as both fighters were already legendary in the sport. 16,000 fight fans crammed into the purpose-built arena to watch the gruelling event, which after 13 rounds, saw Jeffries waning after taking a barrage of hard uppercuts in the clinch. And, in the fifteenth, after being knocked down three times, the referee saved the challenger from further punishment by calling an end to the fight. Amusingly, Arthur Conan Doyle was invited to umpire the bout – he respectfully declined.

The film of the event had reached British shores within a week. However, fight fans in London were denied the chance to see it as the London City Council used the Cinematograph Act as a way of banning its screening in the capital. It seemed 'barbaric bloodsport' was not an acceptable form of entertainment for the masses. The Trojan horse of the Cinematograph Act was now in full effect. Fight fans had to abandon all hope of ever seeing it.

CHRONOLOGY, 1911–2018

Dante's Inferno (1911)
(Original title: *L'Inferno*)
Dir: Francesco Bertolini, Adolfo Padovan & Giuseppe De Liguoro /Italy

With the introduction of the Cinematograph Act in 1910, the authorities in Britain suddenly found themselves armed with the power to cut and ban movies on a whim. The infamous prize fight between James Jeffries and Jack Johnson was banned in London, for example. Other councils across the country seemed to approve of the move as they also began cutting and banning pictures they disapproved of. Most notably, the epic descent into Hell, *Dante's Inferno* (*L'Inferno*). This, the first feature-length film ever produced in Italy, was a fascinating and technically inspired marvel, utilising many of the sharp cuts and special effects sequences that Georges Méliès had pioneered in the previous decades, not to mention a host of curiosities all of its own, including bizarre sets, winged demons, and a surreal three-headed monster.

Loosely based on the first part of Dante's epic medieval poem, *The Divine Comedy*, the film opens on the scene of Dante (Salvatore Papa) lost in the Dark Forest on the edge of Hell. His beloved, Beatrice, floats down from heaven to limbo where she instructs the Roman poet, Virgil (Arturo Pirovano), to escort Dante out of the inferno and back to safety. Virgil is happy to help, but the only path to light he knows of is one fraught with danger, as it leads right through the inner circles of Hell.

Dante is thus rescued from being torn apart by the demons that surround the inferno, and Virgil leads the weary poet through the darkest pits of suffering, where the souls of the damned dwell for eternity. They cross the River Acheron, or the 'underworld river of pain,' and meet with a group of ancient poets, including Homer, Horace, and Ovid. We learn that, because those men had lived before Christ, their souls are unenlightened, and therefore they too must dwell with the sinners. And though they are never harmed, these famous men are condemned to 'live' without hope.

The souls of the damned, however, are not let off so lightly. Carnal sinners are blown by the burning blasts of wind in great circles above the abyss. Among the thousands cast adrift in such fashion are Cleopatra, Queen Dido of Carthage, and Helen of Troy, historical monarchs whose all-consuming lust had brought down empires. Gluttons are tortured with the torments of eternal rain; blasphemers consumed by eternal fire; and the greedy are condemned to roll great sacks of gold around the labyrinth (that particular torment of endless futile labour may have been influenced by the ancient Greek myth of Sisyphus, who was condemned to an afterlife of pushing a large rock up a mountain, only to watch it roll down to the bottom again – a process that is repeated, over and over, for eternity). In the poem itself, there are numerous other 'poetic justices' meted out to the damned that aren't touched on in the film, such as fortune-tellers, for example, who are made to walk the underworld with their heads on backwards so that they cannot see what is ahead of them.

The city of Dis is located in the innermost circle of the inferno, and the poetic duo must cross a lake of fire to get there. And with flames the size of mountains lashing out in the background beyond the rocks, their boat ride across the water is a perilous one. Throughout this sequence, the imagery shakes unsteadily on screen, as though the layers of primitive overlay effects can barely hold together. When they reach the other side, it isn't long before they are met by winged demons who wield pitchforks and crack their whips against the flesh of sinners who are led to the 'River of Filth' where the damned are left to wash away their sins, all in vain.

Before the end, we come face to face with Lucifer himself, who is depicted as a giant ghoul that feasts on the souls of the wicked. The poets sneak around him and climb down the hair on his mountainous back, which leads to the bowels of Hell. And, finding their way through the dark tunnels, the pair eventually emerge at a cave entrance, bathed in the warm light of salvation. The film-makers seem to have skipped the Purgatory middle and instead opted to deliver the viewers into the heavenly rays of Paradiso.

Dante's Inferno is a sublime film, and one that survives with its poetry and allegorical strengths intact, despite the physical wounds and archaic defacements that have been wrought upon it by the ravages of time. More than a century after its release, this battle-scarred gem remains the most engaging and coherent of all the Dante adaptations ever to hit the screen, and is still worth seeing. Watch the film as it struggles to its feet; marvel at the spectacle of epic cinema born in the hay like a half-blind calf, unsure of its surroundings or purpose, and yet instinctively drawn to the right path. We're treated to a vision of the underworld in all its horrific machinations – the experience of watching the film is like taking a doomed safari ride in a kingdom reserved for the sole purpose of eternally tormenting those who had lost their way in life. And yet the film barely gets a mention in the horror history books. As well as being the first Italian feature film, and the first international hit, *L'Inferno* was also the first feature-length horror movie ever made. And, if not, *why* not? All the elements are there – characters surrounded by evil in a dark netherworld; the demonic imagery; the ultimate triumph of good over evil, etc. It even provided its own *Scream*-like set of rules one must abide by in order to survive the horror movie of Hell. Except, it was actually one big rule: Whatever you do in life, avoid those seven deadly sins at all costs!

This was a horror movie. It always *was* a horror movie, even if it was made at a time when horror movies didn't exist as a genre. If the film was made today, no doubt Dante's character would be re-imagined as a plucky, resilient heroine, while Virgil would serve as the on-off love interest, showing up to lend a helping hand from time to time, but mostly leaving Dante in the knowledge that her strength and wisdom will carry her through in her journey towards the light. In fact, similar such films have already been made; you can see the theme carried through with Milla Jovovich in the *Resident Evil* series (seven movies between 2002 and 2017), and Kate Beckinsale in the *Underworld* series (five movies between 2003 and 2016, with a sixth on the way). Of course, those films aren't set in Hell, but they are worlds of eternal doom and gloom, overrun with hostile beasties, such as zombies, vampires and werewolves.

Interestingly, though both the book and the surface level of *L'Inferno* present themselves as allegorical takes on the individual's search for God and salvation in a life of mortal sin, the film also hints at an uncertain future for Italy. A decade after its release, the world saw the rise of Mussolini and the first fascist state in Europe. Eagle-eyed viewers may notice subtle foreshadows of this in the film, such as in the scene in which the ancient poets bid farewell to Dante and Virgil; the dead poets raise their right arms in what looks to be the time-honoured tradition of the Roman Salute. Another Italian film, *Cabiria* (1914) – penned by the nationalist poet, Gabriele d'Annunzio – also included the salute, and the gesture was famously used when d'Annunzio led the occupation of Fiume in 1919.

L'Inferno also presents scenes which can be interpreted as comments on Italy's fascist future, as if the country itself was about to be cast into Hell. In addition, the last shot in the film is of a monument to Dante in Trento; of the dozens of pillars in the country commemorating the great poet, the film-makers opted to show the one in which Dante is seen with his arm outstretched in an unmistakable Roman Salute. Perhaps the film could be seen as a warning about Italy's descent into the abyss in the decades ahead. No wonder the film has been largely erased from film history. Many years later, Pier Paolo Pasolini broached the theme again, this time in retrospect, with his *Salo, or the 120 Days of Sodom* (1975), in which the fascist Republic is represented in four fragments that were inspired by *The Divine Comedy* – the Anteinferno, the Circle of Manias, the Circle of Shit, and the Circle of Blood.

When the film made its premier in Naples on the 10 March, 1911, no one knows how the audience reacted, as there is so little information in the historical records of the event. However, we can assume it was a success, as print copies were quickly made and shipped off across Europe and the world beyond, ensuring it became the first blockbuster hit in film history. In the book, *Dante on View: The Reception of Dante in the Visual and Performing Arts* (pub. 2007), by Antonella Braida and Luisa Calè, it is suggested that a couple of reels are shown in the wrong order. If true, it isn't noticeable. Far more interesting is the rumour that there was a much longer cut of the film that did the rounds in the early days, which ran up to three hours with two intermissions. *Dante's Inferno* also had a major influence on a little-seen film, *Maciste en el infierno* (*Maciste in Hell*, 1926), in which the Devil uses sexually attractive demons to lure a principled man into Hell. It was a fairly graphic and lurid addition to the Maciste series that later flourished in the late 50s and into the 60s.

L'Inferno had its biggest success in America, where – because of its feature-length running time – picture houses felt justified in hiking up the ticket prices with no let up in those flocking to see the film. For an ordinary short, tickets would cost in the region of between 25¢ and 50¢, but with the success of *L'Inferno*, tickets were selling for as much as $2.50. However, the real trouble began when the film reached the shores of Great Britain...

With the introduction of the Cinematograph Act, local councils in Britain embarked on a power trip. Who would have thought it? Blackburn Council demanded that all films be submitted to the Chief Constable so that they could be inspected before public release. Even the advertisements were held under scrutiny, with many posters removed from billboards for inciting 'the vilest and most poverty-stricken purlieus frequented by the veriest riff-raff of the amusement-going public.' Some council officials wrote reports claiming that cinema 'caused blindness.'

It was into this maelstrom of panic that *L'Inferno* found itself in Britain in 1912. In Blackburn, as well as Leeds, Liverpool, Leicester and other cities, the film was either cut to ribbons to remove the sights of frontal male nudity and breasts, or banned outright. The result of this interference was confusion among cinema-goers as the different cuts in different parts of the country led to inconsistent reports in the press, where scenes were mentioned that were not permitted for public viewing elsewhere. Unsurprisingly, this chaos was very frustrating for those who worked in the film industry. Not only were films chided by the middle-class they were trying to reach, they were also being cut, banned and ruined by hundreds of the country's council authorities, each of whom seemed to subject the films to their own personal rules, based on whatever whims or impulses they felt at any given time.

For the film industry, enough was enough. Something needed to be done to make film censorship more cohesive with a standard set of rules for producers and directors to abide by. And it was around that time in 1912 when prominent members of the industry held a meeting in Birmingham. It was decided that rather than having their films subjected to the arbitrary rules of every Tom, Dick and Harry in the councils, they would instead propose a form of state censorship with a clear mandate that the industry could rally behind to the benefit of the producers, authorities and the public alike. Thus, if the British film industry was to survive, it would have to relinquish its control over the content of films. And, at the time, that idea seemed like a fair compromise.

The head of the meeting, film-maker Cecil Hepworth, along with his delegation of producers and exhibitors, approached the Home Office soon after. They proposed their idea of a Board of Film Censors; it would be financed by the fees generated by film companies seeking a certificate of acceptance from the Board, which would (in theory) prevent the film from being tampered with by the local councils. The Board would also be under the leadership of a chief censor, appointed by the Home Office, whose job would be to work with film-makers to ensure that their productions were acceptable for public consumption. Home Secretary, Reginald Mckenna, accepted the proposal on two conditions: 1) the chief censor's verdict on any particular film would be final, and – *crucially* – 2) there could be no way to appeal the final decision. The two parties were in agreement, and with that, the British Board of Film Censors (BBFC) was months away from being.

However, McKenna neglected to mention the fact that the Board would not be a unifying system which would institutionalise censorship – and thus usher in a unifying consent among local councils, as the delegation wanted – but rather a more elaborate form of business as usual. McKenna was cunning enough to keep the BBFC unofficial, otherwise it would have been answerable to Parliament, and that was something McKenna didn't want. So much for democracy.

From the Manger to the Cross (1912)
(aka *Jesus of Nazareth*)
<u>Dir: Sidney Olcott /USA</u>

From the Manger to the Cross arrived in Great Britain following a trail of glowing U.S. reviews. Here was a film that would surely secure that middle-class audience the film industry so desperately needed for its legitimacy in society. With no expenses spared, the Kalem company went to great lengths to present a 'faithful' adaptation of the life of Christ, rejecting the idea of studio sets in favour of real location shooting in Palestine, including Jerusalem, Bethlehem and Jericho. Scenes were also filmed by the Great Pyramid of Giza and the Sphinx. The end result was sure to turn heads.

With inter-titles made up almost entirely of passages taken from books of the New Testament (specifically, Matthew, Luke and John), the story begins with the virgin birth and continues on, addressing the events of His youth, such as King Herod, the three wise men, and the flight to Egypt. The young Jesus eventually settles in Nazareth, and begins drawing in His disciples and performing miracles – walking on water and healing lepers.

Jesus later enters the temple and violently expels the money-changers by whipping them. And when the scribes and Pharisees hear about this, they set out to destroy Him. Judas then makes his visit to the Priests and betrays his Lord. Jesus is later captured, and Judas plants his treacherous kiss on His cheek as He is led away. Judas sinks into despair, regretting his actions. He approaches the Pharisees and attempts to hand back the 50 pieces of silver they had given him. He pleads for the release of his Lord, but the Priests laugh and mock him. Judas is then seen hanging himself.

Jesus is handed over to the Roman governor, Pontius Pilate, who, after much agitation, agrees to have Him crucified. He is then whipped, beaten, mocked and humiliated by the brutish Roman guards, and made to carry His own cross through the streets. The scene in which Jesus is laid flat on the cross while his hands and feet are nailed is very similar to Mel Gibson's version of the same scene in *The Passion of Christ* (2004), and shot from similar angles. And once the cross is hoisted skyward, Jesus accepts His fate like a champ. Mother Mary crouches beneath Him at the foot of the cross, and an earthquake shakes the land.

Shot in a very closed-in style, *From the Manger to the Cross* is a disappointment; a lacklustre effort that fails to take advantage of its authentic locations and game cast. The producers had spent a fortune on shipping the cast, crew and heavy equipment thousands of miles away to the Holy Land – you would think they would have relished the opportunity of presenting wide shots of the olive groves, rolling plains and vistas, as a way of presenting viewers with the grace and beauty of the land. But, surprisingly, cinematographer, George K. Hollister, leaves viewers with only a vague feel for the locations in which the events unfolded. Many scenes were shot among the bright towns, with steps and narrow pathways leading away beyond the sun-scorched walls of the modest buildings. But it all feels stifled and non-adventurous.

Ironically, the earlier French version of the story, *The Life and Passion of Christ* (*Vie et Passion du Christ*, 1903), with its studio-bound sets and much lower budget, is far superior to this. The French version is *alive* with faith and passion and theatricality, while *From the Manger* just sort of plods along statically without much to commend it. See also the Italian variant, *Christus* (1916), which was also filmed in Palestine (and, like *Dante's Inferno*, contains its share of Roman Salutes) – watch them back to back and be astonished at the difference between Hollister's disinterested vision and Renato Cartoni's epic lens which presents the Holy Land as if it was a central character of the film. In terms of cinematography, they're worlds apart. And, also of the silent era, Cecil B DeMille's classic, *The King of Kings* (1927), takes the better elements of all those aforementioned films and adds the Hollywood gloss treatment.

Still, *From the Manger to the Cross* alarmed audiences of the time in much the same way as Gibson's film did almost a century later. For many cinema-goers it was the first time they had seen the Passion depicted so starkly and brutally, with many ordinary members of the public lacking the imagination to fully appreciate the depth and significance of the sacrifice Jesus had made all those centuries ago. The crown of thorns wasn't just a silly hat His executioners made him wear; it was a fiendish device fashioned from a leather holster and barbed with metallic spikes that was nailed into His skull (in the movies, *Hellraiser*'s Pinhead was designed as the counter-point to Christ as the nail-faced emissary of Hell).

Unlike the other Jesus films of the silent era, *From the Manger to the Cross* ends at the crucifixion (as its title makes clear), while the others go on to present the happy ending of His Resurrection. The overall effect was to leave viewers in a saddened or contemplative frame of mind as they left the theatre. Which is what the film's producers probably intended. However, the sombre ending was also perhaps responsible for the media backlash against the film, which was drummed up by the *Daily Mail* and many local papers. With the country still reeling in the aftermath of the Titanic's doomed voyage in the previous weeks, people flocked to the cinema as a means of escapism, not to be confronted with the brutal reality of the Lord's execution. 'Is nothing sacred to the film maker?' the *Daily Mail* cried, before going on to condemn the producers for taking profits from the picture. Local councils began cutting and banning the film up and down the country, to the point where the only theatre in the land willing to screen it uncut was the Queen's Hall in London. The lure of the forbidden film ensured its lengthy engagement there, playing non-stop for eight months. Most sources claim the film was responsible for the establishment of the BBFC, but the Board was well on its way to being long before the film was released. Tom Dewe Matthew's book on the history of the BBFC, *Censored* (pub. 1994), doesn't even mention the film *once* in its 300 or so pages.

The film disappeared from circulation not long after its initial release in 1912, and remained absent or 'lost' for the best part of twenty-five years. The situation may have remained that way forever more if it wasn't for the efforts of one man of the cloth. In the 1930s, Rev. Brian Hession, a vicar in Aylesbury, Buckinghamshire, was organising a retrospective of religious films from the silent era. And, despite having sourced a number of seemingly lost films with ease, there was one title that had always evaded him. He was aware of *From the Manger to the Cross* from the negative press campaign at the time of its release, but he was also aware of the fact that a number of clergymen were invited to a screening, and they had left the Queen's Hall

satisfied that there was nothing objectionable in the film.

For Rev. Hession, what began as a passing curiosity eventually became an obsession for him. He searched the country top to bottom, inspecting libraries and archives, from universities to picture houses and private collections, investigating every lukewarm lead, only to remain empty-handed. In 1938, he took the unprecedented step of a trip across the pond, and began his search all over again in America. For modern-day film buffs, this may not seem all that impressive; after all, you only have to recall the mammoth efforts of distribution companies such as Barrel Entertainment and their search for lost titles like *Last House on Dead End Street* (1977), or Mark Kermode's obsessive tracking down of the lost and censored footage from *The Devils* (1971) and *The Exorcist* (1973). But way back in 1938, it must have been an investigation worthy of a seasoned pro.

On his arrival, he learned that the production company, Kalem, had been sold to Vitagraph Studios in 1919, and the new owners re-released *From the Manger* that same year. By the time Hession had arrived in the States, however, Vitagraph had been sold to Warner Bros. in 1925. As expected, Hession's inquiries at the major Hollywood studio was a frustrating experience, as dealing with corporations still are today for the little people. He persevered, however, and whether out of luck or skill, or divine intervention, all five reels of *From the Manger to the Cross* showed up in a cellar in Manhattan of all places, thousands of miles away from Tinseltown.

So, it's with thanks to Reverend Hession that today we can revisit the film at our leisure. His thoughts on the film can be heard on the audio commentary he recorded at the same time as the new score which he personally composed for the 1938 re-release. (Ironically, that version seems to be lost.) And you can read more about the story in Leslie Wood's old book, *The Miracle of the Movies* (pub. 1947), which, as its title suggests, puts a divine spin on the tale.

The Birth of a Nation (1915)
Dir: D.W. Griffith /USA

One of the most revered and reviled movies of all time, *The Birth of a Nation* is considered one of the cornerstones of the silent era. Based on the novel, *The Clansman: An Historical*

Romance of the Ku Klux Klan (pub. 1905), by Thomas Dixon Jr., director/producer D.W. Griffith is said to have had no interest in the racial element of the story, and instead decided to bring it to the screen for its dramatic drive and epic potential. And epic it most certainly was; at over three hours in length (a whopping 12 reels), *Birth* was the first historical epic to hit cinema screens, utilising dozens of ground-breaking filming techniques – close-up shots, fluid camera pans, quit-cut editing, an orchestral score, etc – and became a major influence on Hollywood productions for decades to come.

The film tells the story of the American Civil War, and subsequent Reconstruction of the south, through the experiences of two families, the powerful Stonemans in the north, and the less well-off Camerons in the south. The action is set largely in the Piedmont region of Georgia, and a southern town which serves as the cauldron of conflict – a storyteller's microcosm in which the main events of the War are staged.

As the conflict heats up, the Unionists send in a Negro regiment to attack the town. The Confederates immediately come to the rescue and turf them out. Both the Camerons and Stonemans lose sons in the conflict. The fighting continues and gets uglier, as women and children are caught up in the street fighting that rages unabated, leaving an inferno in its wake. Another of Cameron's sons dies.

Meanwhile, the troops on the open plains settle into rugged trench warfare. Soldiers are stabbed in their hearts with bayonets while attempting to capture the enemy's position. These blunt images bring to mind the slaughter that was being carried out in the trenches of Europe at the time in the Hellish No Man's Land. Of course, the Northerners win, and the battleground is left in a Hellish blaze of fire and smoke and piles of dead bodies. A sobering and poignant image.

The film passes into its second hour with the aftermath of the war, as Elsie Stoneman (Lillian Gish) plays the banjo at the local hospital as a way of easing the woes of the wounded soldiers – a scene which serves as the opening chapter of Dixon's novel. Col. Ben Cameron (Henry B. Walthall) regains consciousness only to learn that he is to be hanged as an enemy combatant. His mother visits him, and later appeals to President Lincoln to change his mind. The President – long suspected of being sympathetic to the Confederates, hence his nickname, the 'Great Heart' – agrees to pardon the wounded soldier.

After four long years of bloody battle, the Civil War officially comes to an end with Robert E. Lee's surrender, and the union is reinstated once more. Ben recovers from his injuries and returns home to find his neighbourhood has been devastated – the houses are charred black, the fences are falling apart, and debris litters the roads. His beloved family are now impoverished and wearing rags.

On the fateful day of April 14, 1865, President Lincoln – having earned enemies for his lenient stance on the south after the War – is assassinated during a gala performance at Ford's Theater. This is a chilling, suspenseful – and remarkable – sequence that is often used in documentaries to this day as a way of illustrating the historic event. His assassin, John Wilkes Booth, leaps onto the stage from the balcony and flees backstage to escape before the audience has even realised what is going on.

Lincoln takes his reconciliatory influence to the grave with him, and in his place comes a thinly-disguised vengeance on the southerners as new legislation is quickly brought in to antagonise them. Racial tensions rise immediately as blacks are placed into positions of power. The Stoneman patriarch, Austin (Ralph Lewis), is a U.S. Representative, and he is depicted as a power-hungry vulture willing to betray his fellow whites in order to secure his own position within the government hierarchy. Blacks are given the right to vote, while many whites are disenfranchised and turned away from the voting booths.

By this point, Ben and Elsie, from opposite sides of the tracks, begin to fall in love in true Romeo and Juliet style. Negro occupation troops take over the town and bully and harass whites for not voting Union. They even lynch fellow blacks, or 'Uncle Toms,' for their disloyalties. The Negro Party takes control of the State House of Representatives, outnumbering the whites 101 to 23. And a law is soon passed in which all whites must salute Negro officers on the streets.

What was once a quiet, genteel town before the War was now a festering wound of resentment on both sides. Ben Cameron despairs for the future, but, after seeing a pair of white children scaring off black bullies by covering themselves in a white sheet and pretending to be a ghost, he is inspired to organise an underground resistance movement.

The Ku Klux Klan is thus born – small and tentative at first, but soon growing steadily in numbers. The members create costumes and hoods from white sheets, designed not only to terrify their enemies, but as a way of concealing their identities, too. The costumes are emblazoned with a large crucifix design on the chest, and they are soon roaming the lands on horseback, like ghost riders of the apocalypse, or a Knights Templar of the south. The Klan makes its mark by scaring off a couple of suspected black arsonists (in yet *another* scene from the silent era which shows the Roman Salute).

The mysterious outlaws begin waging a war against Silas Lynch (George Siegmann), who serves as Austin Stoneman's mixed race lackey, and the other carpetbaggers from the north. And when the youngest Cameron girl, Flora (Mae Marsh), is harassed in the woods by Gus (Walter Long), a black officer, she dies after jumping from a rock face to escape him.

Ben has the man captured and executed in the woods after a Klan 'trial.' They then dump his body on the doorstep of Lynch's office in town. In retaliation, more Negro troops are placed on the streets, while the Klan members develop their rituals and ideology in secret. They begin burning crosses – inspired by an ancient Scottish legend – in a symbol of 'outraged civilisation.'

By now, anyone suspected of being a member of the Klan – or even caught in possession of a uniform – is punished by death. The old man Dr. Cameron (Spottiswoode Aitken) is arrested soon after and placed in chains before being paraded through streets of cheering blacks, like some half-dazed trophy. Klansmen infiltrate the event, pretending to join in the mockery and jeers. However, the outlaws – including Stoneman's eldest son – hatch a daring plan to free the doctor, and this results in the death of another black soldier.

Thus, former enemies of the north and south are united in racial solidarity to fend off the armed Negroes who have taken over the town. In retaliation for the stunt, whites are openly mobbed and lynched in the streets. The Klan, which began with just a handful of members a short while ago, has now recruited hundreds of thousands. And they ride en masse into the town for a final all-out war against the blacks and carpetbaggers...

Still mired in controversy to this day for its treatment of slave characters, and how the abolitionist supporters are portrayed as a destructive force responsible for the war. The racial element becomes more apparent in the second half as we witness the rise of the Klan, who are portrayed as heroes and the defenders of civilisation. It feels strange to see the Klan depicted as a force for good, after decades of negative press – the Klan is still trotted out today as media boogeymen when the organisation probably went defunct years ago. There are probably more undercover FBI agents than genuine members in the 'Klan' today.

Looking at the film more than a hundred years after it was made, there are some glaring problems; perhaps it didn't need to be three hours long – a skilled storyteller nowadays could probably do the story justice within two hours. The white actors portraying black people with the aid of black-face – which probably wasn't convincing at the time of the film's release – looks positively ridiculous nowadays. There are also two love stories that struggle to develop throughout the film amid the myriad of events in the story which over-shadow everything else; neither of the love elements could be treated in a realistic enough fashion without adding a further hour to the overall picture. But considering the age in which it was made – and how, even today, the romantic sub-plot is an essential element of any big production – the slight misstep is easy to understand, and forgive.

In its favour, the film holds a temporal importance – the amount of time passed since the film was made is more than twice as long as the time between the War and the creation of the film. And, as such, it feels as though you're watching an historical document rather than filmed entertainment. Griffith denied there being any racial or polemical message in the film on his behalf, but there is an undeniable grandstanding here, as if the film was designed in the same way documentaries are; that is to say, as more of a history lesson than mere spectacle.

In a similar vein, aside from the spectacular action sequences, the film's ripe old age presents a number of cultural customs that are more or less extinct now, such as the sequence in which Flora Cameron makes sure to wear her best dress in order to read her brother's letter that has arrived in the mail, direct from the front line.

The dignity of the event demanded it. She refuses to even take a peek at the letter she has been eagerly anticipating for months, until she has scrubbed up and dressed up. To satisfy her curiosity immediately while wearing her day-to-day dress would have been seen as demeaning the letter. Can you imagine people going to such lengths nowadays in our quick-fix, overly-gratified culture? Back in those days, a letter from a loved one – especially from the front line of a war – wasn't a casual doorstep read, but something to prepare for, as if you were meeting the loved-one in person. A 'ritual' of presenting yourself at your best was called for in such matters, as a mark of devotion and respect.

No doubt, those customs still existed in Europe at the time of the film's release. And 1915 saw many letters arriving home from the boggy trenches, reassuring loved-ones of their sender's well-being and well-wishes. And, of course, many of the soldiers never made it home. The trench warfare seen in the film is particularly heart-wrenching to watch when you consider that very similar bloody scenarios were being played out for real thousands of miles away in the European war-zone at the moment those scenes were being filmed – though, due to the media blackout, the general public had no idea of the true scale of the horrors unfolding on the continent.

'War, the breeder of hate'

The Americans didn't join in the War until April 1917, but D.W. Griffith found himself and his film in a war of their own, having to fend off charges of hate and racism wherever it played. *The Birth of a Nation* opened at Clune's Auditorium in Los Angeles on 8 February, 1915, to warm applause. However, as word circulated concerning the film's content and message, pressure groups – particularly the NAACP (National Association for the Advancement of Colored People) – began organising protests, and calling for a ban. And by the time of its premier in New York on March 3, a couple of States had bowed to the pressure and removed the film from circulation. The NAACP stepped up their efforts and organised a 'public education' campaign, with press articles and petitions objecting to the 'historical inaccuracies' of the film.

Around that time, the *New York Post* published an interview with social reformer, Jane Adams, in which she also attacked the film. 'One of the most unfortunate things about this film is that it appeals to race prejudice upon the conditions of half a century ago, which have nothing to do with the facts we have to consider to-day.' Her argument falls flat, however, in the knowledge that the film was set in the 1860s, and the fact that it was based on a fictionalised novel. Of course the situation was different in 1915. Would she have preferred a film that treated the events with a current-day, sugar-coated viewpoint? Of course she would. Since when have 'progressives' cared about the facts of history or the viewpoints of those they oppose?

Before the summer had arrived, the protests had become full-scale riots, especially in Boston and Philadelphia where the film was a huge hit with white audiences. And, a year later, the violence was *still* raging, with gang fights and interracial murders blamed on the film. By that point, twelve States had banned *Birth* on the grounds that it would 'promote race prejudice,' with three more following suit in the proceeding months. The NAACP's national boycott was deemed a success, although profits generated by the film have been estimated to have reached more than $50 million (roughly $681 million in 2017) on its initial run.

Indeed, Griffith had gone over-budget on the production and couldn't afford to pay Dixon the full amount for the rights to use the author's novel. They reached a compromise whereby Dixon accepted a 25% royalty on ticket sales. A very generous move as it turned out, as Dixon went from being a part-time writer to multi-millionaire within a year. The amount he received for the screenplay is still considered the largest sum for an author in film history. Not a bad day's work for the Southern Baptist Minister.

As for Griffith himself, he was stunned by the hostile reaction to his film. He responded to many critical reviews in the press, particularly a snotty piece in the *New York Globe* by Sherwin Lewis, who accused the film-maker of portraying historical inaccuracies before contending that the picture shouldn't be defended by the Constitution because its sole purpose was to make 'dirty dollars.' Griffith responded by calling the journalist a liar and a coward, and went on to defend the film's legitimacy, writing 'the public should not be afraid to accept the truth, even though it might not like it.'

Griffith felt his reputation was being damaged. He published a pamphlet entitled *The Rise and Fall of Free Speech in America* (pub. 1916), in which he expressed his opinions on the matter, and reprimanded journalists and politicians whom he felt should be in favour of free speech rather than trying to hinder the new art form of the motion picture.

'When the first small board of censorship was established six years ago, we who took it seriously then, expected exactly what has come to pass – that a man of the mental caliber of the captain of police of Chicago can tell two million American people what they shall and shall not go to see in the way of the moving picture.

'They tell us we can not show crime in a moving picture. We cannot listen to such nonsense. These people would not have us show the glories and beauties of the most wonderful moral lesson the world has ever known – the life of Christ – because in that story we must show the vice of the traitor Judas Iscariot. Had the modern censors existed in past ages, and followed out their theories to a logical conclusion, there would have been written no Iliad of Homer; there would not have been written for the glory of the human race that grand cadence of uplift called the Bible; there would have been no Goethe. There would have been no thrilling, beautiful dramas given us as the grandest heritage of the English-speaking race – the plays of Shakespeare. And even today, none of these creations would these worthy censors leave in our possession, had they their way.

'All new things in the world, including the Christian religion and the printing press, at their beginnings have been considered as instruments of evil and subject to suspicion.

'The motion picture has had to undergo the same ordeal that seems to be directed at all new things.'

Griffith demonstrated how the newness of cinema had somehow given the authorities a licence to treat the medium in any way they deemed fit. Unlike the written word, film didn't have a history or cultural importance at the time, so therefore only a small number of willing defenders. Griffith makes it clear that, if the censorship was to continue, then future works of film – which could match or even *surpass* the glories of great literally works – would be banished from public view by people unqualified to judge the significance of what they were seeing. And if that sounds like a snooty attitude, it's basically the same attitude the censors had for the film-going public, in reverse; that the masses were not smart or morally fastidious enough to process what they were seeing, and that would lead to moral harm. Note too his paraphrasing of Nietzsche's tenet: 'All great things must first wear terrifying and monstrous masks, in order to inscribe themselves on the hearts of humanity.'

Later in the pamphlet, he goes on to underline the point in no uncertain terms:

'It is said the motion picture tells its story more vividly than any other art. In other words, we [film-makers] are to be blamed for efficiency, for completeness. Is this justice? Is this common sense? We do not think so.

'We have no wish to offend with indecencies or obscenities, but we do demand, as a right, the liberty to show the dark side of a wrong, that we may illuminate the bright side of virtue – the same liberty that is conceded to the art of the written word – that art to which we owe the Bible and the works of Shakespeare.'

After the hostile reception of *The Birth of a Nation*, Griffith went away and began work on another epic drama, this time as a response to his critics, creating another milestone in the annals of film history, *Intolerance* (1916). But we'll get to that shortly. Regardless of the controversy, Griffith did have some fellow film-makers on his side, including Orson Welles, who commented years later, 'I have never really hated Hollywood except for its treatment of D. W. Griffith. No town, no industry, no profession, no art form owes so much to a single man.'

A Free Ride (c. 1915-1917)
(aka *A Grass Sandwich*)
Dir: 'A. Wise Guy' [unknown] /USA

Considered the earliest surviving adult film from America, *A Free Ride* mixes humour and hardcore sex scenes in a way that pre-dates similar such material that didn't surface until at least a decade later. Being the first of its kind, *A Free Ride* can be considered the porn world's equivalent of *Nanook of the North* (1922), only with erections and pubic hair standing in for the harpoons and furs.

Lasting just shy of ten minutes in length, the film opens on the scene of two young women strolling down a country road in the wilderness. An old style Touring Car approaches from behind and slows down beside them. The driver offers the girls a ride, and they hop in, only to have their breasts fondled immediately ('What a beautiful dairy!'). The girls playfully slap him across the face for his naughtiness, but their protests are minimal.

After pulling over to urinate (knuckles up), the driver is amused to see the 'Jazz Girls' spying on him. They head off deeper into the woods and also urinate, which makes the driver hornier than ever. Back at the car, driver Mike gives the girls liquor before taking one of them into the trees. He strokes her hairy vagina while she pulls out his plonker from his flies. At the car, the other girl grows restless, wondering what her friend is up to. She heads out to investigate. Meanwhile, Mike is balls-deep in girl no. 1 in missionary position, with the camera mounted at the rear so that his cock and balls look like a greasy piston rod plunging in and out of a crankshaft.

Girl no.2 arrives on the scene, lifts up her dress and begins playing with herself. 'Please give me a little,' she pleads. Of course, the driver is happy to oblige, but he insists on bending her over – effectively putting the onus on her anus. The film ends with a collection of montage shots – the girls frolicking in the nude; Mike receiving oral sex; the three of them getting dressed afterwards ('All's well that ends well'). And back to the car they go, tipsy and sated.

A free Ride is an odd little blip in film history as the clip seems to exist as a pornographic fossil in a desert of its own. It appears to have been made in a professional and casual manner, leaving us to assume that other such 'stag' pictures were made around the same time with many of the same cast and crew members. It feels very much like a routine porno flick rather than something new and 'out of the blue.' It's difficult to believe that a film like this could be a uniquely made item of its time.

Film historians (and porno-paleontologists) disagree on when the film was made, with suggestions ranging from 1915 to 1923. However, overall, the general consensus narrows it down to 1915 to 1917. Much of the information available on the film is merely rumour; it was supposedly shot in New Jersey; the performers deliberately attempted to conceal their identities by wearing wigs and hats and a fake moustache, etc, but no one knows for sure. And of course, the film-makers appear on the credits under obvious pseudonyms – the film was directed by 'A. Wise Guy,' and the camera man is billed as 'Will B. Hard.'

The film's distribution is equally mysterious, though it most certainly wasn't submitted to any censorship boards or screened for the general public. It's very much a product of the early days of underground cinema, of which so little information exists. And if it wasn't for the existence of the film itself as evidence, few would believe that such a cinema sub-culture could have existed at all at the time. But here it is for you to watch for yourself.

A Fool There Was (1915)
Dir: Frank Powell /USA
Based on the Broadway play, which was in turn based on the poem *The Vampire* (1897) by Rudyard Kipling, *A Fool There Was* (1915) is about a U.S. diplomat, John Schuyler (Edward José) sent to London. And while on the ship across the Atlantic, he falls for the seductive lure of a mysterious woman in black (Theda Bara). Despite being a married man with a young daughter, John's infatuation gets the better of him. However, Bara 'the vampire' isn't some exotic dream girl but an archetypal femme fatale who has already left a succession of ruined men behind in her past, and John is utterly incapable of not slavishly following the same path as her previous victims. He is systematically drained of his cash, morals, reputation and soul before being spat out on the street.

Sort of a mixed bag, *A Fool There Was* is no way as impressive as its reputation would suggest. It's easy to lose track of what is happening in the story, and who's who, as the scenes are clumsily assembled with nary a thought gone into the narrative whole. It's reputation today rests almost entirely with Bara, who steals the show as 'the vampire,' but of course, this isn't really a vampire movie; Bara may be vampiric in attitude and demeanour, but she's not a literal bloodsucking parasite. John's gradual transformation from fine upstanding member of society to a drunken, slovenly shell of a human being takes little more than an hour. It's quite a horrifying morality tale for its time, with John's inner turmoil visible in the haggard flesh and gaunt features of his face (though John Barrymore would go on to complete a similar transformation in appearance – this time in just three minutes – in *Dr. Jekyll and Mr. Hyde* (1920).

In one of the earliest publicity stunts in film

history, press agents Johnny Goldfrap and Al Selig presented Bara at the press conference in a fur suit as an exotic Arabian actress, 'foreign, voluptuous and fatal.' And by the time the film had reached Britain a few months later, Bara's reputation as a sex symbol had already taken hold. The rumours had gotten out of hand, with journalists claiming that Bara was the love child of a French painter and Arab courtesan (she was actually the daughter of a tailor from Ohio), while others had worked out that her name was an anagram of 'Death Arab.' The BBFC not only objected to the film's immoral content and characters, but also the effect of those behaviours being carried out by a woman with undeniable sex appeal. Not only were audiences in danger of being led astray, but they may also have gotten hot under the collar as well. That wouldn't do. The film was banned outright in the Britain.

Interestingly, the film's ban only inflamed Bara's reputation as a hottie. She became one of the most popular actresses of the silent era, appearing in roughly 40 or so films before retiring from the screen in 1926. Sadly, most of her films were destroyed in the Fox vaults fire in 1937. There's no doubt that the British ban had enhanced the lure of Bara as the forbidden fruit of the silver screen – dark, mysterious and utterly devoid of heart and soul. In *Censored*, Tom Dewe Matthews notes, 'The censor had, in effect, created what was censorable.'

On the Firing Line With the Germans (1915)
Dir: William H. Durborough /USA
On the Firing Line With the Germans was an American production made as a compilation using German newsreel footage, and offering the public a rare look at what was going on in Europe during World War I. Released at a time when the Americans still adhered to their isolationist policies, this film is presented objectively with no intention of steering public opinion, one way or the other. The surviving print is in rough condition nowadays, but it might just be the most objective contemporary film made of the conflict.

Almost completely devoid of combat footage until the end, the film instead shows German troops 'behind the scenes,' building barracks, digging trenches, marching captured French soldiers into captivity, and safely demolishing ruined buildings that had been left in a tottering state after being hit by bombs. It also shows the dark side of war, with harrowing footage of a woman mourning at the sight of a pile of bodies, one of whom was presumably her husband or son.

The film was shot entirely by Wilbur H. Durborough, an entrenched cinematographer who had spent seven months with the German army in Russia, Turkey, France and Belgium. He shot around 16,000 feet of film before it was sold to news agencies in Germany and America. The finished film premiered in Milwaukee on 28 November 1915, and played regularly at the Park Theater in Chicago starting in December of the same year, with all proceeds donated to the American branch of the Red Cross (whose aid and rescue work is shown throughout the film).

The similarly titled *Germany on the Firing Line* (1916) was released in New York in January 1916 and is also preserved today, and can be found in the Periscope Film LLC archive. Less than a year after its release, the Americans sided with the Allies and began pumping out propaganda pieces in the press to demonise the Germans, and the films also went on to reflect that new stance. They were gearing up for war.

Les Vampires (1915-1916)
Dir: Louis Feuillade /France
While Eastern France was coming under heavy conflict from the advancing German army, life in Paris went on as normal. On 13 November 1915, a strange new serial had opened in the capital. Opening with two episodes on the same night, *Les Vampires* included its own Theda Bara-like *femme fatale* as the criminal anti-hero, Musidora as Irma Vep (or 'Vampire'), and went on to become a huge success for the Gaumont company, despite the police temporarily banning a couple of episodes until the furore surrounding their release had died down.

Considered a classic of the early serials by film historians, *Les Vampires* was, at the time, seen as a rather inconsistent series; released in ten parts of varying length, with very little in the way of a planned release schedule – there was no set weekly or monthly instalments; instead, episodes appeared in theatres when they were ready for release. There were no cliffhanger endings and the plots often convoluted, and the series wasn't an immediate hit. However, in its favour, the serial served as an off-shoot of the Surrealist movement, and is said to have influenced the work of Orson Welles and Jean

Renoir.

The plot centres on a gang of criminals called The Vampires, who run amok in Paris while a resilient news reporter tries to thwart their every move. Considered fairly subversive in its time, for its casting of Musidora, a charismatic criminal who utterly outshines the hero and his bumbling sidekick, her charms muddy the central theme of good versus evil, with accusations from some critics that the series was amoral. And this criticism was only given added legitimacy as the supposed good guys are seen using devious methods to defeat their nemeses, and even resorting to massacring them in the end. And this led to further accusations that the series was undermining social order.

However, the series is perhaps best remembered today for its bizarre labyrinthine trap doors and secret compartments which are almost as convoluted as the plots. There are fireplaces which serve as secret passageways into rooms from which the criminals come and go – and, in one memorable scene, a large cannon emerges to shoot at a cabaret club! Taxis are equipped with false floors where fugitives can evade capture by dropping through them and disappearing into convenient manholes on the street. There is also a blatant subtext concerning parasitism and vampirism – how the criminals and the media, along with the pillars of society (the church, the police and the judicial system), turn out to be real vampires. And this vampiric theme may – or may not – have been an influence on Abel Ferrara's *King of New York* (1990).

The critics nowadays praise the early serial to the hilt, but casual fans may find it a torturous six-and-a-half-hours to get through in one sitting, as its average score on *IMDb* demonstrates (6.8 out of ten, compared to *Rotten Tomatoes*' perfect 100% aggregate score among the critics). Other serials of the time include Louis Feuillade's *Fantômas* (1913-1914), a five-part suspense thriller; George Pearson's *Ultus* (1915), a four-part British serial that only survives in fragments today; the German *Homonculus* (1916), in six-parts about a mad scientist who creates artificial people; and the American sixteen-parter, *The Crimson Stain Mystery* (1916), about another mad scientist whose experiments in creating a race of geniuses turns out a mob of unhinged criminals instead.

Where Are My Children? (1916)
Dir: Not credited [Phillips Smalley & Lois Weber] /USA

Inspired by the obscenity case of birth control campaigner, Margaret Sanger in New York, *Where Are My Children?* must surely qualify as one of the earliest exploitation movies ever to hit the screen, as it took advantage of a real-life event/debate and used it as an opportunity to sell movie tickets.

For such a down-to-earth film with a contentious theme, the story opens with an otherworldly sequence set 'Behind the great portals of Eternity,' where the souls of unborn children float around with angel wings in a heavenly pre-incarnation, awaiting their call to enter life. However, the place is becoming crowded due to the amount of unwanted souls who are sent back. It seems something is going on on earth that is preventing the children from being born...

Richard Walton (Tyrone Power) is a District Attorney and a great believer in eugenics. He spends his day at the courthouse watching as young delinquents are sent to prison. He despairs for society as he believes the crime problem could be eliminated by using birth control to put a cap on the 'ill-born.' Walton and his wife (Helen Riaume) don't have any children of their own, and this bothers him, though he is careful to conceal the disappointment from his wife. Mrs. Walton, in turn, seems to spend her days relaxing in the pleasant garden of their California home, and caring for a small pack of four-legged friends that keep her company while Richard is away at work.

Walton's sister visits, bringing along her baby which was born of a eugenic marriage. Richard is pleased to see the infant, but seems more interested in the genetic health of the little one, rather than doting as a normal uncle would. The child is looked upon almost as a scientific experiment. Meanwhile, a court case calls for his attention. A doctor is on trial for distributing 'indecent literature' on birth control. The prosecutor reads out a passage from the offending book. 'When only those children who are wanted are born, the race will conquer the evils that weigh it down.' The accused defends his position by talking about the conditions he sees daily in the slums. This sequence then blends into a dramatic portrayal of the squalid living conditions of the city's poor, with crime, drunkenness, misery, suicide and domestic violence a regular occurrence for him to deal with.

Meanwhile, Mrs. Walton's best friend, Mrs. Carlo (Marie Walcamp), is pregnant, and she is seen on a sun lounger in contemplation. The ghostly apparition of a child appears at her shoulder with angelic wings, letting viewers know that she is with child, and unhappy about it. She is invited to a party by her friends but feels she cannot go because of her pregnant state. And when she confides in Mrs. Walton of her dilemma, her childless friend tries to ease her woes: 'If you are determined to evade motherhood,' she reassures, 'and are willing to take the risk, I would suggest that you see Dr. Malfit.'

Of course, this sets off a chain of events which come back to haunt the characters, as was to be expected in morality tales of the time: Dr. Malfit appears as a genie out of a bottle – he agrees to abort Mrs. Carlo's baby, along with the babies of other friends of Mrs. Walton, including a teenage girl. These actions are decided upon in a whim due to convenience and vanity; the babies must be aborted so that their mothers will look good in a party dress. The decisions are met with dire consequences for the would-be mothers, as though the Devil himself had returned to collect his dues. The characters are left old, lonely, and full of regrets and despair. The most harrowing scene, however – apart from the botched abortion that results in the death of the teenage girl – is saved for the end when Robert learns about what his wife has been up to. He confronts her about her own secret abortions, and his horrified cry gives the film its anguished title.

Where Are My Children? is a remarkably well-made film, and one that manages to handle the delicate subject-matter with a degree of even-handedness, despite its pro-life message. Tyrone Power as the betrayed husband, is excellent in the lead role; a man who is forced to face up to the realities of eugenics when he discovers that his own beloved had practised what he had long preached. It's a film chock full of dark ironies, at odds with the idyllic middle-class suburbia of California and its bright, eternal summer. It's also an incredibly modern film, not just in the way it was written and shot, but also the subject-matter and its treatment wouldn't be out of place on a cinema screen today.

Of course, it's not as outrageous as the Japanese gynae-shocker, *Birth Control Revolution* (*Hinin Kakumei*, 1967), with its mad doctor and sadistic contraception methods, but if *Where Are My Children?* was remade today as a TV movie, shot for shot – and with sound, of course – I'm certain it would still have the power to pique the ire of those who would tune in, regardless of which side of the pro-life v. pro-choice divide they happened to occupy.

The film narrowly escaped being banned in Manhattan following a court case for obscenity, while the State of Pennsylvania called it 'filth' and removed it from circulation. And the ban remained in place even after the producers cut the film of its more contentious scenes. In Britain, chief censor Joseph Brooke Wilkinson also banned the film outright. But while, in America, the film's controversial topic led to heated discussion and successful box-office returns, the BBFC seem to have banned the film in order to *prevent* such a debate in Britain, rather than objecting to the film's message.

Monopoly Wars and the Birth of Hollywood

Like the telephone and the automobile, cinema was becoming ever popular among the masses. And by 1915, these technological conveniences were being accepted by a wider range of people. The convenience of telecommunications and the medium of film were even embraced by the middle-class for the first time, after being shunned in previous years. This new found prestige ensured the longevity of cinema, and predictably, as soon as it became an accepted form of mass communication, the cinema the world over was fully embraced by Jewish businessmen.

Jews had had an interest in film since its inception. Jewish film companies were behind dozens of early cinematic reels and cinema chains. *Les Vampires* was produced by Jews in Paris, *A Fool There Was* by Jews in Florida, and *Where Are My Children?* by Jews in Los Angeles. They were certainly no strangers to the game. However, as soon as cinema became an accepted art form, the Jews began a major push to monopolise the industry. Small companies and those struggling to keep afloat were quickly snapped up by the circling sharks.

In his book, *An Empire of Their Own: How the Jews Invented Hollywood* (pub. 1988), author Neal Gabler tells the fascinating story of

Hollywood's founding, from the arrival in America of Jews from the ghettos of Europe, and their nickelodeon businesses in New York and Chicago. Those early days were marred by conflict as the WASP ruling elite, particularly Thomas Edison, tried to squeeze the newcomers out of the industry.

Edison had played a key role in establishing not only the invention of cameras and film-making techniques, but he was also instrumental in developing the industrial side of the business, too. By establishing a cartel known as the Edison Trust, he made it possible for film-makers to distribute, control and profit from the new industry. Before the arrival of the Jews, the film industry in America was firmly in the hands of the established Anglo-Saxon Protestants. However, when the Edison Trust targeted the Jews, something of an ethnic war broke out. And the WASP's grip on the industry was curtailed indefinitely.

Unlike the white establishment, whose individualism could only survive in a society in which they were the dominant group, the Jewish film pioneers worked together as an ethnic pack. Carl Laemmle was born in a small village in southwestern Germany; Adolph Zukor and William Fox were born in Hungary; Louis B. Mayer was born in Russia; Benjamin Warner – who went on to head Warner Brothers – was born in Poland; and Lewis J. Selznick was from the Ukraine. Together, these immigrant outsiders stuck together as a close-knit group – a strategy that had worked in favour of Jewish survival for millennia – and were determined to build that 'empire of their own' through sheer verve and ethno-tribalism.

When it was discovered that the Jews were using Edison's copyrighted machines without permission, Edison personally went after them with a lawsuit. Rather than facing a fine or being sent to prison, the Jews instead opted to up sticks and head out west. They settled in the Hollywood hills in California, far out of reach of the Edison Trust, where, as the epigraphs in Gabler's book state, they had arrived . . . 'In this magical place that had no relationship to any reality they had ever seen before in their lives, or that anyone else had ever seen, [and] they decided to create their idea of an eastern aristocracy. . . . The American Dream— is a Jewish invention.'

The Jewish film-makers had thus defeated the vigorous attempts by the Trust to maintain its WASP monopoly. The Protestant ethic of the sovereign individual was ultimately swept aside by the collective interest of the ethnically loyal Semites. And during the whole debacle, Edison and his collaborators were only dimly aware that race was a factor in the struggle. Thus, according to Gabler, 'These gentiles never seemed to understand that they were engaged in much more than an economic battle to determine who would control the profits of the nascent film industry; their battle was also generational, cultural, philosophical, even, in some ways, religious.'

Scholar, Robert Sklar, in his book, Movie--Made America: A Cultural History of American Movies (pub. 1975, 1994), goes one further and suggests, 'The American elite classes, once they discovered [their loss of control of the film industry], recognized intuitively that this new medium threatened the liquidation of their heritage' (p. 122). The Jews, however, as ethnic and religious outsiders, were fully aware of the nature of the competition from day one.

In the magical land of Hollywood, Carl Laemmle, along with other Jews who owned smaller companies, joined forces and created the Universal Film Company in 1915. Adolph Zukor established the Famous Players Company (which later became the Paramount Pictures Corporation in 1919). He also purchased hundreds of cinema chains, and is credited with 'pioneering' distribution methods and networks, but really he brought nothing new to the game that Edison hadn't already done before him. William Fox founded the Fox Film Company in 1915; Benjamin Warner helped to establish Warner Bros., a company that was run by his three sons; Louis B. Mayer established the Metro Pictures Corporation in 1916, and later joined forces with Samuel Goldwyn (of Goldwyn Pictures Corporation) and his own L.A.-based company, Louis B. Mayer Pictures Corporation, merging the three to create Metro-Goldwyn-Mayer (MGM) in 1924, the biggest and most prestigious of the Hollywood corporations.

These companies were able to survive in the early days by engaging in nepotism, and largely because they had agreed not to step on each other's toes. Thus, each company specialised in a particular genre or 'flavour' of film. In his excellent documentary, A Personal Journey With Martin Scorsese Through American Movies (1995), Scorsese discusses the differences between the studios' output in the early days; Universal catered for the low-end market with small programmers and B-pictures, and would occasionally produce Gothic chillers with Lon Chaney in the lead role; MGM's pictures were glossy and sentimental, while Fox went for a grittier, socially conscious theme. Paramount, on the other hand, was very much a star maker, and concentrated on promoting the next big players of the screen.

'If you worked at MGM,' Scorsese says, 'you had to adapt to the MGM style. And it was quite different from the Warner Bros. or the Paramount style. If they [the directors] did not conform to the studio 'look,' the mavericks were reigned in. […] On the other hand, those who could work comfortably within the system thrived – they came to define their studios' styles – Clarence Brown at MGM; Henry King at Fox; Raoul Walsh at Warner Bros.. They were Hollywood pros who rose from the ranks. Most of their lengthy careers were spent under one roof.'

Indeed, in the old days the studios insisted on staying true to their distinctive styles to such an extent that film buffs could quickly recognise which company had produced any given film, based on looking at only a couple of scenes. And together, these early moguls and their growing companies recognised each other as friendly business partners and allies rather than rivals to be squeezed out, and they withstood and eliminated any and all competition for decades until the advent of the independent film, which took off in the 1960s.

By the early 1920s, these pioneers had amassed great fortunes and had secured for themselves the means by which to shape the face of American – and indeed, *world* – culture for decades to come. The American Dream had become a reality. Adolph Zukor's life in particular was an enviable one – he built several private mansions across the country, each with its own 18-hole golf course and full-sized cinemas. He had the best job in the world, married the girl of his dreams, lived to the ripe old age of 103, and his descendants are still heavily involved in the day-to-day running of Hollywood to this day. What else could a man ever ask for?

However, success has its dark side. And, as any student of history knows, the Jews' success in business and monopoly often comes with the price of persecution. As we see again and again throughout history, the Jews are quick to gain the levers of power, and yet are not as quick to uphold the responsibility that comes with it. Thus, the wheel of history turns, and the same mechanisms fall into place with a big accusing arrow pointing at the Jew – and the same resentments and fury that had followed them around for millennia would once again rear its head in the years to come.

But for now, despite their tight grip on the industry, there was still room for others to play. Independents like D. W. Griffith were still managing to release their own epic dramas without having to rely on the studio system. *Intolerance* was one of the last independently produced epics made by an Anglo-Saxon, old-school WASP, that is, until billionaire eccentrics like Howard Hughes had a go at film-making in the 1930s and 40s...

Intolerance (1916)

(aka *Intolerance: Love's Struggle Throughout the Ages*; aka *Intolerance: A Sun Play For the Ages*)

Dir: D.W. Griffith /USA

Inspired by the controversy sparked by his previous film, *The Birth of a Nation*, *Intolerance* was designed as a cinematic mirror for his critics to look at, in the hope that they would change their ways and cease their harassment and censorship of works of art and cinema. By far the biggest production in film history at the time of its release, the story is told as four segments from different historical epochs, juxtaposed in such a way that they basically tell the same story.

The film is framed with a modern-day tale about a young man ('The Boy' –played by Robert Harron, who had previously appeared as Dr. Cameron's ill-fated son in *Birth*), and his girlfriend, 'The Dear One' (Mae Marsh, who also appeared in *Birth* as Flora Cameron). Together they flee the town after a mill strike that results in dozens of workers being massacred in the street. Renting a small room, he makes a living by committing petty crime while the Dear One looks after their baby. He is later framed for a theft he didn't commit, and while in prison, Dear One has her baby taken away from her by the same 'uplift charity workers' whose meddling had caused the slaughter of the workers during the strike.

When he is released from prison, The Boy returns home only to find his ex-boss attempting to rape Dear One. In the struggle, the boss is shot by his own girlfriend, but she flees the scene, leaving him to be arrested and tried for murder. After the guilty verdict is delivered, The Boy is sentenced to hang until he is 'Dead! Dead! Dead!' In the meantime, Dear One gets the real culprit to confess her crime, and this leads to the first climactic chase scene in the movies as she and a helpful police officer race a car against the train that is carrying the Governor, who is on his way to witness the hanging. Can they reach the Governor and stop this miscarriage of justice, or will The Boy be hanged?

This simple story is inter-woven with events from the annals of history as a way of driving its point home. In ancient Jerusalem, Christ is condemned to the cross; in ancient Babylon, Prince Belshazzar repels Cyrus the Great of Persia in an epic war at the city walls, only to be betrayed from within by a traitor; and the Protestant Huguenots of France are slaughtered by those loyal to the Catholic royals – the St. Bartholomew's Day Massacre. And, added to this are the brief breaks between segments which show the symbolic image of the mother rocking the cradle of her infant, as a representation of eternal motherhood and the passing of generations (the film spans thousands of years).

The film cross-cuts back and forth between the stories, interweaving them and gradually speeding up the process until the last half hour becomes almost collage-like in its depiction of events. For instance, when The Boy is sentenced to hang, the next scene cuts to the crucifixion of Christ; and when the Dear One and the police officer are in pursuit of the train across the wide open spaces, the scene is inter-cut with the Catholics racing on horseback to massacre the Huguenots. Thus, the race against time of the modern-day story is juxtaposed with historical events in which the fates of the persecuted ones were not in their favour. It was an innovative method designed to merge real historical events with a fictional centre-piece, but unfortunately, Griffith doesn't quite manage to execute it as well as he intended. Instead of merging as a seamless whole, the stories tend to intrude on each other to a degree. Indeed, the final film wasn't a hit. Griffith later cut the film down and re-released the modern-day story as a stand-alone film entitled *The Mother and the Law* (1919), and the Babylon epic was re-released as *The Fall of Babylon* (1919).

However, the complete film is essential viewing for those with an interest in the history of film. It may not sit together perfectly as a work of art (though many regard it as a masterpiece today), but it haunts the memory unlike any film of the silent era. Once it's over, the themes and striking imagery tends to settle into a timeless vision of an age gone by. The scenes of worship in the Temple of Love look similar to the scenes of child sacrifice in *Cabiria* (1914), and the battle sequences are astonishing. Utilising more than 3000 extras, the siege of Babylon was easily the most ambitious war sequence ever filmed. And the scenes include some gruesome details, too – soldiers literally bite chunks out of each other, heads are chopped off, and bodies are thrown from the walls, so great was their hatred of each other.

The film is perhaps best remembered today for its incredible sets. The replica of the encircling wall of Babylon was enormous, with a walkway along the top that was wide enough for chariots to cross. The Babylon sets in particular are nothing short of breath-taking, with gigantic pillars and structures as tall as skyscrapers. There are statues of Ishtar and elephants that are 60 feet high, a flight of stairs as wide as a landscape flanked on either side with mysterious tunnels and walkways decorated in cuneiform. It's a huge bustling vista with viaducts and pillars, and balconies of people on top of the pillars, and billowing flags marked with sigils reaching to the heavens. It was a spectacle that Hollywood could only dream of replicating for decades. Never had the camera had the pleasure of soaking up such an epic sight. Not only was it a feast for the eyes, but it was also an architectural marvel, too. Those sets remained intact and became a tourist attraction before the authorities in Los Angeles deemed the ruins a danger to health and safety, and ordered their dismantling.

Intolerance was released on 5 September, 1916, to rave reviews. Eminent critic, Theodore Huff, even compared it to Michelangelo's ceiling paintings of the Sistine Chapel. This very warm reception didn't translate to ticket sales, however, largely because of its length and unorthodox narrative structure. Griffith had mostly financed the project from his own pocket, and its failure at the box-office contributed to his financial ruin. Still, the film's reputation has remained solid in the decades since it was made; communist film-makers, such as Sergei Eisenstein, and even future propaganda Minister of Germany, Joseph Goebbels, admired the film for its persuasive powers. In 1980, an article in the *New Yorker* described *Intolerance* as 'Perhaps the greatest movie ever made. In it one can see the source of most of the major traditions of the screen: the methods of Eisenstein and von Stroheim, the Germans and the Scandinavians, and, when it's bad, de Mille.'

Somme (1916)

(aka *The Battle of the Somme;* aka *Kitchener's Great Army in the Battle of the Somme*)
<u>Dir: Not credited [G.H. Malins] /UK</u>
If there was a war going on in Europe, you wouldn't have known it from the cinematic output of Britain during those years. *Somme* was released almost two years into the conflict, and only given the stamp of approval for its strengths as a propaganda tool for the War Office after the disastrous battle that gave the film its title.

The public was crying out for information on the conflict, and the British High Command eventually allowed cameras to record the offensive at Somme – but only so long as they kept a tight control of the finished film. The documentary opens in late June, 1916, while the British were preparing for the assault, which would commence on 1 July. Much like the previous war film, *On the Firing Line With the Germans* (1915), *Somme* concentrates on activities behind the front lines, with troops unloading wagons, eating and marching. Most of the combat footage is filmed from a distance, with heavy shelling of German trenches across the vast wastelands. In the aftermath, the camera prowls the devastation of a captured dug-out, with dead soldiers lying in the dirt, alongside the fatally wounded dogs and horses.

At last, the public was given a brief taste of the horrors of war – 'At a signal,' the screen reads, 'along the entire 16 mile front, the British troops leaped over the trench parapets and advanced towards the trenches, under heavy fire of the enemy.' Cue the now infamous footage of the Tommies going 'over the top' into No Man's Land, disappearing into the haze and smoke and barbed wire mesh – most of them running head-long into German machine-gun fire. It was surely one of the dumbest – and costliest – disasters in British military history.

For the first time, Britain's war dead were also shown on screen in British territory, albeit with a victorious inter-title down-playing the losses, 'after a glorious and successful charge on the Ridge near Mametz..' The victory is presented as though only a few minor casualties and fatalities were suffered. In reality, the British lost more than 57,000 men on that first day alone. One historian worked out that two soldiers were killed for every yard gained.

Indeed, even after a century since the event took place, the film is still a sad and sobering document. Those men, who were utterly devoted to their respective homelands, were treated as literal machine-gun fodder. They knew their mission would cost them their lives, and yet there was no hesitation to follow orders and charge down those merciless guns. Europe will never live down the shame of what it did to those gallant men. After the cameras stopped filming in early July, the Battle of the Somme continued until 18 November, amassing a death count of more than a million, making it one of the bloodiest battles in history.

The finished film was released in August 1916, and was a huge success. Up to 20 million Brits saw the film on its initial theatrical run, not to mention millions more in the wider Empire. Even the Royal Family watched it in a private screening at Windsor Castle. An unnamed critic of *The Times* summed up the mood of the country soon after its release, noting how audiences 'were interested and thrilled to have the realities of war brought so vividly before them, and if women had to sometimes shut their eyes to escape for a moment from the tragedy of the toll of battle which the film presents, opinion seems to be general that it was wise that the people at home should have this glimpse of what our soldiers are doing and daring and suffering.'

However, the reception wasn't entirely welcoming. A cinema manager in Hammersmith, W. Jefferson Woods, refused to screen *Somme*, and instead put up a notice outside the premises which read, 'This is a Place of Amusement, not a Chamber of Horrors.' Woods was later confronted by a reporter form the *London Evening Standard*, to which he commented, 'I don't think [the film] is suitable for those who have lost relatives. I think it is harrowing and distressing... The papers are full of it every morning. We see for ourselves the wounded walking about our streets...'

Many years later, film historian Kevin Brownlow uncovered a collection of mock-up shots which suggest that the 'over the top' scenes were actually faked. He went on to suggest that the scenes were shot, not on the front line of the trenches, but at a battery school away from the danger zone. If those infamous scenes *were* faked, then not only was it on the orders of the War Office, but it also marks the first time in which sensationalist footage was fabricated on film – a trick that was later embraced for the notorious mondo movies from Italy in the 1960s and 70s.

Director/cinematographer, Malins, returned to the front in August with King George V, Prime Minister Herbert Asquith, and David Lloyd George. The tour resulted in another film released in October, *The King Visits His Armies in the Great Advance* (1916). And by the end of the year, he had shot enough footage for a third film, *The Battle of the Ancre and the Advance of the tanks* (1917), which was released in January the following year. Also in January, the Germans released *With Our Heroes on the Somme* (1917), which recycled much of the same footage from *On the Firing Line With the Germans* (1915). In June 1917, Malins released his final film of the conflict, *The German Retreat and the Battle of Arras* (1917) – none of them, however, came close to the success of *Somme*.

The Cabinet of Dr. Caligari (1919)
(Orig title: *Das Cabinett des Doktor Caligari*)
<u>Dir: Robert Wiene /Germany</u>
'See the sleepwalker, floating down the street, ripped from some nightmare! A street of misshapen houses with brooding windows, streaked by dagger strokes of light and darkened by blots of shadow! You will immediately feel the terror in the movements of that floating grotesque!' – Tagline for *Caligari*

Considered the first feature-length horror movie ever made – though there are a handful of others which pre-date it – *The Cabinet of Dr. Caligari* is nonetheless a milestone in fantastic cinema, and an early example of the melding of film and art. Linked to the German Expressionist movement, *Caligari* was deliberately designed as a hyper-stylised nightmarish twisting of reality, with its bizarre sets, absurdly high stools, shadows literally painted on the walls, and demented performances.

From the outset, writers Carl Mayer and Hans Janowitz wanted to set the story in a timeless, otherworldly realm, where the surrounding buildings and landscapes reflect the agitated state of the character's minds, with sharp, jagged edges and architecturally absurd shapes – insanity literally reflected on the world as 'emotional ornaments'. Fritz Lang was originally set to direct, but he later abandoned the project, largely due to fears that the radical visual style would be too much for audiences to take. Robert Wiene eventually took to the helm, and he embraced the concept with a willingness to try something new.

The result was a story in which a cruel charlatan, Dr. Caligari (Werner Krauss) mesmerises a zombie-like somnambulist, Cesare (Conrad Veidt), into committing a series of murders in the small fictional town of Holstenwall – with a final twist revealing that Cesare is actually an asylum inmate who had dreamt the whole thing. Furthermore, characters from his real life appear in his dream as sinister interlopers – including Caligari himself who is shown to be a decent person in real life, with his patient's best interests at heart. The problem is, however, that the bizarre sets of the real asylum are identical to the ones in the dream, which sort of undermines the plausibility of the whole film. Indeed, Kim Newman commented, 'by revealing its expressionist vision to be that of a madman, the film could even appeal to conservatives who deemed all modernist art as demented.'

The film's reputation as an expression of irrational authority is largely down to the work of Siegfried Kracauer, whose book, *From Caligari to Hitler: A Psychological History of the German Film* (pub. 1947), was very influential over the years. In the book, Kracauer suggests that the film reflects an unconscious desire in German people for a tyrant, and that Cesare serves as a stand-in for the Germans who were more than willing to bow to authority and engage in mindless murder for the sake of the insane authority figure. Of course, in retrospect it was easy for him to view the film in such black and white terms immediately after World War II. As a supposed premonition of the rise of Hitler, and the guilt of the German people for their willingness to go along with the Nazi Party, there are interesting parallels to be made, but that's all they are. Study of his book nowadays reveals more holes than Caligari's sweatpants.

For a start, he had always insisted that there was no framing device in the original screenplay, and that the one seen in the finished film was forced upon it by the producers, much to the protests of the script writers. And, as a result, this potentially revolutionary film was rendered merely a 'conformist' one in his eyes. However, we now know that there *was indeed* a frame to the story from the beginning – a surviving copy of Werner Krauss' original script was made available to the public in 1995, proving Kracauer to have been wrong the whole time. Therefore, the entire theory on which his reputation rests stumbles at the first hurdle.

Indeed, in an age in which even Freudian theory itself is now looked upon with suspicion, the many off-shoots in the fields of psychology and film theory interpretation have come under increasing scepticism, too. Kracauer's claims that films can provide insight into the 'unconscious motivations and fantasies of a nation' can be seen as little more than an indulgent guessing game – and the conclusions drawn were later proved to be not only recklessly assumptive, but ultimately incorrect.

In the introduction to the book, Kracauer writes, 'American audiences receive what Hollywood wants them to want,' a statement that makes perfect sense. But then he goes on to write *in the same sentence*, 'but in the long run public desires determine the nature of Hollywood films.' So he basically presents his readers with a contradiction. If the public's desires are shaped by Hollywood movies, then in the long run, those same desires are *still what Hollywood wants them to want*, because it has already instilled those desires in the public in the first place. He effectively undermines his entire theory in the first few pages. Make no mistake; *all* film is propaganda, one way or another. It isn't the collective unconscious one sees projected on a cinema screen, but rather the film industry's (i.e., the establishment, or the elite's) propaganda – their desires for *you*.

Caligari premiered at the famous Marmorhaus theatre in Berlin on 26 February 1920 to mixed reviews. Some celebrated it as the first true art film ever to hit the screen, while others dismissed it for not being arty enough. Herbert Ihering's contemporary review branded it an artistic failure: 'If actors are playing without energy and are playing within landscapes and rooms which are formally 'excessive,' the continuity of the principle is missing.' The film was due to play at Miller's Theater in Los Angeles in May the following year, but the screening was cancelled due to protests of American workers objecting to the import of German films, which they feared would threaten their jobs. Many in the American film industry expressed similar fears and wanted the film banned. However, the American press was less hostile, with the *New York Times* praising the film as a piece of modern art, while *Variety* magazine published a glowing review which praised everything from the tempo, the direction and sets that 'squeeze and turn and adjust the eye, and through the eye the mentality.'

Director Robert Wiene continued with his expressionist experiments, delivering the lesser-known *Genuine* (1920), a puzzling horror story of a painter whose portrait comes to life and tries to flee, and *Rakolinikow* (1923), an early adaptation of Dostoevsky's *Crime and Punishment*, in which the killer's delirium is reflected in the twisted set designs. Both of these films are much more overtly avant-garde in style compared to the popular *Caligari,* and Wiene also adds surrealist touches, too. The latter is especially worth a watch as it has been unfairly neglected over the years.

As for *The Cabinet of Dr. Caligari*, perhaps the biggest tribute paid to the film was David Cronenberg's *Videodrome* (1982), which updates the scenario to the video age. This time it's the shadowy 'Corporation' that is responsible for controlling the masses via satellite television broadcasts, and James Woods stars as Max Renn, a Cesare-like pawn who is coerced into committing murders while he seems to lose touch with reality. *Videodrome* was arguably just as revolutionary in the early 1980s as *Caligari* was in the early 1920s, albeit for entirely different reasons. But both films seem to concentrate on the themes of sanity and insanity, subjective reality, the duality of human nature and perception itself. Cronenberg's film also seems to be a deliberate inversion of Kracauer's theories, and is one of the most individualistic and anti-mainstream titles of the 80s.

J'Accuse! (1920)
(*I Accuse!*)
Dir: Abel Gance /France

In a small village in the south of France, two men are in love with the same woman, the beautiful Édith Laurin (Maryse Dauvray). One is her husband, François (Séverin-Mars), a full-blooded Frenchman who is prone to jealousy and violence, and the other is Jean (Romuald Joubé), a pacifist poet. When François learns that Édith has been having an affair with Jean, he sends her away to live with his parents. And, with the outbreak of World War I, the two love rivals end up in the same regiment. During the conflict, the men learn to put aside their hostile resentment of each other for the greater good of the woman they love.

However, while staying in Lorraine, Édith is raped by a group of German soldiers, and when Jean returns home on leave, he discovers that she has given birth to baby girl. François returns home soon after, and when he eventually discovers the truth, the two men agree to return to the front line and seek vengeance on the Germans. As the war grinds on to its horrific conclusion, François is wounded and later dies, while Jean is affected psychologically. He returns home once again, this time traumatised to madness. He gathers the villagers together and rants at them of his vision of the war dead coming back to life. The villagers look upon their broken hero with pity at first, that is until zombie-like soldiers show up outside, banging on the windows in a defeated, shuffling horde, baring their rotten flesh, sullied wounds and defacements. The residents are horrified and faced with a reckoning: with the return of the war dead limping and mourning in the neighbourhood, the villagers are forced into asking themselves whether the soldiers' sacrifice was worth it.

For such a simple and devastatingly effective story, writer/director Abel Gance sure took his time in telling it. At almost three hours in length, the film doesn't quite succeed in its horrific build-up, and would have been far more effective at half the length. The film seems to have been structured more as an epic novel than a tightly-packed cinematic polemic, and suffers somewhat because of it. It moves along almost as slowly as the dead soldiers traipsing through the mud. Like the late Michael Cimino's Vietnam epic, *The Deer Hunter* (1978), the first hour or so – as important as it was in establishing its central characters – could have been dropped without having much of an impact on the tale, and making for a much more concise and devastating whole. But whereas *The Deer Hunter* offered up an incredible two hours of trauma and trepidation after its slow start,

J'Accuse never recovers from its agonisingly slow pace.

Having said that, the film is certainly worth watching if you get the chance. There are lots of poetic and artistic visual flourishes throughout, such as Jean's poems which come to life with the image of the ghostly Édith wandering around in pleasant meadows, and – in a darker tone – the rape scene, which is presented almost entirely in silhouette as the shadows of the German soldiers, in their sinister, 'Hun'-like caricature helmets, reach out for her until she is fully engulfed in darkness. Of course, the film will always be remembered for its walking dead sequence, which adds a dream-like surrealism, and is perhaps the most arresting aspect of the film. Not only were the war dead returning to confront the villagers, they were also Gance's way of confronting the French cinema-going public with the horrors of war and the true cost of the – then – recent conflict. Around 2000 French soldiers on leave agreed to be filmed for the sequence. And, according to Gance, around 80 percent of them died in the weeks following the film shoot, as they returned to the front line at Verdun. 'The conditions in which we filmed were profoundly moving,' he said. 'They played the dead knowing that in all probability they'd be dead themselves before long.'

Abel Gance had served as a cinematographer for the French Army during the War, but was discharged early due to ill health. He came up with the idea for *J'Accuse* when he learned that most of his friends had died in the conflict. He found himself wondering whether his ill-fated friends would have approved of the patriotic war fervour that had gripped the country, and imagined the dead coming back to life and returning home to scare the public into peace and sanity. After writing out a draft script, Pathé agreed to finance the film. And his experience as a front-line camera man afforded him the first-hand knowledge of what life was like for the soldiers in the trenches. Shooting began in August 1918, and Gance even secured new footage of the war which he edited into the final film for added authenticity.

J'Accuse premiered in France on 25 April 1919 and was a huge success, raking in 3.5m francs, far outstripping its lavish 525,000 francs budget. In Britain, the film was praised by the critics, despite it playing unregulated as the BBFC had initially refused to grant a certificate as it had violated one of T. P. O'Connor's 43 censorship rules (no. 18 – 'Realistic horrors of warfare'). Pathé's representative in London sent a telegram to Gance which read, 'Your name in England is, at present, more famous than Griffith's.' Griffith himself got to see the film when it played in America, and is said to have been 'deeply moved' by it. He even went to the trouble of arranging its distribution through United Artists, as most channels had refused to touch it because of its pacifism – a very unpopular belief in the States at the time.

However, for all the praise he had received for his film, Gance himself was never entirely satisfied with it. Over the coming years, he would chop and edit the film, releasing many different versions of varying length, ranging from three-and-a-half hours to 100-minutes. A more clearly anti-German version with a happy ending was released in America in 1921, and there are many other surviving prints with alternate endings. He even re-visited the film afresh for a drastically different 'remake' that was released in 1939, on the eve of World War II, but we'll get to that later. The Lobster Collection issued a restored print in 2008 which combines the best surviving elements from four different versions of the film that were stored in archives in Europe.

As for the legacy of *J'Accuse*, it has certainly left its mark on cinema history. From anti-war movies, such as *All Quiet on the Western Front* (1930) and the aforementioned *The Deer Hunter*, to art-house shockers like Bruno Dumont's *Flandres* (2006), and even exploitation and zombie movies, such a *Deathdream* (1972), *Zombie Lake* (1979) and *Les revenants* (2004), each with varying degrees of dream-like surrealism and social commentary.

The Hollywood Scandal Sheet

The early 1920s saw a number of scandals involving Hollywood, both in front and behind the camera, bringing the whole industry into shame and disrepute. But none caused more of a sensation than the manslaughter case of Roscoe 'Fatty' Arbuckle. Most modern-day film fans have never heard of him, but Arbuckle was as famous as Buster Keaton and Charles Chaplin in the early years of cinema. He was the first major comedy star of the screen, the archetypal 'jolly fat man,' whose slapstick antics had amused audiences long before the days of Laurel and Hardy, Abbott and Costello and The Three Stooges.

He made his screen debut in 1909 in a short skit, *Ben's Kids*, for the Selig Polyscope Company. More films followed, and he was eventually signed up to The Keystone Film Company (later an imprint of Universal), delivering a slew of crazy comedies that proved hugely successful, including *The Gangsters* (aka *Peeping Pete*, 1913) and *Fatty Joins the Force* (1913). In the following year, Paramount offered him a very generous contract of $1000-per-day, plus 25% royalties on all profits and complete artistic control, to make comedy shorts for them. Those films not only made him a mega-star, but they also provided a vital platform for new talents, including Mabel Normand, Al St. John, Buster Keaton and Charles Chaplin. A typical scenario for the films was the 'first-day-on-the-job' gag, in which Arbuckle and a co-star would cause chaos in the workplace – the film's titles were often self-explanatory enough, such as *The Butcher Boy* (1917) and *The Cook* (1918), the former includes a dog on a makeshift treadmill and a sticky hat gag with Keaton that is still laugh-out-loud funny to this day. In 1918, Paramount extended his contract to three more years, worth $3 million (the equivalent of around $48 million in 2017).

All was clearly on the up and up for Arbuckle. However, his fame and fortune came crashing down after a fateful binge of drunken debauchery. In early September 1921, Arbuckle and a number of friends from the industry checked into the St. Francis Hotel in San Francisco. Their intention was to take a break as they had just worked on three productions back-to-back. But their 'winding down' became a full-on party that lasted for three nights. With crates of bootleg liquor (it was during the prohibition era), young women were invited to the rooms, including 26-year-old aspiring actress, Virginia Rappe. What followed is still not entirely clear to this day, but Rappe fell ill, and her friend informed the police that Arbuckle had raped the actress.

Rappe died a few days later, and the autopsy revealed she had died of complications brought on by a ruptured bladder. And, as Arbuckle weighed around 266lbs at the time, it was suggested that it was his hefty weight that had caused the internal damage while he was on top of her. The resulting trials for manslaughter were almost as clownish as Fatty's films;

Rappe's reputation was dragged through the mud, with accusations that she was not only promiscuous, but also looked upon abortion as a convenient contraception method. She was also a heavy drinker and suffered an illness which caused her physical pain whenever she was drunk. How much of this information was true or just a smear on her character is still unknown, but we do know that the prosecutor, Matthew Brady, had pressured witnesses into making false statements.

However, despite the fact that most of the witnesses had been known liars – including Rappe's friend, Bambina Maude Delmont, who had raised the first rape accusation and was later shown to have been involved in fraud and blackmail – the nation's newspapers went into overdrive, more or else declaring Arbuckle's guilt in order to sell more papers. William Randolph Hearst in particular seemed pleased with his efforts in this regard, even going on to proudly claim that the trials had 'sold more newspapers than any event since the sinking of the *Lusitania*.' Indeed, the whole sensationalist coverage, or 'yellow journalism,' fuelled the fire, and despite being found not guilty on all charges, Arbuckle's reputation was in ruins. His films were banned, Hollywood studios forbade their stars from defending him in public, and Arbuckle himself never appeared in a major production again. For the rest of the decade, he turned to directing (under his father's name, 'William Goodrich,' which led to him being nicknamed 'Will B. Good' in the industry), and he even made the minor classic, *The Iron Mule* (1925), starring his old friend and nephew, Al St. John. His directorial efforts proved successful enough for Vitagraph Studios (an imprint of Warner Bros. since 1925) to offer him a contract in 1932 to make short films for them. And that he did, producing six such films before dying of a heart attack in the following year.

According to biographer, David Yallop, in his book on Arbuckle, *The Day the Laughter Stopped* (pub. 1976) – which lends a great amount of coverage to the case and its aftermath – a number of original film prints in which the comedian had starred were incinerated and lost forever. The BBFC even banned his films in Britain. His wife filed for divorce in 1923, and he hit the bottle hard. In an interview with film historian, Kevin Brownlow, actress Louise Brooks described working with him at this time: 'He made no attempt to direct... He just sat in his director's chair like a dead man.' After his death, little effort was made to preserve his surviving films, and many only exist today as worn-out negatives, often with foreign subtitles, and are watched primarily by those who are willing to undergo a deep excavation of film history.

If Arbuckle was destroyed by the very same media machine that had created him, he certainly wasn't the only casualty. Like the comedian's case, The Paramount Picture Company was related to four other scandals at the time, such as the murder of director William Desmond Taylor. Still unsolved to this day, Taylor – perhaps best known for working with Mary Pickford and Wallace Reid – was shot dead in his apartment in Los Angeles on 2 February 1922. And though a large sum of cash was stolen from the scene of the crime, the investigators suspected that robbery was not the prime motive. Actress, Mabel Normand (Arbuckle's regular co-star), was in a relationship with Taylor, and he was worried about her cocaine addiction. After several relapses, Taylor met with Federal prosecutors in an effort to put the coke dealers behind bars. A few days later he was murdered. There were several suspects linked to the murder, but the mysterious drug dealers seem to be the most likely culprits. Still, questions were asked: if Taylor *was* gunned down by Normand's cocaine suppliers, then who gave word to them that he was in contact with the Feds? Normand's career dwindled in the years after the killing, and she died in 1930 of tuberculosis. Numerous books have been written about the case, including Robert Giroux's *A Deed of Death: The Story Behind the Unsolved Murder of William Desmond Taylor* (pub. 1990) and the 1000+ paged *Taylorology*, (published in 98 fanzine volumes from 1985 to 2009) which is a collection of contemporary articles from the press. Films were also produced, such as the classic, *Sunset Boulevard* (1950), which was inspired by the case and even includes a character called 'Norma Desmond,' and Universal's *Hollywood Story* (1951), which is a more faithful treatment of the case, even if it includes a fictional ending.

In 1920, the blossoming career of silent movie star, Olive Thompson, was cut tragically short when she drank from a flask containing mercury bichloride which slowly poisoned her to death. The concoction was used as a treatment for syphilis, and the media frenzy speculated that her husband, John Pickford (Mary's younger brother), had given her the disease and she had committed suicide out of shame. Others suggested that she had drunk the poison accidentally while intoxicated. Either way, Hollywood's pristine image was hit hard. In 1923, Wallace Reid, who had appeared in *The Birth of a Nation* and *Intolerance*, died in a sanitarium while trying to overcome an addiction to morphine. Actress Barbara L. Marr was another who succumbed to the Hollywood lifestyle, becoming hooked on cocaine, alcohol and heroin. And, after she was dropped by MGM, she went off the rails completely, and later died of tuberculosis and nephritis in 1929. And Jeanne Eagels' life ended in similar circumstances.

The Hollywood scandal sheet was thus born, and the studios attempted to clean up their image by introducing contracts that included 'morality clauses,' or 'moral turpitude clauses,' which would enable bosses to fire those who breeched them. But it was too late, the damage was done. There was a growing hostility towards Hollywood among religious groups and the press, and even William Randolph Hearst was given a taste of his own medicine when film pioneer, Thomas H. Ince, died under mysterious circumstances on his private yacht. In the aftermath of the tragedy, the press ran wild with speculation and accusations, many of them suggesting that Hearst was directly responsible for the death. Thus, Hearst was in danger of falling victim to the vast corporate media machine he had helped to establish.

However, there was another industry mogul in Detroit who took against Hollywood. Henry Ford of the Ford Motor Company began sponsoring the newspaper, *The Dearborn Independent*, to publish a series of weekly articles that were critical of what he saw as the negative Jewish influence on American society. The articles, published every week from 1920 until 1922, quickly grew into an openly anti-Semitic screed in which Jews were to blame for everything. Articles entitled *The Jewish Aspect of the "Movie" Problem* and *Jewish Supremacy in Motion Picture World* (both published in February 1921), focused specifically on the Hollywood studio system.

'It is not that producers of Semitic origin have deliberately set out to be bad according to their own standards,' the article states, 'but they know that their whole taste and temper are different from the prevailing standards of the American people; and if censorship were established, there would be danger of American standards being officially recognized, and that is what they would prevent. Many of these producers don't know how filthy their stuff is – it is so natural to them.'

Other journalists began airing their worries about the actual content of films, such as Frederick Boyd Stevenson of the *Brooklyn Eagle*:

'On the other hand the reels are reeking with filth. They are slimy with sex plays. They are overlapping one another with crime... From bad to worse these conditions have been growing. The plea is set up that the motion picture industry is the fourth or fifth in the United States, and we must be careful not to disrupt it. A decent photoplay, it is argued, brings gross returns of, say $100,000, while a successful sex play brings from $250,000 to $2,500,000.'

Henry Ford again:

'[Carl] Laemmle, it will be remembered from a former article, said of his company, "The Universal does not pose as a guardian of public morals or of public taste." This is probably the attitude of other producers, too. But though they avoid any responsibility for taste or morals, they consistently fight all attempts of the state to set up a public guardianship in those regions. A business that frankly brutalizes taste and demoralizes morals should not be permitted to be a law unto itself.'

The Dearborn Independent was estimated to have a readership of around 70,000 in the Michigan area, and Ford himself insisted that copies be available for all the workers at his production factories and plants. It is not clear what impact the articles had in America, but if they were written ten years later during Hollywood's pre-code era, they may have resonated more effectively with readers, as, for all the scandals drummed up in the press, the studios were actually remarkably well behaved in the early days. However, the message went down very well on the other side of the Atlantic.

The *Dearborn* articles were collected and published in Germany in four volumes, entitled *The International Jew: The World's Foremost Problem*. The books had a big impact on the growing number of anti-Semites in Germany, including an angry young man named Adolf Hitler, who later acknowledged Ford favourably in his own book, *Mein Kampf*, which was published a few years later. Hitler later claimed to keep a life-sized portrait of Ford next to his desk and, after he became Chancellor, oversaw the development of the Volkswagen, ensuring that the vehicle resembled Ford's own Model T.

It's interesting to note that Henry Ford was friends with both Thomas Edison and D.W. Griffith, Aryan men who had had their own run-ins with the Jews in the past, as we have seen. And it isn't much of a stretch to suggest that the *Dearborn* articles were merely a continuation of the monopoly war that the WASPs had waged back in 1915. With that in mind, we may even be permitted to stretch this theory a little farther: Though I have never known of an historian put it so directly, perhaps Edison's little tussle with the Jews was the catalyst that shaped the entire century – from the establishment of Hollywood, to the Ford articles, to the influence on Hitler, to the Third Reich and World War II. Of course, there were many stepping stones that led to the war, but this particular route may be worth studying in greater detail.

But let us not get carried away, and let us not get too far ahead of ourselves. We now enter 1922. And, speaking of Germany, the disastrous circumstances of the Weimar Republic seemed to collude to bring the public face to face with one of the darkest and most morbid pictures ever to grace the German cinema screen. On 4 March 1922, the first genuine horror anti-hero was unleashed among the public...

Nosferatu: A Symphony of Terror (1922)
(Orig title: *Nosferatu, Eine Symphonie des Grauens*)
Dir: F.W. Murnau /Germany
On the chilly night of 4 March, a large crowd had gathered at the Marmorsaal, or 'Marble Hall' of the Berlin Zoological Garden. Those in attendance had arrived in coded dress – vintage Biedermeier costumes – as instructed in their invitations. They had arrived for the premier of a new picture film by the German artist, F. W. Murnau, who had gone to the expense of investing in a large advertisement in the *Bühne und Film* magazine. The ad promised a 'Festival of Nosferatu', and included a plot summary, production reports and essays on the history of the vampire myth. Most intriguing of all, however, was the fact that the ad also included a series of photographs of a creature unlike anything ever seen on a cinema screen – a pallid, sick-looking demonic entity with sharp pointy teeth and ears, and an icy stare. Little did the attendees know that what they were about to see on the big screen was the result of a myth that had evolved over the course of thousands of years.

Vampire tales first emerged in Western Europe during the Enlightenment era. However, the myth of the malignant bloodsucker actually dates back to ancient times. In ancient Greece there were tales of succubi, such as Lamia and Empusa. These creatures were often portrayed as female demons who had sex with humans before drinking their victim's blood and devouring their corpses. The Strige also has its origins in Greece – a bloodsucker who could transform into a pterodactyl-like flying creature after feeding on human blood. Elsewhere in the ancient world, there was Ekimmu from Assyria and Babylon – Ekimmu were said to be the souls of the dead that were condemned to dwell on earth and draw blood sustenance from the living for having committed transgressions in life. In Imperial Rome, the legend of Ekimmu lived on in the form of Lemures, who were said to be restless spirits that drained the living of their essence.

In Pagan Ireland, Druids would tell tales of evil bloodsuckers whom they called 'Dearg-duls,' and in Indian mythology there are accounts of reanimated corpses that could assume a bat-like form after being revived by the demon, Baital. Also from India was Vetala, who was said to be an old crone who would drink human blood, while in China they had their own version of the vampire in Chiang Shih, an horrific-looking ghoul who could also revive (and possess) corpses and feed on both the living and the dead. Malaysian vampires came in different forms and were almost exclusively female; the most well-known among them was Pontianak. In contrast to the Chiang Shih, the Malaysian bloodsuckers always appeared as beautiful and sexually attractive.

As Christianity conquered Europe, various vampiric strands of folklore emerged from Eastern Europe and the Balkans: there was Vrykolaka from Greece; Obour from Bulgaria; Strigoi from Romania; Paugri from Hungary; Upir, or 'Oupyr' from Russia and Ukraine; Upior from Poland; Vikodiak from Serbia; Vurdolak from Morlacchia. Modern scholars have tried to account for these myths and why the 'vampire' could have emerged from various cultures and geographical areas simultaneously – some draw on Jungian archetypes and the 'collective unconscious,' while others put it down to repressed sexuality, backward superstition, or 'fear of the other'.

The vampire myth eventually weaved its way into Western Europe sometime in the 18th Century. There were tales of the Vampyr, or 'Nachzehrer' from Germany, the Vampiro in Spain and Italy, and of course, the Vampire, or 'Vampyre' in France and England. The vampire began appearing in lurid tales and often printed in the form of 'Penny Dreadfuls,' which were crudely written and cheaply produced pamphlet-like stories that were sold on news stands in the 19th Century. Novelist Bram Stoker became familiar with the vampire myth some time later, and he began amassing data and research. He found 'true' stories from Eastern Europe – one in particular was the account of villagers who were convinced that a recently executed criminal was returning from his grave at night to cause havoc in the area. They assumed the criminal to be a vampire. His grave was dug up, and a brave man from the village drove a stake through its heart, which supposedly gave off a puff of smoke (though, if the story was true in any way, the 'smoke' could have been dust emitting from the body by the force of the stake).

Nevertheless, Stoker felt he was onto a good thing. He immersed himself deeper into the vampire myth, drawing inspiration from the ancient succubi of Greece and Babylon, while also adding his own flavour with the introduction of the historical figure, 'Vlad the Impaler.' Vlad's nickname was Dracul (meaning 'Son of the Devil'), and Bram simply added an 'a' to the name to establish the title of his novel's fearsome anti-hero. Written mostly in the form of a series of letters between characters, Bram Stoker's classic novel, *Dracula* appeared in 1897. And though the book was light on dialogue, there was a heavy emphasis on description, lending it a strong visual quality which would be perfect for the silent cinema screen.

The vampire on film dates back to 1909 with *Vampire of the Coast* (though a supposed 'vampire bat' shows up in the early Méliès short, *Le Manoir du Diable*, 1896). Over the next thirteen years, around two dozen vampire films were made worldwide, often short one-reelers, and most of them are considered lost today. However, in 1922 there was a controversial film from Germany that sealed the vampire myth forever on the silver screen, *Nosferatu*.

Having already made a name for himself in German Expressionist circles, director F. W. Murnau decided to tackle Stoker's novel and bring the story to the screen with a grim and morbid visual style. The threat of a lawsuit from Stoker's estate didn't deter him. In order to get around the copyright issues, he simply changed the names of the key characters and altered a few plot points before continuing with the production – thus, Dracula became Count Orlok, Jonathan Harker became Hutter, and Van Helsing became Professor Bulwer; and Orlok stalks the streets of Bremen rather than Victorian London. However, Murnau's naïve ploy didn't work. Stoker's widow, Florence Balcombe, was entirely dependent on the revenue generated by her late husband's work, and she sued Murnau's production company, Prana-Film, for copyright infringement.

The lawsuit was filed by the British Society of Authors. But, unfortunately for Florence, by the time the case arrived in court, Murnau had already squandered most of his finances on the film's lavish publicity campaign. His Prana-Film company was in receivership by that point, and he was broke. This didn't stop Florence from having the film banished, however; she pursued the case relentlessly, and in 1925 a German court ordered that all prints of the film be destroyed. Fortunately for film fans, several prints survived, despite Florence's best efforts. And when a print showed up in America in 1929, it was game over.

Almost a century on since it was made, *Nosferatu* stands as the resurrected, mouldering, rat-plagued ancestor of the vampire film. But it wasn't always looked upon in a positive light; the horror genre's first well-known historian, Carlos Clarens, dismissed the film as 'crude, unsubtle and illogical,' when he reviewed it in his landmark book, *An Illustrated History of the Horror Film* (pub. 1967). Back in a 1928 issue of *To-Day's Cinema*, the film was described as 'interesting, though not altogether impressive.' In the following year, it was reviewed unfavourably in the *New York Times*: 'It is the sort of thing one could watch at midnight without its having much effect upon one's slumbering hours.' However, there is at least *one* contemporary review that was positive, and it came from *Die Lichtbild-Buhne* in March 1922, around the time of its German release:

'*Nosferatu* is a sensational film, mainly because it departs so radically from the well-worn path of a hundred highly polished romances and machine-made adventure stories [...] Max Schreck's Nosferatu is brilliant both in make-up and movement. Henrik Galeen's scenario provides a firm framework. And in staging it, F W. Murnau has created a masterpiece.'

Due to the poor state of the surviving prints, *Nosferatu* was restored in 1994 in painstaking effort by a team of scholars who spent months carefully cleaning up the sound and audio quality and editing together the best preserved parts of the five remaining prints into a spanking new transfer. And though the restored version isn't perfect, it most certainly looks much better than those battered old prints that were smuggled out of Germany and played in New York in the late 1920s. Available nowadays on DVD, and crystallizing the vampire myth's long and varied evolution over the centuries, from the demonic succubi of ancient Greece and Babylon, to the predatory Count of Stoker's novel, the modern-day vampire was immortalized once and for all in Murnau's fright-fest.

Interestingly, with this film, Murnau also introduced a significant addition to the myth: the vampire's vulnerability to sunlight. In the novel, Count Dracula could emerge during the day suffering only a minor decrease in his powers, such as transformation. However, Nosferatu is destroyed when exposed to the rays of sun. And this susceptibility has since become an accepted norm in vampire films, in everything from *Near Dark* (1987) to *John Carpenter's Vampires* (1998) and dozens of others.

Perhaps the most impressive aspect of the film is Nosferatu himself, the pallid, fright-faced bloodsucker played by Max Schreck (whose surname translates as 'fear'). The eponymous creature of the night gives off a stark, frozen posture, like a frightened tree. Whether appearing as a long-clawed silhouette ascending a staircase, or as a balding demonic predator rising out of the hold on the Death Ship eager to be let loose among the unsuspecting public, once seen he is not so easily forgotten. The name Nosferatu derives from the Slavic word for 'plague bringer,' and with his army of scurrying rats amassing around his ankles, the vampire serves as a living embodiment of death itself. The pointy ears, jagged teeth and piercing eyes lend the creature an icy menace which still

looks particularly creepy almost a century later. Indeed, as far as horror anti-heroes go, Nosferatu must surely rank in the top ten creepiest and most iconic of all time.

Friedrich Wilhelm Murnau went on to make more movies in Germany before having a shot at the Hollywood big time. His other notable works include the Faustian effort, *The Last Laugh* (1924) and the classic, *Sunrise* (1927). He died in a car crash in Santa Barbara in 1931. He was just 43-years-old. Of the 21 films he made, 8 are considered lost or destroyed.

Haxan (1922)

(aka *The Witches*; aka *Witchcraft Through the Ages*)

Dir: Benjamin Christensen /Sweden /Denmark

Released on the 18 September.1922, just as the nights were drawing in in Northern Europe, *Haxan* was a film that captured the magic and menace of All Hallows' Eve and gave *Caligari* and *Nosferatu* a run for their money on the creepy horror front, and even managed to surpass those previous releases in many ways.

Danish film pioneer, Benjamin Christensen's infamous film is part documentary, part horror and part academic exercise that explores the themes of witchcraft and the diabolical from ancient times up until the – then – present day Europe. Still very much worth seeing today, *Haxan* comes on as a bizarre oddity that doesn't sit comfortably in any genre. Many modern film scholars view the work as a correlation between ancient superstition and misunderstandings about mental illness, but the film also works as demented entertainment in its own right. Everything from still images, stock footage, clay models and dramatic re-enactments are used to visualise the film, and this results in many bizarre images, such as an old witch revealing a rotten severed hand from a bundle of sticks; a woman giving birth to large demons; a witch's Sabbath; inquisition tortures; animalistic demons in the form of pigs and cats and birds, and even an appearance from Satan himself. The Surrealists especially appreciated the film, and it even gained a new lease of life in the late 60s when it was re-released on the midnight movie circuit with a new narration by cult writer, William Burroughs.

The film is arranged into seven chapters and begins with a documentary-style introduction that focuses on the history of superstition, from the ancient beliefs on the structure of the earth and the heavens, to the advent of witches in the Middle Ages. This sequence is illustrated entirely with images from history books, with visions of Hell, damnation, and sorcerers dancing with the Devil after dark. The inter-titles inform the viewers that 'All the witches had to show the Devil their respect by kissing his behind.'

Chapter 2 jumps right into a dramatic re-enactment set in the region of Brocken in North Germany. A maiden visits a witch called Karna at her den, which resembles a typical witch's lair with its boiling pots and unsavoury atmosphere. Karna is in the middle of using the stolen body parts of an executed thief to use in one of her spells. The maiden enters the dark den and asks for a potion that will win over the love of a pious man of the Church. Karna recommends that she 'Take a potion of cat feces and dove hearts, and boil them in the moonlight.' Cut to a later scene in which the maiden offers the foul concoction to a monk. He drinks it, not knowing what it is, and transforms into a sex fiend and forces himself upon her.

As word of the bewitching spreads, the Pope sends Inquisitors out to the town to investigate. Meanwhile, an old lady is accused of having 'evil eyes,' and is immediately imprisoned in a dungeon as a witch. Chapter 4 looks at how the Inquisitor judges determine a woman's guilt. First, they check the suspect's hair for witch's powder to ensure that there is no hocus pocus to protect her from justice. Then they lead her into the 'interrogation' room – they lead her in backwards so that she is unable to cast spells on the judges. Of course, her pleadings of innocence are not accepted as it could be the trick of the Devil talking through her, but a confession of guilt is *always* accepted as the truth. And, after having her feet crushed in a medieval block device, she confesses her sins. Not only does she admit to her own involvement in witchcraft, she also names other members of the coven, including Karna.

Viewers are then shown images of the coven flying over the town on their broomsticks. It's a primitive overlay shot (similar to the scene of the flying angels at the end of *Cabiria*), but there is a vintage, surreal charm about it as a nostalgic shot of days lost. Into this dream-like sequence, we see a naked young witch nestling in the woods at twilight as the coven flies above her head. The witch's are shown to be a figment of the girl's imagination – a bitter-sweet memory

of a sisterhood that is about to be destroyed by the Inquisition.

Next up, we're shown a re-enactment of a Witch's Sabbath and a dance with the Devil ritual in which the coven lands in the woods and frolics with demons. The women move in a circular dance while the demons pass among them and beat drums. Black rituals are also shown, under the leadership of a large ugly demon that is referred to as 'the Devil's Grandmother.' The misty twilight air hangs heavy, and there are also candles and skulls, pentagrams and ancient grimoires, and the witches gather around – 'the black mass spat on all that is holy.' Unchristened infants are tossed into a cauldron, and the witches engage in an orgy with the demons while the innocents are boiled alive. Finally, as a parting gesture, Satan bends over, and the witches line up to kiss his bare behind. Some kiss the left buttock, others the right, and one even puckers up and plants her lips right in the bull's eye.

Chapter 5 sees the rounding up of the coven by the Inquisitors. And meanwhile in the monastery, a young monk confesses his own sinful feelings of the flesh. His elder tries to remedy this with an act of 'Faith Healing,' in which the younger man is stripped and whipped. This sequence hints strongly at an S&M dynamic. The monk knows exactly the punishment that is to be dished out to him, and yet he insists on going through with the procedure, as if the punishment was the desired end all along. And the close-up shots of the monk's face as he finds exquisite pleasure in each sharp sting of the lash is unmistakable.

As British film-maker, Michael Reeves, demonstrated many years later with his *Witchfinder General* (1968), Christensen shows how the torture of witches was so vicious and lacking of any mercy or presumed innocence of the accused, that only a sadistic monster could possibly go ahead with such a profession. In fact, the more sadistic and fanatical the monk, the higher he was destined to rise through the ranks of the Church hierarchy. So, the most vicious monks made it to the top while the most marginalised and maligned women found themselves at the bottom – thus, medieval society effectively tied together its loose ends with the practice of the witch hunt. The criminals on top were unleashed on the criminals at the bottom in a convenient sado-masochistic purge that kept society on the pious path, like a snake constantly gnawing at the dead skin on its tail. It is mentioned in the film that it was mostly ugly old women who were accused of being witches, and also the young and pretty. Therefore, the witch burnings can be seen as a way of keeping the populace as a mediocre flock in which those who sunk too low, or those who were in danger of 'rising above their station' with their talents or pretty looks, were cast out of the fold and disposed of in brutal ways.

The world was clearly a very dangerous place in the days when superstition ruled. However, in the twentieth century, in an era when rationality had supposedly triumphed over folly, and atheism reigned supreme over religious dogma, the world was no closer to finding peace and harmony. Human conflict would always find a way to manifest itself, and just a month after the release of *Haxan*, the world saw the establishment of the first fascist state with Benito Mussolini's March on Rome in October 1922. The rise to power in Italy of fascism was symptomatic of a crisis that had gripped countries across Europe during the inter-war period. The gap between the wars was marked with class conflict, communist agitations, inflation, opposition to the liberal state, strikes, land occupations, and – in opposition – an increasing and aggressive nationalism, and a growing resurgence of the influence of the Church. The Bolshevik-style revolutionaries had misjudged and underestimated the patriotism and adherence to tradition of the Italians, and they were soon rounded up by the new regime for interrogation and imprisonment.

The final chapter of *Haxan* suggests a link between witches of the Middle Ages and the – then – modern-day phenomena of 'hysteria.' Hysterical women are shown to be in the possession of their fears and desires, a contrasting mix that leads to madness. Christensen gives an example of a sleep-walker who can't resist striking matches in her sleeping state – a dangerous act, and one made all the more puzzling as the woman had an intense fear of fire since her home burned down when she was a child. He also makes connections between the sexual lure of the Devil and repressed desires – how the Church had linked sex with the 'sins of the flesh.' Thus, repressed sexuality manifests itself in forbidden ways, such as when women are sleeping in bed; the object of their

desires – who is often made up of the same fear and desire, or 'sin' and 'flesh,' Devil and lover – takes possession of their psyches while they're in a vulnerable and unguarded state.

Of course, it's useful to remember that psychology is almost as slippery a concept as superstition itself. As an applied science, it is always morphing and changing, and theories that are celebrated one year are debunked and ridiculed the next. Also of note is how this hysteria was kept alive in art and film in the 20th and early 21st centuries, even if the field of psychology had long since left it behind. Notable films that later dealt with hysteria include Ken Russell's *The Devils* (1971), in which Sister Jeanne of the Angels (Vanessa Redgrave) becomes so obsessed with Father Grandier (Oliver Reed) that her desires become twisted by the Church teachings she had received all of her life, resulting in a madness of conflicting fears and desires. Sexuality is an evil sin, and she cannot stop fantasising about him, so therefore Father Grandier must be the Devil in the flesh. Similar hysterical female characters later showed up in Andrzej Zulawski's *Possession* (1981) and Lars Von Trier's *Antichrist* (2009), each one more explicit in their central theme.

In 1922, when *Haxan* was released, areas of Germany were also becoming a battleground for the Nazis and communists. Each group viewed the other as the ultimate evil coven of the day, and viewed themselves as the real pious ones; the men of knowledge and authority – same old story, different stripes.

Dr. Mabuse, Der Spieler (1922)

(*Dr. Mabuse, The Gambler*; aka *Dr. Mabuse, Parts 1 and 2*)
Dir: Fritz Lang /Germany
A huge hit in its native Germany at the time, this epic two-parter (totalling 195 minutes) includes everything a thrill-seeking audience member could possibly want – it's part thriller, part horror, and part political satire which includes sex and nudity, magic, art, comedy and impressive special effects. This early silent film was the first feature to introduce Dr. Mabuse, the super-villain and master of disguise who seems to embody the social ills of the era.

Mabuse's gang steals a trade agreement between Holland and Switzerland, as a deliberate ploy to cause a stock market crash, which the mastermind then capitalises on,

Rothschild style, by buying up all the dirt cheap shares and bagging himself a fortune in the process. He also ropes in a group of blind men to counterfeit bank notes, a sequence which must have hit quite a nerve with German viewers at the time as they were struggling in the post-WW1 Weimar Republic, where hyper inflation had rendered the Deutsche Mark all but worthless. Mabuse even orders the blind men to forge U.S. Dollars, as even fake American notes were worth more than genuine German currency. Of course, this being a Mabuse movie, you can expect lots of disguises as the villain selects a new identity for every day of the week.

Director Fritz Lang returned to the anti-hero more than a decade later with the talkie, *The Testament of Dr. Mabuse* (1933). Indeed, Lang waited until 1933 – when the Nazis had gained power – before he fled the country. Dr. Goebbels is said to have held a begrudging respect for his film-making talents, and even considered hiring him to direct films for the new regime. However, this didn't stop Goebbels from using *Dr. Mabuse* as an example to show how corrupt and degenerate the Weimar era was.

Raskolnikow (1923)
(aka *Crime and Punishment*)
Dir: Robert Wiene /Germany
Based on Fyodor Dostoevsky's classic novel, *Crime and Punishment* (pub. 1866), *Raskolnikow* seems to pick up right where *The Cabinet of Dr. Caligari* left off, dropping the viewers in the same twisted world of psychological nightmare. One of the greatest novelists of all time, Dostoevsky created characters that would dwell on philosophical and ideological matters, especially theology, morality and psychology. His stories are often shaped by ideological conflicts as philosophical problems are put to the test in the real world. And the conflict often results in strangely irrational behaviour in his protagonists as their actions betray the depths of their souls.

Rakolnikow is just such a character, a young student (though actor, Gregori Chmara, looks a little long in the tooth for the role), who gets an unshakeable idea in his head: murder is morally justified so long as the victim is a blight on society. With his judgement clouded by hunger and poverty, the young man selects as his victim the local slum lord and pawnbroker, Aliona (Toma), a miserly old crone who lives on the top floor of a run-down boarding house.

Raskolnikow pays her visit after dark and smashes her head in with an axe. However, Aliona's sister walks in on the act, and so Rasko ends up killing her, too. What follows is a fairly close adaptation of the book as the student's mind gradually disintegrates into a delirious state as both the police and his own guilty conscience round up on him.

Crime and Punishment was tailor-made for the German Expressionist treatment, and director Robert Wiene never lets the story stray too far from its central premise, making for a gripping cinematic experience. One of the great art directors of the Twentieth Century, André Andrejew, was in charge of the set designs, and he did a remarkable job. With its twisted buildings, misshapen windows, crooked staircases and grim tones, the film is actually far more effective than *Caligari* in reflecting the despair and psychological turmoil in a physical space. And, added to the torment is Wiene's deliberately avant-garde directorial style and the uncredited – and unnerving – jazz improvisations, which are effective in setting the viewer's nerves on edge from the opening shots.

Of course, the film didn't go down too well in its native land. Not only did the growing Nazi movement single it out as an example of the degeneracy of modern art, and accused the film of being populated entirely with drunks and maniacs, but even the art world stayed away from it as being too grim to bear. Which is unfortunate as the film certainly marked the next step on Wiene's artistic progression. In the following years, his work was kept deliberately tame in comparison with his earlier films, though he did deliver the influential horror classic, *Orlacs Hände* (*The Hands of Orlac*, 1924), in the following year. Still, he was later forced to flee Germany as the Nazis came to power. However, the German Expressionist influence lived on in everything from the avant-garde art films to the Universal horror cycle of the 1930s, the film noir trend in the 1940s, and beyond.

Married Love (1923)
(aka *Maisie's Marriage*)
Dir: Alexander Butler /UK
In 1918, Marie Stopes became a household name after the publication of her book on birth control, *Married Love, or Love in Marriage*. Hugely popular (it had sold out its six editions in a fortnight, and went on to 19 editions by

1931), she wrote the book to explain how women could indulge in the joys of sex without the unwelcome intrusion of pregnancy. The book was met with much derision in the British press.

With a wealth of royalties behind her, Stopes announced in 1922 her intention of making *Married Love* into a fictional drama film that would explore the concept of birth control in a dramatic setting. The BBFC rejected the script outright, but this didn't stop Stopes from launching her project into its production phase. What happened next did a lot to illustrate the changing times, as the British censors struggled to keep control and ultimately lost the battle. For a start, Stopes' worldwide reputation as a social reformer protected her work from being discarded outright. Therefore the censors had to be seen as taking her seriously. But chief censor, T. P. O'Connor, was also a Roman Catholic, and is said to have been personally appalled by the very idea of the film. He decided to handle the situation in a more sneaky manner by trying to unite the local councils on his side in a coordinated effort to bring down the ban hammer.

The film itself centres on Maisie Burrows (Lillian Hall-Davis), a parlourmaid in South London who is reluctant to marry her boyfriend, Dick (Rex Davis), due to concerns that doing so would result in a large brood of offspring, just like her own parents who had many children. Maisie's employer eventually has a word with her, and assures her that being married doesn't necessarily lead to an oversized family. Dick is later reunited with Maisie when he rescues her boss from a house fire, and in the aftermath of the blaze, they agree to marry.

The BBFC took more than six weeks to decide on the film's fate, during which time, O'Connor had invited members of the London City Council, along with an official from the Home Office (Sidney Harris, who later became chief censor of the BBFC in 1947), to view the film at BBFC headquarters in Soho. It was the fourth time the film had been screened in the office in as many weeks, and the attendees still couldn't decide on a way to proceed. Had it been an unknown film from an unknown producer, they could have banned it outright. But because Stopes was a name to be reckoned with, they knew they had to approach with caution. Over the next two weeks the parties agreed to several cuts and a title change before it could be granted a BBFC certificate.

The cuts themselves are quite revealing; O'Connor insisted on relegating Maisie's character a few rungs down on the class ladder. Thus, she was no longer a girl from Camberwell, but from a South London slum. Presumably he figured that if birth control was to be promoted in a picture film, it would be best if the film's protagonist was from the lower class. He also insisted that the film's title be changed to *Maisie's Marriage* as a way of avoiding the perceived effrontery of its original title. Finally, in a BBFC first, he also ruled that advertisements and posters for the film were forbidden from including the title of Stope's book on which the film was based.

However, cinema chains ignored the rulings by not only showing the film uncut, but also displaying its original title in large lettering outside theatres and on the marquees, no doubt with the hopes of cashing in on its relation to the infamous, best-selling book. Even the government was outraged by the blatant disregard of the BBFC's ruling, and a secret memo quickly circulated warning cinema licensees to obey the Board's recommendations. And when Stopes found out about this, she threatened to take the Home Office to court as she had never agreed to any of the cuts in the first place.

A meeting was arranged between Stopes and Harris, where he assured her that there was no intention of removing her name from the film or its advertising, but he refused to withdraw the memo. Marie Stopes' influence had therefore won over the combined powers of both the government and the BBFC in this instance. However, this was only a one-off case. Once the situation had blown over, the Board simply continued to work as it had done before. In fact, the *Maisie's Marriage* incident only cemented the BBFC's rule and influence, and by the end of the 1920s it was nigh on impossible for the public to see uncut films as the local councils had fallen in line and agreed to carry out the Board's ruling to the letter. From now on, if a film wasn't accompanied by a BBFC certificate, it would never see the light of a projector bulb.

Human Wreckage (1923)
Dir: Dorothy Davenport /USA

After the death of movie icon Wallace Reid in 1923, his widow Dorothy Davenport set out to produce a film with the hope of scaring the public away from narcotics. The result was *Human Wreckage* (1923), a very controversial film about a heroin addict (George Hackathorne) who later gets clean and testifies against his suppliers in court. Davenport herself co-stars (under her exploitative pseudonym, 'Mrs. Wallace Reid') as Ethel McFarland, who encourages her lawyer husband to defend the ex-junkie in court.

Unfortunately, the film is lost today, which isn't surprising considering the unorthodox way it was presented to the public. President of the MPPDA, Will Hays, had his concerns with the film, but ultimately let it go, presumably because the protagonist manages to clean up his act and is seen to be working for the good of society in the end. However, the film wasn't permitted to be screened in cinema chains. Instead, Davenport toured around the country with the film, screening it on the roadshow circuit (a distribution method later to be followed by Dwain Esper's *Maniac* [1934] and Tod Browning's *Freaks* [1932]). Meanwhile in Britain, BBFC secretary, Joseph Brooke Wilkinson, referred to *Human Wreckage* as 'the most dangerous film ever made,' and it was banned outright.

The Hands of Orlac (1924)
(Orig title: *Orlacs Hände*)
Dir: Robert Wiene /Germany
Perhaps Robert Wiene's most accomplished work as a director, *The Hands of Orlac* was the first of a much-imitated tale of a concert pianist (Conrad Veidt again) who loses his hands in a train crash only to have them surgically replaced by the hands of a recently executed serial killer. Much to his sorrow, Orlac can no longer play the piano, and worse, his new hands seem to have a mind of their own and seem to be hell-bent on strangling the woman he loves...

Much more conventional in style than his previous works – *Caligari*, *Genuine*, and *Raskolnikow* – *The Hands of Orlac* avoids the Expressionistic flourishes for the most part and succeeds in imbibing the film with a grittiness that helps to cement the story in a realistic way. Indeed, Wiene seemed much more concerned with atmosphere in his telling of Maurice Renard's dark tale, and there's barely a shot in the film that hasn't been designed to instil dread in its audience. Many modern-day viewers may find it a tad on the lengthy side, and the editors could have easily dropped a good 10-15 minutes

of extraneous footage for a much tighter pace, but nonetheless, Wiene succeeds in creating – and sustaining – an uneasy atmosphere throughout. The scenes in which Orlac examines his stranger's hands in horror are some of the most unnerving moments of 1920s cinema, with the protruding veins and tendons signifying the evil force that has invaded his flesh. Of course, the story has been re-told many times in the cinema in various ways, from the Hollywood classic, *Mad Love* (1935) and cheapjack B-pictures, such as *Hands of a Stranger* (1962), to the Hammer-esque variation in *The Hands of Orlac* (1960), and even Michael Caine coming under attack from the malevolent limb in *The Hand* (1981). Elsewhere, Jeff Fahay cops for a killer arm in *Body Parts* (1991), and a brain transplant leaves a reanimated corpse with a serial killer's brain in *Frankenstein* (1931). Also, there are a number of films that deal in eye transplants from killers, including *Body Bags* (1993), *The Eye* (2002) and *In the Eyes of a Killer* (2009).

Strike (1924)
(Orig title: *Stachka*)
Dir: Sergei Eisenstein /Soviet Union
Strike is, to this day, one of the most astonishing debut features ever made, and one chock full of innovative ideas, creative camera work, visual quirks and editing techniques. The story isn't necessarily anything new (it's basically an update of Zola's novel, *Germinal,* pub. 1885), but it attains an almost mesmerising quality thanks to director Sergei Eisenstein's cutting edge rhythmic montage-style. Set in and around a factory in Russia, the film kicks off with the theft of an expensive micrometer, and an innocent worker hangs himself after being accused by the factory bosses of stealing it. The worker's comrades immediately spring into action, and begin smashing the factory windows and confronting the police. A formal strike ensues, and the fat cat shareholders are shown to be greedy and hopelessly out of touch with the workers on the ground. With a stalemate reached and starvation looming, the military is finally sent in to deal with the strikers, and this results in a wholesale massacre inter-cut with images of a cow being slaughtered, to drive its message home.

With this, the first of the classic Soviet propaganda movies, the masses are presented as cyphers rather than fully fleshed-out characters (perhaps owing to the government edict of the time that forbade artists from venerating individual heroes of the struggle). And this results in a film that feels far more mythical than historical, as the story takes place in an unspecified past when the revolution was still in its infancy. The capitalists are shown as shady criminals in well-furnished rooms, consuming a seemingly endless supply of food and drinks while they plot their next move on countering the strike. They are portrayed as grotesque caricatures in top hats; overweight, greedy, and exposing rotting teeth as they smile. The horrors unfold in rhythmic fashion, leading to the massacre which, decades on, has been thought of as equally an indictment of Stalin as it is with the evils of capitalism. However, Lenin was still in charge when the film was made, and Stalin didn't take over as dictator until Lenin's death months later.

Battleship Potemkin (1925)
(Orig title: *Bronenosets Potyomkin*)
Dir: Sergei Eisenstein /Soviet Union
Strike was followed by the classic, *Battleship Potemkin* (1925). Also directed by Eisenstein, the film takes its inspiration from a real-life mutiny in which the crew of the Russian battleship *Potemkin* rebelled against the officers. The ship then arrives at the docks of Odessa, where the public greets the sailors as heroes, and honour the fallen comrade, Vakulinchuck (Aleksandr Antonov), who was shot dead by the villainous officer during the struggle. However, Cossack troops, loyal to the Tsar, arrive on the scene and open fire on the spectators, indiscriminately murdering men, women and children in a marching robotic fashion. Cue one of the most famous sequences in film history, as a mother is shot dead and her pram rolls perilously down the stairs to a fateful end (though not quite as shocking as the toddler being thrown off the roof in *Strike*). The sailors vow revenge for the massacre, and a fleet of ships pursue them on the ocean. The crew prepares to fire on the ships, but much to their joy, those vessels look to have undergone their own mutinies, and the comrades celebrate together.

Nothing more can be said about these films that hasn't already been said hundreds of times before since their release, except that though *Battleship* is a masterpiece of propaganda, *Strike* is actually the better made film. Of course, the British censors had expected these types of productions for years, but I'm certain that O'Connor and Brooke Wilkinson never anticipated such highly polished and technically accomplished works to arrive at their offices in 1926, as Russia was still seen as a backward country that was yet to fully reap the benefits of the industrial age. The BBFC didn't waste any time in banning the films outright. They would have been banned regardless, but 1926 was an especially volatile time as in May there was the General Strike, and the fear of working-class insurrection was palpable.

In opposition to the ban was the Film Society that was founded in 1925 by the Marxist aristocrat, Ivor Montagu. The Society included as members a who's who of intellectual heavyweights of the time, such as Bertrand Russell, Julian Huxley, John Maynard Keynes, G. B. Shaw, Roger Fry and Ellen Terry. H. G. Wells was their most vocal advocate, and he openly declared of the BBFC, 'we cannot allow ourselves to be ruled by a gang of mystery men.' In France, the police were ordered to burn every copy of *Battleship* they could get their hands on, which caused no end of problems, while in Germany both films played uncut. And this led to a young Nazi by the name of Joseph Goebbels to remark on *Battleship*: 'This is a marvellous film without equal in the cinema. The reason is its power of conviction. Anyone who had no firm political conviction could become a Bolshevik after seeing the film. It shows very clearly that a work of art can be tendentious, and even the worst kind of ideas can be propagated, if this is done through the medium of an outstanding work of art.' Goebbels' speech presumably explains why the Nazis had continued throughout the 1920s and early 1930s to violently disrupt screenings of the film in German cinemas.

Eisenstein himself visited London in 1929 and tried to have the film unbanned, but to no avail. Amusingly, he later recalled the time in his memoirs, *Beyond the Stars* (pub. 1995), in which he singled out Brooke Wilkinson and O'Connor of the BBFC for special attention: 'One of them is blind,' he wrote, 'and probably deals with the silent films; another one is deaf and so gets the sound films; the third one chose to die during the period that I was in London.'

Joyless Street (1925)

(Orig title: *Die freudlose Gasse*; aka *The Street of Sorrow*)

Dir: G. W. Pabst /Austria

In Austria, G. W. Pabst directed *Joyless Street*, a controversial drama starring a young Greta Garbo. Set in a town in Vienna during the Weimar Republic where hyper-inflation has caused mass hunger, the film is almost as pro-communist as the Soviet classics in the way it juxtaposes the lives of the rich and the poor. Like *Strike*, the rich shareholders sit around plotting on how they can up their profits, while the poor find themselves reduced to taking extreme measures in an effort to stay afloat.

The plot follows two women who live on Melchiorstrasse, one of the poorest streets in the neighbourhood. Marie (Asta Nielson) lives in a run-down apartment with her parents, while upstairs, Greta (Garbo), lives with her retired father and younger sister. Marie believes her boyfriend has been unfaithful, and accuses him of a murder she knows he didn't commit. Meanwhile, Greta collapses of hunger and exhaustion after queuing all night outside the butcher's shop, whose well-fed owner seems to take a perverse pleasure in the suffering all around him. Marie is gradually drawn into prostitution at Madame Grill's, a cabaret club that also serves as a discreet brothel for the rich men from out of town, and Greta is fired from her office job after rejecting the sexual advances of her lecherous boss. 'Get out!' he screams at her. 'I don't want girls of your kind here!'

To make matters worse, Greta's father has cashed in his entire pension fund and used it to invest in the shares of a mining company. He is certain that the family's financial woes are behind them, but little does he know that there are rich speculators working hard behind the scenes, manipulating the markets – they set off a rumour that the mining firm is about to be hit with strikes. And this causes the shares to plummet dramatically overnight. The shareholders make a killing by buying up all the shares at rock-bottom prices, while the old man loses everything and is left destitute. With no income whatsoever in the household, Greta takes a dancing job at Madame Grill's, just one step away from becoming a prostitute like Marie.

Events come to a head with murder – the butcher had accepted sexual favours from the local women in exchange for frozen meat, and after having his wicked way with a mother with a young child, he reveals that he has no more meat left to give. So she kills him in fury. The masses revolt against the nightclub and burn it to the ground, killing many inside, and Greta is saved from of a life of prostitution by a former lodger who works for the American Red Cross.

The first of a string of controversial films by Pabst which helped to launch the careers of Garbo, along with Nielson, Louis Brooks and Leni Riefenstahl, *Joyless Street* was one of the most censored films of the decade, and exists in dozens of different versions that vary wildly in length. Surprisingly, the BBFC passed it but with extensive cuts, while other cuts are almost incomprehensible due to the amount of footage snipped from the prints. In its original form, the film ran for two-and-a-half-hours, but for many years it was only available in a paltry 60-minute version, which not only dropped the entire story of Marie, but also the entire ending, too.

Perhaps for this reason, the film isn't as well-known as Pabst's later efforts, such as *Pandora's Box* (1929) and *Diary of a Lost Girl* (1929), from his early period, but *Joyless Street* can certainly stand shoulder-to-shoulder with them in every way, especially in its uncut form. For all its bleak mood and misfortune, the film was at least honest enough to portray a realistic view of its time and place. And look out for an appearance from Dr. Caligari himself, Werner Krauss, in typically chameleon-like mode as the proud Metzger von Melchiorstrasse. Thanks to the efforts of Austrian Filmarchiv, the full 151-minute uncut edit is now fully digitized and available on DVD.

The Phantom of the Opera (1925)

Dir: Rupert Julian [and Edward Sedgwick, Lon Chaney, and possibly others, uncredited] /USA

In 1920s Hollywood, Universal studios began experimenting with horror films by taking European Gothic stories and adapting them for the screen. According to horror historian, David J. Skal, head honcho at Universal, Carl Laemmle, had no interest in horror or the macabre at all; in fact, he found the idea distasteful. It was actually his son and heir, Carl Laemmle Jr. who had developed a fascination for Gothic horror stories, having read the old classics of Stoker, Shelley and Stevenson in his childhood. The young Carl Jr. was being primed to take over the corporation, and in the years running up to his inheritance in 1929, he was encouraged to take more of an unofficial front seat role in the day-to-day running of the studio.

'Junior's' eventual running of Universal proved disastrous in the long term, despite producing a string of classics in his time. The problem was, he spent far too much money on projects with not enough returns. For every blockbuster hit like *Dracula* (1931) and *Frankenstein* (1931), there were a number of flops, and by 1936 he was removed from his position indefinitely. The signs of his extravagance were clear to see in *The Hunchback of Notre Dame* (1923), a project he had practically begged his father to produce. The film was a hit, grossing around $3 million on its initial run, and this success seemed to spur the Laemmle's on to take a chance on another Gothic novel, Gaston Leroux's mystery, *The Phantom of the Opera* (pub. 1910).

'You're dancing on the tombs of tortured men!' The first feature film adaptation of Leroux's novel is fondly remembered today for its impressive – but brief – Technicolor sequence in which the phantom shows up at the masked ball dressed as Edgar Allan Poe's Red Death (Poe was another of Junior's childhood literary heroes). Other stand-out moments include the falling chandelier scene, the trips down into the strange underworld beneath the Paris Opera House, and of course, the phantom's unmasking which is hands down the scariest moment of the silent era. The scene in which Mary Philbin reaches out and snatches the mask away while the phantom plays the organ is still a very tense moment to this day. That scene alone ensures the film's rightful place in this book – audiences were literally terrified by Chaney's grotesque and nose-less make-up effects. Ray Bradbury later admitted that the scene traumatised him for life!

If Leroux's novel remains utterly unconvincing in its plot turns, director Rupert Julian does little to paper over the cracks in this screen adaptation – though it later became clear that others had intervened in the making of the picture, so it would be unfair to lay the blame entirely at Julian's feet. The beautiful set of the opera house still stands intact to this day at Universal Studios – it's the oldest film set in the world, and remains out-of-bounds to the general public (the curious can, however, enjoy a brief tour of the set by watching the documentary, *Universal Horror* [1998]). Lon Chaney's performance as the doomed phantom is also one of the most fondly remembered of the silent era

– the smartly dressed violent ghoul, racked by his own mental tortures as he attempts to lure his favourite soprano into the rat-infested sewers is as memorable a villain as they come.

A Page of Madness (1926)
(Orig title: *Kurutta Ippeiji*)
Dir: Teinosuke Kinugasa /Japan

As early as 1926, the influence of experimental European cinema was having an impact in the Far East. Young pretender, Teinosuke Kinugasa, had absorbed the worlds of Robert Wiene's *The Cabinet of Dr. Caligari* and Sergei Eisenstein's *Battleship Potemkin* (despite those films being banned in Japan), noting the 'Montage of Attractions' and the dark psychological expressionism therein. He attempted to combine those artistic elements with a kabuki sensibility, creating a uniquely Japanese art film.

A Page of Madness tells the story of an old sailor who takes a janitor's job at an insane asylum. His wife has been a patient there since attempting to drown their son years earlier. To explain any more about the plot would be altogether pointless, as it's very much a film that runs less on narrative than on the deranged mood and performances, as the tale is pretty much viewed through the eyes of madness.

Inspired by Murnau's *The Last Laugh* (1925), Kinugasa opted to tell his story without the use of inter-titles, and instead communicated with audiences purely on aesthetics using montage, superimposition, cross-cutting, and distorted images as a way of shifting between different layers of reality. The result is perhaps the only surviving example of Japan's avant-garde output of the 1920s. The film was considered lost for around 45 years, and during that time it garnered a legendary reputation among cineastes worldwide. The idea of *A Page of Madness* seemed to haunt the blunt monochrome visuals of *Titicut Follies* (1967), the whimsical surrealism of the work of Seijun Suzuki, and the elaborate theatrics of Shuji Terayama.

Miraculously, a print showed up in Kinugasa's garden shed in the early 1970s. Prints were made and the film was re-released in theatres across the world, albeit in shortened form. The original cut of *Page* was 500 metres longer than the one available today. Most sources – *Wikipedia*, *IMDb*, *AllMovie*, etc – list the running time as 60-minutes. However, a 78-minute version was made available in 2007. Whether it's the same version at a different speed is unclear, but it's a miracle that the film survives at all. Indeed, one of the great tragedies of early film is how many prints have been lost or destroyed. Japan was hit hard in this regard, and there is next to nothing left of Japanese film before 1923 when the Kanto earthquake destroyed the Nikkatsu film depot (Nikkatsu's archives were destroyed a second time at the end of World War II). Of the roughly 7000 films made in Japan in the 1920s, only around 1% of them survive today. *A Page of Madness* was only saved from oblivion because Kinugasa owned the materials and kept them in his shed.

The re-release of *A Page of Madness* coincided with a slew of other madhouse flicks unleashed around the same time, from the Hollywood favourite, *One Flew Over the Cuckoo's Nest* (1975) and the anti-Franco Spanish oddity, *Mansion of Madness* (1973), to the drive-in chiller of *Silent Night, Bloody Night* (1972) and the British art-house shocker, *The Other Side of Underneath* (1972).

Mother (1926)
Dir: Vsevolod Pudovkin /Soviet Union

Set in 1905 during the upheaval of the Revolution, *Mother* is similar to *Battleship Potemkin* in the way it uses a simple story to propagate a message of defiance and struggle designed to boost the morale of the victorious working class. It was a transgression that kept the film out of British cinemas for forty years.

Bosses at a local factory learn that a strike is immanent. They furtively hire a group of thugs to disrupt the action, but the strike goes ahead. After a tense stand-off in the street, violence breaks out, and the strikers are forced to flee when gun shots are fired. A worker is cornered in a bar and beaten to death, but not before he unloads a pistol on the thugs, fatally wounding an older man.

One of the organisers of the strike, Pavel Vlasov (Nikolai Batalov), later learns that it was his drunken, abusive father who was killed – and who was recruited by the thugs in exchange for drinks. Father's body is brought home just as Mother discovers a small cache of firearms under the floorboards. Government troops are brought in to 'restore peace,' but are soon behaving as a strong arm of the state when they invade Pavel's home. The guards seize him, and Mother panics and reveals the hiding place of the weapons in the hope that the Officer will show leniency and let her son go. However, not only are the weapons seized as evidence, but Pavel is arrested, too.

Sentenced to a term of hard labour (the Judge doesn't say for how long), Pavel is visited in the holding cell by Mother. She tells him that his comrades at the factory have arranged a march on the prison as a front for him to escape. However, as word spreads in the factory, the bosses get wind of it. And this sets up the tragic finale: The prisoners stage a violent riot and are massacred by the armed guards. Pavel manages to escape, and he runs for his life through the slush and snow, dodging the guards' bullets until he reaches the oncoming march of his comrades. He embraces Mother for the last time when Tsarist troops arrive on horseback and mercilessly open fire on the workers. Mother embraces her dead son and then rises to her feet. Surrounded by dead bodies and chaos on all sides, she holds her flag aloft and stands defiantly as the Tsar's horses gallop towards her at breakneck speed. She has no intentions of stepping aside, and the troops have no intentions of manoeuvring the horses around her. And when she is felled, her body is trampled on by hundreds of racing horses to the strains of The Internationale.

Based on the novel by Maxim Gorky (pub. 1905), *Mother* was the first of Vsevolod Pudovkin's 'revolution trilogy,' that continued with *The End of St. Petersburg* (1927) and *Storm Over Asia* (1928). The film portrays the communist workers as plucky underdogs even though communism had reigned victorious in Russia for almost a decade when the film was made. The political left still view themselves much in the same way today, even though their ideas are held as the universal standard in institutions the world over. And it's interesting to see how this strange dichotomy had set in to the culture so early. The lifeblood of the left depends on its self-image as the 'outsider,' the dogged hero fighting against the system. Even if communism conquered the entire world, it would still see itself as the underdog, and never the establishment. And that's probably why the Soviet classics are invariably set in the past during heroic times of struggle.

Mother is one of the better films to come out of the Soviet Union during that era. It isn't held in quite the same high regard as Eisenstein's ground-breaking efforts, but it has been very influential on world cinema, going on to influence social realism and neorealism in Italy, as well as a diverse group of film-makers. Sergio Leone in particular drew a lot from this early classic, and you can see the clear influence in his spaghetti westerns of the 1960s, especially in the stand-off scene between the strikers and thugs; combining wide shots and intense close-ups, the tension is expertly sustained as the opposing forces are seen gritting their teeth and their hands hovering close to their weapons, ready to strike in a split second. Also, the finale set on an open street looks like a Leone set, with sleet and snow banks standing in for the sun rays and desert dust. It's the original *The Good, the Bad and the Ugly* of the wild East. But, while Leone used water and scorching heat as metaphors for strife and salvation, Pudovkin's original used breaking ice as a similar visual metaphor to symbolise the breaking down of the Tsarist regime.

Mother's treatment in Britain was indicative of the increasing cooperation between the BBFC and local councils. While only three years previously the London City Council and Home Office opposed the planned banning of *Married Love*, and instead settled on the compromise of extensive cuts and a title change. With *Mother*, it was the other way around: chief censor, T. P. O'Connor, watched the film at home and concluded that the harsh, unflattering scenes of poverty and despair would ultimately discourage Brits from the path of communism, and he intended to pass the film uncut. Whether his judgement was borne of sympathy for the Mother character (who is heard early on referring to the strikers as 'those trouble makers'), or a case of the growing sophistication of the subversive elements of Soviet propaganda, in the way its subtle message almost fooled the President of British film censorship, is difficult to say. But one thing for certain is the fact that when word got round of O'Connor's intended leniency on the film, the Home Office immediately piled on the pressure, and just a few days later O'Connor agreed to ban it outright.

Socialist philosopher, Bertrand Russell, was particularly annoyed by the news of the ban, and he arranged a secret screening at the Film Society. Spurred on by this, the workers' film society, the Masses Film and Stage Guild, approached the London City Council for permission to screen *Mother*, along with other banned Soviet works. The request was denied, however, as it was considered a 'breach of the peace' to screen the films, whether in public or private. The uproar against the decision was met by the Conservative chairwoman of the Council's entertainment committee, Rosamund Smith, who issued a statement in which she justified the decision: 'I don't think anyone could be more opposed to censorship than I am,' she insisted. 'But I think we are up against something quite different in these Russian films. I feel that communism is a great deal more than the doctrine of a political party, and I am not prepared to give the authors of these films any right to publish their propaganda in this country. [...] I do not think we should give any preference to people whom we thoroughly distrust.'

With that, *Mother* was barely seen in Britain for the next forty years until it was restored with a new soundtrack and re-released in the late 1960s. By that time, of course, the film was considered one of the classics of the early Soviet period. Indeed, it's often overlooked compared to *Potemkin*, *October* and *The New Babylon*, but *Mother* can stand as one of the finest films of its time. The scene in which prisoners huddle and cower in a corner with nowhere to run while the guards casually shoot at them is one of the most haunting scenes of the silent era.

Flesh and the Devil (1926)
Dir: Clarence Brown /USA
The year 1926 went out with a bang and another tragic ending involving ice. *Flesh and the Devil* premiered on Christmas Day and shows Greta Garbo behind the scenes struggling to adjust to the MGM way of doing things. But, by the time the film was raking in its profits, Garbo had successfully navigated the terrain of Hollywood's star-maker system, and she became one of the highest earning actresses of the time.

A lurid tale of love and death, *Flesh and the Devil* centres on the dangerous temptress, Felicitas (Garbo), whose stunning beauty and powers of persuasion helps to ruin the lives of a succession of fawning men. The first to fall is her husband, a Count, who catches her smooching with a young man on their bed. Infuriated, he challenges the man, Leo (John Gilbert) to a duel. And in a remarkable sequence shot in silhouette, Leo survives the encounter victorious (the duel scene inspired a similar sequence in Howard Hughes' *Hell's Angels* [1930]). However, the death of the Count doesn't go unpunished; despite winning the duel honourably, Leo is court marshalled and sentenced to spend five years in Africa. Hopelessly in love with Felicitas, he asks his childhood friend, Ulrich (Lars Hanson), to look after her while he is gone. Ulrich honours his old friend's request, and even ensures that his sentence is reduced to three years. However, when Leo returns home, his dreams of being reunited with Felicitas are shattered when he learns that Ulrich has been looking after his beloved far too much – they are now *married*. And, to make matters *more* agonising, Felicitas seems open to having an affair with Leo. Thus, the twisted love triangle spirals out of control, leading to an unavoidable tragic finale...

A solid hit for MGM, ensuring a healthy profit margin for the studio's risky gamble of green-lighting such a sultry enterprise, the film's success only convinced the studio heads that sex was a sure fire way to sell tickets. Garbo and director Clarence Brown, along with expert cinematographer William Daniels, collaborated on further projects in the ensuing years, including *A Woman of Affairs* (1928), *Anna Christie* – their first 'talkie' together – (1930), *Romance* (1930), and *Inspiration* (1931) – all box-office hits, but none of them lived up to *Flesh and the Devil*, a pure one-off that casts a dark spell that has rarely been replicated in the cinema since.

The film is best remembered today for the sizzling screen chemistry of Garbo and leading man Gilbert, as the pair became romantically involved on set (quite literally, according to Brown, who claims that the scene on the bed was left to play out in real life, with the staff leaving the building to allow the love-birds an hour of privacy. 'I didn't even call "cut," he insisted. 'I just shut the camera off, and we left them to it.'). However, watching the film all these years after the fact, and viewers will be stunned, not just by the performances and impressive visual ideas, but also by how much the look of the film made its mark on Hollywood productions for the next decade and beyond. It holds a uniquely pining atmosphere, where nothing ends well, and all of life's dreams end in disaster and heartache. As such, the film serves as a forerunner of the lurid tales that would proliferate the screen in the pre-code years ahead. And Daniels' photography is so sharply contrasting of light and dark, you'd be forgiven for thinking you were watching a film noir from the 1940s.

In Paul Rotha's book, *The Film Till Now: A Survey of the Cinema* (pub. 1930), he praised *Flesh and the Devil*, describing it as 'A film of more than passing cleverness... the theme is sheer undiluted sex, and [Clarence] Brown uses a series of close-ups to get this across with considerable effect.' Many years later, even the legendarily stuffy Leslie Halliwell offered a begrudging recommendation, calling it a 'hokey but good-looking melodrama.' As expected, the BBFC wasn't so kind; they insisted on cutting around twenty-three minutes of footage (about a quarter of the film's running time) before granting a certificate.

Metropolis (1927)
Dir: Fritz Lang /Germany

The word 'metropolis' derives from the Greek for 'mother city,' and Fritz Lang's silent epic is certainly the mother of sci-fi cinema; a landmark film whose chequered history has been marred by missing reels, censorship and studio interference. However, each new generation of film-goers were treated to a new piece of the puzzle, to the point where today 95% of the film that originally premiered in Berlin in January 1927 is available for the curious to see for themselves.

Based on the serialised novel by Thea von Harbou (who was married to Lang at the time), *Metropolis* opens with a panoramic view of a gleaming Futurist city with pristine skyscrapers fashioned in Bauhaus and Cubist designs. It's a world in which the elite and their families live on high, while the underclass are forced to toil away in underground labour to keep the city running. The protagonist is Freder (Gustav Fröhlich, of Lang's epic, *Die Nibelungen* [1924]), who's father had built the city. When Freder sets eyes on the beautiful Maria (Brigitte Helm), he follows her down to the underworld where she comes from, and sees for himself the gruelling labour that goes into making his existence a pleasant one. Meanwhile, his father, Frederson (Alfred Adel), strikes up a delicate alliance with his former love rival, Rotwang (Rudolf Klein-Rogge, who later showed up in Lang's *The Testament of Dr. Mabuse* [1933]). Both men had loved Freder's mother who died giving birth, but while Frederson has learned to forget the past, Rotwang seems to have been driven slightly mad by her death and continued absence.

Rotwang has created a mechanoid robot to

replace his lost love, and Frederson convinces him to give the 'bot Maria's face. Maria holds influence over the workers underground, and the plan is to install a robotic version of her as a replacement as a way of controlling the workers and igniting their revolutionary fervour so that they can be crushed by the state. However, in the meantime, Freder falls in love with the real Maria, and when the robotrix is unveiled on a stage performing an erotic dance routine, the workers are driven into a sexual frenzy, and they destroy the machines – which, in turn, causes the vast reservoirs nearby to burst and flood the city. Freder and Maria manage to rescue the workers' children from their homes, and in the end, the devious Frederson comes face to face with the mob whose misery he is responsible for...

The film opened on the 10 January in a 153-minute director's cut. And though the critics of the time wrote positively about it in the press, *Metropolis* tanked at the box-office. If it was just another film, the producers may have simply shrugged and moved on to the next project. But because Ufa – Germany's biggest film company – had spent around 5 million Reichsmarks on bringing it to the screen, they panicked and set about chopping it down to a more user-friendly running time in the hope of recouping some of the losses. So, the film was practically gutted – Gottfried Huppertz's score was scrapped, many sub-plots were cut, and even the heroic ending in which Freder finally gets to shine was dropped onto the cutting room floor. However, the tampering only made things worse, as the film was now overly silly, simplistic and trailing many loose ends. Ufa narrowly avoided bankruptcy as the paltry profits from the film's initial run amounted to little more than 75,000 Reichsmarks.

A 115-minute edit was released in America and the UK in March 1927, while an even shorter (91-minute) version was re-released in Germany in August. Those truncated versions were famously hammered in the *New York Times*, whose critic Mordaunt Hall called it a 'technical marvel with feet of clay.' H. G. Wells wrote a particularly angry response after a screening, summing up his opinion that it was 'quite the silliest film.' Other contemporary reviews objected to the lewd dance scene, and indeed, for this reason – as well as for its scenes of workers raging against the machine – the BBFC demanded substantial cuts before

granting it a certificate.

In Germany, the Nazis were fascinated by *Metropolis*; particularly its final message of harmony between the workers and the bourgeoisie – future propaganda minister, Joseph Goebbels, made a speech in the following year in which he paraphrased the final inter-title of the film, alluding to the workers and government as the 'head and hand' of the state. Lang himself divorced von Harbou soon after as she had become a fanatical member of the Nazi Party. And while other names in the film industry began fleeing the country – such as Marlene Dietrich, Robert Wiene, Carl Mayer, and many others – Lang stayed behind, and only reached for his passport in 1933 when Goebbels expressed an interest in recruiting him to make films for the new regime.

Speaking of fascism, the Italians had largely ignored the potential propaganda power of fictional films up to that point, and instead concentrated much more on taking control of the country's newsreels. However, after viewing *Metropolis*, Mussolini himself personally ordered the censoring of the film. Specifically, he objected to the scenes in which 'the workers slowly walk to work,' and demanded that all such scenes be cut. The fact that a future fantasy film could include such blatant communistic connotations seemed to be a wake-up call for the Italian regime, as they immediately began clamping down on any such messages, whether the directors of films had intended such messages to be there or not. Also in 1927, the regime made it mandatory for all cinemas in the country to screen the fascist *LUCE* newsreel prior to every feature film.

As for *Metropolis*, the BBC broadcast a version with an electronic score by William Fitzwater and Hugh Davies in 1975. It was very well received, unlike Giorgio Moroder's colourised version in 1984 (at 83-minutes) which included a pop soundtrack with the likes of Adam Ant, Freddie Mercury and Bonnie Tyler. Of course, by the 1980s the film's reputation had improved, and *Metropolis* had entered the popular imagination, with clips appearing in music videos and adaptations showing up in comic book form. Even the critics had mellowed somewhat, perhaps out of nostalgia for its epic Jazz Age vision. In 1982, *The New Yorker* magazine referred to the film as 'a wonderful, stupefying folly,' while Roger Ebert described it as 'more powerful today than when it was made.'

In 2002, Kino oversaw a drastic restoration with the inclusion of much of the footage that had been discovered in archives and hadn't seen the light of a projector bulb since the late 1920s. This version included the sub-plots involving the characters Josaphat and Worker 11811. Running for 118-minutes, it was still 35 minutes short of Lang's original cut, but it was a revelation to see that the film had far more substance to it than being merely a 'technical marvel on feet of clay.' It was such an overhaul of new material it was like watching an entirely new film, and many critics and fans found themselves having to re-evaluate their opinions on the film. Perhaps the most impressive addition to this version was the reinstatement of Gottfried Huppertz's original score, which is by far the finest musical accompaniment of the silent era, and it's such a shame that generations of film fans never had the pleasure of hearing it – it's a big, booming brass bonanza; operatic, bombastic and quintessentially cinematic. For a while, the Kino version was seen as the last and most complete version of *Metropolis* we would ever see as all other materials were considered long lost. However, a full uncut copy was found in a film museum in Argentina in 2008. It was a very old copy, poorly stored, and some 5 minutes of footage was unsalvageable, but after much restoration work, the final 148-minute version was released theatrically and on Blu-Ray in 2010.

So in 2010, 83 years after its premier, long-time admirers and newcomers alike were able to see the film more or less as Fritz Lang had originally intended. And what a difference the new-old version makes – at last, viewers can finally appreciate how rich a film it is, as the future city is destroyed by one man's love, another's greed and a crazed inventor with a metallic hand. Scenes that had previously been shown out of sequence, if at all, now emerge as vital and necessary to the plot. And by illustrating the many sub-plots and motivations that were previously discarded, the characters now appear to be far more than mere cardboard archetypes.

Also impressive are the special effects, which were all created painstakingly 'in camera,' long before process shots became the norm. And the new-old version of *Metropolis* shows it to be by far the most FX-laden of Lang's career, with a series of complex multiple exposures, stop

motion sequences, incredibly detailed miniature sets, mirrored matte paintings, and the innovative touch of adding boldly animated inter-titles, such as during the 'Moloch!' vision.

Most astonishing, however, is that what was once considered a spectacular but empty fantasy of fairytale simplicity, can now be clearly seen as anything but. With the original cut, we can now see that the film was designed less as a future fantasy than as a mythical statement on the universal themes of power and control. Much like D. W. Griffith's *Intolerance*, made more than a decade earlier, we see present day hi-tech scenarios played out with historical equivalents. But while Griffith had fumbled with the idea in his epic, and failed to execute the concept as well as he would have liked, here Fritz Lang strikes a perfect balance between the past and present – thus, not only are the buildings kept with a deliberate Art-deco design, but we also see the robotrix Maria being burned at the stake by the medieval-style mob, a re-telling of the biblical story, The Tower of Babel, with obvious parallels to the destruction of the city state, and a nightmarish vision of the workers being marched up a flight of stairs and sacrificed into the jaws of Moloch the ancient deity. The Japanese, having a long history of folklore and the mythical, seemed to understand this long-obscured aspect of the film, and the anime remake of *Metropolis* (2001), which was released before Kino's first restoration, instinctively picks up on the mythical elements and retro-future style, and even adds its own unique cultural flavour for a candy-coloured, hi-tech vision of a futuristic Jazz Age.

Indeed, even in its truncated form, *Metropolis* has been hugely influential over the decades. Von Harbou may have lifted one or two ideas from H. G. Wells for her novel and screenplay, but the film version of *Time Machine* (1960) certainly returned the favour with its vision of the innocent Eloi who serve as sacrifices for a race of underground mutants known as Morlocks. Charles Chaplin's *Modern Times* (1936) visually quotes Lang's masterpiece throughout as a lowly factory worker struggles to make it through his shift. Elsewhere, *2001: A Space Odyssey* (1968), *Star Wars* (1977), *Blade Runner* (1982), *Brazil* (1985), *1984* (1984), and *Judge Dredd* (1995), all borrowed elements from *Metropolis*, from the look and feel to the retro-future style, and the idea of the rich living on top while the underclass wage war from below. Perhaps the most interesting update of *Metropolis* is George Romero's unlikely treatment in *Land of the Dead* (2005), in which a fortress city comes under siege from a horde of shuffling zombies who are clearly a stand-in for the climactic flood and rampaging mobs of Lang's classic.

A whole book could be written just on the occult symbolism in the film, the most glaring example of which is the inverted pentagram etched onto the wall behind the Machine-Man's throne. The upside-down pentagram is a symbol of chaos and Satanic disorder, and the robotrix is eventually sent underground to spread discontent among the working class. And its interesting to note the number of pop music videos which include clips from the film and its symbolism, with many pop stars seemingly clued in to some esoteric knowledge as if their musical missions are to spread chaos and disorder among the masses. Beyonce, Freddie Mercury, Kylie Minogue, Lady Gaga, and many many others have performed dressed up as the programmed Robo-Maria. Apparently, there are a lot of 'Marias' out there today stirring things up.

The film has taken a long hard road to near completion over the years, and the characters and iconic images are certainly indelible nowadays; the shuffling slaves changing shifts; the spectacular creation of the robotrix (which was a major influence on a similar scene in James Whale's *Frankenstein* [1931] a few years later); Freder struggling with the arms of the giant clock; Rogge's occult-fixated Frankenstein of the future; Brigitte Helm's mechanical menace driving men insane with lust and leading an apocalyptic riot. Unmissable.

The Unknown (1927)
Dir: Tod Browning /USA

Among the most fondly remembered of Tod Browning's films – alongside *Dracula* (1931) and *Freaks* (1932) – is *The Unknown*, a silent classic which hit screens in June 1927, mere months before the first 'talking pictures' became all the rage. Starring the 'Man of a Thousand Faces,' Lon Chaney, as Alonzo, a criminal with a deformed hand which includes an extra thumb, *The Unknown* sees Alonzo evade police capture by hiding out at a travelling circus. There he pretends to be an armless knife-thrower, and becomes smitten with his assistant, Nanon (a very young Joan Crawford), who is also the daughter of the gypsy circus owner. Nanon just so happens to hold an aversion to being embraced by men – particularly being held by the circus strongman, Malabar the Mighty (Norman Kerry). This is convenient for both characters as it means Alonzo can spend lots of time with her without her fearing being touched by him.

Alonzo ends up killing her father when his secret limbs are seen. And soon after, he undergoes surgery to have his arms removed, out of love for Nanon. Ironically, when he returns to the circus after his lengthy recovery, he is horrified to learn that Nanon has gotten over her phobia and – worse – has now fallen in love with the strongman. What follows is a devious attempt at revenge by the now genuinely armless Alonzo, as he engineers an appalling 'mishap' whereby Malabar will lose his arms in a strongman stunt gone wrong...

The Unknown is one of the great horror films of the silent era, and one that has aged much better than contemporary fright flicks, such as *Phantom of the Opera* (1925) and *The Man Who Laughs* (1928), despite its ludicrous premise and convenient plot turns. Predictably, the critics of the time found much to condemn, particularly Crawford's scantily dressed Nanon, and *The New York Post* famously slammed the film: 'A visit to the dissecting room in a hospital would be quite as pleasant, and at the same time more instructive.' On the 13 June 1927, the review in the *New York Times* objected to Chaney's character, complaining that he 'deteriorates from a more or less sympathetic individual to an arch-fiend.' However, perhaps the most dramatic write-up on the film appeared a couple of weeks later in *Harrison's Reports*: 'One can imagine a moral pervert of the present day, or professional torturers of the times of the Spanish Inquisition... enjoying screen details of the kind set forth in *The Unknown*. But it's difficult to fancy average men and women of a modern audience in this enlightened age being entertained by such a thoroughly fiendish mingling of bloodlust, cruelty and horrors. Such a picture is enough to turn the ordinary person's stomach inside out... Of Mr. Chaney's acting it is enough to say that it is excellent, of its kind. Similar praise might well be given the work of a skilled surgeon engaged in ripping open the abdomen of a patient. But who wants to see it?'

Chaney was famous for playing grotesque and often physically deformed characters, and he would often endure physical discomfort in order to bring those characters to life – for *The Hunchback of Notre Dame* (1923), for example, he endured unhealthy spine contortions as he carried around a 50lb chunk of plaster on his back. However, it wasn't just the physical demands that made his roles challenging; for *The Unknown* he was also compelled to be drawn to the darker realms of the human mind so that he could understand his strange outsider character, Alonzo, the tragic anti-hero whose attempts at a twisted act of evil stems from the cruellest twist of fate.

Like many films from this period, *The Unknown* was long considered lost until a copy was discovered in France in 1968. The director of Cinematheque Francais, Henri Langlois, later gave an amusing lecture in which he recalled the trouble of finding the print. According to him, many of the reels in the archive were listed as *l'inconnu*, or 'unknown,' which made it far more difficult to locate the Browning film among the heaving shelves of anonymous film cans. The version available today is missing a few early scenes, but according to historians, the lost footage does little to obstruct the story.

London After Midnight (1927)
Dir: Tod Browning /USA
The first major American vampire film, and one which is lost today (check those basements and attics!), *London After Midnight* reunited writer/director, Tod Browning, with Lon Chaney for a quirky mystery set in England. Based on Browning's own short story, *The Hypnotist*, *London After Midnight* was likely given the green light by MGM as a way of cashing in on the success of the hit stage play, *Dracula*, starring Bela Lugosi. In 2002 Turner Classic Movies commissioned Rick Schmidlin to re-create the film by piecing together around 200 production stills. The photographs were enlarged and accompanied with dialogue and scene descriptions on inter-titles, with a copy of the original script, and a score by Robert Israel was also commissioned. The 45-minute recreation premiered on Halloween night 2003 to commemorate the 75th anniversary of the original film. The result was far from perfect, but it should give viewers an idea of what Browning had intended.

This time, the 'Man of a Thousand Faces' plays two roles: the suave inspector of Scotland Yard, Edward C. Burke, and the 'Man with the Beaver Hat,' a 'vampire' who dwells in a house with a female vamp, Luna the Bat Girl (Edna Tichenor). The plot begins with the death of a country gentleman of a gunshot wound. A suicide note was left at the scene, but inspector Burke suspects murder. His plan to catch the elusive killer involves a grand charade in which he and a troupe of hired actors masquerade as the ghouls who supposedly haunt the dead man's house. Five years later, the family in the neighbouring house come to suspect that the building next door is indeed haunted after they hear a series of strange sounds coming from there. The servants of the house are horrified to see a pair of ghouls on the grounds – the Man with the Beaver Hat and the Bat Girl ('They're dead people from the grave! Vampyrs is what they are!"). After much stalking and menacing and spooky goings on, Burke captures the killer with the use of hypnotism.

Released in theatres on 3 December to mixed reviews, the film was a hit nonetheless. The film's success was largely down to Chaney's make-up effects as the Man in the Beaver Hat; he had given himself the creepiest look, with sharp pointy teeth, wide, menacing eyes, and a stark death grin leering out from beneath a dark stove-pipe top hat. The surviving stills and publicity shots of Chaney in his costume and leering into the lens are still enough to unsettle film fans today, as the 'vampire's' visage seems to embody the archetype of the eternal boogeyman – the mythical menace that has haunted the dreams of children since time immemorial. Indeed, at the time of the film's release, even fully-grown adults were disturbed out by the look. A young woman was murdered in Hyde park, London, and the killer later blamed the film, insisting that Chaney's make-up in *London After Midnight* had so unhinged his mind that he couldn't be held responsible for the murder. The insanity plea was rejected, however, and he was found guilty of the charges. And, as we see elsewhere in this book, it wasn't the last time a film would be blamed for murder.

The TCM version – and the many fan-made mock-ups available on YouTube; most of them frankly unwatchable – includes odd touches such as the Armadillos scurrying around (in London!). Browning must have had a fondness for the creatures as Armadillos later showed up again in *Dracula* (1931). Browning's film career began in 1913 when he appeared in a series of short nickelodeon comedies with friends he had met during his time at a travelling carnival. After a car accident in 1915, in which one of his passengers was killed, he was hospitalised for a whole year with a shattered right leg, a period he spent writing film scripts. It was around this time when he contributed to the screenplay for D. W. Griffith's *Intolerance*. He directed *Puppets* in 1916, in which actors were used as harlequin puppets. In the following year he directed his first feature, *Jim Bludso*, on the adventures of a riverboat captain. In 1918 Irving Thalberg of MGM signed him up to make pictures with Lon Chaney, and their first collaboration was *The Wicked Darling* (1919), in which Chaney played a pickpocket. It was the start of a partnership that continued throughout the 1920s as they delivered such oddities as *The Unholy Three* (1925), *The Unknown* (1927), and *Where East is East* (1929), their tenth and final collaboration together.

Chaney died in 1930 of a throat haemorrhage. He was perhaps the earliest horror movie 'star,' though the main bulk of his fandom didn't appear until decades later, thanks to obsessive revivalists like Forrest J. Ackerman, who graced his cult magazine, *Famous Monsters of Filmland*, with glowing retrospective reviews of his films. For unknown reasons, Chaney's crypt remains unmarked to this day. Of the roughly 165 shorts and feature films he appeared in, around two-thirds of them are considered lost. His death marked the end of an era in Hollywood, and the beginning of the 'talkies.' Browning remade *London After Midnight* as *Mark of the Vampire* (1935), with Bela Lugosi in the lead. The last known copy of *London* was destroyed in the MGM vault fire of 1967, and is one of the most sought after titles of the silent era. Still, the film haunts modern cinema; Chaney's fright-faced ghoul inspired the pop-up fairytale boogeyman in Jennifer Kent's *Babadook* (2014).

October (1928)
(Orig title: *Oktyabr: Desyat' dney kotorye potryasli mir*)
(aka *Ten Days That Shook the World*)
Dir: Sergei Eisenstein and Grigory Alexandrov /Soviet Union
1928 was the last year in which silent movies were the norm. It was also a year in which the most controversial films were communist in nature. January 20 saw the premier of the latest Soviet propaganda epic, *October*. As expected, director Sergei Eisenstein (and his associate, Grigory Alexandrov) presented another dramatic retrospective of the heroic days of the October Revolution. Made to commemorate the ten year anniversary of the triumph, *October* is a remarkable – if muddled – piece of cinema, which fumbles with historical facts and lacks a clear-cut narrative, but remains a fascinating document of its time.

If Eisenstein's trademark montage style had defined his earlier masterpieces, *Strike* and *Battleship Potemkin*, here the same ground-breaking technique was in danger of overwhelming the film's central message. Indeed, when the director presented the final edit to his associates, many of them suggested that he take it back to the editing room. However, the only subsequent cuts he made were to remove most of the images and references to Leon Trotsky. Presumably, he made the cuts as a precaution, as Trotsky had now become persona non grata for the new Stalin regime: Oceania was at war with Eurasia, therefore Oceania had *always* been at war with Eurasia. Thus, Trotsky was now a non-person, and he was flushed down the memory hole.

The film jumps right into the thick of the action and doesn't let up until the final frame. It was a huge production, with Eisenstein insisting that all scenes be shot at the real locations where the events took place. Not only did this require buildings to be evacuated with all the disruptions to the Soviet officials, but traffic also had to be diverted so that the thousands of extras could flood the streets for the epic scenes. The result was the most ambitious – and ultimately flawed – film project since D. W. Griffith's *Intolerance* twelve years earlier, with no expenses spared and a half-mad obsessive at the helm. The film is widely remembered today for its series of striking images, from the raising of the bridge, in which a wounded horse and its carriage plunge into the sea, to the toppling of the statue, and the 'for God and country' sequence. And the film also presents an impressive storming of the Winter Palace sequence, making up for Pudovkin's feeble attempt at the same in his *The End of St. Petersburg* in the previous year. Indeed, on completion of the film, Pudovkin remarked, 'How I should like to make such a powerful failure.'

Since there was no actual footage of the 1917

Revolution, for many years scenes from *October* were used in newsreels and documentaries to illustrate the historical event. And this led many to believe that stock footage had been used to authenticate the film. However, no such footage was used; Eisenstein and Alexandrov directed every shot themselves.

The Seashell and the Clergyman (1928)
(Orig title: *Le coquielle et le Clergyman*)
Dir: Germaine Dulac /France

An utterly bizarre, 33-minute short by Germaine Dulac, which is said to have been inspired by Artaud's *The Thearte and its Double*, but actually owes far more to Freud by way of André Breton and the Surrealist movement. It's a dream-like descent into a timeless twilight zone as a clergyman struggles to assert his desires in a strange, irrational world.

The film opens with the clergyman sitting in a laboratory and pouring chemicals into volumetric flasks. He then holds the flasks to the side and nonchalantly allows them to drop and smash on the floor, one by one. A General in full uniform strides down a long corridor in slow motion before entering the lab and striking the chemicals with a sword. This act of violence seems to affect the clergyman and brings on a delirious state.

He is next seen crawling on his hands and knees through the streets, until he catches a glimpse of a beautiful woman in a horse-drawn carriage. He rises to his feet and pursues the carriage, running with his arms kept tightly by his sides in an odd manner. And after tracking it down to a church, he enters only to discover that the beautiful woman is the wife of the General. Angered by this, the clergyman lunges forward and attempts to strangle the General. However, the dream alters, and the General is now a Priest in full habit. The clergyman attempts to drag the Priest out of the confession box by his collar, but try as he might, he just can't summon the strength to do so. However, the Priest's head mysteriously splits down the middle, and the beautiful wife barely reacts. The rest of the film continues to follow the clergyman as he explores his strange world and pursues the woman – and in the end he 'captures' an imaginary version of her and places her into a large glass bowl; the only glass object in the film that doesn't get smashed.

Far more radical and engaging than Dulac's previous playful attempts at surrealism in *The*
Smiling Madame Beudet (*La Souriante Madame Beudet*, 1922), *The Seashell and the Clergyman* is an early classic in which the director doesn't hold back on exploring the free-form possibilities to the full. There are lots of pretentious and long-winded interpretations of the film to be found in books and online, but the most obvious reading would be to see the film as a reaction to Freud's *The Interpretation of Dreams* (pub. 1899). The constant motif of breaking glass represents the clergyman's frustrations and his giving up on his dreams; his longings and desires are embodied in the form of the wife; and the obstacles that prevent him from seizing his dreams are personified in the General/Priest, whom the clergyman succeeds in throwing off a cliff, only to see the tormentor return all over again.

The ballroom scene in particular is an interesting one as the female dancers wear dresses that are cut in such a way that exposes their left breasts'. The celibate man of the church finds himself drawn to the dance as it represents a world that is alien to him; a world of physical contact, hedonism, fun and courtship and sex; and those desires are a constant torment for him – there is even an under-shot with the camera looking up at the clergyman as he is seen fiddling with his groin with both hands like a child while ogling the women. And, despite being overshadowed by the release of Luis Buñuel's *Un Chien Andalou* (1929) in the following year, *The Seashell and the Clergyman* has clearly made its mark on cinema, with its influence felt in everything from the dream sequence in Ingmar Bergman's *Wild Strawberries* (1957), to David Lynch's dark and troubling dream, *Eraserhead* (1977), and the cyberpunk nightmare of Shinya Tsukamoto's *Tetsuo: The Iron Man* (1988).

Unsurprisingly, this free-wheeling style didn't endear Dulac in the eyes of the censors. The BBFC considered the film to be just as subversive as the Soviet propaganda films of Eisenstein and Pudovkin, though they couldn't point to any particular rules the film had broken on T. P. O'Connor's 43 rules. Even with the most explicit scene cut out by the director himself (in which the protagonist tears off a woman's bra and exposes her bare breasts), the censors banned the film outright. Indeed, the BBFC was met with ridicule when the film's rejection slip was made public by Ivor Montagu. It read: 'This film is so cryptic as to be meaningless. If there is a meaning, it is doubtless objectionable.'

Eveready Harton in Buried Treasure (1928)
(aka *Pecker Island*; aka *Les misadventures de Monsieur Gross' Bitt*)
Dir: 'E. Hardon' (unknown/various) /USA

Long before the advent of *Fritz the Cat* (1972), *Down and Dirty Duck* (1974), and the rise of Japanese hentai porn, there was a legendary underground cartoon that was infamous for its wacky humour and explicit nature. *Eveready Harton* is still shrouded in mystery to this day, and though no one knows for sure who was responsible for unleashing the film, speculation has run rampant over the years, implicating such renowned illustrators and animators as Winsor McCay, George Vernon Stallings, George Canata, Rudy Zamora, and even *Woody Woodpecker*'s Walter Lantz!

Lasting just six minutes, *Eveready Harton in Buried Treasure* follows the well-endowed title character whose penis seems to have a mind of its own, and leads its protagonist through a series of hilarious and unlikely sexual encounters on a farm. First, he tries his luck with a woman who is masturbating in the wilderness; then he sees a rancher making love to a donkey; he wants in on the action, and when he attempts to have his wicked way, the animal steps aside, and Harton's penis thrusts into a cactus plant instead. However, the horny little man – whose penis is almost as big as him – *does* get his satisfaction in the end when he is orally stimulated by a cow through a hole in a fence.

Apparently, film labs in America were so incensed by the material that they refused to touch it, and the film-makers had to get the film processed in Cuba. According to Disney animator, Ward Kimball, it was made in New York. '[the film] was made in the late 20's, silent, of course – by three studios. Each one did a section of it without telling the other studios what they were doing. Studio A finished the first part and gave the last drawing to Studio B […] Involved were Max Fleischer, Paul Terry and the Mutt and Jeff studio. They didn't see the finished product till the night of the big show. A couple of guys who were there tell me the laughter almost blew the top off the hotel where they were screening it.'

Eveready Harton was by far the most explicit American film of 1928, even more so than the handful of topless wonders that were released underground in the same year, such as *Betty's Bath, Sirens of the Sea, Hollywood Sand Witches* and *Desert Nymphs* (all 1928). While these equally mysterious live-action shorts were also playful routines that showcased the forbidden sight of female nudity, none of them could match the riotous laughter and outrageous visuals of the ground-breaking cartoon. *Betty's Bath* sees a young woman disrupted from her bathing by the intrusion of a rat. She calls out for help (and, this being a silent film, her cries for help are illustrated with the words 'Help!' gliding over the surface of the walls in an animated fashion). A man arrives and saves Betty from the rat by killing it. They then have a conversation in her huge, castle-like sitting room, and the man imagines what she looks like naked – complete with quick-cut edits that show Betty's clothing removed.

For the record, it's worth noting the other entries in this short series as there is so little information available about them. Interestingly, unlike *Eveready Harton*, these films have a clear feminist angle to them. In *Betty's Bath*, for instance, the title character can sense the man's eyes piercing right through her dress and objectifying her as a desirable 'object.' She is unnerved by this, and calls out to her pet dog which frightens the man into fleeing the house and running away down the street. *Hollywood Sand Witches* shows a pair of naked women playing a practical joke on a man whose interest in them is unwelcome, and he is seen running into the sea at the end, much to their amusement. *Sirens of the Sea* and *Desert Nymphs* celebrate the female form, with the nudes shown to be at one with untrammelled nature.

On the Beach (1930) is the most explicit of them all, and one that seems to have taken inspiration from *Eveready Harton*. It's the short tale of a young man who can't believe his luck when a trio of women show up on the beach and strip off their clothes. He tries to hold their wares to ransom, and will only return them in exchange for sex. One of the girls agrees to sex, but on condition that he do it through a hole in a high fence. However, when the horny young man puts his penis through the makeshift 'glory hole,' the girls at the other side lift up a goat's bottom for him to make love to.

As for *Eveready Harton*, the film was an underground staple for decades, showing up in one-off screenings and flourishing on the VHS bootleg market in the 1980s and 90s, before being granted an official home video release when it was included on *The Good Old Naughty Days* DVD compilation in 2002. Less known is the fact that the film also showed up in France in the late 1920s, under the title *Les misadventures de Monsieur Gross' Bitt*, with many believing it to have been a French production as the Gallic version was routinely included on vintage French porn compilations of the time.

The 1920s – When French Porn Ruled the World

If Brazil and Argentina had dominated the porn world back in 1910, it was certainly the French who had taken that mantle in the 1920s. Dozens of French pornos survive to this day – some in better condition than others – and if the early French erotica reels produced by Pathé were mostly quite tasteful and even artistic in their aesthetics, the batch that was produced in the 1920s were anything but. This was real low-down dirty porn, the kind which nowadays you'll see uploaded onto amateur tube sites online, with next to no production values or even a competent camera man.

Titles such as *Le Satyre Casimir*, *Seduction* (aka *Bastille Day*), and *Au clair de la lune* (*In the Moonlight* – all c. 1920s) are theatrical in nature, with the use of pretty locations, sets and costumes. *The Satyr Casimir* sees a pair of young women pleasuring themselves with a Roman 'statue' in a nature park. Interestingly, the park looks very similar to the one seen in Buñuel's *L'Age D'Or* (1930), with its trimmed privets and ornaments on plinths – perhaps both films used the same area for shooting? The girls soon get bored and begin pleasing each other on the grass, to which the statue becomes erect and joins in the fun. *Bastille Day* is set in the famous prison in which two men in white wigs (one of whom may or may not be a character based on the Marquis de Sade), have their way with a pair of young women. *In the Moonlight* sees a female clown serenade a woman with a ukulele. Their sexual tryst is interrupted, however, by the arrival of a male clown who enters the frame and gets busy with both of them. *Les deux colombines* (c. 1920) features another costumed ménage à trois (though the costumes don't stay on for long). Even Father Christmas gets his end

away in *Petite conte de Noel* (aka *A Christmas Tale*).

Of the dozens of reels I watched (and the dozens more untitled ones), none of them shows what would become the routine in porn decades later – namely, the one-on-one scenario of one man and one woman. And this is surprising, considering that such scenarios are considered the 'entry-point,' or ground zero in modern porn films. But, alas, the French films of the age had already abandoned such a vanilla concept. Instead, threesomes are the norm, usually one guy with two girls. *Trio*, *Le chauffeur de ces dames* (*The Ladies' Driver*), and *Gisele et la groom* (c. 1925) are all based on the ménage à trois. *Le relour de L'exporate* (*The Return of the Exporter*) shows two women together with a trader who has brought a pet monkey along to join in the fun, played by a man in a monkey suit. And *La Pédicure* is remarkable not only for having two guys on one girl, but also because the men turn their attentions on each other, too.

Indeed, such bisexual offerings were surprisingly common at the time, though straight-up gay reels – if any were made – have never surfaced. Perhaps the most famous of all the French porn films made at this time is remembered *because of its* bisexual content, and is regarded as the first of its kind ever made. *Le ménage moderne du Madame Butterfly* (c. 1920) is the oldest known sex film that includes bisexual and homosexual content. It's based on the famous opera and sees an American sailor engaging in a number of encounters, including being sodomised while in missionary poistion with the title character. The man then pulls out and heads round to the front for oral while the sailor continues to service the woman.

The film has been credited to the Romanian Jew, Bernard Natan, who is said to have relocated to France after the War and made dozens of bisexual movies at the time. He was also credited with performing some of the sex scenes himself, but this information has since come into contention since all the male performers involved are brandishing uncut penises. What is remarkable, however, is that Natan's films didn't seem to hold him back at all in his career aspirations – and it's perhaps a testament to France's open-mindedness to sex that, by the end of the 1920s, Natan had assumed the prestigious ownership of Pathé.

Many of the films have surfaced from archives and private collections. Some are pristine, and no doubt ready for the HD treatment, while others are so grainy and jumpy that it's difficult to tell whether you're watching a hairy vagina or a bird's nest in a monsoon. A great number are untitled and are bereft of inter-titles or even a title screen. It is agreed, however, that the purpose of the films were to play in brothel lounges across Europe to get the clientele in the mood. In terms of subject-matter, the clips are remarkably mordern – there are pick-up artists on the waterfront luring women back to their rooms, like something you see in modern-day Brazzers' videos; there are also strange and subdued entries set in opium dens in North Africa; bondage scenarios played out with nuns and clergymen; even comedic routines in which a lucky Frenchman grins in feigned astonishment into the camera lens while enjoying a host of women.

Thunderbolt (1929)
Dir: Joseph von Sternberg /USA
Paramount's loose remake of its own *Underworld* (1927), in sound. This time the gangster's moll is 'Ritzy' (Fay Wray), an unhappy young woman who is seeing a young bank teller on the side. The gangster, Thunderbolt (George Bancroft), is eventually sentenced to death for murder and armed robbery, and this leads to the familiar – but much less action-packed – finale in which the criminal seeks redemption, not by busting out of death row and shooting it out with the police (as seen in *Underworld*), but by forgiving Ritzy and the bank teller (who occupies the cell next to him) and facing up to his fate. The film starts out lively enough, and there is a great scene early on set in a Harlem night club with black jazz musicians, but it soon becomes dull. And things aren't helped by the atrocious wooden acting, especially from the leading lady, Wray. Not Paramount's finest hour.

Half Marriage (1929)
Dir: 'William J. Cowan' [William J. Cohen] /USA
This early RKO production stars Olive Borden and Morgan Farley as Judy and Dickie, a young couple who are in love. She wants to marry, but he's reluctant because his pay packet isn't enough to support them both. As a compromise, they agree to a 'half marriage,' which means hopping over a state border, getting hitched, and returning to New York where their friends and

families will be none the wiser.

At the risk of disappointing her parents and losing her allowance, they go ahead with the ceremony. However, their honeymoon is interrupted by Tommy (Anderson Lawler), Judy's designated suitor, as chosen by her parents. Therefore, Dickie has to climb out of the window and hide on the ledge out of sight while Judy entertains her mother and the smarmy rich boy. Of course, this secrecy causes jealousy and arguments between the couple, as she is continually wooed and charmed by the young men in her life who think she is still available. Would it be a spoiler if I told you that true love triumphs in the end? Well, yes and no. The unexpected ending comes right out of leftfield and is surprisingly tragic.

A fairly routine but memorable comedy-drama that passes by in a brief but entertaining 68-minutes. There is even a death in the film (at the hands of the leading lady, no less), which was certainly a break from the norm in romantic comedies of the time. And, perhaps it was the uneasy mix of laughter and heavy-handed lessons in honesty that kept the film from being the hit it may have been otherwise. A silent version of *Half Marriage* was made simultaneously, but it's probably lost today.

Most tragic, however, is the true story of what became of Borden; she dropped out of Hollywood in the mid-30s and turned to alcohol. She died in 1947, aged 41, in utter poverty. The only possession she had left in the world when she died was a signed picture of herself.

The Trespasser (1929)
Dir: Edmund Goulding /USA
Gloria Swanson experiences a series of highs and lows in this Oscar nominated melodrama that spans the course of six years. When a young typist, Marion (Swanson), elopes and marries Jack Merrick (Robert Ames), the son of John Merrick, a wealthy tycoon, the father strongly disapproves of the marriage. And he makes his opinions known in no uncertain terms to her face, calling her 'some low-down, low-life, fortune-hunting parasite.' The comments are so hurtful to Marion – combined with the fact that Jack fails to defend her – that she takes her leave. Eighteen months later, and Marion struggles as a single mother raising a baby. She faces mounting debts and yet can somehow afford the services of an au pair. She later learns that Jack has been seriously injured in a car

accident.

Two and a half years after that, Marion dates her old attorney boss. However, just as their romance gathers steam, he suffers a stroke and is left in a delirious and confused state. He later dies, and Marion inherits around half a million dollars. By this time, she has piqued the interest of the press, and stories are printed about her as a mysterious married woman eloping with wealthy men. Other stories appear accusing her of baring an illegitimate child, and of being a cold-hearted gold-digger. Upset by this, she gives up the entire fortune, and also the apartment that was left for her, and instead returns to her humble life of a typist. Jack is eventually united with his son, and he is keen to rekindle his relationship with Marion, but she's reluctant as she fears the Merrick family is planning on taking her boy away...

Told with delicate framing, an easy pace, great performances all round, and even a tempered artistic direction from Goulding, *The Trespasser* is a solid, workman-like picture of its time. Of course, this being an early 'talking picture,' the musical accompaniment is scarce, with lengthy moments of silence in the latter stages as Marion's dilemmas become increasingly difficult for her to bear. The story certainly swoons along with a predictable series of events, but it remains an engaging film nonetheless. There are even subtle expressionist moments, such as the scene in the office where rain patters against the window while Marion worries that she may be on the verge of a nervous breakdown.

The film was made back-to-back with a silent version (this entry refers to the sound one), which effectively doubled the production costs. However, the investment paid off as *The Trespasser* was a resounding hit for United Artists in both formats. Unfortunately for Swanson, this was her only successful 'talkie' until she made her comeback in *Sunset Boulevard* (1950) more than twenty years later. Immediately after *The Trespasser*, she starred in a number of flops that hurt her career, such as *What a Widow!* (1930), *Indiscreet* (1931), *Tonight or Never* (1931), *Perfect Understanding* (1933), and *Music in the Air* (1934). Director Goulding revisited similar territory in *That Certain Woman* (1937).

Un Chien Andalou (1929)
(*An Andalousian Dog*)
Dir: Luis Buñuel /France

A man slices through a woman's eye with a straight razor. Then, a guy struggles with his desires, and he is constantly thwarted by absurd interventions from ants, an androgyne toying with a severed hand, dead donkeys on pianos, churchmen, and a doppelgänger. The protagonist strolls along a beach with his female companion, and they spring out of the ground...

Every art form has to push its own boundaries as a way of challenging, questioning and provoking a response, otherwise the art form becomes too safe and predictable; it withers and dies. In order to survive, art must be constantly redefined. The best film-makers have always striven to push things that little bit further. Sometimes, this is done purely for the notoriety and sensationalism, but there are also true artists whose aims are to explore and expand the possibilities of their chosen medium.

In 1929, ambitious young film-maker, Luis Buñuel and painter Salvador Dali worked together on a twenty-one-minute short which would become the most essential film manifestation of the surrealist movement. But *Un Chien Andalou* also works as an effective pastiche and parody of Hollywood conventions of the time, especially in its anti-narrative approach. The seemingly happy ending with the couple strolling into the sunset is intercepted at the last moment with an intrusive fade-out shot of the couple having transformed into frightened human trees. The film opens with the caption, "Once upon a time," a phrase borrowed from countless fairytales, but here given an added playfulness and sarcastic edge – it was Buñuel subverting the age of innocence: cinema as harmless escapism which Buñuel and Dali intended to change forever. And that is exactly what they did with *Un Chien Andalou*.

The next scene remains shocking to this day – perhaps even more so than its imitations in Lucio Fulci's *Zombie Flesh Eaters* and Toshiharu Ikeda's *Evil Dead Trap* – as Buñuel sharpens the blade, tests it on his thumbnail, forces open a woman's eye, and in stark close-up, slices through the eyeball. This incredible special effect, which still looks genuine today, was created by superimposing shots of animated clouds passing across the moon, and an overlap shot of a dead calf's retina being cut. Almost a century later, and that scene is still a seminal moment in cinematic gore. The eye is the primary tool by which we appreciate cinema; a shot of one being cut forces us to do one or two things – look away, or look at things in a different light.

After decades of speculation on what the film-makers used for the eye, Buñuel revealed in an interview in the mid-70s that he had used a dead calf as his stunt double. He even admitted going to the lengths of actually bleaching the calf's skin to make it lighter, to give the area around the eye the appearance of human skin.

Like Germaine Dulac of *The Seashell and the Clergyman*, Buñuel and Dali based the entire film on their dreams and urges, drawing on anything which may have held significance. This seemingly random way of piecing together their film in the hope of uncovering – or experimenting – with the unconscious mind, has led to decades of analytical interpretation from generations of fans and critics, many of whom see the film as the tale of a man struggling with sexual impulses and frustration, his own psychological draw-backs and the disapproval of society (many have also interpreted their later film, *L'Age D'Or*, in much the same way). "Nothing, in the film, symbolizes anything," Buñuel claimed. "The only method of investigation of the symbols would be, perhaps, psychoanalysis."

When *Un Chien Andalou* premiered at Studio 28 in Paris, André Breton and his followers in the surrealist movement attended the screening with the intention of "sabotaging" the event because they had never heard of Buñuel or Dali. The film's makers, in turn, were disappointed when the audience looked to be enjoying the film. Buñuel went as far as saying that the positive reaction "ruined the evening." After all, they had both armed themselves with rocks which they carried in their pockets to throw at anyone who tried to attack the screening. Rather than causing the calculated outrage they had intended with their film, *Un Chien Andalou* was actually greeted with a positive reception from the bourgeoisie, and this made Buñuel sick to his stomach. "What can I do about the people who adore all that is new, even when it goes against their deepest convictions, or about the insincere, corrupt press, and the inane herd that saw beauty or poetry in something which was basically no more than a desperate impassioned call for murder?"

After the premiere, Dalí and Buñuel became the first film-makers to be officially welcomed into the Surrealist movement by leader André Breton. Lookout for Dali who appears in the film as one of the confused priests being dragged along the floor, and Buñuel who does the eye-slicing. Tragically, both lead players committed suicide; Pierre Batcheff took an overdose of barbiturates in April 1932, and Simone Mareuil set herself on fire with petrol in a public square in Dordogne.

The Dance of Life (1929)
Dir: John Cromwell /USA

One of the earliest pre-code movies. Nancy Carroll and Hal Skelly star as a comedy-dance duo who land a gig at a burlesque theatre in Chicago. The first hour focuses on the backstage drama as the characters work through their differences and the company struggles to stay afloat. Bonny King (Carroll) and Skid (Skelly) eventually marry, but Skid's drinking habit causes friction between them. In the second hour, Skid travels to New York and becomes a big name on the theatre circuit. However, his hard drinking and womanising ensures his ultimate failure. The couple are reunited in the end, and when Skid collapses on stage during a performance, Bonny nurses him back to health...

A charming little film that really ought to be rediscovered by a modern audience. Paramount didn't renew its copyright, and so the film belongs in the public domain nowadays, which sadly means we won't see a decent home video transfer anytime soon. Lookout for old slapstick favourite, Al St. John, as 'Bozo,' the clownish performer who serves as a peacemaker early on in the story. The film was remade as *Swing High, Swing Low* (1937) and *When My Baby Smiles at Me* (1948). The original was shot with Technicolor segments, but only the black and white work print survives.

Woman to Woman (1929)
Dir: Not credited [Victor Saville] /UK /USA

Set in 1918 at the height of World War I, a British Officer, David (George Barraud), falls in love with a Parisian cabaret performer, Lola (Betty Compson). The pair agree to marry, but plans are scuppered when David's leave is cancelled and he is immediately sent back to the front line. Lola is unaware of this, and spends the whole day waiting for him to return, much to her disappointment. David is badly wounded in the trenches, and suffers such bad affects of shell-shock that four years of his memory are wiped clean.

Upon his recovery, David returns to London where he continues in his role as an engineer. And this is when we learn that he is now married to Vesta (Juliette Compton), a society girl who thinks of David as 'old fashioned.' Their difficult relationship causes much discontent between them. However, in another convenient twist of fate, Lola shows up in England to perform at a charity concert. Now billed under the stage name 'Deloryse,' she sings an old song that was a favourite of theirs in their Paris days, and this helps to jog David's memory of the romance they had once shared. However, he also learns that he has a son, and Lola receives terrible news about her health. David's memories come flooding back, but will the passion of his love return?

This is the sound remake of the lost silent version, *Woman to Woman* (1923, which was co-scripted by Alfred Hitchcock). The film was remade again in 1946, though the 1929 version is considered the best. Some have criticised the film's look (certainly, the DVD transfer was copied from a worn-out print), but even through the hazy visuals, the cinematography is actually quite warm and nicely framed. Others have accused the production of being 'cheap,' and again this isn't entirely true. For while the trench scenes are disappointingly short, the sets are marvellous, such as David's luxury mansion in London, and the location shots in Paris are remarkably well done.

On the downside, Compson's terrible French accent is so bad that the actress abandons it entirely around half-way through the picture, and Barraud's performance is a little on the stuffy side – his interactions with his son come off as quite cold, for instance. However, as a routine weepy of its time, it's not so bad at all, and director Saville deliberately fades to black during the film's most sombre moments.

All Quiet on the Western Front (1930)
Dir: Lewis Milestone /USA

All Quiet on the Western Front was released on 21 April 1930 to stunned audiences and critics, prompting the *New York Times* to respond, 'most of the time the audience was held to silence by its realistic scenes...' Indeed, it was the first time a civilian audience had seen such chaotic and vicious war sequences, including the sounds of screeching bombs whistling through the air, and a group of young men screaming in terror as they realise that war is not the world of romanticised heroism their professor had promised it to be. Such appalling scenes of brutal conflict wouldn't be replicated in a fictionalised film until the release of *Saving Private Ryan* (1998) sixty-eight years later.

A remarkably faithful adaptation of Erich Maria Remarque's legendary pacifist novel (pub. 1928), the film opens on the day of the outbreak of World War I, with thousands of enlisted soldiers on parade through the streets to a heroes' send-off (as seen previously in *J'Accuse!* [1920]). Told from a German point of view, specifically through the eyes of sensitive youth, Paul Baumer (Lew Ayres). He and his friends enlist in the German Army and are trained by Himmelstoss (John Wray), who was a pleasant neighbourhood postman in civilian life, but now is a by-the-book, no-nonsense corporal who refuses to even acknowledge that he has known the recruits personally after delivering their mail for years. Before long, the recruits are sent to the Western Front for a first-hand taste of blood and smoke, and violence and death. As the conflict grinds on, Paul teams up with a tough veteran and is taught how to survive the horror of the trenches. By now, the idealistic naïvety which had led the youngsters into the war zone is thoroughly eaten away by the harsh realisation that there is no 'good fight' to be fought, only a pointless confrontation with death.

Unlike *Journey's End* (1930), the British-American co-production which somewhat sugar-coated the trench horrors, *All Quiet on the Western Front* offered no such niceties as the film depicted enemy combatants. And this allowed Universal to explore the conflict in all its harsh details without the danger of a backlash from the Allied veterans. Therefore, producer Carl Laemmle Jr was free to create another of his trademark epics with no fear of objection from the more sensitive members of the public. The result was a war film that was the most emotionally draining ever screened until *Come and See* (1985) came along, the devastating Soviet production that owed a thing or two to Milestone's masterpiece. The battle scenes alone are reason enough to see the film, as Milestone (himself a veteran of the conflict) even went as far as aiming the camera at the charging soldiers as though the lens itself was a weapon, and fatally wounding the oncoming soldiers as it passes along the tops of the trenches. Junior spared no expense to get the film on screen, and went to the trouble of converting more than 20 acres of a California ranch into bleak battle-zones, and recruited around 2000 veterans to serve as extras.

However, for all the wonders of the film, one of the most affecting scenes is the one in which Paul ducks for cover in a bomb crater. There he attacks and stabs a French soldier. And as the man slowly dies, Paul is overcome with remorse and rifles through the victim's pockets looking for a name – something to differentiate his victim from the other dead troops that lie in the battlefields above them. And, of course, there is also the much-celebrated final shot of Paul's hand reaching out for the butterfly as he is fatally wounded.

All Quiet on the Western Front was met with stunned silence on its initial release, with *Variety* magazine publishing a sober reflection: '[there is] nothing passed up for the niceties; nothing glossed over for the women. Here exhibited is war as it is: butchery. The League of Nations could make no better investment than to buy up the master-print, reproduce it in every language to be shown to every nation every year until the word "war" is taken out of the dictionaries.' Universal Pictures wouldn't risk such a large production again until the 1960s, but the gamble did pay off as the film was a hit. It was also only the third film to win an Academy Award for Outstanding Picture (and Milestone was awarded his second for Best Director).

The film was greeted much less favourably in Poland, where it was famously banned for being 'pro-German.' Ironically, the growing Nazi movement didn't think it was pro-German at all, and they held violent demonstrations at cinemas when the film was passed uncut, setting off stink bombs and attacking audience members. Goebbels even publicly slammed the film in a speech. But, perhaps the most ironic twist came a decade later when actor Ayres was publicly shunned in Germany as a conscientious objector during World War II, a defiant stance that ultimately cost him his career.

A lesser-known sequel followed, *The Road Back* (1937), directed by James Whale, this time combining a pacifist message with a warning about the rise of Nazism in Germany. The original was remade less successfully as a TV movie in 1979, starring Richard Thomas. As for the original classic, it has been released in various cuts over the decades; first appearing with a running time of 140-minutes (the silent version is said to have had a running time of 152-minutes), some versions floating around were cut down to as much as 90-minutes. A VHS version was released in the 1990s at 130-minutes. However, in 1998 the Library of Congress undertook a major restoration of the film, discarding the music at the end and using the best surviving elements to create a 149-minute cut that was much closer to the way Milestone had intended the film to see seen.

Her Man (1930)
Dir: Tay Garnett /USA

With the world-shaking events of the Wall Street Crash in October 1929, Hollywood studios responded immediately to the threat of the Great Depression by churning out a series of lurid pictures designed solely to sell tickets. Among the early entries in this field were the scheming and cynicism in Cecil B. DeMille's *Dynamite* (1929); the verbal tirades of leading lady, Nancy Carroll, giving as good as she gets in *The Dance of Life* (1929); the contentious subject-matter of prostitution – and the lying and scheming characters – in *Party Girl* (1930); and the weaponised sexuality of Norma Shearer's bed-hopping antics in *The Divorcee* (1930). Such films became known as the 'pre-code' cinema, a trend that lasted from October 1929 until the summer of 1934 when Will Hays finally succeeded in uniting the studio executives to get behind the Production Code, a set of guidelines that were created to uphold morality in the cinema.

What is far less remarked upon, however, is the fact that Hollywood cinema was already heading in a more adult-themed direction quite naturally, regardless of the economic necessities that hastened its path in this direction. The early Austrian films of G. W. Pabst (*Joyless Street* [1925], *Pandora's Box* and *Diary of a Lost Girl* [both 1929]) showcased strong, quick-witted leading ladies (such as Louise Brooks and Greta Garbo) combined with a racier, darker thematic content. Added to this was the fact that musicals had saturated the cinema screens, and audiences were now deliberately avoiding them. Studios found themselves having to delete the musical numbers from their films in an effort to recoup some of the lost profits at the box-office. The pre-code films were much cheaper to produce than the extravagant musicals, and this was manna from heaven for studio heads who were looking for ways to cut corners and keep afloat as the Depression loomed. Therefore, the stage was set for the 'pre-code' avalanche.

One of the best of the early entries in this field is *Her Man*, a seedy little romance set on a mythical 'paradise' island where violence and vice threatens to ruin all who are drawn to its shores. The mysterious island is clouded in a perpetual gloom where the only laughs come in the form of drunken pratfalls. It's a place where American tourists are given free licence away from home to indulge in all of their forbidden desires, and the streets hang heavy with a depressing mood as drunken sailors stagger around looking to get laid. The film opens on the scene of an ageing prostitute, Annie (Marjorie Rambeau), attempting to escape the island. However, she is apprehended by U.S. Customs officials who recognise her immediately, and show no hesitation in turning her away.

So, back to the island she goes to drown her sorrows at Thalia, the dive bar where she plies her trade. Meanwhile, the local pimp, Johnnie (Ricardo Cortez), who has just committed a cold-blooded murder during a bar room brawl, has a word with Frankie (Helen Twelvetrees), his star hooker. She is terrified of him, and his sweet-talk and empty promises does little to settle her nerves, as even the slightest hint of wanting to leave the island is met with a fierce and threatening response. Hope for Frankie comes in the form of Dan (Philips Holmes), a young American sailor who shows an interest in her and offers to take her away from the miserable island. However, she is reluctant to go with him as she is afraid that Johnnie or one of his cronies will put a knife in them both rather than see them leave...

Loosely based on the controversial stage play, *Frankie and Johnny*, *Her Man* is an unlikely love story between a cocky young sailor and a life-long thief and prostitute. Director, Tay Garnett, perfectly captures the mood of late night, end-of-the-party debauched atmosphere (as was also seen in the previous year's *The New Babylon* [1929], specifically the scenes set in the Paris Commune). Frankie is the most interesting character as she was born on the island and raised her entire life to pick pockets and sleep with drunks in order to line Johnnie's pockets. That depressing life is all she has ever known (she doesn't even know her own date of birth), and yet beneath the tough exterior there is an anxious and loving heart just longing to be set free.

Unfortunately, Annie's character isn't as well developed. And that's a shame as the film opens on the scene of her arriving on U.S. soil, only to be turned away, with viewers assuming the film is about her. She is easily the most colourful character in the bar, and she could have easily carried a feature film that focused specifically on her story, which sadly we don't get to learn much about here. She has an uneasy relationship with Frankie – she's much older, is a drunk, and seems to resent the fact that Frankie is being wooed by Dan. She also seems to be mildly astonished that a true romance could blossom on an island so rife with sin. It's certainly something she had never seen before in her years working there. Even at the violent finale when she plays a part in helping the couple to escape, she addresses the balance by admitting, 'You know, I had plenty of reasons to get Frankie out of here.'

The film was shot in Havana, which has led some to assume the story is set there, but the true location of the tale is never made clear. To this day, the *IMDb* plot summary suggests that the film is set in Paris, but that is clearly not true. And this false information only goes to show just how neglected the film has become over the years (though a copy is preserved at the Library of Congress). Of course, *Her Man* was met with hostility by international censors, and was banned in many U.S. States. In Britain, BBFC chief censor, T. P. O'Connor, had died in November 1929, and replaced by Sir Edward Shortt. And one of the first things Shortt did while in office was ban the film outright. The Cuban government also complained about the film, as they had given permission for Pathé and MGM to shoot in Havana, but had no idea of the true nature of the film until after the finished product had been released. The film's tagline only rubbed salt in the wound: "Born in the Scarlet Streets, this hard boiled woman of the night knew no ten commandments – taking suckers was her game." Twelvetrees and Cortez later reunited with director Garnett for the gangster film, *Bad Company* (1931), and the actress went on to play her most fondly remembered role as the twice betrayed, bed-hopping heroine in *Millie* (1931).

L'Age D'Or (1930)
(*The Golden Age*)
Dir: Luis Buñuel /France
A man and a woman are determined to strike up a relationship regardless of the disapproval of society, the police and the Church, and they engage in strange and perverse romantic interludes.

After they had shocked the world with their previous short film, *Un Chien Andalou* (1929), film-maker Luis Buñuel and painter Salvador Dali collaborated on this, intended to be their first talking picture. However, the pair fell out during the making of the film, and Buñuel soldiered on alone, creating a blasphemous classic of surrealism boasting some of the most extreme imagery of his long career.

Buñuel's dark humour cushions some of the more outrageous scenes (in the credits, one of the characters is billed as 'Defenestrated Bishop'), but *L'Age D'Or* remains one of the most elegant and mischievous attempts to assault bourgeois sensibilities ever committed to film. The show kicks off with a scene of scorpions attacking each other and a rat (this footage was taken from a 1912 nature documentary, *Le Scorpion Languedocien*), then goes on to show human scorpions and evil churchmen. The film is supposedly set in Imperial Rome, but actually looks a lot like contemporary Paris where the film was shot. The man and the woman roll around in mud and excrement; the police do all they can to break them apart; they suckle and nibble each other's fingers; the man is distracted from snogging by a marble statue, so the woman begins to suck its toes in a sensual manner. Amusingly, the scene cuts to a 'reaction' shot of the statue's face as she sucks away. She later declares such classic lines as "Oh, what joy in having killed our children!" A government official makes a phone call to the man, but he doesn't give a damn about an impending scandal about to break. The minister shoots himself, and his body slumps on the ceiling. The most risqué scene is saved for the end, and is based on a scene from the Marquis De Sade's outrageous book, *120 Days of Sodom*, in which evil aristocrats peel away from an orgy of sexual violence. Sade's character Duc de Blangis is the leader, and Buñuel models him on Jesus Christ. An injured girl is stabbed to death by Jesus, and the scalps of his other victims hang from a crucifix.

During screenings of *Un Chien Andalou*, Buñuel is said to have put small stones in his pockets so that if the crowd showed their disapproval at the end of the film, he would go up front and throw the stones at them. For *L'Age D'Or* he would have needed a more substantial weapon due to the hostile reception which greeted the film. It sparked organised riots in the cinema. The film was given a screening permit from the censors for the premier at Studio 28 in Paris, in November 1930. Just four days after its initial screening, cinemas across the city were attacked by the right-wing followers of Ligue des Patriotes ('League of Patriots'), who did all they could to disrupt the screening by throwing ink at the screen and physically assaulting viewers who opposed their protests. Screenings often resulted in violent pandemonium. In addition, they also destroyed artworks by Dali and other surrealists, including Man Ray, Yves Tanguy, Joan Miró and others. During this time, the Prefect of Police of Paris, Jean Chiappe, requested that the censors remove the film from circulation. And soon after, *L'Age D'Or* was officially banned in France.

A Spanish newspaper condemned the film and Buñuel and Dalí, and described the content as "...the most repulsive corruption of our age... the new poison which Judaism, Masonry, and rabid, revolutionary sectarianism want to use in order to corrupt the people". In response, the de Noailles family (who had financed the film) withdrew *L'Age D'Or* from cinema exhibition for more than forty years. Nonetheless, three years later, in 1933, the film was shown at the Museum of Modern Art in New York City in a private screening. The film wasn't legally exhibited in America until November 1979, where it 'premiered' at the Roxie Cinema in San Francisco. Despite being constructed as a series of vignettes, *L'Age D'Or* has more of a narrative structure than the previous *Un Chien Andalou*. But it still feels bizarre. This is because while *Un Chien Andalou*'s surrealism is more locked within its own rigid formalities, offering up one bizarre image after another that forms a barely comprehensible link, the surrealism of *L'Age D'Or*, on the other hand, is much more detached, with the strange and bizarre moments standing out from the otherwise simplified, mundane form. Surrealism emphasizes the bizarre that can be found in a perfectly normal situation, and while *Un Chien* does this to a great extent, there is still very little normal or mundane in that film's 'plot'. Not to say that it is any less inspired than *L'Age D'Or*, quite the contrary, but ironically, it is the use of plot and the director's attempts at a loose storyline that infuses the film with a stronger and more prominent feel for the bizarre and surreal.

The 'plot' of *L'Age D'Or* is about how we are forced to compromise ourselves in the society we live in, and more specifically, how we are forced to compromise our *sexual* desires. The man and the woman at the centre of the film are trying desperately to overcome the social obstacles to consummate their love, but whether they are actually 'in love' is never made clear. But interestingly, they suffer the same barriers that couples find in society today. Much of the humour in the film comes from the way in which the lovers disrespect this need to compromise, and the sexual weirdness that results when they are forced to abide by it (the toe fellatio scene in particular), and this does much to offer up a satirical and devilishly mischievous comment on the mores of society itself. Another recurring theme addressed in the film is that society is built on this compromise, and due to it, is always positioned on the edge of madness and hysteria.

L'Age D'Or was a film that dared to goad the upper class culture and depict them as a race of people too sexually inhibited and frightened by their peers to explore Buñuel's revolutionary ideas: that in order to have your own mind you have to free yourself of the Church and its tightening grip. Buñuel's religious pessimism was the result of a strict childhood regime of daily worship and a rigorous religious education in school. It bred in him a derisive perspective on religion where he perhaps conjured negative surrealist ideas and thoughts from his troubled days at school. And the product is this authentic classic. It is through this film that he becomes the teacher of his own beliefs; the idea that the audience no longer needed to be told what to believe, but to make up their own minds, as opposed to Catholicism or any form of organised religion. The man and the woman (played by Gaston Modot and Lya Lis) symbolise Buñuel's radical 'sacrilegious' thinking and are his model couple. Contrasting the original Man and Woman, (Adam and Eve) to his carefully chosen archetypes, we have a greater knowledge about the director's surrealist tendencies and his interest in not the images but the ideas they represent.

The couple are often separated, and the man is taken away by the police. This scene is quite funny because Buñuel and Dali (both co-writers) are implying that society would imprison the man for the most innocent of crimes: to be free and in love. The couple have to surpass the very obstacles that Buñuel faced in making the film: the Church, society and even his – or *their* – own psychological problems.

'Talkie Terror': The Painful Transition to Sound

With the release of Warner Bros.' *Don Juan* (1926) and *The Jazz Singer* in late 1927, Hollywood studios went about a deliberate makeover of the medium, designed to stifle their rivals in the industry with the introduction of sound. In 1928-29, most Hollywood productions were talkies, even the low-budget B-pictures. The scheme worked to a certain extent as many European states were unprepared for the change, especially France. Buñuel's *L'Age D'Or* was released as a talkie, but there are only a handful of dialogue scenes in the entire film. Independent U.S. film-makers were also caught unaware, most famously Howard Hughes, who was forced to re-shoot much of the footage for his epic, *Hell's Angels* (1930), as the transition came along mid-way through filming.

Both Britain and Germany coped with the change remarkably well, especially Germany, as their film industry rapidly turned the situation to its advantage with trademark efficiency. The Brits had been working independently on sound systems and were also well prepared (Hitchcock's first talkie, *Blackmail*, was released in June 1929, for example). However, the BBFC resisted the change for an incredible amount of time. The BBFC offices were not equipped with sound systems, and this meant that the films under consideration had to be viewed in silence while a member of staff narrated the story and dialogue via the screenplays. The British censors continued with this silly practice until 1930 when they finally accepted the fact that talking pictures were not merely a passing fad but a permanent change to the way films were viewed.

The biggest resistance to the change, however, came from cinema chains themselves. To have their theatres upgraded with the latest sound equipment was a costly expense, and many chains simply bypassed the talkies at first, in the hope that silent cinema would return. Of course, there was to be no silent revival for decades yet, and so those who wanted to stay afloat in the business made the investment in the end, no matter how much it pained them to do so.

Warner Bros. meanwhile had perfected the techniques of sound to such an extent that by January 1931 the release of *Little Caesar* felt so naturally at home in the format that it appeared as though cinema had *always* consisted of talking pictures.

Little Caesar (1931)
Dir: Mervyn LeRoy /USA

Inspired by the rise and fall of Al Capone, *Little Caesar* stars Edward G. Robinson as Rico Bandello, a small-time crook and killer who ruthlessly works his way up the crime ladder in Chicago before his ego leads him into an ill-advised shoot-out with police. Early on, he attaches himself to a crime outfit and rises through the ranks, dispensing with the 'criminal code' in order to get what he wants. He makes his biggest mistake early on, however, by killing the city's crime commissioner. This incident brings the heat on the gang in the form of Lt. Flaherty (Thomas Jackson), a cunning Irish detective who seems to know exactly what kind of personality type he is dealing with in Rico (what later became known as the 'dark triad' type). Flaherty is constantly showing up at unexpected moments and putting the spanner in on the gang's capers. And in the end, he uses Rico's own sense of self-importance to lure him out of the shadows after having a humiliating front page article published about him in the press.

Based on the novel by W. R. Burnett, *Little Caesar* was released after the arrival of only a handful of talkie gangster films, such as *Thunderbolt* (1929), *The Racketeer* (1929), and *Doorway to Hell* (1930). What separated *Caesar* from the pack was summed up by co-producer, Darryl F. Zanuck, who commented, 'Every other underworld picture has had a thug with a little bit of good in him. He reforms before the fade-out. *This* guy [Rico] is no good at all. It'll go over big.' Indeed, with its criminal protagonist with a clear hatred for law and order, and its portrayal of a vicious, dog-eat-dog world, the film was sure to make its mark on audiences during the struggle of the Depression.

The snarled street talk, screeching car tyres and deafening tommy guns and explosions introduced many audiences to the wonders of talking pictures for the first time. And, after it, there was no going back.

Serving as the vanguard for a slew of rowdy gangster flicks that followed in its wake, *Caesar* itself quickly became outmoded in terms of gritty realism by later entries in the field, such as *The Public Enemy* (1931), *City Streets* (1931), *Scarface* (1932), and *The Petrified Forest* (1936). But *Caesar* was the first to focus on the exploits of an unrepentant criminal, and its influence has been felt in the cinema ever since. Owing just as much Macbeth as Julius Caesar, the gangster genre that spawned in its wake made a habit of basing its anti-heroes on the same ambitious archetypes whose violent rise to the top is met with an equally bloody fall. And *Little Caesar* catapults its anti-hero from the gutter to the stars and back again in the course of a swift-but-brutal 80-minutes.

Robinson's performance remains as strong as ever, with his quick talk and domineering presence dwarfing those around him. It was his first lead role after years playing heavies on stage and screen, usually in bit-parts. Lew Ayres (who had appeared in *Doorway to Hell*) was originally considered for the role, but was dropped in favour of the unknown Robinson. Incredibly, the 37-year-old actor was considered a quiet and sensitive soul off screen, at complete odds with the loud and aggressive Rico. Of course, Robinson found himself immediately type-cast after the film's release, and he continued to play the bad guy for years.

The Man Who Came Back (1931)
Dir: Raoul Walsh /USA

The son of a wealthy Wall Street tycoon, Steve (Charles Farrell), wakes up with a hangover one evening only to learn that he had married a 'scarlet woman' the previous night while he was steaming drunk. The scandal has made it in the next day's papers, and his father, Thomas Randolph (William Holden), is livid at his son's drunken and reckless behaviour. After a midnight breakfast, Mr. Randolph hands Steve a cheque for $5000 and sends him off to labour on the docks of San Francisco with the hope that his spoiled son will work his way up to respectability from scratch, as he himself had done when he was a young man. Of course, Steve is unhappy with the arrangement, and out of anger, threatens to drag the family name through the mud.

So, Steve begins his voyage of discovery, staying away from the docks and instead boozing his money away in high society circles on the west coast. Fuelled by resentment for his father, Steve drags his wife, Angie (Janet Gaynor), along with him on his destructive journey, going from cocktail parties in San Francisco to the dark and dingy opium dens of Shanghai, looking increasingly dishevelled and emotionally fragile as the seedy underworld threatens to swallow the pair whole, body and soul. However, the odd couple's love seems to be genuine when, even after he almost strangles her to death to 'save' her from her opium addiction, she rescues him, and together they escape their hellish environment and set up home in Honolulu. But will they succeed in conquering their addictions, or will the drink and drugs defeat them in the end?

The happy ending is given away in the film's title, but *The Man Who Came Back* is a little-known pre-code production from Fox that somehow escaped the scandal sheet, despite portraying the spectacular fall from grace of a society rich kid. A modest production, given only a limited release in selected theatres, the film is ripe for a revival and fresh evaluation. Perhaps the most haunting aspect of the film isn't Steve but Angie, the stoic wife who vows to pursue her husband to the depths of despair and help him to pull through – her heroism and support was, frankly, more than the man deserved. 'I don't know where I'm going,' she states early on, 'but I'm on my way to Hell.' She knows it's going to be a rough ride in the company of a self-loathing drunk, but her commitment is unshakeable.

The film takes a particularly dark path to redemption and recovery, and viewers may be stunned by its willingness to probe the difficult fall-out of alcoholism and opium addiction – especially in a production released in 1931. The scenes set in China are the darkest, and there are moments when Steve can't quite believe that Angie has followed him to such desperate lengths; he refers to her as his 'little saint of the shadows' more than once. The ending is the most troubling scene as it throws the whole story into a tangled web of deceit, leaving viewers to ponder the questionable ethics of such a 'happy ending.' A Spanish-language version was released in February 1931 under the title *Camino del infierno* (*Road to Hell*, 1931), a month after the original.

M (1931)
(Orig title: *M - Eine Stadt sucht einen Mörder* — '*M – A city looks for a murderer*')
Dir: Fritz Lang /Germany

The police are on the hunt for a child killer in Düsseldorf. And when the killer strikes again, the investigation becomes so intense – and police officers so intrusive in their crackdown on crime – that the criminal underworld sets out to find the culprit themselves, as his activities have become a hindrance to their own criminal enterprises...

No stranger to portraying shady underworld characters on screen, director Fritz Lang made this – his first talkie – as a return to the crime genre after his *Dr. Mabuse, Der Spieler* (1922). However, this time instead of depicting a mastermind super-villain, he instead brought the genre much closer to the lurid newspaper headlines of true crime. Partly inspired by the crimes of the 'Vampire of Düsseldorf,' Peter Kürten, Lang and his then wife, Thea von Harbou, began piecing together a gripping tale that drew on the press clippings of the Kürten killings. They also found inspiration in the vigilante actions of the beggars' union in the musical, *The Threepenny Opera* (1931). They were even granted access to case files at Scotland Yard and the Alexanderplatz police headquarters, and consulted with experts on how law enforcement would organise a manhunt, taking into account not just good old-fashioned police work but also forensics, too. Lang even took the unprecedented step of visiting asylums and interviewing the inmates – many of whom were psychopaths and sexual sadists (including Kürten himself) – in an effort to try to understand what makes the monsters tick.

Germany's biggest film studio, Ufa, turned down the project because of its dark nature, but the director and his wife had already invested too much into the project to see it shelved. Instead, Lang made a compromise whereby he scaled the project down considerably, using only a fraction of the resources he had grown accustomed to. Eventually signing a deal with the lesser-known Nero-Film company, Lang was given a tight schedule of just six weeks to shoot the film, between January and March of 1931. Reuniting with several trusty crew members, including DP Fritz Arno Wagner (who had previously lensed *Destiny* [1921] and *Spies* [1928]), and set designer, Karl Vollbrecht (of *Metropolis* [1927]), the film-makers were undaunted by the schedule, and even went to the trouble of constructing the huge office block set in a disused zeppelin hangar – the set that would yield the film's most intense scenes as the killer is captured there by a small army of criminals.

Lang later admitted that he had invented the story about the owner of the hangar being a Nazi and ordering the director to change the film's original title, as he considered *Murderer Among Us* to be in reference to Adolf Hitler and the growing Nazi movement. He also claimed that he cast real-life beggars and thieves as extras in the underground jury of the killer's 'trial' at the end. He even claimed that he had lied to the police so that his extras could disappear back into the underworld from whence they came, without being apprehended by the law. And these are just a couple of the director's claims which, true or not, have passed into legend. What *can't* be disputed, however, is the film's impassioned plea against the death penalty, voiced by the underworld 'lawyer' who defends the killer during the finale.

Peter Lorre as the killer is nothing short of astonishing. Lang deliberately cast him because of his soft, baby-face looks, as a way of demonstrating how even innocent-looking humans can be far more dangerous than any big bad wolf. Lorre's character, Hans Beckert, may have abducted and murdered eight children, but he is shown to be a man in overwhelming psychological anguish; Lang allows viewers to witness his characters' torments as he tries – and fails – to escape the voices in his head that command him to kill. But crucially, the film is not a sympathetic portrayal of a child murderer, but a humanistic one. This misunderstanding led the Nazis to use clips from *M* in the propaganda films, *Juden ohne maske* (*The Jew Unmasked*, 1937) and *The Eternal Jew* (1940), as a way of condemning the 'degeneracy' of the Weimar Republic.

Released in May 1931, *M* found itself in trouble with the British censors who objected to the scenes in which Beckert makes his 'excuses' for his crimes, and this resulted in extensive cuts which robbed the film of it most powerful sequence; Beckert stands before his accusers in the abandoned factory and tries in vain to express the horror of his compulsions – how he is haunted by the ghosts of his victims, and how

the voices only leave him alone when he kills. Such humanistic portrayals of killers has resulted in many haunting classics over the years, from *Peeping Tom* (1959) and *Tenderness of the Wolves* (1973), to *Henry: Portrait of a Serial killer* (1986) and *The Ugly* (1996).

M had a much better reception in America where it became a hit and was celebrated by the critics for its gritty realism and as an innovative crime film in its own right. MGM's Irving Thalberg even screened the film for his writers and directors before encouraging them to go out and produce films that could rival the innovation and box-office receipts. However, it would be another decade before Hollywood studios would catch up with Lang's dazzling feat, with the release of *Citizen Kane* (1941). In the year 2000, Criterion released a DVD edition of the original 110-minute cut which had never been seen in the English-speaking world (most of the prints outside of Germany ran for 99-minutes). Lang went on to make *Fury* (1936), which was perhaps the closest he got to recapturing the feel of *M* in his later works. A faithful – if ultimately flawed – American remake appeared in 1951.

Are These Our Children (1931)
Dir: Wesley Ruggles [and Howard Estabrook, uncredited] /USA
High school student, Eddie (Eric Linden), has everything going for him; a steady girlfriend in Mary (Rochelle Hudson), a loving mother, and a good-natured outlook on life. One day, he flunks a speech contest at school, and the humiliation is too much for him to bear. He drops out and tags along with a cynical group of tearaways. And before long he's out boozing all night at the local jazz clubs and robbing strangers at gunpoint to keep his friends supplied with hooch. One night, he and his drunken friends rob his stepfather's delicatessen, and Eddie shoots the man dead when he refuses to hand over a crate of booze. The police eventually close in on the gang, and Eddie is sentenced to death. The film ends with a remorseful Eddie pleading with his younger brother to be good and to look after their mother. 'I picked the wrong side,' he mourns, as he is led away to the gallows.

Okay, so Eddie's final speech isn't in the same league as Hans Beckert's in *M*, but this is a particularly sleazy little pick for its time and is worth a watch. Like other pre-code movies released in the same year, such as *Night Nurse*,

Street Scene and *Night Life in Reno* (all 1931), *Are These Our Children* starts off as a light drama before darkening in tone with each passing reel. It can be seen as a forerunner to the 'delinquent youth' exploitation craze that was just around the corner. The film also pre-dates the sensationalised television movies of the 1970s and 80s that served as warnings for school kids to stay on the right path, such as *Just Ask Alice* (1973) and *The Day My Kid Went Punk* (1987).

Interestingly, Hollywood had until then always portrayed the flappers in a positive light, as outspoken young ladies willing to shirk the conventions of the time. However, with this film, the flappers are shown to be a menace to social order, leading bright young men to their doom. Arline Judge steals the show as 'Flo,' the vampish drop-out who lures Eddie into a life of jazz, booze, casual sex, robbery, nihilism and murder. Judge and Linden reunited in the following year for *Young Bride* and *The Age of Consent* (both 1932). When RKO attempted to re-release *Are These Our Children* in 1937, it was banned by the tight new regulations of the production code.

Safe in Hell (1931)
Dir: William A. Wellman /USA
After murdering one of her ex-clients with a wine bottle and burning down a hotel, prostitute Gilda Karlson (Dorothy Mackail) flees New Orleans to a Caribbean island with sailor Carl (Donald Cook), a love interest of hers. The plan is to sit it out in the tropical 'paradise', exempt from extradition, while Carl heads back to duty on the high seas. However, the island is also home to a number of other fugitives, from pickpockets and fraudsters to cold-blooded killers. And Gilda has a tough time fending off the lewd advances of an array of dangerous, immoral men...

Sounding much more edgy and daring on paper than it actually is to watch, *Safe in Hell* provoked most of its controversy for the skimpy outfits worn by the leading lady which exposed her long sexy legs, particularly in the opening scene as she is shown sitting back on a chair with her legs resting on the table in front of her. The story had so much potential to be a lurid thriller, but unfortunately, even for a pre-code movie, it's far too tame for its own good. Indeed, the story of a lone woman forced to flee to an island, far away from the protection of the law,

and at the mercy of sex-starved savages against whom she must pit her wits – even with a mediocre script, this should have been far more interesting (or at least entertaining) than it turned out to be. The biggest surprise, however, is that *Safe in Hell* was never remade, not even as a cheap TV movie for bored housewives. And, considering the dramatic potential here, it's certainly a loss. Even today, a remake could be quite interesting if done right. Clearly, the usually reliable Wellman didn't have his heart in the job. It's difficult to believe that the same director went on to make such classics as *Wild Boys of the Road* (1933) and *Looking For Trouble* (1934). *Safe in Hell* had a troubled pre-production; Wellman took over the helm at the last minute when original choice for director, Michael Curtiz, pulled out.

Frankenstein (1931)
Dir: James Whale /USA
One of the most important horror movies ever made, *Frankenstein* is perhaps the first true horror classic of the 'talkie' era. Vastly superior to Tod Browning's *Dracula*, which preceded it by a mere ten months, this film shows how quickly Universal mastered the techniques of sound.

Frankenstein was brought to the screen by director James Whale, who had discarded much of Mary Shelley's rambling source novel in order to focus on the central theme of the obsessed scientist who succeeds in re-animating a childlike monster – a confused outcast made up of stolen body parts and a criminal's brain, or 'dysfunctio cerebri.'

Though Shelley's novel had already been adapted to the screen previously, first in Edison's short, *Frankenstein* (1910), and then in the Golem-inspired *Life Without a Soul* (1915), and the long-lost Italian variant, *Il mostro di Frankenstein* (1921), it was Universal Pictures, under the auspices of producer, Carl Laemmle Jr, who managed to capitalise on the story's full screen potential. Still fairly new to the cinematic medium, director James Whale nonetheless presents a remarkable technical mastery of his craft, as well as a willingness to explore the imagination and break the rules wherever necessary. His background in theatre shines through here in many wonderful scenes, such as the monster's introduction: the ghoul backs in from a doorway as the viewer's curiosity peaks. The creature slowly turns around to face the camera, and Whale cuts to intense close-ups of the monster's face.

Make-up legend, Jack Pierce, created the famous and iconic – and copyrighted – visage of the monster, with its flattop, neck bolts, and droopy eyelids, while Whale himself selected the wardrobe – a tatty old hobo suit – to complete the iconic look. But it was Boris Karloff – billed under the '?' on the title credits – who brought the ghoul to life, from a confused monster to a sympathetic, yearning pariah. The marvellous make-up perfectly suits the film's blend of fantasy and science, while managing to highlight Karloff's expressive features. This was the role that launched Karloff – real name Henry Pratt – to legend status overnight.

Elsewhere on the casting front, Whale ultimately rejected the original choice for leading man, Leslie Howard, and instead opted for fellow Englishman, Colin Clive, whose stark accent sounds strangely out of place in the film's quasi-European setting ('It's alive!! It's alive!!'). Both Edward Van Sloan and Dwight Frye were brought in from *Dracula*; Sloan would now play Dr. Waldman, Frankenstein's cautious, disapproving mentor at the Goldstadt Medical College, and Frye took on the crazy role of the hunchbacked dwarf assistant, Fritz, whose incompetence leads to the dysfunctional brain blunder.

The campy humour that typified Whale's later work is less apparent here, but there are moments of comic relief, such as the scenes with Frederick Kerr as Dr. Frankenstein's doddering father. But overall, the humour is mostly subdued. The scene in which the monster encounters an eight-year-old girl by the lake was perhaps inspired by *Der Golem* (1920), and the scene is just as moving, horrifying and cathartic as Paul Wegener and Carl Boese's silent expressionist classic. Universal famously discarded a line from the film in which Frankenstein boasts 'now I know what it feels like to be God,' but they did add a rather quaint disclaimer (featuring Van Sloan) warning viewers of the horrors to follow.

The film premiered in New York on 4 December, 1931, to mostly positive reviews. *Harrison's Reports* commented, 'The film holds one's attention from the beginning to the very end. It is so artistically produced that the story does not seem fantastic.' However, the review went on to question whether or not the film was suitable for Sunday showings, as 'it is a very strong picture.' In January 1932, *Film Weekly* summed up its response: 'It is no idle exaggeration to say that *Frankenstein* is the most revoltingly gripping melodrama of the macabre since John Barrymore gave his hair-raising impersonation of Mr. Hyde.' Likewise, this review heaped on the praise before adding a cautious caveat at the end, suggesting that 'in some ways [the film-makers] have gone a little too far.' Indeed, just a day after the premier, the director of the Studio Relations Committee, Jason Joy, lamented on the slew of horror films that were possibly a oncoming trend of the near future. 'Is this the beginning of a cycle,' he wrote, 'that ought to be retarded or killed?' However, considering the fact that the film raked in more than a million dollars in its first few months (during the Great Depression, mind), the concerns of the moral guardians held no weight whatsoever with the studios. Horror movies were indeed the next new cycle.

Apart from the slew of Universal horrors that would be unleashed in the following years – *The Old Dark House* (1932), *The Mummy* (1932), *The Invisible Man* (1933), etc – direct sequels to *Frankenstein* began with *The Bride of Frankenstein* (1935), which was also directed by Whale. The sequel's opening scene contradicted the ending of the original film in which the doctor and the monster seemed to perish in the burning windmill. However, all prints of *Frankenstein* were later re-edited with a happy ending instead. After *The Bride*, Whale abandoned horror movies as their reputation became increasingly unsavoury in Hollywood. Karloff, however, embraced the genre, and returned for a second sequel, *Son of Frankenstein* (1939). After that, it was Lon Chaney Jr. who took on the role of the monster in *Ghost of Frankenstein* (1942), and Bela Lugosi in the disastrous *Frankenstein Meets the Wolf Man* (1943). Even stunt man, Glenn Strange, got to don the make-up in *House of Frankenstein* (1944) – in which Karloff plays the mad doctor – and *House of Dracula* (1945), before the series turned to all-out farce in *Abbott and Costello Meet Frankenstein* (1948).

DVD editions of *Frankenstein* reinstate the cut footage – the girl tossed into the lake, the 'God' line, etc – as well as the original ending. For modern audiences, the film still holds up extremely well. Many argue that the sequel, *The Bride of Frankenstein*, is the superior to this, but it's a debate that will surely rage on until the end of time. However, there can be no denying the power of this fine film; from the grave-robbing scenes, to the monster's encounter with the girl, to the classic resurrection scenes in which the monster is brought to life in the lab with the lightning and cracking thunder, and the ending, set in the burning windmill, which was one of the earliest fiery finales of the genre. Truly electrifying stuff.

Horror historian, Carlos Clarens, wrote of the film: 'The horror is cold, chilling the marrow but never arousing malaise,' in his book, *An Illustrated History of the Horror Film* (pub. 1967), and in the following year, Les Baxter referred to the film as 'still the most famous of all horror films, and deservedly so.' Indeed, the long shadow *Frankenstein* has cast on cinema over the decades cannot be overstated; not only did it help bring about Hammer films (*The Curse of Frankenstein*, [1957] was released almost three decades later), but also any number of mad doctor flicks, sympathetic monsters, spoof, satire, and even everyday pop culture. Kim Newman wrote, 'Without *Frankenstein*, there wouldn't be a genre called the horror film.' I would go one further: the world just wouldn't be the same without this extraordinary fright film.

The Blonde Captive (1931)
Dir: Clinton Childs, Ralph P. King, Linus J. Wilson, and Paul Withington /USA
Pre-dating *Mondo Cane* (1963) by more than thirty years, *The Blonde Captive* was one of the first 'documentaries' to hit the screens as a slice of sensationalised anthropological exploitation. Made with the pretence of presenting viewers with a scientific investigation into the descendants of neanderthals, the film was actually just an excuse to ogle at primitive tribes in the Pacific Islands.

Members of the 'The Explorer's Club' set off with a film crew from America's west coast and head first for Hawaii, then to Bali, Fiji, New Zealand and finally to Australia. En route, viewers are presented with all the usual elements that flourished in the mondo movies of the 1960s, such as the casual and oblivious racism of the narrator, an abundance of bare-breasted women, primitive customs, and the usual animal slaughter. A turtle's heart is cut out and placed on the deck of a boat – and the heart is still beating. We're informed that the heart continued to beat for another twelve hours

before it 'gave up the struggle,' and this demonstration was designed to show the secret of the turtle's longevity in life. A young Aborigine boy has his front teeth knocked out by his father as part of a coming-of-age warrior ritual. The boy doesn't even flinch as the man uses a bone chisel and a rock to loosen the gnashers, and the kid is then seen bowing his head while a heavy stream of blood flows from his mouth. In another mondo moment, the film-makers supposedly discover a blonde woman with the natives at the end – actually, she looks like a dark-skinned member of the tribe in a white wig. And the expedition pleads with her to return home to civilisation with them, but the woman refuses as she is now married to the tribe leader and has a – blonde – daughter with him.

Owing an obvious debt not only to the vastly superior – and haunting – *Nanook of the North* (1922), but also other doctored documentaries, such as *Gow The Head Hunter* (aka *Cannibal Island*, 1928), *Afirca Speaks* (1930), and *Ingagi* (1931), *The Blonde Captive* was originally made as an hour-long documentary film on the study of Aboriginals which was released into theatres by National Geographic in 1931. After the film's initial run, Columbia Pictures obtained the rights, and they re-edited the footage, adding the voice-over and the fictional scenes of the Explorer's Club and the blonde captive at the end.

The new version of the film with its new title was met with controversy, especially in Australia where many viewers objected to the racism of narrator, Lowell Thomas. By comparing primitive tribes with monkeys, and often sarcastically remarking on the tribe's beauty while the camera zooms in on aged women's sagging breasts, many accused Thomas of being unprofessional and insensitive. At one point in the film, the narrator is heard remarking on 'barbaric customs,' and noting 'here is human life at its lowest.' The scientific community also came out against the film and accused the producers of promoting their picture as an educational film in a cynical way of getting around censorship.

The film did immense damage to American-Australian relations in the sciences as those who had helped the film-makers felt betrayed by the sensationalised money-maker the project turned out to be. *The Blonde Captive* was therefore banned in Australia, and the film disappeared in 1947 for more than fifty years before it was discovered in an archive in 2001. It was released on DVD in 2010.

The Old Dark House (1932)
Dir: James Whale /USA

"No beds. You can't have the beds!" Three stranded travellers, who have narrowly avoided being crushed to death in a mudslide due to torrential downpours, stop by at an old dark house to seek shelter for the night. Inside, they meet a family of creepy eccentrics headed by Horace Femm (Ernest Thesiger), who, along with his aggressive sister, Rebecca (Eva Moore), and the mongoloid servant, Morgan (Boris Karloff), host an awkward dinner in which the lights seem to have a mind of their own. Shortly after, another pair enter the house seeking shelter, and things become even more sinister when characters go walkabout, the mongoloid downs a bottle of gin, and the psychotic, pyromaniac brother is released from the attic... *The Old Dark House* was Universal's affectionate lampooning of British manners. The script was based on J.B. Priestley's novel, *The Benighted* (pub. 1927), with all the philosophical elements scrapped in favour of colourful characters and mordant humour. The result isn't as memorable or as iconic as the other Universal hits of the time, like *Frankenstein* (1931), *Dracula* (1931) and *The Invisible Man* (1932), but is an off-beat classic in its own right, and has influenced dozens of 'crazy family' pictures and TV shows over the decades, among them *Eraserhead* (1976), *Spider Baby* (1964), *The Texas Chain Saw Massacre* (1974), *The Munsters* (1964-66), *The Adams Family* (1964-66), *The 'Burbs* (1989), *Calvaire* (2004), and even the eccentric British sitcom, *The League of Gentlemen* (1999-2002).

Freaks (1932)
(aka *Nature's Mistakes*)
Dir: Tod Browning /USA

Freaks incited so much controversy it was banned in the UK for thirty years. The film is set in a travelling circus where trapeze artist Cleopatra (Olga Baclanova) and strongman Hercules (Henry Victor) become lovers and are the only physically normal members of the act. The rest are all sideshow freaks; midgets and the physically deformed, including a human torso (who in real life is said to have fathered fifty children!). The story centres on Hans (Harry Earles), a dwarf who is in love with Cleopatra.

She is beautiful but also cruel and mocking, and she openly laughs at him. But when she learns he has inherited wealth she begins to see him in a different light.

Hans' friends try to warn him about Cleopatra but he is too smitten with her to listen. Cleopatra and Hercules devise an evil plot – she will marry Hans, slowly poison him to death, and then make off with his fortune. At the wedding reception the freaks welcome her into the fold with chants of "We accept you. One of us, one of us." Cleopatra shrinks back in disgust, and Hercules finds it all highly amusing. She tells them she'll never be grotesque like them. She then humiliates Hans by kissing her strongman lover in front of him, and the community realises there is a threat in their presence.

A few weeks later and the plot to kill Hans is already in action. The freaks become increasingly suspicious when Hans falls ill, and they discover the poison plot. Meanwhile, Hercules is frustrated that he can't have his way with Cleopatra, so he turns his sights on another woman and attempts to rape her. But Phroso intervenes and wounds him with a knife. Hercules escapes to find shelter in the forest. It's nightfall, and the rain beats hard. Hercules stumbles around in the mud, and the freaks pursue him relentlessly. The human torso drags himself through the mud with a knife clenched between his teeth. And when Hercules is dealt with, they return to inflict a horrible, ironic revenge on Cleopatra. As they close in around her, their chant rings out again: "One of us... one of us..."

With a running time of just over an hour, and with an equally slim plot, *Freaks* is a genuinely startling film even today. This film will always be remembered for one thing: the casting of genuine circus freaks. At once a demented work of genius and one of the most memorable exploitation movies ever made, *Freaks* is a film whose horrors are absolutely real. Fake scenes of sex and blood and violence are one thing, but real genetic deformity is something else entirely. The only special effect in this film is at the end: the final shot is of Cleopatra, her whole body mutilated and deformed, and her face mangled beyond recognition, presented as the most horrifying exhibit at the circus's next venue.

Back in the 1930s this film caused such a scandal it effectively ruined the career of its director, Tod Browning. Only in the previous

78

year he had introduced the horror film to the talkie age with the hugely successful *Dracula* (1931), the Bela Lugosi classic. He had made over fifty films dating back to 1915, but after *Freaks* he never made another serious film. Browning had always wanted to make a movie about the sideshows at carnivals, and of course he was a 'carny' himself at one point. As a teen he ran away from home and joined a travelling circus. So on the one hand he had that personal connection with those people which perhaps explains how he managed to get them to agree to appear in the film and relax in front of the camera. And on the other, his own experience as a carny had taught him that those people weren't monsters to be hidden away, but decent people with hopes and dreams and aspirations. The problem was that the everyday movie-going public didn't have that personal connection with circus 'freaks', and they were horrified at what they saw on screen. I suppose Browning's only fault was that he took his own acceptance of those people for granted, assuming that others looking in from the outside would see them in the same way he did. Alas, he was wrong, and sorely punished for it.

Freaks was made by MGM as a way of getting in on the horror boom that was started by their rivals, Universal Studios. Films like *Dracula*, *Frankenstein*, and *The Mummy* had made a fortune and had made stars out of Bela Lugosi and Boris Karloff, and had captured the imaginations of an entire generation (and many more to come over the decades, too). MGM decided they would hire the director of *Dracula* to make a film for them, hoping to ape the financial success of Universal's horror movies. But when the film was completed, the studio was so shocked and horrified that it declared the film 'unacceptable,' and sold the picture off to independent distributors who, rather aptly, toured it around carnival tent shows under the title *Nature's Mistakes* (Dwain Esper, of *Maniac* [1934] infamy, also screened the film in roadshows and burlesque houses in America, further adding to this cult classic's notorious reputation).

Freaks shows an obvious compassion for its carny cast, imbibing the plot with vignettes about the Siamese twins' love life, how a man with no legs gets about by walking on his hands, or how a man with no legs and no arms can manage to light a cigarette. It's an oddly charming film for much of its length, showing its human oddities as innocent and childlike – such as the bearded lady, the bird girl, the hermaphrodite, the human skeleton, and the pinheads – to see how they move, how they feel, how they love. But the ending is an unforgettably nasty nightmare that, to a certain extent, seems to undermine everything else that had occurred in the film up to that point, as the freaks crawl very menacingly through the mud with murder in mind, becoming the very monsters the world thinks them to be. Nonetheless, this is a one-of-a-kind landmark in the horror genre and is still well worth seeing.

The siamese twins, the Hilton Sisters (1908-1964), later hit the stage circuit as a singing duet. They also appeared in the exploitation/revenge film, *Chained For Life* (1951).

Scarface (1932)
(aka *Scarface: The Shame of a Nation*)
Dir: Howard Hawks /USA
A masterpiece from director Howard Hawks, and a major landmark of the gangster genre, *Scarface* takes its cue from the previous hits, *Little Caesar* and *The Public Enemy*, and ramps up the violence and body-count as another Al Capone attempts to climb the crime ladder in Chicago, with bloody results.

The film opens with the scene of 'Scarface,' Tony Camonte (Paul Muni), in Nosferatu-like silhouette, whistling a few bars of an Italian song before gunning down a victim and calmly walking away. We later learn that Tony is a typical gangster type – reckless and arrogant, with next to no impulse control. Francois Truffaut later claimed that Hawks wanted an ape-like performance out of Muni, while others claim he wanted his actor to impersonate Mussolini. And in a subtle way, Muni's superb performance rings true on both counts.

Unlike previous crime films, there is very little back-story on Tony, and no attempts to blame his actions and attitude on his circumstances or environment. Instead, the film-makers present the fully-developed monster without any explanation, for better or worse. And this allows viewers to piece together their own theories on why Tony became such a brutal homicidal maniac. His love for loud guns, flashy cars and expensive suits was a fairly common trait for many young men of his time, but his jealousy of his sister's (Ann Dvorak's) love life borders on the incestuous. And it's this vulnerability which brings about his downfall.

Tony works for Johnny Lovo (Osgood Perkins), a more experienced and rational hoodlum who, in turn, answers to Big Louis (Harry Vejar), Chicago's top crime boss. (Perkins' character was based on Johnny Torrio, the real-life hoodlum who established organised crime in America, and Veja's was based on former Chicago crime lord, Big Jim Colosimo). When Tony is arrested for the murder of the opening scene, a mob lawyer on the inside has him released on a special writ. Tony wants Lovo to kill Big Louis as he is holding the gang back by not getting involved in the bootleg business. And when Lovo sees that Tony has his sights on the North Side crime boss (Boris Karloff), he warns the maniac to leave him alone. However, Tony also has his eyes on Lovo's sexy mistress (Karen Morely), and the stage is set for a bloody climax...

Scarface was the most violent film the cinema had seen up to that point. It also boasted the largest body-count of a non-war movie, with 28 on-screen deaths and many more off-screen. In one sequence, there are consecutive tit-for-tat drive-by shootings with machine guns, in which rival gangs show up at each other's hang-out spots and riddle the buildings with bullets. Hawks certainly went the extra mile, mounting his cameras on dolly wheels and bringing back the fluidity of camera movement after a momentary stay with the early static talkies. Also of note is the 'X' symbol that shows up throughout the film to foreshadow death (the ceiling rafters, Karloff's bowling score, Tony's X-shaped scar on his left cheek, and George Raft's apartment number, for example). Co-producer, Howard Hughes, spared no expense in helping to bring the film to the screen, but he also made his regular habit of interfering with the day-to-day shoot, and requesting that Hawks consult him on all decisions being made on set. The production was almost scrapped altogether due to the constant disagreements between Hawks and Hughes.

Very little of Armitage Trail's source novel made it into the final film except for the title. Instead, Hawks seemed to use the book more as a template on which he placed his own idea of portraying Tony and his sister as modern-day Borgias. The incestuous obsession was perhaps inspired by *Little Caesar*, which featured another gangster who seems to come undone via a forbidden love – in his case a homosexual desire for a friend whom he can't bring himself to kill at the end.

Scarface hit the cinemas on 9 April 1932. The release was delayed while the film-makers added some extra scenes to help cushion the blow of such hard-hitting fare. One of the scenes showed Tony being tried, convicted and hanged (though it was obviously shot after the production when Muni wasn't available, as he never actually appears in this sequence.). All subsequent releases, however, stuck with the originally-intended finale in which Tony, like 'Little Caesar' before him, goes out in a hail of bullets beneath an ad board that reads, 'The World is Yours' (which was recycled from a similar billboard seen in *Underworld* [1927] which reads, 'The City is Yours' – both screenplays were penned by Ben Hecht).

One post-production scene that *did* remain in all subsequent editions is the one in which the Chief Detective snaps at a news reporter for describing Tony as a 'colourful character.' 'Colourful?' he replies. 'What colour is a crawling louse? Say, listen: that's the attitude of too many morons in this country. They think these big hoodlums are some sort of demigods. What do they do about a guy like Camonte? They sentimentalise, romance, make jokes about him. They had some excuse for glorifying our old western bad men; they met in the middle of the street at high noon, waiting for each other to draw. But these things sneak up, shoot a guy in the back and then run away... colourful. Did you read what happened the other day? A car full of them was chasing another down the street in broad daylight. Three kiddies playing hopscotch on the side walk got lead poured in their little bellies. When I think what goes on in the minds of these lice, I want to vomit.'

The Hays office had strongly objected to the film while it was still in script form, which led Hughes to famously order his director to 'screw the Hays office, make it as realistic and grisly as possible.' The American critics were almost universally positive in their reviews, while in Britain, the BBFC passed it with cuts, only to see Beckenham Council ban it outright (along with around 200 other films between 1932 and 1934).

However, such hassles were nothing compared to what was going in Italy. The advent of talkies had introduced a major problem: the censorship of foreign languages. With Italy going through a strong nationalistic phase, and the techniques of dubbing still unheard of, the fascist state found itself having to deal with the 'invasion' of foreign language films. In *Street Scene* (1931), an Italian character has a political debate with a Marxist Jew: 'If Mussolini heard you say that,' the Italian fumes, 'he'd turn you into a casserole.' It is not known how Mussolini had reacted to the scene, but foreign languages were immediately banned in Italian cinema. And this resulted in a brief period of 'sonorisation' which was the process of trying to make silent films out of foreign talkies. To do this, the censors substituted dialogue scenes with captions of translated content. Of course, this clumsy tampering was deeply unpopular with audiences, and the practice was abandoned in 1933.

Scarface in particular was subjected to negative scrutiny in Italy. The head of film censorship until 1939, Luigi Freddi, praised the film's qualities but objected to the fact that 'all the criminals that supported the structure of the terrifying main character, even if they lived in America, were scrupulously and deliberately Italian.' Both *Scarface* and *Little Caesar* were also accused of portraying villains who mimic Mussolini, and were banned.

Vampyr (1932)

(aka *Vampyr der Traum des Allan Gray*; aka *Castle of Doom*; aka *The Strange Adventure of David Gray*)
Dir: Carl Th. Dreyer /Germany /France
'Imagine we are sitting in an ordinary room. Suddenly, we are told there is a corpse behind the door. In an instant, the room is completely altered; everything in it has taken another look; the light, the atmosphere have changed, though they are physically the same. This is because we have changed, and the objects are as we perceive them. That is the effect I meant to get in my film.' So said director Carl Theodor Dreyer on the impetus behind *Vampyr*, a morbid fever dream which was designed solely to put dread in its audience.

Shot in sound but effectively coming across as a silent film, *Vampyr* was shot in France in the summer of 1930 when the rest of the world was appreciating talking pictures for the first time. And by the time the finished film was released in May 1932, the horror genre had already produced such classics as Universal's *Dracula* and *Frankenstein* (both 1931). However, neither of those films could match the strange, otherworldly atmosphere of *Vampyr*, and Dreyer's dark and troubling fever dream tanked at the box-office. Indeed, even today the film isn't an easy ride, and most casual viewers will be put off by the film's refusal to play by the conventional narrative rules.

Vampyr was fully financed by Parisian aristocrat, Baron Nicolas de Gunzburg, and he also took the lead role under the pseudonym 'Julian West'. He drifts through the story like a ghost, observing a spate of vampire attacks in the town of Courtempierre. He's at once fully involved in the action and yet strangely detached from it, like a sleep-walker going through the motions. Upon the death of an aristocrat, the protagonist, Allan Gray, opens a package that the deceased had left behind to be opened after his death. The package contains a book on the history of vampirism. And in the pages, both Gray and the viewers learn that the town was previously attacked by vampires years earlier. In a remarkable dream sequence, Gray's spirit gets loose from his body and wanders the grounds as a faint spirit, where he witnesses his own corpse in a coffin. And at the end, the evil doctor – who has been poisoning the residents – is locked in a flour mill and suffocated to death.

If that brief synopsis sounds kind of vague, the film itself is deliberately enshrouded in mystery and dread, and with little interest in telling a straight forward story. In his book, *Studies in Terror* (pub. 2011), Jonathan Rigby describes the film's confounding descent as 'a dream on the edge of consciousness – not a fully fledged nightmare, but the strangling sensation of swimming up from the depths while not quite managing to surface.' Allan Gray takes a room in spooky old inn that is decorated with a framed picture of a victorious skeleton in the midst of a plague. The protagonist hears strange mumbling sounds coming from the hall, and when he goes out to investigate, he is met by a grotesque man with no eyes. The bizarre occurrences only increase as keys turn of their own accord, a policeman's shadow wanders around with a life of its own, and there are even nods towards F.W. Murnau with several shots borrowed from *Nosferatu*.

The film's most famous set-pieces include Leone (Sybille Schmidtz) slowly transforming into a vampire and baring her teeth at her younger sister; Allan's (possible but not certain) 'death dream' in which he embodies his own corpse and watches on helplessly through a small window in his coffin while the lid is screwed down; and the female vampire peering in through the hole for a closer look. There is also the dramatic finale in which the Renfield-like doctor succumbs to a merciless cascade of flour in the mill. However, the film's quieter moments can be just as unsettling, such as the scene in which the vampire's voice can be heard trying to lure Allan after he has donated blood to Leone: 'Follow me,' the voice says. 'Death is waiting...'

Though officially based on Sheridan Le Fanu's classic anthology, *In a Glass Darkly* (pub. 1872) – particularly the stories *Carmilla* and *The Room in the Dragon Volant* – Dreyer's real intent seemed to be an exploration of the book's intriguing title. And in doing so, he transforms the French wilderness into a dark and menacing netherworld, anchored in nightmare. Laden with surrealism, expressionism, and gloomy atmospherics, the film really does feel as though there is a corpse lying in wait behind every door. The female vampire bears so little relation to the one in Le Fanu's classic tale – or any vampire seen in the movies for that matter. To call *Vampyr* a 'vampire film' would be like calling *J'Accuse!* a war film. In fact, by depicting the voluptuous seductress of *Carmilla* as a white-haired old crone, Dreyer's film fits more comfortably in the realm of witchcraft than vampires, though it fits in no particular genre. The vampire in *Vampyr* more closely resembles the witch who is burned at the stake in Dreyer's *Day of Wrath* (1943) rather than the one imagined by Le Fanu.

Perhaps unsurprisingly, the first to be exposed to *Vampyr* were not altogether impressed. A review appeared in the *New York Times* in July 1932 in which the unnamed critic wrote, 'Although in many ways it was one of the worst films I have ever attended, there were some scenes in it that gripped with a brutal directness...' The critic then went on to completely misjudge and misrepresent the film: '[the set-pieces] have depth and a simplicity of style which is seldom achieved in the hurried world of the film studio. But, for all that, it was a peculiarly irritating picture. The scenario was so bad that the author had to excuse it by pretending it was a dream. It was merely a tritely developed, muddled treatment of the old vampire theme.'

Such casual dismissals were not uncommon among the critics, and *Vampyr* failed to make much of an impact at the box-office. On the censorship front, it was the BBFC once again who objected most strongly to the picture. However, instead of banning it, the Board released it uncut with the newly-created 'H' (for 'horrific') certificate which forbade children from attending the screenings. The certificate was brought in partly in response to the Universal monster movies which were beginning to flourish in the early 1930s. But still, the H certificate wasn't enough to save horror films from the censor's shears; Rouben Mamoulian's *Dr. Jekyll and Mr. Hyde* (1931) lost around a quarter of its running time, resulting in a confusing mess of a film. *The Gorilla* (1930) and *J'Accuse!* (1920) – the latter having being banned in Britain for around thirteen years – were granted H certificates in 1933. *Island of Lost Souls* and Tod Browning's *Freaks* (both 1932) were banned outright. The H certificate was replaced by the 'X' in 1951.

Vampyr's poor reception contributed to Dreyer's nervous breakdown, and he didn't return to film-making until a decade later when he delivered the classic *Day of Wrath*, and from there he went on to become one of the most respected director's in film history. Baron Nicolas de Gunzburg later became the editor of *Vogue* magazine, while actress, Sybille Schmidtz, developed a fan-base that included Joseph Goebbels as one of her admirers. She later committed suicide. As for the film itself, by the mid-1970s *Vampyr*'s reputation had undergone a major turnaround, thanks in part to Dreyer's subsequent works. The critics were then much more inclined to view the film as a masterpiece, with the *Sunday Times* using it as an example to bash Hammer films; '[*Vampyr*] makes our contemporary, explicit Draculas look like advertisements for false teeth.'

In *Vampyr*, viewers may notice little nods and winks, not only to *Nosferatu*, but also to the work of Bunuel and Dali, *Haxan* (1922), *The Seashell and the Clergyman* (1928), and back even further into cinema history, with scenes borrowed from *Dream of a Rarebit Fiend* (1906), Victor Sjöström's *The Phantom Carriage* (1921), and even Henry Fuseli's oil painting, *The Nightmare* (1781). A remake appeared, *Vampyre* (1990).

Red-Headed Woman (1932)
Dir: Jack Conway /USA

Jean Harlow landed her first lead role as the good girl Cassie in *Three Wise Girls* (1932), but the image never really suited her. Her voice was far too catty; her expression too stern; and her overall presence was far too sensually aware to carry off the innocent damsel routine. *Variety* magazine recognised this at the time: 'It is a physical impossibility for Miss Harlow to assume the straight ascetic outlines which are the basis of virtue.' In the same year – in perhaps the wisest move of her career – Harlow signed up to play Lil Andrews, the amoral schemer in *Red-Headed Woman* – a role that not only matched her image like a glove, but also changed her life forever as it propelled her to stardom.

Lil begins by seducing her boss and breaking up his marriage. She then marries him in turn, but finds herself ostracised by his family and circle of friends in high society. When a local coal tycoon catches her eye, she sees him as a ticket to reach higher on the social ladder. She seduces him, then uses cunning tactics to get him to host a party at her place. However, the stunt turns out to be a humiliating one as all the guests leave early to attend another party across the street. She leaves for New York in a huff.

Meanwhile, her former boss and current husband (Chester Morris) gets his son to hire private detectives to keep an eye on her. And it isn't long before they discover that Lil is involved in two affairs – not only is she seeing Charles the tycoon, but his chauffeur too. Seeing the evidence with his own eyes, William reconciles with his ex-wife, Irene. And when Lil returns to him, he rejects her, to which she responds by shooting and attempting to kill him. William survives the attack, and years later while attending a race track in the French Riviera, William catches a sight of Lil in the stands. He sees that she is accompanied by an elderly French gentleman. In the final scene, William watches as Lil and the Frenchman get into a car that is being driven by Albert the chauffeur!

Based on the novel by Katherine Bush (pub. 1931), MGM rushed this film to the screen amid much fall-out from those involved. F. Scott Fitzgerald and Marcel de Sano were hired to write the screenplay, but they despised each other. And despite completing the script in five weeks, producer Irving Thalberg wasn't happy with it, insisting that it was too serious and in need of a streak of humour. Therefore he hired Anita Loos to add the comedy touches. Predictably, the Hays office was not impressed with the film; they suggested seventeen cuts to remove the scenes of a partially undressed Harlow and also lines of dialogue that were considered far too sexual in nature. And even though Thalberg agreed to the cuts, the film was still the subject of much controversy when it was released into theatres.

Red-Headed Woman is an interesting time capsule but isn't considered a game-changer (Harlow was immediately relegated into second place by the arrival of another blonde bombshell, Mae West, in the following year). However, it's certainly worth a watch for the curious. With a change of hair colour, Harlow effortlessly plays up to the archetypal femme fatale; the wise-cracking, gold-digging predator who thinks nothing of wrecking the lives of those who get in the way of what she wants. What makes the film stand out from the batch of other movies of its kind at the time is the fact that instead of getting her comeuppance in the end, she is instead shown to be profiting pretty nicely from her life of sin.

Chief censor of the BBFC, Edward Shortt, personally examined the film – he was so appalled by what he saw that he simply banned the film outright without even consulting his colleagues. And the ban remained in place until 1965, by which time the film was mostly forgotten.

Doctor X (1932)
Dir: Michael Curtiz /USA

A rare sojourn into the horror genre for First International (a production company that was later swallowed up by Warner Bros.), *Doctor X* became one of the great lost films after its release, and garnered a legendary reputation as a risqué early talkie during the decades it went unseen. A major contributing factor to the film's mythic status – aside from its unavailability – was the press reviews at the time of its release, which emphasised the horror in exaggerated ways, such as a write-up in the *New York Times* declaring that *Doctor X* 'almost makes *Frankenstein* seem tame and friendly.' When a black and white print of this two-colour Technicolor film was discovered in the late 1970s, some found it to be a disappointment.

However, now that decades have passed since its rediscovery, those of a younger generation who haven't had their expectations blown out of proportion, may find *Doctor X* to be a finely-honed product of its era.

The story is set in a creepy old mansion that is perched atop the cliffs of Blackstone Shoals on Long Island. Lionel Atwill plays the title character, the obsessive Doctor Xavier, the proprietor of the research lab where most of the horror unfolds. It seems a member of the research team has discovered a synthetic flesh substitute which enables its user to unleash terrifying powers. To make matters worse, the culprit transforms into a monster and strangles people during the full moon. The survivors attempt to expose the creature by recreating the murders, but all does not go according to plan...

Director Michael Curtiz (who went on to make the classic, *Casablanca* [1942]), shows a particular flair for lighting, and does a remarkable job of creating an expressionistic atmosphere, in keeping with the 'haunted house' feel of the story. The film perhaps lacks the dark humour and iconic visuals of James Whale, but makes up for it in the grotesque moments, such as the monster running amok in its synthetic skin suit. Lee Tracy and Atwill are great in their roles as the bothersome reporter and Doctor X, respectively, and newcomer, Fay Wray, in her unknown, pre-*King Kong* days, is also memorable as X's daughter. The highlight of the film is no doubt Atwill's casual discussions of topics ranging from cannibalism and rape, to prostitution and murder, and there are also several eerie set-pieces to marvel at, including the scene with the skeleton and recreation of the final murder in which the killer makes an unexpected appearance.

The Most Dangerous Game (1932)
(aka *The Hounds of Zaroff*)
Dir: Ernest B. Schoedsack & Irving Pichel /USA
One of the landmark titles of the 1930s, not to mention one of the most influential, *The Most Dangerous Game* has seen its central themes echoed in everything from radio shows (including an episode of Orson Welles' *Suspense* in 1943), television, and movies, from *A Game of Death* (1945) to *The Hunger Games* (2012). However, the 1932 version is still the best.

The Most Dangerous Game was originally made as a product of convenience. During the making of the big-budget *King Kong* (1933),

cast and crew members found themselves spending a great deal of time sitting around and waiting for scenes to be set up. Ray Harryhausen's meticulous stop-motion effects sequences turned out to be far more time-consuming than expected. So, in order to keep spirits up among the bored staff, producers, Merian C. Cooper and Ernest B. Schoedsack, simply decided they would tackle a more modest project on the side. They chose Richard Connell's classic short story, *The Most Dangerous Game* (pub. 1924). Schoedsack agreed to direct – with actor, Irving Pichel, helping out. So, while Harryhausen's effects technicians were lumbered with the painstaking work of bringing King Kong to life on screen, many of the same cast and crew spent their off-time making *Dangerous Game* on the same jungle sets. And the end result turned out to be far greater than anyone expected.

If you have read Connell's short, you'll already know the story: a sadistic Russian Count, Zaroff, targets shipwrecked survivors who wash up on his island. He hunts them down through the jungle terrain, armed with a war-bow, henchmen and a pack of dogs. For the first film version, the producers brought in British actor, Leslie Banks, to play the depraved lunatic. And with his absurd – and, it must be said – pretty terrible cod-Russian accent, Banks brings to the role a smarmy arrogance that suits Zaroff's barely disguised sexual sadism. And the way he unconsciously strokes the old hunting scar on his forehead – not to mention the unorthodox way he clutches his cigarette – offers none-too-subtle clues for psychoanalysts to ponder upon.

Zaroff's blood-lust is an extension of his sexual sadism, and so it's fitting that he would prefer to hunt humans rather than animals. He also keeps a trophy room in his castle, into which the film's protagonists, Bob and Eve (Joel McCrea and Fay Wray), find their way while trying to escape. Bob's candle illuminates a blackened, rotten human head mounted on the wall, and Eve discovers a glass tank which displays another human head floating around in preserving fluid. But these were only hints of the horrors seen in the forbidden room; the original cut of the film included the sight of dozens of severed heads all lined up and mounted on the wall, but RKO decided to cut the footage, along with the bloodier shots of the shark attacks at the beginning, as those scenes were considered far too horrific for the time. It is estimated by film historians that approximately 13 minutes of footage was discarded from the original cut, and unfortunately, the forbidden footage is probably lost forever.

Nonetheless, what remains is 63-minutes of classic film-making that passes by in a breeze. The morose edge is constantly off-set by the peculiar asides, such as the wonderful sets – including Zaroff's open-plan room, with its six-foot-tall fireplace and fine decorations – Zaroff's odd lines of communication and his way of lying in wait like a deadly spider, just waiting for the next unfortunates to hit the dangerous reefs and become entangled in his jungle web, and of course the thrilling chase scenes at the end. Unlike the original short story, directors Schoedsack and Pichel dwell on the hunt, showing Bob and Eve fleeing for their lives through the brush and trees, while also avoiding the claws of the wild animals and deadly traps lurking in the terrain.

Though it's now considered a classic, initial reaction to *The Most Dangerous Game* was fairly mixed. *Variety* magazine slammed it as, 'a futile stab at horror film classification, ineffective as entertainment and minus cast names to compensate.' Little did the unnamed critic know that Fay Wray would become an overnight sensation with the release of *King Kong* just a few months later. Meanwhile in the UK, *Film Weekly* called it 'strong meat.' In November 1932, the *New York Times* printed a positive review: '[the film] has the much-desired virtue of originality, which, in no small measure, compensates for some of its gruesome ideas and its weird plot.' And in February of 1933, *Picturegoer* recommended it: 'The whole thing is most colourful, and Zaroff's human hunt is finely directed; thrilling and bizarre in turns. The interest is exceptionally well held, and the thrills, while occasionally forced by artificiality, are much more realistic than the majority seen in this picture's prototypes.'

One of those prototypes was Paramount's *The Cheat* (1931) from the previous year, which also features Pichel, this time in front of the camera. Here he plays Hardy Livingstone, a very strange fellow who seems to worship Yama – the Hindu God of destruction. He also keeps a trophy cabinet in which he stores porcelin dolls that represent the women he has trapped and abused. Livingstone shares many characteristics with Zaroff, and enjoys raping and branding his victims with a hot iron. The film isn't mentioned at all in discussions about *The Most Dangerous Game*, but there's no doubt that it had a major influence on the RKO classic. Another interesting side note is the fact that, before *Dangerous Game*, McCrae had just finished working on another RKO film in which his character narrowly avoided being eaten by a shark, only to wind up being terrorised in the jungle, in King Vidor's *Bird of Paradise* (1932), a film which caused controversy for the scenes in which Dolores Del Rio – one of the most beautiful actresses of the era – swims naked. These films would make for an excellent triple-bill.

As for *The Most Dangerous Game*, the film was restored in 1995 by The Roan Group in a crisp transfer which did the rounds of the revival houses and was released on Laserdisc. However, that version was quickly made obsolete by the Criterion DVD release in the late 90s which presented a new transfer with astonishing detail in both the audio and visual quality, along with a brand new audio commentary. It was later released on Blu-Ray in the States, with *Gow The Headhunter* (aka *Cannibal Island*, 1928) included as a bonus feature. A colourised version was released in 2007 to celebrate the film's 75th anniversary.

On the Influence of
The Most Dangerous Game

The influence of this modest little gem has been immense over the decades. The central theme of the obsessive and unstable man-hunter has been updated and re-shaped to fit the current times to such an extent that almost every film genre and television series has its own take on the 'the game.' Not to mention other forms of pop culture, such as comic books and video games. And if the original Zaroff was portrayed as a fiendish Russian aristocrat who had escaped the upheaval of the Bolshevik Revolution, the future Zaroffs would undergo all manner of changes to suit the ever-changing times, and whose face would be altered to fit the big boogeymen of the day.

The trend began in the following decade with *A Game of Death* (1945), which appeared in theatres just as victory in Europe was assured. It's the same scenario that plays out again – with much of the same footage – with a slight change in that Zaroff is re-imagined as a dangerous German called Erich Kreiger. In the 1950s, Count Zaroff hit screens in a very short – 7 minutes – and very obscure film, *The Dangerous Game* (1953), before he was reincarnated again, this time as a William Joyce-style British Nazi called Mr. Browne (Trevor Howard), in *Race For the Sun* (1956). Browne is hiding in the Mexican countryside with a group of fellow 'war criminals' and a vicious pack of bloodhounds. And when wholesome – but flawed – Americans, Mike and Katie (Richard Widmark and Jane Greer), crash land a glider plane in the nearby wilderness, they are eventually forced to run for their lives while being pursued by Browne and his mini-Reich. The 'game' doesn't get started until after the hour mark, but it remains one of the most gruelling and realistic survival runs in history. It is also the most lavish production of the tale ever to hit the screen, and the first in colour.

The production quality dropped considerably for *Bloodlust!* (1961), a low-budget – if spirited – B-movie in which a group of youngsters are washed up on an island owned by Dr. Balleau (Wilton Graff), a seemingly hospitable host who welcomes the teens into his home. However, we soon learn that his wife, Sandra (Lilyan Chauvin), is having an affair, and the doctor's mild-mannered facade – which matches that of Count Zaroff, right down to the peculiar accent, smoking habit, love of chess, and the silk dressing gown – is just a mask to conceal his true nature: that of a deeply traumatised war veteran. His home may not be as impressive as Zaroff's sprawling castle, but his trophy room certainly is – it's a dark, cave-like space in which the bodies of his past victims are displayed in their frightened death poses. And when the game begins, there's very little sadism in Balleau – in fact, the doctor seems to use the hunt as a way of re-visiting his traumatic memories, as if by killing the youngsters he can somehow 'cure' his afflictions. It's a compulsive act of madness he is drawn to, again and again; an indulgent treadmill of pain that yields nothing but the horrors he wants to cleanse himself of. Fittingly, Dr. Balleau becomes the latest exhibit at his own macabre museum – cured at last.

In an episode of *Voyage to the Bottom of the Sea*, entitled *The Enemies* (season 1, episode 29, 1965), the Seaview submarine leads Admiral Nelson and his skipper to a mysterious island run by General Tau (guest star, Henry Silva). And, with this going to air just as the Vietnam War was heating up, it's no surprise to see that the day's contemporary boogeyman, Tau, also leads an army of 'gooks', as well as a crazed scientist (Malachi Throne). However, the twist here is that Nelson and his underling are psychologically manipulated into hunting each other through the jungle terrain.

Of course, it wasn't long before Zaroff was subjected to the spoof treatment, most famously in the secret agent show, *Get Smart*. In the episode, *Island of the Darned* (season 1, episode 11, 1966), agents 86 and 99 are stranded on an island and menaced by the now cartoonish psycho hunter, played by guest star Harold Gould. Also played for laughs was the episode of the sitcom, *Gilligan's Island*, entitled *The Hunter* (season 3, episode 18, 1967), in which Rory Calhoun gets to chase Gilligan around with a rifle after learning there are no animals to shoot. And the canned laughter may as well have continued with the typically camp *Lost In Space* entry, *Hunter's Moon* (season 3, episode 4, 1967), in which John Robinson is hunted by Megazor, a hostile alien creature who happens to speak perfect English. Like Zaroff, Megazor has a fondness for coldly observing what it sees as human weaknesses (or 'defects'), such as compassion, love and loyalty, and yet exhibits a strange sportsmanship while arranging 'the game.' This episode is just as clumsy and flimsy as the doddering cardboard androids that populate the series, but at least Megazor has the decency, or 'defect,' to programme his mechanoid helpers with a self-destruct button, which is activated as soon as the game is lost.

Twenty years later, and the hunter alien arrived on earth packing a thermonuclear self-destruction device in *Predator* (1987), where the ten foot tall warrior-from-outer-space tests its hunting skills against a troop of mercenaries in the Guatemala jungle before meeting its match in Arnold Schwarzenegger. Though much less verbose than Megazor, Predator does at least live by a code of honour – it only attacks armed men. In fact, this species of alien becomes even more sympathetic in the sequel, *Predator 2* (1990): This new predator seems to take great delight in skinning and hanging a bunch of criminal yardie boys in the concrete jungle of Los Angeles, and earthling Danny Glover is even forgiven for killing the alien by its intergalactic brethren. However, the Predators that arrange the game in *Predators* (2010) revert back to the ice-cold methods of Zaroff, as they kidnap elite fighting forces of earthlings and dump them in a jungle in some far-flung galaxy before mercilessly hunting them down. Interestingly, the mercenaries of the original film are on the hunt for communist guerillas in the jungle, so it's fitting that the Marxist Hollywood system would have these men wiped out by a hostile Hollywood creation.

Punishment Park (1971) put a blatant pro-communist spin on the idea as the story was re-told in faux-documentary style with new boogeymen – the military, or, more specifically, Nixon's Republican establishment. A group of peaceful hippies are released from the over-crowded prisons so that they can be hunted to their deaths in the desert. The film-makers were accused of being communists, and of projecting their own side's crimes onto the sanity of conservatism, with a hollow anti-war and anti-American message. However, the film was made in the aftermath of the Kent State shootings, giving it an air of validity. Also alluding to the Vietnam War is the very last episode of *Bonanza*, entitled *The Hunter* (season 14, episode 16, 1973). Tom Skerritt guest stars as Bill, a psychotic prison escapee who targets the show's hero, Michael Landon, for a most dangerous game in the vast wilderness of the wild west. Along with Zaroff-style musings on the pleasures of the hunt, we get a villain who is racked with inner anguish for his past crimes, which include massacring women and children during the American Civil War. As the game begins, Landon's retort of 'we're men, not animals,' is met with derisive laughter from the dangerous lunatic. And even after a four hour head start, it isn't long before Bill is on his heels, personifying the animalistic nature of Man, and unconsciously just begging for a bullet between the eyes to end all the pain in his mixed-up mind. It was a great send-off for the series, just as *Westworld* (1973) reached theatres, and is perhaps the finest televised version of the story ever to hit the small screen, far outshining its big screen counterparts, such as the weak sexploitation quickies, *The Suckers* (1972) and *The Woman Hunt* (1972), and the messy TV movie, *Maneater* (1973). Also from 1973 is Jess Franco's underrated *La Comtesse Perverse*, which includes a Count and Countess Zaroff targeting a young Lina Romay on a beautiful tropical island – the film is reviewed later in this book.

In the following year, the Zaroff character was embodied by Christopher Lee as Scaramanga in the Bond caper, *The Man With the Golden Gun* (1974). And, aside from him owning a car that transforms into a plane, Lee's dead-eyed assassin actually holds a sneaking admiration for Bond, even if the 'empathy' he shows to his prey is all a scam. He also shares with Zaroff a weird perversity; if Zaroff's remarks sometimes revealed the barest hints of deviancy and even necrophilia, Scaramanga's sexual proclivities, on the other hand, are far more openly evident. A few years later, and the pilot episode of *Fantasy Island* (1977) kicked off the series with another jaded hunter who becomes the hunted, before David 'Bennet' found himself lured to a private island and at the mercy of a maniac in *The Snare* (1979), season 3, episode 9 of *The Incredible Hulk*. Interestingly, the maniac here (guest star, Bradford Dillman) doesn't have a trophy room like Zaroff – instead, his sadistic chess-play consists of taking polaroid snapshots of his victims before the hunt begins. However, it later becomes clear that Dillman has no interest in David – it's the Hulk he wants to hunt.

Dangerous games of the 80s got off to a great start with *Southern Comfort* (1981) and *Turkey Shoot* (1982), the former pitching National Guard trainees against a bunch of heavily armed Cajun warriors deep in the woods for a bloody fight for survival, and the latter an underrated future fantasy in which a prison camp commander and his elitist pals play Zaroff against a batch of new inmates (*Turkey Shoot* is covered in depth later on in this book). Another dangerous game by way of future fantasy is *Slave Girls From Beyond Infinity* (1987), a cleavage-and-laser-guns exploitation favourite, written, produced and directed by Ken Dixon. Blonde hotties, Daria and Tisa (Elizabeth Cayton and Cindy Beal), escape from a slave colony in a spaceship and crash land on a nearby planet that is ruled over by Zed (Don Scribner), a typical Zaroff clone, going through the motions of faux-hospitality – not to mention paraphrasing his forebear, almost verbatim – before unleashing the girls on a wild hunt through the nostalgic indoor jungle sets. It's a lot of fun, but is let down by a lack of imagination – the trophy room is just a carbon copy of heads mounted on the walls, though the ancient Mayan-type sets are different, and there is also

Zed's throne-like chair that is adorned with alien looking skulls. Perhaps Zed had a victorious encounter with a Predator in his past? If so, his space cred is assured beyond infinity. Also in the 80s was an episode of *Hart to Hart* entitled *Hunted Harts* (season 4, episode 11, 1983), in which the husband and wife team are lured to South America by a big game hunter who intends to make them his prey by using one of their acquaintances as bait.

Next up, we go from the deepest depths of space and the darkest depths of the jungle, to the deepest pits of Hell for *Angel Heart* (1987), Alan Parker's scorching hot tale of the damned. If the film's theme of a private eye detective (Mickey Rourke) being hunted down through the metaphysical realm of eternal damnation, seems a little stretched in its relation to *The Most Dangerous Game*, a closer look at the arch-villain should help to put things in perspective. Louis Cyphre (or, 'Lucifer'), is so clearly modelled on Zaroff – from the sharp, pointy beard, and the strange – possibly demonic – ring on his finger, not to mention his fondness for chess and philosophical ramblings, De Niro's monstrous character is an aristocrat of the demonic spirit. The way he muses on the egg as being a 'symbol of the soul,' and the way he then devours it whole after meticulously picking away at the shell, demonstrates not only what he intends to do with Mickey Rourke's poor soul, but also how he is going to gain a great deal of satisfaction while doing it. Zaroff himself would no doubt approve. However, the most chilling aspect of Louis Cyphre is that there's no getting away from him; there's no way to escape from his 'island' unscathed – his hunting ground goes far beyond mere earthly realms. Once the Devil has his sights on you, your choices are extremely limited, because he deliberately picks his victims from among those he knows he can ensnare. Thus, the moment you know of his existence, you're as good as finished. And this brings an interesting thought to mind – perhaps *The Most Dangerous Game* itself plays as a metaphor on the struggle to keep out of the Devil's clutches while lost in the 'jungle' of life, with Zaroff just a stand-in for Satan himself?

In the ludicrous guns-and-mullets fest, *Deadly Prey* (1987), innocent members of the public are kidnapped and taken to a remote Army base where they are used as forest prey for trainee marines to test their skills on. The Zaroff character behind all this is Col. John Hogan (David Campbell), a cold-hearted deviant who, for all his tough guy talk, is initially disinclined to get his hands dirty, and instead stays behind the scenes while a team of errand boys arrange and conduct the hunts for him. However, when Mike Danton (Ted Prior) – a Rambo-type veteran and survival expert – is unleashed into the woods as an intended target, the Colonel is forced to join the hunt as his men are systematically slaughtered. And in the following year, the tables were turned in *Lethal Woman* (1988), as a group of marines are lured to an island, only to be hunted down by their past rape victims. And, in *Betrayed* (1988), a black guy is hunted by racist Texans in the woods at night. They even arm him with a pistol – how sporting of them!

The most interesting Zaroff clone to emerge in the 90s was Osirius in the excellent TV movie, *Deadly Game* (1991). Borrowing just as much from Dr. Anton Phibes as he does from the Count, Osirius is a badly burned recluse who invites all of the people who have wronged him in life to his exclusive island with the intention of hunting them down with his dogs and henchmen. And the victims must face up to their past mistakes in order to find a way to stop him. Direct-to-video fare, such as *Death Ring* (1992), brings nothing new to the game as another ex-marine is kidnapped and dumped on an island where a bunch of rich maniacs – overseen by Billy Drago – go after him in a deadly sporting contest. *Hard Target* (1993) pits a martial artist, Jean-Claude Van Damme, against ruthless criminals, Lance Henriksen and Arnold Vosloo, who enjoy playing cat-and-mouse with the destitute of New Orleans. And in the following year, another homeless man, Ice-T, becomes the target of another group of rich degenerates in *Surviving the Game* (1994). *The Pest* (1997) serves as a 'comedic' version of the story, in the same way *The Cable Guy* (1996) is the comic version of the stalker/interloper movie. And its protagonist, Pest Vargas (John Leguizamo, who later showed up in *Land of the Dead* [2005]), is by far the most annoying character in the genre's eight-decades-long history. An insufferable jock-itch of a man, I'm certain that most viewers would be happy to pay the big bucks to blow his brains out themselves.

In the 90s reboot of *The Outer Limits*, the episode entitled *The Hunt* (season 4, episode 2, 1998) is set in the near future where animal hunting is now a crime. An underground culture has developed in which redundant androids are hunted by humans for fun. The androids eventually learn that running away is useless, and so they remove their inhibitors (the devices that disable them from retaliating against human abuses), and begin trying to defend themselves. What follows is an interesting – if overly explored – sci-fi staple of the humanoids behaving in a more civilised manner than their flesh-and-blood antagonists. 'As machines grow more human, we must be wary that we do not become... less so,' the voice-over warns at the end, as the only surviving android gives itself up for a complete reprogramming – a willingness to have its entire thoughts and memories wiped, in utter disgust at the human monsters.

In the classic, *Battle Royale* (2001), it's the state itself which channels the spirit of Zaroff – an unknown, unseen, all-powerful entity that punishes school children by dumping them on a volcanic island to kill each other off until only one 'winner' remains. The system isn't interested in reforming the children; it just wants to see them die. Meanwhile on television, a couple of tough heroines were on the run in their own dangerous games. Xena of *Xena: Warrior Princess* was embattled with Morloch in *Dangerous Prey* (season 6, episode 11, 2001), a bloodthirsty medieval warlord with a taste for hunting women in the woods. And after being informed of Xena's prowess in battle, they go head to head in the passages of a dark cave, before settling their differences by sword. Also proving handy in battle against sinister psychos was Sydney Fox (Tia Carrere) of *Relic Hunter.* In the episode *Run Sydney Run* (season 2, episode 15, 2001), the female Indiana Jones takes a trip to Russia to find an ancient sword, but her team is ambushed by gunmen. Her captor, Tsarlov, is a vintage Zaroff – cold, cultured and full of empty platitudes. He also owns a hundred acres of land, a kennel full of hounds, and a collection of firearms. Of course, he proposes a dangerous game: If Sydney really wants the sword, she can take it and leave. However, he'll be coming right after her with guns blazing...

In *Mindhunters* (2004), a group of would-be FBI profilers head off to an island for a training exercise – the name of the game is to hunt for a serial killer in a simulated environment. However, when members of the group are killed for real, it becomes clear that there is a genuinely deranged Zaroff wannabe among them... What could have been a fun body-count movie – the death-by-cigarette scene is pretty gross – very quickly descends into a contrived puzzle piece that substitutes human ciphers for believable characters. The prime suspect changes with each gruesome death until only the most autistic viewers give a damn who the killer really is. As in countless television series,' the film-makers here make the usual pig's ear when portraying FBI characters – they're badly written, empty shells of human beings; one moment they're the oh-so-important and rational professionals, and the next they're emotionally vulnerable children who just want to have good careers. And in the meantime, their social interactions and flirtations are so off. The film-makers want to make their characters appear normal and relatable, but as usual, it's far too forced, and as a result the characters come off as a group of oddball misfits. None of these cretins should be working for the FBI.

The Eliminator (2004) brings us back to routine territory as former UFC heavyweight champ, Bas Rutten, faces off against the sinister Michael Rooker and his henchmen in another island showdown. Rooker and his associates are your typical rich deviants, the likes of whom would later show up in *Hostel* (2005) as the thrill-seeking sadists looking to torture innocents in exchange for cash. Interestingly, the evil company in *Hostel* is called Elite Hunting, and its emblem is a dog's head, which their customers have tattooed on their flesh. It's an obvious reference to the hounds of Zaroff. Also, in *Hostel: Part II* (2007), the deviants wind up being torn to shreds by their own attack dogs, and Elite Hunting's trophy room, with its rows of mounted human heads, is almost identical to Zaroff's.

The Backwoods (*Bosque de sombras*, 2006) is set in the Basque region of Spain in the late 70s. Gary Oldman plays Paul, a British ex-pat who spends a few idyllic days with his wife and visiting friends. One afternoon, Paul discovers a deformed, terrified girl locked in a cabin in the middle of the woods. He takes her home, and his wife bathes her. After dark, they set off on the long drive to the nearest police station, but their jeep breaks down. Of course, the next morning they are visited by a gang of suspicious hunters with a dangerous game in mind. And what follows is a desperate fight for survival... Owing just as much to *Straw Dogs* (1972) as it does to

The Most Dangerous Game, *The Backwoods* is a worthy addition to the backwoods horror genre. The remote Spanish setting is as beautiful as it is menacing, and the stranded characters are made extra vulnerable as their cottage doesn't have electricity, or even a phone line.

Also set in the 70s is *Manhunt* (*Rovdyr*, 2008), which borrows a leaf from *The Texas Chain Saw Massacre* (1974) before the game begins. A group of bickering youngsters in a mini van in the Norwegian countryside pick up a weirdo hitch-hiker who promptly entraps them in an ambush further down the road. Later, the remaining youngsters awaken, dazed and confused in the woods, to the sounds of a hunting horn and gunshots. It doesn't take them long to figure out they're the intended prey... The hunters are a silent, cold-blooded lot – they seem to act as a brutal, animalistic force of nature, rather than acting on any kind of grievance or philosophy. They don't seem to derive much pleasure from what they do, either. For them, it's just a routine hunt – an everyday function of what they do. They remain just as cold and implacable at the end as they did the moment they first appeared on screen. For another terrifying clash of cultures, Mel Gibson's *Apocalypto* (2006) winds the clock back even further, dropping its viewers off in ancient Mayan times as a young hunter narrowly avoids having his heart cut out in a sacrifice to the sun gods. When the man is no longer useful, his captors set him loose and relentlessly pursue him through the jungle, armed with deadly accurate spears.

In continuing the trend of re-marketing Zaroff for each new generation to fit the perceived boogeyman of the day, by the turn of the millennium it was the turn of the rural white man – or 'white trash' – to cop the blame for society's ills. Thus, in *The Benders*, an episode of *Supernatural* (season 1, episode 15, 2006), the show's protagonist, Dean (Jensen Ackles), teams up with a female Sheriff's Deputy to capture an evil family who hunt kidnapped humans for sport in Minnesota. In the *Criminal Minds* episode, *Open Season* (season 2, episode 21, 2007), the BAU investigate a pair of hunter-killers who operate in rural Idaho, while in *Law & Order: Special Victims Unit*, *Hunting Ground* (season 13, episode 15, 2012), we get a psychopathic serial killer who lures prostitutes and runaways to his grounds, before hunting and killing them.

New Town Killers (2008) transports the classic game to Edinburgh for a noirish take in which a young man agrees to be hunted through the city streets until dawn, where, if he survives the night, he will use the £12,000 prize money to get a drug smuggling gang off his sister's back. An episode of *Dollhouse*, entitled *The Target* (season 1, episode 3, 2009), also strays into classic Zaroff territory as Echo (Eliza Dushku) is lured into the wilderness by a handsome man, aptly named Richard Connell. And little does she know that Connell's favourite past-time is to hunt humans for sport. *Are You Scared 2* (aka *Tracked*, 2009) sees the game taking place online where treasure hunting gamers are monitored and pursued by psychopaths. And in *The Tournament* (2009), the world's deadliest assassins converge on an unsuspecting town to kill each other off in a battle royale where the last man standing bags himself $10 million in cash. Meanwhile, in Taiwan, *Invitation Only* (*Jue ming pai dui*, 2009) is the type of film *Murder Party* (2007) should have been, as a young chauffeur is lured by his boss to a high society party on the promise of sex, only to discover that he and several others are the intended targets of super-rich sadists who play deadly games of cat-and-mouse with the lower classes for fun. The shadowy organisation behind all this is the Weida Group, an Elite Hunting-type corporation whose deceptively cruel motto is, 'May Your Dreams Become a Reality.'

The Syfy TV movie, *Red: Werewolf Hunter* (2010), takes the game into other legends, straying into *Little Red Riding Hood* and *Dog Soldiers* (2002) territories. When Virginia (Felicia Day) takes her FBI fiance, Nathan (Kavan Smith), home to meet the folks, he is bitten by a werewolf while strolling in the woods at night. Virginia's family just happen to be werewolf hunters, so she refuses to tell them about the incident. Instead, she keeps an eye on her beloved before the full moon comes around and the dangerous lycanthropy takes hold. In the meantime, however, they go a-werewolf hunting in a nearby ghost town, where a pack of beasties are holding humans captive. After dark, the captives are let loose, and they have to make it back to civilisation while being picked off by the pursuing werewolves... The leader of the pack is Gabriel (Stephen McHattie), a pure breed of predator who teaches his 'clan' how to transform themselves at will, so that they can attack their prey at any time without having to depend on the full moon.

The new decade brought more Zaroff influences. Even animation joined the fun with an episode of *Archers*, entitled *El Contador* (season 3, episode 5, 2012) for a comedic take, and also a couple of episodes of *Psycho-Pass* (2012-13), the excellent Japanese anime. Big budget Hollywood movies were also released which owed more than a passing influence to *The Most Dangerous Game*, such as *The Hunger Games* (2012) and its sequels. And even bigger budgets were spent on hugely popular television shows, such as *The Blacklist* (2013-), *Game of Thrones* (2011-) and *The Walking Dead* (2010-), which in turn borrowed elements from the classic tale. *The Blacklist* includes an episode called *The Mombasa Cartel* (season 2, episode 6, 2014) in which government agents are hunted by animal poachers in the wilds of Sierra Leone. Ramsay Bolton of *Thrones* would gain immense pleasure from hunting young women through the woods, and allowing his starving dogs to tear them to shreds. And, like Zaroff, Bolton was eventually served as a just desert for his own hounds. *The Walking Dead's* The Govenor would sit in a darkened room gazing at his collection of trophies – severed zombie heads bobbing away in fish tanks. He was clearly lost in madness, like a Zaroff without a castle. The 'evil white men' media narrative was churned out again with *Green Room* (2015) – this time more blatant then ever, as a nomadic punk rock group is targeted by cartoonish neo-Nazis in rural Oregon, while *Hounds of Zaroff* (2016) goes back to basics as an adaptation of Connell's original story, only this time it's a heroic female, Rachel Schrey, who battles it out against the evil Russian. And, as of this writing, an official remake of the 1932 version is on the cards, *The Most Dangerous Game* (TBA), which, judging by the trends thus far, will no doubt portray Zaroff as a Donald Trump-type crazed traditionalist whose hunting grounds are surrounded by a huge insurmountable wall.

I am a Fugitive From a Chain Gang (1932)
Dir: Mervyn LeRoy /USA

Perhaps the hardest hitting of Warner Brothers' 'social problem' films of the early 1930s, which also included *The Big House* (1930), in which an armed prison riot is put down by tank fire, and *Hell's House* (1931), the story of a teenage orphan who is sent to reform school after getting himself roped into a bootleg racket. *I am a Fugitive From a Chain Gang* is based on the autobiography of Robert Elliot Burns, a real-life escapee who went on to become a successful magazine editor while continuing to live with the threat of being recaptured. Even today, the film is uncompromising and brutally honest in its depictions of the penal system of post-World War I Georgia.

The film tells the story of James Allen (Paul Muni), a man who is framed for the robbery of a hamburger stand and sentenced to ten years hard labour. And after gruelling away in the system until he is thoroughly exhausted – and slowly stripped of all dignity – he resolves to make a break for it. After he succeeds in escaping, he becomes a respectable citizen. However, his vindictive wife reports his whereabouts to the authorities, and James soon finds himself back on the chain gang to serve out his sentence.

The film-makers deliberately avoid mentioning the state in question (Burns' book was called *I am a Fugitive From a Georgia Chain Gang*, pub. 1932), but never skirt on the vicious organised cruelty it seeks to condemn. The convicts are whipped with leather straps while they slave away with their sledgehammers, and are even requested to ask permission to wipe the sweat from their eyes. Director and lead actor, LeRoy and Muni (both fresh from *Little Caesar* and *Scarface*, respectively), pull no punches, with almost every scene designed to instil a sense of social outrage in the audience.

On the film's release in November 1932, *Variety* magazine called it 'a picture with guts,' and audiences flocked to see the gritty, semi-documentary shocker. However, the film was banned in Georgia, and the state also filed a libel suit against the studio. Prison wardens also filed unsuccessful million-dollar lawsuits against Warner Brothers, based on the film's portrayals of them as 'vicious, brutal, and false attacks.' And the publicity generated by the film seemed to motivate the state of Georgia into recapturing Burns; they began a relentless pursuit of him. Warner Brothers made the bold move of asking Burns to visit Hollywood and serve as an advisor on the project. Using an assumed name, Burns did just that, and not only suggested ideas for the story but also helped out with the dialogue before having to flee back into obscurity. In Britain, the film was passed with minor cuts and an added preface that assured viewers that 'Prison conditions revealed here could never exist in Great Britain.'

I am a Fugitive had a major impact on the many prison movies to come, from *20,000 Years in Sing Sing* (1932), *Laughter in Hell* (1933), *The Mayor of Hell* (1933), and *Each Dawn I Die* (1939), to the escape through the swamps scene in Edward G. Robinson's *Blackmail* (1939), the escape truck in *Cool Hand Luke* (1967), even *Sullivan's Travels* (1941) and *O Brother Where Art Thou?* (2000). Mervyn LeRoy continued in his socially conscious vein and released *They Won't Forget* (1937), this time focusing on the lynching of Leo Frank. And *I am a Fugitive* was later remade as a TV movie starring Val Kilmer, *The Man Who Broke 1000 Chains* (1987).

Island of Lost Souls (1932)
Dir: Erle C. Kenton /USA

Freaks wasn't the only controversial horror film made by a major studio in 1932; in December, Paramount released *Island of Lost Souls*, another doomed attempt to cash in on the horror boom that centres on the theme of genetic oddities. And, just like Tod Browning's film, *Lost Souls* was similarly derided in the press and was banned for decades in Britain. Even H. G Wells – who had previously criticised the BBFC's censorship policies – was happy with the ban as he regarded this film adaptation of his novel as 'embarrassing' and a 'bastardisation.'

Based on Wells' celebrated sci-fi novel, *The Island of Dr. Moreau* (pub. 1896), *Island of Lost Souls* follows a shipwrecked man, Edward Parker (Richard Arlen), as he washes up on a tropical island in the South Seas. The island is populated with hairy and deformed 'natives,' who are under the rule of an obsessive doctor, Moreau (a bloated Charles Laughton). Eventually, Parker discovers that the inhabitants are actually mutants created by Moreau, whose fiendish experiments in genetics and vivisection have created a breed of animal-human hybrids, or 'beast-men.' To make matters worse, the slightly unhinged Moreau seems interested in forcing Parker to breed with a 'panther-woman,' Lota (Kathleen Burke). In the end, the monsters rebel against their master and corner him in his lab – known as the 'House of Pain' – where they exact a bloody revenge with scalpels...

Following Dr. Frankenstein and Doctor X, Dr. Moreau was the latest in a line of mad scientists

who ended up paying the ultimate price for playing God. Dressed in a white suit and brandishing a bull whip, the master of 'freaks' also gives off a friendly-but-fearful demeanour, like Count Zaroff, which makes it difficult for Parker to know whether he's dealing with an eccentric genius or dangerous madman. Bela Lugosi is almost unrecognisable as the Sayer of the Law, the leader of the mutants, who is buried beneath hair and make up. During the rebellion, when the creatures gang up on the doctor, he addresses Moreau in pained fury: 'You made us in the House of Pain,' he cries. 'You made us – *things*! Not men! Not beasts! *Things*!'

Now impervious to pain, the creatures lunge forward ignoring the cracks of the whip. They charge through the iron gate that the doctor had slammed behind him in his bid to escape. Amid a monstrous din of wails – an unnerving mix of hostility and heartache – the beast-men swarm on the House of Pain. Now cornered, Dr. Moreau foolishly commands them to stop in a stern tone, but instead the creatures continue to press forward like outraged and super-smart primates. Lugosi commands the horde to grab the knives, to which they respond by breaking the glass doors of the surgical cabinet and seizing handfuls of scalpels. Moreau is then pinned onto the operating table and dissected alive. Cue one of the most appalling sounds of 30s cinema as the doctor screams in mortal terror.

If *Freaks* was the most viscerally haunting horror show of the decade, then *Island of Lost Souls* was certainly the most gruesome. The film-makers seemed to have deliberately ignored the anti-colonial subtext of Wells' novel and instead focused fully on making its audience's skin crawl. Jonathan Rigby suggests that the film was made as a parody of Shakespeare's *The Tempest* – with Moreau serving as a deranged Prospero surgically crafting himself a race of mutant Calibans.

Following the box-office failure of the film, Paramount found itself in financial difficulties. However, Philip Wylie, who was a co-writer on *Lost Souls*, came to the rescue with *Murders in the Zoo* (1933), starring Lionel Atwill. The Halperin brothers (of *White Zombie* [1932] fame), delivered *Supernatural* (1933), their first Hollywood film, which helped to keep the studio afloat. Meanwhile, H. G. Wells saw another of his novels brought to the screen, Universal's *The Invisible Man* (1933), directed by James Whale in blackly comic style. As for Dr. Moreau, he was brought back to the screen again many years later in *The Island of Dr. Moreau* (1977), with Burt Lancaster giving the villain a more quietly unhinged quality. Pam Grier revived the panther-woman role in *Twilight People* (1973), while Marlon Brando played the doctor in an extended cameo form in the $50 million flop, *The Island of Dr. Moreau* (1996).

Ecstasy (1933)
(aka *Extase*; aka *Ekstase*; aka *Symphony of Love*)
Dir: Gustav Machatý /Czechoslovakia /Austria
Highly controversial in its day for being the first non-pornographic film to show nudity, sex and the female orgasm, *Ecstasy* begins on the passionless wedding night of Eva (Hedy Lamarr – née Kiesler), and her much older husband, Emil (Zvonimir Rogoz). While she lounges on their honeymoon bed waiting for him to join her, he spends his time in the bathroom meticulously carrying out some kind of OCD grooming rituals. At one point she fiddles around with her wedding ring, and though Emil is a wealthy man, the harsh realisation of the life he has in store for her brings little comfort.

One day while out in the country, Eva takes a swim in the lake. Her clothes are left on the horse, and when the animal decides to go galloping across the fields, Eva has little choice but to chase it down – in the nude. However, just across the way, there is a small community of workers, and a handsome young man manages to capture the horse. Eva hides among the foliage and doesn't come out until she puts on her dress. The young man, Adam (Aribert Mog), helps Eva when she falls and hurts her ankle. She makes a show of rejecting his hands-on approach. However, during a stormy night of passion, Eva finds herself drawn to him, and she shows up at his house. They make love in Adam's bed, and her face is the picture of sexual ecstasy. For a brief moment, Eva is fulfilled, but once the post-coital cigarette is extinguished, she must head back home to face the music.

When Emil learns about Eva's infidelity, he attempts to plough his vehicle into a moving train – an act designed to kill both himself and his passenger, Adam. However, he slams his foot down on the brake at the very last moment. A distraught Emil takes a room at an inn later that day, and slumps into a deep depression.

Adam and Eva now openly flaunt their relationship, and celebrate at the inn. And, as the festivities heat up after dark, a loud bang is heard, and Emil is found dead of a self-inflicted gunshot wound to the head. The small town immediately turns on the couple, and they find themselves having to flee. Adam falls asleep at the station while they wait for the train. And when it arrives, Eva doesn't wake him – instead she climbs aboard alone and leaves him behind.

With very little dialogue throughout its 88-minute running time, *Ecstasy* shows how many parts of Europe were still struggling to catch up with the Hollywood talkies. And while the major studio productions were often brief and snappy in their pacing, *Ecstasy* deliberately keeps things more subtle and subdued, and even flirts with expressionism and the avant-garde. The original script was just five pages long, and director Machatý somehow managed to spin a simple but sweeping tale of love, loss and regret that still has the power to deflate the hearts of even the hardiest viewers to this day. Shot simultaneously in three languages – French, German and Czech – and in various locations across Europe, including Prague, Slovakia, Ukraine and Austria, the end result is a film which was very much a product of its place and time.

Ecstasy premiered in Prague on 20 January with no problems. However, the scheduled release in Germany on Valentine's Day was delayed due to censorship problems. And the problems only continued as the film prints began making their way across the globe. The film wasn't submitted to the BBFC at all, as the producers knew that it would be banned outright. If any print reached Britain during those days, it would have played underground, but no records have emerged. U.S. Customs seized any copies of *Ecstasy* they could get their hands on – and this prohibition was upheld on appeal, with one official calling the film 'highly – even dangerously – indecent.'

Meanwhile in Italy, Mussolini himself personally banned the film, but not before he remarked on Lamarr's nudity: 'Wow! What a beautiful woman!' Indeed, Il Duce had his own screening room at the Villa Torlonia where he examined the content of the *LUCE* newsreels. Occasionally he would step in and take action against films that he felt were unsuitable for the masses. He ordered the Charles Chaplin comedy, *Modern Times* (1936) to be cut a few years later.

She Done Him Wrong (1933)
Dir: Lowell Sherman /USA

If Jean Harlow was the Queen of cinematic amoral gold-diggers in the early 1930s, her crown was taken in 1933 by Mae West. Like Harlow, West had very little experience in the film world before landing her big break. However, her success was short lived, as despite rescuing Paramount from the brink of bankruptcy, the Hays Code would effectively shut down her career in the years to come.

This gaudy and playful hit showcases West's talents unlike any other film she ever appeared in. As a recreation of her successful Broadway play, *Diamond Lil* from 1928 (which landed the actress in jail for ten days), she flaunts her way through suggestive blues numbers, seduces Cary Grant's young Salvation Army saviour, and delivers some of the most fondly-remembered lines of the decade. Little-known director, Lowell Sherman, does a fine job of replicating the squalor of the late 19th century Bowery, and West effortlessly establishes herself as the new Queen of cool, perfectly at home among the schemers and loan sharks.

West was around 40-years-old when Hollywood came a-calling (she would never reveal her real age), and appeared in a cameo role opposite George Raft in *Night After Night* (1932). *She Done Him Wrong* proved a huge hit, and she became an overnight sensation. She went on to make eleven more movies before retiring from the screen, many of them she wrote or co-wrote with collaborators. Shot in just 18 days after one week of rehearsal, *She Done Him Wrong* presents West as one of the first truly liberated women ever to grace the screen.

Lady Lou (West) runs a Bowery saloon for the owner, Noah Beery, Sr. (Gus Jordan). Cummings (a young Cary Grant) is a captain at the next door's Salvation Army office, and he seems to spend all of his time in the bar in what seems to be an attempt to save Lou's soul. Lou eventually falls in love with the young man of God, and this makes her a little uneasy at first as she has been plied with diamonds from Beery, so much so that they no longer hold the same charm for her as they once did. It later becomes clear that Beery is running a counterfeit racket and sending young women out to San Francisco as pickpockets. A jealous battle results in the death of Russian Rita (Rafaela Ottiano), and Cummings reveals himself to be an undercover fed. The saloon is raided by the police. And while the criminals are rounded up into custody, Cummings has different plans for Lou...

The film caused controversy before it was even shot. The original draft screenplay was rejected by Will Hays of the MPPDA, prompting Paramount boss Adolph Zukor to personally step in and try to salvage the project. Hays relented on condition that all references to prostitution (or the 'white slave trade') be dropped, along with the Salvation Army and the Brazilian heritage of Gus's partners in crime. Hays also suggested that the film should be written more as a comedy than a melodrama. Paramount agreed to the proposals, and this put West in the spot of having to temper her one-liners, though such classic lines as 'You can be had,' and 'Why don't you come up sometime and see me?' made it onto the screen.

Released on 27 January 1933, *She Done Him Wrong* was a huge hit, grossing more than $3 million from its $200,000 budget, breaking box-office records and easing Paramount's financial woes in the midst of the Great Depression. However, despite a smattering of positive reviews in the national press, the film couldn't escape the ire of religious groups and moralists who condemned the picture. Censorship boards across America attempted to have the film cut, banned, or restricted in any way they could. In New York, mobs had formed outside of cinemas where the movie was playing, and hundreds of police officers were called in to get the situation under control. Religious leaders were outraged by the film's nationwide appeal – they had previously objected to DeMille's *The Sign of the Cross* (particularly the scenes of a woman bathing in 'asses milk') and the violence and amorality in Howard Hawke's *Scarface*, but neither of those films had such a large impact at the box-office.

Individually, these films may have slipped through unnoticed if they hadn't been rewarded with such a vast dollar endorsement, but because these pre-code problem films seemed to arrive all at once in a great big pile-up, Church representatives across the country took it upon themselves to present their own approval guidelines in the various states. Publishing lists of safe films for their congregations to consume as early as 1922, by 1934 the Church organised a new pressure group in direct response to *She*

Done Him Wrong, the Catholic Legion of Decency (LoD). The group even provided its own strict ratings system for the public. The 'A' rating meant the film was morally okay for general viewing; 'B' meant it was partly 'objectionable;' and 'C' stood for 'condemned,' designated for films that should not be seen under any circumstances.

Meanwhile in Britain, *She Done Him Wrong* had already been cut by around eight minutes by the distributors prior to its submission to the Board. The BBFC cut a further six minutes, though many of West's innuendos surprisingly escaped the censor's wrath, especially in the songs 'I Like a Man Who Takes His Time,' and 'I Wonder Where My Easy Rider's Gone.' But it was West herself who stole most of the headlines, for her daring performance and one-of-a-kind delivery style that made her the first female superstar of the talkies era. She teamed up once again with Grant in *I'm No Angel* (1933), released in October. In the following year, however, *It Ain't No Sin* (aka *Belle of the Nineties*, 1934), coincided with the strict enforcement of the Production Code, and her short-lived and dazzling career slowly fizzled out. 'I believe in censorship,' she later said. 'After all, I made a fortune out of it.'

Gabriel Over the White House (1933)
Dir: Gregory La Cava /USA

Released on 31 March 1933, less than two months after Hitler became Chancellor of Germany, *Gabriel Over the White House* is a bizarre, pro-fascist American picture that was supported by Franklin D. Roosevelt, his First Lady Eleanor, and media mogul, William Randolph Hearst, who even helped to fund it. Head of MGM, Louis B. Mayer is said to have been so furious when he saw the final cut he wanted the film to be banished. However, after much wrangling behind the scenes, a version did get a small release – though it was barely advertised and struggled to make back its budget costs. It remains a cult item to this day.

The story begins with the inauguration of Judson Hammond (Walter Huston), the new President of the United States. Early on in his administration the President almost dies in a high-speed car crash. And when he awakens from his coma weeks later, he's a changed man. The first thing he does upon his recovery is purge his party of its big business lackeys, which brings about his impeachment. He then simply dissolves the judicial branch and declares himself dictator. He nationalises all the major industries, violates civil rights, and declares martial law. Pretty soon, the Constitution is scrapped, and brown-shirted storm troopers patrol the streets. Interestingly, the only major resistance against these actions comes from the world of organised crime, as criminal gangs begin attacking the President's business interests. Hammond responds by rounding them up and having them executed by firing squads. To cap things off, Hammond's top scientists invent and develop a weapon of mass destruction which he then uses as a cudgel to frighten the other nations into disarmament. And the world lives in peace and prosperity, happily ever after...

As far as totalitarian propaganda goes, *Gabriel Over the White House* is jaw-droppingly blatant in its message, and was designed to spread fascist ideology across North America by portraying an heroic President as a fascist dictator. March 1933 saw other releases with a fascist bent, such as *Black Shirt* (*Camicia nera*), an Italian propaganda production that was released a week earlier, and the American feature-length newsreel-style *Mussolini Speaks*, that was released the day before that. However, none of them can match the quirkiness and audaciousness of MGM's wrong-headed misfire. None of those involved in the making of the film worked for the studio again.

S. A. – Mann Brand (1933)
(aka *Storm Trooper Brand*)
Dir: Franz Seitz /Germany

The Nazi regime produced 1,090 feature films between 1933 and 1945. To this day, dozens of those films are banned in Germany and other European countries, even though the German constitution forbids political censorship. Only a handful of them – including *Titanic* (1943) – have been released on any home video format or broadcast on television. In some cases, the films can be shown at scholarly events, but only under strict rules which includes having an expert introduce the films before they play. Unauthorised screenings are against the law in Germany. Many of the films were made by Ufa, Germany's biggest film studio that had previously produced such classics as *Dr. Mabuse, der Spieler* and *Metropolis*. However, the company was nationalised by the new regime, and from then on, all film production was under the full control of the Nazis.

Opening on 14 June, during the summer of book burnings, *S. A. – Mann Brand* was the first of the official Nazi films to hit the screens. It was also the first part of the 'Kampfzeit trilogy' (or, 'Times of Struggle'), followed by *Hitlerjunge Quex* and *Hans Westmar*, which were released later in the year. The films portrayed Nazi martyrs in the early years of the National Socialist movement before Hitler had come to power, and are mostly remembered today for their scrappiness as early attempts to propagandise the German masses through the medium of film. However, played side by side with the early Soviet films of Eisenstein and Pudovkin, this early trilogy comes off as hopelessly amateur and artless, in comparison. The story of *S. A. – Mann Brand* is a simple one: it's basically a prolonged street war as the S. A. grows in membership and fends off violent and fanatical communist agitators.

From the opening scene of a meeting attacked by the enemy, breaking the windows and kicking in the doors, to the last triumphant march through the streets, the film has little interest in subtlety or nuance – the confrontation between the groups is starkly black and white. The Stormtroopers (or, Sturmabteilung) are portrayed as the Aryan ideal where every one of them is the righteous role-model for decency and wholesomeness, while the communists live in filthy underground squalor, and their ranks are full of drunks and resentful thugs. Interestingly, Brand's father is depicted as a Social Democrat (a drunk and emotional one at that), while his mother somewhat hovers in between her son's fanatical devotion to Hitler and the father's hatred for it. This family situation was exactly the same in the next film in the trilogy, *Hitlerjunge Quex*.

The film was not well received by many in the Nazi movement. A review appeared in Goebbels' Newspaper, *Der Angriff*, which pointed out the many faults: '...the director, Franz Seitz, has attempted to produce an epic account of the Unknown SA Mann, and in doing so, to recreate the glorious myth of the SA for the cinema screens. Unfortunately, Seitz and his team have neither the talent nor the competence necessary for a film of this importance. To capture the epic qualities of the SA requires a vision of the grandest scale.' Indeed, the flat directorial style and lack of memorable set-pieces creates an awfully dull, made-for-TV vibe, long before the advent of television. The characters too are astonishingly one-dimensional, even the forgettable Brand, who, in his final moments as he addresses his comrades while clutching his mortal bullet wound, feels like an amateur dramatics class rehearsing for a Lord Nelson death scene.

Baby Face (1933)
Dir: Alfred E. Green /USA

One of the most controversial of all the pre-code movies, and one that helped bring about the strict enforcement of the Production Code in the following year, *Baby Face* is a simple but effective story of one woman's mission to get rich at the expense of all who get in her way, using her admirers as convenient stepping stones to climb to the top.

Pretty Lily Powers (Barabra Stanwyck), works at a rowdy bar, or 'zoo,' where she is constantly having to fight off being man-handled by leering drunks. An elderly patron gave her a copy of Nietzsche's book, *The Will to Power* ('the greatest philosopher of all time'), and though she claims she didn't understand the book's contents, a tragic change in her circumstances prompts her to take another look. Her father dies horribly in a fire, and she finds herself alone. And, with a sharp tongue and stunning beauty as her weapons of choice, Lily fully embraces a will to power as a matter of survival. Accompanied by her maid, Lily hops on board a freight train heading for New York. A crew member spots them and threatens to have them thrown off, but Lily changes his mind by sleeping with him. When they arrive in the big city, Lily sleeps with a secretary at a large bank in exchange for a filing job. And it doesn't take her long to bonk her way to the top of the firm, where she develops genuine feelings for a more senior member of staff, Courtland (George Brent). In the end, Lily is torn between helping him out of a legal scrape (which will cost her a million dollars), or leaving him in the lurch. However, no matter how risky the situations become – with jealousy, murder and suicide all playing a part – this predatory feline always lands gracefully on her feet.

Made by Warner Bros. as a response to MGM's hit, *Red-Headed Woman*, *Baby Face* was based on an idea by Darryl F. Zanuck, who later became the head of 20th Century Fox. He wrote the treatment under the pseudonym 'Mark Canfield,' and sold it to the studio for a dollar (he was already on a pretty lucrative salary at the company). It was a fairly rushed production, made during the Great Depression when every penny counted, and every box-office flop was enough to put a company in the black. However, the film was a modest success, making a sizeable profit on its meagre budget, despite the negative reception in the press.

While previous hits such as *She Done Him Wrong* and the aforementioned *Red-Headed Woman* were mostly praised by the critics for their daring performances and challenging themes, *Baby Face* was accused of going too far, and it was only a matter of time before the studios were forced to put a stop to such amoral productions, largely out of fear that the Federal government would step in and enforce their own rules. To avoid this, the studios instead adhered to Will Hays and his Production Code in the following summer, which at least gave Hollywood a say in how its productions would be treated during the development phase. And this effectively put an end to the risqué pre-code era, at least until film noir became popular in the next decade.

Variety magazine, which had often published positive reviews of the pre-code movies, was very critical when it came to *Baby Face*. '[the film is] blue and nothing else. It possesses no merit for general or popular appeal, is liable to offend the family trade and can't count on any juve attendance.' The unnamed critic went on to discuss an earlier print of the film which was cut for being 'too hot.' 'Anything hotter than this for public showing would call for an asbestos audience blanket.' In the film's defence, it features a superb performance from Stanwyck as the leap-frogging villainess, whose sweet and innocent looks belie a cunning and ruthless nature (Jennifer Jason Leigh had a remarkable resemblance to her, and may have even took inspiration from Lily when she played the predatory reporter with a southern twang in the retro-inflected *The Hudsucker Proxy* [1994]). The film also moves at a tremendous pace, and passes by in a flash. For all the criticisms the film faced in the press, no one ever said it was boring.

In 2004, the original cut of the film, which includes Lily studying up on Nietzsche and some sexually suggestive material, as well the original ending that was cut by the New York State Censorship Board, was discovered in an archive in Ohio and released in the following year.

Hitler Youth Quicksilver (1933)

(aka *Hitlerjunge Quex*; aka *Our Flag Leads Us Forward*)

Dir: Hans Steinhoff /Germany

The second in Nazi Germany's 'Kampfzeit trilogy,' following *SA-Mann Brand* earlier in the year, *Hitlerjunge Quex* is perhaps the most engaging entry in the series. This time the martyr is Heini Völker (Jürgen Ohlsen), a working-class boy in Berlin. His father is a devoted communist and a veteran of the War. He is also a drunk, and he beats the boy until he sings the communist anthem, The Internationale. Heini is sent to a communist youth camp as a way of steering him away from the Nazis. However, the boy has a miserable time as the communists are made up of louts who seem to sit around doing nothing but drinking. Heini sneaks away through the woods and discovers a Hitler Youth camp nearby. He watches from afar and sees the youths engaged in various disciplined activities. He decides right then and there that he wants to join the group.

Heini endears himself to the Nazis by foiling a terrorist plot – the communists were plotting to set off a bomb at the Hitler Youth headquarters – and this makes him a dangerous enemy of the communists as they are fearful of how much more he knows about their plans. The communists decide that he needs to be dealt with, once and for all. Meanwhile, Heini's mother is so terrified of revenge attacks by the communists that she leaves the gas on over night in an attempt to kill both herself and her son. Heini survives, however, and he leaves his father and moves in to the Hitler Youth headquarters. His comrades soon give him the nickname 'Quicksilver' for his speed in carrying out orders. And while distributing Nazi pamphlets in a communist controlled area, he is spotted and pursued by his enemies. The men capture the boy in a deserted fairground and stab him to death.

Based on the novel by Karl Alois Schenzinger (pub. 1932), which was in turn based on the real-life Nazi martyr, Herbert Norkus, *Hitlerjunge Quex* was one of the most popular movies produced by the regime and played non-stop in theatres for the best part of a decade. It was shot in the same middle-of-the-road directorial style as *SA-Mann Brand*, as a flat kitchen sink drama, but the propaganda element was improved considerably with the use of manipulative, gut-punch emotionalism that ensured it became a hit with the public. Here, the communists are mostly portrayed as lost souls, as too swamped by their own drunkenness and unemployment to see the errors of their ways – the victims of their own ideologies rather than the purveyors of evil. The film also stays faithful to the book, even though the propaganda value of the film could have increased by changing a few sequences. For example, had the bomb plot been successful, the communists would have been responsible for the killing of children. However, the plot is discovered and the tragedy is avoided, and the film-makers missed out on an opportunity to demonise their ideological enemies.

Hitlerjunge Quex was the only film in the trilogy that Goebbels was happy with. He was so pleased with the result that he personally wrote a letter to Ufa, praising the company and its staff. It was also one of the major propaganda tools that helped in recruiting youngsters into the Hitler Youth movement. By 1936, the movement had swelled to more than 6 million members. It was also one of only two films that young actor Ohlsen appeared in (the other was *Wonder of Flying* [*Wunder des Fliegens*, 1935]). He too joined the Hitler Youth in the year following the film's release. He was suspected of being a homosexual, and – ironically – later became a figure of fun in the movement. The Gestapo had Ohlsen sent to a concentration camp in the early 1940s. According to Gestapo records, he was to be 'liquidated.' However, because of the war effort, his execution wasn't high on the list of priorities, and he managed to hang on until the Allies liberated the camp. He died in obscurity aged 77 in 1994.

Wild Boys of the Road (1933)
Dir: William A. Wellman /USA
Released ten days after *Hitlerjunge Quex* in September 1933, Warner Bros.' *Wild Boys of the Road* presents a bleak vision of Depression-era American youth. Directed by William A. Wellman in his typically gritty, documentary-like style, the film caused much controversy for its scenes of juveniles living in garbage dumps and brawling with the police.

The film begins just as the Depression hits ordinary workers, and two young friends, Tommy and Eddie (Edwin Phillips and Frankie Darro) decide to drop out of high school and look for work to ease the strain on their newly unemployed families. They hop on board a freight train destined for Chicago, and there they meet Sally (Dorothy Coonan), who is heading to her aunts in the hope of staying there for a while. And meanwhile, other youngsters show up on the train, each with their own reasons for breaking away from home.

The police intercept the young hobos on their arrival in the city, and most of them are sent to a detention centre. Sally, however, has a letter from her aunt, and the policeman lets her go after being informed that Eddie and Tommy are her cousins. Now close friends, the trio arrive at her aunt's apartment, but the police raid the place soon after – it turns out that the aunt has turned to prostitution to survive – and they are forced to flee. They continue heading west where, en route, they witness the rape of a young girl. The man responsible – the brakeman – is beaten up and thrown off the train to his death. As the train approaches Cleveland, Tommy jumps off and runs into a post which almost knocks him unconscious. He collapses on the track, disorientated, and is unable to crawl away in time before a train heading in the opposite direction runs over his leg.

One of the most prominent directors of the pre-code years, William Wellman had previously made *Public Enemy* (1931) and *Safe in Hell* (1931), and went on to make *Looking For Trouble* (1934). His knack for finding heart-wrenching drama whilst refusing to sugar-coat the lives of his characters ensures his cult following to this day among off-beat film fans. And *Wild Boys* remains perhaps his most technically accomplished and well acted film. Some have criticised the ending with the judge as unrealistic, but the film has its place in cinema history for being one of only a few contemporary films that had the courage to show the true horrors and hardship of the Depression. Films such as *The Grapes of Wrath* (1940) and *The Bicycle Thieves* (1948) take the credit for establishing the neo-realist movement that flourished in years to come, but *Wild Boys* pre-dates them both.

Land Without Bread (1933)
(Original title: *Las Hurdes*; aka *Unpromised Land*)
Dir: Luis Buñuel /France
In stark contrast to Buñuel's surrealist films, in 1933 he presented *Land Without Bread*, a

dispassionate 28-minute documentary on the inhabitants of a small town in the mountains of Northern Spain. It was a region that had been blighted with stigma for centuries, as a backward outpost of civilisation whose people didn't even know how to make bread, hence the film's English title.

Described by *Time Out London* editor, Geoff Andrews, as 'strangely beautiful, and as pungent as sulfur,' and by novelist Graham Greene as 'an honest and hideous picture,' *Las Hurdes* was greeted with hostility on its release, especially from those who lived in the region. And the film was banned in Spain from 1933 to 1936. After all, Buñuel was only too willing to show the poverty and disease that had ravaged the town for centuries, with some stunningly unpleasant images for its time, such as a donkey being stung to death by thousands of wasps (Buñuel was accused of staging the scene deliberately by smearing the animal with honey and disturbing the hives nearby, as well as the shot of the goat tumbling down the mountain side to its death – the film-maker is said to have kicked the goat to force it over the precipice).

The town's only source of income is a state subsidy for taking in abandoned and orphaned children, but disturbingly, the inhabitants are clearly unable to care for them properly, and the children are malnourished and left to suffer alone in the streets. One little girl actually died of a mouth infection while the film was being shot. Early on, we see a strange ritual in which the eligible men of the town ride through the streets on horses and tear the heads off roosters that are tied upside down between the buildings. The residents are then treated to a rare glass of wine. Later in the film, we meet the 'cretins,' a small incestuous clan that are considered outcasts in a town full of outcasts. These near-feral humans survive by scavenging and hand-outs. And finally, the film wraps up with the death of a baby, and how the town deals with such a tragedy.

The story of how the film came into being is a bizarre one. Buñuel's anarchist friend, Ramon Acin, told him that if he won the lottery he would fund one of his films. As luck would have it, he did win a large sum, and gave the film-maker twenty-thousand pesetas for his next project. By that point, Buñuel was engrossed in an ethnographic study on 'human geography,' and he explored his curiosity in this field with the making of the film. La Hurdes was still a seldom seen region in those days; and was thought of as a dangerous, inhospitable land of savages – an unflattering reputation not helped by hundreds of years of rumour and stigma. And while other film-makers would travel the world far and wide to document the strange rites and customs of distant tribes, Buñuel made a point of discovering an equally unknown culture on his own doorstep.

Hans Westmar (1933)
(aka *Horst Wessel*; aka *Hans Westmar: Einer Von Vielen – Hans Westmar: One of Many*)
Dir: Franz Wenzler /Germany

The third part of the 'Kampfzeit trilogy' depicts the life and death of the most infamous of all the Nazi martyrs, Horst Wessel. As a member of the SA, Wessel had been successful at converting communists to the Nazi cause. He also wrote poems, and his *Die Fahne Hoch* was re-worked into Germany's second national anthem during the Nazi years, which became better known as *Horst Wessel Lied*. He was just 22-years-old when he was gunned down by a communist. And the Nazi regime used his death as a recruitment drive for nationalism and anti-communism.

Commissioned by the regime, *Hans Westmar* was banned on the day of its premier in December 1933, mostly due to Goebbels' personal disagreement with the film. He accused it of being '...detrimental to the memory of Horst Wessel.' Goebbels knew Wessel personally, and went on to say, 'the figure in the film neither resembled him nor conveyed his character.' However, perhaps the real reason he objected to the film was because it wasn't particularly good. It was let down by the same dispassionate directorial style as the first two films in the trilogy, and looks more like a cheap poverty row production rather than a grand eulogy to a fallen comrade. Interestingly, Goebbels wasn't in full control of Germany's propaganda at this point, and he seemed to deliberately criticise all propaganda efforts that he wasn't directly involved in, no doubt as a form of political manoeuvring to consolidate his power within the Party.

Goebbels was eventually forced to release the film as there had been a backlash among the public who were upset by the ban. However, before he allowed it to be seen, he insisted that the film should hold no allusions to Wessel. Thus, the film underwent a re-edit, and the title was changed from *Horst Wessel* to *Hans Westmar*. Set in the late 1920s before the Nazis had gained power, Wessel is portrayed as more of a street preacher for working class solidarity rather than the fanatical thug he was in real life. In the film, Westmar is killed by the communists because they were afraid of his success in converting enemies into comrades, while in reality, he was killed in retaliation for his own violent crimes. Beginning in Weimar-era Berlin where communists march through the streets singing their anthem, The Internationale, their leader is portrayed as a Jewish caricature, with all the ugliness that implies. Westmar sees Berlin in a state of 'cultural promiscuity,' and he loses his temper when he sees his friends dancing to a jazz band made up of black and Jewish musicians.

Scenes sometimes cut to shots of the graves of German soldiers who had been killed in World War I, as if to imply that the war heroes are spinning in their graves at the rotten world they died for, and the typical Nazi idea of the Weimar Republic as a den of filth and degeneracy is heavily reinforced here. The government had permitted foreign and destructive influences to corrode the culture, seducing the German people from healthy and wholesome Aryans into sex-obsessed degenerates. In real life, a group of 100 fanatical Nazis managed to win over Berlin while being heavily out-numbered by thousands of communists. Yet the film misses the opportunity to gloat over this fact. In the film's finale, the Jewish communist leaders are seen fleeing the country – they can no longer influence the proletariat, and this results in German workers giving the Roman Salute and joining the Nazi struggle.

By this point, there were other Nazi propaganda films that had become more subtle and technically proficient. In the same week, Gustav Ucicky's *Flüchtlinge* (*Refugees*) was released. With a lavish budget and a more focused production, the film follows the struggle of German nationals trying to flee Manchuria while being persecuted by Soviet communists. Their saviour arrives in the form of Hans Albers, a strong Aryan type who was an obvious representation of Hitler himself – the 'saviour' of the German people. Meanwhile in America, film-makers Herman J. Mankiewicz and Sam Jaffe announced that they intended to produce an anti-Hitler film entitled *Mad Dog of Europe*.

Jaffe had even quit his job at RKO in order to focus his full attention on the project. However, studio heads were nervous as Hitler had threatened to seize all Hollywood property in Germany if the project went ahead. He also threatened to ban American films from the German market. Head of the MPPDA, Will Hays, held a meeting with the film-makers in his office and convinced them to scrap the project. However, in the following year a couple of independently-financed, anti-Hitler movies made it onto the screens, albeit for a short time before they were banned – the faux-documentary, *Hitler's Reign of Terror*, and the drama, *Are We Civilized?* (both 1934). Later on, *The Road Back* (1937) was originally intended to be a blatant anti-Nazi picture. However, Universal's new management (the Laemmles had been ousted in the previous year) buckled to Hitler's threats of a German boycott of Universal Pictures, and they ripped the guts out of the film. Director James Whale was so disgusted by this that he walked away from the studio and never worked with them again.

As for *Hans Westmar*, it was described by David Welch in his book, *Propaganda and the German Cinema: 1933-1945* (pub. 1983) as 'a classic portrayal of the archetypal NSDAP hero,' and though the film may be just as scrappy and uneven as the other early entries churned out by the regime, *Westmar* proved to be very popular among ordinary Germans whose labour was already being sought after for the re-armament campaign that was about to get underway.

The Road to Ruin (1934)
Dir: 'Mrs.   Wallace   Reid'   [Dorothy Davenport] /USA
With the Production Code only months away from being strictly enforced, Hollywood studios began to back away from its more risqué productions, leaving the way open for the smaller independent companies to fill the gap in the market. Cinema of the 1930s is littered with odd little movies that were passed off as 'educational' but were actually exploitation through and through. There had already been lesser-known releases at the time, such as the nudist camp short, *Elysia: Valley of the Nudes* and *This Nude World* (both 1933). However, *The Road to Ruin* was the first indie exploitation film of the talkie era to receive a widespread release and no end of censorship hassles.

Written and directed by Dorothy Davenport

under her pseudonym, 'Mrs. Wallace Reid,' *The Road to Ruin* was a film that fit the niche she was already familiar with. She had made her directorial debut with *Human Wreckage* (1923), an early exploitation film that was designed to steer youngsters away from drugs. She was also drawn into making these films after the death of her famous husband, whose name she would use to help promote the pictures. With *Road*, Mrs. Wallace Reid attempted to push the envelope further than ever before, by borrowing elements from pre-code 'problem films' such as *Are These Our Children* (1931) and *Wild Boys of the Road* (1933), combining the themes of delinquent youths and social concerns to strike home a hard-hitting message to the youngsters who flocked to the drive-ins.

Surviving nowadays in its censored, 67-minute version, the story is a simple one: teenagers get drunk, smoke dope and have sex before they are faced with the consequences of botched abortions and an untimely death. If the film feels rather tame by today's standards, it may have something to do with the fact that *Road* was the most heavily censored film of the year, losing up to 12 minutes of footage in some states. The stripping game between the two girls at the party was heavily censored – there is an abrupt cut to the next scene just as one of the girls is about to remove her skirt. Though, amusingly, bare breasts are clearly on view as the party-goers strip off their clothes and jump into the pool.

The Review Board in Virginia requested a record number of cuts, while in Detroit the Catholic Legion of Decency was out in full force, picketing the venues where the film was being played. *Road* made its biggest impact, however, at the drive-ins and on the roadshow circuit, where Davenport would take the reels on tour with her while also promoting a novelised version of the story. Despite all this, she still managed to find the time to make another film in the same year; *The Woman Condemned* (1934) – a much more sensible yarn about a man trying to save an innocent woman from the electric chair – which was probably influenced by *The Sin of Nora Moran* (1933).

Meanwhile, the exploitation boom continued in earnest with Dwain Esper's amusingly inept *Narcotic* (1934), in which a quack doctor gets high on his own supply and eventually commits suicide when he hits rock bottom. And, of course, his most infamous offering, *Maniac.*

Maniac (1934)
(aka *Sex Maniac*)
Dir: Dwain Esper /USA

In recent times, cult movie fans have succeeded in making auteurs out of previously maligned directors, such as Edward D. Wood, Herschell Gordon Lewis, and even Andy Milligan, where their short-comings become attributes, and 'bad' films become 'good.' However, any attempts to revive Dwain Esper and his work in the same way has been doomed to failure. Working on the extreme fringe of the exploitation industry in the 1930s, Esper directed nine films between 1930 and 1948, and only a handful of them are readily available today. He remains a shadowy figure, a possibly deranged maverick who had made a much bigger impact on the world of exploitation than many have given him credit for.

The most detailed account of his life and work can be found in Eric Schaefer's book, *Bold! Daring! Shocking! True!: A History of Exploitation Films, 1919-1959* (pub. 1999), which goes to great lengths to show how difficult it was to produce films that were in breach of the Production Code. With only a very limited access to funding, equipment, talent and distribution networks, and consequently, very limited time for rehearsals, set-ups, shooting and editing, it's no surprise to see the result as a series of films that fall short of the mark. A typical budget for an Esper film was around $8000, a paltry sum that would barely pay for the services of a bit-part player in a Hollywood movie. To get around this, Esper would make his films as eye-catching as possible by promoting and exploiting the salacious content that was forbidden in mainstream studio films.

The Story of *Manic* sees Don Maxwell (Bill Woods) on the run from the police. He hides out in the lab of a crazed scientist who has little idea that Maxwell is a paranoid schizophrenic. The hunted man helps the scientist in his experiments to revive the dead. Maxwell is also a former Vaudevillian who can impersonate others with remarkable accuracy. Having already stolen the corpse of a young woman for the experiments, Maxwell and the doctor fight over him returning to the morgue to pick up another. Maxwell then kills the doctor and conceals his body in the basement behind a brick wall.

The Vaudevillian then uses make-up to change his appearance, and he impersonates the dead doctor when a woman shows up for the weekly injection for her brother who is afflicted with a mental disorder. Maxwell has no idea what medication the man was proscribed, and so administers a massive shot of adrenaline and hopes for the best. The following scene must surely rank as one of the most deranged and histrionic of all time as the patient growls and gnashes his teeth, chewing up the scenery as the adrenaline takes hold. Like Mr. Hyde times by ten, the patient tears up the lab and then makes off with the now resurrected corpse of the young woman, and he carries her into the dark wilderness outside, presumably to molest her (though neither character is seen or heard of again). Meanwhile, Maxwell's ex-wife discovers that he has come into a large amount of money, and she decides she wants to get her hands on it...

No plot synopsis can adequately convey the lunacy that is *Maniac*, but, as is so typical of exploitation films, it is only minimally concerned with story, and the narrative is employed merely as an excuse to deliver a series of lurid scenes. This is cinema as crude spectacle, hung loosely on a flimsy and awkward production that knows full well that its target audience isn't so interested in formal storytelling anyway. The audience wants to see the forbidden sights of death and gore and sex. And Esper, with his meagre resources, does all he can to deliver. One of the most infamous sequences in the film – besides the patient flipping out – is the one in which Maxwell, in his doctor's disguise, chases a black cat through the house and plucks out its eyeball. He then eats it, proclaiming, 'Why, it is not unlike an oyster or a grape.' A cut-away shot shows the one-eyed stunt cat (whose fur is much lighter in tone to the black cat he was chasing earlier) jumping through a sugar-glass window to escape. Thus, the cat lives on, and will exact its revenge later on in the story.

Of course, the cat and the doctor's body hidden behind the wall in the basement was clearly taken from Poe (Universal's adaptation of the story, *The Black Cat* [1934] was released earlier in the year in May). Esper borrows ideas and imagery from other horror movies, too, from the aforementioned *Dr. Jekyll and Mr. Hyde* (1931), to *Frankenstein* (1931), *Murders in the Rue Morgue* (1932), and even *Haxan* (1922). Bizarrely, the film's third act strays into *Gold Diggers of 1933* (1933) territory, with the scheming ex-wife and the scantily-clad young women desiring a 'rich husband,' all used as a pretext to add some 'pre-code' sexiness to the picture.

Maniac was Esper's most successful film, and the one he is most remembered for. He toured it around America on the roadshow and Burlesque circuits, along with other films he had made (*Narcotic*) or bought the rights to (*Freaks, or Nature's Mistakes*, as he had re-named it). These became some of the earliest productions to be given the mystique of 'cult,' gaining an underground reputation like a lurid carnival sideshow with the curious spectators not quite believing their eyes that what they were seeing was real, let alone legal. The film had travelled a bumpy road over the decades, often talked about but seldom seen. By the 1990s, media academics such as Jeffrey Sconce were screening the film for their undergrad students, not necessarily in acceptance of it, but as a way of demonstrating how *not to* make a film. '*Last Year at Marienbad* may ultimately be more interesting to students,' wrote Sconce, 'once they have seen and discussed a film like *Maniac*.'

The Bride of Frankenstein (1935)
Dir: James Whale /USA

After the classic *Frankenstein* (1931), it took four long years before director James Whale was persuaded to film a sequel. It was well worth the wait. With producer, Carl Leammle Jr., away in Europe, the director had all but complete control of the project. The sequel – which was originally to be titled 'The Return of Frankenstein' – was to be more epic in scope, with more lavish sets, and the humour brought very much to the fore.

The film opens with a dramatised account of the famous meeting between Mary Shelley, Percy Shelley, and Lord Byron, in Switzerland in the summer of 1816. Byron had arranged a competition to see who among them could write the scariest ghost story. Thought to be a casual way to spend a few hours in the Villa Diodati, I'm sure none of them had any idea at the time that the seeds of their competition would produce the tree of Gothic literature, and – consequently – the horror genre as a whole. Byron wrote a short vampire tale that his friend and physician, John Polidori, expanded further, entitled *The Vampyre*, which went on to inspire Bram Stoker's novel, *Dracula*. And Mary – who was still Mary Wollstonecraft Godwin until she married Percy in December of that year –

produced the outline of *Frankenstein*, the tale of an obsessed doctor who succeeds in creating a monster from stolen body parts. Over the next two years, Mary worked on the story, expanding it to a full-sized novel that was published in 1818. And at the time of its publication, she was still only 19-years-old.

In the original cut of *Frankenstein*, both the doctor and his creation perished in the windmill fire at the end. But in order to get the sequel to work, all prints of the first film were altered to make it clear they survived. Thus, once the action starts, *The Bride of Frankenstein* picks up right where the original left off, with the injured doctor stretchered back to his castle to recuperate, while the monster wanders the countryside with the torch mob still after him. And it's here where we first meet the eccentric Dr. Pretorius (Ernest Thesiger), an alchemist who has managed to 'grow' miniature people in bottles (including Henry VIII, which is said to be in tribute to Lanchester's husband, Charles Laughton – and the entire sequence serves as a tribute to Georges Melies). Pretorius blackmails Frankenstein to assist him in creating a bride for the monster, which they eventually do. However, the results of their new creation don't turn out as planned...

A classic combination of Gothic horror and sly wit, *The Bride of Frankenstein* is one of the great films of the horror genre, and has been hugely influential over the decades. It's an unforgettable visual experience with its expressionist sets, pioneering special effects, and fluid camera work. Also, Franz Waxman's compositions are magnificent – this was the first American film to utilise a full orchestral score. Colin Clive is great once again as the unhinged doctor, and Boris Karloff dons Jack Pierce's make-up once more, adding a touching pathos to his performance and even expanding his vocabulary. It was now Elsa Lanchester's turn to be credited with the '?', and she's equally outstanding – though a tad underused – in her double role as both Mary Shelley in the prologue and the marvellously appropriate manifestation of her story, the bride. However, it's Thesiger who steals the show as the waspish Dr. Pretorius – his campy charms and pithy one-liners do little to conceal the menace that lurks beneath. It's difficult not to see him as an exaggerated version of Whale himself, though the biopic, *Gods and Monsters* (1998) – its title taken from one of Thesiger's lines in *Bride* –

was not the most flattering.

The arresting moments come thick and fast – the monster's encounter with the blind hermit is especially moving. The badly burned pariah can only mutter a faint wail when asked if he's okay, and the hermit seems to be just as lonely as the creature. When Pretorius meets the monster in the crypt, he offers the ghoul a false friendship in order to lure him back to the castle. There are also expressionist moments dating back to the silent era, such as the way the forest morphs into a twisted, nightmarish landscape of stark, frightened trees as the monster flees from the mob – his panic and terror reflected in the environment around him. And of course the ending is at once tragic and cathartic as he is rejected by the bride – her repulsion let out in a startled scream. Shunned by the world and its unlovely people, the monster destroys the lab, burying himself, Pretorius and the bride under tonnes of debris. 'We belong dead,' he mourns.

If the film itself is essential viewing, then Universal's DVD edition is the essential way to see it. Presented in a spotless, remastered print, the feature is accompanied by David J. Skal's excellent documentary, *She's Alive! Creating The Bride of Frankenstein*, which includes lots of new information on the creative partnership – and disagreements – between Whale and Karloff. Scott McQueen also contributes the fascinating commentary track that includes an astonishing amount of knowledge and research – he is clearly a man who has spent a lot of time in the studio archives to find every script change and uncredited bit player.

Triumph of the Will (1935)
(Orig title: *Triumph des Willens*)
Dir: Leni Riefenstahl /Germany
Leni Riefenstahl's career as a film-maker began with her documentation of the Fifth Nazi Party rally in Nuremberg, *Der Sieg des Glaubens* (*The Victory of Faith*, 1933), a parade of triumph for the new regime. Nazi high command was so impressed with her film that Hitler personally recruited her to do it all over again, this time in epic proportions for the Nazi Party Congress in Nuremberg in the summer of 1934. The result was a technically accomplished propaganda epic, *Triumph of the Will*.

Opening with aerial shots on a plane above Nuremberg, we are then shown footage of the Führer passing through the streets in an open-top car saluting his adoring public who are out in droves. Hitler Youth camps are filled with thousands of youngsters smiling for the camera. Soldiers admit to never firing a shot in their lives, but are excited about the future, and we are also presented with lengthy enthusiastic speeches from the chief members of the Nazi party themselves. The Nazi Party Congress was attended by more than 700,000 supporters, and they watch in awe as their political heroes – Hess, Goebbels, Rosenberg, and Hitler himself – take to the stand and promise a glorious new age.

At the time of production, *Triumph of the Will* was one of the most ambitious films ever attempted, and is still considered by some to be one of the greatest and most important ever made, with a technical virtuosity years ahead of its time. With its roving camera shots capturing the adoring crowds, aerial photography, grand use of Wagner's music, and 500mm lenses, the finished film could not help but look astonishing, and it did much to cement the belief that Germany was one of the most technologically advanced nations on earth. Director Leni Riefenstahl was afforded the kind of film crew and equipment that would make Hollywood blush today in order to bring the Nazi dream onto the big screen; her crew consisted of around 172 people, with 10 technicians, 36 cinematographers and assistants (16 teams with 30 cameras), 9 aerial photographers, 17 newsreel staff (and a further 12 crew), 17 lighting technicians, two photographers, 26 drivers, 37 security officers, 4 labourers, and 2 office assistants. Occasionally, her staff would even dress in SA uniforms so that they could blend into the crowds. And, as editor, Riefenstahl also had the daunting task of condensing the estimated 61 hours of film into a final cut of just under two hours. She laboured through a seemingly endless string of days and nights to complete the film before the deadline, even sleeping on the editing room floor that was littered with thousands of feet of celluloid.

Hitler – who served as executive producer – praised the finished film, calling it an 'incomparable glorification of the power and beauty of our movement.' But, of course, elsewhere in the world the response was far less enthusiastic. During the war, Frank Capra contributed to a series of newsreel films called *Why We Fight*, commissioned by the United States government, and those films contained snippets of footage from *Triumph of the Will*, with an altered context to make it a piece of Allied propaganda instead. Capra later commented on *Triumph*, observing that the film 'fired no gun, dropped no bombs. But as a psychological weapon aimed at destroying the will to resist, it was just as lethal.'

Riefenstahl is often considered to be one of the greatest female directors of the twentieth century. She only made eight films during her lifetime, and only two of those were screened outside of her native country. Her work was admired by critics for the rest of her life, and much of her reputation rests on *Triumph*. But, perhaps inevitably, the film was equally damaging to her reputation as it was helpful in establishing it. She was imprisoned by the Allies for four years for being a Nazi sympathizer, and was forever blacklisted from the film industry after the war. In 2003, almost seven decades after the premier of *Triumph*, Riefenstahl died. Some of the most eminent publications in the world gave coverage of her passing – the *New York Times, Wall Street Journal, Associated Press, The Guardian* – most of them acknowledging the importance of *Triumph* as a technically innovative historical document.

Just like American film-maker D. W. Griffith and his *Birth of a Nation*, made 20 years earlier, *Triumph of the Will* has been condemned for using spectacular film-making to seduce the populace into a deeply unethical world-view. In Germany, this movie is officially classified as Nazi propaganda, and screenings are restricted in a partial ban under post-war de-Nazification laws, but it may be shown in an educational context. In 1985, trash film fanatic and former gravedigger, Johannes Schonherr, rescued a print of *Triumph of the Will* from oblivion, and while every other cinema in the land was afraid to screen it, he held a screening at the 'Kino im KOMM' cinema in Nuremberg. By law, he had to introduce the film as a way of putting it into context as an educational and historical 'exhibit,' and he did this by informing the assembled audience that *Triumph of the Will* was the only noteworthy film ever made in their city! (see his book, *Trashfilm Roadshows*, for the full story).

The images presented in the film are what we equate with pre-war Nazi Germany today. But, perhaps most dramatically, Hitler's descent from the clouds as he lands in Nuremberg to his adoring public leaves viewers in awe at how such a spectacle came to be. Der Führer is shown exactly how he wanted to be seen, and no other film was made about him after that (though he did appear sporadically in the newsreels, *Die Deutsche Wochenschau* [1933-1945], as well as *Olympia* [1938] – also by Riefenstahl – and *Wort und Tat* [1938]). There was simply no need to openly extol Hitler any further. He was now Germany's messiah.

Dante's Inferno (1935)
Dir: Harry Lachman /USA

Spencer Tracy stars as an out-of-work sailor who helps a carnival barker turn a museum of horrors into an innovative underground theme park based on Dante's circles of Hell. Unfairly maligned over the decades, *Dante's Inferno* is a wonderful little film that suffered from a critical mauling in its day, save for Leslie Halliwell who hailed it as 'one of the most unexpected, imaginative and striking pieces of cinema in Hollywood's history.' Indeed, there are a couple of sequences set in the 'hell' of the museum that are as visually striking as anything seen in 1930s cinema.

The Devil-Doll (1936)
Dir: Tod Browning /USA

Fraudster, Paul Lavond (Lionel Barrymore), escapes from prison and heads for Paris amidst the police manhunt disguised as a sweet old lady, 'Madam Mandelin.' He was also in contact with Marcel (Henry B. Walthall) and his witchy wife, Malita (Rafaela Ottiano), who have mastered the technique of shrinking dogs and humans down to miniature size. Lavond seeks vengeance on the bankers whom he blames for his imprisonment, by having them murdered by his miniature 'dolls,' while also trying to build a rapport with his long lost daughter, Lorraine (Maureen O' Sullivan), who now works as a lowly scrubber in a backstreet laundry...

Browning's penultimate film (his last was *Miracles For Sale* [1939]) is also one of his best, infused with the themes he had explored previously, such as disguise and unrequited love of *The Unknown* (1927). Barrymore is superb as Lavond and Madam Mandelin, a role that no doubt would have been a challenging one, even for the 'Man of a Thousand Faces,' Lon Chaney, who had died years earlier. The special effects are remarkable for the time, with one sequence showing one of the dolls stealing jewelry and tossing it out of a bedroom window – it has a genuine 'land of the giants' feel with the vastly oversized furniture making the room seem like an intimidating world of its own. A minor classic ripe for rediscovery.

Slaves in Bondage (1937)
Dir: Elmer Clifton /USA

When a teenage girl, Mary Lou (Louise Small) escapes from a shady group of men by jumping out of a speeding car, an ambitious news reporter, Phillip Miller (Donald Reed), investigates and tips off the police the location of the prostitution racket. Meanwhile at the Berrywood Roadhouse, viewers are privy to the ins and outs of a whore house where scantily-clad prostitutes make fun of their clients and the house pimp, 'Good Looking Freddie' chastises them for it. The police raid the building in connection with the kidnapping of Mary Lou. The girls are taken down town, but the crooks manage to escape. Freddie's mug shot appears in the papers, and the higher-ups in the shady organisation get rid of him and dump his body on the street.

A new pimp takes over Freddie's side of things, and he opens a new house in a new location and seeks a new roster of girls to work for him. Miller is framed for holding counterfeit notes, and, while in jail, the new pimp preys on his girlfriend, Dona (Lona Andre). She is lured into enslavement and prostitution by the pimp and his Madam who masquerade as the owners of a manicure shop. By offering genuine work to naïve young women from out of town, the crooks purposely put them in debt with a convenient way to settle what they owe – by sleeping with strange men at the roadhouse...

One of the most engaging and competently made of all the exploitation films of the 1930s, *Slaves in Bondage* takes the sensationalism of previous oddities, such as *Cocaine Fiends* (1935) and *Gambling With Souls* (1936), imbues those lurid tales with a more salacious storyline, and adds genuine talent on both sides of the camera. The result is still unmistakably exploitation, but here the quality of the production looks like something a major studio could have churned out, and this time the film-makers have the budget and the personnel to show that they know what they're doing. And, besides being a competent film, it is also one of the earliest to show spanking and light S&M scenarios, played out in the 'Oriental Room,' and 'cat fights,' in which men pay to watch the prostitutes rolling around on the floor and pulling hair, which the clients find titillating.

The white slave trade had been depicted in the movies as early as 1913 with the release of *The Inside of the White Slave Traffic*. But the subject-matter had never been broached on film as openly as this.

Elmer Clifton made the less impressive *Assassin of Youth* (1937) in the same year, in which another young reporter gets the scoop on the local 'marijuana menace.' Elsewhere in the exploitation craze, *Damaged Goods* (1937) and *Sex Madness* (1938) tackled the syphilis menace; *Rebellious Daughters* (1938) dealt with teenage runaways; *Delinquent Parents* (1938), illegitimate children; and *Marihuana* (1936) and *Reefer Madness* (1938) were self-explanatory. All this in the guise of public education. Perhaps the most bizarre of them all – and one that held no such claims about being an 'educational' picture – was *The Terror of Tiny Town* (1938), a ramshackle western cast almost entirely with dwarves, most of whom went on to play Munchkins in *The Wizard of Oz* the following year.

Dead End (1937)
Dir: William Wyler /USA
The great William Wyler wasn't the kind of film-maker to allow the strict new enforcement of the production code to impede on his knack for creating gritty, hard-boiled slum dramas. And in 1937 he ran into trouble, not with Bill Hays and MPPDA, but with the censors across the pond. The BBFC kept a close eye on the development of Wyler's latest project, *Dead End*, pouring over every script change and line of dialogue while trying their damnedest to make the film as tame as possible for the British market. Understandably peeved at this level of interference, in the end Wyler and his producer stopped cooperating with the Board as it had become more trouble than it was worth. The film-maker went ahead with his project, the British market be damned, and helmed this one-of-a-kind gritty masterpiece on his own terms.

The opening shot shows the gleaming towers of New York City standing against the skyline. The camera then lowers beneath the railway bridges and below the rooftops of the tenement slums of the Lower East Side. The area is undergoing gentrification, as the wealthy have begun buying up apartments that overlook the river. The establishing shots juxtapose the lives of the rich and poor. The story centres on a group of street kids who pass the time by getting

themselves involved in bullying and petty crime. Meanwhile, a sinister gangster type, 'Baby Face' Martin (Humphrey Bogart) shows up out of nostalgia for the place he grew up in, And, after being rejected by his mother who accuses him of being a murderer, Martin's identity is eventually discovered, and the police are called in to deal with him in bloody fashion...

Described by *Variety* as 'tense and accurate, but sordid and depressing,' *Dead End* is part gangster film and part coming-of-age drama. It's an easy watch with the story taking place almost entirely on a single large street set, not unlike the similar *Street Scene* (1931). Based on Sidney Kingsley's 1935 Broadway play, there is an undeniable theatricality here whilst still retaining the intimacy that only cinema can bring. The film is most famous, however, for kick-starting the *Dead End Kids* series, of which this was the first of many featuring the young tearaways. Other films to feature the hooligans include *Crime School* (1938), *Angels With Dirty Faces* (1938), *They Made Me a Criminal* (1939), *Hell's Kitchen* (1939), *Angels Wash Their Faces* (1939) and *On Dress Parade* (1939). Subsequently the boys broke up into the *Little Tough Guys* (1939), the *East Side Kids* (1940-1946) and *The Bowery Boys* (1946-1958).

J'Accuse (1938)
(*I Accuse*)
Dir: Abel Gance /France
As the powers of Europe were rushing towards World War II, director Abel Gance decided to update his classic, *J'Accuse!* (1920) – a film he was never entirely happy with – for a new generation. This time, however, he emphasised the horrors of conflict with a more urgent plea for peace than ever before.

An excellent anti-war film, this remake of *J'Accuse!* is all the more poignant considering it was released in France shortly before the Occupation. The story is also a little different: Victor Francen (Jean Diaz), the only survivor of his regiment in World War I, invents a device he believes will stop war forever, only to see it used by his government as a defence measure against the enemy. Driven mad by this exploitation, Francen decides only the war dead marching through the streets will stop the people's thirst for an upcoming war. In his delusion, bodies rise from their graves, and the sight of war's actual horrors so terrifies the patriotic countrymen that all thoughts of war are abandoned.

What makes this film so remarkable is the aforementioned sequence in which the bodies of the war dead rise from their graves. Many of the those used for this stunning sequence were injured veterans of the War who would ordinarily have been killed. But, due to the increasing sophistication of medicine, many of the heroes survived their horrific injuries and physical defacements, and lived on as a warning to others. We see veterans with missing limbs, shattered bones, and even a few who have their noses missing, and parts of their faces almost completely obliterated. It's difficult to imagine what audiences must have made of this back in the late 30s with World War II rearing its ugly head on the horizon. Gance's plot is a very simple one, but told with enormous power and passion for peace. The ravaged faces of the war dead are still disturbing today; they remain very powerful images not so easily forgotten. The message is conveyed clearly, without preaching, and with a sensitivity towards pacifism, which even in the late 1930s was still very much frowned upon by patriots on all sides of the upcoming conflict. Like so many films of this nature, its message was considered unsuitable by Nazi Germany, and the film banned in that country.

The film premiered in France on 30 October 1938, just as Orson Welles and his team at CBS Radio were going through the final rehearsals for their live rendition of H. G. Wells' *War of the Worlds* broadcast scheduled for the following night. It was a broadcast that went down in infamy with its director having to publicly apologise...

War of the Worlds (1938)
Dir: Orson Welles and Paul Stewart /USA
'We interrupt this programme to bring you a special news bulletin...' Orson Welles' infamous live broadcast of *War of the Worlds* was one of the earliest examples of media manipulation, and the ensuing chaos it sparked among the public brought to an end the age of innocence.

The show began at 8pm eastern time (or should that be ET?), and opened as a light evening of jazz. However, the music is constantly interrupted by news-flash inserts as a reporter interviews the Princeton professor of astronomy, Carl Phillips (Frank Readick). They discuss the strange gas clouds that have been emitting from planet Mars. During the

conversation, the professor is handed a note, and, after reading it, he passes it on to the reporter who then reads it aloud on the air. Apparently, an alien spacecraft has landed in the small town of Grover's Mill in New Jersey, not far from where they are. The pair head on over to the site, and after much speculation and pontification, the craft comes to life and sends out an army of aliens to destroy the human race...

The young Orson Welles, who was just 23-years-old at the time, and who had already made a name for himself in theatre, found himself tackling H. G. Wells' classic sci-fi novel, *The War of the Worlds* (pub. 1898). And though Wells' work had already been adapted for the screen before, successfully with James Whale's *The Invisible Man* (1933) and controversially with *The Island of Lost Souls* (1932), *War of the Worlds* was set to be the first major rendition of his work to hit the airwaves. The book was forty years old by that point, and many in the industry were sceptical about the success of a radio play based on a story that most Americans were already familiar with. However, the ambitious Welles had a trick up his sleeve. He wasn't so much interested in re-treading the story in a conventional way. Instead, he transferred the tale from Victorian London to modern-day New Jersey. And, crucially, he chose to tell the story as a series of news-flash bulletins live on air.

This innovative approach was inspired by real-life events, such as the infamous Pathé newsreel from the previous year, which captured the Hindenburg Disaster; the way the reporter's cool and professional manner was shattered once the huge zeppelin burst into flames sent shock-waves across the world. Americans had also become accustomed to the news-flash phenomenon, in which radio programmes would be routinely interrupted to bring them information from Europe, whether it be the soap opera that was Wallis Simpson's relationship with King Edward (and his subsequent abdication), to Anschluss, and the touch-and-go Munich Agreement. Something big was brewing across the pond, and Americans were transfixed to their radios, keeping their ears peeled for the breaking news.

Such a documentary-style horror had never been attempted before, and Welles and his team at CBS managed to create a real sense of verisimilitude. The sounds of shouting and screaming in the background as the sinister threat becomes all too real; the professor and the reporters loosing their professional courtesies as the danger threatens them personally; and the trick of gradually upping the ante and building the tension, from mild bewilderment to outright terror, was expertly done. Forty years later, George Romero managed to capture that sense of panic – albeit briefly – for the opening scenes of *Dawn of the Dead* (1978) in which a television station fell apart live on air as the living dead laid waste to civilisation. As for *War of the Worlds*, another aspect that played in the show's favour was the fact that many had tuned in late, and were unable to separate fact from fiction. The unknowing listeners, who were enjoying some light jazz just a few moments ago, were now being informed by reporters that New Jersey was under attack from Martians.

While the programme was still on the air, CBS was inundated with calls from terrified members of the public, and the panic seemed to spread like wildfire across the country. Some packed their belongings and headed for the hills with their families, while others locked all the doors and windows of their homes and hunkered down for the night with their guns loaded, ready to fend off the invaders. The papers were full of it the next morning – almost every major newspaper in the country ran a front page headline, from the *New York Times* to the *Associated Press*. Though undoubtedly exaggerated, the stories are worth a read if only as an example of the media helping to fan the flames for their own ends. There were reports of heart attacks, stampedes and suicides. Amusingly, an elderly man unloaded his shotgun on a water cooler tower thinking it was an alien spacecraft; many of those who fled from their homes wore damp cloths over their mouths to protect them form 'alien gas'; and there were reports that one man tried to sign up to the Marine Corp. in the middle of the night to help fight the Martians. Orson Welles and CBS sure had a lot of explaining to do.

A dishevelled Welles was paraded in front of a press conference the next morning. The folks at CBS were nowhere to be seen, and the young dramatist was left to face the music alone. To his credit, Welles accepted full responsibility for the broadcast, and he answered the reporters' questions with a doe-eyed innocence, and he was happy to apologise to all concerned on behalf of CBS. However, this wasn't enough for the Federal Communications Commission (FCC), who demanded a strict new censoring body, and called for all future radio plays to be approved by the government prior to broadcast. After a lengthy investigation, the FCC found that the media had indeed grossly exaggerated the panic of that night, and Welles was cleared of all wrong doing. Government censorship was thus avoided, but radio networks were now warned to abide by self-censorship policies. And it was around this time that disclaimers were brought in ahead of programmes, warning listeners of forthcoming scenes that some may find disturbing or unsuitable for children.

In a strange twist, *War of the Worlds* was adapted once again for radio broadcast in Ecuador in 1949, utilising the same 'live on air' gimmick, causing mass unrest in the country. This time, even the police and fire brigades came out to fight the Martians. When the public learned that they had been duped, a group of vengeful citizens stormed the broadcast studio and burned it to the ground, killing six people in the process. Of course, by that point, Welles had long since been signed up by RKO, and he had delivered his masterpiece, *Citizen Kane* (1941), which is still considered one of the greatest films ever made. Less known is the fact that the script was written by Howard Koch, who went on to write such classics as *Casablanca* (1942) and *Letters From an Unknown Woman* (1948) before falling afoul of the House of Un-American Activities. And the conductor on *War of the Worlds* was none other than Bernard Hermann, who went on to RKO with Welles and scored some of the most memorable themes in the movies.

The craze for docu-horror continued for decades, with items such as *Snuff* (1975), purporting to be a document of a real crime (the film included no end credits as a way of boosting its supposed 'authenticity'), *The Blair Witch Project* and *The Last Broadcast* (both 1998) that played around with the documentary format to confound fact and fiction, scaring millions of viewers in the process. In the UK, *Ghostwatch* (1992) borrowed heavily from Welles' work; broadcast on the BBC on Halloween night, live from 'the most haunted house in Britain,' this live show scared a whole generation of British youngsters as they thought that the ghostly 'Mr. Pipes' was real. Once again, the tabloids whipped up a storm of controversy, and the BBC was forced to apologise. *The Night America Trembled* (1957 – an hour-long episode of *Studio One*) and *The Night That Panicked America* (1975 – also penned by Koch) are entertaining TV movies based on the *War of the Worlds* broadcast.

Son of Frankenstein (1939)
Dir: Rowland V. Lee /USA

Dr. Frankenstein's son (Basil Rathbone) takes his wife to his father's old castle in Europe. The locals shun him as soon as he steps off the train, but Frankie Jr is determined to continue the experiments of resurrecting a human corpse, this time without the dysfunctional brain blunder. Conveniently, the Monster (Karloff again, in his last Monster role for Universal), remains on the grounds of the castle, and Frankenstein's old assistant, Ygor (Bela Lugosi), roams the area after surviving being hanged. He now has a broken neck with a chunk of bone protruding out. Frankie Jr discovers that the Monster's blood is superhuman, and thus a far greater danger than he had initially assumed. He vows to destroy the creature, but Ygor overhears his plans and sets the Monster loose, with the intention of killing the jurors who had him hanged... This third entry in Universal's *Frankenstein* series is not quite in the same league as the first two, but is a wonderful addition nonetheless. Fans get the rare opportunity to see Karloff and Lugosi in the same scenes. Other things to look out for include the Gothic castle that has strange, modernist interiors; Lionel Atwill as the police inspector who had his arm torn off by the Monster when he was a child, and now carries around a bionic – and malfunctioning – limb; and the familiar torch mob ending. *The Ghost of Frankenstein* (1942) followed.

Rebecca (1940)
Dir: Alfred Hitchcock /USA

Hitchcock's landmark Oscar winner, and his first Hollywood film made under the auspices of legendary producer, David O' Selznick, was also his second stab at adapting the work of Daphne Du Maurier (the first was the coldly received *Jamaica Inn* [1939]). *Rebecca* is a superb Gothic potboiler though Hitch himself had always dismissed the film as a work-for-hire project for which he was unable to add his own trademark style. Nonetheless, it remains one of his most fondly remembered works, and is essential viewing for anyone interested in film.

Joan Fontaine stars as the unnamed narrator,

the shy second wife of the handsome and brooding Maxim de Winter (Laurence Olivier). They meet on the Riviera and quickly fall in love before returning to Mandalay, Maxim's beautiful, sprawling sea-side estate in Cornwall. The wife is introduced to the servants who immediately display an air of hostility towards her, as they had adored Rebecca, Maxim's first wife whose death is shrouded in secrecy. The servants become ever more sinister, and Fontaine becomes ever more withdrawn and afraid, until she learns exactly what happened to Rebecca...

Rebecca was a prestigious project for Selznick who was still riding high on the success of *Gone With the Wind* (1939). And, just as he had done with that film, he conducted a lavish publicity campaign for *Rebecca* and a meticulous casting process for the lead players. Many names circulated in the press, including Loretta Young, Margaret Sullavan, Olivia de Havilland, Vivien Leigh, and Anne Baxter, but it was the 22-year-old Fontaine who won the part in the end. Depending on your own feelings, you may find her character to be either sweetly endearing or annoyingly naïve and submissive, but no one can deny she was born for the part.

A masterpiece with lavish production values and haunting atmospherics, *Rebecca* is also notable for how civilised its characters are – there's no screaming or hysteria here. The only time one of the characters loses his cool is when Maxim socks a would-be blackmailer on the jaw – and the man's reaction is to down a glass of bourbon and get back to business. The characters remain stoically composed as the world crumbles around them. Perhaps the most remarkable character is Rebecca herself who died before the story begins, and yet haunts the entire film, as if channelled through the mean (and possibly lesbian) Mrs. Danvers (Judith Anderson). For many years, Du Maurier's original ending was dropped in favour of a scene that implies that Rebecca had died after falling and hitting her head. British television versions – from 1978 and 1997 – stuck to the original ending, and Anchor Bay's DVD release of *Rebecca* reinstates the original ending, too.

Jud Suss (1940)
(*Jew Suss*; aka *Suss the Jew*)
Dir: Veit Harlan / Germany

In 1934, a British propaganda film was released entitled *Jew Suss* (aka *Power*), which satirised the German oppression of the Jewish people. Based on true events (and also a couple of novelised accounts), the film depicted the rise of a court Jew who wins favour in high society. His plan is to help out his fellow Jews with his new found power. However, he later discovers that he is in fact a gentile. The film's message about the pointlessness of racial distinctions so enraged Joseph Goebbels that six years later, after the outbreak of World War II, he personally commissioned a re-telling of the tale, this time from the Nazi's perspective. The result was also entitled *Jud Suss*, but as a play on words in German ('suss the Jew'). Films historians today tend to view the film as little more than a vicious piece of anti-Semitic propaganda, with many overlooking the fact that it was made primarily as a way of settling scores with the British propaganda ministry. In the same year, the Nazi regime released *Die Rothschilds* (1940), which was made partly in response to the Hollywood production, *The House of Rothschild* (1934), a film which depicted the banking dynasty in a positive light.

Set in Stuttgart in 1733, the German version of *Jud Suss* tells the disturbing story of a Jewish swindler, Joseph Seuss Oppenheimer (Ferdinand Marian), who flatters the new Duke of Württemberg, Karl Alexander (Heinrich George), with lavish gifts. His plan is to play up to the man's greed and vanity in order to be granted political powers in return. Jews are officially banned from the city and live in ghettos surrounding the state. Oppenheimer worms his way through the city gates and presents the Duke with gifts of jewelry and women (the women are actually whores from the ghetto, unbeknownst to the Duke). In return, Seuss is granted control of all the roads in the city, and the first thing he does while in charge is to impose tolls on all the main thoroughfares. This causes much anger among the populace as food prices rise considerably overnight to compensate for the extra costs. Later, he manages to convince the Duke to lift the ban on Jews, and they immediately begin pouring in from the nearby ghettos. By now, Oppenheimer has also gained control of other areas too, such as setting the tax rates on salt, beer, wine and grain. And the anger of the masses continues to rise...

Members of the city council attempt to talk some sense into the Duke (one of them even reads to him a passage from Martin Luther's notorious book, *On the Jews and Their Lies*), but the cunning Oppenheimer sees to it that the council is dissolved. With the help of his fellow Jews, most notably his secretary, Levy, and his Rabbi (both played by Aryan actor, Werner Krauss), Seuss raises enough funds to pay for an army to repel the furious townsfolk who are now baying for the Duke's blood. In the meantime, several council members are imprisoned and tortured. The wife of one of them (played by Aryan beauty, Kristina Soderbaum) pleads with Seuss for his release, only to be raped. And after her ordeal she drowns herself in a nearby lake. Events come to a head when the Duke suffers a fatal heart attack, and this leaves Oppenheimer exposed and without protection. The council legally resumes its rule, and the Jews are immediately expelled from the city once more. And Seuss is publicly executed in the city square.

Jud Suss premiered at the Venice Film Festival to rave reviews, and became one of the highest grossing German films of the Nazi era, drumming up 6.5 million Reichsmarks, far outstripping its lavish $m2$ million budget. The film was deliberately designed to be a more 'subtle' form of anti-Semitic propaganda, avoiding the harsh realism and heavy-handedness of the less popular documentary, *Der Ewige Jude* (*The Eternal Jew*) that was made around the same time. Goebbels personally oversaw numerous re-writes of the script, insisting that it wasn't anti-Semitic enough for his liking – he was even personally involved in the writing of Suess' final lines of dialogue as he awaits his fate in the cage ('I'm just a poor Jew!'). Oppenheimer's body was left hanging in a human-sized bird cage (gibbeted) in the square for six years before his rotten skeleton was hastily buried below the gallows. That part isn't addressed in the film.

According to the Wikipedia, '[Oppenheimer] gained a prominent position as a court Jew and held the reins of the finances. He established a duchy monopoly on the trade of salt, leather, tobacco, and liquor and founded a bank and porcelain factory. In the process, he made a number of enemies who claimed, among other things, that he was involved with local gambling houses.' He as also accused of fraud, embezzlement, treason, 'lecherous relations with the court ladies,' accepting bribes, and trying to undermine the state by furtively stirring up conflict between Protestants and Catholics.

The Jews raised a ransom fund in an attempt to secure the freedom of Oppenheimer and bring him back to the ghetto, but it was turned down flat. The Wikipedia entry continues, 'after a heavily publicized trial during which no proofs were produced, he was sentenced to death.' The page also adds that the whole event was a 'relatively obscure event in German history.' Unfortunately, court transcripts of the case no longer exist, and so nothing can be verified. However, this 'obscure' historical event has nonetheless produced two drama films, several documentaries about those films, a dramatized making of the film, numerous novels, plays, history volumes and biographies – not to mention a memorial sculpture by an artist called Angela Laich.

After the war, director Veit Harlan stood trial for "crimes against humanity," only avoiding the death sentence because the anti-Semitic content of the film was in the full control of Goebbels. But boy did the new regime want him dead – they tried him *three* times. Heinrich George, who played the pompous and easily manipulated Duke, was a former communist who went on to embrace national socialism. His Soviet captors must have had a field day at having found one of their prized traitors. God knows what kind of horrific treatment he suffered at the hands of his Soviet enemies – he was held at the notorious NKVD special camp no. 7 where being starved to death was seen as the easy way out. All that is known about his imprisonment there is that he died in September 1946.

Kristina Soderbaum, who played the ill-fated wife, Dorothea, was married to Harlan. She had become something of an icon in Germany at the time, having played several roles as the ideal Aryan woman of beauty and innocence and purity. She appeared in 11 films during the Nazi era, the most famous of which, besides *Jud Suss*, also includes Anna in *Die goldene Stadt* (*The Golden City*, 1942). Both roles end with her tragic drowning. She was known by her fans as 'the quintessential Nazi star,' and by her enemies as 'the drowned corpse of the Reich.' After the war, she escaped prosecution after her husband's testimony that it was Goebbels who insisted that she appear in his films. Nevertheless, she had a miserable time in the 50s and early 60s as she was often pelted with rotten vegetables while performing on the theatre stage. She later became a photographer,

and appeared in minor roles for the rest of her life. Her last film role was alongside Hugh Grant in *Night Train to Venice* (1993). She died in obscurity in a nursing home in 2001.

Werner Krauss played the roles of Levy and the Rabbi, along with up to eleven other Jewish bit-parts in the film, all of which amplified ugly stereotypes. Krauss was openly anti-Semitic and a supporter of the Nazi Party. In the postwar years, all of his films were banned in Germany and he was held in detention and forced to undergo a de-Nazification programme. He re-emerged in the mid-50s and was permitted to attend the occasional film festival as a guest. He died in Austria in 1959. Ferdinand Marian, who played Oppenheimer, was also banned from the film industry after the war. He turned to alcoholism, and is said to have regretted his role in *Jud Suss*. He died in a car crash in 1946. It was thought to have been a drunken accident, but some believe he committed suicide.

As for the fate of the film itself, *Jud Suss* was not only banned in 1945 by the Allied Military Occupation, it was also banned throughout the western world. All seized prints were destroyed, but there was at least one print that existed in East Germany and was being screened illegally. Copies were made and distributed in the Middle East with Arabic subtitles. Whether the copies were made by the KGB or underground Nazi sympathizers to stir up anti-Semitism in the region remains unknown.

However, those bootlegged copies are the only ones available today. The picture and audio quality is a little rough at times, but it holds up quite well compared to other German films of the era, many of which were destroyed or considered lost. The German government holds copyright ownership of these films to this day, but I wouldn't hold my breath for a digitally remastered Blu-Ray release any time soon.

The Eternal Jew (1940)
(Original title: *Der Ewige Jude*)
Dir: Fritz Hippler /Germany

When Germany invaded Poland in September 1939, the army was accompanied by a newsreel crew headed by Fritz Hippler. It was their job to document the blitzkrieg tactics and to glorify the Nazis' mastery of warfare for the weekly newsreel, *Die Deutsche Wochenschau* (1933-1945). However, the amount of footage gained from the advance was enough to produce an entire feature film, *Der Feldzug in Polen* (*The Campaign in Poland*, 1940), which was the first time the world had seen the terrifying efficiency of the Nazi blitzkrieg in action. Poland was decimated in a matter of weeks, and put up very little resistance. But instead of heading back home, Hippler and his crew chanced upon a Jewish ghetto in Warsaw, and began documenting their findings. Hippler had intended to use the footage as part of a future instalment of the weekly newsreel, but like the blitzkrieg, the amount of footage gained from the exercise was expanded into another feature – one of the nastiest and most mean-spirited films ever made.

Released into theatres on 28 November 1940, just two months after *Jud Suss*, these films marked a stark difference in the Nazi's depiction of Jews on film. Previously, the likes of *Linen From Ireland* (*Lienen au Irland*, 1939), *Vom Bäumlein* (1940), and *Die Rothschilds* (1940) portrayed the Jews as either comical villains or unscrupulous swindlers, but with *Jud Suss* and *The Eternal Jew*, the 'warm-up' phase of the propaganda had ended, and the German public were now presented with a much more sinister form of demonization. *The Eternal Jew* purports to be a documentary on the life of a Jewish community in Warsaw, but quickly expands to show them as part of an international conspiracy, with members holding high office in the worlds of banking, media and entertainment. They are said to be remarkably wealthy and yet several generations live under the same roof in the cockroach-infested slums. As the film progresses, the Jews are likened to a plague of rats in human form, as cunning underground animals that bring disease and destruction wherever they roam. And finally, the film ends with a disturbing scene of 'kosher' slaughter, in which a cow has its throat cut and is left to bleed out.

Hitler himself took a personal interest in the production of the film. However, the success of Goebbels' *Jud Suss* wasn't replicated with *The Eternal Jew*. In fact, the film wasn't a hit, and audiences stayed away. It was described as 'a strain on the nerves,' while another complained, 'We have seen *Jud* [*Süß*] and we've had enough of this Jewish filth.' The one place where the film *was* well-received was among the Party faithful, as it covered just about everything the Nazis ever claimed about the Jews. The marked differences of opinion between Hitler and

Goebbels on how a propaganda campaign should be properly conducted was never as evident as here with these two films. Goebbels' 'subtle' and fictionalised approach was a hit with the masses, while just a few weeks later, Hitler's brutally frank and blunt documentary-style left the same masses cold.

In his book, *Propaganda and the German Cinema: 1933-1945*, David Welch coins the terms 'Lie Direct' and 'Lie Indirect' to pertain to these differing opinions. 'Lie Direct' refers to the blunt, no nonsense, in-your-face approach of disseminating ideas to the public. As Hitler himself wrote in *Mein Kampf*, 'It makes me sick when I see political propaganda hiding under the guise of art. Let it be either art or politics.' On the other hand, 'Lie Indirect' is the type of propaganda that Hitler was complaining about; political ideas dressed up as escapism or as something other than what it purports to be. And it was this method that was supported by Goebbels. The Minister of Propaganda felt that the people needed to be slowly indoctrinated into accepting ideas that at first seemed alien or immoral to them, and that's why the anti-Semitic films made in Nazi Germany gradually became more sinister with each passing year (and this 'warm-up' style was also utilised in films concerning the sterilisation and ultimate 'liquidation' of the mentally handicapped and criminally insane). According to Goebbels, overtly political films had their place, but should be offered sparingly, '...because the moment a person is conscious of propaganda, propaganda becomes ineffective.'

Just like Veit Harlan, director Fritz Hippler was put on trial for the film after the war and was found not guilty (though he was sentenced to two years in prison for other charges). He was never on friendly terms with Goebbels, who, in his diary, described the film-maker as 'intelligent but cheeky, and totally contradictory.' He expressed regret for his involvement in Nazi films in interviews over the years. He died in May 2002, aged 92.

Ohm Kruger (1941)
(*Uncle Kruger*)
Dir: Hans Steinhoff /Germany
The life and times of South African politician, Paul Kruger, who was eventually defeated by the British in the Boer War. Told as a series of flashbacks while Kruger (Emil Jannings) is on his deathbed, the story charts the provocations

of the British as Cecil Rhodes uses cunning tricks to gain access to the gold mines in South Africa. However, Kruger has tricks of his own up his sleeve, and he imposes high taxes on the TNT needed to blow up the mines. The British attempt to buy him off, but Kruger stands by his people and refuses to be corrupted. So, Rhodes (played by Ferdinand Marian of *Jud Suss* infamy) hits back by showing him a long list of Boer council traitors who secretly work for the Brits. War eventually breaks out, and the British massacre thousands of Boers and imprison men, women and children in – the world's first – concentration camps. Back in the present day, and on his deathbed, Kruger predicts the destruction of Britain before he dies... Looking back, it's incredible to think that such a large production got underway in the middle of the war – there are epic battle scenes involving thousands of soldiers and horses and explosions, and no doubt used up a lot of manpower and resources that were needed for the war effort. The film was made to stir up anti-British sentiment among the Germans. Indeed, throughout the film, the British are often referred to as 'those Jewish lackeys.' Goebbels removed the film from circulation in 1944 for purposes of morale as German towns and cities were being destroyed. Incredibly, in 1944 just as Germany was on its last legs, another massive film production was given the green light, *Kolberg* (1945), in full colour, as a final show of defiance as the nation was defeated.

Citizen Kane (1941)
Dir: Orson Welles /USA

You may ask yourself why *Citizen Kane* would be included in a book about cult and controversial cinema. After all, the film is a mainstay of mainstream discourse and widely considered to be one of the finest pictures ever made. However, you'd be surprised by how many film fans – especially among the younger generations – who have yet to see Welles' innovative classic, and its inclusion here is largely due to how different the film was to the norm when it first hit cinema screens back in May 1941.

Opening on an ominous twilight, the camera closes in on a tall wrought-iron fence that is decorated with the initial 'K.' And beyond the gate spreads Xanadu, a vast, deserted estate that belongs to one of the richest men in the world. The camera slowly surveys the grounds, with its deserted gardens, empty gondolas on a haunted lake, and monkeys lounging around in a private zoo. Above this fog-enshrouded land is a man-made mountain upon which sits a castle with a single delicate light shining from within it. Inside the castle we see a dying man clutching a crystal snow ball of a winter scene. He utters his final word, 'Rosebud,' before death takes him, and the ball drops from his hand and breaks on the stairs into tiny pieces.

So begins the legendary *Citizen Kane*, Orson Welles' stunning debut feature. After several projects failed to get off the ground, including a planned adaptation of Joseph Conrad's *Heart of Darkness*, the 24-year-old *wunderkind* Welles, who was already well-known in the world of theatre and radio (as we have seen), embarked on this most audacious and ambitious project. A milestone in the history of film, not least for its vast array of technical and visual innovations, such as quick cuts, clever dissolves and even the utilising of an iris device that was popular in silent films, *Kane* used every trick in the book – and invented many new ones along the way – to get its epic story up on the big screen. Gregg Toland's expert deep-focus photography (that had been pioneered by James Wong Howe) is so impressive that *Kane* is every much Toland's film as it is Welles'.

Though Welles was co-credited with the screenplay, the real bulk of the story and the clever, incisive dialogue was from the pen of Herman Mankiewicz, brother of Joseph. That's not to take anything away from Welles. His real masterstroke was in his handling of the script, and the way he successfully turned the complex story into a free-flowing, daring and cohesive piece of cinema. The story isn't complicated – it's about a newsreel journalist on a quest to find the meaning behind a media mogul's final word, 'Rosebud.' But the way it was written as a patchwork chronicle of a man's life, with all the biographical scrappiness and mysterious asides, the project could have been a real mess in lesser hands, but Welles succeeded in creating a deeply compelling film that is so tightly constructed that it resembles a perfectly-crafted jigsaw puzzle.

When all is said and done, *Citizen Kane* is a classic story about the corruption of power. The young Charles Foster Kane inherits a media empire and he begins as an idealist, even publishing a front page notice in his paper vowing to serve the public with the truth. But, as the realities of back-biting and inter-personal conflicts escalate, the media world gradually eats away at him until his Inquirer is no different from the rival papers that twist the truth on a daily basis. Late in life, Kane retreats to his unfinished castle high up on the mountain at Xanadu. There, living in near seclusion with his unhappy wife, Susan (Dorothy Comingore), and a small team of staff, Kane is full of regrets and longs for the childhood simplicity that was abruptly cut short. In reality, Kane's last days were spent alone where even the movement of a teacup would echo loudly from the vast walls, spelling emptiness, loneliness and isolation. The defeated king of an empty, hollow empire.

The film concludes on a scene in which reporters are gathered at Xanadu. They walk through a huge warehouse that is to be cleared of its mountains of stored items – stacks of antique furniture, statues, toys, gramophones and crates and boxes full of old gifts and art works. Thompson (William Alland) remarks: 'Mr. Kane was a man who got everything he wanted, and then lost it. Maybe Rosebud was something he couldn't get, or something he lost. Anyway, I don't think it would have explained everything. I don't think any word can explain a man's life. No. I guess Rosebud is just a piece in a jigsaw puzzle... a missing piece.' The camera slowly pans above the heaps of Kane's belongings until it meets a blazing furnace where workers throw a sled into the flames – the same sled that belonged to Kane as a boy in Colorado. Then there's a close-up on the underside of the sled as it succumbs to the flames – the name 'Rosebud' is revealed as the plastic coating bubbles in the heat. The scene cuts to an outdoor shot of the castle as the chimney pours out the thick black smoke of Kane's lost youth. And the final shot takes us back to the iron gate where the film began.

Citizen Kane premiered at the Palace Theatre, Broadway, on 1 May 1941, despite the efforts of William Randolf Hearst who saw parallels between himself and Kane, and did all he could to stop the film from being made. The critics, however, were largely on Welles' side, and the film was a hit, even if Hearst damaged the film's publicity campaign by refusing to carry ads or reviews in his papers. The reviews that were published elsewhere were overwhelmingly positive, heralding the arrival of an instant classic. 'The most surprising and cinematically exciting motion picture seen in many a month...' noted the *New York Times*, 'it comes close to being the most sensational film ever made in Hollywood.' C. A. Lejeune gushed that it was 'probably the most exciting film that has come out of Hollywood in the last twenty-five years. I am not sure it isn't the most exciting film that has ever come out of anywhere.' The *New York World-Telegram* said that it 'belongs at once among the great screen achievements,' while Penelope Houston opined, 'if the cinema can do *that*, it can do *anything*!'

But despite the excellent notices in the press, *Kane* lost out on Oscar night. Not that it made much difference. The film's success, and Welles' free-wheeling style was a gamble that paid off well. By now, Welles was a film-maker who commanded a strong bargaining position in future battles with studio heads. But this new-found freedom didn't last long. His next film, *The Magnificent Ambersons* (1942), was beset by studio interference and given an upbeat ending. And the disappointing box-office returns saw several RKO executives lose their jobs as the company set about a drastic re-shuffle. Alas, in the cut-throat world of Hollywood it didn't take long for Welles and his unorthodox style to be treated with suspicion and panic. Subsequent generations of film-makers, once they reached positions of power in the industry, were quick to pay their respects to Welles, and Alan Yentob even commissioned a documentary for the BBC's *Arena* series on Welles, entitled *The Orson Welles Story* (1982), which to this day remains the finest film ever made about the man and his work. *Kane* reached the number 1 spot on *Sight & Sound*'s 1962 poll on the greatest movies ever made – a position it held on to until it was surpassed by Hitchcock's *Vertigo* (1958) in the 2010s.

Watching *Citizen Kane*, whether for the first time or the tenth, is a vital experience for any film fan. The infinite possibilities of the medium are laid out bare before your eyes. Welles' performance as the title character often gets ignored when discussing the film's achievements, but it was a magnificent performance that covered a lifetime of success and regret. And his triumph in front of the camera serves to reinforce the genius behind the scenes. Not a single shot or line of dialogue is wasted in this masterpiece. It's as near to perfect as any film in history. The casual audacity with which Welles went about the project – breaking the rules whenever they got in the way – made it all look so easy. He continued making films for the next forty-four years, presenting such classics as *The Lady From Shanghai* (1947), *Touch of Evil* (1958) and *F For Fake* (1974), but none of them quite captured the remarkable achievements of his debut. Essential viewing.

Cat People (1942)
Dir: Jacques Tourneur /USA

New York fashion designer, Irena Dubrovna (Simone Simon), marries an average-Joe, Oliver (Kent Smith), but their matrimony comes under strain due to her belief that she is afflicted with an ancient curse – she will transform into a killer panther whenever her emotions are aroused...

By the early 1940s, the horror genre had descended into a furry and melodramatic hokiness. Universal's hit, *The Wolf Man* (1941), introduced all the clichés that helped to shape the face of werewolf movies for decades to come, with Lon Chaney Jr buried under a coat of Jack Pierce's yak hair. *The Wolf Man* was a huge hit, and other studios were keen to cash-in on its success. In the following year, RKO Pictures was still in recovery after supporting Orson Welles' *Citizen Kane* (1941), much to the chagrin of William Randolph Hearst who had smeared the company and tried to have the film shut down. Welles' follow-up, *The Magnificent Ambersons* (1942), brought more problems for the company as executives were fired, and the new bosses instituted a policy of 'showmanship, not genius.'

Into this maelstrom came Val Lewton, a producer hired by RKO whose job was to churn out a series of horror films in the mould of the Universal monster movies. Studio boss, Charles Koerner, supplied Lewton with a title for his first project in the series: Cat People. The reasoning was: if a man transforming into a werewolf could make for a hit film, then how about a woman who turns into a panther? Lewton accepted the project, but instead of churning out a horror quickie as expected, he set out to make a genuinely scary film. He brought in screen writer, Homer DeWitt Bodeen and French film-maker Jacques Tourneur, and together the three of them set out to make a unique film that wasn't just one of the first supernatural horrors to be set in the modern-day, but also one that was at pains to probe the psychological depths of its characters.

The fact that *Cat People* takes place in modern-day New York and addresses a failing marriage sets it apart from the Universal horrors from the outset. Irena is convinced that sexual passion turns her into a black panther. Husband Oliver becomes somewhat estranged and gravitates towards his co-worker, Alice (Jane Randolph), who is far less emotionally complicated. In the end, Oliver and Alice plan to have Irena committed to an asylum. But is Irena really mentally disturbed, or is she a genuine panther-woman? Viewers don't find out until the final scene.

Cat People is chiefly remembered today for playing with audience imagination by refusing to reveal its monster. Instead, the film-makers created lots of mood and shadow for its most celebrated sequences, with DP Nicholas Musuraca's camera work something of a precursor to the film noir style that became popular in years to come, or, as Lewton himself described it – 'patches of prepared darkness.' Those set-pieces remain quite chilling to this day – Irena stalking Alice along the path in Central Park at night, with the jarring cat-like 'hiss' of the air-brakes of the bus, and the haunting sequence at the basement pool with the cries of the ferocious panther. The latter sequence was clearly an influence on Dario Argento's *Suspiria* (1977), in which Suzy Banyon and her ill-fated friend have a secret conversation in the swimming pool at night, only for their presence to be haunted by some witch-like omnipresence that overhears every word.

Despite being a hit with audiences, *Cat People* wasn't so popular among the critics on its first run. On 7 December 1942, during the week of the film's release, the *New York Times* called it 'strangely embarrassing' and 'tedious and graphically unproductive.' Amusingly, the same critic, Bosley Crowther, went on to write an unintended double-entendre: 'Ladies who have such temptations – in straight horror pictures, at least – should exercise their digits a bit more freely than does Simone Simon in this film.' He meant that Simon should have used her claws to kill more victims, but as the film dealt with sexual repression, his words took on an ambiguous meaning. Forty years later, and Paul Schrader's remake of *Cat People* (1982) includes a scene in which Nastassja Kinski 'exercises her digits' in an overtly sexual way.

Val Lewton went on to make eight more pictures for RKO, beginning with Tourneur (the incredibly eerie *I Walked With a Zombie* and *The Leopard Man* [both 1943]), then with Mark Robson as director on *The Seventh Victim* (1943), *The Ghost Ship* (1943), *Isle of the Dead* (1945) and *Bedlam* (1946), and finally, two more with Robert Wise – *The Curse of the Cat People* (1944) and *The Body Snatcher* (1945). Together these films represent one of the most impressive horror series' in the genre. Lewton's career was cut tragically short when he died of a heart attack in 1951, at just 46-years-old.

The Ghost of Frankenstein (1942)
Dir: Erle C. Kenton /USA

Picking up right where *Son of Frankenstein* (1939) left off, Ygor (Bela Lugosi) rescues the Monster from the sulfur pit, and together they make their escape just as the angry villagers destroy the castle. Meanwhile, Dr. Ludwig Frankenstein (Cedric Hardwicke) – another son of Victor – is a successful brain surgeon who discovers that the maniac imprisoned for murder in the town jail is none other than the creature his father had created. The ghost of Victor shows up in the lab and convinces Ludwig to give the creature a normal brain and prove to the world that his scientific work was legitimate. The sly Ygor volunteers to have his own brain transplanted into the body, and the chaos ensues all over again... Enjoyable but a major step down for Universal's *Frankenstein* series. In this fourth instalment of the franchise, the Wolf Man himself, Lon Chaney Jr, steps into the Monster's shoes, and it just doesn't hold the same magic as the earlier films. Lugosi is as fine as ever as the shifty and cunning Ygor; Lionel Atwill – who played the police inspector with the malfunctioning bionic arm in *Son* – returns as the concerned and seemingly level-headed doctor's assistant. But all in all, it's at a loss. In the first two films, we watched the Monster develop as a character in his own right, learning empathy and how to talk all over again, but here the creature just seems to serve as a mute oaf for others to manipulate. The Monster gets dumber and dumber, and the lynch mob surrounding the lab at the end is getting old. The Monster showed up next in *Frankenstein Meets the Wolf Man* (1943).

Child Bride (1943)
(aka *Child Brides*; aka *Child Bride of Ozarks*; aka *Dust to Dust*)
Dir: Harry Revier /USA

An early exploitation effort that was quite controversial in its day. A school teacher, Miss Carol (Diana Durrell), heads to the backwoods town of Thunder Mountain with the intention of putting a stop to the practice of child marriage. One night, she is abducted by a torch-carrying mob who plan on teaching her a lesson in minding her own business. She is rescued by local good guy, Mr. Colton (George Humphreys), and his dwarf buddy, Angelo (Angelo Rossitto). Soon after, however, local girl Jennie (Shirley Mills) finds her father – Mr. Colton – dead and suspects foul play. With no man in the house, Jennie has little choice but to marry one of the leering hillbillies...

Child Bride is a surprisingly well made film with solid production values and a technical proficiency to match contemporary Hollywood products. Like many exploitation flicks of its time, the film was distributed independently to avoid the wrath of the Hays Code. Nonetheless, it did manage to get itself banned in several states for its scenes of wife beating and the notorious nude swimming scene by Mills, who was only 12-years-old. The film was also famously rejected by *Mystery Science Theatre 3000* because of its disturbing and unpleasant subject-matter. The show's presenter, Kevin Murphy, said that he needed 'a good cry and a shower' after seeing it. Mills' most famous role was in *The Grapes of Wrath* (1939). Angelo the dwarf went on to play Master in *Mad Max Beyond Thunderdome* (1985).

The Outlaw (1943)
Dir: Howard Hughes /USA

'"The Outlaw" is a story of the untamed West. Frontier days when the reckless fire of guns and passions blazed an era of death, destruction and lawlessness.'

Billy The Kid (Jack Beutel) and Doc Holiday (Walter Houston) get into a tussle with Sheriff, Pat Garrett (Thomas Mitchell) and his men over a stolen horse. Once wounded, Billy is sent to recover in the care of Doc's girl, Rio (the beautiful Jane Russell), and the two fall in love. When Doc returns, he learns that Billy and Rio are now married. Their enmity is delayed, however, as the men find themselves having to work together to evade lawman Garrett.

After the falling outs on the set of *Scarface* (1932), with director Howard Hawks accusing producer Howard Hughes of interfering in the project, it was a surprise for many in the industry when Hawks signed up to direct *The Outlaw*. Had the pair patched up their differences, or were they simply gearing up for round two? Actually, Hawks walked before shooting began, and Hughes took over the reigns for his first time in the helmer's seat since his World War I epic, *Hell's Angels* (1930). The screenplay by Jules Furthman held much promise (the script was co-written by an uncredited Ben Hecht), and Hughes made no secret of his intention to create a lavish production of *The Outlaw*.

It's unclear why Hughes decided to helm the picture himself, but he may have been swayed by his interest in the leading lady. Hughes discovered Jane Russell while she was working as a dentist's assistant. And, at just 19-years-old, she was made a star. Hughes became obsessed with her – or, obsessed with her *breasts*, truth be told – and who could blame him? He adorned his ramshackle western with lots of suggestive shots of Russell's mesmerising cleavage. Hughes also spent tens of thousands of dollars on the ad campaign, with the purpose of agitating the moral guardians. And it worked. The film was released briefly in San Francisco in 1943 after United Artists refused to distribute it, and was quickly removed from screens due to protests by civic groups. *The Outlaw* didn't see a nationwide release until 1946, and during the years of limbo, huge billboard ads were erected across the country showing off the leading lady's assets. And this led to a sure fire hit and the famous newspaper ads that read: 'What are the two reasons for Jane Russell's rise to stardom?'

The Outlaw isn't a great film. It's certainly no *Hell's Angels*. In fact, it's overlong and surprisingly amateurish in places. Of course, the controversy is all very tame by today's standards, but this was about as risque as it got in 1940s American cinema.

Frankenstein Meets The Wolf Man (1943)
Dir: Roy William Neill /USA
A pair of seedy grave-robbers enter the Talbot crypt after dark and disturb the resting place of werewolf Lon Chaney Jr. The Wolf Man comes to life and heads for Europe in search of Dr. Frankenstein's notebook which he hopes will contain a cure for his lycanthropy. However, an obsessive doctor also wants to use the notes to restore the Frankenstein Monster to its full strength...

This fifth entry in Universal's *Frankenstein* series is also a direct sequel to *The Wolf Man* (1942). It was also the first movie to pit horror heroes against each other, as was later seen in *King Kong vs. Godzilla* (1962), *Godzilla vs. The Smog Monster* (1971), and of course, *Freddy vs, Jason* (2003). Picking up after the events seen in *The Wolf Man* and *The Ghost of Frankenstein* (1942) – in which Chaney Jr played the monster in both films – here he reprises the Wolf Man role while Bela Lugosi steps into the Monster's shoes. And this is a convenient turn of events since, in *Ghost*, Lugosi's character Ygor had his brain transplanted into the monster. The end result is a silly but entertaining piece of fluff that includes a weird gypsy woman, musical numbers, Lionel Atwill this time playing the town Mayor, and a final battle between the monsters in the crumbling castle that is about to be swept away by a flood.

The original film was drastically cut and altered after a preview screening where production staff burst out laughing at Lugosi's thick Hungarian accent as the Monster ('Don't leave me, don't go. I'm weak, they'll catch me and bury me alive!'). Panicked by the reaction, producer George Waggner had editor Edward Curtiss removed all of Lugosi's Monster dialogue. Most of the scenes were cut, while some remain with the volume lowered so that even though we see the Monster's lips moving, no dialogue can be heard. As a result of this, all references to the Monster's blindness was lost (at the end of *Ghost of Frankenstein*, the Monster – with Ygor's brain – is blinded as the body rejects the brain). Blindness is the reason why the Monster stumbles around with arms outstretched, but now there was no justification for such movements in the altered cut. *House of Frankenstein* (1944) followed.

Meshes of the Afternoon (1943)
Dir: Maya Deren & Alexander Hammid /USA
Perhaps the strangest and most perplexing art film of the 1940s, *Meshes of the Afternoon* is a 15-minute short starring co-director, Maya Deren, as a young woman undergoing all manner of surreal goings on in and around her home in Los Angeles. Structured like a recurring nightmare, *Meshes* sees its heroine follow a sinister being that is dressed in a black robe with

a mirror for a face. Borrowing just as much from the early shorts of Dali and Bunuel as it does from contemporary noir and the avant-garde, this film – for all its 'classic' status – is still relatively unknown to film fans and is rarely included in film guides beyond those that deal with 'out there' experimental pics. The film has long been championed by feminists as a work that deals with 'woman's gothic experience,' but, according to Stan Brakhage, *Meshes of the Afternoon* was largely the brain-child of Deren's husband and co-director, Alexander Hammid. Whatever the truth is, it can't be denied that *Meshes* is a remarkable achievement, with many of its themes and images passed on throughout the decades, from Deren gazing out of the window (which was later repeated in *Alphaville* [1965] and *Romance* [1999]), to the winding road, dual roles and dreams within dreams which David Lynch later used in his own surrealist works, *Mulholland Drive* (2001) and *Inland Empire* (2006). See also *At Land* (1944), a less known but equally troubling short.

The Curse of the Cat People (1944)
Dir: Robert Wise & Gunther von Fritsch /USA
An off-beat classic from RKO which serves as a very loose sequel to producer Val Lewton's *Cat People* (1942). The story centres on Amy Reed (Ann Carter), a troubled young girl who is prone to flights of fancy and fantasy, and who has become persona non grata for the other kids in the area where she lives. Her concerned father, Oliver (Kent Smith), encourages his daughter to not be so introverted and reach out to others, but Amy struggles to connect. That is until she befriends an old lady, Julia (Julia Dean), a former actress. However, when Amy's family learn of her new friendship, she is quickly brought back home and alone again. Amy reacts by retreating even deeper into herself, and finds another friend – albeit an imaginary one – with whom she spends a great deal of time. And when it is discovered that Amy's new friend is in fact Irena – her father's dead wife – Oliver and his new wife, Alice (Jane Randolph), suspect that Irena has passed on a curse to the child...

Lewton brings back key cast and characters for this sequel that is very different from the original film. The dull protagonists, Oliver and Alice, have now moved to upstate New York, right next to Washington Irving's *Sleepy Hollow* territory, where they intend to raise the troubled Amy, whose imaginary friend is the cat girl of the original film. Crucially, this isn't really a horror film, but rather a psychological character study that ensures a chilly realisation that Amy's future is going to be far from bright. And this sentiment is deftly echoed in the scenes in which Amy visits the nearby old house of the retired actress, Julia, who seems to despise her own daughter and begins menacing the young Amy.

The film's troubled shoot began in August 1943. The shooting schedule was originally set for eighteen days, but a series of unforeseen problems kept the production in limbo for much longer. Lewton fell ill quite early on, and while in hospital he requested that his cast members not memorise their lines as he was intending to re-write them. However, his recovery took longer than expected, and the producers grew impatient, insisting that work needed to be done immediately. This meant that the actors had to quickly memorise their lines on set, almost scene for scene in some instances, which caused lots of frustration among the cast.

Added to the problems was director, Gunther von Fritsch, who was far too meticulous a film-maker for his own good – this was to be his feature debut, and he didn't want to make any mistakes. However, he worked so slowly on set that the executives lost their patience once again and fired him. (RKO officially announced that he was dropped from the film as he had been drafted into the U.S. Army, but it was later discovered that he didn't actually enlist in the Army until December, almost four months later). With the production falling even further behind schedule, the producers entrusted the film's editor, Robert Wise, to take to the helm and finish the picture. And the initial shoot finally wrapped up on 4 October, 1943. However, there were re-shoots in November as Lewton insisted on altering the scene in which Irena's ghost traps Barbara in the basement, allowing Amy to escape.

The result was a very low-key film that nonetheless won favour with the critics. James Agee, one of the most influential film critics at the time, remarked that the film was 'full of the poetry and danger of childhood,' while Bosley Crowther – who had hated the original *Cat People* – wrote a glowing review for the sequel in the *New York Times;* '[the film] emerges as an oddly touching study of the working of a sensitive child's mind.' Indeed, for all the wonders of this film, from its magical and nightmarish fantasy world, to its nods towards the Headless Horseman in a particularly remarkable scene, and even the tagline ('A tender tale of terror!'), the real heart of the film lies in Ann Carter's remarkable performance as Amy. Complex, effective and seemingly effortless, hers is perhaps the finest child performance of the era. I would recommend watching this on a double-bill with the rare and sadly little-seen *Friday the 13th: The Orphan* (1977), which revisits similar territory, this time from a troubled young boy's perspective.

Ann Carter appeared in a number of small roles as a child, such as *Last of the Duanes* (1941), *I Married a Witch* (1942), and *Ruthless* (1948). Many other bit-parts she played were uncredited. She was just seven-years-old when she appeared in *Curse*. Perhaps her most famous role was as Humphrey Bogart's daughter in *The Two Mrs Carrolls* (1948), which earned her a Critics Award for Top Juvenile Performance, aged ten. She fell ill with polio in 1952, and upon recovery, turned away from film and instead married young and became a schoolteacher. She lived in the Seattle area for most of her adult life, happily married, with three children and two grandchildren. She died in January 2014 of ovarian cancer, aged 77.

On returning from the Army after World War II, Gunther von Fritsch made short films – and the occasional feature, *Cigarette Girl* (1947) and *Snow Bear* (1970) – before he retired from the business. He settled in Pasadena, California, and died of a stroke in 1988.

Double Indemnity (1944)
Dir: Billy Wilder /USA

A masterpiece of murder, and one that helped to establish film noir in America, *Double Indemnity* is a starkly realistic nerve-shredder from the pen of Raymond Chandler that has since been described by Charles Higham as 'one of the highest summits of film noir... without a single trace of pity or love,' and by critic Richard Winnington as 'the sort of film which revives critics from the depressive effects of bright epics about the big soul of America or the suffering soul of Europe and gives him a new lease of faith.' All of which should leave viewers in no doubt of the ghastly spell this film weaves.

Based on the novel by James M. Cain, the story begins with Walter Neff (Fred MacMurray) bleeding from a bullet wound. He

staggers into an office building and speaks into a dictating machine. In flashback we learn that he is an insurance salesman who, out of greed, falls into the deadly trap of Phyllis Dietrichson (Barbara Stanwyck). She convinces him to not only help her take out a life insurance policy on her husband without his knowledge, but also to help her take him out so that they can collect on it. In order to qualify for the 'double indemnity' clause in the contract, the deadly duo must stage the murder on the back of a moving train and make it look like an accident. Once the deed is done, however, the pair must face Barton Keyes (Edward G. Robinson), Walter's boss at the insurance firm whose razor-sharp intellect and years of experience in the game tells him that something suspicious is afoot...

Director Billy Wilder's pacey and unpretentious style fits beautifully with this dark tale, and Chandler, on his first studio assignment, sharpened the script with Cain's pessimism and hard-boiled dialogue. But it's the trio of central players that lend bite to this cynical crime classic. Stanwyck, in a blonde wig, re-set her career with her portrayal of the scheming femme fatale whose boredom and insecurity fuels murder and intrigue. MacMurray, in a change from his comedic roles for Disney, gives the performance of his career as the smart loner drawn into the deadly game. However, outshining them both is Robinson, the conscientious elder who gives the film its heart. In stark contrast to his previous bad guy roles, such as the ruthless gangster in *Little Caesar* (1931), and later as the annoyingly naïve schmuck in *Scarlet Street* (1945), here he plays the level-headed Barton Keyes whose rational, mechanical way of thinking allows everything to 'fit together like a watch.' The scene in which he accurately describes the foul play death of Mr. Dietrichson in the presence of Walter is a great one that nicely blends Wilder's comedic instincts with the dark undercurrents of Cain and Chandler.

With World War II slowly reaching a brutal conclusion in Europe, it wasn't much of a surprise for film fans when *Double Indemnity* missed out on the Oscar to *Going My Way*, the cosy story of a priest. The American mood was in need of a lift, and there was nothing to feel good about in Wilder's unwieldy noir. Less forgiveable is the fact that Stanwyck missed out on the Oscar to Ingrid Bergman in *Gaslight*. Which is a shame as Stanwyck's Phyllis

Dietrichson was at the vanguard of a new breed of cynical super-bitch in the movies, far out-stripping her previous role of the amoral schemer in *Baby Face* (1933) over a decade earlier. Coldly calculating yet opportunistic, distant yet passionate, smart, patient and calm yet utterly petulant and spoiled, Phyllis was a product of the sheltered middle-class lifestyle where boredom and greed unleashes monsters – the ultimate 'Stepford wife' of the 1940s. 'I never loved you, Walter,' she states in a particularly memorable line, 'not you or anybody else. I'm rotten to the heart.'

kolberg (1945)
Dir: Veit Harlan /Germany

While the Soviets were closing in from the east and the Allies pressing hard in the west just miles from the German heartland, the Nazi regime went ahead with an epic film production shot in Agfacolor – a colour film technique that died with the regime – as a final hurrah containing a message to the German masses that they should fight to the death and never surrender.

The first German film released in theatres after the Nazis were elected was *Morgenrot* ('Morning Red,' aka *Dawn*, 1933), just three days after Hitler became Reichskanzier. And though the film wasn't made by the regime, the Nazis nonetheless held it in high regard for its themes of heroism and self-sacrifice, as the crew of a German U-boat in World War I accept their fate of dying together and go down bravely with the stricken vessel. The day after that, another film appeared: *Der Choral von Leuthen* (*The Hymn of Leuthen*, 1933), which depicted Frederick the Great as an influential Prussian leader. The latter was one of Hitler's personal favourite films. By the end in 1945, Goebbels seemed to draw on those earlier examples of German cinema by combining the themes of heroic self-sacrifice and heroic leadership for his own historical allegory, *Kolberg*.

The story is based on the defence of the town during the Franco-Prussian War of 1806-07. With Napoleon and his army fast approaching, the citizens debate whether they should surrender or fight on to the death. In the end, more than 30,000 French troops with 500 cannons obliterate the town that is defended by just 2000 soldiers and 5000 civilians, including women and children. *Kolberg* was never given a full release; there were one-off screenings in France and Germany – under constant threat of bombing from the Allies. At the end of World War II, there were 50 countries attacking Germany, and *Kolberg* was made chiefly to rally the German citizens into mobilising against the invaders, and to battle on against all odds. The film is a little long-winded (the action doesn't begin until after the hour mark), and, as a result, the simple theme of whether the characters should surrender or die fighting is a little trite in places.

The film's hero is the Mayor of Kolberg, Nettelbeck (Heinrich George), who is dead set against surrender, no matter how disastrous it will be for the town. Towards the end of the film, Nettelbeck pleads with the army general, Gneisenau, to stand and fight: 'we haven't fired our last bullet yet! and Blücher didn't have to forfeit his birthplace, and you weren't born in Kolberg. You were ordered to Kolberg, but we grew up here. We know every stone, every corner, every house. We're not letting it go even if we have to claw into the ground with our bare hands. In our town we don't give up. No, they'll have to cut off our hands to slay us one by one. You can't disgrace me by surrendering our town to Napoleon. I even promised our King that we would rather be buried under the rubble than capitulate. I've never pleaded to anyone, but I get down on my knees, Gneisenau. Kolberg must not be surrendered!' The general then gently lifts the Mayor to his feet and embraces him. 'That's what I wanted to hear from you, Nettelbeck,' he smiles. 'Now we can die together.'

Of course, Kolberg and Germany both fell, despite the legions of fanatics who continued the fight. *Kolberg* the film perhaps had its biggest influence on the psychology of the Hitler Youth. After the war, there were hundreds of orphaned Nazi children surviving on the streets. These so-called 'Wolf Children' lived in tunnels that had been dug through miles of rubble in Berlin. Sympathetic neighbours would leave food outside by the bins, and the feral children would come out after dark and take it. They remained utterly devoted to Hitler, and would pelt American soldiers with rocks – the only weapons they had left. Those dust-covered, half-starved fanatics were still being picked up by Allied troops as late as 1947, two years after the war. Their rehabilitation to a de-Nazified Germany was a long and painstaking process, and I mention it here to illustrate just how

120

powerful a hold the regime had on the young – the Third Reich was the only way of life those children had ever known. Perhaps one day someone will make a film about the 'Wolf Children.'

Detour (1945)
Dir: Edgar G. Ulmer /USA
This classic film noir unfolds with the logic of a nightmare. Utilising 'night-for-night' cinematography, this genre landmark stars Tom Neal as Al Roberts, a down-on-his-luck drifter who recounts his story via voice-over. Told mostly in flashback, the story covers the chain of unlikely events that landed the protagonist in a Hellish diner in the back end of nowhere. A pianist at a club in New York City, Roberts stays behind when his fiance goes to Hollywood in search of fame as a singer. Robert later decides he wants to go through with the marriage, and so follows her across the country, hitch-hiking from New York to California. However, his outstretched thumb catches the attention of Haskill (Edmund McDonald), a crooked businessman whose hands are covered in scratch wounds, and Roberts' life is about to be changed forever... A superb example of talent triumphing over budget restraints, this Poverty Row cheapie was made in just six days, and director Ulmer not only managed to create a uniquely sleazy look for his film, but he also inserted his own brand of Freudian allegory in the protagonist's Oedipal rage and distrust of women. The remarkably prolific Ulmer made 10 more movies in the same year.

The Lost Weekend (1945)
Dir: Billy Wilder /USA
Perhaps the hardest hitting of the 'problem films' of the 1940s. Though highly regarded nowadays, *The Lost Weekend* narrowly avoided being shelved by Paramount due to fears of how audiences would respond to such harrowing material. The script by regular collaborators, Billy Wilder and Charles Brackett, certainly keeps things balanced, with Wilder's trademark humour and Brackett's poetic flair rescuing the film from what could have easily been an unrelenting descent in hell.

Struggling alcoholic writer, Don Birnam (Ray Milland), promises to stay off the booze while his brother Nick goes away for the weekend. However, after discovering a bottle of liquor hanging out of the tenement window on a piece of string, Nick retrieves it and pours the contents down the sink. Once Nick and his girlfriend leave, Don learns that there is $10 hidden in the cookie jar in the kitchen that is owed to the building's cleaning lady. So he takes the money and heads out for a weekend bender. And it's all downhill from there as Don hits the gutter, desperately tries to pawn his typewriter to buy more booze, gets caught stealing a purse, bullies a store clerk into handing over a bottle for free, spends the night in an alcoholic's ward, suffers DTs and hallucinations, and contemplates suicide before embarking on a cautious redemption.

While previously, alcoholics in the movies had almost always been depicted as lovable wisecracking rogues (with the exception of RKO's *Are These Our Children?* and Fox's *The Man Who Came Back* [both 1931], the latter adding heroin addiction to the woes of its characters), but *The Lost Weekend* was the first mainstream hit to tackle the subject seriously, with a grim and unsettling look at life on the edge. Wilder and Brackett not only dared to show the harrowing side of alcoholism, they were also willing to show the appeal of such a lifestyle, by addressing the way alcohol can sometimes work as a 'cure' for writer's block and a way of lifting the drinker's spirits. But, of course, it's all a vicious cycle. For example, Don acknowledges the damage that alcohol has had on his physical health while also celebrating the way that drink empowers his mood: 'It shrinks my liver, doesn't it? It pickles my kidneys, yeah. But what does it do to my mind? It tosses the sandbags overboard so the balloon can soar. Suddenly I'm above the ordinary. I'm competent, supremely competent. I'm walking a tightrope over Niagara Falls. I'm one of the great ones. I'm Michelangelo, moulding the beard of Moses. I'm Van Gogh, painting pure sunlight. I'm Horowitz, playing the Emperor Concerto. I'm John Barrymore before the movies got him by the throat. I'm Jesse James and his two brothers – all three of 'em. I'm W. Shakespeare. And out there it's not Third Avenue any longer – it's the Nile. The Nile – and down it moves the barge of Cleopatra.' It's a piece of dialogue reminiscent of the nameless narrator in Dostoevsky's *Notes From Underground*, who comprehends the underlying irrationality of mankind – 'Is my liver failing? Let it get worse!'

Having previously carved a niche for himself as a likeable lead of light comedies and romance, Ray Milland was initially reluctant to take on the serious role of a destructive drunk. However, encouraged by his wife's insistence that he try something new, and also spurred on by the fact that Wilder and Brackett had never had a box-office flop, Milland took the chance. And the gamble paid off in the form of critical praise and an Oscar for Best Actor. The prominence of the Hays Code ensured that the film had to end on a positive note, but the film-makers deliberately set out to make a movie as harsh and realistic as they could get away with at the time. Of course, Paramount bosses took one look at the film and were deeply concerned. The studio was inundated with protests from prohibition advocates who felt that the finished film would encourage alcoholism. Major lobbyists for the liquor industry offered $5 million for the negative of the film so that they could destroy it. But Wilder's influence won out in the end, and *The Lost Weekend* was released on a limited engagement in New York City where the critical praise ensured it became one of Paramount's highest grossing films of the year.

Leave Her to Heaven (1945)
Dir: John M. Stahl /USA

A rare film noir in colour (should that be film coloeur?), *Leave Her to Heaven* – based on the novel by Ben Ames Williams – sees the beautiful Ellen (Gene Tierney) dump her politician fiancé (Vincent Price) and move in with successful novelist, Richard (Cornel Wilde). Enchanted by Richard's resemblance to her late father, Ellen sets about removing anyone and everyone from her life who gets in the way of Richard's affections for her.

Previously known for his women's films, *Imitation of Life* (1934), *Magnificent Obsession* (1935) and *Holy Matrimony* (1943), director John M. Stahl established himself as one of the heroes of the Hollywood golden age with this unnerving classic. Serving as a forerunner to the 'interloper' sub-genre that picked up with *Play Misty For Me* (1971) and *The Babysitter* (1980), before exploding in the wake of *Fatal Attraction* (1987) with a slew of cautionary horror stories in which loving partners and trusted companions gradually reveal themselves to be cold-blooded psychopaths, *Leave Her to Heaven* set the template in a coldly sublime style.

Perhaps where the film succeeds the most is in Ellen's chameleon-like behaviour: the way she is able to remain an alluring figure and barely skip a beat, whether she's seducing Richard in a swimming pool, watching a disabled boy drown in the lake, or throwing herself down a flight of stairs to terminate an unwanted pregnancy. The more her dark side is revealed the more she steps up her desirable qualities as a way of masking and shielding her true nature. And similar traits were also explored by Tierney in other noir classics, such as *Laura* (1944) and *Whirlpool* (1950).

Over the years the film has been disparaged as 'tatty,' and the psychological angle described as 'preposterously simplistic.' Nowadays, however, in an age familiar with Borderline Personality Disorder – particularly cluster B types – Ellen's destructive behaviour rings alarmingly true. There is a general consensus among psychologists that if you have encountered one cluster B type in your life then you have basically encountered them all. Their behaviour in certain situations is reassuringly similar to all cluster B types, therefore easily predictable beforehand. These people *are* preposterously simplistic! Their patterns of behaviour cannot be broken, they are programmed psychopaths through and through. And, for the record, if you're interested in seeing a real life cluster B type in action, watch the horrifying documentary, *Dear Zachary: A Letter to a Son About His Father* (2008). While watching it, think of Ellen's behaviour in *Leave Her to Haven*, and you'll realise you are basically observing the same person, out of place, out of time.

Leave Her to Heaven isn't perfect. The courtroom scenes dampen the ending somewhat, with a dull, anti-climactic showdown, but at least those scenes illustrate the inter-personal damage the psychos leave behind in their wake. Alfred Newman's score, on the other hand, is a marvel, a grand orchestral piece punctuated with loud foreboding drums that set the uneasy mood from the outset. And, of course, there's Leon Shamroy's Technicolor cinematography that captures both the beauty and menace and isolation of the lonely Back of the Moon homestead where Ellen's dangerous fixations take hold. Williams' book was adapted for the screen again as *Too Good to be True* (1988), for television, a light and mellow rendering this time with Loni Anderson and Patrick Duffy as the doomed lovers.

Scarlet Street (1945)
Dir: Fritz Lang /USA

Edward G. Robinson stars as Chris Cross, a humble cashier for a large New York retailer who enjoys painting in the bathroom in his spare time. At a company banquet held in his honour for twenty years of loyal service to the company, Chris is gifted a gold watch. On quietly leaving the party so as not to raise a fuss, Christopher walks the rain-swept streets looking for a cab, and there he witnesses Kitty (Joan Bennett) being harassed in the road. Chris then beats the attacker with his umbrella and befriends Kitty. They go for a quiet drink at a bar, and Chris becomes immediately infatuated with her. He can't bear to tell her what he really does for a living, so he lies and lets her believe that he is a renowned painter. Chris is married to Ivan, a shrieking old crone who constantly henpecks him and chips away at his self esteem. It isn't long before he falls in love with Kitty, and she continues to lead him on, not telling him about her relationship with her pimp/partner in crime, Johnny (Dan Duryea).

Now recognised as a naïve mark blinded by love, Kitty and Johnny convince Chris to rent an expensive studio apartment where the 'love birds' can meet for their trysts. The gullible man also uses the space to store some of his art works after Ivan threatens to chuck them out with the garbage. Johnny shows the paintings to a renowned art critic, and the man is impressed. However, the cost of renting two separate residences is now eating away at Christopher's savings. Johnny puts Kitty's signature on the paintings and sells them. This annoys Chris until he learns that the works have been acknowledged to be works of genius. Taking solace from the fact that his art is finally appreciated (even though it's Kitty who is taking the credit), Chris begins stealing cash from the company safe where he works. Meanwhile, Ivan's first husband, who was thought to have died at sea, returns to New York, alive and well. This means that Chris can divorce Ivan and marry Kitty. However, after racing to the studio to inform her of the great news, he finds her and Johnny in a love embrace. He watches from the shadows as his world falls apart and his betrayal becomes clear. And later, when he confronts Kitty, she laughs and mocks him with the accusation that he was just a weak, pathetic patsy all along. 'I've been wanting to laugh in your face ever since I met you,' she taunts.

'You're old and ugly and I'm sick of you – sick, sick, sick!' The quiet, mild-mannered Chris then snaps, grabs an ice-pick and stabs her to death. Johnny is found guilty of the murder and is executed, and Chris spends the rest of his days as a homeless, suicidal wreck.

Despite including one of the bleakest denouements of 1940s cinema, *Scarlet Street* is a classic noir based on the novel and play, *La Chienne*, by Georges de la Fouchardiere (a story that had already been filmed in 1931 by Jean Renoir). Having built up momentum on the previous year's thriller, *The Woman in the Window* (1944), here director Fritz Lang teamed up once again with indie producer, Walter Wanger, and actors Robinson, Bennett and Duryea, for another classic that this time incorporated a chilling Expressionistic slant, especially in the final scenes. But while *The Woman in the Window* includes a cop-out ending in which the protagonist's nightmarish predicament turns out to be nothing more than an elaborate daydream inspired by a painting in a shop window, there's no such last minute relief for Robinson's character here (and that goes for the audience, too). Rarely has a character been put through the noir mincer as mercilessly as Chris in *Scarlet Street*, and rarely has a character broken free from the femme fatale's wicked spell as brutally as Chris and the ice-pick. Initially portrayed as naïve and gullible, once Chris discovers the truth of his betrayal, Lang's contempt for the man's impotence is unleashed in a shocking act of violence. Film critic Ian Freer noted Lang's personal insight in the project: by portraying a character like Chris as an artist whose works have been exhibited under another's name, the 'Master of Darkness' had found himself in a similar situation at Universal. However, by teaming up with Wanger, Lang found himself a new lease of artistic freedom. Little wonder *Scarlet Street* was one of his personal favourites.

The Spiral Staircase (1946)
Dir: Curt Siodmak /USA

With the real life horrors of World War II, Hollywood horror had descended into a jokey, non-threatening farce, with such palatable camp as *The Wolf Man* (1942), *Son of Dracula* (1943) and *The Monster Maker* (1944), all seemingly designed to reassure a target teenage audience. Until 1946, Val Lewton was the only producer willing to attempt genuine chills in such eerie classics as *Cat People* (1942), *I Walked With a Zombie* (1943) and *Isle of the Dead* (1945). The exception was David O' Selznick and *The Spiral Staircase*, a Gothic masterpiece – also for RKO – which was years ahead of its time as a contemporary fright-fest that influenced dozens of psycho movies, from *Black Christmas* (1974) and *Deep Red* (1975) to *Mute Witness* (1995) and *The Ugly* (1996). The result is a quintessential 'old dark house' movie of the early post-war years.

Mute from childhood and constantly on edge thanks to the activities of a vicious serial killer who targets women with physical imperfections, Helen Capel (Dorothy McGuire) serves as a companion to the ailing Mrs. Warren (Ethel Barrymore), a difficult woman who despises her weak sons, one of whom is a nerdy scientist and the other a womanising dolt. A thunder storm traps the residents in the Warren mansion for the evening, and a death in the household reveals that the killer must be among them. Could it be one of the sons, or the cook (Elsa Lanchester), or the sexy Miss Blanche? In the end, Helen squares off against the maniac in the dead of night as the storm reaches a full-on crescendo.

Rivalling Hitchcock's *Rebecca* (1940) for its Gothic atmosphere, *The Spiral Staircase* is a remarkably powerful film that can stand shoulder to shoulder with the Master of Suspense's output of the time. Ironically, such a forward-looking film drew much of its style and inspiration from the past, with stark Expressionist visuals combined with cracking thunder, whistling winds, creaking doors, billowing curtains and close-up shots of the killer's intense, bloodshot eye. All of which combined to produce a milestone in atmospheric Gothic horror. As if to emphasise the film's debt to the past, director Robert Siodmak also incorporated references to the birth of cinema itself, perhaps as a way of reinforcing the predicament of Helen's vulnerability. In the source novel, *Some Must Watch* by Ethel Lina White (pub. 1933), Helen was a cripple but able to speak, whereas here in the film version she is able-bodied yet unable to scream. And the trip to the silent cinema emphasises the restrictions that anticipate her forthcoming peril. In addition, the motif of mirrors, glass and windows in the mansion were also inspired by cinema's past, particularly the German films of Fritz Lang who was the top director at Ufa when Siodmak began his career, and whose expert use of light and shadow, mood and atmosphere, had a huge impact on the Universal monster movies of the 1930s.

The Spiral Staircase often gets lumped in the film noir cannon, and indeed, besides the chiaroscuro visuals there is also a blatant psychological angle. The then-fashionable Freudian themes are certainly there, with Helen's affliction stemming from childhood trauma, and the Warren sons under the domineering thumb of the bed-ridden mother (for a real life expose of the destructive nature of the Oedipus complex, there is no better – or more chilling – example than in the documentary, *Crumb* [1994]). Less obvious is the film's treatment between the killer's motive and the Nazi experiments in eugenics, with both the killer and the Nazis driven by a disgust for weakness and a devotion to natural law, even if it means conducting themselves in the cruellest ways imaginable. And this theme of eugenics as an undercurrent for horror cinema had also been drawn upon by RKO in contemporary hits, such as Hitchcock's *Notorious* (1946) and – more explicitly – in *The Master Race* (1944).

Decoy (1946)
Dir: Jack Bernhard /USA

If *Detour* and *Double Indemnity* emerged as dangerous puzzle boxes seemingly crafted by the Devil himself, with all the infernal clockwork of the Faustian nightmare unbound, then *Decoy* took film noir even further to its most cynical extremes, and chances are viewers won't realise just how radical and heartless this film is until the very last line of dialogue.

A man with a bullet wound struggles to keep his composure as he walks the streets in broad daylight. He has a task to complete before he succumbs to his fatal wound. He enters an apartment block and shoots a woman, and then dies just as the detective arrives on the scene. The injured woman, Margot Shelby (Jean Gillie), knowing she only has a short amount of time left on this mortal coil, begins telling the story of how she ended up in such a sorry state. And so begins the lengthy flashback in which she revives a dead man (!) so that she can discover the whereabouts of a buried loot of cash. Once she gets her hands on the treasure map, she begins ruthlessly killing off her helpers so that she can keep the $400,000 for herself...

Many noir classics built up their reputations over the years thanks to late night television screenings and home video, but *Decoy* missed out on such exposure as the print had gotten lost in the vaults for more than three decades, and the film itself had garnered a legendary reputation during its long absence, even if very few film fans had actually seen it. The fact that it re-emerges now as one of the cornerstone classics of the mid-1940s serves as a testament to how effective the film is. Even for modern audiences, *Decoy* still packs one helluva punch. Once the print was rediscovered, it was released as part of Warner Brothers' fourth *Film Noir Collection* DVD box set in 2007. It was also shown on a one-off screening at the American Cinemateque where, according to reports, it 'brought down the house.' Unfortunately, the rescued print is the censored version which trims some of the violence, such as the scene where Gillie's character drives over a man (in the original theatrical version, she drove over him four times!). Nonetheless, this long lost Monogram classic of greed, double-crossing and revenge makes a welcome return, with its Poverty Row status worn like a badge of honour.

Decoy was devised as a showcase for British actress, Gillie, and her director husband, Jack Bernhard. However, they divorced soon after, and Bernhard moved away from directing in 1950 while Gillie died of pneumonia in 1949. This film is easily their finest hour, with Bernhard rivalling the great Edgar G. Ulmer for the gritty, no-nonsense style, and Gillie serving as one of the most memorable – and utterly ruthless – femmes fatale ever to (dis)grace a cinema screen.

The Chase (1946)
Dir: Arthur D. Ripley /USA
How about a 'Lynchian' movie that was made before David Lynch was even born? *The Chase* stars Robert Cummings as Charles Scott, an honest former marine who returns a lost wallet to Eddie (Steve Cochran) at his luxury home. In return for his honesty, Scotty is given a job as driver for Eddie and his men. But little does he know that Eddie is actually a ruthless gangster who deals with his enemies by feeding them to his pet Alsation. And, in a genre mainstay since the days of *Underworld* (1927), Scotty falls for the beautiful blonde moll, Lorna (Michelle Morgan). Together the love birds flee to Havana, but when she winds up dead with a knife in her back, the police assume that Scott is responsible. The former marine cooperates with detectives at

first, but once he's satisfied that sinister forces are out to frame him for Lorna's murder, he makes a run for it. However, that turns out to be only *half* the story as things only get *weirder*...

Released less than a year after the British portmanteau horror, *Dead of Night* (1945), *The Chase* takes a similar theme of the recurring nightmare and uses it to bookend a B-movie 'gangster' flick. Except, of course, that *The Chase* isn't really a gangster movie at all. Nor is it a horror film. Rather, it's a strange noir hybrid that sits uncomfortably in any pigeon hole. Little wonder that the ideas and concepts here would later crop up in the work of David Lynch. Eddie the 'friendly' but brutal gangster who takes Scotty under his wing by giving him a job was probably the inspiration behind the Nice Guy Eddie character (played by Robert Loggia) in *Lost Highway* (1997), over half a century later. And if that seems like a stretch, then consider Eddie's car that is fitted with a super-accelerator peddle that can be controlled from the back seat. In *Lost Highway*, Nice Guy Eddie's car had a similar turbo-charged engine that allowed him to accelerate at incredible speed so that he could catch up with – and terrorise – a fellow motorist who had aggressively cut him off on the road. There is also the blonde moll, the noir shadows, and sense of impending doom and gloom, and the longing to escape to a better world, all of which was later emphasised in Lynch's classic.

Finally, there's Mr. Scott himself who, in typical Lynchian tradition, seems to have a side to his character that the viewers aren't privy to. He suffers from strange and terrifying dreams that could in fact be premonitions. It is also hinted that 'Chuck' has a history of mental health problems, but this area is deliberately left blank by the film-makers, and we never find out who Mr. Scott really is. Even the ending is straight out of the twilight zone: is the premonition coming true, or was the entire story just a figment of a troubled mind? Indeed, the film begins with Scott standing aimlessly on a street. He stares into a restaurant window, watching in hunger as the staff flip burgers on a grill. And then he just happens to find a wallet by his feet that contains around $80 – the beginnings of an elaborate daydream fantasy?

If *Lost Highway* is about a character (Bill Pullman) who steps into a black hole and emerges as an entirely different character, then *The Chase* plays out a similar scenario: Mr.

Scott is seen at first as a kind and naïve pleb, but then he enters the criminal underworld (his own black hole) and emerges as 'Chuck,' a brooding and violent film noir anti-hero, willing to flout the law and live on the risky edge of society.

Based on the novel, *The Black Pearl of Fear*, by crime writer Cornell Woolrich, *The Chase* has all the markings of a cult classic, but is all but lost in obscurity these days. It's certainly no masterpiece, but there are enough interesting ideas and sinister twists and turns in the plot that it should lure the more adventurous film fans off the beaten track. Also, kudos goes to Peter Lorre who plays Gino, Eddie's right hand man. And he's just as terse and heartless here as he was in other roles he played at the time, such as the sly gangster in *Black Angel* (1946) and the sadistic boss in *Island of Doomed Men* (1940). Here, however, he is utterly overshadowed by the 'nice guy,' Eddie, the smiling maniac.

Secret Beyond the Door (1946)
Dir: Fritz Lang /USA

While on holiday in Mexico, Celia (Joan Bennett) falls in love with the morbid and mysterious Mark (Michael Redgrave). They soon marry, and she moves into his huge mansion. An architect by trade, Mark's hobby is to reconstruct rooms from history where bloody psycho-sexual murders took place. Hubby's 'collection' of rooms alarms her at first, but there is also a secret room that Mark forbids her entry. However, she has a key cut to the mysterious place and sneaks in to take a look for herself. And what she finds there does little to settle her nerves... Though it's now considered a classic, *Secret Beyond the Door* was met with largely mixed reviews at the time of its release. Otis J. Guernsey Jr called it 'a dog-wagon *Rebecca*,' while James Agee dismissed it as a 'pig's ear' of a movie. Universal re-edited the film prior to its release, cutting it down to 100-minutes and re-arranged many scenes. But this interference ironically only added to the dream-like mood. The film occupies an uneasy limbo between Lang's more outlandish epics like *Metropolis* (1927) and *Moonfleet* (1955), and his more grounded efforts like *M* (1931) and *The Big Heat* (1953). It's not a particularly original film, and it does owe a huge debt to *Rebecca* (1940), but *Secret Beyond the Door* is nonetheless a solid noir that works as both a serial killer mystery and a Freudian case study, as well as a good old Gothic potboiler in its own right. The

ending is a little weak, and a bit of a cop-out, but the first 90-minutes more than make the trip worthwhile.

Duel in the Sun (1946)
Dir: King Vidor [and Joseph von Sterberg, William Dieterle, B. Reeves Eason and David O' Selznick, uncredited] /USA

Described by the *Daily Mail* as 'cornography,' by *Time* magazine as 'a knowing blend of oats and aphrodisiac,' and by influential critic, Pauline Kael, as 'a cartoon passion,' *Duel in the Sun* mixes sexuality and violence to such an extent that the concepts become disturbingly undifferentiated. Pre-dating the contentious themes that showed up in Sam Peckinpah's *Straw Dogs* (1971) a quarter of a century later, King Vidor's epic dared to present a borderline sadomasochistic relationship between a 'half breed' girl, Pearl Chavez (Jennifer Jones) and the cruel sadist, Lewt (Gregory Peck), whose sexual savagery is not only tolerated but welcomed.

Standing out from the pack in 1946, not only for its perverse elements, but also for its garish Technicolor template, *Duel in the Sun* is set against the backdrop of the old West, and strings together a series of melodramatic set-pieces concerning a land dispute. But that's just window dressing. The real dark heart of the story is of two brothers divided by their desires for the dancer, Pearl. In one of many unsubtle scenes, Pearl is seen drinking from a mountain stream next to her horse – it's an obvious demonstration of the woman's 'untamed' nature. The brothers fighting over her are polar opposites, and this is where the clichés come thick and fast. Jesse (Joseph Cotton) is kind and sensitive, while Lewt is brutish and quarrelsome. Guess which one she falls in love with?

The consummation between Pearl and Lewt is one that straddles the line between desire and disgust, and the film-makers keep the scene as ambiguous as possible. Unlike *Straw Dogs*, which – in the uncut version – shows Amy's rape to be an ordeal she ultimately rejects, here in *Duel* Lewt forces himself on Pearl, and her reaction – though she resists him at first – is one in which she responds positively, despite him treating her like dirt. And if *Straw Dogs*' flirtation with the 'no means yes' rape myth got the film in an endless amount of trouble with censors and critics, *Duel in the Sun*, on the other hand, treats the matter so casually that many modern audiences may be outraged by the scene. And though the film did cause a scandal at the time of its release, the lurid qualities were largely disarmed in the grand spectacle of a candy box entertainment.

The most memorable sequence, however, is saved for the finale. By now, Lewt has killed both his brother and another of Pearl's suitors, and she lures him out to the desert mountains for revenge. After shooting and wounding him, Lewt collapses into a ditch and returns fire. But even while blasting each other to smithereens, their mutual desires will not die. Instead, bloody and torn, and with death enveloping them, the pair struggle through the dust in agony while espousing words of love and hatred for each other. Finally, they embrace weakly as they take their dying breaths in each other's arms.

Duel in the Sun was David O' Selznick's ode to the allure of Jennifer Jones in much the same way that *The Outlaw* (1943) was Howard Hughes' hymn to the titted goddess, Jane Russell. So seriously did he take the film that he couldn't resist interfering with the production and pushing director Vidor aside while he obsessively fine-tuned the film like a man possessed. Uncredited directors who were roped in to complete the picture include Joseph von Sternberg, William Dieterle, B. Reeves Eason and even Selznick himself. Gregory Peck was cast after first choice leading man, John Wayne, turned it down and is said to have been made to feel squeamish by the dubious screenplay. How different the film would have been if John Wayne had taken the lead role can only be guessed at. But as it stands, initial audiences were completely unprepared for the events that unfolded on screen. Critics of the day dubbed the film 'Lust in the Dust.' Selznick spent a lavish $6 million on the production, and a further $2 million on the scandalous publicity campaign to promote it, with a heavy emphasis on the twisted sex angle. And this caused much commotion among moralist groups. Storms of protests from both Catholics and Protestants, however, failed to steer Selznick off course. And even when *Duel* found itself banned and censored in Memphis and Hartford, Connecticut, Philadelphia and other American cities, the film seemed unstoppable. The public lapped it up, and Selznick raked in around $12 million in profit.

Duel in the Sun is a true one-off cinematic experience in which the darker themes nestle uncomfortably among the candy-coloured charms of the epic western. But everyone should watch it, at least once. Martin Scorsese claims he first saw the film when he was four-years-old, and that the experience haunted him for life. 'It's a flawed film,' he said, 'but nevertheless the hallucinatory quality of the imagery has never weakened for me over the years. It seems the two protagonists could only consummate their passion by killing each other.'

Black Narcissus (1947)
Dir: Michael Powell & Emeric Pressburger /UK
A classic from one of the most revered collaborations in film history, Michael Powell and Emeric Pressburger, and one of the most atypical movies ever made in Britain. *Black Narcissus* came after such daring classics as *The Life and Death of Colonel Blimp* (1943), *A Matter of Life and Death* (1944), and *The Red Shoes* (1945), as a lightning strike of creativity that reached its zenith with this story about a group of nuns who attempt to open a convent high in the Himalayan mountains. The mission ultimately fails, however, due to a growing sexual tension that finally manifests itself in the form of madness and murder. The result is a masterpiece that effectively reinvented British cinema, and is as bold and daring a film as you're ever likely to see.

Deborah Kerr is brilliant as the enterprising Sister Clodagh, embracing her new-found authority but succumbing to the overwhelming climate, the locals, the British agent Mr. Dean (David Farrar) and her own emotional instability. Veteran actor, Sabu, in his last major movie role, plays Dilip Rai, a wealthy narcissistic general who wears Black Narcissus perfume. Highly effeminate, he falls in love with the untamed native girl, Kanchi (a young Jean Simmons), who wears a jewelled snail on her nose. And, of course, events reach a climax when Sister Ruth (Kathleen Byron) is driven insane by her sexual obsession with Mr. Dean and her jealousy of Sister Clodagh.

The film can be read as a cautionary lesson on the dangers of both restraint and unchecked passion, and also as an allegory on the fall of the British Empire, coming as it did just two years after the end of World War II. It's also one of the most stunning films ever shot in colour, and set designer Alfred Junge's incredible constructions of the Himalayas (built in the home counties) are still jaw-droppingly impressive to this day. Years ahead of its time, *Black Narcissus* went on to influence everyone from Martin Scorsese and Douglas Sirk, to Fassbinder and Ken Russell. It also inspired many of the sleazy nunsploitation movies that assaulted cinema screens in the 1970s. Alfred Junge and Jack Cardiff deservedly picked up Oscars for Best Color Cinematography and Best Art Direction, respectively. The BBFC initially removed the sequence in which Sister Clodagh recalls her happy days of romance before entering the convent, but all home video editions are uncut.

Nightmare Alley (1947)
Dir: Edmund Goulding /USA

An ambitious young carnival worker, Stan (Tyrone Powers), uses devious means to rise to the top of his profession, eventually becoming one of the top psychics/confidence tricksters in America. During a reading at a high-class gathering, he meets the ice-cool Lilith (Helen Walker), a clinical psychologist. Upon learning that Lilith records her patient's psychiatric couch talk on vinyl records, he devises a blackmail scam to increase his wealth by threatening to reveal the embarrassing psycho-sexual secrets of the patients if they refuses to pay up. However, before the plan is put into action, Lilith indulges in a scam of her own which sees Stan eventually crawling back to the carnival as a defeated drunk and fugitive begging to be accepted back into the fold...

Not since the days of Tod Browning had the cinema showcased the 'carny' lifestyle in such a crude and cynical way as this. And not since Browning's *Freaks* (1932) did a film so unflinchingly expose the Faustian comeuppance of its central villain, as we watch Stan's disgraceful rise and fall as he ends up living out the rest of his days as that which he had always feared the most – namely, as a carnival freak forced to eat live chickens for the amusement of the paying public. Noted critic, James Agee, said that the film was worth watching for its 'two or three sharply comic and cynical scenes,' but really, the entire film is one long cynical sick joke that barely skips a beat as it goes from one strand of warped behaviour to the next. Stan's character is portrayed like a tragic gangster figure of old in the way he rids the world of his rivals (in one scene giving an alcoholic a bottle of moonshine that he knows will probably kill him). And even when he

makes it big as a household name, his ambition and greed knows no end – and this ultimately proves to be his downfall as a flurry of poetic justices rain down on him and destroys his life, just like Paul Muni in *Scarface* (1932) and James Cagney in *The Public Enemy* (1931) and *The Roaring Twenties* (1939). Even Leslie Halliwell – who always had an aversion to off-beat cinema – called it 'a striking oddity.' It's a sadly little-seen film these days but no cult movie fan should miss it.

Women in the Night (1948)
Dir: William Rowland /USA

In comparison with the 1930s, exploitation films of the 1940s were just as cheap and amateurish, but now the films also lacked the passion and wackiness of the ones that appeared in the previous decade. *Mad Youth* (1940), *Escort Girl* (1941), *I Accuse My Parents* (1944), *Delinquent Daughters* (1944) and *Test Tube Babies* (1948), are all let down by atrocious acting, non-existent production values and a dull-as-dishwater visual style. *Test Tube Babies*, however, did at least hold a modicum of educational value despite its shoddiness, but the 1940s sorely lacked a Dwain Esper toiling away on the fringes. The only exploitation film of the decade to hold any long-lasting value is perhaps the little-seen *Strangers in the Night* (1944), about a kooky old lady who pretends to be much younger so that she can be pen pals with an American soldier who is about to return home. Somewhere in the middle, nestled between the amateur dreck and the more respectable fair is *Women in the Night*, a rather silly but entertaining drama about a group of women in Shanghai who are being held in a Nazi-run detention centre. Set in the summer of 1945, just as the Americans have dropped the A-bomb on Nagasaki and the Japanese are on the verge of surrender, the Nazi officials try their best to keep order whilst knowing deep down that the war is lost and that they will soon have to flee China. If nothing else, *Women in the Night* can lay claim to being the first Nazisploitation film ever made, pre-dating the Italian shockers that flourished in the 1970s, such as *Salon Kitty* (1975), *The Beast in Heat* (1977), and *SS Experiment Camp* (1977). *Women in the Night* doesn't sink to the same unsavoury depths as those films mentioned above (in fact, it probably has more in common with *Tenko* [1981-1985] than, say, *The Red Nights of the Gestapo*

[1977]), but surprisingly, most of the elements that made up the Italian films can be seen here, albeit in a much tamer fashion. The following year brought more exploitation trash, such as *She Shoulda Said No!* (1949) and *So Young, So Bad* (1949), the former revisiting the previous decade's 'marijuana menace,' and the latter laying claim as the first women-in-prison exploitationer ever made.

Los Olvidados (1950)
Dir: Luis Buñuel /Mexico

By the mid-1940s Luis Buñuel had spent 15 years in the cinematic wilderness. When the civil war broke out in Spain, he found work as a spy in Spain and France, spent some time unemployed, then crossed the Atlantic for New York and Los Angeles where he wrote and translated screenplays. His career as a once great film-maker seemed to be long gone. As a youngster, Buñuel had often joked to his friends that he wouldn't be seen dead in Mexico, but by the mid-40s that was the only place where he'd stand a chance of directing another film.

Reluctantly, he drifted south to Mexico City which had become a haven for Nazi's, spies, communists, anarchists, and intellectuals of all stripes who had been hounded out of their own countries. Mexico's non-involvement in World War II meant there was plenty of money around, and wealthy film producers still remembered Buñuel and his surrealist classics, *Un Chein Andalou* and *L'Age D'Or*, and it was Oscar Dancigers who finally offered him the opportunity to get back behind the camera. After helming a couple of cheap programmers (*Gran Casino* [1947] and *El Gran Calavera* [1949]), Buñuel had dispelled the ring rust and felt ready to tackle something more substantial. The result was *Los Olvidados*.

After escaping from a reform school, El Jaibo (Roberto Cobo) returns home to the shanty towns of Mexico City where his loutish behaviour gains him a reputation. Young street waif, Pedro (Alfonso Mejia) looks up to him with a nervy respect until Jaibo sleeps with his mother, Marta (Estela Inda). An infuriated Pedro then dobs him in to the police for killing a member of a rival gang, and so Jaibo seeks revenge.

Buñuel combines his love of surrealism with Italian neo-realism in *Los Olvidados*, and keeps the former to a subtle minimum whilst embracing the latter to stunning effect. He dispensed with the norm by hiring a largely professional cast (Inda and Cobo, and also Miguel Inclan as the blind beggar), and found it difficult to resist injecting his trademark flights of fancy (producer Dancigers had to talk him out of hiring a 100-piece orchestra that would play in the background of the scene where Jaibo kills Pedro). It's a hard-hitting film for its time, a tale of low-life criminality and all-consuming lust that leads to anger, death, and despair. The script was based on Buñuel's own observations during his time spent in Mexico City, and also on real case studies from reformatories which he used to cement his screenplay in its realism. The film was shot in the director's typical haste in just 21 days, well ahead of schedule, despite some troubles during production, with crew members objecting to the harsh subject-matter and quitting. The film's hair stylist objected to a scene in which Marta refuses to feed Pedro ("No Mexican mother would do that!"). Buñuel stuck to his guns though, and refused to change anything in the script.

Indeed, the film's unflinching depiction of abandoned kids having to fend for themselves in a cruel world devoid of any moral guidance was always going to be controversial. And when *Los Olvidados* premiered at the CineMexico, the critics were outraged that their city and its inhabitants had been depicted in such a harsh and unflattering way. Buñuel was criticized for perpetuating misery on the citizens, some of the actors who appeared in the film were so scared of the hostile reception that they fled the city, and producer Dancigers, who had invested a large amount of money in the film, felt intimidated enough to remove it from circulation after only two days (it premiered on a Thursday and was withdrawn on the Saturday). Of course, Buñuel was no stranger to this type of thing; some of his earlier films had provoked organized riots in the cinema, and he seemed to take the whole debacle in his stride; just another day at the office!

The tide turned, however, in the following year when *Los Olvidados* played at Cannes to a rapturous reception. It seemed the French had missed the *enfant terrible* (it had been more than two decades since *L'Age D'Or* and his controversial documentary, *Las Hurdes*), and the Spaniard was bestowed with the Best Director Award, and had that much needed career resurgence.

Los Olvidados has since become an accepted

classic, with its gritty template passed down the decades, with film-makers as diverse as Hector Babenco (*Pixote*), Alan Clarke (*Scum*), Ulrich Edel (*Christiane F.*), Walter Salles (*Central Station*), and of course, Larry Clark and Harmony Korine (*Kids*), all willing and proud to display their influences. As for Buñuel, *Los Olvidados* marked the beginning of the third part of his career after his promising start in Paris, and 20 years spent mostly in limbo. This fresh new start lasted for the rest of his life where he made 26 fascinating films in 27 years, securing his reputation, once and for all, as one of the most important film-makers of all time.

Riot in Cell Block 11 (1954)
Dir: Don Siegel /USA
Prisoners stage a riot and hold several guards hostage while they try to negotiate to abolish the brutal conditions of the institution. Sort of like a prison version of *Battleship Potemkin*, *Riot in Cell Block 11* is a barely disguised call to arms for working class insurrection. Banned in Britain and viewed with suspicion elsewhere in the world. In America, it was a miracle that the film avoided getting caught up in the 'red scare' panic as a pro-communist picture, as anybody watching it must have been blind to not recognise the film's message. Senator Joseph McCarthy is generally looked upon nowadays as a paranoid loon who engaged in a witch-hunt against imaginary communists who had infiltrated government, media and the entertainment industry. However, with films like this and *Blackboard Jungle* (1955), many viewers couldn't help but notice the blatant Marxist message as the prisoners literally lose their chains and attempt to overthrow the bourgeois prison authorities. Of course, back in the 50s it was a risky business to indulge in such subject-matter, even in allegorical form. And, with many in the film industry finding themselves blacklisted by the House of Un-American Activities Committee, director Don Siegel went on to make the classic, *Invasion of the the Body Snatchers* (1956) – an almost as blatant *anti*-communist picture – perhaps as a way of safeguarding his career against the scrutiny of the Committee. As for *Riot*, it's not too bad a film. The prisoners aren't entirely convincing as hardened criminals (despite the film being overwhelmingly cast with former and current convicts), and the preachiness of its message hasn't aged very well at all. However,

the use of real locations (at Folsom State Prison) and great performances from Neville Brand and Emile Meyer, more than make it a worthwhile watch. The critics were overwhelmingly positive, with just about every contemporary review singing its praises. The *New York Times*' A. W. Weiler was no less enthusiastic, assuring readers that the film 'punches and preaches with authority.' But hey, Senator McCarthy was just silly and paranoid!

Them! (1954)
Dir: Gordon Douglas /USA
An influential 50s creature feature which begins in the desert with a decimated caravan, a stink of formic acid, stolen sugar and a traumatized little girl afraid of "them." The FBI and insect experts arrive on the scene and trace a mysterious footprint to a nest of giant radioactive ants that have mutated thanks to A-bomb tests. *Them* is a superb documentary-style horror flick which charts America's defence against the commie ants, and features an unforgettable finale set in the L.A. storm drains. It's one of the very best creature features of its time, and was Warner Bros' biggest box-office draw of that year. With savvy dialogue, restrained performances and sharp photography embellished with a newsreel documentary feel, the crazy proceedings nonetheless have an alarming air of authenticity. The only let down is Dick Smith's 15-foot-long model ants, which – though cutting edge for the time – look incredibly silly six decades on.

Blackboard Jungle (1955)
Dir: Richard Brooks /USA
An idealist teacher, Richard Dadier (Glenn Ford), starts a new job at a tough inner-city school. Of course, his fist day on the job is marred by the students pushing their luck and misbehaving as a way of testing the man's mettle. However, Dadier's by-the-book discipline fails to get through to the kids. And, before long, the back-and-forth aggitations between the teacher and his students turns to all-out war when Dadier's wife is targeted.

Based on the novel by Evan Hunter, which in turn was partly inspired by real-life newspaper headlines, *Blackboard Jungle* set the template for delinquent youth 'social problem' movies for decades to come. The story of a mild-mannered teacher holding true to his convictions while the class troublemakers escalate their confrontations finds a surprising amount of social commentary and emotional depth to tap into. The film sparked controversy for corrupting the nation's youth. MGM denied the allegations, but with its rock 'n' roll soundtrack by Bill Hailey and His Comets, and its inclusion of street slang in the teen dialogue, helped to convince many that the film was indeed aimed at youths in order to inflict social harm and delinquency. The fact that the film also inspired street violence and vandalism by youths didn't do it any favours, either.

Interestingly, *Blackboard Jungle* marked the first manifestation of what conservatives call 'Cultural Marxism' that can be identified in the movies, along with culture and academia as a whole. In just the previous year, *Riot in Cell Block 11* was still stuck in the Eisenstein stage of promoting class conflict (albeit in a disguised prison setting). However, traditional Marxism had lost favour among the masses, partly because of the horror stories that were trickling out of the Soviet Union. The idea of *Cultural* Marxism, on the other hand, was nothing more than a shameless sleight of hand. This morphing of communist ideology was developed at the Frankfurt School where academics agreed to abandon the workers and instead push for revolution by promoting minorities in academia and entertainment. It was still the same old game being played, but the chess pieces were altered to suit the academics' new preference.

To explain this more clearly is important because most people have no idea that this is going on in Western societies. The traditional Marxists pitted the workers (proletariat) against the capitalists (bourgeoisie) in a class conflict, whereas this new breed of *Cultural* Marxists began pitting ethnic minorities, feminists and – decades later – transgender minorities (the new pawns) against white men of any class (the new bourgeoisie). The justification for this new strain of conflict stemmed from what the Frankfurt academics referred to as 'the authoritarian personality' – i.e., the fact that white German workers shunned communism in favour of Hitler and fascism. Since the end of World War II, the Cultural Marxists have slowly and steadily taken charge of universities, media, governments, the Church, televison, radio, Hollywood, and even major corporations such as Google and Microsoft. They refer to this as 'the long march through the institutions' (i.e., infiltration). And once in positions of power

they begin 'deconstructing' (i.e., destroying) everything that makes Western civilisation great – art, literature, science, institutions, capitalism, social cohesion, etc. And *Blackboard Jungle* marks the first example of this in the movies. You've got to hand it to those maniacs; what better way to kick-start this corrosive ideology than to make a movie set in an inner-city school with a cast of multi-ethnic hoodlums? Indeed, just by typing these paragraphs, I probably qualify for the 'authoritarian personality' type. I am also a white male, so I guess I'm destined for the gulag either way. But make no mistake: the idiotic theories of the Cultural Marxists hold no scientific value whatsoever, despite them parading their work as 'social science'. They despise white men because Germany voted for Hitler. And that is the reason why they are destroying our societies. There is nothing scientific about these people; they are mad with resentment and desperate for revenge. But hey, Joe McCarthy was a paranoid loon, don't forget!

The Curse of Frankenstein (1957)
Dir: Terence Fisher /UK

Disgraced doctor, Baron Victor Frankenstein, is behind bars for murder. With the guillotine awaiting him, he tells a Priest of how he and his assistant, Paul Krempe, had conducted illegal experiments and resurrected a dead body...

Frankenstein's monster was by far the biggest horror icon of the 1930s and 40s, having been the subject of numerous films, gradually watering down the horror elements until *Abbott and Costello Meet Frankenstein* (1948) gave up all pretence of it being a horror picture. The early 1950s had more or less abandoned the Gothic horrors of yesteryear, and were instead replaced with alien invasion movies and mutated bugs from Atomic bomb blasts. By the mid-50s, a small British production company, Hammer Films, had an unexpected hit on their hands in *The Quatermas Experiment* (1956), and immediately set out to recapture the success by tackling Mary Shelley's classic novel.

Initially, the film was to be entitled *Frankenstein and the Monster*, and was originally envisaged as a low-budget, black and white quickie to be completed in just three weeks. American writer, Milton Subotsky, had hastily stitched together a script that was a fairly uninspired re-tread of the Frankenstein story (he later became the successful Amicus producer of horror anthologies, such as *Vault of Horror*

[1973], *Tales From the Crypt* [1972] and *The Monster Club* [1981], etc). However, Universal Pictures began throwing its weight around, threatening legal action. For, though Shelley's novel was in the public domain by that point, Jack Pierce's make-up design for Boris Karloff in *Frankenstein* (1931) was protected by copyright, along with several plot points that Universal had introduced to their version of the story. Thus, Hammer found itself having to tread very carefully.

Consequently, Subotsky's script was rejected, and Jimmy Sangster was brought in to come up with something new, and which avoided all references, verbal or visual, to the Karloff classic. Thus, 'the Monster' became 'the Creature,' and the main thread of the story was shifted from the exploits of the Creature to the mad doctor's incessant meddling with the unknown. Of course, re-writing the script had a knock-on effect, and the entire production was altered; not only was the shooting schedule extended, but the film's budget was increased to £70,000. And it was around this time that Hammer decided to try something else: they would shoot the film in full-bloodied colour. Thus was born *The Curse of Frankenstein*, which was not only the first Frankenstein movie in colour, but also the first *British* horror movie shot in colour. And this helped immeasurably to make the film a box-office success.

As with the previous *Quatermass* films and other B-movies, Hammer's American financiers suggested an American actor play the lead, as this would ensure the film's distribution in the States. However, Hammer was reluctant, and eventually took a chance on an actor who was unknown in the States, Peter Cushing. Nonetheless, the Americans seemed happy with the casting choice as they upped their investment to 50% of the film's overall budget (for a 50% return of profits). The other half came from smaller companies, such as ABPC – which owned the ABC Cinema chains – and Hammer themselves.

Cushing signed up to play the amoral meddler in October 1956, a role that would not only make him an international icon, but one he would go on to reprise no fewer than five times in *The Revenge of Frankenstein* (1958), *The Evil of Frankenstein* (1964), *Frankenstein Created Woman* (1967), *Frankenstein Must Be Destroyed* (1969), and *Frankenstein and the Monster From Hell* (1974) – and all but one of

them were also directed by Terence Fisher. The other cast members were still being carefully selected, but there was still one very important role to fill; that of the Creature itself. Initially, it looked like future *Carry On* star, Bernard Bresslaw, would land the role. However, his agent was demanding too much money, and so Hammer took another chance, this time on an unknown actor, Christopher Lee, to take on the role that would change his life. And, coincidentally or not, Cushing and Lee just happened to have the same agent.

To direct the film, Hammer chose Terence Fisher, for no other reason than the company owed him the job under the short contract they were under at the time. Little did anyone know that Fisher would go on to become perhaps the finest director of the Hammer stable. Fisher deliberately refused to see Universal's *Frankenstein* as he didn't want the film to influence him in any way.

From the opening shots, with the blood red background, it was clear that British horror would never be the same. For the first time, here was a horror film willing to present close-up shots of the macabre details that cinema had always shied away from up to that point – dead bodies, eyeballs, severed hands and brains were displayed in all their gory glory, delighting young fans and infuriating the critics. Christopher Lee's grotesque make-up is horrific in its own right, for a 50s horror movie. The 'look' was created by Phil Leakey, the man responsible for Victor Caroon's transformation in *The Quatermass Experiment*. Here he gives the Creature a rotten, waterlogged face, looking like something that has stepped out of a plane crash.

The finished film was quickly picked up for worldwide distribution by Warner Bros. And when *The Curse* opened at the Warner Bros. theatre in London's West End in May 1957, the punters were queuing around the block, despite the hostile reviews from the press. C.A. Lejeune fumed, '[*The Curse of Frankenstein* is] among the half-dozen most repulsive films I have encountered in the course of some 10,000 miles of film reviewing. I can only think of two which sickened me more,' while *Harrison's Reports* commented, 'In black and white photography it might have proved acceptable to those who seek horror entertainment, but in color it seems as if it will prove too gory for them.' The lobby at the Warner theatre was decorated to look like

Frankenstein's lab, while ticket sales broke the venue's box-office records. And in the following weeks, the crowds only got bigger as word of mouth helped to ensure that Hammer became the horror buzz-word of the year.

Even the British censors were uncharacteristically kind to the film; it was granted a – no doubt desired – X certificate, and suffered very little in the way of cuts, save for the shot in which Dr. Frankenstein drops the highwayman's mangled head into a vat of acid (the shot has since been restored on DVD and Blu-Ray releases). Even the close-up shots of severed body parts made it through the censor's office intact.

However, the film really hit it big when it reached America in June 1957. 'Full week's business in two days!' the trade ads gloated, while the pressbook for the film encouraged cinema managers to 'feature the creature and go!' Amusingly, the pressbook also encouraged cinema chains to screen the film 'around the clock' in special 'horror-a-thon shows,' in which there should be 'ambulances outside, smelling salt displays, money back if you faint tickets, and nurses in attendance.' Makes you wonder if the marketing ideas were written by William Castle! *The Curse* took around £2 million worldwide, a huge profit on its £70,000 budget. Not bad business for a small independent production house who, up until then, had been struggling to get by in the B-movie market.

Modern-day viewers may find the film a little slow going at first – the first third is filled with lots of boring 'drawing room talk,' but things pick up when the dead body of the highwayman is brought back to the lab. The Paul Krempe character, as Frankenstein's bothersome assistant, wears thin fairly quickly, but *The Curse of Frankenstein* set the template of things to come in the following years, revitalising Hammer into an internationally acclaimed Gothic horror house. *Curse* was followed by Terence Fisher's brilliant *The Revenge of Frankenstein* (1958), coming on the heels of the prestigious *Dracula/Horror of Dracula* (1958). Jimmy Sangster went on to write *Blood of the Vampire* (1958) in the same year, a film which shares similarities with his script for *Revenge*. *The Curse of Frankenstein* also had an immediate effect in America; *I Was a Teenage Frankenstein* (1957) was hastily put together as a sequel to the minor hit, *I Was a Teenage Werewolf* (1957), while legend Boris Karloff himself returned with *Frankenstein 1970* (1958).

The Abominable Snowman (1957)
(aka *The Abominable Snowman of the Himalayas*)
Dir: Val Guest /UK

Not long after the success of *The Curse of Frankenstein* (1957), Hammer produced this film based on Nigel Kneale's 1955 TV play, '*The Creature*', starring Peter Cushing. Shot in atmospheric black and white, and avoiding the colourful excesses of *Curse*, this film nonetheless offers up a certain degree of tension and unease, and is still worth a watch on a cold winter's night. The story centres on a Himalayan expedition headed by an American entrepreneur (Forrest Tucker) and an English doctor (Cushing), who are out to discover evidence of the Yeti's existence. And it isn't long before their party is picked off, one by one. Though it was largely shot on the backlots at Bray Studios and Pinewood, the film also has the added benefit of location shots in the Pyrenees, managing to convince viewers of its Himalayan setting. There's also a Tibetan monastery set designed by Bernard Robinson which offers acute details, and a wise old Llama who seems to know more than he lets on about the elusive Yeti. Audiences at the time who were expecting a typical 'monsters-on-the-rampage' type of horror show were largely disappointed by the film's thoughtful, character-driven, philosophical approach, but the film's overall message – basically, a rumination on the destructive nature of mankind – was a refreshing one for its time, as noted in the *Sunday Times*; "For once an engaging monster is neither bombed, roasted nor electrocuted. For this welcome courtesy, as well as its thrills and nonsense, I salute *The Abominable Snowman*."

The Blob (1958)
Dir: Irvin S. Yeaworth /USA

Jack H. Harris, the cheapjack producer who went on to make the forgettable 'comedy', Mother Goose a Go-Go (1965), struck it rich with this film that gave Steve McQueen his first lead role after a few supporting stints in *Somebody Up There Likes Me* (1956) and *Never Love a Stranger* (1958). This is a classic teen terror movie with McQueen and Aneta Corsaut trying to convince the folks in their small Pennsylvania community that they've seen a huge reddish-purple intergalactic gloop eating people alive. And of course, just like in countless other creature features over the years, no one believes them until it's too late. Boasting a classic theme tune by Hal David and Burt Bacharach, and one of the greatest moments in 50s horror when the blob invades a packed movie theatre, this film also gets away with many eccentricities of the time (such as the casting of leads in their late-twenties as teens, repressed authority figures, etc), but *The Blob* remains one of the most memorable B-movies of its time. It was followed by a sequel, *Beware! The Blob* (aka *Son of Blob*, 1971).

Eyes Without a Face (1959)
(Orig title: *Les yeux sans visage;* aka *The Horror Chamber of Dr. Faustus*)
<u>Dir: Georges Franju /France</u>
Les yeux sans visage is one of the most shocking and beautifully poetic horror films ever made. Scalpel-sharp and soft as velvet, its twisted charms have been hugely influential over the years. It's a black and white masterpiece which puts the hokey horrors of contemporary hits to shame with its morbid atmosphere and graphic bloodshed. Forget the flash-trash of modern-day hokum, this is the real deal in hair-raising terror, a true landmark in post-war Euro-horror. Prepare to be blown away by the grim elegance of *Eyes Without a Face*.

Adapted from Jean Redon's novel by Pierre Boileau and Thomas Narcejac (the pair who wrote *Vertigo* and *Les Diaboliques*), *Les yeux sans visage* was director Georges Franju's most ambitious film to date. Having started his career as a subversive documentarian with the unforgettable *Le sang des betes* (*Blood of the Beasts*, 1948), which juxtaposed the beauty of Paris with the graphic animal butchery of the city's slaughterhouses, Franju felt ready to tackle a feature film. The French critics had always been down on horror, and Franju claimed he wanted to add a seriousness to the genre, to help lift it out of its silly rut of ridiculous space monsters and creaky sets, and to add his own unsettling blend of compassion and cruelty, terror and tenderness, and cold blunt visuals. Suffice it to say he succeeded. But alas, the critics weren't ready for such stark realism, and they panned the film on its initial release (much like Charles Laughton's earlier film, *The Night of the Hunter* [1955], which is also considered a masterpiece nowadays but was given a harsh critical drubbing at the time of its release).

The plot concerns a guilty surgeon, Genessier (Pierre Brasseur), who crashed his car, severely disfiguring his daughter's face, and who runs his own sinister clinic with the aid of Louise (Alida Valli, who would later show up in Dario Argento's *Suspiria* [1977]). Genessier attempts to restore his daughter's beauty with disastrous skin grafts, but he can only continue in his guilt-racked obsession by procuring skin donors. Louise prowls the streets of Paris and kidnaps pretty young girls whose faces Genessier surgically removes and places onto his daughter Christina (Edith Scob) with increasingly reckless results.

The film caused much controversy in Europe; *L'Express* noted that viewers "dropped like flies" during the graphic face removal scene. The French critics were united in their disgust and condemnation of the film. Elsewhere, seven people collapsed during its screening at the Edinburgh Film Festival, prompting critic Isabel Quibly to brand it "the sickest film since I started film criticism." In America, the film was cut, dubbed into English, and given a new title, *The Horror Chamber of Dr. Faustus*, as a way to bring in some revenue and distance it from its reviled status in Europe.

The long and lingering surgery sequence is still quite shocking today, but it's also a master class in tension-building and editing. There are also more subtle moments in the film which disturb and haunt viewers long after the end credits roll, such as the opening scene where Louise drives a corpse out into the wilderness and dumps it in the river (this is played out to Maurice Jarre's bizarre waltzy score). Genessier's misguided love also haunts; he wants the very best for his daughter, but he also wants to ease his own guilt by throwing himself into his research. His desire to restore the innocent beauty of Christina sends his moral compass into haywire; his ice-cold mannerisms and facade of dignity and professionalism dissolves into a slushy mess of heartache and torturous guilt whenever he is in his daughter's company. Christina, in turn, doesn't openly blame her father for the incident which destroyed her face; she's just fed up and depressed at being hidden away in her room the whole time. But it's clear that Genessier blames himself for his daughter's miserable situation. Also, Alida Valli's twisted smile as she lures the young women to their deaths is not easy to forget; it just adds to the overall unsettling atmosphere of the film. Franju himself described the film's unease as "Anguish... it's a quieter mood than horror... more internal, more penetrating. It's horror in homeopathic doses".

Incredibly, it was only in the late 90s when the film was finally released uncut in the UK. And horror fans who for years knew nothing about the film other than the precious write-up in Phil Hardy's *Aurum Encyclopedia of Horror* finally had the opportunity to see the faceless horror icon, Edith Scob, whose blank mask had influenced Jess Franco's *The Awful Dr. Orloff* and John Carpenter's *Halloween*. The film's influence spread further, with its heart-rending storyline imitated in Anton Guillio Majano's *Atom Age Vampire* and Franco's *Faceless*, and the sailing white doves and graphic face removals were updated to stunning effect in John Woo's *Face/Off*. Quite a legacy indeed, but very few film-makers have managed to match Franju's classic, which along with *Psycho* and *Peeping Tom*, laid the foundations for the sleazy slasher boom which became all the rage a couple of decades later.

Peeping Tom (1960)
Dir: Michael Powell /UK

Critically reviled on its initial release for its morbid and disturbing voyeurism, Michael Powell's *Peeping Tom* is now held in very high regard as one of the finest British movies ever made.

A psychologist (played by director Powell himself in a knowing bit of casting) subjects his young son to nightmarish experiments in his studies on fear. Inevitably, the child grows up to become a voyeuristic cameraman/serial killer (Carl Bohm) who stabs his pretty young victims with his spiked tripod and films the terrified expressions on their faces at the moment of death. He then goes home and watches the footage over and over again. Bohm conceals his derangement with a polite manner and clean-cut appearance, but it isn't long before his neighbour's suspicions encroach on his personal space.

This film is much more restrained than its reputation suggests; none of the overtly gruesome bits are displayed on camera. Horror fans who are more accustomed to the latter day excessive bloodletting of the sleazy 'stalk and slash' formula will probably be disappointed

with the steady pace and lack of graphic dismemberment, which is ironic considering that *Peeping Tom* played a big part in kick-staring the slasher boom of the late 70s/early 80s.

Peeping Tom was also one of the first films to depict a somewhat sympathetic killer, and this aspect has been imitated over the years in everything from *Martin* (1976), *Mosquito the Rapist* (1976), and *Henry-Portrait of a Serial Killer* (1986). The stunning Eastmancolour photography with its bold and punchy colour palette has been much imitated too, as has Gordon Watson's creepy piano score. Director Donall Cammell paid homage to the film in his 1982 horror classic, *White of the Eye*, and also Italian horror auteur Dario Argento touched upon many similar themes in his excellent late 80s shocker, *Opera*.

Michael Powell deserted the earlier grand qualities which earned his reputation with Emeris Pressburger in the preceding years when the pair produced such classics as *The Red Shoes* and *A Matter of Life and Death*, and instead turned his attentions onto something altogether removed from the pleasantries of his earlier output. In one scene he goes as far as casting Moira Shearer, the dancer in *The Red Shoes* as a whore who gets stabbed to death by Bohm, and he even casts himself as the deranged psychologist whose sadistic experiments turns his son into a twisted murderer. The choice of casting himself in the role was clearly designed to express the obsessive and ruthless nature of all great artists, and also as a comment on the scoptophiliac nature of cinema-goers themselves, with Otto Heller's 'killer's eye' camera work imitated to death ever since.

Unsurprisingly, the critics were not impressed. They didn't just dislike the film, they actively hated it and decried everything about it. *Peeping Tom* premiered in March 1960, just three months before Hitchcock's *Psycho*, and it was immediately panned. Derek Hill of *The Tribune* suggested that "the only really satisfactory way to dispose of [the film] would be to shovel it up and flush it swiftly down the nearest sewer." Some other loser called it "the sickest and filthiest film I remember seeing." The film's hostile reception brought its theatrical run to an immediate end when it was pulled from cinemas. And like Todd Browning before him, whose *Freaks* had been met with a similar outraged reception in the 1930s, Michael Powell's career effectively came to an end as a direct result of all the negative press. Alfred Hitchcock seemed to take an important lesson from this, and he rather wisely released *Psycho* without a preview press screening – smart move.

In America, the film played in a black and white version that was cut down to 86 minutes. But even in this shoddy form *Peeping Tom* managed to gain a cult following around New York's Alphabet City district in its limited theatrical run. Film student Martin Scorsese was suitably impressed, and his dogged devotion to *Peeping Tom* helped to save it from oblivion, even providing his own full-colour 35mm print for future screenings and a DVD release. "I have always felt that *Peeping Tom* and *8 1/2* say everything that can be said about film-making," he said, "about the process of dealing with film, the objectivity and subjectivity of it and the confusion between the two. *8 1/2* captures the the glamour and enjoyment of film-making, while *Peeping Tom* shows the aggression of it, how the camera violates... From studying them you can discover everything about people who express themselves through film."

The City of the Dead (1960)
(aka *Horror Hotel*)
Dir: John Moxey /UK

A moody, atmospheric gem which shares similarities with Mario Bava's *Black Sunday*, which was made around the same time. The film opens on the scene of a suspected witch being burned at the stake during the Salem witch-hunts of 1692. She curses the townspeople and laughs as the flames rise around her. It then cuts forward to modern-day Massachussets where Christopher Lee plays a history professor who encourages his favourite student, Nan (Venetia Stevenson), to visit the strange misty town of Whitewood, the place where many a witch burning took place. Her trip will not only help her in her studies, but will also feed her own personal fascination with witchcraft. Things get creepy as soon as she enters the town, as her mysterious 'tour guide' disappears into the night. She takes a room in a spooky hotel and begins to uncover some horrific home truths... But that turns out to be only *half* the story. With its dry ice and perpetual darkness, *City of the Dead* is one of the great horror movies of the early 60s, despite its low-budget. The 'town-full-of-

hooded-Satanists' sub-genre flourished in the 70s, but this understated classic got there first.

Jigoku (1960)
(aka *Hell*; aka *Concepts of Hell*; aka *The Sinners of Hell*)
Dir: Nobuo Nakagawa /Japan

After a hit 'n' run accident, a pair of Japanese students – one with a conscience, the other without – agree not to speak about it, and are eventually targeted by relatives of the victim before being plunged into hell for their transgressions... Unreleased outside of Japan for the best part of 40 years, *Jigoku* has developed a legendary reputation over the decades as one of the earliest gore movies ever made. On the surface, *Jigoku* resembles many other Japanese horrors of the early 60s, with its lethargic pacing, poetic flourishes and the philosophical/existential angst of its central characters. What sets the film apart from the norm, however, is the hell sequence – in full colour, mind – that recalls the desolate landscapes of *Dante's Inferno* (1911) and the impressive sets of *Dante's Inferno* (1935), the latter producing some of the most striking imagery of the 1930s. The hell sequence also pre-dates the full-colour damnation scenes in *This Night I'll Possess Your Corpse* (1966), Jose Mojica Marins' excessive shocker which owes a thing or two to Nakagawa's pioneering film. *Jigoku* is no masterpiece, and newcomers to Japanese cinema are advised to start elsewhere, but it does at least show Nakagawa and his producer willing to try something new. They knew that their film wouldn't be a hit, and indeed, producer Mitsugu Okura was initially upset that the finished film concentrated exclusively on hell rather than a combination of heaven and hell, which the film-makers had originally decided upon before the shooting went ahead. As for the infamous sequence in question, the hell scenes – and remember, this is a Buddhist hell – includes such graphic sequences as flaying, beheading, a victim sawn in half, hands cut off, etc. All fairly graphic but let down slightly by the not-so-convincing special effects. *Jigoku* was remade under the title *Jigoku: Portrait of Hell* (1969), and again in 1979 by the Toei studio. Teruo Ishii took another stab at the story with *Jigoku: Japanese Hell* (1999).

The Day of the Triffids (1962)
Dir: Steve Sekely [and Freddie Francis, uncredited] /UK

Meteorites stream across the night skies, delivering dangerous killer plants to earth with fatal stingers. The glare of the meteorite shower has blinded those who witnessed the spectacle. Meanwhile, Bill Mason (Howard Keel) is recovering in hospital after an eye operation, and ironically, he's only one of very few people left who can actually see what's going on. As the chaos spreads across London, Bill rescues a young schoolgirl, and together they flee to France and Spain hoping to escape the alien threat, only to learn that the disaster is global...

This adaptation of John Wyndham's classic novel starts with a great opener, but ultimately disappoints as the story progresses. The pointless trips to Paris and the Spanish countryside serve only to dish up scenarios that could have easily taken place back in London. There are also visual inconsistencies concerning the Triffids (in some scenes they look like giant alien orchids with creepy tendrils, and in others they sort of resemble spiky, hopping Christmas trees). Director Steve Sekely's original cut of the film was deemed so bad that Freddie Francis was brought in to shoot a new sub-plot in which a couple of characters are trapped in a lighthouse having to fend off the pesky plants. And this made way for the silly ending in which they use plain old seawater to destroy the pests (as was later ridiculed in Tim Burton's *Mars Attacks!* [1996], though M. Night Shyamalan later recycled the idea again un-ironically in *Signs* [2002]).

The film became much talked about thanks to its regular screenings on late-night television, and has influenced various film-makers over the years (including the 'main-character-awakens-in-hospital' opener in Danny Boyle's *28 Days Later* [2001], Rick Grimes in *The Walking Dead* [2010-], and the scenario of Fernando Meirelles' *Blindness* [2008]), but it was the power of Wyndham's original plot that seems to have resonated the most, rather than its lacklustre screen adaptation.

Mondo Cane (1962)
Dir: Gualtiero Jacopetti and Franco Prosperi /Italy

The shockumentary, or 'Mondo' movie has existed since the dawn of cinema itself, and these films have outraged viewers worldwide for as long as films have been exhibited. It's certainly not a recent phenomenon. The word 'mondo' is Italian for 'world,' and it became the by-word for a genre of fact-based shock movies and documentaries made by Gualtiero Jacopetti and Franco Prosperi that flourished in the 1960s. But in truth, the mondo movie can be traced back as far as 1900 to Thomas Edison's glimpses into the forbidden in a couple of his one-reelers which show an execution and an elephant being electrocuted.

The 1930s saw the first heyday for this kind of fare when sideshows would screen all kinds of this stuff – alongside Todd Browning's *Freaks*, the paying punters could lay eyes on all manner of sensationalist films, such as William Campbell's *Ingaji* (directed under the name 'William Alexander') which ended with 'real' footage of natives sacrificing a member of their tribe to the gorilla god, Ingaji. *Armand and Michela Denis Among the Headhunters* was a film made by a husband and wife collaboration that also spent time with the natives, and these films made a fortune.

By the early 60s, Jacopetti had written the narration for *Mondo Di Notte* (*World By Night*), a documentary exploring the weird and bizarre from the exotic parts of the world. It was quite successful, and this encouraged Jacopetti to take the format further. He teamed up with film-maker Franco Prosperi, and together they travelled the world documenting the strangest rites in the most far flung cultures. The result was *Mondo Cane* in 1962.

"All the scenes you will see in this film are true and are taken only from life. If often they are shocking, it is because there are many shocking things in this world. Besides, the duty of the chronicler is not to sweeten the truth but to report it objectively". This quote is from a caption that appears on the screen at the beginning. A dog is led into a pen that contains hundreds more dogs who seem quite hostile, and is then set free from its chain and allowed to wander inside the enclosure to check out the other hounds. And this probably serves as a visual metaphor for the journey we the viewers are about to take. The next sequence shows an 'appreciation ceremony' where a man called Brazzi inherits Rodolpho Valentino's fortune. He visits New York and is mobbed by adoring women.

The film continues in a similar vein for the next 100 minutes as we're shown the strange rites of various cultures from across the world. We head to the jungle of East New Guinea and witness a tribal pig feast where the animals have their heads beaten in with lumps of wood. A pet cemetery in California next, then on to an East Asian island where the locals eat dog meat. Back in Italy, it's Easter season and hundreds of chicklets are warmed in the ovens and are then dipped in coloured ink. In Japan, farmers massage the buttocks of bulls and make them drink 6 litres of beer per day, as apparently it makes the meat taste better. In Africa, native women are fed in a fattening process. Back in America, we visit a gym for elderly widows who want to lose weight so that they can re-marry. To Hong Kong next where the locals basically eat any animal they can get their hands on, even crocodile. Rattlesnakes, muskrats, bugs and worms are also eaten. And this stuff is then sold to New York restaurants where the rich wine and dine in their plush surroundings. And much more.

This is quite a tame 'documentary' compared to the modern standards of the shockumentary, but many scenes in *Mondo Cane* must have been quite an experience for audiences in the early 60s. There's little rhyme or reason between the footage here to link it all together other than having bizarre cultures and ceremonies from across the globe paraded before our eyes. *Mondo Cane* was a sensation. Shot in full colour in beautiful scope, and featuring a grand score from Riz Ortolani (the man responsible for the classic 'soap opera' theme of *Cannibal Holocaust*), the film was pure spectacle and made a fortune. It's a gleefully leering and voyeuristic tour around the world that distorted reality any way its makers saw fit. It caused outrage among the critics who generally dismissed it as a vile form of sensationalism, and of course, having read this condemnation in the press, the punters came thick and fast to see this film that everyone was complaining about. Italy has always been a land of imitation as far as cinema goes, and film-makers from that part of the world were soon churning out their own mondo movies, such as *Mondo Freudo, Mondo Balordo, Malamondo*, and *Women of the World*, where every bizarre activity known to man was exploited on film. But it was Jacopetti and Prosperi once again who steered the genre to where it needed to be when they released their official sequel, *Mondo Cane 2* in the following year.

The Mondo Movie and Shockumentaries

Most of the mondo movies that flourished in the 60s had one thing in common; they all had scenes that were staged for the effect of the film. The film-makers wanted sensationalism, and if they couldn't find it in the reality of the things they were filming, they would simply create the shocking material themselves. Truth wasn't always stranger than fiction when it came to the mondo film. Pretty soon, the Americans jumped on the bandwagon and produced their own entries that documented the hippy movement with the same familiar air of crude sensationalism in the free-love and drug havens of the late 60s. But all this led to the saturation of the genre, and it was Jacopetti and Prosperi, as conscious as ever of the fast-changing world, who came to the rescue once again and offered *Africa Addio* in the mid-60s. They instinctively knew that the old format of the mondo movie had run its course, and they decided to up the ante as a way of presenting things that were forbidden on television.

Africa Addio went further than any mondo film before it, and ultimately dispensed with the fun and light-hearted feel of their earlier films, and instead showed their viewers a grim and pessimistic view of hell on Earth. Rumours circulated that the film-makers had organized a real execution for the sake of the film, and the critics were once again outraged as they had been with the release of *Mondo Cane* almost decade earlier.

As the 70s progressed, the mondo film became increasingly extreme, making their 60s predecessors look almost tame in comparison. *Savage Man, Savage Beast* was cut to ribbons by the British censors who objected to the animal violence. Strangely, scenes of wild animals catching and feeding on their prey were cut on the advice of the RSPCA, while scenes depicting the practice of fox hunting were passed unscathed. Elsewhere around the world, the film became notorious, chiefly for the scenes which supposedly show a man being eaten by lions in a zoo, and mercenaries castrating a native. It was later confirmed that both of those scenes were in fact dramatic reconstructions made purely for the exploitative factor. The film was made by Alferdo and Angelo Castianalli, who along with Mario Mora, overtook Jacopetti and Prosperi and became the new leaders of the genre. Their work also includes *This Violent World*, *Sweet and Savage*, and *Shocking Africa*. The latter is to this day still widely regarded as one of the most unpleasant films ever made. Other mondo-flavoured titles came along which revelled in gruesome death and explicit sex, such as *Shocking Asia* parts 1 and 2, and *This Is America*. And the public's fascination for death and disaster was also catered for in *Days of Fury*.

The 1970s also saw a rise in popularity of the sex education film. Film-makers were keen to exploit the fact that sex films that served to educate the viewer could be much more explicit than would be acceptable otherwise. Shaun Cunningham's *The Art of Marriage* and *The ABC's of Love and Sex* were both tremendous box-office draws before hardcore porn became popular. But this type of fare had a negative effect on genuine sex education films, as they were all treated as exploitation garbage, particularly in the UK where the Swedish production, *The Language of Love*, was banned.

Faces of Death came along in 1979, and was the single most successful mondo film since *Mondo Cane* in the early 60s. This international hit was a co-production between American and Japanese financiers, and wallows in footage shot at a kosher slaughterhouse, the eating of monkey brains, autopsies, and death by electric chair. Like the earlier mondo films, many of the scenes here were faked, but it isn't always easy to know what is real and what isn't. My guess is that most of the footage is genuine but is not as graphic as you would assume. For the record, it's safe to say that the electric chair sequence was probably faked, and the eating of monkey brains was most certainly staged.

Faces of Death was huge in Japan, it was a bigger hit than *Star Wars*. In the UK, the film got caught up in the 'video nasties' debacle and was banned for years (even today the UK DVD is missing a couple of BBFC cuts to remove the sight of a dog fight and the killing of a monkey). The film also spawned numerous sequels, cash-ins, and rip-offs, such as *The Shocks*, and *Death: The Ultimate Horror*.

The success of *Faces of Death* and the rise of home video in the 80s led to a renewed interest in the genre, with sequels to the *Mondo Cane* series appearing on video along with sequels to *Shocking Asia* and *This Is America*. The Japanese and American financiers collaborated again for the production of *The Killing of America* as a way of trying to ape the success of *Faces of Death*. But this film is actually a different breed from the usual mondo fare; *The Killing of America* is a genuinely uncomfortable look at the state of the modern world, and serves as the high water mark of the genre. And unlike the previous mondo entries, all of the footage is as real as it gets.

Home video allowed the mondo movie to flourish in cheapo productions where the staged sequences were banished altogether in series like *Faces of Gore*, *Traces of Death*, and *Banned In America*. These direct to video abominations took the exploitation factor to unprecedented levels, and feature bizarre voice-overs that mock the carnage on display. But there were others who took the genre elsewhere, such as the rare and barely seen *Army Medicine In Vietnam*, which stands as a serious look at the botched surgery of marines, including one soldier who has his face blown off, pieced back together, and then after recovery he is sent back to the front line.

In the mid-90s, the Brits added their own entry in the field with *Executions*, a video release that caused outrage in the press but was unbelievably passed uncut by the BBFC. I vividly remember reading the lurid tabloid headlines and scare stories about the film (which I took as recommendations!). According to the papers, *Executions* showed footage of people having their heads drilled. I eventually did get to see it, and it's actually a serious intended documentary exposing the barbarity of the death penalty. Many of these films I find difficult to watch nowadays. I recently re-visited *Executions* for the sake of writing this piece, and although it's certainly not an easy film to watch, there's very little there footage-wise that can't be shown on broadcast news reports. The ending, however, shows a guy being machine-gunned in the face at close range. It takes him a long time to die and the camera never flinches from the gruesome horror on display as he takes his dying breaths. I love horror and gore movies as much as anyone, but the real stuff like this is something different; a boundary has been crossed here. I had to look away from that scene this time around.

The Video Diary of Ricardo Lopez

The most recent shockumentary I saw was *The Video Diary of Ricardo Lopez*. In this DIY mondo oddity we follow the last few weeks in the life of Bjork obsessive, Ricardo Lopez. He was confident and articulate, but his world is turned upside down when he discovers that his favourite pop star is dating a black guy. He then sets about documenting the last moments of his life on video in his New York apartment, and we follow every step of the way as his mind disintegrates.

He refers to Bjork as a "nigger lover" and relates his own race theories in which he explains that white women make up only 5% of the world's population, and that white women are too precious and unique to be going with black guys. He purchases a vat of very strong concentrated acid with the aim of making an acid bomb that he hopes will be opened by Bjork herself. He mails it to her (the parcel was intercepted by the police). And then, like a real life Travis Bickle, he flips completely, and shaves his head, paints his face, and blows his brains out on camera. *The Video Diary of Ricardo Lopez* is an extremely disturbing and humbling viewing experience. Lopez, for all his faults, was a bright kid; he was only 19 but his mannerisms and intelligence gives the impression that he could be at least ten years older. The film as a whole stands as a chilling look at the fragility of the human mind, and that of the obsessive stalker personality. But also, one can't help but feel some sympathy for Lopez; he had quite clearly lost his marbles, and the last shots of the film which sees him sitting with the gun in his hand are especially powerful. He barely utters a word throughout this long sequence, but his facial expressions tell their own story; as he contemplates the end of his life he seems afraid and perhaps even remorseful. He hadn't touched his medication for weeks and yet there seems to be a moment of clarity right at the end; it's as if he doesn't want to pull the trigger, but at the same time he realises the enormity of his crime; whether or not Bjrok opens the package he has sent to her is irrelevant in the eyes of the law. He knows that there's no turning back for him, and even if he had doubts about ending his life, he also seemed to be driven by demons that were ultimately beyond his control.

The police recovered the tapes when they raided his apartment and the footage was kept by the FBI for a number of years. Copies of the tapes were made and given away to those who requested the footage (and this in itself says something about our jaded sensibilities when we have to contact the FBI for our latest DVD fix). This casual distribution of such sensitive footage has caused much criticism of the FBI and those hoping to cash-in on the tragedy. Indeed, even watching films like this nowadays feels like an intrusion for me. There's something borderline obscene about watching this stuff. Lopez, like many other victims in these films, was somebody's son, somebody's loved one. He had dreams and aspirations. Yes he was a flawed individual, but all of us are.

Having said that, I still believe that more than any other type of documentary style of film, the mondo movie, in its many and varied forms, is a powerful medium for information. And for that reason alone I refuse to condemn them completely. No matter how crude or uncomfortable they may be for us to watch, they are only a reflection of the world we live in. And if they are offensive, then we must look back at ourselves and change the way we live. As the caption says at the beginning of the original *Mondo Cane*, "The duty of the chronicler is not to sweeten the truth but to report it objectively."

Dementia 13 (1963)
Dir: Francis Ford Coppola /USA
Based in Los Angeles, Roger Corman's production/distribution company, New World Pictures, served as both a production house and an invaluable training school for gifted young film-makers. He would buy cheap sci-fi movies from Russia, edit them together to create a new story, and then release them in America as new and improved products. When he recruited Francis Ford Coppola from UCLA, it was Coppola's job to edit the footage together. Coppola eventually pitched an idea for a film: "As I described it," says Coppola, "a man goes to a pond and takes off his clothes, picks up these dolls, ties them together, goes under the water, dives down... And Roger says, 'change the man to a woman and you can do it.'"

Corman insisted that his film-makers shoot fast and include regular shots of female flesh in order to keep viewers interested. But other than that, they were free to put their own personal stamps on the pics. Coppola went away and made *Dementia 13*, a crafty *Psycho* rip-off about a young woman who visits her dead husband's family in Ireland, only to learn that there is an axe murderer on the loose. While hardly a masterpiece, the film is worth a watch nowadays for the flashes of visual brilliance throughout which hint at Coppola's future visual style. Those with a keen eye for the auteur will also spot thematic details which would later crop up in his work, such as twisted loyalty and family conflict. Later in his career, Coppola reverted to the tricks of the trade as taught to him by Corman by filming *The Outsiders* and *Rumble Fish* back-to-back in 1982, using many of the same locations for both films, and saving a small fortune on production costs.

Black Sabbath (1963)
(aka *The Three Faces of Fear*)
(Orig title: *I tre volti della paura*)
Dir: Mario Bava /Italy
Tagline: "This is the night of the nightmare... when a headless corpse rides the cold night wind, when a woman's soul inhabits the body of a buzzing fly."

Black Sabbath is right up there with *Kwaidan* (1964) as one of the finest – and most visually arresting – horror anthologies of the 1960s. It's a trilogy of spooky tales introduced by Boris Karloff, who also appears in the *Wurdulak* segment. The first story, *Telephone*, is an early giallo-flavoured tale starring Michelle Mercier as an up-market call girl who is pestered by threatening phone calls while she lounges around in her luxury apartment. In *The Wurdulak*, a headless corpse is discovered by a man at the side of a country road. The man heads for a nearby house to raise the alarm, and when he gets there he discovers that the family therein are awaiting the return of the father, played by Boris Karloff. And later, the patriarch shows up clutching a severed head which he claims belonged to a 'wurdulak,' a vampire. And in the final segment, *The Drop of Water*, a young woman (Jacqueline Pierreux) is left to prepare the corpse of a woman who died during a séance, and is unnerved by the cold dead eyes. However, this doesn't stop her from stealing a valuable ring from the deceased lady's finger. And soon after, she experiences very strange goings on as loud drops of water can be heard, and a restless fly buzzes about the room...

Black Sabbath is one of Mario Bava's finest achievements, a masterpiece of style that has influenced everyone from Dario Argento to Quentin Tarantino. The Anglicized title of the film also inspired the name of Tony Iommi and Ozzy Osbourne's band. Here, Bava embraces metaphor like never before. For example, *The Drop of Water* plays like a Poe tale come to life as the young nurse pockets the ring and is immediately plunged into *Tell-Tale Heart* territory as her unconscious guilt distorts her perception in disturbing ways. In America, the film was released by AIP in a drastically altered form. It was toned down and new intros were added. The *Telephone* segment was re-edited into a ghost story, *The Wurdulak* had its more graphic moments censored, and even the order in which the stories were presented was shuffled. And Les Baxter provided a new score. Nonetheless, even in its butchered form, *Black Sabbath* proved to be such a powerful film that it quickly became a cult classic in the States thanks to its regular screenings on late night TV. At the turn of the millennium, Image released the film on DVD, reinstating Bava's original cut, uncut and in the correct order with Roberto Nicolosi's original – and subtle – score, and the bizarre original ending which includes Karloff on a prop horse in a film studio.

Blood Feast (1963)
Dir: Herschell Gordon Lewis /USA
Peoria, Illinois, 1963. It was a Friday night at the local drive-in theatre. Dozens of cars were lined up facing the huge whitewashed wall which suddenly burst into life as the projector light beamed upon it from across the parking lot. The audience, usually made up of courting couples making out on the back seats, were immediately distracted from their semi-private activities by events playing out on screen; within moments of the film starting, a blonde woman taking a bath is attacked by an intruder with dark, blueish hair, and he proceeds to hack off her leg in full-bloodied colour. The drive-in patrons were stunned. It was the first time in movie history that an audience had witnessed graphic gore on a cinema screen, and it wouldn't be the last.

The film they were watching was *Blood Feast*, a low-budget horror quickie produced and directed by Herschell Gordon Lewis and David F. Friedman. The pair had previously churned out nudie cuties like *Living Venus* (1961), *Daughters of the Sun* (1961) and *Nature's Playmates* (1962), but decided out of sheer boredom to try something new. They had noticed that horror movies had always shied away from showing gruesome death; characters either died cleanly and quietly with their eyes closed, or the screen would fade to black just at the moment the killing started. And having noticed this strange discrepancy, they decided to shatter the taboo in full-on *grand guignol* style. With a budget of $24,000 and a Playboy pin-up girl (Connie Mason) for their lead actress, this bloody-minded duo set to work.

The plot of *Blood Feast* concerns a young woman, Suzette (Mason), who dates the local shit-for-brains cop, Pete. They attend a lecture on Egyptian cults. Meanwhile, young women are being butchered by the local caterer, Faud Ramses (Mal Arnold), who sets his eye on Suzette becoming the latest sacrifice to the Egyptian god, Ishtar.

Lewis and Friedman decided to premier their blood-drenched movie in Peoria, where, according to Lewis, "If the film dropped dead, no one would know." *Blood Feast* opened on a Friday, and the film-makers deliberately stayed behind in Chicago unaware of how their pic was being received by audiences. The following day, anticipation got the better of them and they decided to take a drive to see for themselves, and what greeted them was a spectacle of unprecedented chaos. Speaking to John McCarty (author of *The Sleaze Merchants*), Lewis revealed, "Even though there was a major fair in town, theatre traffic was backed up so far the State Police were directing it. We were still about a quarter mile from the theatre when I turned to Dave, held out my hand, and said 'I guess we've started something.'" People were so grossed-out by the film that they went and told their friends about it and returned the following night, en masse, with those who wanted to see what all the fuss was about. Local residents complained that 60 foot images of women being mutilated were visible from their bedroom windows and giving them nightmares.

Blood Feast is at once funny and revolting, the acting terrible, the lighting flat, the camera almost completely static throughout. Lewis described the film as an 'experiment' project, and admitted to directing it in four days in a rushed, careless manner, aware that the finished product could easily sink without trace in its opening weekend. However, despite its many faults, this film will always have its place in horror history for daring to try something new,

and for its defiantly in your face, gore-for-gore's-sake attitude. Tongues are ripped out, legs cut off (see the newspaper headline!). We also get to witness tabletop eviscerations, skulls ripped open and entrails fondled in loving close-up. John Waters later used bloody clips from *Blood Feast* in his suburban satire, *Serial Mom* (1994). He also claims to have used binoculars to spy on screenings of *Blood Feast* at the drive-in near his home in Baltimore as a child, to which Lewis commented, "If John did that, he's a bigger masochist than I thought!" Lewis and Friedman became exploitation legends overnight, and their film enjoyed a huge success in the American underground and the drive-in circuits, with Lewis later christened as 'the Godfather of gore'. The pair returned the following year with *Two Thousand Maniacs!*

The Blancheville Monster (1963)
(aka *Horror*)
Dir: Alberto DeMartino /Italy
Emily has a lot of growing up to do. She returns to her family castle after completing her studies to discover that her home life has drastically changed. Her brother is now in charge of the estate, the servants and maids whom she knew for years and were almost part of the family have died and been replaced by new members of staff who are cold and unfamiliar. Her father, Count Blancheville, has been horribly disfigured and lives secluded in one of the castle's isolated towers. Count Blancheville believes that the family curse will be lifted if Emily dies before her 21st birthday (this belief is based on an ancient 'prophecy'). Emily is 20 years old, and her birthday is only five days away. To make matters worse, her father escapes from the tower and disappears, only to show up trying to convince Emily to embrace 'sweet death'.

This underrated and rather obscure oddity still hasn't received its due on DVD but is worth hunting down for fans of Eurohorror and the cine-bizarre. It has an eerie atmosphere and a grand Gothic setting, reminiscent of Roger Corman's Poe adaptations of the early 60s. Emily returns home as the picture of youth; one can only guess how much fun she had while away at college, making new friends and having the space and the freedom to shape her own ideals and identity with her whole life ahead of her.

Time brings inevitable changes to any household, and in this film those changes are exaggerated. Death has taken away the servants from old age, her father has been "horribly disfigured", but in a metaphorical sense, this disfigurement is simply old age. Many youngsters are forced into adulthood due to circumstances beyond their control; debilitating terminal disease and death itself can alter family life beyond recognition (the new members of staff are blank faced and unfamiliar, and this could represent a personification of this change).

Much of the film centres on the struggle of Emily to stay young and irresponsible and fight against the changes which demands her to grow up and allow her youthful spirit to die. The 'family curse' is of course death itself, the curse of every family. The bed-ridden father sends out a phantom shape of himself to stalk and harass Emily, trying to lure her by guilt and pity into giving up her life to care for him and to keep the family unit going. It seems appropriate that the father's method of 'killing' Emily are by poisoning, because in situations where youths are expected to take on the responsibilities of adulthood, many feel they are being poisoned with duties and burdens. When the doctor informs Emily's brother that she has been poisoned, he adds "It's not her body that is threatened, it is her spirit". Whilst in bed sick with the delirium brought on by the poison, her fever dreams represent the adolescent battle between freedom and responsibility. In these dreams, Emily wanders around the desecrated ruins of the castle dressed in a swirling and virginal white dress, seemingly looking for a way to escape, but instead she always bumps into her father who whispers things like "You have reached the eternal lair. You are dead Emily, you are dead".

It all ends in the nightmarish finale where Emily is comatose at her own funeral. Not literally dead but spiritually nullified. "Why can't you hear me?" she calls out to the mourners, "I'm alive! I'm alive!" She is then entombed in the mausoleum in a splendid metaphor of the painful birth of the adult. And of course, the 'family curse' continues... In the coda, Emily escapes from the nightmare of the mausoleum, but finds herself in wedlock; her youth and vitality gone, replaced by conformity and boring old adulthood.

Mondo Cane 2 (1963)
(aka *Mondo Pazzo*, '*Crazy World*')
Dir: Gualtiero Jacopetti and Franco Prosperi /Italy

Starting eerily similar to the original *Mondo Cane*, this sequel opens with a scene involving caged dogs. But this time they are locked up in individual cages with bandages on their throats. The dogs are seen to be barking, but only let out faint squeaks – this is because their vocal chords have been cut prior to vivisection. An Alsation under anaesthetic has an operation on its abdomen. Of course, this being a mondo movie, it's always wise to question the authenticity of what is happening on screen, and *Mondo Cane 2* is no exception. Jacopetti and Prosperi are simply up to their old tricks of shaping the 'reality' around them for their own ends. They even go as far as to poke fun at the British censors who had banned *Mondo Cane* (although it was screened illegally several times in the UK). The narrator asks if the censors would like to cut this sequence in the same way as the vet cuts the dog's voice.

It's clear that Jacopetti and Prosperi wanted to take the mondo format further than their previous film, and with the political upheaval at the time, they had the perfect opportunity to out-shock the original *Mondo Cane*. About halfway through this sequel is a scene that was shot in Saigon in 1963. It's a scene which supposedly shows the infamous suicide of the Buddhist monk, Quang Duc, who was protesting the Vietnamese government's suppression of Buddhism. At first glance, this all looks horribly real, and for years many had assumed it to be genuine footage of the event – the man sits in the middle of a public square, a fellow monk pours petrol over him then pours a trail away from Duc to a safe distance. The crowd of protesters and police watch on in horror as the monk sets fire to the trail of flammable liquid, and Duc is engulfed in flames. The stoic monk sits calm and lotus-like as the fireball ravages his flesh, putting years of meditative power to the ultimate test. According to a *New York Times* reporter who had witnessed the incident, Duc remained unmoved throughout. "As he burned, he never moved a muscle, never uttered a sound, his outward composure in sharp contrast to the wailing people around him." And because Duc was assisted in his death, this makes the incident technically murder.

On first viewing, you could be forgiven for

thinking it was real footage. However, in their book, '*Killing For Culture*', David Kerekes and David Slater compare the footage with the original photograph from the Associated Press to argue that the scene was faked. In addition to noting a suspicious edit in the film when a spectator backs into the lens, obscuring the view just before the fire is lit (the perfect place to sneak in a cut and replace the man with a mannequin 'double' to burn), they also point out that in the real photo (which is helpfully printed side by side with a still from a scene in the film) there doesn't look to be a trail of fuel there at all. They go on to add, "Furthermore, the petrol container is positioned about a metre behind Duc, while in the film, the canister is taken away and placed in the vicinity of the vehicle visible in the background. The assisting priest, kneeling by the vehicle in the film is not evident in the photo. As the fireball engulfs the man it travels from the right, yet the photograph shows the right side of Duc's face and shoulder to be free of flame."

Kerekes and Slater put forward some interesting points, and viewers should bare those in mind while watching the film. The photo – which was later used as an album cover by Rage Against the Machine in 1992 – shows various inconsistencies when compared with the scene in the film. Self-immolation was a common form of protest used by Buddhists in Vietnam at the time, and for that reason alone the scene does at least have some credibility (many similar types of protest were also filmed, if not for the purpose of entertainment). But whether real or not, it's unlikely that the scene in *Mondo Cane 2* shows the burning of Quang Duc.

The rest of the film presents the usual bizarre practices from across the globe, including American cops disguised in drag as a way of capturing street muggers and sex offenders, a brief S&M sequence shot in a torture dungeon, Indian fakirs demonstrating various stunts, such as having pins pushed into flesh, and, in the final sequence, we get to witness a supposed real slave auction in the Congo; drought and destitution has led to many villagers deciding to sell themselves as labour. The villagers are beaten by their potential owners as a way of testing their strength. Real or staged, this is all very depressing, especially when the slaves smile throughout their ordeal to show that they're a tough and durable slave force.

Mondo Cane 2 (pronounced 'Mondo Cannay' by the way) comes across as even more sensational and exploitative than its controversial predecessor. But surprisingly, the film didn't receive the same kind of world-wide press coverage as the original film. International journalists were perhaps aware of how their collective column inches dedicated to the first film had helped to catapult it to box-office gold (as the famously stuffy critic, Leslie Halliwell noted, "It's huge commercial success made one worry for the world"), and this time decided not to aid the sleazy sequel in achieving the same goal.

No matter how much the critics disliked the film, Jacopetti and Prosperi did at least have inexperience and naïveté on their side, which perhaps spared them from the ultimate condemnation by the press. This sequel, however, shows the film-makers more in their true colours – as a pair of immoral opportunists prepared to orchestrate anything for the sake of sensationalism, no matter how crude or debased it may be. Ultimately, *Mondo Cane 2* does a lot to drop the pretence of it being a factual documentary, and instead seems happy enough to parade its shock sequences with a gleeful edge. It's a film which wears its vulgarities on its sleeve. The pair returned with the even more disturbing *Africa Addio* in 1967.

Gualtiero Jacopetti

I suppose the worst thing you could say about *Mondo Cane 2* is that it presents to us the pessimism and inhumanity that Jacopetti himself was often accused of in his private life – the fact that he personified the very evils that he purported to condemn in his films. Born in Northern Italy in 1919, Jacopetti was the only child of a wealthy middle class family. His childhood fascination with Italy's colonial wars in Africa led to his life-long passion for travel and adventure. He volunteered as a soldier in Mussolini's army. Jacopetti was then stationed in Albania, an experience which opened his eyes to the cruelty of his fellow man as he witnessed various atrocities as part of serving in the fascist army. According to The Center for Relief to Civilian Populations (Geneva), Albania was one of the most devastated countries during the war.

During the early post-war years, he tried his hand at acting but wasn't very successful. He later spent some time as a globe-trotting photo-journalist, where his intention was to shock by travelling to the most war-ravaged parts of the planet and documenting everything he saw there. His work for the Italian 'News From Around the World' newsreel service made him famous. Those featurettes which made his name were similar to the British Pathé reels (1910-1970), except the Italian versions often included lots of explicit violence – and naked women – to spice things up. Working freelance in a very freewheeling way, Jacopetti was very much his own boss. After years out in the wilderness of the world he secured his reputation of being a seasoned veteran, a hard-nosed pessimist who would venture absolutely anywhere to find 'newsworthy' shots. Even at this point of his career, sensationalism was the only thing that seemed to interest him. Anything sleazy or offensive and Jacopetti was there, camera in hand. Fellow cynic Bill Landis described him as "the eyeball peeking into hell and bringing it home."

It's easy to view Jacopetti as a glamorous adventurer. He had that restlessness and danger about him. Indeed, he seemed to live his life much in the same way as Candide in Voltaire's novella (which happened to be his favourite book). He was a free agent, a lone maverick travelling the world, doing as he pleased, and getting paid for it; the envy of millions. But he was also the subject of many a scandal in his time, which in retrospect makes his constant travelling look like he was running away from something. And his behaviour – both with a camera and behind the scenes in his private life – makes it difficult to admire him. He hit the headlines in Italy in the mid-50s when the father of his thirteen-year-old 'girlfriend' coerced them into marriage. He later told the papers he was impotent, even though the girl was pregnant with his baby.

Jacopetti got involved with feature production in the late 50s; he wrote the narration and also shot some of the footage for *Mondo Di Notte* (*World By Night*). During this time, he was in a casual relationship with British actress Belinda Lee, who had appeared in the *St. Trinians* comedies. She remained romantically attached to him even though he was caught in a hotel room in Hong Kong with two girls aged just ten and eleven. He spent time in jail in 1960, but was typically defiant, arrogant and in denial about the seriousness of his crime (a trait not uncommon in paedophiles). He insisted he had done nothing wrong, claiming "the two girls were prostitutes and I paid." A year later, while drunk-driving to Los Angeles, he was involved in a high-speed collision which killed Belinda Lee and injured members of his film crew who were also in the car. Jacopetti himself badly injured his arm and almost had to have it amputated. In the aftermath of the accident, he received much attention from the paparazzi who photographed him attending events accompanied by women who were much younger than him.

It was also in the early 60s when he teamed up with Franco Prosperi, and together they created *Mondo Cane*. And the rest is history. The power of their mondo movies came from avoiding the Italian traditions of neorealism, a filmic trend pioneered by people like Luchino Visconti, Roberto Rossellini and Federico Fellini. They abandoned the neorealist principles in favour of 'hyper-realism', often referred to as 'shockumentary' because of its brutal edits ("shock cuts", Jacopetti once called them), rapid zooms, heightened post-production sound effects and sharp contrasts between the rough and ready *mise-en-scène* and Ritz Ortolani's hauntingly beautiful music scores.

After *Mondo Cane 2*, the mondo genre flourished across the world, reaching a saturation point in 1967, just in time for the dubious duo to return once again with *Africa Addio*. This book is filled with characters whom straight society would call shady – Jodorowsky, Buttgereit, D'Amato, et al – people of supposed 'ill-repute' who shouldn't be doing what they're doing; people who use film-making as a smoke-screen for other – sometimes illicit – purposes. Buñuel made his movies as a way of attacking bourgeois values; Todd Solondz makes his films to highlight the overall crumminess of humanity. During the late 70s and early 80s, Ruggero Deodato and Umberto Lenzi looked to be in some kind of competition to see who could create the most outrageous film. But even among such outrageous company as those mentioned above, Gualtieri Jacopetti is still among the most disagreeable men to have ever held a movie camera; a "depraved hedonist" and heartless narcissist – he not so much attracted controversy as actively sought it, which made him the perfect individual to head out into the big bad world with a big bad attitude, to 'document' the worst he could find in human nature, and shove the results in our faces. As Bill Landis put it, "He was born for the job."

Jacopetti died in 2011 aged 91. Upon his death, he received many write-ups in the press, including the *Guardian*, but none of them addressed his darker side. All the articles I read had smoothed over his convictions for sleeping with under-age prostitutes and his inhumane activities in making his films. Perhaps the most fitting tribute to Jacopetti was paid by JG Ballard in his novel *The Atrocity Exhibition*, in which he included a fictional "Jacopetti exhibition" which incorporated his aggressive filming style.

At Midnight I Will Take Your Soul (1964)
(Orig title: *A Meta-Noite Laverei Sua Alma*)
Dir: Jose Mojica Marins /Brazil
Welcome to the strange films of Jose Mojica Marins, a heady mixture of Gothic horror and desolate cruelty, wanton surrealism and German Expressionism, Catholic guilt and Nietzschean nihilism. He wrote, directed, produced, and starred in Brazil's first ever horror movie, and created that country's most infamous character, the cackling gravedigger known as *Ze do Caixao* (or 'Coffin Joe').

His horror career began in 1964 with *At Midnight I Will Take Your Soul*, which offers up two introductions before the film itself begins; one from Coffin Joe himself, and another from an old gypsy woman who urges viewers to leave the theatre before it's too late... Coffin Joe is the undertaker of a desolate village who attacks the residents for his own warped amusement. He keeps the local women in bondage and tortures them with deadly spiders, picks fights in bars, eats meat on Good Friday, and cuts off someone's finger with a broken bottle. Turns out that Coffin Joe is looking for the perfect female to be the mother of his son, but the residents don't seem to offer any suitable candidates, that is until the beautiful Terezinha shows up.

Shot in thirteen days, *At Midnight* is a remarkable achievement for a home-made horror movie. Taking its inspiration from the Universal horror cycle of the 30s and the EC comic books of the 50s (especially *Tales From The Crypt*), it also bares a close resemblance to the work of Mario Bava (the graveyard scenes in *Black Sunday*), and Terence Fisher (whose 50s Hammer horrors were also a big influence on Marins). All of the actors used in the film were non-professional, either friends or relatives of the director, and they did a remarkable job, especially the young women who underwent all

manner of discomfort and humiliation in the making of the film.

It is Marins himself though who deserves the bulk of the credit for single-handedly creating the Brazilian horror genre and creating its most infamous son, the maniac with long curly fingernails, top hat, and piercing eyes (you only have to look at pictures of Coffin Joe and Strewwelpeter to know who Freddy Krueger's parents really are). *At Midnight* became a huge hit with audiences in Brazil where it played non-stop for sixteen months in Sao Paulo alone while Catholics complained of its blasphemous content. But this kind of interference from the nation's Catholics did nothing to quell Marins' thirst for the forbidden; he would return a couple of years later for the even *more* outrageous *This Night I'll Possess Your Corpse*.

Two Thousand Maniacs! (1964)
Dir: Herschell Gordon Lewis /USA
While driving out in the country, three couples end up in a strange town called Pleasant Valley where the whole community gives them a warm welcome and free lodgings. When the visitors begin to disappear, however, the remaining couple suspect that all is not well and begin plotting their escape. Turns out that the whole town is populated by Confederate ghosts of those slaughtered during the American Civil War, and who re-appear every one hundred years to exact revenge on the Yankee tourists.

Though technically more proficient than the earlier *Blood Feast*, *Two Thousand Maniacs!* holds back on the gore in comparison with Lewis' earlier outing, but there are still some wonderful murder set pieces here – the thumb-slicing and subsequent dismemberment with an axe isn't just graphic; the camera seems to linger on the scene for much longer than any other film-maker would deem necessary. More sadism ensues with some poor guy being drawn and quartered between two horses pulling in opposite directions; another man is forced into a spiked barrel and rolled down a hill; and a woman is crushed to death by a huge boulder during a strange game of dare. And all of these atrocities are committed in front of the local yokels who clap and cheer the proceedings like enthusiastic parents at a school sports day gathering. With this film, HG Lewis chooses to build up to the murder scenes to give them more impact rather than bombard the audience with blood and guts, and the film is all the better for it. This time the horror is drawn-out and more disturbing, resulting in a vast improvement over *Blood Feast*.

Color Me Blood Red (1965)
Dir: Herschell Gordon Lewis /USA
A troubled production, this tells the tale of Adam Sorg (Don Joseph), a frustrated artist who resorts to using human blood in his paintings. And before long, he ends up on a killing spree, wiping out his girlfriend and local residents for the sake of his art. Inspired by Roger Corman's *A Bucket of Blood* (1959) and going on to inspire Abel Ferrara's *The Driller Killer* (1979), *Color Me Blood Red* sees a definite drop in quality since the previous *Two Thousand Maniacs!* (1964). It's a claustrophobic take on encroaching madness that lacks the style and energy of his earlier films. Lewis and his producer, David F. Friedman, parted ways, and the movie was finished in post-production without their involvement, and that could perhaps explain the subdued mood and visual inconsistencies. Friedman continued in film production for years, with softcore credits like *The Erotic Adventures of Zorro* (1972), horror items such as *She Freak* (1967), and the notorious *Ilsa, She Wolf of The SS* (1975). Lewis continued making movies but didn't return to the gore genre until 1967 when he unleashed *The Gruesome Twosome*.

The 10th Victim (1965)
(Orig title: *La decima vittima*)
Dir: Elio Petri /Italy /France
Perhaps the closest thing to a snuff theme in 60s cinema was *The 10th Victim*, an Italian/French co-production set in the near future where the Big Hunt is a popular form of televised entertainment. Contestants are given weapons to hunt victims, with the opportunity – for both the hunters and the surviving victims – to earn a fortune. Ten years later and Paul Bartel took a similar theme of televised murder entertainment and added a welcome dose of graphic gore and satire in the cult classic *Death Race 2000* (1975). And the hunting theme was later updated in minor gems like *The Running Man* (1987), *Hard Target* (1993), *Battle Royale* (2000), *Slashers* (2001), *The Condemned* (2007) and *Series 7: The Contenders* (2001), the latter updating the reality TV satire to great effect.

The Wild Angels (1966)
Dir: Roger Corman /USA
The biker movie was a short-lived genre which came roaring into the American drive-in theatres in the mid-60s and went crashing to a halt in the early 70s, leaving behind a brief but brilliant back catalogue of atrocities and a reckless amoral culture whose grubby outsider characters would often burn out in a blaze of nihilistic glory. Forerunners to the genre were everywhere, from studio releases (*The Wild One*), exploitation road movies (*Faster Pussycat Kill! Kill!*), to underground mythologising (*Scorpio Rising*). But with the publication in 1965 of Hunter S. Thompson's landmark book, *Hell's Angels: The Strange and Terrible Saga of the Outlaw Motorcycle Gangs*, the public's interest in these shady characters had elevated the gangs into pop heroes, and it was only a matter of time before some bright spark in the movie business came along and put their crude and dangerous exploits onto the big screen. Enter Roger Corman.

Perhaps the most important figure in the history of indie film, producer/director Corman and his AIP production house unleashed *The Wild Angels* in 1966. With its amoral anti-heroes, grim and gritty style, and overall unredeeming stories supposedly based on true events, the critics at the time labelled the film as dangerous garbage. The punters didn't agree though, and *The Wild Angels* was soon breaking AIP's box-office records and inspired a whole slew of imitators over the following years, but none of them could match the gruelling charm of Corman's epic which to this day remains the greatest biker movie ever made.

From its opening shots, *The Wild Angels* is a grim and nasty joyride with the film's only positive statement coming from its leading man, Peter Fonda ("We want to be free to ride our machines without being hassled by The Man. And we want to get loaded"). Fonda is the leader of his gang, The Heavenly Blues, a ragtag group of social misfits and psychos who tear through the land and get into fights with gangs of "taco benders" and rednecks. A nurse gets KO'd, and there's much looting and dope smoking as the outlaw riders thrive on defying the authorities.

The film culminates in the outrageous funeral scene where Fonda's deceased buddy, Loser (Bruce Dern), is laid to rest amid bongo drum beats and sloshes of cheap plonk. But the service soon becomes a full-scale riot as the boys systematically destroy the church, sit Buddy's corpse up with a joint in its mouth, rape the poor widow, and beat the crap out of the priest before dumping his body into an empty casket.

On the casting front, Fonda stepped up for the role after first choice actor George Chakiris dropped out after refusing to ride a chopper, and he looks born for the part with his uber-cool line deliveries, backed up by his horde of delinquents in black leathers and sporting swastikas which add to the transgressive shenanigans on display. Bruce Dern is also great as Loser, a snarling scumbag who is shot by a cop and whose last words ("I just want to get high") would echo throughout the whole counter-culture movement. Lookout for Nancy Sinatra who seems to be around to confirm that she can't act for shit. And also Peter Bogdanovich helped out behind the camera, and who of course would go on to bigger and better things in the following years.

The film was unique for its time in that the entire movie is seen from the perspective of the gang members themselves with no outsider characters present to offer an objectified and/or moral counterpoint. Ironically, *The Wild Angels* played at the Venice Film Festival in 1966 as the only American film entry that year. And the film's box-office kerching meant that the floodgates were opened for a slew of oddball imitators, from the good (*Hells Angels On Wheels*, 1967), the bad (*Angels From Hell*, 1968), and the downright crude (*Satan's Sadists*, 1969).

The biker film was a passing fad which came and went, having given a leg-up to rising stars like Fonda and Dern, and also Jack Nicholson and Dennis Hopper, before revving off into oblivion. The posters and ad campaigns were aggressive and sleazy, the entertainment was built on wanton cruelty and debased behaviour, the anti-heroes were cool but also dirtball scumbags, but for the exploitation crowd it was filmic heaven. Those films prided themselves on violence, sex, and chaos, and delighted in driving a wedge between the fans and the mainstream of society. And that is something to be celebrated indeed.

Django (1966)
Dir: Sergio Corbucci /Italy /Spain

Made to cash-in on the runaway success of Sergio Leone's Dollars trilogy with Clint Eastwood, *Django* is an altogether more downbeat affair with a bloody and pessimistic viewpoint making it legendary among spaghetti western and cult movie fanatics. A major success across Europe at the time, *Django* failed to make much of an impact in America but has gradually won the hearts and minds of Stateside fans in the ensuing years, and was recently 're-imagined' by Quentin Tarantino for his major production, *Django Unchained*.

The film opens with the title character walking through a bleak and desolate landscape dragging a coffin behind him. And after rescuing a woman about to be burned alive, he strolls into a whorehouse and gets himself in trouble with the local bandits who shoot Mexicans for fun. And after dealing with the red-hooded bad guys in bloody fashion, he finds himself caught in the middle of a war between a crooked Major and a group of Mexican outlaws, all of whom are interested to find out what Django keeps in his coffin.

This is a rough and dirty piece of work, both in terms of its themes and its look. But what it lacks in polish and sophistication is more than made up for in its grubby and downbeat edge. The title character is a quietly sinister rogue, a true anti-hero. Whereas Eastwood's 'man with no name' character was likeable despite his moral ambiguity, it's difficult to feel the same about Django because it's obvious from the start that he is a heartless and selfish bastardo. He's no different from the wily scum he's fighting against; he's just as much concerned with greed and lust, except he's cooler and more laid back about it.

The violence was, um, cutting edge for its time, especially in the scene where a man has his ear sliced off and is forced to eat it, and the Gatling gun massacres pre-date the excessive violence of Sam Peckinpah's *The Wild Bunch*. Franco Nero is in fine form in the lead role (Tarantino later gave him a cameo in *Django Unchained*), Loredana Nusciak is passable as the lovelorn redhead even though she doesn't have much to do except be humiliated by Django and shot. José Bódalo, who plays General Hugo Rodriguez, is also pretty good in an over-the-top kind of way. And curiously, in some scenes his chubby cheeks look like buttocks, so it's difficult to concentrate on his performance without thinking his mouth is about to flatulate at any moment. But face-farting aside, *Django* is a diamond in the rough and still packs a punch today.

Titicut Follies (1967)
Dir: Frederick Wiseman /USA
Appearing in the early 90s after a mysterious 25 year ban, Frederick Wiseman's feature debut, *Titicut Follies*, is a documentary set in the Bridgewater State Hospital, Massachusetts, where the criminally insane go about their daily bouts of injustice and humiliation alongside the mentally ill. There's no structure to the film as such, no story to follow, no voice-over to tell us what's going on; just grainy black and white images capturing the incompetence and despair, fly-on-the-wall-style, in a mental institution.

There are some disturbing moments – a clearly distressed inmate gets naked and goes berserk in his cell, frank exchanges about mutual masturbation between inmates and screws, and what appears to be a deceased inmate propped up in a chair being shaved, presumably to smarten his appearance for the funeral. But there's nothing sensationalist or exploitative in the approach of the film-makers. Alongside the sporadic hygiene of the institution, hunger strikes, force-feeding through tubes inserted down the throat, and general victimization, the patients and guards put on their annual show, the Titicut Follies, a musical play which offers a brief respite from the daily horrors.

The controversy started just prior to the film's premier at the 1967 New York Film Festival when the government of Massachusetts tried to have the film banned on the basis that it violated the patients' privacy and dignity. In watching the film, however, one can't help thinking that it was the detached observations that served as a shocking indictment of the institution that was causing the real concern, not the welfare of those depicted. And the film was allowed to be shown. But in the following year, the Massachusetts' Superior Court ordered all copies to be removed and destroyed after a social worker complained of a scene which shows a naked man being tormented by a guard. Director Wiseman appealed against the decision and a compromise was reached whereby only doctors, lawyers, and healthcare professionals were permitted to view the film. Wiseman

appealed again, this time to the Supreme Court, but he was basically shunned. This was the first time that a film was banned from the general public on grounds other than obscenity, immorality, or national security in America, with Wiseman frustrated that the court restrictions were "a greater infringement of civil liberties than the film was an infringement on the liberties of the inmates."

It wasn't until 1991 that the film was deemed acceptable for public consumption, by which time the damage had already been done. Whereas contemporary films like *Cathy Come Home* did a lot to change British attitudes towards poverty and the working classes, *Titicut Follies* could have had a similar impact on American attitudes towards incompetent institutions and the mentally ill, were it not for the authorities being terrified of being portrayed in a bad light, and scurrying around trying to have the film banished to save their own reputations rather than their most vulnerable citizens. Shame on them. Indeed, had the film reached its rightful audience in the first place, there's a good chance that institutions like the Bridgewater State Hospital would have been either closed down for good or had their services dramatically improved. But the place remained open for decades, stacking up case after case of death and neglect; the most infuriating being the case of an inmate who, according to his representative, Steven Schwartz, was "restrained for two and a half months and given six psychiatric drugs at vastly unsafe levels", and who eventually "choked to death because he could not swallow his food". That's censorship for you; rarely makes things better, often makes things worse.

At least now the film has its rightful place in cinema history, with luminaries such as Nick Broomfield and Marc Singer accepting Wiseman's compelling film as a crucial document of its time, with Singer's 2000 documentary *Dark Days* taking inspiration from Wiseman's work and cementing its long overdue legacy for the downtrodden masses. Tough stuff then, but honest to a fault.

Branded To Kill (1967)
(Orig title: *Koroshi no rakuin*)
Dir: Seijun Suzuki /Japan
Japan has produced many risque and unique film-makers over the decades, from Koji Wakamatsu (*The Embryo Hunts In Secret*),

Teruo Ishii (*Horrors of Malformed Men*), and Norifumi Suzuki (*School of the Holy Beast*), to latter day saints like Shinya Tsukamoto (*A Snake of June*), Takeshi Kitano (*Violent Cop*), and Takashi Miike (*Gozu*). But nowhere will you find a more unique talent under such restricted conditions as Seijun Suzuki, an uber-prolific artist who was as inventive as anyone working in the medium, and who was producing up to four movies per year at the height of his powers whilst maintaining a distinctly wacko style all of his own.

Branded To Kill is his finest hour, a strange nihilistic hitman movie made in the late 60s for the Nikkatsu Corporation, Japan's biggest film studio that released a couple of new movies every week due to their frantic schedule. Nikkatsu demanded that their film-makers have only one week for pre-production, three weeks to shoot the film, and three days for editing. Ironically, working under such hectic circumstances seemed to bring out the best in Suzuki who thrived on a spontaneous approach to film-making, and he would add all kinds of surreal and perverse touches to his pictures, much to the annoyance of the execs at Nikkatsu who had continually warned him against it. But the great Suzuki would just carry on regardless.

The plot of *Branded To Kill* concerns lone hitman, Hanada Goro (Jo Shishido), who is ranked third in his assassination organisation but is under some stiff competition. He becomes obsessed with Misako (Annu Mari), a femme fatale who has her own fixation on dead birds and butterflies. She recruits him for a seemingly impossible contract killing, and when he fails in his mission due to some blackly comic timing, he becomes the target of the Number One ranked hitman, known only as The Phantom, whose methods of hunting threaten Goro's sanity just as much as his life...

Branded To Kill borrows elements from classic American noir, French new wave, and the expressionistic style of *The Cabinet of Dr. Caligari*, but Suzuki blends those disparate elements into something fresh, exciting, and original. It's a confusing tale for many, but it's also astonishing to look at; almost every frame in the film is perfected to Kubrick-esque proportions, even if many of those frames contains images of demented sexuality and shockingly casual violence. The result is a feast for the eyes and the brain, as beautiful as it is outrageous, seductive and repulsive,

entertaining and appalling.

The executives at Nikkatsu were not impressed with Suzuki's freewheeling style, and they immediately fired him for making "movies that make no sense and no money." But in the meantime he became something of an icon among the counter-culture movement, and after much prompting from fellow film-makers, like-minded students, and the general public, Suzuki successfully sued Nikkatsu for wrongful dismissal. Suzuki was henceforth blacklisted and unable to direct another feature for years.

Branded To Kill's reputation has gradually flourished over the decades into cult classic status, and is generally considered to be an 'absurdist masterpiece', and has achieved a certain level of international art house acclaim, with luminaries like Jim Jarmusch, John Woo, and of course Quentin Tarantino all citing Suzuki's film as an influence on their own works.

Theatre of Death (1967)
(aka *Blood Fiend*)
Dir: Samuel Gallu /UK
A Paris-set mystery which offers one of Christopher Lee's finest performances. The grumbly-voiced actor plays a theatre director who puts on macabre, *grand guignol*-type shows about the occult. When a wave of vampiric murders sweeps the city with bodies turning up drained of all their blood, Lee and his team fall under instant suspicion. *Theatre of Death* has been a cult favourite for decades, a film which soaks up every tired cliché of the horror genre and then turns them on their heads for the spectacular finale. It isn't as bloody or as delirious as Herschell Gordon Lewis' similarly themed *The Wizard of Gore* (1967), which was made around the same time, but it has its fair share of camp charms all of its own.

The Gruesome Twosome (1967)
Dir: Herschell Gordon Lewis /USA
This looks to be a gory spoof on *The Adams Family*. The story follows the criminal escapades of a wig store owner, Mrs. Pringle (Elizabeth Davis) and her retarded son, Rodney (Chris Martell) who lure college girls into the shop so that Rodney can scalp them in graphic detail with an electric carving knife. Heavy on jokes and silliness this time around, *The Gruesome Twosome* is the one which includes the legendary opening scene of two styrofoam

heads having a conversation before one of them is stabbed. Lewis claimed he shot that sequence simply to bring the production up to the required feature length. Another troubled production, the cast and crew were thrown out of one particular shooting location after the 'electrician' accidentally set fire to the place.

Goke: Body Snatcher From Hell (1968)
(Orig title: *Kyuketsuki Gokemidoro*)
Dir: Hajime Sato /Japan
In the early 00s, DVD and video companies were falling over themselves to uncover and release the most bizarre and twisted treasures they could find. And DVD addicts were spoilt for choice with the sheer amount of cult material on the shelves. And when Quentin Tarantino paid homage to *Goke: Body Snatcher From Hell* in a key sequence in *Kill Bill Vol.1* (look for the red skies), it was only a matter of time before a company came along and released the film in an anamorphic, digitally-remastered transfer. *Goke* is an obscure sci-fi/horror/disaster movie from Japan that somehow manages to cram a jetliner diverted by a bomb threat, a fleeing political assassin out to prolong the Vietnam War, a close encounter with a UFO, and a crash in the wilderness into the first ten minutes pre-credits sequence. After that, things become even more bizarre as blue jello creatures ooze in and out of vertical slots in character's heads, which turns them into vampiric aliens who lament on mankind's destructive ways. Long live DVD!

The Devil Rides Out (1968)
Dir: Terence Fisher /UK
One of the high points of British horror in the 60s, Christopher Lee gets to momentarily drop his Dracula cape and take on the hero role in this Richard Matherson-adapted tale based on Dennis Wheatley's novel about a naïve young man, Patrick Mower, who dabbles with evil. It was brought to the screen by director Terence Fisher, a man who had a knack for creating unmatchable scenes of delirious Satanic rites. Wheatley was the Stephen King of his day, and sold paperbacks by the shed load. He wrote before, during and after the war, but hit paydirt in the 50s and 60s with the arrival of the mass paperback market. His books can be on the lengthy side, but he was one of the first modern novelists to explore the themes of Arthur Machen and Arthur Collier. And he took his subject seriously enough to include a preface

warning his readers not to mess around with the black arts. The film reaches a climactic point of full-on allegorical melodrama with the night of the pentacle during which the forces of evil are met head-on by Lee. *The Devil Rides Out* is also notable for introducing aspects of mythology that the cinema had completely ignored up to that point.

Night of the Living Dead (1968)
Dir: George Romero /USA
Often described as the first truly modern horror film (although a case can be made for the early gore films of Herschell Gordon Lewis), George Romero's *Night of the Living Dead* began a turning point in genre film-making and introduced thousands of movie-goers to verite ambiance for the first time. But horror fans often need reminding that *this movie is not perfect*. It was a cheap, low-budget B-movie with a non-professional cast and largely inexperienced crew who just so happened to catch Vietnam and the civil rights struggle on TV news reports, and set about creating lurid documentary-like images for a true nightmare on film.

Barbra and her brother John visit a cemetery to place flowers on a relative's grave; but they are attacked out of the blue by a lumbering zombie. Barbra flees to a farmhouse where she meets a group of survivors, and together they are forced to put their differences aside if they are to fend off the hordes of flesh eaters who are trying to force their way in, before the shockingly casual and nihilistic ending.

Barbra isn't a tough heroine ready for battle against the undead, she spends much of the movie in an almost catatonic state; this being Romero's way of taking away viewer control. By focusing on a surrogate character who sinks into a helpless state, Romero succeeds in irritating the viewers and making them feel uncomfortable by not being able to control what's happening on screen. And when Barbra does finally pull herself together and finds the courage to take a stand against the ghouls, she is rather ironically eaten by her zombified brother. This was a real break from the norm in horror films at the time. With this film the floodgates of modern horror were opened: Heroes, heroines, and good people of all kinds are just as likely to be killed as anyone else; everything was not going to be okay in the end; our fellow humans could be just as monstrous as the monsters. The film's bad guy, Harry Cooper, insists on having everyone hide in the basement in the farmhouse, but the black hero, Ben (Duane Jones), refuses to be holed up down there – an understandable decision. However, this turns out to be a big mistake later on. – the bad guy is later proved to have made the right choice by offering to barricade everyone in the basement.

Perhaps Romero's central message was that *we are the zombies*, you and I, our friends and loved ones. On DVD, be sure to stick with Romero's original version and avoid at all costs the 30th Anniversary Edition which includes a terrible synth piano score and some dreadful extra scenes that were shot 30 years later and do nothing but obstruct the story.

Also contrary to popular belief is the fact that although *Night of the Living Dead* is one of the greatest and most influential horror films ever made, it didn't have an immediate impact on the zombie movies that followed in its wake; *Tombs of the Blind Dead*, *Messiah of Evil*, *Shockwaves*, *The Living Dead at the Manchester Morgue*, *Sugar Hill and Her Zombie Hitmen*, etc; all of those films differed radically in zombie lore from Romero's shuffling rotting corpses of *NOTLD*. It wasn't until Romero unleashed the second part of the series, *Dawn of the Dead*, a decade later did we see other film-makers following suit, with Lucio Fulci's *Zombie Flesh Eaters* (released in Italy as an unofficial sequel to *Dawn*), *City of the Living Dead*, and Jean Rollin's *Grapes of Death* and *Zombie Lake* willing to promulgate Romero's basic vision of the zombie as a walking corpse that dines on warm human flesh. But still, even after *Dawn of the Dead*, other film-makers continued to take the myth elsewhere – Fulci with *The Beyond* and Gary Sherman with *Dead and Buried*, for example.

Over the years *NOTLD* has been rejected, celebrated, over-analysed, discovered, rediscovered, colourised, remade, extended, re-released, sequelized, ripped off, and spoofed to such an extent that it's difficult to make sense of its initial impact. The film is widely accepted now as a bona-fide genre classic, but for many years it was accused of having a negative effect on viewers. Produced for less than $150,000 and rejected by Columbia because it was in black and white, and rejected by AIP because it had no love story and a downbeat ending, *NOTLD* was then relegated to playing at matinees where it scared the crap out of an entire generation before showing up on the midnight circuit, becoming one of the most successful indie movies of all time.

Flesh (1968)
(aka *Andy Warhol's Flesh*; aka *Flesh 18*)
Dir: Paul Morrisey /USA

As Andy Warhol recuperated from the gunshot wounds inflicted by Valerie Solanis, his Factory associate Paul Morrisey took the chance to emerge from under the master's cloak and directed this drowsy, picaresque tale of a henpecked male prostitute in Manhattan, the first of several 'Warhol' films that are actually part of Morrisey's equally interesting *ouevre*.

Joe (Joe Dallesandro), a virtually affectless but oddly charming creature of the East Village, drags himself out of bed to hustle tricks on 33rd Street. His girlfriend Gerry (Geraldine Smith) has demanded cash to pay for an abortion. During a long day of entrepreneurial improvisation Joe encounters a variety of Warhol regulars, including legendary transvestites Jackie Curtis and Candy Darling (who, along with Dallesandro, were later immortalized in Lou Reed's classic tune '*Walk On the Wild Side*'). Although *Flesh* displays many of the hallmarks of Warhol's non-narrative Factory style (endless takes, speed-fuelled improvisation, casually amateurish lighting and sound, etc), Morrisey is already experimenting with the kind of traditional film-making techniques that Warhol pretended to dislike – at least until Morrisey's increasingly polished movies began turning nice profits.

Viewers today will still find this film to be quite shocking in places, and many will struggle to handle the fact that the film was made entirely in-camera (basically, the whole film is presented as exactly the way it was shot; in sequence, with lots of very long shots, jump cuts, etc) but this is the film that made an underground star of Dallesandro, and was widely considered a ground-breaking revelation on first release for portraying New York's underground life.

In interviews, Morrisey's opinions on drug culture, art-groupies, Andy Warhol, and sex movies in general can sound quite harsh and hypocritical at first, but his conservative stance doesn't contradict his films. His values may lean to the right but his manner and opinions on art are actually very liberal. Rather than lecturing his viewers on morality, he allows liberal ideals to express themselves in his films, and watches as they consequently contradict themselves in the process (as they do in the sequel, *Trash*, for example, specifically the scene in which a government health worker visits a family home).

Morrisey rejects the idea of censorship, even in cultural forms he strongly disapproves of, and is happy to challenge the so-called freedoms we take for granted. Ultimately, his films are loaded with a strong sense of humanity and sympathy, even when depicting characters whose values he disagrees with. And it's perhaps his stubbornly individualistic stance that led him to be regarded as uncool among the clingers-on at the Warhol Factory back in the old days.

The best option on DVD is the box set from Tartan which also includes the loose sequels, *Trash* and *Heat*, and an audio commentary. This is an old 16mm film so don't expect to impress your friends with super-duper audio/visual quality, but is the best transfer of the film you'll probably ever see, considering the source materials. And it is at least tons better than those old VHS copies that were floating around back in the day.

Targets (1968)
Dir: Peter Bogdanovich /USA
Peter Bogdanovich got his start in the movie industry at AIP as a protege of Roger Corman. Recognising him as the writer of film articles in *Esquire*, Corman invited him to write film scripts. And in a very short space of time, he landed the gig of Corman's assistant on *The Wild Angels* (1966), perhaps the greatest biker movie ever made. Years later, Bogdanovich acknowledged the importance of the experience on his film-making career: "Although I worked 22 weeks – pre-production, shooting, second unit, cutting, dubbing – I haven't learned so much since."

Corman gave Bogdanovich his directorial debut with *Targets*, which has since become a minor classic in its own right. The film only came into being because Boris Karloff owed Corman two days shooting work. He also had around twenty minutes of unused footage from an earlier horror film, *The Terror* (1963), which he encouraged Bogdanovich to use. Corman assumed that the young film-maker would fashion a Poe-like tale, but instead he delivered an original modern-day scenario in which Karloff basically plays himself as an old horror icon called Byron Orlok. Bogdanovich plays a young director trying to make a horror movie, and this is cross-cut with a parallel story about a madman who murders his family and then goes on a shooting rampage, firing from the top of a water tower, and later from behind a drive-in movie screen where Orlok is making his guest appearance. And it's this latter sequence in which Bogdanovich inserts the previously unused *Terror* footage.

The debut film-maker managed to pull it off thanks to the encouragement of his mentor whom Bogdanovich quotes as saying, "You can shoot 20 minutes with Karloff in two days. I've shot whole pictures in two days!" *Targets* is very much inspired by the French new wave movement, and specifically by film-makers like Francois Truffaut and Claude Chabrol. He also draws on the time he spent as an auteur film critic in *Esquire*, offering subtle references to Hitchcock's *Psycho* (1960) and Orson Welles' *Touch of Evil* (1958). The film is loosely based on the true case of the Texas tower sniper, Charles Whitman, a former marine who shot dead his mother and fourteen random strangers in August 1966.

The Bird With the Crystal Plumage (1969)
(aka *Phantom of Terror*; aka *The Gallery Murders*)
(Orig title: *L'uccello dalle piume di cristallo*)
Dir: Dario Argento /Italy
Argento's debut sees American writer, Sam Dalmas, staying in Rome with his girlfriend (Suzy Kendall) and who becomes an eye-witness to an attempted murder in an art gallery late one night. Sam becomes convinced that in the back of his mind lies a clue that could lead to the identity of the assailant, but he can't quite figure it out (a theme that would later crop up again in *Deep Red* a few years later). After being informed by the police that the attempted murder was probably the handy work of a serial killer who has been hacking and slashing his way across Rome, Sam decides to investigate on his own, in parallel to inspector Morrisini's official investigation...

Boasting a cool, modernist photography by Vittorio Storaro, and a ground-breaking squawky score by Ennio Morricone (featuring Edda dell'Orso on vocals), *The Bird With the Crystal Plumage* introduced us to the motifs which would refigure the giallo and become prevalent throughout Argento's career. In this film, knives are no longer plain old murder weapons, but cherished instruments of death kept in cases to be admired and fetishized as well as to slice and dice the victims.

Sam Dalmas was the first of Argento's characters to fail to recognise the 'fairer sex' of being capable of pre-meditated murder – women as victims by the very nature of their gender. When Sam witnesses the attempted murder in the art gallery, he assumes that the aggressor is male, and automatically sets out to rescue the 'damsel in distress'; it isn't until the end of the film that he realises his own gender-related preconceptions have thwarted his pursuit of the killer. It was the woman, Monica, who was brandishing the blade. Even the experienced Inspector Morrisini assumes the killer to be male. Argento transforms the typical conventions of the thriller/giallo by reversing the trend of aggressive and masculine men, and passive, helpless women. And a rather clever move by Argento is that he knew that we too, the viewers, will instinctively assume the killer to be male, perhaps because of movie trends just as much as our own gender-preconceptions.

This was the first in Argento's 'Animal Trilogy' which continued with *The Cat O'Nine Tails* and *Four Flies On Grey Velvet*. The 2-disc set from Blue Underground is the best option on DVD, the best this film has ever looked on home video. The DVD promises "Recently discovered, never-before-seen footage of explicit violence," but this is actually just a couple of seconds at the start of the slashing on the stairwell scene.

The Oblong Box (1969)
Dir: Gordon Hessler /UK
In this tale of witchcraft, disfigurement, murder and grave-robbing, aristocrat Julian (Vincent Price) keeps his mutilated brother, Edward (Alister Williamson), hidden in the attic. And when Edward instructs his lawyer to bring to England the African sorcerer responsible for his disfigurement, Julian refuses to allow them to meet. So, to get round this problem, the lawyer pretends that Edward has died, and the 'body' is removed from the house in an 'oblong box,' a coffin. However, a real dead body comes into the possession of a research pathologist (Christopher Lee). In a panic, Edward pays a doctor to live in the attic and pretend to be him while wearing a scarlet mask to conceal his face. Edward then goes on a killing spree in the nearby town, and things become even *more*

convoluted for the final third... *The Oblong Box* is remembered today primarily as the first film which paired Vincent Price and Christopher Lee together in the same scene. It also has a sombre tone as scriptwriter, Lawrence Huntington, died not long after he completed the screenplay, and the film's original director, Michael Reeves (of *The Sorcerers* and *Witchfinder General*), committed suicide. Gordon Hessler took over the project as producer/director, and he brought in Christopher Wicking to re-write the script. The result is an interesting – if flawed – entry in the British horror tradition of its time that also marks an ambitious attempt to keep the tragedy-stricken project afloat.

Scream and Scream Again (1969)
Dir: Gordon Hessler /UK
The police trace a spate of bloody murders to Vincent Price, a mad scientist suspected of creating a Frankenstein-like race of super-humans constructed from stolen body parts. Set in modern-day London, *Scream and Scream Again* contains lots of action, weird science, super-long car chases and shady bad guys, all designed to cash-in on the Bond craze which was at full-swing at the time. This atypical Brit horror sees the re-teaming of scriptwriter Christopher Wicking and director Gordon Hessler (the pair also collaborated on the troubled *The Oblong Box* in the same year). Here they serve up another complicated tale of madness, murder and body-snatching. Those accustomed to Hammer horrors of old may be less than impressed with the idea of their beloved horror heroes engaging in such modern-day tomfoolery, but others will appreciate the film as an ambitious attempt to keep the slow death of British horror at bay. The producers were not impressed with such modern-day material, and they oversaw a drastic re-cut which the film-makers were deeply unhappy with.

Mark of the Devil (1969)
Dir: Michael Armstrong /West Germany
With a theme tune similar to Ritz Ortolani's for *Cannibal Holocaust*, *Mark of the Devil* presents the activities of an evil, bloodthirsty witchfinder whose devious work is upstaged by an even more sadistic aristocrat who acts in the name of the Church. This is a nasty period horror that was heavily influenced by Michael Reeves' *Witchfinder General* (released the previous

year), but *Mark of the Devil* ups the ante by lingering on graphic scenes of brutal torture – hacked off limbs, burnings, brandings, beatings, rape, tongues "removed by the root," etc. It claims to be based on cases 'taken from historical documents', but the end result looks more like an exploitative cash-in on Reeves' film. *Mark of the Devil* was banned outright in the UK, and an unregulated VHS release quickly disappeared in the 80s. Sick bags were handed out to audiences when the film played in America.

Seven in Darkness (1969)
Dir: Michael Caffey /USA

A group of blind folks on a plane heading for a convention crash land in a stormy wilderness and have to make their way back to civilization on foot. Not only do they have to navigate the hostile terrain, but they are also being picked off by a pack of wolves. This film is absolutely riveting for all the wrong reasons; we have blind people tapping around with their sticks, slipping and rolling down hills, walking into trees and falling through the gaps on railroad bridges. It's played completely straight but feels like a politically incorrect slapstick comedy. I'm surprised it doesn't have more of a cult following among fans of wrong-headed cinema. Maybe it would have if more people actually saw it.

The Honeymoon Killers (1969)
Dir: Leonard Kastle /USA

Bad tempered, overweight nurse, Martha Beck (Shirley Stoler) lives at home with her overbearing mother. Ray Fernandez (Tony Lo Bianco), is a Spanish immigrant and a slimy rat who rips off lonely, middle-aged women of their life savings. The pair meet when Martha decides to join a lonely hearts club at the prompting of her friend Bunny (Doris Roberts, who later showed up in the American sitcom *Everybody Loves Raymond*). Raymond (another one whom everybody seems to love) answers her letters and worms his way into her life. After spending the night with her he steals her cash and bails. However, when Martha discovers how Ray makes his living, she contacts him and arrives at his apartment with mother in tow. She doesn't care how he fucks people over for a living, she is in love and desperately needs him.

At the suggestion of Ray, Martha agrees to put her mother into a nursing home, and the pair hit the road together, swindling more women with Martha posing as his sister. Ray promises to never sleep with any of their victims, and this seems to reassure Martha at first, but her jealousy simmers under the surface. Her jealous rage soon enough boils over, and she crosses the line into murder. And before long, Ray joins in the killing spree, strangling the victims and looting their homes for anything of value.

Sticking fairly close to the real life case in the 1940s on which it is based (in real life, Martha actually dumped her kids to be with Ray, not her mother), this sole directorial outing for opera composer Leonard Kastle is right up there with Charles Laughton's *The Night of the Hunter* and Robin Hardy's *The Wicker Man* in the 'one-off wonder' horror classics. The blunt monochrome imagery, music cues by Gustav Mahler, and powerful performances from the two leads, combine to produce a filmic experience which remains just as raw and visceral today as it must have been for audiences back in the late 60s when it was first released. Actress Stoler, in her debut performance, embodies the role of the vicious Martha with ease, and went on to appear in bit-parts as lesbian prison guards, and also landed herself roles in *The Deerhunter* and *Seven Beauties*. Lo Bianco as Ray matches her all the way, and he went on to bigger projects like *The French Connection, God Told Me To*, and *Nixon*. The rest of the cast members aren't so good. In fact, if they were any more wooden they'd give you splinters.

Director Kastle admirably refuses to romanticise the brutally cold-blooded criminals at the heart of this film. The result could be read as an anti-*Bonnie and Clyde* as it deglamorizes the murders after years of movies that portrayed outlaws as 'cool' and sympathetic. Kastle also adds subtle visual tricks without overdoing things. He allows the incredible story to tell itself with very little in the way of fanfare or sensationalism. The scene where Ray and Martha murder an old woman is presented in a cold, detached manner, with the camera poised on the crime like a fly on the wall. "I need a drink" Ray deadpans after strangling her. Indeed, it's this kind of blunt, no-nonsense imagery and down-at-earth realism which has influenced many other film-makers over the years, such as John Waters and John McNaughton, whose *Henry - Portrait of a Serial Killer* is especially indebted to Kastle's minor classic.

The Honeymoon Killers was originally set to be directed by Martin Scorsese, but he walked off the set due to 'artistic differences' after shooting only a small amount of footage. Kastle was then enlisted to the helm, and he re-wrote the script and stuck to the docu-drama style that Scorsese had initially established. Most of Scorsese's scenes made it into the final cut.

Perhaps people were more trusting of strangers in the 1940s, but even so, the scams Ray and Martha pull off on these women defies belief. If the film wasn't based on a true story, you'd call bullshit when one of the marks hands over $10,000 in cash to a stranger like Ray, who looks like a greased-back porno gigolo, and not a very trustworthy one at that. Lonely or not, it's difficult to feel sympathy for many of these women when they are so blindly gullible.

The couple manages to pass themselves off as brother and sister, and this is also hard to swallow – she's an overweight, explosively jealous Grotbags, and he's a slimy Casanova wannabe with a thick Spanish accent. As blood siblings, they're slightly less convincing than Arnold Schwarzenegger and Danny DeVito in *Twins*. And as a couple, they're about as compatible as shit and strawberry shortcake.

Both Martha and Ray were executed by electric chair at the cheerfully named Sing Sing Prison in 1951. Ray had to be carried to 'Old Sparky' as he was terrified, whereas Martha stubbornly denied doing any wrong, insisting theirs was a love story, and stomped her way to the hot seat without a care. She was too big for the seat, and a team of guards had to wedge her in. Her brains cooked up nicely though.

Horrors of Malformed Men (1969)
(Orig title: *Kyôfu kikei ningen: Edogawa Rampo zenshû*)
Dir: Teruo Ishii /Japan

A film that remains as fierce and offensive now as it did more than forty years ago when it first hit screens in Japan, *Horrors of Malformed Men* gained an instant notoriety in its native land but sadly saw little exposure anywhere else. Made during the late 60s when 'Pinky Violence' was reaching the heights of its popularity, Ishii's seminal shocker is brimful of grotesque imagery, bizarre plot twists, colour-coded flashbacks, and a gleefully un-PC attitude. The film's scandalous reception did nothing to halt the blazing career of one of Japan's foremost purveyors of exploitation, and is essential viewing for anyone interested in the stranger side of celluloid.

Based on the disturbing novel, *The Strange Tale of Panorama Island*, by celebrated horror maestro Edogawa Rampo, the film follows medical student Hirosuke Hitomi (Teruo Yoshida) on his surreal journey to trace his doppelganger who died under mysterious circumstances. His search eventually leads to a strange volcanic island populated by deformed and disfigured humans who seem to be under the rule of a mad scientist with webbed fingers. In a series of flashbacks we learn more about this madman who may or may not be Hirosuke's father, and also other bizarre and grotesque bits like evil cross-dressing prison wardens, flesh-eating crabs, incest, and hunchbacked freaks raping imprisoned women.

Right from the get-go the film is a disorientating experience, with the curtain-raiser set in a sexually-integrated insane asylum. The plot throws up some amazing scenes, one after another, with little rhyme or warning, such as the half undressed women being whipped, the graphic scene of a woman having her breasts sliced open with a knife, and the colour-tinted episodes which accentuate the mood of the back-story. Although it's not as graphic or extreme as some of the more outrageous Japanese offerings that flourished in the 70s (many of which were also directed by Ishii), *Malformed Men* nonetheless boasts some freakish imagery and a whacked-out psychedelic edge. It's perhaps best described as a cross between *Freaks* and *Island of Dr. Moureu*, as directed by Seijun Suzuki.

After a very short-lived theatrical release, the film had caused so much outrage it was promptly banned by the Japanese authorities. Even the film's title was something of a cultural taboo but that didn't stop it from being a much discussed hot topic, conferring upon it an almost mythic reputation in the ensuing decades for those who didn't get to see it. And this legendary status was bolstered by the subsequent work of its director who became known as 'The King of Cult' in his homeland after a series of unforgettable entries in the notorious Ero guro sub-genre, such as *Shogun's Joys of Torture*, and of course, *Female Yakuza Tale: Inquisition and Torture*.

Beyond the Valley of the Dolls (1970)
Dir: Russ Meyer /USA

"You shall drink the black sperm of my vengeance." Russ Meyer's *Beyond the Valley of the Dolls* is an outrageously entertaining cult classic, and one of the sleaziest mainstream movies ever released by a Hollywood studio up to that point. Crucially, this is not a sequel to *Valley of the Dolls*, but rather a demented rehash of Jacqueline Susann's trashy bestseller, alternating psychedelic hipness and bland moralizing. The film is also strangely bereft of Meyer's usual love of nudity and big-boobed women, but is just as insane as his other works like *Mudhoney* and *Vixen*.

Eager to break into the big time, an all-girl rock group consisting of Kelly (Dolly Read), Casey (Cynthia Myers), and Pet (Marcia McBroom) heads for Los Angeles accompanied by their manager, Harris (David Gurian), who is also Kelly's lover. Kelly's aunt introduces the girls to record producer Ronnie 'Z-Man' Barzell (John LaZar), who turns the band into stars. As they become successful, Kelly abandons Harris for playboy Lance Rocke (Michael Blodgett), Harris is seduced by a porn star, and Pet falls in love with a law student. Casey, who gets hooked on pills and alcohol, is attracted to Kelly's aunt's lesbian employee. Things reach a head when Lance and the band members attend a party at Bartell's house; 'Z-Man' freaks out and attacks his guests one by one whilst dressed as a super-heroine named 'Superwoman'.

After losing a fortune on epic flops like *Doctor Doolittle*, 20th Century Fox enlisted Russ Meyer – who had earned millions with low-budget exploitation flicks – to make a film for them. The result was a movie that outraged the industry but turned a huge profit on its $1.2 million budget, despite Fox's trepidation in promoting it. Technically, Meyer's films were always top-notch, and in this, his first widescreen movie, he and cinematographer Fred Koenekamp create some stylish comic-book compositions, splashed with Day-Glo colours.

In addition to the cast of former playboy models and other non-actors, there are wild orgies, drug parties, Nazi butlers, and a gruesome Manson-like massacre that reaches a manic pitch of surreal hysteria. *Beyond the Valley of the Dolls* is often repellent and demented – which is to say it's typical Meyer – but it's also a funny psychedelic time-capsule which has joined the likes of *Psych-Out*, *The Trip*, and *Head* as one of the great cinematic legacies of the acid years.

And would you believe that this drug-laden, sex-engorged camp masterpiece was written by none other than Roger Ebert? Sure, the guy turned into a stuffy old square later in his career, and he may have felt embarrassed by his association with the film, but you've got to admire anyone who can churn out lines like "This is my happening, and it's freaking me out!" or "I want it. I need it. I love it when a beautiful woman licks between my toes." The British censors demanded cuts to the opening credits sequence in which guns are used to stroke breasts; the implied connection between sex and violence is still a big no no for the BBFC, and the cuts remain in place to this day. But hey Russ, thanks for the mammaries!

Savage Intruder (1970)
(aka *Hollywood Horror House*; aka *The Comeback*)
Dir: Donald Wolfe /USA

This film opens on a glitzy scene of a movie premier in Hollywood in the 1930s with full press attendance and clamouring crowds. It then cuts to the quiet, eerie credits sequence set in the modern day, with the camera probing around the abandoned Hollywood sign in the hills; the large iconic letters have fallen into disrepair with the paint peeling off, bits of the rotten sign swinging loose and creaking in the breeze – it's a picture of rot and rust, an all too obvious symbol of the rot and corruption of modern times. The camera then pans down to reveal the head and severed body parts of a murdered woman.

As the film starts proper, it is revealed on a television screen in a bar that the murder victim was a Hollywood actress. A woman in the bar finishes her drink and leaves. She is stalked by a mysterious figure on her way home, and brutally hacked to death by the maniac who carries around with him a box containing various implements such as an electric carving knife and a meat cleaver. Meanwhile, a Hollywood tour bus does the rounds in the neighbourhoods of the rich and famous, and the young maniac hops off the bus and promptly enters the home of another ageing actress, Katherine Packard (Miriam Hopkins). She's a little kooky, an alcoholic who is hung up on her past glories, and likes to fantasize about still being popular and successful. The man introduces himself as 'Mr. Laurel and Hardy,' and somehow lands the job of household nurse to help Katherine recover from her broken leg after falling down the stairs.

Her initial hostilities towards the young man are thawed when he wins her over with his clowning antics. They spend a lot of time together watching her old movies and reminiscing about the good old days. Other members of staff in the house have their reasons for mistrusting the man, but the kooky old timer won't listen to their concerns. And before long, the disruptive Vic (David Garfield) has corrupted and knocked up the quiet maid, Greta, has the house gatecrashed by a group of drug-addled hippies, injects himself with some kind of hallucinogen which causes intense psychedelic trips (with hallucinations which reveal lurid details about his troubled childhood), and anyone who gets in his way ends up meeting the business end of his trusty meat cleaver...

Sort of a slasher version of *Sunset Blvd* (1950), *Savage Intruder* is an interesting little film that was shot almost entirely in the Hollywood mansion of a real ageing actress, Norma Talmadge. There are a few lapses in logic and common sense here and there; for instance, how Vic can just walk into the home of a wealthy actress and become a part of her life with no background checks or anything (especially at a time when a maniac is stalking the Hollywood hills and killing off the starlets!). But this is only a minor quibble to what is otherwise an enjoyable and quirky little pot-boiler. The final 20 minutes enters into some very strange and twisted territory, and the film echoes the fears felt by the Hollywood establishment in the wake of the Manson murders which were just coming to court as the film was released.

The Devil Came From Akasava (1970)
(Orig title: *Der Teufel Kan aus Akasava*)
Dir: 'Jess Frank' [Jesus Franco] /W. Ger /Spain
Jess Franco turns his hand to a *Krimis*-like tale with *The Devil Came From Akasava*, made for the German market. The story revolves around a stone that holds mystical powers; it can turn metal into gold, and can even transform humans into shambling, zombie-like ghouls. Lots of twists and turns, crossing and double-crossing ensues as various characters plot and scheme to get their hands on the stone, including Franco regulars, Paul Miller, Howard Vernon and

Soledad Miranda. This film will be more of interest to fans of Euro crime thriller and Edgar Wallace adaptations as the horror elements are kept to a minimum here. Nonetheless, Franco turns out an entertaining and energetic movie that is worth watching if only for the performance of Miranda.

Emperor Tomato Ketchup (1970)
(aka *King Ketchup Tomato*)
(Orig title: *Tomato Kecchappu Kôtei*)
Dir: Shuji Terayama /Japan
This cinematic attack on Japanese state policies and culture of the time is wild, shocking, and even a bit dull in places. However, some of the imagery here is jaw-droppingly risque. It's a film about an imaginary revolution where the children have seized control of the country and have condemned their parents to death for restricting their free-expression and sexual freedoms. Many themes that subsequently cropped up in Terayama's later work are also included here – adults raping young boys, white powdered faces, clocks, and studio sets falling apart. Many scenes of disturbing and playful decadence look to be ad-libbed and were probably drawn from Terayama's own experiences in the theatre.

In the opening sequence we watch people doing seemingly random and mundane things like climbing up buildings, pulling an old boot out of the toilet, dancing in a garden, someone standing in the middle of a sun dial, body builders flexing their muscles, a goat wandering around aimlessly in some bleak and desolate wasteland. This intro lasts for about ten minutes and has a green tint on the lens. The soundtrack is brooding and rhythmic like we're anticipating something to happen.

Next we get a pink tinge on the lens for the opening credits which show still images of historical figures, children in school photos, and artist's impressions of historical events played out to traditional Japanese music, presumably as a way of showing a bygone era. Then the screen turns black for a few seconds and we can hear a high-pitch noise. Something's wrong, but what is it? Well, there are street riots, and historical faces are crossed out with children's crayons (Karl Marx, et al), and a jangly guitar on the soundtrack culminating in victorious kids standing on street corners in military uniform, waving flags; the winners of some kind of revolution. The rest of the film is tinged in a dull sepia tone as the kids have taken over and are now in power. The adults are stripped, tied up, and used as sex slaves.

The most notorious scene in the film is undoubtedly where a trio of women pin a young boy onto a bed, strip him, and stroke, tickle, and roll around with him on the bed whilst they too get naked and simulate playful sex positions. It is a scene that will offend and infuriate many, and should make any normal person feel uncomfortable. And it's hard not to conclude that the kids were exploited by the adults in the making of the film in the same way the adults were exploited in the film by the kids, making any message that Terayama intended to convey all the more difficult to accept.

At the end of the film, three youngsters put on fake beards and mustaches as a way of making themselves seem more grown up and authoritative, and putting their mark over the new regime. This looks like a pointless recap of Orwell's *Animal Farm*, with the revolutionaries exploiting the situation for their own self-interests in a similar way as the animals in Orwell's book who gradually expose their hunger for power by adopting human traits; the very same 'evils' that they had successfully overthrown in the revolution.

There are two versions of this film doing the rounds; a black and white 'highlights' version which was produced in Germany for the European market (under thirty minutes running time), and Terayama's full version which runs for about an hour and is mostly in sepia. This latter version also has two short films spliced into the footage, bringing the total running time to around 88 minutes. Those shorts are *The Cage* and *Paper-Scissors-Rock-War* which plays out the destructive finale.

Director Shuji Terayama (1936-1983) was also a poet, playwright, essayist, and theatre director with a healthy interest in all that is strange and chaotic. He made a number of films in the 70s, and his style and attitude matured considerably during that decade, becoming one of Japan's most revered artists. He was involved in naive revolutionary provocations for many years (*Emperor Tomato Ketchup* was only a part of it), and preferred practical knowledge rather than books, which is strange coming from a writer. *Pastoral: To Die In the Country* is a Fellini-esque mix of childhood memories, symbolism, and bizarre surrealism, and is generally considered to be his masterpiece,

although a case can be made for *Fruits of Passion* (1983).

Eugenie de Sade (1970)
(aka *Eugenia*)
Dir: Jess Franco /Liechtenstein

Young Eugenie (Soledad Miranda) becomes besotted with her deviant stepfather, Albert (Paul Muller), a writer of erotic literature. After browsing his library of 'erotic' books, rather than being repulsed by the sexual sadism found in the works of the Marquis de Sade and other writers, she is instead aroused by them, and begins a pseudo-incestuous relationship with Albert. Not content with this, Albert eventually draws Eugenie in to a dark world of lust and murder, picking off prostitutes and hitchhikers and often recording their dreadful deeds in the form of photographs and snuff movies. However, the couple are being followed by another writer, Tanner (Jess Franco), and when the pair organise the snuff murder of a sulky jazz musician, their plans are thwarted by jealousy, treachery and more murder...

After the success of *The Honeymoon Killers* (1969) in the previous year, director Jess Franco set out to cash-in on the crazed-killer-couple craze by making this bizarre and misty slice of Euro-horror. Inspired just as much by the Marquis de Sade as Leonard Kastle's true crime classic, *Eugenie* adds a decisively kinky twist to the already contentious themes, making for an uncomfortable portrayal of the blackest hearts imaginable – lovers whose lust depends on the sadistic slaying of innocent victims. Franco cushions the blow somewhat with a deliberately hazy and dreamy style, and none of the murders are too graphic. But nonetheless, this film is as daring a work as any from the early 70s. It may have also influenced other shockers that arrived in its wake, such as *Love Me Deadly* (1973) and *Assault! Jack the Ripper* (1976), films which explore similar themes while also adding their own perverse twists.

A recurring theme in Franco's work is the idea of Sadean libertines running amok and treating the world and its human beings as their very own playthings for their sadistic urges. The world becomes an amoral playground for deviants whose only code is to indulge in as much pleasure as possible, even if that pleasure comes at the cost of innocent lives. The coldness of this world is even presented literally, as *Eugenie* is one of only a handful of Franco films that is set in a snowy winter time. Yet, time and again, Franco shows the viewers how this lifestyle choice is doomed to failure: all such alliances and love affairs built upon torture and death are betrayed by one or the other because it is always selfishness that leads the way. Like many of Franco's Sade-inspired works, *Eugenie* makes it clear that such a destructive path in life will be at the cost of any genuine friendship – betrayal is inevitable, and no one can really trust anyone else, and even the trust between a father and daughter is no exception.

Eugenie de Sade slipped under the radar when it first hit cinema screens, but has since become a cult favourite over the years thanks to home video and the pristine DVD release from Blue Underground. It's one of the many gems to be found in Franco's filmography for those who are willing to dig through the dirt. The beautiful Soledad Miranda certainly adds to its continued appeal as she steals every scene she is in. And the film was ultimately her swansong. The daughter of a gypsy, the Spanish beauty was originally a flamenco dancer. Franco had cast her in a couple of small roles in the past, mostly to help her out as she couldn't afford to eat. The director left the country for filming in France and elsewhere, and upon his return to Madrid five years later, he met up with her again and began casting her in more prominent roles in *She Killed in Ecstasy*, *The Devil Came From Akasava*, and *Vampyros Lesbos* (all 1970). Tragically, after filming *Eugenie de Sade*, Miranda died in a car accident. She was just 27-years-old. She was travelling with her husband on the Costa do Sol highway between Estoril and Lisbon, and died on the same stretch of road she had travelled on in a scene in an earlier film, *Un dia en Lisboa* (1964). She was on her way to meet Franco and his producer to sign a 10-movie deal that would no doubt have made her a star.

El Topo (1970)
(*The Mole*)
Dir: Alejandro Jodorowsky /USA/ Mexico

Alejandro Jodorowsky is a Chilean native who caused artistic controversy in the 60s with his 'Panik Movement' in Mexico and Paris. Although he is nowadays remembered for his work in film, *El Topo* didn't actually premier until he was in his forties. His work in music and theatre is still unknown to most, but his films, which include *El Topo*, *The Holy Mountain* and *Santa Sangre*, will forever cement his place as a legend among fans of incredibly strange cinema.

Jodorowsky teamed up with Fernando Arrabal and Roland Topor in Paris where they were involved with André Breton's surrealism group. The trio quickly became bored and decided to break away and form their own movement which they called 'Panik'. The Panik movement had its first 'Happening' in 1965 at the 2e Festival de la Libre Expression. The gathering crowd was much bigger than anticipated, and at the last moment both Topor and Arrabal lost their nerve, and Alejandro was left to improvise the whole show by himself. Later, Topor and Arrabal began joining Alejandro in the Happenings; it was wild, chaotic street theatre/performance art inspired by Antonin Artaud. Artaud rejected traditional Western ideas of theatre in favour of a theatre that would "make itself the equal of life," and in which themes "will be cosmic, universal, and interpreted according to the most ancient texts." As far as Artaud was concerned, a Theatre of Cruelty was to be "bloody and inhuman" for it to exorcise the viewer's repressed impulses – a notion Jodorowsky fell in love with.

During the Happenings, they would do things like release a thousand birds in the theatre, break bottles, cut the throats of wild geese, and Jodorowsky did all this while wearing a complete costume made up of beef steaks – beat *that*, Lady Gaga. Throwing live snakes at the audience was not an uncommon practice, and they would also decorate the area of performance with human-shaped casts of plaster. The events would often be attended by Beat writers like Allen Ginsberg, Lawrence Ferlinghetti and Gregory Corso. André Breton himself would even show up to see what all the fuss was about. Some of the Happenings were captured on film, but Jean Jacques Lebel, a jealous rival who organized the cameras, alleged to have destroyed the reels (some of this legendary footage does appear in Jodorowsky's earlier film, *Fando and Lis*, and the documentary, *Constellation Jodorowsky*). As if the Happenings weren't challenging enough for the everyday public, Jodorowsky planned to crucify two horses in public, "a black horse and a white horse." He also expressed an interest in walking through the streets with a real human corpse strapped to his back as part of a performance.

In the late 60s, Jodorowsky tried his hand at film-making, and when he showed up in New York with a copy of *El Topo* in 1970, he had no reason to doubt he was on the verge of international superstardom. His debut feature, *Fando and Lis* (1968), received global recognition when the Mexican government banned it. Just weeks before its premier, Mexican police fought running battles with student protesters, resulting in hundreds dead or wounded. *El Topo* begins with the leather-clad title character (played by Jodorowsky himself) riding into the desert with his naked son, Brontis, who then commands him to bury his possessions so that he can become a man. Soon after, they chance upon the aftermath of a village massacre where the dead, mutilated bodies litter the streets and blood literally flows in the gutters. El Topo vows to track down the Colonel who is responsible for the deaths, and abandons his son in his quest for vengeance. The Colonel's missus, Mara Lorenzio, informs him of the 'Four Masters' who control the territory, and encourages him to kill them all. El Topo encounters the Masters one by one, and each of them shows off their philosophies and abilities before they are taken out. And it's at this point when things become increasingly convoluted and bizarre, with the inclusion of plot twists, jumps in time, a sequence involving underground freaks, and the fully-grown Brontis. And all of this leads to the appropriate Zen-like finale.

Jodorowsky takes top honours for *El Topo* which is very much an auteur piece all the way; not only did he star in the film, he also wrote and directed it, did his own production design, and composed the catchy soundtrack which can be described as 'Morricone on acid.' The end result isn't too dissimilar from *Fando and Lis*, but the addition of full-colour photography certainly helps to bring out the trippiness of the more acid-infused sequences (despite Jodorowsky claiming he has never touched psychedelic drugs in his life). Those new to Jodorowsky often start here, and it's easy to see why; it's a dazzling treat for the eyes and ears. But if you're looking for something that is more narrative friendly, try *Santa Sangre*, and those looking for something visually striking to show off on their massive TV's, try *The Holy Mountain*. *El Topo* was a huge success in New York where it played non-stop at the Elgin theatre for more than a year and became the first ever 'Midnight Movie,' kicking off a cult movie phenomenon that would last for decades.

10 Rillington Place (1970)
Dir: Richard Fleischer /UK

Based on Ludovic Kennedy's book, which itself was based on the true crimes of British serial killer Reginald Christie, *10 Rillington Place* opens in 1944 in the middle of an air raid. A young woman knocks on his door. Once inside, we learn that Christie has promised this woman a cure for her bronchitis, which involves breathing deeply through a mask. Turns out that she is breathing gas fumes and begins to struggle. When she falls unconscious, he strangles her with a length of rope, molests her body and later buries her in the back yard.

Cut to 1946. Christie has advertised a flat for rent upstairs in the house. A young couple, Tim and Beryl (John Hurt and Judy Geeson) and their baby eventually move in. These scenes set in the aftermath of the war look very grubby and bombed-out; the walls of the house are filthy, and the kitchen is particularly grim – the walls are charcoal black as if there has been a fire in the house – probably caused by chimney soot from the local factories (the interior scenes were shot next door to the actual house where the murders took place). Beryl falls pregnant, but they know that their financial hardship could never stretch enough to feed another mouth. Christie talks the couple into aborting their baby, a procedure he assures them he can perform (he lies that he was in medical training before the war). And while Tim is out at work one day, he sets to work. He terminates her baby all right, but he also terminates her with his trusty dose of gas. Tim gets home to find his wife dead, and Christie subtly informs him that if the police get involved they will both surely hang. So Tim agrees to pack some belongings and disappear from London for a while (he was not too bright, IQ of only 70), but not before helping Christie to remove the body. Later that night, once Tim has gone, Christie strangles the baby with a necktie.

Richard Attenborough's performance as the egghead psychopath is chillingly realistic. With his calm effete and very softly spoken voice, he embodies that old adage, 'look out for the quiet ones'. A typical predator, he would prey on those weaker and less intelligent than himself. He was no criminal mastermind, but was very cunning and always several steps ahead of his victims while leading them to believe he was ultimately harmless and inconspicuous.

Timothy John Evans was found guilty of killing Beryl and his baby Geraldine. He had changed his story of what happened so many times that the police and the jurors no longer believed a word he said (not to mention his history of violence and tantrums). He was eventually hanged at Pentonville Prison in March 1950.

Giving evidence in court, Christie wriggles his way out of any implications in the case and manages to convince everybody of his failing health and his calm and kindly nature. And despite having previous convictions for theft and fraud, he leaves the courtroom as a model citizen. Interestingly, during the court scenes we see a very British class division as court officials are seen to treat people very differently according to their social standing; Christie copped for some mustard gas during his duty in the First World War which left him blind for several months (just like Hitler). He also served as a member of the War Reserve Police during the Second World War. Curiously, those facts seem to absolve him of any wrong-doing in the eyes of the law.

The scene where Timothy feebly tries to convince medical examiners of his innocence during his appeal is especially powerful – his lack of intelligence and mounting confusion about the whole thing makes you wish you were there to state his case for him and get him off the hook – but all he can muster is "Christie done it. I say Christie done it." Two years later and Christie's wife is finding it very difficult to cope with living in the house; tenants stay away knowing the flat has a sinister past, and none of the neighbours will talk to her anymore. She also suspects her husband of being involved with the murders. Late one night, Christie is shown disposing of her corpse. And after adding another to his list of victims, the police finally catch up with him. He was hanged at Pentonville in July 1953. Rillington Place was bulldozed in the 70s, much like Fred and Rosemary West's house of horrors, and was renamed Ruston Place.

Don't Deliver Us From Evil (1970)
(Orig title: *Mais ne nous delivrez pas du mal*)
Dir: Joël Séria /France
Banned in its native France for blasphemy, and heavily censored elsewhere for the graphic scenes of child molestation, *Don't Deliver Us From Evil* is about a pair of Catholic schoolgirls who make a pact with Satan. They ride around the country lanes on their bicycles and make life hell for the repressed men in their rural village. In the end they burn themselves alive on stage as part of a macabre ritual, influenced by their forbidden literary heroes, Charles Baudelaire and Comte de Lautréamont.

Described by Nathaniel Thompson as 'one of those movies that might send you to hell just for watching,' this is very loosely based on the Parker/Hulme case (which was later adapted to film more faithfully in Peter Jackson's *Heavenly Creatures* [1994]). *Don't Deliver Us From Evil* was the debut feature of Joël Séria, and is by far the most controversial film he ever made. Like *Heavenly Creatures*, it's a film that plays around with fantasy and reality, and the blurring of the two, especially during the 'black wedding' ceremony sequence. It's also a film that portrays men as primitive sexual predators who cannot control themselves at the sight of young flesh. It is simultaneously blatant in its digs at the Catholic faith while also cynically subversive in the way it exposes the underlying corruption of Man.

The film quickly became a cult classic, especially in the UK where the censored version was often screened in art colleges and halls of residence. However, the lack of a VHS release saved the film from the 'video nasties' panic of the 80s. In the mid-2000s, Mondo Macabro released the uncut version with a bunch of extra features, including an interview with Séria himself. Some reviews claim that no animals were harmed during the making of the film, but I'm not so sure: canaries cannot flop around and play dead. Nor can they jerk around the bird cage pretending to be in the grip of death spasms. The birds were probably crushed and poisoned for real.

The Ravager (1970)
Dir: Charles Nizet /USA
An American soldier, Joe (Pierre Agostino), becomes separated from his platoon in Vietnam. He wanders lost in the jungle and witnesses the rape and murder of a Vietnamese woman (the rapists then shove a stick of dynamite up her twat, and detonate it). Later, back home in Nevada, Joe is a fragile, traumatised vet obsessed with explosives, and a very short fuse on his temper. He sets about blowing up

unsuspecting couples to satisfy his twisted sexual urges... *The Ravager* is a very obscure exploitation film. It was even considered lost in some circles until Something Weird Video released a scrappy version on DVD-R in the late 00s. With its bizarre 50s style voice-over – sounding like an old public educational film – and booming operatic music, it was a surprise to see the film released at all. Fans of *Combat Shock* (1986) and *The Mad Bomber* (1973) may get a kick out of this, but it's also worth pointing out that *The Ravager* lacks an ongoing narrative, and instead plays out the same scenario over and over again: we simply follow the bald anti-hero as he stalks his prey, watches them making out, and then blows 'em up! The maniac takes extra care when dealing with a lesbian couple – he even douses one of the girls in gasoline and burns her alive, which led one reviewer to call the film "porno for pyros." The transfer looks very rough in places, with permanent vertical lines hovering on screen, but it's certainly watchable. Besides, considering how obscure this film is, and its status as a genuine curio – even among the large number of oddball 70s exploitationers – it's worth a look. I also think a remake of this would be interesting.

Night Slaves (1970)
Dir: Ted Post /USA

Sinister aliens show up in *Night Slaves*, in which James Franciscus deals with sinister body snatchers. After recovering from a near-fatal car accident, Franciscus moves with his wife to a – literally – sleepy town where the locals are constantly yawning and nodding off. After a bit of sleuthing, he discovers that the town is surrounded by an invisible force field, a solid shell that makes it impossible for anyone to leave. Turns out that a 'psychokinetic' race of space aliens, disguised in human form, have colonised the town, enslaving the locals in nocturnal hard labour. To make matters worse, the populace doesn't seem to mind their exploitation, and they walk around espousing their mindless, stupidly proud, self-congratulatory work ethic of being unthinking drones (Jeez, sound familiar?). *Night Slaves* is an interesting little TV movie which is perfect for watching in bed while in a drowsy state of mind. There seems to be a conservative stance here about the perceived dangers of trade unions and organised labour, in keeping with the 'red scare' subtext of this film's biggest inspiration, Don Siegel's classic, *Invasion of the Body Snatchers* (1955).

The Wizard of Gore (1970)
Dir: Herschell Gordon Lewis /USA

Perhaps the most bizarre film of HG Lewis's career. With self-parody taking centre stage, we're introduced to Montag The Magnificent (Ray Sager), a hammy stage magician who performs tricks whereby audience members are sawn in half with a chainsaw or forced to shallow a sword. After the grisly 'illusions' have taken place, the volunteers seem to be okay at first until hours later when they turn up dead with their sloppy innards strewn across the floor. The master of *grand guignol* later finds himself on a live television show demonstrating an existential stigmata sequence. And if this film doesn't leave you questioning your sanity then nothing will.

Bigfoot (1970)
Dir: Robert F. Slatzer /USA

A couple of smarmy opportunists and a biker gang come under attack from a family of large bipedal beasties deep in the woods. It's all very tame by today's standards, this is the film which helped kick-start a slew of bigfoot-themed movies in the 70s (*The Legend of Boggy Creek* [1972], *The Legend of Bigfoot* [1977], *Snowbeast* [1977], *Mysterious Monsters* [1975], *Curse of Bigfoot* [1976], etc). The film picks up on the remnants of the dying hippie movement – there are moments of 'free love,' but the bikers here aren't good enough to be hippies, nor are they bad enough to be dirtball Hell's Angels types, either. Most disappointingly, the bigfoot creatures are far too nice, and instead of killing off the characters – as any decent horror movie should – they are instead carried off deep into the woods and tied to stakes with the intention of breeding with them!

Nightmares Come at Night (1970)
(Orig title: *Les cauchemars naissent la nuit*)
Dir: Jess Franco /Liechtenstein

From 1968 to1975, Jess Franco produced some of his finest films. This isn't one of them. Diana Lorys plays Anna, a cabaret stripper who suffers from recurring nightmares. Convinced she's going nuts, she seeks the help of a doctor (Paul Muller) while her dreams seem to bring about the deaths of several men, and the whole scenario has been masterminded by armed robbers who use Anna's instability so that they can kill off their rivals and keep the loot for themselves... This slapdash quicky from Franco was pieced together from a couple of failed projects that were left unfinished. And even with the added voice-over designed to paper over the cracks, this is still a largely incomprehensible mess. Of course, Franco fans will find much to savour here, like the clumsy crash zooms, an abundance of bare skin and a swinging score from Bruno Nicolai, which combines groovy free-form jazz and a bongos and Spanish guitar freak out. Newcomers to Franco are advised to start elsewhere; try *Venus In Furs* (1967) or *A Virgin Among the Living Dead* (1973).

Blood Mania (1970)
Dir: Robert Vincent O'Neill /USA
Far more entertaining and competently made than its trashy reputation suggests, *Blood Mania* centres on a sleazy, crooked doctor (Peter Carpenter) who needs $50,000 to pay off a blackmailer who is threatening to inform the authorities of his past activities, such as conducting abortions to pay for medical school. Meanwhile, the daughter of one of his patients (Maria de Aragon) has the hots for him, and she deliberately speeds up her father's death so that she can get her hands on the inheritance money. However, after his death she learns that she has been cut out of the will, and the doctor – who is now sleeping with her sister – learns that she's a schizophrenic, and feels that he could be her next victim... Yes, it's certainly trashy, predictable and talky in places, and the body count is disappointingly low, but on the plus side, *Blood Mania* includes Bava-esque hallucinatory dream sequences, lots of nudity and a 'far-out' rocking soundtrack courtesy of Don Vincent, whose eccentric scores were also heard in other early 70s horror outings, such as *The Night God Screamed* (1971), *Point of Terror* (1971), and *Happy Mother's Day, Love George* (1973). The film looks fantastic on DVD, though it runs for only 80 minutes, same as the VHS releases – the original press book for the film claimed an 88-minute running time.

The Andromeda Strain (1970)
Dir: Robert Wise /USA
A satellite falls out of orbit and crashes in the desert town on Piedmont in New Mexico, killing everyone. The U.S. Airforce calls an emergency as the satellite was part of project Scoop, created to gather alien micro-organisms from outer space. Mankind now faces extinction as an alien virus is unleashed, and to combat this, a team of expert scientists are hastily assembled to try and contain the outbreak before it's too late... Based on Michael Crichton's great novel about the dangers and accomplishments of science, this atypical invasion movie posits the idea of aliens posing an unseen, microscopic threat. The film works wonders at wringing dramatic tension, both as a conventional thriller and also as an intellectual puzzle for the characters to solve. The action kicks off in the devastated town of Piedmont, where the local's blood has turned into powder; it then moves along to the enormous underground research lab where the decontamination process is explored in detail; and the final act reverts to more conventional means as the virus – dubbed the Andromeda Strain – breaks out of the facility. What separates this film from most of its kind is the way it depicts scientists; they are presented as what they are – intelligent, rational people faced with a crisis. And the casting of unknowns instead of the usual Hollywood stars also helps. Director Robert Wise, who also brought us such classics as *The Body Snatcher* (1945), *The Day the Earth Stood Still* (1951) and *The Haunting* (1963), presents his film as a possible reality rather than mere escapism – as often befell most disaster movies as they flourished in the 70s. And Crichton's moral message about how science should always be subservient to mankind – as echoed in many of his books – is delivered here in full.

The Act of Seeing With One's Own Eyes (1971)
Dir: Stan Brakhage /USA
Stan Brakhage was the creator of *Dog Star Man*, a 75-minute avant-garde epic that was required viewing for anyone who went to film school in the 70s and 80s. Made between 1961 and 1964, *Dog Star Man* was an experimental art piece that fused various cinematic techniques, brazen colours, overlaps, and only a bare minimum of traditional photography – shots of Brakhage walking through the snow with his dog, for instance. This artistic masterpiece influenced the next generation of film-makers and artists while Brakhage himself remained an underground figure, creating more than 400 films that varied in length before his death in 2003.

Around this time, Criterion compiled a

retrospective of twenty six of his most important works for a double-disc DVD release entitled *By Brakhage: An Anthology*. Included were some of his most pioneering and innovative works, such as *Desistfilm*, a study of life and form through architecture and anatomy; *Wedlock House*, which was shot on inverted black & white, and shows Brakhage and his wife engaging in explicit sex; almost two dozen shorts that vary in length from 18 minutes to 9 seconds, including *Black Ice* and *The Dark Tower*. *Dog Star Man* is also included in the package and is split into five separate chapters. All very well and good. But for fans of extreme cinema, the real curio here is the notorious Brakhage film from 1971, *The Act of Seeing With One's Own Eyes*, a 32-minute delve into death.

Along with *Deux Ex*, *The Act of Seeing* forms part of the 'Pittsburgh Documents,' a trilogy filmed in 1971. For eyes, Brakhage was given permission to film at the Pittsburgh Police Department. *Deux Ex* was filmed from within the West Pennsylvania Hospital, and *The Act of Seeing With One's Own Eyes* at the Allegheny Coroner's Office. The title is a literal translation of the word 'autopsy', and this should give you an idea of where the film is coming from. This latter part of Brakhage's trilogy has been an underground classic for decades (indeed, it is featured prominently on the DVD bonus features on the German release of Nacho Cerda's *Aftermath*; both Cerda and Jorg Buttgereit discuss the film at length while clips are played in the background during an interview with Cerda). Filmed on hand-held 16mm, it's a sobering documentation of death without the crux of a voice-over or anything to let us know what's going on. Just the dead bodies of the city's recently deceased laid out in the morgue. The corpses are sliced open in a routine, unceremonious manner. The cold flesh is peeled apart to reveal the forbidden sight of organs riddled with tumours, hearts clogged up with fatty deposits, and layers of blubbery intestines, like something seen at the back of a butcher's shop. Skulls are opened up, faces are peeled off, and brains are examined.

The first ten minutes or so shows the pathologists preparing for the procedure and arranging the cadavers and metallic instruments of dissection. This long build-up to the first autopsy is effective at instilling a morbid anticipation in the viewer. And when the scalpel first makes contact with the body, the effect is at once a feeling of pain and relief, such is the intensity of the film, despite its cold and clinical style. The close-up shots of the internal organs of human cadavers becomes a hypnotic – if disturbing – thoroughfare of colour and form, and recalls Brakhage's other work which deals with light and texture, such as the aforementioned *Desistfilm*, and also *Cat's Cradle*.

In a letter to a friend, the poet and author Robert Creeley, Brakhage explained how he had originally intended to insert soothing shots of "mountain ranges, moons, suns, snow, and clouds," to allow the viewer a respite from the stark images of death. But once the lab had processed the film and he watched it, he decided against the idea, "one good look at the footage… and I knew it was impossible (for me at least) to interrupt THIS parade of death with ANYthing whatsoever".

The Act of Seeing With One's Own Eyes may have lost some of its disturbing power over the years (after all, autopsies have been broadcast live on TV in the UK conducted by the eccentric German artist, Gunther Von Hagens), but back in the 70s and 80s this film sure had the power to freak people out, and is still heavy-going for most audiences to this day.

Requiem For a Vampire (1971)
(aka *Virgins and Vampires*; aka *Caged Virgins*)
(Orig title: *Requiem pour un Vampire*)
Dir: Jean Rollin /France
The story is simple: Two young girls (Mireille Dargent and Marie-Pierre Castel) are involved in a shoot-out with criminals and end up having to burn the body of their male accomplice who was fatally wounded. And while dressed as clowns, the girls trek through the wilderness, robbing men and visiting a graveyard before they chance upon an old crumbling castle. Inside they are captured by a den of vampires and coerced into using sex as a way of luring in men for the bloodsuckers... With barely a word of dialogue for the first 45 minutes (and not much more after that), *Requiem For a Vampire* plays like a surreal fever dream that glides by in a flash thanks to its expressionistic images and poetic feel. The girls are resilient and likeable, and they relish the opportunity to provide their vampire master with fresh blood in the form of unwitting men. Castel's character becomes attached to one of her victims, and she decides

to defend him at the last moment. However, perhaps the most interesting character in the film is the master vampire, or 'le vieux vampire' (Michel Delesalle), who must face up to the fact that his time on earth is coming to an end. And it isn't just a personal decision as he also feels responsible for his fellow vampire breed, including Erica (Dominique Troussaint) and the melancholic piano-playing Louise (Louise Dhour). But ultimately the master accepts his fate and that of his undead followers. He lies in his coffin for the last time as Louise closes the lid and guards over him until he perishes of blood-thirst. Director Jean Rollin's obsession with young sisters had provided other films like *Les Demoniaques* (1974) and *Shiver of the Vampires* (1970), and the basic plot would be later recycled in the less impressive *Schoolgirl Hitchhikers* (1973) and *Two Orphan Vampires* (1997). The British censors cut around 10 minutes of blood and nudity on its initial release, but all DVD releases are fully intact.

Let's Scare Jessica To Death (1971)
Dir: John Hancock /USA
Recently released from a psychiatric institute after a nervous breakdown, young Jessica (Zohra Lampert), and her husband, Duncan (Barton Heyman), move into a rural house in Connecticut where she can recuperate in peace and quiet. They are joined by their mutual friend, Woody (Kevin O'Connor), and, not long after arriving they are startled to find a squatter in the premises, Emily (Mariclare Costello). Jessica takes a liking to the hippie girl and asks her to stay. It later turns out to be a bad decision as both Duncan and Woody get 'woody' for her. In the meantime, however, Jessica finds an old framed photo in the attic which includes an image of a young woman with a chilling resemblance to Emily.

An antique dealer in town informs Jessica and Duncan that a young girl called Abigail, who lived in the house in the 1890s, had drowned in the nearby lake. This information disturbs Jessica as she has seen a mysterious figure in a white dress lurking on the banks. She sees other things too; dead bodies that mysteriously vanish, and she also hears voices in her head. Emily becomes increasingly sinister, and Jessica feels that her husband is becoming distant and unsupportive – and all of this inevitably takes its toll on her fragile state of mind...

Let's Scare Jessica to Death is a slow-paced, dreamy character study which owes just as much to the post-hippie movement as it does to George Romero. The film charts the mental disintegration of its central character, and it also carries a charged sexual and emotional undercurrent. Much of the film was shot in broad daylight, and yet there is a strange twilight quality to its overall effect – the exterior shots of the house are shrouded in mist and look to be under a brewing storm cloud. The film also has a sober, end-of-an-era feel to it, filmed as it was during the fall out of the hippie dream. The cause of Jessica's initial breakdown is never explained, but she has a delicate air about her, a 'burned-out' look as if she took a trip too far on mushrooms or LSD. Duncan drives a large black hearse with the word 'LOVE' stencilled on the side; this perhaps another nod to the counter-culture. And interestingly, the locals in town can barely suppress their hatred of the hippie outsiders.

However, much of the film also hints at the return to conventional ways after the days of hippie yore; the idea of buying a home and settling down – even jealousy marks its gnawing return after the blissful days of 'free love.' Both men are attracted to Emily, and Jessica can sense it. A tension becomes apparent between the men as they quietly compete for Emily's interest. The film is viewed almost entirely from Jessica's perspective, so that as her psychological condition worsens, the sounds and images become increasingly bizarre and horrifying. And all of this culminates in the climactic sequence in which she is almost drowned in the lake by Emily. She makes a run for it into the town where more horrific visions await her. And the ending is one that George Romero would have been proud of.

The Headless Eyes (1971)
Dir: Kent Bateman /USA
A delirious grindhouse gutter-piece, *The Headless Eyes* opens on a scene in which a burglar loses an eye when his victim awakens and gouges it out with a spoon handle. The would-be robber then staggers out of the tenement window and down the fire escape while screaming 'MY EYE!! UUHHH UH! My eye!' This incident seems to affect our anti-hero for the worse, and he embarks on a killing spree, removing the ocular orbs of his victims and storing them in clear perspex cubes so that he can exhibit them in his backstreet art store... If

you want to delve into the scuzzier side of the grindhouse exploitation experience then this is a must-see. Seemingly directed in a couple of days without a script or even so much as a competent camera man, this film nonetheless possesses a certain unruly charm. In many ways it's perhaps the archetypal grindhouse movie – cheap, nasty, lurid, leering – and it looks exactly the way you would imagine grindhouse movies to look. It boasts more chaotic energy and finesse than the entire filmographies of H. G. Lewis and Andy Milligan combined, and like those films, *Headless Eyes* was also shot guerilla-style in and around New York's 42nd Street with the nearby slums adding a gritty verite ambiance of rot and decay. Don't expect this one to hit Blu-Ray any time soon.

I Drink Your Blood (1971)
(aka *Phobia*)
Dir: David Durston /USA
A Manson-like Satanic cult, led by the charismatic Horace Bones (Bhaskar), arrives on the outskirts of a run-down town in up-state New York. After a twilight ceremony in which the cult drops LSD, a local girl is spotted spying on them in the woods. Horace has the girl captured, and she is sent back home bloody and beaten. Later, the girl's elderly father finds out what happened to her, so he grabs his shotgun and confronts the Satanists at their hideout. However, the old man is easily overpowered and abused in turn – they dose him with LSD. The grandson, Pete (Riley Mills), seeks vengeance on the cultists by injecting rabid dog's blood into their meat pies. And inevitably, the cultists are quickly transformed into bloodthirsty hydrophobic maniacs – and all hell breaks loose!

I Drink Your Blood is a sure-fire cult classic, a wild and delirious party movie, and is a must-see for anyone interested in 70s indie horror. Described by Stephen Thrower as a 'cocktail-shaker blend of horror and sly send-up,' and by Bill Landis as 'the pinnacle of the blood horror movie,' the film is memorable for its vivid, colourful photography, strong bloody violence, and bizarre soundtrack which is unlike anything heard in a 70s horror movie.

The film's journey to the big screen began in 1970 when producer Jerry Gross approached up-and-coming writer/director, David Durston, with a proposition. 'He asked me if I could top *Night of the Living Dead* for graphic horror and original plotting,' Durston recalled. 'Jerry never minced words. What he had to say he came right out with. He said he wanted to make the most graphic horror film ever produced, but he didn't want any vampires, man-made monsters, werewolves, mad doctors or little people from outer space. He said he would double [the pay] what my last writing and directing project was... It was a challenge, but I said I would like to try.'

Over the next few weeks, Durston was trying to think of a new and unique spin on the horror genre. Then he chanced upon a newspaper article which detailed the story of a pack of rabid wolves attacking a school in a rural village in Iran. Durston then began researching rabies and hydrophobia, and its effects on the human central nervous system. He even contacted a Canadian doctor who had helped treat those Iranian children. They met in New York, and the doctor screened some 8mm films of the children locked in cages and foaming at the mouth. 'They were gripping the bars of the cage,' Durston remembered, 'and raving like maniacs. It made the hair on the back of my head elevate. I had never seen anything so horrible, yet so real, in my life.' And when Durston proposed his story outline – that of a small town under attack from a rabies epidemic – Jerry Gross was elated. 'Oh, shit!' he exclaimed. 'That's it! Go home. Go to work. You're on salary as of now!'

Of course, around this time there was another story making the headlines; the capture and conviction of Charles Manson and his followers. This provided extra inspiration, and Durston simply put two and two together – infusing his rabies idea with a dangerous Satanic cult, and inventing the charismatic leader, Horace Bones, as the final piece of the puzzle.

The film was shot in eight weeks, and though the project went over budget by $100,000, the producer didn't complain as he knew he had a gem on his hands. The film's original title was *Phobia*, and Durston was particularly annoyed when Jerry changed the title to *I Drink Your Blood*. The producer was also sitting on another film, a low-budget black and white voodoo flick entitled *Zombies* (1964), which he couldn't sell. The resourceful Jerry Gross then simply renamed it as *I Eat Your Skin*, and released the films on the drive-in and grindhouse circuits on a double-bill with the now infamous poster blurb: '2 Great Blood-Horrors To Rip Out Your Guts!' Needless to say, no blood was drunk and no skin was eaten in the films, but it didn't matter. The punters were queuing around the block, making it perhaps the most famous – and ingenious – exploitation double-bill in American indie horror history.

The films played non-stop, nationwide, throughout the 70s, and, according to Bill Landis in *Sleazoid Express*, they also played at several grindhouses in New York for six months at a time. It was still playing on a double-bill with Ruggero Deodato's *Carnivorous* (aka *Last Cannibal World/Jungle Holocaust*, 1977) at the Deuce in 1979 where Landis claimed he first saw it. 'The impact was like a brick in the head,' he wrote. 'Audience members were stunned into silence and there was even the occasional sound and odour of vomiting in the dark.'

I Drink Your Blood was the first film to be given the X-rating by the MPAA on the basis of violence alone. An edited R-rated cut did the rounds for a while and even shipped up on home video, running around 8 minutes shorter. However, DVD editions are all uncut.

Durston – who had worked in television and radio since 1947 – made his debut feature, *Felicia*, in 1964, a romantic mystery. He followed it up with the ultra-rare *The Love Statue* (1966), which explored the free love and drug scenes of the counter-culture. It was around this time when he met Jerry Gross, and it wasn't until 1970 that he returned to the big screen with *Blue Sextette*, a giallo-flavoured film in which a group of characters remember their recently deceased friend. Durston wasn't entirely happy with any of his films up to that point, and refused to release them on home video format right up until his death in 2010. After *I Drink Your Blood*, he returned with *Stigma* (1972), a fairly underrated film about the dangers of venereal disease. Unfortunately, his talents as a writer and director were never fully realised. After *Stigma*, Durston's film-making career went fully underground as he found himself churning out hardcore gay porn movies under pseudonyms such as 'David Ransom' and 'Spencer Logan.'

For all the fun to be had from watching *I Drink Your Blood*, there is also a tinge of sadness for the array of talents on screen who never reached their full potential. Alongside Durston, there is also the underrated actress, Lynn Lowry, who went on to appear in David Cronenberg's *Shivers* (1975) (she's the one who makes the 'everything is sexual' speech) and

George Romero's *The Crazies* (1973), and whom sadly little has been seen since. Most tragically, however, is what happened to the Indian actor who played Horace Bones. Bhaskar (full name, Bhaskar Roy Chowdhury) was a professional dancer by trade. And not long after the film was complete, he was paralysed from the waist down after an accident in which he landed in an orchestra pit after someone switched off the lights during a dance rehearsal. He was confined to a wheelchair for the rest of his life, and took up painting – he sold around forty paintings and had an exhibition in New York. He died in 2003. Durston paid tribute to his old friend in *Nightmare USA*: 'He was one of a kind. In the face of his misfortune, his spirit and zest for life was an inspiration to all of us.'

The Devils (1971)
Dir: Ken Russell /USA /UK

Ken Russell's masterpiece was based on Aldous Huxley's 'true life' account of demonic possession in France in the 17th Century. It was Russell's only political film and called for a distinct secularism between Church and State. Oliver Reed delivers a career best performance as the rebellious priest Father Grandier who is burned at the stake after urging the citizens to resist the destruction of their city. The film boasts many blasphemous scenes and orgies involving the Ursuline nuns who believed to have had their bodies possessed by Grandier, encouraged by the visions of Sister Jeanne.

The head of British censorship at the time, John Trevelyan, had some reservations about the film, and it was obvious it was going to cause much controversy. Set in the 17th Century Loudon, a French city that was causing problems because it was contained in a walled fortress. The king wanted the walls to be taken down, as this would strengthen his position. But, aware of how unpopular this move would be among the townsfolk, he instead decided to distract the denizens by fabricating a story in which the much-loved priest was accused of being the ringleader of a Satanic cult. Cue lots of horrendous torture as the king's henchmen are sent to Loudon to purge Father Grandier of his demons, and to bring down that defensive wall. Oh, and the film also contained a sequence in which a group of nuns tear down a life-sized effigy of the crucified Christ and pleasure themselves with it.

The new head of British censorship, Stephen

Murphy, insisted on substantial cuts, including that of the infamous 'rape of Christ' sequence. It was then released by Warner Brothers with an X certificate. The political pressure group, NFL (the National Festival of Light), vehemently disagreed with the decision, and they descended on the film and campaigned to have it banned. The British censors refused to budge on their ruling, and so the NFL decided to take a back route instead; members of the NFL had discovered a loophole that would help them; by putting pressure on local councils, they succeeded in having Russell's film banned in many regional provinces. This was particularly upsetting for Russell, who considered himself a devout Catholic. "For myself," he later said, "although I am not a political creature, I always viewed *The Devils* as my one political film. To me, it was about brain-washing, about the state taking over." The NFL may as well have thrown Russell in the river to prove he was a witch. Although *The Devils* had been censored before its theatrical release in the UK, it was the film's own financial backers who objected to it the most. When Ken Russell took the film over to America for a screening for the financiers, their horrified reaction was to label it as "disgusting shit." They promptly removed whole chunks of the film before sending it out in a limited theatrical run.

Film critic Mark Kermode was a good friend of Russell's, and he spent a long time searching for the 'lost' footage which included the infamous 'rape of Christ' scene. After a long search, the footage later surfaced in the Warner Brothers' vaults. This restored director's cut was then screened at the National Film Theatre in London in 2004. Kermode also put together the excellent documentary, *Hell On Earth: The Desecration and Resurrection of the Devils*, in which the cast and crew were interviewed at length on the film's background and production. Both the film and the documentary were broadcast on Channel 4, with the BBFC giving the original version of *The Devils* an uncut 18 certificate.

So, we had the restored version of the film in a gorgeous 35mm print, and some invaluable bonus feature material which would make for an excellent special edition DVD release. But all hopes were dashed when the American backers put their foot down again and banned the film for a second time. The version screened on Channel 4 looked astonishing, it was a beautiful and pristine print. A version was leaked onto download sites which was missing the 'rape of Christ' scene, and that version looked absolutely dreadful and should be avoided at all costs. It's a sad fate for one of the finest British films of the 70s. *The Devils* has since been officially released on DVD with Kermode's *Hell On Earth* documentary included as a bonus feature. However, this version is still missing the 'rape of Christ' scene, but it is shown in its entirety in the documentary.

Straw Dogs (1971)
Dir: Sam Peckinpah /USA
Straw Dogs is one of Sam Peckinpah's finest films, a relentless study in violence and machismo that is shocking, not only for its violence, but the degree to which it manipulates 'civilised' audiences. Even the most passive viewer may find himself silently cheering on the carnage at the film's finale – an act that, in retrospect, gives much cause for discomfort.

David Sumner (Dustin Hoffman), a quiet mathematician, and his wife Amy (Susan George) seek to escape urban violence by moving to her birthplace, a small Cornish village. They hire four locals to construct the garage roof, and it isn't long before they begin making life unpleasant for David. Led by Charlie (Del Henney), an ex-boyfriend of Amy's, the four workers ridicule David while chipping away at his masculinity and ogling Amy, who seems to encourage their attentions. David, in an attempt to win their acceptance, joins them on a hunting trip; but they desert him in the wilderness, and two of the men return to the cottage and rape Amy, who is ambivalent about the experience and doesn't tell her husband.

Some time later, the couple attends a local church function where Amy, haunted by memories of the rape, breaks down. Driving home in the dense fog, they knock down Henry (David Warner), the town's simpleton. Unbeknownst to the couple, Henry has just strangled a young girl. They take the injured man back to their home and, when an angry mob (which includes David's tormentors) learns of Henry's whereabouts and lay siege to the house, David resolves to stay put and fight them off. What follows is a brilliantly edited, spectacularly violent climax.

Straw Dogs generated tremendous controversy upon its release in 1971. Many found the violence too graphic and gratuitous, as well as taking offence at the film's neolithic sexual politics: by resorting to brutal, deadly violence, the man proves himself true master of his 'property' – his house and his wife. The film is played as a power struggle between David and Amy (they play several symbolic games of chess during the story), with Amy pushing her partner's tolerance to breaking point. Her strategies include teasing the workers and disrupting David's work, while he counters by abusing her cat and accepting the hunting invitation. But David's checkmate comes when – after he has killed a few men and become quite abusive – he compels Amy to shoot one of the assailants. David has thus 'won' the game, losing everything he stood for in the process. This cynical premise, combined with the fact that David has actually relished in the violence, is difficult to swallow for many viewers.

Straw Dogs contains one of Hoffman's most layered performances, with the final explosion of violence all the more believable thanks to his initial, mild-mannered quietude. George combines suggestive sexuality with spitefulness to create an equally unforgettable character. Peckinpah handles everything with consummate skill, exerting complete control over his audience's responses. *Straw Dogs* is full of arresting images (the mesmerizing opening dissolve was borrowed by David Cronenberg for the beginning of *The Fly*), perfectly complemented by Jerry Fielding's eerie, Oscar-nominated score. Whatever your reservations about its content and philosophy, *Straw Dogs* remains one of the strongest and most memorable statements about violence ever put on screen.

Based on Gordon Williams' novel, *The Siege of Trencher's Farm*, it was Peckinpah himself who chose the title *Straw Dogs*, inspired by the Chinese proverb, "Heaven and Earth are not humane and regard people as straw dogs." And this does much to clarify the attitude towards violence in the film, and indeed, the *nature* of the violence. Even from the opening scenes it's clear that all is not well between David and Amy. He is immediately disliked for his nerdy status, while she flaunts her body and teases the villagers, and this culminates in the oft-discussed double rape scene, in which she is seen – at first – as a willing participant. Crucially, it isn't the rape which leads to the bloody showdown – David never actually learns

about the incident – but their sheltering of the town simpleton, who has accidentally killed a young girl, like Lennie Small in *Of Mice and Men*, by not knowing his own strength. Throughout the film, David's masculinity has been goaded to the point where he decides he will defend his home from the lynch mob, even if it means resorting to murder. This is all the more shocking because of his quiet, pacifist, non-confrontational manner which the yokels misread as a weakness. Many critics over the years have felt uncomfortable with the way Peckinpah manipulates his audience into endorsing David's actions and cheering him on in the cinema. Pauline Kael famously described the film as "fascist." Even producer Daniel Melnick felt unnerved by audience reactions, "It was certainly an anti-violent statement we all wanted to make," he said. "But when I saw the adolescents in the audience screaming 'Kill 'em! Kill 'em!' I thought, Jesus, what have we unleashed?"

Despite its powerful merits as a work of cinematic art, *Straw Dogs* – along with *A Clockwork Orange* and *The Devils* – remains one of the most notorious mainstream movies ever shot on British soil. Co-scripted by Peckinpah and David Zelag Goodman, the story unfolds in a primordial moral fog where men abuse women and women are turned on by it. Before long, it feels like a tour around the darkest parts of the director's psyche, since he was no stranger to violent outbursts and raging jealousy – he even went as far as auditioning one of his ex-girlfriends for the role of Amy. The fact that he added an extra rape to Williams' novel only added to the suspicion that he was an unrepentant misogynist. However, Katy Haber, Peckinpah's ex-girlfriend and assistant on *Straw Dogs*, defended him, saying, "Sam loved women but he resented his need for them. He feared the control they had over him. But frankly, in the relationships I've had in my life, I don't think that's an uncommon feeling in men."

Wild Bunch actor, Strother Martin, once described Peckinpah as a "dirty psychiatrist" who got what he wanted from actors by getting inside their heads and searching for strengths and weaknesses (during the filming of the church party scene, Peckinpah told Susan George that her father was dying in order to elicit the troubled and conflicting emotions from her as she recollects her traumatic rape). At the height of his powers in the late 60s, he was vilified as an alcoholic, drug-abuser, bully, womanizer and sadist. He was infamous for being very difficult to work with: volatile, terse, confrontational, uncooperative, even violent (Hoffman tried to get him fired from *Straw Dogs* after a rowdy party turned violent. Charlton Heston even threatened him with a sword during the making of *Major Dundee*, due to the director continuing to goad him when he was warned to stop). If he wasn't such a damn fine film-maker, Hollywood studios would have given him the boot long ago. But he had a knack for screen writing and a visceral flair behind the camera which meant he was much in demand. In 1969, he made *The Wild Bunch*, a critically-acclaimed, extremely violent western which set a new standard for action films while re-writing the rulebook in the process. His now trademark style involved quick-fire edits and bloody violent set-pieces presented at varying speeds. His films were often provocative, violent and preoccupied almost exclusively with masculinity.

Straw Dogs isn't Peckinpah's best film, but the finale presents us with a self-assured ferocity that suggests he knew exactly what he was aiming for. He was also disheartened with audiences when they cheered along with what he always saw as catharsis. "Sam worked from instinct," says his biographer Garner Simmons. "He saw the world in shades of grey and he used the film to examine things that he didn't understand – to see if they came out any clearer. He says that *Straw Dogs* is about the violence in all of us, but one of the first things he changed in the script was the lead character's name, from George to David – his own real name."

For its US release, the film was trimmed of the second rape which actually undermined the film for decades, as editor Roger Spottiswoode explains, "The first rape is more of a seduction, the second real, terrible rape. But shortening the terrible rape, of course, made it seem like Sam was saying rape was OK." During a hostile preview screening at the North Port Theatre in San Francisco in September 1971, in which there were jeers and walkouts, an enraged man who claimed to be a "pacifist" physically attacked the director. Peckinpah had to run for his life, and luckily for him, his driver was waiting in the car out front, and they fled.

Before its UK release, the British censors demanded cuts to the film even to secure the X rating. Producer Daniel Melnick recalls, "The

big issue was in the rape scene, whether it was pure rape or sodomy. So here were a group of grown-up men running a sequence of a few seconds back and forth on a Moviola, all looking at the angle of penetration, arguing that it couldn't be sodomy because of the position."

Upon release in the UK, the British press was merciless. Derek Malcolm of *The Guardian* called it "a brilliantly made, thoroughly bad film [which] leaves a bad taste in the mouth but only numbs the brain." *The Daily Telegraph* dismissed it as "ridiculous, pretentious and very nasty indeed, both artistically and morally." Thirteen UK film critics wrote an open letter to the *Times* condemning the film.

Straw Dogs appeared on VHS in 1980 just as the moral panic about 'video nasties' was brewing. Under the 1984 Video Recordings Act, all tapes had to be re-submitted to the BBFC for classification before 1988. But the successive distributors of *Straw Dogs* over the years refused to comply with any further cuts, and this left the film in limbo for the next 15 years. It was revived theatrically in the UK in 1995, but any hopes of a home video release were quickly dashed when in 1999 the BBFC made their position clear: "The issue of sexual violence has become of greater concern to the Board than 20 or 30 years ago [...] The clear indication that Amy comes to enjoy being raped is grounds for continued censorship." This ambivalent position on the no-means-yes 'rape myth' remains the most controversial aspect of the film to this day. "That's the acceptance of rape people find unacceptable," says Haber. "When Amy reaches up and kisses him, I can see why it angered people, but I can also see what Sam was doing. If ever there was a rejection of her relationship with David, it was at that moment." Daniel Melnick has always claimed that the rape was "totally organic" to the story, although he later admitted regretting Amy's enjoyment in the scene.

Straw Dogs was eventually passed by the BBFC in July 2002 with an uncut 18 certificate on its seventh time through the censor's office. Ironically, it was the reinstated footage of the double rape scene which made all the difference, as a BBFC spokesman explained: "The ambiguity of the first rape is given context by the second." Previously, the British censors had always been presented with the American R-rated version which loses the second rape, thus making the first one seem even worse. In 2002, however, the Board was shown the original uncut version which vigorously downplays any eroticism. Or, as the BBFC's Sue Clark explained: "The second rape now makes it clear that sexual assault is not something she welcomes." Fundamentally, this was the culmination of a cultural shift at the BBFC. Former chief censor, James Ferman, held a nannying, dictatorial stance on censorship in the UK, and was rumoured to have had personal issues with films like *The Exorcist* and *Straw Dogs*. And it's certainly no coincidence that the moment he retired in the late 90s, his successor, Robin Duval, gave *The Exorcist* a long-overdue amnesty on home video. Many of the 'video nasties' soon followed. Around the turn of the century, public consultations informed the BBFC that the way they ran the organisation was "old hat" and "po-faced." They thus decided it was time to instil a new order of transparency and consultative censorship, a far cry from Ferman's isolated in-house decisions process. The changes were indeed radical, and helped towards putting film censorship more in line with European law. This was encouraging news for anyone interested in films like *Straw Dogs*, as Ken Law of Freemantle Media says, "To move from a situation where *Dogs* was rejected with three minutes of recommended cuts to passed uncut in three years was a tall order but it was worth pursuing." He also praised what he saw as a new accountability at the BBFC, and welcomed the dialogue between distributor and censor.

Submitted in July 2001, it took the BBFC a whole year to decide the fate of the film. They consulted with psychologists specializing in sex offenders, and a focus group of 26 video-renters to inform their decision (20 accepted the uncut version). "If something is contentious, we'll seek advice," said Clark at the time. "The decision-making process is for the public, not some in-house arbitrary decision." And with that, the *Dogs* were finally unmuzzled.

A Clockwork Orange (1971)
Dir: Stanley Kubrick /USA
Stanley Kubrick's most controversial film follows Alex (Malcolm McDowell) as he leads his gang of young rogues through nightly rounds of "ultra-violence," with beatings, rape, stolen cars, and breaking and entering, all for kicks. They wear white jump suits, codpieces, and black bowler hats, and communicate in a strange lingo made up of broken Russian and cockney slang called "nadsat." Alex dislikes school but has a passion for Beethoven and sexual violence. The victims include subversive writer (Patrick Magee) who is severely beaten before his wife (Adrienne Corrl) is gang-raped.

After violently dealing with insubordination among his "droogies" (Russian for friends), Alex is smashed in the head with a milk bottle and left for the police during a raid on a house. In police custody he learns that his beating of a woman with a huge phallus has resulted in her death, and pretty soon Alex finds himself in prison. In order to shorten his sentence, he volunteers to undergo a radical new treatment for violent criminals, or 'aversion therapy'. The treatment is still in its experimental stages, and although Alex has a torturous experience, by the end of the therapy he does seem to be cured. He still has the violent urges, but those feelings are countered by extreme nausea.

Released back into society, Alex is no longer a natural being with free will, but a technologically manipulated drone (hence 'A Clockwork Orange' of the title), and even the thought of his beloved Beethoven is enough to make him physically sick. The outside world suddenly becomes very menacing to Alex, where vengeance is visited upon him by his ex-droogies who are now policemen, and his old victims (including Magee, who has some special payback in mind). After a suicide attempt, the media make Alex into a celebrity, and the shadow Prime Minister uses him as proof of a broken society in a cynical ploy to win votes. But perhaps the biggest cynic is Alex himself, whose phrase "I was cured all right" ends the film on a morally dubious note.

Kubrick's free-thinking, anti-authoritarian take on Anthony Burgess' novel on Catholic redemption is extremely effective, regardless of what allegorical take you put on it. It's visually astonishing, disturbing, ever quotable, and features one of the most memorable portrayals of evil in the history of film. With his lurid narration which is at once intimate and engaging, it's difficult not to feel sympathy for Alex, especially when you consider the dreary leap-frog games going on around him in the political sphere, with power-hungry parasites using him as a pawn in their reckless antics.

With *A Clockwork Orange*, Stanley Kubrick even surpasses the directorial virtuosity that he displayed in his previous film, *2001: A Space*

Odyssey; almost every trick in a film-maker's arsenal is utilized, with fish-eye lenses, beautifully choreographed set-pieces, expert use of lighting and arrangement, fast motion, slow motion, etc. McDowell puts on the best performance of his career, gleefully reeling off Burgess' self-invented slang terms (good is "Horrorshow", sex is "The old in-out-in-out") with a sadistic glint in his eye, and perfectly capturing the faux-innocence of youth ("It wasn't me, brother, sir").

A Clockwork Orange was released in the UK in January 1972, not long after the controversies which met Ken Russell's *The Devils* and Sam Pekinpah's *Straw Dogs*. A wave of media-led controversy shot the film to box-office success, and this in turn led to some imitative behaviour among young fans who began wearing the white boiler suits and bowler hats as a way of emulating their anti-heroes. The media leapt onto 'copycat' crimes, such as a Dutch tourist who was gang-raped by youths who sang *Singin' In the Rain* (a song Alex sings during a gang-rape in the film) whilst they did it. And the case of a 16 year old youth who kicked a homeless man to death. The press described the kid as being fascinated by *A Clockwork Orange*, although it later turned out he was obsessed with the book and had never seen the film.

The controversy escalated when the British censors were seen to be lenient on the film, and unlike *The Devils* and *Straw Dogs*, *A Clockwork Orange* was passed uncut with an X rating. This led to calls for the head of censorship, Stephen Murphy, to resign. Even the government got involved when the Home Secretary, Reginald Maudling, demanded to view the film at the BBFC headquarters before its release, and this led to accusations of state censorship. However, while all this hassle was going on, something very strange happened; director Stanley Kubrick simply banned the film himself due to concerns of copycat violence, and that ban remained in force for almost 30 years until he died in 1999. Still a hot topic today, no film fan should miss it.

Daughters of Darkness (1971)
(Orig title: *Le Rouge aux Levres*)
Dir: Harry Kumel /Belgium /France /W. Germany
Elizabeth Bathory was a Hungarian Countess who discovered, quite by accident, that the blood of young women helped to restore the youthful vitality of her skin. This idea later became an obsession for her, and in the decade from 1600 to 1610, she slaughtered and 'milked' at least 600 young women (possibly more than 700) with the aid of her household servants. She would bathe in the warm blood of her victims, convinced that she had found the secret of eternal youth. By 1611, the rumours of her evil deeds had become so widespread that King Mathias II of Hungary investigated the atrocities and brought her to trial. Bathory declined to appear in court, and, with overwhelming evidence stacked against her, she was found guilty and imprisoned in her castle. The outside doors and windows of her home were bricked up, and she was left inside to rot.

The legend of Bathory has become part of European folklore, along with the grisly deeds of other historical figures like Gilles de Rais and Vlad the Impaler. In 1971, two feature films came along which were based on Bathory; Hammer's *Countess Dracula*, starring Ingrid Pitt, and Harry Kumel's art-house favourite, *Daughters of Darkness*, which is set in modern-day Europe. The story of *Daughters* follows young newly-weds, Stefan and Valerie (John Karlen and Dannielle Ouimet), as they stop by at an eerily unoccupied hotel whose only member of staff seems to be the receptionist. While eating supper in the huge deserted hall, they notice the arrival of Countess Elizabeth Bathory (the stunning Delphine Seyrig, of *Last Year at Marienbad* fame) and her lesbian companion, Ilona (Andrea Rau) check in to the hotel. These new arrivals are immediately drawn to Valerie, and Bathory strikes up a conversation with the couple, and it isn't long before her intentions are made clear: she wants to seduce Valerie and take her away from her husband, a man who also holds some dark secrets of his own...

Daughters of Darkness is a masterful film, and one that radiates elegance and quality from every frame. The story unfolds from a realistic, down-at-earth position, yet somehow manages to feel strangely surreal, thanks to the haunting imagery and bizarre, dream-like pacing, not to mention the setting – a grand, empty hotel in the middle of winter. And, as others have noted, Seyrig steals the show with her superb performance as Bathory, the original 'Countess Dracula' who had somehow survived her imprisonment in 1611, and still lives on in modern times, leaving a trail of blood-drained bodies behind. She's perhaps the greatest female vampire in film history, emanating a deep, dark wisdom and world-weary attitude that could only come from the mind of a centuries-old bloodsucker.

The film is much more explicit in its themes than Hammer's *Countess Dracula*, in that it depicts Bathory as both a vampire and a sexual deviant. In one scene, she talks about her medieval days, claiming she drained "the blood of three hundred virgins to bathe in and drink." Emphasis on the word 'drink,' as the film portrays her as a blood-lusting vampire in the traditional sense. She attempts to seduce rather than attack her victims (as was later echoed by the immortal Miriam in *The Hunger* [1983]), to make loving companions rather than destroying them. The ending also adds a new twist to vampiric lore as Bathory seems to take possession of her latest consort at the moment of death, thus ensuring the ultimate immortality of evil.

Born in 1940, director Harry Kumel began experimenting with film as a child at the prompting of his father, producing dozens of 8mm shorts. He won numerous prizes at amateur film festivals as a teen, and at just 21-years-old he landed a job at the Belgian television channel, BRT. He spent much of the 1960s working in Belgian and Dutch television, making documentaries and programmes for *Premiere*, Belgium's popular series that was still running in the late 90s. His first big screen effort was *Monsieur Hawarden* (1968), a box-office flop that nonetheless garnered some strong critical support, and it helped secure the funding for *Daughters of Darkness*. *Daughters* was a financial success, particularly in the UK and US. And this afforded him an even bigger budget for his next fantastical film, *Malpertuis* (1972), another horror classic which, at the time, was the most expensive Belgian movie ever made (2.5 million guilders). Unfortunately, United Artists shelved the film for years for tax-dodging purposes, and this effectively stunted Kumel's promising career. He was later drawn back to the small screen, making TV movies for the rest of his career.

W.R. Mysteries of the Organism (1971)
Dir: Dusan Makavejev /Yugoslavia /W. Germany

Yugoslav twenty-something Malena envies her room-mate's lack of sexual inhibition, and ignores the attentions of her ex, Radmilovic. She instead tests out her belief in the ideas of Wilhelm Reich by sleeping with Russian ice skater Vladimir Ilyich, who is compelled by the power of his orgasm to decapitate her with his skates.

Dusan Makavejev had read Wilhelm Reich's *Dialectical Materialism and Psychoanalysis* as a student and had been fascinated by his assessment that what Marx had done for economic society, Freud had done for the human organism. But he was also aware of the ironies within Reich's life, which saw him exiled from both Soviet Russia and Nazi Germany for wanting to break down the barriers that limited creativity. He was eventually persecuted in America for being a medical charlatan, and spent much of his later life in a mental hospital. Indeed, Reich, who had dedicated his life to human liberty, died alone in a federal prison in 1957, having had his books burned in an incinerator in New York.

In the late 60s, Makavejev was commissioned by German television to make a film about Reich's theories. But he soon realised that the documentary approach he had in mind would not be sufficient enough to do the subject justice. In order to side-step the problem, he simply devised a framing story set in Yugoslavia that would serve as part of a collage of fact and fiction designed to subvert the repressed masses with an anarchic sense of humour. In addition, the film would also present to viewers the pleasures to be had through physical and psychological freedom. And by leaving many of the sequences unresolved, he thus encouraged viewers to actively engage with the film and arrive at their own conclusions.

Unsurprisingly, the finished film found itself ostracised in Eastern Europe, and its distribution elsewhere was severely limited. The fact that it was almost universally billed as a porn flick didn't do it any favours, either. And at the time, very few audiences got to see it. Overflowing with interesting ideas, the critics were largely dumbfounded and divided as to what it all meant – they described it variously as a treatise on applied sexology, a political satire, a doomed romance, Pop Art posing, and even as a new form of autobiography. They did, however, agree on one thing; Makavejev as a film-maker had a fine command of his craft, and he handled the humour and montage elements with an assured artistic manner. Yet, in poking fun at Lenin and Stalin and Mao, many Western critics also missed the point of how balanced this film was, and they championed it as an anti-communist satire. It never occurred to them that, although Makavejev may have mocked the communists, he also attacked America in the film for what he saw as its misuse of freedom and the vulgar manner in which it had allowed sex to be commercialized and turned into just another capitalist commodity, like everything else.

WR: Mysteries was passed in its entirety for a cinema release in the UK (it was the first film ever to get through the censor's office with the sight of an erect penis intact). On home video, however, it was altered to obscure the more explicit moments. After the opening credits sequence, a B&W Soviet sex-education film viewed through a kaleidoscope lens is obscured by animations of goldfish. This supposed act of censorship hasn't completely obscured the action and an erect penis can still be seen. Wall paintings of men and women masturbating were blanked out. A sequence showing Jim Buckley having a plaster cast made of his erect penis has all the tumescent shots obscured by animated stars. On UK video, Buckley's penis is covered up with psychedelic colours added in haste. It was the artist Nancy Godfrey who made the cast of the famous man's penis, and she was among a loose group of practitioners called Plaster Casters.

In the 90s, FilmFour broadcast the video version on UK TV. Head of British censorship at the time, James Ferman, claimed that the original version would have probably passed uncut, but the version submitted to them was the same as that which was censored back in the early 70s, and they had no choice but to pass it in its truncated form.

The Cat O'Nine Tails (1971)
(Orig title: *Il gatto a nove code*)
Dir: Dario Argento /Italy
The second in Argento's 'Animal Trilogy' which kicked off with *The Bird With the Crystal Plumage* and continued with *Four Flies On Grey Velvet*, *The Cat O'Nine Tails* has long been seen as one of the weakest entries in the Argento

cannon (but is actually a masterpiece compared to later turds like *The Card Player*, for example), but there's still much to be marvelled here as he simply refuses to abide by genre conventions.

A blind, retired reporter named Franco Arno (Karl Malden) overhears a blackmail conversation while taking a walk with his niece, Lori. A genetic research institute is broken-into, and one of the top research experts is pushed in front of a passenger train the next morning. Arno discovers that the victim was one of the men he had overheard the previous evening, and so he joins up with newspaper reporter, Carlo Giordani (James Franciscus), to help track down the killer who is always one step ahead of them, using a garotte wire to wipe out anyone who could jeopardise his freedom by revealing his identity...

Argento throws out all the usual giallo requirements of the time – the whodunit three-act plot structure, romantic interest, and so on – and instead has a field day playing around with the murder mystery template. In fact, the unmasking of the killer seems to be Argento's way of showing contempt for the usual by-the-book guidelines, as the killer turns out to be the least developed character. In this film, the killer seems to be everywhere, a shadowy omni-presence, he seems to know everything, and is right there at the right time to witness important details of the investigation, and is then able to keep the sleuths at bay by killing off those who may know too much.

Deep Red, *Suspiria*, and *Inferno* all feature buildings where the architecture becomes a puzzle to be solved; where the bricks and mortar almost become like a living and mysterious being. In *Cat O' Nine Tails* we see the beginning of this idea: Although it's less developed here, the Terzi Institute of Genetic Research becomes a cache of information, a place where all nine clues are yielded.

Ennio Morricone provides another wonderful score; this is actually one of his best – a sweet lullaby theme that breaks off into some dark jazz improvisations. Lookout for a gravestone which reads 'Di Dario!' as Arno and Giordani search for Bianca Merusi's tomb at the cemetery. Along with *Four Flies On Grey Velvet*, this was the most difficult of Argento's films to see for many years. The Anchor Bay version is the best option for DVD so far, but even here the intro and credits sequence looks a bit rough – it may have been taken from another print – and a couple of seconds are missing from the beginning of Morricone's theme. But as for the rest of the print, it looks pristine and all of the violence is intact.

Short Night of the Glass Dolls (1971)
(Orig title: *La Corte Notte Delle Bambole Di Vetro*; aka *Malastrana*; aka *Paralyzed*)
Dir: Aldo Lado /Italy

A man (Jean Sorel, star of Lucio Fulci's *Perversion Story*) is found unconscious one morning by a street sweeper, and is rushed off in an ambulance. He is pronounced dead on arrival at the hospital and his body is stored away in the morgue. However, it turns out that the man is still very much alive and conscious but in a completely paralyzed state due to a drug he was given. Through voice-overs we listen to his thoughts as he desperately tries to piece together the events which led to his nightmare predicament, and flashbacks are interspersed with medical professionals trying to work out why his body temperature hasn't dropped and why rigor mortis hasn't set in. We soon learn that the man's name is Gregory Moore, an American journalist reporting on the political situation in Prague, and whose girlfriend, Mira (Ringo Star's wife, Barbara Bach) had vanished. While investigating her disappearance, Gregory stumbles upon murder, a sinister cult, black magic, ritualistic orgies and human sacrifice. It's no spoiler if I tell you that Gregory is in for an excruciating fate.

An underrated and fairly obscure offering from writer/director Aldo Lado (whose only other horror movie was *Night Train Murders*), *Short Night of the Glass Dolls* is a tightly-structured horrific thriller which kicks off with a nightmarish scenario – conscious paralysis, and medical professionals casually discussing your impending post-mortem procedure – and only ratchets up the tension as it goes. With stunning cinematography from Giuseppe Ruzzolini, which captures the beauty of Prague, an effective score from Ennio Morricone, which begins with a simple riff before reaching intensity as the strings come thick and fast, and lots of bizarre and unsettling set-pieces – such as the scene on the railway bridge, the catatonic audience watching the musicians play, the sinister cult orgy, etc – *Short Night of the Glass Dolls* does a great job of keeping the viewers mesmerized throughout before the infamous 'autopsy' at the end, a scene so intense you'll be gripping your arm-rest for sure.

Sweet Sweetback's Badasssss Song (1971)
Dir: Melvin Van Peebles /USA

In the early 70s, a new strain of exploitation movies found their way into the grinders. And unlike the short-lived genres of yesteryear, like beach party flicks and biker epics which played mostly at drive-in theatres, this new breed of films played almost exclusively within urban areas. Blaxploitation had arrived with its kick-ass brothers and sisters, pimps, pushers, and super studs. Audiences flocked to the grindhouses excited to see black heroes finally make it to the big screen. The white middle class critics were scared shitless by these films, and they were also frowned upon by many in the black community who accused them of playing up to racial stereotypes and conveying the wrong type of messages. Nevertheless, for the next few years Blaxploitation dominated the inner-city screens with its funky threads, soul music, and 'kill whitey' revenge scenarios.

There had been a few forerunners to the genre, such as *The Black Klansman* and *The Bus Is Coming, Honky*, but things really kicked off in 1971 with the release of a couple of films that, although seemed to attract a similar audience, were very much polar opposites in terms of their origins and overall messages. One was MGM's *Shaft*, a slick detective yarn starring Richard Roundtree as a black crime fighter that boasted a super-cool soundtrack by Isaac Hayes. The other was much more raw, angry, and confrontational; Melvin Van Peebles' *Sweet Sweetback's Badasssss Song*.

Written, directed, produced, and starring Peebles himself, and dedicated to "All the Brothers and Sisters who've had enough of The Man", *Sweetback* opens with the title character working in a brothel doing live sex shows. He is hassled by a couple of cops and witnesses a fellow black man being abused. He decides to take action and attacks the cops, bashing their heads in before fleeing on foot. The rest of the film follows Sweetback on the run through the backstreets and urban decay of Ghettoville, USA.

When the film made it into theatres audiences were dumbfounded. They had seen nothing like it before. Peebles didn't sugar-coat the film at all; it's a grim, gritty, angry, and unrelenting tirade and a call for social change. And there's nothing in the style or performances or overall message that even attempts to lighten the blow. This uncompromising stance was rewarded with an X rating from the American censors ("An all white jury" as the ads put it) who were threatened by the fact that a black anti-hero had brutally attacked the police and then successfully crossed the border into Mexico at the end, his crime going unpunished. The epilogue warns us to "Watch out... a badasssss nigger is coming back to collect some dues". It was the first in a new wave of Black Rage films and audiences were lining around the block to see it.

This ground-breaking film raked in more than $10 million in its first year (a profit margin which outstripped its big-budget counterpart, *Shaft*, which managed $12 million), and became one of the most financially successful indie movies of all time, prompting producers to embrace black actors and turn them into screen heroes with a healthy box office kerching making it all worthwhile. Thus Blaxploitation was born, but none of the subsequent productions (often starring icons such as Jim Brown, Jim Kelly, Pam Grier, and Fred Williamson) could quite live up to the original double-whammy of *Sweetback* and *Shaft*. The main reason being that *Sweetback* was for real, it was a film that came from the heart of Peebles, not from a lust for profit, unlike the other films in the genre. He washes the screen in pain in order to move audiences into action, and announces that black militancy has reached your neighbourhood and that the times they are a-changing.

The British censors passed *Sweetback* uncut and it remained that way for three decades until 2003 when the docudrama *Badasssss!* was released. Peebles had written to the BBFC assuring them that a scene in which a young boy loses his virginity to a prostitute in *Sweetback* was played by a man called Hubert Scales who was over eighteen at the time. However, *Badasssss!* makes it quite clear that it was actually Melvin's son, Mario, who played the part, and he could not have been older than fourteen, thus putting the film in breach of the Protection of Children Act. The BBFC had no choice but to review their rating, and on the advice of a lawyer, they cut the scene to keep the film within the bounds of UK law. .

The Night Evelyn Came Out of the Grave (1971)
(Orig title: *La notte che Evelyn usci dalla tomba*)
Dir: Emilio P. Miraglia /Italy

After suffering a mental breakdown and spending time in a psychiatric hospital, a degenerate English Lord, Alan (Anthony Steffen) procures redhead prostitutes to torture and murder in his own private dungeon. He seems to act in this way in order to soil the memory of his deceased wife (who was also a redhead), as he believes she was having an affair before she died. Alan's doctor suggests he should get remarried, and this he does. Then both he and his new bride see Evelyn's ghost. And meanwhile, the bodies continue to pile up... A guilty pleasure for fans of Euro-horror, *The Night* sets up an interesting premise as a psychological character study before shifting into sub-par giallo territory (those paying attention should spot who the killer is quite early on). Like other gialli of the time, this remains utterly unconvincing in its English setting and English characters (see also *Cold Eyes of Fear* – supposedly set in London). But nevertheless, the film is put together quite well with good production values and a plethora of memorable set-pieces. Look out for the fox cage scene.

The Devil's Nightmare (1971)
(Orig title: *La plus longue nuit de diable*)
Dir: Jean Brismee /Belgium /Italy

A group of tourists – each of whom represents one of the seven deadly sins – arrive at an old dark castle where they are picked off by a sultry succubus (Erika Blanc). And a Priest makes the dumbest of deals with the Devil in an attempt to save their souls. Of course, all does not end well for him... A classic Euro-horror offering that includes baby sacrifice, softcore sex, bloody demises and the most unlikely Devil in the movies. This also includes an insanely catchy theme tune courtesy of Alessandro Alessandroni.

The Velvet Vampire (1971)
Dir: Stephanie Rothman /USA

Just as the hippy dream had turned sour, film-makers were keen to examine the fallout of the flower power movement. And though *The Velvet Vampire* does have its contemporaries in Harry Kumel's *Daughters of Darkness* (1971) and Jose

Larraz's *Vampyres* (1974), this film – which sees a bisexual vampire riding through the Californian desert in a dune buggy, picking up couples to feast on their blood – was a definite break from the norm at the time. *The Velvet Vampire* takes its time to bring the audience down from its hippy high and confront them with the base, animal instincts of human nature: the need for chaos, violence, control and domination. The vampire, Diane LeFanu (played by Celeste Yarnall) is obviously named in tribute to the author of the classic vampire story, *Carmilla*. She is calm and seductive and lays on the heavy innuendo, she perhaps represents the modern-day feminist female, in contrast to her female victim (Sherry Miles), a sexually-repressed, pre-feminist screamer.

The Abominable Dr Phibes (1971)
Dir: Robert Fuest /USA
"Nine killed her. Nine shall die. Nine eternities in doom!" After a team of physicians fail to save a woman's life following a car crash, her husband, the horribly disfigured Dr Anton Phibes, engineers an elaborate scheme of revenge, murdering each of them in the style of the Old Testament biblical plagues of Egypt: hence rabid rats, frogs, bees, locust's blood, hail, etc. *Phibes* sees Vincent Price's third term as the horror anti-hero of choice after doomy 50s fare like *House On Haunted Hill* and *House of Wax*, and the 60s flamboyance of *The Fall of the House of Usher* and *Masque of the Red Death*. By this time in the early 70s, Price had embraced the gothic roots of horror with this Hammer-esque madcap caper which mixes slick art deco stylings with a British-style gallows humour. The detectives on the case constantly hit a brick wall due to their belief that Phibes is dead, but the avenging doctor is still very much alive and communicates through a victrola via a cord, and drinks wine through a hole in his neck. It was followed by the sequel, *Dr Phibes Rises Again* (1972).

The Demons (1972)
(*Les Demons*; aka *Las poseidas del Demonio*)
Dir: Jess Franco /France /Portugal
In 1968, director Jess Franco teamed up with notorious producer, Harry Alan Towers, and together they made several films for the international market. One of those films was *The Bloody Judge* (1969), an historical drama starring Christopher Lee as a vicious Old Bailey judge who deals with political opponents by accusing them and their loved ones of being criminals or witches, and watching them burn. Though well received, *The Bloody Judge* was a tempered affair, with Franco on his best behaviour as he attempted to recapture the international success of Michael Reeves' *Witchfinder General* (1968). In the early 70s, however, Franco teamed up with French producer, Robert De Nesle, and decided he would tackle the theme of witch persecution all over again in a project entitled *The Demons*. This time he didn't have the star power of Christopher Lee, but, to compensate, he was afforded unlimited freedom behind the camera to explore the sordid tale in all its graphic and horrifying detail.

The Demons opens on the torture of a suspected witch. After the title credits, she is burned in the town square, but not before she curses her accusers in typical witch movie fashion. Lady De Winter (Karin Field) is a sadistic aristocrat who's superstitious side has been spooked by the witch's curse, and who attempts to put her mind to rest by rounding up the witch's estranged daughters and having them condemned, too. This she does by visiting the Blackmoor Nunnery and pointing her finger at Kathleen (Anne Libert), an innocent nun who has no recollection of her mother. After a lengthy ordeal at the hands of the torturers where she is pricked and scalded, local astronomer, Malcolm (Howard Vernon), bribes the dungeon guards into setting her free. Kathleen wanders through the woods in her injured state and stumbles into the den of a blind witch. It seems the witch had expected her arrival, and knows exactly who Kathleen is (presumably this blind witch was part of the same coven as Kathleen's mother who was burned in the prologue, but this is never made clear). The blind witch begins instructing Kathleen on the powers of sorcery to enable her to exact a supernatural revenge on De Winter and her associates. Perhaps unsurprisingly, Lady De Winter – easily the most cunning and ruthless character in the film – also turns out to be a witch. She has the power to turn men into smoking skeletons just by kissing them on the lips. And the stage is set for a fiery finale...

No other witch movie has as many sex scenes and burnings as *The Demons*. And no other witch movie is available in so many different versions. The victim of countless censorship cuts over the years, *The Demons* was banned outright in the UK in 1972, and remained outlawed for 36 years until the Redemption DVD release in 2008. During those years, the film turned up in any number of versions on VHS, at various lengths and in various languages, sometimes without English subtitles, intriguing and frustrating film fans who could sense they had stumbled upon a neglected gem. A restoration job was attempted in the late 2000s, by gathering together all of the different versions and constructing as close to an uncut version as possible. However, even the supposed 'director's cut' on DVD contains blatant cuts, and it's clear that much censored material has yet to surface.

The version that survives today seems to have most – if not all – of the sex scenes intact, while the more violent shots look to have hit the cutting room floor. The burnings are similar to the ones seen in *The Bloody Judge*, with the condemned tied to ladder-like wooden structures and dropped into the flames, but here the camera lingers on the horrors for much longer, and very little is left to the imagination. And, in addition to the witch craze kick-started by *Witchfinder General*, *The Demons* also looks to have been influenced by Ken Russell's *The Devils* (1971) (and, by extension, Huxley's novel on which it was based), which was a controversial hit in the previous year. Franco borrows not only the 'nunsploitation' elements of Russell's film, but also the socio-political themes too, with the Church and judicial institutions depicted as rotten and corrupted by evil. An establishment lackey is even named Renfield in reference to the vampiric nature of the wicked aristocracy.

The Demons, even in its incomplete form, is not too bad a film, but newcomers to Franco are advised to start elsewhere (try *Venus in Furs* [1967] or *Necronomicon/Succubus* [1968] for examples of the director at his best). At this stage in his career, Franco was much more willing to churn out pure exploitation films with no more of an objective than to satisfy his producer's wishes and to explore his own strange obsessions. The film is supposedly set in a medieval English town, but looks a lot like sunny Portugal where it was shot. And the director even collaborated with his regular composer, Daniel J. White, to produce the wah-wah guitars and free-form jazz improvisations – an odd choice of music for an historical drama, to be sure (some of those jam sessions were later recycled in other Franco films, particularly *La Comtesse Perverse*). All in all, *The Demons* isn't all that dissimilar to *Haxan* (1922), which was made fifty years earlier and explores the same psycho-sexual undertones and employs a similar exploitation film-making method.

The Last House On the Left (1972)
(aka *Sex Crime Of the Century*; aka *Krug and Company*)
Dir: Wes Craven /USA

Although he's more well-known nowadays for his 'postmodern', self-referential slasher movies of the *Scream* franchise, and the surrealist horrors of *A Nightmare On Elm Street*, which gave the world a new horror icon in the form of Freddy Krueger, there is something altogether more dangerous and sinister tucked away in Wes Craven's filmography which for more than thirty years was considered harmful and obscene by the British censors. *Last House On the Left* is an uneasy melding of art house seriousness and grindhouse sleaze which continually throws viewers into confusion by adding a bizarre banjo soundtrack and moments of ill-advised comedy. Just like *The Texas Chain Saw Massacre*, *Last House* had long been outlawed in the UK, and it wasn't difficult to see why; the BBFC have never been kind or lenient on films which flaunt chainsaw mayhem and death by blowjob. Even hardened New York exploitation fans on the 42nd Street Deuce were appalled, with audiences invading the projection booth and knifing the film print to shreds. This was all publicity heaven for the film-makers who marketed *Last House* with the much-borrowed tagline: "To avoid fainting, keep repeating, it's only a movie… only a movie…"

Right from the very beginning, Craven and his producer, Sean Cunningham (who later went on to launch the *Friday the 13th* series), knew exactly what they intended to do with their film, "One of the key aims was to show the harsh, brutal reality of interpersonal violence." They weren't interested in giving viewers ninety minutes of cosy, perilous fun. Instead, they wanted to send their audience home truly disturbed and afraid. Back in the days of the 'video nasties', *Last House On the Left* was one of the sickest puppies in the litter. An ugly, harrowing cult favourite which is much more complex (albeit crudely made) than its reputation would suggest. Loosely based on Ingmar Bergman's *The Virgin Spring*, Wes

Craven's film depicts the atrocities committed by a 'family' of Manson-esque rootless criminals led by Krug, who kidnap, rape and torture two teenage girls before murdering them. The sadists then make their way through the dense New Jersey woods and take refuge with a suburban couple, posing as a family whose car has broken down. Little do the killers know that the house they have picked for their refuge is owned by Dr. and Mrs. Collingwood, the parents of one of their victims. After discovering the truth, the nice, liberal, middle-class couple exact savage revenge on the Krug and co, with the husband wielding a chainsaw and the wife her teeth for an unhappy ending.

Made on the tiniest of budgets, this drive-in exploitation pic decisively transcends its limitations. The intense violence is never played for thrills; indeed, Craven has said he wanted to "re-sensitize" Americans to the reality of violence in the wake of the Vietnam War. Craven – who would go on to polish his themes in the slicker *The Hills Have Eyes* (1977) – never for a moment allows the viewer to sympathise with the killers, but he does provide a window of understanding into how seemingly senseless acts of violence occur. The killers initially toy with the girls, as if playing a game; but when the game gets out of hand and the girls end up dead, the killers look at their corpses with saddened confusion, like children who have broken a favourite doll. Some have seen the film as a critique of the nuclear family, exploring the threat of patriarchal violence that lies beneath traditional structures of domestic authority. Undeniably, the good Dr. Collingwood's behaviour, from his surreptitious appraisal of his daughter's figure to his spectacularly violent revenge, is not the kind of behaviour you would expect from a liberal. And like David in *Straw Dogs* – which was made at around the same time – we see an otherwise sane and benign character resorting to savage behaviour. Both *Last House* and *Straw Dogs* make you think about how you'd react if you found yourself in a similar situation.

And now for the long history of censorship. *The Last House On the Left* was banned outright in the UK when it was submitted for a planned theatrical release in 1974. The British censors claimed that no amount of cuts would make it acceptable for public viewing. In June 1982 it was released briefly on VHS by Replay Video, and in little over a year it fell afoul of the 'video nasties' panic and was prosecuted and banned on video, too. In 1999, Feature Film submitted the film for classification, and although the BBFC were now prepared to lift the ban, they would only do so if the distributors agreed to around 90 seconds of cuts "to remove images of the horrific stripping, rape, and knife murder of the two women." And after Feature Film declined to cooperate with cutting the guts out of the film, the censors simply kept it on the banned shelf. Not long after this, Exploited Films – a subsidiary of Blue Underground – began holding public screenings of *Last House* in the UK in uncut form. The idea was to show that the BBFC was out of touch with public opinion (*The Texas Chain Saw Massacre* had also been subjected to illegal screenings in the UK, and this had resulted in its eventual uncut release after being banned for around twenty-five years). *Last House* was shown ten times at the ICA in London without a public outcry or police intervention, and this convinced the folks at Blue Underground that the film was now considered acceptable for adult audiences. But still, chief censor, Robin Duval, insisted on cuts. By now, the situation was beginning to look like Duval had a personal problem with the film; for horror fans at the time, Duval's unmovable stance was reminiscent of former chief censor, James Ferman, and his strong dislike for films such as *The Texas Chain Saw Massacre* and *The Exorcist*, both of which were only okayed in the UK after he resigned from the Board.

Blue Underground was informed that sixteen seconds of cuts were needed to secure a DVD release in the UK. But, spurred on by the encouraging words of film critic Mark Kermode, the distributors decided to go to the Video Appeals Committee (VAC), where concerned bods heard arguments for releasing the film uncut on the grounds of its great historical importance – this was also known as the 'Last Appeal On The Left'. Central to Blue Underground's case was an essay written by Kermode – the 'specialist witness' – which put the troublesome film into context as a legitimate work in the evolution of the horror genre, and verified its importance as a work of American independent cinema. "It was a bravura polemic," Kermode later joked, "weighty, profound and forthright." However, after considering the evidence, the VAC announced that in their opinion, the sixteen seconds of cuts being contested were actually *too lenient* for such a harrowing and disturbing film. And accordingly, the BBFC prevailed in their ruling. Kermode was particularly disheartened by the outcome; after all, it was his erudite and informed essay which was all but ignored in the lead-up to the decision. "The BBFC not only held up the cuts – they doubled them!" he later said.

It was a bad day for horror fans, as Blue Underground's Carl Daft made clear, "I'm frankly astonished and appalled at the VAC's decision. Not only is it incorrect on the basis of the evidence put before them, it makes a mockery of the established rules of fairness on conduct applicable to public bodies such as the BBFC. Contrary to what we might expect under Article 10 of The European Convention of Human Rights, we are a very long way from having our right to free expression in this country guaranteed. Such actions make us the laughing stock of the rest of the Western World. The right to free speech in the United Kingdom died today, and for that I have to say that I am ashamed to be British."

The late 00s saw the release of the violent video game, *Manhunt 2*, which the BBFC immediately banned. However, the developers, Rockstar Games, appealed their decision, and ultimately, the Video Appeals Committee voted that the game could be released with an 18 certificate. The case was taken to the High Court and the game granted a release. Central to the decision was the Board's 'sexual violence policy tests' which consisted of in-depth research carried out by Ipsos MORI which looked at the potential for sexually sadistic images to cause harm to viewers. In 2008, Second Sight submitted *Last House On the Left* to the censors, and the film was finally given an uncut bill of health. Interestingly, it was the furore surrounding *Manhunt 2* which altered the censor's guidelines, as a BBFC statement points out, "On the basis of the authoritative interpretation of the harm test as directed in the High Court in the *Manhunt 2* case, the Board considered that the dated nature of the work had reduced much of the impact of the sexual violence previously cut. The Board's sexual violence policy tests had been applied afresh since the previous submission, and the Board did not now believe that the work posed a realistic possibility of harm, so it was classified '18' uncut."

BBFC director, David Cooke, claimed that the High Court case which saw the release of *Manhunt 2* had actually helped the Board. "We actually got a fairly substantial benefit from the *Manhunt* episode," said Cooke. "We went to the High Court, and it clarified the harm test – actually a benefit that flies across a whole range of games and film. It all gets quite technical, but for instance, it showed it was not necessary for us to show devastating effect, which was what the arguments had said previously. So we've ended up with a clearer legal definition of that test than we had before the case started."

As for *Last House On the Left*, director Wes Craven had always described the film as an angry response to TV images of the Vietnam War, and addressed the more contentious elements in terms of confrontation and catharsis. Of the film's many vocal detractors, he has always supported the audience's right to destroy film prints if they felt compelled to do so, whilst disagreeing with the official censors for being so biased against low-budget, independent films. "[*The Last House On the Left* is] a protest against real violence in the world," he has since stated, "and the downplaying of the reality of violence in films. We showed violence in its true ugliness, rather than taking the usual Hollywood path of making it glamorous and exciting and entertaining, which is in essence a lie. I've had many people over the years tell me it's my strongest film and most truthful film. And I think there is a sense that the film was 'pure' in that it didn't pull any punches or cater to any form of censorship."

The Gore Gore Girls (1972)
Dir: Herschell Gordon Lewis /USA
The Gore Gore Girls is upbeat fun from start to finish, with its catchy rock 'n' roll grindhouse numbers, amusing script and the bickering lead players who are on the hunt for a serial killer, and who gradually warm to each other as things progress. It's also a film packed with outrageous gore and splatter, including the sight of a woman having her face hacked up with a meat cleaver, in close-up, until there's nothing left but a mound of red pulp; another girl is beaten on her derriere with a meat tenderiser, to which the killer adds salt and pepper to the pulverised mess; another victim has her nipples snipped off with scissors, resulting in streams of white milk and chocolate milk; one girl takes a whack to the back of the head while blowing bubble gum, and the bubble fills with blood; one victim has

her head shoved into a deep fryer, and another has her face scolded with a hot iron. Yet despite all the gratuitous nastiness on display, it's so over-the-top that it can't be taken seriously. Lewis went on to make his fortune in advertising and stayed away from film-making for decades until he returned for the ill-advised *Blood Feast 2: All You Can Eat* (2001).

Pigs (1972)
(aka *The Killer*; aka *Blood Pen*; aka *Daddy's Deadly Darling*)
Dir: Marc Lawrence /USA
At the grubbier end of the grindhouse exploitation movies is *Pigs*, a lurid, low-budget weirdy about a cafe owner, Mr. Zambrini (Marc Lawrence) who feeds dead bodies to his porkers. A psychotic young runaway, Lynn (Toni Lawrence), joins him at his run-down ranch, and after she murders a lecherous truck driver, the farmer helps her to dispose of the body, and of course, more bodies are added to the count. Meanwhile, a kooky neighbour is suspicious of the pair's behaviour, and she constantly pesters the local Sheriff to investigate the pig pens for evidence of murderous behaviour, but the lawman always comes up short, until the end when Lynn's psychotic rage spirals out of control...

Pigs is a good place to start if you're new to 70s grindhouse horror; it includes all the things that make these films so well loved (and hated) by fans of the genre – strange, morbid storyline, oddball characters, technical limitations and general all-round weirdness. Actress Toni Lawrence (the director's daughter in real life) does a fine job in her role, alternating between child-like innocence and knife-wielding psychotic. Her father, Marc, isn't quite as good in his role as Mr. Zambrini, but his adequate performance shows how each of the doomed souls are also victims in their own right: Lynn's psychosis stems from being raped by her father, and Zambini's own oddness seems to have been brought about by the local residents in the area who try all they can to make life difficult for him.

Stephen Thrower described the film as "a love story between a psychotic teenage girl and a grave-robbing pig-farmer," which is quite accurate, but despite the pair recognising each other as kindred spirits, their relationship doesn't have time to develop fully as a succession of outside threats encroach on their lives. Perhaps the biggest impression the film leaves behind is a misanthropic one; it is hinted throughout that the pigs in the pen are just an extension of the bestial, crummy behaviour of human swine. There are constant references to humans as pigs, and in one nightmare sequence in particular, Lynn's screams are merged with the sounds of squealing pigs.

Deep Throat (1972)
Dir: Gerard Damiano /USA
The world's first porno blockbuster, *Deep Throat* tells the tale of Linda Lovelace who visits her doctor (Harry Reems) complaining that she cannot reach orgasm. After some tests, Reems discovers that the reason is because her clitoris is located deep down in the back of her throat. Cue much hilarity as a newly cured Lovelace gobbles every cock in sight and has that long sought after orgasm after all...

Not exactly the best place to start if you're getting into 70s porn, for although *Deep Throat* is one of the most well-known pornos of all time, the film itself looks bloody awful. The lighting and sets are flat and completely uninteresting, and as for the sex scenes themselves, they're all rather boring. The film serves as nothing more than a curiosity nowadays. To have it available on DVD is surprising because I can't imagine why anyone would want to watch this more than once. The sex scenes are also ultimately a turn-off after hearing the awful rumours and allegations concerning the making of the film, such as the rumour that Lovelace was under-age when the film was shot, and the alleged practices of Chuck Traynor. The DVD presentation is disappointing, with print damage and speckles galore. It was shot for $22,000 and the cast and crew had to hitch hike from New York to Miami where the shooting took place.

The film has a sinister dark side due to the involvement and practices of Lovelace's then husband/manager, Chuck Traynor, a hate figure not only among the anti-porn movement and feminists, but even among long-time porn fanatics and many who have worked in the industry. Lovelace later spilled the beans and accused Traynor of beating and coercing her into selling her body and appearing in porn films. Feminist author Andrea Dworkin helped Lovelace to put a case together and took the matter to court where she accused pornography of being a violation of women (see also her scathing book on the subject; *Pornography: Men Possessing Women*). In a 2000 documentary for Channel 4 entitled '*The Real Linda Lovelace*', Traynor was interviewed and confronted with the allegations that he had ordered his own wife's gang rape and had forced her at gunpoint to have sex with a dog on camera in a Miami motel room. His reaction to these claims was horrifying; he seemed basically nonplussed by the idea and acted like it was no big deal, and didn't really deny anything.

As for Linda Lovelace, I think her sad story has more to do with the fact that she had found herself in an awful relationship rather than being a victim of porn per se. She married a man who battered and abused and exploited her for a couple of years, ironically making her a star. To put a ban on porn won't make it go away, it will only make it more difficult to regulate and drive it underground. Nor will it put an end to the violence and abuse of women.

Scream Bloody Murder (1972)
Dir: Marc B. Ray /USA
A young boy, Matthew, runs a bulldozer over his father, killing him. He then falls from the seat and has his hand crushed beyond repair in the vehicle treads. Ten years later, and Matthew returns home from a mental institution with a hook in place of his mashed up hand. But his Oedipal rage starts anew when he discovers that his mother is now remarried. Matthew murders his mamma's new hubby with an axe, and when mother intervenes, he throws her to the ground and she bashes her head on a rock and dies (presumably). Matthew flees home and hits the road accepting a lift from a young couple. He hallucinates that the girl is his mother – hallucinations which continue to torment him throughout the film – and of course, he ends up killing them too. The movie continues to follow Matthew on his murderous journey; an artist/prostitute, a sailor, housemaid, a pet dog, an elderly woman, a house caller – everybody gets it. The plot steers into other areas in the second half, exploring kidnap, mental abuse, and sexual intimidation.

This is a pleasingly nasty and violent little film considering it was made in 1972 and I'm surprised it doesn't have a much larger cult following. There's lots of gruesome death scenes filmed with trippy wide-angle lenses and hosts a tense, downbeat ending making it top-of-the-

range exploitation. Matthew isn't a glamorised and unstoppable killing-machine like Freddy, Michael, or Jason; he's a pathetic, single-minded mamma's boy who deflects all of his own problems onto others (like many real life killers), and it's these lurid qualities that make the film all the more interesting to watch, as far as I'm concerned.

The UK video version loses a small cut during the axe murder scene, and is also trimmed of the aftermath of the pet dog butchered with a meat cleaver. The American video version (which is also available in an awful looking transfer on cheap horror DVD box sets) is fully uncut. This film is in desperate need of a proper DVD release, so until then, happy hunting.

The Case of the Bloody Iris (1972)
(Orig title: *Perche quelle strance gocce di sangue sul corpo di Jennifer?*)
Dir: 'Anthony Ascott' [Giuliano Carnimeo] /Italy
Known primarily for spaghetti westerns like *Find a Place to Die* (1968) and *Sartana the Gravedigger* (1969), director Giuliano Carnimeo teamed up with horror writer, Ernesto Gastaldi, in 1972 for a stab at the giallo, delivering a competent if unremarkable murder mystery. The bulk of the plot takes place in a luxury apartment block where English girl, Jennifer (Edwige Fenech), moves in with her friend, Marilyn (Paola Quattrini). Murders were committed in the building before they moved in, including a black nightclub dancer who was drowned in their bath tub. And as the police investigation gets underway, Jennifer and her friend suspect that they could be next on the killer's hit list... The film throws up enough red herrings, with character's whose words can be misconstrued in a negative way, thus casting themselves under instant suspicion. In fact, all of the characters at some point are portrayed in a sinister way, even the beautiful leading lady, Fenech. Of course, this makes the whole film feel overly contrived to fit the giallo tradition. However, there's enough twists and turns and nudity to keep fans amused. Bruno Nicolai also contributes the luschious, string-heavy pop score.

Tombs of the Blind Dead (1972)
(aka *The Blind Dead*; Orig title: *La noche del terror ciego*)
Dir: Amando de Ossorio /Spain /Portugal

During a trip to Portugal, Spanish friends investigate the disappearance of Virginia (Maria Elena Arpon), who had stormed off in a huff, and learn that she was killed by 'the Knight's Templar,' blind zombies on horseback, after she had awoken them from their tombs in the ancient ruins of a monastery. And, soon enough, the Knights target the friends – and anyone else who gets in their way – as they saunter on through the plains using their swords and teeth to finish their victims... *Tombs of the Blind Dead* is a slow-moving but haunting and stylish little zombie flick, but beware of the censored version which has all the bloody stuff cut out, including the torture scene in the opening prologue. Fans of 70s Euro-horror – and Jean Rollin in particular – should find much to savour here. It was followed by three loose sequels; *Return of the Evil Dead* (1973), *The Ghost Galleon* (1975) and *Night of the Seagulls* (1976). Though interesting, none of them are as good as the first.

Haunts of the Very Rich (1972)
Dir: Paul Wendkos /USA
This TV movie – based on a story by T.K. Brown – sees wealthy passengers on a luxury airliner travelling to a mysterious destination called Portals of Eden. They arrive at the tropical paradise and are greeted by Seacrist (Moses Gunn), a white-suited black man who serves as their tour guide. The passengers argue about where they are; some reckon Central America, others the Caribbean. They stay in a grand, opulent hotel, where they're free to pamper themselves and enjoy their luxurious surroundings. However, the characters soon begin to question the reality of their environment while the lecherous millionaire, David Woodruf (Lloyd Bridges) tries to sleaze his dick into every female he meets, even when he knows they're married. A thunderstorm cuts off the electricity, which means no phones, no TV and no air conditioning. Food supplies are also running low. And their tropical paradise slowly darkens into a hellish nightmare as they realise they could all be dead.

It's a real shame that this film is only available nowadays in horrid-looking bootleg copies that were obviously recorded from television and ripped from an old, worn-out video cassette. It's one of the best ABC 'movies of the week,' from a series of TV movies which ran from 1969 to 1976, delivering such classics as Steven Spielberg's *Duel* (1971), *Death at Love House* (1976) and *Trilogy of Terror* (1975). Frustratingly, ABC seem very reluctant to delve into their archives as only a very few of their titles have ever made it onto disc

The Folks at Red Wolf Inn (1972)
(aka *Terror at Red Wolf Inn*; aka *Terror House*; aka *Terror on the Menu*)
Dir: Bud Townsend /USA
College girl, Regina (Linda Gillen), arrives home one day to discover she has won a competition. Her prize? A vacation at Red Wolf Inn, a mysterious 'resort' run by a seemingly wholesome elderly couple, Henry and Evelyn (Arthur Space and Mary Jackson), and their grandson, Baby John (John Neilson). For the first couple of days, Regina enjoys herself and makes friends with other competition winners, Edwina and Pamela. However, when they leave without saying goodbye, Regina becomes suspicious of the place and its increasingly controlling owners. She eventually discovers the severed heads of Edwina and Pamela in the pantry, and soon after she is taken prisoner and forced to eat strange meat. Baby John has become smitten with her, and her only hope for survival is with his help. But is he willing to betray his grandparents to save her? *The Folks at Red Wolf Inn* wouldn't have been out of place as an ABC Movie of the Week, alongside equally off-beat treats like *Crawlspace* (1972) and *Haunts of the Very Rich* (1972). And even though it plays like a made-for-TV movie, meaning there is very little on-screen bloodshed and the cannibalism angle is kept a little too subtle, it can be quite a gripping little thriller if you go in with low expectations.

Blood Sabbath (1972)
(aka *Yyalah*)
Dir: Brianne Murphy /USA
One of the better witchcraft-themed movies of the early 70s is *Blood Sabbath*, which despite the wrong-footings on the casting front, and its slim running time of just over an hour, is well worth a watch. The story follows David (Anthony Greary), who is sort of a hippie fresh from a stint in Vietnam. While on a hiking trip through Mexico with his acoustic guitar, David bumps his head and knocks himself unconscious in the wilderness. A beautiful young nymph called Yyalah (Susan Damante-Shaw) nurses his wounds, and when David recovers he becomes

obsessed with her. It turns out that Yyalah is part of a witch cult run by the Priestess Alotta (the brilliant Dyanne Thorne), and she informs him that they cannot be together because he has a soul. So David pleads with Alotta to sacrifice his soul so that he can be with Yyalah... The casting of Greary in the lead role was a terrible decision, and this diminishes much of the film's mystic spell; he's so unconvincing as a war veteran and his naïve and lovelorn clumsiness gets quite irritating at times. However, the same can't be said of Dyanne Thorne, who steals the show effortlessly as the wicked Priestess – her charismatic portrayal of evil renders all the other players redundant, and she single-handedly rescues this strange little tale from oblivion.

Diabel (1972)
(*The Devil*)
Dir: Andrzej Zulawski /Poland
Set during the Prussian occupation of Poland in the 1790s, a black-cloaked stranger sets a prisoner free. The prisoner, Jakub (Leszek Teleszynski), eventually gets back home across the snowy wilderness only to find that his family has fallen apart. He then finds himself embarking on a vicious killing spree. Still one of the most criminally overlooked film-makers in cinema history, Andrzej Zulawski is only familiar to the most adventurous of film fans. *Diabel* was his second feature after the controversial World War II epic, *The Third Part of the Night* (1971), and here he confirms his early promise with an allegorical tale about the monstrousness of the – then – current communist rule. Zulawski's quirks for which he is most well known for are all in evidence here: shrieking, hysterical women, rapid hand-held camera work, interesting use of music, political provocation and strong bloody violence. Unsurprisingly, the communist authorities didn't look too kindly on the film, and promptly banned it for many years. The DVD looks a bit rough in places, especially around reel changes, but it's a minor miracle that this film still exists at all.

Crawlspace (1972)
Dir: John Newland /USA
A retired couple are set on edge when a strange young man is found sleeping in the cellar. After the old man padlocks the doors, the bedraggled youngster flees into the night. The following evening he returns and tries the doors again. The couple hear him while in bed, and hug each other for comfort. In the morning they take food down to him, but the kid, Richard, doesn't seem interested in conversation. The old couple don't know where he came from or what his intentions are, and are reluctant to call the police for fears of antagonising him. So they try their best to ignore him. However, there is a bad smell coming up from the cellar... Eventually Richard begins to ingratiate himself into the household by helping out with the chores; chopping logs for the fire, shovelling snow, making morning coffee. The couple welcome him into their home, but Richard's violent streak ensures a lynch mob arrives on the doorstep to take him out... *Crawlspace* is more of a tragic story than out and out horror, which is a shame because the subtle rise in tension is expertly handled, but the horrific ending expected by the audience fizzles out in the final moments.

Blood Freak (1972)
(aka *Blood Freaks*)
Dir: Steve Hawkes and Brad F. Grinter [Frank Merriman Grinter] /USA
A strapping young man, Herschell (co-director Steve Hawkes), is caught between two sisters; one is a nice Christian girl, and the other is a pot-smoking trollop. He is lured into bed by the latter after she gets him stoned by the pool, and later he allows himself to be the subject of genetic experiments which go horribly wrong – the experiment causes his head to mutate into a giant turkey's head. The mutated monster then goes on a killing spree, slaughtering the local dope fiends in the area, and all the victims share the same hilarious looped screams... *Blood Freak* is such a badly made film that the film-makers must have been in on the joke. It comes on like a fanboy's tribute to Herschell Gordon Lewis, and there is also a religious slant with some anti-drug propaganda thrown in. The film's other co-director, Grinter, appears at regular intervals talking directly to camera about the dangers of drugs and encouraging viewers to find salvation in God, while he chain-smokes cigarettes. All in all, it's a bad movie classic which includes some of the most ludicrous anti-drug preaching since *Reefer Madness* (1936).

Lemora: A Child's Tale of the Supernatural (1973)
(aka *Lady Dracula*; aka *The Legendary Curse of Lemora*)
Dir: Richard Blackburn /USA
At the invite of a mysterious woman called Lemora, young church singer, Lila, takes off in the middle of the night to Lemora's house on the promise she will get to meet her father who is on the run for shooting his cheating wife. Lila passes through the town witnessing all manner of lecherous drunks and abusive pimps. And when she finally arrives at Lemora's homestead, she meets the prim and softly-spoken woman, and is alarmed when her reflection doesn't appear in the mirror ("the mirror is broken, dear"). She also appears to have an aversion to Lila's crucifix necklace. Even stranger are the ghoulish creeps who stalk Lila through the house, and the sinister children who laugh mockingly at her every word... *Lemora* is an unsung masterpiece of 70s horror and the only film by writer/director Richard Blackburn (he also plays the seedy Priest in the film). It's an eerie, dream-like vampire flick that was released on murky VHS transfers for years until Synapse unleashed an astonishingly rich and detailed DVD in the mid-00s. For the first time, audiences could fully appreciate how beautifully shot and lit the film is, with the striking visuals reminiscent of Mario Bava's candy-coloured Gothic chillers of the 1960s. Lesley Gilb is great as the seductive vampire, all clad in black and exerting a devious, predatory relish in grooming her young victim. Cheryl Smith is also great in her first starring role as the good Christian girl, Lila. Surprisingly, she was 18-years-old at the time, though she looks much younger in the film. She went on to appear regularly in exploitation movies like *Massacre At Central High* (1976) and *The Swinging Cheerleaders* (1974). She also appeared in Jonathan Demme's drive-in classic, *Caged Heat* (1974).

Forced Entry (1973)
Dir: 'Helmuth Richler' [Shaun Costello] /USA
The deranged Vietnam veteran has turned up in all kinds of films over the last few decades, from silly comedy-horror (*The Vagrant*), all-out action movies (*Rambo First Blood*), and home invasion movies (*Naked Massacre*), to intelligent horror fantasy (*Deathdream*), the ultra-obscure (*The Ravager*), and stomach-churners like *Combat Shock*. But nowhere will you find a darker, more twisted version of the psycho 'Nam vet than in Shaun Costello's directorial debut, *Forced Entry*.

With a prologue that opens with stock footage of atrocities in the Vietnam war zone, the film proper begins with gas station attendant Harry Reems (without the moustache), who tricks young women into giving him their addresses. He then follows them home, peeps through their windows, and then forces them at knife or gunpoint to perform sexual favours on him while he cuts them down with speeches of pure hatred before stabbing them to death. It's a lurid horror/porn hybrid with unsimulated sex scenes that is much closer in spirit to Lee Cooper's *Wet Wilderness* and Costello's own *Waterpower* rather than Gerard Damiano's *Deep Throat*, and Reems looks to be relishing the opportunity of playing the bad guy; he's clearly enjoying it but few viewers will be laughing.

Forced Entry does have humour all right, moments where you laugh out loud, such as the scene where Reems has finished raping a woman from behind and then gets angry, teasing her and screaming "You made my prick all full of shit, didn't you?! You made my prick all full of shit!!!" But it's the laughter of sheer cruelty and you need to be in that frame of mind to go along with it. Also, the seemingly endless repetition of the dubbed line "Fucking hippies coming into my station. Scummy hippies!" is amusing, if not a little bizarre.

Viewers who can't handle the entertainment value of brutal rape and murder are advised to stay away from this one as there is more provocative mayhem here to fill a hundred controversial movies. It has a real bad attitude and stands out like a sore, um, thumb. Even in those glory days before the PC spoilsports came along, this film stood out from the unruly crowd. Amazingly, it was originally marketed as just a typical porno; just what the audience must have thought as this nasty piece of work played out on the big screen is anyone's guess.

Completely banned in the UK and something of an underground video title in the States for years, *Forced Entry* made it to DVD courtesy of Alpha Blue in their Costello/Avon box set. That version looks to have been taken from a muddy VHS transfer. A much better presentation is the Afterhours DVD taken from possibly the only print of the film still in existence. Image quality isn't perfect but it's the best we'll ever see it considering the scarcity of the source materials.

186

An indefensible horror/porn shocker then, but it succeeds in highlighting the nasty bitterness and anger felt by devalued soldiers who returned from Vietnam only to be treated like garbage after being conscripted into the hellscape of state sanctioned atrocities. You have been warned.

The Mad Bomber (1973)
Dir: Bert I. Gordon /USA

A twisted moral crusader plants a series of bombs in L.A.. He targets a school, a hospital, and a feminist meeting in revenge for the death of his daughter. Meanwhile, an overworked detective tries to track him down. A vile rapist had witnessed the attack at the hospital, and he must be captured as his description of the bomber's appearance is a vital clue as to the killer's identity... The Mad Bomber is a sleazy classic from the notorious Bert I. Gordon, and was made to cash in on the success of Dirty Harry (1971). It's one of those blunt, no-nonsense exploitation epics that could only have been made in the cynical 70s. The film also boasts no less than three cinema psychos; the lieutenant is played by hard-boiled Vince Edwards, the rapist is Neville Brand (who went on to play the psycho killer in Tobe Hooper's Death Trap [1976]), and Chuck Connors is the title character, and he also went on to play Slausen in Tourist Trap (1979). Be sure to watch the uncut version from Code Red as there are a number of watered-down TV prints available on video that tones down the violence and the rape scene. A classic.

The Sinful Dwarf (1973)
(aka Abducted Bride)
Dir: Vidal Raski /Denmark

The sleaziest dirty dwarf movie ever made. This film follows the depraved title character (former kids TV favourite, Torben Bille), who lives in a crummy, dilapidated boarding house with his equally messed up mother. His favourite past-time is to lure young women into the house (including a teenage girl who is taken against her will after following a wind-up toy puppy to her doom). Once the women are inside, he strips them, locks them in the attic, gets them hooked on smack, and then pimps them out to a group of shady clients. Meanwhile, a young couple have booked a room at the place, and when wifey disappears, it's up to the husband to find out what the hell is going on in the house of

horrors...

With a title that is both crude and accurate, The Sinful Dwarf has been an underground video hit for years, enticing and amusing jaded horror and sleaze buffs for the best part of three decades. And the film itself doesn't disappoint in the way it lives up to its salacious name and sick reputation. Bille is spot-on as the titular dwarf who procures the unwilling smack whores with a leering cheeky-chappy smile on his lips. The other cast members aren't so good, but most of 'em are only there to writhe around naked, suffering withdrawals and rape. The set 'design' works perfectly; the dirt, decay and overall grimness of the boarding house reflects the whole premise and mindset of the film (why anyone would pay to spend the night in that shit hole is beyond me). These aesthetics of filth were later replicated in Joel M. Reed's Bloodsucking Freaks, especially the scenes featuring the caged women who look like they've just stepped out of Raski's film, with the same grubby lighting and dirty decor.

After a lukewarm reception in its native land, The Sinful Dwarf was picked up by exploitation legend Harry Novak for a Stateside release under his company, Box Office International (under the new title Abducted Bride).Whether the film's original makers saw a pay day from the American drive-in theatres is unknown, but Novak was notorious for ripping people off, so I wouldn't bank on it.

Something Weird Video released the film on DVD-R because apparently it proved to be too outrageous to be released as part of their official stock. Severin released two versions of the film; the original cut, and also a hardcore version that runs for an extra four minutes and includes some very unattractive body-double shunting (this version was also released in Denmark as a 2 disc set). In the UK the film simply went under the radar, freaking out many a viewer when it was broadcast on cable TV in the mid-00s.

The Killing Kind (1973)
Dir: Curtis Harrington /USA

A young man, Terry (John Savage), is released from prison after being bullied into raping a girl on a beach. He goes to stay with his mother, Thelma (Ann Sothern), in her large house while he tries to rebuild his life. However, the young man has been mentally scarred by the experience, and is a sexual deviant with a sadistic streak. He sets about attacking the women around him – he stalks his old rape victim, harasses an aspiring model who rents a room at the house, shuns a neurotic woman who lives next door, and terrorises his lawyer whom he holds partly to blame for his incarceration. As the bodies pile up, his mother becomes suspicious of his erratic behaviour, but ultimately helps him to dispose of a corpse, and seems resigned to the disastrous consequences...

The Killing Kind is one of Curtis Harrington's finest films, though personally, I feel that the eerie Ruby (1977) is his crowning achievement. The film has a strange incestuous vibe to it, and leaves many questions unanswered, such as why does she help him get rid of the body? Is it loyalty born out of familial love, or is there some kind of psycho-sexual incestuous undercurrent at play? Does she blame herself for Terry's condition, and so feels partly responsible for clearing up after his murderous deeds? Those aspects are never made clear, but viewers can clearly see that there is much more than meets the eye in this strange tale. The history between the mother and son is another area that is barely touched upon, with viewers only receiving minimal details (we learn that Thelma was a whore in her younger days), and we're left to piece together the emotional puzzle in our own minds. Terry's inappropriate kissing of Thelma goes beyond mere affection and into creepier areas as he sensually kisses her neck. Thelma responds with laughter like it's some kind of joke ('You're too much, Terry. You're too much!'), but she puts up very little resistance. It's a fairly low-key, melancholic film with a melodic – but sadly underused – score by Andrew Belling, daring performances from Savage and Sothern, and has much in common with Claudio Guerin Hill's Spanish oddity, The Bell From Hell (1973), which was made around the same time.

Love Me Deadly (1973)
Dir: Jacques LaCerte /USA
Lindsey (Mary Wilcox), a troubled young woman with daddy issues, falls in with a coven of evil Satanists whose deranged activities include embalming live humans and gang-banging fresh cadavers. Lindsey desperately tries to repress her necrophiliac urges by dating a regular guy and even marrying an older man. However, one sniff of dead man's balls, and she's riding them like Frankie Dattori on a prized stallion. Things end tragically when her husband inevitably discovers her secret. Love Me Deadly feels very different to most American horror movies of the time. Much of the drama takes place in and around the Morningside Mortuary, with its morbid props of casks and coffins and mourners. And Lindsey's perversion is treated as an excuse to wring every last drop of soap opera-style tension from the narrative. The film clearly had a big influence on Lynne Stopkewich's Kissed (1996).

The Exorcist (1973)
Dir: William Friedkin /USA
Still one of the most controversial films of all time, The Exorcist centres on Regan (Linda Blair), the twelve year old daughter of a famous stage actress (Ellen Burstyn). She begins to suffer from unexplainable seizures and displays some very odd behaviour. Regan is taken to doctors, but examinations fail to pinpoint any physical or psychiatric abnormalities. Her condition worsens, and she begins to transform physically, taking on an ugly, demonic appearance. In desperation, and with all rational possibilities exhausted, Regan's mother begs the help of a young priest, Father karras (John Miller). Realising that Regan is possessed by the Devil, and knowing that his own faith is too weak for him to deal successfully with the problem all by himself, Karras turns to Father Merrin (Max Von Sydow), a more senior priest who has experience in exorcisms. And the showdown begins.

Based on William Peter Blatty's best-selling novel (which itself was based on the true case in 1949 in Maryland of a fourteen-year-old boy who exhibited bizarre behaviour that led to his 'exorcism' by Father Raymond J. Bishop and Father William S. Bowdern), The Exorcist shrewdly exploits the fears and frustrations of parents. The film is an intense ride, a marvel of audience manipulation, with director William Friedkin pushing all the right buttons to ensure his film became a genre landmark. It's a perfect mixture of its then state-of-the-art special effects and good old-fashioned atmospheric horror to produce two hours of dread and unease.

Whilst the film was still in production, rumours circulated about the 'Curse of the Exorcist', in which supposedly dark supernatural forces were to blame for the death of actor Jack McGowran (whose character also dies in the film), and the house interior set mysteriously burning to the ground. The deaths of nine people connected to the making of the film only intensified the rumours, quickly becoming the stuff or urban legend. Director Friedkin even tried to have the set exorcised!

The Exorcist reached the UK amid reports that American audiences had been fainting and vomiting at Stateside screenings, and the hysteria continued unabated on these shores. There were calls to have the film banned, evangelist Billy Graham claimed that the film itself was evil and that demonic forces were trapped in the very celluloid. Newspapers ran stories about people being driven to madness by the film, pregnant women miscarrying, and a spate of crimes – from shoplifting to murder – all blamed on the film. Nuns would show up at UK screenings and sprinkle the queuing punters with holy water to protect them from the evils they were about to be exposed to. Silly but true.

Linda Blair had reportedly received numerous death threats from a bunch of dangle-mouths ever since she appeared in the film when she was just fourteen years old. Incredibly, some movie viewers have a difficult time distinguishing reality from fiction, and thus Blair's superb performance as a possessed child led some to believe that she was actually Satan. According to legend, throughout this insanity the police sent out a special agent to live with the Blairs, to protect her from the unwanted attentions of an assortment of sinister psychos. Even today, there are still those who believe – and report as fact – that Linda Blair was driven insane as a direct result of appearing in *The Exorcist,* that she ended up in an asylum and her mother was struck by lightning. Of course, it isn't true.

She lived a bizarre life in the wake of the film; people would recognise her in the supermarket and run away screaming into the street. "I was a normal kid," she said, "and I wanted to be pretty. But all people ever said to me was 'Wow, can you really spin your head around and throw up?'" When asked how she feels about her association with the film today, she says "Well, you know, there isn't a day goes by that someone doesn't ask me about that film. So to me it's like my left arm – it's just there."

Although *The Exorcist* did get a video release in the UK in the early days of home video, it was short-lived. The head of British censorship at the time, James Ferman, had his own personal problems with the film and was determined to keep it out of our homes. For years, the only way to catch *The Exorcist* was on the occasional 'Midnight Specials' screenings up and down the country. The film was shrouded in controversy. It became this mythical thing, a forbidden fruit that seemed to be something genuinely sinister and dangerous. The film harmed people! They were carried out of the theatre on stretchers! And like *The Texas Chain Saw Massacre* and *A Clockwork Orange*, *The Exorcist* became one of those legendary 'banned' films that younger generations thought they'd never get to see.

There was hope, however, in 1998, the year of *The Exorcist's* 25th anniversary. The media frenzy that anticipated the re-release was extraordinary; books were published about the film, documentaries were broadcast on TV, hundreds of articles and columns were written. The film itself was re-visited, and the general consensus was that *The Exorcist* was just as powerful then as it was back in the early 70s. But despite all the excitement, in a strange twist of fate, James Ferman of the BBFC yet again refused to pass the film for home viewing. "The problem with *The Exorcist,*" he said, "is not that it's a bad film, it's that it's a very good film – one of the most powerful ever made." Ferman had his own – possibly religious – reasons for restricting the film (the ending implies that 'evil wins', or at least has the victory of killing one of the priests; something writer Blatty had always been concerned about in Friedkin's film version).

So, despite all the hype and excitement concerning the re-release, *The Exorcist* remained outlawed on home video in the UK. The film's mythic power of unattainability remained so. The following year, however, saw another twist in the saga when Ferman retired and was replaced by the much less stuffy Andreas Whittam Smith, and he promptly passed *The Exorcist* uncut for home video without further ado. The spell was finally broken at long last, and out came the video and the DVD and the laserdisc.

Nowadays *The Exorcist* lurks in high street stores, that iconic image on the DVD sleeve of Father Merrin standing outside Regan's house, bathed in light that radiates from an upper window, satchel in hand. The DVD sits right there on the shelves across the country, nestled between *Shrek* and *Back to the Future*, with kids as young as Regan able to pick it up and have a read about the synopsis on the back cover. Does the film then lose any of its power by being as free and as widely available as *Shrek*? The answer is no. *The Exorcist* is a genuinely scary movie.

For all the wonders of this film, from the magnificent performances of the cast, the impressive special effects, and its story grounded in gritty realism, the most effective element is the sound: There's Mike Oldfield's *Tubular Bells*, and there's also Jack Nietzsche's eerie sounds that underscore some intense scenes. But beyond the music there's also the incredibly effective sound design by Robert Knudson and Chris Newman, and this is where the horror truly lies: the eerie scuffling in the attic, the traffic noise, the rising wind and fighting dogs in Iraq. Also, the demon Pazuzu itself, voiced by actress Mercedes McCambridge. Her gutteral tones provides much of the unease; her voice is filtered through sound effects, loops, and animal noises combined for the full effect. Also, one of the creepiest scenes in the film is when Father Karras plays back a tape recording in his room.

Film critic Mark Kermode deserves much praise for his dogged devotion to the film. It was Mark who unearthed the rare deleted footage, that included Linda Blair's legendary 'spider walk' down the stairs. It was Mark who made the excellent documentary, *The Fear of God*, for the BBC. He has also written books about the film, helped organise its re-release, fought long battles with the BBFC over its ban, and believes it to be the greatest movie ever made. "I have seen *The Exorcist* about two hundred times," he admits. "I stopped counting after the first hundred. I've stood outside that house on Prospect Street, stepping in the shadow of Max Von Sydow, putting myself into the picture that haunted my childhood and which will surely follow me to my grave. Worse still, I have forced my entire family to make the pilgrimage to Georgetown just to parade up and down the precipitous steps which plummet from Prospect Street to M Street and which feature so prominently in the film – first my long-suffering wife Linda, then more recently my kids and my mother who haven't even seen *The Exorcist*. Friedkin was once quoted as saying that on his gravestone would be engraved the words 'The guy who made *The Exorcist*'. He meant it self-deprecatingly, but at least he made the damn film, of which he should be proud. On my gravestone it'll just say 'The guy who bored his family and friends to death with *The Exorcist*.'"

The Last House On Dead End Street (1973)
(aka *The Cuckoo Clocks of Hell*; aka *The Funhouse*)
Dir: Victor Janos [Roger Watkins] /USA
Upon his release from jail, a minor drug dealer, Terry Hawkins (played by director Watkins under the pseudonym 'Steven Morrison') is determined to avenge the porno peddlers whom he worked with and who have pissed him off in some way by gathering together a group of low-lives whose job it is to film a string of tortures, disembowelments, and murders. A group of victims are quickly assembled and lured to an old abandoned building where the filmic misadventures begin.

Straight up porno is not good enough anymore, people want their movies to be gruelling and nasty, and Mr. Hawkins decides to give the people what they want. Terry tortures and kills the 'performers' while his female assistants stand by in ghoulish masks. The end result is similar to Joel M. Reed's *Bloodsucking Freaks* but lacks that film's silly *grand guignol* style, and opts instead to play up the awful seriousness of a snuff film, for better or worse..

Lots of vileness ensues as the slaughter reaches overdrive – men and women are tied up, branded, have their faces cut off, and eyeballs skewered. One woman has her leg cut off while she is unconscious, only to be brought around again with the aid of smelling salts so that she can fully comprehend the horror of her situation. She is then subsequently disembowelled. And much of the film is narrated by the psychopaths themselves...

Made on a shoestring budget of $800, this heavy-duty horror of nihilism and misanthropy is told in an icy and clinical way with its low lighting and technical limitations adding to its harrowing atmosphere of dread. It isn't a snuff film, but that kind of nasty, cynical attitude needed to make a snuffy is in full force here as Watkins' performance as the troubled film-maker is one of the most memorable and evil in all of 70s horror.

Speaking of evil, *The Last House On Dead End Street* also features one of the most freakishly evil soundtracks in the history of film, made using old classical library music slowed down, played backwards and channelled through a guitar phasing effects peddle. The result is simply mesmerizing. Adding to the hostilities are the artistic flourishes throughout the film; it's cheap and nasty for sure, but there's nothing corny about the performances or script or overall tone of the project, unlike many films of its era. I can't think of any other film that oozes such pure hatred in every frame, except maybe Shaun Costello's horror/porn hybrid, *Forced Entry*.

The murders become a strange kind of ritual towards the end with the use of knives, mirrors, masks, and other objects. Those familiar with the magickal arts and Satanism will notice that a magick symbol is used as a branding iron, and deer hooves are used for sexual excitation in the victims, and Hawkins even wears a God mask during the slaughter sequences.

It may come as no surprise to learn that Watkins was heavily into amphetamines during the making of the film. Speed leaves its users in a state of social dislocation, and all feelings of empathy towards our fellow human beings are shut down in that highly-charged state. And that mindset is suitably mirrored in the film's grim and heartless hostility.

The Last House On Dead End Street was completed as early as 1973 under its original title, *The Cuckoo Clocks of Hell*. That version had an epic running time of almost three hours (and right up until his death in 2007 Watkins had always insisted that that version was the definitive cut). The film was reluctantly cut down to 115 minutes for a planned screening at Cannes which never actually happened due to an actor filing a lawsuit after he was fired from the set. This kept the film in litigation for years until the case was thrown out of court.

Watkins was then finally free to secure some distribution, and he struck a deal with Warmflash Productions. For a while things seemed to be working out well until he discovered that the company had cut his film down to 77 minutes, re-arranged scenes, created a fake credits sequence, changed the title to *The Funhouse*, and even added a 'bad-guys-get-their-comeuppance' coda at the end. Understandably peeved and disillusioned, Watkins moved away from feature production and carved out a career in the porn industry instead.

Meanwhile, the 77 minute cut was raking in large sums of money on the drive-in circuit when it was re-titled again as *The Last House On Dead End Street* to cash in on Wes Craven's classic *Last House On The Left* title. And then the film simply disappeared, leaving only a handful of rave reviews in its wake. On home video it was released in the States on Betamax and VHS by a company called Sun Video, and in Canada by Marquee, but both releases were fleeting and short-lived. Due to the rarity of the film and the mysterious nature of its director (billed as 'Victor Janos') and everyone else involved, *Dead End Street*'s reputation began spiralling out of control. Some of the more spurious rumours going around were that it was a genuine snuff film, and it wasn't long before the movie had garnered a legendary reputation. Bootleg copies from an awful looking Venezuelan videotape were selling on eBay for as much as $100 per tape, and this led Watkins' then girlfriend Suzanne to post a message on an internet horror forum enquiring about fans of the film. This post caught the attention of Headpress honcho David Kerekes, and the rest is history. He met up with Watkins for a lengthy interview (see *Headpress 23*) and arranged to get the movie out on DVD.

This holy grail amongst horror movie collectors was then dragged out into the light when Kerekes managed to source an incomplete 35mm print belonging to FantAsia's Mitch Davis. It was missing the extended disembowelment scene but the folks at Barrel Entertainment located a super-rare copy on VHS, and they inserted the scene for a Special Edition DVD release. It isn't the long lost 3 hour director's cut, but Barrel did a fantastic job of rescuing this caustic gem from oblivion, and they should be commended for making an uncut release a priority.

Abducted (1973)
(aka *Schoolgirls in Chains*; *Girls in Chains*; *Let's Play Dead*)
<u>Dir: Don Jones /USA</u>
Two retarded brothers are 'instructed' by their twisted, domineering mother to abduct young women and bring them back to their underground lair in the backyard. There, the unfortunate girls are subjected to rape and other 'games' like doctor and hide and seek, while they are restrained with collars and chains around their necks. However, one day the simple brains kidnap a feisty blonde who isn't in the mood for their shit... *Abducted* is an underrated backwoods horror of the post-*Psycho* (1960) variety that nonetheless absorbs its inspiration to successfully ring a few changes

on the familiar theme. It isn't often that you'll find realistic acting abilities in grindhouse exploitation movies, but this film boasts impressive performances all around. There are no hammy psychos here; from the retarded games of the brothers to the fearful, captive women desperate to escape, all of the performances ring true. John Stoglin's role as the frustrated child in a man's body is superb, and all the more creepy as viewers are subjected to his rape fantasies from his own childish perspective. Gary Kent – an exploitation regular who also crops up in the works of Al Adamson and Ray Dennis Stekler – offers a more subtle form of madness inflicted by the monstrous mother who sexually abused him, even into adulthood. The result is a film which, despite all the leering, grindhouse sleaze, is actually an emotionally-driven film rather than one built purely on visceral shocks. Similarly-themed movies include *Deranged* (1974), *Mother's Day* (1980) and *Barn of the Naked Dead* (1974).

The Holy Mountain (1973)
Dir: Alejandro Jodorowsky / Mexico/ USA
Dazzling. Demented. Disturbing. Deranged. These words have been bounded around for years as a way of describing Alejandro Jodorowsky, the Chilean artist, mystic, and film-maker who generally shows up on the scene every decade or so to make a movie and then disappears again. He first made a splash with *El Topo*, the first ever 'midnight movie', in which he also cast himself in the lead role as the leather-clad gunfighter on a mystical tour through the desert lands. The phenomenal success of *El Topo* allowed him to make a follow-up film which would be bigger, badder and more epic, thanks to former Beatles manager, Allen Klein, giving him a generous budget to go off and capture his vision in ambitious, Cinemascope style. The result is a mind-blowing feast for the eyes and the brain, a hallucinogenic smorgasbord of religion and weirdness and dazzling imagery.

A bearded man awakens from a coma and wanders into a town populated with freaks and crazies – we see flowers growing through stigmata wounds; skinned rabbits are crucified and carried through the streets by an army wearing gas masks; birds take flight from human bullet wounds; a man plucks out his glass eye and hands it to a young girl; a chimpanzee accompanies a group of prostitutes

to church; peasant women are raped by soldiers for the amusement of tourists; costumed frogs re-enact the bloody Spanish invasion of South America. The bearded man soon finds himself being used as a body mould for the production of hundreds of life-sized plaster casts of Christ. And when he ventures back out into the streets, he ascends a mysterious tower with the aid of a golden hook which is dangled from the top.

Once inside the tower, the bearded man meets the White Master. And after a fight – which he loses – the bearded man has a blue octopus removed from a lump on the back of his neck. Soon after, the pair have amassed a group of thieves, each one representing a particular evil of modern society; Venus is a stud of the cosmetics industry who uses mechanical devices to animate dead bodies so that they can do things like kiss their loved ones goodbye at funerals, or a dead Bishop can give himself his own last rites; Mars is a woman who creates weapons of mass destruction; wealthy 'artiste' Jupiter has his quirky artworks mass-produced on an assembly line; Saturn is a government official whose job it is to brainwash children into extreme xenophobia; Uranus is the President's financial advisor, and he orders mass genocide to save the crippled economy; Neptune is the chief of police who castrates criminals and preserves their testicles in jars; and finally, Pluto, a crude architect who devises a budget housing scheme whereby all the homes in the land resemble upright coffins. The White Master's plan is to scale the Holy Mountain and steal the secrets of the wise men. However, his band of thieves must first learn wisdom by shaving their heads and burning all their money…

Allen Klein and Jodorowsky had their differences which eventually became all-out hostility, and Klein did all he could to have the film banished by refusing to release it in America, a place where most of the film's profits would have been generated. To make matters worse, John Lennon stopped speaking to Alejandro (they had become friends after *El Topo's* theatrical run in New York) when the *Village Voice* published an article claiming that he had criticized John and Yoko's artworks. Nevertheless, *The Holy Mountain* was successful across the rest of the globe, especially in Italy where it became the second highest grossing film of the year behind the Bond caper, *Live and Let Die* (with that film's classic theme tune provided by another ex-Beatle, Paul McCartney).

In the UK, the British censors employed an optical 'fogging' on the castration, and gave the film an X rating for its 1974 cinema release. All subsequent releases on VHS and DVD are fully uncut and unfogged.

The ending of the film is magnificent; the audience has spent two hours following the characters on their journey, and we've become the White Master's disciples just like the followers in the film. We've seen the beauty and the chaos, and we've been led to believe that the ending will grant us some kind of knowledge, some wisdom. We've reached the point where we're expecting magic to happen before our eyes. However, at this point Jodorowsky simply 'pulls the plug' and breaks the fourth wall by addressing the viewers and banishing the whole idea of magic. It reminded me of the ending to Mario Bava's original cut of *Black Sabbath* where Boris Karloff is seen riding a horse in the dark, with the camera pulling back to reveal that he is actually stationary on a prop horse with a wind machine blowing in his face on a busy movie set. But the finale here is much more powerful.

La Grande Bouffe (1973)
(aka *Blow-Out*)
Dir: Marco Ferreri /France/Italy

Four middle class men choose to escape the restless futility of city life and retreat to an isolated mansion where they indulge in an experimental feast. An airline pilot (Marcello Mastroianni), a judge (Philippe Noiret), a cook (Ugo Tognazzi), and a TV producer (Michel Piccoli), seem to have everything going for them, but the boredom of modern life has taken its toll on their well-being. They greedily devour mountains of food, sit around watching vintage porn loops, and bring along call girls to quench their lusts. All of this indulgence is part of their grand scheme; it's a suicide pact whereby the gentlemen will quite literally die on the excess of pleasure.

This visually stunning film nevertheless picks at themes that should offend everyone at some point or another. The grim tone of the setting and savage humour is dished up with very little in the way of subtlety, much like the constant mounds of food that are offered up for the feast. All four of the men represent an evil of modern life – the corruption of the judicial system (the judge), the wasteful and greedy nature of the West when many in the third world are starving (the cook), the thinly-disguised imperialism of the modern world 'village' which exists purely to conquer and exploit weaker nations, made easier by the miracle of aviation (the pilot), and the mind-numbing emptiness and cultural wasteland perpetuated by television (the TV producer).

The film also boasts four of the finest actors in Europe at the peak of their powers, and they're clearly having a good time misbehaving while entrusting their director's impeccable eye to bring all the chaos together into a sumptuous whole. It's certainly not a traditional kind of film, but fans of subversive cinema will find much food for thought here.

La Grande Bouffe premiered at the Cannes Film Festival and caused an immediate firestorm of controversy, and divided audiences down the middle. Mastroianni's girlfriend at the time, Catherine Deneuve, is said to have been so offended at the screening that she wouldn't talk to him for a week. Meanwhile, mass brawls broke out in the cinemas in France between those who loved and loathed the film, and the violence continued in Paris throughout its lengthy theatrical run (ah, the 70s).

Elsewhere around the world, the critics were equally divided in their reactions, with some declaring it a triumph as a fierce attack on the appetites of the bourgeoisie, and others a tasteless sick joke. American critic Terry Curtis Fox famously summed up his reaction to the film in no uncertain terms, "This re-affirms my faith that it is possible to be offended by a film." This kind of blunt opposition between viewers surprised even director Marco Ferreri, but it didn't make him temper his work; his next film, *Don't Touch the White Woman!*, was released the following year and also taunts the easily offended with its biting humour and twisted allegory on American colonialism (not surprisingly, it wasn't released in America).

The influence of *La Grande Bouffe* was felt soon after its release when fellow Italian auteur, Pier Paolo Pasolini, paid tribute to the exploding bowels and broken toilets in his equally subversive attack on modern society, *Salo, Or the 120 Days of Sodom*. But it was perhaps British art-house favourite, Peter Greenaway, who has provided the most obvious homages over the years with his mixture of sex, death, and food in *The Cook, the Thief, His Wife, and*

Her Lover, in which he replicates the trick of naming his characters after the names of his cast members. He also cast Andrea Ferreol in a similar role in *A Zed and Two Noughts*. And like Greenaway's *The Cook, Thief, La Grande Bouffe* was also slapped with an NC-17 rating in America in the late 90s, surprising those who had believed the film to have grown much more mellow with age.

Nowadays while watching *La Grande Bouffe*, or indeed any of Ferreri's films, the action on screen is always tinged with a touch of sadness that this extraordinary film-maker has never received his full dues as an artist. His talent was the equal of greats like Pasolini and Fellini, and yet his work is ignored by all but the most adventurous of film fans. When Ferreri died in May 1997 it was the end of an era. He should be considered one of the giants of cinema, yet the event of his death amounted to little more than a brief mention in the obituary sections of a few newspapers. The reason for this lack of respect is a mystery to me; maybe it's because he was an Italian who made most of his films abroad, or the fact that his films were distributed in shoddy fashion (his VHS filmography was a joke with most of the titles hard to find and quickly going out of print, and presented in dreadful pan-and-scan jobs). Some of his films saw no other form of distribution beyond the festival circuits. Who knows. At least with the advent of DVD, his back catalogue is slowly reaching a wider audience, and perhaps one day soon Ferreri will get the respect he deserves.

La Comtesse Perverse (1973)

(aka *The Perverse Countess*; aka *Les croqueuses*; aka *Sexy Nature*)
Dir: 'Clifford Brown' [Jess Franco] /France
When a naked and terrified woman washes up on the beach, holidaying couple, Bob and Moira (Robert Woods and Tania Busselier), take her inside for safety. There, the woman (Kali Hansa) breaks down and struggles to explain how she was the victim of a pair of deranged sadists on a nearby island. She claims she was raped and tortured by the Count and Countess Zaroff (Howard Vernon and Alice Arno). She is also adamant that the vicious pair cannibalise their victims after hunting them down on the island with a war-bow. However, little does the petrified victim know that Bob and Moira actually work for the Zaroffs, and supply them

with their prey. And once she has been dealt with, the deviants set their eyes on the young and innocent Silvia (Lima Romay) to be the next victim of their hunt...

Shot back-to-back with *Plaisir à trois* (*Pleasure For Three*, 1974) in the spring of 1973, *La Comtesse Perverse* is another of Jess Franco's erotically-charged horrors set on the Canary Islands where the sun, sand and sea are intermingled with sex, sadism and death. Even by Franco's standards, this is a remarkably stripped-down film with only the barest of plots. However, the Spanish director simply shoots on the fly, using every opportunity to infuse his project with the unmistakable Franco atmosphere that pervades in his finest films. And, like *Plaisir à trois, La Comtesse Perverse* presents a bright tropical paradise that is eclipsed by the darkness of the souls of its twisted characters. An ongoing theme in Franco's work is that the sea serves as a symbol of death. So many of his films were shot near the coast, and the ocean is a constant reminder of the characters' mortal danger. This idea is seen most blatantly in films such as *Venus in Furs* (1967), *Vampyros Lesbos* (1970) and *La Comtesse Perverse*, where the sea is an almost constant presence in the background: a vast dreamy nothingness, a blank void lying in wait to engulf the doomed characters, body and soul.

Made during his most productive period, with an almost unlimited freedom behind the camera, Franco used the opportunity to combine his fascination for the works of the Marquis de Sade with the helplessness and isolation of *The Most Dangerous Game* (1932). And the end result stands out as one of his most striking efforts, using the stunning locations to his advantage. The prolific director completed no less than seven films in 1972, eleven in 1973 (with a further three that were never finished), and seven in 1974, and many of them are remarkably accomplished with a frenzy of creativity he would never match for the rest of his career. Of course, working at such an incredible speed ensured that the rough edges were always apparent, but *La Comtesse Perverse* is one of the many gems that can be found in the director's filmography, for those who are prepared to dig a little deeper than *Vampyros Lesbos* (1970) and *Bloody Moon* (1981).

Franco's future wife, Lina Romay, appeared in just about every film he made in 1973, and it was also the year in which they met. She began acting in theatre before the pair had a chance encounter in a lift and became inseparable until she died of cancer in 2012. Within a fortnight of meeting, she appeared in a bit-part role in *The Sinister Eyes of Dr. Orloff* (*Los ojos del Dr. Orloff*, 1973). Just weeks later she appeared in *Plaisir à trois*, playing the mentally-handicapped girl. *La Comtesse Perverse* was only her third time in front of the camera, and she delivered a fine (and completely uninhibited) performance as the doomed Silvia. And a couple of months after that, she had her first starring role as *The Bare-Breasted Countess* (*La Comtesse Noire*, aka *Female Vampire*, released in 1975). For this most exhibititionistic performer and voyeuristic director, theirs was a match made in celluloid heaven.

Interestingly, the first person to object to *La Comtesse Perverse* was the film's producer, Robert De Nesle. He was disgusted by the idea of cannibalism in a sex movie, and wanted Franco to add more sex scenes and lighten the mood as he felt the film was far too grim and unappealing. And, much like the producers at RKO who balked at the original cut of *The Most Dangerous Game* forty years earlier after preview screenings proved too horrifying for audiences, Franco saw his film slip out of his hands where it was drastically re-cut to 73-minutes and spiced up with inserts of hardcore sex. Franco's original 87-minute cut was thought to be long lost until Mondo Macabro finally released it on DVD in 2012. In the meantime, fans had to make do with bootleg copies taken from an old French version entitled *Les croqueuses*, and there was also a 100-minute version doing the rounds on VHS entitled *Sexy Nature*, with even *more* unnecessary scenes of near-hardcore sex.

However, even in such a compromised condition of dupe copies with no subtitles, film fans have always found much to marvel at in *La Comtesse Perverse*; from the beautiful locations and quick-fire cinematography of Gerard Brisseau, to the stunning Xanadu building which served as the Zaroff's lair (and which was also used as a location previously in Franco's *She Killed in Ecstasy* [1970]), the dazzling red staircase with its modernist geometric design, the eclectic score by Olivier Bernard and Jean-Bernard Ratieux which mixes fuzzed-up guitars with menacing strings, eerie organs and blasts of bongo drums, and the final shot that was recycled for the equally bizarre *A Virgin Among the Living Dead* (1973). All in all, it's quite an experience – easy to watch yet strangely haunting, and almost immediately beckoning the viewer to sit down and watch it again and again.

The Baby (1973)
Dir: Ted Post /USA
One of the most politically incorrect films to appear in the early 70s was *The Baby*, a bizarre tale about a government aid, Ann (Anjanette Comer), who visits the home of Mrs. Wadsworth (Ruth Roman), a mother of three whose youngest is a fully-grown man who has been kept in a state of infancy all of his life. He can't walk or talk, and his mother and older sisters keep him bottle fed and in nappies. Ann vows to take the 'baby' away from his unhealthy surroundings, and this ensures a bloody climax when Wadsworth and her daughters break into Ann's home in the middle of the night... *The Baby* is one of those films that could only come from the 70s, the decade which produced an abundance of weird and strangely disturbing titles such as *Night Hair Child* (1971), and *The Witch Who Came From the Sea* (1976). Quite what audiences must have thought of this as it played out on the big screen is anyone's guess, but Leslie Halliwell at the time described it as 'grotesque.' The *Monthly Film Bulletin*'s Tom Milne was also unequivocal in his verdict, commenting 'ultimately, this is a long walk around a very sick joke.' Indeed, the ending throws up some pretty twisted surprises, so be sure to stick with it to the end.

Turkish Delight (1973)
(aka *The Sensualist;* Orig title: *Turks Fruit*)
Dir: Paul Verhoeven /Netherlands
The censor's scissors are always at hand when Paul Verhoeven makes a new film, and his erotic drama *Turkish Delight* was snipped of around six minutes of offending footage by the British censors on its initial release. The problematic areas were in the many sexual encounters of Erik (Rutger Hauer), a young sculptor whose bed-hopping antics allowed him briefly to forget about his insecurities and broken heart due to the loss of his love, Olga (Monique van de Ven). Erik reminisces on their fractured relationship which ended in tragedy; Olga is involved in a road accident, and Erik gently nurses her back to health in his flat. The couple eventually get

married, but their happiness comes to an end when her father (Wimm van dern Brink) dies, taking his calm influence to the grave. Much heartache and arguments ensue, and the couple split. Olga emigrates to America and re-marries. They eventually do get back together, but Olga collapses and is diagnosed with a brain tumour. Erik decides to stay with her to the end.

This collaboration between Paul Verhoeven and screenwriter Gerard Soetman was a splendid meeting of minds; Verhoeven supplied the risque and plentiful sex scenes, and Soetman provided the bitingly satirical script targeted at the Dutch establishment. Indeed, Verhoeven would carry the mantle further in his future work, repeating the cheeky swipes at the rampant commercialism and the status quo in the 'news flash' clips and mock-ad propaganda in Hollywood hits like *Robocop* and *Starship Troopers*. Ultimately though, *Turkish Delight* is a touching portrayal of a loving relationship, despite all the casual sex and scatalogical madness on display.

If censorship wasn't enough of an obstacle for this modest gem to contend with, *Turkish Delight* opened in theatres in the same month as a trio of classics; *Serpico*, *Papillon*, and *Westworld*. Over time, the film has enticed a fair deal of interest and has been influential over the years; echoes of the doomed lovers can be felt in such art-house triumphs as Lars Von Trier's *Breaking the Waves*. Steven Spielberg is said to have been so impressed with Verhoeven's previous film, *Soldier of Orange*, that he even recommended him to George Lucas as a potential director of *Empire Strikes Back*. He quickly retracted that enthusiasm though once he clapped eyes on *Turkish Delight*, a film much more in keeping with the Dutchman's sleazily evocative aesthetics. One can only imagine how different the *Star Wars* saga would have been had Verhoeven taken to the helm...

The Boy Who Cried Werewolf (1973)
Dir: Nathan H. Juran /USA
Kerwin Matthews is attacked by a werewolf while strolling in the woods with his son one night. Matthews becomes infected and transforms into a lycanthrope himself. Of course, no one believes the son's claims that there is a werewolf on the loose. And when daddy takes chunks out of a nearby Christian hippy camp, the boy is torn between wanting to help his father and slaying the beast. This is

typical furry nonsense with a hackneyed plot and transformation sequences that date back to Lon Chaney Jr in the 1940s. There still hasn't been a completely satisfying werewolf movie.

Trapped (1973)
Dir: Frank DeFelitta /USA
In this TV movie by Universal, James Brolin is mugged and beaten unconscious by two men in the toilets of a department store. When he awakens in the middle of the night, he discovers that the security guards have unleashed a pack of killer dogs to roam free throughout the store. So Brolin spends the rest of the night trying to keep the feeding frenzy away from his protein-packed genitals. *Trapped* is a fun but little-seen movie that would make for a great double-bill with Jim Wynorski's *Chopping Mall* (1986). As far as I'm aware, this hasn't been released on DVD, but catch it if you can. Also check out another TV movie of the same name, Fred Walton's *Trapped* (1989), in which Kathleen Quinlan is locked overnight in her work place, and is pursued through 40 floors of bland office space by a knife – and bat – wielding nut job.

Theatre of Blood (1973)
Dir: Douglas Hickox /UK
Refreshingly gruesome for its day while managing to maintain an air of early 70s camp, *Theatre of Blood* sees Vincent Price at his hammiest as a sour actor who embarks on a dramatic murder spree. Having been the butt of many critics' jokes throughout his career, Price murders his detractors using Shakespeare as a bloody template. One scribe donates a pound of flesh, *Merchant of Venice*-style; another is repeatedly stabbed, a la Julius Caesar. Other murders include tributes to Cymbeline (nocturnal decapitation) and Titus Andronicus (the poodles scene). The film doesn't quite share the same madcap vibe as the earlier *Dr Phibes* movies but still, it boasts a 'knowing' humour which pre-dates *Scream* (1996) by more than 20 years.

The Satanic Rites of Dracula (1973)
Dir: Alan Gibson /UK
A Satanic cult revives Count Dracula (Christopher Lee again, in the last time he ever donned the cape for Hammer) who blends into the community by posing as a wealthy property developer. However, when Scotland Yard finds evidence of vampiric murders, Peter Cushing's

Van Helsing is called in to help with the investigation and dissolve Dracula one last time. *The Satanic Rites* is one of the few Hammer horrors set in the modern day, and relies heavily on a 'scientific' approach to telling the story, and borrows many of its narrative contraptions from action capers, like Bond movies which were very popular at the time. And Dracula also finds a modern, scientific way of spreading his deadly plague.

Terror on the Beach (1973)
Dir: Paul Wendkos /USA
Duel's Denis Weaver takes his family on vacation in a camper van where they're initially mocked by a group of degenerate low-lives. When the family ignores them, the teasing turns to all-out hostility as their RV is vandalised and bugged through a PA system where loud animal noises are played all night, keeping the family awake. They are then terrorised by the thugs on dune buggies. Like *Duel*, Neil (Weaver) is subjected to an unprovoked series of attacks in the American wilderness. And like *The Hills Have Eyes* (1977), Weaver plays the confused pacifist at a loss as to why anyone would get pleasure out of tormenting a lone family. And also like *Hills* (and *Straw Dogs*, 1972), the mild-mannered family man is gradually drawn into a savage battle with the low-lives, becoming a bloodthirsty homicidal maniac to protect his loved ones. The film's status as a TV movie ensured it could never compete with *Hills* or *Straw Dogs* in terms of sheer visceral horror and bloodshed, but *Terror on the Beach* is a decent little pic – save for the cop-out ending – which hit the screens almost half a decade before Wes Craven's film.

Badlands (1973)
Dir: Terrence Malick /USA
A teenage girl (Sissy Spacek) and a garbage collector (Martin Sheen) take to the road together and travel across America on a vengeful murder spree. This cult classic has been hugely influential over the years, with the template of 'young lovers on the run' used by subsequent film-makers who have made use of its engaging power. The story is told mainly through the eyes of Spacek's Holly, who sees Kit's actions as endearingly romantic; she's blinded by her unquestioning, adolescent crush on him, and the stark dislocation between her dreamy, 'head in the clouds' acquiescence and the downbeat horror of the couple's actions gives the film a deftly disturbing power, which flits between feeble fantasy and earth-shattering reality. The film is based on the crimes of Charles Starkweather and Caril Fugate's killing spree in the Dakota badlands in the 1950s.

Arnold (1973)
Dir: Georg Fanady /USA
A tale of revenge from beyond the grave that serves as a cross between *The Abominable Dr. Phibes* (1971) and *The Horror Star* (1981). Upon the death of an eccentric English aristocrat, Lord Arnold Dwellyn, his family converge on the sprawling estate for the reading of the will which is played as a series of audio recordings read out by the dead man himself. Lord Arnold's corpse winds up marrying his mistress, much to the annoyance of his widow who is left with one lousy share in the late Lord's textile business. And meanwhile, other friends, family members and servants plot against each other for the inheritance and are killed off, while others hunt for the treasure that is believed to be hidden somewhere on the grounds of the manor house. And Arnold's corpse lays in state the whole time with a wry smile on his lips while the chaos erupts all around him... *Arnold* is a bizarre curio that never made it to DVD, perhaps because it's not a well-known film. It wasn't a hit when it was originally released due to the amount of morbid humour which makes *Dr. Phibes* seem rather quaint in comparison. The film was produced by Bing Crosby Productions, a company that specialised in B-flicks in the 70s (they also produced *Williard* [1971], *Ben* [1972] and *Terror in the Wax Museum* [1973], the latter also directed by Fanady). On the casting front, there's Bernard Fox (of *Hogan's Heroes*) as a bumbling constable, Roddy McDowell as one of the schemers, Victor Buono as the minister, and the Bride of Frankenstein herself, Elsa Lanchester, as Arnold's sister who meets the sorriest fate at the end. Thankfully, the lousy theme tune – which is played prominently in the trailer – is kept to a bare minimum in the film itself.

The Barn of the Naked Dead (1974)
(aka *Terror Circus*; aka *Nightmare Circus*)
Dir: Alan Rudolph /USA
Three showgirls on their way to Vegas are picked up by a strange man after their vehicle

breaks down on the desert road. The man takes the girls back to his isolated ranch where he already has several women held captive in the barn. And before they can flee, the showgirls are chained up and added to his collection. Soon after, the girls are forced to endure the horror and humiliation of being paraded around the grounds like circus animals and being hunted down by the lunatic's pet cougar. Of course, the man has some serious psychological issues, and becomes convinced that one of the girls is the reincarnation of his dead mother. As the girls plan to escape, their plight is made all the more hopeless as there also lurks a brutish mutant in a nearby shed... This sleazy little drive-in effort is let down by its sluggish pace and its insulting disregard for characterisation and logic. The women are portrayed as frustratingly dumb, and the lunatic (played by 70s exploitation regular, Andrew Prine, of *Grizzly* [1976], *The Town That Dreaded Sundown* [1976] and *Simon, King of the Witches* [1971] fame) somehow manages to keep the women enslaved without even possessing a gun. The Nevada desert location looks impressive with its lonely desert plains and deep blue skies, and there's also a hopeless, downbeat mood that is sustained throughout, but this is strictly second-rate stuff compared to other 70s psycho movies like *Abducted* (1973), *Deranged* (1974), and of course, *The Texas Chain Saw Massacre* (1974). Director Alan Rudolph has refused to even acknowledge this film since he went on to direct more mainstream fare in the 80s, which is a shame because *Barn* has since been issued on DVD by Shriek Show (under its *Terror Circus* title) with a great transfer and with many of the cast and crew re-uniting for the audio commentary and featurette.

Hardgore (1974)
(aka *Horrorwhore*, aka *Sadoasylum*)
Dir: Michael Hugo /USA
A young nymphomaniac who suffers from hallucinations is put into a rehab centre, but little does she know that the proprietor is the leader of a Satanic cult who indulge in murderous after hour orgies(!) Well, it's certainly unique! Running around an hour in length, *Hardgore* is one of the more well-known horror/porn hybrids of American exploitation of the 70s. None of the actors are very attractive, the soundtrack, though pretty decent in places, has the annoying habit of recycling the same old tune until your ears feel like they're gonna pop.

The sex scenes are all rather bland and unimaginative, and the horror sequences are few and far between. The Satanic 'orgies' are almost completely static with very little of interest going on (except for the scene where a woman is guillotined the moment her partner reaches orgasm). The hallucinations are silly and mostly quite laughable (dildos on strings spurting semen?), the leader of the cult wears a red Satanic mask and robe and puts on a deep booming voice which is also unintentionally hilarious ("Nirvana!!!"). The girl does get some revenge at the end in the form of an axe rampage, but even this is quite dull and over before it really starts.

The Texas Chain Saw Massacre (1974)
Dir: Tobe Hooper /USA
A group of fresh-faced youths journey to rural Texas in a camper van to find the ransacked graveyard where a relative is buried, and to make sure the grave has remained unmolested. On their way back home, they run across an isolated farm and discover to their horror that it houses a family of homicidal cannibals. Meanwhile, running riot in a mask made of human skin, a butcher's apron, and a revving chainsaw, Leatherface attempts to fill his deep freezer with the unlucky travellers.

The Texas Chain Saw Massacre is one of the most notorious horror films ever made, a landmark of terror which was outlawed by the British censors for nearly twenty five years, and which still cuts straight to the bone all these years later. According to former chief censor, James Ferman, it's 'an exercise in the pornography of terror'; for genre film-maker John Carpenter, it's 'a classic that rides along the very edge of taste'; and for film critic Kim Newman, it's quite simply 'a masterpiece which is totally committed to scaring you witless.'

The Texas Chain Saw Massacre was based on the activities of grave-robber-turned-murderer, Ed Gein, whose crimes (which included skinning, eating, and even *wearing* bits of his victims) had previously inspired such classics as *Psycho* and *Deranged*. Directed by Tobe Hooper, who later went on to make *Death Trap*, *Lifeforce*, and *Poltergeist*, *The Texas Chain Saw Massacre* was sold to its audience with the poster blurb '...it happened', a claim that was bolstered by the gruelling docu-drama style which gave viewers the impression that what they were watching was real. Shot largely in and around a claustrophobic house which designer Robert A. Burns had decorated with entrail artworks, the movie literally put viewers right inside the mouth of madness, where Marilyn Burns and her unfortunate compatriots discover the dark side of the myth of the American family. And everyone screams... a lot.

Unemployed since the closing down of the local slaughterhouse, this family stick to their old ways by bumping off strangers and tourists in the same way they would deal with beef cattle. These nameless maniacs (they were later named the Sawyers in the first sequel) resemble a bizarre parody of the sitcom family, with the long-suffering patriarch who tries to keep some kind of 'order' (Jim Siedow), the bewigged, apron wearing Leatherface as 'mom' (Gunnar Hansen), and the unruly, long-haired hitch-hiker (Edwin Neal) as the son. And their degraded household serves as a cracked mirror of the ideal home. There are skeletal and entrail remains, and feathers everywhere, and an armchair that looks to have human arms. An interesting point made by Kim Newman in *Nightmare Movies*: In Texas you're allowed to shoot dead anyone who steps foot on your lawn. These youngsters are trespassing, so this massacre probably isn't even illegal!

The black humour is often overlooked, building a powerful parody of the nuclear family, represented by the grim and efficient Leatherface, who picks off the touring party to feed his retarded, cannibal clan. The film's low-budget production values and cast of unknowns gives it a verite frisson, particularly during the closing scenes when it becomes clear that the cuts and bruises on Marilyn's face are actually real, and it's a mark of the film's plausibility that ever since his move to Hollywood, Tobe Hooper has never matched it, not even with the most state-of-the-art special effects money can buy. People talk endlessly about the damaging effects of horror movies, but too little is heard about the life-affirming power of being scared out of your skin.

If the events of *The Texas Chain Saw Massacre* were shocking enough, the way the British censors dealt with them was even worse. When the film was shown before the Board in March 1975, trailing glowing US reviews, the BBFC were so appalled that they simply banned it outright. Two years later, the film found its way back to the BBFC where James Ferman, embarrassed by its growing popularity, spent

some time with a chainsaw of his own, attempting to cut out the very few shots of explicit violence. When he'd finished, he learned what we all knew in the first place; that the film was indestructible, or more accurately, censor-proof. 'The cuts made no difference at all,' Ferman huffed before giving up and banning it again. It wasn't until Ferman resigned from the Board in the late 90s (by which time the *TCM* had been banned again for the third time) that the film finally earned itself a long overdue amnesty from the new chief censor, Andreas Whittam Smith.

The version now available is exactly the same as that which was first outlawed in 1975, with no cuts, just pure, undiluted terror.

The Night Porter (1974)
(Orig title: *Il Portiere Di Notte*)
Dir: Liliana Cavani /Italy

Vienna, 1957. At an upmarket hotel, head porter, Maximilian (Italy's chief British Nazi, Dirk Bogarde), is shocked when he locks eyes on a female guest, Lucia (Charlotte Rampling). Max is considered a vitruous and hard-working man, but it soon becomes clear that he was once a Nazi SS officer who engaged in a torturous, semi-sadomasochistic relationship with Lucia while she was held in a concentration camp. Upon meeting again at the hotel, Max is surprised when she seems willing to continue in her submission to him, and they become so carried away in their passion that they lock themselves in a room and explore the darkness that draws them together. Meanwhile, Max's former colleagues are being tracked down by Nazi hunters, and are worried that Max and Lucia's relationship will reveal the details of each of their dark pasts, and so they conspire to have the lovers killed.

The Night Porter is a meditative drama that mixes stylish, erotic scenes with a background of concentration camp ugliness, resulting in a disturbing and prurient fascination. While many subsequent Italian movies took 'Nazisploitaton' down some very unsavoury paths, descending to the pits of tastelessness (*The Beast In Heat*, *The Gestapo's Last Orgy*, etc), Liliana Cavani's film remains perhaps more controversial because of the seriousness with which she treats her subject-matter. And though it was Tinto Brass's *Salon Kitty*, made a couple of years later, which really kicked off the Italian Nazi cycle, this earlier film is much more concerned with mood and – sometimes unconvincing – psychology rather than bombarding the audience with ludicrous and tasteless thrills. But anyone watching the film expecting an easy ride will be shocked by some of the kinky goings on here, such as broken glass and a severed head on a platter used as a means of dominance and sexual excitation.

Along with the rare and hard to find *Beyond Good and Evil* (1977), *The Night Porter* shocked and offended many bourgeois Italian critics at the time (which is no doubt what Cavani intended). Back in the 70s, Cavani was a serious film-maker who had much to say on the subject of sexual transgression, so it's a shame that much of her subsequent work consisted of mediocre TV movies, clearly not the place where her heart was. Both Rampling and Bogarde had previously starred in Visconti's Nazi-themed soap opera, *The Damned* (1969).

Exorcism (1974)
(Orig title: *Exorcismes et messes noires*; aka *Demoniac*; aka *The Sadist of Notre Dame*)
Dir: Jess Franco /France /Spain
In 1974, in response to the controversy that greeted *The Exorcist* in the previous year, British director Pete Walker, and writer David McGillivray, unleashed *House of Mortal Sin* (1974), this time flipping the theme of good and evil on its head by portraying a homicidal Catholic Priest who targets the local sinners after they reveal their transgressions to him during Confession. The film-makers were surprised to find that the film had barely raised an eyebrow among the public, and that much sought after publicity-by-way-of-controversy never materialised. This despite including a scene in which the Priest clobbers a man to death with a flaming censer. Meanwhile on the continent, Spaniard Jess Franco was tackling similar subject-matter in his film, *Exorcism*, about another homicidal Priest – or near Priest – and the director was much more willing to acknowledge the hypocrisy and sexual repression of his unhinged maniac, unleashing a grim and truly nasty little film that was actually much closer to Pete Walker's cold grey style than Franco's own previous efforts.

Exorcism opens on an extended scene in an S&M dungeon where a nude Anne (Lina Romay) is chained to a cross and slowly tormented by a knife-wielding blonde, Martine (Catherine Lafferiere). The two women turn out to be actors performing a late-night show for an audience. However, there is a puritanical maniac on the loose, Mathis Vogel (Jess Franco), a failed Priest who was banished from the Church for his extremism, and who may have also been a mental patient in his recent past. Declaring himself 'The Grand Inquisitor,' Vogel sets himself the task of cleansing the streets of what he sees as an insidious demonic influence spreading throughout society. And his way of dealing with the problem is to kidnap sinners and cut out their hearts to save their souls. Meanwhile, the local police – in a coordinated effort with Interpol – attempt to track the maniac down, but it isn't easy as he seems to select a new name and identity for each town or country he visits on his crusade...

Set in a grey and perpetually overcast Paris, *Exorcism* is a cold and sobering exercise in horror, as demented hedonism is stopped ruthlessly in its tracks by an even more demented fundamentalism. It's a film which perfectly illustrates the decadent world from which a crazed killer such as Vogel could emerge. And in this sense, the film has much in common with William Friedkin's *Cruising* (1980). For Vogel, sexual impropriety is detrimental to the soul, therefore murder is a perfectly legitimate act of sanctity, for he is freeing his victims' spirits from the filth of their flesh. Of course, this is the kind of reasoning that he uses to justify his transgressions, but it's also fairly obvious that Vogel is guilty of the very same carnal impurity – he lusts after his victims, and gains a great deal of sexual satisfaction in cutting up young women with a blade.

Thanks to the extensive research by *Video Watchdog*'s Tim Lucas, we now know that Franco shared some interesting parallels with his twisted character. Franco had moved to France to make freer and more challenging movies, and Vogel had arrived in Paris for his own sinister ends; Vogel writes S&M-themed stories under pseudonyms such as 'Laforgue,' and Franco often credited himself in his films under aliases including 'Clifford Brown,' and screenplay credits such as 'David Khune' (sometimes 'Khunne') to escape being identified; Franco playing Vogel means he gets to torture his beloved, Lina Romay, a corrupted soul whom Vogel wants to 'save'; and perhaps most amazingly, Vogel abducts and tortures a prostitute on his own deceased mother's bed –

the victim was played by Caroline Riviere, the real-life daughter of Franco's second wife, Nicole Guettard! And, in the hardcore version, Franco/Vogel even gets to perform cunnilingus on her! All of which makes for a very sinful collision of reality and fiction.

Franco was never entirely happy with *Exorcism*. In 1979, he re-cut the film with additional scenes and re-released it under the title *The Sadist of Notre Dame*. In the 80s, there were numerous versions available on VHS, including hardcore versions. However, the most widely seen copy during that time was the heavily censored edit entitled *Demoniac*, which was released by Wizard Video in the States. On DVD, Synapse released the most extensive cut of the film, compiling all of the available footage and discarding the hardcore shots that were added by the producers. That same version was re-issued on eye-popping Blu-Ray by Kino in 2012, and is now widely regarded as the definitive version.

Film fans who for years had been comparing notes on the lookout for the most complete version of the film could now rest assured that they had found it. But be warned: *Exorcism* is not an easy ride. There are moments to be enthralled and appalled by, such as the near constant nudity, the impressive soundtrack (some of which was carried over from Franco's previous *Les Gloutonnes* [1973]), also the beautiful Romay in her prime, some graphic torture, torso carving, and some of the nastiest anti-Christian sentiments ever committed to film.

The Centerfold Girls (1974)
Dir: John Peyser /USA
1974 saw the release of two films that dealt with twisted puritanical killers – Pete Walker's *House of Mortal Sin* and Jess Franco's *Exorcism*. These were films that portrayed serial killer Priests who attempted to combat evil by murdering sinners. Their self-righteous killing sprees were also conveniently in synch with their own sexual sadism and impotence. Far less known is another film released in the same year that portrays a similar messed-up maniac, *The Centerfold Girls*. This time, however, the religious angle is dropped, and the story is told in the style of an anthology film.

The killer, played by Andrew Prine (in the second of his maniac roles after his stint as Andre, the mother-fixated psychotic in *The*

Barn of the Naked Dead [1974]), selects his pretty young victims from a calendar in which they posed topless. In the first segment of the trilogy, the killer stalks one of the models, Jackie (Jaime Lyn Bauer), a nurse who is duped into allowing a seemingly innocent girl stay at her home, only for the girl's reckless friends to show up in the middle of the night... The second segment plays like a giallo, and sees several models, along with agents and a photographer, stop by on an island for a photo shoot where they are executed, one by one... And the last segment charts the misfortunes of another model, Vera (Tiffany Bolling), who heads out of town to escape the killer, only to find him stalking her anew at a hotel. She accepts a ride from a couple of drunken sailors, and they slip a roofie into her beer and rape her. However, the next morning her ordeal is far from over.

The Centerfold Girls deserves a much larger audience as it's one of the great unsung gems of the mid-70s, but barely gets a mention in horror fan circles. The film boasts a no-nonsense, matter-of-fact immediacy in the way the devious killer serves as an evil omnipresence trying to eradicate the impurity of his desires by slaughtering pretty young women. The music is also quite atypical of the horror genre at the time, mixing strange harpsichord chimes with acid rock. One of the most unnerving aspects of the film is its cynicism – almost all of the characters serve as friendly-faced predators. This was director John Peyser's only stab at horror genre. A veteran of more than a thousand credits for television since 1947, he made *The Centerfold Girls* as a favour for his producer friend, Arthur Marks. He died in 2001.

Flavia the Heretic (1974)
Dir: Gianfranco Mingozzi /Italy /France
One of the most infamous entries in the Italian nunsploitation series of the 70s, *Flavia the Heretic* mixes religion-bashing with sleazy grindhouse aesthetics, an unholy combination that kept it away from home video for years in anything resembling an uncut copy. Most often seen released in blurry, censored form, Synapse came along and offered the full uncut version on DVD in the early 00s in a beautiful, razor-sharp transfer. Suffice it to say, it remains the only version of the film you should see.

Flavia (Florinda Bolkan) is sent off to a remote convent after witnessing her father decapitate her friend. And it's there she lives under the rule of the cruel Mother Superior. She takes her chance to leave and meets a Hassidic scholar, but soon finds herself back at the convent under the power of the sisters. Later, freedom looks to be at hand when a Muslim sect rolls by, known as the Tarantulas, and Flavia becomes the leader of a bloody revolt from within the convent walls. Flavia cuts off her hair when she becomes attracted to the leader of the sect (Anthony Corlan, of *Vampire Circus* fame), and then sets out on a fateful journey that leads to much more violence and gruesomeness.

Flavia the Heretic remains notorious to this day for its depraved and sadistic ending, but the sleaze-factor is present throughout the entire film. Within the first five minutes we're witness to much disarray as women in the convent run wild, playing with themselves and encouraging the sisters to join in while chanting "Tarantulas!" over and over, and sensually caressing the walls like Britt Ekland in *The Wicker Man*. It's a scene reminiscent of the nun pandemonium in Ken Russell's *The Devils*, and shares with that film the uninhibited performances of the cast. Those expecting something along the lines of Joe D'Amato's *Images In a Convent* or Bruno Mattei's *The Other Hell*, however, will be in for a surprise here as *Flavia* is a competently made drama with characters the audience can feel for and believe in. Indeed, the film has a warm 70s vibe to it and radiates quality from every frame, which makes it all the more startling when things turn nasty and graphic.

In addition to scenes of bull castration, bloody massacres, suicide victims swinging from the rafters, severed heads, and a Fernando Arrabal-esque sequence in which a couple have sex within the hollowed-out carcass of a cow, the film also includes a magnificent performance from Bolkan, whose assured presence is engaging from start to finish. Whether she's lusting after Corlan or gripped in a homicidal frenzy, it's difficult not to feel for her, and this only makes the inevitable ending all the more horrific to watch.

Caged Heat (1974)
Dir: Jonathan Demme /USA
Roger Corman's greatest contribution to film was his willingness to nurture new talents. In the 60s, his AIP studio was crammed with up and coming young directors including Martin Scorsese, Francis Ford Coppola, Peter Bogdanovich, Joe Dante, and Jonathan Demme, film-makers who would go on to define the age of modern cinema. So just remember, if it wasn't for Corman we would probably never have had *Raging Bull*, *The Godfather*, or *Silence of the Lambs*.

Jonathan Demme's stint as a writer/producer for Corman put him in good stead to make his debut feature, *Caged Heat*, a women-in-prison title for the drive-in market, whose memorable tagline ('Rape, riot, and revenge. White hot desires melting cold prison steel') sounds very typical of the exploitation angle of many similar types of films. However, Demme's take on the sleazy genre manages to strike an impressive balance between violence, nudity, and sadistic authority figures, whilst keeping the proceedings in line with the popularity of feminist ideology.

Jacqueline Wilson (Erica Gavin) is sentenced to a spell at Connorville Women's Prison for armed robbery. The institute is run by the crippled Governess, McQueen (Barbara Steele), and her cronies, including her side-kick, Pinter, and a neo-fascist doctor, Randolf. She befriends inmates, and together they hatch an escape plan which sees them back on the streets. Together with 'Crazy Annie,' an old friend of Jacqueline's, the gang pulls off a bank robbery, stealing the thunder from a couple of male would-be robbers. The escapees then decide to return to Connorville to save their captive friends from the sadistic experiments of the evil Dr. Randolf...

All the usual women in prison ingredients are here – the obligatory shower scenes with full frontal nudity, the violence and bitching, the riots and rebellions, and fiendish personnel – but Demme expands on this limited genre by centring on a likeable bunch of renegade women, and stylistically he pushes the boundaries for such fare; legendary DP Tak Fujimoto supplies the eye-popping visuals, John Cale the unorthodox score, Erica Gavin a rousing lead performance, and horror starlet Barbara Steele presents her usual iconic campy quality, all adding to the legitimate proceedings of a prison film which is far greater than the sum of its exploitation parts.

The US drive-in crowd always had a taste for dangerous foul-mouthed women, and this has resulted in a few strange concoctions over the years, such as Russ Meyer's *Faster Pussycat, Kill! Kill!*, but very few were as interesting or as unique as *Caged Heat*. I'd settle for this over *Silence of the Lambs* any day.

Black Christmas (1974)
Dir: Bob Clarke /Canada
"Ho ho ho, shit!" An icy gem that continues to scare the hell out of each new generation of horror fans. It's Christmas Eve, and a group of college girls are preparing for the holidays. The festivities are soon spoiled, however, when they're pestered by obscene and threatening phone calls – possibly the creepiest and most disturbing phone calls in film history. The killer's voice yelps and shifts tone so crazy and spouts incomprehensible gibberish of pure malice it will put you on the edge of your seat right away. One of the girls is murdered and dumped in the attic. The police are quick to link her disappearance to a spate of attacks on young girls in the local area, but as is the way with any seasonal slasher, the killings continue...

There are lots of jump-out-of-your-seat moments in *Black Christmas*, a film which, along with Mario Bava's *A Bay of Blood* (1971), served as a blueprint for the slasher movies that followed in the late 70s and early 80s. The spooky close-up shots of the killer's eyes recalls taut classics like *The Spiral Staircase* (1946) and *Profondo Rosso* (1975). John Carpenter's *Halloween* takes credit for kick-starting the slasher boom, but that film owes a huge debt to Bob Clarke's underrated masterpiece. It is also laced with a biting sense of humour that inspired the later unfunny slasher imitators; the ongoing fellatio joke ("I know, it's something dirty ain't it"), and the killer's obscenities on the phone ("Let me lick it! Let me lick your pretty pink cunt!"). It also had an influence on another underrated gem, Fred Walton's *When a Stranger Calls* in 1979.

Axe (1974)
(Orig title: *Lisa, Lisa*; aka *California Axe Massacre*)
Dir: Frederick Friedel /USA
Not your typical video nasty. For, although it was made on a tiny budget of $25,000 and is a fairly grim and downbeat affair, *Axe* is nonetheless an atmospheric mood-piece that possesses genuine artistic merit, despite its lurid title.

Three criminals are on the run after a killing and a bungled robbery. They race their getaway car to a remote farmhouse where they intend to hideout until the dust settles. The people who live in the house – the wheelchair-bound mute grandfather, and a disturbed teenage girl, Lisa – seem like easy prey to the trio of hoodlums, but this kind of cocksure bravado overlooks just how dangerous Lisa is...

Axe was written and directed by former fashion photographer, Frederick Friedel, who was just 25 years old when he shot the film. His naivete and inexperience ironically helped rather than hindered the proceedings; he kept the production on a minuscule basis, with just a handful of sets and characters, and his way of stretching the running time to meet the 'feature length' requirements was frankly ingenious – he allowed the scenes the space to breathe in the editing room, and allowed the end credits to run their full course, creating an intense atmosphere to prevail throughout. And this also offered composers George Newman Shaw and John Willhelm the chance to shine with their fantastic score that plays uninterrupted at the end. The result is a beautiful, poetic mood-piece that is unlike anything else ever shown at a drive-in theatre. Friedel (who cast himself in the role as Billy, one of the crims) is also aided by some decent performances from Jack Canon who plays the leader of the gang, Leslie Lee who plays the withdrawn Lisa, and Douglas Powers as the grandfather whose mute and crippled existence limited his role to his intensely expressive eyes.

All was going well for the film when it played a few dates under its original title, *Lisa Lisa*, until Friedel secured a distribution deal with Harry Novak and his Box Office International company. *Lisa Lisa*, along with Friedel's follow-up film, *Date With a Kidnapper*, had their titles changed to *Axe* and *Kidnapped Coed*, respectively. Novak was also skilled at ripping people off, and Friedel barely saw a penny of revenue from the film's modest success at the drive-ins. Stung and disillusioned by the experience, Friedel backed away from the movie business and was unable to pay back his financiers, and this resulted in family members of those who bankrolled the film committing suicide, and Friedel wanting to murder Novak. That's the tragic side of indie film-making for you (see Stephen Thrower's excellent book, *Nightmare USA*, for the full story).

In the UK, *Axe* found itself on the 'video nasties' list and was kept out of our homes for years until the BBFC relented and passed it uncut in 2005, allowing us to finally lay eyes on this idiosyncratic gem. Sometimes referred to as 'America's answer to *Repulsion*', *Lisa Lisa* works best at night in a hazy frame of mind. Don't expect a traditional 'join-the-dots' type of narrative, but a dark and troubling dream, and you're on the right track.

God's Bloody Acre (1974)
Dir: Harry E. Kerwin /USA

A trio of men fed up with the modern world have ditched their jobs and now live in a makeshift shack in the woods. Their peaceful habitat comes under threat, however, when land developers show up with their bulldozers, cutting down trees to make way for a public park. The anti-social woodsmen, Monroe, Ezra and Benny (William Kerwin – the director's brother – Daniel Schweitzer and Sam Moree) attempt to disrupt the workers by pelting them with rocks. And when one of the workers is killed, the men decide they should continue 'God's work' and terrorise the outsiders until they leave... Supposedly based on 'true events' (the end credits make it clear that the film is entirely fictional), *God's Bloody Acre* is a lacklustre and mostly forgotten little backwoods horror. In its favour, there are some glorious, politically incorrect moments with racist outbursts, an extensive rape scene, and all of the black characters are portrayed as savage thugs. In order to drag the film out to feature length, there are lots of scenes on the road played out to a bunch of acoustic numbers from forgotten folk singers. Also, the initial attack on the bulldozer drags on for much longer than necessary. The film could have easily been cut down to an hour for a much tighter, well-paced flick. It's a technically proficient, middle-of-the-road, workman-like approach from director Kerwin (who had worked on movies and television since the mid-50s). This is perhaps his finest hour. He died in 1979 after delivering his swan song, *Baracuda* (1978). As for *God's Bloody Acre*, there's an obvious message about the destruction of nature and the downfall of civilisation, and during the rape scene the same library cues that George Romero later used in *Dawn of the Dead* (1978) are played on the soundtrack!

The Killers Are Our Guests (1974)
(Orig title: *Gli assassini sono nostri ospiti*)
Dir: Vincenzo Rigo /Italy

After a bungled diamond heist, armed robbers make their getaway and arrive at the home of a doctor and his wife. One of the crims has taken a bullet in the shoot-out and needs urgent medical attention. And though the doctor does what he can to save the injured robber, the criminals target the couple for rape and other forms of abuse... *The Killers* is a home invasion movie which pre-dates *House on the Edge of the Park* (1980). And though it never quite reaches the levels of degradation found in Deodato's film, this is still a fairly watchable addition to the Italian exploitation cycle.

Zero Woman: Red Handcuffs (1974)
(Orig title: *Zeroka no onna: Akai wappa*)
Dir: Yukio Noda /Japan

The film opens in a go-go dancing club where the sexy Miki Sugimoto, dressed in red, attracts the attention of a sleazy white man, and they are soon back to his hotel room. Foreplay over with, he decides to make her his latest victim in a series of brutal rape and murders. However, Sugimoto, an undercover cop, confronts him with photographic evidence of his previous victims, and while he finds it all very funny, he completely underestimates her, and winds up taking multiple bullets to the groin. Her superiors at the station are infuriated with Miki's rough justice, and they summarily strip her of rank, send her to jail, and leave her there to rot.

Sugimoto soon finds herself back on the streets when a situation arises that requires her services. The engaged daughter of a politician has been kidnapped and held to ransom. The politician father wants her back and her affair kept hush hush. At the father's instigation, Sugimoto is released from prison and becomes an unofficial agent of the government with a license to kill. She now calls herself 'Zero Woman', and is sent out to infiltrate the gang of kidnappers, a bunch of bumbling hoodlums led by the lunatic Nakahara, and attempts to rescue the girl, and see to it that none of the hoodlums make it out alive.

It's a great premise and with such a simple plot that may have been an influence on Luc Besson's *Nikita*. The problem is that neither Zero Woman nor the gang are interesting enough to help the film transcend its limitations. Zero Woman starts out as a tough, take-no-shit, kickass heroine, but as soon as she falls in with the gang of scumbags she immediately becomes weak and passive. The audience knows she is capable of wiping out the bad guys while hardly breaking a sweat, and yet frustratingly, she continues to allow herself to be abused at the hands of the scumbags. The sex and violence can only carry the film so far. Aside from the fact that she is a cop, we learn very little about her. Don't get me wrong, I like mysterious characters but not so much when they do absolutely nothing. And as a result, she appears more dull than mysterious.

On the plus side, *Zero Woman*, like many exploitation pics from Japan at the time, looks astonishing, and the violence is often strong and bloody. The gruelling finale set in a wasteland of swirling newspapers is also exceptional, and the film is worth watching for that reason alone.

The Bloody Exorcism of Coffin Joe (1974)
(Orig title: *Exorcismo negro*)
Dir: Jose Mojica Marins /Brazil

Marins finds himself under threat from his fictional alter-ego in this blatant cash-in on William Friedkin's *The Exorcist* (1973), which at least has the distinction of pre-dating such post-modern horrors as *Wes Craven's New Nightmare* (1994) and Lucio Fulci's *A Cat in the Brain* (1990) by almost two decades. Marins spends Christmas with friends working on the script for his latest horror film, 'O Exorcismo negro,' (or 'The Black Exorcism'), and soon uncovers strange demonic possessions, treachery, sacrificial rituals, murder and witchcraft in their midst. Who could be behind all this skullduggery? Why, it's the one in the top hat with the long, curly finger nails, of course.

The Brazilian media had vilified Marins for years, accusing him of desecrating gravestones, sleeping in graveyards, abusing his actresses, being a drug addict (he was heavily into amphetamines at one point), and even necrophilia. Perhaps with this film, Marins was attempting to balance the issue by drawing the very distinct separation between his real identity and his fictional persona. But it made no difference. Upon the release of *The Bloody Exorcism*, the media accused him of being insane, and the censors banned his film for years. Highlights include a crying girl holding a dead fox while the adults stand around gawping at each other; the zombie-like possessed ones who look like they've just stepped in from George Romero's *The Crazies* (1973); and the bloody axe dismemberments and group tortures in the finale.

The Cars That Ate Paris (1974)
(aka *The Cars That Ate People*)
Dir: Peter Weir /Australia

Overblown and typically overrated since the director moved on to bigger things. Peter Weir marked his directorial debut with this black comedy which went on to inspire *Mad Max 2: The Road Warrior* (1981) and a homage in Quentin Tarantino's *Death Proof* (2007). Taking inspiration from rebel pics like *The Wild One* (1953) and westerns, such as *High Noon* (1952), here we have spiked car wrecks driven by fun-seeking youths through the streets of Paris, Australia, causing smash-ups. Turns out that the collisions are actually planned ahead and are engineered by the vulturous populace for economic and medical reasons. The looters profit by selling the salvage, and the town doctor performs immoral medical experiments on the victims. The film culminates in a bloodbath between the youths and the townsfolk.

Shivers (1975)
(aka *The Parasite Murders*; aka *They Came From Within*)
Dir: David Cronenberg /Canada

"I love sex, but I love sex as a venereal disease. I am syphilis. I am enthusiastic about it but in a very different way from you."

So said David Cronenberg on the rationale of his first commercial feature, *Shivers*, which caused an almighty stink in his native Canada but has since become regarded as one of the highlights of 70s horror. It's original, inventive, controversial, ironic, dangerous, and caused an instant notoriety. The film unfolds entirely in and around a luxury apartment block as the residents therein are infected by slug-like parasites that invade the human body, turning the hosts into sex-crazed maniacs. These creatures invade through any bodily orifice available – usually the mouth, but in a scene featuring scream queen Barbara Steele, the parasites are happy to make entrance through more private areas too. Of course, mass panic ensues as the uninfected try to escape and hide away from the hordes of horny homicidal sex addicts who run riot through the corridors and apartments, and Cronenberg has a blast playing against society's sexual taboos.

Shivers is as much Cronenberg's ironic comment on society as it is a horror film, laced with gross black humour and clever invention. It also displays his usual themes which would crop up again in his later work (and in that sense, the film is similar to George Romero's *Night of the Living Dead*). His previous underground films like *Stereo* (1969) and *Crimes of the Future* (1970) were also brimming with his warped body-horror ideas, but *Shivers* took those obsessions and unleashed them on a mainstream audience. The film's isolated setting brings on a claustrophobic edge, and the 'monster' represents our own sexuality which was definitely a break from the norm at the time (and this also relates to *Night of the Living Dead* in which the monsters in that movie was our fellow man; even our neighbours, or loved ones, or ourselves). Cronenberg toys around with the antagonistic characteristics of the movie monster to an unsettling effect, and he's clearly having a good time subverting our biological needs. Even in today's climate of remake mania in Hollywood, no one has yet attempted an updating of *Shivers*; if a remake was done correctly, it would no doubt cause just as much controversy now as the original did back in the 70s.

Cronenberg struggled for years to find financing for the project, and had almost given up on the idea and was preparing to go to Hollywood to work with Roger Corman when the Canadian Film Development Corporation (as they were then known) stepped forward and offered the relevant funding. However, even before the film had been released, Cronenberg found himself and his film in hot water as *Shivers* became a scandal in the Canadian press and would remain his most controversial film until *Crash* caused a similar stir in the British tabloids a couple of decades later.

The trouble started when film critic Robert Fulford was invited to a preview screening of the film as a gesture of goodwill by the producers at Cinepix. They had hoped for some mainstream acceptance for their exploitation title by having a renowned critic provide a review prior to its official release. The move horribly backfired when Fulford (under the pseudonym 'Marshall Delaney') wrote a damning piece entitled 'You should Know How Bad This Film Is. After All, You Paid For It', in which he accused *Shivers* of being the most despicable and repulsive film ever made. He also pointed out that tax payer's money had financed the film and that it was a completely unacceptable way to spend public money. This

moral panic spread like wildfire, and other so-called film critics attacked *Shivers* for similar reasons in the *Toronto Globe and Mail*, and the *Montreal Gazette* (who, to be fair, did allow Cronenberg to publicly defend his film in print). The scandal reached parliament, Cronenberg became a celebrity, and *Shivers* became the most successful home-grown movie in Canadian history. When people learned that *Shivers* was the only film funded by the CFDC that actually turned a profit for the taxpayer, the furore quickly died down, making Cronenberg the most bankable director in the country. And this allowed him to explore his obsessions further in projects like *Rabid* (1976) and *The Brood* (1979), each with a more generous budget than before.

There were exceptions to the bad press though; *Cinema Canada* published a glowing review praising *Shivers* as a masterpiece of horror, and Cronenberg himself managed to turn the tide of criticism in his favour when asked to account for his work, "The true subject of horror films," he said, "is death and anticipation of death, and this leads to the question of man as body as opposed to man as spirit."

Shivers has since been accepted as an innovative genre classic, with its daring and unflinching probe into social-sexual taboos of the time – promiscuity, lesbianism, homosexuality, and even paedophilia and incest. The film can also be seen as a journey through the historical evolution of the horror movie as a legitimate art form in its own right. On home video, the film has more or less managed to stay intact in most territories. The best option is the Region 0 DVD from Image; it's uncut and presents the best looking transfer of the film so far. Arrow Video released the Blu-Ray in 2014.

The Beast (1975)
(Orig title: *La béte*; aka *Devil's Ecstasy*)
Dir: Walerian Borowczyk /France
Talented Polish painter Walerian Borowczyk moved to France in the 60s taking with him a Buñuellian sense of mischief and a strong desire to use erotic cinema as a way of attacking and undermining bourgeois values. His early films were animated and well received, such as *The Theatre of Mr. and Mrs. Kabal* (1967), but he soon moved onto live action with his impressive *Goto, Island of Love* (1968), and the ambitious medieval epic, *Blanche* (1971).

He returned three years later with *Immoral*

Tales (1974), a quartet of erotic stories which earned him a solid reputation among the art house elite. But all of that positive acclaim came crashing down with his next film, *La béte*, which features a sequence in which a pretty young woman is chased through the woods and ravished by a well-endowed hairy beast, complete with wild prosthetics and cum shots.

The story of *La béte* focuses on Lucy Broadhurst (Lisbeth Hummel), an English woman who travels to the L'Esperance estate where she intends to marry the brutish son, Mathurin (Pierre Benedetti). Whilst the family await Lucy's arrival, members of this deranged household have sex and plot murder, all in the guise of social respectability. Lucy is welcomed to the estate by the sight of horses copulating on the driveway, and she takes a polaroid snapshot for herself. After finding an illustrated diary belonging to the lady of the estate, Romilda, Lucy has a nightmare of being chased through the woods by a humongous beast with a huge erection. Mathurin dies the next day just as Lucy's sexuality awakens. And when the Cardinal arrives explaining his own ideas on bestiality, Lucy is sped away in her chauffeur-driven car.

A horny and explicit piece of incendiary film-making, *La béte* explores the sexual subtexts of classic fairytales like *Little Red Riding Hood* and *Beauty and the Beast*. The infamous 20 minute segment featuring the monster in the woods was originally envisaged as being part of Borowczyk's previous film, *Immoral Tales*, but instead seemed to develop a life of its own and became the centrepiece of an entirely new film. Whether seen as a horror film, a satire, dark fantasy, or erotica, Borowczyk clearly delights in stripping away the facade of polite convention. It's a film that uncovers the bestial nature of polite society, as seen in the horses breeding on the drive, and taking inspiration from Luis Buñuel for an amusing comedy of manners spiked with a subversive edge. The Spanish surrealist's *The Discreet Charm of the Bourgeoisie* (1972) looks to have been used as a healthy template.

The film caused an almighty stink when it first hit screens, and found itself banned and censored all across the world. The critics who had previously championed Borowczyk's work turned against him and felt personally insulted by the film, and for years it was almost impossible to see in anything even resembling

an uncut copy. An English language version appeared on VHS under the title *Devil's Ecstasy*, but most of the offending footage had been removed (including the horses). An uncut French print played at UK and American art house cinemas in 2001 in a limited run, but on DVD it was Cult Epics who came to the rescue with a 3 disc set of *La Béte* in a Director's Cut which is actually missing around four minutes of dialogue that Borowczyk himself cut out of the film (the third disc presents the original fully uncut version with English hard subs).

Wet Wilderness (1975)
Dir: Lee Cooper /USA
This sick little porn film pays homage to the sadism and murder scenes in Wes Craven's *Last House On The Left*, but those expecting a climatic rampage of revenge will be disappointed as this film wraps up on an unredeeming note.

A pair of hippy throwbacks take a wander through the woods and are accosted by a dangerous sex maniac. Armed with a machete and wearing a bright yellow and black ski mask, the madman forces the peace-loving stragglers to perform sexual acts on him and each other whilst waving his blade around like he's conducting some kind of depraved orchestra. One of the girls escapes but the other is not so lucky and she meets the sharp end of the maniac's weapon. The escapee returns to the scene with the aid of more cardboard characters who serve as nothing more but slabs of meat to be treated in a similar way. It's no spoiler if I tell you that all does not end pleasantly for the hippies. More nastiness, murder, and forced-incest ensues...

Made for spare change in the woods in a single afternoon, *Wet Wilderness* is a 'roughie' that lacks the zesty zeal of *Widow Blue* (1970) and the darkly comic tirades of Harry Reems in *Forced Entry*, but makes up for it in its casual and gleeful degeneracy. Daymon Gerard does an adequate job of playing the maniac, even though his face is hidden throughout the entire running time. The yellow and black ski mask seems almost illuminated among the dull and hazy foliage, and brings on a slight phobia in some viewers; but make no mistake, this backwoods killer is far more dangerous than any wasp or hornet, and he has one hell of a nasty sting in his 'tail'. The film's biggest let down is the 'gore' which amounts to some light plywood in the shape of a machete or axe glued to the victim's head or torso with a dollop of ketchup. But I suppose the FX are no worse than in *Last House On The Left*.

Another disappointment is that *Wet Wilderness* doesn't come close to matching the gruelling sadism of Craven's classic; the killer is a nasty piece of work all right, but he doesn't share quite the same array of sick ideas as Krug and Weasel and co. Maybe it's because in Cooper's film we're dealing with a lone psychopath and he doesn't have any evil buddies to help bounce ideas around?

Wet Wilderness appeared on a double-bill with Gil Kenston's *Come Deadly* (1974) (they were also paired up together on the Afterhours DVD), and played to some moderate success before shipping up on VHS by VCA. Now, the original soundtrack was loaded with uncleared music taken from the classic themes of *Jaws* and *Psycho*, and in order to get the film back into the public eye without facing legal action, the folks at Afterhours had to re-dub the entire audio track. And although this tampering isn't really much of an artistic violation, those who remember the original version of the film should bare that in mind (that version is still lurking around if you know where to look). But in terms of visual quality, the Afterhours DVD – though bedecked with speckles and print damage here and there – looks pretty good considering the film's origins.

Salo, Or the 120 Days of Sodom (1975)
Dir: Pier Paolo Pasolini /Italy

Towards the end of World War II in Fascist-controlled Northern Italy, a pack of sadistic libertines coerce a group of young teenagers into a nearby castle where a bunch of equally ruthless women 'entertain' them with tales of sexual debauchery. Any kind of sexual activity is forbidden without the libertine's permission, and the often naked captives are used in a series of cruel and degrading social experiments, such as an ugly marriage ceremony, a disgusting dinner banquet, and other unpleasant past times.

Salo is one of the most shocking, disturbing, repellent, and subversive movies ever made, and marked the end for director Pier Paolo Pasolini whose mutilated body was discovered on the outskirts of Rome just days before its premier. The film's initial release was overshadowed by lurid tabloid headlines and sensationalist photographs of the director's corpse. A rent boy

confessed to the murder, but circumstantial evidence suggested the involvement of others, possibly right wing extremists threatened by his Marxist leanings and open sexuality. And whilst the confusing and mysterious nature of his death would continue to be debated for decades by fans and conspiracy theorists alike, the film itself was almost universally reviled by critics and the Italian government first time around.

Based on an equally controversial book by the Marquis de Sade with its relentless detailing of the most extreme and disgusting sexual fantasies reaching an almost nullifying effect, *Salo* is a stomach-churning experience but stands as an essential classic of world cinema. It's certainly not family viewing, but the camera work, music (by Ennio Morricone!), and stunning performances more than make the trip worthwhile. Often compared both favourably and unfavourably to films like Liliana Cavani's *The Night Porter* and Lina Wertmuller's *Seven Beauties*, *Salo* has an ice-cold approach to sexuality; there are no conventional characters, there's no psychological angle, no realism as such. Instead, Pasolini seems determined to unveil all the niceties conferred upon sexuality in romance, erotic softcore, and plain old pornography, and presents everything – including nudity, sadomasochism, and sexual sadism – in a way that is both sensually reductive and stunningly subversive. He also rather crucially shifts the historical setting of Sade's original to the 20th Century in order to exemplify further the targets of his transgressive classic. The insatiable greed of the powerful is brutally satirised in the 'Circle of Shit' segment in which manufacturers force consumers to dine on industrial food; namely crap.

Pasolini claimed that *Salo* was his first film about the modern world, and indeed it is an unflinching look at the world of neo-capitalism and takes Karl Marx's warnings about the commodification of man to an almost literal extreme as characters in *Salo* are reduced to nothing more than slabs of meat to be exploited by members of the 'establishment'. The film's finale adds further to the subversive nature when the libertines use binoculars to view their victim's excruciating rape and torture. This violent massacre merges the view from the binoculars with that of the camera lens, thus merging our gaze with that of the sadists, and uniting our voyeuristic complicity with degradation and death.

Of course, this did not go down too well with international censors, and *Salo* has been banned and cut to ribbons the world over. Only in the mid-00s did the BBFC finally lift its thirty year ban and pass *Salo* uncut for home viewing. But elsewhere, the film has been treated even less favourably, especially on home video; a gay bookstore in America was famously raided by police when the uncut version was discovered to have been on sale there.

The Image (1975)
(aka *The Punishment of Anne*; aka *The Mistress and the Slave*)
Dir: Radley Metzger /USA
Released shortly before *The Story of O*, Radley Metzger's less famous *The Image* is an altogether more graphic and extreme variant on a similar theme. Reporter, Jean (Carl Parker), arrives in Paris and meets an old friend, Claire (Marilyn Roberts), at a high society gathering. Claire happens to be sadistic bitch who lords it over a young blonde, Anne (Rebecca Brooke). The 'story' follows this pair through a series of increasingly lewd and depraved acts against Anne, such as forced urination, whipping, needling, public sex and humiliation. In the end it's all so depraved and pointless that most viewers will have switched off long before the end credits. There are some great shots of 70s Paris – courtesy of DP Robert Lefebvre – with all the landmarks and monuments looking beautiful in scope. There are also decent performances all round. However, this film rubbed me the wrong way (for want of a better phrase). And I'm not exactly sure why. I found it irritating and offensive, and the bath tub scene was the final straw. Viewers don't find out until the end whether Anne puts up with the abuse out of masochistic desire, or whether Claire has some kind of hold over her (in the same way that Frank Booth has a hold over Dorothy in *Blue Velvet*, by threatening to hurt her family, for example). And it's perhaps that uneasy uncertainty that makes this film uncomfortable viewing. Also, the heavy-handed dubbing doesn't help. Of course, the power dynamics of this troubled trio shifts radically at the end; during the scenes in the Gothic Chamber, one of the sadists gets a bit carried away with the abuse, and the other targets the abuser with a bull whip (makes me wonder whether George Lucas saw the film and gained the inspiration for the scene in *Return of the Jedi* [1983] in which Darth Vader takes pity on Luke Skywalker and chucks the evil old Sidious over the precipice. Hey, stranger things have happened!). Unsurprisingly, *The Image* was banned in Germany and France, and heavily censored the world over. The DVD and Blu-Ray releases from Synapse are uncut.

The Story of O (1975)
Dir: Just Jaeckin /France
This softcore classic was banned in the UK for 25 years and was only deemed fit for consumption in the year 2000 when it was the subject of some illegal screenings. The BBFC were then forced into making a decision, and like *The Texas Chain Saw Massacre*, which had been outlawed for a similar length of time and had also been screened without a certificate, both films were then passed uncut by the Board.

The Story of O followed in the footsteps of director Just Jaeckin's previous film, *Emmanuelle* (1974), which was a big hit and helped secure some mainstream acceptability for softcore sex, and spawned countless sequels, cash-ins and foreign rip-offs. But whereas *Emmanuelle* was a delicate adaptation of Arsans cult novel, Jaeckin decided to up the ante next time around by focusing on Pauline Reage's scandalous tale of a woman's journey into sexual awareness through the dangerous pleasures of sadomasochism. By taking another explicit novel, Jaeckin hoped to ape the success of his previous film, but instead it was banned outright by the British censors who accused it of being "utterly filthy."

It's not a great film, but it does stick quite closely to Reage's text (except for the ending which sees O commit suicide in the novel). The film's strength lies in its beautiful soft-focus visuals and the fact that former fashion photographer Jaeckin adds a sweeping and epic quality to the story and is quite an ambitious and audacious attempt to break away from the run-of-the-mill softcore erotica which was being churned out en masse during the 70s. The film was quite popular with audiences (despite one critic who famously complained that it bared so much flesh he was considering vegetarianism), and has become a landmark in softcore, finding echoes in later works like Stanley Kubrick's *Eyes Wide Shut* and (more explicitly) in Catherine Briellat's *Romance*. Indeed, it was successful enough to warrant a sequel in 1984, *Story of O 2*, which, the less spoken about the better. Reage even followed up O with *Return to Roissy*, which was very loosely adapted for the screen by Japanese provocateur Shuji Terayama in the early 80s for the unforgettable *Fruits of Passion*, which goes to show that there was still much life in the legend yet.

Mysteriously, the BBFC still hasn't made it clear why *The Story of O* was banned in the UK for so long. It's no more explicit than Jaeckin's other work like *Emmanuelle* and *Lady Chatterly's Lover*, both of which suffered some slight trims by the censors. One can only assume it was the sadomasochistic angle which offended the Board. The British have had a long and difficult relationship with the idea of consensual mutilation, with real life scandals like the Spanner Case in the 90s and the filmic misadventures of Barbet Schroeder's *Maitresse* and David Cronenberg's *Crash* all provoking the wrath of the authorities on these shores. This in contrast with the French whose main objection to the film was in its depiction of women, with France's First Minister for Women's Affairs criticising Jaeckin and his film for presenting a harsh and stifling depiction of feminine sexuality; which is ironic considering how liberal the film is compared with Reage's book.

Island of Death (1975)
Dir: Nico Mastorakis /Greece
Christopher's 'girlfriend' Celia refuses to have sex with him, so he goes outside and fucks a goat before cutting its throat. Meanwhile, Celia goes and fucks a guy whom the couple had met the previous evening, a man whom Christopher took an instant dislike to. Christopher spots them having sex in a field and takes a few snapshots with his camera. Then with the aid of Celia he pins the man to the ground with nails through his hands before pouring a tub of white paint down his throat. Interestingly, Celia joins in excitedly like it's a game, whereas Christopher feels that the murder is justified because he is helping to "punish perversion". The deranged couple continue on their killing spree on the island, targeting everyone in their path. Towards the end when the couple are on the run, Christopher shows vulnerability by seeking shelter in a shepherd's barn. In Celia's eyes he is no longer that domineering male that she longs for. He affections and loyalties shift to the shepherd when he shows up and rapes them both. Christopher couldn't defend her or himself from being raped, so now Celia has found her

new man. The shepherd manhandles Chris with ease and throws him into a lime pit (after cocking a leg and farting at him). Christopher calls out to Celia for help, but she doesn't want to know. His pleading only shows weakness, and she doesn't do weakness. The shepherd is her new protector, and Chris can go to hell. "It needs a strong man to get you out of there", she says as she leaves with her new man, seemingly turned on by Christopher's screaming "Help me! I'm burning!! I'm burning!!!"

Island of Death reached UK cinemas in April 1976 under the title *A Craving For Lust* in a heavily censored print. The film later surfaced at the onset of the video boom of the early 80s in an uncut cassette from the AVI label. It then found itself on the 'video nasties' list and was prosecuted under section 2 of the Obscene Publications Act in 1985. *Island of Death* was later re-submitted to the censors under the title *Psychic Killer 2* and was banned outright. Throughout the 80s and 90s, bootleg copies were selling on VHS for as much as £50 each. Vipco released a BBFC-approved version in 2002 which had more than four minutes of footage missing, and it wasn't until a few years later that the British censors finally relented and passed the uncut version, available from Allstar Pictures.

Wedding Trough (1975)
(aka *Pig Fucking Movie*; Orig title: *Vase de noses*)
Dir: Thierry Zeno /Belgium
A lonely farmer courts his pig. He then has sex with it, producing mutant offspring who insist on eating from his plate. The stresses of fatherhood are all too much for the farmer; he has a mental breakdown and kills his children by hanging them in the yard. Poor piggy mother dies of a broken heart, so the farmer buries her and buries himself at the same time... However, while waiting for death he has some kind of religious epiphany and decides to stay alive for a while longer so that he can drink urine and spread handfulls of feathers around before he eventually hangs himself.

Wedding Trough opens with a man seen placing a severed doll's head onto a flapping bird for some reason, perhaps as a way of illustrating how strange this guy is. And then we're immediately thrown into the next scene in which he sits on the floor gently caressing a pig's udder. And, considering the film's

210

giveaway title, I don't think he has anything noble in mind while he strokes away. This weird fellow looks to be a lonely farmer; he looks harmless enough, but so did Norman Bates. He ploughs his field and plays a game of blind-man's-bluff with the farmyard animals – and he's the one wearing the blindfold! He captures the pig, escorts it into the barn, strips off naked, and then attempts to have sex with it, but she turns him down. So the farmer sits there feeling sorry for himself (aww, chin-up lad, maybe she's just a bit frigid). The animals, including the farmer, spend the rest of their day farting and defecating and staring at each other. The next day he tries his luck again, chasing the pig around the yard with his pants around his ankles (not the best way to woo your sweetheart), but still, the heartless swine has better things to do with her time, like shoving her snout into a huge mound of manure, for instance. Talk about rejection!

The non-love story continues, interspersed with footage of an ongoing gang-war between rival groups of feathered fiends who attack, mount, and peck at each other over food and sex. On the third day, the farmer finally has his wicked way with the pig, and they make passionate love in the middle of the yard. The ducks catch wind of this incident and they don't seem to approve one bit; they congregate and communicate in duck language, probably making snark comments about the pig being a no-good whore for sleeping with such a creepy and desperate perv like the farmer. Presumably, the man and the pig become 'an item' at long last, and he gently covers his porky mistress in straw to keep her warm while she sleeps. She gives birth to a litter of piglets and daddy holds one; he seems happy but slightly worried as though he's wondering why the little one doesn't look like him; is he really the father or has she been unfaithful? The latter half of the film concentrates on the farmer's stress and strain as he raises three boisterous piggies. Tragically, the farmer is driven nuts and he hangs his piglets in the yard, much to the mother's dismay. She dies, so he places her body into a grave and buries himself alive beside her. He soon claws his way out though when he gets cold due to a bizarre vision of being stuck in the middle of nowhere. He indulges in a bit more bizarre behaviour before he hangs himself from a ladder.

Filmed on black and white 16mm film, and containing absolutely no dialogue whatsoever,

unless you count a bunch of ducks quacking at each other as legitimate conversation. Instead, we get a constant barrage of choral music, religious-type monk-rocker-anthems, and bizarre, space-age synthesizer noodling. A strange mix indeed. It's not a particularly graphic film, you'll be glad to hear; this is not some hardcore bestiality video. That would be a step too far, even for me. But the 'love' scenes between the farmer and his barnyard babe are shown on camera, albeit in a simulated fashion. But anyway, this film is disturbing because for much of the time our anti-hero is balls-deep in his beloved ones. You don't see *that* in *Babe*.

The film could be seen as an allegory on human relationships, and if this is so then not only is *Wedding Trough* a rare milestone in cinematic bestiality, but also outrageously misogynistic too. Double whammy! But before you get offended it's important to note that this film doesn't seem to take itself seriously at all, so why should you treat it any differently? Think of it as a visual sick joke. Distribution, not surprisingly, has been kept to a minimum, and the film to this day is still much talked about but little seen. The lead actor wasn't credited and I've no idea who he is and have never seen him in any other films after his appearance here (perhaps he died of shame when he sobered up?). The DVD implies that writer Dominique Garny 'features' in the film, but this is not made clear in the credits. In terms of cinematic reference points, *Wedding Trough* comes across as a perverted hybrid of Orwell's *Animal Farm* and Herzog's *Even Dwarfs Started Small* (1970). Both Zeno and Garny had worked together previously on *Of The Dead* (1972), a deeply disturbing and graphic mondo shocker about how different cultures deal with the deaths of loved ones.

As for *Wedding Trough*, you've probably gathered by now, this film is nuts, but it really does have a deranged charm about it. I can't help thinking if this was made by someone like Luis Buñuel it would be hailed as a deranged, absurdist masterpiece nowadays. But because it was directed by an unknown Belgian who was quite possibly insane, the film was instead greeted like a senile grandfather showing up to a family dinner with his soapy hardon in hand, with all the shrieking, yelling, and crying you would expect from such a scene, as embarrassed relatives quickly banished him from the festivities promising to never speak about it

211

again. Ever. And this is exactly the kind of greeting the film received when it played at the Perth International Film Festival in the mid-70s, where it caused such a scandal the Australian censors pulled it from the screens and banned it outright, hoping it would just go away. But it didn't. It was later banned for a second time in Australia.

If *Wedding Trough* piques your interest then I suggest you go the whole hog and team it up with an episode of *Black Mirror* entitled *The National Anthem* for a double-bill of pig-fucking fun! *The National Anthem* is a 'political thriller' in which the British Prime Minister is blackmailed into having sex with a pig live on TV after the Princess has been kidnapped and held to ransom by a crazed artist/terrorist. Pop these DVDs on at Christmas time for all the family to enjoy. I dare you.

Who is the Black Dahlia? (1975)
Dir: Joseph Pevney /USA
TV movie mystery based on the true – and still unsolved – case of Elizabeth Short, a young woman whose bisected body was discovered under shrub growth in California in 1947. The story of her life is then told in a series of flashbacks. Turns out that Elizabeth was an aspiring actress from Maine who picked up the moniker 'The Black Dahlia' because of the dresses she wore. The film-makers portray her in a good light while acknowledging her flaws; i.e. that she was a fantasist and a compulsive liar. Disappointingly, the film-makers are less than faithful when it comes to portraying the disgusting behaviour of journalists swarming the police over the case, as a reporter for the *Los Angeles Daily News*, Gerry Ramlow later stated: "If the murder was never solved it was because of the reporters... They were all over, trampling evidence, withholding information." It took several years for the police to take full control of the investigation, during which time reporters roamed freely throughout the department's offices, sat at officer's desks, and answered their phones. Many tips from the public were not passed on to the police, as the reporters who received them rushed out to the get the 'scoops.' *True Confessions* (1981), starring Robert De Niro and Robert Duvall, is loosely based on the same case, as is Brian DePalma's *The Black Dahlia* (2006).

Trip With the Teacher (1975)
Dir: Earl Barton /USA
An old grindhouse exploitation fave, *Trip With the Teacher* sees four girls and their teacher terrorised and molested by biker thugs out in the Arizona wilderness. The leader of the bad guys is Al (Zalman King), a hook-nosed, snickering sadist who sports a Syd Barrett hairdo. He's no Krug, but he's a nasty piece of work, nonetheless. The film was made ultimately to cash-in on the success of *Last House on the Left* (1972). *Trip* also has much in common with *Weekend of Terrors* (1970), in which three nuns travelling on a desert road are terrorised by crooks when their car breaks down.

The Joy of Torture 2: Oxen Split Torturing (1976)
(aka *Shogun's Sadism*)
(Orig title: *Tokugawa onna keibatsu-emaki: Ushi-zaki no kei*)
Dir: Yuji Makiguchi /Japan
This sequel to Teruo Ishii's classic, *Shogun's Joys of Torture*, focuses on the persecution and corruption throughout the history of Japan. Christians, adulterers, criminals, samurai, etc. We're treated to a couple of stories from different epochs, but don't expect any soapbox moralizing here as this film is just an excuse to indulge in scene after scene of mindless ultra-violence.

The film opens with bizarre moog music and stills of war atrocities, and then we're introduced to snake torture, a heavy mallet to the foot, men and women being burned and boiled alive. In one scene a woman is hung, and while she's still hanging there she is cut in half at the waist with a samurai sword. A 12 year old girl is forced to confess to crimes she didn't commit, but she refuses to talk, so she is beaten and branded across the eyes with a hot iron, blinding her. The film attempts some sub-plots along the way, but all very quickly descend into more torture scenes. The latter half brings on some silly slapstick comedy reminiscent of a Cat III movie. The production values are very impressive too, with lavish sets, great location shooting, costumes, and superbly gruesome special effects.

There's not a single redeeming factor among the characters (except for the good Christian girl who sucks the poison out of a man's arm after he is bitten by a snake), but we do get what the title promises – torture, and lots of it. Also gang rape, crucifixions, stabbings, burnings, a woman being torn apart by wild oxen, blasphemy, foot-stomp abortion, ears and dick cut off... Fun for all the family!

The Japan Shock DVD looks superb. Someone has obviously taken good care of the negative over the years (if only American and Italian exploitation films were so well preserved). The colours are bold and punchy, and there's not a speck of damage on the print. This is top-of-the-range Japsploitation, essential viewing.

Shoot (1976)
Dir: Harvey Hart /USA /Canada

A fascinating and largely underrated thriller about a group of hunters who come under attack from another group in the woods. The men return fire and end up killing a man. So they flee back to their lodge cabin and decide not to report the killing in the hope that the rival group will report it as a hunting accident. However, when the news breaks, Rex (Cliff Robertson) visits the dead man's widow, and comes to suspect that the rival group are planning to come after him and his hunter friends for bloody revenge... Amazingly, this film has never been released on DVD (at the time of writing, VHS copies are selling on Amazon.com for $40 a pop), which is a shame as this is a fairly original paranoid thriller with a gritty edge, realistic characters, and an all-round Peckinpah feel. It's a film about pride and machismo, and interestingly, some of the hunters actually *welcome* the idea of being attacked as it would give them the perfect excuse to draw their weapons and wage a manly war. The hunters meticulously plan how they will counter an attack, but only one of them (movie veteran, Ernest Borgnine) pauses to consider the overall picture and how there is a very good chance that their lives are going to be destroyed. Kim Newman described the drunken speech of the dead man's widow as 'one of the bitterest, most hateful scenes in the movies.'

Maitresse (1976)
Dir: Barbet Schroeder /France

Young man, Oliver (Gerard Depardieu), arrives in Paris and breaks into a building to discover that the place is a brothel. He gets into a relationship with Arian (Bulle Ogier), a professional dominatrix who owns the house. Pretty soon he finds himself assisting her in her work and becomes uneasy with the differences between her relationship with him and her clients. Inevitably, he decides he should take her away from it all. But will she go?

Maitresse is an unlikely love story, and a blackly comic look at the world of sadomasochism. Director Barbet Schroeder, the man behind *Single White Female* and *Reversal of Fortune*, presents this ice-cold romance as a painful and destructive affair with a heavy emphasis on the rituals of S&M, and is not recommended to the squeamish. The film was shot in a real brothel and portrays real *clientele* going through real acts of painful submission under the authority of S&M queen Bulle Ogier. And this makes for some unforgettable scenes of unashamed masochistic ecstasy. Ultimately though, it's a film which forces viewers to face up to their own relationships, with the material on screen serving as nothing more than an extreme form of the furtive mind games and power struggles that exists in the most normal and everyday of relationships.

In America *Maitresse* went X rated, but in the UK it was initially banned in its entirety in October 1976. The film was re-submitted to the censors five years later and heavily cut, mostly on scenes depicting real footage, like nipple piercing, genital needling, heavy spanking, and most notoriously, a penis being nailed onto a chair. The BBFC have always been outraged by the idea of consensual mutilation (and it's still against the law in the UK), with films like *Blue Velvet*, *The Story of O*, and Cronenberg's *Crash* being the subject of much controversy over the years. But even in its censored form, *Maitresse* proved to be too much for some viewers. In 2003 it was finally passed uncut with an 18 certificate.

Salon Kitty (1976)
(aka *Madam Kitty*)
Dir: Tinto Brass /Italy /West Germany /France

Salon Kitty is a Berlin brothel run by Madam Kitty (Ingrid Thulin). The venue holds regular cabaret events and is popular with the locals. However, in September 1939, the clients and staff sit in the lounge and hear a news report on the radio that includes a speech by Hitler declaring war. The staff attempt to carry on as usual by hosting a champagne party, but the festivities are soon dampened when a pair of Gestapo officers arrive and announce the Reich's plans to commandeer the place. Madam

Kitty is far from happy about the government intrusion on her business, so she pays a visit to the local SS officer, Biondo (John Steiner), a man who seems to have his own psycho-sexual hangups. Kitty continues with the day-to-day running of the brothel, but the Nazi officials replace the hookers with their own lady spies and bug the place in an attempt to catch any disparaging comments about Hitler or the regime. Meanwhile, one of the troubled clients, Hans (Helmut Berger), confides in one of the girls, Margherita (Teresa Ann Savoy), of his discontent with the regime, and his horrifying experiences of the war...

Based on the true story of the Kitty Kellermann incident in which her Berlin brothel was used by the Nazi regime to spy on various clients, *Salon Kitty* was the breakthrough hit of director Tinto Brass, who went on to helm the equally controversial *Caligula* (1979), in which Malcolm McDowell, John Gielgud and Helen Mirren found themselves in the world's biggest hardcore historical epic. And, like *Caligula*, *Salon Kitty* treads an uncertain path between lurid exploitation and a genuine exploration of its subject-matter, and is sure to offend most viewers. Those who can get past the disturbing themes of Nazis, perversions, autopsies, sadism and swastikas, however, may find an underrated gem with a feather-full of camp charms all of its own.

Following the likes of Visconti's *The Damned* (1969) and Liliana Cavani's *The Night Porter* (1974), it was actually the cult success of *Salon Kitty* that led to the short-lived fad for Nazi-exploitation films in Italy, which offered up such unruly items as *SS Experiment Love Camp* (1976), *The Beast in Heat* (1977), and *Deported Women of the SS Special Section* (1977). Bruno Mattei's *The Private House of the SS* (aka *SS Girls*, 1977) was a cheap and nasty remake of *Kitty*, while *The Gestapo's Last Orgy* (1977) and *The Red Nights of the Gestapo* (1977) also borrowed many themes and scenes from Brass' film. However, none of those imitators could hold a candle to *Salon Kitty*, a film that wavers between sadism and sentimentality, high quality visuals and gutter aesthetics, anti-war drama and soap opera shenanigans. It's a bumpy ride indeed, and one not suited to all tastes, but it is at least the best of the disreputable bunch.

The original cut of the film found itself in trouble with magistrates in Italy, and was cut to shreds in America and given a new title, *Madam Kitty*. In Britain, the BBFC imposed a number of cuts on the theatrical version, snipping the near hardcore shots, scenes of S&M, and most bizarrely, shots of a man throwing a jumbo-sized sausage at a woman's crotch that had been painted as a target. BBFC records state that the film's running time was left at 129-minutes after the cuts. However, a version appeared on VHS in the 90s which was shorter than that, but contained some of the material that was censored in the 70s, including the scenes of pig slaughter in the abattoir, and the man with the sausage. In 2003, all such confusion about censorship was put to rest when the full uncut version (133-minutes) was released on DVD by Blue Underground, and in 2010 on Blu-Ray in a spanking new transfer. And this original cut reinstates footage that had never been seen before outside Italy, including the disturbing scene in the aquarium.

Alice, Sweet Alice (1976)
(aka *Communion*; aka *Holy Terror*)
Dir: Alfred Sole /USA

Alice (Paula Sheppard), a disturbed, destructive, foul-mouthed little girl loves making life hell for her family members and the residents in the area. Her mother (Linda Miller) is a devout Catholic who prepares for her other daughter, Karen's (Brooke Shields') communion. But Alice's nasty streak gets out of hand, and when good girl Karen is brutally murdered in church, the finger of blame is pointed at Alice. Throughout the police investigation and the intervening of nervous relatives suspicious of her, Alice doesn't show a glimpse of sorrow for her dead sister, runs rings around the police, and continues her spiteful attacks on the neighbours (most notably the obese Mr. Alphonso, played by *Blood Sucking Freaks*' Alphonso DeNoble), and more murderous mayhem ensues...

Through a string of excellent performances, complex plotting, and scenes of brutal violence, *Alice Sweet Alice* is a blatant attack on Catholicism. It's a film whose sociological viewpoint actively demands viewer participation, despite its roots in low-budget horror. The film's low end scale actually helps the proceedings, with its New Jersey setting offering up some believable locations and a sense of stuffy religious repression and the eruption of household tensions. Organised religion is the film's central target point, with its double-crossings, maliciousness, and ruthless treatment of its characters, randomly picking them off regardless of whether they deserve their fates or not.

The knife attacks are spectacular, as good as anything seen in 70s horror, and it isn't just the special effects that make the stabbings impressive, it's the overall execution of performances, editing, and the build-up, too. Many horror fans of the time would have put money on director Alfred Sole becoming the next big thing in American horror, but that honour went to John Carpenter instead, even if his first big hit, *Halloween*, owes much to Sole's masterpiece. It's a shame there wasn't room at the top for both of these talented film-makers. Sole's future genre offerings were scarce with the jokey slasher spoof *Pandemonium* not even coming close to the greatness that is *Alice, Sweet Alice*.

The film was originally released theatrically as *Communion*, then on video in edited form as *Holy Terror*. Alfred Sole was never happy with the cuts of either of those presentations, and was eventually given the chance to tighten up his film in the editing room. But this new version has caused controversy with some fans annoyed at the deletion of a scene where Dom receives a phone call from his latest wife. The Anchor Bay DVD reinstates the footage, offering something of a definitive cut, and thus making everyone happy.

Death Trap (1976)
(aka *Eaten Alive*; aka *Starlight Slaughter*; aka *Horror Hotel*)
Dir: Tobe Hooper /USA

Deep in the Louisiana swamplands, a prostitute (Roberta Collins) is fired from a brothel for refusing to have anal sex with a client (Robert Englund). She packs her things and leaves, taking a room at a creepy hotel down the road, The Starlight, whose owner, Judd (Neville Brand), winds up brutally killing her with a garden rake and feeding her corpse to his pet alligator. A family later stops by, and all pretence of a respectable establishment falls apart when their pet dog gets eaten by the 'gator. From then on, Judd the maniac has his hands full trying to keep control, with trussed-up victims, runaways, and a very hungry 'gator all vying for his attention, until the sister of the murdered prostitute shows up to save the day...

Death Trap was the follow-up to director Tobe

Hooper's masterpiece, *The Texas Chain Saw Massacre* (1974), and one that continues to live in the shadow of its flawless predecessor. It was also the first of many Hooper films to be beset with studio interference and an all-round troubled production. And though it can never live up to the sheer visceral power of *Chain Saw*, this film really isn't as bad as the many negative reviews would have you believe. Neville Brand is great as the deranged maniac, a man who is so far gone he doesn't even *pretend* to have an ounce of sanity or goodwill towards his fellow man, and Marilyn Burns reprises her role as the trussed-up victim at the mercy of a backwoods maniac, as she did in *Chain Saw*. The film is said to have been influenced not only by EC comic strips of the 1950s, such as 'Country Clubbing' and 'Horror We? How's Bayou?' (from *Haunt of Fear*), but also the true case of Joseph Ball, a sadist who ran a gin mill in the 1930s and is suspected of having killed 25 women and fed their remains to his pet alligators. So, if you enjoyed your stay at the Bates Motel, and Marc Lawrence's pig farm in *Pigs* (1971), or Mr. Slausen's mannequin museum in *Tourist Trap* (1979), then there's no excuse for not visiting The Starlight.

Assault! Jack the Ripper (1976)
(Orig title: *Bôkô Kirisaki Jakku*)
Dir: Yasuharu Hasebe /Japan

A young couple agree that they both feel sexually aroused by the act of murder and bloody mutilation, and so they embark on a sex and killing spree. I'm not sure what Jack The Ripper has to do with any of this, but hey, the Ripper still sells, right? This couple seem to get along fine until the boyfriend (Yukata Hayahashi) ventures out alone for his own thrill-kills, and leaving his girl behind.

The roof-top crotch-stabbing and unplanned escape debacle says a lot about a killer's complacency and arrogance that sets in if they're not careful. The girlfriend sees news reports of his murders on TV and goes ape shit until she realises she may lose him, then calms down a bit. The absurdity of this sequence is that she feels so jealous of missing out on the action (not necessarily the violence, but missing out on *him*, knowing that he's been out there getting his sick kicks without her) that it feels like a dark send-up of the dynamics of the modern relationship. She tries to show him what he's been missing and unbuttons his jeans; we're expecting a nice blowjob scene but she pulls out his murder blade instead (symbolic?).

Before long, it becomes clear that it's the boyfriend who has the real murder-lust, and the girl just agrees and tags along with him out of a desperate and deranged love (shades of Brady and Hindley, moreso than Jack The Ripper). We get oodles of soft core sex scenes which usually get pretty boring in this type of fare, but here they're done quite well, and the girlfriend (played by Tamaki Katsura, who was requested to sport an afro hairstyle for the film by director Hasebe) has the most beautiful breasts, which makes it all the more easy on the eyes. The body count rises dramatically at the film's finale and we're even offered a warped tragedy of sorts (although I'm sure many viewers certainly won't see it that way).

Emerging as the second part of Hasebe's 'Violent Pink Trilogy' which kicked off with *Rape!* and concluded with the notorious *Rape! 13th Hour*, *Assault! Jack the Ripper* was received the most positively by the critics. It was still treated as an outcast movie by the mainstream public, but the producers at the Nikkatsu studios were so happy with the critical appraisals of their film that they decided to up the ante and push the rape theme into overdrive with their next Roman Porno offering, *Rape! 13th Hour*. It was a move that backfired horribly when *13th Hour* was widely deemed to be one of the most offensive movies of all time and almost ruined the Nikkatsu Corporation. The fact that the very same critics who hated *13th Hour* for its ugly misogyny but were happy to write lovingly about a film which depicts a pair of deranged sex killers beggars belief.

Assault! Jack The Ripper is arguably the best in the trilogy, and includes many odd little quirks that make Japsploitation all the more interesting, like the connection between food and sex that is always hinted at throughout the film, the scene in the abandoned bowling alley – was that an actual police car siren, or was it the film-makers inventing their own sound effects on the cheap? Also, the crazy self-mutilating girl in the taxi at the beginning – perhaps a little homage to *The Texas Chain Saw Massacre*? And the crotch-stabbing scenes give *Giallo a Venezia* a run for its money.

Mosquito the Rapist (1976)
(aka *Bloodlust*, aka *Mosquito The Desecrater*)
(Orig title: *Mosquito der Schander*)
Dir: Marijan Vadja /Switzerland

Mosquito the Rapist tells the tale of a deaf mute who is fixated on death. He has a job in an office where his co-workers show nothing but open contempt for him. In a series of flashbacks we discover how this man has been victimised throughout his life; the death of his mother at a young age, abuse from his alcoholic father, bullying at school. His death obsession leads him to take nocturnal trips to the local mortuary where he defiles the corpses and drinks their blood through a glass straw.

The film has a grim and morbid atmosphere similar to Joe D'Amato's *Biou Omega* and Augustin Villaronga's *Tras el cristal* (both of which were made after Vadja's film). Mosquito returns to the mortuary and removes the eyeballs from a female corpse. He is also obsessed with dolls; a necrophiliac's substitution? People in the town are warned to stay away from the creepy Mosquito, but one young woman (played by Birgit Zamulo) flirts with him occasionally, but he more or less ignores her. Back at home, Mosquito puts the eyeballs in a jar of formaldehyde and adds them to his collection.

Werner Pochath's performance as the title character reminded me of Carl Bohm's outstanding role in Michael Powell's *Peeping Tom*; his smart appearance, quiet nature, and icicle features all giving the impression, on first glance, that something is not quite right about this person. His antiseptic cleanliness conceals the murky waters beneath.

He just cannot keep away from the mortuary. His next visit ends with him stabbing another corpse. Mosquito's behaviour becomes increasingly erratic when a policeman catches him snooping around. He strangles the copper and escapes. Zamulo, the flirty dancey girl, falls from the roof of a building and dies. He seems afraid of sex, or more accurately, uncomfortable with human intimacy (his collection of body parts and dolls is perhaps a way for him to have 'companionship' on his own warped terms). This aversion to human intimacy is a big frustration for Mosquito and he trashes his room.

After Zamulo's funeral, he returns and caresses her corpse. The warped tragedy of the film is that Mosquito (billed here as 'The Man') can only allow himself to become intimate with her once she's dead (and thus non-threatening).

It's only during this scene that we realise how much The Man liked and cared about her; her beauty, her careless attitude, and free spirit something he admired and perhaps even envied – he genuinely mourns that loss. And after that sad encounter, Mosquito seems to lose control altogether and sets his sights on living victims with his trusty straw, reaching a full-on Ed Gein mode.

If you're a fan of dark, morbid cinema then *Mosquito the Rapist* will have you transfixed for the entire 90 minute running time. Funny thing is, there's no rape in this film at all; Mosquito the Vampire, Mosquito the Necrophile, or Mosquito the Bloodsucking Corpse Raider would all have been more accurate titles (the German DVD release shortened the title to *Mosquito*). Made around the same time as George Romero's *Martin*, this film shares its sympathetic depiction of a vampiric ravager, and also offers a darkly romantic lullaby theme courtesy of Dafydd Llewelyn, that adds to the cracked innocence and strange morbidity of the film.

Loosely based on a true story of a deaf and mute worker in Nuremberg who drank the blood of corpses and who eventually turned to murdering women to satisfy his blood thirst in the early 70s, and clearly a big influence on the filmography of Jorg Buttgereit, the film continues to captivate unsuspecting viewers to this day. Look out for some fine performances from Pochath and Zamulo, and the unflinching graphic scene of a particularly troublesome flashback in which Mosquito's young sister is groped very unnecessarily by their wretched father. This lone gem from Switzerland has left legions of fans and future film-makers with new and darker paths to explore.

Rabid (1976)
Dir: David Cronenberg /Canada

Following the scandalous triumph of *Shivers*, writer/director David Cronenberg extended his cold, detached vision on sexualised horror in the following year with *Rabid*. This time, however, instead of focusing on the residents of an enclosed apartment block, we're invited to follow the deadly STD through the wintry streets of Montreal.

Employees at a medical clinic witness a motorcycle crash, and one of the accident victims, Rose (Marilyn Chambers), undergoes radical surgery at said clinic involving new

techniques in tissue regeneration. But when she awakens from her coma, she is in an agitated state, seemingly hungry for something. We soon discover she has developed a strange vaginal cavity in her armpit from which a spike protrudes to pierce her victim's flesh and feed on their blood. Rose then wanders the hospital trying to 'seduce' everyone in sight, and each of her victims develops highly contagious rabies. It isn't long before the outbreak reaches epidemic levels, with the dazed and lumbering diseased foaming at the mouth and attacking the public in violent frenzy. The National Guard is called in to try and quell the epidemic and bring back some law and order, but the situation spirals even further out of control, and the city becomes a battleground with survivors trying to fend off the infected and stay alive.

David Cronenberg first wrote *Rabid* as a tale of modern-day vampires called *Mosquito*, but due to his own misgivings about the project (his producer Ivan Reitman had to talk him out of scrapping the whole idea), *Rabid* altered form a couple of times before he was entirely happy with the script. The Canadian Film Development Corporation once again financed the film, even though his last effort, *Shivers*, caused much controversy in the press. The result is another for the pantheon of 70s horror and remains one of the most nightmarish and action-packed films of his career. He has a field day showing us a series of grim, disturbing, and darkly humorous imagery, such as the persistent frothing at the mouth that spells immediate mayhem, a Santa Claus getting machine gunned in a busy shopping mall, monsters preying on their victims in a bizarre form of sexualised 'intercourse', and Rose's visit to a porno cinema which seems to encapsulate the director's *raison d'etre* in a single extraordinary scene.

Reitman suggested the casting of porn legend Marilyn Chambers as her name alone would secure distribution for the film worldwide. Incidentally, Chambers (who had starred in the hardcore classic, *Behind the Green Door*) was looking to appear in something more mainstream, and although her performance in *Rabid* is pretty good, she returned to porn immediately after the film wrapped up production. Cronenberg returned with more body horror mayhem in 1979 with *The Brood*.

The Omen (1976)
Dir: Richard Donner /USA

The genesis of Richard Donner's *The Omen* had begun with hits like *Rosemary's Baby* (1968) and *The Exorcist* (1973), but hysterical diabolical horror hit its high water mark with the *Omen* series, which followed the rise of the Antichrist with some of the bloodiest murder set-pieces ever seen in a Hollywood film up to that point. American ambassador to Great Britain, Robert Thorn (Gregory Peck), agrees to switch his wife's stillborn baby with a healthy orphan, without her knowledge, in order to protect her fragile mental state. Their son is named Damien (Harvey Stephens), and on the boy's fifth birthday, his nanny hangs herself in front of the horrified party guests. Many more 'accidents' occur, such as an animal attack at a zoo and a Priest impaled by a falling church spire. Robert is warned that Damien is the son of Satan and can only be killed with the seven daggers of Meggado. He doesn't take the claims seriously at first, but as the body count rises, he is forced to confront the diabolical truth...

Like *The Exorcist* and *Rosemary's Baby*, *The Omen* hints at an unconscious subtext concerning the anxieties of parents, and the anxieties of *failing* as parents. In the year before the film was shot, Gregory Peck's son, Jonathan, committed suicide. Peck was on holiday in France at the time, and blamed himself for not being in California with his son. When offered the role of playing Robert Thorn (after first choice actor, Charlton Heston, turned it down), the role no doubt held a certain cathartic appeal for him.

David Seltzer's script is said to have been inspired by an Antichrist passage in the Book of Revelations: 'When the Jews return to Zion, And a comet rips the sky, And the Holy Roman Empire rises, Then you and I must die. From the eternal sea he rises, Creating armies on either shore, Turning man against his brother, 'Til man exists no more.' Actually, the Bible contains no such passage, but this didn't stop the publicity department at Twentieth Century Fox from attempting to give their film a feasible religious legitimacy. And, predictably, the Vatican was less than impressed; the film-makers were denounced on Vatican radio for making a movie 'for reasons and towards ends absolutely consumeristic and economical.' And, as the film grossed more than $100 million from its $8.8m budget (including its lavish $6m ad campaign),

Twentieth Century Fox had clearly hit on a winning formula, even if they were laughing all the way to Hell.

The Omen also shares with *The Exorcist* its own 'dark curse.' 'The curse of The Exorcist' saw several people associated with the film dying in real life, and a studio set was mysteriously burned to the ground. And *The Omen* has its own share of legends pertaining to *Omen*-like tragic accidents and near-misses, with its cast and crew: Seltzer's plane to London was hit by lightning; Peck cancelled a flight to Israel, only for it to crash, killing all on board; director Richard Donner copped for an IRA bomb while staying in a hotel; senior crew members survived a head-on car collision on the first day of the shoot. And later, members of the special effects team were injured and killed during the making of *A Bridge Too Far* (1977).

However, no amount of real-life tragedy was going to stop Twentieth Century Fox from having a second bite of the cherry. *Damien: Omen II* (1978) hit the screens a couple of years later, and is surprisingly even-handed, even if it does re-tread much of the same territory as the original. The now thirteen-year-old Damien (Jonathan Scott-Taylor) enters military school under the supervision of his wealthy uncle. And, as usual, those who come to suspect his dark origins find themselves on the receiving end of Satan's wrath – cue the fatal 'mishaps,' including death by toxic fumes, a character trapped under ice, and – in the film's most spectacular moment – another character has a deadly encounter with a lift. Scott-Taylor manages to add a human dimension to Damien, delving a little deeper than the icy glare of Damien in the original film. There is a great scene in which Damien discovers the 666 birthmark on his scalp and runs terrified into the woods screaming 'why me?!' The disciplinarian Sargent (Lance Henriksen) points him in the direction of God, but once Damien accepts his dark destiny, the film has nowhere else to go beyond an effects-laden body count picture.

In *Omen III: The Final Conflict* (1981), Sam Neill plays the fully-grown Damien Thorn who is now the head of a multinational corporation, Thorn Industries. Seven Italian monks, led by Rassano Brazzi, form an assassination squad and set out to kill the Antichrist using the holy daggers of Meggado. And meanwhile, an astronomical presence sees the birth of the new Messiah on earth, so Damien orders his followers to murder every baby that was born on that day... This second sequel is a bit of a mess, discarding the lean and mean plots of the first two films and instead adding a bible-thick chunk of extraneous nonsense. *Omen III* does at least make the connection between big business and diabolical evil, as was later expanded upon in films like *Wall Street* (1987) and *The Devil's Advocate* (1997), but here it all feels a bit glib. On the plus side, Jerry Goldsmith's booming, operatic score is given free reign once more.

Ai no Corrida (1976)
(aka *In the Realm of the Senses*)
Dir: Nagisa Oshima /Japan

Based on the true story of a woman who in 1936 was found wandering the streets of Tokyo with a severed penis tucked into her kimono, Nagisa Oshima's sexually explicit and deeply disturbing *Ai no Corrida* became infamous when it was seized by US customs in 1976, delaying its screening at the New York Film Festival.

In 1930s Japan, ex-prostitute Sada (Eiko Matsuda) gets a job at an inn owned by Kichizo (Tatsuya Fuji) and his wife. Kichizo begins an affair with Sada, eventually leaving his wife so that he can be with her. They stay at a geisha house in the red light district and indulge in constant sex. Their shenanigans are enough to even embarrass and shock the other prostitutes. In need of money, Sada agrees to become a prostitute herself and resumes contact with an ex-client of hers, who was once her school principal, and Kichizo has sex with a maid at the geisha house. Their sexual escapades become increasingly bizarre and dangerous, as they experiment with domination and strangulation before the grisly finale...

Blurring the line between pornography and art, *Ai no Corrida* was tailor-made to break taboos. With graphic scenes of unsimulated penetration and fellatio, the film was nonetheless not intended to arouse sexual desire in the audience, and was instead created by writer/director Oshima as a completely honest depiction of encroaching madness brought on by an insatiable sexual mania. Fuji and Matsudo are haunting in their roles as the doomed lovers, and Oshima takes great care in presenting the scenes in a serious manner with a delicate visual beauty of sparse colour, decor, and composition. And this sensitive approach is aided by an aesthetic which borrows from classical Japanese block prints and Kabuki theatre, combined with themes of sadomasochism and voyeurism. Oshima once remarked on Japanese culture, saying "People hurry to live and hurry to die", and *Ai no Corrida* ultimately serves as a mirror on the ceremonies of the society which spawned it.

The film premiered in Japan in 1976 with black optical blocks concealing the sexual details on screen (which for many years was a customary part of Japanese censorship). Oshima side-stepped the problems of making an 'obscene' film in Japan by having the footage processed in France, but this didn't stop the authorities from charging him with obscenity, and for years he was left to defend his film and his reputation in the courts.

When *Ai no Corrida* reached the UK, it was denied a certificate by the BBFC but was allowed to play under a club license at the Gates Cinema Club in Notting Hill in the late 70s. By this point, the head of British censorship, James Ferman, had successfully altered the law with the introduction of the Obscene Publications Act. But even with the new bit of leniency brought in by the OPA, *Ai no Corrida* was not granted an official BBFC certificate until 1991.

Ferman, who was clearly an admirer of the film (although you certainly couldn't say the same of *The Exorcist* or *The Texas Chain Saw Massacre*, both of which he happily banned in the UK), personally approached Oshima for permission to employ an altering to one of the most problematic scenes in the film in which Sada reaches out and tugs at a young boy's penis. The scene caused problems for the British censors because, although Sada's character is clearly insane at that point in the film, the scene could not be passed intact because she grabs the boy's penis for real. With very good reason, UK law forbids any kind of sexual involvement of children in films, however integral to a plot such things may be, but Ferman re-set the scene by zooming in onto the top half of the screen. Thus, in his words, "You see her intentions, but you don't see the contact."

Due to the Video Recordings Act, it was almost a decade later when *Ai no Corrida* was finally passed for a home video certificate in the UK in 2000, with the only form of censorship being the aforementioned optical zoom.

To the Devil, a Daughter (1976)
Dir: Peter Sykes /UK /W. Germany

A fallen Priest (Christopher Lee) has amassed a Satanic cult behind the facade of respectability. And the daughter of cult member Henry (Denholm Elliott) has been scheduled to a Satanic ritual on her eighteenth birthday, which is only a matter of days away. However, Henry has a change of heart, and he contacts an occult author, John Verney (Richard Widmark), offering him some juicy information for his next book if he agrees to protect his daughter, Catherine (Nastassja Kinski). Verney accepts, and with the Satanic Priest hot on their heels, the author finds himself in conflict with the forces of evil that want to transform Catherine into Satan himself... Being a European co-production, *To the Devil a Daughter* was afforded a bigger budget than the usual Hammer films, and is cast with lots of familiar faces and makes use of extensive location shots in London and Germany. The filmmakers also up the ante on the visceral front, in an attempt to compete with contemporary American hits like *The Exorcist* (1973) and *The Texas Chain Saw Massacre* (1975), by including a scene in which Kinski handles a grotesque demon child and inserts it into her womb. It was Hammer's second stab at the work of Dennis Wheatly after *The Devil Rides Out* (1968), and the author is said to have hated the film. For all its modern trappings and interesting plot, *To the Devil* struggles to hold together as a film, and Hammer just couldn't adapt to the changing face of modern screen horror, and sunk soon after.

Savage Weekend (1976)
(aka *The Killer Behind the Mask*)
Dir: David Paulsen & Jason Mason Kirby /USA

A group of couples head for the wilderness of upstate New York for a fishing trip while one of them also uses the opportunity to fix his boat. While there, they employ the services of local farmhand, Otis (*Fight For Your Life*'s William Sanderson), to carry out menial tasks. Otis is also known to have a violent past, and of course, it isn't long before a masked maniac begins offing the tourists with a variety of farmyard implements and stringing them up in a nearby barn... *Savage Weekend* was made primarily to cash-in on the success of grindhouse hits like *Last House on the Left* (1972) and *The Texas Chain Saw Massacre* (1974), complete with isolated setting and an excessive banjo soundtrack. The difference here is that the film-makers attempt to add some depth to the characters by giving them lots of extraneous dialogue, but all this does is set up the usual roster of red herrings while the actual murders are postponed until the 50-minute mark. This isn't the worst of the backwoods slasher movies, but the sluggish pace and technical shortcomings sure make it feel that way. The film was released in 1979 but was actually completed three years earlier under the working title, *The Killer Behind the Mask*.

Death at Love House (1976)
Dir: E.W. Schwakhamer /USA

Robert Wagner moves with his wife (Kate Jackson) into a Hollywood mansion to write a book. But the house is haunted by the spirit of a dead actress, Lorna Love, whose body is entombed in a glass shrine on the grounds. *Death at Love House* is a lacklustre TV movie which pre-dates – and also anticipates – certain themes that cropped up in Stephen King's *The Shining*, such as the ballroom scene in which Wagner dances with ghosts. Other similarities include Wagner slowly transforming into his father, the betrayal of his wife, his finding 'comfort' in the arms of a haggard old ghost, his writer's block and lack of progress on his book; and his slow psychological breakdown. Also, the film shares a gas poisoning scene with *Burnt Offerings* (1976), which was made around the same time.

The Child (1976)
(aka *Children of the Night*)
Dir: Robert Voskanian /USA

A dreamy little film in which a child minder, Alicianne (Laurel Barnett) is hired to look after a little girl, Rosalie (Rosalie Cole) at a secluded house in the woods. She arrives at the eerie, fog-bound setting and soon learns that the girl's mother had died under mysterious circumstances. Her father is a bit loopy, and seems to be losing his mind altogether. And if things aren't weird enough, Rosalie is in contact with sinister zombie-like ghouls that dwell in a nearby graveyard. As Alicianne tries to make friends with Rosalie, her friendliness is met with mockery and the summoning of her 'friends' from the cemetery via telekinesis, whom she leads on a killing spree of those she believes have killed her mother...

After years of watching horror movies, I have

learned through experience that certain films have to be watched while in a certain frame of mind, otherwise the magic can be lost. And for me, *The Child* is one of those movies. Like, say, *Eraserhead* (1976) or *Axe* (1974), I knew within the first five minutes that this is a film best suited to late night viewing. The mind is much more willing to latch onto strange movies, and be taken on a peculiar journey while in a sleepy haze. And *The Child* doesn't disappoint. From the opening shots, viewers are immediately plunged into a world that seems to exist in another slightly warped dimension. The music score (by Rob Wallace and Michael Quatro) alternates between eerie electric organ and wailing synthesizer effects; the camera is consistently posited at odd angles; the performances are stilted and defiantly drab; the 'plot' takes strange little detours that – interesting though they are – seldom lead anywhere, and the whole production walks a tightrope between amateur and avant-garde. Even the scratches and speckles on the print transfer somehow add to its vintage charms. Many horror fans have dismissed this film over the years, but if you sit back and relax, this weird and wonderful little gem might just work its peculiar magic on you.

Satan's Slave (1976)
(aka *Evil Heritage*)
Dir: Norman J. Warren /UK
A young woman, Catherine (Candace Glendenning), is horrified to learn that she was born into a Devil-worshipping cult. Her uncle and cousin try their damndest to ease her into his Satanic Majesty's service in their plans to resurrect a long-dead relative, but Catherine has other plans... This is perhaps Norman J. Warren's weakest horror effort of the 70s and early 80s (which also includes *Terror* [1978], *Prey* [1981] and *Inseminoid* [1981]). The production values are impressive, but it plays like a bad soap opera with the added bonus of bizarre Satanic visions, incest and graphic gore. For a more interesting take on a similar theme, see the obscure American TV movie, *The Devil's Daughter* (1973) – here, the daughter turns the tables on her Satanist guardians by embracing the dark side much more than anyone around her had dared. As for *Satan's Slave*, in an interview with *Flesh & Blood* magazine in 1995, Warren confirmed rumours that there was a bloodier cut of the film made for the Japanese

market. That version included a flashback sequence in which the blonde girl tied to the tree is stabbed to death. Horror fans immediately went on the hunt in the Far East and rescued the only print known to exist of that version. It was later issued on DVD.

Barbed Wire Dolls (1976)
(aka *Caged Women*; Orig title: *Fraunengefangnis*)
Dir: Jess Franco /Switzerland
Women! Prison! A sadistic wardress! Jess Franco! Lina Romay plays Maria de Guerra, a woman who is jailed for killing her abusive father. So, off to prison she goes, where she's faced with all manner of corruption, perversion and brutality. And when the evil Dr. Moore (Paul Muller), shows more than a passing interest in Maria, she decides to use her sexuality as a way of hatching an escape plan... Romay undergoes more torture and degradation than usual here, as director Franco thinks up more depraved ways of amusing his audience (look out for the electric shock 'treatment'). Still, *Barbed Wire Dolls* is one of the more fondly remembered women-in-prison movies of the 70s, alongside *The Big Doll House* (1971) and *Caged Heat* (1974). Trivia fans will be interested to know that, though the film is set in South America, most of the filming took place in an old military compound in France. Also, look out for Franco himself as he makes a cameo appearance as Maria's abusive father!

Eraserhead (1977)
Dir: David Lynch /USA
David Lynch's debut film, which he himself called "a dream of dark and troubling things," is a disturbing, hallucinatory chiller set in a decaying dystopia where madness rules and practically defies synopsis. John Nance is Henry Spencer, a strange man who undergoes all manner of surreal goings on when he is left holding his girlfriend's mutant baby. A fat-cheeked woman emerges from the radiator and sings songs, the lights seem to have a mind of their own, and Henry himself meats the mind-boggling fate that explains the title (not pretty). Whether this is supposed to be a view of post-apocalyptic America is unclear. Nevertheless, Lynch mixes ingredients from horror, science fiction, fantasy, and the avant-garde to create some of the most striking images ever to grace a cinema screen.

David Lynch said at the time, "*Eraserhead* was made in Los Angeles and most of the shooting took place at night on sets built in the attic of a mansion. The amount of tools and hardware used would make a normal hardware store look barren, and the five or six of us on the crew worked every night for over a year. Jack Nance said to me, making a film with you Lynch is one frame at a time."

The film rapidly gained cult status with favourable comparisons to *Un Chien Andalou*, and Lynch was praised for his daring as a first time director, and rewarded with the chance to write and direct *The Elephant Man* which went on to earn him an Oscar and BAFTA nominations. If you ask Lynch what *Eraserhead* is about he'll tell you it's about 89-minutes. "I felt *Eraserhead*," he once said. "I didn't think it." And he also claimed it was a film to be experienced rather than explained. Certainly, no one has ever managed to adequately describe this confounding descent into nightmare, least of all Lynch who playfully called it "My version of *The Philadelphia Story*, only without Jimmy Stewart." Lynch even refuses to explain the monstrous baby at the heart of this dark film, with many rumours claiming that it's actually an animated bovine foetus! All we know for sure about Lynch's extraordinary film is that it has become a landmark of modern surrealist cinema, a midnight movie hit in America which quickly bloomed into an international cult classic and which remains essential viewing for anyone interested in incredibly strange films.

Although it first surfaced in the late 70s, *Eraserhead* was actually made over a period of five years, during which time Lynch was in the US Film Institute Centre in Los Angeles. According to Lynch, he presented the AFI with a 21 paged script, looted through their equipment department, and promptly set up shooting in some deserted stables in which he subsequently lived during production. Shooting began in June 1972 and proceeded through an endless run of nights, with Lynch dashing off in the early hours to do the *Wall Street Journal* paper round which was providing his income. After the first nine months of shooting (already longer than the average film shoot), DoP Herbert Cardwell died in his sleep, leaving Frederick Elmes to take over camera duties. But no such substitution was possible for leading man Jack Nance, who was forced to keep his trademark, electrified hairstyle unchanged for years so that a set-up

shot eighteen months apart could be edited together to make a single sequence. And throughout this tortuous process, Nance's wife, Catherine Coulson, worked as a waitress by day and first assistant, financier, hairdresser, and general problem solver at night, spurred on by Lynch's insistence that he had a vision of her holding a log in a TV series – a vision which actually came true many years later when Lynch himself finally cast her as the 'Log Lady' in *Twin Peaks*. Strange but true.

Although it's now regarded as a masterpiece, the first people to be exposed to *Eraserhead* were more appalled than impressed. Both the Cannes and New York Film Festivals turned it down flat, while *Variety* magazine slammed it as "a sickening exercise in bad taste" when it premiered in LA. Wounded, Lynch panicked and cut out three or four scenes, bringing it down to the current cut which was then championed by late night guru, John Waters. And the rest is history.

No matter how many cheesy pop videos or arty horror movies come along ripping off its late-70s aesthetic of slimy industrial decay, *Eraserhead* remains as powerful and original and disturbing as ever. Whether the finished film is a gory homage to *Sunset Blvd.* or, as Lynch's daughter Jennifer suggested, a horrified reaction to the stresses of fatherhood, is up to you to decide. One word of advice: for all the on-screen wonders, the real heart of this film lies in Alan Splet's throbbing, industrial soundscapes, which are among the strangest things you'll ever hear in a movie.

Emanuelle In America (1977)
(aka *Brutal Nights*)
Dir: 'Joe D'Amato' [Aristide Massaccesi] /Italy
Sex, nudity, hardcore sex, more nudity, bloody violence, bad dubbing, groovy music, censorship troubles, snuff footage, torture, hairy porn, bad acting, bad clothes and bad hair, bestiality, lesbianism, orgies, sleaze, blowjobs, penetrations, secret brothels, freakish fantasies – this film has everything you could possibly want from 70s exploitation.

Exotic beauty Laura Gemser stars as the nympho Emanuelle who embarks on her international jet-set lifestyle as a globe-trotting photo-journalist doing all she can to find the latest scoop. No danger is too great for her if it means getting hold of a good story or two. En route, she witnesses all manner of lusty perversions, from horny aristocrats to sleazy snuff movie dealers, but her 'undercover' work is about to get her into big trouble...

Emanuelle In America is part of a range of Italian exploitation pics that were made to cash in on Just Jaeckin's 1974 film, *Emmanuelle*, which was an international box-office success in softcore erotica. The Italian versions were often made by Joe D'Amato and starring Laura Gemser in the lead role, and these films were much more exploitative, adding all kinds of bizarre elements and hardcore sex into the mix.

The film stomps through the narrative with very little method, but D'Amato wasn't famous for his pacing skills, so the film's series of mini-structures allows him to get away from traditional narrative constraints. Some may still find it plodding of course, but in the vast jungle of 70s exploitation you could do a hell of a lot worse. D'Amato never claimed to pursue any artistic notions in his epics, he always made his intentions clear: to entertain the fans. And this remains the sleaze standard to which all exploitation aims to match.

Made during a time when film-makers were free to explore the darkest areas of human behaviour and have the results played out on the big screen in glorious 35mm celluloid, *EIA* is still a jaw-dropping experience for jaded fans today. The hardcore scenes, the castration, gyno shots, orgy dinner parties, gruesome and graphic snuff footage, 2 on 1 interracial action, cumshots, and even a pornstar (Paula Senatore) jerking off a horse; all these sequences are shown so casually from one scene to the next in D'Amato's usual blase manner – just another day on a movie set! The only disappointment is that we never see Gemser in any hardcore action.

Controversy surrounded the film while it was still in production; legend has it that one actress was so distressed by the awful screams coming from the snuff set that she thought it was real and informed the police. The producers had to prove that no one was being hurt or killed. The snuff footage looks amazing; the dirty, grainy shots of girls having nipples hacked off, meat hooks inserted into vaginas, and huge dildos filled with red hot tar forced down their throats; it has that awful air of authenticity about it and looks exactly the way you would imagine a snuff movie to look. Not pretty. And these brutal sequences are said to have influenced David Cronenberg's *Videodrome*. D'Amato himself has said that the snuff footage was shot in 35mm and then the negative was scratched to make it look rough, printed in 8mm, and then blown up again.

Look out for sleaze veteran Lorraine de Selle (*Cannibal Ferox*) as the lesbian in the steam room, and Gemser's real life husband, Gabriele Tinti, as the host of the decadent party at the Venetian mansion. The 100 minute full uncut version is available on DVD from Blue Underground, and looks tons better than those old bootleg tapes. Included are interviews with D'Amato and Gemser (the latter is audio only).

Shock (1977)
(aka *Beyond the Door 2*)
Dir: Mario Bava /Italy

Dora (Daria Nicolodi), her new husband Bruno (John Steiner), and Dora's young son, Marco (David Colin Jr.) move into a new house where she recovers from having a nervous breakdown. Things don't go to plan though as the boy is easily bored and quite a prankster in the household. Turns out that Dora's ex-husband was a heroin addict who committed suicide seven years previously, and new hubby Bruno is keen to keep the cellar door locked... Meanwhile, Marco's pranks become increasingly disturbing and perverted; he invades his mother's bedroom drawers, cuts up her panties, and utters casual sentences such as 'Mama, I have to kill you.' Has her son been possessed by the evil spirit of her ex-husband, or is Dora simply having another breakdown?

A Bay of Blood may have been more graphically gruesome, *Rabid Dogs* more claustrophobic, and *Black Sunday* more influential, but *Shock* is easily Mario Bava's creepiest and most disturbing film. A masterpiece of psychological horror that boasts a career-best performance from Nicolodi, a superb and haunting theme tune by I Libra, and a tightly woven script by Dardano Sacchetti. Just like Joe D'Amato's *Buio Omega*, *Shock* was also released on dreadful pan-and-scan VHS copies that looked awful and muggy, and this led to many fans and critics dismissing the film. The DVD release by Anchor Bay, however, is a revelation (but currently out of print); the colours and image are fully restored, adding to the unsettling mood.

Bava was aided in this his last film by his son, Lamberto (who went on to direct *Macabre* and *Body Puzzle*), and the pair offer up some of the most effective scares of their careers; there's the sequence near the end where little Marco runs towards his mother on the landing, and I guarantee that scene will scare the crap out of you. That scene alone has had a clear influence on Japanese scare-monger, Hideo Nakata, whose *Ringu*, and especially *Dark Water*, are loaded with similar chills. There's also the very creepy scene where the little boy softly strokes his mum while she sleeps, and then the camera cuts to his perspective, or perhaps the perspective of her deceased husband, Carlo, whose large rotting hands caress her neck... The scene with the wardrobe is reminiscent of Roman Polanski's *Repulsion*, and the ambiguities relating to Dora's mental health relate to that classic American horror, *Let's Scare Jessica to Death*. Dora's hallucinations are all expertly done and produce quite a chill. Whether her son is possessed, or if she is insane, or if Bruno is helping or harming her, are never really made clear, and the ambiguities are admirably kept at a knife edge until the very end.

The hint of possession led to the film being re-titled *Beyond the Door 2* for its Stateside release, implying that it was a sequel to Ovidio G Assonitis' *Beyond the Door*, a cheesy *Exorcist* clone, and of course this did Bava's underrated classic no favours at all.

Rape! 13ᵗʰ Hour (1977)
Dir: Yasuharu Hasebe /Japan

Hasebe's most controversial film follows a bored shop assistant who tags along with a fugitive rapist and helps him in his crimes. And that's basically it. They rough 'em up, rape and rob them, and then move on to the next victim. The kid does have pangs of conscience here and there but one sight of the opposite sex and he can't control himself, and he's onto them, with or without consent. Some of the women enjoy the experience and even take control of the situation for a bit of reverse cowgirl! One woman even hands over a wad of cash and asks them to come back very soon! The rapist is also being hunted down by a posse of homosexual vigilantes, and the film ends with a nasty and violent poetic justice.

Rape! 13th Hour is a trashy piece of misogynistic mayhem that is at least completely honest in its exploitation triumphs and doesn't try to justify itself unlike many similarly themed Western movies of the time. The downside is that, because of this approach, the film dispenses with any kind of insight into the psychological effects of violence and rape on the victims, and instead serves as a lewd, crude, and shameless comic book caper, for better or worse.

Emerging as part of Nikkatsu's Roman Porno series, *Rape! 13th Hour* was the final film in Hasebe's 'Violent Pink' trilogy which kicked off with *Rape!* and continued with *Assault! Jack The Ripper*. It's a film which almost single handedly helped ruin the Nikkatsu Corporation with many critics complaining that the film "went too far" in its outrageous fun. Personally, I think the previously released *Assault! Jack The Ripper* is just as twisted as this but the Japanese critics saw nothing wrong in that film's depiction of a deranged couple who are aroused by bloody murder.

When approached by Nikkatsu and asked if he would make violent pink movies, Hasebe famously replied "Are you sure you want me? You must be aware – my craft is very bloody." But Nikkatsu were adamant that he make a trilogy of films that would push the boundaries of rape and misogyny. Well, Hasebe certainly delivered, and the execs were very happy with the results until the scandal became too much. Nikkatsu found themselves taming down their future releases for a while until the success of Koyu Ohara's *Zoom Up: Rape Site* in 1979.

As for *Rape! 13th Hour*, it remains one of the key texts in the violent pinky genre, throwing in all the ingredients that make these films so compelling for cinema miscreants everywhere – beautiful photography, beautiful women, lively soundtracks, oddball characters, and of course rape and gleeful sleaziness.

The Beast In Heat (1977)
(Orig title: *La Bestia In Calore*; aka *SS Hell Camp*)
Dir: Ivan Katansky [Paolo Solvay aka Luigi Batzella] /Italy

After a short-lived video release in Britain, *The Beast In Heat* was swept up in the moral panic that was the Video Recordings Act 1984, and has been an outlawed 'video nasty' in the UK ever since. But its 'banned' status may be just down to the fact that no distribution company has submitted the film for classification in this country since those draconian days. In any case, I wouldn't expect a deluxe Special Edition of this title to hit the shelves any time soon.

The haphazard 'plot' to *Beast In Heat* centres

upon a Nazi torture chamber run by the fiendish Macha Magall with the aid of an aphrodisiac-fuelled troglodyte, all in the name of science, whilst a group of resistance fighters struggle against the Nazi Storm troopers in the surrounding countryside. If the film lacks coherence overall, that's because it's basically two movies spliced together; director Luigi Batzella recycled some footage from his 1970 war film, *When the Bell Rings*, added the new sequences featuring Magall, and bingo, he had a sleazy new cine-product on his hands. The old footage takes up around 60% of the film's entire running time, but it holds together quite well, much better than many would have you believe (heck, we've all sat through Marino Girolami's *Zombie Holocaust* which was pasted together in a similar fashion). The intro credits come and go whilst a red swastika is flaunted before our eyes accompanied by wonky sounding electronic music. This most despised symbol of the 20th Century seems to linger on the screen forever before the movie starts proper; and it's then that we're led into the torture chamber where the evil Dr. Kratsch commands the tasteless and ludicrous proceedings (the old UK video version is amusingly dubbed and offers up some insane dialogue). We get rape, baby shooting, a woman being eaten alive by rats, another woman tortured with electrodes attached to her vag, a fat hairy man strung upside down and whipped (long rumoured to have been played by the film's producer, Xiro Papas!), and a young woman having her fingernails ripped off. But the real show-stopper is Sal Boris who plays the caged troll forced-fed on aphrodisiacs; it's basically a reprise of his similar role in Tinto Brass' *Salon Kitty* (1976), taken to the extreme. It's one of the most ludicrous performances in the history of shock cinema, and makes this film essential viewing for that reason alone. As punishment, women are thrown into the cage where the eponymous 'Beast' attacks and rapes them with gusto. At one point he gets so carried away in his frenzy, he even rips out a bunch of pubic hair from his victim and proceeds to eat them, leaving behind a raw bloody patch. The DVD is available uncut on Region 1 under the title *SS Hell Camp*, in Italian with English subs. This is Nazisploitation at its nuttiest.

Suspiria (1977)
Dir: Dario Argento /Italy

Suspiria is a dose of vintage Italian terror from the king of modern horror, Dario Argento. Shot in the late 70s in the aftermath of his international breakthrough hit, *Deep Red*, and anticipating his later shockers such as *Inferno*, *Tenebre*, *Opera*, and *The Stendhal Syndrome*, *Suspiria* is a sensory overload of black magic, madness, and death. It's a film which dispenses with his earlier giallo preoccupations and instead plunges the viewer into a dazzling technicolour nightmare where the irrational and supernatural evils are given free reign. Little wonder that Argento has since become widely regarded as the quintessential Italian horror auteur.

The plot of *Suspiria* is deceptively simple; an American student, Suzy Banyan (Jessica Harper), arrives in Germany to enrol at the Tansakademie, an internationally renowned ballet school, where she eventually discovers that the place is run by an evil cabalist organisation headed by the 'Black Queen' Helena Markos. But it's the way Argento tells the story that makes the film so daring and innovative. The fluid and intoxicating camera work, the extreme expressionistic style, and bold primary coloured lighting scheme lead the viewer mesmerized through a labyrinth of stylish sets and beautifully balletic murder set pieces. It's a film in which the character's physical realities are less important than their psychological states which are echoed in the meticulous set designs.

After the success of *Deep Red*, Dario Argento had become an avid reader of H.P. Lovecraft whose tales of cosmic terror were often linked with the author's own expansive mythology. A recurring theme for Lovecraft was an array of extremely powerful beings whose practice of the dark arts had led them to the outer realms from where they would inflict insanity, mutation, and chaos in the human and material world. Argento had never planned on bringing Lovecraft's work to the big screen, but after listening to stories from his wife (actress Daria Nicolodi) about her grandmother's troublesome experiences at a school with occult connections, Dario put two and two together, and the stage was set for his most ambitious film to date...

Suspiria was radically different from the horror hits of the time in that it lacks the rationalist social minutiae that was the backbone of other supernatural sagas like Stephen King's early novels, *Carrie* and *Salem's Lot*, and William Friedkin's *The Exorcist* (also that film's original novel by William Peter Blatty). Those tales prided themselves on creating everyday characters set in realistic backgrounds, ensuring that the sceptical reader/viewer would go along with the outlandish elements once firmly planted in the normal, everyday settings. Well, Argento certainly banished that idea (as did Stanley Kubrick a couple of years later with his adaptation of King's third novel, *The Shining*), and we're plunged almost immediately into the cinematic storm in *Suspiria*, where magic and menace is quite literally everywhere.

Music is also a key element in the film's audio-visual delirium, with Argento encouraging the prog rock group Goblin (credited as 'The Goblins' here) to freak out, resulting in one of the most memorable soundtracks in horror history. It's a tinkling nursery rhyme that builds with a mocking voice imitating the tune, and then reaches a crescendo of metallic drums, scary synths, and agonised screams. It's a perfect melding of sound and vision, and perhaps one of the film's greatest achievements overall, with the camera hungry for images that can match the heightened threat of the sounds. It's a sensory overload that strives to attain that "rational derangement of all the senses" that French poets like Rimbaud and Baudelaire were so fond of.

The all-female coven are in complete control, and all of the male characters are missing something (which amounts to a symbolic castration according to some of the characters); a young male dancer with no money is at the receiving end of cruel gossip and bad jokes, handyman Pavlos has no teeth due to a bout of gingivitus that Miss Tanner (Alida Valli) seems suspiciously amused about; pianist Daniel (*Night Train Murders'* Flavia Bucci) has no vision because he's blind ("Can't you see that?!"); and Little Albert, the young boy, seems to have no voice. The film as a whole lacks that male rationality that so typified the giallo in previous years (although it did come under threat from Daria Nicolodi's character in *Deep Red*). In *Suspiria*, it's the feminine irrational that rules, and is considered for the most part to be destructive of the individual and of social structures as a whole. Men have absolutely no power in the film and at the same time it is

unflinching in its depiction of feminine evil.

Whilst many are quick to pick upon gender issues relating to Argento's films, very few are willing to acknowledge the magical beliefs which adorned his work around this time. Gender studies and psychoanalysis are the critic's main tools of deduction when deciphering a film. However, they often come unstuck in their attempts to analyse the unruly mysticism in films like *Suspiria* and its follow-up, *Inferno* (also Kubrick's *The Shining* which left many scratching their heads when Jack Torrence's character is freed from a storage room by a ghost, thus dispensing with the idea that all ghostly apparitions and 'bumps in the night' can be blamed on everyday 'rational' occurrences like hallucination and mental illness, etc). Maitland McDonagh's book on Argento, *Broken Mirrors/Broken Minds* is a case in point; here she completely ignores the conversation between Suzy and Mandel (played by *The Exorcist's* Rudolph Schündler) in which he talks about the power of the occult: "They're malefic, negative, and destructive. Their knowledge of the art of the occult gives them tremendous powers. They can change the course of events, and people's lives, but only to do harm". This kind of dialogue is blasphemy for those devout materialists who rely on rational explanations in order to make sense of anything.

Overall then, *Suspiria* is a tremendous achievement, a feast for the eyes and ears, so full of mystery and wonder: Why is Miss Tanner smiling all the time? Does she know something we don't? Was that really red wine that Suzy poured down the sink, or was it something more sinister? And what's the deal with that beam of light that is shone into Suzy's face and causes immediate migraine and eventual collapse? And what about Little Albert – was he named after that most notorious cabalistic grimoire, *Petit Albert* (c.1702)? Who knows. It's a film in which every door and curtain leads to more darkness and more mystery, and we're treated to some of the most extravagant murders in film history as Argento continues his obsession into the beautiful and sacrificial destruction of human bodies and minds.

A rare hit in the US for Argento, *Suspiria* was released by Twentieth Century Fox in an R-rated version that was trimmed of some of the violence. It became a collector's item in the 80s with the Venezuelan VHS and Japanese laserdisc both uncut. Magnum Entertainment later released the complete version in a widescreen transfer (it has since been released by Anchor Bay in a definitive 3 disc set). In the UK it wasn't passed uncut by the BBFC until the 90s.

Planet of Dinosaurs (1977)
Dir: James K. Shea /USA
Space explorers crash-land on a distant, earth-like planet that is populated with dinosaurs, huge spiders and a stop-motion T-Rex. The survivors – a group of blank Tarzans and Jaynes – trek through the jungle struggling to survive while talking endlessly about nothing in particular. Yes, it's silly, but this film is endearingly eccentric, and includes a marvellous soundtrack that was put together with primitive electronics and synthesiser melodies. While watching this you can imagine audiences back in the 70s howling with laughter at this one. It's the epitome of cheesy 70s drive-in dreck.

Rituals (1977)
(aka *The Creeper*)
Dir: Peter Carter /USA /Canada
A group of doctors head out to the vast isolated woods in Northern Ontario for a holiday armed only with a hatchet. On the day of their arrival, their boots are stolen from the camp, which leaves them pretty much immobile. While one of them sets off alone to seek help, the remaining men stay put and are viciously killed off by a disgruntled Army veteran who knows the terrain like the back of his hand... Taking its cue from John Boorman's *Deliverance* (1972), which sees a group of urban professionals forced to engage their savage instincts in a fight for survival against wood-dwelling maniacs, *Rituals* re-visits the concept and adds a stalk 'n' slash flavour (the film pre-dates the slasher boom that was kick-started by *Halloween* in the following year). The maniac is rarely seen but serves as a blood-thirsty omnipresence in the way he toys with his victims and leaves cryptic clues as to his motivation for killing. He also seems to enjoy leaving severed heads behind for his victims to find. The result is a decent little film that bridges the gap between *Deliverance* and *Southern Comfort* (1981).

Ruby (1977)
Dir: Curtis Harrington /USA
One of the great benefits of sifting through thousands of horror movies is that, occasionally, you come across gems that have been all but ignored by fans and critics. And for me, *Ruby* is one of those gems, a supernatural shocker starring Piper Laurie as an ex-gangster's moll. Sixteen years previously, she had betrayed her lover to the merciless guns of his gangster rivals. And now their daughter, who hasn't spoken a word since birth, is behaving very oddly. It soon becomes clear that the dead man has returned in ghostly form and is using their child as a vehicle for vengeance. This is downright eerie stuff, with much of the content filmed at twilight in a decrepit drive-in movie theatre which is owned by Laurie's character. The plot shares similarities with Mario Bava's classic, *Shock* (1977), which was made at the same time. A remastered Blu-Ray release would be most welcome.

The Possessed (1977)
Dir: Jerry Thorpe /USA
Alcoholic priest James Farentino shows up at a girl's Catholic boarding school to conduct an exorcism on Joan Hacket. There's no scepticism here; as soon as a couple of items catch fire – including Joan's dress – the exorcist is called in immediately. The highlight for me is undoubtedly the scene in which Harrison Ford's legs are set on fire and he proceeds with a slow and awkward tap dance of the damned. In fact, there are so many fire outbreaks in this film, the staff would have been wiser to call the fire brigade instead of a priest. A lame *Exorcist* clone.

Kingdom of the Spiders (1977)
Dir: John 'Bud' Cardos /USA
A blonde entomologist investigates a series of spider bites on animals at an Arizona ranch while William Shatner tries to get into her panties with lines like 'you're kinda pretty, for a girl.' And soon enough the furry arachnids turn their attentions onto human prey, killing off the characters with venomous bites and wrapping the bodies in cacoon-like webs. By the hour mark, the whole town is overrun with the silent killers that serve as a stand-in for the killer flocks of *The Birds*. It's a decent little creature feature which is basically a re-run of the classic Hitchcock film.

The Mafu Cage (1978)
(aka *Deviation*)
Dir: Karen Arthur /USA

Featuring a powerhouse performance from Carol Kane, who went on to appear in Fred Walton's *When a Stranger Calls* (1979) and the American sitcom, *Taxi* (1978-83), *The Mafu Cage* centres on Cissy (Kane), a psychotic spoilt brat who lives with her older sister, Ellen (Lee Grant). They live together in a large house in California and regularly engage in incest. Cissy is obsessed with primates and African culture, perhaps stemming from her late father who was a hunter of wild animals. Before his death, the father pleaded with Ellen not to have Cissy locked away in an institution, insisting that she's just a little 'eccentric,' and she should be allowed to create her own environment and be given the freedom to create her art in peace. In keeping with her father's wishes, Cissy is given free reign of the house to do as she pleases, and this sees her dress in bizarre African costumes and transform the place into an indoor jungle with tropical vines and African sculpture. After throwing numerous child-like tantrums, and even threatening suicide, Ellen gives in and allows Cissy to have a pet orangutan that she keeps in a steel cage at the back of the sitting room. However, Cissy isn't merely a bit 'eccentric,' she's actually a full-blown psychotic. And when the sweet, placid animal upsets her, it sets off a vicious homicidal rage, and she kills the poor thing by repeatedly beating it with an iron chain. Later, Cissy learns that Ellen is attracted to a colleague at work. And when the man visits the house one day, Cissy's psychotic streak rages like a wild animal...

The Mafu Cage is a little seen but excellent movie about a destructive and sadistic control freak. By focusing on only a handful of characters in a tight, claustrophobic setting, director Karen Arthur does a fine job of developing the characters – each player in the film is so vastly different that the glaring contrasts between them give the impression that it's almost like watching the interactions of different species. The power games between the sisters are at once sad and disturbing, and extremely realistic. Ellen is also an intriguing character because, despite wanting to care for and protect her sister, she is also lonely and incredibly frustrated with her selfish sibling; she seems to be on the verge of giving up on her and starting a new life with her colleague, David.

There are also moments of subtle black comedy in the scenes in which Cissy flips out – her uncontrollable rage is so over-the-top and shriekingly hysterical, it's difficult not to smirk, especially as her favourite put down is call everyone a 'dumb shit!' over and over.

The Forbidden (1978)
Dir: Clive Barker /UK

It's a rare thing for a film-maker to release his or her early experimental works on video for the public to view and judge, but in the late 90s this is what Clive Barker did when he unleashed *Salome* and *The Forbidden*. But as it turned out, this pair of early films from Barker have since provided inspiration for thousands of young film-makers to launch their own careers. *Salome* is a black and white treat that Barker made in the 70s and includes some strikingly dark images, but it is *The Forbidden* that remains the most interesting of the pair as it addresses many of the prevalent themes and ideas that would crop up time and again in his films, novels, and paintings.

In *The Forbidden* Barker takes his time to present his images and takes his artistic preoccupations up a notch. The result is a twisted version of the *Faust* tale in which a man's sadomasochistic desires leads him to being skinned alive. The film begins with a man in a mask and the creation of a bizarre painting. A bearded man (played by Barker's friend and *Hellraiser* scriptwriter, Pete Atkins) looks to be locked in a kind of cell, and he gazes at the painting. The film was printed almost entirely on inverted black and white negative, and with the strange music that accompanies the film, this gives the proceedings an otherworldly edge. Pete Atkins begins putting together pieces of the puzzle which could make up a map, but it's difficult to define exactly what it is. A woman shows up and pierces Atkins with needles. Clive Barker himself then makes an appearance with his face painted silver; his penis is covered in blood and he hops around in a bizarre dance routine, probably a demonic ritual of some sort. Meanwhile, Atkins is still being mutilated by the woman, and while this is happening, more people show up to help her – these mysterious hands from another dimension begin cutting into Atkins' flesh and eventually peel back his skin, revealing the bloody figure of muscle and bone beneath the flesh (much like Frank in *Hellraiser*). The pieces of the puzzle are then discarded and blown away.

With *The Forbidden* Clive Barker demonstrates that even at an early age he had a fantastic ability to create a dark and eerie mood with only the simplest of sets and props to work with. And it's great to see him working on a project in which he had a free artistic rein which was eventually somewhat thwarted when Hollywood signed him up to make *Hellraiser*. Here, Barker explores his obsessions with the rituals of the macabre in his own way, with no interest in making compromises to suit his producers, no interest in financial reward or making it palatable to any 'target audience'. This is Barker at the closest he ever got to being a true film artist, *Hellraiser* not-withstanding. And the film remains much more dark and disturbing than anything in his *Books of Blood* series.

It's clear to see in this little 8mm film many of the ideas Barker revisited in his later works, such as the puzzle that leads to hell, the ghouls that seem to appear from another world, another dimension (much like the Cenobites). Also, the recurring Faustian theme of a man's complicit relationship with hell and damnation; here it is Pete Atkins who solves the puzzle because *he desires* to know what lurks on the other side, and desires his gruesome fate. And this idea links *The Forbidden* to *Hellraiser*, in which Frank solves the mysterious puzzle box because of his own masochistic curiosities. Also, in *Candyman* the curious must stare into a mirror and chant his name five times before he'll come and get you; in other words, you have to be curious enough to bring hell upon yourself. Even in Barker's novels and stories he sometimes bases the entire plot on this very simple yet very frightening idea, such as the evil Shadwell in *Weaveworld* who dazzles his victims into submission by giving them a glimpse of something they desire in the magical lining of his jacket.

Barker admits that his early shorts were heavily influenced by Andy Warhol and Kenneth Anger, but you'd never assume it if you didn't already know. In fact, *The Forbidden* is unlike anything I've ever seen, despite it being a testing ground for many themes that would help to define modern horror. Barker also reports that one potential investor actually backed out of funding *The Forbidden* because he couldn't understand what the director meant when he described the "sublime and wonderful unveiling of the central figure," and demanded to know

exactly what is so wonderful about being skinned alive.

I Spit on Your Grave (1978)
(Orig title: *Day of The Woman*)
Dir: Meir Zarchi /USA

A film that has always provoked a passionate reaction from those who see it, *I Spit On Your Grave* is one of the most well-known movies to come out of the controversial rape-revenge genre, and has been cited in countless books and articles on feminism.

The simple story sees New York writer, Jenny (Camille Keaton, granddaughter of Buster), driving out to the sticks where she rents a house in the woods. She plans on settling down there for a few months, where the peace and quiet of country life will allow her to concentrate on writing her debut novel. However, her presence in the rural area drives a group of local yokels to a sexual frenzy, and while walking in the woods one day, she is attacked and raped. On her way back to the house, she is ambushed by the same men and raped a second time – this time anally. And when she makes it back to the house, the men show up once again; and this time they coax a bespectacled simpleton, Matthew, into raping her. During the third rape she is battered and bruised, and is also violated with a wine bottle. She is pretty much terrified and puts up very little resistance. As the men leave, Matthew is given a knife and ordered to go back to the house to finish her off by stabbing her in the heart. But instead, Matthew just wipes some of her blood onto the blade to make it look like he has committed the deadly deed as instructed.

Jenny cleans herself up and then visits the church where she asks God for forgiveness in advance before embarking on a brutal retribution mission in which she uses her sexuality to lure the scumbags to their grisly demise (the church forgiveness theme was also touched upon in other rape-revenge thrillers, such as *Thriller: A Cruel Picture* and *Ms.45*, for example). Matthew, the slack-jawed imbecile, is hung from a tree in an implausible scene which would require super-human strength from the heroine to execute sufficiently; the first rapist – and assured leader of the gang – has his dick cut off in the bathtub; the final two men are dispatched with an axe and a speed boat propeller, respectively.

The film's original title was *Day of the*

Woman, but was given the more lurid namesake by distributor Jerry Gross (producer of the cult classic, *I Drink Your Blood*), for a very successful theatrical run at the grindhouses and drive-ins across America. The film's huge success brought it to the attention of mainstream critics like Roger Ebert (who hated it; he was particularly appalled by the audience indifference he saw during the screening, and their jaded attitude towards Jenny's suffering), and this has given the film more attention over the years than it perhaps deserves. It's a competently made production; there's nothing wrong with it as such. But it also has a flat, middle-of-the-road vibe about it; there's no ambition here at all from the film-makers, it's just a straight-up, low-budget cheapie made to cash-in on the *Last House On the Left* controversy. There is very little in the film that could lift it above the sum of its exploitation parts... save for the rape scenes.

The rape scenes are long, sustained and harrowing, with the camera never flinching from the horrors of Jenny's ordeal. And the revenge scenarios are equally drawn-out, with the yokels thinking that they're being invited by Jenny for some consensual sex, when in fact they're being lured to their deaths (except for Matthew, who for some reason, she consents for him to "come inside her" before she hangs him). And while it's impossible to understand how anyone could sympathize with this bunch of cud-chewing, dangle-mouthed low-lives, there is undoubtedly an element here of the film-makers attempting to excite and titillate the audience with Jenny's rape scenes.

In her book, *Men, Women and Chainsaws*, Carol Clover argues vehemently against the idea that viewers take pleasure in the rape and consequent vengeance in films like *I Spit On Your Grave*. She also points out the 'city/country axis', as the city girl invades a rural area, suggesting a cultural 'rape'. And in addition, she suggests that city folks are usually presented as sophisticated and affluent, whereas the country folks are more often presented as a menace due to their indiscipline and lack of law and order.

For many years, *I Spit On Your Grave* was considered by many as a radical feminist film. But it falters in too many areas for it to hold up to scrutiny. Writer/director Meir Zarchi delivers too much of the exploitation elements, like nudity and violence, thus giving his critics lots of ammunition to accuse him of not bringing to the subject-matter the seriousness it deserves. The film also includes many flaws which are apparent throughout the rape-revenge genre. A film which depicts a woman getting even with a bunch of chauvinistic rapists does not in itself denote its legitimacy as a feminine 'text'. Some of the most prurient movies around adopt a superficial level of feminism as a way of gaining kudos, when usually, the opposite seems to be the case (see Jess Franco's *Faceless*, for instance). As Clover says, "Horror is built on exploitation and appropriation, and *I Spit On Your Grave*'s exploitation and appropriation of feminism are no cause for surprise."

Much of Clover's work is concerned with responsibility, and who is to blame for rape, claiming "if a woman fails to get tough, fails to buy a gun or take karate, she is, in an updated sense of the cliché, asking for it". In the movies, it is often the women who are blamed for their rape because they are beautiful or they make themselves vulnerable, or dress in a skimpy, revealing way, inviting violation. In *I Spit On Your Grave*, Jenny's second victim bases his entire excuse on this idea, claiming "That thing with you was a thing that any man would have done. You coax a man into doing it to you... You come into the gas station and expose your damn sexy legs to me, walking back and forth real slow, making sure I see 'em good... And then, you're lying in a canoe in your bikini, just waiting, like bait." By allowing the scumbag to assert such a pitiful defence, films like *I Spit On Your Grave* simply invalidates them. Clover's assertion, however, is that the rape-revenge genre tends to justify the rape scenes through the female character's refusal to get tough.

One of the principal titles on the 'video nasties' list, *I Spit On Your Grave* was banned in the UK for around 22 years. The BBFC passed it with 7:02 cuts for the Anchor Bay DVD release in 2005, removing all of the heavier rape footage but leaving the revenge killings intact. The film was submitted to the censors again in 2010 prior to the 101 Blu-Ray release, and some of the cuts were waived, leaving it still missing almost three minutes of footage. This latter version was banned in Ireland in 2010.

Dawn of the Dead (1978)
Dir: George A. Romero /USA
In the late 60s, a zombie movie called *Night of the Living Dead* changed the face of modern

horror forever. With its mixture of creepiness and a sharp social satire, this lurid black and white classic introduced audiences to a new master of horror, George A. Romero. Across the decades, Romero would occasionally return to his living dead roots, and alongside such classics as *The Crazies* (1973) and *Martin* (1976), he would add to his zombie series, and each film seemed to pick up on some social dislocation that was relevant for the time. And as a whole these films served as a cracked mirror reflecting back on the era in which they were made.

In the 60s with *Night of the Living Dead*, it was the Vietnam War and the civil rights struggle which was strongly hinted at (despite Romero himself who had always denied that he intended any such 'messages' in the film). In the 80s, *Day of the Dead* presented scientific progress hijacked by the military for the purpose of conflict and destruction. *Land of the Dead* (2005) focused on the callous conservatism of the Bush administration, *Diary of the Dead* (2008) on the information overload of the YouTube generation, and *Survival of the Dead* (2010) on man's lack of progress since the days of the 'wild west'. But it was in the 70s, with its mindless consumer culture, that Romero offered up the blackly comic gore-fest, *Dawn of the Dead*.

The film opens on a chaotic scene in which a TV station struggles to make sense of the situation as they see the living dead chomping their way through civilisation. Fran (Gaylen Ross) and her helicopter pilot boyfriend, Stephen (David Emge) decide to flee before the mayhem takes over. Meanwhile, a brutal SWAT team including Peter (Ken Foree) and Roger (Scott H. Reiniger) launch an assault on an infected housing project, which expands upon themes in *NOTLD* in which, in the eyes of the law, there is no difference between racial minorities, political radicals, and flesh-eating zombies; they are all gunned down in cold blood.

Pretty soon, Peter and Roger join Fran and Stephen (or 'Flyboy') for a chopper flight into the wilderness where they hover above fields crawling with gun-toting rednecks before settling down in a huge shopping mall. It's here that the gang of human survivors stay put surrounded by zombies who are seemingly drawn to the comforting consumer paradise by a faint nagging memory that continues to possess

them, post mortem. Interestingly, the zombies here aren't as menacing as they are in *NOTLD*; they're slow, pathetic parodies of humanity, stumbling around dazed and confused, and falling into water fountains whilst instinctively gnawing at useless consumer products. The survivors aren't much better; they whine and argue amongst themselves endlessly in their materialistic haven as they load up all the products they can until a marauding biker gang turns up and spoils all the fun. And then the situation spirals completely out of control...

In a market swarming with glossy Hollywood horrors, *Dawn of the Dead* was something of a controversial hit. The film's huge success in Europe and Asia put other horror efforts of the time (like *Nightwing* and *Prophecy*) to shame. Romero's sly take on 'retail therapy' and the pleasure of blowing lots of cash still rings true today. It would make for a great double-bill with Philip Kaufman's remake of *Invasion of the Body Snatchers* (1978) which was made around the same time and also touches upon themes of mindless conformity (or even a triple-bill with Willard Huyck's *Messiah of Evil* [1974] which pre-dates *Dawn* and also has much to say on the subject, too).

It's also worth noting that *Dawn* was the first film to fully explore the concept of a man being bitten and slowly turning into a zombie himself. *Night of the Living Dead* hinted at the idea with the sick girl in the basement, but *Dawn* presents us with the slow, harrowing details, from delirium to the cooling down, to death and transformation. And this idea has been duplicated in countless zombie movies ever since. But even here, Romero remains disinclined to reveal whether the zombie pandemic is something that affects a human corpse, or is a contagious disease that affects the blood. Decades later, when new classics like Danny Boyle's *28 Days Later* and Zack Snyder's *Dawn* remake hit the screens, this idea had become so confused that, technically, the 'zombies' weren't really zombies at all. Almost every single zombie movie has to tussle with this idea to a certain extent, to gauge its path and find its feet in zombie lore.

Dawn of the Dead exists in at least three different versions, all of which were the subject of controversy with the censors. The European print, which was put together by none other than Dario Argento, is the shortest, but ironically, caused the most offence to the BBFC. This version concentrated more on the gore, and dropped much of the satirical stuff, and for this reason it was heavily censored. Romero's preferred 128 minute final cut was treated less harshly but still it didn't escape unscathed. For, although the censors seemed to 'get' the joke, they remained insistent on locking out some of the more extremely gory moments. This same version was released unrated in America as Romero feared the MPAA would give it an X rating (to most Americans an X means porno). A longer 'Festival Version' was shown at Cannes and did the rounds in 16mm format. This version includes many extended and alternate sequences, but the Goblin soundtrack is missing, and it runs for 140 minutes.

On home video, the film has suffered a lot with the UK censors, with the 'Director's Cut' being shorn of a few seconds up until 2003 when it was finally passed uncut. Say what you will about Mr. Lucas' many re-releases and special editions, but as far as George's go, it's actually Romero who takes the biscuit with endless DVD repackaging. After numerous bootlegs and not-quite directors' cuts (including that in the *Trilogy of the Dead* box set), the fully uncut edit of his zombie masterpiece is here in all its glory. Okay, so those extra few seconds of gore don't make much difference to what was already one of the finest horror movies ever made, but it's a welcome addition to any self-respecting horror fan's collection, nonetheless. With a budget of $1.5 million, and boasting the very graphic head-popping special effects by Tom Savini (who also cameos as the leader of the biker gang), *DOTD* went on to become one of the most profitable indie movies in history. Essential viewing.

Black Friday is an exciting day for consumers in America, as on the day after Thanksgiving the nation's superstores drastically reduce the prices on all of their snazzy products, and the public arrive in droves to take advantage of this special day on the calendar to load up their shopping baskets with mountains of gadgets, LCD TV's, and designer label clothes. In November 2011 we witnessed a more crazy Black Friday than usual; in addition to the stampedes and fisty-cuffs and hair pulling and general greed, one woman resorted to using pepper spray on her rival consumers, and one man, when cornered by armed robbers in an outside car park, refused to hand over his precious bargains and was shot dead on the spot.

Say what you want about the rampant consumerism of the 70s, but things nowadays have escalated to the point where people are willing to die over a few cheap products. What can you say about a culture in which a man feels that his shopping goods are more important than his life? George Romero has said that the scariest thing about *Dawn of the Dead* was watching an American audience 'getting off' on the fantasy of running riot in a shopping mall, and it was only then that he realised how raw a nerve he had struck with his film.

The World Beyond (1978)
Dir: Noel Black /USA

The second of two pilot TV shows (the other is *The World of Darkness*) about a sports writer who has a near death experience, and returns with the power to hear the voices of spirits. The spirits guide him to solve supernatural crimes. In this episode (titled on screen as '*Monster*'), he is sent to deal with a Golem-like creature made of mud that has been terrorising a small fishing community in Maine. The show lacks energy and interest, the protagonist lacks personality, and the monster – though noisy enough – looks like Godzilla ate the Swamp Thing and shat it out whole. No wonder the shit-caked wailing bum is so pissed off. Unsurprisingly, the networks passed on it and consigned this nonsense to oblivion.

Microwave Massacre (1978)
Dir: Wayne Berwick /USA

An unhappy building site labourer resolves to deal with his nagging wife by beating her to death in a drunken rage. The next morning he cooks her body in a huge microwave and hands out her remains to his co-workers as foil-wrapped lunch time treats. And through a series of mishaps, he adds a few prostitutes to the list of victims, and this ensures he has a seemingly endless supply of cold cuts to dish out... *Microwave Massacre* is bloody awful. The synopsis sounds like it could be an entertaining low-budget comedy horror, along the lines of *The Gore Gore Girls* (1972) or *Living Doll* (1990), and indeed it *could have been* were it not for the torrents of *Kentucky Fried Movie*-type goofy humour. There are scenes where the killer (comedian Jackie Vernon) is shown alone with the body parts of his victims; we get to see how he hacks them up and stores them in the basement refrigerator. And instead of acknowledging the grim reality of such grisly deeds, the film prefers to keep it strictly tongue-in-cheek.

The Evolution of Snuff (1978)
(aka *Confessions of a Blue Movie Star*)
Dir: Andrzej Kostenko & Karl Martine /W. Germany
Film-makers sometimes promote their movies with claims of a factual basis. Michael and Roberta Findlay's *Snuff* (1975) was the first snuff-based horror film to adopt such marketing tactics, but it wasn't the last. Just a few years later and along came *The Evolution of Snuff* (aka *Confessions of a Blue Movie Star*), an amusing mockumentary about the making of a porn movie which came to an end when the lead performer committed suicide. The film includes a talking head sequence with Roman Polanski and the discovery of a snuff film which is passed off as genuine and is shown at the end (it's actually footage of David Hess as Krug killing one of the girls in a deleted scene from *The Last House On the Left*).

House of the Dead (1978)
(aka *Alien Zone*)
Dir: Sharron Miller /USA
An anthology horror that has nothing to do with aliens, in case you were wondering. A mortician tells four tales about how the latest bodies have wound up in his establishment. The first story is about a highly-strung school teacher whose home is invaded by sinister masked children. The third story depicts a battle of wills between two of the world's finest detectives. And the fourth sees a journalist trapped in a basement of horrors after he falls down a lift shaft. But it's the second story which is the most unusual. It's about a serial killer who lures women back to his house so that he can strangle them to death in front of his video camera. Though the acting and dialogue is often clunky, this segment stands out from the other routine stories as it just doesn't sit right with the usual horror fair of the time. The other stories wouldn't have been out of place in an Amicus production, but the story here, however, explores much more down to earth horrors, and by default this gives it a disturbing edge. Too bad it was directed with little care as a throwaway piece. In its favour, *House of the Dead* stands as one of the earliest narrative films to explore the snuff legend just as home movie cameras were becoming much

more readily available to the public. It's a difficult film to track down nowadays. Have fun trying to find it.

The Last House on the Beach (1978)
(aka *Terror*; Orig title: *La settima donna*)
Dir: Franco Prosperi /Italy
A trio of violent armed robbers flee the scene and hold up at a beautiful beach-side home where a nun (*Flavia the Heretic*'s Florinda Bolkan) and her young students are rehearsing a play for an up-coming Shakespeare festival. The robbers force their way into the house and spend a few days tormenting and raping the women at gunpoint before the nun resorts to brutal righteous vengeance... This is yet another *Last House on the Left* (1972) rip-off from Italy which makes other variants like *Night Train Murders* (1975) and *House on the Edge of the Park* (1980) look like sleazoid masterpieces. Though beautifully shot and well acted for the most part, this is extraordinarily dull and tame.

The Death Train (1978)
Dir: Igor Auzins /Australia
An investigator for an insurance firm enters a strange town called Clematis to ascertain the cause of death of a man who had died three months earlier. The townsfolk prove very unhelpful to outsiders, and so the investigator trudges on alone (with a little help from a horny, van driving chick), and uncovers a legend about a phantom train that has been passing through the town and flattening the locals. Like a *Scooby Doo* episode, we get the usual goofy humour and ghostly goings on that turn out to have an all-too-human explanation.

Avere Vent'anni (1978)
(*To Be Twenty*)
Dir: Fernando Di Leo /Italy
Two beautiful young women meet on a beach and discover that they have something in common – they're both "young, hot, and pissed off." So they head off to Rome, and their attitude gets them into all kinds of adventures. They stop by at some commune of low-life hippies and indulge in sex, fights, tantrums, and lesbianism (but this is 70s lesbianism, which basically means lots of kissing and stroking and little else). Whilst staying at the commune they're asked to pay their way, so they reluctantly agree to go door to door selling encyclopedias, and this leads to more fun and

games. It's supposed to be a comedy but the gags are old and worn out for the most part. The 'La la la la la' on the soundtrack becomes annoying very quickly, as do the two young leads (Gloria Guida and Lilli Carati). Much of the film plays like a tourist's travelogue. Anyway, after cavorting with stoned radicals and a pretentious film-maker, the commune is raided by the police, and the girls are ordered to get out of Rome or face being arrested. So they decide to leave, but on their journey home something dreadful happens...

There seems to be some kind of vague socio-political message here but it's never made clear (perhaps a comment on the death of 60s idealism and a rude wake up call to the violence and cynicism of the 70s?). The ending of the film is notorious, but be sure to catch the uncut version as the American version has a completely different ending, apparently. The last ten minutes are very dark but it's not enough to save it.

Death Moon (1978)
Dir: Bruce Kessler /USA

A workaholic is forced by his boss to take a vacation, so he chooses Hawaii. And while he's there trying to relax and chatting up the women, the full moon transforms him into a werewolf. He spends the rest of his holiday intermittently perusing the island, and killing people with his furry face. The closest we get to a transformation sequence here is close-up shots of the protagonist's face straining as if he's taking a shit or on the verge of sexual climax, or both. And crucially, the man's lycanthropy wasn't triggered by a werewolf bite, but a curse; turns out his ancestors were missionaries who destroyed a sacred temple on the island in the late 19th Century. For die hard werewolf freaks only.

Don't Go in the House (1979)
(aka *The Burning*)
Dir: Joseph Ellison /USA

One of the great unsung gems of the stalk 'n' slash heyday, and also one of the grubbiest and most downbeat, *Don't Go In the House* will have little interest for those looking for something along the lines of fun-time slashers like *Halloween* or *Prom Night*, but for fans of darker and more disturbing fare like William Lustig's *Maniac* and Gerald Kargl's *Angst* will find much to savour here in this tale of a madman who abducts women and burns them to death with a flame-thrower in a makeshift steel room in his house.

Donny Kohler (Dan Grimaldi) was the victim of horrendous abuse at the hands of his cruel mother as a child. She would hold his arms over the hob of a gas cooker, and severely punish him for every little misdeed he committed. Now a grown man, Donny is constantly plagued by visions and flashbacks to his troubled past, and suffers from acute psychological problems, including pyromania. When he returns home from work one day, he discovers that his mother has died. But rather than being upset, he instead jumps for joy and plays loud music. However, his new found freedom doesn't last very long as he soon begins to hear voices that command him to kill.

He wastes no time in converting one of the bedrooms in the house into a fire-proof cell, and then goes on the hunt for his first victim. He manages to lure a young woman back to the house, and he beats her unconscious. She later awakens chained to the ceiling by her wrists in the steel room, completely naked. Donny appears in the doorway wearing an asbestos suit and a welding mask. He slowly and methodically pours petrol on his victim. His mask serves as a perfect metaphor for the unreasoning psychopath – no matter how much she begs and pleads, there's no getting through to him; his blank mask remains completely inscrutable. And after a short pause, he blasts her with the flame-thrower. We watch in horror as she dangles there, writhing in the flames and screaming in terror and agony – the camera never flinches, it shows everything in one horrific take. It's one of the most shocking scenes of the slasher era, right up there with the scalping of the prostitute in *Maniac* and the nail-gun shooting in *The Toolbox Murders*.

Donny continues on his killing spree, and he keeps the charred bodies of his victims in the house; he dresses them in his mother's old clothes and sits them on sofas in the living room. Each corpse communicates with Donny via the voices in his head, and he has regular 'conversations' with them. Even Donny himself becomes uncomfortable and freaked out by spending too much time in his house of horrors, and decides he should sort out his social life. He accepts an invite from a work-mate for a double date, but this turns into a nightmare as another flashback to his youth causes him to lose control and toss a candle stick at his confused date. Her hair catches fire and she leaps screaming onto the dance floor. Donny is chased out of the club and given a beating, but on his way home he finds a couple of drunken women and invites them back to his place…

As you've probably gathered by now, *Don't Go In the House* is not a cheery kind of film. And why should it be? We're not dealing with some unstoppable boogeyman from the *Halloween* and *Friday the 13th* franchises; horror fans should welcome this slice of badly burnt exploitation cinema because it delivers on the essential elements that makes these movies so compelling – it has a bleak, despondent edge, and a morbid curiosity value in that we see how a deranged serial killer lives and goes about his business when he isn't killing; it has its shock elements with the burning of the girl; it has a twisted psychological edge in that we get to hear the voices in Donny's head, and we see his visual hallucinations as the charred corpses rise from their seats and slowly shuffle toward the camera, and so on. Horror movies should make us feel shocked and disturbed and horrified; your head should be spooked out for days after watching a real good horror movie, and *Don't Go In the House* is one of the precious few that actually delivers.

Donny is a pathetic loser and the product of an unstable mother; a man who can't even light the oven without suffering severe flashbacks to his childhood traumas. His psychological damage serves as his prison from which he can never escape. And, suffice it to say, it's extremely unlikely that anyone could look up to someone like Donny for their sadistic kicks. He's too feeble; he's clumsy and awkward; the film often makes fun of him in several scenes. He's frightening for sure, but only because of his pre-meditated conniving. He knows exactly what he plans to do to his victims before hand – but he's also banal and nervous and… well, he's basically a pussy. And as such, he doesn't have the bulk or the unstoppable ruthlessness of a Michael Myers or Jason Vorhees. What I'm trying to say is that Donny more closely resembles the pathetic and chilling characteristics of real-life serial killers, and this helps to lift the movie up and above the usual body count fare.

Cannibal Holocaust (1979)
Dir: Ruggero Deodato /Italy

When a group of immoral American documentarians vanish in the Amazon jungle, a rescue team led by Professor Monroe (Robert Kerman), trace their footsteps in order to locate them and bring them home. And after some gruesome animal butchery and false starts, the expedition finally come in contact with the Yamamomos tribe (or "the tree people"), who indulge in such pleasant activities as raping and murdering an adulterous woman with a stone dildo for punishment, and shoving a newborn baby in the mud to die. When the expedition gains the trust of the Yamamomos, the team is given the film reels belonging to the missing film-makers, whose rotting corpses are enshrined by a tree.

Back in New York, the footage is shown to TV executives who are interested in making a documentary about the missing Americans. But their reaction is one of horror as the footage shows the film-makers engaging in ruthless, reprehensible acts against the tribe, and who finally meet their grisly end at the hands of the natives they were exploiting.

Still an unbearable viewing experience today for most people, and very much ahead of its time in terms of narrative construction, *Cannibal Holocaust* is the high-water mark of the short-lived Italian cannibal sub-genre which came and went in the late 70s and early 80s. While most of these films can be dismissed as tasteless fun due to the campy acting, bad dubbing, and cheap gore effects on display, *Cannibal Holocaust* is an altogether different animal; a film viewed through the lens of its amoral, nihilistic director who presents his grim and misanthropic worldview with a casual viciousness rarely seen before or since.

Just like Joe D'Amato's *Emanuelle and the Last Cannibals* (1977), *Cannibal Holocaust* begins pleasantly enough in New York in glorious 35mm celluloid, giving the impression that we're watching a big international co-production. However, when it cuts to the jungle scenes, with the arrogant film-makers shooting on rough, hand-held 16mm, the experience becomes much darker and unremitting as the quartet stomp through the 'green inferno', committing brutal atrocities against the "little mud people" and slaughtering animals. Of course, killing animals for the sake of entertainment is completely unacceptable, but unlike other films in the genre – *Cannibal Ferox*, for example – in which the mondo footage served as nothing more than shameless gratuity, the animal death in *Holocaust* leaves viewers with the disturbing thought that the whole film could be real. Indeed, the special effects are so realistic that director Ruggero Deodato was charged with murdering his cast members and had to stand trial in an Italian court.

The notorious shot of the native woman impaled on a sharp pole led many to believe it was a genuine image, and also a later scene in which a man has his penis cut off. Deodato demonstrates an extraordinary eye for visual detail as he successfully blurs the line between fact and fiction, and effectively toys with viewer's preconceived ideas about the mondo movie. It's a film which celebrates the mondo style while at the same time devouring itself in the process. Deodato seems to be saying 'you like mondo movies? You wanna see something shocking? Well, here it is in all its brutal glory'. Like it or loathe it, *Cannibal Holocaust* is an essential work of horror, and a milestone in the mondo genre. If you were to receive this film out of the blue, having never heard of it or knowing anything about it, part of you would seriously question whether the whole thing is real or not. Rarely has a film managed to convey the feeling of being stranded in the middle of nowhere and being hunted down by people whose sole intent is to kill you and eat you.

Italy has always been a land of imitation as far as cinema goes, but the Italian cannibal cycle didn't take its inspiration from Hollywood movies or American indies (which was usually the case). Instead, it owes its debt to the home-grown Italian tradition of the mondo film. Certainly, the cannibal movies' reliance on a fabricated reality, driven home with the inclusion of genuine atrocities, such as animal violence, does lend itself to the sensationalist trend which started with *Mondo Cane* in the early 60s. And the barbaric, primitive savages depicted in *Cannibal Holocaust* are almost unique to the cannibal sub-genre.

Before Deodato's film came along, there were other epics, such as Joe D'Amato's aforementioned *Emanuelle and the Last Cannibals* and Sergio Martino's *Mountain of the Cannibal God* (1978), starring Ursula Andress and Stacy Keach. The latter film would mark the prestigious highlight of the genre with its big budget and epic style. But even that film had its detractors due to the uneasy mix of star names, bestiality, and graphic violence. Deodato himself had already dipped his toes in the genre previously for 1977's *Last Cannibal World* (aka *Jungle Holocaust*) which is about a man who is captured by a tribe of cannibals after being stranded in the Malaysian rainforest following a crash landing. With his next film, *Cannibal Holocaust*, Deodato attempted another spin on the 'western civilized man meets a backwards, flesh eating tribe' by giving it a strong *cinema verite* style and an unrelenting nihilism that has kept the film mired in infamy to this day.

The film starts on the busy streets of New York, and the visual comparison between the modern metropolis of the Big Apple and the primitive way of life in the South American rainforest seems to be asking viewers which 'jungle' is the more dangerous. Joe D'Amato had already toyed with this idea in *Emanuelle and the Last Cannibals*, and Umberto Lenzi would later approach it again in *Cannibal Ferox*, but Deodato's take on this theme is the most effective.

Aside from the animal slaughter, *Cannibal Holocaust* does have other points of contention, such as the fictional violence and viewer alienation; the very first act of human on human violence is a punishment dished out on an adulterous woman. She is raped with a stone dildo and then beaten to death with a rock. Later, we see a pregnant native giving birth. The newborn is dumped in the mud without any explanation, and the mother is subsequently beaten to death. Again with no explanation. The American film crew are cocky and arrogant, thoroughly unlikeable, and prone to horrible acts of sadistic savagery. However, the film's most recognisable image, that of the native woman impaled on a sharp pole, was done at the hands of the tribe. There are no moral characters in the jungle for audiences to identify with, and this does much to make us feel lost and dismayed. Indeed, in the eyes of some viewers, Deodato's depiction of the natives as barbaric savages makes *Cannibal Holocaust* not only extremely disturbing and morally bankrupt, but racist too. By presenting us with a conservative standpoint, and showing Third World primitives indulging in rape and cannibalism as 'normal', everyday activities, *Holocaust* is dismissed as a repulsive carnival attraction with the animal cruelty completing the spectacle.

The live animal cruelty was part and parcel of the cannibal sub-genre – although there were a couple of movies at the time that managed to avoid it, such as the Spanish oddity *Cannibal Terror* (1981), and the zombie/cannibal hybrid, *Zombie Holocaust* (1979). As yet, no one, not even the film-makers themselves, have offered a reasonable explanation as to why audiences should see a turtle being decapitated and gutted on screen. Presumably, they did it for reasons of verisimilitude, and while this excuse would never make it acceptable, it would make more sense in this light. Incredibly, some of the film-makers have attempted to deflect the blame away from themselves; in an interview with *Gorezone* magazine in the early 90s, Umberto Lenzi even went as far as claiming that scenes of unmistakable animal deaths in *Cannibal Ferox* were fake. "I don't want people to think that I torture animals," he said. "Most of what you see [in the film] is special effects, and if you look carefully, it shows." If he really thought the horror community would buy that bullshit, then he clearly has fewer brain cells than a steak-and-ale pie. Over the years, Deodato has stuck to blaming the producers of *Holocaust*, insisting that they demanded the animal footage because it would make the film more marketable in Asia and Germany.

Nowadays, however, Deodato seems more willing to accept responsibility: "Now, if it was possible to turn back time, then I would not shoot any scenes with the animals because it was stupid to do that [...] I was born in Rome, and many times my family would go out to the country. The country people, the farmers, they would kill the pigs. They would turn them upside down, and the blood... it was normal to see the pigs killed, the rabbit killed, the chickens... but now this is not normal. Now you do not see anything. Who killed your chicken? Now we don't know. But before, you saw the women in the village do it, so for me it was natural."

There are stories of Deodato trying to bully his cast members into committing animal atrocities for the camera. Actor Carl Gabriel Yorke recalls, "The only thing I can think is that Ruggero wanted to be as shocking as possible. I brought it up when they killed the monkey. I said 'This is a movie, you can fake it. That's what movies are all about'. I said this to Salvatore Basile, the assistant director, who also starred in the picture as Felipe, but he just said

'That's the way it is'. It came to a head over the pig. Ruggero called me a pussy when I wouldn't pull the trigger with live ammo in the rifle, and after that we all kept up a civil working relationship. I didn't feel like Ruggero and the crew respected me anymore, but that could be my imagination."

Actor Robert Kerman also grew more upset as the true nature of the film became apparent. One of the local natives arrived 'on set' carrying a live chipmunk. Kerman asked "What's going on here?" and Deodato replied "Don't you worry." Kerman became angry, "You're going to kill this animal, aren't you?" He then begged and pleaded with the director not to kill it, but to no avail. "The idea of really killing it on film was a pleasure to him," Kerman has since said. "I think it came from the film *Mondo Cane*, but that was like really watching people who were killing animals for a living, it wasn't for the camera, the camera is a detached spectator. It's like taking the camera to a slaughterhouse to see what happens. But Deodato *made* it happen. In Hollywood, the chipmunk would have had his own dressing room with his own handler."

Added to the mondo mayhem was the 'Last Road To Hell' sequence, made using real newsreel footage of a military coup in Africa, and which shows real executions of political opponents by firing squad, and a man who has a car tyre placed around his neck and set on fire (a barbaric execution method known as 'necklacing,' which was devised by Winnie Mandela, of all people). This sequence was edited into the film as belonging to the Americans as a part of their previous documentary before they entered the jungle. But Deodato wasn't alone in this kind of practice; his fellow countryman – and respected art house director – Michelangelo Antonioni used a similar shock tactic in his 1975 classic, *The Passenger*, where he inserted real footage of political uprising and human executions.

The mondo movie, with its accusations of fakery, is strangely what Deodato seems to be criticising in *Cannibal Holocaust*. And if this is so, then this is ultimately where the film fails. As with many titles in the shockumentary canon, the director fails to practice what he preaches and condemns the horrors on screen through the character of Professor Monroe, who is supposedly the film's 'voice of reason'. And at the same time, he doesn't hesitate in showcasing these horrors for the audience. It's this contradiction which makes *Cannibal Holocaust* guilty of the atrocities it seeks to condemn. The killing of the turtle on camera doesn't benefit anyone, but the director succeeds in making us feel sick to our stomachs, and ramps up the edgy nature of the fictional documentary footage. In addition, it's by showing the long and drawn out killing of an endangered animal that Deodato and co expose themselves as being the very same environmental terrorists that they seek to criticise through their portrayal of the wretched documentarian characters in the film. The truth of the matter is that the makers of *Holocaust*, toiling away in their capitalist, profit-hungry industry, had invaded a foreign land and bled the area's resources for all it's worth. The local natives were cast in degrading roles as barbaric gut-munchers, and animals were captured and slaughtered, their needless suffering recorded on film. All this to remind viewers of just how cruel and cold-blooded the world is. It's a perverse way of going about things, isn't it? For Deodato, he may as well have made a hand-wringing film about the horrors of domestic violence by bullying his cast members into drop-kicking women down the stairs for real, or a World War II epic given extra realism by having the Allies murdering a bunch of Jews and gypsies, and then having one of the characters muse "hmm, I wonder who the *real* Nazis are..." for some added stupidity. It sounds ridiculous but the contradictions are the same.

Animal cruelty was a rare thing to see on screen at the time. There was the documentary *The Animals Film* (1981), which showed endangered turtles being killed for food, and this was only a year after *Cannibal Holocaust* was released. But rather than merely shocking its audience, the harrowing documentary *The Animals Film* – which was narrated by Julie Christie – served the purpose of educating the viewers. Most of us have no problem with buying packaged meat from supermarkets, and the reality of how the product got there (or the lab animals suffering for our cosmetics and medicines, and washing powder) rarely crosses our minds. But the reality of actually seeing animals killed on camera, as we do in *Cannibal Holocaust*, the effect is extremely disturbing. Without making excuses for the film, *Cannibal Holocaust* does at least have the power to remind us that death is far from pretty.

As a work of horror cinema *Cannibal Holocaust*, for better or worse, has few rivals; when Deodato gets things right the results are astounding. There is the scene where the film crew arrives at a small village inhabited by peaceful Indios. They force the villagers into their straw huts, and then set the huts ablaze as a way of starting a tribal war ("just like in Cambodia"). With this powerful scene, Deodato proves he didn't need to kill animals to make a thoroughly disturbing scene; he perfectly captures the American invaders' cruelty and inhumanity, with the sight of women and children gripped with terror as they are burned alive. Ritz Ortolani's score is also praise-worthy; a sweepingly epic romantic ballad that reminded me of the theme tunes of American soap operas like *Sons and Daughters* (remember that one?). Deodato had requested Ortolani to score the film because he was impressed with the composer's sterling work on *Mondo Cane* (and this adds another connection between *Holocaust* and the mondo cycle). And Ortolani delivered the goods by offering up a sweet, hum-along chorus that is constantly at odds with the shocking imagery on screen. Even the film's smaller details can pack quite a wallop, such as Faye, the only female member of the documentarians, and the only one in the group who refuses to partake in the violence; she is rewarded for her non-violent approach by suffering the most long and drawn out death of all the crew members (and her harrowing rape and murder is captured on film by her fiance).

Cannibal Holocaust caused widespread controversy across the world. After being released in Italy for just ten days, the courts banned it. "I had many problems with this film," Deodato has said. "At the box-office it was taking millions and millions of lira, it was fantastic, but after ten days it was gone." Deodato faced prosecution and stood trial for murder in Italy where it was believed that he had killed off his cast members for real. The scene showing the native woman impaled was so realistic the court didn't believe him when he assured them it was just a special effect, made using balsa wood and an old bicycle seat. The actors were contracted to "disappear for one year" as a way of generating the film's mondo reputation (a trick utilised by Michael and Roberta Findlay for *Snuff*, and later by Myrick and Sanchez for *The Blair Witch Project* – both these films were advertised with their cast members listed as 'Missing, presumed dead').

However, with the prosecution looming over his head, Deodato had to track down his actors and present them to the tribunal, live and well. "I called one of the Italian actors who worked with me, Luca Barbareschi. I said 'you need to come to Milan and I need to present you at the tribunal because you're still alive!' The idea was fantastic but not for me... The young people who shot *The Blair Witch Project*, when they did this the internet had arrived and it was fantastic, but for me, no. It only caused trouble."

Deodato was soon acquitted of murder, but was almost sent to prison for the animal killings. If the film had been shot in Italy he would most certainly have spent time behind bars. Instead, he was given a suspended sentence and the production company given a hefty fine for cruelty to animals. Looking back to those days, Deodato admits he got a kick out of watching jury members squirming in their seats when *Cannibal Holocaust* was screened for them, "The jury had two women on it and they screamed through the film!"

Despite the fact it was banned in its native Italy for obscenity, *Cannibal Holocaust* made a fortune in other territories such as France, Spain, Germany and Asia. In Japan it was a massive hit, even out-grossing Spielberg's *E.T.* at the box-office. In America, the film was barely released at all, except for a battered print which did the rounds at the Deuce on New York's 42nd Street, playing to outraged audiences at the grindhouses (as noted by Bill Landis in *Sleazoid Express*: "It branded you with its mark for having watched it"). In the UK, *Cannibal Holocaust* was released on VHS in cut form in the early 80s. Its availability was only brief though as the government soon clamped down on unregulated video tapes, and *Holocaust* became one of the most infamous 'video nasties'. The UK ban was lifted in 2001, albeit with five minutes and forty four seconds of cuts which removed all of the animal abuse.

Due to its banned status in the UK and its unavailability in North America in the 80s and 90s, horror fans had to make do with bootleg versions copied from the Venezuelan VHS and Japanese laserdisc (the latter had all the nudity blurred out). The best option for home video nowadays is undoubtedly the two disc DVD set from Grindhouse. This incredible package took five years to put together and contains everything you could possibly want from the film. The discs include both the uncut version and an 'animal cruelty free' version for when you're not in the mood to stomach the animal slaughter. The main feature is presented in an anamorphic transfer, and there's also a shed load of bonus features, including audio commentaries from Deodato and Robert Kerman, trailers, featurettes, music videos, DVD-Rom material, and no less than eight hidden Easter eggs.

This set also dispels the rumours concerning the legendary 'piranha bait' scene, which over the years had grown to mythic status. Although no one ever saw that sequence (it wasn't even filmed due to the 'misbehaviour' of the piranhas and the camera breaking down as soon as it was submerged in the water), some horror fans thought it was a missing scene that was deleted for being too gruesome. The idea was to show a member of a tribe suspended in water and slowly eaten alive by the piranhas. In fact, all that remains of the scene is a few still photos as part of the DVD supplements, and to be honest it doesn't look all that bad. Perhaps it was just a case of fan expectation getting carried away with itself, as there is nothing in those photos to make us believe it could have been any more shocking than the film's other imagery.

Cannibal Holocaust's legacy has spread far and wide over the decades, with films as diverse as *Cannibal Ferox*, *Man Bites Dog*, *The Blair Witch Project*, and *Welcome to the Jungle* all displaying the influence of Deodato's mondo shocker. The best tribute was paid by Zack Snyder in his remake of *Dawn of the Dead*, during the end credits sequence where the last survivors sail a yacht to an island hoping to distance themselves from their flesh-eating menace. But as soon as they step foot on the island they are ambushed by a horde of zombies, and devoured in gruesome detail as one of the unlucky travellers records the atrocity on video camera.

Deodato's film was also subjected to a spoof treatment in the low-budget *Isle of the Damned* (2008), which was given the amusing ad-line "Banned in 492 countries!" Hollywood horror maven Eli Roth is a big fan of *Cannibal Holocaust*, and he gave Deodato a small role in *Hostel 2* as the bespectacled torture tourist seen at the table (he also cast another Italian exploitation legend, Edwige Fenech, in a role that looks to have been inspired by Elizabeth Bathory, as she lays in a bathtub and literally bathes in her victim's blood). And Roth paid further tribute to *Holocaust* with his cannibal film, *The Green Inferno* (2013).

Beyond the Darkness (1979)
(Orig title: *Buio Omega*; aka *Buried Alive*)
Dir: 'Joe D'Amato' [Aristide Massaccesi] /Italy
A morbid and graphic shocker from the king of sleaze, Joe D'Amato, *Beyond the Darkness* follows the exploits of a disturbed young man, Frank (Kieran Canter), who recently lost his girlfriend. Taxidermy just happens to be his favourite past time, and so he tries to preserve his beloved by embalming her. But, as in any self-respecting horror movie, Frank's plans to live happily ever after with his doll are quickly dashed when stragglers and strangers become suspicious of his weird behaviour, and pretty soon he finds himself on a graphic and gruesome murder spree, wiping out those who may know too much. Cue burnings, dismemberments, fingernail-ripping, eye-gouging, and an acid bath.

Boasting a creepy and morbid atmosphere, and a downbeat soundtrack courtesy of Goblin, *Beyond the Darkness* marks one of the highlights of D'Amato's long and varied career. For years this film was really only available in horrible looking VHS bootleg copies where the picture quality was so dark and scrappy that many of the scenes were barely visible, and reviewers trashed it as a cheap and nasty piece of garbage (the video version was also cut). However, the DVD release was something of a revelation as the original source materials were used to re-master the footage. Not only were the legendary gore scenes reinstated and now clearly visible, but also other more subtle qualities could be appreciated for the first time for many viewers, including the beautiful interiors of the inherited villa where Frank lives, and Enrico Biribicchi's creative and intriguing camera work.

Beyond the Darkness ultimately stands as a tragic and twisted love story with a necrophiliac edge (though Frank doesn't have the time to get *too* intimate with his girlfriend's corpse as he's too busy murdering and dismembering those who enter his life). It's an insane and desperate love that spirals out of control, and not even his dead mother's housemaid (with whom he has a perverse sexual relationship, and who helps him to dispose of the bodies) can talk him into letting go of his beloved Anna.

Joe D'Amato perfectly combines the fever dreams of Edgar Allan Poe with the down-at-earth morbid realism of Marijan Vadja's *Mosquito the Rapist* for a true nightmare on film. Younger horror fans who are more accustomed to the flash-trash style of many modern films will probably find it difficult to deal with the laid back tempo and eerie mood, but they sure don't make 'em like this anymore. British film-makers George Dugdale and Peter Mackenzie Litten later explored similar territory in blackly comic style with *Living Doll* in the early 90s.

Guyana: Crime of the Century (1979)
(aka *Guyana: Cult of The Damned*)
Dir: Rene Cardona Jr. /USA
Of all the destructive cults that arose out of the chaotic 60s and 70s, Jim Jones and his Peoples Temple cult were second only to Charles Manson's family in terms of creepiness. Even by today's standards, the mass suicide at Jonestown remains one of the most disturbing images of group hysteria ever to burn its way into the collective consciousness. Perhaps inevitably, the morbid fascination surrounding the event would be the springboard for many media cash-ins. Books about Jones and the cult were rushed into publication, and press coverage leeched onto the sensationalism of the event. Even a tape recording of the mass suicide and Jones's final sermon was released, and advertised for sale on the cover of the *New York Times*. The event was given the docu-drama makeover treatment for television in *Guyana Tragedy: The Story of Jim Jones*, and that version had an awfully safe and respectful TV movie vibe about it. On the big screen, however, there came a quick exploitation effort by Rene Cardona Jr. entitled *Guyana: Crime of The Century*, which remains one of the finest true crime exploitation movies ever made.

Cardona Jr. was no stranger to exploitation movies, he had previously written *Survive* (1976), the first film about the Andes plane crash survivors who were forced to cannibalize the dead passengers in their efforts to stay alive (and this was later remade as *Alive* in the early 90s). For *Guyana*, Cardona was shooting the film within four months of the tragedy, and the result is a movie that is undeniably compelling, even if it is frequently sleazy and shocking.

Based on news reports and audio tapes of Jones's sermons (including the notorious suicide tape), Cardona documents the final two years of the People's Temple, though the names of characters have been changed. *Guyana* starts in

1977 with 'Jim Johnson' (Stuart Whitman) leading his followers from San Francisco to a 27,000-acre compound in Guyana, Central America. He's already teetering on the edge – perpetually wearing dark shades, he is paranoid, sadistic, and constantly taking pills as he puts his followers through mass suicide rehearsals. Meanwhile, Congressman Lee O'Brien (Gene Barry) has received numerous complaints from cult members claiming that Johnson is unstable and out of control. So he organises a trip to Guyana accompanied by the media to bring back home any cult members who wish to leave. The arrival of O'Brien and the clamouring press sends Johnson over the edge as he sees their presence outside the compound as a threat, and he fears the media will discover the horrors of Johnsontown. And this sparks a series of events that head towards tragedy for all, and culminates in a re-enactment of the infamous mass suicide in which Jim orders his congregation of some nine hundred followers to drink cyanide-laced Kool-Aid.

With a running time of almost two hours, *Guyana* boasts the same kind of morbidly fascinating atmosphere that fuelled the media frenzy in its reporting of the event. With not a shred of taste or decency or sensitivity here from the director in his handling of the material, Cardona nonetheless re-creates that awful sense of hysteria, and puts his viewers right there in the middle of the compound. Gene Barry is superb as Congressman O'Brien, whose crusading heroism is really quite touching in a way you wouldn't expect in this type of exploitation fare. However, the true star of the show is Stuart Whitman as Jim Johnson, in the greatest performance of his career. There are scenes in which he rants on at his followers at length, delivering each brimstone-drenched tirade with the fervour of an actor chuffed to have some decent material to work with. By the time the mass suicide comes along, Whitman has transformed Johnson into a nasty, demonic force of self-obsessed evil whose frightening power helps to elevate the film up and above the usual exploitation movies of the time.

No one will ever confuse this with great art – it's way too tacky and insensitive for that – but the dark subject-matter is given a solid treatment with a grim tabloid style and some fantastic performances. There is actually another version of *Guyana* floating around, an American version called *Guyana: Cult of the Damned*.

This version was assembled by Universal and was cut down to 90 minutes and given an added narration by a surviving member of the cult, a character who never actually appears on screen. Many believe it to be the superior version but is still unavailable on DVD, and is extremely difficult to find. Missing from this version is the opening scene of a man blowing his brains out in front of a mirror. Interestingly, *Cult of the Damned* received an R-rating in America but includes the scene of a little boy being punished for stealing by having electric shocks to his genitals. And that same scene is cut from the DVD version of *Guyana: Crime of the Century*.

Caligula (1979)
Dir: Tinto Brass, Bob Guccione & Giancarlo Lui /USA

When *Caligula* premiered in 1980, it did so amongst a chorus of outrage from people who described it as anything from "a revolting work" to "an unmitigated disaster," and that was just the people who made it. Director Tinto Brass disowned it, writer Gore Vidal washed his hands of it, Sir John Gielgud called it "my first pornographic film," British customs officers called it "obscene" and sequestered it. Only Penthouse mobile turned film producer, Bob Guccione, seemed happy with *Caligula*. After all, he'd sunk $17 million of his own hard-earned money into it. But he still found the time to tell the press that Tinto Brass had mishandled and brutalised the film's sexuality, that you never see actor Peter O'Toole sober, and that Malcolm McDowell was "shallow and manipulative."

The story of *Caligula* the movie is every bit as intriguing and confusing as that of Caligula the Roman Emperor who, according to legend, slept with his sister, made a consul of his horse, and forced his senator's wives into prostitution... and that was *before* he went insane and was assassinated and replaced by Claudius.

Caligula (Malcolm McDowell) is next in line as Emperor of Rome. He has an affair with his sister, Drusilla (Teresa Ann Savoy), and orders the assassination of the corrupt Emperor Tiberius (Peter O'Toole) to be carried out by his bodyguard Macro. He then ascends to the throne. Caligula soon develops a God-complex and exploits his position of power in every way he can as a way of offending and antagonizing his senators who he feels dislike him. He casually indulges in much violence and sexual debauchery as a way of crushing his enemies. He marries "the most promiscuous woman in Rome," Caesonia (Helen Mirren), sleeps with Macro's wife, his half-brother, and even his horse. After lingering near death, due to a feverish disease, Caligula goes completely off the rails, and this leads to more madness, more butchery, and more debauchery, before he and his family are finally dealt with, once and for all, in brutal fashion.

Originally written as a historical morality tale about the absolute corruption of absolute power, *Caligula* began its journey to the big screen in 1976 when Italian exploitation artist, Tinto Brass, was enlisted to make the film. Marshalling an extraordinary key cast of celebrated British screen thespian, with bit-parts divided out to semi-famous European actors and glamorous 'Penthouse Pets'. Brass set to work at Rome's Dear Studios, where Oscar winner, Danilo Donati, conjured up a sweep of breath-taking sets which ranged from a gigantic boat-shaped brothel, to a shocking, mechanized 'Wall of Death' which decapitated those who fell before it. The film could not help but look stunning, and with Brass working on his own as director of photography, the end result was sure to turn heads.

Armed guards kept the inquisitive away from the set while the Italian director and American producer fought over the nature of the film. But the real trouble began after Brass had finished shooting, when Guccione sneaked back onto the sets with Giancarlo Lui and shot around six minutes of hardcore footage, which he then edited into Brass's savagely unsexy movie, provoking two years of litigation before the film finally saw the light of day. The result of this painfully protracted birth is a cinematic cyclops, an unwieldy beast described at best as "a hideously deformed masterpiece," and at worst as "a multi-million dollar monstrosity."

Originally released in an unrated American print of around 156 minutes with a self-imposed X-rating, this version was cut by a whopping 55 minutes for the R-rating. The cuts included shots of a woman bathing her face in semen, bestiality, babies sucking phallic-shaped bottles, lots of sex scenes with hardcore inserts, female nudity, and most of the graphic violence. In the UK, the film was cut to 149 minutes by the BBFC who removed all of the hardcore shots, and also removed scenes of child abuse before giving it a theatrical X-rated certificate. The

head of the BBFC at the time, James Ferman, commented: "Even before it could be considered for a certificate, some eight and a half minutes had to be cut to make it legal. There are scenes of perverted violence that I wouldn't have thought would ever have been seen in this country, in clubs or anywhere else. A lot of the sex was just straight sex, but more explicit than has ever been passed here. They took out another three or four minutes and replaced it with lesser material to make it acceptable for the X certificate." This version then played a lengthy engagement at the Prince Charles cinema in London, whilst a massively truncated print did the rounds in the provinces before shipping up on Electric Blue Video, complete with oodles of now softcore sex and sadly little of Brass's original ambitious vision which, like its inspiration, simply passed into legend.

In 1999, FilmFour prepared a version of the film which wasn't the two-and-a-half-hour theatrical cut, but was much closer in spirit to Brass's original than the VHS certificated version. For years it was almost impossible to see in anything even close to an uncut copy until the advent of DVD. The fully uncut 156 minute version is available on DVD on the Dutch Filmworks label in an anamorphic transfer, and this includes the revealing documentary on the making of the film, 'Gore Vidal's Caligula', with lots of talking heads and previously unseen footage, including McDowell bashing in a senator's head with a sledgehammer.

Whether *Caligula* has gained any more friends since the uncut version has been available remains to be seen. Personally, I like to believe that somewhere in there is a savage celluloid soul struggling to escape from its porno strait-jacket.

Zombie Flesh Eaters (1979)
(aka *Zombie*; aka *Zombi 2*)
Dir: Lucio Fulci /Italy
A seemingly abandoned boat floats along at a New York harbour. A couple of police officers climb on board to investigate. A quick snoop around reveals the place to be empty of occupants. But when one of the officers checks below deck, he is met with the sight of a bald, flesh-munching zombie chewing on the innards of a crew member. The policeman backs off in horror, and the zombie rises to its feet. The officer opens fire, but the ghoul is impervious to bullets and continues lurching towards him…

It later transpires that the boat had drifted from Matoul, a Caribbean island, and a newspaper article written about the incident catches the attention of Anne Bowles (Tisa Farrow, Mia's sister, who also appeared in Joe D'Amato's *Anthropophagus The Beast*). Her curiosity concerning the mysterious boat stems from her anxieties for her father, who is a scientist conducting experiments on the island. One night, she visits the harbour to gain some clues from on board the boat, and she is approached by reporter Peter West (Ian McCulloch), and together they head for the island to find out what's going on… En route, they meet a couple on a boat, Brian (Al Clive) and scuba diver Susan (Auretta Gay), and she is attacked underwater by an aquatic zombie. When they arrive on the exotic island of Matoul, they find it to be a paradise wasteland ravaged by an evil contagion, and the walking dead have overwhelmed the place. Turns out that Anne's scientist father had been attempting to cure leprosy with the practice of voodoo (as you do), and this has resulted in disastrous consequences as he summons up the dead. Soon enough, zombies are breaking out of the earth, and the heroes try to escape from the island by using weapons and molotov cocktails to ward off the hordes of rotting corpses.

Zombie Flesh Eaters is perhaps Lucio Fulci's most famous – or infamous – film, especially in America where it was given a generous Stateside distribution deal by Jerry Gross, in which it played a successful run in grindhouse theatres, complete with a lurid ad campaign with huge billboards in Manhattan displaying the rotting face of a zombie, with the words "We are going to eat you" plastered across it. At the time of its release, this was probably the goriest movie ever unleashed on a mainstream audience. Director Fulci successfully blends the contemporary gore of George Romero's *Dawn of The Dead* with the nostalgic themes of tropical voodoo epics of the 1930s and 40s (*White Zombie* and *Isle of the Dead*, etc) for an interesting take on the zombie mythos (it was marketed as a sequel to *Dawn of the Dead* in Italy). Fulci side-stepped the satirical, modernist style of Romero, and instead concentrates on excessive gore, allowing FX master, Giannetto De Rossi, to have a field day. The zombie make-up style, which effectively shows the walking cadavers in various states of decomposition, is superbly done, and puts Tom

Savini's pale blue zombies (as seen in *Dawn*) to shame. Rossi's vision of the zombie apocalypse is one of ugly rot and decay, with the zombies' flesh infested with maggots and worms, and their very presence radiating with the ungodly plague. Gory highlights includes an ancient zombie breaking out of the ground and towering over the terrified Susan before leaning in and biting a chunk out of her throat, with the camera closing in on the gaping wound flowing with blood. Also, the controversial scene where the scientist's wife is dragged towards a broken door by a zombie, and a long sharp splinter slowly punctures her eyeball.

The latter scene is not quite as squirm-inducing as the eyeball trauma seen in Bunuels' *Un Chein Andalou*, but the explicitness of the scene led to it being banned during the 'video nasties' scare in the UK. For years, British horror fans had to make do with imported bootleg copies of the uncut US version from Wizard Video, or the watered-down BBFC-approved version released in the late-90s by Vipco (billed as the "Extreme Version"). The British censors finally passed it uncut in 2005 when Anchor Bay UK submitted it for a planned release as part of the 'Box of the Banned' DVD set, which included five other 'video nasties', including cut versions of *Last House on the Left* and *I Spit On Your Grave*, and also a fascinating documentary about UK censorship.

Zombie Flesh Eaters marked the first of Fulci's celebrated zombie quartet which continued with *City of the Living Dead*, *House By the Cemetery*, and *The Beyond*. All the regular crew members who helped to make these films so memorable are here too, such as the aforementioned FX wiz, Rossi (who went on to work with Umberto Lenzi in *Cannibal Ferox* and Alexanda Aja in *Haute Tension*), DoP Sergio Salvati, whose impressive scope photography was overlooked for years due to the bleary, pan-and-scan VHS versions destroying his compositions, and composer Fabio Frizzi offering up one of his catchiest tunes.

The Brood (1979)
Dir: David Cronenberg /Canada

Controversial psychiatrist, Dr. Hal Raglan (Oliver Reed), has created a treatment called psychoplasmics whereby his patients are taught how to manifest their anxieties into physical mutations spawned through the pores of their skin. Sometimes the teachings of this method brings out sores and cancers in his patients, and his treatment of Nola (Samantha Eggar) unleashes mutant killer humanoids who murder those responsible for the 'mother's' rage. Her ex-husband, Frank (Frank Hindle of *Black Christmas* fame) becomes suspicious of Raglan and his methods, and he attempts to find out why his daughter is covered in bruises and why people are falling victim to a clan of pint-sized killers. He eventually discovers that Nola can project her hostilities in physical form by giving birth to furious mutant offspring, and the showdown begins...

The Brood presents a typical Cronenbergian scenario; a mad doctor creating radical new techniques that goes badly wrong and have an ambiguous effect on the human body. I use the word 'ambiguous' because the body horror elements that Cronenberg unleashes on his characters aren't necessarily destructive of the human host, but serve rather as an altering of the biological make-up of the victim. The disease sits in its own warm human shell, beyond good and evil, and unleashes its life-force as needs must. In *Shivers* it was a slug-like parasite that invaded the human body and turned its hosts into sex-crazed maniacs; there was no real damage done to the hosts other than wanting to have sex all the time. In *Rabid* it was a spike which emerged from a woman's armpit and fed on the blood of her victims with the unfortunate aside of infecting her 'partners' with rabies; she still wanted 'intercourse', but her idea of sex had become radically different from the rest of society, and crucially, her new biological disposition didn't really do her any harm. The virus, or disease, or (in the case of *The Brood*), the physiological mutations taught by Raglan are only evil in relation to other humans (and their nervous systems), and their attempts to hit back against the alienating condition and resist the 'orgy'. But beyond that, Cronenberg always treats his body horror scenarios and bizarre diseases with respect. He famously proclaimed "I am syphilis" whilst promoting *Shivers* a few years earlier, and has since commented that he would be interested in seeing a beauty contest based on the internal organs of humans, and a reality TV show of terminal patients angled on the perspective of the cancer (and Cronenberg is one of the sanest and most intelligent directors in this book!).

Cronenberg wrote the script for *The Brood* in an agitated state in the middle of a nasty divorce and custody battle. And it's these autobiographical details combined with his obsessions on the bizarre mutations of the human body that led to the birth of his most quintessential film. Amazingly, *The Brood* was originally only a side project; he was supposed to be working on a script called *The Sensitives* (which later became *Scanners*), but because of his ongoing divorce and parental strife, he found it difficult to concentrate on writing it, and instead tried to deal with his anxieties by developing a whole new screenplay that was much more in tune with the way he was feeling at the time. He has since described *The Brood* as "My version of *Kramer Vs. Kramer,*" adding that he seriously wanted to kill his ex-wife.

What follows is a nasty and poignant little movie set in the bleak of winter. It's a much more character-driven piece than his previous work, but there are still some fantastic set-pieces of brutal carnage, such as the murder by mallet and the scene where a playschool teacher is beaten to death in the presence of her traumatised pupils. Reed is as good as ever as Raglan, Hindle is likeable as the concerned father, and Samantha Eggar is superb and way over the top in her role as the dangerous mother, Nola. Also lookout for Cronenberg regular, Robert Silverman, as a disgruntled ex-patient, listen out for Howard Shore's modest but effective score (the first of many for Cronenberg), and marvel at the dark subtext concerning familial anguish, child abuse, domestic hell, and of course, the revolt of one's own body.

Giallo a Venezia (1979)
(aka *Gore In Venice*)
Dir: Mario Landi /Italy

Generally regarded as one of the sleaziest gialli ever made, *Giallo a Venezia* opens at the aftermath of a double murder on the banks of Venice. A man has been stabbed to death with a pair of scissors, and a woman has been drowned. Not only does detective DePaul have to find the killer, but one of the clues may become clear if he can work out why the woman's body was pulled out of the water after her death. Much of the story is told in flashback, and it's here we learn that the murdered couple were husband and wife, Fabio and Flavia. Fabio was a sex-crazed coke head who got his kicks from the violence and voyeuristic cruelties he inflicted on Flavia. And meanwhile a killer is doing the rounds of Venice.

There's very little suspense in this 'murder mystery'; director Mario Landi seems much more interested in showing dull sex scenes and even duller police procedures. The violence is nowhere near as shocking as some would have you believe (the notorious crotch-stabbing of the prostitute is an exception though); Giordano having her leg cut off, and the burning of Marizia's lover are quite well done, but I personally found the simple and unexpected discovery of a body in a fridge to be more effective – it's such a startling image. The long overdrawn sex scenes are nowhere near as explicit as some have said, either, but the cat 'o nine tails and the cinema scenes are good for a giggle.

Overall it's not too bad a film, but if you watch it having heard all the hype then you may be disappointed. If Landi really was more interested in showing blood and sex rather than a tightly constructed giallo, then he ultimately fails there too. He should have given us more. And the film is still unavailable on DVD. It was released on DVD-R on the Cult Action label. And that version looks to be taken from from the same muddy transfer as the other bootleg copies.

Mad Max (1979)
Dir: George Miller /Australia

Australia in the near future. Road cop, Max Rockatansky (Mel Gibson), spends his days racing up and down the endless highways in pursuit of reckless criminals in a world in which law and order is hanging by a thread. Not only do the criminal elements roam free to kill and harass innocent members of the public, but Max's own police force is hopelessly corrupt, too. To make matters worse, a biker gang from Hell roars into town, leaving death and carnage in its wake. After his partner is severely burned by the maniacs, Max takes his girlfriend and young child to a remote location to escape the chaos. However, it isn't long before trouble catches up with them. And once his loved ones have been taken away from him, it's No More Mister Nice Guy Time as Max embarks on a ruthless revenge mission against the biker thugs...

This debut feature by writer/director, George Miller, cost just $400,000 to produce, and went on to make over $100 million, becoming one of the most financially successful films of the decade. In fact, the budget restraints were so tight that Miller even volunteered to wreck his own car for a scene in the film. He also wisely focused the money where it mattered – on the action and the stunts – rather than trying too much to convince the viewers of its post-nuclear, apocalyptic setting (and this trick was later utilised by Paul Verhoeven during the making of *Robocop* (1987) – he only made minor changes to the look of Detroit of the future, and instead concentrated the bulk of the budget on his impressive hi-tech killing machines).

It was also the screen debut of twenty-three-old actor, Mel Gibson, who is said to have stood out during the auditions due to having a black eye, which he sustained during a bar fight the night before. Here he does a remarkable job as the less than verbose, leather-clad super-cop. He's utterly convincing in his portrayal of a character who transforms from a duty-bound family man to cold-blooded killer. Of course, it wasn't the first time audiences were presented with a man-of-the-law driven to extremes; Don Siegel's *Dirty Harry* (1971) springs to mind. However, Harry Callahan, for all his ruthlessness in dealing with psychopathic killers, there was always a core of humanity beneath his hard boiled shell; and what compelled him to act more than anything else was his hatred for the weak bureaucrats and their timid philosophies which he felt were causing more harm to society than good. Max Rockatansky, on the other hand, is eventually driven to the point where he no longer gives a damn about society at large, nor the corruption within his own force – by the end of the film, all he cares about is making his enemies suffer as much as possible. His humanity is extinguished like the flick of a light switch once his loved ones have been killed. And thenceforth, *Mad Max* goes about his brutal business with a cold, dead-eyed efficiency. And the viewers, who have followed his dark journey up until that point, are with him every step of the way.

Unsurprisingly, both George Miller and his rising star, Mel Gibson, were signed up to Hollywood immediately on the strength of this low-budget thriller alone. And they moved on to bigger and better things in the new decade. *Mad Max* became a cult classic on home video in the 80s, though the U.S. version was initially dubbed with American accents as the distributors felt the Aussie accents were a little too difficult to follow. Thankfully, DVD editions and the more recent Blu-Ray release stick with the original cut. But, as impressive as this film may be, it serves as little more than a teaser of what was to follow. The sequel would be even bigger and badder, with a budget ten times the size of this, for one of the greatest and most influential post-apocalypse movies ever made, *Mad Max 2: The Road Warrior* (1981).

The Driller Killer (1979)
Dir: Abel Ferrara /USA

The Driller Killer became infamous in the UK in the early 80s as a principal title on the 'video nasties' list. But was the film really all that bad? Well, the answer is simply no because despite all the negative attention heaped on the film at the time, and the original VHS cover which graphically shows a man being drilled through the forehead, *The Driller Killer* actually bares a closer resemblance to the art films of Andy Warhol rather than a sleazy stalk and slash epic.

However, the film nonetheless got swept up in the controversy and was prosecuted under the 1984 Video Recordings Act, a farcical piece of legislation which Ferrara's film, ironically, was partly responsible for bringing about, and which affected home video viewing in the UK for the best part of two decades.

Often wrongly listed as Ferrara's debut feature (he actually directed and performed in the earlier XXX porno, *Nine Lives of a Wet Pussy*), *The Driller Killer* stars Abel Ferrara himself as Reno, a struggling artist living in a squalid apartment in New York surrounded by bums, druggies, and a noisy rock band next door. His lack of concentration drives him to madness, and he eventually goes on a killing spree with a portable power drill.

Many have dismissed the film (including Ferrara himself on the Cult Epics DVD commentary), mainly because it doesn't pander to any notions of popular taste or commercial manners (slasher or otherwise). The film instead makes great use of gritty realism and a DIY punk aesthetic in the harsh natural light, improvisation, and location shooting which no doubt has left many slasher movie fanatics scratching their heads over the years. But all this is really just bleak window dressing, and what Ferrara and his writing partner, Nicholas St. John, really concentrated on was the crumbling psychological state of Reno's mind.

The painting of the buffalo is a work in progress – Reno's art represents his mind's eye. As the painting develops, incidents which annoy or distract Reno have a direct effect on the painting. Early in the film, Ferrara employs quick-fire edits between the drill and the buffalo's eye; these cuts express the simmering rage that is gathering in Reno's head. The buffalo also represents Reno as he would like to be; a wild, free, and careless animal instead of a starving artist in a crummy apartment. When he fantasizes on future success, the buffalo is proudly displayed in the background like a thought-bubble on the verge of breaking free. But in reality, Reno is faced with tensions from the other members of the household, an art dealer who doesn't understand his work and refuses to buy his paintings, a dreadful rock band who live next door and insist on rehearsing late into the night, financial troubles, and the homeless bums (one of whom is Reno's father) who are a constant reminder that he too could soon be joining them on the streets. And of course, at this stage the painting becomes increasingly frayed and off-balance, reflecting the building tensions in his mind.

When the painting reaches its conclusion, the distractions and annoyances continue to irritate Reno, and instead of starting afresh with a new canvas and a new painting, he snaps – and this is the most important part of the film – the negative urges and demons which he had channelled into his art have now broken loose into reality. And he immediately sets forth to drill those who represent his fears and anxieties. The beast breaks out of the painting and onto the seedy streets of New York.

The Driller Killer was originally promoted with lurid artwork and posters which implied that half-dressed bimbo's would be drilled by an unhinged psychopath, but this exploitation tease couldn't be further off the mark. For a start, all of the on-screen killings are dealt out to male victims, and overall the film stands as a rumination on the sometimes torturous process of creativity and as a study on encroaching madness. It's a film that is actually closer in spirit to Roman Polanski's *Repulsion* (1965) than to big apple sleaze like William Lustig's *Maniac* (1980). Indeed, Ferrara's follow-up to *The Driller Killer, Ms.45* (1981) (which also found itself on the DPP's 'nasties' list), revisits similar territory from a female perspective.

The film was re-released in the UK in the

late 90s with 54 seconds of violence cut by the distributors themselves. The BBFC's chief censor at the time, James Ferman, suggested that the uncut version probably would have been passed had the film been submitted to the Board intact. And it wasn't until 2003 that *The Driller Killer* finally received an uncut 18 certificate. The film's salacious reputation has roped in many horror fans over the years only to leave many of them disappointed with the overall lack of bloodshed (there are a couple of great scenes of violence in the film though, such as a bum being drilled through the forehead that looks very realistic; but I suppose it's the scene where Ferrara eats a pizza that remains the most disgusting), but *The Driller Killer* is not the film many think it to be.

Scum (1979)
Dir: Alan Clarke /UK

The violence and fear of borstal life is explored in Alan Clarke's extraordinary *Scum* which began life as a TV drama only to be shelved by the BBC for being "too realistic." Clarke and co remained undeterred in their attempts to expose the abuse and corruption in British institutions, and instead remade that caustic drama a couple of years later for the big screen. The result was unlike anything else seen in British theatres.

Young thug Carlin (a very young Ray Winstone) is sentenced to imprisonment at a young offenders institute. He is immediately assaulted by officers and beaten up by the 'Daddy' of A-wing, Pongo. Initially Carlin steers clear of trouble and takes his abuse on the chin, but once he gets to know the ropes and understands whom he can trust and whom he can't, he sets about a violent rise to the top, wiping out Pongo and his cronies one by one (including the use of snooker balls in a sock as a weapon, which has been imitated in other films over the years). Once Carlin proclaims himself Daddy of A-wing, he takes over Pongo's cut of the drug deals and other contraband, and protects the few friends he has made on the way. However, his new authority doesn't reach high enough to deal with the officers whose abuse and neglect crosses the line when a young inmate commits suicide after being raped. A full-scale riot ensues...

With largely the same cast who appeared in the BBC *Scum*, this later version is no less unnerving in its depiction of a brutal authoritarian system that seems utterly unconcerned with reforming the young inmates. It was also shot in Clarke's usual stark and grounded style that would typify his later works such as *The Firm* and *Rita, Sue, and Bob, Too*. Ray Winstone's performance as Carlin is assured and totally believable as the first of many big-screen roles to come, and he's also aided by the superb Mick Ford who plays Archer, a much more ingenious rebel who devises many non-violent ways of making life as inconvenient as possible for the screws, such as pretending to be vegetarian in order to disrupt the prison menu, and then showing an interest in converting to Islam in the presence of the chief warden who happens to be an intolerant idiot and devout Christian. The film is also very unflinching in its violence and disturbing details, with the desperate suicide of a young man being difficult to watch due to its gritty realism. The film's most notorious scene though is the rape in the greenhouse which was trimmed by the BBFC for its initial release and early home video editions. It has since been passed uncut by the Board.

During preparations for the TV version, Alan Clarke and writer Roy Minton spent six weeks researching on borstal life and spent time visiting the institutions and interviewed many ex-inmates in order to construct as real a drama as possible, and many of the stories and tidbits of information gathered were worked into the script, not only forming the narrative but also serving as a damning indictment in the troubled 70s. It's no surprise that the BBC refused to broadcast the result until the 90s, by which time this latter version had secured its reputation as being one of the finest and harshest British films of the 70s. Thank goodness that important research didn't go to waste.

Beautiful Girl Hunter (1979)
(aka *Star of David - Hunting For Beautiful Girls*)
(Orig title: *Dabide no hoshi: Bishôjo-gari*)
Dir: Norofumi Suzuki /Japan

A twisted war veteran intrudes on a home, ties up the couple who own the place, robs them of their savings, and then subjects the woman to forced deep-throating and rape. Later, when the ordeal seems to be over, the partner cruelly lashes at the woman with a bull whip, accusing her of enjoying the experience. And his rage only intensifies when she reveals to him that she is pregnant with the rapist's baby...

A few years later and the household is fast deteriorating. The 'father' can barely look at the youngster because he reminds him of the rapist, and constantly slaps, threatens, and abuses the boy, much to the dismay of the mother. He often subjects his wife to brutal S&M sessions, involving another woman whom he ties up, whips, abuses, and forces to urinate on each other. The boy, Tatsuya, witnesses much of this by spying through the keyhole. Wife can't handle it anymore, and she commits suicide by plunging her own throat down onto a blade (similar to the suicide of a murder suspect in David Cronenberg's *The Dead Zone* [1983] in which a man plunges himself face-first down onto a pair of opened scissors).

Not surprisingly, Tatsuya grows up to become a deeply disturbed sadistic sex maniac, partly because of his traumatic childhood experiences, and (according to the film) partly due to his own wretched gene pool. He spikes a lady's drink and then carries her unconscious body down into his basement that he has renovated into his own secret torture dungeon that resembles the spacious lab in Paul Morrissey's *Flesh For Frankenstein* (1974) He strips and rapes her, and when she regains consciousness he berates her and blames her for his own emotional turmoil. His deranged activities go unchecked, even using his own birthday party as an alibi so that he can escape down into his basement to indulge in his sick urge to rape and murder his captives.

Meanwhile, Tatsuya's biological father is still up to his old tricks. He may be older but he still has no trouble in overpowering young girls and savagely raping and strangling them out in the wilderness. And like father like son, Tatasuya becomes bolder in his kidnapping antics, and in a scene which serves as a chilling reminder of the crimes of Ted Bundy, he approaches a high school girl pretending to be a photojournalist and manages to lure the poor girl into his car. Back at the basement she is abused and forced to masturbate.

Through a series of short flashbacks we get some more back-story on Tatsuya; as a school student he became obsessed with the Nazi's and Auschwitz, and is seen jerking off to images of Jews being hung and gunned down by firing squads (Ian Brady displayed similar traits). He deflowers the school girl and she eventually becomes completely subservient to him, willing to do absolutely anything for her 'master'. It's interesting to note here that director Suzuki composes the sex scenes in such a way that there is no need for those distracting 'blurs' that crop up all the time in Japanese sex movies. Here Suzuki pushes as much as he could get away with in this type of soft core fare.

Next up, Tatsuya kidnaps a pop star (Hiromi Namino, who was Miss Japan at the time in her first film role in which her nudity caused much fuss in the Japanese press) and her assistant. By treating the pop star mean and treating her assistant with a bit of care and kindness, he succeeds in exposing a knot of resentment between the two, and the master-slave dynamic is reversed when the assistant bull-whips the pop star to within an inch of her life.

In perhaps one of the most offensive sequences in the film, Tatsuya seems to take pity on the schoolgirl, and he dumps her on a beach in the middle of the night. And in a later scene he spies on her while she's back at school, and she seems to have rebuilt her life. Not only is she more popular than before, but she looks to have developed a new lease of life; she's happy, smiley, care-free, and the centre of attention. The implications of this scene are very dubious. And dangerous. To suggest that her awful experience at the hands of a madman who had deflowered and turned her into a nervous subservient wreck, and then showing her to have gained from it and even to have *appreciated* the experience – this sequence gives the film one of its most authentic notes of misogyny.

Anyway, the pop star makes an unsuccessful escape attempt. And while an injured Tatsuya is dealing with her, the assistant manages to escape from the house. But in a cruel (and ludicrous) twist of fate, she runs directly into the arms of Tatsuya's father. Cue a long-overdue family reunion as father and son meet for the first time and team up for more depraved fun involving the captives, an Alsation, and of course, rape, torture, and murder.

Throughout the film, Tatsuya has been courting a pretty young girl; they go on dates, go horse riding, and generally spend a lot of time together. He tells her that he keeps birds in his basement, and the girl is keen to see them but he always avoids taking her home. Indeed, viewers are not sure whether Tatsuya is just luring her along as part of another of his twisted games, or whether he genuinely cares for her. But in a nasty and cruel finale, we discover that yes he really *does* care about her, but he has a funny way of showing it... But as it turns out, this girl has her own warped agenda to deal with involving her faith, incest, and the Star of David. A touch of redemption maybe? I don't think so!

When asked why his films contain so many images and references to Christianity, director Norifumi Suzuki replied "I suppose sacred things are actually quite erotic. The idea of defiling something sacred like a nun or a nurse or a schoolteacher is very erotic". Certainly, if you look through the films of Suzuki (*Truck Yaro* and *School of the Holy Beast*, for example) you'll find that the defiling of sacred things is an ongoing theme in his work, and *Beautiful Girl Hunter* is no exception. Having worked for the Toei studio for a number of years, Suzuki was eventually head-hunted by the Nikkatsu Corporation who offered him bigger budgets and a free choice to make whatever kind of film he liked, just as long as it would fit in with the 'Roman Porno' tradition. Suzuki settled on *Star of David*, a Manga by Masaaki Soto, and in just 19 days he had written, directed, and edited the film in a flash. The result is a vile and misogynistic piece of trash that perhaps isn't supposed to be taken seriously. But it's also beautifully shot with neon-lit photography, and permeates a dark and brooding atmosphere, and boasts some fantastic performances. The film echoes Jess Franco's *The Sadistic Baron Von Klaus* (*Le Sadique baron von Klaus*, 1962), with its Sadean streak passed down the generations of the family bloodline, and the grandson who is compelled to kidnap young women and torture them in the basement of the family chateau. Also, similarities can be found in Koji Wakamatsu's *The Embryo Hunts in Secret* (*Taiji ga Mitsuryō Suru Tokl*, 1966) and Mario Bava's *The Whip and the Body* (1962). For all the shocking and disagreeable elements the film may possess, it's certainly never boring and is expertly made. In today's PC climate, nobody makes big-budget shock films like this anymore. Suzuki once described *Beautiful Girl Hunter* as a film which "deals with the joys of being evil."

Bloodline (1979)
Dir: Terence Young /USA
Bloodline sees Aubrey Hepburn inherit a multi-national corporation when her father dies. It later turns out that her father's death was no accident. Numerous shareholders within the company are suspected of the murder, and when prostitutes are brutally murdered in a series of snuff clips, Hepburn realises her own life is in danger. *Bloodline* was a shoddy production; underfunded and brimming with hilarious gaffs, underwhelming performances, terrible FX sequences and studio interference. The film was made during the breakdown of Hepburn's second marriage. She accepted the role of Elizabeth on a whim, and became very upset when she learned about the film's murky snuff movie sub-plot. She initially washed her hands of the project, only to return in a bid to honour her contract with Paramount. Many of her fans never forgave her for appearing in such R-rated filth. Television prints of *Bloodline* include an extra 40 minutes of footage which helps to clear up some of the more confusing loose ends of the theatrical version. But that extra footage has never been included on any of its home video or DVD releases.

Ring of Darkness (1979)
(aka *Satan's Wife*; aka *Un'ombra nell'ombra*)
Dir: 'Peter Karp' [Pier Carpi] /Italy /UK
Carlotta (Anne Heywood) is a member of a secretive Satanic sect. She and other members of the cult become increasingly worried by the exploits of Daria (Lara Wendel), Carlotta's teenage daughter, who has developed terrifying powers, and thinks nothing of casting evil spells on those around her whom she is upset with, including members of the sect. Carlotta and others renounce their pacts with Satan, and in desperation seek the assistance of a Priest to help rid Daria of the evil that has consumed her soul... *Ring of Darkness* is better than the usual *Exorcist* rip-offs, even though the performances are a little stilted at times. The film has a cold, gloomy, paranoid vibe to it, and Stelvio Cipriani provides the Goblin-esque, prog-rock score that works wonders at enlivening what is essentially a cheap exploitation pic. The film is shrouded in controversy to this day for the casting of Lara Wendel; she also appeared in the notorious *Maladolescenza* – both films were shot in 1977 when she was just thirteen-years-old, and both films contain scenes in which she is naked for much of the time. *Ring of Darkness*, in particular, includes the outrageous scene in which mother and daughter have a cat fight in the middle of a pentagram in a church, in the nude.

Bloodrage (1979)
(aka *Never Pick Up a Stranger*)
Dir: 'Joseph Bigwood' [Joseph Zito] /USA
"I'm tired of people pushing me around. I'm gonna start pushing back now. Only, I'm gonna push harder. They won't fuck with me anymore, I'll make sure of that." A disturbed young man flees to New York City after accidentally killing a prostitute. There he takes out his frustrations on other prostitutes, making sure to abuse and humiliate them before taking their lives. And meanwhile, a cop who was a regular client of the first hooker, tracks him down... This grimy little slasher movie mixes the grim voice-over and urban squalor of *Taxi Driver* (1976) with the 'bird's eye' horrors of Alfred Hitchcock, but ultimately fails to rise above its micro-budget limitations. The film pays tribute to *Psycho* and *Rear Window*, with the killer's meticulous clean up after the first murder, and his obsessive voyeurism as he watches the prostitutes in the opposite building. The look of the film rivals *Basket Case* and *The Headless Eyes* in terms of its grotty urban decay, with litter-strewn sidewalks and flea-pit apartments. Unfortunately, there's not enough of a psychological angle on the killer and his motivations, and the project probably ran out of funding before the shoot was complete, as the ending is quite sketchy with many crucial plot points taking place off screen. The UK video version runs for around 70 minutes, while the US VHS release (reviewed here) clocks in at 82 minutes. Director Joseph Zito's next project was the much more polished *The Prowler* (aka *Rosemary's Killer*, 1981).

Tourist Trap (1979)
Dir: David Schmoeller /USA
An impressive, atypical effort from the slasher movie heyday, *Tourist Trap* sees a group of teens arrive at a mannequin museum whose kooky owner uses telekenesis to puppeteer the dolls to kill. Similar to *Psycho* (1960) in many ways; the insane Mr. Slausen (Chuck Connors) shares a similar, Ed Gein-like psychosis as Norman Bates in the way he channels split personalities to commit the deadly deeds. And just like the Bates Motel, the museum is located in a backwoods area that has been cut off from the rest of civilisation by a newly constructed motorway nearby, causing the tourist trade to bypass the museum. Includes an eccentric score by Pino Donaggio.

Human Experiments (1979)
(aka *Beyond the Gate*)
Dir: Gregory Goodell /USA
A rushed women-in-prison pic hastily cobbled together to cash in on the exploitation craze of the time, *Human Experiments* starts with a string of very bad luck for Rachel (Linda Haynes), a nightclub singer who finds herself charged for a mass murder of which she is innocent. She is sent off for a lengthy custodial sentence where she becomes the centre of unwanted attention from the prison psychiatrist, Dr. Kline (Geoffrey Lewis). Those expecting fiendish medical experiments carried out on female prisoners, as seen in movies like *Caged Heat* (1974), *Barbed Wire Dolls* (1976) and any number of Naziploitation pics will be disappointed, as the experiments here are mostly of the psychological kind. The film starts off with a lightning pace, and doesn't waste any time in slamming it heroine behind bars. But, once there, the tempo begins to lag quite badly, and the film-makers struggle to hold the viewer's attention. It's also disappointingly sleazeless for a 70s babes-in-the-slammer pic, but the lead performance from Haynes is quite good; she's totally believable as the street-wise tough cookie struggling to cling onto her sanity as her ordeal becomes increasingly unbearable. The film is certainly worth a watch, but ultimately, it's far too tasteful for its own good.

Zombie Lake (1979)
(aka *Lake of the Living Dead*; aka *Le lac des morts vivants*)
Dir: 'J. A. Laser' [Jean Rollin and Julian de Laserna] /France /Spain
Taking its cue from *J'Accuse!* (1920) and *Shock Waves* (1977), *Zombie Lake* centres on a rural French town where green-faced Nazi ghouls emerge from the nearby lake to chew on the flesh of the living. That's about as close to a plot the film gets as much of it plays as a series of vignettes. A troubled production, Jess Franco was originally set to direct, but he was swamped with other obligations and had to drop out (though he did return with a Nazi zombie movie of his own a couple of years later, *Oasis of the Zombies* [1981], also for Eurocine). Frenchman Jean Rollin and Spaniard Julian de Laserna took over directorial duties, and though the film does have its moments, the film-makers' hearts clearly weren't in it. It's a slow, maudlin flick, almost as slow as the ghouls, but is enlivened

somewhat thanks to Daniel White's eerie score, which mixes such avant-garde elements as atonal chimes, weird organs and the haunting, romantic interludes carried over from Franco's *Female Vampire* (1974).

The Exterminator (1980)
Dir: James Glickenhaus /USA

After a prologue in which the protagonist endures *Deer Hunter*-style torment at the hands of the Vietcong, before his buddy, Mike (Steve James), initiates a daring escape, we cut to modern-day New York City where 'Nam vet, John (Robert Ginty), works as a van loader at a food distribution depot. After being rescued a second time by his old 'Nam buddy when thugs are caught stealing, John is horrified to discover that Michael has been jumped in a revenge attack and paralysed. And, with no build-up whatsoever, we simply cut to the next scene in which John is threatening a suspected gang member with a blowtorch! This guy doesn't mess around! And from then on, we simply follow John (or, as the papers have now dubbed him, 'The Exterminator'), as he embarks on a ruthless vigilante mission to rid the streets of the criminal 'ghetto ghouls' who are a plague in the area.

Cue car wrecks, shootings, a mob boss lowered into an industrial sized meat grinder, sadistic perverts burned alive, and a bleak ending that strays into dirty politics territory. And meanwhile, the detective on the case, Dalton (*City of the Living Dead*'s Christopher George), spends most of his time trying to bed the pretty night doctor, Samantha Eggar, rather than catching the culprit. *The Exterminator* was made primarily to cash in on the success of *Death Wish* (1974) and *Mad Max* (1979). And the anti-hero here even shares the same character traits as the vigilantes in those films, from Paul Kersey's mild-mannered liberal at the end of his fuse, to Max Rockatansky's psychotic and traumatised avenger. If Mad Max was driven insane by his inability to protect his loved ones, John instead has untreated PTSD as a result of his 'Nam days when he witnessed a fellow marine having his head cut off by the enemy – a bloody fate that he himself was only seconds away from. Thus, John's madness becomes enmeshed with his humble, liberal outlook, combining to produce a street thug's worst nightmare, as all the wrong-doers he encounters trigger those awful flashbacks to those desperate days in the jungle. *The Exterminator* was a cult classic on 80s home video, but it hasn't aged too well. It's not bad, but Ginty, for all his good work, has nothing on Charles Bronson or Mel Gibson. The soundtrack mixes dull acoustic ballads with Joe Renzetti's frenzied, horror-themed string arrangements, while Robert M. Baldwin's camera work only comes to life during the title credits helicopter shots over New York, and there are far too many blatant swipes from *Death Wish*, right down to the flick knife waving bandanna thugs mugging innocents in Central Park. Be sure to watch the full cut (104-minutes), as there have been a number of censored versions released over the years.

Eaten Alive! (1980)
(Orig title: *Mangiati vivi!*)
Dir: Umberto Lenzi /Italy

Umberto Lenzi's finest film sees New Yorker, Janet Agren, head out to New Guinea to find her sister whom, it is feared, has gotten herself mixed up in a dangerous pain-worshipping cult out in the jungle. The cult leader, Jonas (Ivan Rassimov), is a bloodthirsty maniac who subjects his followers to rape, beheadings and castration. While Janet tries to rescue her sister, Jonas keeps control over his flock by threatening to banish all wrong-doers out of the community and into the jungle surrounding them which is teeming with savage cannibals. When things slip out of his control, he encourages a Jim Jones-type mass suicide, and those who refuse to die are stabbed to death. *Eaten Alive!* is an underrated curio, which – despite the oodles of stock footage of tribesmen hanging on meat hooks, fire walkers, and the usual animal footage – is far more riveting and enjoyable than it had any right to be. The direction is well handled, and the sense of foreboding and being isolated with lunatics is evident throughout. Footage is also taken from *Mountain of the Cannibal God* (1978) and Lenzi's own *The Man From Deep River* (1975). Also, Me Me Lai runs around with her tits out again in footage taken from Deodato's *The Last Cannibal World* (1977).

Maniac (1980)
Dir: William Lustig /USA

Frank Zito (Joe Spinell) is a very sick man. He stalks, murders, and scalps young women. He is not necessarily guided by particulars either, any will do; prostitutes, nurses, couples on the beach or on lover's lane – anyone who catches his eye is in serious danger. He lives in a crummy basement flat surrounded by his beloved mannequins, and often falls into deep depression, struck by guilt for his awful crimes. But his resentment and mad urges to kill just won't go away. He strikes up a relationship with beautiful photographer, Anna (Caroline Munro), and they genuinely like each other, but Frank can't hide his sickness from her for very long...

If you're a fan of 'fun-time' slashers like *Halloween* and *Friday the 13th*, then William Lustig's *Maniac* may come as something of a shock to the system. It's about as much fun as being stalked through a deserted subway after dark. Instead, we're invited to join the company of a miserable, self-loathing psychopath who prowls the seedy streets of New York's red light district in search of his next kill, or sulks almost in his squalid flat, mumbling to himself whilst nailing the scalps of victims onto the heads of his mannequin collection. It's a grim, nasty, and unsettling film, but also perhaps one of the finest slasher movies ever made. I just wish there were more films like this that refuse to glamorise the killer and is prepared to get down and dirty with the harrowing bleakness of what happens behind the headlines in serial murder.

Inspired by the panic and paranoia of big city life, *Maniac* boasts the greatest sequence in slasher movie history in which a young nurse (Kelly Piper) is followed down into an empty subway station by her killer and is slaughtered in the toilets. It's a long and painfully protracted scene that will leave you with clammy hands thanks to some superb pacing and editing techniques, before the pay-off when Zito rams his 'chete through her spine (this sequence is said to have influenced Alexandre Aja for the public rest room scene in *Haute Tension*).

An earlier scene in which Frank visits a prostitute is difficult to watch because it's played out so unsettlingly straight. It's easy to imagine a real life murder taking place in an almost identical way as the scene in which the hooker (Rita Montrone) begins servicing her client, only to be thrown down onto the bed and strangled. And it's here that Frank takes out his hunting knife and proceeds to cut away at her scalp, taking his souvenir with him from the crime scene.

Jay Chattaway's downbeat score adds to the bleak and harrowing nature of the film, as does

Tom Savini's gruesomely realistic special effects (although Savini himself is said to have felt uncomfortable being associated with the film after it grew and generated its notorious reputation). Trivia fans will be interested to know that the character Frank Zito was named after director William Lustig's friend, Joseph Zito, who directed a couple of nice slasher movies himself around that time, *Bloodrage* (1979) and *The Prowler* (1981). But neither of those comes close to the urban nightmare that is *Maniac*, a film so ruthless and bleak it sent many a movie-goer leaving the cinema in fear, especially those who were planning on taking the train home.

William Lustig was a frequenter of the Deuce and the grindhouses of 42nd Street; he would skip class and soak up as much sexploitation and import horror as he could. He made his directorial debut in 1977 (under the name 'Billy Bagg') with *The Violation of Claudia*, a porn effort. He eventually teamed up with executive producer Judd Hamilton and actor Joe Spinell to make their masterpiece, *Maniac*. His career ran steadily throughout the 80s, offering up genre classics like the *Maniac Cop* series and *Relentless* before he retired from directing to concentrate on releasing his favourite grindhouse movies on DVD with his label, Blue Underground (much in the same way as fellow New Yorker Frank Henenlotter, who gave up film-making for his own label, Something Weird Video, although he did return to the director's chair for the insane *Bad Biology* in 2008).

When *Maniac* was released in the early 80s it was accused of being symptomatic of everything that was 'sick', 'grim', and 'irresponsible' about modern horror films. Even many horror fans at the time felt that the film had gone too far in its depictions of cold-blooded murder, but in more recent years with films like John McNaughton's *Henry-Portrait of a Serial Killer* and Gerald Kargl's *Angst* gaining reappraisal, even exploitative shockers like *Maniac* have had a partial acceptance with special edition DVDs and red carpet treatment on Blu-Ray. For many though, *Maniac* still remains a sick no-go area.

The Shining (1980)
Dir: Stanley Kubrick /USA
The Shining is a masterpiece of horror cinema, and one that never gets old. No matter how

252

many times you re-watch it, you'll always find a new nugget of interest that you hadn't considered before. It's a timeless classic which only gets better with age, whilst still retaining an air of mystery and wonder, and dread.

Jack Torrance (Jack Nicholson), a former school teacher hoping to find the space necessary to write a novel, applies for the job of winter caretaker at a Colorado hotel, The Overlook. The snow storms are so fierce that the hotel remains isolated from the rest of civilisation throughout the winter months. After a successful interview at the resort, Jack is warned that the isolation of being stuck out in the middle of nowhere for months at a time can be a psychological ordeal (the previous caretaker was driven stir crazy and chopped up his wife and daughters with an axe). However, Jack accepts the responsibility of his new position, and pretty soon he and his wife, Wendy (Shelley Duvall), and their son, Danny (Daniel Lloyd), travel by car to the foreboding hotel.

Danny possesses a psychic gift that the hotel's head chef, Halloran (Scatman Crothers), refers to as 'the shining' – he can 'see' events from the future and the past. He can also project his thoughts into the minds of others, and both he and the chef share a playful psychic communication while the family are being given a tour around the building. Later, Danny sees something evil about the hotel, and while pedalling his toy trike through its labyrinth corridors, suffers grisly visions of past murders. His only playmate in this isolated environment is his imaginary friend, Tony. Meanwhile, the emotionally vulnerable Jack – a recovering alcoholic with a history of violent episodes – is also afflicted by the visions. And before long he begins to succumb to the dark, supernatural forces of the hotel, and is consumed by thoughts of dismembering his family with an axe...

According to his then secretary, Stanley Kubrick first encountered Stephen King's source novel in the late 70s while perusing the latest paperback releases. He would sit in his office with a stack of books, reading the first few pages of any given title before getting bored and throwing it at the wall with a loud thump. However, one afternoon the thumps had stopped, and she saw that her boss was deeply engrossed in a new novel entitled *The Shining*. Kubrick had stumbled upon what would be one of the finest novels in the 'haunted house' tradition, and he immediately set out to bring the

spooky tale to the big screen.

The young, up-and-coming author, Stephen King, was understandably pleased to have his work validated by such a giant of cinema as Kubrick. However, the good relationship between the two didn't last very long; King was annoyed at the casting of Jack Nicholson, as he felt the role should have gone to someone like Michael Moriaty or John Voight, actors whom he felt would do a better job of portraying the mild-mannered side of Jack Torrence's character. He also received phone calls at 3am from the notoriously obsessive director during the shoot to enquire whether or not he believed in God. Add to this the fact that Kubrick and his co-screenwriter, Diane Johnson, purged whole chunks of the book, discarding the more formulaic elements in favour of a loose study on encroaching madness, and by the time of the film's release, King made no secret of his dislike for the film, describing it as a 'big and beautiful car. Ultimately a piece of machinery with neither heart nor soul.'

Kubrick's perfectionism was legendary, and he often made actors repeat the same scene more than a hundred times. Actors in *Dr. Strangelove* (1964) were requested to throw 1000 pies per day for a week for a scene that he eventually dropped from the final cut. And that meticulousness was taken to equally staggering levels during the filming of *The Shining*. Shelley Duvall was regularly forced to do no less than 127 takes of certain scenes; Nicholson was requested to eat endless cheese sandwiches so that he would develop an 'inner sense of revulsion,' veteran actor Crothers had to endure more than 140 takes of his character 'shining' in the hotel room, and at one point Nicholson felt the need to step in and talk the director into limiting Crother's climactic death scene to a mere 40 takes! Kubrick also insisted on shooting the entire film chronologically, which meant that all the sets had to be built and ready to go at a moment's notice. And though the shoot was a gruelling one for all involved, the end result was a precision-perfect masterpiece of horror.

The film opens with beautiful aerial footage of the Torrence's car driving on the isolated mountain roads accompanied by Wendy Carlos' eerie and mournful electronic score. There's also some impressive Steadicam work (by its inventor, Garret Brown), as the camera follows directly behind Danny riding his trike along the corridors, creating a rhythmic pattern of sound and vision as he pedals over the rugs and hard wooden floors. Kubrick's regular DP, John Alcott (of *A Clockwork Orange* and *Barry Lyndon*) offers up his usual outstanding work in many key sequences. Nicholson's performance was key to the success or failure of the film, and Kubrick wisely allows him the room and the freedom to improvise, and this culminates in the most famous line in the film where an axe-wielding Jack peers in through the broken bathroom door and snarls 'He-e-e-re's Johnny!' (a line taken from the intro to NBC's *The Johnny Carson Show*).

Kubrick wanted to take the horror film away from its conventions, cheap tricks and tired clichés, and instead build his film on atmosphere and symbolism. There are no silly jump scares here, no pointless 'shocks.' Kubrick's take on *The Shining* is quite insidious in the way it gets under the skin. There's a strong theme which runs through the film concerning the frustrations with family. From the opening scenes it's clear that Jack isn't all that happy – as he is escorted around the hotel, he can't resist ogling the backsides of women. Then there's the quiet frustration with his son, Danny. He has to spend several months alone with these people – a wife that looks like Olive Oil and a son who talks to his finger.

When Jack seeks solace in the large ballroom (or 'the Gold Room'), he perhaps enters the dark realm of his own psyche, and he is told 'Your credit's fine, Mr. Torrence.' Indeed, it's never made clear whether it's Jack's growing insanity or the dark forces of The Overlook (or a combination of the two) that are responsible for gripping his soul. The previous caretaker, Grady, also makes an appearance, and he tells Jack 'You have always been the caretaker.' Thus, Grady is suggesting that the hotel is merely awakening an evil that has always existed deep within him. So it seems The Overlook serves as an isolated, inescapable maze that draws madness to the surface.

The tortures of the creative process is another element that seems to contribute to Jack's mental crumbling. He struggles to make progress with his novel – he stares at a blank page a lot (a writer's worst nightmare); he tries to break the deadlock of writer's block by rhythmically throwing a tennis ball against the wall in the main hall; and when he does get down to writing, he is interrupted by his wife, which causes him to lose his temper and speak to her in an appalling manner.

Jack's true feelings are revealed when he chats to the bartender, Lloyd. It's here we see that Jack and Wendy's marriage is under strain – she has never forgiven him for accidentally hurting little Danny. And it's here we learn just how crazy Jack is, if we hadn't already. He's talking to ghosts. Many fans and critics believe the ghosts to be merely figments of Jack's imagination for there are often mirrors behind the apparitions, and so he is effectively talking to himself. But I'm not so sure – after all, in a later scene, Jack is released from the locked storage room, not by Wendy or Danny. If the ghosts in this film are just mental emanations of Jack's then how the hell could he have freed himself from the storage room so that he could terrorise his family all over again? Of course, no 'trendy' psychological horror buff cares to explain *that*.

The real star of the show is Kubrick himself. His command of lighting is impeccable – just marvel at the scenes in the Gold Room; his use of music – a soundtrack built on the electronic whirls of Wendy Carlos and the alarming, spine-chilling compositions of Krzysztof Penderecki; the way he tackles the scene in Room 237, and how he avoided an easy 'jump scare' and instead used it as a moment to show Jack's willingness to be unfaithful; the many unanswered questions – does evil exist in all of us, does it wait for an opportunity to come to the surface? What is the significance of the framed picture on the wall at the end? Has Jack's soul been consumed by the building, just like the family in *Burnt Offerings* (1976)? Kubrick never explains. Indeed, he would often quote HP Lovecraft when dealing with actors and journalists and their questions, saying 'In all things that are mysterious – never explain.'

The scene which shows the torrents of blood gushing out of the lift doesn't seem to have any real purpose to the film except it's an amazing visual (and one that was used in a very effective teaser trailer). Other visual wonders include the aerial shots at the beginning, the hedge maze which seems to symbolise the character's predicaments; a ghost receiving a blowjob from another ghost in a bear costume; and of course, the page after page of a typed phrase which is perhaps the creepiest moment in the entire film.

The Shining was released in May 1980 in the US in an epic 142-minute cut. However, it wasn't long before Kubrick re-cut the film, discarding the 2-minute epilogue in which Wendy is treated in hospital and informed that no trace of her husband has been found on the grounds of the hotel (and this final scene will probably never be seen again, unfortunately). For European audiences, the film was drastically cut down to 119-minutes by the director himself as he assumed a more psychological spin on the tale would be better appreciated across the pond. So much for a 'definitive' director's cut then. The American longer cut is the best option, and it's only available on Region 1 DVD.

Cruising (1980)
Dir: William Friedkin /USA

Al Pacino plays an undercover cop in pursuit of a vicious serial killer who is targeting members of the gay community in New York. And, of course, as with any obsessed cop, the more embroiled in the case he becomes, the more his private life falls apart. *Cruising* – based on true events that took place in New York between 1962 and 1979 – was always going to be a controversial film. During filming, gay protesters turned up on set chanting slogans and throwing bags of urine at the crew members. And when the film was finally released – after United Artists literally destroyed around 40-minutes of footage – the protests only got bigger, with cops from the NYPD joining the pickets, outraged at the way their force was depicted in the film.

  Cruising isn't the disaster many film critics would have you believe, nor is it anything special. Take away the gay angle and seedy setting, and you have a typical incognito cop movie, like a sub-par *Serpico* (1973) or *The French Connection* (1971). The film also has much in common with William Lustig's *Relentless* (1989), in that the killer in that film shares a similar psychosis to the one in Friedkin's pic. Pacino's investigation into the slashings is depicted as being like a literal descent into hell. The gay clubs he visits are dark, subterranean pits. Disturbingly, the man awaiting trial for the real-life murders, Paul Bateson, had previously appeared in a small part in Friedkin's earlier film, *The Exorcist* (1973). Friedkin even visited him in prison and used their conversation to help flesh out his film script.

  Interestingly, during the making of *Dog Day Afternoon* (1975), Pacino famously refused to kiss his co-star on the lips as he felt it would

have been a bit gay. However, just a few years later, during the making of *Cruising*, he seemed happy enough to get down and dirty with leather bars, mascara and anal fisting. Anal fisting! Blimey, talk about becoming comfortable with one's sexuality.

The Beasts (1980)
(Orig title: *Shan Koa*)
Dir: Dennis Yu /Hong Kong

A Hong Kong take on the rape-revenge thriller, *The Beasts* follows a group of friends on a camping trip deep in the backwoods, and before you can say 'I Spit On Your Grave', these youngsters are terrorized by a gang of degenerate human monsters who make Krug and Weasel and co seem like a charming, misunderstood bunch. They rape and murder the teens, and the local police force seem utterly unconcerned with the violence and savagery going on in their midst. However, the father of one of the victims decides to take the law into his own hands, and he heads out to bring some brutal vigilante justice down on the scumbags, by luring them into makeshift booby traps – including the use of a wooden box with nails hammered into it for a particularly ghoulish trap, which I guarantee will make you cringe – and one by one, the ruthless "disco boys" are slaughtered in satisfying fashion.

  Despite pre-dating the CAT III rating by almost a decade, *The Beasts* is often cited alongside other examples of Hong Kong nastiness, such as *Her Vengeance* and *Suburb Murder*. Likewise, it's easy to spot the influence of Western exploitation flicks in this film, such as *Last House On the Left* and *I Spit On Your Grave*. And alongside *Devil Fetus* and *Dangerous Encounters of the First Kind*, this is one of the most outrageous films to come out of Hong Kong in the 80s. Much of the film is shot in 'stalker vision' with lurid, POV camera angles and has a tense and intimate feel overall. The bad guys are a cruel and nihilistic bunch, with one of them brandishing a knife and making silly growling noises. They're perhaps the ugliest set of villains you'll ever see, and would make the elephant man puke down his face-bag. The growling one looks like a freeze-frame snapshot of a horse's head imploding; the chubby one resembles Asia's answer to the marshmallow man in *Ghostbusters*. As for the rest, well, they're so grotesquely ugly it's difficult to make out which way up they are; you have to look for noses and mouths and work it out from there.

Bad Timing (1980)
(aka *Bad Timing: A Sensual Obsession*)
Dir: Nicolas Roeg /USA
Still a disturbing viewing experience to this day, Nicolas Roeg's *Bad Timing* was the subject of much controversy when it opened back in 1980. It's dark, depressing and grim as it tackles such contentious themes as obsession and necrophilia.

Roeg was no stranger to cinematic controversy. His debut feature, *Performance* (1970), was shelved for two years by Warner executives for its seedy nature; *Don't Look Now* (1973) found itself at the centre of speculation concerning the sex scene with Donald Sutherland and Julie Christie, with many believing that the actors were engaged in real intercourse; and *The Man Who Fell to Earth* (1976) was awarded with the X rating by the BBFC, effectively shifting the film beyond the reach of leading man, David Bowie's, army of devoted teenage fans who were too young to see it. However, it was *Bad Timing* that did the most to push the boundaries, and is still one of the bleakest movies of the early 80s.

Described by Kim Newman as 'almost like a Burroughsian cut-up of a *Columbo* episode,' *Bad Timing* is set in Cold War Vienna where a troubled young beauty, Milena (Theresa Russell), is rushed to hospital after taking an overdose. Art Garfunkel plays Alex Linden, a psychoanalyst who had an on/off relationship with Milena. Harvey Keitel plays the shrewd detective, Netusil, who suspects foul play and casts a suspicious eye on Linden from the outset. Over the course of the next two hours, the film flashes back and forth in time, eventually revealing a fiery relationship built on obsession and manipulation – a relationship that spirals out f control for the pessimistic finale.

Clues as to the central motif of the film are spread liberally throughout, from the book titles on view, the picture of the maze, Gustav Klimt paintings, and even the musical choices, from Tom Waits and Billie Holiday to The Who. Leading players, Russell and Garfunkel found filming a difficult experience and were on the verge of quitting the shoot within four days of filming. Roeg convinced them to stay by insisting that his film-making style was 'a maze, but there is an end to it.' However, executives at Rank were not so forgiving, with one of them famously describing *Bad Timing* as 'a sick film made by sick people for sick people.' Initial reviews were not much kinder; Leslie Halliwell called it 'weird and unsympathetic,' while *Variety* magazine called it 'an enervating experience. Technically flashy, and teeming with degenerate chic, the downbeat tale is unrelieved by its tacked-on thriller ending, and deals purely in despair.' You have been warned.

Out of the Blue (1980)
Dir: Dennis Hopper /Canada
Tagline: "*Her dad's in prison... Her mom's on drugs... the only adult she admires is Johnny Rotten.*"

Troubled teen, Cebe (Linda Manz), finds life difficult with a drug-addled mother and alcoholic, sexually abusive, ex-con for a father. She finds solace in the night life and seething nihilism of the local punk scene in Vancouver.

Dennis Hopper, God rest his soul, was always a contrary so and so; a man whose remarkable talents both in front and behind the camera were constantly off-set by his wild and self-destructive behaviour through drink, drugs, and pretentions, and whose steps up the filmic ladder were often met with sudden falls from grace. So much so that many times throughout his career he was considered basically unemployable by producers and directors, and Hollywood would often avoid him like the plague. The fact that he was also capable of a well-timed genius, combined with his engaging personality, offered him many 'second chances' that mere mortals like us could never hope to be granted. And right up until his death in 2010 he was always a firm fan favourite.

Hopper's career began in the 50s alongside James Dean in *Rebel Without a Cause* and *Giant*. This bright start soon drifted into improvisational chaos and 100-take madness that infuriated those around him, and banished him from the Hollywood hills. He returned in the late 60s with the low-budget *Easy Rider* which made a fortune and catapulted him to stardom, becoming one of the most bankable icons of the counter-culture era. But all of that success came to an end when he committed a second career suicide by heading deep into the jungle to make *The Last Movie*, with too much booze and drugs, but very little in the way of a script, or plan, or cohesion. By the late 70s he was referred to as "that photographer nutcase from *Apocalypse Now,*" and his once promising career seemed to be well and truly over.

Surprisingly, another comeback was on the horizon in 1980 during the making of *Out of the Blue*. Hopper had originally signed up to play Cebe's depraved father, but after writer/director Leonard Yakir jumped ship, Hopper was entrusted to take over the reins of the project. And much to everyone's surprise, he took to the helm with a sane and sober professionalism, managing a re-write of the script which incorporated his own dark vision, and remaining even-tempered throughout. He delivered the film on time, in budget, and with no complaints. The producer's gamble had paid off, and this independent Canadian feature was a hit with critics, despite its grim tones and punk aesthetics.

Hopper was rewarded with a Palm D'Or nomination at Cannes, and for a while seemed to be back in contention. But for all the modest success of *Out of the Blue*, he still hadn't fully purged his demons, and it wasn't until a few years later when he made yet *another* comeback as the psychotic Frank Booth in David Lynch's *Blue Velvet* did he finally reach some kind of contentment in his life and embraced the straight and narrow.

Out Of the Blue was described by *Time Out* magazine as "a film about extremes directed by an extremist", and indeed the film opens with Hopper crashing a truck into a bus load of school kids, and culminates in his daughter Cebe embracing the wreckage of human life in the city's punk clubs. The heart of the film lies in its cathartic energy, a destructive cry of anguish in the face of boredom, banality, poverty, and domestic hell; where the obliteration of self-destruction and a raw passion for noise and chaos is preferable to the quiet misery of trying to fix a broken home. Something Hopper could no doubt relate to (he certainly had no trouble in filling the role of the drunken wretch of a father!). An important and much overlooked gem.

Spetters (1980)
Dir: Paul Verhoeven /Holland

A flashy, fast-paced drama, *Spetters* is the story of Dutch teenage motocross enthusiasts Eve (Toon Agterberg), Hans (Maarten Spanjer), and Reen (Hans Van Tongeren), all of whom dream of being as tough and successful as motorcycle champ Witkamp (Rutger Hauer). Their youthful rebellion ends tragically for both Reen, who is crippled in an accident, and Eve, who is raped, beaten, and killed by a gang of violent homosexuals. Providing a sexual outlet for the teenagers, and just about every other biker on the wharf, is Fientje (Renee Soutendijk), a conniving creature who runs a greasy spoon with her gay brother.

Spetters is a violent, action-packed assault on the sensibilities of all but the most hardened filmgoers, not surprising given that it was directed by Paul Verhoeven, who would go on to score major successes in Hollywood with *Robocop*, *Total Recall*, and *Starship Troopers*, all of which were pretty excessive for mainstream audiences. With *Spetters* he demonstrates his penchant for startling visuals, explicit sex, and graphic violence, though his intelligent direction is anything but careless or irresponsible. Soutendijk and Joroen Krabbe would later co-star again in another classic Verhoeven film, *The Fourth Man* (1983). The film caused a scandal in its native Holland where critics, financiers and the public slammed Verhoeven for his harsh depictions of homosexuals, Christians, the police, and the press. The film was described as "perverted" and "decadent," but despite the controversy *Spetters* was a hit with audiences.

The Nesting (1980)
Dir: Armand Weston /USA

Director/producer Armand Weston made two great movies in 1980; *Night of the Demon*, a delirious 'bigfoot' caper, and *The Nesting*, which is one of the quintessential haunted house movies of the early 80s. The story follows Lauren (Robin Groves), an agoraphobic novelist. She visits the countryside with her friend, Mark (Christopher Loomis), and while walking in the wilderness they come across a crumbling old mansion. Lauren is startled by the building as it perfectly resembles the old house she had imagined while writing her novel, even though she has never seen it before. She and Mark enter the building to have a look around, and it seems to be deserted. They track down the owner, an old man ill of health (John Carradine), and Lauren convinces him to rent the house to her for a few months while she writes her next novel. On her first night alone in the spooky old building, she has a weird dream about stroking herself in front of a tall mirror, and very soon some ghostly goings on make her re-think her decision to stay – could she be losing her mind, or are there really ghosts in the house who want to communicate something to her?

The Nesting is a perfectly-paced little spooker that really ought to have a larger audience. If you enjoyed *Death at Love House* (1976), *The Shining* (1980), or *Heart of Midnight* (1988), then here is another movie in which a writer/lone woman experiences some creepy goings on while staying in a large empty building. Throughout the film we learn that the house was once a brothel in the 1940s, and a mass murder took place there. And during the climax, we learn just who Lauren really is – and this makes events leading up to the finale all the more poignant, such as Carradine's character collapsing when he first sets eyes on Lauren. Also, the house itself is very impressive; a large Victorian octagonal shaped structure, which, in its rotting derelict state looks like the ideal dwelling place for lost spirits. On the gore front, there are some nice surprises too. Lauren's psychiatrist comes to a sticky end when he falls – or is 'pushed' – off the roof and impaled through the eye; and a particularly odious character cops for a scythe in the face. Also, the horny handyman meets a nasty fate after trying to force himself on Lauren: an entity torments him by throwing him around the room. The dirty old man does manage to get his dick wet though when the ghosts of dead hookers drown him in a nearby lake. Weston started out in the porn industry, churning out nasty sado efforts like *The Defiance of Good* (1974) and *The Taking of Christina* (1976), before trying his hand at indie horror. It's a shame he didn't stick to the genre as his horror efforts still hold up quite well today. He died in 1988.

Altered States (1980)
Dir: Ken Russell /USA
Tortured by the idea of God after the death of his father, Professor Jessup throws himself into researching the idea of altered human states by experimenting with hallucinogens and submersing himself in a sensory deprivation tank with the purpose of experiencing the de-evolution of his own body. He soon finds himself altering beyond prehistoric man and into a form unknown by human knowledge or science. Yep, even beyond *Daily Mail* readers and chavs.

Never one to allow gripping tension or convoluted mystery to get in the way of colourful frenetic tricks and extremely extravagant imagery, Ken Russell came across a tale that was seemingly tailor-made to suit his wild style, with its delirious excesses and blasphemous content. The story is based on Paddy Chayefsky's novel (he also wrote the screenplay before disowning the film), and is quite frankly insane, but Russell earnestly delivers the movie version with such a gleefully outrageous style and aesthetic abandon it's like a grand ode to Kubrick's *2001* psychedelic showreel by way of *Dr. Jekyll and Mr. Hyde*. The end result is a delirious head-trip with enough clashing colours to make your eyeballs vomit.

The idea behind this lunacy is that man will regress to a primordial state without the outward stimulants of companionship, love, science, or even God. William Hurt in the lead role remains completely po-faced throughout, even while enacting the hilarious scene where he shifts about in his regressed state like a rampaging chimp. The mixing of the peyote with sensory deprivation is a recipe for a special effects light show bonanza in Russell's eyes, and it still looks pretty 'far out' even after three decades. During this trippy sequence, Russell intends for the screen to serve as a representation for the outer limits of human experience and understanding, and yet Professor Jessup could have achieved the same results by simply watching Russell's entire filmography on a loop.

Altered States is a horror movie at heart, with its religious iconography re-arranged and defiled before our eyes (including the sight of a goat with seven eyes). Even with such a ludicrous 'science-based' premise, there's still much in this film that is likely to offend, especially among those who are in any way religious. During the moments when all is seemingly back to normal, director Russell can't resist a devilish poke of fun here and there. The film ultimately stands as another in the long line of movies which depict doctors and scientists meddling with the forces of nature, and producing horrific results. The proposal scene is particularly funny as Jessup declares his love for his sweetheart in a psychiatric ward as a lunatic in the background is force-fed on hallucinogens. On the casting front, look out for Bob Balaban who went on to direct *Parents* (1989), Blair Brown who basically plays a pair of naked tits, and also a tiny Drew Barrymore in her first movie role.

Abnormal: The Sinema of Nick Zedd (1980-2001)

Dir: Nick Zedd /USA

This 2-disc set from the man who coined the term 'Cinema of transgression' includes a dozen short films mostly shot on 8mm that span twenty years of his career. They're presented chronologically but in reverse order for some reason, and are a hit and miss collection displaying the difficulties of being a super low-budget filmmaker whose main objective is to shock, provoke, and push the boundaries.

Tom Thumb In the Land of the Giants (1999) was shot in Copenhagen and is fashioned in a faux trailer style (a la Jim Van Bebber's *Chunk Blower* and Richard Gale's *The Horribly Slow Murderer With the Extremely Inefficient Weapon*). A child is running through a graveyard and is followed by a being in black. The voice-over is very tongue-in-cheek and sells the film well. The kid (played by Zedd's son) crawls into a huge vagina at the end. Running time: 3 minutes.

Ecstasy in Entropy (1999) 17 mins. This looks like a tribute to the old grindhouse movies of the 60s with its gritty style and constant barrage of tinny pop music. A bunch of strippers get into a fight and a man receives a blowjob before unloading half a bucket of (fake) spunk onto a woman's face. Then we switch to a colour scene where someone dressed in black and wearing a mask, strips and attempts to rape a woman (Annie Sprinke), but she fights back and amusingly drops some huge tit-bombs on his head while she rides on his back.

Why Do You Exist (aka *Screen Test*) (1998) 16 mins. This starts out quite fun and entertaining but outstays its welcome by a good ten minutes. It basically presents a group of people in front of the camera; a large woman puts squirty cream all over her tits, along with cinnamon and cherries, and then licks it off (or as Zedd puts it, "consuming a picnic on her tits"). More people posing and smoking a lot. The woman painted in blue and strumming an acoustic guitar (the 'Blue Lady,' Kembra Pfahler) was another highlight, but overall this isn't up to much. The film also features other underground personalities, including Brenda Bergman and Dr. Ducky DooLittle.

War Is Menstrual Envy (1992). Perhaps the highlight of the whole set. This excerpt from Zedd's feature film ranks among the finest work he has ever achieved. A woman painted almost entirely in blue (except for the pink nipples, reminiscent of Barbara Steele in *Curse of the Crimson Alter*) unwraps a mummified figure to reveal a man who has severe burns to his head, face, torso, and arms. It's clear that this guy is a real burns victim, and this makes the clip uneasy viewing. This sequence is played out to a light flute arrangement like from an old Disney movie, and this gives the proceedings a dark fairytale edge. In the next scene, the man is encountered by the infamous fetish porn actress, Annie Sprinkle, and she dresses him in a gun holster, a head scarf, and a pair of shades, takes them off again, and then kisses and licks his melted flesh. The man then sucks her tits for a while and tries to caress them, but finds it difficult because all his fingers have been melted together, and he struggles to make that lustful contact he so desires. I'm not sure what this clip means but it's mesmerizing stuff. The end credits are displayed with graphic footage of real eyeball surgery.

Whoregasm! (1988) 12 mins. A short collage/experimental film which juxtaposes images of hardcore sex and war footage through a process of tricky and inventive editing and over-lapping techniques. Perhaps Zedd's most technically impressive film to date. Again, there's no narrative here to speak of but it's quite engaging and much more interesting than some of the crap that gets passed off as 'experimental.' Includes graphic shots of fellatio, explosions, in-and-out penetration close-ups (some performed by Zedd himself), more explosions, and an image of a young boy whose hand is being held by a man who has an erection (whether this is a 'doctored' image or a real one I've no idea but it certainly adds to the transgressive nature of the film), a transvestite sucking a foot, a policeman screaming into the lens (that shot was taken from Zedd's previous short, *Police State*), and the transvestite receiving a blowjob from a woman.

Police State (1987) 18 mins. This micro-budget slice of punk nihilism could have been so much better, but as it stands it's a scrappy and uneven piece that at least adds a few nuggets of interest on repeat viewings. Perhaps the most disappointing film of the set due to the potential at its disposal, *Police State* is about a young man (played by Zedd himself) who is cornered and harassed for a while by a cop before he is taken to the station, interrogated, beaten by more cops, and eventually castrated. It shows an obvious disdain for the police and an Orwellian warning about where we're at as a society, sleep-walking into totalitarianism, which is a valid point to be made, but the acting, camera work, and script could have been so much better. According to the interview on the second disc, Zedd and his cohorts were almost caught by the cops vandalising police cars with spray paint during the making of the film.

Kiss Me Goodbye (1986) is another disappointment, but at least this one only takes up three minutes of your time. A man (again played by Zedd) wanders into a room to find a woman reading a book. He kisses and then strangles her. The end. Zedd appears as 'B.D. Shane', a 'dead star', and he apparently strangles one of his fans.

Go To Hell (1986) 11 mins. This one isn't much better. Zedd wanders around and sees a woman dressed in white and some junky shooting up into her arm. The junky follows the woman and beats her unconscious, and then Zedd shows up and kisses her as an atomic bomb blast goes off in the background. Music by The Swans who sound like an 80s version of The Doors.

Thrust In Me (1985) 8 mins. Things improve a lot with this one. This time Zedd plays two roles. Co-directed with Richard Kern (it's also included on Kern's *Hard Core Collection*). A tranny reads a book on suicide. Zedd walks the streets. Tranny gets into the bath and slashes her wrist. Zedd enters the apartment and takes a shit without noticing the bloody corpse in the tub. He takes a picture of Jesus off the wall and wipes his arse on it, and then notices the dead tranny. He then fucks the corpse in the mouth and shoots half a gallon of spunk on its head. He walks out onto the rooftop of the apartment and gazes at the New York skyline. Aww, who said romance is dead. It's a shame that Zedd and Kern ended their friendship over a "misunderstanding" as this film shows potential. Yes it's childish and you get the impression that they're trying really hard to offend you whilst at the same time pretending not to care what you think. But there is an undeniable power to this clip that probably stemmed from a competitive streak between the two. It would have been interesting to see more collaborations. A stunt porn star was also used.

The Wild World of Lydia Lunch (1983) 20 mins. Someone once dubbed this 'The Incredibly Dull World of Lydia Lunch', and to

be honest, I can't argue with that. Even many of Lunch's fans find this a crushing bore. It starts in a dark room where she reads a letter from someone complaining about being stranded in London with increasing money problems. Then it cuts to scenes of Lunch walking the streets of London (well, we see a red phone box so I assume it's somewhere in England), and a voice-over talks a lot of nonsense. She teases a cute dog, hangs out in the park, stands on street corners, and stares a lot into the camera lens. It's as if she is trapped in some kind of post-punk-pre-goth limbo.

The Bogus Man (1980) 11 mins. A satirical pseudo-documentary with weird clips of rehearsed and repeated voice-overs. A man in a ski mask tells of his warped ideas about the American President being a clone. He explains his conspiracy theory and shows us footage of a doctor under interrogation who shoots himself when asked why he has blood on his hands. We also see footage of the kidnapped President (actually, some dude in a Jimmy Carter mask). He is tied to a strange vaginal chair that has phallic prongs sticking out at either side, and someone cuts his finger off. We're told that the tissue from each finger will be used to generate more clones... The most disturbing scenes though are the ones featuring the woman (or is it a man?) in a full body suit dancing around in a room with an American flag displayed in the background. One of the freakiest things you'll ever see. This film is also notable as an early outing for special FX legend, 'Screaming Mad George' of *A Nightmare On Elm Street* (1984) and *Society* (1989) fame.

1 of K9 (2001). This last clip is in black and white and lasts just a couple of minutes. There looks to be an orgy going on in the background, and a woman takes hold of a dog's face and starts kissing it on the mouth with tongues and everything. The Doberman doesn't look to be too happy about being slobbered on (I suppose it makes a change, it's usually the dogs who slobber on us), and looks to be on the verge of chewing her face off at any moment. But then a man enters the frame, shoves the woman out the way, and then *he* starts to kiss and lick the dog's mouth; he almost has his tongue down its throat at one point. An amusing clip but I've no idea what it means.

So there you have it, 12 shorts that vary in terms of quality and re-watchability set over a twenty-one year period of film-making history.

None of them can really live up to the scummy triumphs of Zedd's debut feature, *They Eat Scum* (1979), but there are a few clips here that are worth a re-visit from time to time. It's a good place to start if you want to know what all the fuss was about in the New York underground. I should also point out that the extras on the second disc includes a very strange interview with Zedd taken from some old cable TV show. See it to believe it.

Nick Zedd made his debut feature, *They Eat Scum*, in the late 70s. Starring Donna Death as Suzy Putrid, she leads her Death Rock band, The Mental Deficients, to world domination when she kills her family and causes a core meltdown at a nuclear power station. The film features murder, cannibalism, bestiality, and a girl being forced to eat a live rat. It was broadcast on cable TV in 1982 causing much controversy when the *Wall Street Journal* condemned the screening with a damning front page article. The following year, Zedd returned with his second feature, *Geek Maggot Bingo, Or, The Freak From Suckweasel Mountain*. Coming on like a twisted take on the Universal monster cycle of the 1930s, *Geek Maggot Bingo* saw the return of Donna Death, along with Brenda Bergman and Richard Hell, and depicts an evil doctor who uses a slave to procure victims for his fiendish experiments.

In 1985 Nick Zedd wrote *The Cinema of Transgression Manifesto* for his fanzine, *The Underground Film Bulletin*. Written under the pseudonym Orion Jericho, Zedd calls for a rejection of traditional film theory and instead declares that he and his fellow underground filmmakers, including Richard Kern, intend on breaking every taboo they can in the name of freedom. His next feature, *War Is Menstrual Envy*, appeared in 1992, and is the first of his full-length films to break away from traditional narrative storytelling.

The Strangeness (1980)
Dir: David Michael Hillman /USA
An exploration party visits an old mine, Gold Spike, that has been closed for almost a hundred years. And while they explore the dark maze of rocks and tunnels, they spook each other with tales of urban legend about a creature that is said to have lived in the cave and killed dozens of miners back in the days of the gold rush. And in the final reel, the impressive monster makes an appearance... Released on VHS in Europe and North America in the mid to late 80s, *The Strangeness* was actually completed as early as 1980. It isn't the greatest monster movie ever made, but, considering how few people have seen it, this is well worth a watch, especially since it was re-issued on DVD. It boasts good characterisation, heavy atmospherics, and a Giger-esque clay-motion creature complete with a phallic-like head, creepy tentacles and a large, meaty vagina for a face.

The Babysitter (1980)
Dir: Peter Medak /USA
A much-ado-about-nothing TV movie about an interloper child minder who drives a family apart. We know she's a little loose in the head when she moans in orgasmic pleasure while clubbing a fish to death. She flirts with the husband (William Shatner) while wearing his wife's little black dress; she encourages mom to relapse into alcoholism; and when her concerned doctor investigates her past, he discovers she may have been responsible for the death of a baby. And when the family learn of her ways and try to oust her from the house, she figures if she can't be part of the family, then they all must DIE HORRIBLY. But fortunately, the Loomis-like Dr. Linquist shows up to save the day. Bloodless and derivative but watchable on a slow afternoon.

Last Rites (1980)
(aka *Dracula's Last Rites*)
Dir: Dominic Paris /USA
After a road race leads to a fatal crash, one of the surviving girls has her throat bitten and is then staked through the heart by medical staff at the hospital. The son-in-law of a recently deceased woman becomes suspicious when the staff refuse to hand over the body. He eventually uncovers a vampire conspiracy which also involves the town coroner and local Sheriff. *Last Rites* is a heavy-handed critique of corporate health institutions, but is a decent little vampire flick which has much in common with Peter Weir's *The Cars That Ate Paris* (1974). The film also pre-dates such similarly themed movies as *A Return to Salem's Lot* (1987) and *Blood on the Highway* (2007).

Prom Night (1980)
Dir: Paul Lynch /Canada
Starting with a prologue in which children cause a fatal accident while playing in an abandoned

building, the film cuts to six years later with Jamie Lee Curtis and her high school buddies preparing for the prom. Meanwhile, a detective hunts for a maniac whom he believes will strike again. With its Haddonfield-like suburban setting, *Prom Night* is a shameless Canadian cash-in on the success of John Carpenter's *Halloween* (1978), and features a godawful shit disco soundtrack and a bunch of super-annoying characters. *Prom Night* is a real chore to sit through; the first killing (after the death in the prologue) doesn't occur until the hour mark, and is a disappointingly bloodless throat slashing. In the meantime, we have to put up with time-padded dance scenes in which the mediocre students prance around like desperate animals on the dance floor, and the girls get bitchy with each other in their bathroom mirror congregations. Turns out the killer's psychosis was brought on by the guilt of witnessing the death of the child in the prologue. Pfft! *Prom Night* was followed by two sequels, *Hello Mary Lou: Prom Night II* (1987) and *Prom Night III: The Last Kiss* (1990). A disastrous remake appeared in 2008.

Effects (1980)
Dir: Dusty Nelson /USA
The long unreleased *Effects* is a calmer, more contemplative version of *The Last House On Dead End Street*. A filmmaker shows his cast and crew a realistic film of a woman being tortured and killed by a fat guy in a mask. When the viewers express their anger at being subjected to the footage, the director assures them that it's all fake. However, the camera man is not entirely convinced, and, after snooping around on set, he discovers that there is another film being made behind the scenes, something truly sinister which endangers everyone on set. *Effects* is a nicely subdued take on the snuff myth, avoiding all-out blood and guts in favour of a slow, horrific build-up and psychological tension. It has a slow start but patient viewers are rewarded with a great final third when the shit hits the fan. Fans of George Romero will spot a few familiar faces from his films, such as the director played by John Harrison who went on to compose the music for *Day of the Dead* (he also composed the score for this film, too, which sounds similar to Joe Delia's score for *Ms.45*, made around the same time). Also look out for Joe "Choke on 'em!!!" Pilato as the camera man who went on to play Captain

Rhodes in *Day of the Dead*. Tom Savini also appears as Mick, a hard partying coke-head who turns very nasty. *Effects* was never released in any format and basically sat gathering dust on a shelf for 25 years before being released on DVD by Synapse in 2005.

Stage Fright (1980)
(aka *Nightmares*)
Dir: John Lamond /Australia
Opening with a prologue/flashback sequence set in the early 60s, this film presents us with a young girl whose mental anguish at the hands of her abusive father causes her to lose her mind altogether when her mother dies in a car crash. She lashes out in a psychotic rage, stabbing her father in the throat with a broken glass. Cut to the present day, and the young girl, Helen, is now a grown-up actress who lands a role in a theatrical play called 'Comedy of Death.' Helen tries to live a normal life, and goes steady with a boyfriend. However, during moments of intimacy, she suffers flashbacks to her mother's affair with a strange, shadowy figure, and of course, the cast members are sliced and diced with glass shards by a maniac who stalks the backstage area...

Hailing from Melbourne, *Stage Fright* is a pretty solid Aussie entry from the slasher movie heyday, delivering its fair share of flesh and blood and intrigue. Though the film offers up some not very convincing red herrings, such as the pompous director and the snide theatre critic who are constantly at loggerheads, these setbacks are made up for with a rousing lead performance from Jenny Neumann as the quietly deranged Helen, lots of bloody kills, with the maniac using broken shards of glass as weapons, and lots of sex scenes which are fairly graphic for an early 80s slasher movie. On the music front, the grand orchestral score was provided by Brian May (no, not the Queen guitarist), who was one of Australia's finest film composers, and whose other credits include *Patrick* (1978), *Mad Max* (1979), *Snapshot* (1979), *Thirst* (1979), *Harlequin* (1980), *The Survivor* (1981), *Mad Max 2: The Road Warrior* (1981), *Escape 2000* (1982), *Freddys Dead: The Final Nightmare* (1991), and *Dr. Giggles* (1992).

Alligator (1980)
Dir: Lewis Teague /USA

This formulaically-plotted creature feature manages to rise above its lesser rivals thanks to a witty and engaging script by monster movie maven, John Sayles. Set mostly in downtown Chicago, this film pits a beleaguered cop (Robert Forster) against a gigantic, rampaging 'gator that has been living in the sewers since it was flushed down the toilet in the late 60s. For more than a decade it has been feeding on dead animals that were experimented on with illegal growth hormones, and now it has emerged from underground to terrorise the city... Of course, in Sayles' eyes, the monster here is one that gains viewer sympathy for devouring an assortment of shady characters; a pet thief (Sidney Lassick), who sells animals for illegal experiments, is taken out in the sewers while he tries to discard of some dead dogs, a smug hunter (Henry Silva) is eaten whole in a darkened backstreet, and in the finale, the 'gator (dubbed 'Ramon') emerges at a pool-side wedding reception and gloriously devours the tuxedoed guests who represent the city's corrupt side, from bad cops and self-serving politicians to members of the evil chemical corporation responsible for Ramon's condition.

He Knows You're Alone (1980)
Dir: Armand Mastrioianni /USA

A notorious serial killer whom detectives have failed to catch over the years, returns and continues his killing spree while setting his sights on a young woman who is soon to be married. This is a routine slasher movie which starts out quite promising. The opening scene set in the cinema with the film-within-a-film gimmick proved so effective an idea that the producers secured funding to make the film based entirely on the pitch of that opening scene. Spanish film-maker, Bigas Luna, was so impressed he stole the idea and managed to wring an entire tension-packed 90-minutes from the same idea for the excellent *Anguish* (1986). As for *He Knows You're Alone*, the bright start is soon muddied with a lacklustre and charmless middle and end.

The Hearse (1980)
Dir: Goerge Bowers /USA

Divorcee Jane (Trish van Devere) leaves San Francisco to move into her late aunt's country house that she has inherited. Early on, she finds the locals to be quite rude and unwelcoming, and there are rumours going around that the old house is haunted and that her aunt was a Devil worshipper. Others in the community also resent her moving in, such as a local lawyer who feels he should have inherited the property, and the only person willing to give Jane a helping hand is the shopkeeper's son who becomes somewhat infatuated with her. However, Jane's problems only get worse when a sinister-looking hearse repeatedly crawls up her driveway after dark and stalks her on the roads. She eventually strikes up a romance with a handsome stranger who, rather suspiciously, only ever shows up at night... *The Hearse* is a pretty solid effort, despite being a generic ghost story. All of the elements come together quite nicely: Jane's likeable and engaging heroine; the mournful score by Greg Poree, which is made up of strings and piano (and which also rips off the classic four-note refrain from *The Twilight Zone* theme); the large menacing hearse which looks similar to the demonic vehicle in *The Car* (1977); and a terrific lead performance from van Devere (who also appeared in Peter Medak's *The Changeling* in the same year). The ending is a little too open-ended, and modern horror fans may grow impatient with its laid back tempo, but for those who enjoy spook shows of old, with the quiet country setting and pervasive Gothic atmosphere, this comes recommended.

Demented (1980)
Dir: Arthur Jeffreys /USA

In the prologue, Sallee Elyse is gang-raped by country boys wearing tights on their heads. She has been badly affected by the experience, and is edgy and suffers from constant flashbacks. She begins to rebuild her life with the help of her cheating scumbag husband (Harry Reems). However, when intruders break into her house one night with the intention of raping her, she finally snaps altogether and gets even with the assailants by hacking at throats with a meat cleaver, and offing another's testicles with cheese wire. *Demented* is essentially an also-ran of the rape/revenge sub-genre, thanks to an awful performance by leading lady Elyse, and the pedestrian directorial style by one-time helmer, Arthur Jeffries. However, the film is worth a watch if only for the demented finale in which Elyse goes all twisted on us; she laughs whilst playing with the blood of her victims, and dresses in lingerie while humming a happy tune.

Like *I Spit On Your Grave* (1978), *Demented* is basically a melodramatic version of Zarchi's film; the castrated character even gets to vent his sorry excuses for wanting to rape the woman ("We just wanted a bit of fun"). But after listening to Elyse's annoying tirades in this film, it's easier to admire the way Zarchi decided to keep Camille Keaton's character mostly silent during her revenge spree in *I Spit On Your Grave*.

Fiend (1980)
Dir: Don Dohler /USA

The corpse of a recently-deceased music teacher is possessed by a demon and breaks out of the ground to attack a couple who are smooching nearby. The demon drains them of their life essence, and then moves into the local area, continuing as a violin teacher under the name 'Mr. Longfellow.' However, when more women are murdered in and around the neighbourhood, mustachioed Gary (Richard Nelson) investigates, casting a suspicious eye on the oddball Longfellow... This is one of Don Dohler's finest films with a creepy synth score by Paul Woznicki and a decent performance from Dohler regular, Don Leifert, as the demon corpse. If *The Alien Factor* (1977) was a little silly, and *Nightbeast* (1982) a little too subdued, then *Fiend* is nicely balanced in the middle, allowing it to be enjoyed by young monster fanatics and older horror aficionados alike. If there's anything wrong with the film, for me it would be the over-long scenes of dialogue between Gary and his wife. The film could have been shaved of a good ten minutes of extraneous padding for a much tighter film.

The Unseen (1980)
Dir: 'Peter Foleg' [Danny Steinmann] /USA

A TV reporter and her two assistants find themselves stranded in a town with no motel. So they spend a few nights at a house owned by a local museum owner, whose sister is severely withdrawn. On day two of their stay, one of the unlucky girls discovers that in the basement dwells a bloodthirsty being out to kill them all... This film plods along familiar territory up until the last half hour when the heroine gets locked in the basement. Things pick up immediately from there on in, with a blackly comic revelation as to the identity of the Sloth-like killer, which astute viewers will suspect long before the reveal. Director Steinmann was so disappointed with the final cut of the film that he had his name removed from the credits, but *The Unseen*, for all its faults, is worth a watch just for the crackpot ending. The film also pre-dates Wes Craven's *The People Under the Stairs* by more than a decade.

Zombie Holocaust (1980)
(aka *La regina dei cannibale*)
Dir: 'Frank Martin' [Marino Girolami] /Italy

An investigation into missing body parts leads a New York doctor (*Zombie Flesh Eater*'s Ian McCulloch) and his assistants to a tropical island where they are attacked by a savage cannibal tribe. And their day goes from bad to worse when a horde of shuffling zombies show up for a nibble. Turns out that a mad doctor is draining humans of their blood and reviving corpses by transplanting live brains into dead bodies. McCulloch and what's left of his team try to stop the experiments by befriending the cannibals and laying siege to the doctor's hideout... Something of a guilty pleasure, *Zombie Holocaust* works as a mish-mash of Italian exploitation cinema, appealing to zombie and cannibal freaks as well as fans of 'bad' films. The first half hour or so of the film was shot in New York by Roy Frumkes, making this a cut and paste job of two films spliced together. The entertainment value picks up considerably when the story reaches the island, and the action rarely lets up from there. There's lots of blood and gore as bodies are torn apart, and hearts and eyeballs are ripped out, and the beautiful assistant, Lori (Alexandra Delli Colli), has no qualms about getting her kit off. The film borrows elements from Ruggero Deodato's *Cannibal Holocaust* (1979) and Lucio Fulci's *Zombie Flesh Eaters* (1979), while also pilfering much of Nico Fidenco's score from *Emanuelle and the Last Cannibals* (1977). It was originally marketed as a zombie movie, and then later did the rounds again under its alternate title as a cannibal movie, effectively doubling the film's revenue.

Forest of Fear (1980)
(aka *Toxic Zombies*; aka *Bloodeaters*)
Dir: Charles McCrann /USA

A group of marijuana farmers with a secret dope field deep in the Pennsylvania woods, come under attack from a couple of trigger-happy cops. Once the officers have been garrotted to death, the remaining criminals decide to harvest their crops before any more law officers show up. Meanwhile back at the police headquarters, the Chief of police hires an alcoholic crop-duster pilot to spray the area with toxic pesticide, and the dope farmers find themselves transforming into lumbering ghouls. Of course, it isn't long before campers, hikers and more cops fall victim to the zombies... No one could possibly love this movie; you'll either hate it or be mildly amused by it. I fall into the latter camp. Overall, this is a real let down with weak, half-arsed zombie attacks and a muddled story line that runs out of steam before the 40-minute mark. However, for fans of early 80s video dreck laced with a synth-heavy soundtrack, and lots of screaming chicks in peril, you may find it tolerable. Also, fans of Jean Rollin's *The Grapes of Death* (1978) might get a kick out of it. Director Charles 'Chuck' McCrann died in the twin towers terrorist attack on September 11, 2001.

Revenge of the Stepford Wives (1980)
(aka *Terror in New York*)
Dir: Robert Fuest /USA
TV journalist Kay Forster moves into the town of Stepford to investigate why it has the lowest crime and divorce rates in America. There she befriends Megan, another outsider of the town whose husband is there on a work assignment. And it isn't long before Kay encounters the weirdness when she is almost run over by a droid-like, mechanized lady, who later has no memory of the incident. Kay digs deeper and discovers a populace of servile women (or, as she puts it, "an empty-headed bunch of plastics") who are obsessed with cleaning, and tuppaware, appliances and domesticity. And if everything's a little out of whack in the strange town, things only get worse when she is attacked with a meat cleaver, and, to her horror, sees that the usually witty and no-nonsense Megan has become just another bubble-headed part of the community. Kay then sets out to rescue Megan from the white-washed suburban hell. Although it feels like a TV movie and is quite predictable, this is actually a decent sequel to the mid-70s classic, *The Stepford Wives*, that continues the original's theme of how people in affluent neighbourhoods become monstrous snobs.

Dark Night of the Scarecrow (1981)
Dir Frank De Felitta /USA
When a little girl is mauled by a dog, the local town retard, Bobba, is blamed for her injuries. A lynch mob with sniffer dogs hunt the man down to a corn filed and they find him hiding in a scarecrow. They open fire on him. And after the men are cleared of murder, Bobba's mother breaks down in court and utters a veiled threat: "There is another justice in this world besides the law!" Meanwhile, the little girl makes a full recovery, and though no one has told her about what happened to poor Bobba, she insists that they still play together. And the men responsible for Bobba's death begin dying off in a series of brutal 'mishaps'... *Dark Night of the Scarecrow* is a bone-fide cult classic and one of the most memorable TV movies of the early 80s. It went on to inspire other classic like *Scarecrows* (1988) and *Pumpkinhead* (1988). There's no blood or graphic gore here, but the story unfolds in a gripping and believable way, with a deliberate ambiguity to it; are these evil men really being killed off by an avenging scarecrow, or are they simply unravelling psychologically due to paranoia and unconscious guilt? Charles Danning steals the show as the bigoted town mail man and leader of the posse. He's much smarter and more cunning than his fellow conspirators, but his attempts to cover his tracks only leads him into making an even dirtier mess, like a good old EC comics villain of old.

Tales of Ordinary Madness (1981)
Dir: Marco Ferreri /Italy/France
Charles Bukowski is among the most translated and respected American writers in Europe, but for many years he was almost completely ignored in his homeland. Barbet Schroeder's *Barfly* (1987) soon helped to change all that, but *Tales of Ordinary Madness*, an Italian-French co-production, was the first to bring his wino wisdom to the big screen. This is a hit and miss effort though, and almost completely disowned by Bukowski.

Adapted from the collection of stories, *Erections, Ejaculations, Exhibitions, and General Tales of Ordinary Madness*, Marco Ferreri seemed like the perfect director to tackle Bukowski's prose (he had previously made *Bye Bye Monkey* and *The Last Woman*). Ferreri had a deft touch for perversity and excess that a screen adaptation of Bukowski would require, but the finished film just doesn't quite work. Ferreri insists on adding a mushy, sentimentality to the film and goes for a mildly uplifting ending, and it was this that caused Bukowski to abhor the end result (though it didn't stop him from reaping every penny he could in royalties). The author does have a point though; the film barely gets to grips with the dark and twisted humour of his writings, and portrays Bukowski himself as overly-sensitive and overly-pretentious. But despite these missteps, *Tales of Ordinary Madness* is definitely worth a look.

After delivering a brilliant drunken speech, Charles Serking (Ben Gazzara) takes us on a lurid trip through LA with his trusty six pack of beers by his side. He touches up a thirteen year old girl, spots a blonde woman on a swing ("she had an ass like a wild animal"), follows her home and then 'rapes' her. He later catches the eye of the beautiful, masochistic Cas (Ornella Muti, who also appeared in Ferreri's *The Last Woman*). Cas is a prostitute and she performs an impromptu cheek-piercing stunt at the bar with the aid of a giant safety pin by way of introduction. Charles is immediately smitten but when he takes her back to his place he refuses to sleep with her until dawn. A drunken writer and a beautiful, self-mutilating woman doesn't exactly sound like a match made in heaven, and no sooner have they got together and Charles begins slapping her and treating her mean. Cas responds by using the extra-large safety pin to pierce her labia as a way of closing her vagina in a symbolic gesture of love.

Tales of Ordinary Madness is not for all tastes, but for anyone curious about the work of Marco Ferreri this is perhaps the best place to start as it's his most accessible film. Overall, the film lacks the outrageousness of *La Grande Bouffe*, and it fails as an adaptation of Bukowski (also Muti's performance is pretty bad – her acting range basically amounts to two different ways of pouting), but still there is much to keep viewers engaged here.

Mad Max 2: The Road Warrior (1981)
(aka *The Road Warrior*)
Dir: George Miller /Australia
If the original *Mad Max* was a gritty and personal example of the darkness of 70s cinema, *Mad Max 2* is very much a product of the 80s – an operatic, excessive and sometimes silly grand spectacle. And this clear contrast between the films and the decades in which they were produced, is all the more remarkable considering the films were made just two years apart.

Picking up not too long after the end of the first film, we find Max scavenging for food and fuel, both of which are now in very short supply. Max has witnessed the total collapse of civilisation since we last saw him, and he is still very much a lone warrior – though he does have a companion, his pet dog, that he presumably picked up on the road during his aimless travels. He is no longer a man-of-the-law as there are no longer any laws to defend. Instead, the desert wasteland is now ruled over by an army of violent barbarians who roam around raping, killing and pillaging anyone who isn't them. And though Max is still burned out and badly affected by the deaths of his girlfriend and child, he does at least find a spark of humanity left within himself to help a small community fend off the savage barbarians who have laid siege to their compound with demands for their precious oil...

The Road Warrior reveals its hand quite early on as a continuation of the western. The time and place may have been altered and updated for modern audiences, but the traditions are the same. And this new frontier is just the same old outpost community struggling to survive in a Hellish land devoid of law and order. And the besieged homestead is populated with the same old archetypes: Max is the world-weary anti-hero – the mysterious 'Man With No Name' in classic Clint Eastwood tradition. Those around him can sense that he has emerged from a traumatic past, but they fail to get him to talk about it. By the end of the film, they know just as little about him as they did before. The leader of the bad guys, Humungus (Kjell Nilsson), is an updated version of the ruthless Apache leader. And, of course, the mohawked, feral bad guys are a stand-in for the savage native Indian tribe. Only, instead of roaming around on horseback, they get to fire their arrows from hotrods and futuristic armoured vehicles.

In the westerns, the Indians attacked a wagon train for the precious whiskey cargo in *Hallelujah Trail* (1965); they attacked a peaceful Texas homestead in *The Searchers* (1956); fortified wagon trains were their targets in *Red River* (1948) and *Winchester '73* (1950). Also, a group of travellers came under threat from Geronimo in *Stagecoach* (1939), and peaceful settlers were raided and killed by the savages in *Hondo* (1953). The peaceful community in *Mad Max 2* remains just as bewildered and fearful as the victims in the films mentioned above, and director George Miller portrays them with compassion, making sure to reveal their moral core, *as well as their fighting pioneer spirit*, despite facing off against a horde of vicious sadists in a lonely, isolated outpost of the new 'wild west.' This allusion to the westerns of old is also echoed in Max's friendship with the feral boy, which recalls Alan Ladd's gunslinger and his idolising young buddy in *Shane* (1953). Miller wasn't the first film-maker to update the western for modern audiences; Wes Craven had already done so a few years previously with *The Hills Have Eyes* (1977). In Craven's horror film, the vulnerable wagon of the western was replaced with a trailer as a family is attacked in the desert wilderness by an inbred tribe of savage mutants. The family under siege were likewise just ordinary Americans who had suddenly found themselves isolated from the moral decency of the civilisation they had previously taken for granted. And we the viewers are forced to watch on as morality is ultimately forced into the back seat while the family embraces a brutal and savage instinct in their efforts to stay alive.

This contrast between 'society-as-it-should-be,' compared with the reality of 'society-as-it-really-is,' has since moved away from the western and the post-nuke worlds, and found new life in recent times with the advent of the zombie apocalypse. Most notably in *The Walking Dead* (2010-), where Mad Max is reincarnated as Rick Grimes, a former lawman who awakens from a coma one day to find that civilisation has collapsed. Throughout the series, Grimes – like Max – loses the woman he loves, which in turn causes him to go 'mad' for a while, before he finds his humanity again, just in time to defend a prison homestead from the reincarnation of his old enemy Humungus, The Governor, who has appeared behind the fortifications with his feral army, demanding their precious resources. Just like George Lucas with his *Star Wars* movies, George Miller was also fascinated by myth (he was a devotee of scholar/guru, Joseph Campbell, long before those ideas became a cinematic trend), and he deliberately infuses his film with a connotative richness that borrows from the heroic tradition and Homer's *Iliad*.

Critics sometimes bemoan the overblown nature of the film, and the lack of character development for Max since the original (in *Nightmare Movies*, Kim Newman joked that the killing of Max's dog 'robbed him of a significant part of his identity'), but *Mad Max 2* is most certainly a film for fans rather than critics. The final 20-minutes of *Mad Max 2* features a wagon ride through Hell as we get to see more thrills, spills, wreckages and daring stunts than a dozen other action movies combined. And don't forget, all of this was filmed for real, with none of that fancy CGI nonsense. This 'carmageddon' took weeks to shoot, and every painstaking shot is expertly choreographed by Miller (who, astonishingly, was working on only his *second* feature film at the time). In *Destroy All Movies!!! The Complete Guide to Punks on Film*, Rob Fletcher contributed a glowing, nostalgia-filled review for *Mad Max 2*: 'Growing up, this is what I hoped the future would be like,' he wrote. 'Custom-fitted cars with mounted weaponry; dune buggies filled with angry pro wrestlers; crossbow battles on motorcycles.' All I can say is, with the world heading in the direction it is right now, his old childhood hopes may become a reality yet.

The Road Warrior has had a huge influence on cinema over the years – the Italians made an entire movie industry out of ripping it off! There was *1990: The Bronx Warriors* (1982), *The New Barbarians* (1982), *2020 Texas Gladiators* (1982), *2019 – After the Fall of New York* (1983), *Blood Rush* (1983), *Exterminators of the Year 3000* (1984) and *A Man Called Rage* (1984), as the most glaring examples among them. Elsewhere, other low-budget imitators include *Battletruck* (aka *Warlords of the 21st Century*, 1982), *Stryker* (1983), *Wheels of Fire* (1985), *Hell Comes to Frogtown* (1987) and *Steel Dawn* (1987), the latter ditching the vehicles for martial arts. Even the Japanese got on board with ultra-violent anime fare, such as *Violence Jack 3: Hell's Wind* (1990). Actor, Vernon Wells, who played the psychotic Wez, went on to reprise his memorable role in John Hughes' *Weird Science* (1987). Hollywood borrowed the plot, though they did change the locations to a lonely ocean apocalypse, for *Waterworld* (1995), and a distant waste disposal planet for *Soldier* (1998). And the studios recycled various odds and ends for other hits, including *Robocop* (1987), *The Crow* (1994) and *Demolition Man* (1993), before George Miller returned to the fray with *Mad Max: Fury Road* (2015).

Escape From New York (1981)
Dir: John Carpenter /USA

Set in the future, 1997, where crime has gotten so out of control that Manhattan island has been sealed off as a maximum security prison surrounded by federal law enforcement. It has become the dumping ground for all the country's undesirables and criminal waste. The President's plane has been hijacked by members of a criminal gang, and crash-landed in the rotten heart of the city. The maniacs are now holding him to ransom. The police – headed by Commissioner, Hauk (Lee Van Cleef) – recruits a moody, eye-patch wearing bank robber, 'Snake' Plissken (Kurt Russell), to head into the danger zone to rescue the President and save the day. But he only has 22 hours to do so. His reward? If successful, Snake will be pardoned by the state. And if he fails? He will be killed by the poison the authorities have injected into his neck.

So, off he goes, landing atop of the World Trade Centre in a glider plane in the dark. And pretty soon, Snake is traversing the debris-strewn streets and fighting against various street punks, savages and scavengers before he comes up against 'Duke' (Isaac Hayes), the top gangster of the lawless city who has the President in his custody, and who is surrounded by an army of maniacs...

John Carpenter's decimated Manhattan is a perpetually dark and gloomy vision of a comic book caper brought to life. Pre-dating *Blade Runner* (1982) by a year, Carpenter manages to pull off an epic scale future fantasy with only a fraction of the budget Ridley Scott had at his disposal. Carpenter also contributes to the soundtrack which mixes mellow synths and disco beats. The opening scenes have an apocalyptic vibe about them, reminiscent of the opening scenes of George Romero's *Dawn of the Dawn* (1978) – a chilling vision of society in meltdown and the authorities struggling to cope.

Kurt Russell was never the best action hero in the movies, but his turn here is very well done. Of course, he would go on to damage his credibility after a string of indifferent action roles and ill-advised romantic comedies, but *Escape From New York* (along with Carpenter's *The Thing* [1982] remake the following year), saw him in his element, as a resourceful, no-nonsense badass. Interestingly, Snake, as the archetypal rugged anti-hero, is a throwback to Sergio Leone's spaghetti westerns, specifically Clint Eastwood's 'Man With No Name,' and the moral ambivalence and laconic line deliveries of Snake may as well have been uttered from Eastwood's cigar-chomping lips. The loner-warrior role would be later embraced by the post-apocalypse genre that flourished in the 80s, with everything from the *Mad Max* movies to *Future-Kill* (1985), and even Japanese anime flicks, such as *Fist of the North Star* (1984) and the *Violence Jack* series (1986-1990), all featuring protagonists whose moral stances are compromised by their deviant nemeses and Hellish surroundings. And this link between Snake and the 'Man With No Name' is underscored by Carpenter in his choice of casting Lee Van Cleef in the role of the Police Commissioner, whose sly and ugly conduct (having Snake injected with poison), leaves viewers very much on the side of Snake.

Elsewhere on the casting front, Oscar winner, Ernest Borgnine plays the strangely upbeat cab driver; Harry Dean Stanton appears in a more familiar role as 'Brain,' one of Snake's shifty old accomplices from his bank robbing days; Donald Pleasance plays the U.S. President, which is fairly odd, considering he doesn't even pretend to conceal his English accent; Adrienne Barbeau doesn't have much to do besides show off her cleavage; Frank Doubleday is notable for his wardrobe alone – here he plays Romero, one of the Duke's top cronies, with his hair spiked a foot high and the rest of him clad in punk-style get up; and there's even an appearance from Tom Atkins as one of the police officials – he would later go on to take the lead role in the underrated *Halloween III: Season of the Witch* (1982).

Escape From New York is a true off-beat classic. And the film's solid reputation is no doubt helped considerably by Carpenter's typically straight forward approach – there are no sub-plots here to bog things down and disrupt the rhythm; instead, the scenario is allowed to play itself out for maximum tension and effect. Carpenter even began the trend of naming his supporting characters after famous genre film-makers, such as Romero and Cronenberg. George Romero himself returned the tribute in *Creepshow* (1982) the following year, as a 'Mrs. Carpenter' is devoured by an ape. Sam Raimi placed a torn poster for Wes Craven's *The Hills Have Eyes* on the set of *The Evil Dead* (1982), to which Craven returned the jibe by showing a poster for Raimi's film in a scene in *A Nightmare On Elm Street* (1984). And the insider name-checking trend continued into the 00s with films such as *Sleepwalkers* (1992), *The Dead Hate the Living!* (1999), *Hack!* (2007), and many others.

The influence of Carpenter's film had an immediate impact on the slew of apocalypse movies that were churned out in the 80s, particularly those made by the Italians – *The Bronx Warriors* (1982), *Escape From the Bronx* (1983), *Exterminators of the Year 3000* (1983), etc, all took turns at pilfering as much of the plot as possible from Carpenter's film without crossing over into plagiarism. *Con Air* (1997) was a big-budget mainstream flick that also borrowed elements from the film. But it was perhaps George Romero who paid the ultimate tribute by turning the premise on its head; for *Land of the Dead* (2003), he re-imagined the future city as a luxurious prison for the rich, this time with undesirables in the form of zombies trying to break *inside*. Carpenter later returned with the less successful sequel, *Escape From L.A.* (1996).

The Burning (1981)
Dir: Tony Maylam / USA

A prank misfires at an upstate New York summer camp, leaving the caretaker, Cropsy, badly burned. Five years later, and a whole bunch of odious, over-confident high school kids arrive at the summer camp to indulge in their care-free fun and pranks and bitching. Meanwhile, Cropsy has undergone the agony of failed skin-grafts, and is lurking in the nearby woods with a pair of shears, just waiting to send the little bastards to hell…

While there can be no denying the influence of *Friday the 13th* here, *The Burning* actually took its biggest cue from 'Cropsey', an age-old American campfire legend about a disfigured doctor or judge seeking revenge on subsequent generations of young campers after a gone-wrong prank (it was also the inspiration behind another slasher movie, 1982's *Madman*). This film actually surpasses *Friday the 13th* in terms of tension, atmosphere and creepiness. It also gets down to the nasty bits in good time (whereas *Friday* seems to take an age to get going). Rick Wakeman provides the quirky electronic score which serves as a nice backdrop to the slaughter. *The Burning's* ace card, though, is the casting; these young characters are so teeth-grindingly annoying it's a joy to watch

them being cut, stabbed, and slashed to ribbons by the crazed killer.

It isn't the best slasher movie from that period (William Lustig's *Maniac* beats it in every department); there are numerous plot-holes and nonsensical asides. It's also chock-full of just about every slasher movie cliché of its time, with characters saying things like "I'll be right back" just before they venture off to meet their doom, the usual conservative hang-ups about sex and freedom that must have had Kevin Williamson popping a hard one while researching *Scream*. There are also the annoying point-of-view stalking shots that flit between Cropsy and having viewers believing it to be Cropsy when it isn't, kind of thing. This being a low-budget slasher movie, logic and sophistication are at the bottom on the list of priorities here, but for the sheer thrill of watching a group of morons get slaughtered, *The Burning* gets the job done. The most notable deviation from the *Friday the 13th* template is that the heroic virgin who is terrorized throughout but perseveres to become the sole survivor of the slaughter is a geek boy (played by Brian Backer) rather than the usual plucky and resilient Jamie Lee Curtis clone in the 'final girl' situation.

The most famous sequence in the film – and the one which helped to get it outlawed as a 'video nasty' in the UK – sees Cropsy leaping onto a raft on the river, and in about 30 seconds (and with just as many quick-fire edits) a group of teens are butchered with a pair of shears; chests and throats are stabbed, heads slashed open, and one unlucky kid grimaces in terror as his fingers are lopped off. We have special effects legend, Tom Savini, to thank for this memorable sequence. Savini once created a severed head that looked so realistic the police took it in as evidence of a genuine murderous decapitation. Fact.

Directed by Englishman Tony Maylam, who had previously scored a modest success with *The Riddle of the Sands* (1979), *The Burning* marked the pinnacle of his film-making career as he hasn't been up to much in the movie world since. Maylam's film also 'crops' up on embarrassing credits forums; lookout for early appearances from Holly Hunter in a bit-part role (she would go on to win a Best Actress Oscar for her performance in *The Piano*), Fisher Stevens as 'Woodstock' (who later showed up in *Short Circuit*), and Jason Alexander of *Seinfeld* fame who here serves as the token blobbo boy. Furthermore, the screenplay was co-written by future Miramax boss and Oscar winner, Harvey Weinstein.

The controversy surrounding the film in the UK in the 80s was triggered by the distributors accidentally releasing the uncut version on video after the theatrical version had already been sheared of it bloodiest bits. This led to the tape being included on the Department of Public Prosecution's 'video nasties' list, and the film was effectively banned on VHS in 1983. It was later passed by the censors in 1992 in a cut version and was released on Vipco Video. Those cuts were eventually waived by the BBFC in 2001. In America, *The Burning* was initially cut by the MPAA of just over a minute of footage to secure the R-rating, and it was later released unrated on video and DVD.

Cannibal Ferox (1981)
(aka *Make Them Die Slowly*)
Dir: Umberto Lenzi /Italy

Perhaps the most outrageous entry in the Italian cannibal cycle of the late 70s and early 80s, *Cannibal Ferox* was part of that list of banned movies – the 'video nasties' – which assaulted viewers and censors alike in the 80s. The film caused much controversy in America where it was released under the title *Make Them Die Slowly*, complete with a sleazy and graphically violent trailer. News media and current affairs programmes paraded its shocking images on television as an example of how depraved modern horror had become, with claims that the nation's youths were being corrupted by this type of fare. And when Elvira, Mistress of the Dark refused to film an introduction for its Thriller Video release, this eventually led to the MPAA tightening its restrictions on screen violence. The word 'ferox' is Latin for 'ferocious', and this should give viewers a good idea of what to expect here, as its catalogue of carnage – including real animal killings and gruesome death – makes it one of the most deeply unpleasant viewing experiences you'll ever have.

A couple of hard-boiled New York cops led by Robert Kerman harass a local drug dealer, Mike (John Morghen, aka Giovanni Lombardo Radice). Meanwhile, grad student Gloria (*Emanuelle In America's* Lorraine De Selle) is writing her thesis on the premise that cannibalism is just a myth, and heads off to the rainforest in South America. She is joined by good guy Rudy (Danilo Mattei) and the promiscuous Pat (*New York Ripper's* Zora Kerova). After their jeep breaks down in the mud, they're forced to trek through the jungle on foot, and this is when they bump into Mike and his pal. Turns out this dodgy duo have just escaped death at the hands of a cannibal tribe who have killed and eaten their friend. But Mike's sinister manner leads us to believe there's more to the story than he lets on. Pat beds down with Mike that same night, and in the morning he encourages her to molest and torture one of the native girls. So now we know for sure what decent a guy he is. And soon we learn that Mike and his buddy had ripped off some mobsters in New York and then fled to South America in search of emeralds and cocaine. After a drug-fuelled sex scene and some pointless animal killing, the cannibals soon descend on the Americans to inflict some graphically gruesome punishment – Mike is tied to a tree, has his dick cut off, is then relieved of the top of his head and has his brains eaten. Pat is subjected to an excruciating death which involves being suspended in the air with metal hooks through her breasts. A sympathetic native leads Gloria out of harm's way and is killed as a consequence. She eventually makes it back to New York and receives her doctorate in which she still insists that cannibalism doesn't exist, and keeps the horrors she had witnessed in South America to herself.

While many viewers were rightly appalled by the animal butchery on display here, many also see it as a camp classic due to the awful dubbing and amusing dialogue ("They, they... ATE HIS GENITALS"). The animal scenes are, of course, sickening and tasteless, and turns what could have been an over-the-top gore movie into something altogether more dangerous and indefensible. Whereas Ruggero Deodato had crafted a more serious and intricate film with *Cannibal Holocaust*, in keeping with his bleak and nihilistic worldview, Umberto Lenzi, on the other hand – who was never a fan of horror movies – simply trudges through the jungle, camera in hand, in an attempt to film anything that will keep the gorehounds happy without any regard for anything or anyone. For all the atrocities on show in *Cannibal Holocaust*, its director did at least have a vision, albeit a depraved immoral one. But Lenzi shot *Cannibal Ferox* with nothing in mind other than creating a quick exploitation pic that would out-do *Holocaust* in shocking and tormenting its audience. And that to me is an extremely messed-up thing to do. Indeed, during this period, Lenzi and Deodato seemed to be in some sort of gross pissing contest to see who could make the most shockingly outrageous film, and this only came to an end when Deodato found himself on trial for murder. And for a horror film, *Cannibal Ferox* never feels authentic in the way Deodato's movie does; as a genre novice, Lenzi clearly didn't have a clue what he was doing out there in the jungle, and was always much more interested in crime thrillers and *gialli*.

Shooting on location in the Amazon rainforest turned out to be almost as gruelling an experience as the doomed characters face in the film. There was the humidity and heat, the isolation and makeshift living conditions, and of course the strange exotic wildlife all around them, as Giovanni Lombardo Radice explains: "It was just terrible. When the Almighty invented the Amazon he must have been very upset. It's not a place for human beings to be in. Everything is so rough; the weather, the humidity, the animals, the insects, the snakes. Even dolphins are bad in the Amazon. Once, I was on a canoe with Zora Kerova and we were having lunch, which consisted of the two sandwiches they gave us. All of a sudden, there was this big huge fish a bit far away that was jumping in and out of the water as a dolphin would do, but it was red. Zora said 'oh c'mon, let's go and see the fish'. Just to please her I started rowing, and in a minute there was another canoe with Indios following us and saying 'no no no no no' and making big gestures. Then they explained that this 'fish' was a kind of dolphin, but it's nasty and would try to turn the canoe upside down and bite you. It's a terrible place."

And it wasn't just the strange tropical creatures and harsh environment that was hostile; many of the cast and crew members took an instant dislike to the director, and would undermine him at any opportunity. During the filming of the scene in which an anaconda crushes a small caoti, Lenzi was dismayed when the snake seemed to get bored and released the critter. And when the director ordered his assistant to step in and somehow force it to swallow the poor thing, the cinematographer switched off the camera and shouted "Cut, that's

enough," and this caused fisty-cuffs between the enraged Lenzi and his DoP.

After a moderately successful theatrical run in Europe, *Cannibal Ferox* opened at the Liberty grindhouse in New York (which specialized in Euro-sleaze), complete with lurid ad-mats displayed in the lobby showing giant stills of some of the gruesome scenes in the film. Even the hardcore 42nd Street crowd was repulsed by what they saw, as Bill Landis noted in *Sleazoid Express*: "There wasn't one member of the Liberty Theatre audience who didn't holler or groan aloud during the course of the movie."

In the UK, *Ferox* was released on VHS in 1983 in an edited form with most of the animal footage dropped. Trims were also made to scenes of sexual violence and excessive gore. Prior to the Video Recordings Act of 1984, these cuts were considered "informal" by the BBFC. But once the VRA came into effect as a piece of legislation, all such 'informally' classified videos had to be submitted to the BBFC again and judged anew in accordance with the precise terms of the VRA. By this point, both the cut and uncut versions of *Cannibal Ferox* had been deemed 'video nasties' and prosecuted under sections 2 and 3 of the Obscene Publications Act, and it wasn't until the year 2000 that the ban was finally lifted. The distributors had hacked out around five minutes of footage and submitted it for classification, with the BBFC cutting a further six seconds to remove the "sight of small animal on end of rope banging against side of a jeep." And this is the version that remains legal in the UK today.

Trapped (1981)
(aka *Baker County, USA*)
Dir: William Fruet /USA

Backwoods horror of the post-*Deliverance* (1972) variety which sees a group of youngsters out camping in the woods witness a brutal murder at the hands of Henry (Henry Silva), an angry hillbilly who had caught the man in bed with his wife. The kids make a run for it to the nearby shack town to report the crime, but the locals are Henry's friends, and the kids soon find themselves trapped in a cellar beneath a convenience store awaiting their fate at the hands of the increasingly unhinged Henry... *Trapped* makes great use of menacing wilderness locations, and there is a complicated morality at play, which was quite rare in horror films of the time. Silva stands out as the star of the show – he's easily one of the finest redneck maniacs in film history – as the unstable patriarch of the town who is having one of those days where everything goes wrong. Admirably, the film-makers keep things tense and deadly serious; these yokels aren't picked out as figures of fun, unlike many more recent films which deal with backwoods maniacs. And there is a very plausible feel for the outer realms of 'white trash' culture.

The Appointment (1981)
Dir: Lindsey C. Vickers /UK

A very obscure and intriguing oddity starring Edward Woodward as a father who embarks on a business trip after premonitions that he will crash his car on the mountain roads and die. An odd and dreamy little film where the plot holes serve as mysterious asides rather than a hindrance to the overall atmosphere that the film creates. There are enough clues to suggest that the finished film turned out to be very different from the original script – perhaps the film-makers ran out of funds before some of the key sequences were shot, and had to make do with the footage they had. But, considering how little information there is about this film (even *IMDb* is severely lacking even some of the most basic information), the truth can only be guessed at. The opening scene shows a schoolgirl falling victim to a serial killer. However, this plot-line is then dropped entirely in favour of the relationship between Woodward's character and his teenage daughter, with disturbing and incestuous undertones. Utterly bizarre but certainly worth a watch

Ms.45 (1981)
(aka *Angel of Vengeance*)
Dir: Abel Ferrara /USA

One of the finest urban revenge movies of all time, *Ms.45* finds director Abel Ferrara dispensing with the macho vigilante likes of Charles Bronson and instead opting for the silent flower of Zoe Tamerlis. The results are frankly mesmerizing.

Young mute Thana (Tamerlis), is dragged into an alley and raped and robbed by a masked assailant (played by Ferrara himself under his pseudonym, 'Jimmy Laine'). Bloody and bruised, Thana arrives home only to be attacked again by an intruder. But this time she fights back and ends up killing the scumbag by bashing his head in with an iron. Rather than call the police, Thana drags the corpse into the bath tub and saws it into little pieces that she then wraps into paper packages and attempts to dispense in the waste bins of New York City. However, her plans for disposal are risky, and her pretty looks draws much attention from the male members of society. Unable to cope with the stress any longer, Thana snaps and goes on a killing spree, culling the male population of Manhattan. By the film's finale, Thana dresses as a nun and attends a work party with a loaded pistol and a bloody massacre in mind...

Ms.45 was Ferrara's follow-up to *The Driller Killer*, and like that previous film it got caught up in the 'video nasties' panic and was banned in the UK due to the 1984 Video Recordings Act. It became an urban classic and one of the most hotly debated titles of the 80s. Even with its grubby roots mired in exploitation, the film was taken deadly seriously, not only because it was played out so straight and convincingly as a piece of cinema, but because it also played a key part in the 'gender wars' of cinema. In her book *Men, Women and Chainsaws*, feminist academic Carol Clover cites *Ms.45* as introducing the notion that "we live in a 'rape culture' in which all males – husbands, boyfriends, lawyers, politicians – are directly or indirectly complicit and that men are thus not individually but corporately liable".

Personally, I don't think that the film really has that much of a deliberate feminist stance other than the fact that the one doling out the punishments just happens to be female. At the end of the film Thana is systematically destroyed for her attempts at playing God. The final scenes at the party show that she is clearly insane and unloading her pistol indiscriminately on both men and women, perhaps 'blinded' by her rage to the point where she had lost sight of who the real perpetrators are.

Ms.45 is often compared with Martin Scorsese's *Taxi Driver* (1976) and Michael Winner's *Death Wish* (1974), but the film is actually much closer in spirit to Euro-horrors like *Repulsion* (1965) and *Thriller: A Cruel Picture* (1973). Joe Delia provides the squawky jazz score that kicks in at the most dramatic points, and the film is also awash with surprising touches and interesting visual ideas. The true star of the show is Zoe Tamerlis (nee Zoe Lund) who was just seventeen years old at the time of filming, and whose assured performance made her an instant icon among lovers of cult movies. She later teamed up with Ferrara once again more than a decade later when they collaborated on the script for *Bad Lieutenant* (in which she also made an appearance as Harvey Keitel's junky lover). Tragically, her career was cut short when in 1999 she died of heart failure, leaving us with a precious few films in her back catalogue. As the angel of vengeance in *Ms.45*, it's perhaps her most iconic moment.

Ms.45 was cut by one minute and 42 seconds by the BBFC. The first rape loses shots of Ferrara undoing his jeans and then pulling down Thana's panties. The second rape loses shots of the intruder bashing his gun against the floor as he ejaculates. Shots were also removed from the scene where Thana dismembers his body in the bath tub, including an expression of pleasure on her face while she does it. The use of nun-chucks was removed from the scene with the gang of would-be rapists. In America, the film was subjected to similar cuts, but the uncut version was leaked into circulation when Warner Brothers' Maverick Collection accidentally released the full version. The tapes were quickly removed from stores after a week, but a number of them were sold and can be identified by the duplication date code on the sleeve; 082897. Drafthouse Films released the uncut version in 2013.

The Beyond (1981)
(Orig title: *L'Aldilà*; aka *Seven Doors of Death*)
Dir: Lucio Fulci /Italy

Italian gore maestro, Lucio Fulci, is best known for his quartet of extremely violent and gory zombie movies, which includes *Zombie Flesh Eaters*, *City of the Living Dead*, *House By the Cemetery*, and of course, *The Beyond*. It's a series of films in which all of the elements come together in a perfect way, and everyone involved in the making of the films were at the top of their game; from the performances of the cast, to the stunning photography and lighting effects of Sergio Salvatti, the gruesome and innovative special effects of Gianetto De Rossi, Dardano Sacchetti's nightmarish scripts, Fabio Frizzi's haunting music, and the meastro himself, Lucio Fulci, tying it all together in a masterful way. And even among such grisly company as *Zombie Flesh Eaters* and *City of the Living Dead*, *The Beyond* remains not only the finest film Fulci ever made, but also a landmark of Italian genre cinema. And of all the spaghetti

horrors out there, only Ruggero Deodato's *Cannibal Holocaust* can rival *The Beyond's* grim spectacle and gut-punch nihilism.

The film opens with a sepia prologue set in 1927 Louisiana in which a torch-carrying lynch mob enters the Seven Doors Hotel, make their way to room 36, and chain-whip the room's occupant, Schweick, a painter and "ungodly warlock," before they nail his wrists to the wall and pour acid in his face. While this is going on, a woman reads from the *Book of Eibon* (pronounced 'A-ban'), an occult text that catches fire as Schweick's face dissolves into an acidic mess.

Cut to modern day 1981 where the long-abandoned hotel has been inherited by New Yorker Liza (scream queen Catriona MacColl). One of the workers helping to renovate the building falls from the scaffold after seeing a pair of evil eyes, and John McGabe (exploitation favourite David Warbeck) arrives on the scene to try and keep things under control. Strange occurrences and more nasty goings on begin to happen in and around the hotel, including an unfortunate plumber who has his eyeball ripped out, dead bodies rising in the morgue, and an extended spider attack in the local library. Liza first meets Emily (the woman reading from the *Book of Eibon* in the prologue) on an eerily deserted stretch of road, but Emily's eyes have turned a milky white. Turns out that the book holds a dark secret concerning the gates of hell which are located somewhere within the Seven Doors Hotel. Soon enough, Liza and John are fighting off hordes of walking corpses, and this leads to the film's stunning finale in which the characters seem to plunge into hell.

As with many of Fulci's films, *The Beyond* is often accused of being a confusing mess, especially by those who rely on mainstream storytelling where everything comes together with a satisfying 'click' at the end. Fulci has little concern with traditional filmic manners or the niceties of character development or rationality. However, true fans of Italian terror and Fulci in particular, know that those odd peculiarities are what makes these films so interesting and so different. If you want proof that Fulci was a talented film-maker, you only have to look at the last few minutes of *The Beyond*. Everything in the Fulci cannon suddenly makes perfect sense in the film's finale; a nightmare logic that spirals into hell as the heroes find themselves eternally trapped in a dark netherworld.

In the prologue we're led to believe that Schweick was an innocent painter hunted down by a superstitious lynch mob. The themes of good and evil are muddied though when we see that the hell-scape at the end looks identical to Schweick's painting. This supposed innocent painter, it turns out, really was responsible for opening the gates of hell. At the beginning and end of the film we're shown two forms of evil; the physical and the metaphysical. The lynching and the walking corpses represent physical evil and earthly horror, whereas the closing scenes shows evil as a vast nothingness. The blank eyes of Liza and John express an existential terror rather than physical horror at their comprehension of an infinite emptiness. And this idea is made clear in the film's grim voice-over that declares "And you will face the sea of darkness and all therein that may be explored."

Fulci's masterpiece was neglected for years with a heavily censored American VHS under the title *7 Doors of Death* was the only way for fans to see it. In the UK it was added to the 'video nasties' list and banned until 2001 when the BBFC finally passed it uncut, by which time the film's reputation had rocketed thanks to the uncensored Japanese laserdisc and American midnight screenings by Grindhouse and Quentin Tarantino's Rolling Thunder Pictures. For the first time, fans were at last given the chance to fully appreciate Giannetto De Rossi's stunning visual effects which include an eyeball being ripped out of a plumber's head, an Alsation biting a chunk out of a woman's throat with blood gushing out of the gaping wound, a little zombie girl getting her head blown off, and a bunch of creepy-crawly tarantulas chewing on a man's face. It was only then that the film secured its long-overdue status as a cult classic. Oh, and Fabio Frizzi's excellent score was reinstated too.

Scanners (1981)
Dir: David Cronenberg /USA
A homeless man scrounges for scraps of food in the dining court of a shopping mall. He is then spotted by an elderly diner, and the man engages in some kind of psychic activity: he seems to involuntarily 'lock on' to her thoughts and nervous system, causing the woman much pain and distress. The alarm is raised, and the homeless man is pursued up the escalator and detained by armed security.

The man, Cameron Vale (Stephen Lack), is brought into the custody of Dr. Paul Ruth (Patrick McGoohan), a man who is sponsored by the shadowy ConSec corporation. Here we learn that Vale is indeed a psychic/telepath, or 'scanner,' and that Dr. Ruth was responsible for creating the scanners with the use Ephemorol in the 1940s, which resulted in many women giving birth to psychic mutants. There are also a group of evil scanners on the loose, led by Darrell Revok (Michael Ironside). And this group has infiltrated the ConSec corporation through bloody means, and seem to be hell bent on destruction. Revok and Vale just happen to be brothers, and Dr. Ruth happens to be their father. Ruth then convinces Vale to engage Revok and his group in a brutal psychic war...

It's incredible to look back at *Scanners* as a classic of the sci-fi/horror genre, as the film stands as an abject lesson in how *not* to make a movie. Writer/director, David Cronenberg, first came up with the idea for *Scanners* in the late 70s after he had wrapped up production on *Rabid* (1976). He originally referred to the project as 'The Sensitives,' and intended to flesh out a script treatment inspired by a section of William Burroughs' novel, *The Naked Lunch*, which included a group of telepathic terrorists called 'The Senders,' who were trying to take over the world. However, real life problems interrupted, and Cronenberg found himself dragged into a difficult divorce and bitter custody battle. And it was during this time that the script for 'The Sensitives' was abandoned in favour of a new project which allowed him to work through his mental anguish and parental strife for the semi-autobiographical *The Brood* (1979).

In October 1979, Cronenberg felt ready enough to have another look at 'The Sensitives,' and during a meeting with producer, Claude Heroux, he explained his idea for the film in a single sentence: 'a psychic war between telepaths in Montreal.' Heroux responded enthusiastically. 'Yes!' he beamed. 'This could be very commercial.' The project was immediately put into production, and shooting began just a fortnight later – even though there wasn't a script!

Now under great pressure, Cronenberg had little choice but to write the script on set. He would type up a few pages at dawn and then spend the rest of the day shooting those scenes. '*Scanners* was made in a very crazed way,' he later admitted,' and it's a miracle that it made any sense at all.' According to initial reports, the early rough cut was incoherent, and the production – which was already running over budget – was delayed further as Cronenberg insisted on several re-shoots to fill in the blank spots.

However, much to everyone's relief, *Scanners* was a hit with audiences, hitting the #1 spot in *Variety* magazine's film chart, and raking in more than $14 million dollars on its modest $2 million dollar budget. The reviews weren't so enthusiastic, however, as Roger Ebert bemoaned the genre's abandonment of audience participation in favour of bland plot mechanics. 'The problem with *Scanners*,' he wrote, 'is really very simple: It is about its plot rather than about what happens to its characters.' For Ebert, *Scanners* was just an FX-laden conveyor belt of a film, in which cut-out characters are paraded for the audience and expected to go through the motions before arriving at a 'predestined' conclusion. And, looking back at the film, it's hard not to agree with that opinion. It's difficult to feel anything for the characters and their predicaments – they simply pass through the narrative of cinematic convention, doing all the things heroes and villains are expected to do before the perilous finale. It's a film of pure spectacle and pure action. And that's not necessarily a bad thing. Cronenberg even executed his first ever car chase (though *Fast Company* was shot in 1977), and delivered his most infamous special effect sequence, too.

Indeed, *Scanners* is best remembered today for the exploding head sequence, which was created by special effects pioneer, Dick Smith (along with his assistants and technicians, Tom Schwartz, Chris Walas, Gary Zeller and Stephan Dupuis). The achievement of the effect was surprisingly simple: a gelatin cast was made of the actor's face. The head was filled with vegetables and dog food. Dick Smith laid on the floor behind the mannequin body and blew its head off with a shotgun. Only one take was needed, as the gruesome sight of the cranium splitting open and discharging its bloody contents while the face peeled off and the skin flopped down, was pretty spectacular. Smith was pleased with the result: 'I was in Vietnam,' he said, 'and that is how it really looks, man!'

Scanners also includes the tense psychic battle at the end between the estranged brothers, which boasts the often overlooked – and eye-popping – effects sequences that were overshadowed by the earlier exploding head scene. Those familiar with Cronenberg's *Stereo* (1969) will notice that Darrell Revok is actually the same psychic character who had attempted suicide by taking an electric drill to his forehead, leaving him with a 'third eye' scar. And this puts *Scanners* into context as a loose sequel to that early experimental short. So, if *Scanners* is something less than an artistic triumph, its box-office success did at least ensure the funding for Cronenberg's follow-up film – his masterpiece, *Videodrome* (1982). And that is something to be celebrated indeed.

Sequels followed: *Scanners II: The New Order* (1991) and *Scanners III: The Takeover* (aka *Scanner Force*, 1992). Also, spin-off movies set in the same universe: *Scanner Cop* (1993) and *Scanner Cop 2: Volkin's Revenge* (1994). They were all released direct to video.

Bloody Moon (1981)
Dir: Jess Franco /Germany

This *Halloween*-inspired Euro-slasher would sit perfectly on a bouble-bill with Juan Piquer Simon's *Pieces* (1982), a film which in turn owes a chromosome or two to this deranged offering from cult legend, Jess Franco.

Facially-disfigured Miguel is an unwelcome lurker at an evening pool party. The object of his affections rejects him in favour of another guy, so Miguel dons a Micky Mouse mask and tries it on with her. Not knowing who he is, she succumbs to his advances, and pretty soon they're back to her room for some fondling on the bed. But when she removes the mask, she is horrified when she discovers who she's been canoodling with. Outraged by this indignity, Miguel grabs a pair of scissors and stabs her to death.

A few years later, and the disturbed young man is released into the care of his sister, Manuela, who along with their wheelchair-bound mother, operate the day to day running of a language school. Pretty soon we learn that Miguel and his sister had an incestuous relationship before the murder, and when little sister refuses to rekindle their sex frolics, poor mother meets a fiery death. Meanwhile, another pretty girl, Angela (Olivia Pascal of *Behind Convent Walls*) is being stalked by Miguel, and no one believes her when her hot young student friends are offed in grisly fashion.

The most shocking thing about this film for

many viewers was the fact that director Jess Franco delivered a pretty solid body count movie. Having earned himself an unflattering reputation as being one of the most prolific but incompetent film-makers of all time, some dismiss his entire filmography on the basis of having seen only one or two of his movies. But true fans of this maverick of schlock know that his back catalogue of around 180 features contains dozens of surprisingly accomplished films, and even a handful of absolute gems. And it has become something of a rites of passage for Franco fans to wade through all the crap to find the treasures.

Bloody Moon is far from being a masterpiece but is entertaining from start to finish, with a barrage of T&A, inventive murder scenes, ludicrous dialogue ("So, where's the cadaver, honey?"), and tributes to John Carpenter's *Halloween*. One topless chick is stabbed in the back and the blade exits her body through the nipple; another woman is tied down onto a rock and sent hurtling into the path of an oncoming circular saw. A young boy tries to save her but the maniac scares him away, and the woman is decapitated, complete with blood spurting from the neck wound (this scene was inserted into the gore montage in Pedro Almodovar's *Matador* a few years later). The young boy is squished when he runs in front of a passing Mercedes. Another of Angela's friends is strangled with a pair of fire tongs; a snake is unnecessarily decapitated with a pair of shears; and a man is brutally cut wide open across the chest with a chainsaw.

After an extremely limited theatrical release, *Bloody Moon* was released on VHS at the dawn of home video, but uncut copies weren't available for long in the UK due to the arrival of the 'video nasties' fiasco. All of the tapes were removed from circulation when the film was prosecuted and banned. The Canadian VHS by CIC was uncut but difficult to get hold of on these shores. UK fans had to make do with the diluted version by Vipco (which was missing 80 seconds of gore) until it was passed uncut by the BBFC in 2008. The Severin DVD is the best option to date with the best transfer from the original negative, the complete cut of the film, and a fantastic audio commentary by Franco (who cameos early in the film as the psychiatrist).

Pixote (1981)
Dir: Hector Babenco /Brazil

Shot on the mean streets of São Paulo, *Pixote* (pronounced 'pee-shot') is a bleak and harrowing depiction of the lives of a group of Brazilian street kids, many of whom were non-professional actors from the shanty towns. Over the three decades since the film was made little has changed in the country's treatment of its wayward youths, despite Brazil's economic boom in the last few years. Directed by Argentina-born Hector Babenco whose previous film, *Lucio Flavio* (1977) caused a scandal due to its portrayal of Brazilian death squads; this later effort was no less controversial.

In *Pixote* we get a harsh snapshot into the lives of homeless street kids. A judge is murdered, and armies of young delinquents are herded into a reformatory. One of the new inmates is Pixote (Fernando Ramos de Silva), a young boy who bares witness to the murder suspect being executed without trial, and a pair of homosexuals murdered for no other reason than their sexuality. Pixote joins a gang and together they escape their incarceration and pretty soon they're back on the streets committing petty crimes. The lure of the money encourages them to get involved in pimping and drug dealing, but after they are ripped off, they seek revenge. The boys become friendly with a prostitute (Marilia Pera), and she helps them to get organised as a crime unit and eventually becomes Pixote's lover. A brief spell of happiness follows before the bleak denounement.

The first choice actor for Pixote missed a rehearsal, so eleven year old de Silva stepped up and won the lead role, becoming an icon among lovers of off-beat cinema. His savvy nature and mature, no-nonsense performance seems to have stemmed from his own experiences as a homeless street waif, which demanded an instant growing up and an assured confidence which helps to cement the film in its effective documentary realism. The gritty style was also helped tremendously by Rudolph Sanchez's impressive camera work. Director Babenco once again took a text by Jose Lozero (after his previous *Lucio Flavio*), and adapted its plot structure with an urgent, hand-held immediacy, giving the proceedings a grim air of authenticity.

International censors were not too kind to the film. In the UK, the BBFC cut *Pixote* by 27 seconds under the Protection of Children Act to delete the scene which shows a child in the same frame as a sexual act taking place. The cuts were similar to those imposed on Larry Clark's *Kids* more than a decade later, and whose writer, Harmony Korine, was hugely influenced by Babenco's films. When *Pixote* premiered in Brazil, a retired court judge requested that Babenco be held to account under the law of national security for condoning the use of drugs, encouraging the corruption of children, and undermining social institutions.

Most tragic, however, is the true story of what happened to the young actor Fernando Ramos de Silva; having made such an impressive impact in Babenco's film, he was later shot dead by Brazilian police in a bungled armed robbery. A grim fate indeed, and one which continues to haunt viewers three decades later, as the gun-toting eleven year old pimp in his trademark woolly hat igniting the screen and bringing the grittiness of Babenco's film crashing into reality.

Pixote is not for all tastes, but those looking for something as tough as nails and with no hope of redemption, will find much to be enthralled and appalled by here.

Christianne F. (1981)
(aka *We Children of Zoo Station*)
(Orig title: *Wir Kinder vom Bahnof Zoo*)
Dir: Uli Edel /W. Germany

Many first encountered this film on the back of the David Bowie soundtrack and had no idea what was in store for them. It's a disturbing classic that has left scores of film fans reeling over the decades as this bleak narrative features youngsters falling to the depths of debauchery with no redemption in sight. Along with *Requiem For a Dream*, *Christiane F* is one of the most effective anti-drug movies of all time. The plot is based on the true story of a thirteen year old girl who arrives in Berlin after her parents' divorce, and whose desire to be accepted by the local youths leads her to becoming a desperate junky and street prostitute.

Even before her addiction to heroin, life isn't exactly much fun for Christiane; she lives in a grim tower block that "stinks," her sister moves away to live with their dad, and her mother is rarely there for her. On the positive side, she's a big Bowie fan and she hangs out at a local night club called Sound, a place where fellow Bowie fanatics hang out, do drugs and watch *Night of the Living Dead* in a conjoined cinema club.

Christiane becomes attracted to Detlev, a young homeless kid who is part of the scene at Sound. He introduces himself to her after she spots a junky on the nod in a toilet cubicle (she thought he was dead). Her relationship with Detlev means she gets to hang out with druggies, wastoids, and punks, and go on petty crime sprees to pay for their kicks. This early part of the film bristles with a positive vibe of youthful optimism. But perhaps inevitably, dropping LSD becomes passe for the group, and when Christiane learns that Detlev and his buddies are hooked on smack, she is tempted to try it for herself...

Christiane (based on real-life counterpart Christiane Felscherinow, on whose autobiography this film is based) dyes her hair pink on her fourteenth birthday and uses her birthday money to buy heroin and shoots up for the first time using a kit borrowed from a complete stranger. And it's all a slippery slope from there – street hooking for dirty and abusive scum at Zoo station, shooting up in filthy toilet cubicles, needles clogged with blood, and the nightmares of withdrawal are all par for the course. We see Christiane transform from a bright and pretty young girl, to a sick and repellent, greasy street bum in less than two hours. Heroin chic it most certainly isn't.

If the powers-that-be were serious about their anti-drug campaigns, they could simply make it mandatory for all impressionable teens in the country to watch this film, because believe me, after watching this harrowing masterpiece only the stupidest of the stupid would consider the lifestyles depicted here as cool or hip. The drug abuse explored in the film is so unglamorous that it makes viewers shake their heads in disbelief when Christiane goes right ahead and gets herself hooked on heroin, despite the degenerate junkies that surround her and who should have made her realise what damage the drugs can do. But having said that, Christiane seems to drift in to her addiction by just going along with the flow, by not having any kind of motivation either way except that she wants to be with her new boyfriend, or as William Burroughs puts it in his classic novel, *Junky*; "junk wins by default." She isn't forced by bullying or by peer pressure into taking drugs. In fact, when Detlev discovers that she has taken H, he goes mad and gives her a harsh telling off. Parental neglect is an issue that is dealt with in subtle fashion in the film by director Edel; Christiane's mother is rarely ever at home and generally has no idea what her daughter gets up to while she stays out all night. Even when she does learn of Christiane's habit (after the girl OD's in the bathroom), her way of dealing with the situation is suspect at best.

The David Bowie soundtrack – which comprises some of his most new-wavy stuff taken from such classic albums as *Station to Station*, *Low*, and *Heroes* – is nothing short of incredible; we have *TVC15*, *Look Back In Anger*, *Warszawa*, *V-2 Schneider*, *Stay*, and *Helden/Heroes*, the latter becoming the theme tune to Christiane and Detlev's co-dependency. Bowie even makes an appearance as himself in a live performance of *Station to Station* in which he looks to be just as wasted as his audience. And it's a credit to the Thin White Duke that he accepted the role, despite the inevitable controversy of the subject-matter.

Natja Brunckhorst's performance as Christiane is astonishing; she has an assured manner and maturity which far exceeds her years. In fact, the entire cast of young actors in this film do not put a foot wrong – each and every one of these performances is astonishingly good. The aforementioned Bowie tracks are also perfectly woven into the dark fabric of the film, wearing off as each reel becomes bleaker and more depressing until we reach the equally downbeat ending. Uli Edel's sleek and detached direction is also expertly done, as is Pankau and Jurges' mesmerizing camera work; they manage to make late 70s Berlin look like a neon-lit hellscape. Quite simply one of the bleakest movies ever made. Unmissable.

The real Christiane F has been on and off drugs since the late 70s. She was in a band called Sentimentale Jugend with her then boyfriend, Alexander Hacke, with whom she appeared in the early 80s cult movie, *Decoder*, alongside fellow junky William Burroughs and Genesis P. Orridge. She lost custody of her son in 2008 when it was discovered that she was back on drugs.

Porno Holocaust (1981)
Dir: 'Joe D'Amato' [Aristide Massaccesi] /Italy
This goofy piece of exploitation trash from the uber-prolific 'Joe D'Amato' mixes monster mayhem, hardcore porn, and sunny beach locations, but ultimately fails to satisfy on any

level. The horror fans hated it, the raincoat crowd took it as a sick joke, and anyone else who saw it probably thought they were on drugs. However, believe it or not, it does have a tiny cult following among those who can't resist its sleazy, exotic charms.

A group of male and female 'scientists' travel by boat to an island to investigate radioactivity. Their research doesn't go as planned though as these people just seem to spend their time fucking on the beach. And unbeknownst to them, they're also being stalked by a radioactively mutated monster who goes on a killing spree and rapes the women!

Still unavailable to this day in any kind of legitimate English language version, *Porno Holocaust* was shot back to back with *Erotic Nights of the Living Dead*, using the same cast (with the notable absence of Laura Gemser), crew, and location. This has led to more than a few film guides and filmographies confusing the two. The sex and horror sequences are measured out fairly equally but monster fanatics will probably be bored to tears because the creature doesn't make its appearance until well over an hour into the film (it does manage to wipe out all but two of the cast members though). The sex scenes are long, dull, and boring as hell; we get a crappy lesbian scene, and then two black guys on one white woman (and this section will always be remembered for one of the guys who stays limp throughout the whole scene!). And when the monster does show up, it's a disappointment as it's basically a black guy with dried porridge stuck to his face. His first scene is pretty cool though as he drowns a man in the sea and then coerces the girlfriend into giving him head! The monster continues on its rampage, smashing a man's head in with a rock, and another with a lump of wood. Dead bodies are eventually found scattered across the island, and when the captain has finished doggy-styling his lady friend, he decides to investigate...

The action is played out to a backdrop of sickly sweet pop music and disco tunes courtesy of D'Amato's regular tunesmith, Nico Fidenco (of *Black Emanuelle* fame). The *Anthropophagus* monster himself, George Eastman, is responsible for the script, and he seems happy to appear in the film but wisely stays away from the hardcore stuff (as he did in *Erotic Nights*). Those of you who first encountered the film on dodgy bootleg video will be astonished by the German DVD from

Astro. Picture quality is crisp and colourful, and the somewhat exotic feel of the film (which was lost on the murky VHS versions) is fully restored here. It's also uncut and runs for the full 110 minutes. It's just a shame the dub tracks are in German and Italian only.

No Mercy, No Future (1981)
(aka *The Heiress*; Orig title: *Die Beruhrte*)
Dir: Helma Sanders-Brahms /W. Germany
A suicidal schizophrenic wanders the streets of Berlin looking for Jesus and having sex with strangers until she is eventually institutionalised. Based on the true story of 'Rita G', a schizophrenic woman who is said to have written letters to director Sanders-Brahms pleading with her to make a film about her plight, *No Mercy, No Future* is a bleak docu-drama that offers a superb performance from Elisabeth Stepanek as the doomed Veronika. Viewers are taken on a dark journey alongside the protagonist as she finds herself trapped in a miserable cycle of abuse, self-abuse and the psychiatric clinic. She seeks love but finds sex; she wants acceptance but gets exploited; she wants to find solace in God but instead finds a collective of downtrodden, broken people. In the end, she decides she wants to escape life entirely, and she cuts her own throat in the shower. Her parents find her and send her back the hospital, and when she is released, the bleak cycle continues all over again... This is a little-seen film that will be hell to sit through for fans of mainstream cinema, but for those with an interest in downbeat, disturbing films with an edge, *No Mercy, No Future* offers a fiercely uncompromising study on insanity that presents a plethora of shocking and disgusting images and a cold, detached directorial style.

Der Fan (1981)
(aka *Trance*)
Dir: Eckhart Schmidt /W. Germany
One of the most disturbing films to come out of Germany in the 80s was *Der Fan*, a study on obsession, madness and murder which reaches the heights of full-blooded horror. The story follows Simone (Desiree Nosbusch), a seventeen year old loner who has an intense obsession with 'R' (Bodo Steiger), a bland, new-wave pop singer. Her passion for him is so strong that she physically attacks her father when he changes channels during a performance of one of his televised songs. Simone sends fan letters to 'R', and though he never responds, she tells herself they are soul mates and will eventually be inseparable. She manages to blag her way into a TV studio where 'R' is recording a music video, and this means we're forced to listen to the same bloody awful tune played over and over again, *ad nauseam*, complete with low-budget 80s lighting effects and bald mannequins. After taking her back to his place and spending the night together, he tells her he is going away on vacation, but because she is better than the average groupie, he tells her she is welcome to stay at his house until he gets back. Simone doesn't like the idea of being left alone, and just as 'R' is about to leave for his trip, she creeps up behind him and cracks his skull open. What happens next is an unforgettable art house nightmare as Simone turns to some extremely twisted measures to ensure they'll never be apart again.

Made shortly after Uli Edel's *Christiane F.* and Helma Sanders-Brahm's *No Mercy, No Future* (*Die Berührte*), *Der Fan* was the latest in a line of German movies which showed youth as being anything but pleasant, with characters plunging to the depths of madness and degradation. *Der Fan* looks like it could have influenced Jorg Buttgereit's *Nekromantik 2* which was made almost a decade later and shares with Schmidt's film the themes of obsessional, twisted love and dismemberment (not to mention the surprise ending).

Possession (1981)
Dir: Andrzej Zulawski /France /Germany
If you enjoyed *Antichrist* (2009) and *The Brood* (1979), then you really ought to see *Possession*, an incredibly strange film which features another case of female 'hysteria' with a stand-out performance by Isabelle Adjani. It's also a film that remains as enigmatic today as it was on the day of its release. It makes a mockery of Freud, gender studies and the fabric of reality itself, and is resistant to all forms of analytical inquiry.

Government spy, Marc (Sam Neill), returns home one day from a work assignment to discover that his relationship with Anna (Adjani) has broken down beyond repair. He hires private detectives to follow her, and soon learns that she has been having an affair with an older man named Heinrich (Heinz Bennett). However, when confronted in his apartment, Heinrich tells Marc that Anna has *another* lover, and that they meet for sex in a grubby apartment. And, upon further investigation, it becomes clear that her second lover is not even human...

With its cold blue colour palette and wild camera work, *Possession* is an astonishing film, with director Zulawski managing to bring out the very best in his small cast of characters. Interestingly, the themes of love triangles, Eastern mysticism, doppelgangers, fading love and the fight over the same love object had existed in Zulawski's work from the very beginning. His earliest short films, *The Story of Triumphant Love* (*Piesn triumfujacej milosci*, 1969) and *Pavoncello* (1969) had explored these areas more than a decade before *Possession* hit the screens.

One of the most underrated film-makers to have ever worked in the medium, Zulawski's career was beset with often painful set-backs. His feature debut was set to be a big budget adaptation of Joseph Conrad's novella, *Heart of Darkness*, but like Orson Welles' doomed attempt before him, the project eventually fizzled out to nothing, thanks largely to the faults of producer, Jeffrey Selznick (David's son), who didn't inherit his father's talent for film production. Zulawski got his career off the ground with *The Third Part of the Night* (*Trzecia czesc nocy*, 1971) and *The Devil* (*Diabel*, 1971), the latter incurring the wrath of the communist authorities in Poland, and was banned as an anti-communist picture.

After several other failed projects, Zulawski began work on the sci-fi epic, *On the Silver Globe* (*Na srebrnym globie*, 1977 [released in 1988]). It was the most expensive film ever shot on Polish soil up to that point, and was a hugely ambitious undertaking (the finished film was expected to be more than 3 hours long). Unfortunately, the communists once again suspected that the director was making a subversive anti-communist film, and the project was shut down with only 85% of the footage in the can. Not only was he forbidden from completing the film, he was also locked out of the editing room, the sets were destroyed, materials were confiscated, and the props and costumes were hidden away. To see such a huge project – into which he had put his heart and soul – come to an end just as he was approaching the home stretch, was devastating for Zulawski. And it was that profound disappointment that seeped into his artistic mindset when he began work on *Possession*.

Amazingly, the communists gave Zulawski a passport and allowed him to leave Poland for France. Stephen Thrower has suggested that this rare case of granting permission to leave was perhaps a mere excuse for the communists to get rid of him.

Just like David Cronenberg's *The Brood*, where the writer/director inserted auto-biographical elements into the story on his bitter divorce and custody battle, Zulawski approached *Possession* from a similar angle. His marriage to Malgorzata Braunek (star of *The Third Part of the Night* and *Diabel*) had broken down. In the late 70s she met a Swedish journalist, Andrzej Krajewski, who was a Zen Buddhist. This had a profound effect on her religious beliefs, and she became a Zen Buddhist for the rest of her life. Zulawski was open about the autobiographical elements in *Possession*, and he even based much of the explosive dialogue between Marc and Anna on his memories of his arguments with Braunek. Of course, such a traumatic and personal screenplay full of rage, frustration and confusion was destined to explode on the screen. And, in retrospect, it's difficult to imagine any other film-maker coming close to replicating the sheer pain and insanity this film basks in.

Initially, *Possession* didn't fare too well in the English-speaking world. It played for just two weeks in UK theatres, picking up just a handful of thoughtful and balanced reviews amongst a deluge of hostile write-ups from critics who accused the film of being 'hysterical.' In America, it fared even worse; for a start, the Stateside distributors cut it down from 123-minutes to a bastardised 79-minute version, with the loss of around 44 minutes of footage. And, to add insult to injury, this version was also puffed up with generic 'horror' themed music on the soundtrack. Of course, that desecrated version of *Possession* was met with even *more* confusion in the States. Nonetheless, the uncut version slowly developed a cult following on home video, with the UK VHS version (released by the VTC label) bootlegged and traded in America for years, especially in the aftermath of the 'video nasties' scare, of which *Possession* found its way onto the long list of films deemed potentially impeachable by the Director of Public Prosecutions. By the 90s, the film was already quite legendary in cult and horror fan circles, with 'zines such as *Eyeball* and *Slimetime* dedicating memorable articles to the film, from both the art-house and exploitation perspectives, respectively. And it was Anchor Bay who came to the rescue around the turn of the millennium, and they released *Possession* uncut on DVD, in a beautifully crisp, widescreen transfer and with an audio commentary track by Zulawski himself. In the following decade, a limited edition was released on Blu-Ray, too.

Possession is, on one level, an exploitation film (Zulawski himself playfully described it as 'a film about a woman who fucks an octopus'). It certainly has enough weirdness, blood and madness to alarm many viewers. But it's also clearly a European art-house work. Adjani picked up the Best Actress award at Cannes, and the film was taken seriously enough in art-house circles, and yet ended up consigned to the 'video nasties' dungeon. It's a film that challenges viewers by pushing at the limits of human understanding. It seems deliberately designed to sit awkwardly at the threshold of the indescribable and the ineffable – that uncanny realm where language breaks down and our understanding of ourselves constantly slips out of reach.

I'll leave you with what Stephen Thrower had to say in summing up *Possession*: 'There's a quality of a journey to the underworld in the film, which perhaps stems from the *Heart of Darkness* story, this time about a man who goes into the blackness of the soul to look for and find a 'rogue' woman (in this case), and attempt to bring her back. So there are themes from his earlier films and failed projects which are still kicking around in *Possession*. It's too extreme for the naturalistically inclined art-house crowd, and yet too intellectually and verbally complex for the horror hounds. So the film works best with both heads on.'

The Loch Ness Horror (1981)
Dir: Larry Buchanan /USA
Scummy scuba divers steal a Nessie egg in the hope that it will bring them riches, but what it brings instead is a very angry monster mother who savages the locals with her big rubber head. Featuring bad acting, bad dialogue and atrocious 'Scottish' accents (which amounts to American actors over-pronouncing their 'R's'), the most unforgivable sin in this film is that it wasn't filmed in Scotland but in sunny California. Sacrrrrrilege!!

The Forest (1981)
Dir: Don Jones /USA
Two California couples take a camping trip to the Sequoia National Park. A pair of ghostly children warn them not to stick around. And when the campers fail to heed the warning, a cannibal madman begins offing the couples with a hunting knife... *The Forest* is an eerie slasher movie from the early 80s which has as much in common with supernatural shockers like *The House By the Cemetery* (1982) as it does with the usual backwoods slashers of the time, like *Don't Go In the Woods* (1980) and *Friday the 13th Part 2* (1981). Although the film was made on a low budget and is let down by some awful songs with dreadful lyrics, *The Forest* is worth a watch for its 'out there' supernatural angle, and for the interesting back-story: Here we learn that the killer had fled to the woods with his children after killing his cheating wife. He survived by killing and eating backpackers. The kids couldn't take it any longer and committed suicide. Since then, the maniac has survived alone in the woods with his insanity going unchecked, while the ghosts of his children try to warn travellers to stay away. Writer/director Don Jones re-mortgaged his house to finance the project, only to be burned by crooked distributors on both its short theatrical run and on home video. Not only did he make no money for his efforts, but he lost his house too.

New Year's Evil (1981)
Dir: Emmett Alston /USA
Typical 80s slasher nonsense about a misogynistic maniac in various disguises who targets a television station broadcasting a musical showcase on the countdown to midnight. The slashings are fairly graphic and bloody, but none of the characters are particularly likeable. The film is worth watching if only for the roster of forgotten punk and new-wave bands (including Made in Japan), and the lift sequence at the end is exceptionally well done. Director Emmett Alston's only other credit of note is the underrated video gem, *Demonwarp* (1988).

Final Exam (1981)
Dir: Jimmy Huston /USA
What is it about films in which American college kids walk around carrying stacks of books? Have they never heard of a rucksack? Anyway, *Final Exam* is a routine slasher movie

from the early 80s. The murders don't really begin until close to the hour mark. In the meantime we're forced to endure the lives of a bunch of frat pricks and their friends with endless pranks and general tomfoolery on campus. In the film's defence, the characters here are not as annoying as usual, except for 'Wildman,' a blonde dummy whose windpipe you'd love to pinch just so you could watch him squirming on the ground, gasping for breath. Also, the film is endearingly earnest, and there is an innocence to it, hailing as it does from an era before the corrosive strangle-hold of Cultural Marxism had fully taken hold of our culture and educational systems in the West. Interestingly, the killer doesn't turn out to be a psychotic student or authority figure (teacher, Sheriff, etc); in fact, viewers have no idea who he is or what his motivation for killing is! He just shows up on campus with a large knife and begins stabbing the teens until he meets his match with the 'final girl,' Cecile Bagdadi.

Burned at the Stake (1981)

(aka *The Coming*)
Dir: Bert I. Gordon /USA

By Bert I. Gordon's usual standards, *Burned at the Stake* is not a bad movie at all, despite the fact that no witches were ever burned at Salem. After a prologue set during the height of the witch trials in 1692, we cut to modern-day Salem where a morbid teenage girl – who looks a lot like one of the accusers in the prologue – is harassed by the ghostly father of an accused woman. And the girl, who could be the reincarnation of the accuser, is captured and somehow hypnotised into committing evil deeds. According to this film, it wasn't necessarily superstition that was to blame for the tortures and executions of those times, but rather malicious accusations that got out of hand. The bureaucracy of the Church-sanctioned laws were exploited by deviant folks with petty grievances, and the authorities had no choice but to act on the accusations as instructed in the law books. That's not to say that those holding the trials were entirely reasonable or rational; while one man pleads his innocence while heavy boulders are crushing his chest, the man conducting the torture says, "If you were innocent, why would God allow you to be treated in this way?" Chilling. How can you argue with such lop-sided thinking? Such twisted 'logic' runs through many witch-themed movies, such as *Witchfinder*

General (1968), *Mark of the Devil* (1969), and *The Bloody Judge* (1970). Bert I. Gordon, known affectionately as the 'Notorious B.I.G.' to his fans, may not have been the greatest filmmaker around, but when he had interesting material to work with, the results were often quite enjoyable.

Dead and Buried (1981)

Dir: Gary Sherman /USA

Surprisingly loved and dismissed in equal measure by horror fans, *Dead and Buried* is an EC comics-inspired atypical zombie movie set in the quiet town of Potter's Bluff. James Farentino plays the perplexed Sheriff who investigates a series of grisly murders, only to find that the victims are seen alive and well soon after their deaths. The 'twist' ending can be seen coming from a mile away, but this is a very well made spooker of its time with some remarkably nasty death scenes, including a photographer tied to a post and burned alive as the locals gather around, *Wicker Man*-style, and celebrate. Director Sherman never topped this.

The Secret of Seagull Island (1981)

(aka *Seagull Island*; Orig title: *L'isola del gabbiano*)
Dir: Nestore Ungaro /UK /Italy

A five-part mini-series made for cable TV. A British woman, Barbara (Prunella Ransome), heads to Rome in search of her blind sister, Marianne, who has mysteriously vanished. After alerting the police, the body of a blind woman is discovered on a rubber dinghy adrift at sea. But when it comes to identifying the body, Barbara is relieved to find that it isn't that of her sister. However, when she learns that the boat victim was murdered, she suspects that the killer may also have something to do with Marianne's disappearance. And so she does a bit of giallo sleuthing, and all clues lead to a mysterious island... This lightweight mystery has nothing going for it beyond the splendid underwater photography and early 80s fashion atrocities. The performances are lacklustre, as is the script, and the direction by the unknown Nestore Ungaro only comes to life when scenes take place below the ocean surface (I suspect underwater photography was Ungaro's day job, and the main reason he got this gig). Beyond that, the 'mystery' takes all of ten minutes to solve, and the heroine pretends to be blind so that she can get close to the sight-phobic maniac and save the day. Okay, so there's slightly *more* to the story than that, but the revelations really aren't worth sticking around for. Recommended only to die-hard giallo completists.

Darkroom (1981-1982)
Dir -Various- /USA
"You're in a house, maybe your own. Maybe one you've never seen before. You feel it, something evil... You run, but there's no escape, nowhere to turn... You feel something beckoning you, drawing you to the darkness, to the terror that awaits you in the darkroom." *Darkroom* was a short-lived horror anthology series that aired on America's ABC network in the early 80s, and disappeared pretty fast. A silver-haired James Coburn introduces the lacklustre short tales, most of which weren't worth the paper they were written on, let alone going to the trouble of assembling a cast and crew to film and broadcast them to a nation.

'*Closed Circuit*' stars Robert Webber as an employee of a TV studio who returns to work after suffering a minor stroke to discover that his identity has been stolen by a computer programme. '*Stay Tuned, We'll Be Right Back*' shows a man becoming obsessed with a transistor radio when he discovers he can pick up morse code and radio broadcasts from the 1940s. And even though it's forty years later, he convinces himself that he can end the war by intercepting German U-boat communications. In '*The Bogeyman Will Get You*,' a girl suspects an old family friend of being a vampire, but he turns out to be a werewolf instead. In '*Uncle George*,' a man convinces a homeless guy to live with him and his wife to take the place of his recently deceased uncle. In '*Needlepoint*,' a black pimp visits a witchdoctor who is also the grandmother of a recently killed hooker. He pleads with her to end the curse that was placed upon him, but to no avail. In '*Siege of 31 August*,' a young boy's toy soldiers come to life and attack the family farmhouse. '*A Quiet Funeral*' sees a murderer get the surprise of his life when he visits the open casket of his victim. '*Make Up*' stars Billie Crystal as a young man who acquires a make-up kit from the widow of a dead film actor whom no one has ever heard of. '*The Partnership*' stars David Carradine as a hitch hiker who befriends a talkative loner in a diner, and together they visit a deserted fairground called 'Happy Land,' with deadly consequences. In '*Daisies*,' an adulterous lab technician is shot dead by his wife. In '*Catnip*' (penned by *Psycho*'s Robert Bloch), a young biker thug is terrorised by a witch's black cat. '*Lost In Translation*' sees a man hired by an archaeologist to translate an ancient Egyptian scroll which happens to be stolen, and cursed. In '*Guillotine*,' a French criminal desperately tries to avoid his execution by exploiting a loophole in the law. An untitled story stars Samantha Eggar as an influential theatre critic who comes face to face with an actor she had slagged off in the press. In '*Who's There?*' a man tries to talk a friend out of shooting dead his cheating wife. And finally, '*The Rarest of Wines*' sees two rich siblings squabbling over the details of their late mother's will.

With sixteen stories spread over six hour-long episodes, *Darkroom* never reaches above mediocre levels. *Daisies*, in particular, is especially bad; a dull, three-minute scene of a woman entering a science lab and shooting her husband dead. The acting and direction is flat and feels rushed, like we're watching loose rehearsals rather than the finished product. Amazingly, some episodes were considered too shocking for TV at the time, and were cobbled together for the anthology feature, *Nightmares* (1983).

Blood Beach (1981)
Dir: Jeffrey Bloom /USA
Detectives in search of missing women discover that they were the victims of a creature that dwells under the sand of the local beach, dragging its prey below the surface to their doom. The search for the mysterious carnivore leads to a subterranean cave where the remains of sixteen bodies are found... Despite a welcome dash of deadpan humour, *Blood Beach* is a dull and uninvolving creature feature that bites off more than it can chew, what with the string of pointless plot-lines going nowhere, and the creature itself only makes an appearance at the end, and it's a real disappointment; it's hard to make out through the shadows, and it appears very briefly, but it sort of resembles a screaming organic satellite dish, or a grisly, bowl-shaped thing with a phallic prong jutting out in the middle.

A Day of Judgment (1981)
(aka *Stormbringer*)
Dir: C.D.H. Reynolds [Christopher Reynolds] /USA

Set in the 1920s in a small American town, the church is almost empty during Sunday Service. The local Pastor despairs for the community, whom he feels have turned away from God and embraced the evils of the modern world. However, the local townsfolk succumb to violent deaths as evil poisoners, unscrupulous bankers, adulterers and a heartless son are all sent to Hell on a day of judgement as the Grim Reaper pays them a visit, one by one...

Slow moving at times, and with some shaky acting here and there, *A Day of Judgment* is nonetheless worth a watch. The 20s setting is nicely done, and there are sparse sets and an obvious message here about where Western Civilisation is heading (down the toilet, fast). From a 21st Century perspective, where you'll be hard pushed to find anyone with religious convictions, let alone a firm moral grounding, there's a mourning here for a society that has lost the battle between good and evil – and the realisation that only extreme fundamentalism and cold-blooded murder could have any hope of revitalising the community and the Church. Depressing indeed.

If you look online for the handful of reviews for the film, a common thread among them – besides bemoaning the lack of blood and tits – is a sneering smugness as they look down in disdain at the religious aspects of the story, confirming director Reynolds' concerns expressed in the film. Apparently, the director's real name was Charles Reynolds (he also played Reverend Cage in the film), and the horror elements were forced on the production by the Earl Owensby Studio in order to spice things up a bit. The original ending was also scrapped, and a new director was brought in to film the silly ending we are left with today in order to market the product as a horror film. I imagine the irony of Reynolds' warnings about the modern world went over the distributor's heads as they butchered the story for their own greedy ends. The mysterious Reynolds never made another film. See also *Grim Reaper* (1976), another religious-themed horror movie featuring the scythe-wielding avenger of death.

Videodrome (1982)
Dir: David Cronenberg /USA

"I've got something I want to play for you". One of the most puzzling and extreme movies ever released by a major Hollywood studio, *Videodrome* sees director David Cronenberg continuing with his body horror themes and social satire that he had developed throughout the 70s, but this time he also adds a welcome dose of surreal, hallucinatory weirdness to the mix.

The plot of *Videodrome* centres on obscure cable channel entrepreneur, Max Renn (James Woods), who inadvertently stumbles upon a strange broadcast whilst checking a pirate satellite. The show, known as Videodrome, depicts women being tortured on camera by masked men, and Renn becomes obsessed with finding out the truth behind the mysterious channel – Is it real or fake? Who's behind it? And where does the signal come from? To find the answers to those questions leads him to a roster of dangerous characters, including kinky lover Nicki Brand (Debbie Harry), media commentator Brian O' Blivion (Jack Creley), his daughter Bianca (Sonja Smits), and eyewear tycoon, Barry Convex (Lewis Carlson).

Max's fascination with the videodrome signal isn't necessarily based on any moral crusade to put an end to the abuses on screen, it's selfishness and greed that pushes him on with the lure of making a profit, until he discovers that watching Videodrome causes him to suffer bizarre and often violent hallucinations and bodily mutations. Turns out that Videodrome is a corporate enterprise, a secret TV broadcast that causes its viewers to develop brain tumours that can be used to control perception itself, all hidden behind images of extreme pornography. The idea is to create a society that is completely dependent on the signal, a nation of TV addicts who are enslaved to whatever agendas the corporate powers see fit. Thus, Max Renn eventually becomes an assassin and is used as a pawn by warring factions to do their dirty work, before the violent and baffling finale.

Released in the UK in 1983, *Videodrome* coincided with the emergence of home video and the fast transformations of television itself at the time. Channel 4 appeared in 1982, and we had breakfast TV for the first time ever. The home video explosion was well under way, with VCR's being sold in this country at twice the rate of America, but this private home viewing also had a negative effect on those who wanted to control what we saw on those machines. The 'video nasties' fiasco was just around the corner, with uncut and unregulated videotapes widely available in the nation's stores, such as *Cannibal Holocaust*, *The Driller Killer*, and *I Spit On Your Grave*, with fears that those tapes, with their grim content and salacious sleeves, would have a negative effect on the nation's youth. Suddenly, your television wasn't safe anymore, and the powers that be decided that those videos needed to be legislated against. That square box that sits in the corner of your living room was causing anxiety and was increasingly being treated as some sinister thing. So it was ironic how Cronenberg's film – which ultimately rejects the idea of censorship – was subjected to censorship itself at the time, with fearful distributors cutting out whole chunks of the film to avoid the 'video nasties' scandal.

The themes explored in *Videodrome* have become more relevant with the ensuing decades since the film was made, especially with the rise of the internet and the way it is slowly taking over our lives and creating a very public consciousness. The media conglomerates manipulating and controlling the populace with their not-so-subtle propaganda (sometimes amounting to an altering of consciousness itself in the process).

Back in the early 80s *Videodrome* was often dismissed as an eccentric take on the new video age, but if you consider Cronenberg's later film, *eXistenZ*, which was released in the late 90s (and also touched upon some similar themes as *Videodrome*), critics were accusing Cronenberg of losing his vision and running out of steam. It's hard not to conclude that it's the technology and mindset of our modern age that is slowly catching up with Cronenberg's vision, making his ideas seem less outlandish nowadays, or as Jean Baudrillard suggested: we are entering an age of "the implosion of science fiction," whereby the expanse of the human imagination will one day be eclipsed by the technological realities of our darkest dreams. Pretty scary nonetheless.

Indeed, Cronenberg's film is prophetic in many ways; notice how the character Brian O' Blivion seems to represent the modern-day web-savvy technocrat; he is a 'media expert' who only exists as a huge library of video cassettes through which he communicates with the world.

With the internet, we are all media experts nowadays, we're all promoting ourselves online in one way or another, whether it be socially through Facebook, or globally on YouTube, our lives are more documented and exposed than ever. Even O' Blivion's name relates to the latter-day trend of online 'usernames', the pun-laden alias' of anonymous web forum members.

Another example would be the growing sophistication of TV commercials over the decades since the film was made; the colours, the jingles, the psychological manipulation of the whole thing. Brand names with their logos symbolising 'the things you want in life', 'the things you *need* in life', the media and advertisers have learned how to seduce that part of our brains that compel us to go out and buy the latest 'thing', or to vote for this or that political party. The 'brand name' seduces the viewer, it plays up to their sense of being, their sense of wanting to belong, to fit in with a society that deems the brand name to be 'cool' and 'normal', and as such, it also plays up to our anxieties of existing in the world without those things, without the 'coolness', without that social acceptability. Actually, your TV has indeed become sinister, it has been made dangerous and unhealthy by the very people who outlawed the 'video nasties', and who regulate what we can and cannot watch 'for our own good'. And *Videodrome* picks up on both the seductive and repulsive aspects of this modern-day corporate control. Notice the health warnings that are everywhere; everything is suspected of causing cancer nowadays – the very products and gadgets and 'telly addict' lifestyles of late capitalism radiated from our TV screens – the fast food, the mobile phones, the comforts and inertia. It's ironic how Max Renn develops a brain tumour after being exposed to the evil corporate signal of *Videodrome*.

This exploration of the seduction and repulsion of the TV lifestyle is symbolised perfectly in the scene where Max is lured to his throbbing television screen by Nicki Brand. Sex has always been a big selling point in advertising, a way of gaining an audience's attention. The sex appeal aspect of television plays on the viewer's desire to bypass the threshold of possibility; the screen lurches out at you with its seductive images, it invites you along ("C'mon Max, come to me"). To be absorbed by the TV screen and transported into the world of perfection and sex and splendour has become one of the true motivators of mankind. But of course, Nicki isn't really there luring Max along, it's just an image, a hallucination. Regardless of Renn's altered state of mind brought on by his brain tumour, the image on his screen isn't real; the image is actually made up of thousands of electronic dots, or 'cells' through the manipulation of quantum mechanics and digital processing which, in their entirety, results in an approximation of an image.

With *Videodrome*, Cronenberg is clearly taking his subject-matter much more seriously than in his previous work. He even dishes out some just deserts on his negative characters, EC Comics-style. Of all the supposed 'bad' guys in Cronenberg's films up to *Videodrome*, none of them were truly evil. Dr. Emil Hobbes of *Shivers* was definitely a madman, but he genuinely believed his experiments with parasites would help mankind; Dr. Hal Raglan of *The Brood* was shrewd and arrogant, but he was also driven to make up for his mistakes. And *Scanners*' Darryl Revok was motivated by a justified vengeance. Barry Convex, on the other hand, the implacable corporate manipulator of the Videodrome signal, seems to be Cronenberg's first truly negative character with not a shred of human decency. The director relishes the opportunity to give him an awful and gory death. But was Convex real or just another hallucination emanating from Max's damaged mind?

This confusion and ambiguity concerning the levels of reality explored in *Videodrome* can also be found in the work of one of Cronenberg's major influences; writer William Burroughs. In his books and other experiments using film, tape recorders, and 'cut-up' texts, Burroughs (along with friend and cohort Brion Gysin) demonstrated the idea of reality being a construct (or 'Reality Film') which can be manipulated in the minds of others for good or bad. This theoretical terrorism encouraged readers to conduct their own experiments with drugs and tape recorders as a way of slashing and discombobulating reality itself ("cut the words and see how they fall"). Thus *Videodrome* is more Burroughsian than his own future adaptation of *Naked Lunch* a decade later.

Rick Baker provides the outstanding special effects work with throbbing TV screens, a stomach opening into a gaping vaginal cavity, and the extended death sequence of Barry Convex which almost out-does the exploding head scene in *Scanners*. DP Mark Irwin lends his usual cold and sardonic eye to the proceedings, and Cronenberg's regular composer, Howard Shore, contributes the dark and eerie synth organ score. The film was cut by the MPAA for its theatrical release but has been left fully intact on all DVD editions. Another masterpiece from Cronenberg then. Essential viewing.

The New Barbarians (1982)
(aka *Warriors of the Wasteland*; aka *Metropolis 2000*)
(Orig title: *I nuovi barbari*)
Dir: Enzo G. Castellari /Italy /USA
Set in 2019 after a nuclear holocaust has ravaged the earth, a group of refugees are huddled in the wasteland trying to make radio contact with other possible survivors in the area. However, their camp is brutally attacked by a group of misanthropic nihilists, known as The Templars, who roam the wasteland and get off on massacring any survivors they come across. Into this environment steps a 'Man With No Name' type lone warrior, Scorpion (Giancarlo Prete, here billed under his Anglicised pseudonym, 'Timothy Brent'). It's his mission to wipe out The Templars. And after being saved from decapitation by rotary blades attached to the side of one of the Templar vehicles, we learn that Scorpion has an ally in Nadir (Fred Williamson, in perhaps one of the most bizarre outfits he ever wore on screen). Nadir is armed with his trusty weapon – a crossbow that fires explosive arrows. Of course, you can probably guess what happens next: the heavily outnumbered warriors go to battle against The Templars when a new group of refugees are targeted...

Despite the ludicrous sound effects, oddly customised vehicles, ridiculous futuristic gadgets, and huge purple mohawks, *The New Barbarians* is far more entertaining than it had any right to be. The music certainly helps; a synth-heavy blitz of 80s pop lunacy, courtesy of former Goblin member, Claudio Simonetti (he also composed the catchy theme tune for *Tenebrae* in the same year). The film is basically a carbon copy of *Mad Max 2: The Road Warrior* (1981), with a bit of *Death Race 2000* (1975) and *Seven Samurai* (1954)/*The Magnificent Seven* (1960) thrown in. Director, Castellari, even reprises a couple of scenes from his own previous western, *Keoma* (1976), this time shifting the action from a 19th Century town ravaged by plague and bandits, to a 21st Century wasteland ravaged by nuclear fallout and futuristic bandits, or, *new* barbarians.

The film opens on the scene of a Japanese-style miniature model city that looks like it is about to be stomped on by Godzilla. Instead, a bright flash of light and a loud boom signals nuclear warfare and the end of civilisation. After the title credits, the camera pans along the wreckage of rusty old vehicles and skeletal corpses wearing bizarre perspex helmets. But despite the devastation, there are survivors, even if their numbers are steadily dwindling thanks to the lawless bandits who are terrorising the area. The Templars are the most entertaining aspect of the film. They ride around in custom-built battle vehicles, and wear white plastic armour, probably inspired by the Stormtrooper outfits in *Star Wars* (1977).

Their leader, Supreme One (played by the 6 foot 5 badass, 'George Eastman'), is the Darth Vader of the group, a megalomaniac who orders his troops to 'exterminate' innocents. Early on in the film, there is a July Plot against him as several troopers scheme behind his back. However, this vague sub-plot is merely an excuse on behalf of the film-makers to show how ruthless Supreme One is. He deals with the insubordination by burning the traitors alive and raping them in the arse! However, the leader's madness also reveals itself in more subtle ways, too, such as in the moments where we see him lounging around and listening to bizarre audio recordings about taking over the skies. Supreme One serves as the archetypal villain – the vintage comic book bad guy of old who seems to thrive in the future apocalypse when mankind has found itself at its weakest and most vulnerable. Indeed, the same character seems to spring up regularly in pop culture, from the aforementioned Darth Vader, to Flash Gordon's arch-nemesis, Ming the Merciless, to more recently – and in more down-to-earth mode – as the Governor in *The Walking Dead* (2010-). And, interestingly, these types of characters first emerged in the 1930s, just as Adolf Hitler rose to power.

Tenebrae (1982)
(aka *Unsane*)
Dir: Dario Argento /Italy
Best-selling crime author Peter Neal (Anthony Franciosa) arrives in Rome to promote his latest novel, Tenebre, but soon receives a threatening phone call and learns that there is an obsessed killer on the loose using his book as a blueprint for a string of murders. Inspector Germani informs him that a young shoplifter (the gorgeous Ania Pieroni) has been found with her throat cut and pages of his book stuffed into her mouth. Meanwhile, the killings continue to mimic events in the novel and Neal receives pictures of the murder victims in the post with quotes from his own work. His agent, Bullmer (exploitation legend John Saxon), and his assistant Anne (Daria Nicolodi, Argento's wife at the time) try to persuade him to leave town, but Neal decides to stay put and help out with the investigation. Even when the killer is finally dispatched, there still seems to be no end to the bloodbath.

Seemingly constructed from a mountain of ideological influences, *Tenebrae* actively demands its viewers to engage in subjective interpretation. Such a challenging assortment of interpretative texts is unheard of outside of art movies – Freudian angst, perception, psychoanalysis, gender studies, identity, an awareness of the work of Michelangelo Antonioni, etc. And it's interesting to note that Argento's creativity only started to dwindle once his films were taken seriously by intellectuals.

The word 'tenebre' literally means 'darkness', but the film itself is brightly lit with sunny outdoor locations and light modern interiors. Dario was referring to the darkness of the mind, or the subconscious, in the film's title (the bright aesthetic and colour schemes were also designed so that the victim's blood would be as visible as possible). And again, as with his previous work, Argento prefers to construct stories which self-consciously embrace the process of deduction and interpretation, and in the process anticipates the viewers' and critics' own analysis as it goes, subverting the thriller/giallo conventions and playing around with our preconceptions of gender and misogynous screen violence; victims scream and moan aloud as if they're having orgasms while they are cut, stabbed ('penetrated'), and strangled in stylish hyperreality, and the film is awash with surreal symbolism.

One of the greatest psycho movies ever made, *Tenebrae* reunited Argento with DP Luciano Tovoli who lensed *Suspiria*, and Claudio Simonetti of Goblin who composed the catchy soundtrack. Argento was inspired to write the script after receiving threatening phone calls from a fan while in Los Angeles. And, as is the way of any artist of the macabre, he took that basic premise to its most startling extremes for a nightmare vision on film. His usual technical invention is also in full force here with a single crane shot that anticipates a double murder scene in which the camera ascends a building, peers into the windows at the lives of the future victims, travels over the roof, and then descends down the other side. It's an audacious move and very typical of Argento at the time.

In the UK, the film was swept up in the 'video nasties' controversy and banned in the mid-80s. It was passed by the BBFC in 1999 with cuts, and then passed completely uncut in 2003. In America, it was badly truncated and even re-titled *Unsane* by the film's Stateside distributors for a limited release. The Anchor Bay DVD is fully uncut.

Amityville II: The Possession (1982)
Dir: Damiano Damiani /USA

The Amityville Horror (1979) was supposedly based on fact, though Jay Anson's bestselling paperback turned out to be a cynical, money-spinning pack of lies. It put many of the clichés found in spooky house TV movies up onto the big screen, and was a hugely successful theatrical hit. It wasn't until a couple of years later when Stanley Kubrick adapted Stephen King's *The Shining* for the big screen did we really see how powerful the old 'possessed-father-in-a-scary-house' scenario could be, but for *Amityville*, hack director Stuart Rosenberg simply wasn't up to the task, and he delivered a rather lacklustre tale of the Lutz family moving into a suspiciously affordable mansion (bargain of the century at just $80,000), the place where a previous tenant had murdered his entire family, and the father is possessed by an evil, malevolent spirit.

Anson's book concerned George and Kathy Lutz – and Kathy's three children – who bought the house at 112 Ocean Avenue in Amityville, Long Island, in the summer of 1975, and moved in later that year. They only spent a month there before they upped and left, insisting that they had been driven from their home by an evil spirit. The story soon made the papers, and it became ever more strange and far-fetched as it captured the imaginations of millions, to the

point where the family were offered publishing deals and a movie contract.

By the time the sequel was proposed in the early 80s, the Amityville story had become more complicated. The Lutz family had been sued by the new owners of 112 Ocean Avenue, who were fed up of being bothered by trespassers and ghost hunter tourists who would show up at the house all the time, day and night. Those who took an interest in the Lutz story also noticed some glaring differences between the hardback and paperback versions of the book, and even the Lutz family themselves would alter their version of events each time they were interviewed. William Weber, who was the defence lawyer for the mass-murderer Ronald DeFeo, also filed a lawsuit against the Lutz family for stealing his story; the story that would form the basis of *Amityville 2: The Possession*.

The DeFeos were a troubled family who lived at number 112 prior to the Lutz's. The eldest son Ronald was always up to no good, and after holding up his own father's car dealership with a friend, both Ronald and his father came to blows during a basement row. Just a week later, on the 13th of November 1974, Ronald shot his entire family to death with a rifle. And that's why the house was sold at such a reasonable price to the Lutz family the following summer. At first, Ronald told police that he had been asleep and knew nothing about the incident. He later claimed that the mafia was involved in the murders. On one occasion, he even boasted that he would be released in just two years if he pleaded insanity. He even had the gall to enquire how much of his inheritance he was entitled to. Six consecutive terms of 25 years to life is what he got instead.

The idea of a prequel to *The Amityville Horror* was met with less than an enthusiastic response from horror fans at the time. But producer Dino De Laurentiis somehow turned the prospect of a run-of-the-mill horror quickie into an exciting and disturbing film, thanks to his hiring of Italian director, Damiano Damiani. With a script loosely based on the DeFeo murders, and with the ghostly possession theme thrown in to keep it in synch with the original film, the scene was set for an American horror with a distinctly Italian vibe. Trust the Italians to add some nastiness and perversity to the proceedings. *Amityville 2* offers a dark and moody atmosphere, and in retrospect looks and feels very similar to the work of Lucio Fulci, especially *House By The Cemetery* and *The Beyond*. Both of which were also penned by Dardano Sacchetti.

Whereas in the first film, the menace posed by the evil force was manifested through financial woes and the dream of owning a home – a pattern that led to the destruction of the patriarchal unit. This prequel instead shows its teeth in the form of domestic meltdown and incest within a family that was already dysfunctional before they even moved into the house. The relationship between the father and son is especially volatile and resentful, with the father's aggressive bullying causing a dangerous friction in the psyche of his unruly son. The mother of the house is a devout Catholic, the eldest daughter has reached the age of adolescent sexual awakening, and the two youngest children only adds to the tragedy that is about to unfold.

So, this troubled family move into number 112, the spooky old house on Ocean Avenue with its foreboding presence and eye-like windows. And within the first fifteen minutes we're witness to blood gushing from the taps, crude graffiti on the kids' bedroom wall ("dishonor thy father – Pigs!"), and people spattered with fecal matter. But the real point of interest in this film is the eldest son, Sonny (Jack Magner, who later appeared in *Firestarter*). We watch as his life falls apart due to a malevolent force that possesses him; he becomes increasingly alienated from his family, has sex with his teenage sister, and eventually goes on the rampage with his father's rifle. The evil force communicates with him through the earphones of his Walkman, giggling and hissing murderous suggestions in his head. The film is so gripping and intense throughout the whole possession and murder sequences that it fails to live up to its lively promise in the finale. Instead, the movie blows its wad at around the hour mark when Sonny is led away from the house by the arresting officers.

The gun rampage starts with Sonny – in an ugly, demonic appearance, similar to Regan in *The Exorcist* – blowing his dad's brains out (in a scene which was initially cut by distributors on its first release, and is still missing from many subsequent VHS and DVD releases). He then creeps through the house... Mother is shot in the stomach. The kids see her bleeding on the floor and they start to scream. The youngest sister is

then shot. The little brother tries to hide, but is spotted and shot in the back of the head. His incestuous sister is next; he catches up with her on the stairs, lowers the barrel of the gun between her breasts, and then pulls the trigger. The speed at which this household is destroyed is one of the most appealing – and disturbing – aspects of the film. Usually, haunted house movies take an age before they get into gear and begin delivering the thrills and chills, but director Damiani manages to keep things moving at an exciting pace throughout, despite the final third running out of steam.

Unfortunately, once Sonny is arrested, the film descends into a lights and smoke special effects fest, with silly theological nonsense and the usual *Exorcist* rip-off style as the priest attempts to wrestle the demon from Sonny by re-visiting the house and inviting evil upon himself in an altruistic self-sacrifice to save the kid – a rather pointless endeavour as Sonny is looking at spending the rest of his days behind bars, regardless of what the outcome is in this fight between good and evil. Even with the demon ousted from his body, Sonny will never be free again.

The Lutz story is nowadays treated as nothing more than a hoax. The truth is, the house was too expensive for George Lutz, even with the drastically reduced price tag following the DeFeo murders. He and Kathy tried to make a go of it but couldn't manage, and ended up staying with relatives after leaving. And it was around this time that they concocted the whole haunted house story. The couple pestered William Weber for information about the DeFeo case, and worked the killings into their story. Weber was particularly annoyed at this because he had planned to write his own non-fiction account of the DeFeo killings, and he sued the Lutz's for snatching his story.

The Amityville movie franchise continued throughout the 80s, 90s and beyond; *Amityville 3-D – The Demon* (1983) is the one in 3D where Meg Ryan drowns. It was also directed by Richard Fleischer of *The Boston Strangler* and *10 Rillington Place* fame. *Amityville 4: The Evil Escapes* appeared in 1989 (the one with the ugly, cursed lamp), *The Amityville Curse* (1990) was based on one of the paperback cash-ins and was the first in the series that was released direct to video. The next few sequels were based on accursed items that were purchased at Amityville yard sales, such as a clock in

Amityville 1992: It's About Time, a mirror in *Amityville: A New Generation* (1993), and a dollhouse in *Amityville Dollhouse* (1996). An abysmal remake of the original *Amityville Horror* was released in 2005 and is best avoided, as is *The Amityville Haunting* (2011), an absolute stinker that attempts to base its plot on Anson's book.

Café Flesh (1982)
Dir: 'Rinse Dream' [Stephen Sayadian] /USA
Most porn movies are made purely for two reasons: to make the viewers horny and to make the producers wealthy. Of course, there are those who claim there is some artistic merit to be found in some hardcore porn, but they're just kidding themselves while they beat the meat. But having said that, *Café Flesh* just happens to be the exception to everything above. One of the great hardcore films of the 80s, with more imagination and carefully thought-out ideas than dozens of other XXX flicks, *Café Flesh* is basically a bizarre sci-fi pic with lots of weird fantasies and cum shots.

Set in the near future after a nuclear holocaust, radiation has left 99% of the surviving population unable to have sex. These impotents are known as 'Sex Negatives' who torment themselves with memories before the bomb by hanging out at Café Flesh, an apocalyptic nightclub where 'Sex Positives' – made up of the remaining 1% of the population who can still make it – perform live sex shows, much to the audience's mounting frustrations. The live shows include bizarrely detailed fantasies, such as in the scene where a housewife is raped by a milkman dressed in a rat costume while three oversized 'babies' sit in high chairs holding bones. And just like any other XXX feature, we get all the usual explicit sex and cum shots, and girls bending over as if they're inviting us to inspect whether they've wiped themselves properly. While most narrative-based pornos of the time looked so obviously choreographed, here with *Café Flesh* it's supposed to look that way. The film is loaded with style and humour, and on the technical front, it's equally impressive – there's neon-lit photography, impressive sets (which look like they could have been an influence on Crispin Glover's *It Is Fine. Everything Is Fine*), and strange soundscapes all adding to the eerie ambiance.

The characters in this apocalyptic world include the host of Café Flesh, Max Melodramatic (Andrew Nichols), who impersonates Elvis and Marlon Brando in between teasing the Sex Negs in the audience; Angel is a naïve virgin from Wyoming on her first excursion to the big bad city; Nick and Lana (Michelle Bauer, under the pseudonym 'Pia Snow,' who later showed up in classic exploitation movies like *Reform School Girls* and *Hollywood Chainsaw Hookers*) are a couple on the brink – he's a Negative, she's a secret Positive, and they're both hoping to save their relationship; and there's also Johnny Rico (whose namesake would later crop up in Paul Verhoeven's *Starship Troopers*, not so coincidentally) the super-stud who's so cool he doesn't remove his shades, even while eating pussy.

This is all well and good, but one of the major differences here from the usual XXX fare is how *Café Flesh* is so blatantly derisive towards its audience. The film works as a mirror reflecting back on the jaded raincoat crowd who are the main consumers for hardcore porn. During the more graphic moments, the director cuts to the audience who all look like leering, libido-punished slobs, and it's then that we realise we're just like those poor fuckers, by watching *Café Flesh* on the screen we're unable to get involved in the action.

Overall, *Café Flesh* is a vision of despair which has often been interpreted as a metaphor for the AIDS pandemic, even though in 1982 when the film was made, nobody knew about the virus. Would you believe it, a thought-provoking, sci-fi porno movie.

The New York Ripper (1982)
(Orig title: *Lo squartatore di New York*)
Dir: Lucio Fulci /Italy
Perhaps Lucio Fucli's most controversial film, *The New York Ripper* follows detective Williams (a scary-looking Jack Hedley) on the hunt for a nasty serial killer who, according to witnesses, quacks like a duck while he hacks and slashes his prey. We soon find out this is no lie as we see for ourselves some young woman being slashed to death in a parked car on a boat while the killer goes "quack quack!"

The killer mostly uses a handy cutthroat razor to slay his victims, but broken bottles and other sharp implements are wielded, too. Each murder sequence is more graphic and gruesome than the last, and the soundtrack startles with its absurd and ridiculous blasts of quack quack! Most of the killings are of women, and this has led to accusations of misogyny at director Fulci, but the film is actually a pessimistic barrage of misanthropy and nihilism; the target of the film isn't women, but the whole of mankind.

After a university professor (Paolo Malco) helps out with the case, and a young woman narrowly escapes the killer with her life (in a superb dream-like sequence), the mystery begins to unfold. And when the killer strikes closer to home, detective Williams becomes increasingly obsessed with finding the maniac, and the final revelation explains the madness behind the killer's motive.

The New York Ripper touches on almost every convention of the giallo formula, and also boasts an excellent jazzy score by Francesco De Masi. Made around the same time as Dario Argento's *Tenebrae* and Brian De Palma's *Dressed to Kill*, Fulci's film takes a grittier approach to similar themes. Indeed, it's remarkable how many similarities there are between this film and Argento's masterpiece in terms of structure and female butchery (also, the film has a sleazily evocative style similar to the New York scenes in Umberto Lenzi's *Cannibal Ferox*, too). With *Zombie Flesh Eaters*, Fulci effectively turned a tropical island into a plague-ridden wasteland of the living dead. And with *House By the Cemetery*, he turned a spooky Lovecraftian sensibility into a ghoulish nightmare. With *The New York Ripper*, however, he brings a gritty and grounded roughness to the project, making New York feel like a cold and hostile place. Many of Fulci's critics have accused him of being unable to tell a simple story without it falling into incohesion, but here (as elsewhere) he proves them wrong; *New York Ripper* has a gripping, disturbing narrative, and is very well put together (most of the film was shot in Italy except for a few brief location shots, and this only makes the film even more impressive, considering how closely it resembles early 80s downtown New York).

The film's hostile reception is not surprising, even many of Fulci's fans object to much of the material on screen here. But even with such misgivings, and flaws, there are still numerous noteworthy elements to keep fans of Euro-horror interested, such as Luigi Kuveiller (of *Profondo Rosso* fame), whose camera work is quite impressive, and much of his scope compositions were lost in murky and badly cropped VHS and bootleg copies. The actors do a decent job despite the clumsy dubbing here and there, adding much in the way of unintentional humour. Jack Hedley's detective Williams is of the old-skool, un-PC variety, and he seems just as interested in sleeping with hookers as he is with finding the killer. Also of note is the ending which probably inspired the 'bullet through the cheek' sequence in Argento's *The Stendhal Syndrome*.

The New York Ripper was banned outright in the UK in 1984, with all prints escorted out of the country. The BBFC later passed it with 22 seconds of cuts in 2002, removing the close-up shots of the woman tied to the bed being cut up with a razor blade (as a side note, Shameless released the film in the UK on DVD in 2007, and that version has 34 seconds of footage missing, even though the censors did not require any additional cuts). The 2011 DVD and Blu-Ray release is missing 29 seconds that were imposed on the same notorious scene. In America, the MPAA left all the violent scenes intact but insisted on the removal of sex; the scene in the Puerto Rican bar in which the wife of a wealthy sleazeball is toe-fucked under the table was missing on American prints for years. It wasn't until 2009 that a legitimate uncut copy was released on DVD and Blu-Ray by Anchor Bay, and that version reinstates all the footage – good news for toe-fuck fans.

In Germany, *New York Ripper* was subjected to a bizarre form of censorship; the film could be legally shown in theatres, but because of the extreme nastiness on view, it was illegal to mention the title in the ad campaign. This, of course, led to some odd poster blurbs, such as one which read, "An Italian horror movie made in the early 80s about a New York serial killer." Horror fans knew which film was being described, but advertisers and cinema chains were forbidden from actually mentioning the title. Ridiculous. Unsurprisingly, this silly form of censorship didn't take off.

1990: The Bronx Warriors (1982)
(aka *Bronx Warriors*; Orig title: *Il guerriri del Bronx*)
Dir: Enzio G. Castellari /Italy
By 1990, the law has given up on the Bronx, and the place has become an official no go zone, or 'no man's land.' The territory has been completely abandoned by the authorities, and is now ruled over by warring gangs of creeps and

maniacs. Into this mess comes Ann (Stefania Girolami), the daughter of a corporate boss. She is harassed on her way home one night and ends up getting lost in the derelict slums. Luckily for her, she runs into nice guy, Trash (Mark Gregory), the leader of a biker gang called The Riders, and he protects her from the assortment of savages in the area. Meanwhile, her worried father sends out a helicopter search squad to track her down. And when this yields no sign of her, he sends in a lone assassin, Hammer (Vic Morrow), who had grown up in the area and knows the terrain like the back of his hand. Hammer begins eliminating the gang members, and even pits the rival gangs against each other by framing them for a series of killings. However, Ann has grown to despise her father and his unscrupulous corporation, and refuses to be rescued. In the end, her powerful father loses all patience and sends in a deadly assault squad to get the job done...

Surprisingly light on action until the finale, *1990: The Bronx Warriors* is nonetheless a spectacular urban warfare epic, and perhaps the best of the Italian apocalypse movies that flourished in the 80s. The film borrows just as much from quirky gang pics, such as *The Warriors* (1978) and *The Road Warrior* (1981), as it does from mainstream fare, like *Escape From New York* (1982). Mark Gregory (real name, Marco di Gregorio) as Trash is actually pretty good here, so it's a mystery why he seemed so horribly miscast in the following year's loose sequel, *Escape From the Bronx* (1983). Perhaps you could lay the blame at the feet of director Enzo Castellari, who was growing tired and wearisome of apocalypse movies after churning out three of them in quick succession. However, *Bronx Warriors* catches the director at the beginning of the loose trilogy, and there is an infectious spark of energy and creativity here that the other movies severely lack.

Trash's biker gang, The Riders, travel around with huge blades sticking out of each side of their bikes, as a way of slicing through their enemies as they ride by. Unfortunately, the other gangs aren't as cool; there are tap dancing swordsmen in top hats who synchronise their fight moves like a dance troupe; there is also a dusty clan of subterranean cannibals and a hockey team on roller blades! Fred Williamson even appears as The Ogre, the leader of a rival gang who drive around in a convoy of Rolls Royce's, and who wear colourful silk suits, looking like pimps who have just rolled out of a blaxploitation pic. And while The Riders may not be the most flamboyant of gangs in the area, they do at least have the coolest dress sense – their uniforms loosely consist of black, sleeveless t-shirts emblazoned with SS skulls, and swastika armbands and various other Nazi emblems.

Typical of Italy's cinematic mimicry, even the film's tagline was stolen from Wes Craven's *The Hills Have Eyes* (1977). Thus, 'The Lucky Ones Died First,' becomes, 'The First To Die Were the Lucky Ones!' But it doesn't really matter in the grand scheme of things. *Bronx Warriors* is a must-see for exploitation fans, and walks a tightrope between amateur clumsiness and expert efficiency, dazzling its audience with unexpected set-pieces and memorable characters. There is a segment in which The Riders are forced to make it to the other side of the Bronx, and this means having to run the gauntlet through a seemingly endless array of enemies who want them dead. The sequence was probably inserted into the script as a way of adding an extra bit of action to spice things up, but for me, the sequence is even more fun to watch than the finale. Fans of Lucio Fulci will spot many familiar names on the credits – screen writing veteran, Dardano Sacchetti (*The Beyond* [1981], *City of the Living Dead* [1980]) co-wrote the script; Walter Rizzati (*The House By the Cemetery* [1981]) provided the memorable guitar wails and funky bass score; and the whole project was seen through the lens of legendary DoP, Sergio Salvati (*Zombie Flesh Eaters* [1979]). Also, lookout for other Italian legends, such as the Anthropophagus monster himself, 'George Eastman' (real name, Luigi Montefiore), and the late Ennio Girolami (*Tenebrae* [1982]). Interestingly, the Japanese biker epic, *Burst City* (1982), was made in the same year as this, and shares many odd similarities.

First Transmission (1982)
Director Not Credited /UK

I still don't know what to make of this. Maybe if I was able to ascertain the facts concerning the making of this film, and who exactly was involved, and what's real and what isn't, then it would probably be easier to make sense of the whole thing. However, considering how little information there is out there, and how even some of the most basic 'facts' about the film are constantly being debated three decades after its release, then perhaps the ins and outs of these tapes will be shrouded in mystery forever.

All I know for sure is that First Transmission offered me one of the strangest, most mesmerizing, freakiest, and disturbing viewing experiences in my life so far. It's not a 'good' film by any stretch of the imagination, but even with the truly objectionable images on display here (and their supposed authenticity), it cannot be shrugged off as useless junk like so many other shockumentaries out there. If Videodrome wasn't made in the same year as this I would have sworn it had influenced Cronenberg's film. But here, it isn't just the traditional mondo stuff that's disturbing, but also the weird attempts at trying to brainwash the audience by showing mysterious logos that appear on screen for minutes at a time.

Whatever the intention was of including those images, it had an almost hypnotic effect, alluring and off-putting in equal measure. There's an image of the Virgin Mary with a radiating heart and a dark shadowy halo behind her head that became freaky after a while; simultaneously sacred and profane in both spiritual and symbolic terms, it was perhaps the uneasy balance between the innocence of love and the blasphemy of pure evil that became uneasy. The radiating heart became like the Leviathan in Hellraiser 2; it can expose the blackness of your own heart, and the words 'Psychic TV' suddenly made sense to me! Or maybe I just get freaked out by religious iconography. Whatever, it made me feel as uncomfortable as watching a young man volunteering to have his dick cut off.

First Transmission was a collection of video tapes that were made available through Psychic TV's mail order system in the early 80s. Fans of the band had to own all of the albums in order to qualify to be given the videos as a gift. The tapes consisted of almost four hours of footage assembled by the band members themselves, and included an initiation ritual of a new member into the cult of Thee Temple Ov Psychick Youth, of which band member Genesis P. Orridge was a founding member. Thee Temple Ov Psychick Youth (or TOPY) was founded in the early 80s by members of Psychic TV, Coil, Current 93, and others. They allegedly practised magik "without the worship of gods," and focused on the psychic energy of "guiltless sexuality."

Cassette no.1 starts with an image of a skull that hovers on screen accompanied by weird and wonky orchestral music. Then we meet a spokesman for Thee Temple who gives a speech concerning strange sexual pressures, the stifling nature of society, and how to use your body wisely. We then cut to the initiation ritual; shot on video, it looks more like an underground S&M clip more than anything. It depicts a man whose hands are chained to the ceiling and who has a black sack on his head. He is covered in blood but it's difficult to see where his wounds are. Some dude rubs his cock into another dude's eye. More guys walk around naked and covered in blood; they are aroused and chanting some kind of mantra or incantation. By this point, the soundtrack has changed from a piano ballad to something that sounds like a dozen moaning trumpets.

The inductee is unchained from the ceiling and tied to a bed and has talcum powder rubbed onto his genitals. He is then subjected to needle torture/pleasure (he doesn't resist or even flinch, so I assume he likes that kind of thing). Symbols are scratched onto his torso with a knife and the blood is smeared across his body. The man with the knife then turns the blade on himself. And after some genital torture, it's time for some good old fashioned fucking. It's then the turn of a young woman to experience the cutting blade, and she doesn't mind letting out a few moans of pain/pleasure. The ceremony wraps up with an enema and close-ups of injections (of what I don't know), whipping, dildo play, and the inductee gets pissed on.

The clip finishes with anal sex and lots of blood. This whole sequence is dark, disturbing, and difficult to watch in places, and is undoubtedly 100% real. Then comes the aforementioned Virgin Mary scene before we cut to a shot of a guy or girl pulling down their panties to reveal... err, I don't know what! Some have said it's a girl with an unfortunate protruding labia, which may well be so, but it could just as easily be a guy showing off an ugly cock stump after castration.

Cassette no. 2. According to a caption on screen, this footage came from 'contacts' in San Diego. We're in a car driving through the city. Then we arrive at some hotel room. This footage was shot on 8mm and the cameraman stands in front of a tall mirror and exposes his cock. Back outside again at some California skate park with shots of youngsters whizzing by on their skateboards. Now we reach the most problematic scenes in the whole film; we see a bunch of drowsy kids laid out on beds in the hotel room with what look to be needle wounds in their arms. At first we're thinking junky children, but between more random cuts of driving on the freeway, an older man appears wearing a white surgical overcoat, similar to the kind worn by surgeons and lab technicians. The man cuts into a teenage boy's arm with a scalpel and the kid seems okay with this. He is then connected to an electrical device with a wire that is inserted into the wound, and the man shocks the kid with a few vaults of electricity, causing him to wriggle around like he's having a fit. The kid then uses the device to shock himself, and he keeps on zapping away with the currents until he ejaculates.

In a later scene, another kid is laid face down on a table and the strange doc cuts him open at the base of his spine and inserts the electrodes. After feeding him a few currents of electricity, the kid goes limp, presumably dead. The doc packs his stuff away and still the kid doesn't move... (Did I detect a bit of bad acting from the doc here? There's something about his mannerisms during this sequence that looks like he's basically chewing the scenery; theatrically sharpening his posture into panic mode and exaggerating the look of surprise on his facial features like a bad thespian. I don't know about the rest of the scenes on cassette 2, but I'd bet my house that this 'death' sequence is fake).

It's now that we reach the most infamous scene in the entire film: A kid lies on a bed and the reckless and amoral Dr. Benway character enters the frame and proceeds to sever his penis with a scalpel. It's all filmed in one long take with the camera remaining completely static throughout. With blood spurting everywhere, Benway hurries with a rushed stitch-up. Afterwards, the kid explores his cock stump and his testicles are still intact - stupid boy. He eventually tries to take a piss but finds it difficult and makes a mess (I should also point out that there is no live sound on the San Diego footage. Instead we get a mariachi tune and what sounds like Mexican radio commercials).

Next up is a quirky revolving logo in shades of grey that serves as some kind of subliminal invitation. Created using blocky computer graphics, this hypnotic scene pulsates with a foreboding kind of ambience like a TV commercial transmitted from another world. It's very much a product of the 80s, but aesthetically it oozes a warped perfection of its era, with its stark video glow, VHS tracking lines, and cubic vortices combining to produce a timeless glitch of eternity. It genuinely feels like it was created by some 80s retro freaks from the distant future. Absolutely spellbinding, and probably unlike anything else seen from the 80s, completely untouched by the ages of re-mastering and enhancing, it sits in its own dark void of perfection. No amount of modern day tinkering could quite capture that kind of fuzzy analogue magic. It looks simultaneously dated, contemporary, and futuristic; it has a modest and grandiose presence, it moves but stays still, changes but stays the same, fluid but concrete. You look into it and it looks back into you as it sails on its postmodern loop. It belongs in an art gallery (see what I mean about the brainwashing elements?)...

Anyway, next up is a segment entitled 'Brion Gysin's Dream Machine' in which we enter a room filled with Arabic music. A man stares into one of those psychedelic cylinders (the dream machines also appeared in Gysin and William Burroughs' excellent short film, Towers Open Fire). The camera stays focused on the spinning wheel and the whole screen is enlivened with trippy psychedelic colours and random abstract patterns, and the Arabic music picks up in intensity. The whole idea of this clip is to try and induce a hallucinatory experience in the viewer, and I tried to play along, but in the end with those patterns rushing across the screen, I found it difficult to focus on without feeling nausea.

Cassette no.3 starts with a clip called 'Thank You Dad' and features Jim Jones of The Peoples Temple Cult spouting his nonsense. Picture quality is unwatchably bad in this one but the images are quite random and unimportant. Audio is crystal clear though, and we can listen to the rantings and ravings of a guy who somehow brainwashed hundreds of people and talked them into committing mass suicide in Guyana in 1978. He had a fake laugh which sounds like Flipper the dolphin which I hadn't noticed before... Then we go to an 'Intermission' that is basically a short segment in which a woman gets dressed in front of an open window...

Then the skull logo appears on screen once again and a narrator informs us about cognitive brain theory; the individual(s), and our personalities, and the "traps of time." We are encouraged to describe ourselves as "we" as part of being "multi-dimensional individuals." And this philosophy is basically the raison d'etre of artists like Genesis P. Orridge who reinvented himself from Neil Andrew Megson into the artist-as-metaphor-itself. In the postmodern contemporary world, the metaphorical multimedia artist Genesis P. Orridge was created in order to experientially immerse himself into the artistic formulae, regardless of the results and consequences. Thus, his art must reflect back on himself both physically and cognitively. Unlike previous artists whose paintings cause controversy, the person responsible can sneak away. Not so with Orridge; his art is part of his whole being, and if it goes wrong, or is unpopular, or causes outrage, there is nowhere for him to hide. Thus he is lauded in the underground art and music scenes but demonized in the tabloid press.

The next clip is a strange series of scenes designed to shock with its grotesquely surreal and sexual symbolism. Masked faces, weird pictures, a woman sitting on a toilet and snipping her pubes. A man blows smoke out of his eyes. The woman puts a long black centipede onto her vag... We see some pretty graphic photos of genitals with venereal disease... The centipede is not impressed and wanders off onto the floor... So the woman pokes herself with a vibrator instead. Image of skull shattering on ground. Woman lubes herself up and inserts a long stick-type thing into her cooch... A guy with a massive hole in his cock uses a hooked metal instrument to pick at the hole – he pulls out a bunch of live maggots from the wound... Effigies are burned... The end. This is all played out to an ambient/industrial soundtrack reminiscent of Throbbing Gristle, and sounds like rhythmic factory machinery. And I understand that most of the action in this clip was performed by members of the COUM Transmissions, a group of performance artists with close links to Throbbing Gristle, Psychic TV, and Orridge himself was also a member.

Cassette no.4 opens with an excerpt from a BBC documentary on Psychic TV. Genesis and Peter 'Sleazy' Christopheson are interviewed before we're shown a short clip from a music video. Then there's more discussion on the 'multi-personality' aspect of Thee Temple Ov Psychik Youth (Psychic TV were allegedly considered to be the propaganda wing of the cult)... 'Psychoporn' is another music video with strange tribal rhythms and colourful abstract imagery. When specific images do come into focus, we can make out various sexual positions. A psychedelic blowjob and penetration shots are also included; this latter piece was most definitely not part of the BBC coverage.

A paraphrase from Nietzsche appears on screen, "Those who don't remember the past are condemned to repeat it," and then we're introduced to some kind of experimental music video that basically serves as the band's manifesto. The Burroughs influence is apparent again as the words 'The Naked Lunch' are displayed, and then the tape reaches a crescendo of sounds and visions from the previous cassettes arranged into a 'cut-up' style montage with the moaning trumpets, the face of Jim Jones, the emblematic skull, the electric orgasm device, and various other bizarre imagery crops up again. The tape concludes with the reappearance of the spokesman with some final words.

I mentioned earlier that First Transmission reminded me of Videodrome, and if you consider that Orridge and other band members were involved in radical performance art as part of the COUM Transmissions troupe, the subject inevitably brings us back to Cronenberg. For years, Cronenberg has worked on a screenplay entitled Painkillers which centres on a group of performance artists. The script still hasn't been filmed as yet but it's interesting to know that Cronenberg has had a fascination with this shadowy subculture. He felt compelled to write Painkillers after a friend told him the story of how a man surgically removed his own hand in the name or art. Cronenberg's research into the minutiae of this kind of activity would no doubt have led him onto the COUM whose public performances have become the stuff of legend. And this would have led him onto Orridge, Psychic TV, Throbbing Gristle, Thee Temple Ov Psychik Youth, and perhaps even First Transmission.

The release of Videodrome in 1982 coincided with First Transmission, and although it seems unlikely that Cronenberg's film could have taken inspiration from those tapes, there are nonetheless some interesting comparisons to be made. Both films attempt to induce a hallucinatory experience in the viewer through the manipulation of the electronic cells on your television screen (and it's important to note that Videodrome built up its considerable cult following by its regular broadcasts on late night cable TV); some will argue that *Videodrome* is a metaphorical piece of sci-fi/horror make believe, which of course is true, but if you consider the implications of that metaphor and the overall meaning of Cronenberg's film (namely that it's an exploration and a prophetic look at how 'reality' can be manipulated in the minds of others, for good or evil), the implications aren't too dissimilar. Indeed, whilst watching *First Transmission* you'll probably feel a bit like Max Renn who has stumbled upon a strange and violent broadcast from a pirate satellite, and you'll be asking yourself similar questions like who's behind this? What's real and what isn't? And where did all this footage come from?

First Transmission was created and compiled by people who were influenced by artists and writers such as Brion Gysin, William Burroughs, and JG Ballard; and they in turn have had a big impact on Cronenberg's work. In First Transmission a kid has electrodes inserted into the base of his spine, and in Cronenberg's *eXistenZ* characters are injected with 'Bioports' in the same sensitive/dangerous area. Also, characters in *eXistenZ* are hooked up to 'fleshy game pods' through an attachment of organic wires, and they manipulate the pods with their fingers in order to arouse the game into action. Compare this to the scenes in *First Transmission* where the kids are hooked up to electronic devices which they manipulate with their fingers as a way of increasing and decreasing the voltage in order to arouse themselves, and you'd perhaps be forgiven for thinking of it as a direct influence as Cronenberg's film was released fifteen years later.

British tabloid paper The People published a scathing sensationalist 'article' on Genesis P. Orridge in the 90s, accusing him of corrupting the nation's youth. And among the range of accusations of Satanic rites, sadism, greed, and general foulness, there is a brief mention of First Transmission and it is described as showing "scenes of a pregnant woman being tied to a dentist's chair and raped and a man being urinated on by Orridge". The pregnant woman being raped is nonsense, and although a man does get pissed on in the film, I'm pretty sure it wasn't Orridge who did the pissing. And if this

so-called journalist did actually watch the tapes, I'm certain that those scenes he described above would have been the least of his concerns. The infamous 'castration' scene alone would have stolen the headline.

Now, the 'castration' (technically a de-penising as the kid's testicles remain intact) looks to be genuine. In fact, the whole film looks to me to be genuine except for the aforementioned 'death scene' and bad acting of the doc on the second tape. And though there aren't many reviews of this film around (write ups are scarce even on the web), every one I have read so far has assumed the footage to be real. There are rumours circulating, however, that the footage was faked, and that the special FX were created by artist/madman Monte Cazazza, but I've been unable to confirm this. And to be honest, I'm not convinced it was faked (I wish it was!). It would take a dedicated and precise effort to produce that kind of illusion; the transition from the real penis to a prosthetic substitution would have to be absolutely perfect, and there are no cuts or edits (the version I watched had a slight damage on the tape which fuzzed up the screen for a second before the scalpel makes contact, and I know some will say that's all you need to sneak in an edit, but no, I still don't believe it was faked). The craft of special effects in those days weren't really up to much unless you had a Hollywood-sized budget and a good team of technicians, but for a cheap bit of shock footage shot on 8mm with no chance of financial reward, the chances of creating something that has that awful air of authenticity (even with someone like Cazazza on board) are pretty slim. Even today with the best FX team on the planet working with unlimited resources would struggle to replicate that scene. So if that footage does turn out to be faked then I'd be absolutely gob-smacked.

If the people involved in *First Transmission* weren't so tight-lipped when it comes to discussing the film then maybe things would be much clearer – its makers would then either be in jail or in Hollywood giving Tom Savini and Screaming Mad George some FX tips. But strangely, the rumours and hearsay surrounding the film elevate it into that uneasy blur between fact and fiction, a place where all the Blair Witches and Texas Chain Saw Massacres in the world can never hope to situate themselves. Not even the power of the internet can dispel the myths concerning this fucked up little film, and the mystery deepens...

One of the most ludicrous rumours surrounding First Transmission is that Orridge had to flee the UK because the police were onto him about the tapes. Now, I'm no expert on international law, but he only emigrated to the USA, and it wouldn't be difficult for the British authorities to have him extradited.

Made in Britain (1982)
Dir: Alan Clarke /UK

After the BBC refused to broadcast *Scum* in the late 70s for being "too realistic," director Alan Clarke (along with writer David Lelend) was given another opportunity to explore the dark side of youth a few years later when he was invited to film a project for a short-lived TV series, '*Tales Out of School*.'

The result was an episode entitled *Made In Britain*, a no less realistic depiction of a rebel without a cause, featuring a powerhouse performance from Tim Roth as the troubled Trevor, an angry skinhead with a Swastika tattooed on his forehead. The film follows this deeply disturbed kid on his destructive path as he hurls racist abuse, vandalizes homes and businesses, and crashes a van into the local police station. His social worker tries desperately to calm him down and plays on the boy's intelligence but to no effect. Trevor seems determined to spiral even further out of control, and sinks deeper into his own rotten sense of hatred before his rampaging behaviour lands him in police custody.

With its stylish mix of neon-lit streets and natural daylight, director Alan Clarke shows more willing this time around to experiment here than with his previous *Scum*s, even trying out Steadicam for the first time to stunning effect. The way the camera prowls along, keeping up with the fiercely energetic Trevor has the effect of turning even the most ordinary scenes into provocative and poetic flourishes (he would use Steadicam later on in his career for *The Firm* and *Elephant*).

Actor Tim Roth in his first role is absolutely superb as the young Trevor spiralling out of control. Roth went on to carve a pretty decent career for himself on the fringes of Hollywood, working with such luminaries as Peter Greenaway and Quentin Tarantino, and has always been willing to offer a leg-up to up and coming filmmakers such as Buddy Giovinazzo when Roth agreed to play a role in his film, *Life*

Sentences. But nowhere has he found a more meaty, grittier role than as Trevor in *Made In Britain*, one of the most honest and compelling of all young rebel movies.

One of the most fascinating scenes in the film shows Trevor in debate with a youth worker who scribbles his warnings on a blackboard about the dangers and idiocies of a life spent in the criminal justice system. What's so extraordinary about the scene is that the film doesn't choose sides, and both sides of the argument have their own understandable (if disagreeable) logic, and both are passionate and ring true. The youth worker literally spells out to Trevor that if he continues the way he is he'll find himself going "round and round" the system with no escape, and Trevor retorts, accusing the youth worker of being just as racist as him but hides it because he's a coward. Now, with the undercurrent of racism that existed in Britain during that time (and perhaps things haven't really changed too much since), Trevor could indeed have a point there. It's interesting how the youth worker doesn't explain to him how racism is stupid and wrong but instead simply sighs, "no one cares about your little protest, Trevor."

Regardless of the racist subject matter (they could have been arguing about politics or football, or music or women, etc), this scene represents a classic case of young versus old. The older man has probably come into contact with many tearaways like Trevor in his time; his pleadings for a quiet life of order and stability constantly falling on deaf ears. And Trevor is the youth whose misguided and chaotic passion is outraged by the fact that he feels surrounded by cowards who are too afraid to fight his cause. It's the idealism of youth and the 'anything-for-a-quiet-life' of age that are at loggerheads in this scene, and it is one of the finest of its kind in the history of film.

With a slim running time of 73 minutes, *Made in Britain* is one of the finest TV movies ever made; it's gritty, honest, provocative, but full of style, courage, and compassion in everything from the camerawork and performances to the script and overall message: I'm sure most of us have had our Trevor moments in our pasts where we've been insanely passionate about things we cared about, whether it be football, movies, or a girl, etc, and Clarke shows us that 'growing out of it' isn't always a matter of maturity, but more often a case of having to take responsibility and make compromises just so that we can live a 'quiet life'.

The film also ends on an interesting note: For all the trouble that Trevor has caused he was never physically hit; he took some harsh bollockings from the people around him who were trying to steer him onto the straight and narrow, but he was never given a hiding. At the end of the film, however, when Trevor finds himself in police custody, his mouth infuriates one of the policemen who promptly wacks him with his truncheon. Trevor has no answer for that, he seems a bit stumped for the first time in his life. And it's there that the film ends. Make of that what you will.

Basket Case (1982)
Dir: Frank Henenlotter /USA
Basket Case hit the screens in the early 80s as a sort of grindhouse alternative to Spielberg's *E.T.*, where surgical masks were handed out to audiences "to keep the blood off your face." Dedicated to Herschell Gordon Lewis, this film purposely mixes horror and humour in a way that Lewis only managed by accident. The story starts with Duane (Kevin Van Hentenryck), a young man who arrives in NYC carrying a locked wicker basket. He checks into a run-down sleazy hotel, and a succession of characters come to regret their curiosity as to "what's in the basket?" as, to their horror, they discover that it contains Belial, a razor-toothed mound of deformed flesh with an unholy temper and an appetite for eating people's faces. Turns out that Belial was formerly Duane's siamese twin. They were attached at the waist until they were surgically separated against their wishes, and now the twins are seeking the surgeons for bloody revenge...

Paying homage not only to H. G. Lewis' bloody gore effects and sadistic sense of humour, but also to other sleazy 42nd Street wonders like *Nightmares In a Damaged Brain* (1981), *The Headless Eyes* (1971) and the early films of John Waters, writer/director Frank Henenlotter was a true student of the Deuce. But rather than simply regurgitating the cinematic influences he had developed in his misspent youth, he also adds a genuine compassion for his monster and a heartfelt sense of familial love; there is a flashback scene in which Duane finds his little brother outside disposed in a bin bag and left to die after their separation. Duane

rescues his twin and they develop a telepathic bond. It's a poignant scene – so rare in grindhouse flicks – that adds an emotional undercurrent to the bloody humour and cynicism. Fans of the film often complain about the scene in which Belial murders the heroine and molests her dead body, insisting that it adds a bitterness to the film, but as pointed out by Stephen Thrower, it's worth noting that Belial is simply acting out what he is: an unnurtured 'beast,' as was alluded to in the scene where the twin's aunt reads to them Shakespeare's *The Tempest* as a bedtime story. The Bard's tale includes the character Caliban, a feral human who rapes Prospero's daughter. Like Belial, he is a character who was never taught to unlearn his savage instincts.

Basket Case 2 (1990) picks up right where the original left off, as Duane and Belial are whisked off into the protective custody of their aunt, a 'freak's rights' activist whose remote country house serves as a safe haven for a variety of genetic oddities. However, when a prying reporter gets too close, all hell breaks loose once again. Not in the same league as part one, this sequel concentrates more on the satirical aspects of the genre, from political correctness and the increasingly tabloid-centric American culture, and the battle for social justice in a post-Regan, conservative climate. It was followed by more of the same in the second sequel, *Basket Case 3: Progeny* (1992).

Pieces (1982)
Dir: Juan Piquer Simon /USA/Spain/Puerto Rica
A young boy kills his mother with an axe and cuts her body into pieces after being caught with a nudy jigsaw puzzle and porn mags. The police assume the killer to be some madman who has fled the scene, and so the kid gets away with murder. Forty years later and there is a chainsaw-wielding maniac on the loose at a college campus, slicing and dicing the pretty students and collecting their body parts. But who could be responsible?

This is one of those so-bad-it's-good early 80s slasher movies; we're bombarded with bad acting, a boring police investigation, and all kinds of bizarre and insane moments that appear out of nowhere ("BAS-STAARRRD!!!"). There's also the usual share of cat-out-of-the-bag jump scares, but I've never seen any who know Kung Fu, until now. The film's real saving grace though is the extreme violence and gore, and we're treated to a nice amount of the red stuff in the film's numerous graphic slayings.

There are also many blatant tributes to Dario Argento and giallo movies that are spread liberally throughout; shades of *Deep Red* and *Tenebrae* (the latter was made around the same time); the reliance on childhood sexual trauma as the springboard for a psychopath; the stylized POV shots of the black-gloved killer who seems to be omnipresent, stalking and slashing his victims (usually beautiful young women); the red herrings and heavy bloodshed (the stabbing on the waterbed is textbook Argento). But not even the great Dario have a chainsaw-swinging maniac his films. Even the music is Goblin-esque – tension building bass notes and swirling synths.

Although shot in Spain, *Pieces* is also very much an American slasher movie of its time, with the usual ingredients of teens, sex, nudity, slaughter, and a boring police investigation (Christopher George of *City of the Living Dead* fame plays the film's detective, Bracken), it's all here. There's some hilarious goofs and cringe-inducingly bad acting on display (look out for Jess Franco regular Jack Taylor who plays a smug professor), but you can't miss it if you're a fan of slasher movies.

Director Juan Piquer Simon is no cult favourite like a Jess Franco or even a Joe D'Amato. The rest of his filmography is absolutely dire with the godawful likes of *The Pod People* and *Cthulu Mansion*. Only his late 80s effort, *Slugs*, can live up to the deranged promise of *Pieces*.

Mysterious Two (1982)
Dir: Gary Sherman /USA
An intrepid journalist follows a mysterious couple who claim to be evangelists. Turns out they're cult leaders who have convinced their followers that they're from another galaxy. They then encourage the faithful to join them on a spaceship and journey back to their home planet. The unquestioning followers are soon selling all of their possessions in preparations for the 'trip,' while the journalist and local Sheriff investigate why people are disappearing. This TV movie was written and directed by the underrated Gary Sherman – of *Death Line* (1972) and *Dead and Buried* (1981) fame – and is far better than expected and still largely unseen by horror fans. The film does a fine job of exploring the mindsets of those who are suckered in by charismatic leaders, and does a lot to foreshadow the tragedies of real-life cult suicides. The film is loosely inspired by Marshall Applewhite and Bonnie Nettles, also known as 'The Two,' a couple of supposed UFO contactees who built a considerable following in California in the 1970s before disappearing. Applewhite showed up again in the early 90s (Bonnie died of a brain tumour in the 80s), as the leader of Heaven's Gate, surgically castrated and claiming that a spaceship was awaiting him and his followers behind the Hale Bopp comet to take them to a better world. When the police broke into their commune-like home in March 1997, they discovered the cult members' bodies laying in their beds. All had killed themselves by drinking a poisonous concoction.

Turkey Shoot (1982)
(aka *Escape 2000*; aka *Blood Camp Thatcher*)
Dir: Brian Trenchard-Smith /Australia
This wildly entertaining Ozploitation classic from Brian Trenchard-Smith (of *Stunt Rock* [1980] and *Dead End Drive-In* [1986] fame), is still criminally underrated to this day. It often gets completely overlooked, even in cult movie guides, but make no mistake, this is future fantasy entertainment at its wackiest, and is well worth picking up on DVD.

Set in a future prison colony for 'deviants' (i.e. enemies of the state, or anyone the authorities don't like), we witness the arrival of three new inmates, Chris and Rita (Olivia Hussey and Lynda Stoner) and Paul Anders (Steve Railsback). Dressed in bright yellow jumpsuits, the new arrivals are quickly inducted into the brutal, Big Brother-type setting, with sadistic guards and Newspeak slogans. And after watching a fellow inmate being humiliated and burned alive, the newcomers are offered the opportunity to leave the camp. They are invited into the office of the camp commander, Thatcher (Michael Craig), and he lays down the rules: five inmates will have a head start to escape the compound and to start a new life of freedom. The catch is, they will be hunted down by an elite group of heavily-armed sadists who just love hunting their inferiors for sport.

Thus, the 'turkey shoot' begins, as Thatcher's friends set off in pursuit of the fleeing inmates, including Michael Petrovich, a giggling maniac who drives a custom-built bulldozer complete with a mounted machine gun and rocket launcher turrets. Also accompanying him is a hairy, cannibalistic circus freak called Alf (Steve Rackman), who has a thing for eating people's toes. Other hunters include Carmen Duncan as the cold, pampered, sadistic bitch, Jennifer, whose weapon of choice is a crossbow that fires explosive arrows (just like Fred Williamson in *The New Barbarians* [1982]). Her character was perhaps inspired by the veiled and mysterious super-sadist, the 'Lady On the Train' (played by Macha Meril) in *Night Train Murders* (1975). And just like that character, Jennifer also wears a veil to help conceal the dark depths of evil in her eyes (a similar deviant character later showed up again in Ridley Scott's *The Counselor* [2013], with the 'famished' Malkina, decorated in cheetah tattoos that represent her predatory nature, and played with a cold-hearted finesse by Cameron Diaz).

The inmate's break for freedom sees them trudging through the hostile terrain of the wooded and mountainous landscape. Annoyingly, instead of staying hidden among the trees, most of the them stay out in the open, with their distinctive yellow suits easily picked up in the crosshairs of the hunters. However, what follows is a gripping adventure, full of tension and struggle and graphic gore, all played out to Brian May's glorious score which mixes big brass arrangements with booming bongos and swirling synthesizers.

Turkey Shoot takes it biggest inspiration from *The Most Dangerous Game* (1932), and its offshoots, *A Game of Death* (1945), *Run For the Sun* (1956) and *Bloodlust!* (1961), along with that other hunting-for-humans classic, *Punishment Park* (1971). It also has much in common with *Terminal Island* (1973), and adds a delirious dose of exploitation and other popular sub-genres, such as future fantasy and women-in-prison, to jungle adventures and war-era POW escape movies. The red haired Dodge (John Ley), with his thick bifocals and nerdy demeanour, is reminiscent of Dustin Hoffman in *Papillon* (1973), another escape-from-a-prison-colony classic. And, with all this commingling of influences, it's difficult to get of a sense of the film's legacy, or if it even has one. Arnold Schwarzenegger would go on to wear a yellow jumpsuit while being pursued by leering maniacs in the film version of *The Running Man* (1987), and a sub-genre of futuristic prison escape movies flourished in the 90s and beyond, which provided the likes of *Fortress* (1992) and *Fortress 2* (2000), which were also shot in Australia. *Turkey Shoot* is clearly a film that has borrowed from cinema much more than it has given back, but its current neglected status as a barely talked about oddity is a fate far worse than it deserves.

Blood Beat (1982)
Dir: Fabrice-Ange Zaphiratos /USA

Blood Beat is a micro-budget supernatural slasher that attempts to add a degree of respectability by concentrating on things like back-story and character development, which is all well and good, but by the half hour mark the average viewer will be crying out for blood. Enough with the ponsy pretentiousness and give us some slashings! The story is about a family of hunters with a psychic mum, hunter-gatherer father, and overly sensitive daughter who constantly shuns her boyfriend's sexual advances. At the 40-minute mark one of them snaps and goes on a rampage with a Samurai sword. And the stabbings seem to project psychic orgasmic thrills in the daughter, and we never find out why. And meanwhile, the house is also under attack from a dark demonic force... Director Zaphiratos demonstrates a knack for interesting visual angles (especially in the outdoor scenes), and the special effects are quite impressive for an early 80s amateur horror, but don't be fooled by the classical music and arty technique; this is an incredibly dumb movie posing as something smart and sophisticated.

Scarab (1982)
Dir: Steven-Charles Jaffe /Spain /USA

A physicist summons an ancient Egyptian demon which grants him unlimited power in his quest to assassinate a number of high-profile political figures. A clumsy news reporter investigates the deaths after noticing scarab-like insects left behind on the bodies, and his sleuthing leads him to uncover a sinister underground cult that is bent on world domination. Hard to find on any kind of home video format these days (the version I watched was dubbed in Spanish with French subtitles), *Scarab* isn't really worth any major effort in tracking down as it's a badly made, lightweight horror with lots of silly attempts at humour and many loose ends. On the plus side, there are some individual moments that work, such as the scene in which a woman's body is transformed into a giant slimy bug, and the ritual scenes at the end are deliriously over-the-top.

Superstition (1982)
(aka *The Witch*)
Dir: James W. Roberson /Canada

The evil spirit of a witch that was drowned to death by the Church in 1692, returns to the 'black pond' almost three centuries later to dish out some revenge on the descendants of the original townfolk... Anyone familiar with movies like *Black Sunday* (1960), *Mark of the Witch* (1972) and *Burned at the Stake* (1981) will have seen it all before. But in its favour, *Superstition* takes the hokey theme and delivers the story with an urgent, action-packed appeal. Barely a minute passes without a character revelation or the lead-up to a vicious death scene. And the production values are very impressive for a low-budget fright flick of its time, and looks wonderful on DVD all these years later. Gory highlights include a human head exploding in a microwave, a body torn in half on a window pane, a Priest having his chest ripped open by a runaway circular saw, and a young woman graphically staked through the forehead.

Mongrel (1982)
Dir: Robert A. Burns /USA

The directorial debut of Robert A. Burns, the set designer on *The Texas Chain Saw Massacre* (1975) and *The Hills Have Eyes* (1977). After a vicious dog is shot dead during an attack, a young man has recurring dreams about the beast coming back to life and attacking the residents of a run down guest house. And when the dreams turn out to be somewhat true, the remaining guests club together in their efforts to kill the pest. *Mongrel* is the kind of film that is populated with so many annoying characters, it's a joy to watch the dog snap and tear them to pieces. Even the main protagonist is a lumbering dangle-mouth. And things are not helped with the casting of an obviously timid dog, who – despite all the posturing and dubbed 'growling' sound effects – looks like it's just dying to roll over so you can tickle its belly.

Incubus (1982)
Dir: John Hough /Canada

A doctor (John Cassevetes) and local Sheriff are puzzled by a series of rape-murders in a small New England town while a young man has severe nightmares about black-cloaked figures conducting evil Satanic rituals. The vicious killings continue, and the perpetrator looks to be inhuman, some kind of incredibly strong beast that fires such a high volume of spunk that the coroners believe the girls to have been gang-raped. *Incubus* is an ever so tasteful approach to the monster rapist horror sub-genre, but is worth a look if only for the monster itself; a kind of bald-headed toothy ogre who could probably father a whole squad of Wayne Rooneys with one load. Now *that's* scary.

The Slayer (1982)
Dir: J. S. Cardone /USA

A surrealist painter, Kay (Sarah Kendall), endures recurring nightmares about a demon killing her friends. And when her husband arranges a vacation for them and their buddies, Kay's protests against the trip fall on deaf ears. And, sure enough, not long after they arrive on the fishing island, someone – or some*thing* – begins wiping out the cast members, one by one... The concept of a dream demon coming to life and murdering the heroine's friends while she desperately tries to stay awake to avoid confronting the ghoul, may seem hokey nowadays, but *The Slayer* pre-dates Wes Craven's *A Nightmare on Elm Street* (1984) by a couple of years. The film can be commended for having adult characters instead of the usual teens, and for adding a supernatural twist to the 'slasher' movie template. Memorable death scenes include one character getting his head trapped and slowly decapitated by his own bodyweight, and a pitchfork murder which rivals the ones seen in *The Bogey Man* (1980) and *Friday the 13th Part 2* (1981).

One Dark Night (1982)
Dir: Tom McLoughlin /USA

A young Meg Tilly is so keen to join 'The Sisters,' a high school girl gang, that she agrees to spend the night in a crypt at the local funeral home as part of her initiation. However, a recently deceased telekinetic practitioner has been entombed there, and he returns from the dead, unleashing a horde of 'zombie' minions from their coffins to terrorise the girls. *One Dark Night* is a slow-paced, damp squid of a movie which is worth a watch if only for the final 20-minutes when the re-animated corpses are unleashed. Crucially, these aren't zombies in the traditional sense of running on some deep primal instincts, but literally dead meat puppeteered by telekinesis. The upright coffins open up like mummy's tombs, and the bodies –

dressed in funeral suits and with stitched up, yellowy eyes – clamber out at the terrified girls. Fans of *Children Shouldn't Play With Dead Things* (1972) should lap it up.

Oi For England (1982)
Dir: Tony Smith /UK

A subversive TV play written by the openly communist Trevor Griffiths. Centring on a punk band called 'White Ammunition' (they sound a bit like *Live at the Witch Trials*-era The Fall), we watch as they audition for a shady, sharp-suited A&R man, known only as 'The Man.' He is looking for a band to perform at an upcoming far-right political rally. The group blasts out a couple of songs in the dank Manchester cellar while the Moss Side riots rage outside. *Oi For England* is one of those micro-budget television productions that takes place on a single set. The cast members do their best to look and sound like angry northern skinheads, but their middle-class, drama school pedigree shines through in every scene. It's not enough for the teens to be proud of their race; consequently, they must also be shown to be evil. Thus, the angriest of the skinheads reveals that he has just mugged a black guy for his wages. Ultimately, their racism stems from unemployment and poverty, and the lead singer, Fin (Adam Kotz), ultimately rejects racism when he befriends a black girl.

I Was a Zombie for the F.B.I. (1982)
Dir: Marius Penczner /USA

Retro-inflected nonsense in the style of a 50s B-movie. A crashed UFO gives off radiation which causes the dead to walk. 'Zombie' criminals are sent by the F.B.I. to infiltrate and destroy the alien invaders, or something like tht. Just like the 30th Anniversary Edition of *Night of the Living Dead*, this film was later re-released on DVD with 'improved' special effects, extra scenes and a dreadful new soundtrack which obliterates the 50s illusion and ruins what was already a pretty terrible movie in the first place. Crucially, these are not rotting, flesh-eating ghouls, but mute, catatonic in-patients.

Burst City (1982)
(Orig title: *Bakuretsu toshi*)
Dir: 'Sogo Ishii' [Gakuryu Ishii] /Japan

This follow-up to Ishii's *Crazy Thunder Road* (1980) is set in some kind of future Tokyo wasteland where rival gangs of bikers race each other in the streets before the epic finale in which an army of riot police descend on their fortress hideout. Unfortunately, the film doesn't quite live up to its cult classic reputation; the frantic energy and pacing of the film becomes irksome after a while; the performances of the bands throughout are never more than mediocre (one of the bands sing 'White Riot in the Supermarket,' an odd medley of Clash covers); the storyline is rarely coherent, etc. However, the film's saving grace is the assorted fashions on display – clearly based on the UK's mods and rockers fad, these wayward youths also sport a variety of bizarre outfits, from the run-of-the-mill 50s-style flick knife greasers, to leather-and-spikes-studded street punks, and others who look like they have just stepped out of a *Mad Max* movie. At around two hours in length, the film is perhaps a tad over long, but it's worth sticking around for the ending – more than 6000 punks were used for the final battle sequence, and though it's certainly great to watch, it could have been so much better. The film-makers clearly went for an 'anything goes,' punk rock style approach to the showdown, letting total chaos reign, but perhaps if they had organised the shots better (or at least planned them out on storyboards beforehand), the end result could have been ten times better. As it stands, *Burst City* remains a minor cult item rather than the classic it ought to have been. On the plus side, we do get to see a cop being decapitated by a drum cymbal that is frisbee'd into the crowd. Punk rawk!

Visiting Hours (1982)
Dir Jean Claude Lord /Canada

Michael Ironside plays a misogynistic psychopath who targets a women's rights campaigner. And when he learns that she has survived the vicious attack, he heads to the hospital where she's recovering to finish what he started... *Visiting Hours* is an above-average slasher movie with lots of suspense and impressive set-pieces, the most memorable of which is the initial attack sequence in which the victim tries to hide in the laundry chute.

The Deadly Spawn (1982)
Dir: Douglas McKeown /USA

A sleepy American town is awoken by the arrival of a meteorite carrying a spawn of toothy alien creatures that feast on human prey. A young monster movie fan discovers the creatures in the family basement. And, with the help of his older brother and friends, he sets to work eliminating the pests... *The Deadly Spawn* is a pean to the monster movie, and is a must-see for fans of *Critters* (1986) and *Phantasm* (1979). For such a low-budget film, this boasts a superb score and sound design, along with a great imagination, likeable characters, gruesome special effects, and a genuine love for monster movies of old. Most of the budget was wisely spent on the creation of John Dods' space alienss; the FX guy did a marvellous job of constructing the critters, which look like giant reddish mouths with row upon row of uneven teeth dripping with alien slime. In their infant stages, the baby spawn look like oversized tadpoles, or the blood parasites in Cronenberg's *Shivers* (1974), slithering around in the waterlogged basement. The result is a 50s-style invasion movie by way of HR Giger.

Bloodtide (1982)
Dir: Richard Jeffries /UK /Greece

A bog-standard monster movie in which James Earl Jones uses a chunk of semtex to blow up a cave. It turns out to be a silly move as he uncovers an ancient sea-dwelling demon. Not only does he have to fend off the bald, diseased dog of a beast, but he also has to appease the locals on a Greek island who are prone to offing outsiders in sacrificial rituals to keep the demon's hunger sated. The only good thing I can say about this film is that it's better than *Demon of Paradise* (1987). But that isn't saying much.

The Fourth Man (1983)
(Orig title: *De Vierde Man*)
Dir: Paul Verhoeven /Holland

Alcoholic gay writer, Gerard (Joroen Krabbé), is troubled by premonitions. During a speaking engagement at a sea-side town, he finds himself so attracted to a man called Herman (Thom Hoffman) that he romances his wife as a way of getting close to him. However, the wife is a witchy minx who may be responsible for the deaths of her previous three husbands, and may have her sights set on a fourth...

'The blueprint for *Basic Instinct*'. That's the description most often bounded around by film fans when discussing Paul Verhoeven's *The Fourth Man*. Made in the early 80s in the period between the opening of the controversial Dutch shocker, *Spetters*, and the start of production on his first Euro-American project, *Flesh & Blood*, *The Fourth Man* found Verhoeven in his element, crafting a stylishly slick, erotic thriller which blended elements of tortured Catholicism and perverse sexuality into an exquisitely twisted cocktail of sex and death.

Based on the novel by Dutch writer Gerard Reve, of whom you'll hear more of in the movie, *The Fourth Man* confounded critics who had Verhoeven down as a brash populist. Yet here he was trading on the name of one of Holland's most respected literary figures, the celebrated artist who had both supported the film during production and later declared it to be the very best screen adaptation of any of his writings. The fact that it took less money at the box-office than Verhoeven's previous movies mattered not a jot – this was a project that marked him out as a filmmaker worthy of serious attention, and he has never looked back. Part of the attraction of *The Fourth Man* is in its unrepentant ambiguity, as it follows Gerard's seduction by the archetypal femme fatale who may or may not have murdered her previous partners.

Pre-figuring the rows which greeted *Basic Instinct* ten years later, Verhoeven casually throws together unashamedly contradictory gay and straight, sacred and profane images which imply – but never clarify – their humorously heavy-handed themes. The film also combines multi-sexual eroticism, strange religious imagery (including a crucified gay poster and an appearance by the Virgin Mary), Argento-inspired horror elements and gore (a memorable eye-gouging after a car crash springs to mind) and some biting black humour. Soutendijk gives a fine performance – her tightly tied-back hair and blood-red lips make her an unusual satanic seductress. Krabbé is also in fine form as the obsessive Gerard who persists in finding decency in his extraordinarily sleazy character. The film moves along as a dark fantasy, offering up several genuinely surprising plot twists and moments of shock-power.

Form a stylistic point of view, the film is seen through the eyes of action-packed cinematographer Jan De Bont, who would later lens *Die Hard* and direct *Speed*. There are movie nods too to the works of Luis Buñuel, Alfred Hitchcock and – oddly – John Landis. And, of course, there's religious allegory aplenty, even if it does come wearing a pair of bright red swimming trunks.

In Holland, *The Fourth Man* was declared to be the first home-produced 'magic-realist' thriller, and it was also the winner of the Los Angeles Film Critics Association Award in 1984 for a foreign language film. Here in the UK, it remains a much talked about but still fairly little seen milestone in violent erotic cinema.

Escape From the Bronx (1983)
(aka *Bronx Warriors 2*; aka *Escape 2000*; Orig title: *Fuga dal Bronx*)
Dir: Enzo G. Castellari /Italy
Mark Gregory is a poor Kurt Russell substitute in this Italian *Escape From New York* (1981) clone. Set in the near future, Gregory stars as 'Trash,' a bike riding urban warrior who seeks vengeance on the GC Corporation that is responsible for incinerating his parents with flame-throwers. The corporation wants to relocate the residents of the Bronx to New Mexico so that the buildings can be demolished to make way for a state-of-the-art super-city. The company sends the DAS (or 'Disinfection Annihilation Squad') – a ruthless team of corporate lackeys who are ready and willing to murder those who refuse to leave their homes – into the slums to clear out any stragglers. However, Trash teams up with an outraged journalist and a gang of underground rebels, and together they embark on a campaign of guerilla warfare against the murderers...

This sequel to *1990: The Bronx Warriors* (1982) was director, Enzo Castellari's third apocalypse movie in a row, and the fatigue was beginning to creep in. The bad dubbing, crazy clothes, awful soundtrack – disco jazz, composed by Francesco Masi – are shoddier than usual. Add to this a simple plot that is needlessly convoluted simply as a way of stretching out the film's running time, and you've got a recipe for one helluva bad movie. The same scenario of tit-for-tat attack and counter-attack between the heroes and villains goes back and forth in the same slummy surroundings until the boredom becomes too much. Perhaps the biggest problem with the film is the casting of Gregory in the lead role. He comes across as more of a bit player than a leading man – his angelic features and lack of all-out aggression are at odds with his supposed 'tough guy' image of the rugged underdog action hero. He's more of a young pretender rather than the real McCoy. Still, some may find the film entertaining if they catch it in the right mood. Look out for Henry Silva as the sadistic boss of the DAS.

The Dead Zone (1983)
Dir: David Cronenberg /USA
Tagline – 'In his mind, he has the power to see the future. In his hands, he has the power to change it.' Christopher Walken stars as Johnny Smith, a quiet, reserved school teacher who leaves his fiance's house one night during a rainstorm and suffers a near-fatal car accident. Five years later, and Johnny comes out of a deep coma, his life irrevocably changed. He learns that his fiance has married another man, and his mother has turned to religious fundamentalism. But that's not all. He also discovers that he has developed a psychic 'gift' which enables him to experience visions of the past and future. However, each call on his services drains him, so he decides to ration himself. After assisting the police in the hunt for a serial killer, and saving the life of a child he 'saw' trapped under ice in a vision, Johnny attends a political rally. There he shakes hands with local candidate, Greg Stillson (Martin Sheen, in a very different political role prior to *The West Wing* [1999-2006]), and experiences a terrifying vision: Stillson will become President and bring about the apocalypse through nuclear war. And as the politician gains power and influence, Johnny resolves to assassinate him...

David Cronenberg's first mainstream film, *The Dead Zone*, was a surprise to horror fans at the time who were expecting the director to embrace his usual outlandish style. And while *The Dead Zone* is most certainly part of his body horror cannon, the scenario here is much more down to earth than the previous year's *Videodrome* (1982). The obsession with disease, mutation, and sexuality take more of backseat while Cronenberg tackles Stephen King's source novel to explore themes of social alienation and perception itself.

Cronenberg had considered adapting *The Dead Zone* to the screen a couple of years earlier, but had initially turned it down. However, after the box-office disappointment of *Videodrome*, the writer/director was in need of a hit. And though he had never worked on anothers writings before, especially a well-known novel by a well-known author, he decided to give it a shot. In the introduction on the DVD, Cronenberg commented, 'it immediately became apparent that the most honest and straight forward way to approach it was to strip away all of the stuff in the book that really didn't interest me or convince me.' Five scripts were written for the project, and Cronenberg decided to proceed with Jeffrey Boam's treatment which managed to capture the various elements – the sci-fi/horror and political thriller – for a screen-friendly story.

The result is a genuine fusion of Cronenberg and King, and remains one of the finest King adaptations to hit the screen, alongside *Misery* (1990) and *The Green Mile* (1999). Kim Newman initially dismissed the film as a 'clumsily strung procession of episodes,' but changed his mind when he revisited the film almost three decades later, calling his comments 'harsh,' and admitting that he actually found the thread-line of the film 'compelling.' Indeed, the film has aged very well, with its snowy New England setting (actually shot in Ontario), and its subtle, emotionally-driven through-line makes a change from the usual roughshod King adaptations that proliferate the screen. If there are any criticisms, for me it would be the clichéd right-wing political villain.

Christopher Walken is superb in the lead role – his vulnerability coming to the fore as he realises that his new 'gift' could actually be a curse. The underrated Brooke Adams is also great as Johnny's ex-fiance. Elsewhere, look out for the solid supporting cast which includes Tom Skerritt, Herbert Lom and Anthony Zerbe. Cronenberg fans will also spot Cindy Hines and Nicholas Campbell (of *The Brood*), and Les Carlson (of *Videodrome* and). However, for all the wonders of *The Dead Zone*, the most compelling aspect is the sense of longing and lost love that haunts the film. The psychic pain that Johnny suffers is always underscored by his sudden alienation in dealing with a world that had passed him by for five years while he was in the 'dead zone' of a coma. 'The reason that his love is lost,' Cronenberg said, 'is because of Johnny's new awareness. It's as though he becomes an artist and is therefore not fit to integrate in human society. Before the accident, he was a normal guy about to get married, and afterwards he's this strange man seized by visions, and he can't relate to people, and things are always too complex for him.'

The notorious scene in which the serial killer commits suicide with a pair of scissors was censored in many territories, but DVD editions are fully uncut. *The Dead Zone* was later brought to the screen again, this time as a TV series starring Anthony Michael Hall, which ran for 6 seasons from 2002-2007.

Endgame (1983)
(Orig title: *Endgame – Bronx lotta finale*)
Dir: 'Steven Benson' ['Joe D'Amato,' – Aristide Massaccesi] /Italy

Set in a post-nuclear police state in 2025, where squads of gas masked Nazi cops roam the rat-infested streets hunting illegal mutants. The national sport is Endgame, a televised slaughter fest in which a posse of bad guys (including Bobby Rhodes as 'Woody,' and George Eastman as 'Karnak') hunt down volunteers with guns for prize money. In tonight's show, we have a Mad Max/Clint Eastwood-type loner, Ron Shannon ('Al Cliver,' real name Pier Luigi Conti), who volunteers for the game. And off he goes, with a few minutes head start, disappearing into the foggy darkness, armed with only a hunting knife. After making quick work of the bad guys, Shannon ends up killing a bunch of cops and helping a telepathic mutant girl, Lilith ('Moira Chen' – Laura Gemser of the *Emmanuelle* series) and others to get to a safe haven 200 miles out of the city. However, their journey is a dangerous one as they encounter hostile mutants while the cops hunt them down every step of the way...

Surprisingly action-packed and much less cheesy than one would expect from an early 80s Italian *Mad Max* knock-off, *Endgame* is one of the better apocalypse movies that showed up on VHS. In fact, director and exploitation legend, Joe D'Amato – whose filmography includes around 200 titles – always insisted that *Endgame* was his favourite. Some of the action scenes are a little flat, and the editing could have been tighter, but the pacing is generally spot on, never losing a beat as the band of heroes make their way through the radioactive wasteland. En route, they encounter various creeps, including a commune of blind worshippers in black robes (which looks to be an inversion of a sequence taken from John Wyndham's novel, *The Day of the Triffids* [pub. 1951]). They also run into an army of *Mad Max 2*-style punk barbarians in armoured cars and riding dirt cross bikes ('Look at me while I rape you, dammit!'), before the final ambush by the Nazi cops. It's the kind of film in which a karate chop to the collar bone is enough to finish a man, but you'll be hard pushed to find a more fun and exciting future fantasy. Also of note is Carlo Maria Cordio's typically eclectic score which mixes synthesizers, church organ, and other eerie sounds, all set to pulsating electronic beats.

For all the film's future-bound setting, *Endgame* borrows just as much from cinema's past as it does from the present. The film could have been set in the mid 19th Century in the wild west, with only minor changes needed in the script. Much of the film plays like a future update of the old bounty hunter movies by Sergio Leone, Andre de Toth and Sam Peckinpah, in which renegade characters roam the lawless land making pacts and alliances with those they know will ultimately betray them in the end – see *The Good, the Bad and the Ugly* (1966), *The Bounty Hunter* (1954), and *Bring Me the Head of Alfredo Garcia* (1974). In one scene in particular, Shannon is seen clutching a thin, Eastwood-type cigaro between his teeth while he negotiates a pact with gold-hungry bandits, as if to press the point home to viewers that even in the distant future, the bad and ugly side of human nature will always be there.

Endgame also belongs to a family of films set in bleak times ahead. Aside from its obvious debt to *Mad Max* and its first sequel, the other filmic reference points are many and varied. It owes an obvious debt to *The Most Dangerous Game* (1932), *The 10th Victim* (1966), *Death Race 2000* (1975), and its follow-up, *Deathsport* (1978), films in which hunting humans becomes either personal or televised entertainment. It also borrows from the early work of Stephen King; the sub-plot involving the telekinetic kid whose very existence is regarded as a national threat by the authorities, relates to the young girl, Charlie, in *Firestarter* (first published in 1980), and in a less direct way, to his debut novel, *Carrie* (pub.1974) and even David Cronenberg's *Scanners* (1980); while the televised blood hunt inspired by *The Running Man* (first published in 1982 under his pseudonym, 'Richard Bachman') also provided the basis for the film version starring Arnold Schwarzenegger in 1987. And, after that, the mantle was carried further with any number of movies borrowing liberally from this cluster of ideas, such as *Cyborg* (1989), in which a less-than-verbose warrior agrees to protect a life-like 'female' cyborg while journeying through an apocalyptic landscape teeming with bloodthirsty bandits; *Total Recall* (1990), with its emphasis on a community of persecuted mutant telepaths; *Hard Target* (1993), which revisits the concept of the hunters and the hunted; and *Battle Royale* (2000), which broadcasts the slaughter as prime time television; also *Slashers* (2001), *Series 7:*

The Contenders (2001), and *The Condemned* (2007), among others. And in my opinion, *Endgame* can tough it out with the best of them.

Aristide Massaccesi was born in Rome in 1936. The son of an electrician at the Cinecitta studios, he got his first gig in the film industry at 16-years-old as a stills photographer on the set of *La carrozza d'oro* (*The Golden Coach*, 1952), an experience which helped to fuel his passion for film and photography. Throughout the 60s, he worked with cinematographers as an apprentice and camera operator, before landing his first DoP job at the end of the decade with *Pelle di Bandito* (1969), a little seen true crime caper. By the early 70s, he was working regularly with directors such as Demofilo Fidani (*Django Meets Sartana!*, 1970), Massimo Dallamano (*What Have You Done to Solange?*, 1972), and Alberto De Martino (*The Killer Is On the Phone*, 1972), before taking to the helm as director with *More Sexy Canterbury Tales* (1972), under the pseudonym 'Romano Gastaldi.'

Throughout the rest of his career, his films branched out in all directions, from westerns to swashbucklers, war movies to peplum fantasies, nunsploitaion to gialli, horror and porn, to horror/porn hybrids, and other genres and sub-genres, often under a variety of pseudonyms, the most infamous of which was 'Joe D'Amato.' He is the most prolific director ever to come from Italy, with 198 known credits (and 166 as cinematographer). His most well-known films include the 'video nasties,' *Absurd* (1981) and *Anthropophagus, The Beast* (1980), the morbid horrors of *Beyond the Darkness* (1979), glossy softcore efforts like the *Black Emanuelle* series, and the horror/porn hybrids of *Emmanuelle In America* (1977) and *Porno Holocaust* (1981). By the time of his death in January 1999, he was the most successful hardcore porn director in Italy.

Angst (1983)
(aka *Fear*; aka *Schizophrenia*)
Dir: Gerald Kargl /Austria
One of the most disturbing and realistically executed killer movies of all time. In this straight forward story we follow a nameless criminal who has just been released from prison for stabbing his mother. But there's not a trace of guilt or remorse at all. In fact quite the opposite; in a series of fascinating but twisted voice-overs we soon learn that this creepy little man has no

thoughts of trying to build a new life; the only thing that's on his mind is the search for new victims.

'Addicted' to and aroused by the fear he sees in his victims' eyes, we're challenged to tag along with this maniac as he goes about his work. He gets into a taxi and eventually tries to strangle the female driver. But because of his suspicious behaviour before-hand, she seems ready for anything, and manages to fight him off and escape. So he wanders through the woods until he arrives at a large family home. He breaks in and snoops around, and discovers a man in a wheelchair who appears to be both physically and mentally disabled ("I knew I would kill him, but not immediately"). And when the rest of the family gets back from a shopping trip, they're completely oblivious to the monster who is lurking in their home. The maniac then sets about a series of deeply unpleasant murders. The disabled son is slowly drowned in the bath tub in a truly agonizing scene, the middle-aged mother is strangled, and the young daughter is repeatedly stabbed and mutilated. He then rapes her bloody corpse in a frenzy (in the first full-on depiction of necrophilia in film history). And all of this is shot more or less in real time.

Unsurprisingly, this film is often referred to as 'Europe's answer to *Henry-Portrait of a Serial Killer'* (even though it pre-dates that film), but unlike John McNaughton's masterpiece, we get to see everything in unflinching detail in *Angst*. It's also based on the crimes of convicted mass murderer, Werner Kniesek, who killed three people in Slazburg, Austria in 1980 (and who, incidentally, made a failed escape attempt during the film's production). Quotes are taken from real life killers throughout; "I just love it when women shiver in deadly fear because of me. It is an addiction which will never stop." Those are the words that Kniesek used when addressing the Judge in court. Quotes are also used from the true confessions of the 'Vampire of Dusseldorf', Peter Kurten (true crime buffs will also spot similarities in the film relating to the later case of Jack Unterweger).

Erwin Leder's central performance as the crazed killer is so full of bug-eyed, manic energy and unpredictability, it reminded me of Klaus Kinski at his nuttiest, or even an actor from the silent era. It's the shifty and erratic behaviour that draws so much attention to this character, and is ultimately his downfall. And Leder captures that fear and twisted excitement so well. In real life, psychopathic killers are usually very good at concealing their sickness to appear quite normal to the everyday public. Even moments after committing the most horrendous crimes, the psycho killer can revert back to outward normality in a flash. But the killer explored in this film seems to lack that self-consciousness.

A major influence on Gaspar Noe, especially his *Seul contre tous*, *Angst* features a soundtrack which is more well-known than the film itself. Klaus Schulze of Tangerine Dream provides the ominous electronic score, of which the track '*Surrender*' seems to be playing constantly, complimenting the ice-cold set decoration, colouring, and lighting of the film. Kudos to Zbigniew Rybczynski, whose hand-held camera work was really quite innovative for the time. In fact, his work is so impressive that it's easy to forget that much of the film was indeed shot in real time. He also co-wrote the script and edited the film (according to French filmmaker, Pascal Laugier, he even directed the movie too! Apparently 'Gerald Kargl' was just a pseudonym used by Rybczynski so that he could avoid facing responsibility if the film were to cause outrage! Unfortunately, I've been unable to verify this as fact).

Angst was released theatrically in Austria in the early 80s to some good reviews, but made no money and disappeared pretty fast. It then turned up in France on VHS under the title *Schizophrenia* and even garnered a bit of a cult fan base. In the UK, it was the 'video nasties' era, and potential distributors felt it would be a waste of time and money to release it here only to see it banned immediately, so the film was deemed 'too outrageous' and distributors wouldn't touch it. In America, the film was slapped with a XXX rating, usually given to hardcore porn titles, so the market potential there was pretty slim... Over the next couple of decades, *Angst* became a much talked about but little seen film, with awful looking scuzzy bootleg videos being the only way for horror fans to see it. Barrel Entertainment announced that they would release *Angst* uncut on DVD, but the company went bust soon after, and it wasn't until 2005 that we saw a significant release of the film when German DVD label Epix Media issued the full uncut version in a very satisfying transfer.

Kargl (or Rybczynski, or whoever he is) fully financed the film on his credit card, and after completion he found himself stuck making TV commercials for years while he paid off his debts. He sacrificed a potentially great career to bring us this masterpiece.

Kniesek's psychiatrist described him as "extremely abnormal but not mentally ill". The real life Kniesek was mixed race but is white in the film. When released from prison, he drove to a town called Poelton, broke into a villa owned by a widow, Gertrud Altreiter, and found the son in a wheelchair. Later the mother and daughter returned from a shopping trip. He tied them up and gagged them, and dragged them into different rooms in the house. The daughter actually tried to seduce him as a way of softening him up, but he was having none of it. He strangled the son and displayed his corpse to the mother and daughter before strangling the widow. The 25 year old daughter was then tortured and raped for hours before she too was murdered. He also killed the family cat, whereas in the film it's a pet dog which he takes with him and treats nicely. He also spent the night in the house with the bodies. "I killed them simply out of lust for murder," he claimed, "I even gave the elder woman some medicine so that she would live longer." He tried to commit suicide in his prison cell but failed. A few years later he made an escape attempt, but failed.

Screamtime (1983)
Dir: 'Al Beresford' [Michael Armstrong & Stanley Long] /UK
Screamtime is a horror anthology comprising three short films that were cobbled together with a wraparound plot shot in New York. The film starts with two youths stealing a bunch of video tapes from a store. They later show up at a girl's apartment and play the tapes. The first video is about a middle-aged man who runs a Punch & Judy show on Brighton beach. His family doesn't share the same enthusiasm for the puppets as he does. And after his son burns down the theatre stand, a slightly charred Mr. Punch goes on a killing spree, beating people to death with a plank of wood...On the second tape, a married couple move into a new house, and the wife sees strange, ghostly figures in and around the place. The husband becomes concerned for her mental health, and even the local ghost whisperer think she's nuts. And when she is finally sent to the nuthouse, viewers will find that perhaps she isn't insane after all (this second segment was released as a stand alone short film entitled *Dreamhouse* in 1982). And in the third tape, a young motorcross enthusiast, who needs money to repair his bike, accepts the job of handyman for a pair of kooky old ladies who believe in fairies. One night, he takes his brother and mechanic friend to the house. They break in with the intention of stealing a treasure-trove of silver and cash. However, the garden gnomes and fairies come to life and murder the intruders, one by one... *Screamtime* was an attempt to recapture the glory days of the British anthology horror as popularised by Amicus and *Hammer House of Horror.* The film is partly successful – the *Dreamhouse* segment manages to sustain a sense of uneasiness and suspense – but the low budget and lack of directorial skill ensured that this feature will be forever languishing in video hell, where only the most rabid of horror fans will get to see it.

Zombie Bloodbath (1983)
Dir: Todd Sheets /USA
Amateur zombie flick made on a cheap camcorder. When a housing project is built on the grounds where a nuclear power station once stood, it's no surprise when the leftover radiation causes the dead to walk. The local residents band together and fend off the plague of flesh-eating ghouls... Made at a time when DIY filmmakers actually put a lot of effort into their backyard epics, *Zombie Bloodbath* is an entertaining video, despite being utterly crude in all departments. There's lots of effort here in everything from the lighting, the editing, quirky camera angles, the blood and gore effects, and even an original score which is pretty decent. There is also a very large cast of characters, even if most of them serve as zombie extras. The main cast are generally terrible, but they do at least give it their all. Respect! According to IMDb, this film cost $30,000 to make. I call bullshit on that. $30 max! The scene in which the mother and son argue over the death of the husband/father is one of the all-time great moments of bad movie history – it's a scene in which director, Todd Sheets, tries to drum up some emotional impact in the audience while a cheesy synth ballad plays in the background. Needless to say, the fluffed lines and astonishingly bad acting from the 'mother' make it pure comedy gold. Sequels followed, *Zombie Bloodbath 2* (1995) and *Zombie Bloodbath 3:*

Zombie Armageddon (2000), if your brain can handle it.

Scalps (1983)
Dir: Fred Olen Ray /USA

A group of college students take a field trip out to the California desert plains for a spot of artefact hunting. However, one of the them disturbs an old burial ground near to the sacred 'black trees,' and he is possessed by 'black claw,' the vengeful spirit of a native American. And when night falls, he sets about slashing and scalping his classmates... With its effectively doomy synth score, isolated setting, and grisly death scenes, *Scalps* is a must-see for fans of early 80s slasher flicks. It boasts a lurid 'video nasty' appeal and a strange, otherworldly atmosphere in some parts. And even the teens aren't as annoying as usual, and viewers can enjoy their company as they trek their way to oblivion without wishing death upon them from the outset. Forrest J. Ackerman makes an early cameo appearance as a professor chastised for reading monster mags. An unofficial sequel followed, *Dream Warrior* (1988).

The Keep (1983)
Dir: Michael Mann /USA

German troops in 1942 occupy a citadel in the mountains of Romania. A pair of soldiers attempt to steal silver from the tombs and unleash a vengeful, Golem-like entity that begins murdering the troops. When the SS arrives to investigate the deaths, they release a Jewish scholar from a concentration camp to help them deal with the crisis. However, the scholar and the Jew entity form an alliance to eliminate the Nazis... For the first 50-minutes of its running time, *The Keep* plays as a marvellous, visually-stunning, haunting masterpiece-in-the-making. But then things go seriously to pot in about five minutes flat, and the film never recovers. And what's left of the plot limps along in a frenzy of silly melodrama and even sillier special effects. The film is based on the vampire novel by F. Paul Wilson (who famously hated the movie so much, he later went on to write *Cuts*, a story about a writer who puts a voodoo curse on a film director who mangled his work), and also shares similarities with *Castle Keep* (1969) – also set during World War II in which American soldiers occupy a 10th Century castle and defend it with their lives... Or, perhaps they were dead the whole time? As for the entity itself, director Michael Mann – himself a Jew – has clearly drawn on the ancient Jewish legend of the Golem, a being made of clay and lacking a soul, which seeks vengeance against its creators. The film's central message – whether Nazi or Jew – is a warning of how raw power ultimately corrupts. It's just a shame that the message is easily lost among the daft dialogue and billowing dry ice.

Adam and Eve Versus the Cannibals (1983)
(aka *Blue Paradise*; Orig title: *Adamo ed Eva: La prima storia d'amore*)
Dir: 'Vincent Green & John Wilder' [Enzo Doria & Luigi Russo] /Italy

After a snake leads them to eating the forbidden fruit, Adam and Eve are cast out of the Garden of Eden and are left to wander in a desolate wilderness while having to fend off various beasties and warring tribes of cannibals and neanderthals. This little-seen biblical fantasy lacks any memorable set-pieces but lingers in the mind like a weird dream. The film was shot on beautiful scope and looks great on DVD. It's fun to watch Adam and Eve take a tumble into *Hills Have Eyes* territory, but this is more of a lavish love story than out and out horror.

The Demon Murder Case (1983)
Dir: Billy Hale USA

TV movie based on a 'true story' that supposedly happened in Brookfield, Connecticut. The film borrows heavily from the previous year's *Amityville II: The Possession*, and, like that film, this is basically just post-*Exorcist*, child possession shenanigans, with Satanic forces sending the boy's belongings violently hurling across his bedroom, as he convulses and makes growling noises while family members struggle to pin him down to the bed. At least this film doesn't waste any time in getting down to the good stuff: The child changes, and the demonologist is called in within the first twenty minutes. After that, things lead to an unintentionally amusing showdown in a church. This movie is goofy as hell with its levitations, a sceptical priest who refuses to believe that the child is possessed, yet has no trouble believing in a magic being in the sky. Add to this some horse shit dialogue, lame, *Omen*-inspired 'accidents,' an evil madness that seems to hop from one person to another, and you've got a real 80s shitter. At one point, a lady reporter asks a priest what's going on, to which he deadpans, "What's going on? A divine comedy." No shit, Father! But I suppose the silliest aspect of the film is that top-billed actors, Kevin Bacon and Liane Langland, play the teenage love birds and do nothing but sit around the house looking stoned.

The Hunger (1983)
Dir: Tony Scott /USA

A stylish, dream-like vampire movie in which Catherine Deneuve plays Miriam, a bisexual bloodsucker. Throughout the course of thousands of years, the immortal Miriam repeatedly falls in love with her consorts and promises to give them eternal life. However, unlike her, they eventually die of old age after a few centuries. She keeps her lost loves in coffins in the cellar of her New York apartment. Her latest soulmate, John (David Bowie), is rapidly reaching the end of his tenure on earth, and he urgently seeks the help of Sarah (Susan Sarandon), a doctor who is researching how blood diseases relate to the ageing process. After John's disintegration, Miriam falls in love with Sarah. And when Sarah learns of Miriam's vampiric ways, she resorts to drastic measures to put an end to the vampire queen... *The Hunger* was Tony Scott's first mainstream movie, and is based on the novel by alien abductee, Whitley Strieber. It's a moody, visually-dazzling, pop promo of a film, where the billowing curtains, swirling dry ice and neo-noir shadows rarely get in the way of what is essentially a solid story told in the style of a modern-day Gothic fairytale. Abel Ferrara borrowed the look of Scott's film for his crypto-vampire tale, *King of New York* (1990).

Blood Rage (1983)
(aka *Nightmare at Shadow Woods*)
Dir: John M. Grissmer /USA

A pair of twins, one of whom is an axe murderer, blame each other for a series of brutal slayings. The evil twin's psychosis seems to stem from the mother's promiscuous behaviour, in the way they would see her fucking random guys at a drive-in movie theatre. Memorable killings include a guy having his beer-holding hand lopped off, a woman in the woods chopped in half at the waist, and the axe-to-the-face murder in the prologue. Add to this a synth-heavy soundtrack, big hair and scream queens, *Blood Rage* is the perfect item for those looking for some early 80s slasher nostalgia. But beware, an edited bloodless version is doing the rounds under the title *Nightmare at Shadow Woods*.

Cujo (1983)
Dir: Lewis Teague /USA

While chasing a rabbit in the wilderness, a family dog, Cujo, pokes its head into a warren and is bitten by a bat. The dumb hound then develops rabies and begins savaging the locals at an isolated community. Meanwhile, a mother and her son run out of fuel nearby, and they find themselves in a lengthy stand-off with the dog while they are stranded inside the vehicle in the blazing heat... This would be a good movie to screen for anti-gun campaigners; if the lead heroine had a pistol in the glove box, the situation would have been over in no time. Instead, Donna (Dee Wallace) and her boy, Tad (Danny Pintauro), are forced to endure days of stalking fear, vicious attacks and severe dehydration while they try to figure out a way to deal with the persistent pest. Stephen King managed to write a fairly tension-packed story for the source novel, and screenwriters, Don Carlos Dunaway and Lauren Currier (King also helped out with the script) sure use up a lot of time establishing the lead characters – Donna has been having an affair, and her husband's advertising firm is under fire after reports that a breakfast cereal his company is involved with has caused internal bleeding in children. The ending is a bit abrupt, and the pacing is a little off at the start, but the film soon picks up by the half hour mark, and is helped tremendously by Jan De Bont's superb photography and a great performance by Cujo the dog! Actually, five dogs were used during filming, and they had such a good time on set that crew members had to tie their tails to their legs because they were wagging them too much! Director Lewis Teague returned to King territory a couple of years later with the entertaining *Cat's Eye* (1985).

Curtains (1983)
Dir: Jonathan Stryker [Richard Ciupka] /Canada

An ambitious method actress, Samantha (Samantha Eggar), pretends to be psychotic so that she can experience life in a mental asylum in preparation for a future theatrical role. The only person who knows about her performance is her director husband, Jonathan (John Vernon). And of course it's no surprise when he abandons her to the asylum so that he can audition a group of pretty young actresses for the part instead. And when Samantha cottons onto the fact, she escapes, and someone shows up at the mansion where the auditions are taking place, slicing and dicing the hopeful candidates... Despite the unconvincing set-up and lack of all-out graphic bloodshed, *Curtains* is an effective little slasher movie. The ice skating scene is one of the great murder sequences of the slasher movie heyday, and the film boasts a streak of sardonic Canadian humour. It was a troubled production, with one actress fired for refusing to do a nude scene. This meant that much of the film had to be re-shot with the new actress, causing a sour mood on set with cast members turning against the director.

Suffer, Little Children (1983)
Dir: Alan Briggs /UK

A mysterious mute girl shows up at a children's home and causes demonic havoc among the other children and staff before Jesus Christ makes an appearance to magically banish her back to hell. *Suffer, Little Children* is a 'home movie' shot on video at a London drama school. The 'direction' is non-existent; the camera is almost completely static in every shot, the performances are generally terrible, etc. Nonetheless, it got a video release in the 80s, and was available to rent up and down the country. The video even got caught up in the 'video nasties' panic when police raided the offices of distribution company, Films Galore, and seized the tapes. The company hit back by threatening to sue the OPA's Public Prosecutions' goons for £3000 a day, arguing that the police had acted beyond their powers by purposely misinterpreting the Video Recordings Act (VRA) and acting on a film before the BBFC cuts were made. The tapes were not available to the public at the time of the raid, so Films Galore had every right to sue. Unsurprisingly, neither the police nor the Director of Public Prosecutions would comment on the matter, though James Ferman (who was head of the BBFC at the time) admitted in a letter to the company that there were inadequacies in interpreting the VRA. The Meg Shanks drama school was immediately closed down as a direct result of the negative press (headlines included 'School of video nasties'). Oh, feel that rush of pipsqueak power coursing through your veins. Congratulations, you quashed a bit of fun!

Spasms (1983)
Dir: William Fruet /Canada

Western anthropologists argue over whether or not to destroy a demonic monster that was summoned by African tribesmen. Millionaire Oliver Reed wants to keep it alive for research purposes, while Reed's wife and psychologist Peter Fonda set out to destroy it before any more people are killed. Of course, Satanic forces are also at work, and after a spate of *Omen*-inspired fatal 'accidents,' the demon escapes and rampages through the city. Meanwhile, a group of Satanists also want to be in possession of 'the great serpent' for their own sinister purposes. *Spasms* is a watchable, if disastrous, production which ran out of money before many of the key sequences were shot. The filmmakers had to make do with padding things out with extraneous footage and outtakes. Had the film been completed in its intended form we may have had a minor gem on our hands. But as it stands, it often gets branded with 'worst movie ever' stigma on *IMDb*. It certainly isn't the worst. Nowhere near the worst. Only today I watched *Slash Dance*, and that's a hell of a lot worse than this, believe me.

Attack of the Beast Creatures (1983)
Dir: Michael Stanley /USA

A group of wedding guests lost at sea in a rowing boat are washed up on a strange island. One unfortunate guest has his head melted in an acid river, and another has her hand bitten while picking berries. Meanwhile, an injured member of the group is found in skeletal form on the beach – it appears something has devoured the poor guy, leaving nothing but the bones behind. The remaining characters seek shelter for the night and are attacked by dozens of pint-sized carnivorous critters whose eyes glow in the dark... This was unknown director Michael Stanley's only film, which though fails to live up to basic standards (there's bad pacing, poor editing, unrealistic dialogue, etc), nonetheless serves up some nice 'bad movie' charms all of its own. The film is quite typical of American indie horror of the time, meaning it can be enjoyed if you know what to expect and are in the right mood, despite the tiny budget and technical limitations. None of the characters stand out – there are no obvious heroes or heroines here – they all just seem to serve as bland, bickering fodder for the beasties. As for the critters, well, they kind of resemble the folkish creature seen in *Trilogy of Terror* (1976), but here they appear on camera much more often, which ruins the sense of menace – in the cold light of day, they clearly look like children's toys carved out of wood. Kudos to John P. Mozzi whose creepy synth score enlivens the slower, more repetitive moments. For some reason, the film is set in 1920, but this has no bearing on the story whatsoever, apart from giving the cast members the opportunity to dress up in fancy frocks and vintage style tuxedos. I liked it. And I'll probably watch it again some day. Fuck *you*.

A Blade in the Dark (1983)
(Orig title: *La casa con la scala nel buio*)
Dir: Lamberto Bava /Italy
Lamberto Bava's second feature after the superb *Macabre* (1980) was originally intended to be a four-part mini-series for Italian television, which is surprising considering the amount of blood spilled on camera. The film is about a composer, Bruno (*The New York Ripper*'s Andrea Occhipinti), who agrees to create a horror score for his film-maker friend, Sandra (Anny Papa). She lets him stay at her isolated villa in the hope that it will inspire a spooky composition. However, there is a blade-wielding killer on the loose, and as various characters are bloodily dispatched in and around the villa, Bruno does a bit of investigating and realises the murders may have something to do with the recordings he is working on...

For a project set almost entirely on the grounds of a country villa, *A Blade in the Dark* manages to wring a great deal of suspense and tension from its limited means. Bava shows great confidence with pace, atmosphere and extended murder set-pieces, putting those years he had worked as an apprentice to his father Mario (and also as an assistant director for Dario Argento) to fruition. The film tips its hat in homage to Argento with its musician character trying to solve a string of murders (see *Deep Red* [1975]), and the light interiors of the open-plan villa and its illuminated leafy gardens recalls Peter Neal's house in *Tenebrae* (1982). The murder scene in the bathroom in which a woman is suffocated and has her throat cut looks to be Bava's way of trying to out-do the 'drowned-in-scolding-bathwater' scene in *Deep Red*. Also of note is Guido and Maurizio De Angelis' brilliant score which, once heard, is not so easily forgotten – just watch the trailer if you don't believe me. The 109-minute cut from

Anchor Bay is the longest version, though shorter cuts have all the violent scenes intact.

The Exterminators of the Year 3000 (1983)
(aka *Gli sterminadori dell'anno 3000*)
Dir: 'Jules Harrison' [Giuliano Carnimeo]
/Italy /Spain
In a deserted, post-apocalyptic landscape, a couple of road cops find skeletal remains in an abandoned car. And while they look on in horror as a snake slithers out of the corpse, they are attacked by an armour-plated vehicle driven by a Mad Max-type drifter. One of the cops manages to flee, and a lengthy chase sequence ensues along the bleak mountainous roads, played out to Detto Mariano's electronic score that sounds similar to Vangelis' music for the previous year's *Blade Runner* (1982). Meanwhile, a small survivor community hidden away in a secret fortress have run out of water, and one of them volunteers to lead a group out beyond the walls of their compound with a tanker truck to find fresh supplies. However, their dangerous mission is made altogether hopeless when a crooked convoy of customised death machines, led by the shaven-headed maniac, Crazy Bull (Fernando Bilbao), terrorises them on the road. Thus, it's *Road Warrior* time all over again as the peaceful survivors cling to life while the marauding maniacs attack them with machine guns and sticks of dynamite. After the men from the compound are killed, a young boy, Tommy (Luca Venantini), manages to escape unseen. The kid meets up with the Mad Max wannabe (turns out his name is Alien), while scavenging among the rusty vehicles. They eventually make a deal to locate a large reservoir of water while Crazy Bull and his henchmen hunt them down...

This fairly entertaining Italian/Spanish co-production was a VHS staple for years, though Code Red later released a better edition on DVD. The story is bogged down a little by a silly sub-plot in which the kid gets his mechanised arm fixed, but once the action picks up, it's certainly fun. I must admit, the ending was very unexpected – and not just once, but twice; the end scenario goes from extremely bleak to insanely positive in the space of less than a minute! Like many post-apocalypse movies of the time, this borrows just as much from Sergio Leone's westerns as it does from sci-fi comics and the *Mad Max* series. And Alien (Robert Iannucci) is even more selfish and immoral than usual, as he intends to betray the kid every step of the way. However, his time we also get a feisty heroine called Trash (Alicia Moro) who occupies the moral centre ground between the innocent Tommy and the corrupted Alien.

Eyes of Fire (1983)
Dir: Avery Crounse /USA
Set near the American frontier in 1750, a preacher is persecuted from his town for polygamy and witchcraft, so he escapes with his children to a remote forest deep in French colonial territory. After surviving out in the wilderness for months, they find themselves at battle with an evil spirit that dwells among the trees. *Eyes of Fire* is a beautiful, absorbing period fantasy that has been unfairly overlooked for years. It isn't a particularly scary movie, but it balances wonderful flights of fancy with grim period details, producing magic and menace at every turn. Highly recommended.

Exterminator 2 (1984)
Dir: Mark Buntzman /USA
This time, producer of the first film, Mark Buntzman (who also appeared as one of the thugs in the original), returns to direct this largely plotless sequel which sees Ginty don his familiar green marine jacket, along with body armour and a welder's mask, as he stalks the lawless streets of New York at night, using a flame-thrower to reduce evil thugs to smouldering, crispy carcasses. Meanwhile, 'X' (Mario Van Peebles), declares war on the city's cops, and his army of maniacs terrorise the streets. They shoot a police chopper out of the sky and watch on as the pilot burns to death. They also kidnap another cop, pin him onto the subway tracks in crucifixion pose, and watch as a train comes along and runs over him. They also beat John's new girlfriend with baseball bats, paralysing her from the waist down, before finally killing her and John's other friend, Be Gee (*A.W.O.L.*'s Frankie Faison). They're just begging for a pissed off white guy to show 'em who's boss.

What could have been a pointless, crushing bore, is instead a lively and brilliantly paced catalogue of carnage, as the bad guys are thrice as mean and numerous, and The Exterminator is thrice as ruthless in dealing with them. John may have been reduced to a mere symbol of righteous vengeance here, rather than a fully fleshed-out character, but as far as 80s VHS wonders go, this is well worth a watch. The BBFC imposed 2:39 of cuts, mostly on violence and the scenes with the nunchucks, for the UK video release. In America, similar cuts were needed to secure the R rating. Even the DVD releases are taken from the same censored R rated transfer.

Angel (1984)
Dir: Robert Vincent O'Neill /USA
A demented necrophiliac serial killer targets L.A.'s street hookers. Donna Wilkes plays the title character, a 14-year-old student who moonlights as a street walker to fund her education. She has seen several of her friends fall victim to the killer, and the only people looking out for her are a no-nonsense transvestite (Cliff Gorman) and a detective concerned for her well being who urges her to stay away from the streets. But instead, Angel arms herself with a pistol and confronts the maniac, who has by now disguised himself in Hare Krishna garb. This is a routine, join-the-dots killer movie that nonetheless outshines most others of its like thanks to some decent production values, a well-observed grim humour, and a roster of unforgettable characters, including Susan Tyrell's ludicrous lesbian who has the best line: "You can't die. You still owe me $147, you fucking faggot."

Mutant (1984)
(aka *Night Shadows*)
Dir: John 'Bud' Cardos /USA
A pair of knucklehead brothers visit a small country town and are run off the road by a truck-full of hostile rednecks. To make matters worse, the town is overrun with mutants, transformed by a chemical spill at a local corporate plant. The remaining brother teams up with a hot blonde barmaid, and together they hold up in a hardware store and fend off the ghouls. *Mutants* is a typical, join-the-dots monster movie in the 50s tradition, and is enjoyable for what it is. It is also infused with the post-*Night of the Living Dead* tradition, meaning the mutants are grey-skinned and prone to gurgling and traipsing the streets in mobs, just like the zombies in George Romero's films.

Surf II (1984)
Dir: Randall Badat /USA

A zombie punk infection spreads through a beach party after a vengeful chemistry nerd (*Grease*'s Eddie Deezen) contaminates the Buzz cola drinks. Before you know it, the revellers are scoffing down garbage, rioting, and have somehow grown multi-coloured mohawks and are suddenly clad in spikes and pins and leather. It's the kind of film that defies all synopsis' and criticism, but if you enjoyed *Street Trash* (1987), then chances are you'll like this too. The video cover sums it up best: "Menlo Schwartzer – the geekiest mad scientist of all – wants to rid the world of surfers by transforming them into garbage-ingesting zombie punks! But no way dude can he stop their most awesome party!" A timeless classic that was never released on DVD.

Night of the Comet (1984)
Dir: Thom Eberhardt /USA

A passing comet turns most of the population of earth into crumpled cloth bodies. A cinema projectionist and an usherette, Regina (Catherine Mary Stewart) have survived the apocalypse by spending the night in the projection booth with steel walls. The man is soon beaten to death outside by a mutant beastie, so Regina escapes on a motorcycle and sees that the entire city of Los Angeles looks to be deserted of people, and the skies are glowing a hellish red. She finds that her sister Samantha (Kelli Maroney) has also survived, and, together with a trucker they meet at a radio station, they battle for survival against the mutants and the underground coven of scientists who are on a mission to suck the blood of survivors to ensure their own survival... *Night of the Comet* is a cult classic that takes its cue from an assortment of sci-fi and horror movies of the 50s and 60s (chiefly *Target: Earth* [1953] and *The Day of the Triffids* [1962]), while also borrowing elements from Richard Matheson's *I Am Legend*/*Last Man On Earth*/*Omega Man*. Eberhardt's witty script also has the survivors indulge in some *Dawn of the Dead*-type fun in a deserted shopping mall, and somehow making the post-apocalyptic fantasy seem like utopia. We also get a constant barrage of cheesy 80s pop music and Mary Woronov as a suicidal scientist. Personally, although I like this film, I think it could have been so much better; it lacks the all-out mutant mayhem, and instead concentrates on the evil scientists and their immoral behaviour. There are also loose ends here and there; it is never made clear why some people were vaporised and others were transformed into mutants.

Razorback (1984)
Dir: Russell Mulcahy /Australia

One of the great horror debuts of the 80s which saw director Russell Mulcahy signed up to Hollywood almost immediately after the film was released in the States. *Razorback* starts with a man standing trial for the murder of his grandson. He is adamant that the child was carried away by a wild boar. Meanwhile, an American television journalist catches wind of the story and heads over to Australia to get the scoop. However, she soon falls victim to the creature. Next, her husband Carl (Gregory Harrison) arrives in town looking for her, and he ends up teaming up with a couple of locals to track down the elusive beast... Inspired by the Dingo baby case, *Razorback* is a stylish treat for horror fans, boasting strange backlighting effects, arresting images (a car stuck in the branches of a tree, a man watching TV has half of his house torn away), and a marvellous score by Iva Davis which is a throwback to 50s monster and disaster movies punctuated with synths and piano. The scenes where Carl falls into the lake from the windmill tower, and his hallucinatory trip through the desert, pre-dates the slapstick weirdness inflicted on Ash in *Evil Dead II* (1987) and *Army of Darkness* (1992). Screenwriter, Everett de Roche (of *Long Weekend*, 1977), continued to churn out movie scripts based on killer animals – *Frog Dreaming* (1985) and *Link* (1986) – but none of them are in the same league as *Razorback*.

Manson Family Movies (1984)
Dir: John Aes-Nihil /USA

Created to stimulate the rumours that Charles Manson and his gang actually filmed their murders on stolen television equipment, serial killer aficionado, John Aes-Nihil, created this cheap, deliberately grotty-looking faux-snuff footage of the cult murders which has been an underground video staple for years. Interestingly, the footage in this film was shot in the same locations where the events actually took place, and Manson himself even contributes to the soundtrack, along with Aes-Nihil's band, Beyond Joy and Evil, and the punk group, Sloppy Titty Freaks, whose song. *'Die Bitch,'* is played over a particularly tasteless scene in which the pregnant Sharon Tate is repeatedly stabbed in the stomach.

Body Double (1984)
Dir: Brian De Palma /USA

A struggling actor (Craig Wasson) catches his wife in bed with another man. And while drowning his sorrows at the bar, he encounters a fellow actor who gives him the job of looking after a friend's apartment for a few days. He accepts the job and becomes obsessed with the mysterious woman who lives in an opposite apartment, and who gives a striptease in front of the window every night. However, when she is murdered by an ugly intruder with a power drill, Wasson becomes chief suspect... One of De Palma's finest films, and one that is light on plot but heavy in style and memorable set-pieces. One of the better 80s time capsule movies, this one borrows elements *Rear Window* and *Vertigo* and yet also manages to display a unique voice of its own. The stalking scene in the shopping mall and beach is an extended dream-like sequence, and an exercise in pure film-making. A classic.

Special Effects (1984)
Dir: Larry Cohen/USA

A recurring theme in fictional snuff-based movies is the megalomaniac filmmaker; from Terry Hawkins in *Last House On Dead End Street*, Boris Arkardin in *Snuff-Movie*, Vukmir in *A Serbian Film*, Brauth in *Melancholie der Angel*, Bill in *The Great American Snuff Film*, Jefe in *The Counselor*, 'The Wall Street Butcher' in *The Poughkeepsie Tapes*, and many others. These characters may vary in their backgrounds and outward aggression, but they're united by a common attitude which places themselves above everyone else: They harbour Sadean philosophies and hold their fellow humans in outright contempt. Many of these types of characters also view their film-making as ongoing artistic projects and view everyone who doesn't share the same opinions as weak and dumb. Larry Cohen's *Special Effects,* a hitchcockian B-movie, focuses on a reclusive sicko filmmaker who is obsessed with the meaning of reality. Zapruder happens to be his favourite 'director'. And when runaway wife, Maryjean (*Ms.45*'s Zoe Tamerlis) breaks away from softcore films to work with him, he murders her in his bed while covertly filming the crime through a one-way mirror. The police suspect Maryjean's redneck husband of killing her, and when the filmmaker decides to make a movie about her death, those involved in the production soon begin to learn what a sly, manipulative scumbag he is.

Clash of Warlords (1984)
(aka *Mad Warrior*)
Dir: Wilfredo Milan /Philippines

Utterly bizarre, micro-budget radioactive waste from the Philippines. You know you're in for a lousy time when a film opens on the scene of a supposed nuclear explosion that looks like someone has lit a large bonfire. The screen freezes on the 'mushroom cloud,' while the cheesy upbeat music plays on. This is where you'd expect to see the title credits appear, but nope, we don't get any. That would be far too professional. Instead, we're forced to watch a still frame of a bonfire for several minutes.

Set in a post-apocalyptic world ruled over by the evil warlord, Malzon, we first meet the protagonist, Rex, as he is forced into an axe duel to the death. If he refuses to fight, Malzon will kill Rex's wife and young boy. And when Rex finally kills his opponent, this sets off a chain of hysterical laughter among Malzon's men. Rex manages to escape the compound with his wife and child, and they are immediately pursued by the evil warlord's army. However, the production couldn't afford a fleet of *Mad Mad 2* style armoured vehicles and dirt bikes for the bad guys. What we get instead is a micro-budget fleet, which amounts to a glorified go-cart and about half a dozen men on horseback. Anyway, his wife and child are murdered by Malzon's men, but this doesn't seem to bother the hero in the slightest. He simply moves on with his life in greener pastures where women are constantly throwing themselves at him. The plot pretty much gets stuck in the mud at this point, as nothing much happens for the next 20 minutes, except for a bunch of Filipino punks kicking the crap out of each other in the woods. However, things do pick up a little in the finale when Malzon's men are mowed down by machine gun fire...

This is the type of dreck that makes the Italian *Mad Max* clones look like cinematic master works. Even the future barbarians here are disappointingly well behaved – they are ordered and disciplined, they walk in formation, and they only speak when they're spoken to. I don't about you, but I prefer my future barbarians to be out-of-control, feral lunatics. The entire soundtrack was dubbed in post-production, and those responsible did an awful job; the scenes in which the characters scramble through the woods and branches sounds like someone is rubbing sandpaper on the mics. Beyond this, there are some of the most hilariously bad martial arts sequences you'll ever see, a terrible soundtrack that endlessly repeats an annoying marching beat, silly sound effects, scenes abruptly cut off, insane dialogue, appalling dubbing, a man whose head melts during a full moon, and a lightsaber battle in the finale that lasts about 10 seconds. If this all sounds like bad movie heaven to you, then go ahead, knock yourself out. You might get a giggle out of it. But don't say I didn't warn you. See also *Warriors of the Apocalypse* (1985).

Rocktober Blood (1984)
Dir:Beverly Sebastian /USA
Rock singer, Billy, loses his mind and goes on a killing spree, murdering his manager and others in the recording studio. Two years after his execution, Billy's ex-girlfriend, Lynne, attempts to rebuild her life by joining a new group called Headmistress. However, the trauma of having escaped death is too much for her to bear. And when Billy returns from the dead to stalk and harass her with obscene phone calls ("I want your hot, steaming pussy blood all over my face, ha ha ha ha ha!!!"), her friends fear that she could be losing her mind, too. That is, until the finale when Billy shows up at a Headmistress gig with murder in mind... The first and final ten minutes of this video are glorious snippets of bad movie heaven – we get silly death scenes, half-arsed line deliveries, abysmal songs, and cat screams that go on and on forever. The middle chunk of the film sits in a much more ordinary bad movie realm, but is still entertaining. If you want to remind yourself of how awful the 80s were, there's no alternative.

The Key (1984)
Dir: Tinto Brass /Italy
A tale set against the backdrop of Musolini's rise to power, *The Key* centres on an art professor who keeps a diary detailing his frustrations over his wife's prudery. She, in turn, begins her own diary detailing her affair with her daughter's boyfriend. Typical softcore nonsense from Tinto Brass, who is to arses what Russ Meyer is to big tits, except this particular film addresses such themes as transvestitism, necrophilia and urolagnia, and includes a scene where Franck Finlay dresses in bra and suspenders, and who suffers a heart attack while having sex. As the *Virgin Film Yearbook* put it best: "Where there's muck there's brass; and where there's cinematic muck, there's Tinto Brass."

Zombie Island Massacre (1984)
Dir: John N. Carter /USA
Tourists on a Caribbean island witness a voodoo ritual in which a dead body is brought back to life. And, of course, it isn't long before they're having to fend off dozens of ghouls that have overrun the tropical paradise... Not quite in the same league as *Isle of the Dead* (1945), or even *The Serpent and the Rainbow* (1987), but *Zombie Island Massacre* boasts plenty of campy charms of its own. There's barely a dull moment here as the tourists are picked off by the barely-seen zombies in a variety of ways – one guy has head beaten in with a stick; other unfortunates are dragged into the river; and one has his head sliced off with a machete. In the end, the handful of survivors hold out at a nearby house, a la *Night of the Living Dead*. Harry Manfredini provided the quirky score.

Children of the Corn (1984)
Dir: Fritz Kiersch /USA
Many Stephen King stories have been murdered on screen in cheapjack, 'couldn't-give-a-shit' cash-ins on his good name, and *Children of the Corn* was perhaps the earliest example of this shoddy treatment of his work. The story is set in an isolated town called Gatlin where the children have turned to a strange religion, murdered all of the adults, and worship 'He who walks behind the rows.' A young couple driving through town witness a murder and come up against the mad children when they try to report it. King's original message about the damage religion can have on inexperienced minds is almost completely lost in the fake storms, rubber monsters and over-acting,. But the film was a cult success on home video, spawning no fewer than six sequels. See also the Spanish oddity, *Who Could Kill a Child?* (1976).

Beautiful Teacher In Torture Hell (1985)

(Orig title: *Oniroku Dan: Bikyoshi jigokuzeme*)
Dir: Masahito Segawa /Japan

Beautiful Teacher In Torture Hell is a typical entry in Nikkatsu's Roman Porno series of the time. It's simple premise sees a newly recruited teacher, Ran Masaki, subjected to a barrage of nasty goings on from both the pupils and the teachers, including violence, rape, and imprisonment. Masaki is picked up on her first day at the train station by a fellow teacher, and their drive through the isolated mountain roads is blocked by a group of thugs who attack the women. Masaki just happens to be a fencing teacher, and she puts her sword skills to use by beating off two of the thugs with a stick. She then rescues the other teacher from rape by beating the third yobbo into submission.

Despite the incident on the journey to her new job, Masaki seems to settle into her new role. That is until she is bopped on the head and knocked unconscious in the basement. She awakens in a hospital ward surrounded by a pupil and a couple of creepy looking teachers, but she has no memory of what happened to her. She has marks on her wrists which suggest she has probably spent some time tied up somewhere. She settles at her friend's house to recuperate, but the event has clearly affected her deeply. The two women then get naked and have a sexy bath time together, but Masaki rejects her friend's sexual advances. She wakes up in the middle of the night to find her house-mate in an S&M session with the creepy looking dude. She spies on the action for a while until she is spotted, and then goes back to bed.

Back at school the following morning, the creepy dude enters Masaki's classroom and hands her an envelope containing naked photos of her that were obviously taken while she was unconscious in the basement. She flees the school premises and confronts the young pupil, Yuki, about the incident and to find out who is responsible for her ordeal, but to no avail. After burning the photos, she enters the gym one night after school to find Yuki being tied up and tormented by the thugs who attacked her on the mountain road at the beginning. They threaten the girl with a knife and cut off her panties. Yuki pleads with her teacher to help her, and Masaki reluctantly obeys the boy's demands that she take off her clothes and have a fencing duel with one of the thugs. After beating the thug's arse with the stick she is set upon by the other boys

and gang raped whilst a third records the event on film.

After the ordeal, Masaki takes the girl home and ends up staying the night at her house. However, it soon becomes clear that Yuki's father is the school headmaster, and the whole episode that night was just a ploy to get her to the house. Yuki, the gang of thugs, the creepy guy, and even her own house-mate were in on the conspiracy. Masaki is then trussed up in the basement for more depraved fun where everyone gets in on the act; bondage, tit-slapping, forced fellatio, vibrator fun, an enema, and a hanging. Even the young pupil gets in on the action when she climbs into an aquarium for a bit of teacher molestation.

With a running time of just over an hour, *Beautiful Teacher In Torture Hell* is a silly piece of brainless exploitative garbage. But if you're a fan of Japanese Pink films then you'll probably lap it up anyway as this is no better or worse than the usual Nikkatsu fare of the time. The script was written by Nikkatsu veteran Oniroku Dan, and the visuals are typically stunning and put most American and Italian exploitation pics to shame with the beautiful lighting, textures, framing and photography. The story is deliberately stripped down to its basic essentials so that we're basically left with a string of sleazy sex and bondage scenes. And it's this latter element that perhaps puts the film into context as a precursor to the whole 'torture porn' movement of recent years.

Even by the Japanese standards of the time, this is an extremely cynical and pessimistic film. We can't even rely on the innocence of youth here as the young pupil Yuki turns out to be just as messed up and debased as the adult characters. The film is populated almost entirely with sly and manipulative scumbags, and the only decent character is subjected to all of the vile abuse! Even many of the most disreputable Pink films of the era had their bad guys getting their comeuppance at the end, but not so here; actually quite the opposite; in the coda we see another young teacher arrive at the train station, and it's clear that this new recruit will be subjected to the same abuse.

Day of the Dead (1985)

Dir: George Romero /USA

The third instalment in George Romero's living dead series is a moody, claustrophobic gem set almost entirely in a huge subterranean storage compound in Florida that serves as a makeshift laboratory and military base. The army has been ordered to protect a small group of scientists who are trying to find a solution to the zombie pandemic. Hordes of walking corpses have been penned into an enormous cave, and the scientists use them as guinea pigs for their research. The chief scientist, Dr. Logan (Richard Liberty), nicknamed 'Dr. Frankenstein', tries to domesticate the zombies so that the human survivors (who are now outnumbered by 400,000 to one) can keep them under control. One zombie, 'Bub', shows promise and responds to various influences like music and hand gestures, and offers hope to the ever-dwindling civilization. But the army, led by Captain Rhodes (Joseph Pilato), puts an end to the research and takes over with reckless abandon, ultimately leaving themselves exposed to the millions of hungry zombies who are waiting outside...

George Romero's initial living dead triptych offers up three of the greatest zombie movies ever made. *Night of the Living Dead* (1968) was the first truly modern horror film with its verite ambiance and savage social commentary. *Dawn of the Dead* (1978) attacked the mindless consumer attitude of the 70s and beyond, and *Day of the Dead* (1985) took us underground to explore the pseudo-scientific engineering being hijacked for murderous military deeds. The film also follows on from his earlier efforts like *The Crazies* and *Martin* in the way it addresses the lack of communication as being a big problem to any kind of solution.

Romero originally intended to create an epic three hour movie of *Day*, but financiers would only pay up if he agreed to tone down the blood and gore (1985 was the year that the MPAA started clamping down on movie violence). Fortunately, Romero saw sense and slashed his budget and script in half, brought back effects maestro Tom Savini, and delivered hell on earth as mankind makes its last stand against the living dead.

Looking back, it's incredible how Romero decided to scrap his "mainstreamed" idea for the script and plunge into a much more darker and bleaker territory, because not only was his third instalment set to compete with his earlier *Night* and *Dawn*, but there were also a couple of contemporary zombie movies competing at the box office around the same time, Dan O'Bannon's *Return of the Living Dead* and Stuart Gordon's *Re-Animator*. And, as mentioned before, the MPAA was tightening its restrictions, and its interference would have a negative effect on those who enjoyed watching violence on the big screen for years to come (notice how slasher franchises became increasingly silly and 'comedic' in the latter half of the 80s, the *Friday the 13th* and *Nightmare On Elm Street* sequels, for example).

Fans and critics treated the film with disdain on its initial release, and *Day of the Dead* quickly died at the box office, only to break out of the grave as the film earned a huge cult following thanks to home video and late night cable screenings. It is now generally regarded as one of Romero's finest films, with many hardcore horror fanatics ranking it in their top five greatest movies of all time. It's interesting how opinions can change like that; from disappointment to admiration in a few short years. Indeed, Romero's latest trilogy of the dead, consisting of *Land of the Dead*, *Diary of the Dead* (dubbed 'Diarrhea of the Dead' in some circles), and *Survival of the Dead* have been treated non too favourably in recent years, and perhaps that too will change a little further down the line. In Romero's defence, it's important not to forget that he no longer has complete control of his finished films anymore; his latest efforts have been studio financed, thus he has the bigwigs to answer to nowadays. Even a masterpiece like *Martin* was greeted with boredom and confusion on its initial release.

It's no coincidence that *Day of the Dead* was made right after *Creepshow*. The characters in *Day* seem to have stepped out of an E.C. comic strip, with the sly, nasty, perverted bad guys meeting their grisly fates. Romero perhaps wasn't through with that side of things. And how could he be? *Creepshow* is a piece of juvenile garbage and a waste of Tom Savini. But rest assured, Savini sure wasn't wasted on *Day of the Dead*, he really went to town on this one; characters are literally torn apart before our eyes, arms are hacked off, heads blown to pieces, and guts are literally spilling out onto the floor.

Although the film has been available uncut in the UK since 1997, the BBFC initially snipped out 30 seconds of gore for both film and video, including the shot of one of the soldiers having his back bitten by a female zombie, the close-up shot of the machete cutting through Miguel's arm when he has his limb amputated, the scene where a zombie is decapitated with a shovel, a soldier having his fingers bitten off, and the zombies feasting on the innards of Captain Rhodes.

Come and See (1985)
(Orig title: *Idi i smorti*; aka *Kill Hitler*)
Dir: Elem Klimov /Soviet Union

Produced to mark the 40th anniversary of Russia's victory over the Nazi invaders in World War II, and based on the novella *The Khatyn Story* by Ales Adamovich who was a partisan himself during the conflict, *Come and See* follows young teenager, Flyora, who joins the Soviet partisans in the woods near his home. With a naïve sensibility Flyora reckons on being a hero with an easy triumph over the Nazi's but, as the film progresses we witness his descent into trauma and madness as the Byelorussian holocaust literally tears his world apart. It's a horrendous coming-of-age story, from naïve innocence to blind hatred to costly experience, his face physically alters throughout the film from fresh youth to haggard old war veteran.

Made during the Perestroika period, *Come and See* is perhaps the most brutal and emotionally draining war film you'll ever see. Director Elem Klimov was obsessed with authenticity in the making of his film, and he went to some alarming extremes in order to replicate the harsh environments of war. The explosions weren't created with safe pyrotechnical trickery, they were real. The bullets were also real. And it's astonishing to see lead actor Aleksei Kravchenko running around with real explosions going off around him, sometimes as close as three feet away. In some scenes he has live rounds just missing his head by centimetres. All weapons used here (guns, bombs, flame throwers, etc) are genuine. Even the uniforms in the film are 100% authentic originals. Adding to the realism is Aleksei Rodiomov's hand-held camera work which gives the proceedings an intimate edge. Real footage showing the aftermath of Nazi atrocities in the area is inserted into the film to drive the authenticity home.

Originally entitled *Kill Hitler*, *Come and See* is a hallucinatory, heartbreaking, traumatic, and uncompromising experience – not for all tastes. There's a scene where civilian villagers are rounded up and forced into a barn by German soldiers where they await their fate with dread. An officer appears at the window offering the chance for anyone to leave, but on condition that the children are left behind. Of course, no one is prepared to desert their children to die alone. And unlike the Jews in Spielberg's *Schindler's List*, there's no respite at the final moment. No, the barn is then merrily set on fire by the Nazis. And while the civilians are screaming and burning alive, the Nazis shoot at the barn with machine guns and flame throwers, and we are forced to watch all of it.

For a while this film was used as propaganda to warn citizens of the Eastern Block about the dangers of fascism, but it certainly wasn't made with propaganda in mind. There's no nationalistic one-upmanship to be found here, the 629 villages decimated are well documented. There's no communist rhetoric either, and many of the partisan heroes in the film are flawed characters. It's a film about the suffering of ordinary people during wartime. In fact I would say there is ten times as much propaganda in films like *Saving Private Ryan*.

In the UK, *Come and See* was given an uncut 15 certificate, which may puzzle some readers, but it's one of those films that really ought to be seen by the largest possible audience, even school students. However shocking the film may be, it's never gratuitous and certainly not exploitative, and the British Board of Film Classification have recognised this.

The Kino DVD release is disappointing – it looks to be a rushed job, presented with very little care in full screen format, and appears to have been lifted from the VHS version with no attempt at re-mastering. The film is also split over two discs which means having to change discs midway through viewing (like VCDs, or having to flip over a laser disc in the old days). Such an important film treated in a cheap and shoddy fashion is not good enough. However, the film later released by Artificial Eye in 2011 in a much better presentation, and in one piece.

The Devil's Experiment (1985)
(aka *Unabridged Agony*)
(Orig title: *Za Ginipiggu: Akumano Jikken*)
Dir: Hideshi Hino /Japan

Devil's Experiment was the first entry in the *Guinea Pig* series from Japan, and one of the first shot on video shockers ever made. Nowadays 'torture porn' is everywhere, a cheap and simple way for filmmakers to make an impact, rather like the power chord in punk rock. With the advent of the camcorder which became widely available in the early 80s, the everyday public was able to contribute to the medium with home-made amateur epics like *Boarding House*, *They Don't Cut the Grass Anymore*, and *Black Devil Doll From Hell*. Over in Japan meanwhile, there was a growing market for micro-budget shot on video dreck; the burgeoning AV (adult video) market was becoming ever popular, with specialist superstores filled to the brim with amateur and very small production companies filling the shelves with assembly line trash. These videos were mostly porno products, but with the natural evolution of the horror genre, it was only a matter of time before a company came along and injected a bit of grue and nastiness into the market.

At the auspice of producer Satoru Ogura, *Devil's Experiment* was made back to back with the second in the series, *Flower of Flesh and Blood*, and like that film it's a plotless exercise in cheap and nasty sadism. And although Hino's *Flower of Flesh and Blood* is open to interpretation as far as those interested in subtext are concerned, there's really none of that to be found here. What we get is quite literally torture porn in its most stripped down and obscene basics. Three young men kidnap a woman and spend the next 40 minutes torturing her before finishing her off with some nasty and graphic eyeball needling. The eyeball trauma is the single most impressive and realistic looking scene in the entire *Guinea Pig* series, but the rest of the film ranks among the poorest, too.

The film's insistence on scene after repetitive scene of slapping the captive woman across the face becomes irksome very quickly; the oft-quoted "banality of evil" is in full force here as we're witness to a seemingly endless display of slaps (the actors are clearly seen just slapping their own hands, and it's so lame and unconvincing) that reach an almost nullifying effect on the viewer. But rather like the scene in Mariana Peralto's *Snuff 102* in which a woman is repeatedly punched in the face, this silly and clearly unrealistic violence ultimately curtails the edgy nature of both films, and instead serves as a disturbing realisation that we the viewers are simply wallowing in the lowest detritus of 'shock video', for better or worse.

Oh, but it definitely gets worse; the three villains put the woman in a swivel chair and spin her around. And around, and around. She is also kicked around on the floor, has the skin on her knuckles twisted with a pair of mole grips, is forced to listen to white noise on headphones at very high volume for 20 hours, has her finger nails ripped off, is hung from in a tree in a hammock, is burned, covered in maggots and animal guts, is cut open with a scalpel, and then the nasty eyeball trauma. And that's it. It's interesting how Japanese censorship forbids the sight of pubic hair, and yet has no problem with the most vile and misogynistic nonsense like this (another example is Tamakichi Anaru's *Tumbling Doll of Flesh* which mixes pixelated sex scenes with graphic tongue torture!). Along with the rest of the *Guinea Pig* series, *Devil's Experiment* became an underground cult collector's item in the west, but I'm sure that many of those who hunted high and low for the bootleg VHS would have been disappointed with the end result. The whole series is available uncut from Unearthed Films.

Flower of Flesh and Blood (1985)
(Orig title: *Za Ginipiggu - Chiniku No Hana*)
Dir: Hideshi Hino /Japan

This is the most notorious entry in the *Guinea Pig* series, and the only one truly deserving of its nasty reputation. Directed by Hideshi Hino, *Flower of Flesh and Blood* is a short, 44-minute video about a madman who stalks and kidnaps a young woman and takes her home before dismembering her and placing her body parts in a backroom with the rest of his 'collection'. The film is remembered primarily for its remarkable special effects (which looked so realistic on bootleg VHS that Charlie Sheen thought it was a genuine snuff tape and reported it to the FBI; of which more later), and we get to witness the graphic dismembering in full detail thanks to Nobuaki Koga's FX work.

The tape comes with its own legend: Manga artist Hideshi Hino allegedly received an 8mm snuff film in the post along with a letter and photographs. After alerting the Tokyo police (who took away the evidence), *Flower of Flesh and Blood* was conceived as an attempt to re-enact the scenes in the snuff tape. This was more than a decade before *The Blair Witch Project*, and the intriguing back-story was bought wholesale by the Japanese AV addicts, and the tape became a hit (the film is actually entirely fictional and based on Hino's own Manga).

Flower of Flesh and Blood is often accused of being utterly repellent, tasteless, and misogynistic. Others have read it as a journey into spiritual nirvana! Personally, I have always viewed the film as a savage satire on the masculine idea of sexuality: It is often remarked how women seek 'soulmate' qualities in potential partners, whereas stereotypical men are happy with surface requirement (legs, breasts, etc); this goes towards explaining why men are more likely than women to enjoy the visual stimulants of porn. The deranged samurai goes on the prowl; he sees his desired love object in a young woman walking the streets, and decides she will be the satisfactory candidate for a 'one-night-stand'. Of course, our madman will fail to lure this girl with his charm alone, so what better way to win her body than to smother her unconscious with a rag of chloroform?

After tying her down to the bed, the samurai proceeds to inject her with some kind of sedative to make her drowsy and docile (an alert, intelligent woman has always been the arch nemesis of full-blooded males!); he drugs her at the outset as a way of turning her into a passive object, to rid the room of the other consciousness. What follows is a literal joke of the blackest kind. The graphic dismemberment can be seen as a comment on the male habit of breaking down the attractive female into mental body parts (in fact, the whole film could represent this whole thought process as viewed from inside the male psyche).

"In the love relationship the tendency to break the object down into discrete details in accordance with a perverse auto erotic system is slowed by the living unity of the other person." – Jean Baudrillard

It's worth noting too that although our anti-hero doesn't get sexually intimate with the body parts, he does pause briefly between amputations in order to caress and admire the pieces lovingly as if the segments of her body have become his own personal property; her will can no longer operate or manoeuvre her limbs when they have been sawn off. The samurai, however, now has complete control of them without any possibility of her consciousness resisting (possessiveness taken to the literal extreme).

The blood and gore and drama are simply genre requirements – the essential thing here is the samurai representing the phallus (check out that helmet!), and the phallus as libido, rummaging and ransacking the desired love-object in the male imagination, taking each bodily segment and assessing its sexual value. For the grand finale we are invited to a backroom where we get to view the 'collection': Various macabre artefacts, mutilated corpses, hands, limbs, eyeballs, maggots and worms kept in old fish tanks, jars, hanging on the walls and generally scattered about the place. We are also treated to a poem of sorts about falling to the depths of hell. Can you guess where we are yet? The subconscious of course! We followed the libido back behind the curtain where, to quote the poem, "The darkness is boundless."

Flower of Flesh and Blood was directed by Hideshi Hino, a creator of comic books who has been churning out lurid Manga horror such as *Panorama In Hell* and *Hell Baby* for more than forty years. He was approached by cheapjack video producer Satoru Ogura and offered the chance to direct a miniscule horror film based on Hino's own comic, *Flower of Flesh and Blood*. Hino, whose childhood dream was to direct samurai films, immediately set to work, recruiting actor friends from the underground theatre, and an ambitious team of special effects technicians led by Nobuaki Koga. The tape hit Japanese video stores in the mid-80s and became one of the biggest selling titles of the month (Don't forget, Japan is a country where *Faces of Death* out-grossed *Star Wars* at the box-office and *Cannibal Holocaust* out-stripped *E.T.*). The *Guinea Pig* films soon became the subject of much controversy when a serial child killer seemed to be re-enacting scenes from *Flower of Flesh and Blood*, and the police investigation led to the questioning of the film's makers. But even when the culprit, Tsutomo Miyazaki, was apprehended, the tabloid frenzy only intensified, accusing Hino and his films of being to blame for the depravity and sickness of Japanese society.

Meanwhile in America, *Deep Red* fanzine editor, Chas Balun, had VHS bootleg copies of *Flower* and *Slaughter Special* (aka *Guinea Pig's Greatest Cuts*), and as a favour to a writer friend, Dennis Daniel, he agreed to make a compilation tape comprising the bloodiest and most graphic sequences from the films to be shown at Dennis' birthday party. The video played at the party and was a success, but copies were made and swapped hands for a while until one of the tapes came into the possession of Charlie Sheen and film producer Adam Rifkin.

They watched it and were horrified, thinking it was real. They contacted the MPAA and the FBI. An investigation was launched, and everybody basically snitched and ratted on their friends until the trail led back to Chas. But Chas also just happened to have a copy of *The Making of Guinea Pig*, a tape which shows behind-the-scenes footage and outtakes of a smiling actress doing re-takes, and the special effects team demonstrating their cable-controlled illusions, proving once and for all that the 'snuff' video wasn't real. The whole episode became an embarrassment for everyone concerned.

In the UK, 26 year old Christopher Berthould was prosecuted for importing *Flower of Flesh and Blood* (along with *Infant Brain Surgery* and *Faces of Dissection*) into the country. The prosecution at Southward Crown Court knew the contents of the tape were fake, commenting that the film was "so well simulated that [snuff] is the impression it creates." Berthould was given a £600 fine and a ludicrous newspaper headline ("DEATH CRAZE MAN'S SNUFF MOVIE SHAME"). The film is still outlawed in the UK today but is available uncut from Unearthed Films in America. I would say import at your own risk but things have moved on a lot since Berthould's day in the dock, haven't they?

Bits and Pieces (1985)
Dir: Leland Thomas /USA

At the bottom of the 80s slasher movie barrel you'll find *Bits and Pieces*, another micro-budget, 'damaged-by-mummy' schizo killer movie. Like Joe Spinell in *Maniac* (1980), this maniac keeps a collection of mannequins which serve as clothes props for dressing in the souvenirs he has taken from his victims. And like Norman Bates in *Psycho* (1960) and Dan Grimaldi in *Don't Go in the House* (1979), he is still tormented by his mother by way of the ghostly voices in his head. When he was a child, his mother would make him watch her have sex with random guys (a form of abuse experienced by the real life serial killer, Henry Lee Lucas), and the killer takes out his frustrations by kidnapping women, torturing them in his basement, and dumping their dismembered remains in dumpster bins for anyone to find. But for all the film's attempts to create a serious character study, the amateur feel of the production is a major let down.

Wife Collector (1985)
(aka *Rotten City*; Orig title: *Hitozuma Korekuta*)
Dir: Hisayasu Sato /Japan

Japanese society's passive attitude towards rape never ceases to amaze me, particularly when portrayed so openly in film: here in the West, where the crime is considered marginally less abhorrent than murder, the traumatised victim is, more often than not, depicted wreaking savage revenge with a variety of sharp implements (at least in the films I tend to watch); in Japan... well, let's say that the woman's reaction is often less bloody, but certainly no less shocking.

Wife Collector is a tale of a deviant taxi driver who kidnaps and molests young women and records his crimes on video. In one sequence a girl is raped by two louts out in the rain. Afterwards she takes a cab home and then masturbates in the shower. And if that isn't un-PC enough, the cabbie drives around playing his own rape tapes on a little monitor, and records himself molesting some chick in the back seat in full view of the passing traffic while wearing a gas mask! Two sisters find themselves competing over the 'affections' of the scumbag taxi driver, and the girls eventually find comfort in each other's arms...

Wow. This is one of Sato's better films of the Pinku eiga era that wraps up with the director's trademark 'guerrilla-style' street filming in which the everyday public become unknowing extras in a sleaze epic. With a running time of just over an hour, *Wife Collector* passes by in a brief but brilliant flash, and is sure to amuse those who think they've seen it all. The film also boasts an avant-garde jazz/rock soundtrack courtesy of Ginza Sound who sound like a cross between Can and The Fall, in Japanese.

Cut and Run (1985)
(Orig title: *Inferno in diretta*)
Dir: Ruggero Deodato /Italy

A TV news reporter and her camera man head to South America to track down the son of a television executive who is being held against his will by drug barons. And meanwhile, Richard Lynch makes an appearance as a cult leader in the vein of *Apocalypse Now*'s Colonel Kurtz, who was Jim Jones' right hand man at Jonestown... This is more of an action flick than out and out horror, but genre fans should get a kick out of the memorable set-pieces – including beheadings, stabbings, and one unfortunate getting himself 'wishboned' in half. Also,

Michael Berryman shows up as a sinister jungle assassin who leads a group of silent natives into attacking camps and making off with cart-loads of stolen cocaine.

Mad Max Beyond Thunderdome (1985)
Dir: George Miller & George Ogilvie /Australia
This second sequel also happens to be the least popular of the *Mad Max* saga. However, it does have its charms on repeat viewings. Max is back to being the directionless drifter who has his supplies stolen. So he wanders in the desert and chances upon Bartertown, a shanty haven for criminals and scumbags. He seeks shelter there and becomes entangled in a power struggle. And after narrowly escaping with his life, he discovers a cavern populated by orphaned children.

For the longest time this film had suffered a barrage of abuse from fans and critics for its abandonment of the rough and ready edges that helped make the first two films such classics. And though I agree with those criticisms, newcomers may find that *Thunderdome*, for all its faults, is not such a bad film if you go in with low expectations. By far the most expensive of the first three films in the series, this offers up its fair share of amazing stunts, while also exploring the wider terrain of the post-apocalyptic world that Max inhabits. And while there are clearly all the signs that Hollywood had intervened in many key areas, the core of the film manages to withstand the tampering and find its feet as a more laid back entry, which takes the time to show Max's gradual path back to sanity.

Thunderdome can be broken up into three segments. The first sees the arrival of Max into Bartertown where he confronts Aunty (Tina Turner), the self-styled matriarchal monarch whose attempts to uphold the fragile rule of law ensures her villainous demagoguery. Thus, Max soon finds himself at battle in the Thunderdome – a huge dome to which he is harnessed with elastic and forced to fight 'Master-Blaster,' a WWE-style champion. In the second segment, we drift into *Peter Pan*-inspired territory as Max encounters the lost children. Presented as a kind of infant cargo cult, the orphans look up to Max as their divine saviour. It's that helpless need of the children and their desire for guidance that ultimately brings Max back to humanity. And this sets up the final segment in which he protects them while confronting a horde of bandits from Bartertown.

The end result is a mythical future fantasy, in which Miller and his co-director, George Ogilvie, explore the netherworld like never before; Bartertown is fuelled by the methane extracted from pig droppings; the old train that remains from a distant, unknown past, becomes the source of much fascination. It's a fully realised world of make believe, and – dare I say? – fun for all the family.

The Dark Power (1985)
Dir: Phil Smoot /USA
In the darkest corners of the VHS dungeon you may be lucky enough to find a dusty old copy of *The Dark Power*, a fun but bloody awful movie hailing from North Carolina. Toltec zombies are the name of the game here as a cursed house that was built on Totem Hill, an old burial ground, has been transformed into a sorority house. The residents are made up of young students, including the openly racist Lynn (Cynthia Farbman), who objects to having a black girl move in with them. Thus, she invites her brother and his friends – a group of drunken obnoxious goons – to move in with the hope that the girl will be driven to leave. And meanwhile, an old man who tames wild animals with a whip (Lash LaRue), turns up to save the day when the Toltec ghouls break out of the ground and begin murdering the teens with axes and bow and arrows! I wanted to hate this movie so much, but by the time we reached the whipping contest in the finale, it had won me over. Plus, there is a great gore moment when one of the ghouls rips off the face of one of its victims. I may even unearth this long-forgotten weirdy and watch it again some day.

Trancers (1985)
Dir: Charles Band /USA
Taking elements from *Blade Runner*, *The Terminator*, *Omega Man* and any number of rogue cop movies, *Trancers* centres on Jack Deth (former comedian, Tim Thomerson), a detective based in a future Los Angeles where much of the city is submerged under water. Jack is sent back in time to 1985 to track down an evil criminal who has transformed much of the populace into brainwashed, slave-like zombie creatures who blend into society but become extremely violent when their true natures are exposed. Deth teams up with a pretty young side-kick (Helen Hunt), and together they comb

the city looking for trancers while slyly poking fun at 80s cultural trends like hair gel, fashion and punk rockers... *Trancers* is a pretty solid sci-fi B-movie which has become a cult favourite on home video over the years, spawning no fewer than six sequels. It's well worth a watch but unfortunately, just like *Night of the Comet* (1984), the film lacks the all-out zombie/mutant mayhem which could have made this a real treasure.

Blood Tracks (1985)
Dir: 'Mike Jackson' [Hal Elge] /Sweden
A mother escapes an abusive relationship by stabbing her husband and taking her large brood of children to hide out at a snowed-in abandoned factory. The family survive by picking off travellers and intruders. And when the famous rock band, Solid Gold (real name Easy Action), stop by to shoot a music video, the group and their entourage are attacked. *Blood Tracks* is a Swedish take on the Sawney Beane legend by way of Wes Craven. It has a wonderful 80s synth score, clumsy dubbing, atrocious fashions and ugly, mutant-like creatures. A more accurate title for the film would have been *The Snow Has Eyes*.

Cannibal Ferox 2 (1985)
(aka *Massacre in Dinosaur Valley*; Orig title: *Amazonas*)
Dir: Michael E. Lemick [Michele Massimo Tarantini] /Italy /Brazil
A paleontologist visits Brazil with a group of tourists. They're heading for 'The Valley of the Dinosaurs' to collect pre-historic fossils. However, their propeller plane crash lands in cannibal territory deep in the jungle. With Kevin's expertise on tribes, and 'Nam veteran John's survival knowledge, the small group trek through the wilds avoiding the deadly snakes and piranhas and crocodiles before falling foul of an unscrupulous slave driver. *Cannibal Ferox 2* offers up some solid B-movie fun, and is even better than the original in many ways. Thankfully, there's no animal abuse this time, but there's no cannibalism either. Like Me Me Lai in Deodato's *The Last Cannibal World* (1977), the women in this film are made to run around topless for much of the running time. In the original *Ferox*, the tribe is portrayed as retaliating to the Westerner's nastiness, whereas this time they're depicted as evil from the start, kidnapping and murdering members of the group without any provocation. We get some great jungle locations, great use of Kevin's 'boomstick' which confuses the tribe as they've never seen a gun before, but, like I said, Cannibalism is disappointingly off the menu here.

Noir et blanc (1986)
(*Black and White*)
Dir: Claire Devers /France
This black and white art-house oddity appeared in the UK surprisingly uncut. Films which deal with the subject of sadomasochism are notoriously frowned upon on these shores by everyone from critics, to censors, tabloid papers, and politicians. But Claire Devers' directorial debut seems to have completely bypassed the kind of moral panics which greeted Just Jaeckin's *The Story of O*, David Lynch's *Blue Velvet*, and Barbet Schroeder's *Maitresse*. The reason for this may be because *Noir et blanc* looks at first glance to be a mild and non-explicit depiction of submission. But make no mistake, this film certainly takes its themes of pain and pleasure to fatal extremes, and leaves very little to the audience's imagination.

Loosely based on a short story by Tennessee Williams called *Desire and the Black Masseur*, *Noir et blanc* centres on young accountant, Antoine (Francois Frappat), who takes a new job at a leisure centre. He is out of shape and prone to migraines, so co-worker, Dominique (Jacques Martial), offers to give him a massage after office hours. With his masochistic desires awakened, Antoine continues with the massages, and they get rougher and rougher until his arm is broken. Dominique shows up at the hospital ward after dark and takes him to a hotel room – and later an abandoned factory – where they can indulge in their passion uninterrupted to its chilling conclusion. Their desires become increasingly extreme and destructive as the pair reach into the realms of lethal eroticism. Claire Devers won an award at Cannes in '86, but the film's risque reputation kept it away from any kind of English language distribution until the early 90s when a subtitled print appeared uncut in American arthouse cinemas. Devers' public profile continued to grow with her next film, *Chimere*, earning a Palm D'Or nomination at Cannes, and in 1994 *Noir et blanc* was passed uncut for home video in the UK. This vital release did little to bolster the film's reputation, and it remains much talked about but barely seen.

Silip: Daughters of Eve (1986)
<u>Dir: Elwood Perez /Philippines</u>
Unlike many modern shock movies that display a cynical edge to the cinematic extremes they delight in showing us, *Silip* is a whacked out movie hailing from a time when the shocking material on screen was depicted quite innocently. This little known gem is the perfect movie to show those who think they've seen it all; a bizarre blending of cheesy melodrama, steamy sex, and gratuitous violence. It's like a tawdry old soap opera gone very very wrong.

In an isolated salt-making community under a baking hot sun, a group of children desperately plead with the local stud Simon (Mark Joseph) to spare a buffalo from being slaughtered. Simon ignores their cries and proceeds to beat the buffalo's head in with a club before skinning it and preparing lunch. The kids are so distraught at losing their pet in such a brutal way that one young girl is induced into having her first period. Simon spends his off-time sleeping with the local women in the village, and when happy-go-lucky Selda (Sarsi Emmanuelle) returns from a trip from Malta with her American boyfriend, she also tries to get him in the sack.

Meanwhile, Selda's devout sister, Tonya (former Miss Philippines, Maria Isabel Lopez), runs a bible class for the kids, and punishes her own feelings of sexual desire by rubbing handfuls of salt onto her cooch. And it isn't very long before the eccentric little village is torn apart by uncontrollable lusts, brutal bloody violence, gang rape, and misguided mob justice.

If Alejandro Jodorowsky and Fernando Arrabal were to remake *The Wicker Man* with a bit of *Who Can Kill a Child?* thrown in for good measure, chances are it would look something like this. A couple of scenes stray very close to hardcore, but this is not a straight-up sex movie, it's far too bizarre and disjointed for that. Sarsi Emmanuelle steals the show as the Westernised and outspoken Selda, whose promiscuous dalliances cause the delicate mores of the village to collapse. Lopez is also fantastic in her role as the devout Tonya, with her hysterical preaching and patronising ways coming across like Dr. Quinn Medicine Woman on drugs. Her warning to the young girl who has just started menstruating typifies the crackpot mentality of the whole film:

Tonya - *"We all reach the age where we're easily tempted. The Devil is constantly around us. He is always waiting for a mistake so that he can... so that he can tempt us into... into committing a mortal sin. And the ones that he tries most to tempt are girls having their first period, like you."*

Girl - *"But how do you know who the Devil is?"*

Tonya - *"He appears in the form of a young man. Those with large organs are devils, that is the true source of the Devil's evil powers here on Earth."*

Girl - *"Huh? Does that include my father too?"*

Made at a time of relaxed censorship in the Philippines under the rule of Imelda Marcos, *Silip*, along with better-known titles like *Scorpio Nights* and *Snake Sisters* (also starring the beautiful Lopez) were being churned out by filmmakers who were given the green light to explore the seedier side of life in their movies. Bizarrely, the profits gained from those sleazy epics were channelled into funding various cultural schemes throughout the country.

The film barely saw any distribution outside of its native land except for a scarce VHS release that was dubbed into English, but very few people saw it before it sunk into oblivion. Mondo Macabro released it on DVD in the late 00s in a nicely framed transfer that restores the rich colours, the original language with English subs, and also Lutgardo Labad's original score, all of which were lost in that horribly brown, VHS pan-and-scan job. The DVD also includes the hilarious dub track; just check out the scene where Selda's American boyfriend has a fight with Simon and then storms back to his shack and demands a blowjob from Tonya – absolutely priceless dubbing.

In a Glass Cage (1986)
(Orig title: *Tras el cristal*)
<u>Dir: Agustin Villaronga /Spain</u>
One of the most intense, courageous, and disturbing films of all time, *In a Glass Cage* ranks alongside *Salo* and *Cannibal Holocaust* as a superbly made shockfest.

Klaus, a Nazi paedophile, suffers pangs of guilt and attempts suicide by jumping from the roof of a building. He doesn't die but ends up paralyzed from the neck down at his family home in Spain where he is confined to an iron lung in need of round-the-clock care. A creepy young man, Angelo, enters the family home and lands himself the job of full-time carer to Klaus. We soon learn that Angelo is a very disturbed individual and subjects Klaus to near-suffocation by unplugging the iron lung as a way of demonstrating his total power over his new 'employer'. Things become even more desperate when Angelo reveals Klaus' wartime diary and reads aloud the entries where Klaus sadistically abused and tortured young boys in a concentration camp; all this whilst masturbating onto the old man's face. Angelo then turns up the heat by threatening his wife and daughter and bringing young boys back to the house where he intends on re-enacting the most harrowing tortures of the diary – the most appalling of which includes injecting petrol directly into the youngster's heart for a truly agonizing scene, before the depraved ending.

Very few films touch on the subject of child murder, and fewer still dare to breach the taboo in such detail as this. Added to the disturbing subject-matter is the way director Villaronga presents the action; he uses classic genre tricks like intensely claustrophobic chase scenes, graphic murders, and a 'thrilling' soundtrack reminiscent of all manner of stylish 80s horror. He also steers dangerously close to viewer implication as he toys with the dynamics of sadistic and masochistic sexual fantasies; make no mistake, this film has the potential to unleash some dark desires in some viewers: Approach with caution.

The murder scenes in *Tras el cristal* are very difficult to watch. We're not shown much in the way of blood or violence or gore; it's in the extremely effective build-up to the scenes that make them all the more hard to deal with. The scenes are also cruelly fascinating in the way Villaronga exposes our complicity with the shocking tortures on screen; through his eyes we're not just watching evil events being played out, we're in fact reminded through our willingness to go along with genre conventions, that the dark side isn't just limited to sadistic murderers, but is present within all of us to a certain degree.

Stylistically, *In a Glass Cage* is part art-house exploration and part horror, like a cross between Dario Argento and Luchino Visconti. Thematically, the premise is very similar to Stephen King's *Apt Pupil* (1981), whether the director was aware of this or not. *Apt Pupil* is about a teenage boy who blackmails an ageing Nazi war criminal into helping him with a school essay on the nature of evil. King's novel can be interpreted as an interrogation of Satan himself, but in *Tras el cristal* the two central characters are just as evil as each other. Whatever your opinion is on this film, it is at least a gruelling but vital alternative to those cheap and nasty Naziploitation films of the 70s.

Tras el cristal was shown at the London Film Festival and produced mass walk-outs. It was then shown at a gay film festival in Tyneside, and even billed as a gay-friendly title. Unsurprisingly, the film was met with anger and *more* walk-outs. It was later discovered on video by adventurous horror hounds (along with *Salo* and Andrzej Zulawski's *Possession*) and quickly rose to notoriety on the bootleg video circuit before Cult Epics came along offering the full uncut DVD.

Violence Jack (1986)
(aka *Violence Jack: Slum King*)
(Orig title: *Baiorensu Jakku: haremu bonba-hen*)
Dir: Ichiro Itano /Japan

Set in the future after a series of natural disasters have destroyed civilisation, *Violence Jack* depicts the chaos of life on earth as roaming gangs of sub-humans enslave and rape young women. Violence Jack, a ten foot tall badass, serves as a lone vigilante dishing out street justice on the scumbags, and who also loses an arm and an eye for his troubles. Banned in Australia for its graphic depictions of rape, this 37-minute video stood out from the usual anime fare due to its extreme violence, and became a cult item on home video in the early 90s. *Violence Jack 2: Evil Town* (1988) is based on another of Go Nagai's manga comics that ran from the mid-70s until the early 90ss. Here Violence Jack seems to have miraculously grown back a new arm. This time, the giant breaks out of concrete and takes on a predatory gang leader called 'Mad' while earthquakes ravage the lawless town. This sequel is a little less action-packed than the original, and takes a while to reach full throttle. But once it gets going, the violence is just as extreme, and includes a graphic massacre of innocent children, pixelated sex scenes, cannibalism, and a bloody showdown between Jack and his nemesis. And finally, in *Violence Jack 3: Hell's Wind* (1990), a ruthless motorcycle gang, Hell's Wind, lays waste to a peaceful community, terrorizing the locals and cutting them to pieces with chainsaws and raping the women., until Jack shows up and unleashes his now familiar brand of brutal justice. At just short of an hour, this third and final entry in the series reveals its influence as a future western set in a post-apocalyptic Tokyo.

52 Pick-Up (1986)
Dir: John Frankenheimer /USA
An exceptional thriller based on the novel by Elmore Leonard. When successful business man Harry's (Roy Schneider's) infidelity is caught on camera, he is blackmailed into paying $105,000 to a shady trio of thugs. When he refuses to pay up, however, the gang resorts to murdering his mistress on camera by shooting her in the chest and framing him for her murder. In order to save his skin and his wife's political ambitions, Harry refuses to inform the police and instead sets out to play the thugs at their own game, using his intelligence to drive the blackmailers apart. But the gang's leader, Allan (John Glover), proves himself to be much more dangerous and cunning than he lets on... *52 Pick-Up* was one of the last films made by Cannon before the company went bankrupt, and was given very little in the way of an ad campaign, disappearing from theatres pretty fast before becoming a cult classic on home video. It's a hard boiled 70s crime thriller lost in an ocean of 80s sleaze, and can't be recommended highly enough.

The Fly (1986)
Dir: David Cronenberg /USA
Fascinated with the horrific implications of a combination of science, technology, mutation and disease, director David Cronenberg has created highly personal films over the years. While the body horror concepts of his films were often under-budgeted and sometimes deliberately obscure, with *The Fly*, Cronenberg presented his ideas to the wider population, and it remains his most mainstream movie to date.

With his decision to remake the 1958 classic, *The Fly*, Cronenberg had found a perfect outlet for his ongoing interests, creating a more complex and more scientifically plausible version of the story than the original film. The new version of *The Fly* teams up a young science magazine reporter, Veronica Quaife

(Geena Davis), and a shy, awkward scientist, Seth Brundle (Jeff Goldblum), who is conducting secret experiments to transport matter that will revolutionise world travel. A long-time sufferer of motion sickness, Seth hopes to create the first ever teleportation system that will allow individuals to cover vast distances at the touch of a button. The idea is, instead of physically travelling from point A to point B, the teleportation system will break down the organic matter of the individual to atoms, and instantly reconstruct those atoms at point B.

Though a brilliant scientist, Brundle has a hard time with the standard social protocols, and his clumsy efforts to woo Veronica look like a high school nerd trying to impress a cheerleader with his science project. The pair do eventually fall in love, however. Actually, it's probably safer to assume that *she* falls in love with *him*. Anyhow, their relationship seems to motivate Seth's research more than ever. First, he attempts to transport a baboon (with horrific results), before he steps into the teleportation chamber himself. And, in typical 'mad scientist' mode, Seth makes the very bad mistake of not noticing that a common house fly has entered the chamber with him. Thus, when he goes ahead with the teleportation, both he and the fly are broken down and reconstructed in the second chamber at the other side of the lab. Seth then steps out of the chamber, assuming the experiment has been successful. But little does he know that his DNA has now been spliced with the fly...

The Fly is one of the great horror movies of the 80s, and also one of only a few horror remakes that is actually better and more thought provoking than the original. Cronenberg brings out the very best in his small cast of players. Goldblum offers up the performance of his career in a rare leading role, and Davis is also magnificent as the lovelorn victim, half-enthralled and half-appalled while witnessing Seth's mutation. As a couple, they're appealing and convincing, and this just makes the horrors to come all the more affective for viewers (the two leads were romantically involved in real life at the time). This version of the story transcends the original, taking it in new directions and introducing the audience to new potentials along the way that the original had skipped over. And it's those underutilised elements where Cronenberg finds himself at his most comfortable as a story teller. If the original descended into a playful fly hunt, the remake instead opts for a gradual metamorphosis of its main character, from healthy human being to grotesque man-fly (or 'Brundlefly'), that develops in the same way a disease might. And it's this latter element that sees Cronenberg in his element, as he gives himself the time to examine the horrific implications of such a physical process, while meditating on death and change which eventually affects us all.

Special effects technicians, Chris Walas and Stephan Dupuis (who were previously part of Dick Smith's FX team that worked on *Scanners* [1981]), picked up an Oscar for Best Make-Up. And their sterling work on *The Fly* ranges from an arm wrestler's broken arm to the final shots of the grotesquely mutated Seth, along with all manner of transformation, including the scene in which Seth tears off his own finger nails. Unsurprisingly, the film went down with audiences much better than with the critics. To this day, some still regard the film as a love story as well as a comment on the AIDS pandemic that was headline news at the time of the film's release. This despite Cronenberg always insisting that it wasn't a love story at all – in fact, quite the opposite; one of narcissism and selfishness – and that he intended no such messages with the film. *Variety* magazine gave *The Fly* one of its trademark backhanded compliments: 'One does not have to be totally warped to appreciate this film, but it does take a particular sensibility to embrace it.'

Indeed, this version of *The Fly* even strays into *Beauty and the Beast* territory, albeit in reverse, as Veronica falls in love with the man knowing that he will one day become an unlovable beast. The film also has its roots in the tradition of the 'mad doctor' flick, specifically *Frankenstein* (1931) and *Dr. Jekyll and Mr. Hyde* (1931). Dr. Frankenstein created his monster to satisfy his overwhelming obsession to play God, while Seth Brundle – like Dr. Jekyll – takes it a step further as his obsession leads him into 'creating' a monster of himself.

Blue Velvet (1986)
Dir: David Lynch /USA

It seems incredible now to think of him as the saviour of 80s American cinema, but David Lynch emerged on the scene with *Eraserhead* in the late 70s, a surreal and disturbing dream of dark and troubling things. It was a midnight movie favourite that became an international cult classic and allowed him to head towards the mainstream with his follow-up, *The Elephant Man*, which in turn earned him a BAFTA and an Oscar nomination. The Hollywod A-list seemed to be within his grasp for a while until he helmed *Dune*, a multi-million dollar disaster which could have ended his career. But two good things came out of *Dune*: Actor Kyle MacLochlan and producer Dino De Laurentiis. De Laurentiis never lost faith in Lynch, and gave him $6 million to make his next film. And while Coppola was skint, Scorsese tired, and Spielberg adapting literary works, David Lynch quietly went about filming his own script, *Blue Velvet*, a nightmare voyage through the underworld of suburbia.

College student Jeffrey Beaumont (MacLachlan) heads home after his father suffers a heart attack, and whilst walking through a clearance in the woods he discovers a severed human ear. He takes the evidence to the police, but his curiosity overwhelms him and so he teams up with sweet-natured school girl Sandy (Laura Dern) to help him find out more about the ear, and who it belonged to. Their sleuthing leads them to nightclub singer Dorothy Vallens (Isabella Rosselini). Jeffrey sneaks into her home in search of clues but ends up having to hide in the wardrobe as Dorothy's psychotic 'boyfriend' shows up. Frank Booth (Dennis Hopper) subjects Dorothy to bizarre sexual games and sadism, and Jeffrey has to play peeping tom through the slats in the closet doors while all of this is going on. It soon becomes clear that Frank holds a terrible secret over Dorothy...

The late great Dennis Hopper steals the show as Frank. His daring performance is a stunning creation; terrifying, perverse, and brutal. His snarling delivery and child-like tantrums are enough to put viewers on the edge of their seats more than three decades later. Lynch picked up his second Best Director nomination at the Oscars, his long-time composer, Angelo Badalamenti, provides the grandiose Hermann-esque score, and film fans the world over were relieved that, at last, a true film-maker was back to his full strengths, leaving the likes of contemporary hits like *Top Gun* and *Back To the Future* paling into insignificance. But it wasn't all praise from the critics; horror expert Mark Kermode was physically assaulted in a pub after he wrote a damning review of *Blue Velvet*, and Stateside critic Roger Ebert famously hated it, and argued that the scenes of sexual despair should have featured in a sincere film, not a bubblegum pop movie. He did at least acknowledge the film's strong sexual horror, but was angry that the power of the scene was squandered in its half-arsed context.

Blue Velvet opens with a superb visual metaphor as we see the white picket fences, green lawns, and friendly neighbourly faces passing by and tending their gardens. It's a dream-like sequence of middle America perfectly encapsulated. But then the camera dips and we're suddenly faced with the underbelly that is crawling with insect life.

Dorothy's character is perhaps the most haunting in the film; we discover that her husband and child have both been kidnapped by Frank, and he blackmails her into playing along with his strange sadomasochistic games in order to save the lives of her loved ones (he has already cut off one of her husband's ears). Some have suggested that Dorothy takes a masochistic pleasure from her encounters with Frank, and she certainly does seem to be playing along, but is it genuine or is she just playing it safe and giving Frank what he wants so as to save the lives of her family members? Even during the most intense scenes with Frank, there's something not right; she seems totally withdrawn and distanced from herself, perhaps as a way of turning herself into a passive object – dissociation – so that the abuses can almost have the effect of happening to another person, and not herself.

The theatricality of that scene has led psychoanalysts to suggest that the S&M session stems from Frank's impotence. His loud, aggressive manner is almost comical in an old 'arch-villain' way. He bellows "Don't you fucking look at me!" and it seems fairly obvious that he doesn't want to be looked at because he is ashamed; there is nothing there – no erection. He fakes these crazy 'sex' sessions so as to conceal his impotence. All the shouting and wildness and sexual gestures serve as a mask to conceal the fact that he can't get it up! He apparently has no idea that Jeffrey is hiding in the closet and spying on them, but at the same time he seems to be in some kind of exhibitionist performance. But for whom? He doesn't know about Jeffrey, and he doesn't want

Dorothy to look at him, so we can only assume that he is simply performing for himself, so that he can convince himself of his potency with a strange game of sexual charades.

Another late great, Jack Nance (of *Eraserhead*), and Brad Dourif (who provides the voice of Chucky in the *Child's Play* movies) lend good support as members of Frank's gang, and Dean Stockwell plays the doomed detective. But film fans often need reminding that *Blue Velvet* is not perfect. Sure, it's one of the best of the 80s but Lynch has improved in almost all areas in his subsequent efforts. *Twin Peaks* was more effective in exploring the small-town underbelly, and its villain, Leland Palmer, is more dangerous than Frank Booth simply because he conceals his evils and appears quite normal, even friendly, on the outside. In *Blue Velvet* the characters only get into problems when they venture into unknown areas, whereas in *Twin Peaks* evil is everywhere; it's all a part of the character's families and their home lives – a much more disturbing idea. *Blue Velvet's* take on sexual obsession, identity, and even its garish musical numbers were all done to better effect in *Mulholland Dr.* and *Lost Highway*.

Blue Velvet is best viewed today as a Hitchcockian greatest hits package: The aforementioned Hermann-esque score, nods to *Shadow of a Doubt*, MacLachlan's voyeuristic character reminds one of James Stewart in *Rear Window*, and the sexual obsession with Dorothy strays into *Vertigo* territory. This tribute to Hitchcock's greatest achievements is also alluded to when Sally says to Jeffrey, "I can't figure out if you're a detective or a pervert."

Henry – Portrait of a Serial Killer (1986)
Dir: John McNaughton /USA

One of the most harrowing movies ever made, *Henry-Portrait of a Serial Killer* begins as a sleazy 'stalk and slash' caper before settling down into a raw and edgy character study. Loosely based on the confessions of convicted serial killer Henry Lee Lucas, we're invited to join Henry (Michael Rooker), a lowlife drifter whose job as an exterminator allows him to enter people's homes in search of easy prey.

There's no set method to his killing style; whether it be guns, knives, a broken bottle, or even his bare hands, he systematically sets about his brutal and motiveless crimes by whatever means necessary. Henry moves in with Otis (Tom Towles), a degenerate simpleton whom he met in prison, and when Otis' sister Becky (Tracy Arnold) visits Chicago, she stays with them while she looks for work. Henry encourages Otis to join him in his murderous pursuits, and before long Otis is cackling like a goon as he takes to death and destruction like a duck to water. And this culminates in the notorious home invasion scene in which the pair watch their own crimes on videotape after recording themselves in the act.

Things deteriorate even further when Otis goes completely out of control and tries to rape and strangle his sister Becky. Henry stabs him to death and dismembers his corpse in the bath tub. Becky and Henry then leave the area and spend the night in a motel where they are at last free to kindle their tentative relationship uninterrupted. But anyone expecting a glimmer of hope here are left with a final gut-punch as Henry leaves the motel the next morning, alone.

John McNaughton's stunning debut is a masterpiece of horror which presents its sick characters and the world in which they're bred in a chilling but non-judgemental way. It's a film in which there are no cops or good characters to offer hope to the audience, just pure grubbiness and poverty and ugliness, leaving its viewers emotionally drained and depressed. McNaughton's true masterstroke is the way he presents to us our own vulnerability to an unreasoning psychopath like Henry; an idea few will want to dwell upon. It's a grim view that is at once too awful to be a reality, and yet too life-like to be ignored.

Featuring solid performances from Rooker and Towles, who both went on to bigger projects, and also a very impressive turn from Tracy Arnold (who allegedly went into severe shock during the filming of a particularly gruesome scene), whom sadly little has been seen since. Tom Towles as Otis fits into the depraved role with ease, drawing on his background in comedy theatre to add a touch of grim humour to his performance. Otis is such a scuzzy character he even unsettles Henry; his disturbing and erratic behaviour seems to expose Henry's own mask of sanity, something which he feels uncomfortable with – it's clear that Henry doesn't like to face up to the depths of his own sickness, and he alleviates this by putting Otis in line like a father guiding a wayward son with an absurd air of moral authority! ("No Otis, she's your sister")! And it's telling that the most graphic murder in the film

is that of Otis who is stabbed to death and beheaded. But no matter how sympathetic Henry may become, he truly is a lost cause.

Unsurprisingly, *Henry-Portrait* was released unrated in America, but in the UK it was heavily censored, first for its theatrical release and then again for video. The most problematic scene was the 'home invasion' sequence in which Henry and Otis force their way into a random family home and proceed to beat, rape, and murder the occupants (not necessarily in that order). The main problematic area becomes apparent when the camera pulls back, revealing the events to be taking place on a TV screen with the two psychopaths watching their own previous crimes on videotape that they had recorded themselves; watching and enjoying it ("I want to see it again"), thus implicating the viewers who are watching – and at least seeking – entertainment through degradation and death.

It's a scene reminiscent of the sadistic massacre at the end of Pasolini's *Salo* in which the libertines view the carnage through binoculars, merging their perspective with the audience. But whereas *Salo* was outlawed entirely in the UK for decades, *Henry-Portrait* was initially passed with a re-editing of that crucial scene, and lost most of its disturbing and voyeuristic power in the process. The BBFC later relented and granted the film an uncut 18 certificate for home viewing, by which point it had become widely regarded as one of cinemas darkest horror shows. But even with all the censorship hassles, the film is never exploitative or gratuitous, and even won some kind words from mainstream critics. Don't expect an easy ride then, as McNaughton himself has said, "If it becomes too difficult to watch then *Henry-Portrait* has probably served its purpose."

A Better Tomorrow (1986)
(Orig title: *Ying hung boon sik*)
Dir: John Woo /Hong Kong

Hong Kong film-making is among the most extreme in the world. The emphasis is usually on action and violence, usually to the detriment of the plot. And the violence is often graphic, whether it be guns, swords, or hand-to-hand combat. Films rated Category III often add nudity and deeply disturbing themes to the mix, and usually, things are also spiced up with broad farce and slapstick comedy. For years these films only had the tinniest of cult followings in the West, but with the arrival of master film-maker John Woo, all that was about to change.

'Heroic Bloodshed' is a term often used in reference to the sub-genre of Hong Kong action cinema involving excessive gunplay, bloody shoot-outs, and excessive stunts and car chases. It is the genre with which John Woo has become synonymous. *A Better Tomorrow* was the first of his epics to be granted widespread distribution beyond Hong Kong, and did much to cement his reputation as 'The East's answer to Sam Peckinpah'.

The plot centres on two brothers who come into conflict. Kit (Leslie Cheung) is the cop with a good conscience, and whose dedication to his profession crosses the border into obsession. His brother Ho (Ti Lung), and his good friend Mark (Chow Yun-Fat), make a profit from counterfeit bank notes, and Ho manages to keep his illegal activities hidden from his family. But when a transaction goes awry, Ho is betrayed, their father is killed, and Kit's career in the police force is put into jeopardy. When he is released from prison, Ho tries to patch things up with his brother, attempts to help out his struggling friend Mark, and keep out of trouble. However, before long he finds himself drawn back into the criminal underworld.

A Better Tomorrow presents violence as graphic but also stylized, and the perfect example is the sequence where Mark stages a retribution attack against Ho's betrayer, who is seen eating in a restaurant surrounded by friends and bodyguards. Wearing a suit and a full-length overcoat, Mark strolls down a corridor towards the room in the restaurant, hiding a bunch of handguns amongst the foliage of potted plants. He then bursts into the room, executes his victim at close range, and then retreats through the corridor, using the guns he stashed earlier to wipe out the bodyguards who are pursuing him, discarding each pistol as it empties. This is violence as pure visual poetry. Director John Woo's superb use of editing and slo-mo makes him the most successful practitioner of these techniques since the great Sam Peckinpah.

Never one to go lightly on action sequences, Woo's films also go against the traditions of Hong Kong cinema; he always puts plot and characters first in his epics, and – believe it or not – the violent set-pieces never break away from those important elements. He also never uses the silly slapstick humour to keep his audience engaged between shoot-outs, which is extremely rare in Hong Kong film-making. And

crucially, all of his characters pay the ultimate price for their use of violence, much like Peckinpah's characters.

Lucker the Necrophagous (1986)
Dir: Johan Vandewoestijne /Belgium

The subject of necrophilia has cropped up over the decades in many horror films, albeit in mostly tame and metaphorical terms, with the works of people like Mario Bava, Roger Corman, and Jean Rollin all hinting at the twisted sensualities of death. In the 1970s when the gates of excess were thrown wide open, and almost every taboo you can think of were explored by filmmakers willing to obliterate the boundaries, still there was no one brave enough to tackle the subject in a blunt and literal fashion (Marijan Vadja's creepy and morbid *Mosquito the Rapist* and Jacques Lacerte's *Love Me Deadly* were perhaps the closest thing to necrophilia we saw in 70s horror). A few years later, and Joe D'Amato's *Biou Omega* came closer still to a full-on depiction of corpse fucking, but it wasn't until the early 80s that this most enduring and disgusting of taboos was finally broken with Gerald Kargls *Angst*, in which a young woman is murdered and subsequently raped.

Later that decade, a pair of rancid videotapes started floating round Europe via mail order; Jorg Buttgereit's *Nekromantik* and Johan Vandewoestijne's *Lucker the Necrophagous*. And although both of these films have been known to induce actual physical vomiting in their audiences, Buttgereit's film is an arty shocker with warm sweeping music and soft-focus photography which somewhat softens the blow, whereas Vandewoestijne's *Lucker* dispenses with the glossiness and gets down and dirty with the cadavers, and culminates in one of the most repulsive sequences in cinema history.

The film kicks off with *Lucker* on a mad killing spree after a failed murder, suicide attempt, and escape from a mental institution. He stores away his young female corpses and allows them to mature for a while (like a fine wine?) before he samples the earthly delights. And this sets up the unforgettable sequence in which Lucker cuts a woman's throat and watches her bleed to death before covering her with a sheet. We then spend the next week or so with the slobby psychopath as he kicks around in his squalid apartment biding his time...

Eventually he returns to the bed and uncovers

the corpse, but the body laid out before him no longer resembles that of a young woman, but a bloated, discoloured stiff riddled with maggots (you can almost smell it). Undeterred, an aroused Lucker strokes the corpse between the legs, his fingers becoming slimy with the putrid residue of rotting flesh, and then proceeds to lick and suck the ghastly death juice from his hand. It's a scene that is guaranteed to sicken even the hardiest of extreme movie devotees, but that isn't all; Lucker then climbs on top for a bit of penetrative sex. The term 'viewer discretion is advised' has never been so apt. But of course, this murderous necrophile can't continue with this kind of craziness for very long, and it's only a matter of time before death itself catches up with him...

Nick Van Suyt as the title character does a serviceable job of conveying the depravity of a sick maniac, though I very much doubt he put this on his CV when looking for further work. He deserves a ton of respect for having the balls to go ahead and get 'stuck in' to such a scuzzy role. He reminded me of a down-market version of Pep Tosar (of *Aftermath* infamy) in his willingness to disregard everything for the sake of sleaze. And to my knowledge he hasn't appeared in any film since... Hold on a sec, maybe he *did* put *Lucker* on his CV...

Lucker is not a good film, in fact quite the opposite. There's some awful acting, bad framing, and needless time-padding in the film's rather short 74-minute running time. On the plus side, director Vandewoestijne shows some visual flourishes with lighting, spatial composition, and mood, but the very limited budget curtails any serious attempts at style. He also admirably rejects the idea of traditional attempts to try and understand the killer; a nice move considering how alienated this film is from the rest of cinema, and how alienated Lucker himself is from the rest of society. 'Why is it so important to know what makes him tick?' the filmmaker seems to be asking us. 'Lucker just is'.

The film has had a troubled history; the producers destroyed the original negative, the director gave up film-making altogether, and the film's commercial prospects were extremely limited. Nevertheless, a tape did the rounds on the grey market in a 74-minute cut with Dutch subtitles, and this was the only option available for years until Synapse released a Director's Cut on DVD in the mid-00s. This version is copied

from a rare VHS due to the non-existence of the original source materials. And although it looks terrible compared with other Synapse releases, it is at least uncut and trimmed only of a few needless bits of padding by the director himself.

Combat Shock (1986)
(aka *American Nightmare*)
Dir: Buddy Giovinazzo /USA
"Today's one of those days where everything that can go wrong, does." *Combat Shock* is a grim and repellent little movie that was eventually picked up by Troma and given a theatrical and home video release, becoming a cult classic among 80s videophiles in the process.

The DVD box art makes this look like some all-action, gung-ho heroic war movie, but anyone buying or renting the DVD who were expecting a *Rambo* clone or a *Platoon* would have been shell-shocked at what they actually got for their money. Without a doubt, *Combat Shock* is one of the nastiest, bleakest, most depressingly downbeat movies ever released by Troma; and it also happens to be a near-masterpiece of zero-budget film-making. Imagine *Taxi Driver* remade by John Waters with a bit of *Eraserhead* and *The Deerhunter* thrown in, and you should have some idea of what to expect here, but nothing can really prepare viewers for how ugly this movie is...

The Director's brother, Ricky, stars as Frankie, a down-on-his-luck, severely traumatized 'Nam vet who lives in a rank and grubby tenement block with his shrieking wife and mutant baby. They have no money and no food, and he receives a letter from the landlord informing him that his family have been evicted and should vacate the premises by 6pm. To make matters worse, he is in debt to a trio of local thugs who constantly hassle him and beat him up, and his best friend is a sick junky who has resorted to robbing lone women at gunpoint as a way of feeding his addiction. Plagued by constant flashbacks to his traumatic experiences in a makeshift POW camp, and being hunted through the jungle by the Vietcong, this deeply troubled ex-marine – a trained killer – crumbles psychologically, and this leads to one of the bleakest and most shocking movie endings of the 80s.

Combat Shock is a labour of twisted love. Director Buddy G filmed most of the Vietnam scenes on Staten Island, and to be fair it's almost a perfect illusion. Had he decorated the close-ups with exotic plants, those scenes would have been much more convincing as a Vietnam war zone, but he nonetheless captures that sense of hostile terrain perfectly. Buddy earned his living at the time as a music teacher, and most of the cast members (even the extras) were his drum students who agreed to appear in the film in exchange for free drum lessons. The only downside is that most of the amateur actors aren't really good enough to convey the severity and desperation their roles needed, such as Mike Tierno who plays the junky and who uses a rusty wire coat-hanger to manually insert heroin into a raw wound on his arm as he doesn't have a syringe at hand. Also, the hoodlums were a bit miscast and look about as tough as The Village People (they were probably decent drummers though).

On the plus side, actress Veronica Stork who plays the annoying wife is superb in her grating role, and leading man, Ricky G, whose burned-out stare and grubby clothes make him one of cinema's most memorable budget-psychos (he also contributed the quirky and eccentric score). Director Buddy G shows remarkable visual flair with some interesting camera work, tightly-paced editing, and a real knack for picking out shooting locations – we have scenes shot in genuine urban cesspools of grime and squalor, which seems to mirror the fractured state of mind of our troubled protagonist. Needless to say, if you're accustomed to such Troma crappola as *Fat Guy Goes Nutzoid* or *Surf Nazis Must Die*, then *Combat Shock* will come as something of a nasty surprise.

Originally shown on the festival circuit under its original title, *American Nightmare*, it played well at the grinders in New York's Times Square district before Lloyd Kaufman and Michael Herz of Troma offered a distribution deal. The MPAA demanded cuts to the film but the folks at Troma decided to push their luck and release it uncut. They were eventually found out and ordered to remove the more graphic shots or face a hefty fine (in the book version of *Sleazoid Express*, Bill Landis claims that this kind of practice was fairly common for Troma who would release the uncut versions of their films into theatres, regardless of what the censors had to say on the matter). Troma also added the stock war footage which definitely improves the film, especially during the opening

credits. And while we're on the subject of Troma, it's worth pointing out that their DVD release of *Combat Shock* includes an excellent audio commentary by Buddy G, and he is joined by European gorehound Jorg Buttgereit for a fact-filled, laugh-out-loud funny audio track that is worth the price of the disc alone.

Buddy G continues today as a music teacher, and he occasionally teaches video production classes at New York's School of Visual Arts. His career as an indie film-maker has been marred by frustrations since his promising debut. He got the gig to direct the legendary *Maniac 2* but the project fizzled out when actor/producer Joe Spinell died suddenly. Also in the late 80s he wrote a screenplay called *Dead and Married* for Vestron. It was a dark comedy, but in the finished cut of the film all the sick jokes had been watered down to such an extent that the finished product (re-named as *She's Back*) didn't work.

Numerous self-written scripts remain unfilmed, such as the intriguing *Dirty Money*, the controversial *123 Depravity Street*, and even the relatively commercial *Jonathan of the Night*. He has written short stories, poetry, and even novels, the third of which he adapted to the screen himself under the title *Life Is Hot In Cracktown*. The crowning achievement of his career so far is undoubtedly *No Way Home* (aka *Life Sentences*) in which, by a mad miracle, he managed to cast Tim Roth, James Russo, and Deborah Unger in his film which is about a man who is released from jail and who must face the daily grind of poverty, drugs, and violence.

Death Powder (1986)
(Orig title: *Desu pawuda*)
Dir: Shiguero Izumiya /Japan
Running just over an hour, *Death Powder* is a weird, trippy VHS wonder from Japan. The film opens with a prologue in which bizarre, nonsensical images appear on screen – charred human heads in a blazing industrial building; a woman lying on a metal bed frame wearing headphones, shades, and some kind of hi-tech breathing apparatus; and a man vandalising the building with a metal pole. After the title card, we follow a woman as she is chased through a busy shopping mall by sinister looking men, shot in guerilla-style. The woman is captured. She also has a male accomplice. The sinister men exchange a few words with them before leaving, and I have no idea what they were

talking about as, for some reason, their dialogue was subtitled in Japanese. Anyway, I won't go on with the 'plot' as it doesn't make much sense, but from what I can gather, the 'woman' on the bed frame is actually some kind of mechanoid that gives off 'death powder,' a fatal substance that causes the victims to trip their balls off before they expire. There is a group of people trying to protect the cyborg while others want to be in possession of it for their own devious purposes... It's certainly low budget and shot on video, but don't be dismayed, it looks great with its moody shadows and expert lighting, great special effects, and DP Kazuo Komizu (of *Entrails of a Virgin* infamy) shows great inventiveness with his camera work. The subtitles alternate between English and Japanese (at least in the version I saw), and this makes the confusing plot-line even harder to follow. However, fans of cyberpunk oddities like *964 Pinocchio* (1991) and the *Tetsuo* movies should enjoy regardless. Writer/director/producer, Izumiya, inserts clips of one of his music videos, called *Dr. Loo Made Me*, from his earlier days as a rock musician, presumably to help pad out the running time. *Death Powder* has never had an official DVD release.

Zero Boys (1986)
Dir: Nico Mastorakis /USA
A group of Hollywood stunt actors head out to the Californian wilderness and trespass at an isolated cabin. Of course, machete-and-crossbow-wielding maniacs target them, and the youngsters learn the hard way that the cabin is actually a torture house where snuff movies are made... Despite a mediocre set-up, this actually becomes a fairly decent slasher movie by the 45-minute mark. It's also slightly different from the usual by-the-numbers slasher flicks in that the teens are armed with fully-automatic machine guns. Not that it does them any good, as the killers lurk in the shadows and only strike when it's to their advantage. The recent Blu-Ray release makes it clear that the film was shot on the same sets as *Friday the 13th Part 3* (1982).

Captured For Sex 2 (1986)
(Orig title: *Kankin sei no dorei: Ikenie 2*)
Dir: Masaru Ijuin /Japan
The 'plot' is drearily simple: A sadist kidnaps a young couple and takes them back to his lair in the middle of the woods, where the girl is physically tortured and the man psychologically

tormented. Some reviewers have called it an S&M movie, but because none of the victims here are willing participants, that label just doesn't hold up. And what we have instead is a plain old pinku roughy, and not a particularly good one at that. The actresses involved were most certainly there by their own consent (in some scenes you can see the welts and bruising on their thighs during the abuse), and the style of their torture – with the use of whips and candle wax, etc – is the only reason anyone could mistake it for an S&M movie.

The torture seems to bring out the young man's own sadistic side, and he begs the captor to make him his 'apprentice'. And before long, the sap is helping the scumbag to kidnap another girl from a tennis court. Back at the house, the abuse becomes increasingly extreme – we are witness to such past times as anal rape, pixelated sex scenes, candle wax torture, a milk enema (which is then plugged up for weeks with a cork), a demonstration of various pervert tools, including gynecological apparatus and bondage accoutrements, needle pricking, and in the pièce de résistance, a horrid scene involving the use of marbles, wine and a funnel.

The soundtrack consists of bizarre computer bleeps created on primitive electronics, and sounds like an old Spectrum ZX loading up. The title of this film clearly states that it's a sequel to *Captured For Sex*, but it's actually a loose sequel to *Ikenie*. The original *Captured For Sex* was also a sequel to another bizarre pinky film with strange set pieces, *Daydream*. *Captured For Sex 2* is a bizarre ride through lust, pain, and the transgression of normal pain, and was probably an influence on future AV dreck like *Tumbling Doll of Flesh* and *The Devil's Experiment*. Even with the short running time of 67 minutes, you'd have to be a seriously committed bad movie vulture to sit through this to the end. It has all the grace and charm of a glob of phlegm bobbing around in a fetid pub urinal.

April Fools Day (1986)
Dir: Fred Walton /USA
College kids head for a house on an island where they are picked off by an escaped lunatic... This film offers a novel twist on slasher movie conventions, but this doesn't make things any less tedious to sit through. We get a hackneyed script which is heavily influenced by Agatha Christie's *Ten Little*

Indians, a lack of suspense (save for a spooky basement scene near the end), and the most irritating cast of characters this side of *The Burning* (1981); a bunch of 'hark-at-us' show-offs whom you can't wait to see the backs of. In its favour, this does have some good production values for an 80s 'slasher' movie, but of course, the whole film turns out to be a waste of time once we get to the revelation at the end. Check out David Fincher's much superior *The Game* (1997) instead.

TerrorVision (1986)
Dir: Ted Nicolaou /USA

The Putterman family has trouble with their newly-installed satellite dish. And no sooner is the problem 'fixed' when a one-eyed space monster is beamed through their television screen to cause havoc in the household... *TerrorVision* is a fun little flick aimed at teens, and became a cult item on VHS. It's rare for an intentionally campy movie to work, but this one hits the ground running. Everyone on screen delivers the campy goods in spades: Mary Woronov and Gerrit Graham play the swinging parents whose double-date with a suave Greek man and his wife doesn't go quite to plan. There's also Diane Franklin as the teenage daughter, Suzie, a monolith of brightly-coloured hair dye and spandex. Her metal-head boyfriend, O.D., is played by Jon Gries (who also played the legendary arcade maniac, 'King Vidiot,' in *Joysticks* [1983]), here in a slightly more subdued mode. A young Chad Allen is marvellous as the younger brother, Sherman, a resourceful kid who struggles to convince his family of the truth. And then there's grandpa, played by former Robert Altman regular, Bert Remsen, a keen survivalist who has his own underground bunker stock-piled with a shit-load of military hardware. Grandpa also delivers the best line ("Well, do something, you ugly bastard!"). As for the space monster itself, it looks like a giant scrotum dipped in acid, or a slime-drenched gloopy mess, sort of like a cross between Jabba the Hutt and the alien creatures of *The Deadly Spawn* (1983). And its voice sounds like it's talking and burping at the same time.

Blood Cult (1986)
Dir: Christopher Lewis /USA

A bog-standard, shot-on-video slasher from the mid-80s which opens with a *Psycho*-esque bathtub slashing before setting up its hokey premise of a town Sheriff investigating a series of meat cleaver murders on a college campus. With a stilted voice-over, the elderly Sheriff explains what's going on while looking for clues and pestering his librarian daughter. He comes across as a weak and ineffectual man as he allows himself to be manipulated by the college principal. Surely an experienced man of the law would recognise when people are obstructing him and trying to tell him how to do his job. A real man of the law would assert his authority in an instant, but here the bumbling old-timer accepts his lecturing and gets on with his day as a jovial and incompetent fool. In fact, the investigation only makes progress thanks to his daughter's immersive research into symbolism and witch cults. Anyway, at the hour mark, the Sheriff chances upon robed cultists offering up bloody sacrifices in the woods... *Blood Cult* was one of the first SOV projects to be picked up for distribution across America, along with *Boardinghouse* (1982) and *They Don't Cut the Grass Anymore* (1983). It was even released on DVD in 2001. It's quite well made for a micro-budget slasher but it's also very dull. 80s trash maven, Joseph A. Ziemba, summed up the problem with the film in *Bleeding Skull*: "*Blood Cult* isn't slick enough to complement theatrical releases like *The Prowler.* But it's also not distinct enough to provide a lasting trash experience, like *Heavy Metal Massacre.*" The film's best idea is the scene in which the killer murders a college girl by beating her to death with her room mate's severed head, but even that sequence is poorly done. Director Lewis returned with a sequel, *Revenge: Blood Cult II* (1986).

The Abomination (1986)
Dir: Max Raven /USA

A bizarre, home-brewed horror in which a mother coughs up her lung tumour. It then mutates, enlarges, takes control of her son and terrorises a small Texas community. Hmm, I wonder if there could be a message here about the ravages of cancer... This film marks a rare attempt by a low-budget film-maker to tackle Cronenbergian body horror, and if the results are far from successful, this flick does at least have a vicious toothy cancer creature in the mix which looks similar to the critters in *The Deadly Spawn* (1982). Perhaps director Max Raven will return to film-making one day with a movie about gonorrhea in which a town full of dicks and pussies suddenly ooze a thick green slime that dribbles out from the bottom of their hems and leaves trails on the ground. The local virgin follows the tracks while stopping his dog from licking up the gloop, and the trail leads to a Texas barn where unprotected demonic orgies are going on... You know, something with a very subtle social message, like *The Abomination*.

Trick Or Treat (1986)
Dir: Charles Martin Smith /USA
Everything that sucked about 80s rock music is rubbed in your face for 98-minutes in this horrendous time-capsule of a movie hailing from the decade that taste forgot. The spirit of a devil-worshipping rock star comes back from the dead to empower a victimised school kid into getting even with bullies. *Trick Or Treat* is a lukewarm, non-eventful 'revenge of the nerd' movie in the vein of *Evil Speak* (1982), *Christine* (1983) and *976-Evil* (1988). Includes an amusing cameo by Ozzy Osbourne as a Reverend campaigning on TV against 'rock pornography.'

Necropolis (1986)
Dir:Bruce Hickey /USA
In 1686 in New York (or, New Amsterdam, as it was then known), a Christian follows a mysterious blonde through the woods to an underground lair where a Satanic black wedding is taking place. The Christian stays hidden in the shadows as he witnesses all manner of girating and voodoo and human sacrifice. A posse soon shows up, and the blonde Satanist curses at the men and swears revenge... Cut to 300 years later, in modern-day New York, and the blonde sorceress is still around, albeit reincarnated. She's now a punkette who rides a motorcycle and is in search of an ancient ring that will enable her to complete the 300-year-old Satanic wedding we saw in the prologue. However, this strand of the plot is abandoned for much of the film's running time, and instead we follow her as she struts around, leaving a pile of dead bodies behind. And meanwhile, an Italian cop, Billy (Michael Conte) and his British love interest, Dawn (Jacquie Fitz), team up with a black Pastor, Henry (William K. Reed), and attempt to put an end to this nonsense...

Necropolis is typical 80s video swill from Empire (Charles Band served as executive producer, uncredited). There's bad acting, trashy 80s music – much of it borrowed from other 80s flicks, such as *Trancers* (1985) and *Eliminators* (1986) – trashy fashions and big bad hairdos. The Satanic femme fatale isn't very menacing, and the frankly terrible performance by leading lady, LeeAnne Baker, invites nothing but ridicule. Unsurprisingly, Baker swiftly vanished from the movie world in the following year, never to be seen on screen again. But, to be fair to her, *everyone* in this film is just as bloody awful. Still, 80s trash fiends should get a kick out of this, especially the sequence in which the sorceress grows six breasts in some kind of demonic ritual, and a hooded congregation of zombie-like ghouls shuffle in on her to breastfeed a gelatin secretion that holds dark powers of immortality.

Tim Kincaid and Cynthia De Paula produced a slew of low-budget oddball pics for Empire during the period, including *Breeders* (1986), *Mutant Hunt* (1987), *Riot On 42nd St.* (1987) and *The Occultist* (1988). And most of those films included the special effects work of Ed French. Kincaid began his career producing and directing gay porn, under the pseudonym 'Joe Gage.' He later returned to the porn field at the turn of the millennium after a twelve year break from the movie business.

Bullies (1986)
Dir: Paul Lynch /Canada
In every run-down area there is always at least one family whose surname strikes fear in the hearts of the locals, and in the isolated town of Granton, Ontario, that family is the Cullens, a destructive, inbred, psychotic clan who think nothing of terrorising the neighbourhood and even running old folks off the road to their deaths. And when a nice family moves into the area to take over the local grocery store, the Cullens take an instant dislike to them and set out on a vicious campaign of persecution. Meanwhile, the teenage son, Matt (the late Jonathan Crombie), befriends an old native Indian called Will (Dehl Berti). Matt also strikes up a friendship/romance with Becky (pretty Olivia D'Abo), the youngest daughter of the Cullens, and the conflict between the families soon spirals out of control... *Bullies* is a decent and sadly little-seen film (at the time of writing, it only has 8 user reviews on *IMDb*). It's a film which nicely bridges the gap between *Straw Dogs* (1971) and *Eden Lake* (2008), with a man seemingly out of his depth when dealing with a

rival patriarch who encourages his sons to behave in the most vicious and brutish ways. And the only 'language' they seem to understand is violence. This being a backwoods horror show, you can expect lots of eerie slide guitar on the soundtrack, and a brutal showdown towards the end. Oddly, the Indian character, Will, is built up to be a tough and wise old man. Viewers who expect him to show up and play a part in the final showdown will be disappointed, however, because as soon as the Cullens pay him a visit and rough him up a little, he simply packs his belongings and leaves town, never to be seen again!

Cassandra (1986)
Dir: Colin Eggleston /Australia
Tessa Humphries plays Cassandra, a girl plagued by recurring dreams of a shotgun suicide of someone she knew. She suspects the dreams are actually repressed childhood memories of some atrocity she witnessed, but she just can't remember exactly what it was. Her parents aren't very helpful, and they suspiciously do all they can to convince her that her experiences are nothing more than random nightmares. However, when a killer shows up bloodily dispatching a few locals, Cassandra is convinced that she shares psychic links with the maniac. This tense, atmospheric oddity is part mystery, part supernatural chiller, and part slasher movie that boasts superb roving, Raimi-esque camera work and an outstanding, creepy-as-hell synth score. The film owes a debt to other psychic link killer movies, such as *Eyes of Laura Mars* (1978), *Mind Over Murder* (1979), and the bloody awful *Blood Song* (1982). *Cassandra* would sit nicely on a double-bill with another Aussie psycho movie, *Out of the Body* (1989). Tessa Humphries is actually Dame Edna's daughter! Luckily for her, there's no family resemblance!

Witchboard (1986)
Dir: Kevin S. Tenney /UK /USA
House party revellers break out a ouija board and unleash the angry spirit of a young boy. The spirit then engineers a series of brutal 'mishaps' on the party goers, one by one. A collapsed roof, some tossed beer cans, and a dead psychic later, the remaining ones soon learn that a much more powerful spirit, Malfeitor, is actually responsible for the murders. *Witchboard* is your typical 80s teen horror flick which borrows

elements from *The Omen* (1976), 80s slasher movies, and even *The Exorcist* (1973). Silly at times, but also watchable if you're in the right mood, this film also went on to influence the *Final Destination* series years later.

Zombie Nightmare (1986)
Dir: Jack Bravman /Canada
When a baseball player is killed in a hit 'n' run accident, his distraught parents have him resurrected by a voodoo sorcerer called Molly. The ghoul then stalks the streets at night with his trusty baseball bat, taking out the local delinquents who are responsible for his death. 'You're looking for a large angry person,' the forensics guy tells the detective after a young man is found with a broken neck in a sports centre. Lots more deadpan humour abounds in this 80s time capsule that throws up the sounds of Motorhead, Death Mask, very early Pantera, and of course, Thor. Frontman Jon Mikl Thor stars as the ghoul that shows up in green face paint, looking a bit like The Incredible Hulk (he also starred in *Rock 'n' Roll Nightmare* in the following year). It's silly but a lot of fun, and draws on such previous classics as *The Monkey's Paw*, *Deathdream* and EC comics. Also look out for Tia Carrere who plays one of the ill-fated bimbo girls, and who later showed up in *Wayne's World* and eventually landed the starring role in the Canadian TV series, *Relic Hunter*.

House (1986)
Dir: Steve Minor /USA
A successful novelist (William Katt) moves into his aunt's suburban middle-class home after she commits suicide. There he settles down to write a memoir based on his tour of duty in Vietnam, but his work is interrupted by a series of ghostly goings on in the house, with strange apparitions, levitating garden tools and ugly, frog-faced demons showing up to terrorise him... Producer Sean S. Cunningham this time delivers a family-friendly, lightly-toned haunted house movie after the success of his earlier slasher classic, *Friday the 13th* (1980). There is very little to take seriously in this film; it's competently made, and there is the appearance of a seven-foot-tall zombie soldier in the finale, but the script – which constantly hints that the protagonist is suffering from PTSD after his experiences in Vietnam (a subtext which was probably lost on most of its target teenage

337

audience) – is ultimately too afraid to address the subject-matter without sugar coating in a self-defeating, tongue-in-cheek style. *Friday the 13th*'s Harry Manfredini also contributes the score.

Critters (1986)
Dir: Stephen Herek /USA

A group of Krites – sort of furry tumbleweeds with razor-sharp teeth – escape from a prison farm on an asteroid, steal a spaceship, and head for planet Earth while being pursued by shape-shifting bounty hunters. Meanwhile, on a Kansas farm, a family comes under attack from the carnivorous critters, and it's up to a resourceful ginger kid to save the day by fending them off with firecrackers. *Critters* is an endearing attempt to recapture the sense of fun in 50s space invasion movies, such as *Invaders From Mars* (1953) and *It Came From Outer Space* (1953), and for the most part it is successful in its aims. The creatures – their design clearly influenced by Gremlins – are nasty little things, sort of like intergalactic piranhas covered in arse hairs that not only roll around biting chunks out of people, but are also capable of shooting sharp spines as projectiles out of their backs. We get the typical small-town setting, incompetent authority figures (including M. Emmett Walsh as a sceptical Sheriff), and a deliberately tongue-in-cheek script co-written by Don Opper (who went on to co-star in *Critters 3* and *Critters 4: In Space*, alongside newcomers Leonardo DiCaprio and Angela Bassett).

Anguish (1986)
(Orig title: *Angustia*)
Dir: Bigas Luna /Spain

In this unsung horror classic, writer/director Bigas Luna borrows the film-within-a-film gimmick from the humdrum slasher movie, *He Knows You're alone* (1980), and wrings 90-minutes of nail-biting tension, delivering one of the best psycho movies of the late 80s. The film stars Michael Lerner as a psycho eye surgeon who loses his job and crumbles psychologically while his domineering mother (Zelda Rubinstein) convinces him to seek vengeance on the world by carving out eyeballs with a scalpel. *Anguish* is the kind of film that constantly folds in on itself without ever confusing or obstructing the narrative. Like *He Knows You're Alone,* the film opens on a scene in which the camera pulls back to reveal that the events are being played out on a cinema screen, and that a member of the audience is about to be killed for real. However, rather than settling for a William Castle-type fright gimmick, Luna instead keeps it going, and successfully absorbs the peculiar premise into the narrative proper. The William Castle influence is also present during the opening scene in which viewers are warned that they will be subjected to hypnotic suggestions throughout the screening.

Evil Dead II (1987)
(aka *Evil Dead II: Dead by Dawn*)
Dir: Sam Raimi /USA

In the winter of 1981, talented film-maker Sam Raimi and his buddies, Bob Tapert and Bruce Campbell headed out to rural Michigan to make a movie. Braving the sub-zero temperatures, the youngsters overcame their inexperience by sheer verve and spirit. And, by the time the spring had arrived, they had delivered the splatter classic, *The Evil Dead* (1982), which was a huge hit with horror fans, despite being embroiled in the 'video nasties' panic in the UK. According to BBFC chief censor, James Ferman, the problem with *The Evil Dead* was that 'the name of the game was excess,' and that the film was 'too excessive.' And while *The Evil Dead* was faced with mounting cuts and court appearances, Sam Raimi and much of the same cast and crew simply got on with doing it all over again, this time bigger, better, and even *more* excessive, for the delirious *Evil Dead II*.

Much less a sequel than a remake, this time Raimi spends little more than five minutes setting up the story before unleashing hell on his characters. A young man named Ash (Campbell) drives his girlfriend, Linda (Denise Bixler), to a remote cabin in the woods. There, they discover an old tape recorder and play back a recording of a professor who claims to have unleashed demons after studying dangerous passages in the Necronomicon, or 'Book of the Dead.' No sooner have the incantations blared out through the tiny tinny speaker, when the Deadites – a horde of ghoulish demons from Hell – converge on the cabin to prey on the victim's 'fresh souls.' Added to this version is a new sub-plot in which the professor's concerned daughter hires a couple of backwoods types to escort her to the cabin to find out why her parents haven't returned home in so long...

A vast improvement over the original in

every way, with a lightning fast pace and even more inventively daring set-pieces and wacky asides, *Evil Dead II* can rank alongside that rare breed of sequels that are actually superior to their predecessors. What's even more remarkable is the fact that Raimi turned down the opportunity of working with legendary producer Dino De Laurentiis on a big-budget adaptation of Stephen King's *Thinner* (which was later brought to the screen by Paramount in 1996), in order to concentrate on his wacky redux. Incidentally, King had described *The Evil Dead* as being 'like a thunderstorm in a bottle.' *Evil Dead II* was more like a typhoon in a glass house. With a polite nudge from King, De Laurentiis agreed to help fund the project, albeit with a much lower offering than was intended for *Thinner*.

With a budget of $3.6 million, Raimi set out to implement a back-to-basics approach to re-capturing the winning formula that had previously proved successful. Having already felt the sting of a flop in *Crimewave* (1984), the pressure was on, and the focus of the film-makers was concentrated on the most effective aspects of the original *Evil Dead*, utilising a frenetic pace and scenes in which blood literally sprays from the walls by the gallon. Added to this extreme style was an equally off-kilter humour and career best performance from Bruce Campbell as the tormented Ash. Whether he's dismembering his undead girlfriend, or his own hand with a chainsaw, the film never feels entirely disreputable thanks to Campbell's charismatic hero.

The end result was a hit with audiences, much like the original. However, unlike its savagely dismembered predecessor, the censors seemed to get the joke and passed it uncut in most territories, except for the UK where the BBFC cut out the head kicking scene of the Deadite in the fruit cellar for both its theatrical and VHS releases (though DVD editions are all uncut). The cult success ensured another sequel was on the cards, and in 1992 Raimi delivered the third in the series, *Army of Darkness*, a film that picked up right where *Evil Dead II* left off with Ash battling the Deadites with his 'Boom-stick' in medieval Europe. Two decades later, Raimi, Campbell and Tapert (of Renaissance Pictures) produced the remake, *Evil Dead* (2013), a dull and humourless effort that was the most financially successful entry in the series, though it left many fans cold.

As for *Evil Dead II*, Sam Raimi once described it as 'my version of *The Three Stooges*, with blood and guts standing in for the custard pies.' It's a film made almost entirely from bizarre and macabre set-pieces, from the dancing corpse with the loose head, to the runaway hand, and the eye-popping sequence in which an eyeball flies across the room and lands in a character's mouth. Like Stuart Gordon's Re-Animator (1985), Brain Yuzna's *Society* (1989) and Peter Jackson's *Braindead* (1992), the grue and splatter is constantly kept in check with a firm tongue-in-cheek style, a winning formula that has ensured its status as one of the great cult classics of the 80s.

A Short Film About Killing (1987)
(Orig title: *Krotki film o Zabijaniu*)
Dir: Krzstof Kieslowski /Poland

A Short Film About Killing is an extended version of Episode 5 of late director Krzstof Kieslowski's *Dekelog*, a ten-part series made for Polish television interpreting the themes of the biblical Ten Commandments in modern stories. This episode, focusing on the Fifth Commandment ('Thou Shalt Not Kill'), brilliantly portrays the dynamics between the killer, the victim, and the legal system.

Jacek (Miroslaw Baka) is a young thug from the countryside, unhappy and restless, who wanders the city aimlessly. Piotr (Krzstof Globisz) is an idealistic law student who takes and passes his bar exams. Waldemar (Peter Jan Teserz) is a simple taxi driver and a thoroughly unpleasant character. The film inter-cuts the lives of these three apparently unrelated figures throughout the course of the day in which their fates will intersect irretrievably. It is with apparent arbitrariness that Jacek finally hails one cab and not another, instructs the driver to take them on a desolate alternative route, and then brutally murders him. Jacek will be unsuccessfully defended by the young lawyer Piotr, given the death penalty, and hanged by the state.

The relative speed with which the film moves from the murder to capital punishment serves to highlight their moral equivalence. The long build-up that precedes the murders engenders no sympathy but rather adopts the cold perspective of a stranger. In this sense, Kieslowski relies entirely on the crimes themselves to reveal the meanings of the moral commandment. Indeed, the film's cold, detached style and its harshly honest theme owes much to Camus' classic novella, *The Outsider*.

Jacek's feelings of alienation and lack of respect were emphasised by DP Slawomir Idziak who shot the film through a green filter that not only reinforced the contrasting light and darkness, but also gives viewers the sense that Warsaw and its environs was a cold and cruel place to be. Both Jacek and the taxi driver's actions before their meeting shows little in the way of humanity, with Jacek dropping stones onto passing cars and insulting the elderly, whilst Waldemar refuses his neighbour a lift and frightens a man out walking his dogs.

And yet neither of them deserve to die in such a manner – Waldemar being strangled and beaten around the head with a rock whilst begging for his life, and Jacek at the hands of a chillingly merciless hangman. The murder scenes are completely unflinching and are shown for the whole duration – for something like seven and five minutes, respectively – and are among the most harrowing deaths in film history. It is the killings themselves, presented so cold and brutally, that leave the most indelible mark of emptiness and cruelty at the state of society. Poland has since abolished the death penalty since it joined the EU.

Released in Poland in 1988, this film preceded the success of Kieslowski's later French films, such as *The Double Life of Veronique*, and the much acclaimed trilogy, *Red, White, and Blue*, which take up similar themes of contingency, fate, and coincidence surrounding and defining human actions and responsibility.

Hellraiser (1987)
Dir: Clive Barker /UK

Frank, a sexual adventurer in search of new carnal pleasures, purchases a mysterious puzzle box while visiting an unnamed Third World country. Back home in England, he opens the box to discover that he has unlocked the door to hell. Frank is pulled into another dimension, whose dwellers, known as Cenobites, push him over the fine line between pleasure and pain by ripping him apart with fish hooks. Years later, Frank's brother Larry moves his family into the house – to which, through some blood spilled on the attic floor, Frank returns in near-skeletal form. With the help of sister in law Julia – with whom he once had an affair – Frank begins sucking the life out of human bodies in order to

regenerate to his old form. Meanwhile, Larry's daughter from a previous marriage, Kirsty (Ashley Laurence), begins to suspect her hated stepmother Julia of having an affair, and to her horror becomes involved with Frank, the puzzle box, and the Cenobites.

Elegantly portrayed by Doug Bradley, who lends a snarling Elvis lip-curl to this face from beyond the grave, Pinhead was the coolest and weirdest screen monster of the 80s; the being for whom pain was power, and whose orgasmic wounds and physical defacements were not signs of submissiveness, but of wicked strength. Echoing the piercings and scarifications of the modern day primitives who were just starting to become 'hip' at the time, Pinhead was the creation of Clive Barker (with a little help from special FX legend, Bob Keen), the painter turned playwright, novelist, and film-maker, whose efforts to re-define the meaning of monstrosity led Stephen King to comment "I have seen the future of horror, and his name is Clive Barker."

Barker's path to stardom started back in the 70s when, as a student at Liverpool University, he teamed up with Pete Atkins and Doug Bradley, with whom he shared an interest in the macabre. Initially, Barker had explored his sacred obsession through theatre and graphic design, but inspired by the low-budget endeavours of film-makers like Andy Warhol and Kenneth Anger, they decided to try their hand at 8mm art, producing two short films, *Salome* and *The Forbidden*. *The Forbidden* is the black and white short in which many of the skin-flailing, sadomasochistic pleasures of Barker's big screen horror hit were first road-tested. Crucially, in both *Hellraiser* and *The Forbidden*, the apparently horrendous tortures inflicted upon the flesh are seen as transformations rather than degradations – births not deaths.

Barker eventually moved to London and quickly established himself in theatre, where his love for everything bizarre and fantastical found an outlet in such works as *Frankenstein In Love*, *The History of the Devil*, and the wonderfully titled *The Secret Life of Cartoons*. He also expanded on his dark visions in short stories, and soon became one of Britain's foremost horror writers with such classics as 'The Damnation Game' and the 'Books of Blood' series. One of his early short stories, *Rawhead Rex*, and a screenplay, *Transmutations*, were made into films (Barker penned both screenplays), and he was so disappointed with the end results that he vowed to get back into the director's seat himself. And in 1987 he did just that, adapting his own novella, '*The Hellbound Heart*', for the big screen under the title *Hellraiser*.

At the time, the horror genre was dominated by American slasher movie franchises, and international audiences were totally unprepared for the cinematic onslaught that was *Hellraiser*. Was this a revitalisation of the British horror film? An open love letter to S&M sex? Or an attack on the unexpected success of the Rubik's Cube? It was all of this and more. Here was a mainstream movie that dared to link sensuality with fear, a film whose villains were also victims, and who were described by Pinhead as "demons to some, angels to others."

From Nosferatu, Dracula, and Frankenstein, to Leatherface and Michael Myers, the image of the horror film has always been one that thrives on icon-status. The Munch-inspired *Scream* mask is another example. And yet, for a genre that boasts thousands of titles, these key images are difficult to find – notice the countless horror movies out there in which the monster inspires nothing more than casual interest (like the screen version of *Rawhead Rex*, for example). The whole point of designing a screen monster is to come up with something we have never seen before, otherwise what's the point? The best monsters positively revel in their own unlikeliness: that's why low-budget curios like *The Deadly Spawn* and *Godmonster of Indian Flats* work so well. Monster movies should be like beauty contests in reverse; the stranger and uglier the better. And with the Cenobites – Pinhead in particular – Clive Barker understood this perfectly and succeeded in creating a unique horror anti-hero.

"They're like sadomasochists from beyond the grave," Barker once said of the Cenobites. Barker even joked that he originally wanted to call the film 'Sadomasochists From Beyond the Grave'. In the sequels *Hellbound: Hellraiser II* and *Hellraiser III* we learn that Pinhead was Captain Eliot Spenser, a First World War veteran who had discovered the puzzle box, known as the Lament Configuration (or Lemarchand's Box in the novella), and found his own gateway into hell. By exploring Pinhead in his human form, Barker made him more accessible to the audience, and used the old 'war is hell' metaphor

in its most literal extreme.

In the original script, the foremost monster was simply referred to as 'Lead Cenobite'; only after the film's release did the name Pinhead attach itself to the character created by actor Doug Bradley, in reference to the mass of nails that symmetrically encased his head. Pinhead is the voice of the Cenobites, an emissary from hell whose sonorous delivery of lines such as "We'll tear your soul apart" ensured that the threat posed by the Lament Configuration was as real and intense as Barker could make it. "The box. You opened it, we came", Pinhead states succinctly. Most of their contemporaries in 80s horror films conformed to traditional monster-templates, but the Cenobites were the products of a new age of freedom in the arts. Not only was the gore quotient increased, but Barker explored another taboo to the full: sexual perversion.

The slasher sub-genre had always allied sex with death as a prurient excuse to show some naked flesh, but *Hellraiser* had much more than a hint of sex; it positively reeked of it. The Cenobites' conjoining of pleasure and pain raises disturbing implications that intensify the horror and open doors into the soul that few other films dared to attempt, at least until the advent of 'torture porn' and movies like Lars Von Trier's *Antichrist* came along.

"I think what the monsters in movies have to say for themselves is every bit as interesting as what the human beings have to say," Barker once stated. "That's why in stalk 'n' slash films I feel that half the story is missing. These creatures simply become, in a very boring way, abstractions of evil. Evil is never abstracted. I want to hear the Devil speak. I like the idea that a point of view can be made by the dark side." *Hellraiser* is the type of film that lets the Devil speak, a full-on screen shocker in which the almost willfully boring teenage heroes are utterly overshadowed by the twisted monsters. From the skinless body of Frank, to the tooth-chattering torments of Pinhead's Cenobite accomplices, and the sensually earthly corruptions of Julia, who serves up human sacrifices to feed her all-consuming lust, *Hellraiser* is a true landmark of modern horror.

Lolita Vibrator Torture (1987)
Dir: Hisayasu Sato /Japan

Notoriously difficult to find in any English language version, *Lolita Vibrator Torture* follows the escapades of a sick voyeuristic maniac who likes to 'cuff young girls to his bed, titillate them with a vibrator, pour acid into their mouths, and take snapshots with his camera as the girl's throats are burned out. Pretty nasty stuff. A typical predatory paedophile, the man (Takeshi Ito) grooms and sweet-talks his potential victims on the streets, gains their trust, and then unleashes hell on them.

When he captures one particular girl (Kiyomi Ito), he discovers that she is already carrying around her own vibrator that she keeps down her panties! He proceeds to assault her and smears the bloody joy stick across her chest. After the ordeal he seems to take pity on her and keeps her alive so that she can become his accomplice. Another girl is defiled with spray paint, stripped, covered in shaving foam, then given the old buzz-stick treatment and raped. His little helper then takes over the vibrator duties and really goes to town, ramming the victim with all of her little might. Then comes the acid and the camera, and young Ito poses with the bloody corpse as the madman begins clicking away with a photo shoot from hell. The pictures are then used to decorate the walls of his lair – a freight container perched on the top of an apartment block. This couple build a rapport based on sex and secrecy, but perhaps inevitably, things are due to end very badly... and those pesky vibrators just keep on buzzing away.

Even by Sato's sleazy standards this wretched piece of celluloid crosses some serious boundaries. And you thought *Maladoloscenza* and *Emperor Tomato Ketchup* were at the cutting edge of under-age exploitation? Well, wait until you clap eyes on this, because for once, the title of the film actually lives up to expectations. And then some. The national age of consent in Japan is just 13 years old, but from a Westerner's perspective the bombardment of school uniforms, bloody vibrators, and deranged black and white stills of children in their death throes amounts to some truly pathological images.

Unsurprisingly, the film hasn't been officially released in any form outside of Japan, and out of the hundreds of Pinku eiga films that were made over the decades, this is perhaps the most shocking and outrageous (though not the best) of them all. Even the Japanese themselves were outraged, with some claiming it to be the most repulsive film of all time. The film does,

however, have its share of supporters, most notably Pinky legend Yuji Tajiri who praised it as being a major inspiration behind his own directing career.

Made as part of Kan Mukai's Shishi Productions, and released by Nikkatsu as part of a Roman Porno triple-bill, *Lolita Vibrator Torture* features the debut of actor Takeshi Ito who would go on to become one of the most successful Pink film actors of his era, winning the first ever Best Actor Award at the Pink Film Grand Prix for his role in Toshiya Ueno's snappily titled *Keep On Masturbating: Non-Stop Pleasure*. And incidentally, actress Kiyomi Ito (no relation) won Best Actress at the same event for Sato's unforgettable *Dirty Wife Getting Wet*. The original title for *Lolita Vibrator Torture* was *The Secret Garden* (*Himitsu no Hanazono*) under which name it was released on DVD in Japan in 2003.

Crazy Love (1987)
(aka *Love Is a Dog From Hell*)
Dir: Dominique Deruddere /Belgium
1987 was a great year for Charles Bukowski screen adaptations. Barbet Schroeder offered up *Barfly*, a low-life epic of squalor and drunkenness starring Mickey Rourke and Faye Dunaway. In the same year, Dominique Deruddere presented his debut feature, *Crazy Love*, a much lesser-known film that stunned the art house crowd with its darkly amusing and disturbing edge. But since its initial release, this film has gone on to be regarded as one of the finest of the 80s.

Crazy Love began life as a short film entitled *A Foggy Night*, based on Bukowski's taboo-breaking story '*The Copulating Mermaid of Venice, CA*'. Deruddere had wanted to expand the short into a full-length feature, but was also aware of Bukowski's dislike for another film based on his writings (*Tales of Ordinary Madness*). Deruddere and co travelled over to America to meet Bukowski with the hope he would give their little film the seal of approval. The booze-laden author's now legendary response was that he was so pleased with Deruddere's short that he gave the filmmakers his blessing to turn it into a feature, and even declared the short to be better than the original source material.

We first meet Harry as a twelve year old who falls in love with a princess who graces the screen of his local cinema. But after an encounter with an older woman who has had a bit too much to drink, his illusions of love are shattered. In reality, things aren't always as perfect as they are in fairytale movies, and thanks to Harry's older friend, his early attempts at getting laid leave him with experiences of adolescent horror. In the second story, Harry is a nineteen year old ridden with acne, and this has turned him into a romantic pariah. Obsessed with a beautiful classmate, but lacking the confidence to talk to her, he instead turns to the liquor bottle knowing he can depend on it and that it won't judge him because of the way he looks. However, through some drastic circumstances, he does eventually get to dance with his teenage crush, albeit by having his head wrapped up in toilet paper for an oddly touching scene. The third and most disturbing story in the film finds Harry as a fully-grown homeless alcoholic who finally finds his perfect love in the form of a female corpse he steals from a parked hearse.

The synopsis above may sound dark and depressing, but director Deruddere somehow manages to keep things sweet and humorous, thanks in large part to Bukowski's no-nonsense narrative style which Deruddere captures perfectly in this film. The result is a vast improvement over the previous Bukowski adaptation, *Tales of Ordinary Madness*. It's an incredible movie, an emotionally-wrenching but comical portrait of a human being destined for life-long loneliness, and the film simply refuses to be sentimental about its subject. It's honest and unflinching yet still comes from the heart. These cold presentations of estranged love are captured invariably in their settings, usually in vehicles. Car rides, car park rendezvous points, fairground rides and stolen hearses; in a metaphorical sense the car symbolizes Harry's loneliness, and serves as his prison of shame. The only way he can escape is by distancing himself from reality, and with an act of revenge that befits both the fairytale ending and Bukowski's own symbolism, our anti-hero does eventually get to hold his princess in his arms, and finally makes his escape to his dream world.

Nekromantik (1987)
Dir: Jorg Buttgereit / West Germany

The film equivalent of eating a month old moldy sandwich, *Nekromantik* was a popular video that did the rounds by mail-order in Europe before being bootlegged and spreading across the underground of North America like a vomit-inducing plague. By the time *Film Threat* magazine had officially released it on video in America, *Nekromantik* was already a legendary title among 80s videophiles. And for the record, this is the closest I've ever come to being physically sick while watching a movie (though *Forest Gump* and *Waterboy* came pretty close, too).

Forget that slew of German amateur crap that lined video shelves at the time, and which were content in churning out ludicrous and unrealistic blood and gore (*The German Chainsaw Massacre* and the *Violent Shit* trilogy, for example), *Nekromantik*, for all its grubbiness and cheap origins, has genuine artistic merit and was directed by a man with considerable film-making talent. However, if you have a weak stomach you might want to give this a miss, for if any film out there will cause you to puke, this is probably it.

Director Jorg Buttgereit makes it his priority to shock and offend sensibilities as the opening scene drops us into the middle of a bloody car wreck in which a woman's body has been severed in half. Along comes Rob (Daktari Lorenz), an employee of Joe's Streetcleaning Agency, whose job it is to body bag the mangled corpses. Rob just happens to be one of those guys who likes to take his work home with him, and has amassed himself a collection of human organs and eyeballs he preserves in formaldehyde (he must have been pretty legendary during games of 'truth or dare' as a kid). His morbid curiosity is shared by his girlfriend Betty (Beatrice Manowski who, amazingly, made an appearance in Wim Wender's *Wings of Desire* in the same year); only, her death fixation is sexual, so when Rob returns home one night with an entire human body, she's delighted. They take the corpse to bed for a disgusting ménages à trois, where they stroke its decaying flesh and Betty has sex with it, but not before she removes its eyeball and places it in her mouth (yep, that's the bit that almost had me puking).

After this encounter, Rob and Betty's relationship is never the same. She eventually leaves him when he fails to bring home any more bodies, and he sinks into madness and depression, seemingly fully-aware of how sexually jaded he has become. To him, after the arousement of necrophilia, everything else just seems bland and too ordinary to excite him. And so his ever-escalating search for sexual gratification leads him to the ultimate thrill: death itself. He lies in bed masturbating, and just before he comes, he repeatedly stabs himself in the stomach, causing his penis to jettison blood and sperm.

This is a film which notoriously embraces the eroticism of death, and which warrants its repulsive reputation. It's a pean to mankind's darker obsessions, and is told in a lyrical style. It will evoke many conflicting emotions in its audience; on the one hand it will leave you with feelings of shock and revulsion, and on the other, you may even find curiosity and amusement here too. Indeed, for those into morbid movies, *Nekromantik* will be positively hypnotic as it forges ahead into its exploration of the absurd.

The special effects are generally spot on, which was a rarity in micro-budget horror at the time, especially the corpse which looks very real, and this only adds to the viewer's discomfort. The scene involving a head being decapitated with a shovel looks like it wandered in from George Romero's *Day of the Dead*. Buttgereit doesn't shy away from injecting a dose of black humour here either (as he would do again later in *Schramm*), and Rob's expression when he enters a cinema showing a slasher movie is hilarious (the film shown on screen has the soundtrack of Lucio Fulci's *Zombie Flesh Eaters*, and this only adds to the bizarre mix). Without a doubt, *Nekrmantik* would be a much more difficult viewing experience were it not for the superb music score which is co-credited to Lorenz. It's honestly one of the finest horror movie tunes of the 80s. And kudos also goes to whoever arranged the set design (probably Buttgereit himself); Rob and Betty's place is littered with macabe decorations similar to Ed Gein's and Leatherface's homes in *Deranged* and *The Texas Chain Saw Massacre*.

Horror fans had long speculated on Jorg Buttgeriet, trying to work out what type of person would create such a film. Many of them concluded that only a sicko, a man completely ill of mind would make *Nekromantik*. So it came as a surprise when the director turned out to be a fun-loving, well-presented guy with a deep love of horror cinema. There's the story of when Martin Scorsese met David Cronenberg at a film festival. Scorsese admitted that after seeing Cronenberg's films, he was expecting to meet one of those creepy guys you'd rather avoid, "a Renfield catching flies with his tongue", as he put it, but was stunned when a nerdy-looking, bespectacled man in a suit offered his hand with the words "Hi, I'm David Cronenberg". Their meeting lasted several hours, and Scorsese was amazed by Cronenberg's intelligence and easy-going nature. Although we all do it, we shouldn't judge artists on the basis of their work alone. It's extremely rare for a macabre artist to live a macabre lifestyle, and I struggle to think of any examples. Carravaggio often created violent paintings and he eventually committed a violent murder. And there's John Wayne Gacy, of course, a sadistic serial killer of young men who would occasionally paint creepy pictures of sad clowns (if that counts). And, according to Patricia Cornwell in her book, *Portrait of a Killer, we could also add the British artist Walter Sickert to the list too. In the book, Cornwell accuses Sickert of being the real perpetrator of the 'Jack the Ripper' killings of 1888. Many 'Ripperologists' have since dismissed her claims, but it's an interesting read, and I'll never be able to look at his dark self-portraits, such as Jack the Ripper's Bedroom, in the same way.*

As anyone who has listened to his audio commentaries on *Combat Shock* and *Killer Condom* will agree, Jorg Buttgereit is a decent fellow with a wacky sense of humour, despite his films being among the top of the list of those you should never watch with your family, or anybody's family, or anyone who isn't you and your fucked-up movie deviant friends. On the commentary track for *Nekromatik* he explains how he filmed a rabbit being killed and skinned; the footage was shot at a working rabbit farm and is the most disturbing scene in the film because it's real. "Just because we show it doesn't mean we like it", he explains.

Shot on 8mm and blown up to 16 for cinema and video releases, *Nekromantik* is banned outright in the UK even though it was shown uncut at the Shock Around the Clock Film Festival at London's Scala Cinema, causing much trouble when the British bobbies attempted to intercept it.

Bad Taste (1987)
Dir: Peter Jackson /New Zealand

Wellington, New Zealand, 1983. The 22 year old Peter Jackson opens the oven door, but rather than taking out a tray of cakes or cookies, the young kiwi instead removes a baked rubber mask. In the living room, Jackson's parents despair for their only child. With the cooker in use once again, it looks like another cold lunch for mum and dad. Peter remains completely oblivious to his parents' looming starvation. He has a dream, and his home-made rubber masks are only a part of it.

It's difficult to imagine now, but there was once a time when Peter Jackson wasn't the billionaire brown-nose sell-out of *Lord of The Rings* fame. Thirty years ago, he was just a typical horror and sci-fi geek trying to make his debut feature film with his buddies. Back then, he wasn't interested in shooting some silly saga based on an over-long 'celebrated' book. The younger, thinner and less hairy Jackson was working on something much more interesting: An intergalactic sick-drinking home-made epic, appropriately entitled *Bad Taste*.

The plot goes something like this: When aliens arrive at a remote part of New Zealand with the intention of turning the human populace into burgers for their fast food restaurant, Crumb's Crunchy Delights, the authorities send in the 'boys,' a group of incompetent morons, to deal with the situation. A local door-to-door salesman has been captured by the aliens who plan on boiling him alive for lunch, and the 'boys' must try to rescue him and save the day before it's too late.

Bad Taste is one of the finest home-made splatter movies of all time, a cult sensation with its sick, morbid humour, cross fertilization of genres, and an acute awareness of its own craziness. It was four years in the making, and only completed when it was thanks to financial help from the New Zealand Film Commission, whose chairman Jim Booth had been blown away by some of the early rushes. If it wasn't for the grant from Jim Booth, who knows how long it would have taken to finish the film. When it was completed, Peter Jackson was still only 25 years old, the same age as Orson Welles when he made *Citizen Kane*... but um, comparisons get kinda blurry after that. The overall budget for the project is still not clear – various sources claim that it cost anything in the region of $17,000 to $150,000. But regardless, the end result is a remarkable achievement considering that most filmmakers couldn't create anything even nearly as visually accomplished as this, even when they're given several millions to spend. Jackson served as director, actor (two roles), producer, writer, cameraman, special effects supervisor, and he probably did the catering too. It's very much an auteur piece, and as such, *Bad Taste* will probably tell you more about him than his entire *Lord of The Rings* trilogy.

For a start, it has a rampant, diseased sense of humour, and a true love for the stickier side of horror, in the same way as people like Stuart Gordon (*Re-Animator*) and Brian Yuzna (*Society*). The film is anarchic, wild, bloody and gruesome; the movie equivalent of juvenile delinquency, with messy sequences trailing off to the bloody effects as quickly as possible. The early sequence set on the edge of a cliff where the alien swings at Derek wildly with a sledgehammer, is at once hilarious and nerve-racking. It's a scene which is also balanced at the very edge of plausibility – and kept there for quite some time – as Jackson keeps things at a knife-edge, precariously racking up the absurd feeling of suspense before the pay-off when the alien swings too hard, and misses, causing Derek to lose his footing, and then he tumbles down the cliff, crashing onto the rocks below.

The jagged rhythm of the film was necessitated by the use of a wind-up camera that could only film for thirty seconds at a time. But rather than hinder the shoot, it actually helped to create a fast-paced, action-packed scuzzbucket, with Jackson's limited special effects coming at you too thick and fast for you to notice just how crude and amateurish they really are. The rubbery aliens (disguised as humans in the first half of the film) are in need of human meat, especially the 'chunky bits,' for their intergalactic fast food chain. And when the aliens do show their true selves – as butt-ugly balding creatures with their bony bums tearing through the backs of their jeans – the gruesomeness really kicks in, and includes a scene in which a ravenous invader dines on human brains with a spoon, scooping the contents out of some poor guy's broken skull (a scene that was later paid tribute to by Lucifer Valentine in his film *Slaughtered Vomit Dolls*, with the added bonus of having the brain-eater vomit the contents back into the victim's hollowed-out skull. Ah, good old Lucifer Valentine, you can always rely on him to add a touch of class to proceedings).

The acting is stilted at best, but these weren't professional actors, they were actually Jackson's friends. One of them, Michael Minett, who played an alien as well as Frank, recalls, "It took us four years to make. That's a helluva long while. We gave up every Sunday during that period. The worst thing of all was that we had to wear the same costumes all the time." Indeed, the troubles of keeping the visual consistency going in scenes that were sometimes shot years apart became a major problem on set, as Pete O'Herne, who played Barry, points out. "The day I started going in front of the camera, I hadn't shaved for a few days. So at the end of the day's filming, Peter said to me, 'Pete, you're going to have to keep the look 'til we finish'. So for four years, I could only shave once a week!" This reminds me of Jack Nance in *Eraserhead* who was requested to keep his iconic, anti-gravity hairdo in place for several years so that director David Lynch could keep the 'look' of his leading man unchanged between shots that were also shot years apart. Jackson was lucky to have such loyal friends willing to sacrifice hundreds of weekends to help him put his demented vision up on the big screen. But he also asked a lot of himself, too. On the technical side, he basically did everything himself, and *Bad Taste* remains to this day the ultimate example of DIY film-making.

The ingenious Jackson also constructed his own 'Steadicam' for the paltry sum of $15. He created the film's weaponry, too, from the simplest of materials. "I made guns out of aluminium tubing, wood and Fimo [modelling clay]," Jackson explains. "I made exact replicas of Stirling sub-machine-guns. The bolts worked on them – they were neat!" To this most hands-on of directors, invention and micro-budget improvisation was the lifeblood for the entire duration of the shoot. Following George Romero's example in *Night of the Living dead*, where the director procured animal guts from an abattoir for his zombies to feast on, Jackson used sheep's brains and guts acquired from the local butcher's shop to be used in the gore sequences, which makes for an offal lotta fun.

Perhaps the most memorable aspect of *Bad Taste* is in how it revels in brain-mush, bone fragments, gaping wounds, severed body parts and a big bowl of vomit. It's absolutely gross in places, but viewers in the right frame of mind who are prepared to go along with it will be rewarded with a barrel of laughs, non-stop action, a gung-ho cast and lots of sick humour. In one scene, Jackson's character Derek falls 100 feet down a cliff and lands on the jagged rocks at the bottom. He doesn't die, but a large chunk of his brain falls out from the enormous wound in the back of his skull. He simply stuffs it back in and ties his belt around his head to hold it in place. And throughout the remainder of the film, Derek has to battle against the invaders while ensuring that his brain doesn't fall out. If that sounds like fun to you then you'll enjoy this film. But either way, there's no denying the formative talent that was at work here, with its warped imagination, experimentation, difficult special effects sequences, interesting visual ideas, and the pervasive sense of fun to be had from watching a group of friends getting together to make a movie.

Angel Heart (1987)
Dir: Alan Parker /USA

In 1955 New York, a mysterious boss of a law firm, Louis Cyphre (Robert De Niro), sends a seedy private eye, Harry Angel (Mickey Rourke), to investigate the disappearance of a popular singer who is in debt to him. Angel heads off in search of the crooner and meets an odd bunch of occultists and weirdos from New York to Louisiana where he eventually discovers that the missing person had opted out of a pact with the devil. He then seems to plunge quite literally into hell.

Based on the novel *Falling Angel* by William Hjortsberg, *Angel Heart* was met with shock and awe by film fans and critics at the time who were expecting just another *Faust* knock-off, or something similar to Wes Craven's *Serpent and The Rainbow*. The pervading grimness, graphic bloodletting, and spooky twists and turns, however, seemed to be too much for everyday movie-goers. Often accused of being thoroughly unpleasant in detail, which it is, but devotees of the darker side of horror should get a kick out of this scorching hot tale of eternal damnation. It's quite simply one of the greatest horror movies of the 80s. The MPAA demanded cuts to the scene in which Rourke and Lisa Bonet writhe on the bed covered in chicken blood, but the same scene has been reinstated in its entirety on all DVD editions. It's always a sick pleasure to see the innocent Cosby kid, Bonet, getting naked and covered in chicken blood, so fans of celebrity skin watch out for that.

Resembling a cross between a gritty detective yarn, film noir, and full-bloodied horror, *Angel Heart* failed to make much of an impact at the box-office. It raked in around $17 million, just about breaking even with its budget costs. However, it was on home video where the film quickly established itself as a cult classic, with fans around the world appreciating the grim tone and mish-mash of genres.

Zombie High (1987)
Dir: Ron Link /USA

Virginia Madsen and her friends settle in to a new term at a new school where many of the staff and students are cold and emotionally empty. And as Andrea (Madsen) snoops around the building, she discovers a conspiracy involving the faculty who steal the life essence of the young so that they can preserve their own youth. Andrea then teams up with her on-off boyfriend to destroy the evil parasites. *Invasion of the Body Snatchers* meets *The Stepford Wives* meets *Strange Behavior* in this dull and derivative teen horror. The 'zombies' here don't reveal their true putrefied appearance until the end in a short, underwhelming sequence.

Bodycount (1987)
Dir: Ruggero Deodato /Italy

By the late 80s and early 90s, Italian horror production was winding down with lame, half-arsed Fulci efforts (*Aenigma*, *Demonia*) and crude, Bruno Mattei cine-tranquilizers (*Zombi 3*, *Shocking Dark*). Spaghetti horror had turned lukewarm, and things were never the same. *Bodycount* is one of the better Italian horror movies of that era, directed by Ruggero '*Cannibal Holocaust*' Deodato. And though it's a far cry from the best of pasta-land efforts, there is still much to be impressed by here if you accept it for what it is: a routine slasher movie made for the American market. The film pits an all-American cast – which includes Mimsy Farmer and David Hess – against an 'Indian Shaman,' a hulking great Worzel Gummidge on steroids. Cue lots of mayhem as the merry campers are picked off, one by one. *Bodycount* is worth watching if only for the prank scene – which is one of the funniest in slasher movie history – as the gullible fat kid is told that there is an orgy going on in one of the cabins. He immediately strips off his clothes and runs inside with a smile on his face and tiny cock jiggling about, only to be met by a girls' parents who are having a quiet lunch together. He screeches to a halt, apologises and then gets the hell outta there.

Dark Age (1987)
Dir: Arch Nicholson /Australia

A wildlife vet (John Jarratt) teams up with park rangers to kill a giant crocodile that has been eating people, and seems to be impervious to bullets. The local aborigines refer to the croc as 'Numunwari,' and they believe that the creature embodies the spirit of their people. And of course, there's a blatant message here about wildlife preservation and the blah blah 'evil white man.' With good performances, decent production values and some very dangerous stunts along the way, this film failed to reach the audience it deserved, due to distribution company, Avco Embassy, going bust shortly before the film's release. *Dark Age* wasn't officially released in its native Australia until 2011.

Wicked City (1987)
(Orig title: *Yoju toshi*)
Dir: Yoshiaki kawajiri /Japan

A man is picked up in a bar by a hot female. They go back to a hotel room and have sex. And afterwards, she transforms into some kind of demonic, humanoid spider with a toothy vagina... And so begins this lurid tale of sex, death and monsters as a peaceful pact between the worlds of the mortal and the supernatural is put under strain by the arrival of a group of bloodthirsty demons. It's up to a government bodyguard and a female demon to protect a sex-crazed scientist whose job it is to sign a peace treaty between the two worlds. *Wicked City* is more of a laid back effort than the usual anime monster mayhem from Japan. This time the Lovecraft-inflected material is given a deliberately ponderous pace with poetic flourishes. See also *Monster City* (1991).

The Hidden (1987)
Dir: Jack Sholder /USA

This film opens with a superb sequence in which a stockbroker with a distant look in his eyes robs a bank, helps himself to a Ferrari and drives recklessly through police blockades while listening to blaring rock music. It's a sequence I must have replayed two dozen times when I rented the tape as a kid. Finally, the police force the car into a blazing crash that sends the injured driver to hospital. Later on, a mysterious FBI agent, Lloyd Gallagher (Kyle Maclachlan), arrives at police HQ to enlist the help of a veteran detective (Michael Nouri) in tracking down the fugitive. Meanwhile, the bank robber dies, and a slimy slug-like alien creature crawls out of his mouth and into the body of another patient in a nearby bed. And pretty soon the mayhem begins anew... *The Hidden* is a genre hybrid, mixing sci-fi, horror and cop thriller into an exciting and often darkly amusing blend. Filmed on a bigger budget than usual, and offering up decent performances all around, especially from Nouri and Maclachlan, the latter's character feels like a dry-run for Agent Cooper in David Lynch's *Twin Peaks: Fire Walk With Me* (1992). A childhood classic!

Prince of Darkness (1987)
Dir: John Carpenter /USA
An obscure Catholic sect, known as The Brotherhood of Sleep, has guarded a dark secret for centuries. And when a Priest discovers that a canister dripping with green slime could contain the essence of Satan, he invites a group of theologians and scientists and their truck-loads of equipment to spend the weekend in a run-down inner-city church to study the thing. And while the investigators get to work and squabble amongst themselves, a small army of homeless people, led by Alice Cooper, gather outside the church, and the investigators are squirted with goo and transformed into Satanic ghouls... *Prince of Darkness* is a slow-moving and convoluted film that is much better appreciated on repeat viewings. It's heavily influenced by the work of Nigel Kneale (indeed, John Carpenter even wrote the script under the pseudonym 'Martin Quatermass'), and has much in common with Kneale's spooky classic, *The Stone Tape* (1972). The film flopped dead at the box-office, but has developed a cult following over subsequent years thanks to home video.

Slaughterhouse (1987)
Dir: Rick Roesseler /USA
An old man, whose slaughterhouse business faces foreclosure, encourages his huge, retarded, pig-loving son to slaughter the locals as a way of settling his grudge against the Sheriff and court officials whom he blames for his destitution... *Slaughterhouse* is a low-budget 80s rehash of *The Texas Chain Saw Massacre* (1974) which expands on the premise of a family being forced to adapt to the industrial upheaval as the corporate bigwigs squeeze them out of the market, damaging their livelihoods and ensuring a violent reaction (as also seen in

Tobe Hooper's classic). The film is quite well made, with lots of dark humour and a professional sheen that is rare in 80s cheapjack video swill. However, the death scenes – though certainly bloody enough – lack a certain panache; there's barely any musical accompaniment or anything to put an exclamation point on the scenes to separate them from the rest of the picture. Those not paying attention will miss the scenes of the Sheriff's deputy having his hand cut off, and another guy getting his head squashed by the maniac. 80s slasher freaks should get a kick out of it though.

Zombie Death House (1987)
(aka *Death House*)
Dir: John Saxon /USA
A Vietnam veteran, Derek Keller (Dennis Cole), gets on the wrong side of the Mafia and is sentenced to death by electric chair for a murder he didn't commit. While on death row, he learns of a sinister government scheme whereby the inmates are subjected to illegal drug experiments. And when the guinea pigs transform into rampaging homicidal maniacs, Derek and a few remaining uninfected prisoners find themselves trapped as the virus takes over the prison... This interesting concept is let down by a middle-of-the-road directorial style by exploitation legend, John Saxon, who also plays the unscrupulous head of the research programme. A filmmaker like John Carpenter would have had a field day with a project like this, but in Saxon's inexperienced hands the end result is nothing more than a minor cult item. It isn't a *bad* film, but it could have been so much better. Saxon later acknowledged the film's shortcomings, and blamed studio interference for the lacklustre results.

Rock 'n' Roll Nightmare (1987)
(aka *The Edge of Hell*)
Dir: John Fasano /Canada
This film spends no less than 15 minutes on the title sequence and initial establishing shots of an 80s hair metal band arriving at a large house to record a single. And while the band – real band, The Tritons – rehearse their racket, the groupies and engineers are ravaged by hand puppet beasties and shape-shifting demons. For the most part meandering and nonsensical. As far as guilty pleasures go, I'd rather watch Jess Franco's *Killer Barbys* (1996) any day. Now

there's a *real* rock 'n' roll nightmare!

Don't Turn Out the Light (1987)
(aka *Night of Retribution*; *Skull: A Night of Terror*; *One Eyed Killer*)
Dir: Robert Bergman /Canada
It's bad soap opera time as a wife-cheating traumatised cop tries to protect his family from dangerous killers who have busted out of a prison truck. This is a guilty pleasure, an action-packed, Z-grade piece of nonsense, but hey, we can't watch *Straw Dogs* (1971) or *Assault On Precinct 13* (1976) every night, can we? The big, bollock-headed Robbie Rox steals the show as the eye-patch wearing maniac called 'Skull,' who is just as adept at chewing off his intended rape victim's blouse as he is at chewing the scenery. Unintentionally hilarious but endless fun, especially when the cop dresses in pieces of makeshift armour and climbs on his house like some kind of drug-crazed superhero wannabe. The shit movie *par excellence*.

Blood Frenzy (1987)
Dir: Hal Freeman /USA
This film opens with a prologue in which a young boy slashes the throat of his father. It then starts proper with a group of head-cases driven out to the desert in a camper van to undergo 'confrontational therapy' with their doctor. We know that one of the group is the now-grown-up psycho killer, but we – supposedly – don't know who it is until the bodies have piled up. *Blood Frenzy* is the kind of 80s video fare that completely bypassed the DVD boom of the 00s, and it isn't difficult to see why; almost everything about it is wretched, save for a bloody table-top torture scene in an old mine shaft that evokes *The Last House on Dead End Street* (1977). Even among such neurotic patients, the killer here stands out like a clown at a funeral. At first I thought he was a blatant red herring, but no, he's the culprit. A similar concept was explored almost a decade later in the vastly superior *Color of Night* (1994), an American giallo which includes a similar bunch of neurotics (the prude, the 'Nam vet, the alcoholic, the nympho, the lesbo, the chauvinist, etc) who are being picked off by one of the fellow patients. And Bruce Willis tries to nail the culprit while donning an ill-fitting hairpiece. As for *Blood Frenzy*, I read somewhere that the film was intended to be a cross between H.G. Lewis' *Blood Feast* and Alfred Hitchcock's *Frenzy* (1972), but frankly, those comparisons are lost on me.

House II: The Second Story (1987)
Dir: Ethan Wiley /USA
This first sequel is set in a different – but much bigger – house where a young man and his buddy dig up his great grandfather with the hope of finding a priceless crystal skull that they suspect could have been buried with him. However, great gandpa returns as a 170-year-old zombie and is brought back to the house and allowed to stay in the basement. Meanwhile, one of the bedrooms in the house transforms into a vast, *Jumanji*-like jungle occupied by dinosaurs, aztec warriors and other comical ghoulies who are determined to get hold of the precious skull for themselves... This sequel has very little to do with the original film, and all pretences of it being a horror film are dropped after the intriguing prologue. From then on, the filmmakers seem content to churn out a silly adventure yarn, which may be good for adventure fans, but horror nerds were not impressed. Stephan Jaworzyn of *Shock Xpress* summed up his feelings on behalf of many in the horror community: "This is a sluggish, nonsensical and a generally pointless venture, replete with animated monsters, unresolved plot convolutions and totally forgettable characters. Ridiculous."

Blood Lake (1987)
Dir: Tim Boggs /USA
More 80s video trash in which a group of wise-cracking youngsters head out on a weekend trip to a lake. And after much lame innuendo and endless footage of piss-poor water-skiing, a killer finally shows up around the 47-minute mark. The slayings are all of the 'rolling-eyes-and-smeared-ketchup' variety, and the killer's motivation doesn't stem from any deep-seated resentment or childhood trauma. Oh no. He's simply getting even for a bunch of unpaid cabin rental fees!

Beaks – The Movie (1987)
Dir: Rene Cardona Jr /USA
Written, produced and directed by Rene Cardona Jr (the man behind such exploitation classics as *Survive* and *Guyana: Crime of the Century*), this film pays homage to the eye-gouging scene in Hitchcock's *The Birds* within the first ten minutes. *Beaks* stars Michelle

Johnson as an ambitious young news reporter who is given the shitty assignment of reporting on a spate of deaths caused by killer birds. Her scepticism on the subject is soon banished, however, when it becomes clear that the murderous pests have indeed declared war on the human race. Owing just as much to Spielberg's *Jaws* as it does to *The Birds*, *Beaks* is played surprisingly straight considering its amusing title, but can't avoid the inevitable tongue-in-cheek style which is the obvious way to go when dealing with a human bird-feed scenario.

Berserker (1987)
(aka *Berserker: The Nordic Curse*)
Dir: Jef Richard [Jefferson Richard] /USA
Same old story: A group of 'teens' – played by actors in their late-20s, of course – hop into a truck and head out for a camping trip in the countryside, where they drink beer, smoke pot and get themselves murdered by a maniac. Only this time the maniac is supposed to be a Nordic Viking warrior. But it's not exactly clear: It's actually a grizzly bear *possessed* by the spirit of the Nordic Viking warrior that is actually responsible for the killings... Or is it? The death scenes are quite good, and the night scenes with the youngsters wandering through the woods are particularly eerie, but too much time is used up with boring talk and dull games of chess. And the confusion as to the true identity of the killer – is it the bear or the Nordic? – is never made clear. For slasher movie completists only.

I Saw What You Did (1987)
Dir: Fred Walton /USA
A TV movie remake of the 1965 film, itself based on the novel by Ursula Curtis. A prank phone call goes wrong for a couple of teenage girls when a maniac suspects them of listening in to a murder he has recently committed. Directed by Fred Walton, the man behind the other telephone-based horror, *When a Stranger Calls* (1979), this is actually superior to the original, despite its TV feel and sometimes unconvincing plot turns.

Dead Ringers (1988)
Dir: David Cronenberg /Canada
Dead Ringers offered solid evidence of David Cronenberg's maturity and development into a truly great filmmaker, and builds on his previous character study, *The Fly*, and combines it with his interest in the metaphysical, to ultimately create yet another milestone in his exotically extreme *ouevre*. Stunningly powerful, deeply moving, and loaded with bizarre and disturbing ideas, *Dead Ringers'* expose of male fantasies has much to say on the fragility of masculinity, and is presented in the director's usual cold, detached, and unflinching manner.

Based on the book *Twins* by Bari Wood and Jack Geasland (which was in turn inspired by the real life story of respected twin gynaecologists, Steven and Cyril Marcus who in 1975 were both found dead in their littered New York apartment, a double suicide by overdose brought on by their addiction to barbiturates), Cronenberg presents Elliot and Beverly Mantle, a pair of outstanding gynaecologists who open a brand new state-of-the-art fertility clinic and share a luxurious apartment. Although physically identical, the twins have very distinctive personalities; Elliot is a self-assured lady magnet, whereas Beverly is shy and introverted. Elliot is happy to procure women for Beverly by seducing them, having his wicked way, and then passing them off to his brother when he's done, unbeknownst to the women. When famous actress Claire Niveau (Genevieve Bujold) enters the clinic for help with her infertility, she also brings trouble in the form of jealousy; for although both brothers take turns in bed with her, Beverly falls in love, thus driving a wedge between them...

Not your average horror roller-coaster ride then, *Dead Ringers'* shocks are much more suggestive this time, but no less horrifying. Gone are the more overtly grotesque and spectacular shocks of the exploding head (*Scanners*), gaping stomach cavities (*Videodrome*), and squeamish fingernail ripping (*The Fly*), and in their place are disturbing questions on the nature of identity, masculinity, narcissism, eroticism, and misogyny; a far cry from contemporary horror hits like *Friday the 13th Part VII* or *A Nightmare On Elm Street IV*, which were more concerned with churning out bloodless kills and corny one-liners (actually, the biggest screen monsters of the time were the MPAA whose tough new stance on movie violence was strangling the life out of the genre). The censors though couldn't touch *Dead Ringers*, for although it explores some dark and disturbing themes and subject-matter (misogyny, drug addiction, and um, custom-made gynaecological apparatus for 'mutant women', to name but a few), Cronenberg's quietly devastating horrors were simply censor proof.

The true star of the show is Jeremy Ions, whose double role as the twins offers a nuance so perfected that viewers can tell immediately which twin he is playing without him resorting to bug-eyed dramatics or cliched characteristics. And he is aided by Bujold whose striking performance stops her role from becoming a mere plot device.

Mississippi Burning (1988)
Dir: Alan Parker /USA

Two young white civil rights activists and their black co-worker are driving down a road in Mississippi and are pulled over by the law. After being referred to as "nigger lovers" the three men are then shot dead by members of the Sheriff's department, in a barbaric act of mindless hatred made worse by the fact that the murderers use their powerful positions within law-enforcement to conceal their nocturnal activities as high-ranking members of the Ku Klux Klan.

Alan Ward (Willem Dafoe) and Agent Rupert Anderson (Gene Hackman) are sent down from Washington to investigate the disappearance of the three activists, and are immediately made the targets of small-town prejudice. Former Sheriff, Anderson, doesn't seem to take the situation seriously at first; he makes jokes and sings Klan songs on the drive down, much to the annoyance of his partner Ward, a more sensible and by-the-book investigator. However, it isn't long before Anderson realises just how serious and dangerous the situation is when everyone they try to speak to ends up badly beaten and their homes burned to the ground.

Their investigation leads them higher and higher up the social ladder, with some of the most responsible folks of the town implicated in the deep-seated racism and intimidation being carried out on the black citizens; churches are burned, black men are kidnapped and severely beaten or killed by masked men, and a church congregation of black worshipers is attacked by men with bats and clubs. Ward and Anderson gather enough evidence to charge three white men with beating a black kid half to death, but the court case turns into a farce due to the judge being just as racist as anyone else in the town and who sentences the three men to five years suspended sentences.

Meanwhile, Anderson has been sweet-talking the Deputy's wife (Francis McDormand), and she seems sympathetic to the investigation, even informing him of the whereabouts of the bodies of the three activists. This crucial piece of info carries the investigation towards its end, but the two agents decide to employ some pretty nasty tricks of their own to see justice at long last.

Those familiar with the real life case of James Chaney, Mickey Schwener, and Andy Goodman, three civil rights activists who were murdered in Neshoba County in 1964, leading to the biggest manhunt in FBI history, will be left scratching their heads throughout much of this film, as director Alan Parker takes a free-form artistic licence and bends the facts to suit his own vision. On the one hand, Parker can be accused of treating the events as if his own dramatic drive was more important than history, but on the other, he does a remarkable job of re-creating the time and place of Neshoba County of the mid-60s; it's a scary place, and whether you're black or white or in any way different, or have a mind of your own, you seriously wouldn't want to have lived there during those times. That place with its burning crosses, burning churches, and authority figures wearing silly white costumes with pointy hoods and dealing out brutal retributions and death on anyone who isn't just like them – it's a vision of hell on earth. And for a studio film that was made in the late 80s, *Mississippi Burning* does not spare viewers from the truly disturbing and frankly evil goings on of that town. The violence is so one-sided and viciously cruel, and it's agonizing to see these ugly scenes unfold, knowing that whatever else happens on screen for the next couple of hours, it's certainly not going to be for the faint of heart or the easily offended.

No studio would have the balls to unleash a film like this in today's PC climate. And it's a shame because if you are in any way racist in your own heart, this film sure has the power to make you look deeply into yourself and reconsider your own prejudice. It's a film which does much to show how insane things can become when small-town attitudes are allowed to grow unchecked out in the wilderness.

Director Alan Parker, whose previous work includes *Midnight Express* and *Angel Heart*, films which take on a somewhat leisurely pace, but here with *Mississippi Burning* we're treated to a much more tightly constructed film which flies by at a ferocious tempo. Hackman is superb as Anderson, the world-weary Agent who deals with his grim profession with an equally grim sense of humour, and Willem Dafoe as his strait-laced partner who eventually dispenses with common procedure in order to bring justice down on the town. Also look out for a young Michael Rooker as a hick Sheriff, Brad Dourif as a hick Deputy, and R. Lee Ermey of *Full Metal Jacket* fame as Neshoba's hick mayor who is subjected to one of the film's most satisfying acts of revenge.

Men Behind the Sun (1988)
(Orig title: *Hei tai yang 731*)
<u>Dir: T.F. Mous /Hong Kong/China</u>
Not to be confused with your typical Cat III entry, *Men Behind the Sun* reaches a whole new level on the shocking and disturbing meter and is easily one of the most repulsive movies you'll ever see. The film was made by Chinese director T.F. Mous partly because he wanted to draw attention to a barbaric era of Japanese foreign policy during the 1930s and throughout World War II, where Chinese and Manchurian citizens were considered sub-human by their Japanese invaders, and were subjected to horrendously cruel experiments involving the dissection of live humans, the inducing of hypothermia, bubonic plague, and other nastiness, all as a test to discover the extreme limits of human endurance. The experiments were led by General Shiro Ishii at the notorious Unit 731, and even to this day the Japanese remain in denial as to what exactly went on at that place. Mous' film, however, attempts to expose the ugly truth, for better or worse.

The plot centres on a group of teenage Japanese conscripts who arrive in Manchukuo, a Japanese puppet state in north-eastern China. They're freezing cold, hungry, and homesick, but their destination doesn't live up to its promise – they were assured that food and warmth would be plentiful, but when they get there they discover the conditions to be just as harsh as the rest of the empire due to the ongoing war effort. What the boys get instead is brutal discipline, indoctrination into the evils of fascism, and first-hand accounts of one of the most barbaric episodes in history. The rest of the film plays like a catalogue of atrocities.

One of the boys makes a run for it to escape the miserable place. A Japanese soldier opens fire on him with a machine gun and the kid runs into an electrified fence that surrounds the compound. He drops his ball and it rolls down the hill in the snow as he is burned to death. The young conscripts are told very little about the true nature of Unit 731 but gradually discover that something evil is going on. They become friendly with a little mute boy who is often seen over the fence. They throw the dead kid's ball back and forth to each other. Meanwhile, a train load of Manchurian citizens arrive at the unit; a woman has her screaming baby taken away from her and it is buried alive in the snow. The head of the squadron, Sgt. Kowazaki, begins indoctrinating the youths on the Chinese and Manchurians; they are to be considered worthless and sub-human. From now on the kids are ordered to refer to the foreign prisoners as 'maruta', which literally means 'material', and the youths are driven to such frenzy that they gang up on a lone Chinese man and beat him to death with clubs. Meanwhile in a nearby lab, one such 'maruta' has been injected with bubonic plague three times – those running the experiment decide to open him up to discover why he hasn't died.

The Chinese prisoners at the lab try to ascertain what's going on and why they've been held captive, and what would be the best escape plan. Outside in the freezing conditions, a woman is kept in -35 degrees temperature for ten hours and has ice-cold water poured onto her hands and arms. She is then taken back inside to an audience of officers and the Youth Corps, and then has her arms dipped in warm water. General Ishii himself slashes her down each arm and then literally rips off the skin from her limbs like he's removing elbow-length gloves to expose the skeletal stalks beneath. A man is then brought into the room and the audience is informed that his arms have been frozen at -196 degrees; his limbs look like grey blocks of ice. Ishii then starts to chop away at the arms with an iron bar and the frozen flesh and bone shatters into pieces. Some of the new recruits at the Youth Corps buy in to the twisted ideology and tow the line in both word and deed (but whether they act this way out of fear or a genuine support for the cause is not explored in the film). Others are not so cold and heartless though, and they are wary and questioning the whole barbaric idea behind the place.

The technicians succeed in creating plague-infected fleas with the idea of inserting them into bombs and dropping them from planes onto Japanese enemies. But there's a problem; due to the high temperatures that results from exploding bombs, most of the fleas will die before they get the chance to infect anyone. General Ishii comes up with the cunning idea of inserting the fleas into porcelain capsules instead so that they can be easily contained, but also when dropped from a height will be much more effective at spreading death and destruction. When he reveals his idea on the 'porcelain bacterial bomb' to an assembly he is given an ecstatic ovation with cries of "bonzai!"

Another 'experiment': Dozens of maruta are taken out into a field and tied to posts that are strategically placed at specific distances from a bomb that sits in the middle. The bomb is then detonated. And when the smoke clears, a group of boffins inspect the damage; some are clearly dead and blown to pieces, others are still alive and in agony with legs hanging off by a strip of tissue and eyeballs loose from the sockets. The idea behind this pointless experiment is to calculate how close to an exploding bomb a man can be without dying (yep, not very close, apparently).

The next sequence looks disturbingly real but is actually a very impressive special effect that took days of painstaking and tricky work to get right. A naked man is placed into a decrompression chamber and the dial is cranked up to full power. He collapses to the ground and his intestine literally unravels from out of his anus and shoots across the floor. It's such a crude and realistic sequence it has an awful air of reality about it (footage really was taken of the experiments and sent back to Japan for study but none of it has surfaced since).

A Russian woman and her young daughter are encased in an air-tight glass container and gassed. The young recruits surround the box and look on as the pair succumb to the deadly fumes. What the inductees are supposed to be learning by watching these atrocities is unclear. Perhaps the idea is to inure them to the suffering of these people so that in the future they can partake in the experiments directly without feeling any sorrow for the maruta.

Sgt. Kowazaki orders the young Ishikawa to go and bring the little mute boy into the compound. He carries out his orders assuming the kid will be given a medical check-up. But what happens instead is that the boy is stripped, laid onto an operating table, put to sleep with a cloth of chloroform, and then dissected alive. The way the flesh separates as the scalpel cuts

through it exposing the yellowish fat beneath the skin is very real. After years of rumours concerning the authenticity of this scene, it was no real surprise when director Mous confirmed that the footage did contain real elements. With the permission of the parents and the local police, Mous filmed the autopsy of a young boy, and some of that footage was inserted into the fictional film. I suspect that if the parents of that dead child ever saw the finished film they wouldn't be happy about having their son's remains paraded in an action/horror film for the entertainment of others (it would be interesting to know how Mous convinced the parents to allow him to shoot that footage). The heart is still beating as it is removed and placed into a jar of formaldehyde.

Ishikawa discovers what has happened to the mute boy and organises a revolt among the Youth Corps. They confront Sgt. Kowazaki in the disinfectant showers and they severely beat him with planks of wood. But oddly, this scene of violent insubordination is then forgotten about, and the film just carries on as though nothing has happened. The boys are not punished for the attack, and Kowazaki is later seen going about his business unscathed.

General Shiro Ishii drops a cat into a pit of starving rats as a way of demonstrating how power in numbers can defeat a larger opponent. The cat is slowly eaten alive (and this horrible scene is very real and difficult to watch). The Chinese prisoners start rioting in the cells and the Japanese soldiers put an end to this by cutting them down with machine gun fire. When Ishii finds out about this incident he is furious about losing so many maruta ("precious experimental material") in the massacre.

More maruta are taken out into the field and tied to stakes for another close-range bomb test (like the results weren't pretty conclusive the first time around; bombs kill and maim people at close range – case closed). This time, however, one of the prisoners isn't secured properly and he manages to untie himself and helps to free the others. This infuriates the Japanese and they hunt the escapees down in their jeeps and motorcycles whilst firing at them. For a while things become chaotic with lots of action and stunts; the Chinese hit back, collecting weapons from injured soldiers and returning fire. The heroic Chinese are outnumbered and heavily out-gunned, and their brave stance is ultimately short-lived as they are all either run down by a vehicle or shot dead at the scene. Their corpses are then taken down to the incinerator that is run by an old drunken Japanese man who hacks up the bodies like firewood into small pieces to feed the fire whilst he sings traditional songs.

News filters through to the compound that the Soviets have declared war on Japan and that the Americans have dropped atomic bombs on Nagasaki and Hiroshima. The war effort and dreams of empire are over and Japan is on the verge of surrender. Ishii orders that all remaining maruta be exterminated, all buildings in Unit 731 be destroyed, all documents and evidence burned, the Youth Corps be sent back home to Japan, and all officers are ordered to commit suicide.

Ishii's right hand man pleads with him to not be so rash, and argues that the data collected is too precious to be destroyed, and that the officers deserve the opportunity to make it home alive. Ishii relents on the latter but insists on the destruction of all evidence that Unit 731 ever existed. The compound immediately falls into chaos; officers who disobey orders are shot dead on the spot, the maruta are gassed in their cells, labs are destroyed, offices detonated with explosives, other buildings catch fire, soldiers loot the rooms for money and anything of value, hundreds of corpses are thrown into a huge hole in the ground and torched, the lab rats catch fire and scatter around in flames in all directions (symbolic?).

The film ends with the soldiers and their families leaving on trains with an on-screen text revealing how they got back home and what happened to Shiro Ishii (he was later arrested by the Americans and agreed to hand over his collected data in exchange for his freedom. He was also suspected of being involved in the biological weapons programme in the Korean War. He died in 1959).

Men Behind the Sun is basically a catalogue of carnage. We're presented with scene after scene of increasingly nasty and disturbing behaviour (including the immoral decisions of the director himself), and this does come at the expense of the narrative and plot developments. It was shot in glorious 35mm celluloid and the music score is a strange throwback to old skool Hollywood adventure films of the 50s and 60s with its big brass sections and smoochy clarinets making for a bizarre and discomforting mix. Indeed, the plot of the film and the way it is played out and presented is as a conventional Hollywood action film of old. In fact, the disturbing contents, images, and subject-matter are the only things that lift it out of its time warp and convince us that the film wasn't made at least 25 years earlier.

People often ask where the film stands in terms of legitimacy; is it an exploration of those cruel times, or is it just a piece of crude exploitation? I believe it to be a bit of both. Throughout his career in film, T.F. Mous has continually explored and exposed the cruelties of the Japanese during World War II; he obviously feels very strongly about that time in history and has done much to draw attention to those times and educate others on the facts, even uncovering important documents from Russia and America. But even with the best will in the world, his film-making skills are basic at best; his style reeks of classic Hollywood of old, and this, combined with his crude and disturbing imagery, gives his films a clumsy and morally reprehensible edge (where in any Hollywood film have you seen a real autopsy carried out on a little boy, or real footage of a cat being fed to hungry rats?). His directorial skills were not sufficient enough to tackle such weighty themes as the ones explored in *Men Behind the Sun* (or indeed his later film, *Black Sun - The Nanking Massacre*, which serves as a loose prequel that concentrates on the Japanese invasion of China in the 1930s), and this is perhaps the main reason why the whole thing comes across as a piece of exploitative trash.

The film's producer, Fu Chi, grew up in Northern China, and he witnessed first-hand the atrocities committed by the Japanese during the war. He had very personal reasons for investing in the film, and he did so knowing he would probably never get his money back, let alone see a profit, as the film was never going to be commercial. I think it's safe to say that if the film fails as a piece of historical documentation, it's not because the people behind the camera didn't have the right intentions at heart. In fact, T.F. Mous perhaps took things a bit too far in that respect in the way he crossed the moral line himself in order to get his point across.

The aforementioned scenes of the autopsy, the cruel killing of the cat, and the needless burning of rats have for many viewers ruined any chance of this film being treated seriously as a legitimate work of cinematic art. Indeed, Mous' eagerness to present us with a picture of sheer evil and cruelty loses its moral high-ground the moment he starts to engineer real atrocities to put his point across. It's a bit rich to commit morally reprehensible acts in the making of his film to underpin that which he is railing against, and it's these scenes which most obviously bring on the accusations of exploitation. Okay, so no humans were killed or tortured in the making of the film, but a dead child's body was violated, and animals were unnecessarily killed. It reminds me of how Italian filmmakers like Ruggero Deodato and Umberto Lenzi filmed the cruel slaughter of animals in order to address the moral vacuum of the West in their cannibal epics; it just doesn't wash.

Despite all this moral indignation, *Men Behind the Sun* definitely works as a nightmare vision of modern barbarism. Shiro Ishii was one of the most evil men of the 20th Century, and at least his awful crimes haven't been watered down for the sake of 'cinematic manners'. Ishii's character in the film is every bit as cruel and loathsome as the real person whose exploits have been speculated on for decades. Unlike the Nazi 'Angel of Death,' Josef Mengele, who seemed to be motivated by his own sadistic drive, Shiro Ishii gave the impression that his experiments were conducted with a dogged devotion to collecting data that would benefit the Japanese war effort. To be seen to be indulging in the pure sadistic drive for its own sake may have been considered shameful and ignoble by Ishii, and so perhaps he concealed his sick urges under the guise of national duty. Who knows. One veteran member of the Youth Corps who was stationed at Unit 731 during the war gave a speech to university students and explained to them that Mous' film doesn't even begin to address the barbaric acts that were carried out at the compound – a chilling thought.

Men Behind the Sun has been banned and censored the world over, but it was in the Far East where the film caused the most controversy. At a screening in China in 1997, there were mass walk outs and a few viewers even fainted. According to Mous himself, 16 people have died of heart attacks while watching his film in the cinema. Much of the factual information in the film came from witness testimony, as some of the fleeing Japanese soldiers were captured and put on trial in Soviet courts. The film was met with hatred in Japan and has only ever been screened in that country once. It wasn't the nastiness or gore which upset the Japanese, it was the film's taunting as a political hot potato which angered the conservatives and led to right-wing groups threatening to burn down all the cinemas in the country if the film was ever screened again. Mous received numerous death threats and had to flee Japan.

Addendum: *Men Behind the Sun 2: Laboratory of the Devil* was released in 1992. It has a reputation for being one of the most unpleasant movies ever made, but really, it's no more extreme than the original.

Her Vengeance (1988)
(aka *I Piss On Your Urn*; Orig title: *Xue mei gui*)
Dir: Simon Nam Ngai /Hong Kong

Hong Kong's answer to *I Spit On Your Grave*, *Her Vengeance* is an ultra-violent rape-revenge thriller from the late 80s. In Macau, a group of drunken rowdy hoodlums are thrown out of a cabaret show, and later that night after her shift, usher Chieh-Ying takes a walk home from work, but is dragged into a graveyard by the five men, beaten and gang-raped. Left bloody and traumatized, Ying's only clue as to the identity of the rapists is a cigarette lighter that was left behind at the scene. She later discovers that the ordeal has left her infected with AIDS. Leaving behind her blind sister, Ying heads to Hong Kong to contact her uncle, Hsiung, with the hope that he will help her to wreak vengeance on the scumbags...

Uncle Hsiung happens to be wheelchair-bound and he owns a popular bar in Hong Kong. He refuses to help Ying and instead advises her to go back home to look after her sister. But Ying vows to stay put until she gets revenge. Tracking down her wrong-doers, one by one, and exacting a bloody and ruthless retribution, Ying succeeds in putting fear in the gang. The men who raped her are part of the criminal underworld in Hong Kong, and they suspect that they are being picked off by rival gangsters. Cue much ruthless retribution of their own against shady underworld characters, but the attacks on them continue. And after one of the men has acid thrown in his face, they discover that it's actually Ying who is responsible for the attacks. In retaliation, the gangsters head over to Macau and pay a visit to Ying's blind sister. And after the deaths of a couple more people whom Ying is close to, such as her flat-mate Susan and her young admirer Hao, she is at last joined by her uncle Hsiung, and together they hold up in the bar and set dangerous booby-traps and await the arrival of the bad guys for an extremely violent finale.

Unlike many Cat III titles of the time, *Her Vengeance* is completely devoid of the silly slapstick humour that is very popular in Hong Kong cinema, and is instead played absolutely unsettlingly straight. The world of *Her Vengeance* is portrayed in a bleak and brutal way; it's a vicious dog-eat-dog existence, or as one of the characters puts it, "it's a villain's world". The rain-soaked neon-lit cityscape is *Blade Runner*-esque with its dazzling surface veneer of colours and sounds barely concealing the darkness and ruthlessness around every corner. The soundtrack includes a deep droning synth that drops out of tune and is quite unnerving and compliments the sense of decay and the apocalyptic vibe of the film.

In the West, the rape-revenge genre usually sees women acting alone in their quests for violent retribution, and even though in *Her Vengeance* Ying does spend at least two thirds of the running time as the sole avenger dishing out the just deserts, she is joined by Hsiung in the finale. And although Hsiung is confined to a wheelchair, he turns out to be pretty handy in bar room brawls despite his disadvantage, as an earlier scene indicates. But in terms of the 'sex wars' of cinema (in which the rape-revenge movies play a large part in its discourse), feminist-minded viewers will notice that Hsiung's character, despite possessing the 'manly' qualities of being able to defend himself in violent confrontation, ultimately serves as a man who is symbolically sexless, or 'castrated' because of his confinement to the wheelchair. His disabled existence makes him non-threatening to Ying, and therefore he is accepted as a suitable ally in the fight against the enemy.

Most of the other male characters in the film are depicted as pure evil except for Hao, a nice young man who is completely smitten with Ying, and whose love she can never accept due to her AIDS infection that he doesn't know about. The fact that Ying can't allow herself to get close to him no matter how much she'd like to, adds one of the bleakest notes to the film. The rapists couldn't take away her heart; but perhaps even worse, they made it so that she can never truly love again.

Be sure to stick with the uncut version available through Deltamac on VCD, as there is

an edited version floating around on the Joy Sales DVD label which has been stripped down to a Cat IIb rating (even though the sleeve carries the Cat III logo), and this version places heavy cuts on the rape scene.

Tetsuo: The Iron Man (1988)
Dir: Shinya Tsukamoto /Japan

By pure coincidence, 1988 saw the release of two unrelated Japanese films with characters called Tetsuo who mutate into oblivion; Katsuhiro Otomo's cult anime *Akira*, which became the first 'Manga movie' to achieve international recognition, reached its chaotic finale with delinquent teen Tetsuo bloating into a gigantic mess of oozing liquified body-mass, almost filling an Olympic-sized sports stadium with his blob-like enormity. It was Otomo's speciality: body-horror for the wayward teen, and animation as a legitimate filmic art. The other was a no less delirious horror weirdy, *Tetsuo: The Iron Man*, a brutal and perverse meeting of technology, sex, and violence.

Shot in a rough and ready style on scraps of black and white 16mm film, *Tetsuo The Iron Man* makes up for its tiny budget limitations with a hyper-kinetic style and an inexhaustible imagination. The confusing 'plot' concerns a quiet salaryman (Tamoroh Taguchi, who later showed up in the *Guinea Pig* entry, *Android of Notre Dame*) who is freaked out by visions of transmutation, and who apparently killed a child in a hit-and-run accident. He tries to deal with the troubling memories by engaging in strange sex practices with his girlfriend (Kei Fujiwara, who would go on to direct a couple of her own cyberpunk entries with *Organ* and *Organ 2*). It soon becomes apparent that the kid survived the accident and has passed on a highly infectious disease which infects human flesh, transforming man into rampaging machine. And before long, Taguchi mutates into a metallic killing machine with a huge drillbit for a penis that he uses on his girlfriend in a gruesome sex attack before hitting the streets in a war with the now grown-up hit-and-run victim... or something like that.

Director Shinya Tsukamoto, who appears in the film as the self-mutilator who lives in the junkyard and inserts metal tubing into his open wounds, is clearly in his element here. It's a labour of twisted love with its hyperactive camera and rapid editing techniques. He also presents us with wild and unruly montage sequences made painstakingly with stop-motion animation techniques for an insane barrage of twisted nightmarish imagery.

Tetsuo seems to take its inspiration from a wide variety of disparate sources; the most obvious reference points are perhaps as a heady mixture of elements from *Eraserhead*, *Robocop*, and *The Evil Dead*, with a heavy dose of Cronenberg and Jan Svankjmajer thrown in for good measure. But Tsukamoto takes these elements and mashes them into something completely delirious and original. The resulting film re-ignited the fledgling cyberpunk movement and became a midnight favourite in Tokyo before sweeping the globe and capturing the imagination of cult film fanatics the world over. So, if you're in the mood for fetishistic visual overload, the lack of a traditional linear plot, and a pure cinematic experience, then *Tetsuo* is for you.

Faceless (1988)

(Orig title: *Les predateurs de la nuit*)
Dir: Jess Franco /Spain /France
The notorious Jess Franco revisits *Eyes Without a Face* territory (after *The Awful Dr. Orloff* (1962)) for another entertaining and gruesome mad doctor flick. This time the story depicts Dr. Flamand (Helmut Berger), an immoral plastic surgeon who, while heading home with his sister one night, is accosted in a car park by an ex-patient whose facial reconstruction surgery has gone wrong. The irate woman attempts to douse the doctor in acid, but his sister steps in the way and cops for a face-full instead. Flamand attempts to restore his sister's beauty by imprisoning beautiful models in cells below his clinic, in the hope that he can graft a pretty face onto his loved one. But, of course, the operations prove to be unsuccessful. And meanwhile, the father of a missing model hires a private detective to head for Paris and track her down...

Afforded a much bigger budget than usual, Franco here crafts a colourful and wildly entertaining shocker that includes lots of gruesome deaths, awkward dubbing, a cheesy 80s pop tune by Vincent Thoma, but surprisingly very little nudity. Fans of outrageous screen carnage should enjoy scenes of acid burning, hands hacked off with a machete, a syringe plunged into an eyeball (which looks to have been inspired by a similar death scene in *Dead and Buried* [1980]). There is also the disastrous face-removal scene, a patient having her head cut off with a chainsaw while she's still alive, a nasty throat stabbing with scissors, and a woman's head skewered with a power drill. On the casting front, fans of Euro-sleaze will spot many familiar faces, which alongside *Salon Kitty*'s Helmut Berger, also includes Brigitte Lahaie as the mad doctor's sexy assistant, *Dr. Jekyll and His Women*'s Gerard Zalcberg as the hulking great retard who works at the clinic. There's also Caroline Munro as the doomed model, *Kojak* himself, Terry Savalas, as her concerned father, and Chris Mitchum as the tough guy detective. Howard Vernon even reprises his role in a cameo as Dr. Orloff himself, and Lina Romay makes a brief appearance as his wife!

Matador (1988)

Dir: Pedro Almodovar /Spain
A lurid cocktail of sex and death, Pedro Almodovar's *Matador* opens with morbid bullfighting instructor, Diego (Nacho Martinez), jerking off to violent video clips from Mario Bava's *Blood and Black Lace* and Jess Franco's *Bloody Moon*. Apprentice matador, Angel (Antonio Banderas in his least macho role), is a closet homosexual who faints at the sight of blood. He attempts to assert his masculinity by forcing himself on Diego's girlfriend, but this rape attempt turns farcical. Later, a guilt-stricken Angel hands himself over to the police and confesses to a series of murders of which he is innocent. His lawyer, Maria (Assumpta Serna), sees through his lies when she learns that he is haemophobic. She, however, just so happens to have a thing for blood and death, and despite her veneer of elegance and her important profession, likes to indulge in sexualized murder herself, striking like a black widow spider and inserting a long hairpin into the necks of her victims the moment they reach orgasm. Maria recognizes a kindred spirit in Diego, the man who is actually responsible for the murders, and together they consummate their passion in a suicide pact for the ultimate orgasm...

Matador is a tribute to the stylish giallo/slasher movies of Mario Bava and Dario Argento, injected with a dose of Almodovar's usual kinkiness and dark humour for a slice of chic erotic horror. The humour is apparent in the scenes where Angel tries to rape Diego's girlfriend and fumbles around with a Swiss army knife, threatening her with a bottle opener before finding the blade, and later when he goes to the police station to confess, the girl's crazy mother tells him "don't bother, you've done enough already". The film is also awash with ludicrous coincidences, such as Maria being Angel's lawyer whilst at the same time being in cahoots with the real perpetrator (this perhaps another nod towards Dario Argento whose *Tenebrae* includes an absurd sequence where a pretty victim is chased by a vicious dog, ever so conveniently, right into the killer's lair).

Generally though, *Matador* is a much more serious and sombre effort than Almodovar's earlier work, and has more going for it than just a stream of sick jokes. Angel's mother, for example, is a stone-cold religious maniac who has clearly instilled much poisonous guilt into her son's troubled psyche, and even goes as far as to try and persuade Maria that he is anything but innocent, and fails to see that his 'confessions' stemmed from a fractured frame of mind. More tributes abound, such as the amusing catwalk scene which is clearly indebted to Bava's *Blood and Black Lace*, and also the climax which owes a lot to King Vidor's *Duel In the Sun*, in which Maria and Diego kill each other in an elaborate plan of sex and death, with their pursuers distracted by a solar eclipse.

Hellbound: Hellraiser II (1988)
Dir: Tony Randal /UK/USA

Focusing on before and after Clive Barker turned modern horror on its head, following the rip-roaring success of *Hellraiser*, which had given the world a new horror hero in the form of Pinhead, a sequel (or sequels) was pretty much inevitable.

Having served as both writer and director on his ground-breaking original, Clive Barker decided to take more of a back seat for this second instalment, *Hellbound*. Serving as executive producer and general overlooking eye, and handing over directorial duties to Stateside helmer, Tony Randal, and entrusting the script chores to his long-time cohort, Pete Atkins (who was previously skinned alive in *The Forbidden*). If *Hellbound* was something less than an artistic triumph, you could lay the blame at the feet of Mr. Randal, who – with the best will in the world – just didn't have a big enough budget to do justice to the ambitious and grandiose script. And although he was clearly more technically proficient than Barker, Randal lacked that chaotic spark of inexperience which ironically made the original a more unruly delight. But having said that, I've probably seen this film more times than I've seen the original; it's so re-watchable.

Picking up where the original left off, *Hellbound* starts with Kirsty waking up in a psychiatric ward where she is questioned by a detective. The head of the hospital, Dr. Channard (Kenneth Cranham), a man who keeps the most disturbed patients locked up in cells below the hospital basement, just so happens to be obsessed with the puzzle box, the Lament Configuration, and its mysteries. His office resembles a museum of hell, and is decorated with magazine clippings and macabre photographs. He already owns three scale replicas of the boxes which he keeps in glass displays on his desk. With the help of a hospital porter, Kirsty manages to escape after receiving a message, allegedly from her father Larry who is in hell, and she gets back to the puzzle box and gains access to hell by evading the Cenobites once more.

Hellbound is much more epic and grand in scale than its predecessor but tends to lack the claustrophobic terror which helped make the original such a classic. Which is not to say that *Hellbound* doesn't contain its fair share of twisted pleasures; the graphic birth of Pinhead sequence, for example, is a ghoulish, head-hammering treat which no *Hellraiser* fan would want to miss, nor the transformation of mild-mannered Dr. Channard from a wretched human to a beautiful monster, courtesy of some ectoplasmic cheese wire and a brain-hoovering umbilical cord which matches the visual brilliance of anything in part one. Plus, we get to see what Julia looks like naked. And by naked, I mean without the skin. Unmissable indeed.

Intriguing too is the fact that, of all the *Hellraiser* movies (including part four which was disowned by its director), *Hellbound* had the most trouble with censors on both sides of the Atlantic. Released in America were both rated and unrated versions. *Hellbound* was only ever okayed in the UK in its slightly cut form, with the VHS version losing a few seconds from the film's most notorious scene in which a disturbed psychiatric patient sets about razoring his flesh to ribbons as he imagines maggots crawling over his skin. The British censors also removed the sight of bare breasts, which were clearly far more dangerous and offensive than the sight of a man having nails hammered into his head! That you *will* get to see, thanks to the continuing genius of Bob Keen and his Image Animation makeup effects.

There's more of Christopher Young's majestic score which echoes around the labyrinth of hell with all the pomp and circumstance of Lucifer unbound. All of which leaves more than enough encouragement for you to join Pinhead on his return journey to hell.

Deadbeat At Dawn (1988)
Dir: Jim VanBebber /USA

Young film-maker Jim VanBebber became something of a cause celebre of the underground when his debut feature, *Deadbeat At Dawn*, hit the screens. Made over the course of three and a half years, and eventually racking up budget costs of $85,000, VanBebber's film is second only to Robert Rodriguez's *El Mariachi* in terms of boasting some of the most impressive action scenes ever seen in a home-made movie.

VanBebber cast himself in the lead role as Goose, the leader of a gang called The Ravens. They start the film by having a mass brawl with a rival gang, The Spiders, in the middle of a graveyard. Under pressure from his occult-fixated girlfriend, Goose agrees to quit the gang and the violent lifestyle so that the pair can move away from the area and settle down together. However, The Ravens catch wind of this and take it as a betrayal. And while Goose is out one day, a couple of gang members take a visit to his apartment and viciously beat his girlfriend to death with a golf club. How does Goose handle this situation; does he break down crying at the loss of his love? Does he call the police and have the culprits punished by law? No. He simply dumps her body into a trash compactor and swears revenge. The Ravens and The Spiders put aside their differences and team up to pull off a complicated bank heist, and while this is going on, Goose hits the bottle hard and has trippy nightmarish hallucinations, including the sight of his bloody beloved wandering through the graveyard in her white funeral sheet. Goose eventually gets involved in a bloody and extremely violent showdown where he single-handedly takes on both The Ravens and The Spiders for one of the most glorious fight scenes of the 80s.

Jim VanBebber is a rare kind of filmmaker, a true auteur. In addition to writing and directing his films, he also raises his own funding, acts in his films, and edits them into the final products. Based in the mid-western town of Dayton, Ohio,

Jim has often found it difficult to achieve the kind of success he deserves. He's a greatly talented film-maker but the harsh environments of the movie business, combined with his own hard-hitting and uncompromising stance, has made his geographical restraints the least of his troubles. VanBebber's films are among the most ferociously transgressive and brutal of the 80s and 90s, and his budgetary constraints have never held him back from directing some of the most intricate and complicated violent-set-pieces in the history of low-budget film.

With *Deadbeat At Dawn* VanBebber throws together every cliché from the 60s and 70s gang films but the end result is surprisingly fresh and exciting. Visually, he also adopts a retro, backward-looking edge with his use of psychedelic kaleidoscope segues and a crimson-laced backdrop (that would crop up again in his later film, *The Manson Family*) which comes across as being heavily influenced by the works of Roman Polanski and Kenneth Anger. *Deadbeat At Dawn* is also deliberately gritty and grating on the sensibilities of its audience. However, it's the last 10 to 15 minutes of this film which will be remembered the most fondly by cult movie fans – the final showdown with The Ravens and The Spiders is so violent and expertly done it defies belief. These gang members don't just die, they get splattered! Just looking at the intricacies of that final sequence, with the dangerous stunts and tightly choreographed violence (including the use of nunchucks that has kept the film banned in the UK for years), and you know it must have been a real headache to organise all of that chaos, and probably took weeks to shoot. Van Bebber's next feature film, *The Manson Family*, was an even bigger headache for Jim; a nightmare fifteen year voyage through production hell.

Evil Dead Trap (1988)
(Orig title: *Shiryo no wana*)
Dir: Toshiharu Ikeda /Japan

Baring no relation to Sam Raimi's *Evil Dead* movies, *Evil Dead Trap* became something of a cult favourite on the bootleg video circuit in the 90s before being passed surprisingly uncut by the BBFC in 2003.

Television host Nami receives a package in the mail that includes a video tape showing the gruesome murder of a young woman. Desperate to improve the viewer ratings on her show, Nami gathers together a bunch of colleagues to serve as her camera crew, and they venture out to the location where the snuff tape was shot (a large derelict warehouse complex) in order to report on the crime and to look for clues as to the killer's identity. But, of course, things go badly wrong, and the TV crew are picked off, one by one, by the mysterious killer in spectacularly brutal fashion.

The second half of the film takes a detour into supernatural territory, borrowing themes of twisted familial love from classics like *Basket Case* and *Psycho*, and horror fans have always been divided on which half of the film they like best. Slasher fans love the first half with its gruesome and stylish slayings, whereas those who prefer oddball plotting, shunting body horror, and the climactic fireworks of Cat III movies, prefer the latter half. But there are also those, myself included, who enjoy the whole show!

It's very much a feature length tribute to Western horror at its best with the main theme tune reminiscent of Fabio Frizzi's work on Lucio Fulci's *The Beyond*, and John Harrison's synth score on George Romero's *Day of the Dead*. The candy-coloured lighting and gorgeously brutal murder set pieces are very Argento-esque; *Suspiria* and *Tenebre* being the most obvious influences (he even recycles the maggots-from-the-ceiling scene from *Suspiria*). Director Ikeda, who had previously stunned audiences with his entry in the *Angel Guts* series, *Red Porno*, bombards his audience with set-piece after blood soaked set-piece, all mired in a moody ambiance making this feel like a video nasties greatest hits package; we get severe eyeball trauma, rape, impalements, death by crossbow, a shocking strangulation over the roof of a car, and a very gory demon birth. The Synapse DVD includes an audio commentary with Ikeda and special effects guy Shinichi Wakasa. It's one of the strangest and most absurd chat tracks you'll ever hear; unintentionally hilarious!

A sequel came along soon after, *Evil Dead Trap 2*, which is vastly different from the original film and features a strange mix of femmes fatale, a creepy child ghost, perversities, and surreal nightmare visions. The story seems to be based on guilt caused by abortions, but it's all quite incomprehensible. Also a lonely, overweight projectionist who holds some dark secrets, and a celebrity seems to be extremely envious of the projectionist for some reason. It's

visually striking, and has a creepy atmosphere, but these are the only things it has in common with the original.

Elephant (1988)
Dir: Alan Clarke /UK

A ruthless and relentless comment on the troubles in Northern Ireland, *Elephant* is a short 39-minute assault to the senses depicting the seemingly unstoppable tit-for-tat murder and counter-murder in that troubled part of the world at the time. With no real narrative to speak of, the film presents a series of chilling shootings, back to back, with nothing to explain what's going on. Instead we're shown the sickening violence with no context other than the bloodshed itself.

Whether each killing is revenge for another, or a pre-emptive strike, or a punishment is not made clear, nor whether the shootings are being carried out by Loyalists or Republicans or both. Each deadly scenario is played out to such a spot-on and chillingly accurate way it makes big-budget Hollywood gunplay look kind of silly in comparison. With no music on the soundtrack and no dialogue to distract us from the relentless onslaught on screen, director Alan Clarke doesn't allow for a moment's respite from the horrors.

It's also ironic how a film which strives to avoid all artistic notions and entertainment value boasts such superb performances from both the killers and the victims; these 'sketches' of characters nonetheless offer vivid portrayals of cold-blooded killers and desperate victims, the most memorable of which are the shootings at the taxi rank, the football field, and the large abandoned warehouse complex (reminiscent of the warehouse cum squat in Geoffrey Wright's *Romper Stomper*, a later film which was influenced by Clarke's work).

Each scenario is also rehearsed and directed to within an inch of its life. In fact, it might just be the most perfectly directed film of Alan Clarke's career. From a horror fan's perspective, *Elephant* resembles the stripped-down kill-a-thon antics of a lurid slasher movie; but instead of 'stalk and slash' we get 'stalk and shoot'. And the special effects are amazingly realistic and unflinching with trickling blood and exploding squibs adding to the senseless onslaught of this extraordinary body-count movie. All the details concerning the build-up to the killings are discarded as a way of exposing the evil practice of murder. But even the most bland and mundane of the slasher movies had some kind of narrative as a way of 'joining the dots' and making the 'pay off' seem cinematically justified when a dumb jock or bimbo cheerleader meets the sharp end of a blade or axe. Alan Clarke didn't need to play that game, the narrative of his 'story' was headline news, day in and day out.

The slasher film is often accused of being grim and irresponsible – an outcast genre. And Clarke takes that disreputable template and turns it into a political statement that says more about the troubles in Northern Ireland than a dozen other movies. And the reason for its success is simple: Just like the bastard slasher movies, *Elephant* is a purely visceral experience, it is designed to affect viewers on a primordial level, make them gasp, make their skin crawl and their hearts race as the film's perspective changes from predator to prey from one sequence to the next. It's certainly not a popcorn movie, and you won't hear any bad jokes or see any sex scenes or drug taking before the killings start. No, Clarke used the slasher template because it's the most effective way of expressing the startling hunting ground of life and death on the big screen, with the 'boogeymen' often wearing black ski masks and invading the lives of others and taking them out with the cold and precise manner of a gun. And the audience walks away wanting no part of that in their lives.

Necromancer (1988)
Dir: Dusty Nelson /USA
A supernatural rape/revenge flick in which a young blonde college graduate is raped, then unwittingly utilises the help of a demon to get her own back on her aggressors and anyone else she happens to be upset with. The attacks are all bloodless and depicted in the same way: red creature growls and shows its teeth, and the victim's screams echo into the next scene, that sort of thing. The video box claims "A special effects extravaganza in the tradition of *Serpent and the Rainbow*," but actually this is crude and amateurish, and the laughs are all unintentional. It's akin to a real shitty Troma movie, minus the deliberate humour.

Zombi 3 (1988)
(aka *Zombie Flesh Eaters 2*)
Dir: Lucio Fulci [and Claudio Fragasso & Bruno Mattei, uncredited] /Italy

When a top secret military freezer is stolen by armed criminals, the contents – a deadly bio-weapon – are spilled, and the lethal toxin spreads across the nearby countryside. The government attempts to cover up the disaster by secretly cremating the bodies of victims, but the smoke infects a flock of birds which in turn spread the contagion even farther. A zombie epidemic ensues, and the military lose control of the situation. Meanwhile, a group of off-duty soldiers (and the girls they're trying to pull) must fend off the grisly hordes... *Zombi 3* is the first sequel to Lucio Fulci's *Zombie Flesh Eaters* (1979) , which was itself marketed as an unofficial sequel to George Romero's *Dawn of the Dead* (1978) – hence its alternate title, *Zombi 2*. If you're still confused about the *Zombi* sequels, this is the one with the radio DJ who adds a wry commentary on the disaster until he meets his own sorry fate at the end. This film borrows elements from *The Crazies* (1973) and *Return of the Living Dead* (1985), with the military personnel dressed in bio suits and gas masks, struggling to cope, and the idea of toxic smoke reviving the dead. And the machete-wielding zombie looks like it has stepped right out of Dan O'Bannon's film. If this sequel seems a bit haphazard and unfocused, that's because it is; director Lucio Fulci had to pull out of the project after suffering a stroke. Writer Claudio Fragasso and hack director Bruno Mattei were then hired to finish the picture. The pair shot around 40 minutes of additional footage which was then pasted onto Fulci's 50 or so minutes of usable footage. Horror fans at the time were not impressed with the end result, but thanks to home video, the film has built a well-earned reputation over the years as a goofy curio.

Zombie 4: After Death (1988)
(aka *Zombie Flesh Eaters 3*; aka *After Death*; Orig title: *Oltre la morte*)
Dir: 'Clyde Anderson' [Claudio Fragasso] /Italy
On a tropical island, a practitioner of voodoo opens the gateway to Hell in this entertaining but utterly goofy sequel. Twenty years later, a group of armed mercenaries team up with a woman whose parents were killed, and they head to the island to deal with the zombie problem... By this point in the late 80s, the Italian exploitation scene was rapidly declining, but producers would still insist on spending small fortunes on flying their casts and crews and equipment to exotic locations on the other

side of the globe – in this case, the Philippines. If you can tolerate hilariously bad dubbing, over-the-top gore effects and an atrocious theme tune ('living after deeeaaath!'), then give it a try. If not, then stay well clear. Leading lady, Clandice Daly, does a serviceable job alongside porn star, Jeff Stryker, who allegedly landed the role of the gun-toting hero because actor/producer, Werner Pochath, was a big fan of his porno movies! Here he is billed under his pseudonym, 'Chuck Peyton.'

Zombie 5: Killing Birds (1988)
(aka *Killing Birds: Raptors*)
Dir: 'Claude Milliken' [Claudio Lattanzi & Joe D'Amato, uncredited] /Italy
College kids head out to rural Louisiana to help save a rare species of bird from extinction. On their journey, they meet a peculiar blind man who seems to hold a dark secret. They also find a dead body in an abandoned truck before they chance upon a deserted house in the middle of nowhere. Thanks to the trippy prologue, we know that a deranged 'Nam vet had murdered a family in the house years earlier. And, of course, not long after they arrive at the house, the students are picked off by one of the lamest ghouls in zombie movie history... Despite the elaborate set-up and emphasis on birds, this turns out to be your typical 'teens-get-murdered-in-a-spooky-old-house' movie. The dubbing is poorly done, but the performances are okay. There's some decent photography by Fred Sloniscko Jr, a sweet score by Carlo Maria Cordio, and at least one very gruesome death scene in which one of the students gets his chain caught in an industrial grinder. Lara Wendel is pretty good as the lead heroine, and *Man From U.N.C.L.E.*'S Robert Vaugn seems to be slumming it somewhat as the ineffectual blind doctor. It's a good film to watch in bed before you drift off. Oh, and the house used here is the same one that served as the Seven Doors Hotel in Fulci's *The Beyond* (1981).

The Hook of Woodland Heights (1988)
Dir: Michael Savino & Mark Veau /USA
A 40-minute amateur video in which an escaped lunatic goes on a murder spree using his metallic hook on his victims. Despite a variety of creative kills (including a clipboard frisbee'd into a guy's head, and another unfortunate getting genital'd by the hook), this has nothing on other 'killer hook' movies, such as *Scream*

Bloody Murder (1972) and *Candyman* (1992), but could pass as mild entertainment on a slow afternoon.

Patti Rocks (1988)
Dir: David Burton Morris /USA
A northern log worker, Billy (Chris Mulkey), drags his old friend along for a thousand mile drive down to Florida to confront an ex-girlfriend. The woman in question, Patti (Karen Landry), is now pregnant with Billy's baby, and he accuses her of 'stealing' his sperm... A low-key drama that packs quite a wallop, despite a clumsy start, *Patti Rocks* was an obvious influence on Neil LaBute's *In the Comany of Men* (1997). A modest – and still sadly little seen – film that ought to have a far wider audience.

Jack's Back (1988)
Dir: Rowdy Herrington /USA
One hundred years to the day after the original Jack the Ripper killings, the bodies of murdered prostitutes are discovered in Los Angeles, the handy work of a copycat killer. A police manhunt gets underway amid the media frenzy, and meanwhile, James Spader has a nightmare vision of his twin brother (also played by Spader) being killed. Of course, the nightmare comes true, and so he sets out to catch the maniac before he strikes again... *Jack's Back* is a routine thriller that throws in more twists and turns than it can adequately handle, but can be quite enjoyable if you're in an undemanding mood.

Ghosthouse (1988)
(Orig title: *La Casa 3*)
Dir: 'Humphrey Humbert' [Umberto Lenzi] /Italy
A young man receives a strange radio signal, so he and his girl visit the abandoned mansion in the wilderness where it came from. And once there, they soon find themselves terrorised by exploding jars, a rocking camper van, a ghost dog, a makeshift guillotine, and a ghost girl holding a sinister doll. *Ghosthouse* was released in its native Italy as an unofficial sequel to *The Evil Dead*, but let's face it, Umberto Lenzi is no Sam Raimi, and dumpy lead actor Greg Scott is no Bruce Campbell. Even regular fans of Euro-horror tend to dislike the late 80s Italian productions, but personally, I've always had a soft spot for goofy curios like Fulci's *House of*

Clocks (1989), Deodato's *Bodycount* (1987), Lamberto Bava's *Demons* (1987) and especially *Demons 2* (1988). *Ghosthouse* is in the same vein as those mentioned, with the bad acting, bad direction, nonsensical dialogue and all-round cheapness somehow adding to its demented charm. My only gripe is that I wish the filmmakers had included Deadite-like creatures, in keeping with the *Evil Dead* series, but perhaps they were wary of being sued, so they stuck to the pee-brained ghosts instead. Two more sequels followed, *La casa 4* and *La casa 5,* which were equally cheesy and mildly entertaining.

Demon City – Shinjuku (1988)

(Orig title: *Makaitoshi Shinjuku*; aka *Monster City*)
Dir: Yoshiaki Kawajiri /Japan
The influence of HP Lovecraft was also felt in Japanese anime in which tentacled creatures from the portals of hell have long been the norm. *Wicked City* (1987), *Demon City – Shinjuku* (1988), the *Urotsukidoji* series (1988-1996) and *Tokko* (2006), to name only a few. These movies and TV shows share a fondness for sexually-frustrated tentacled demons from hell. The Japanese also add their own perverse touch, which often includes the sight of pretty young females hoisted skyward by the monsters and raped in every orifice by the phallic-like prongs. In a change from the usual demon rape anime, *Demon City* includes a sequence in which a tentacled demoness attempts to have her wicked way with a man in a deserted bar room, only to be overpowered, beaten, and almost drowned with a bottle of whisky poured down her throat. Apparently, only women are permitted to be raped by tentacles in Japanese movies.

Slugs (1988)

(aka *Slugs: The Movie*; Orig title: *Slugs, muerte viscosa*)
Dir: Juan Piquer Simon /Spain /USA
A perpetually pissed-off health inspector tries to convince politicians that his town has been invaded by giant killer slugs. They think he's insane and ignore his pleas until the bodies start piling up... *Slugs* is a low-budget gem and a triumph for fans of creepy bug movies. It takes a while for the action to pick up, but once it does it never falters. We get the usual B-movie characters, such as the sceptical Sheriff, the all-knowing scientist and the teenage lovers joined at the genitals. The slugs themselves are long, black and repulsive, and there are literally *thousands* of them that have been breeding in the sewage pipes. And, unlike normal slugs, these things also have razor sharp teeth and devour flesh while they slither through the eye-sockets of their victims, slowly nibbling away at their internal organs. Mutated bug movies of the 50s and 60s put the blame on radiation (see giant radioactive ants in *Them!* [1954] and radioactive leeches in *Attack of the Giant Leeches* [1960]), and in the 70s it was pollution (see the mutant cockroaches of *Bug* [1975]). But here in the 80s, it's toxic waste that is to blame for the mutations as it is discovered that there is a secret waste dump in town. Gooey moments include a gardener hacking off his own hand with an axe, a man's head exploding in the middle of a restaurant, sending blood and bugs flying across the room, and another character is shredded alive in the sewers. *Slugs* would sit nicely on a tripple-bill with *Kingdom of the Spiders* (1977) and *The Deadly Spawn* (1983).

Ghosts... of the Civil Dead (1988)

Dir: John Hillcoat /Australia
A new prisoner soon learns of the brutal system in an Australian jail by being victimized and having the word 'CUNT' tattooed on his forehead, and who witnesses much more victimisation and injustice behind bars. Filmed in an almost documentary-like style, *Ghosts... of the Civil Dead* is a gritty and downbeat movie that nonetheless offers up some fantastic performances from David Field (who looks a bit like UK MMA fighter, Ross Pearson) and Nick Cave, whose turn as the psychotic maximum-security prisoner, Maynard, is as insane as they come. His performance could have been an influence on Sam Rockwell's turn as 'Wild Bill' Wharton in *The Green Mile* (1999).

The House on Tombstone Hill (1988)

(aka *The Dead Come Home*; aka *Dead Dudes in the House*)
Dir: James Riffel /USA
Enjoyable nonsense from Tromaville in which a group of youngsters set about renovating a newly purchased house whose previous owner, Annabelle, had murdered her husband there in the 1940s. One of the goons smashes a nearby headstone, and this act of vandalism seems to bring back Annabelle's ugly corpse as a frail –

but very deadly – zombie, or ghost, or something. Who knows what she is supposed to be, but the characters are so irksome even the house itself takes an instant dislike to them, and shows its contempt by locking 'em in and leaving them to their fates... Memorable death scenes include one of the 'dudes' losing his hands, and another cut in half by a window pane, complete with twitching severed legs (perhaps in tribute to *Superstition* [1982] which includes a death scene that is very similar). Also look out for the homages to classics like *An American Werewolf in London* (dead friends coming back to life to crack a few jokes) and *The Shining* ("What about MY responsibilities?!!").

Heart of Midnight (1988)
Dir: Matthew Chapman /USA
A disturbed young woman, Carol (Jennifer Jason Leigh), inherits an old nightclub from her uncle. And rather than sell the place, she decides to continue with the refurbishments and keep the place running, in keeping with her uncle's wishes. However, the workmen are an obtuse bunch who refuse to listen to her suggestions on the designs of the bar layout, and they constantly pretend to listen to her while carrying on with the original plans. One night, the workers attempt to rape her, but she makes a run for it and triggers the fire alarm, causing the men to flee. And with her history of mental instability, the experience – combined with the feelings of isolation of living alone in the sinister old building – leaves her feeling very fragile... Similar to Roman Polanski's *Repulsion* (1965) and Stanley Kubrick's *The Shining* (1980), *Heart of Midnight* presents us with a character in a crumbling mental state. She dislikes sex, and she dislikes the fact that men are constantly intruding on her personal space. The film also has some seemingly supernatural elements; a bicycle tosses itself down the stairs, the bathroom mirror cabinet opens by itself. And there are menacing, shadowy figures dashing around the building. Like Carole in *Repulsion*, this Carol also experiences terrifying visions of things breaking through the bathroom door – in this case, a giant eyeball – and strange, psycho-sexual visions, such as the phallic prong which juts out from her bed sheets and closes in between her legs. But unlike *Repulsion*, this time we get a brief back-story on Carol, with revelations that she may have been molested by her uncle as a child.

The Rejuvenator (1988)
Dir: Brian Thomas Jones /USA
A scientist in the closing stages of perfecting a youth-preserving agent, is pressured by his financial backer – an ageing actress desperate to get back into the limelight – to rush through his research and bring immediate results. The serum is administered intravenously and seems to be a success at first. However, there is also the undesired side-effect of an acceleration of the ageing process once the dosage has worn off. Thus, the user must be continuously dosed up like a junky to avoid becoming an ugly, putrefied Andrew Lloyd Webber lookalike. *The Rejuvinator* has its roots in the 'mad scientist' movie, but here the doctor is the sanest, most level-headed character in the film. Instead, it's the madness of our youth-obsessed, brain dead vanity culture that hijacks scientific research for a short, sharp fix, with disastrous results. An underrated curio.

Betrayed (1988)
Dir: Costa-Gavras /USA /Japan
In the late 80s, a number of neo-Nazi and KKK movies hit the screens, from mid-budget theatrical releases (*Mississippi Burning*) to low-budget video dreck (*Surf Nazi Must Die*), each one more ludicrous than the last. *Betrayed* is perhaps the nuttiest of them all. It stars Tom Berenger as Gary, a Texas farmer whose life changes when undercover FBI agent, 'Katy Weaver' (Debra Winger), strikes up a relationship with him. She's digging for evidence of his involvement in a series of political assassinations, and discovers that he's a vicious white-supremacist, Klansman, neo-Nazi, religious bigot, murderer, terrorist, armed robber, – basically the whole works – who enjoys hunting 'niggers' in the woods with his friends. 'Goddamn Jews are running our country with their nigger police,' Gary fumes, after he has just shot dead a black man in cold blood. His objection to ZOG (that's 'Zionist Occupied Government') is robbed of its patriotic charge in the eyes of the viewers who are now reviled by his cruel actions. However, the plot-line becomes ever more complex as Weaver had developed feelings for Gary before she realised just how dangerous he is... An entertaining if way over-the-top crime thriller, even the most extreme of neo-Nazi groups in North America at

the time were no way as dangerous or as organised as this film likes to make out.

Scarecrows (1988)
Dir: William Wesley /USA

Double-crossing criminals in search of a box of stolen money trek through the woods after dark. The area is also guarded by huge scarecrows that come to life and pick off the crummy humans, one by one, EC comics style. *Scarecrows* has much in common with the – then – fading slasher movie tradition, in that it shares with those films a puritan vibe in which the monster seems to feed on sin while the innocent ones are spared. Michael Simms as Curry is the Captain Rhodes of the group, a sinister scumbag whose fate is disappointingly bloodless. The crux of the story could have fit into an episode of *Tales From the Crypt*, but by spreading things out over the course of 83 minutes, the characters are given the chance to dig their holes even deeper, making the pay-off that much more satisfying. A late-80s classic.

Brain Damage (1988)
Dir: Frank Henenlotter /USA

A young man, Brian (Rick Herbst), wakes up one morning with a headache, and discovers a strange, Tingler-like creature in the room. Bizarrely, the creature (named Aylmer) talks to Brian, and even slips a pointy appendage into his neck, administering a potent blue hallucinogen which causes euphoric psychedelic trips. However, Aylmer also has a vicious side, and during a surreal journey to a junk yard, a security guard has his brains devoured. Brian becomes fast friends with Aylmer, completely unaware of the murder and mayhem going on around him. And his relationships with his girlfriend and his room mate brother go to pot as he spends hours splashing around in the bath tub with his little trip-dispenser buddy. Of course, more murders ensue, and Brian's neighbours come to his aid, informing him of Aylmer's true nature and evil past... Like *The Hunger* (1983) and *The Addiction* (1995), *Brain Damage* is a blatant allegory on the dangers of drug addiction. But unlike those films, it's also a fun, anarchic comic strip come to life, sort of like a cross between Ken Russell's *Altered States* (1980) and William Castle's *The Tingler* (1959). Aylmer (pronounced 'Elmer') is a curious little creature and easily the star of the show. Turns out that it's an ancient parasite that keeps its host

sedated in a blissful haze while it feeds on their life essence and keeps them addicted to the process. A mutual dependency is established, and separation from the creature results in horrendous withdrawal symptoms. The MPAA insisted on cuts to secure the R-rating, including two of its most notorious scenes – death by blowjob and brain matter literally pulled out of a character's ear. Synapse later released the film fully uncut on DVD.

Headhunter (1988)
Dir: Peter Scheffer /USA /South Africa

In this routine police procedural monster movie, a detective whose wife has become a "muff diver" investigates a series of brutal voodoo beheadings among the Nigerian community of Miami. The detective (Wayne Crawford) and his colleague Katherine (Kay Lenz) put their own heads on the line in their attempts to track down the culprit, which turns out to be an overgrown, hideous sun demon with a hangover lookalike.

Pumpkinhead (1988)
(aka *Vengeance: The Demon*)
Dir: Stan Winston /USA

A late-80s classic starring Lance Henriksen as a farmer who summons an earth demon to get revenge on the teenagers who accidentally killed his son. But, to do this, he must first head deep into the woods and seek the blessing of old lady Haggis, a reclusive witch who advises him against such drastic action. And sure enough, once Pumpkinhead – a ten foot tall scaly killing machine – is unleashed and begins slaughtering the terrified teens, the distraught father must face up to the consequences of his decision. *Pumpkinhead* is a marvel; a sort of dark fairytale brought to life on screen. It is also beautifully crafted, and director Stan Winston should be commended for never allowing the bloodshed to overshadow the unforgettable storyline.

The Blob (1988)
Dir: Chuck Russell /USA

A faithful remake of the classic 50s B-movie which sticks to the original theme of small-town American teenagers trying to convince the sceptical populace of the arrival of a blob-like invader from another world. This time the blob serves as a genuinely menacing threat, thanks to the vast improvement in budget and special effects since the original was made. The opening scenes of the homeless guy losing his hand, to the *Alligator*-like action in the sewers is tightly constructed and moves at a fair old clip. Director Chuck Russell (the man behind *A Nightmare On Elm Street 3: Dream Warriors*, made in the previous year) pays homage to the first film without crossing over the 'fanboy' threshold, which may well have happened if Rob Zombie got to work on his own remake which he eventually decided against.

Curse of the Blue Lights (1988)
Dir: John Kenry Johnson /USA

A farmer finds a mutilated kitty on his land. His scarecrow then comes to life, foaming at the mouth with yellow bile, and kills him with a shovel. Teens bicker in a car. A trio of overweight ghouls plot in the shadows. Teens track a pair of mysterious blue lights in the woods. They find a frozen creature in the ground called the 'Maldoon Man.' The creature disappears and the cop doesn't believe their story. The teens enter a graveyard mausoleum and discover that a human corpse is being dissolved with acid by the overweight ghouls seen earlier. They're trying to resurrect the Maldoon creature. The kids are spotted and chased out of the graveyard. Things then become even *weirder* when a coin taken from the creature's chest begins to affect the environment, causing objects to levitate. Meanwhile, back in the mausoleum chamber, one of the captured teens is transformed into a snake. The kids take the coin to a witch. She crumbles to her knees at the sight of it. She tells them that the coin is very dangerous as it contains an evil from a dark netherworld. The kids are then picked off, one by one, by the ghouls and their spectral minions while the witch concocts a magic potion in her cauldron which the remaining kids use to battle against a horde of zombies, the Maldoon Man and the fat ghouls.

Heavily inspired by *Children Shouldn't Play With Dead Things* (1972) and EC comics, *Curse of the Blue Lights* is a low-budget horror weirdy which – despite its obvious flaws – is a fun little movie to watch while you're stoned. It has enough green-headed ghouls, macabre reanimated corpses and mystical weirdness to keep viewers occupied for 95 minutes. Things fall apart a little in the third act as the narrative sort of tumbles out of control, but it remains far more engaging than the usual 80s video trash.

And as for the significance of the killer scarecrow and the mysterious blue lights? Who the fuck knows.

Society (1989)
Dir: Brian Yuzna /USA

Many film directors start out in the horror genre as a way of making an immediate impact, and once their credentials are in place they often move on to bigger things, or at least projects that are different (Sam Raimi, Stuart Gordon, Abel Ferrara, et al). Brian Yuzna, however, has always been a true lover of horror films and has always stubbornly stayed within the mushy template of the genre. Even his lesser projects like *The Dentist* and *The Dentist 2* show an unpretentious admiration for the simple mechanics of old skool horror, combined with his love for deranged – but also often sympathetic – monsters, and bold, primary-coloured day-glo aesthetics. He is chiefly remembered today for his racy sequels to *Re-Animator* which heaped on the twitching body parts and sick laughs, but even in his darker films like *Necronomicon* and *Return of the Living Dead III*, his desire to break new ground is always perfectly balanced with a strange satire and morbid sense of fun.

Yuzna's most extraordinary film was his directorial debut, *Society*, one of the many highlights of 80s horror but which remains a much overlooked gem. The plot of *Society* centres on former *Baywatch* boy, Billy Warlock, whose alienation and increasing paranoia makes him afraid and wary of his own family. His friend Blanchard (Tim Bartell) is just as suspicious as Billy, and sets about snooping around the family mansion and gathering audio recordings which seem to suggest that some kind of incestuous orgies are going on. But when Billy's friend dies in a nasty car wreck, the film's hero must continue on his journey alone to find out exactly what is going on, during which he will discover the literal meaning of the word 'butthead' and will get to the guts of the matter as people are literally pulled inside out...

Society is a film which plays on the nightmare of teenage angst, and those feelings of paranoia, persecution, and alienation; not just in society at large, but within the family unit. The film should have propelled Yuzna to the horror A-list but it didn't happen, perhaps because *Society* is also an unashamed attack on bourgeois appetites and the cliquiness of the

Hollywood elite. The special effects were created by Screaming Mad George (of *A Nightmare On Elm Street* fame) whose show-stopping finale has left many viewers gagging in delight and disgust as he graphically obliterates the line between pornography and horror. Surreal, metaphorical, and visually astonishing, this sequence was only made possible with the aid of gallons of KY jelly and tons of special effects goo, and one truly warped imagination. Enjoy!

The Killer (1989)
(Orig title: *Die xue shuang xiong*)
Dir: John Woo /Hong Kong
In the world of John Woo's over-the-top action movies, it seems there's no problem that can't be solved by a hail of bullets. Don't be fooled; *The Killer* is far more than the sum of its plot elements.

Jeffrey Chow (Chow Yun-Fat) is a professional hit man with his own code of ethics and a lethal two-handed draw. Detective Lee (Danny Lee) is a cop at odds with the system: he'd rather get the scum off the streets than play departmental politics. Sydney Fung (Chu Kong), a hit man past his prime, is Jeff's only friend. Jennie (Sally Yeh) is a nightclub singer caught in the crossfire and blinded when Jeff slaughters a room full of gangsters. Guilt-stricken, Jeff befriends and then falls in love with the blind woman. And when he agrees to one last contract killing, with the intention of using the money to pay for a cornea transplant for Jenny, the hit doesn't go off as cleanly as it should, and he gives away his identity. Before long, the criminal underworld – along with detective Lee – vow to hunt him down, using Jennie as bait.

The Killer rings a genuinely delirious set of changes on American movie themes, careening between brutality and mawkish sentiment without missing a beat. Western audiences were almost literally stunned in their seats by the excessive gunplay and extravagance on view; the insistent visual and narrative symmetry, the barely repressed homoeroticism (there are moments of male bonding in this film that looks like the whole thing will descend into some romantic brown-dicking at any moment), the cute comedy of blind Jennie – unaware of the gunplay going on around her – trying to serve tea. One moment Woo's heroes are .44 magnum dervishes, the next they're spinning some outrageous fiction about childhood friendship

and their nicknames for one another – "Tom" and "Jerry". The original title translates as Bloodshed of Two Heroes, and is a more accurate title as the film is just as much about cop Lee as it is the lone 'killer' of the Anglicised namesake.

And the bullets... Ah, the bullets. They fly freely at the drop of a hat, splatter bad guys all over the walls while miraculously missing the protagonists (special credit to the sightless Jennie, who shows a particular flare for dodging speeding projectiles), and generally make the world go round. For Western film fans unfamiliar with Hong Kong gangster films, there's no better introduction. Described by Kim Newman as "a genocidal film with more corpses than *Total Recall* and *Die Hard* combined," *The Killer* is quite simply one of the greatest action movies ever made.

Legend of the Overfiend (1989)
(Orig title: *Urotsukidoji*; aka *Wandering Kid*)
Dir: Hideki Takayama /Japan
Japan is a country obsessed with animation. It's a cartoon culture, and you're never far away from a place where cartoon junkies can get their fix. People read comics, or 'Manga', everywhere; at home, during their lunch breaks, and on the subway. They buy their animated films, or 'anime', in their millions, too. With so many average consumers of cartoons, the market caters for every taste. Each year there are over two billion Manga books sold in Japan. That's almost half of everything printed. If you look at it from a different angle, that's fifteen books per year for every man, woman, and child in Japan. That's a lot of books. And part of this massive market has always been erotic. It started with the woodblock prints in the 17th Century; in amongst the beautiful fabrics and contrasting patterns, genitals are aplenty, and clearly not modelled on the local Samurai, but his horse.

In modern Japan, entrepreneurs were quick to see the opportunities for adult anime. Thus was born the animated feature series *Urotsukidoji*, created strictly for the adult market where it was massively popular. It broke new ground in depicting graphic sex, and initiated a long line of imitators. But when the film first opened, it caused an uproar in Japan. In fact, the Japanese were just as shocked by the film as Western audiences, and it was just as much a landmark title in Japan as it was over here.

Originally released as a serial made up of three episodes – *Chojin Tanjo Hen*, *Chojin Jusatsu Hen*, and *Kanketsu Jigoku* – each running less than an hour, *Legend of the Overfiend* was made up as a compilation comprising much of that material, and re-released as a stand-alone feature. The three original episodes are available uncut on the *Urotsukidoji: Perfect Collection* DVD. *Overfiend* features a typical monster anime plot. You know the kind of thing: a thousand foot high super-being comes down to earth to be reincarnated, destroys the world, and then re-creates it again. Bizarrely, for such a supernatural film, the setting is spookily common place – a city college. There are several candidates for the overfiend (or the person who will father him), and there are also several candidates for the woman who will give birth to the reincarnated overfiend. Meanwhile, ghostly entities, known as Jujin, are keeping an eye on college kid Tatsuo Nagamo, who may be the overfiend (or Chojin), and also protecting him from the Makai, a malignant race of Lovecraftian demons who rape young girls with their long tentacles.

Outrageous, disturbing, and not a little confusing, this bizarre film became the benchmark of provocative animation in the 90s. Like any other porn business, the majority of the viewers for anime erotica are young men. *Legend of the Overfiend* is a sick but clever way of showing not just pornography but also the feelings and fears of an adolescent male. The original author of the film, Toshio Maeda, is a master craftsman at exploiting the moment of standing at the threshold of adulthood. His characters are usually young people, and they see the adult world as a place where everyone is having sex, everyone has power and authority, but they don't. And this triggers a violent reaction.

The Japanese censor is often quite a fussy individual because the job is usually handed out to those who are eased out of the regular police force. And although it isn't law in Japan, there is an unwritten agreement that the censors should avoid showing pubic hair wherever possible, which often results in the use of those optical smudges, or 'pixelations' to blur out any offending pubes on display. It is also standard practice in Japan for censors to blur out the sight of penises on screen. However, *Legend of the Overfiend* found a clever way of avoiding the restrictions by having 50 foot super-beings sprouting strange phallic-like tentacles that penetrate pretty young girls. The tentacles even had glans, but the censors were unable to do a thing about it. And, as if to rub the authorities' face in it, the sequel, *Legend of the Demon Womb* (1993), seemed delighted with its notoriety, and pushed its luck even further with the penis/tentacle ambiguity.

Adding to the controversy was the fact that the animators, knowing that their work was going to be blurred out by the censors, neglected to draw in the pubic hair, and this created more outrage when the uncut version was released and seemed to show apparently under-age youngsters engaging in sexual activities. The BBFC cut over 2 minutes of offensive footage before it was granted an 18 certificate for home video release. Whilst putting together a film show for the British National Science Fiction Convention, Helen McCarthy, co-author of *The Erotic Anime Movie Guide*, opted to screen *Legend of the Overfiend* with an open warning that 'This film will offend everybody.' Yet still, the theatre was packed with those eager to see the notorious film everyone was talking about. And this goes to show how controversy definitely sells.

Indeed, in the wake of *Overfiend*, a whole slew of 'tentacle porn' animation hit the video shelves, with titles such as *Demon Beast Invasion* (1990), *LA Blue Girl* (1992) and *Adventure Kid* (1992-1994), while the *Urotsukidoji* series continued with the equally outrageous *Legend of the Demon Womb*, the two-part *Urotsukidoji III: Return of the Overfiend* (1992-1993), *Urotsukidoji IV: Inferno Road* (1993-1995), the still unreleased *Urotsukidoji V: The Final Chapter* (1996), and the attempted re-hash of the series, *The Urotsuki* (2002). Many of these titles have been heavily censored or banned outright in the UK. The BBFC Annual Report for 1996-1997 condemned the film-makers with the following: 'It is difficult to fathom where such attitudes come from. Male chauvinism is far too mild a term to describe the film-makers' psychology, since many of these cartoons drag misogyny down to the level of atrocity.'

Violent Cop (1989)
(Orig title: *Sono otoko, kyōbō ni tsuki*; その男、凶暴につき)

Dir: Takeshi Kitano /Japan

'Beat' Takeshi Kitano is best known for directing and starring in hard-boiled, minimalist gangster films like *Boiling Point* and *Sonatine*. The latter has its pride of place in Quentin Tarantino's top five favourite movies of all time. His appearance as the ruthless, murderous school teacher in Kinji Fukasaku's *Battle Royale* also raised his profile considerably in the West. Back in the late 80s, however, he was known as a comedian, newspaper columnist and poet. In 1986, a Japanese tabloid paper published pictures of the married Kitano canoodling with another woman. His reaction was to gather together his buddies and storm the paper's headquarters, attacking the staff and causing millions in criminal damage. Somehow, he avoided going to jail, but was later 'kidnapped' by the *yakuza* and forced to have a drink with them. "It can reflect badly on me," he said, "when the *yakuza* go around saying, 'Hey, we like Mr. Kitano." At the height of his powers, Kitano was hosting and appearing in up to eight Japanese TV shows a week, ranging from the familiar *Takeshi's Castle* where he would ride around in an electric buggy shooting contestants with a water cannon, to other more obscure quiz games in which he would drop live scorpions down the underpants of the everyday public, for laughs. He was banned from appearing on the NHK television network in Japan for five years for exposing himself live on TV.

After the motorcycle accident in 1994, which left his face partially paralysed, his film work became increasingly experimental (he also spent his time painting and writing novels), the violence in his work was tempered with warmth and a sentimental sense of humour (see *Hana-Bi*, *Kids Return* and *Kikujiro*). "Films are my hobby," he once said. "I make films for Takeshi Kitano, not the public. For me, it's not about making money [...] People say I have mellowed since my accident and maybe they are right, but I've always had a dual personality. I also like to shock other people's expectations. Before, people talked about the violence in my films. Always the violence. Now they say, 'Hah! Takeshi has gone soft!' That's why I made *Brother* [*an American-Japanese gangster flick set in L.A. with lots of death and carnage. Ed.*]

after *Kikujiro* – to show that I am not part of the establishment. Then I decided to make *Dolls*. Who knows, maybe my next film will be the toughest one yet."

His next film was *Zatōichi*, a blood-drenched Samurai epic. But to this day, Kitano's toughest film remains his directorial debut, *Violent Cop*, a film which starts off in a whimsical, light-hearted manner with Kitano's usual humorous turn. But by the time the end credits roll, however, viewers will be stunned by how dark and downbeat this film plummets during the 98-minute running time. *Violent Cop* stars Kitano himself as Kajima, a police Lt. who walks into a family home and roughs up a delinquent kid who has been tormenting a homeless man with his friends. This type of surreal, day-to-day combating of crime takes on a darker shade every ten minutes or so, especially once Kajima's sister is lured into the criminal underworld and is kept there against her will, gang-raped and hooked on heroin. Things become increasingly grim and desperate until we reach the pessimistic, bleak ending.

With its casual brutality interspersed with scenes of mundane serenity, *Violent Cop* is unlike any other cop movie you'll ever see. Usually, in action-style police movies, chase scenes are accompanied by adrenaline-fuelled pounding rock or percussive-heavy music on the soundtrack. Not so here. With *Violent Cop* we get smooth jazz piano and saxophone during a scene in which a criminal beats up three cops and then flees out the window before attacking more cops with a baseball bat. The overall effect is downright surreal, and a true masterpiece of world cinema.

The Cook, the Thief, His Wife and Her Lover (1989)
Dir: Peter Greenaway /UK

"I'm gonna kill him, and I'm gonna... EAT HIM!!" Perhaps Greenaway's finest film to date, and one of the highlights of 90s cinema, *The Cook, the Thief, His Wife, and Her Lover* centres on Le Hollandais, a lush restaurant owned by gangster Albert Spica (Michael Gambon) whose wife Georgina (Helen Mirren) has an affair with Michael (Alan Howard), a mild-mannered bookish type, before all hell breaks loose. The film boasts excellent performances all round, but Gambon steals the show as Mr. Spica, a foul, obnoxious, ignorant brute whose verbal tirades are blackly hilarious and whose poisonous presence soils the atmosphere of any room he's in. Every time he opens his mouth something vulgar comes out (an accusation he amusingly levels at one of his cronies). There's superb camera work courtesy of veteran DP Sacha Vierney, Jean Paul Gaultier provides the costumes which compliments the decor of each luschious room in the restaurant, and Michael Nyman contributes one of his finest scores.

Often described as a 'Jacobean tragedy,' the film presents a simple story of adultery, jealousy and revenge. However, this is all just window dressing. The film is constructed around the four characters of the title, the separate rooms of the restaurant (each perhaps representing a different historical era), and the central themes connecting food and faeces, mouth and anus, and sex and death, which affectively puts the film in similar territory as Marco Ferreri's *La grande bouffe* (1973). Apparently, Greenaway himself identifies with the cook; by keeping a dignified distance, he observes the growing hostilities, and is ready to spring into action and rescue the lovers from the Thief's wrath by hiding them away in a refrigerated truck.

The director's fondness for structural symmetry is in evidence here with the Lover and Thief characters who represent polar opposites; one is calm and gentle, and the other is loud and aggressive. Mild-mannered Michael doesn't utter a word for the first half-hour or so of the film, and he is later shown to be rational and smart. Mr. Spica, on the other hand, seems to think aloud, and his thoughts are anything but reasonable or even coherent. In the end, Greenaway reveals the Thief to be far more than just another petty criminal; he presents us with a genuinely depraved monster. Many critics read the film as a heavy-handed critique of the greed and consumerism of the Thatcher/Reagan years, but actually the director's wrath seems to be aimed at a target that encompasses far more than mere contemporary culture and politics. Early on, Michael is seen reading a book on the French Revolution (perhaps Edmund Burke's famous critique?), and this enables viewers to see Mr. Spica as a representative of the peasant revolt and subsequent Terror. Thus, the Thief represents Michael's worst nightmare – a big, dumb villain with the mob on his side, who can't even pronounce the names of the expensive dishes he orders for his feast.

Due to the outrageous violence, sex, and nudity, this film (along with Pedro Almodovar's *Tie Me Up! Tie Me Down!*), was one of the first to receive an NC-17 rating in America, prompting Blockbuster Video to destroy all of their uncut copies and replace it with the R-rated alternative, which loses a whopping thirty minutes of footage. Now, the R-rated version implies a more perverse ending than Greenaway had intended; during the cannibalistic finale in which Georgina forces her husband at gunpoint to eat Michael's dead body, she suggests that he "try the cock, you know where it's been," then there's a cut showing Spica eating a piece of meat from a fork, with the audience believing that he is eating Michael's penis. Whereas in the uncut version we know that that particular piece of meat came from Michael's hip area (David Cronenberg's *The Brood* suffered a similar glitch in narrative when British censors demanded cuts to the scene in which Samantha Eggar gave birth to a furious humanoid creature and proceeded to lick away the blood, with the cut version implying that she was eating her child!). However, all censorship hassles are over now, and *The Cook* is widely available on DVD in all its uncut, NC-17 glory.

Psycho Cop (1989)
Dir: Wallace Potts /USA

Teens on summer vacation are targeted by a giggling, Satan-worshipping cop. Bloody awful VHS trash with lame kills and terrible one-liners. Makes *Return of the Family Man* (1989) and *Dr. Giggles* (1993) look like master works. Unbelievably, a sequel followed, *Psycho Cop Returns* (1993) – both films have long since been confined to the VHS dungeon.

The Freeway Maniac (1989)
Dir: Paul Winters /USA

80s video trashola about a psychotic killer, who – institutionalised since embarking on a childhood killing spree – escapes from the nuthouse, leaving a trail of bodies behind as he heads off to a remote movie set in the middle of the California desert. He also has his sights set on a dumb blonde. Like Michael Myers before him, this maniac has superhuman – or plain old retard – strength, and is impervious to bullets. Once the film hits third gear, it's so ridiculous and over-the-top, you'll realise you're watching a spoof on crappy slasher movies disguised as a crappy slasher movie... Or, at least that's what *I* got from it. If that's right, then it's a bloody good disguise.

Meet the Feebles (1989)
Dir: Peter Jackson /New Zealand

A bizarre puppet parody set backstage at a variety show where a lonely hedgehog falls in love with a poodle. Meanwhile, the boss of the theatre is a cheating walrus. There is also a hedonistic rabbit who contracts AIDS, a paparazzi fly who literally eats shit, a rat photographer who appears in a Vietnam flashback, and a bunch of musical numbers and sex and gore. Entertaining and certainly different, *Feebles* is a tad more spiteful than funny (a zen puppet gets its head literally stuck up its own arse, for example), but this is essential viewing for those interested in twisted, off-beat films. The project was fuelled by Jackson's frustrations of being unable to secure the funding needed for *Braindead* (1992).

Down In It (1989)
Dir: Eric Zimmerman /USA

On the music video front, *Down In It* was a promo by Nine Inch Nails that was mired in 'snuff movie' controversy. The video depicts frontman Trent Reznor ascending the stairs of a deserted building, followed by a couple of band members. And when he reaches the top, he either falls or jumps to his death. The directors used helium balloons to lift the camera into the air for the overhead shots, and the balloons were secured to the ground with rope. Somehow the balloons got loose, and the camera – which contained raw, unedited footage of the shoot – drifted over 200 miles from Chicago to Michigan where it landed in a farmer's field. The person who found the camera looked at the tape and, thinking it was real death footage, alerted the police. The FBI launched an investigation under the assumption that the tape contained footage of a genuine suicide. They even declared it to be a 'snuff film.' And even when Trent Reznor was identified as the man on the tape, and that he was still very much among the living, the band's manager had to convince the authorities that none of the musicians were involved in Satanism or any kind of illegal activity.

Out of the Body (1989)
Dir: Brian Trenchard-Smith /Australia

Tessa Humphries returns again after the similarly-themed *Cassandra* (1986), for another *Eyes of Laura Mars*-inspired psychic killer movie. This is also directed by Brian Trenchard-Smith, who co-wrote *Cassandra*. After a spate of killings in which the victim's eyeballs are removed, musician David Gaze believes he may share psychic links with the lunatic who commits his deadly deeds via astral projection. His attempts to inform the police of the killer's plans and his warnings to future victims leaves him labelled as both a weirdo and prime suspect. However, as the killings continue and Gaze's 'predictions' are proven correct, he feels he has no alternative but to track down the killer himself. *Out of the Body* is decently made, but anyone familiar with those films mentioned above will know exactly how the narrative will pan out within the first ten minutes. On the plus side, the film does have a nice giallo feel to it, sharing links with Argento's *Deep Red* (1975) and Lamberto Bava's *A Blade in the Dark* (1983), films in which musicians are drawn into solving murder mysteries. For an even stranger twist on the theme, check out *Spasms* (1983), in which Oliver Reed shares psychic links with a demonic killer snake.

Shocker (1989)
Dir: Wes Craven /USA

Serial Killer, Horace Pinker (Mitch Pileggi), is executed by electric chair and returns in the form of an electric power source to continue on his killing spree. A college football kid, equipped with psychic abilities after bumping his head on a goalpost, teams up with a detective to somehow put an end to the killings. But it's far from easy as Pinker now has the power to shift his being from person to person, literally possessing the bodies of anyone in contact to carry out his evil deeds... *Shocker* is an enjoyable if unremarkable flick. It's lively and action-packed, and moves from one absurd sequence to the next with no concern for practicalities or logic. In one sequence, the teenage hero is pursued by Pinker (in the guise of a cop) through a park, and he is shot at at least two dozen times with a handgun. Of course, every shot misses him while bystanders are picked off with ease. Anyway, minor annoyances aside, *Shocker* is a fun little film if you go in with low expectations. There's a streak of goofy humour throughout, and the film shares the surreal, 'plastic reality' dream-world style with Craven's earlier *A Nightmare On Elm Street* (1984). And, for once, here is a Craven film that doesn't attempt to turn an entire sub-genre on its head in an 'oh so clever, Mr. Craven' sort of way. How modest of him. Look out for bit-parts and cameos from Craven, Heather Langenkamp and Ted Raimi.

Battle Heater (1989)

(aka *Electric Kotatsu Horror*; Orig title: *Batoru Hita*)
Dir: Joji Iida /Japan
Another in the line of homicidal appliance movies which includes deadly fridges in *The Refrigerator* (1991) and *Attack of the Killer Refridgerator* (1990), a homicidal vacuum cleaner in *Tabloid* (1985), a deadly lawn-mower in *Blades* (1989), deadly electrical sockets in *Pulse* (1988), an evil elevator in *Down* (2001), and even deadly mobile phones in *One Missed Call* (2003). From Japan we have *Battle Heater*, a fun film about an electric heater possessed by a demon. It eventually sprouts creepy arms and devours people in an apartment building with plenty of assorted weirdos and killers in residence to keep it well fed for an entire running time. Goofy fun with a touch of satire.

Relentless (1989)

Dir: William Lustig /USA
A New York cop relocates to L.A., and his first assignment is to help track down a vicious serial killer who seems to be selecting his victims at random from the phone book. The killer turns out to be the son of a legendary tough guy cop who had so traumatised his boy by bullying him into a psychotic mess. He now talks to his father's picture, and continues to carry out 'orders' through the voices in his head. This film is disappointingly ordinary from the director of the notorious slasher, *Maniac* (1980). Perhaps director Lustig was aiming more towards the mainstream this time around. But despite the off-beat humour and east coast/west coast rivalries, *Relentless* is a routine police procedural picture.

Skinheads: The Second Coming of Hate (1989)

Dir: Greyon Clark /USA
In this little-seen film, the neo-Nazis are confined to the wilderness of the forest, in an obvious point about their ideology existing on the fringes of society. These Nazis run amok in the area causing as much chaos as possible. As expected, the skins here serve as nothing but caricatures of the dumb thugs the media likes to label them as. There's 'Brains' (Dennis Ott), the

big dumb oaf of the group who serves as muscle; there's also Damon (Brian Brophy), the leader of the group. And he serves as the intense outcast whose simmering rage and mental fallout runs much deeper than mere racism. The other members of the gang do all they can to impress Damon, with one of them going as far as having a swastika tattooed on his forehead in order to win acceptance. They drive around in their 'Death Van' that has a large swastika spray painted on the side. After shooting dead a black guy, they hide out at their shared apartment before going on to cause more trouble with college kids at a remote diner. It's no spoiler if I tell you that all does not end well for the skinheads – they eventually come up against rugged mountain man, Chuck Connors. One of them even ends up as lunch for a grizzly bear... Director, Greydon Clark (of *Joysticks*), turns a low-budget to his advantage by concentrating on just a handful of characters and a limited setting. And, perhaps more than any of his other films, he certainly had his exploitation cap on while working on *Skinheads*; 'Obviously, these are repulsive people with repulsive thinking,' he said in an interview. 'There are some friends of mine that said, "Aw, Greydon, why do you want to do a picture about skinheads?" I said, "Well, come on, they're not going to be the heroes of the picture." I was interested to see if I could make that political statement and still do an interesting action thriller.' So, basically, he wanted to condemn the repulsive skins while riding on their jocks for 90 minutes.

Amok Train (1989)

(aka *Beyond the Door III*)
Dir: Jeff Kwitny /Italy /Yugoslavia /USA
American students on a trip to Europe meet up with their professor (Bo Svenson) in Belgrade. He takes them out to the Serbian countryside and introduces them to a small pagan community. However, the professor is actually an instrument of the Devil, and the community is just a facade for a Satanic cult. The student's cabin is set ablaze after dark, and the handful of survivors who manage to escape climb on board a moving train whose strange passengers sit in deathly silence. Turns out that one of the students, Beverly (Mary Kohnert), has been 'promised' to Satan, and the train becomes possessed by a demonic spirit which sets up death traps to kill off the characters... This Italian co-production was one of the last big-

budget horror films from producer Ovidio G. Assonitis, and one that was always destined to sink with little trace on home video. Of course, it's a silly but entertaining movie filled with ludicrous dialogue, a cast made up of mostly unknown international actors, and a hilarious Satanic ritual at the end. The best part though is the train itself as it veers off the tracks, hurtles at full speed through a densely wooded area, and even crosses a lake! The film was marketed in America under the title *Beyond the Door III*, implying that it was a second sequel to Assonitis and Robert Barrett's *Exorcist* rip-off, *Beyond the Door* (1974). (But at least *Amok Train* has a Satanic element in the plot, unlike Mario Bava's *Shock* (1977) which was released in the States under the title *Beyond the Door II*). VHS releases were presented in ugly, pan-and-scan transfers with much of Adolfo Batoli's superb scope photography lopped out of view. The tapes were also heavily censored. Shriek Show's DVD release in the late 00s was a revelation as they offered a crisp transfer presented in the original aspect ratio, and with all the gory moments reinstated, such as the train driver being run over and decapitated, a girl tearing her own face off, and another character torn in half between train carriages.

Slash Dance (1989)
Dir: James Shyman /USA
A woman undercover, whose "tits are too nice to be a cop," tracks down a serial killer who has been picking off auditionees for a musical. This is an extremely low-budget rehash of Mario Bava's *Blood and Black Lace* (1964), and suffers badly from extraneous exposition, blatant time-padding sequences and spandex overload.

Freakshow (1989)
Dir: Constantino Magnatta /Canada
A mass shooting outside a cinema compels a TV news reporter to investigate. She chances upon the 'Freakshow,' a strange museum whose proprietor tells her a quartet of macabre tales. The first one sees a heroin addict resort to murder and poodle chasing to get his fix. In the second story, a pizza delivery guy stops by at 1313 Bram Stoker Blvd, a large crooked mansion which houses a coven of vampires. Next up, a catatonic girl finds herself in an autopsy room after as it was presumed she had died of a drug overdose. And finally, we get zombies tearing up a golf course in search of the dirt that was stolen from their graves (!). It's strongly hinted throughout the film that the museum's proprietor has the power to hypnotise people into committing heinous acts, such as the cinema shooting at the start. And the film ends with the TV reporter now under his demonic influence. It then cuts to a cinema audience that – presumably – is about to step outside to be massacred by her, which would bring the narrative full circle, as is popular in the anthology horror tradition, dating back to the classic *Dead of Night* (1945).

Freakshow is a fairly ambitious little movie but it never steps beyond trashy fun. None of the stories are anything new to horror fans, and the execution of the tales concentrated more on fancy lighting and a tongue-in-cheek attitude rather than a serious attempt to unnerve its viewers. However, the film is worth a watch today if only for the murder sequence which shares striking similarities to the murder scene of the fat, obnoxious TV guy in *Henry – Portrait of a Serial Killer* (1986) with the stabbed hand and the television set plonked on his head ("plug it in"). Except here it's a microwave that is crashed onto the victim's head and is used to cook his brains.

Elves (1989)
Dir: Jeff Mandel /USA
An evil elf is resurrected from the earth and goes on a killing spree at a department store during the Christmas holidays. A group of teens, an old bearded guy, and a group of shady gangster types spend the night in the store battling against each other while the elf picks 'em off with a switchblade. This is a woeful Yuletide monster movie which moves along slower than a snail on valium, and makes 89 minutes feel like 3 hours. Turns out that the elf is a product of a Nazi experiment to create a silent army of ghouls. And when the chain-smoking hero discovers that the elf plans to rape a virgin on Christmas Eve in order to produce a master race, he sets out to destroy the thing and save the day... Those who are into 'so-bad-it's-good' movies will find much to be amused by here, but those looking for a decent Christmas horror will have to look elveswhere – ho ho.

976-Evil (1989)
Dir: Robert Englund /USA
Trailer quote: "A real man has the nerves to take what he deserves." A victimised nerd, Hoax (Stephen Geoffreys), who is obsessed with his cousin, Spike, finds himself drawn to an evil phone line that can change the future of its callers. Hoax then becomes empowered with the forces of darkness, and his megalomania comes to the fore as he dispatches the bullies who made his life hell. *976-Evil* is the directorial debut of *A Nightmare On Elm Street*'s Robert Englund, and he delivers a pretty decent – if formulaic – slice of late 80s American horror.

House III: The Horror Show (1989)
(aka *The Horror Show*)
Dir: James Isaac /USA
Detective McCarthy (Lance Henriksen) witnesses a notorious serial killer, Max Jenke (Brion James) being executed by electric chair. He hopes to put his recurring nightmares to an end with a sense of closure after watching the scumbag fry. But the execution is horribly botched, and the spirit of the unrepentant killer is somehow revived and set loose to kill again via electricity... If the *House* series couldn't get any more inconsistent, along came part three which is basically your typical 'cop v supernatural serial killer' flick in the same vein as *Shocker* (1988), *The First Power* (1990) and *Seed* (2007). This is perhaps the best of the bunch as a traumatised cop tries to rebuild his life while suffering from hallucinations and flashbacks to the dark days when the killer was still at large. When Jenke makes his return, it puts McCarthy's family life – not to mention his sanity – under severe strain. This is also the bloodiest and most adult-themed entry in the *House* series, with lots of disturbing details and graphic kills. The MPAA enforced a number of cuts to ensure the R-rating. Among them were the removal of scenes in which blood spills from a birthday cake, McCarthy exposes his heart after ripping open his chest, and another character is torn in half. Oddly enough, the scene which shows a little girl being decapitated and her severed head tossed into McCarthy's lap made it into the R-rated cut. To this day there hasn't been an uncut release of *House III*, and it remains absent as a stand alone DVD release. The murky-looking, pan-and-scan VHS and Hong Kong laserdisc releases are very difficult to find nowadays. DVD/Blu-Ray companies

take note.

Angel Cop (1989-1990)
(Orig title: *Enzeru Koppu*)
Dir: Ichiro Itano /Japan
A six-part anime series about an elite police force that is at war with a dangerous communist terrorist organisation called The Red May. Supernatural forces show up, seemingly on the side of the cops, but by episode three the mysterious entities have other motives... An above-average anime for adults, with blood, guts, torture and foul language. The storyine gets a little incoherent towards the end, but anime heads will no doubt know what to expect. The series wasn't released in the West until the mid-90s when an English dub vversion was unleashed on the UK on VHS (in monthly installments). The DVD box set was released a decade later.

Tales From the Crypt (1989-1996)
(aka *HBO's Tales From the Crypt*)
Dir: -Various- /USA
An American horror anthology series made for the HBO cable channel. Running for seven seasons totalling 93 episodes, the show was based on the gory EC comics from the 50s of the same name (plus a range of other comics, including *The Vault of Horror*, *Crypt of Terror*, and *Haunt of Fear*). Each show was presented by the 'Cryptkeeper', a cackling skull-faced puppet that introduced tales in which characters made bad decisions which inevitably led to their gruesome deaths. Memorable episodes include '*You, Murderer*' (season 6, episode 15) in which Humphrey Bogart and Alfred Hitchcock made 'cameo' appearances thanks to the magic of digital technology. It was also directed by co-producer Robert Zemeckis. Other memorable episodes include '*Cutting Cards*', '*The Switch*' and '*Carrion Death*'. The show's broadcast on cable allowed it to be exempt from the strict censorship of regular network television, and this meant that things like graphic violence, bad language and nudity could flourish (though re-runs on regular networks were often censored). Episodes were sometimes directed by established horror film-makers like John Frankenheimer, William Friedkin, Walter Hill, Tobe Hooper and Freddie Francis (Francis also directed the Amicus film, *Tales From the Crypt* in 1972).

Special guest directors also showed up,

including Michael J. Fox, Tom Hanks and Arnold Schwarzenegger, the latter two even making cameo appearances in the show. Numerous spin-offs were made, including movies (*Demon Knight* [1995], *Bordello of Blood* [1996] and *Ritual* [2002]), a Saturday morning cartoon (*Tales From the Cryptkeeper*, 1993), a kiddies game show (*Secrets of the Cryptkeeper's Haunted House*, 1996-1997), a sci-fi variant of the original show (*Perversions of Science*, 1997) and even a radio series.

First broadcast in the summer of 1989, season one gets off to a frying start with Walter Hill's *The Man Who Was Death*, in which Bill Saddler stars as a State executioner whose job it is to pull the lever on the electric chair. When the death penalty is abolished, he loses his job, and he sees the justice system go to pot with murderers walking free from court. Outraged at what he sees as judicial weakness, he resorts to vigilante action, electrocuting to death those he feels have escaped justice. However, karma eventually catches up with him ("Don't worry, boys and girls, I'm sure he never knew watt hit him. Hee hee")... In the seasonal farce, *And All Through the Night* – directed by Zemeckis from a script by Fred Dekker – a woman kills her husband on Christmas Eve by smashing his head in with a fire poker. She plans on fleeing the scene and meeting up with her illicit lover. However, an evil Sanata Claus shows up wielding an axe... This episode was based on the same *Vault of Horror* comic that formed the basis of the Joan Collins segment of Freddie Francis' 70s version of *Tales From the Crypt*. The best episode of season one is undoubtedly Richard Donner's *Dig That Cat... He's Real Gone*, in which a meddling scientist conducts experiments on a homeless man and succeeds in giving him nine lives by transfusing his mortality with a cat. Together they hit the road to fortune as part of a macabre carnival act, astounding audiences with death-defying stunts – drowning, hanging, electro-cution, etc – ("Maybe this dying shit's taking years off my life"). However, it isn't long before greed and literal backstabbing muddies his count of how many lives he actually has left... In the Faustian *Only Sin Deep*, a street hooker called Miss Vane is desperate to live the high life. So she robs and murders her pimp. And when she tries to sell his gold, the owner of the pawn shop instead gives her $10,000 to 'capture' her beauty in a wax cast of her face. And as she spends a few months in

the lap of luxury with the man of her dreams, she notices that her pretty looks are fading fast... In Tom Holland's *Lover Come Hack to Me*, newly-weds Amanda Plummer and Stephen Shellen spend a rain-soaked honeymoon evening stuck in an old dark house where competing murder plots go head to head with a large inheritance at stake... And finally, in Mary Lambert's *Collection Completed*, M. Emmet Walsh stars as a recently retired grumpy old man who finds himself a new hobby to deal with his wife's fondness for taking in stray pets...

Season two (1990) gets off to a great start with *Dead Right* in which Demi Moore stars as a hot barmaid. She allows herself to be 'wooed' into a relationship with a large, overweight man after her psychic assures her that he will come into a fortune. And though she finds him repulsive, she sticks around, spurred on by the psychic's vision that he will die a violent death shortly after they marry. However, destiny doesn't quite go according to her wishes... Arnold Schwarzenegger pops up next to direct *The Switch* – he also makes a cameo appearance in the intro – in which an old millionaire takes drastic measures to restore his youth so that he can win the heart of a much younger woman, with disastrous consequences... Walter Hill returns with *Cutting Cards*, a classic episode starring Lance Henriksen and Kevin Tighe as a pair of stubborn old gamblers who agree to settle their differences with intense games of Russian Roulette and 'chop poker.' This episode was the inspiration for the Tarantino segment in the anthology film, *Four Rooms* (1995), and also includes an appearance from *Crypt* regular, Roy Brocksmith as a bartender. Chris Walas' *'Til Death* sees a wealthy landowner use a voodoo potion to win the lust of a highly-strung English aristocrat. However, when he causes her to overdose on the horny potion, her corpse breaks out of the ground and molests him. The bumbling fool does all he can to destroy the ghoul, but even when she catches fire, her charred corpse still wants nookie ("So much for 'burning desire,'" hee hee)... In *Three's a Crowd*, a man feels that he is losing his wife to his rich best friend. The three of them go on holiday together, and the paranoia brings him to breaking point. The ending of this episode is especially horrific. Next up, Fred Dekker takes to the director's chair for *The Thing From the Grave*, in which a fashion photographer finds himself attracted to a beautiful model. She's attracted to him too, but the problem is she's already in a relationship with her manager, an uber-arsehole. However, their passion for each other is so great that they end up fucking anyway, and so the boyfriend lures the photographer into a death trap and a shallow grave. He then sets up an even more elaborate revenge for the girl who betrayed him. But little does he know that he's in for a ghoulish surprise of his own... In *The Sacrifice*, an insurance agent murders an arrogant client so that he can collect the money and steal his wife. And all seems to be running smoothly until Michael Ironside shows up to blackmail him... In *For Cryin' Out Loud*, the owner of a rock club attempts to steal $1 million in cash from a charity concert fund. He even commits murder to cover his tracks. However, his conscience – voiced by comedian Sam Kinison – delights in tormenting him every step of the way... Tom Holland's *Four-Sided Triangle* sees a young Patricia Arquette as a confused farm girl who is in love with a scarecrow, and is forced to defend herself against her lecherous boss and his wife... Richard Donner's *The Ventriloquist's Dummy* – written for the screen by Frank Darabont – stars Bobcat Goldthwait as an aspiring showman who seeks the advice of a retired master. However, the old man holds a dark secret under his glove... The first weak entry in the series is *Judy, You're Not Yourself Today*, in which a vain housewife has her body stolen by a doorstep cosmetics rep via a magic necklace... Much better is Jack Sholder's blackly funny *Fitting Punishment* which stars Moses Gunn as an evil, penny-pinching mortician whose orphaned nephew comes to stay with him. The old man shows the kid how to cut corners to keep the business running, but his evil ways eventually come back to haunt him... In *Korman's Kalamity*, male fertility pills work wonders at firing up the imagination of a comic book artist. But there also happens to be monstrous side-effects... *Lower Berth* is another below average episode that centres on a carnival freak show host who is duped into buying the cursed remains of a 4000-year-old Egyptian mummy... Much better is *Mute Witness to Murder*, in which Patricia Clarkson witnesses a husband murder his wife in the opposite building. She immediately collapses in a mute and catatonic state. Her husband finds her on the balcony and calls for a doctor. And when the doc shoes up, he turns out to be the same man

who has just killed his wife... The last three episodes of season two are rather silly schedule-fillers – *Television Terror* is about a reality TV show broadcast live from a haunted house, *My Brother's Keeper* charts the fall-out of siamese twins, with very distinct personalities, who go to war over their surgical separation, and in *The Secret*, an orphaned child is sent to live with a weird, childless couple in a huge mansion.

Broadcast throughout the summer of 1991, season three contains fourteen episodes starting with *Loved to Death* – which echoes an earlier episode, *'Til Death* – in which a screenwriter uses a magic potion to win the heart of an attractive neighbour he's obsessed with ("Miranda, I'm fucked-out!"). It was followed by another classic episode, *Carrion Death*, which stars Kyle MacLachlan as an armed robber fleeing to Mexico with a motorcycle cop in close pursuit. Without giving away any spoilers, it's worth noting here that the criminal makes some incredibly dumb decisions in his efforts to be free, but that's perhaps the whole point; he fashions a DIY axe, but uses it to strike the wrong area. And also, the key to freedom is right there the whole time in the dead guy's gut... Anyway, next up Michael J. Fox serves as guest director on *The Trap*, a tale in which an obnoxious man fakes his own death with the help of his wife and brother in order to collect the $500,000 life insurance payout. However, the wife and brother have a thing for each other, and plot a very different outcome... Another great episode is *Abra Cadaver* which opens with a brilliant practical joke in an autopsy room. But the laughs soon turn to horror when the victim suffers a heart attack. Cut to years later, and we learn that the prankster and the victim are brothers who both work in medical research. And the victim decides to get some payback on his little bro... In *Top Billing*, a struggling actor hits rock bottom when he is evicted from his apartment and his girlfriend moves in with another man. He auditions for the role of Hamlet in a run-down theatre, but snaps and becomes a mad murderer when his acting rival lands the part instead of him... In Tobe Hooper's *Dead Wait*, a tale of greed, voodoo and double-crossing, a petty thug (James Remar) gains the trust of a wealthy plantation owner (John Rhys-Davis). The thug manages to steal a valuable black pearl, but a voodoo sorceress (Whoopi Goldberg) leads him into a deadly trap... Elliot Silverstein's spoofy *The Reluctant Vampire* stars Malcolm McDowell as an age-old bloodsucker with a heart. He passes the time by working the night shift as a security officer at a blood bank, and helps himself to the bags of plasma which he drinks from a cocktail glass. Mr. Longtooth's morality, however, is put to the test when the secretary comes onto him... This episode, for all its silliness, has some good ideas, such as the holy water pistols, Michael Berryman as a bumbling vampire hunter, and McDowell's fangs which jut out like pointy erections every time the secretary embraces him... John Harrison's *Easel Kill Ya* stars Tim Roth as a struggling painter who accidentally kills a noisy neighbour. The death inspires a painting which he sells for $20,000, and so for further inspiration he engineers a few more fatal mishaps. But when he tries to save the life of an art student friend, he makes a grave mistake ("Now *that's* a still life, hee hee")... In *Undertaking Palor*, a group of teens break into a mortuary to film a dead body. However, they also stumble upon a murder conspiracy and a mad mortician who beats the corpses with a mallet. The following day, one of the boy's fathers is killed by the crooks, so they grab a video camera and head back to the mortuary with the intention of securing some video evidence. But it isn't easy as the deranged mortician thinks nothing of pouring embalming fluid into the chest cavities of victims that aren't even dead yet... In *Mournin' Mess*, a womanising journalist investigates a spate of killings among the city's homeless. And while digging for clues, he falls into a literal underground conspiracy run by bloodthirsty, bald-headed ghouls that pose as members of a homeless charity organisation... Russell Mulcahy's *Split Second* – written for the screen by Richard Matheson – concerns the boss of a logging firm (Brion James) whose jealous streak gets out of control when his attractive wife turns the heads of his lumberjack workers. A new employee is seduced by the bored wife, and when the boss catches them together he beats the man with an axe, blinding him. After his recovery, the young man's workmates help him to get bloody revenge on the couple in a macabre stunt at a log-cutting tournament... In Walter Hill's *Deadline*, an alcoholic reporter meets a mysterious woman called Vicky in a bar. He quits drinking to show her how serious he is, but she insists on keeping their relationship as a casual fling. One night he

witnesses a cafe owner murder his wife, and after listening to the murderer's story of how his wife would pick up random guys from bars for one-night-stands, he realises that the victim is Vicky. But he also realises that she's not quite dead. And his sense of betrayal overwhelms him as he reaches for her throat ("What some people won't do for a good 'stiff one,' hee hee")... In *Spoiled*, a mad scientist who has been working on reanimating a rabbit, discovers that his fantasist wife has been shagging the cable guy. So he subjects them both to a prolonged surgical procedure in the basement whereby he swaps their heads around and brings them back to life so that they can marvel at his handiwork... The final episode of season three is *Yellow* – it's also longer than usual at 38 minutes – set in France during World War 1. The son of a general (Eric Douglas) is sent on a risky mission to prove that he isn't a coward. However, his cowardly conduct leads to his fellow soldiers being killed. He is court marshalled and sentenced to death by firing squad. However, on the eve of his execution, his father visits him with a cunning plan... *Yellow* also stars Lance Henriksen as an ill-fated soldier, Dan Ackroyd as the General's right hand man, and Kirk Douglas as the father who is determined that his son will be remembered as a gallant man. This episode is different in tone from the usual *Crypt* fare; the tongue-in-cheek style is nowhere to be seen, and instead we get a poignant and sobering tale that ends the season on a sombre note.

The disappointing season 4 (1992) sees the rot setting in with stories watered-down with toothless scripts and weak endings to make the show more palatable for mainstream audiences. Things get off to a choppy start with Tom Hanks' *None But the Lonely Heart*, about an evil man who has made his fortune by bumping off his wives for the inheritance money. He sets his sights on a new companion, a rich elderly widow. He worms his way into her life, and she falls head over heels for him. And after they marry, he puts his murderous plan into place, but comes to a sticky end in a mausoleum. Look out for cameos from Hank's himself as a victim who has his head rammed into a television screen, and Sugar Ray Leonard as a gravedigger... In the disappointing *This'll Kill Ya*, Dylan McDermott takes revenge on his colleagues after they inject him with an experimental virus that has no antidote... Not much better is William Friedkin's *On a*

Deadman's Chest, which sees a rock singer (in a band called 'Exorcist') head to the rough side of town to get a tattoo. However, he hates it. And when he undergoes surgery to have it removed, it just comes back. In the end, the awful tattoo drives him to madness and murder... The rut continues with *Seance*, a tale in which con artists end up killing one of their marks, so they turn their attentions onto the victim's blind wife instead... Slightly better is *Beauty Rest*, in which an actress (Mimi Rogers), jealous of her roommate's success at landing roles, accidentally kills her. She then develops a taste for murder, and bumps off another rival before landing a dream job that soon becomes a nightmare... In *What's Cookin'*, Christopher Reeve serves up his mean landlord's (Meat Loaf's) remains as steaks so that he can keep his struggling diner in business ("The restaurant business is a little hard to swallow")... In Peter Medak's *New Arrival*, David Warner stars as a radio psychologist who visits the home of a mother (Zelda Rubinstein) whose mentally disturbed daughter leads him to a grim discovery in the attic... Richard Donner's western-themed *Showdown* – adapted to the screen by Frank Darabont – follows an outlaw as he shoots dead a Texas ranger and meets a strange Irishman in a bar who offers him a 'medical tonic' that he is assured will quicken his gun-drawing reflexes. However, as soon as he drinks it, his deceased victims appear around him and send him to hell... Tom Holland returns to the director's seat with the lacklustre *King of the Road*, in which Brad Pitt plays a cocky young road racer who meets his match when he messes with the daughter of a road cop, who is also legendary himself behind the wheel. And all leads to a fiery finale ("Now that's what *I* call 'burning rubber,' hee hee")... Next up, John Frankenheimer joins the fray with *Maniac at Large*, in which Blythe Danner plays a nervous librarian who believes that she will be the next victim of a serial killer that has been making the local headlines... In *Split Personality*, Joe Pesci stars as a con man who gets more than he bargains for when he attempts to scam a couple of reclusive billionaire twins... *Strung Along* sees a puppeteer with heart problems – and who also communicates with his doll – suspect his wife of cheating on him. The final image of this episode is brilliantly creepy... In *Werewolf Concerto*, a lycanthrope is on the loose on the grounds of a luxury hotel, and the guests –

which include Charles Fleischer, Timothy Dalton, Beverly D'Angelo and Dennis Farina – have to work out who among them is the beastie... And finally, in Elliot Silverstein's *Curiosity Killed*, a bickering old couple (Kevin McCarthy and Margot Kidder) are camping in the woods. Another couple on the trip lets the old man into a secret concerning a youth potion, and Kidder suspects the men of murder...

Broadcast in the winter of 1993, season five sees a return to form for the series, and includes a couple of gems. First up is *Death of Some Salesmen*, in which Ed Begley, Jr stars as a con man who goes around scamming grieving relatives, and eventually targets the wrong house. This episode is perhaps most notable for the appearance of Tim Curry who plays three roles as members of the redneck family... In Kyle MacLachlan's *As Ye Sow*, a man employs the services of private detectives to snoop on his wife as he is convinced she is having an affair. The investigation leads to a Catholic Priest, and when the husband pays to have him whacked, he soon comes to regret it. This one also features Patsy Kensit as the wife trying – and failing – to perform with an 'Irish' accent... One of the gems of season five is *Forever Ambergis*, which stars Roger Daltery as a combat photographer who ropes a talented young colleague (Steve Buscemi) into joining him on a dangerous assignment in Central America. However, it turns out to be all a ruse so that he can return home and steal the young man's girlfriend... In *Food For Thought*, another character loses his head over a pretty girl when a jealous carnival clown discovers that the psychic lady is in love with the fire-swallower... Next up is Russell Mulcahy's *People Who Live in Brass Hearses*. Perhaps the most memorable episode of season five, this stars Bill Paxton as a foul-tempered thug who ropes his younger brother (Brad Dourif) into helping him get revenge on the ice cream man whose testimony put him behind bars years earlier. However, he doesn't take into account his little brother's trigger-happy ways, and the ice cream man's peculiar secret... In *Two For the Show*, a man tries to dispose of his wife's body after stabbing her to death. A cop shows up on the doorstep after receiving reports of a scream. And after a quick look around the house, the cop thinks all is well and leaves. However, the two men meet again later that night at a train station where the murderous husband is transporting a large, suspicious package... In *House of Horror*, fraternity initiates are challenged to make it to the top floor of a haunted house. However, when they fail to return, the sadistic leader of the club (Kevin Bacon) heads up there only to find that the sorority girls have a nasty little surprise of their own to dish out... In *Well Cooked Hams*, Billy Zane stars as a failing magician who murders a grand illusionist and steals his 'box of death' idea, only to find his work sabotaged when trying to perform the death-defying stunt himself... In *Creep Course*, a high school football player attempts to steal exam questions from the home of his teacher with the aid of a nerdy bookworm. However, once at the teacher's house, the girl is betrayed and locked in the basement with an immortal mummy ("Ewww, I guess that's a wrap for Findlay, hee hee")... Uli Edel's *Came the Dawn* stars Perry King as an outwardly mild-mannered man who picks up a woman in a rainstorm as her truck has broken down. He drives her back to his country cabin for some *Dressed To Kill*-style mayhem... The worst episode of season five is probably *Oil's Well That Ends Well*, which stars Lou Diamond Phillips and Priscilla Presley as con artists who convince a bunch of old men to invest in 'recently-discovered crude oil' found beneath a cemetery. This episode also features John Kassir, who provides the voice of the Cryptkeeper, in a supporting role... Clancy Brown stars in *Half-Way Horrible* as the owner of a chemical corporation with links to macumba voodoo. His colleagues are being killed off by a mysterious assailant. And when he returns home one night to find threatening graffiti on his living room wall, he suspects he could be next on the hit list... And the season ends on a tribute to Amrose Bierce's short story, *An Occurrence at Owl Creek Bridge*, as a young woman imagines her possible future before she is executed by her treacherous gangster lover...

Season six (1994-1995) brings on a surreal, nightmarish quality to many episodes, with strange, oversized, architecturally-improbable rooms, and a bizarre 'plastic reality.' Russell Mulcahy's *Let the Punishment Fit the Crime* is about an injury lawyer who finds herself trapped in a Kafka-esque bureaucratic hell where her past sins come back to bite her on the arse... William Malone's *Only Skin Deep* centres on a man who picks up a mysterious blonde at a fancy dress party. Back at her place, their sexual fling hits the skids when the woman refuses to remove her 'mask'... Next up, Mick Garris chips in with *Whirlpool*, a tale about a comic book artist who is fired and has recurring dreams about shooting dead her editor... In *Operation Friendship*, a computer programmer is tormented by his destructive, *Drop Dead Fred*-like imaginary friend while dating a beautiful neighbour... In *Revenge is the Nuts*, the residents of a home for the blind take sweet revenge on the scumbag owner of the place... Next up, *The Stepfather* himself, Terry O'Quinn, stars in *The Bribe* as a health and safety inspector who makes a deal with a sleazy night club owner to help pay for his daughter's college tuition... In the awful episode, *The Pit*, two martial artists are manipulated by their wives into competing in a no-hold-barred death match in a cage... Bill Saddler returns as the Grim Reaper in *The Assassin*, in which a group of killers terrorize a housewife while searching for her husband who once worked for the US government... *Staired In Horror* stars D. B. Sweeney as a fugitive who hides out in an old lady's house that has a cursed stairway... In Vincent Spano's *In the Groove*, a struggling radio DJ attempts to boost his career by committing murder... In *Surprise Party*, a man inherits an old burned-out building after strangling his father. However, when he shows up he finds the place has been invaded by ghoulish revellers... In *Doctor of Horror*, a deranged 'Dr. Orloff' steals corpses with the aid of a couple of dim-witted security guards so that he can dissect them and 'find their souls'... Next up, Michael Ironside and Bruce Payne star in *Comes the Dawn* as a pair of Army poachers who use a young woman to catch a bear. However, the hunters soon become the hunted when they stumble into a den of vampires. This is a decent episode that was perhaps the inspiration for *30 Days of Night* (2007)... In *99&44/100% Pure Horror*, a pompous, self-absorbed artist murders her rich husband and turns him into soap. She later comes to a sticky end in the shower... And finally, *You, Murderer* stars Humphrey Bogart as a company executive with a violent past whose wife (Isabella Rossellini) threatens to expose his identity.

Season 7 (1996) strays across the Atlantic with 13 episodes set and shot in the UK, and featuring many familiar faces from British film and television. And though there are no masterpieces here, the episodes are consistently good throughout, offering the best tales since season 3. First up is *Fatal Caper*, in which an aristocrat nearing retirement is faced with a dilemma: He wants to pass on his estate to his sons, but they're a pair of irresponsible dunces. Before he dies, he creates a will that includes a clause that states that unless the sons can track down their long lost brother, the inheritance will be donated to charity. This is a strong opening episode with a great twist at the end... Next up, Freddie Francis returns with *Last Respects*, which is basically a re-telling of W.W. Jacob's classic tale, *The Monkey's Paw*. This time, the story is set in an antique gift shop where the three sisters who work there come into contact with a monkey's paw that grants them wishes... In *A Slight Case of Murder*, a novelist is bothered by house callers, including her estranged husband who plans on burying her alive... Martin Kemp stars in *Escape*, a World War II drama about a German POW who also operates as a spy for the British. When a fellow German he had betrayed ends up in the same camp as him, he feels he must make a daring escape before his cover is blown... In Russell Mulcahy's *Horror in the Night*, a wounded diamond thief hides out in a spooky hotel... In *Cold War*, Ewen McGregor and Jane Horrocks show up at a service station to rob the place, only to find that it is already being robbed by a Chinese motorcycle gang. After a shoot-out, they flee to a hotel and are attacked by a vampire... *The Kidnapper* stars Steve Coogan as a lonely proprietor of a pawn shop who allows a pregnant homeless woman (Julia Sawalha) to live with him. After she gives birth, they get into a romantic relationship, but the man becomes jealous of the attention the baby gets. One day, the baby is snatched in the park, and the pawn broker may have had something to do with it... In William Malone's *Report From the Grave*, a scientist violates the tomb of a long dead corpse in his attempts to conduct experimental research, but accidentally kills his girlfriend in the process. Thus, he becomes obsessed with the idea of resurrecting her from the grave... In *Smoke Wrings*, Daniel Craig saunters into an advertising company and blags himself a job. However, the impressed executive has no idea that he is there on behalf of her disgruntled ex partner who is looking for revenge... *About Face* stars Anthony Andrews as a seedy Priest who learns that he has fathered twins, one of whom is a deformed fundamentalist Christian

with a murderous streak. This one shares a similar twist ending with an earlier episode, *People Who Live In Brass Hearses*. *Confession* stars Eddie Izzard as the prime suspect in a serial killer case in which hookers have been decapitated. Detectives oversee his interrogation at the hands of a master criminal psychologist... In *Ear Today... Gone Tomorrow*, a gangster's moll lures a safe cracker into robbing her partner's private vault. However, he is hard of hearing, so before getting to work, he undergoes an operation to fine-tune his hearing to that of an owl... And the final episode, *The Third Pig*, is an amusing and gruesome animation narrated by the Cryptkeeper throughout. It's about three pigs who are targeted by a big bad wolf who has a habit of fluffing his lines. And that's it, boils and ghouls.

Wild At Heart (1990)
Dir: David Lynch /USA

Fans of David Lynch will already be familiar with the writer/director's many nods and winks in his films towards Victor Flemming's *The Wizard of Oz*. That timeless childhood classic has fascinated Lynch since he was a youngster, and has continually wormed its terrifying beauty into his work. *Wild At Heart* still stands as Lynch's most obvious tribute to Flemming's classic fantasy, but ironically it also remains Lynch's most savagely violent film to date.

Loosely based on Barry Gifford's novel, *Wild At Heart* is a deranged road movie that propels through the savage underbelly of modern Americana. Murderous Sailor (Nicholas Cage, doing a permanent Elvis impersonation) and his lover, Lula (Laura Dern), are on the run from a gang of psychotic killers hired by Lula's crazy mother (Dianne Ladd, Dern's mother in real life). Their journey takes them through a series of surreal, violent, and darkly comic escapades, but will their mutual love carry them through?

An exuberant, funny, and disturbing film due to its many scenes of violence and death, *Wild At Heart* takes a detour from Lynch's previous *Blue Velvet* from the outset; whereas *Blue Velvet* centres on a couple of relatively normal characters who find themselves in a web of encroaching evil, *Wild At Heart* begins with the film's hero committing a brutal murder, and events soon become increasingly disastrous and apocalyptic from that point on. There's also a positive and optimistic message in the film that suggests even the most fantastical of fairytale endings really *can* become a reality, just so long as you're prepared to follow the yellow brick road...

Barry Gifford himself loved the film, describing it as "a wonderful thing, like a big dark musical comedy." Lynch called it "a film about finding love in hell" (a few years later the two men would collaborate on the astonishing *Lost Highway*). Many audiences disagreed, and *Wild At Heart* produced mass walk-outs from preview screenings. Lynch panicked and re-edited the film, removing gruesome scenes of torture and murder that were apparently leaving the theatres half-empty due to people leaving in a huff. But even with these tempered scenes, *Wild At Heart* remains well-known for its graphic violence; from the head-cracking opening, to the bungled bank robbery and nasty shotgun mayhem, that annoyed the hell out of the censors and led to critics complaining about film violence, yet again. At the time of its release, the MPAA was reviewing its ratings system, and *Wild At Heart* was slightly trimmed. In the UK, however, the film was left untouched by the British censors, passing with an uncut 18 certificate.

An unofficial sequel followed in 1997, *Perdita Durango*, directed by Spanish maverick Alex de la Iglesia which caused even more of a stink for the censors and critics. As for *Wild At Heart*, lookout for the aforementioned references to *The Wizard of Oz*, listen out for Angelo Badalamenti's dark and achingly beautiful score, and marvel at the unforgettable roster of oddball characters who populate the film, such as Crispin Glover as Lula's strange cousin who keeps cockroaches down his boxers, stays up all night making sandwiches ("I'm making my lunch!"), and is supposedly abducted by aliens wearing "little black gloves." Willem Dafoe is also excellent and almost unrecognisable as the creepy hitman Bobby Peru. Freddie Jones, Calvin Lock Hart, David Patrick Kelly, and Mr. Eraserhead himself, Jack Nance all appear as the gang of killers, and Harry Dean Stanton as an unfortunate victim caught up in all the madness.

King of New York (1990)
Dir: Abel Ferrara /USA

Christopher Walken stars as Frank White, a New York drug lord who is back on the streets after a prison term. He claims to now be a reformed character, and tries to do some good for society by cleaning the streets of rival pushers and pimps, and uses ill-gotten gains to save a Bronx hospital from closure. He is backed up by his (mostly) loyal gang of black maniacs who are happy to unload their weapons on anyone who gets in the way of Frank's dream. Meanwhile, a group of angry cops with a personal vendetta against White decide to take ruthless vigilante action against him and his gang when their efforts to see them back behind bars fails due to legal chicanery and the deaths of important eye witnesses.

King of New York is Abel Ferrara's first foray into the gangster genre with a bleak worldview penned by Ferrara's long-time cohort Nicholas St. John. It's the kind of film where the entire principal cast are wiped out in the most cold and calculated ways (including a cop who is shot dead at his colleague's funeral), and one man's attempts to redeem himself from the errors of his ways is doomed from the start. But for all the film's bleak tone and ruthless slaughter, this is actually one of Ferrara's most optimistic efforts to date. It's also one of his most accessible, boasting a strong neon-lit photography by Bojan Bazelli and one of the most impressive casts of the 90s which, alongside Walken, also features Larry Fishburne, David Caruso, Wesley Snipes, Victor Argo, and Steve Buscemi.

Interestingly, *King of New York* tips its hat to vampiric legend; it's a film which owes more to Gothic horrors like *Nosferatu* and *Near Dark* rather than *Goodfellas* or *Scarface*. It's no coincidence that Frank White constantly states that he is "back from the dead," or that his main enemy is called Bishop; Argo's detective serves as a Van Helsing determined to slay White, the slippery bloodsucker who is never seen in any kind of natural light, and who literally walks on his own grave. Indeed, Ferrara went on to cast Walken a few years later as Peina the philosophising vampire in *The Addiction*.

This vision of New York is dark and complicated. The jumbled scenery juxtaposes criminality and morality, rich and poor, order and chaos, politics and apathy, business and pleasure to such an extent the result is mind-boggling. It's a concrete jungle of racial and cultural diversities where even the cops and politicians roam around in clan-like groups held together by their own sense of loyalty. Ferrara and St. John know the city inside out; the ethnic areas, the subways, districts, tourist spots, hotels, bars, and restaurants. And all of these elements help give *King of New York* a fractured but realistic sense of place. A classic.

Poison (1990)
Dir: Todd Haynes /USA

A controversial, narratively complex triptych of tales that introduced Todd Haynes' work to a wider audience beyond the gay community. Taking its inspiration from celebrated French author/convict Jean Genet, this fiery feature debut does much to create an increasing sense of discomfort while wearing its intelligence on its sleeve.

The first story, *Hero*, is a faux-documentary in which neighbours and family members discuss Richie, a troubled seven year old boy who is said to have murdered his father and then quite literally flown away out the window, never to return. The second story, *Horror*, mimics the style of a 50s black and white sci-fi movie, and features Dr. Graves (Larry Maxwell) who succeeds in isolating the human libido into a handy serum, but accidentally doses himself and mutates into a dangerous and infectious monster. And finally, *Homo* – the most obviously inspired by Genet – tells of the obsessive John (Scott Renderer), a thief whose life in prison is turned upside down with the arrival of Bolton (James Lyons), an object of his desire since their days in reform school.

The three stories are assembled together in a challenging and innovative way, and the disturbing build-up of the scenarios seems to affect viewers on a subliminal rather than a more obvious, narrative based level. And this results in curious afterthoughts as the film slowly settles in viewers' minds long after the movie has finished. The stories vary in their styles and are linked very loosely in their themes of persecution, alienation, and sexual anxiety, and uncovering the film's intriguing and enigmatic connections is left very much up to the viewer to decipher. Rather than allowing the audience to be spoon-fed by a more obvious and traditional narrative style, Haynes' film actively demands its viewers to engage with the action on screen in a subjective manner. If the film has a 'message' it's very much up to you to work out because *Poison* is by no means an explicit polemic.

Poison opened to much hostility when far right religious groups expressed their displeasure that the film received funding from tax payer's money. And this had a crushing effect on the next generation of filmmakers as many funding bodies, such as the National Endowment For the Arts, had their government funding withdrawn as a direct result of the protests, leaving many young filmmakers without a pot to piss in, financially. The film did, however, find much favour with those who actually bothered to sit down and watch it (as opposed to those who just stood outside waving their accusatory fingers), and it eventually picked up the Grand Jury Prize at the Sundance Film Festival.

Director Todd Haynes first made a splash with *Superstar: The Karen Carpenter Story*, a short biographical piece played out with Barbie dolls. It won the Best Experimental Short Award at the USA Film Festival before Karen's brother Richard had the film prosecuted and banned in a lawsuit. *Poison* was his first feature film, and despite the controversy was successful enough for him to continue in his chosen medium throughout the 90s and beyond with films like *[Safe]*, *Velvet Goldmine*, and *Far From Heaven*. None of his subsequent efforts showed the same degree of challenging innovations as his early work, nor sparked such notoriety, but they did at least bring some much deserved attention to *Poison*, a provocative gem steeped in technical virtuosity.

Bullet in the Head (1990)
(Orig title: *Die xue jie tou*)
Dir: John Woo /Hong Kong

Arguably John Woo's greatest and most disturbing film to date, and without question his most violent. *Bullet In the Head* is an Eastern version of *The Deerhunter*, and follows the fortunes – and misfortunes – of a group of friends, Ben, Frank, and Paul. The film begins in Hong Kong where violence is rife, rioting and social meltdown are an everyday thing, and thugs rule the streets. Ben's wedding dinner is disrupted when Paul, who had borrowed the money from a loan shark to pay for his friend's big day, is attacked by triad boss Ringo and his cronies. Paul endures a savage beating rather than settling his debt. Ben and Frank decide to get revenge, and in their attack they end up killing Ringo. So the three buddies flee to Saigon where they come into contact with Luke (Doctor Lam himself, Simon Yam), a dodgy mercenary who is just as likely to kill for money as he is to steal gold in his pursuit of riches.

After what they have already been through, you would think these three men would have taken some very important lessons from their violent experiences back home in Hong Kong, but instead they get themselves involved in robbery and wholesale massacre of anyone who stands in their way of making some dirty money. And this reckless behaviour finds them fleeing deeper and deeper into war-torn Vietnam. And soon their bonds of friendship are frayed when Paul provokes a Mexican stand-off with Ben and Frank due to his greedy obsession with their stolen shipment of gold. Soon after, they are captured by the Vietcong.

In place of the forced games of Russian Roulette in Cimino's film, here the POWs are forced to open fire on their fellow prisoners for the entertainment of the VC. Ben participates in the game as a way of affecting an escape plan – his desire for survival outweighing his morality. Paul's attitude, on the other hand, is even more reprehensible; when making an escape, Frank is injured, so Paul simply shoots his old buddy in the head so that he won't have to deal with the burden of having to assist the injured man out of the war zone! He then goes on to murder a group of unarmed civilians in order to steal an escape boat. The film ends back in Hong Kong with Paul, who has now become a rich and successful businessman, is confronted by Ben over his act of treachery. They subsequently have a fight to the death that is as violent and brutal as anything seen in the history of Hong Kong cinema.

Bullet In the Head is perhaps most notable for the absence of actor Chow Yun-Fat, and for this reason the film seems to be missing a moral centerpoint. In a later film, *Full Contact* (1992), Yun-Fat was mistakenly cast in the bad guy role, and the punters stayed away not wanting to see their hero as the villain, and so the film flopped quite badly at the box office (it's a decent film though, and well worth checking out). Here with *Bullet In the Head*, it comes as a genuine surprise when some of the characters turn bad and others present some deep heroics. All are driven insane with terror and agony, and hysterically do all they can to survive. A classic.

The militarist slant on the 'Heroic Bloodshed' genre can also be seen in Samo Hung's *Eastern Condors* (1986), a film which borrows heavily from Robert Aldrich's *The Dirty Dozen* (1967). But these borrowings often

work both ways; Ringo Lam's *City On Fire* (1987) provides the basis for Quentin Tarantino's *Reservoir Dogs*, and Chow Yun-Fat's two-handed gunplay in *A Better Tomorrow* is said to have influenced Harvey Keitel in Tarantino's film.

Legend of the Demon Womb (1990)
(Orig title: *Urotsukidoji II*)
Dir: Hideki Takayama /Japan

More bizarre mayhem ensues in this sequel to *Legend of the Overfiend* which has only a loose connection to the original film. We get the usual demons and man-beasts with massive tentacle dicks, but also a battle to prevent the son of a crazy Nazi from gaining unlimited powers by murdering the child who is destined to be the overfiend, the ultimate god of gods. Those hoping for a delirious, outrageous anime won't be disappointed as we also get the usual extremely gruesome fantasies, graphic sex, fellatio, masturbation, lesbianism, and rape, decapitations, mad Nazis, multiple bloody murders and human sacrifice. More sequels followed.

Misery (1990)
Dir: Rob Reiner /USA

Writer Paul Sheldon (James Caan) crashes his car off a mountain road during a blizzard. He is later pulled from the wreckage by his number one fan, Annie Wilkes (Kathy Bates). She takes him back to her secluded home and begins nursing him back to health. However, Annie is emotionally unstable and has a violent temper. She could also have been responsible for the deaths of young children who were in her care in her former career as a nurse. And when Annie learns that Paul has killed off her favourite fictional character, she burns his manuscript and forces the bed-ridden writer to start again from scratch. *Misery* is one of the best adaptations of Stephen King source material (the book is also one of King's best). It takes a long, dark look at the price of fame and the nuttiest realms of fandom, and is at times wickedly funny. The film's central premise is perhaps the notion of control – or, in this case, the sudden loss of it – and the film charts the psychological conflict between the two main characters. Annie is a writer's worst nightmare; she is stifling and controlling and anti-intellectual; she is ignorant at the top of her voice; she acquaints morality with a hatred of profanity, and exudes a homicidal rage for anything that doesn't fit into her narrow world view. As a film which examines the relationship between the artist, the critics and the fans, *Misery* has no equal.

Wheels of Terror (1990)
Dir: Christopher Cain /USA
Better than average TV movie in which a filthy black Sudan is driven around the desert roads of Arizona, and its driver is abducting and murdering young girls. And when school bus driver, Joanna Cassidy, witnesses her own daughter taken, she pursues the vehicle along a lonely stretch of road. Like the villain in *Duel*, viewers never get to see the driver. He enjoys toying with his victims, and the car is seemingly indestructible and demonic, just like the sinister vehicle in *The Car* (1977). Miles better than other similarly-themed TV movies like *Road Rage* (1999) and *Death Car on the Freeway* (1979).

Jacob's Ladder (1990)
Dir: Adrian Lyne /USA
Tim Robbins stars as a wounded Vietnam soldier who returns home to New York and experiences terrifying hallucinations. And just as he is about to uncover some evil government conspiracy about US marines being chemically 'altered' with psychedelics, he learns that he is actually dying and watching his possible future pass before his eyes... Loved and hated in pretty much equal measure by film fans, *Jacob's Ladder* is nonetheless a stylish cult classic that depicts hell as urban blight in a perpetually gloomy 1970s. The story owes an obvious debt to Ambrose Bierce's short, *An Occurance at Owl Creek Bridge* (1890), and also to Herk Harvey's horror classic, *Carnival of Souls* (1962), but director Adrian Lyne offers up a fascinating, personal and psychological vision of death. In tune with the Buddhist beliefs, the film is ultimately about the difficulties of accepting death, and the process of coming to peace with it. Independent film-maker, Gaspar Noe, delved even deeper into the subject with his *Enter the Void* (2009).

No Retreat, No Surrender 4 (1990)
(aka *The Kickboxer*; aka *The King of Kickboxers*)
Dir: Lucas Lowe /USA
Martial arts romp with a sinister snuff movie edge. Jake, a policeman and retired kickboxing champion, is sent over to Thailand to investigate a group of shady filmmakers who murder their actors on the sets. Turns out that one of the men responsible for the films had killed Jake's brother ten years earlier. The film is basically a carbon copy of the Jean-Claude Van Damme vehicle, *Kickboxer* (1989) with a darker, more depraved snuff undertone.

Nightbreed (1990)
Dir: Clive Barker /USA
Based on Clive Barker's own novella, *Cabal*, *Nightbreed* was an unmitigated disaster. Originally intended as a two-and-a-half-hour epic monster fantasy, Twentieth Century-Fox aggressively cut the film down to 102 minutes and marketed it as a typical slasher movie. What was left of Barker's ambitious vision flopped dead at the box-office, alienated much of its audience, and sidelined Barker as a director. The plot is about a young man, Boone (Craig Sheffer), who is accused by his psychiatrist, Decker (David Cronenberg), of murdering six families. However, the doc is actually a cold-blooded psychopath, and he arranges for Boone to be executed by the Gestapo-like police. So Boone heads for Midian, a subterranean city of monsters, with Decker and the police in hot pursuit... *Nightbreed* is a study on bigotry and on the acceptance of one's true nature, even if that nature goes against the 'mores' of society. The 'monsters' in Midian are good and kind hearted, while Decker and his all-too-human accomplices reveal themselves to be the truly monstrous. The director's cut was long overdue and released on Blu-Ray in 2014, and includes around 40 minutes of extra footage, including a musical number!

Hardware (1990)
Dir: Richard Stanley /UK /USA
Richard Stanley's debut feature is heavily inspired by *The Terminator* (1984), as a military killing machine plunges itself into the electricity grid and targets a group of friends for extermination. Described by one critic as 'a fascist cyberpunk nightmare,' the cyborg here – named M.A.R.K. 13 – even goes as far as rampaging with a phallic drill, just like Tamora Taguchi in *Tetsuo the Iron Man* (1988). The film had to be drastically cut in America to avoid the X rating, while the British censors left it intact for release on VHS.

The Haunting of Morella (1990)
Dir: Jim Wynorski /USA

A tits and lightning anti-epic produced by Roger Corman and directed by Jim Wynorski. This film is supposedly based on Poe's story, *Morella*, but the end result has more in common with soft core cable TV than any 19th Century Gothic literature. An executed witch who had sworn revenge before her death returns to possess her daughter, Lenore. For all its shortcomings, the film does at least deserve credit as a warm tribute to Hammer, with numerous references to everything from *Countess Dracula* (1970), *The Vampire Lovers* (1970) and *Lust for a Vampire* (1972). And lots of bare tits.

Flatliners (1990)
Dir: Joel Schumacher /USA

Flatliners was perhaps the first anti-yuppie movie, coming after a decade of 'Reganomics' and 'greed is good' mentality. Here, viewers are confronted with horror as metaphysical dread. Embossed with director Joel Schumacher's usual flashy surface style, *Flatliners* is about a group of arrogant med students who embark on a series of dangerous experiments. They each undergo a Near Death Experience, and under those conditions, while their bodies have ceased to function, they experience horrifying, DMT-like trips in which their wrong doings from days of yore come back to haunt them. At heart, *Flatliners* is an old-fashioned morality tale that can be interpreted by Christians as a fable on the afterlife, and by athiests as a purely psychological horror.

Exorcist III (1990)
Dir: William Peter Blatty /USA

This much underrated third instalment in the *Exorcist* saga was directed by Blatty himself and based on his own novel, *Legion*. It's just a shame that the studio hacked it up to meet their 'crowdsourced' demands. Horror fans are still awaiting the release of a director's cut. Set 15 years after the original, *Exorcist III* sees a new evil stalking the rainswept streets of Georgetown with a series of brutal murders. George C. Scott plays Detective Kinderman who discovers that all clues lead to the Gemini Killer (Brad Dourif) and Regan's original exorcism... Warner Bros. insisted that there should be an exorcism in the film, so Blatty's slick serial killer movie went through re-shoots

and had an inferior ending forced upon it to keep the film in line with *Exorcist* tradition. In the original film, the Devil possessed the young and innocent Regan, whereas in this third entry in the series, evil turns its attentions onto society's outcasts – the hopeless, the abandoned, the senile, and the criminally insane. It's a world of cynicism, of society going to pot, of aged men clinging to the past because they have no future, and the present is too bleak to contemplate.

Spontaneous Combustion (1990)
Dir: Tobe Hooper /USA

In 1955, a young couple, Brian and Peggy, volunteer to sit in an underground state-of-the-art bomb shelter in the Nevada desert while scientists carry out hydrogen bomb tests right above them. The couple emerge unscathed, and, thanks to newsreel footage of their days underground, they become national heroes. Peggy later gives birth to a boy they call David. However, the parents burn to death in the maternity ward for no apparent reason. The orphaned baby is re-named Sam, and he grows up to be a struggling actor and divorcee (Brad Dourif), and people around him begin burning to death in mysterious circumstances. Turns out that, not only is Sam responsible for the burnings through some kind of psychic pyromania, but the bomb tests his parents were involved with may also have something to do with it... This film starts off well enough but sags quite badly after the hour mark and never recovers. *Spontaneous Combustion* came along after director Tobe Hooper delivered the late 80s duds like *Invaders From Mars* (1986) and *Texas Chainsaw Massacre 2* (1986), and the rut only continued with turds like *I'm Dangerous Tonight* (1990), *Night Terrors* (1993) and others. This film kind of sits in the middle; it isn't the complete disaster that many have claimed, but nor is it on a par with his better works, like *Death Trap* (1976), *Salem's Lot* (1979) and *Lifeforce* (1985). Taken on its own merits, *Spontaneous Combustion* is your typical direct-to-video horror fare of the early 90s. In its favour, Dourif offers a decent performance as the tortured protagonist, the action comes thick and fast, and almost every character ends up burning to death. Look out for cameo appearances by Hooper, along with John Landis (who is burned to death in a radio studio), and cult legend, 'Buck' Flowers, in a radio voice-over part as a preacher.

The Guardian (1990)
Dir: William Friedkin /USA
A tree-worshipping druid princess called Camilla lands the job of guardian for a baby boy, but she turns out to be an evil interloper, and a powerful woodland tree aids her in offing her enemies in brutal fashion. The couple who hired the strange woman as nanny don't realise the danger they're in until it's too late. *The Guardian* is your typical interloper horror tale, albeit with a supernatural twist. Director William Friedkin has come under attack from many a critic for basically wasting his talents on what is essentially a hokey old tale, but the film does have its intriguing moments; the 'love' scene between the tree and the druidess is very weird, as in some shots it looks like the tree is 'fingering' her. Also, there is an excellent sequence in which an admirer of Camilla follows her into the woods, sees what's she's up to, runs off home, and is then attacked in his home by the wolves. Friedkin once remarked, 'I'd rather work with tree stumps than actors.' Here he got the best of both worlds.

Grim Prairie Tales (1990)
Dir: Wayne Coe /USA
A decent, western-themed anthology horror, the highlight of which is the tale '*Grassy Hills of the Great Divide*,' a creepy and well executed story about a man who encounters a pregnant woman, only to be devoured whole by her vagina. Talk about man eater! The woman then roams around again in her 'pregnant' state awaiting the arrival of her next victim. The other tales include a white man who has a fatal encounter with an Indian rite, a family who head out West after the Civil War and get themselves entangled in murder, and a gunslinger who is haunted by an enemy who is thought to be dead following a shoot-out in the street. The stories are told by men around a campfire in the American West in the 19th Century.

Demonia (1990)
Dir: Lucio Fulci /Italy
Archaeologists unleash hell when they dig at a monastery where evil nuns were crucified in 1486. *Demonia* is as graphic and gruesome as we have come to expect from director Lucio Fulci. There's baby burning, blood draining, tongue hammering, death by cats, and – perhaps most notoriously – the 'wishbone' scene in which a man is strung upside down by his ankles and is literally torn in half. The special effects are quite lousy, however, and the narrative is sluggishly paced.

Dead Girls (1990)
Dir: Dennis Devine /USA
The lead singer of an all-girl goth band is haunted by the suicide of her sister while a skull-faced maniac goes on a killing spree. This is bottom of the barrel slasher nonsense, shot on bleary video, and stuffed with pointless red herrings, needless exposition, zero suspense, lacklustre kills, wooden acting – all the usual.

Child's Play 2 (1990)
Dir: John Lafia /USA
Chucky tracks down little Andy and murders his foster parents. But before the evil doll can take over the child's body in a voodoo ritual, Andy and his foster sister put up a final battle in the Good Guy doll factory. Cue a lethal stitching machine, a vat of melted plastic, and a machine that inserts plastic eyeballs into dolls heads – all used as nasty weapons. A cartoony sequel which is perhaps more enjoyable than the original film. Also look out for the references to *Pinocchio*, the tale of another doll that wanted to be a real boy.

Demon Wind (1990)
Dir: Philip Moore /USA
Now here's a weird one, a visually interesting demon movie with terrible performances, awful dialogue and wonky character interactions. A young man, Corey, and his girlfriend visit a house in the middle of nowhere to look for clues concerning his parent's mysterious deaths. They are accompanied by their friends, a bunch of self-regarding piss-weasels. They arrive at the desecrated house, despite being warned not to go there by the local cafe owner, and immediately stumble upon the skeletal remains of murder victims. And, before you can say 'Evil Dead,' a character reads aloud an incantation scrawled on the wall, and the place erupts into chaos as a demonic force sends the clutter flying across the room. And as they try to flee, a sinister mist pursues them and drops off demonic little girls to terrorise them. And then things just get *weirder...*

Demon Wind is a little-seen effort that was released directly to VHS and has never seen the light of day on DVD. It includes possessions, Deadite-like creatures and other allusions to Sam Raimi's *The Evil Dead* (1983). From the outside, the house the characters visit looks like a single-storey, free-standing wall with a doorway surrounded by desecrated ruins. However, inside it looks like a full-sized house with an upstairs and bedrooms and everything. The main protagonist, Corey, is a dull, humourless oaf, but this is an entertaining and bloody little flick that really ought to be picked up and released on DVD some day. Also, there is a magician character called Chuck who takes out Deadites by decapitating them with spinning roundhouse kicks – It was driving me nuts trying to think where I had seen him before, and of course, he's the 'Fight Professor' himself, Stephen Quadros, perhaps best known for his entertaining commentaries for the *Pride Fighting Championship*!

The Texas Chainsaw Massacre 3 (1990)
(aka *Leatherface: The Texas Chainsaw Massacre 3*)
Dir: Jeff Burr /USA
By the time *Texas Chainsaw Massacre 3* came along, New Line Cinema wanted to turn the films into a franchise in the same vein as the *Halloween* and *Friday the 13th* series'. To do this, they hired splatter punk writer, David J. Schow to pen the script which was to be unashamedly gruesome as an L.A. Girl, Michelle, has to endure a night of horror in the Sawyer's farmhouse. And like David in *Straw Dogs* (1971), Michelle has to learn that pacifism is for pussies, and that violence is the only answer... Entertaining if uninspired, again the filmmakers ignore everything that made the original such a classic, and seem content to heap on the brutal killings. On the up side, there is a particularly ghoulish scene in which a victim is strung upside down while the crazy family members stand around casually discussing which parts of him they would like to eat while the poor guy is still alive and conscious.

Brain Dead (1990)
Dir: Adam Simon /USA
Not to be confused with Peter Jackson's zombie bloodbath, this *Brain Dead* is an intelligent mind-bender that shares similarities with both *Lost Highway* (1997) and *Jacob's Ladder* (1990). Bill Pullman stars as Dr. Rex Martin, a paranoid loner whose life changes irrevocably when he is assigned the task of restoring the mind of a genius who had killed his family and went insane. Penned by *The Twilight Zone* producer, Charles Beaumont, it's a film which reminds us that perspective is all, and that a damaged brain brings on a damaged 'reality.'

Night of the Living Dead (1990)
Dir: Tom Savini /USA
Tom Savini's respectable remake of Romero's zombie classic brings changes on expectations from the very beginning. The first zombie attack in the graveyard is nicely done, as is the follow-up of a recently risen corpse dressed in a funeral suit cut down the back. The suit slips off and reveals the autopsy wounds on its chest. Nice touch. At the farmhouse, Barbara doesn't slip into catatonia this time, she remains logical, gazes through the window, notices how slow the ghouls are, and suggests escaping from the house. Ben (Tony Todd) agrees, but convinces her that they should stay overnight before making a move. Stupidly, the survivors draw much attention to the house by loudly hammering doors and tables across the windows – if this was *The Walking Dead* (2010-) these characters wouldn't last five minutes. When the zombies do besiege the property, Barbara turns into a shotgun-blasting badass, in keeping with the tough heroine characters dating back to Ripley in *Alien* (1979) (she even wears a white vest with a strap of ammo across her shoulder, like Ripley).

We get more stupidity at the gas station. In the original, we never actually saw what happened there, as Tom (William Butler) decides to shoot the petrol pumps, turning himself and his girlfriend into fresh barbecue for the flatliners. Tom Towles portrays the bad guy, Harry Cooper, as even more reckless and aggressive this time around, even going as far as taking pot-shots at Ben when his zombified daughter is about to be brained. The ending is almost as shocking as the 1968 version, and also very different. The updates and unexpected twists on the familiar story may not seem all that important, but they toy effectively with viewer expectations, and continually keep us off-centre throughout.

This remake also contains interesting references to the other films in Romero's series, such as Barbara visiting the redneck picnic – perhaps the very same picnic the characters in *Dawn of the Dead* (1978) fly over in a helicopter on their way to the shopping mall. The helicopter is even visible in one shot. Also, the zombie cage fight in the remake was later expanded upon in Romero's *Land of the Dead* (2005), in which humans are forced to battle the stinkers for lurid entertainment purposes (a similar idea also crops up in *The Walking Dead* season 3).

A Cat in the Brain (1991)
(aka *Nightmare Concert*)
Dir: Lucio Fulci /Italy

While American postmodern horrors like *Wes Craven's New Nightmare* and *Scream* were doing the rounds, Italian horror maestro Lucio Fulci had already mined similar territory years earlier with *A Cat In the Brain*, a gruesome, self-reflexive nightmare of a filmmaker coming to terms with his own macabre brand of art and its effects on society.

Starring Lucio Fulci as himself, a film-maker who suffers from extremely violent hallucinations while directing his latest epic. Fulci compares his fractured state of mind to a cat clawing away inside of his skull, tearing his grey matter to shreds. And this metaphor is gleefully shown in graphic detail (this is a Fulci film, after all). Fulci eventually visits a psychiatrist (David L. Thompson) who puts his troubles down to an 'identity crisis'. However, this psychiatrist just so happens to be a very dangerous serial killer, and he plans on letting Fulci and his movies take the blame for his killing spree by using hypnotism to control the film-maker. And while the doctor continues to slaughter the local women in the area, Fulci's sense of guilt and horror increases as he thinks he could be responsible for the deaths.

A Cat In the Brain is quite simply one of the goriest and most insane movies ever made, and still divides its audience to this day. Most of the footage was recycled from other late-wave Fulci pics, such as *Ghosts of Sodom* and *Touch of Death*, and this footage is inter-cut with new scenes in an attempt to make a cohesive whole. And, to be fair, I think Fulci just about manages to pull it off, even if one or two of the characters – namely Thompson's killer psychiatrist – ages about ten years from one scene to the next due to the mish-mash of old and new footage. Newcomers to Fulci are advised to start elsewhere (try *The Beyond*) as this isn't the best showcase for the director's work; the performances are all quite bad, including Fulci

himself whose acting range basically amounts to him gazing off screen in horror... or is it surprise, or consternation? I've no idea, but I'm sure *he* knew what he was going for!

In addition to the recycled footage, we also get a recycled soundtrack, with Fabio Frizzi's themes taken from previous classics like *The Beyond* and *City of the Living Dead*. Scene for scene, this is Fulci's goriest film, and one of the goriest ever made by anyone. The killer cuts a chunk of flesh from a dead woman's hip, fries it in a pan, eats it while sitting on the couch watching a video tape of the woman, and then cuts the rest of her body up with a chainsaw and feeds her remains to his pigs. The scene where the mad doctor smashes his wife's head in with a lump of wood is extremely nasty; a piece of her brain is knocked out of her skull and lands on the floor pulsating. There's also a very nasty scene of a woman being slowly decapitated with a piano wire used as a garotte.

A Cat In the Brain bares more breasts than any other Fulci film, even if many of the naked women are cut, stabbed, or dismembered with an axe or chainsaw. But it isn't just women who are the victims; in one scene, Fulci runs over a man in his white Mercedes, reverses, and then drives over him again. And again. And just because this is Lucio Fulci we're talking about here, it's no surprise when he reverses once more and runs over the man's torso a fourth time, and then zooms in on all the sloppy intestines and bloody organs oozing from the victim's body. Towards the end, the rickety plot goes out the window completely, and the film just seems to wallow in one gruesome death after another. There are more decapitations in this movie than any other I can think of, and they're all pretty graphic.

But despite the non-linear style and gallons of blood, this film seems to be Fulci's way of exorcising his demons and exploring his anxieties as a filmmaker. He seems to be asking 'Is it irresponsible for an artist to make horror movies?' And at the end of the film when Fulci sets sail on his yacht with a beautiful brunette by his side, the answer seems to be a resounding 'hell no!' And during the same sequence, Fulci brilliantly draws the distinct line between fictional movies and reality when his film crew film him poking fish hooks through severed human fingers. At first we're thinking that Lucio really could have been responsible for the killings, but then the camera pulls back, revealing it to be just a scene from the movie he is currently working on.

This strict differentiation between representation and actuality is something I wish the censors and moralists everywhere would consider much more often, instead of calling for violent films to be banned. The world would be a much saner place, that's for sure. And whether you see this film as an autobiographical piece concerning the dark side of Fulci's chosen profession, or a self-indulgent mess, is entirely up to you to decide.

Nekromantik 2 (1991)
(aka *Return of the Loving Dead*)
Dir: Jorg Buttgereit /Germany

After releasing the sombre and meditative *Der Todesking* in 1990, many believed Jorg Buttgereit's next film would be a sure-fire opportunity for him to head more toward the mainstream as his directorial talent was clearly head and shoulders above most of his peers slogging away in the cine-underground. But instead, he returned the following year with *Nekromantik 2*, a film which manages to be even more outrageous than its perverted predecessor whilst at the same time surpassing the original in both thematic and technical skill. Make no mistake, this sequel to one of the most notorious movies ever made is a bona fide art film, but this didn't stop the German authorities from attempting to destroy the print.

Coming on like one of Sylvia Plath's most morbid poems written on her darkest day, *Nekromantik 2* centres on a twisted necrophiliac nurse, Monika (Monika M). She enters a graveyard in broad daylight and digs up the body of Rob, the anti-hero of part one. She sneaks off home with the putrid corpse and places it in her bathtub. And after dressing him up, she takes a few snapshots of herself posing with the stiff. In an attempt to infuse her life with semblance of normality, she strikes up a relationship with Mark (Mark Reeder), a strange but nice guy who works for a video distribution company dubbing porn movies into German. Monika's attempts to get intimate with Rob in the bathtub ends with her being violently sick, so she decides to spend more time with Mark, tagging along with him to art films and house 'parties' to watch seal brutality videos. Mark's kinkiness means he spends much of his time hanging from the ceiling by his feet. Pretty soon, Monika has Mark playing dead during sex, and with this she feels she has finally found her ideal partner. She wastes no time in dismembering Rob's body, keeping his head and penis as mementos in the fridge. Meanwhile, Mark becomes concerned by how morbid his girlfriend is and he dumps her. They eventually agree to meet up again, only this time Monika has an extremely perverse solution for the men in her life.

The film concludes with one of the most shocking scenes in history: Whilst having sex with Mark, Monika decapitates him with a hatchet and replaces his head with that of Rob's. She tightens a tourniquet around his still erect penis, and with blood gushing everywhere, she finally has that elusive orgasm.

Aside from the aforementioned seal scene, a needless attempt to best the killing of the rabbit in part one, Buttgereit seems determined to avoid any scenes of graphic bloodshed until the finale. And yet it still manages to haunt with its bleak and morbid atmosphere that is sustained throughout. The scenes with Rob's corpse are repulsive, and this is somehow made even more disturbing as there is a strange fairytale quality that lingers like a nightmare of Cinderella discovering her dark side and digging up a sexual playmate from the local cemetery. It leaves you feeling slightly defiled. You know how sometimes people refer to shock movies as leaving them wanting to take a shower afterwards to cleanse themselves of the disgusting imagery they have subjected themselves to? Well, *Nekromantik 2* is one of those movies.

While much of the dense narrative concentrates on mood and plot, Buttgereit certainly delivers on the gorehound's expectations in the last reel for the sequence in which Monika literally swaps her boyfriend's head for that of Rob's. This outrageous scene easily surpasses Daktari Lorenz's 'climax' in part one. And aside from the corpses and the blood and the grim atmospherics, *Nekromantik 2*, like its predecessor, also offers a touch of humour here and there, including the romance between Monika and Mark, and Mark's work which sees him improvising sound effects and dubbing porn very badly into German.

Buttgereit breaks new ground in the horror genre by presenting the story from a feminine perspective. And because we view the film through Monika's eyes, her twisted necrophiliac perversion is presented as perfectly normal (and this is helped tremendously by Monika M's gutsy performance – she also contributed to the music score). Early on in the film when she laboriously digs up Rob's body, Buttgereit films a bird's eye in close-up as it gazes down on Monika's immoral actions. The bird's eye represents us the viewers, the judgemental voyeurs gazing at a transgression over which we have no control. And with this scene we witness a cinematic first – a woman stealing a corpse from a graveyard for her own sexual gratification. The body could be mine or yours, and just like Rob's body and the observing bird, we are completely helpless to do anything about it.

Shot on 16mm but looking superb on the DVD transfer, *Nekromantik 2* is at once a detailed exploration of outsider love and one of the most disgusting and provocative horror movies ever made. It's a masterpiece of horror, but one that is all out to grate on viewer sensibilities; and for this reason it's not a film you could watch over and over again like, say, *Repo Man* or *Evil Dead II*, but you've probably gathered that by now.

In June 1991, *Nekromantik 2* was deemed obscene by the German authorities, and the Werkstattkino cinema was raided by Munich police who had been ordered to seize the print. Director Jorg Buttgereit was facing a custodial sentence, and even the projectionist was threatened with jail for screening the film. The police had a warrant for the film's arrest, apparently, but thankfully someone had the presence of mind to sneak out of the back door with the film cans, leaving the police unable to locate it. If the negative had been discovered it would have been destroyed, but fortunately it survives. I think that little incident speaks volumes about how rigidly closed-minded some people can be when it comes to provocative art; the attempts to destroy the film were eerily reminiscent of the Nazi book burnings of the 1930s, the fascistic purging of 'degenerate art' and literature that didn't sit right with the status quo. The film is still banned in Germany to this day.

Hiruko The Goblin (1991)
(Orig title:*Yokai hanta: Hiruko*)
Dir: Shinya Tsukamoto /Japan
This film is much more conventional than Tsukamoto's other works (*Tetsuo, Tokyo Fist, Nightmare Detective*), even if it does feature

demon spiders with humanoid faces on their backs spilling out of a gateway to hell under a Japanese high school. A student and a professor team up to investigate deaths and eventually go head to head with the Hiruko demon. This is a run-of-the-mill teenage horror flick, presumably made so that the director could head more towards the mainstream. That didn't happen. In the following year, Tsukamoto went back to what he knows best for the delirious *Tetsuo II: Body Hammer* (1992).

Robotrix (1991)
(Orig title: *Nu ji xie ren*)
Dir: Jamie Luk Kim-Ming /Hong Kong
This silly piece of sci-fi mayhem from Hong Kong was sexy and brutal enough for it to be awarded with the Cat III rating. Life-like androids from across the world are demonstrated at an expo. The German and American Robots engage in a battle of supremacy. Both robots malfunction but the American one goes ape shit and starts murdering the spectators. Then Eve R27, the Hong Kong robot, somersaults into action and beats the crap out of the Yankee droid and saves the day. The Sultan of some middle eastern country is in attendance, and the police show up to inform him that his son has been kidnapped by a disgruntled Japanese robot maker, Ryuichi Yamamoto. This Yamamoto character is a bit of a crazed genius and has managed to fuse his own thoughts into a new android that is fully sufficient and is causing a lot of trouble in the city. The remaining scientists give Eve an upgrade by transferring the thoughts of a recently killed police woman into the machine, and then it is sent out to track down and destroy Yamamoto's driod, and save the Prince.

Heavily influenced by Hollywood action movies like *The Terminator*, *Robocop*, *Universal Soldier*, and *Eve of Destruction*, *Robotrix* ups the ante on the sex and violence front, and we're treated to some superb stunts and set pieces. The scene in which Yamamoto's rogue android brutally rapes a hooker until she bleeds internally and then ruthlessly throws her corpse out of the window is extremely nasty, and made even moreso by its inclusion in such a routine actioner as this. And a later scene depicts the brutal and casual killing of a policeman that is not easy to forget. Popular actress Amy Yip (of *Erotic Ghost Story*) plays Eve the sexy cyborg, Japanese AV sensation Chikako Aoyama (of *Edo Rapeman*) plays Eve's trusty sidekick, and both provide plenty of T&A, and Cat III regular, Billy Chow (of *Escape From Brothel* and *Horrible High Heels*) plays the evil robot. All in all it's a fun piece of hokum, an unrelenting and gleefully gratuitous slice of sleaze that mixes sex, violence, and slapstick into a nice little time-killer. But beware, there is a cut version doing the rounds that drops the rape scene.

Popcorn (1991)
Dir: Mark Herrier and Alan Ormsby /USA

A girl who has recurring nightmares about a sinister man teams up with her college buddies to organise a horror film festival. And during a preview screening of an old avant-garde 60s horror flick, she collapses, convinced that the man in the film is the same person who has been haunting her dreams. Later, she learns that the man was a crazed filmmaker who murdered his family on stage at a film festival, and that he was the victim of the 'possessor,' a malignant being that steals human faces and is hell-bent on destruction and murder. And to make matters worse, the possessor shows up at the theatre during the festival and targets the movie-goers... *Popcorn* is a fun little flick aimed at the teenage horror crowd, and is also a lot of fun for those with a nostalgia for watching old horror flicks with William Castle-type gimmicks like a giant mosquito that flies through the theatre, and electric shockers built into the cinema seats. The film manages to create a degree of tension without taking itself seriously, and it also boasts a great heroine in Jill Schoelen as the troubled Maggie. The film died on its arse at the box-office, but became a minor cult item on home video. Another festival-themed horror film is *Nightmare In Blood* (1977).

Deadly Game (1991)
Dir: Thomas J. Wright /USA

A vengeful millionaire by the name of Osirius invites a disparate group of characters to his private island – a Japanese yakuza, a businessman, a Vietnam veteran, etc – and lets them loose on his land while hunting them down with armed henchmen and a pack of bloodhounds. The victims try to work out why they are being targeted this way, and gradually piece together the things they have in common. Turns out that each character committed a deadly act against Osirius in their pasts; Jack

stole a car and crashed it, killing his reluctant passengers; Peterson committed atrocities in Vietnam, and left a fellow soldier burning to death; and Dr. Harrand (*Fright Night*'s Roddy McDowell) failed to restore Osirius' burnt face. *Deadly Game* is a little seen but excellent TV movie which is basically a modern-day update of the RKO classic, *The Most Dangerous Game* (1932). Fans of *Dr. Phibes* and *Battle Royale* should lap it up.

Dolly Dearest (1991)
Dir: Maria Lease /USA

An American family moves down to Mexico to open a doll factory on the cheap. However, the factory is located next to an ancient Mayan tomb, and the young daughter of the family, Jessica (Candy Hutson), comes into possession of 'Dolly,' a doll inhabited by the spirit of an evil force that attempts to create a Devil Child. *Dolly Dearest* is a well-made, haunting little movie that is still very much worth watching today. But the problem is that the film is guilty of the very same faults the film itself is railing against; the film stands as a critique on the American trend of heading south of the border and using their wealth to get rich quick by exploiting the cheap materials, low tax rates and cheap labour. And, as the film itself was made in Mexico where the filmmakers enjoyed the very same cheap labour, the overall message – though legit – can be taken with a pinch of salt.

Ricochet (1991)
Dir: Russell Mulcahy /USA

Russell Mulcahy's *Ricochet* is one of those so-bad-it's-good action thriller/dark comedies that is a must-see if only for John Lithgow's performance as Earl Blake, one of *the* most unhinged psychopaths in the history of film. Denzel Washington plays the cop, Nick Styles, who puts Blake behind bars. And while in prison, Blake learns that Nick has become a successful lawyer. This infuriates Blake, and he decorates his prison cell with newspaper clippings of Nick's achievements, as a way of constantly keeping his rage at boiling point. And, like Max Cady in *Cape Fear* (1991), he is hell-bent on getting out of jail and exacting a terrible revenge on Nick and all he loves.. Those who only know Lithgow as the family man in movies and TV shows such as *Harry and the Hendersons* (1987) and *3rd Rock From the Sun* (1996-2001), will be astonished at his turn here as the utterly ruthless 'Aryan warrior.' His jail-break and subsequent revenge attacks are so casually brutal it defies belief. In the end, it takes the whole of the black community – including Ice-T as a local drug dealer – to band together to stop the white maniac.

The Borrower (1991)
Dir: John McNaughton /USA
A criminal alien is 'genetically devolved' into humanoid form and dumped on planet earth as punishment for some unspecified crime. However, the culprit's head explodes on arrival, and so it resorts to ripping off fresh human heads and wearing them like a series of hats while it causes havoc in downtown Chicago. A tough female cop (Rae Dawn Chong) is assigned the task of tracking down the elusive alien while her sceptical superiors thwart her every move... *The Borrower* is typical monster alien nonsense that is played for laughs. Director John McNaughton brought over much of the same cast and crew that worked with him on his previous film, *Henry-Portrait of a Serial Killer* (1986), most notably script writer Richard Fire, actress Tracy Arnold, and Tom Towles who here plays a hick whose head is stolen early on in the woods. See also *The Hidden* (1987).

Alligator II: The Mutation (1991)
Dir: Jon Hess /USA
A sequel that bears very little connection to the original film other than the alligator-run-amok basis. We get another mutated alligator, this time lurking in a large city pond where a greedy land developer (Steve Railsback) has dumped toxic waste chemicals, and intends on running a carnival in the area. However, when humans fall prey to the beastie, he hires Richard Lynch and Kane Hodder and co as big game hunters to get rid of the problem. And meanwhile, detective Hodges (Joseph Bologna) fails to convince people of the 'gator problem until it's too late... An uninspired, uninvolving film that follows formula in predictable ways, and lacks the wit, satire and pace of the original. Some may want to give it a watch if only for the ridiculous carnival attack at the end, however.

Naked Lunch (1992)
Dir: David Cronenberg /Canada
"*It's impossible to make a movie out of Naked Lunch. A literal translation wouldn't work. It would cost $400 million to make and would be banned in every country in the world.*" – David Cronenberg

One of the most difficult and introverted studio films of the 90s, *Naked Lunch* is essentially a hit and miss affair, exploring the life and work of underground cult hero, William Burroughs.

Former bug powder junky, William Lee (Peter Weller), works as an exterminator and lives with his wife Joan (Judy Davis) who lures him back into the squalid world of addiction. Whilst under the influence of the powder, Lee hallucinates that he is a secret agent for a disgusting horde of giant beetles who order him to kill Joan and flee to Interzone. With an increasing dependency on the powder, and his grip on reality loosening further still, Lee meets some oddball characters, his typewriter mutates into a metallic talking insect, and he indulges in more exotic substances.

Naked Lunch is an amusing and often grotesque concoction, and Cronenberg sidesteps the trouble of bringing an 'unfilmable' text to the screen, and instead concentrates on events and incidents from Burroughs' personal life, combined with Cronenberg's own ideas on the sometimes painful process of creativity itself. The result is a fascinating mess of a film, virtually incomprehensible on first viewing but offering at least a few nuggets of interest on repeat viewings.

On the plus side, *Naked Lunch* is a demanding film that also stands on its own as a personal creation in its own right, boasting some of the most impressive and imaginative hallucinatory imagery in Cronenberg's career. It's also an allegory on the battle against personal demons that vividly expresses the nightmare of drug addiction. The very antithesis of mainstream entertainment, the film nonetheless offers fine performances from Weller, Davis, Ian Holme, and Roy Schneider. The downside is that there's no room for audience participation in the film; it's very egotistic and introverted. But perhaps the biggest flaw is that Cronenberg doesn't explore what Burroughs wrote, and instead seems more content to ask 'why did he write?' And according to the director, he wrote because he shot his wife. And in this decision Cronenberg fails to shed light on the text that graced the pages of Burroughs' books, and thus fails to make clear just what it was that made Burroughs such a giant of 20th Century literature.

The scene that re-enacts the incident where Burroughs shot and killed Joan in a game of 'William Tell' stands as nothing more than a gimmick in Cronenberg's hands. As fascinating as Burroughs' life was, these biographical elements are less interesting than the contents of his texts. Burroughs' work had never been sufficiently explored in the cinema before, so it was exciting for fans to discover that Cronenberg – who cites Burroughs as one of his major influences – would be making a film based on *The Naked Lunch*. The film, however, is not an adaptation of the book but rather a snapshot of biographical elements combined with Cronenberg's own personal flights of fancy. Burroughs' fans were less than impressed.

Another misstep was Cronenberg's rather tame handling of Burroughs' most notorious character, Dr. Benway. Benway is generally considered to represent Burroughs' own dark side; he is a cruel, destructive, power-hungry manipulator whom the author allowed free reign in the safe form of penmanship whilst acknowledging that those negative characteristics were present in him too. Cronenberg, however, restricts Benway to only a couple of disappointing scenes.

Naked Lunch was originally intended to be shot on location in Tangier, but those plans were quickly dashed after the outbreak of the Gulf War. And this halt to proceedings left the director with no choice but to re-write the script (he is no stranger to this kind of pressure though; he basically wrote the screenplay for *Scanners* on set). The major problem was how to deal with Interzone, the international free zone in Tangiers that was a mecca for artists and bohemians of all kinds in the 50s, and is a place where Burroughs spent much of his time in those days. Cronenberg eventually settled on the idea that Interzone would become "a hallucinatory state of mind", and this meant that indoor sets had to be built to replicate the exotic Moroccan settings for a shooting schedule in Ontario, Canada. These unforeseen problems in the film's production led to the project becoming even more introverted. I think it's safe to say that if *Naked Lunch* was shot in Morocco as originally planned, we would be watching a very different film today.

Initial audiences were dumbfounded when the film first hit the screens, and many still are today. But with the subsequent releases of *Crash* and *eXistenZ*, fans and critics were more willing to put *Naked Lunch* into context as being part of Cronenberg's latest phase, following on from his 'humanist trilogy' that includes *The Dead Zone*, *The Fly*, and *Dead Ringers.* Those new to Cronenberg are advised to start elsewhere (try *Shivers*) as *Naked Lunch* is deliberately off-putting for the most part.

Hard Boiled (1992)
(Orig title: *Lat sau san taam*)
Dir: John Woo /Hong Kong

Hard Boiled is a classic piece of Hong Kong action from John Woo. If you like lots and lots of guns and action then you're in for two hours of head-cracking entertainment as we discover that it's okay for today's modern man to be left holding the baby... and a pump-action shotgun.

John Woo's final film before embarking for Hollywood is a typically kinetic calling card, high on style and energy. Once again, Chow Yun-Fat takes the lead playing Tequila, a hard-nosed Hong Kong cop intent on bringing down the arms dealing mobster, Johnny Wong (Anthony Wong), who killed his partner. After his boss takes him off the case, Tequila decides to carry on his investigation unofficially, forging links with Tony, an undercover cop who has infiltrated the gang posing as a hitman who must kill to maintain his cover. To get near the target, Tequila must blur the line between good and evil, gaining support from friends who endanger themselves to keep Tony's secret, and unite to fight against Wong as he holds an entire hospital hostage.

Trivia fans will have a bonanza with Woo's bullet ballet which spent 100,000 rounds of ammunition during filming, culminating in a body count of a record 300 (far higher than its nearest rival, *Die Hard 2*). Yun-Fat's character was named as a tribute to Sam Peckinpah's *The Wild Bunch*, in which a character downs a bottle of tequila prior to the infamous bloodbath ending, while the title is a pun on the Cantonese translation of *Dirty Harry*, another film which provides inspiration here. Woo trimmed his original version after the crew complained about the amount of explosives he envisaged – he later requested only 25% of that total after seeing sense. From there on the production appears to have run smoothly, with the same crew offering to work without pay when money was running low on a key sequence.

Hard Boiled played in UK theatres in the early 90s where its catalogue of carnage earned it the title of 'the most violent film in the history of cinema', and unsurprisingly, the British censors weren't entirely impressed, cutting out three seconds from the cinema release and a further two from video. Although interestingly, the cuts focused on human interactions like chops to the throat and knees to the chest rather than the excessive gunplay of which there is so much. But censor's quibbles aside, *Hard Boiled* was a resounding hit with audiences, giving Woo a platform to launch him to a string of English-speaking blockbusters like *Broken Arrow*, *Face/Off*, and *Mission Impossible 2*, in which glossy Hollywood heroes got to blow each other away in eye-popping style. All well and good, but for some film fans, Woo's best work was done before going to Hollywood in his films up to, and including, *Hard Boiled*.

Born in mainland China in 1948, John Woo started making movies in the 70s, turning out martial arts romps like *The Young Dragons* and *The Dragon Tamers*, and even helping out Jackie Chan's career with a co-starring role in *Hand of Death*. But it was in the 80s when he teamed up with Chow Yun-Fat to produce the internationally acclaimed gangster epic, *A Better Tomorrow*, that Woo's talent first started to be recognised in the West. Subsequent fare like *Bullet In the Head* and *Return to a Better Tomorrow* further raised his profile, with British-based company Palace Pictures picking up *The Killer* for distribution in the UK. But it was *Hard Boiled* which finally secured his reputation as the most exciting director in town, with one critic declaring "John Woo is God!", and notaries like Quentin Tarantino shouting that Hollywood should sign him up immediately. Something Universal Pictures did with *Hard Target*. And the rest is history.

As for Chow Yun-Fat, he subsequently went on to explore a softer side of his personality in Hollywood hits like *Anna and the King*, which proved that there's much more to him than gun-toting machismo. Indeed, as *Hard Boiled*'s ironically sardonic DVD cover shows Chow cradling a baby in one arm and a shotgun in the other, this demonstrates the key to the success of his on-screen persona; it's that strange balance between sensitive vulnerability and ice-cool implacability. He may be hard boiled on the outside but, like Woo, there's a tenderness underneath, even if you do have to run through a hail of bullets to get there.

Beauty's Evil Roses (1992)
(Orig title: *Se jiang II zhi xie mei gui*)
Dir: Lam Wuah Chuen /Hong Kong

This is one of the most insane and schizophrenic movies in the entire CAT III canon. It isn't as shocking or graphic as other films from Hong Kong of the time, but it's a must see for anyone who enjoys outrageous 'WTF?' moments piling up on screen.

The story starts with a young woman (played by the tomboy cop in *The Untold Story*, Emily Kwan) entering the office of a chief of police, seducing him into sex, and passing on some kind of bizarre, sexually-transmitted curse. The plot is then put on hold for ten minutes or so as various hot young women engage in steamy softcore sex scenes. When the story picks up again, there is a man looking for his girlfriend (Wong Wing-Fong), who has been abducted by an evil cult ruled by the leader, Da-Shie, and a police officer (Alex Fong of *Escape From Brothel* fame) is investigating the spate of missing girls, and who had a hot model sweetheart. There's also a Taoist priest who looks to be a down-market version of Lam Ching-Ying from the *Mr. Vampire* movies. He stumbles upon the evil magic of the cult leader, but doesn't make it to the final battle between good and evil… or something like that.

It's a confusing tale for sure, and not helped by the haphazard editing (in fact, the version of the film available on VCD looks suspiciously cut to ribbons by the censors – scenes often cut to the next just as things become graphic and violent – even the soundtrack clumsily breaks off in numerous scenes). I've read various synopses from online reviewers, some of which differ radically, and it's good to know that I'm not the only confused soul trying to work out what the hell is going on in this film. This movie doesn't seem to worry about coherency, it's far more occupied with things like the hilarious tentacle that comes out of Da-Shie's wrist; it looks like a ten foot long, brown crooked turd with a critter face on the end. And she uses said turd as a tool of punishment and enslavement. There is also a fight to the death set in another dimension that looks like something from an 80s TV show with its corny computer graphics and trippy aesthetics.

In terms of entertainment value, *Beauty's Evil Roses* is a riot and gradually becomes increasingly off the wall as it progresses until you reach the point where you're thinking your drink has been spiked with about eight tabs of LSD. The first half-hour is loaded with dull sex scenes (but the women here are hot), and it soon picks up, and before you know it you're assaulted with silly police procedures, even sillier kung fu fight scenes, black magic, witches, violent rape (including a woman having a knife rammed into her flue). There's also some amusing lesbian action, a wacky soundtrack which includes exotically-charged tribal rhythms, and cute girls teasing and whipping each other with what looks like a long, flexible pipe for a vacuum cleaner. And once it gets going, it never gets dull for a minute. There is probably a more graphic cut of this film doing the rounds somewhere, but I'll be damned if I can find it.

Braindead (1992)
(aka *Dead Alive*)
Dir: Peter Jackson /New Zealand
The final part of Peter Jackson's celebrated 'splatter trilogy' which kicked off with *Bad Taste* and continued with *Meet the Feebles*, is also the funniest and goriest. The basic plot concerns Lionel (Timothy Balme), whose tarot reading girlfriend, Paquita (the gorgeous Diana Penalver) joins him for a date at the local zoo. But Lionel's mother Vera (Elizabeth Moody) disapproves of their relationship because she believes the girl to be "experienced," and does all she can to disrupt their date until she is bitten by a Sutran rat monkey and transformed into a contagious zombie. Lionel takes her home but is unable to stop the spread of the undead, and pretty soon he has to deal with a zombified nurse, priest, and a very annoying zombified toddler. And then all hell breaks loose.

Braindead is a bloody spoof which takes a nostalgic look at 50s New Zealand, subverts it with a sharp social satire, and then adds a whole lotta blood. It's a film which marks the zenith of extreme movie gore whilst at the same time is a lot of fun, coming on like a feel good family comedy that just so happens to have sick jokes, hungry zombies, and a lawnmower bloodbath at the end. It's a bizarre mix that has delighted global audiences over the years, but not so much the critics, many of whom failed to see the funny side, like *The Daily Mail*'s Christopher Tooky who sniped "It's a good job the director grew out of making this stuff". Yeah, so that he could bombard us with utter tosh like *Lord of the Rings*, *King Kong*, and *Lovely Bones*? No

thanks, I'd settle for *Braindead* any day. Another critic labelled the film "The end of civilisation as we know it." High praise indeed!

With the international cult success of his home-made debut, *Bad Taste*, Jackson struggled for a long time to find anyone willing to finance *Braindead*, and eventually set out to work on *Meet the Feebles* instead, a strange puppet parody which became the focus of his frustrations as a filmmaker, and the result was a very nasty piece of work which attacked everything from showbiz, to war veterans, to AIDS victims. But none of that spiteful aggression is to be seen in *Braindead*, which despite the high levels of violence and sick gore, is a very upbeat experience. And with this film, Jackson seems to have exorcised some kind of demon from his psyche, because after *Braindead* he seemed to have matured and moved on to more adult-orientated projects like *Forgotten Silver* and *Heavenly Creatures* before selling out to Hollywood.

Incredibly, the BBFC passed *Braindead* uncut whilst films like *Straw Dogs* and *Reservoir Dogs* were still being refused home video certificates. The film did, however, cause much controversy in America when the MPAA cut it to ribbons for an R rating (it was also re-titled *Dead Alive* to avoid confusion with the Bill Pullman film of the same name). The morons at Blockbuster Video refused to stock the unrated version, so video company Vidmark supplied them with the R-rated cut which is just as silly and incoherent as the Blockbuster versions of *The Cook, the Thief, His Wife, and Her Lover,* and *Bad Lieutenant.*

It's a testament to Peter Jackson that he stuck to his guns and made exactly the type of movie he wanted to make without compromise, leaving viewers slack-jawed in amazement as Lionel gets out his lawnmower for the bloody showdown. Often topping polls for being the goriest movie ever made, but there is also a lot of heart here, even if you do have to pass through an avalanche of blood, guts, and body parts to get there.

Hellraiser III: Hell On Earth (1992)
Dir: Anthony Hickox /USA/Canada
"Down the dark decades of your pain, this will seem like a memory of heaven." So says Pinhead, or more accurately, the *dark side* of Pinhead in this much underrated third instalment in the *Hellraiser* saga. Subtitled *'Hell On Earth'*,

Hellraiser III completes the series' strange turn across the Atlantic, centring on a singly American nightclub whose sleaze-bag owner unknowingly unlocks the gateway to the other side while a TV news reporter investigates the puzzle box phenomenon. Pinhead soon appears with a new band of Cenobites, including Mr. CD Head and the Lensman ("Are you ready for your close-up?"), and pretty soon we see a bunch of clubbers get offed in brutal fashion.

Alongside the present-day action which is clearly designed to entice a new teenage audience, writer Pete Atkins and director Anthony Hickox also serve up a smattering of historic back-story in which Doug Bradley has the chance to explore his lighter side in his pre-Pinhead incarnation as Eliot. Here for the first time, *Hellraiser* fans get to see the gallant soldier, who had sold his soul to the Devil in 1920s India to give in to his desires to experience all the pleasures and pains of the flesh to which war had inured him. This marriage of acceptable teen trashiness and slightly more mature movie myth-making is the key to the success of *Hellraiser III*, allowing it to be loved by those who enjoyed the subtextual themes of Barker's original, and those who just want to see a goth nightclub go to hell.

One of the best scenes in the film finds Pinhead performing the blackest of black masses in the suitably desecrated surroundings of a church. The fact that a mainstream horror movie with undeniable teen-appeal could deliver such a blasphemous blow, is one of the true pleasures of *Hell On Earth*. Unlike *Hellbound* before it and *Bloodline* after it, Hickox's vision successfully straddles the two worlds of horror fandom, uniting young guns and old flames in a festival of destructive fun. There's also a smattering of knowing cameos for the hardcore horror fanatics to look out for, including Pete Atkins reprising the skin-ripping antics of *The Forbidden*; here he plays the bartender who has his face graphically re-arranged with barbed wire.

Hellraiser III doesn't deliver quite the same lasting love-bite as the first two in the series, but what it does do is inflict as much damage as possible from within the limited aesthetic of the pop video promo, from which it takes its visual cues. And that is something to be celebrated indeed.

A poor critical reception did not stop the series from marching on with *Hellraiser IV: Bloodline* (1995), which sent the franchise into the past and the future for an interesting tale which explored the origins of the puzzle box from the perspective of the year 2127. Part four was the last in the series to make it to the big screen. *Hellraiser: Inferno* (2000), *Hellraiser: Hellseeker* (2002), *Hellraiser: Deader* (2005), *Hellraiser: Hellworld* (2005), and *Hellraiser: Revelations* (2011) all went straight to DVD and serve as nothing more than morality tales in which Pinhead makes an occasional guest appearance to keep viewers awake. At the time of writing, the long-anticipated remake of *Hellraiser* still hasn't been made.

Man Bites Dog (1992)
(Original title: *C'est arrive pres de chev vous*)
Dir: Remy Belvaux, Andre Bonzel, Benoit Poelvoorde /Belgium

A spoof documentary in which a group of student filmmakers follow a racist, sexist, homophobic, and all round opinionated serial killer called Benoit. He cracks jokes, mocks the public, recites dreadful poetry, and is also a rapist. For all its sharp satirical humour, the film succeeds in wiping the smiles from our faces about two thirds of the way in during a scene of unbelievable debauchery; and it's then that the film attacks its audience, turning uneasy laughter into abysmal horror...

Benoit ogles the camera for most of the running time, giving tips on how to weigh down a corpse, and expressing his views on every subject imaginable between his acts of cold-blooded murder. Nobody is safe from this psychopath – men, women, children, the elderly, everyone is a potential victim. He doesn't stick to a particular murder method either; hence shootings, beatings, strangulations, suffocations, and even the blackly comic act of scaring somebody to death, is all paraded before our eyes. Benoit is soon calling the shots and even using his own cash to fund the impoverished production when funds are running low. And it's only a matter of time before the filmmakers are roped in to helping Benoit in his crimes until there's no difference between student filmmaker and calculating killer.

Shot in hand-held black and white, *Man Bites Dog* is a chilling parody of the Reality TV format which would pollute the world's airwaves for years to come. The filmmakers wanted to expose how easily the appearance of a film crew can alter the behaviour of those being filmed, and how the 'reality' of the film's subjects is nothing more than a performance designed to entertain the viewers. In *Man Bites Dog* that entertainment factor is taken to disturbing extremes, guiding the viewers through its farcical set up and becoming increasingly unsettling as it reaches its conclusion.

As if to confuse the line further between fact and fiction, the cast members appear on screen using their real first names, including Remy, the psychotic moron who is driven into participating in the crimes with dreams of fame and fortune, and director Andre who begins with a strict journalistic distance from Benoit, but is eventually joining in on the mayhem too. And it's here that *Man Bites Dog* turns against its audience for liking and expecting to be thrilled by the exploits of serial killers. It's this latter element that puts the film in the company of John McNaughton's *Henry-Portrait of a Serial Killer* and Michael Haneke's *Benny's Video* and *Funny Games*; films which take on a similar stance and present us with amoral thrills before pulling the nasty carpet from beneath our feet. And like those films, *Man Bites Dog* also succeeds in presenting us with a cracked mirror which reflects on the cynical world view that panders to dumb arseholes (especially nowadays with the real life exploitation of reality TV which glorifies, condescends, and mocks its performers whilst swelling its producers' bank accounts).

Man Bites Dog cast a large influential shadow over the subsequent years. Whether directly or indirectly, the power of this Belgian art-house favourite has made its presence felt in everything from the cheap and shoddy farce-fests of the crudest examples of reality TV, to the big screen skin-crawling horrors of *The Blair Witch Project* and *The Last Broadcast* (compare the last shot of *Man Bites Dog* with that of *Blair Witch*, for example).

In America, the film emerged unrated (except for Blockbuster Video who demanded one of their infamous re-edit jobs to make the film palatable to their customers), and in the UK it was passed uncut for both cinema and video. One of the chief censors at the BBFC later admitted that if they had known how popular the video would become they would have snipped a couple of scenes. Luckily for us it didn't happen, and *Man Bites Dog* escaped intact from their clutches and reached cult classic status before its notoriety would return to haunt the censors.

Bitter Moon (1992)
Dir: Roman Polanski /France/UK

Even as early as 1992, the erotic thriller had seemingly run its course after such lurid hits as *Fatal Attraction, Basic Instinct, Poison Ivy* and the like having worn the sub-genre into the ground with their clichés and dangerous femmes fatale. But Polish director, Roman Polanski, presented *Bitter Moon*, an utterly warped variation on his earlier film, *Knife In The Water*, to show that there was much that had yet to be explored in this otherwise silly and excessive genre.

On board a cruise ship heading for Istanbul, British couple Nigel (Hugh Grant) and Fiona (Kristen Scott Thomas) meet a strange French woman called Mimi (Emmanuelle Seigner, Polanski's wife) and her wheelchair-bound husband, Oscar (Peter Coyote). Oscar begins to tell the story of how he met Mimi, and goes on to describe their highly unusual relationship. And while Fiona deals with her seasickness by taking sleeping pills, Nigel is drawn deeper into the story, convinced that he and Mimi will get to have sex at some point on the cruise. However, Oscar's story becomes increasingly nasty and twisted, and after telling Nigel how he came to be paralysed from the waist down, the scene is set for a disastrous New Year's celebration…

Bitter Moon is a film which plays up to – and parodies – the erotic thrillers that were popular in the 80s and early 90s, and succeeds in spicing things up with a cruel and perverse edge, offering up much in the way of dark humour, while the emotional turmoil of each character is laid bare in sometimes excruciating detail. Much of the story is told in flashback, and this is where we discover the psychological torture that drove Mimi and Oscar's relationship from a mutual harmony to an obsessive and destructive battle of wills.

Fiona's character is a tad underused, but she really comes to the fore in the finale. Coyote is absolutely brilliant as the American writer Oscar, and he demonstrates a convincing transformation from a naïve and ambitious writer who heads for Paris in the footsteps of his heroes, Hemingway and Fitzgerald, and eventually becomes a bitter and twisted loser. Seigner puts on the finest performance of her career, which frankly, isn't saying much, but despite what the critics have said, and despite her bad performances in other movies, she's perfectly cast in *Bitter Moon*, and is totally believable at expressing both vulnerability (when she is bullied, humiliated and abandoned on a plane) and menace (when she decides to dedicate her life to making Oscar's a living hell). Whether she's brandishing syringes, cutthroat razors, or even her own sexuality as weapons, you believe every second of it. And Hugh Grant is his usual self in a typically bashful and awkward role as Nigel, a man so wimpy and spineless he puts up with the silly games and practical jokes that Oscar and Mimi play on him. Any normal person would have thrown them both overboard after the blatant cock-teasing prank in which she invites him to their darkened cabin only for him to find that he had climbed into bed with her crippled husband. Nigel's barely controllable lust for Mimi is quite creepy; his willingness to be unfaithful to his wife at the first sight of an attractive female doesn't really sit right with his character. He just doesn't seem like that kind of guy. Unfaithful ones are usually those who are more forward and self-assured in their pursuit of sexual gratification, but Nigel doesn't have the confidence to talk his way into bed with a beautiful stranger. Besides, he seems far too normal and prudish to be drawn into Oscar and Mimi's twisted games. His idea of a coke-fuelled threesome would be a glass of cola followed by a smoked salmon and horseradish baguette. And the only time you hear him growling the phrase "you know you want it" is when he is offering his wife a sleeping pill.

Hugh Grant made a successful career playing wimpish, floppy-haired Englishmen; he did such a great job of embodying those types of characters that many assumed he must be that sort of person in real life. So it came as a shock to the world when in 1995 he was busted by L.A. cops getting sucked off by a street whore. His mug shot was strewn across news headlines worldwide; he looked like a man who had just been rudely awoken from a great dream, and didn't look to be happy about it at all. I was a teenager at the time, and besides from wondering what kind of bleak world we live in, in which movie stars like Hugh Grant have to pay to get noshed off, I was also reminded of *Bitter Moon* and how Grant's horny rendezvous was exactly the kind of thing Nigel's character would have done the moment the cruise ship docked at Istanbul.

Speaking of scandals – and on a more serious note – director Roman Polanski was no stranger to them, either. He slept with a thirteen-year-old girl after a photo shoot in L.A. in 1977. He was arrested and pleaded guilty to the charge of unlawful sex with a minor. To avoid his prison sentence, Polanski fled to London, and eventually moved to France. More than three decades later, in September 2009, he was apprehended by Swiss police at the request of U.S. authorities, who also asked for his extradition. The Swiss rejected that request, and instead released him without charge. He has never returned to the states since the late 70s. If he ever steps foot again on American soil, he'll be detained at the airport and forced to serve his sentence. He remains a free man in Europe, and continues on his filmmaking career to this day. His classic films, such as *Frantic*, *Death and The Maiden*, and his masterpiece, *The Pianist*, were all shot in Europe, often as big international co-productions. And despite the scandal looming over his head, his reputation as a filmmaker has continued to grow over the decades, with top producers and actors queuing up to work with him.

Anyway, back to *Bitter Moon*. Mainstream critics largely dismissed the film, accusing it of being "crass" and lacking credibility overall. The S&M scenes and pig-mask role-play games were also frowned upon, especially in the UK where *Empire* magazine cried "Don't they believe in divorce in Paris?" *The Observer* called it "the work of a perverse, exhausted talent narrated by a perverse, exhausted talentless writer to trap a dim-witted listener." The reception wasn't much better across the pond; Janet Maslin of the *New York Times* praised Kristen Scott Thomas's performance on the grounds that she wasn't actually present in most of the scenes. She went on to accuse everyone else of "going off the deep end." But still, there was something about the film that has kept people coming back for more over the last couple of decades since its release, making it something of a bona fide cult item nowadays. Indeed, at its best, *Bitter Moon* presents a darkly comic *grand guignol* take on modern relationships, and is ideally suited to repeat viewings. Polanski has since tried his hand at repeating the cult appeal with films like *Death and the Maiden* and *The Ninth Gate*, but they don't come close to the noirish, decadent fun of *Bitter Moon*, whose 139-minute running time passes by in a flash.

Twin Peaks: Fire Walk With Me (1992)
Dir: David Lynch /USA

If your only familiarity with *Twin Peaks* is sitting in puzzled silence for a couple of episodes as some backwards-talking dwarf appears on screen, then there's very little point in seeing this feature-length offering as this does little to shed any light on the saga either. However, if you're one of those who feel that David Lynch's small-screen series was a work of demented genius, then you absolutely must see this, despite the numerous boos and jeers and scathing reviews which greeted its initial release.

Serving as a prequel to the TV series, *Fire Walk With Me* is unconventional from the get-go and is split into two distinctive parts. The first half hour or so plays like a self-contained episode in its own right, as FBI Agent Desmond (Chris Isaak) and dorky forensics guy Stanley (Keifer Sutherland) investigate the murder of Teresa Banks, stopping off at a strange diner and the Fat Trout trailer park run by the shifty owner (Harry Dean Stanton). And it's only now, more than thirty minutes into the film, when we finally get to hear the famous *Twin Peaks* theme tune; those deep, resonating guitar notes which signify sweetness and wonder, in stark contrast to the dark, psycho-sexual menace soon to be explored on screen. The plot then heads off in a different direction and follows high school girl Laura Palmer (Sheryl Lee) on the last few days of her life. It's a disturbing, nightmarish descent into hell as she falls apart psychologically while getting into prostitution and blow. These dark details were only briefly hinted at in the TV show, but here they're presented in much more sordid detail as she heads closer to the Black Lodge, the place of her demise, and the point at which the series began.

But for all the film's freedoms away from the small screen where it was permitted more flexibility in form and content, *Fire Walk With Me* is simply not interested in letting the fans know what happened next after the series finished. There is also the absence of many key characters and locations of the TV show, such as Sherilyn Fenn's Audrey Horne and Lara Flynn Boyle's Donna Hayward, the Great Northern Hotel and the police station. However, we are introduced to several new characters, most notably the oddball apparition Philip Jeffries (an awful – and thankfully brief – performance by David Bowie whose awkward, transatlantic accent shifts between London and Texas from one word to the next), but the real interest here is the sinister mood that Lynch manages to sustain throughout much of the film. Lynch also inserts a little in-joke in the scene where he introduces Agent Desmond and Stanley to the mime girl (Kimberly Anne Cole), whose strange dance reveals a complex set of messages which will help them get started on the case. Desmond later explains to Stanley the significance of the symbolism in her dance, and it's an obvious skit on the way fans and critics tend to pick apart his films in search of symbols and hidden meanings.

I sometimes watch movies late at night with headphones on so that I can crank up the volume. Maybe it's a bit weird, but I find it surprisingly effective as a way of getting drawn in to whatever it is I'm watching. Try it. Of course, it helps when there's a kick-arse soundtrack and score by Angelo Badalamenti. And using headphones is also very effective at accentuating the horror, as in the scene where Laura slowly creeps into her bedroom looking for clues as to why pages from her secret diary had been torn out. As she peers around the door into her room, she sees something which – I guarantee – will make your skin crawl off and hide under the table. But, as I said, the scares work much better when you have loud headphones on for the full effect.

However, the real dark heart of *Fire Walk With Me* rests with Laura and her gradual realisation that the person who has been raping her since she was twelve years old is actually someone very close to home. The film is also notable for the difference in Leland Palmer's character; in the TV show he was depicted as the tragic man of the town, but in this prequel he is shown to be exactly what he is: an outright monster.

Escape From Brothel (1992)
(Orig title: *Hua jie kuang ben*)
Dir: Lung Wei Wang /Hong Kong

A young sports teacher, Sam (Alex Fong), is recruited by his friends to Hong Kong for an armed robbery at a jewellery store that has been pre-arranged by the store owner as a way of cashing in on the insurance payout. However, when the boys give away their identities on their escape from the crime scene, due to a camera, a couple of tourists, and an unfortunate killing, they find themselves on the run and in deep trouble, not only with the local police, but also the jewellery store owner who would much rather have them killed than confessing anything to the police. Meanwhile, Sam's sweetheart, Hung (the late Pauline Chan), works in a brothel, unbeknownst to him. And when he shows up at the house one day looking for a place to hide out, Hung tries to keep her profession a secret so as not to hurt him. When he does eventually discover what's going on, Sam and Hung are forced to flee from the brothel when ruthless criminals show up looking for his blood. Sam attempts to get back to the mainland, but perhaps inevitably, their journey ends in treachery and brutal violence.

Like many other Category III titles, *Escape From Brothel* starts out as a soft and silly sex comedy, but darkens dramatically as it progresses. The humour is apparent in scenes involving a naked white woman who displays some high-kicking kung fu moves, and the "sex maniac" who hangs out in the women's shower room, incognito. But the lighthearted tone soon becomes muddied with the introduction of rape, electro torture, and superbly choreographed bloody violence, including an amazing fight scene in which people attack each other with machetes while climbing a bamboo scaffold. Those who regularly watch these types of films will spot one or two familiar faces, such as Ho Kai Hui of *Daughter of Darkness* who plays a corrupt cop who demands freebies from the prostitutes. Also lookout for Ben Lam (*Police Story* and *Police Story 2*) who plays another bad guy, and Japanese AV star Rene Murakami (of *Sex and Zen* fame) as Hung's sexy sister.

Actress Pauline Chan made such an impact in this film as Sam's girlfriend, Hung, and also in other classics like *Devil of Rape*, *Whores of China*, and *Erotic Ghost Story III*, and became an icon for off-beat film fans in the process. She caused much controversy in the Chinese press during the 90s. Born in Shanghai in 1973, she moved to Hong Kong and entered the film industry in 1991 at 18 years old, and starred in dozens of Cat III films. She was in a troubled relationship with a famous Taiwanese investment tycoon, Huang Jen Chung, who was 33 years older than her. She used drugs and sorcery to ease her emotional pain and to win back his heart when they split up. She attempted suicide during a live television interview,

physically attacked random members of the public, set fire to her home, and was also hospitalised several times for near-fatal drug overdoses. Her career came to an end when she was sent to prison in the UK for assaulting a stranger. Most tragically, Chan later committed suicide by jumping from her apartment window on the 24th floor. She was just 29 years old. In a strange twist, Chinese actress Crystal Sun played Chan in the biopic *Pauline's Life* (2002), and she also took her own life in 2009.

Escape From Brothel is perhaps Chan's finest hour, a challenging mixture of humour, heartbreak, and horror, directed by the ever adaptable Lung Wei Wang who also made the wacky *City Warriors* (1991), and even took up a few minor acting roles, most notably as the gang leader in Billy Tang's outrageous *Run and Kill* (1993). *Escape From Brothel* was cut for its UK release, but is available untouched on VCD on the Ocean Shores label.

964 Pinocchio (1992)
Dir: Shozin Fukui /Japan

Brain-modified sex slave, Pinocchio, can't get an erection and is thrown out by his horny female owners. Lost and vulnerable, he meets Himiko, a seemingly friendly face who offers him food and shelter. Himiko teaches Pinocchio how to walk and talk, but on their heels are the inventors who are in charge of the sex slave industry, and they must capture Pinocchio in order to repair him and spare the blushes of the company. This very odd couple are forced to live in the shadows and they spew forth all kinds of bodily secretions before Himiko reveals her true motives...

Borrowing heavily from the early work of Shinya Tsukamoto, both visually and thematically, writer/director Shozin Fukui creates a volatile cyberpunk nightmare that includes high-powered androids, slimy body horrors, and frantic set-pieces, all shot in a ferocious hyper-kinetic style. This is disorientating stuff, visually astonishing, tirelessly inventive, and includes just about every bodily fluid there is. Due to the film's low budget, many scenes were shot in guerrilla-style, with the normal everyday citizens staring into the camera lens and probably wondering what the hell they are witnessing as Pinocchio staggers through the streets dragging along with him a silver pyramid.

The only downside to this film is that the

characters are so cliched and predictable; we have the inventor who will stop at nothing to protect his investment, the flirty secretary who will do anything for her boss, Himiko who is clearly much more sinister than she lets on, and also the agents who are chasing Pinocchio; they resemble your typical cyber-boffins who are willing to sacrifice anything for the sake of their important research.

On the plus side, we get a director at the height of his directorial powers who wears his varied influences very much on his sleeve; we get elements of *Tetsuo the Iron Man* and *Tetsuo 2: Body Hammer* with the faded comic-book-style colours, frenetic camera work, and the climactic robot march through the city. The scene in which Himiko gets violently ill in the train station and literally vomits everywhere is clearly modelled on the classic scene from Andrzej Zulawski's *Possession*. Fukui returned with *Rubber's Lover* in 1996.

Romper Stomper (1992)
Dir: Geoffrey Wright /Australia

Geoffrey Wright's *Romper Stomper* opened at Leceister Square in the early 90s and was surrounded by controversy when the Anti-Nazi League gathered and protested outside. In an eerie air of deja vu, a similar reception greeted *A Clockwork Orange* 20 years earlier, and like Kubrick's film, the morally outraged protesters had not even seen the film that they were so adamant would encourage imitative behaviour. Those who actually sat down and watched the movie saw nothing that could in any way label it as a pro-Nazi picture, and the wide-spread controversy in the end created a firestorm of publicity, thanks to the tabloid frenzy and the misguided lemmings, and *Romper Stomper* became something of a hit.

The film follows a gang of neo-Nazi skinheads led by Hando (Russell Crowe) who beat and bully the local Vietnamese. They also get into a tangle with the father of a rich white girl (Jacqueline McKenzie), and she runs away to be with Hando, and becomes witness to an array of nasty goings on, and is lectured on the ideology of Hitler's *Mein Kampf*. After a night of sex, violence, and debauchery, the thugs discover that their local pub has been sold to a Vietnamese man. They then converge on the place and brutally assault the new landlord's two sons ("Let's break some fingers!"). A third son manages to escape unseen, and he phones his friends for back up. And before long, cars and van loads of Vietnamese show up brandishing baseball bats and iron bars. A mass brawl breaks out at the back of the pub, and Hando's heavily out-numbered skinheads flee the area, leaving their casualties behind to face their ugly fates. The gang are chased through the backstreets of Melbourne to their dilapidated hideout, a barbed wire fortress where they intend to make a last stand. But the sheer number of enemies forces them to escape through a roof hatch instead as the Vietnamese clobber their way inside and set fire to the building. The skinheads commandeer a nearby warehouse and set up their new base, but the damage is done, and the gang turn on each other as Hando's bully-boy antics spiral out of control, leading to treachery and murder.

Russell Crowe's first lead role is a tour de force in seething hatred as the shaven-headed Hando, and he is also backed up with some solid support from McKenzie as Hando's spoilt brat lover, Gabe, and Daniel Pollock as Hando's second-in-command, Davey, whose secret love for Gabe and his own German heritage adds another angle to the drama, as these things only seem to effect Davey's conscience once the madness has reached irrevocable levels. The thrash punk soundtrack was created by members of Screwdriver, and the oily tunes like '*Fuhrer Fuhrer*' and '*Fourth Reich Fighting Men*' adds to the gritty excitement of the chaotic fight scenes. None of the musicians would accept licensing fees or royalties for their work on the film. The excitement though is ultimately quashed by a sense of dismay for people like the characters in *Romper Stomper*; all the violence and hatred stemming from the sad fantasies of grown men who cannot even take charge of their own destinies let alone a neo-Nazi movement.

Romper Stomper found itself mired in controversy once again in 2000 when the psychotic British prisoner, Robert Stewart, battered to death his Asian cellmate while he slept, only days after watching the film. Stewart idolised Hando, and also Alex from *A Clockwork Orange*, and the numerous letters he wrote contained much hatred and racism. But I think this awful tragedy says more about the failings of the Feltham Young Offenders Institute than it does about the film's supposed racist and amoral stance. The fact that the actions of a psychotic young prisoner, who was already known for being racist before he committed the crime (clue: he had a Swastika tattooed on his forehead) can be used as a further ploy to call for a banning of the film beggars belief. The nutcases of society (and in the prisons and young offenders institutes) can be led to extreme violence by watching Cartoon Network if they're that way inclined, so the argument that *Romper Stomper* can cause imitative behaviour among normal members of society is either moral cowardice, legal chicanery, or plain old stupidity, as far as I'm concerned. Besides, the skinheads in *Romper Stomper* are depicted as a group of dumb and selfish bullies who all turn on each other at the first sign of anyone taking a stand against them; hardly character traits anyone in their right minds would aspire to.

Wright was interviewed by Marcus Stiglegger for *Flesh & Blood* magazine in 2001. Talking about the controversy that greeted his film, Wright pinpointed a fault line of the media. 'The idea of saying, in a creative work, that the appeal of fascism is very much about a licence to act out of control – and making that point on a visceral level that pumps adrenaline for the viewer the same way that the members of the gang pump adrenaline – is just too sophisticated a notion for them to come to terms with. They are not equipped for it on a policy level. What the left and right have in common is a fear that the individual cannot think for themselves and must be organised and saved from themselves. The point is, if the viewer gets excited in the chase scene and the skinheads in the movie also got excited in the chase scene – how different are you fundamentally or physiologically? The answer: not very. And there's the rub, that's what drives detractors of the film crazy. A creative work, to them, should never get this intimate, but remain stand-offish, objective, in the realm of a deep perspective that shows THEM – those evil skinheads from outer space – and US – the good people who would *never* do that and may judge from afar. Huh?! Really? Skinheads are not *that* different from anyone else.'

Like it or loathe it, *Romper Stomper* is here to stay. Director Geoffrey Wright has much to say on the subject of racism, and on its travels across the globe, *Romper Stomper*, despite all the controversy, got people talking about racism and its effects on individuals and on society as a whole. And that can only be a good thing.

Suburb Murder (1992)
(Orig title: *Heung Gong gaan saat kei ngon*)
Dir: Jeng Kin-Ping /Hong Kong

British rule in Hong Kong had always forbid filmmakers from attacking their imperial majesty and from depicting their rulers in a bad light. *Suburb Murder*, however, looks to have escaped the scandal sheet perhaps because it's a tale based on a true story, but the finished film can barely disguise its resentment, and does little to sugarcoat its anti-colonialist stance, and pushes as far as the rule of law will allow.

A young woman and her grandfather stumble upon a mutilated body while jogging in the hills and they report their discovery to the local police. The body is that of a young white woman who looks to have had her face smashed in and her nipple bitten off. An investigation is launched. A tip-off leads the police to the hideout of a wanted gang, and a gun battle ensues with the gang members desperate to escape. One young rogue is captured and beaten by the police. In custody he is beaten some more and interrogated, and he agrees to tell the police the full story of his crimes in exchange for a cigarette. Cue a lengthy flashback as the kid explains his side of the story, a la *Daughter of Darkness* and *The Untold Story*.

Kang's only childhood friend was Chi, a chubby kid who was taken by his father to live in America. Kang plays truant one afternoon and goes home to witness his father catching mum fucking another guy. The guy jumps out of the bedroom window and escapes in his underwear. Mother is slapped and thrown out of the house, and young Kang is also thrown out on his ear and told never to return again. And from then on the kid must fend for himself on the streets.

As a young adult, Kang works as a dishwasher at a restaurant but his boss is an arsehole and is constantly looking for an excuse to dock his wages. Kang and his co-workers have formed a gang and they go out looking for trouble; they find a young couple and beat the boyfriend and gang-rape the girl. They then head back to work and beat the crap out of their boss. A passing policeman sees the incident and gives chase but the boys make their getaway on foot. Kang bumps into his old friend Chi who is back in Hong Kong after the death of his father. Kang takes him back to his living quarters but the other boys are in the middle of a sex sesh with a couple of young women, and Chi is shocked by the unabashed coupling on display.

The arsehole boss sends out some heavies to attack the gang with clubs and iron bars, and a mass brawl ensues in the middle of the street.

The gang go to have some fun at a whorehouse and one of the older hookers turns out to be Kang's mother whom he hasn't seen for years (this only becomes clear after two of his friends have slept with her). Kang feels upset and betrayed, and his resentments begin to simmer under the surface. He and his old friend Chi make a pittance by washing cars, one of which belongs to his father who looks him over like a piece of garbage and throws a couple of dollars in his face. Kang's father looks to have done well for himself over the years since he severed all ties with him and his mother; he drives a nice car and wears an expensive suit. Kang's humiliation continues when he helps a white woman with her bag from the boot of a taxi but she refuses to give him a tip. He shouts abuse at her and then he is arrested by a white man for begging offences. In custody he bumps into his father yet again who looks to be employed by the city, but he refuses to bail out his son.

Kang later gets himself a girlfriend, Kitty, and on her birthday the gang have a little party for her and get drunk (everyone seems to drink San Miguel in Hong Kong). Whilst walking her home, they stop by at King's Park for a drunken sing song; Chi decides he wants some wine and heads off to the shop, Kang and Kitty stay behind and have a smooch, but the merry mood is spoiled when a pair white thugs show up and beat Kang before raping Kitty. Chi returns to the hills to see what's going on and he attacks the thugs with a stick, but he is beaten with a rock and left paralyzed. Kitty runs into the middle of the road and is run over by a passing van and killed.

From now on, Kang is like a time-bomb ready to explode, and when he and his gang get drunk and go roaming the hills at King's Park, they spot a young Western couple sitting on the grass. The boyfriend is badly beaten, and then his hands are tied and Kang finally explodes; he takes a tree branch and repeatedly beats the guy's head in with it. He then approaches the others who are gang-raping the woman, and he pushes them aside and then beats her head in with the stick and even bites her nipple off in a psychotic rage. The others have to drag him away. The girl's lifeless body is then thrown into the tall grass and they flee the area.

After a violent robbery at a gambling den with the use of guns and machetes, the boy's days are numbered. Their pictures are broadcast on the news and they fall out and turn on each other. One of the gang members, Hairy, is captured by CID and he later informs officers of the gang's hideout. And the story comes full circle when the police show up for a blazing gun battle.

This downbeat tale from Hong Kong is atypical of the usual Cat III madness in that it is played unsettlingly straight; there's none of the usual dark humour or hammy psycho performances or bold candy coloured lighting effects to be found here. What we get instead is an absorbing and believable study of encroaching madness brought on by a string of humiliations and bad luck, and has more in common with Fu Lee and Chu Yin-Ping's *Angel Heart* than Herman Yau's *The Untold Story*. It still offers the obligatory Cat III sex scenes and a steady build-up to a grim and violent finale, but at the same time it feels completely out of step with the works of Yau and Billy Tang, and Bosco Lam, et al.

The rape scenes are as graphic and exploitative as most Hong Kong titles, and the killing of the young woman at the end is extremely nasty and disturbing; Kang's resentment has reached such a fever pitch of discontent that even to see an innocent couple spending some time together in the park is enough to make his blood boil and sends him completely over the edge. And director Jeng Kin-Ping should be commended for depicting the seething resentments that simmer under the surface of society in a completely honest and brutal fashion. It's certainly not a film for everybody, and those new to the Cat III phenomenon will be turned off, but those who are familiar with these films may find it a refreshing change from the norm.

Bad Lieutenant (1992)
Dir: Abel Ferrara /USA

"I'm sorry. I'm sorry I did so many bad things". After causing much controversy in the 70s and 80s with a pair of notorious 'video nasties', *The Driller Killer* and *Ms.45*, director Abel Ferrara shocked the world once again in the 90s with *Bad Lieutenant*, an intelligent and fiercely uncompromising journey into the pit of human darkness, boasting a riveting, uninhibited performance from the brilliant Harvey Keitel.

Taking its inspiration from a newspaper headline about the rape of a nun, Ferrara co-wrote the script with Zoe Lund (formerly Zoe Tamerlis who starred in *Ms.45* as the angel of vengeance), and together they fashioned a tale about a New York cop who self-destructs on drink, drugs, and gambling. The nameless cop becomes even more troubled when he discovers that the nun has forgiven her attackers, and the Lt. must try to put aside his own desperate need for vengeance if he is to save his wretched soul.

The resulting film was met with outrage from the press, so much so that it even surprised Ferrara himself who was certainly no stranger to cinematic controversy. For, although *Bad Lieutenant* is a raw exercise in requisite shocks, it's also a classic tale of Catholic redemption. The BBFC recognised this and passed the film uncut for a British cinema release after seeing the light at the end of a very dark tunnel. But when it came to home video classification, Ferrara's film didn't make it through unscathed; a minute and a half of cuts were imposed by the censors due to an altering of legislation that stemmed from the original Video Recordings Act (which Ferrara's films, *The Driller Killer* and *Ms.45*, ironically helped usher in).

In America, the MPAA imposed an NC-17 rating on the film which resulted in Blockbuster Video refusing to stock it, and instead oversaw a drastic re-cut that was so empty and incoherent it has since been referred to as 'the really not that bad at all lieutenant'. The video release was also beset with contractual problems over the Schooly D soundtrack; Jimmy Page of Led Zeppelin had allegedly watched the video and noticed that his song, *Kashmir*, had been sampled without permission in the song *Signifying Rapper*. A lawsuit followed which saw the removal of all home video editions. I think that's a bit cheeky of Jimmy Page – after all, Led Zeppelin ripped off plenty of classic blues numbers themselves back in the day, but I digress.

In the year 2000, Film Four broadcast *Bad Lieutenant* in the BBFC-approved version with the Schooly D track restored. Other video and TV prints include an acoustic track, *'Bad Lieutenant'*, written and performed by Ferrara himself. But it's Harvey Keitel's stunning performance which saves the film and stops it from falling by the wayside. Even with the camera following him and rarely leaving his side for most of the running time, his method master class basically carries the film from start to finish. Whether he's shooting up heroin, jerking off in front of a couple of girls, walking around stark bollock naked whilst drugged up to the eyeballs, or wailing like a sick parrot, he somehow manages to add a touch of humanity to the role which, for many viewers, has made *Bad Lieutenant* just about tolerable.

Look out for the late great Zoe Lund as Keitel's junky mistress, and Ferrara's buddy Paul Hipp who makes a cameo appearance as Christ himself. Despite some of the knee-jerk reactions to the film, and despite what the *Washington Post*'s Desson Howe said about it ("A notch nicer than Satan"), *Bad Lieutenant* has had many good write ups over the years. Martin Scorsese claimed it to be one of the finest films of the 90s. What more encouragement do you need?

Tetsuo 2: Body Hammer (1992)
Dir: Shinya Tsukamoto / Japan

The international success of *Tetsuo The Iron Man* awarded Tsumamoto with something resembling a budget this time around for a sequel-cum-remake. And like Sam Raimi's *Evil Dead II*, Tsukamoto was ready to do it all over again in epic proportions for *Tetsuo 2: Body Hammer*. This time, however, he also presents us with a back-story which helps explain all the chaos.

Borrowing plot elements from Cronenberg's *Scanners*, *Tetsuo 2*'s premise sees a visionary lunatic pitching his rival sons together in a war based on mind power. Tamoroh Taguchi returns as the 'salaryman' who is attacked by a pair of scary looking fellows who belong to a subterranean sect of shaven-headed followers who are prone to mutations. The two men shoot Taguchi in the chest with an infectious rivet gun and kidnap his little boy. In a fit of desperation, he chases the bad guys up onto the roof of a tower block where the kidnappers taunt him by dangling his child over the edge. Taguchi's fears and fury reach boiling point and he begins to mutate, and a strange gun breaks out of his chest. And in his attempts to finish the bad guys, he accidentally shoots his own child, leaving nothing behind but lots of blood and a pair of tiny hands being held by one of the cackling kidnappers. Having to go home and explain all this to his wife understandably puts their relationship under severe strain. And when the kidnappers return and take off with her too,

Taguchi's transmutations reach overdrive as he gradually becomes a human tank who is prepared to put his own loved ones in jeopardy in order to get even with his rivals. The underground sect, meanwhile, sees a new leader (Tsukamoto himself) who forces his way into power, and this man happens to be Taguchi's long lost brother who is no less adept at sprouting firearms from his body. And the war continues...

This time around, director Tsukamoto shot the film in colour with a murky comic book tint; in some scenes (especially the ones played out in broad daylight) he employs a shade filter over the lens giving the shots a strange orange glow. For such a small budget film the visuals are no less than stunning throughout. He also resumes his love for the busy hand-held photography, rapid cutting, and bizarre stop-motion sequences which are perhaps more impressive than those seen in the original *Tetsuo* film. And there's a blatant homosexual subtext made apparent in the scenes featuring the shaven-headed army posing and pumping iron and penetrating their fellows with metal pipes.

The emotional side of the story is also improved upon in *Tetsuo 2* with the back-story adding depth and dimension to the main characters. Most impressive though is the exploration of fury and the desire for revenge that becomes so great that wiping out your entire family is perfectly fine if it means getting one over on those who put them in danger in the first place. It's a trait that pertains the human condition but is rarely explored to any degree in film. It's a 'curse' of masculinity that many men are in danger of jeopardising everything in times of crisis due to feelings of helplessness and a lack of control.

Tetsuo 2 stands as a film unto itself and you don't have to be familiar with the original in order to get to grips with this one. However, if you were impressed by *Iron Man* then chances are you'll be amazed by this full colour offering. Tsukamoto returned with a third instalment of the *Tetsuo* series in 2010 with *Tetsuo: The Bullet Man*. It was shot on DV in English with a largely Western cast. Tsukamoto this time casts himself as the mutating anti-hero, and the film is good fun, although overall it lacks the unruly spark of mayhem and epic quality of the first two films.

Doctor Lamb (1992)
(Orig title: *Gou yeng yi sang*)
Dir: Danny Lee and Billy Tang /Hong Kong

Loosely based on the true case in 1982 of a deranged taxi driver, Lam Go-wan, who brutally murdered several women whom he considered unsavoury. He later told police that he had been instructed by God to kill the women. He was captured after developing extremely disturbing photographs of himself mutilating and having sex with the bodies. Horrified staff who worked at the camera store alerted the police. And Lam was sentenced to life in prison.

The film starts with a flashback to Lam's troubled childhood before the present day action in which cops close in on Lam when he enters the camera shop to collect his photos. The police apprehend him and search his home. After Inspector Lee (Danny Lee of *The Untold Story* and *Love to Kill*, who also served as co-director on this film), finds an incriminating clue, Lam is taken back to the station and placed under heavy interrogation and abuse as a way of getting a confession out of him. He is beaten with a hammer through a phone book, an old police trick to ensure no bruising. He is also beaten with a hammer on the soles of his feet while the Hong Kong press clamour outside. And, using a plot device which would later be imitated to death in future Cat III releases – *The Untold Story, Daughter of Darkness, Suburb Murder*, etc - Lam eventually breaks down under the pressure and reveals his gruesome story to the police in flashback.

Doctor Lamb is one of the more well-known Cat III shockers from Hong Kong, alongside *The Untold Story, Riki-Oh*, and *Ebola Syndrome*. It was Danny Lee's directorial debut (he was helped by the notorious Billy Tang, the man behind *Run and Kill* and *Red to Kill*), and offers up an insane performance by Simon Yam in the lead role. Yam is superb as the maniac, leering at the camera and chewing the scenery like a pro. At various points in this film, his features seem to take on a life of their own, as if at any moment his face will literally leap off his head and go running through the tall grass, attacking dandelions with its teeth. Also lookout for Kent Cheng as the overweight cop, Fat Bing; he would later go on to play the stoic victim in Tang's harrowing *Run and Kill* a few years later. For a double-bill of Cat III mayhem, try lining this up alongside *Crazy Love For You*, another legendary shocker featuring Simon Yam in a

405

maniac role which also offers up many dark laughs.

In its original cut, *Doctor Lamb* proved so extreme the Hong Kong censors insisted on the filmmakers removing the most grisly scenes of mutilation before it could be given the Cat III rating. Both the DVD and VCD releases are cut. The Spanish VHS from Manga is uncut but long out of print and almost impossible to find. And that version runs for an extra 15 seconds.

The Cat III Phenomenon

In 2010, a Cat III movie came along entitled *Dream Home* which focused on the extreme lengths that one crazy woman will go to secure her ideal living space. The fact that the film was also loosely based on a true story only added to the viewer's discomfort as Josie Ho set about her goal with a ruthless single-mindedness.

At its core, *Dream Home* represents a frustrating aspect of Hong Kong life; the poor, cramped living conditions, and busy, almost ruthless lifestyle of its citizens. Of course, all big cities have their daily grind and bustle, but in Hong Kong the environment is more concentrated than your average city. And it's these harsh unnatural conditions and the relentless hyper-capitalist mindset of its inhabitants that make Hong Kong one of the most chaotic cities of the Far East. Anger, madness, and violence is rife, and the tabloid papers are often strewn with lurid headlines detailing the bizarre and shocking crimes of those who have snapped and committed horrible atrocities caused by the pressures of life.

With no safety nets of social housing or even a minimum wage, it's the poor who feel the worst effects of this kind of lifestyle, and they're often the first to crack under the pressure. It's hot, humid, competitive, cramped, and hostile. The streets are a frenzy of traffic and stressed out commuters, the bright neon-lit city scape is littered with thousands of signifiers and advertisements all vying for your attention. And even when you get home you can't really relax due to the crowded living conditions, with families sharing tiny apartments in high-rise tower blocks with barely enough room to stretch their legs. Such breakneck speed and intolerable conditions leave behind a debris of madness and murder.

The main reason for all of this chaos is fairly obvious. In 1947, the British 'borrowed' the island of Hong Kong on a 50 year lease as a way of having access to the 'Tiger economies' of the Far East. Shortly afterwards, mainland China fell under the rule of Communism. Hong Kongers knew that in 1997 their land would be handed back to the Chinese, but very few of them relished the idea of living under Communist rule. And after Margaret Thatcher failed to secure anything in the way of the British having a say in the running of the island once it was to be handed back, the race was on for the citizens to make their fortunes and escape the territory before the handover which would commence on the 1st of July 1997.

This rush to get things done seeped into everything; the day to day running of the city, the financial sector (Hong Kong was one of the world's fastest growing economies), and especially in the cinema. Whether it be the hyper-kinetic Kung-Fu vehicles of Jackie Chan, the fast and furious gunplay of John Woo's action epics, or the lightning speed of the production schedules of the sleazy Cat III movies, this race against time was clear to see in the nation's cinematic output.

Although there had been a few *outre* films released in the 80s, such as *Dangerous Encounter of the First Kind* and *Devil Fetus*, the Cat III rating wasn't officially made law in Hong Kong until 1988. The idea was to give filmmakers the room to produce sex, violence, and horror films with the encouragement of cashing-in on the export (and domestic) potential. A slew of extreme Hong Kong productions hit the screens soon after and caused a scandal the world over.

The Category III rating is similar to the American equivalent of the NC-17 – no one under 18 years of age was permitted to see these films (whereas the NC-17 forbids anyone under the age of 17). In America, films are often drastically cut to avoid the stigma of the NC-17, while in Hong Kong the sleaze and the controversy was worn like a badge of honour. And at their height these films made up around 39% of the country's yearly output.

Early Cat III releases were dominated by sexy thrillers, such as *Erotic Ghost Story*, *Robotrix*, and *Naked Killer* – basically violent softcore films. Just around the corner, however, was a new breed of gruesome ultra-violent killer movies like *Doctor Lamb*, *The Untold Story*, and *Daughter of Darkness*, and these films starred such legends as Simon Yam, Anthony Wong, and Lily Chung. *Doctor Lamb* tells the tale of a psychotic taxi driver who rapes and mutilates young women before taking photographs and hiding the bodies in the confines of his house. *The Untold Story* focuses on the confessions of a man who murdered his restaurant owner boss and his family before serving up their bodily remains to the locals in the form of 'BBQ pork buns'. And *Daughter of Darkness* puts us in the shoes of a young woman who resorts to murdering her entire family after years of rape and abuse from her parents and siblings. All three of these films are spiced up with grim and repulsively dark comedy, and all three are also based on true newspaper headlines.

The Category III ratings system applies to films produced anywhere (the French horror, *Haute Tension,* received the Cat III rating, for example), but the ones produced in Hong Kong have often been clubbed together and treated as a genre unto itself. Thus, many international cult classics, such as *Run and Kill* and *Ebola Syndrome*, are referred to under the umbrella term 'Cat III' movies. The significant cultural impact of these titles cannot be overestimated; there is no such umbrella term for the NC-17 movies in the West, perhaps because they constitute only a fraction of the sheer number of their Hong Kong equivalents.

On the 1st of July 1997, the British handed back sovereignty of Hong Kong to China, and it was around this time that the production of Cat III titles started to dwindle. Hong Kong has since been given some autonomy by the mainland, and been allowed to continue in its capitalist drive, but many citizens have complained that freedom of speech has taken a steady decline ever since. For more than a decade since the handover in '97 Hong Kong has continued to release the occasional *outre* film, such as *Naked Poison*, *There Is a Secret In My Soup*, *Gong Tau*, and *Revenge: A Love Story*, but the Cat III industry is a shadow of its former self. A recent trend in the Hong Kong film industry is to imitate the cinema of the mainland where romantic comedies rule the roost (if a film is a hit in China it can rake in millions in revenue that just isn't available in Hong Kong). Also, the Chinese have a strict censorship, and horror movies are generally outlawed there, which is perhaps another reason why Cat III movies have dwindled since the handover.

It's doubtful that we'll ever see a resurgence in the production of sleazy and extreme horror in Hong Kong while the mainland continues to frown on such films. But with the miracles of the internet and DVD, and indeed VCD (on which format many Cat III titles found a release for home viewing), we at least have a rich and diverse back catalogue to explore with more than twenty years of frantic and outrageous film-making at our disposal.

Gayniggers From Outer Space (1992)
Dir: Morten Lindberg /Denmark

A bizarre, low-budget exploitation spoof about a crew of black homosexual aliens from the planet Anus who arrive on earth with the intention of exterminating womankind. The crew, comprised of Schwul, Captain B. Dick, Sgt. Shaved Balls, Arm In Ass and Dildo, intend to create a gay universe by boldly traversing the stars and zapping bitches with their lethal ray guns. Written and directed by cult Danish musician, Morten Lindberg, this 27-minute short is the only film he ever made, and it remains the perfect item to show those crazy cult movie fans who think they have seen it all. Of course, mockery and satire is the name of the game here, and though there are many racist and homophobic snipes throughout, the film is so deranged and earnestly insincere that only the most sensitive of viewers could be genuinely offended. Blaxploitation and *Star Trek* seem to be the film's main inspirations (and targets). The sets of the spaceship interior looks like they were created in the film-maker's garage; the soundtrack offers up funky wah-wah guitars, bongos and 70s-era crime thriller brass sections; and the sound effects sound like they were fashioned on an IBM machine from the 80s. Look out for 'Dino Di Laurentiis' on the credits as the supposed 'co-producer;' also look out for the huge dildos that decorate the walls of the ship like fire extinguishers in a public building. Ironically, the film inspired the neo-Nazi hacker, Andrew 'Weev' Auernheimer, to create the infamous internet troll groups, Goatse Security and the Gay Niggers Association of America. Quite a strange legacy for a strange little film.

Zipperface (1992)
Dir: Mansour Pourmand /USA

Florida's first female detective (Donna Adams) squares up to the title character, a leather-clad, S&M sadist who wears a gimp mask and enjoys murdering prostitutes. This is routine, police procedural nonsense that has nothing on

Friedkin's *Cruising* (1980). It's a fairly slick and professional-looking production but is cast entirely with planks of wood. And this spoils things. The heroine is so plain she may as well be a glass of water on legs.

Minbo no Onna (1992)
(aka *Anti-Extortion Woman*)
Dir: Juzo Itami /Japan
Follow-up to *Violent Cop*. A female lawyer is brought in to deal with a yakuza gang who are attempting to blackmail the manager of a high-class hotel. This broad satire wastes no time in mocking Japanese gangsters and exposing their methods of extortion, intimidation and other nasty tricks. The film is well known for upsetting the yakuza; six days after its premiere, writer/director Juzo Itami was hospitalized after having his face and throat slashed by gangsters. In a related incident in Tokyo, a man slashed a cinema screen during the showing of another of Itami's films.

Stephen King's Sleepwalkers (1992)
Dir: Mick Garris /USA
Two shape-shifting monsters disguised as a mother and son terrorize a small town in their search for the blood of virgins. But feisty Madchen Amick refuses to give in so easily. A disappointing effort which nonetheless contains its fair share of gruesomeness (cat lovers will be dismayed at the number of dead and mutilated felines on display). Hardcore genre fans will spot familiar faces like Joe Dante, Tobe Hooper, Clive Barker, John Landis and Stephen King (who also wrote the screenplay) in cameo roles.

Ghostwatch (1992)
Dir: Lesley Manning /UK
Ghostwatch was originally aired on Halloween night, 1992, on the BBC as a supposedly real documentary filmed live from 'the most haunted house in Britain.' It was in fact entirely fake, but the viewing public weren't told that. The show was supposed to be a bit of fun, a harmless little spook show for families to enjoy on Halloween. However, just like Orson Welles' *War of the Worlds* radio broadcast from 1938 in which thousands of Americans ran screaming from their homes after believing they were listening to news coverage of a genuine Martian invasion, *Ghostwatch* traumatised a nation's youth in a similar way. Watching it again for the first time in 22 years, it's surprising how much of it I

remember. *Ghostwatch* seems etched on my psyche like an abuse memory. Looking back on it all these years later, it's remarkable how TV has changed; the presenters were much more strait-laced and well-spoken back then, unlike nowadays. I was expecting *Ghostwatch* to be cheesy, but the 'live on air' gimmick is done quite convincingly, with all the real life untidiness, fluffed lines, awkwardness and technical faults all adding to the illusion of authenticity.

976-Evil II: The Astral Factor (1992)
Dir: Jim Wynorski /USA
The evil phone line is pushed more towards the background in this sequel, as we see a school principal held on suspicion of a spate of killings. But while in custody, the killings continue, and the police have no idea what to do. Turns out that the evildoer is using astral projection to free his spirit from the cell and carry on his evil plan. However, a leather-clad burk called Spike and his bimbo blonde sidekick, Robin, discover what he is up to and put a stop to this nonsense. Basically a remake of *Psychic Killer* (1975), *976-Evil II* dresses up the hackneyed script with amusing sequences such as the 'mirror' scene in the motel and the part where one of the characters is somehow sucked into a TV set showing *It's a Wonderful Life*; but while she's there with the characters, they suddenly turn into zombies from *Night of the Living Dead*!

Benny's Video (1992)
Dir: Michael Haneke /Austria /Switzerland
A video-obsessed teen lures home a girl from a video rental store and kills her on camera. In typical Haneke form, *Benny's Video* is about alienation and the questioning of the purpose of video violence in society. Haneke has said that the film is a statement "about the American sensational cinema and its power to rob viewers of their ability to form their own opinions." Like his other films, such as *Funny Games* (1997) and *Code Unknown* (2000), this is a very cold and clinical look at the modern world which, ironically, is sure to alienate many horror fans.

House IV (1992)
(aka *House IV: The Repossession*)
Dir: Lewis Abernathy /USA
In this final instalment in the *House* series, William Katt of the original film is brought back only to be killed off in a car crash in the first ten

minutes. His widow, Kelly (Terri Treas), stays at the house and attempts to renovate it while looking after her daughter who was paralysed in the accident and is now confined to a wheelchair. However, shortly after her brother-in-law shows up to dispute ownership of the property, Kelly is terrorised by blood showers, hallucinations and, uh, a talking pizza. She also develops a passion for stabbing things that upset her, and this endangers her daughter's life on more than one occasion. Out of desperation, Kelly visits a native American, and he informs her that the house was – wait for it... – built on Indian burial ground! Part 4 is on a par with the first two films of the series; the interesting ideas are squandered in favour of slapstick humour. Even *Fangoria* was critical in its review: "It's really sad that given the high-gloss resources afforded this production, the filmmakers couldn't have done any better." The British VHS release was shorn of a few seconds of the shower scene in which the heroine's breasts are smeared in blood. Again, this final entry in the series is only available nowadays as part of the *House* boxset.

Hell Roller (1992)
Dir: G. J. Levinson /USA
A bitter, wheelchair-bound teen goes on a voyeuristic killing spree ("God help the next 'normal' who fucks with me!"). Funny in places, and also aware of its own shortcomings, which means that the performers are permitted to ham it up without ruining what is already sub-standard, amateur fare in the first place. You could team it up with *Feto Morto* (2003) for a double-bill of lame, disabled revenge movies.

The Ages of Lulu (1992)
(Orig title: *Les edades de Lulu*)
Dir: Bigas Luna /Spain
Young Lulu (Francesca Neri) explores her sexuality with an older guy who basically introduces himself by shaving her pussy. And together they experiment with various frolics, including a blindfolded incestuous threesome. They also spend time in bed with a transvestite. Lulu eventually breaks off alone and visits a gay bar where she pays men for sex. And all of this leads to a predictably nightmarish climax... *The Ages of Lulu* was a difficult film to see before the Tartan DVD release in the early 00s. Much of the film plays like a typical European 'erotic drama,' and it's only at the end when the true

horror sets in for a moment that rivals David Lynch for its scenes of twisted evil. The British censors snipped over a minute of footage of a potentially indecent scene of a baby girl lying on her back and pissing in the air.

Love To Kill (1993)
(Orig title: *Ai zhi sha; aka Nue zhi lian*)
Dir: Siu Hung Cheung and Kirk Wong /Hong Kong
Anthony Wong is in typical psycho nutjob mode here as Sam, a cruel, controlling, and possessive husband who subjects his wife Keung (Julie Lee) to brutal rape in their apartment. He likes to suffocate her with a polythene bag while doing it. She manages to fight him off and runs outside into the rain where a passing cop, Hung Lee (Danny Lee, the good cop in John Woo's *The killer*) protects her and savagely assaults Sam.

When Sam leaves the hospital, he escapes prosecution because Keung is too afraid to speak out against him or press charges. The police give him a rollicking but have no choice but to let him go free. Back at home, Sam pathetically tries to make it up to Keung by massaging her feet and being nice to her, but this just has the effect of making her feel even more depressed and uncomfortable. Keung's mother is ill in hospital with cancer and she just about manages to get permission from him to go and visit her, but on condition that he escorts her.

Keung's heartache at seeing her mother in intense pain and being heavily addicted to opium sees her attempting to suffocate mum with a pillow. Now it's the time for the police to give *her* a rollicking, but they also remember her from the incident with Sam, and accuse her of 'liking it rough' due to her not pressing charges. This pushes Keung over the edge and she slashes her wrist with a piece of broken mirror.

Cop Hung Lee takes pity on her, and Keung eventually confides in him that she is terrified of her husband and is afraid for her son's safety. Lee immediately organizes a van and he takes Keung home to collect her son and pack some belongings – he also takes an interest in her panties. Sam arrives home just in time to see them leaving in the van.

Keung and son move into the cop's apartment with his girlfriend Jenny. Meanwhile, Sam stays behind and fantasizes on revenge. He stalks Lee as a way of finding info on his wife's whereabouts. Lee finds himself increasingly drawn to Keung and finds it impossible to stop lusting after her, especially when she does the housework. And just as things look to be calming down and Keung is starting to rebuild her life, Sam turns up to spoil all the peace and harmony.

He checks her mother out of hospital and holds her hostage at their apartment. He orders Keung to come home or she'll never see mum again. And of course, when she gets there, Sam reaches full-on psycho mode. He teases her with a cutthroat razor, accuses her of sleeping with the cop, scrubs her in the bath tub, and chains her to the wall. He then goes out and frames Lee for police brutality. And while the cop is in custody, he takes a visit to his apartment and brutally beats, rapes, and suffocates the cop's girlfriend Jenny, and takes off with his son. Hung Lee rushes to the hospital to find Jenny bloody, bruised, and in a vegetative state on a life support machine. And the scene is set for a bloody showdown...

This is a surprisingly subdued take on extreme domestic violence that in other hands may have become just another sleazy Cat III shocker (Herman Yau, or especially Billy Tang would have had a field day depicting the awful crimes in this film). Don't get me wrong, it was made purely for the exploitation market but at least takes the time to acknowledge just how despicable the human animal can be without resorting to a dramatic 'fun-time' sleaziness like Yau's *Ebola Syndrome* or Billy Tang's *Red to Kill*, for example.

There's very little of the usual slapstick scenes (although there are some comic interludes, such as Lee's lusting after Keung while she does the cleaning, and his awkward relationship with his high-maintenance girlfriend, Jenny). Anthony Wong is at his scummiest and best here as the psycho husband who subjects his wife to a miserable existence. His brutal sexual fantasies (actually, they're probably flashbacks) of the horrendous abuses on his wife are stemmed from his own childhood traumas; as a child, Sam's father savagely beat his mother and attempted to hang the little boy, but the rope snapped. And by the end of the film we can see how this evil behaviour is passed down the generations (Sam's own son witnesses much of the domestic carnage), and although the film refuses to suggest that the little boy will

continue in his father's and grandfather's evil footsteps, you can't help but think that much damage has been done.

If this all seems a bit sensitive for a Cat III title then don't dismay; the film's finale is extremely violent – there's a brutal decapitation, a gruesome and repetitive face-smashing with an axe, a character beaten with a lump of wood that has six inch nails sticking out of it, a near-decapitation on a broken window pane, and some nasty nail-gun mayhem, with one character shot through the eye. Unmissable.

The Untold Story (1993)
(aka *Bunman*; Orig title: *Bat sin fan dim ji yan yuk cha siu bau*)
Dir: Herman Yau /Hong Kong

The first CAT III title to become an international hit, and the one that propelled actor Anthony Wong to cult movie superstardom, *The Untold Story* was directed by former cinematographer, Herman Yau, who used his years of experience in the film industry to fashion one of the most visually dazzling and explicitly graphic crime films in the history of Hong Kong cinema.

Based on a true story that happened in 1978 in which a restaurant cook, Wong Chi-hang, was accused of murdering his boss and his entire family with a meat cleaver, and then serving their body parts to unknowing customers in the restaurant, the film opens with Chi-hang (Anthony Wong) beating a man to death in an apartment and then burning the corpse. Eight years later, body parts are washed up onto the shores of Macau. The police, led by Danny Lee (of *Doctor Lamb* and *Love To Kill*, and who also served as producer on this film) is the police captain who always has a sexy hooker on his arm. There is lots of silly humour from the investigating officers, mostly at the expense of the only female cop who is ridiculed for having small breasts and looking like a tomboy.

Wong has drastically altered his appearance since the murder almost a decade previously, and is now running his own restaurant in Macau. He specializes in selling BBQ pork buns which go down well with the locals and with the investigating officers. But, of course, the buns are not filled with pork but with human remains. After a couple of brutal murders of people who have pissed him off in some way, Wong is eventually arrested. In custody, the police have very little evidence to pin on him so they resort to a long and sustained period of interrogation as a way of getting him to confess to the crimes. He is brutally beaten by both the cops and his fellow prisoners in the holding cell. He attempts a grisly suicide but is saved at the last moment. He is also kept awake for days on end and injected with water which causes painful boils to appear on his skin. Unable to handle the pressure for much longer, Wong breaks down under the mistreatment and agrees to reveal all of the gruesome details of his numerous killings...

If the film hasn't already pushed the boundaries in terms of graphic violence and bloodshed, Wong's flashbacks to the murders of his boss and his family certainly do the trick. There is also a very nasty rape scene and a desperate suicide attempt in a prison cell involving a rusty old slop bucket. The rape scene in particular has been the subject of much controversy over the years; Wong has openly admitted that he dislikes the film for this reason, and director Yau has made his own excuses for depicting the scene in a very crude and voyeuristic way, insisting that he wanted to capture the scene purely from the killer's deranged perspective. But basically, the rape scene is there for the sole purpose of exploitation; sure, Yau may not have intended to arouse the viewer's sexually with this scene, but there's no doubt that he lingers on the victim in her peril and even revels in displaying her naked body, complete with bush shots (which are a rarity even in Cat III titles) before killing her and mutilating her corpse.

The scene featuring the killing of the family is also a long and drawn-out one, and makes for some very difficult viewing. In excruciating detail we watch as they are tied up and graphically butchered, one by one; first the son has his throat cut, then the mother is killed, the father, and then the rest of the petrified children who are cowering near the dining table. One of the little girls is beheaded with the meat cleaver in graphic detail. All seven family members are massacred in this extended and harrowing sequence. Interestingly, Wong doesn't set about the killings in an out-of-control psychotic rage, but in a determined and methodical way which makes the scene all the more disturbing in his calm and pre-determined nastiness. Unforgettable.

The Underground Banker (1993)

(Orig title: *Xiang Gang qi an: Zhi xi xue gui li wang*)
Dir: Bosco Lam /Hong Kong

CAT III movies, I love 'em! Anthony Wong plays long distance truck driver, Tong, who has just moved his family into a small apartment to ease their financial strain. Early in the film he is accosted by petty crims who claim to own the road where he parks, and they demand $200 for him to leave his truck there. Nicknamed 'marshmallow' because of his soft and jovial nature, Tong reluctantly hands over the cash. Later, while eating lunch at an outside cafe, a woman's body falls from a high-rise window and lands on his table. His workmate tells him that the woman probably owed money to the local triad boss, the 'underground banker'.

Tong's wife Chun (Ching Mai) bumps into an old sweetheart, Canner, who is now working for the triads. She takes him back to their apartment to meet Tong and their young son, Tak. Canner informs the family that they're living next door to the notorious serial killer Doctor Lam! The nervous family get to meet Lam (who was originally played by Simon Yam in *Doctor Lamb*, but here he's played in a less evil but more cryptic mode by *Sex And Zen's* Lawrence Ng), and he assures them that he is not a danger anymore. He then expertly kills a chicken with a cleaver for tea, and this does little to settle the nerves of Tong and Chun. Little boy Tak doesn't seem to mind though, and he spends a lot of time round at Lam's flat playing video games.

Tong feels insecure about his inabilities to satisfy his gorgeous wife and so he uses self-help audio cassettes to improve his technique and stamina, and this leads to a hilarious practical joke when his workmate gets hold of the tape. Meanwhile, Canner ropes Chun into investing on the stock market with the hope of easing the family's financial woes. And before long she inevitably finds herself losing the family savings. Canner tells her not to worry because his brother is an usurer and will lend her the money she needs.

With Tong not knowing about her gambling away all the money, she agrees to see Canner's brother for help. Canner's brother turns out to be Chao (Ho Ka-Kui, the psycho nutcase from *Brother of Darkness*), the underground banker, and he agrees to lend her HK$40,000 to be paid back in weekly instalments. A week later she gives Canner 10,000 promising to pay the other 30,000 very soon. But Canner tells her that the debt has increased and that she now owes 48,000. She protests but realises she's been caught in some shady scam. Canner tries to reassure her that everything will be okay, and he gets very close and tries to kiss her. She backs off disgusted, and then Canner tells her that he has spiked her drink with an aphrodisiac. He then rapes her while she's in a delirious state. The rape scene is played for maximum titillation with that 80s chic day-glo lighting and soft drum-machine 80s rock on the soundtrack, and displaying Ching Mai's beautiful naked body in various positions; she tells him to stop but the drug has the opposite effect on her orgasmic moans and sensual body language. He then beats her.

Pretty soon Chun begins selling her body to raise money, and this sees her being tied up and spanked and doggy-fucked by a bunch of strangers with the *William Tell* Ouverture galloping along on the soundtrack, all making light of her desperate situation. Tong's prankster workmate even gets in on the action and sleeps with her, and this makes things awkward in a later scene when Tong brings him home for tea. His friend later confesses that he has slept with Chun but swears blind that he didn't know that she was his wife. Tong beats him up and leaves.

By now, the ruthless triads have stepped up their campaign of intimidation, and begin threatening Chun's family. The outside of the apartment is vandalised with graffiti and the security gate at the front entrance has been chained up and padlocked. The fire brigade have to cut the chains to free the family. Chun enters Chao's office and begs for more time to raise money, and pleads for him to leave her family out of it. She is then drugged and gang-raped, but this time the incident is recorded on video, and Chao informs her that videotapes will be handed out to all and sundry if she doesn't start making payments.

Chun's sister, Chi Kwan, is abducted, and Chao slaps and intends on raping her but she jumps out of the speeding van. She sustains injuries but she still manages to make it to Chun's flat and attacks her for getting her involved in the debt. Tong has to break them apart, and it's only now that he learns the full extent of the trouble that his wife is in. Chun tells him about losing their savings, and Chao, and the prostitution, and the intimidation. Tong

feels he has no choice but to sell his truck. He gets 90,000 for it, and a colleague gives him a further 20,000 to help out.

He visits Chao's office with the 110,000 and offers to settle the debt in full there and then, but Chao instead has him crawling around on the floor in an act of humiliation to amuse his cronies. The triads then play the rape video, and Tong is informed that if he wants to stop it from being seen by anyone else he should pay an extra 100,000. This devastating revelation sees Tong leaving in a huff and refusing to pay a penny. He is then robbed of his money outside by Canner's men on a busy city street and not a single person steps in to stop the attack.

That night while Chun and her young son are sleeping, Chao's men chain up their security gate and pour petrol through the mailbox. They then set fire to the place. Tong returns home to find their flat ablaze, with Chun and Tak screaming for their lives. He rattles at the security gate but it's no good, there's nothing he can do. The fire spreads, and Chun pushes her boy under the bed in a futile attempt at safety. She gets caught in an explosion and Tong can only watch in agony as his wife writhes around in flames and drops to the floor in a burning heap. It's a truly nightmarish scene rarely presented so graphically on film. Dr. Lam shows up with a pair of bolt cutters and opens the gate. Chun is dead but little Tak is rushed to hospital.

Outside, Canner appears and he teases Tong about the death of his wife, to which a normally peaceful Buddhist monk steps up and beats the crap out of Canner to much applause from the gathering neighbours of the block. In a heartbreaking scene, Tong visits the hospital to see his little boy - Tak is badly burned; his head is a bald mess of melted flesh and his face unrecognisable. Lam presents Tak with a gift, a Nintendo Gameboy, but the kid can't play it because his hands now resemble charred stumps of melted flesh. Chi Kwan is furious and swears revenge on the gang. Lam tries to console Tong and offers to help him get some payback on the Triads. Tong the soft 'marshmallow' has doubts and is unsure of himself, but then a tearful Tak encourages his dad to "beat those bastards", and Tong's eyes burn with sorrow and vengeance...

What follows is a grim and glorious revenge attack on Chao and his cronies. It's an extremely violent finale which sees Tong pulling out a meat cleaver and shouting "I'll chop you and make BBQ pork buns" (an obvious reference to the bunman in *The Untold Story*), and Doctor Lam finds his bloodlust renewed bigtime. We get slicing and dicing, meat cleaver fights, dicks blown off, piano wire used as a garrote, and a nasty castration. Director Bosco Lam (who made *A Chinese Torture Chamber Story* the following year) teams up with Hong Kong's 'King of sleaze', producer Wong Jing, and together they have created an almost perfectly crafted piece of audience manipulation; by the hour mark you'll be screaming for the bad guy's guts as insult, rape, and death is added to the character's injuries. Anthony Wong is in fine form in a rare role as the good guy, and Ho Ka-Kui as Chao is also brilliant in his typecast role; he's such a mean and ruthless bastard, always ensuring that Chun's debt can never be settled. And Lawrence Ng as Doctor Lam adds an interesting ambiguity in the middle-ground between good and evil.

The film ends with a disturbing coda that shows Tong to have been radically changed by the ordeal, and not for the better; as the end credits roll he is seen setting himself up as the new underground banker, lending money to someone and laying down his rules for repayment. A classic.

The Baby of Macon (1993)
Dir: Peter Greenaway /UK

In the 17th Century, encouraged by a naive and sadistic prince, a play is performed about a miraculous child exploited by both his sister and the church. Soon enough, the play becomes all too real, and rape, death and dismemberment follows as the events take on the appearance of an actual religious ritual.

This cold, alienating and repetitive film starts with the 'ugliest woman in Macon' giving birth to a beautiful baby. Those who witness the birth cannot believe that such beauty could be spawned by such a wretch, and begin to question God's ways. The woman's virginal daughter (Julia Ormond) has a scheme in mind whereby she convinces the town that the child is her own, a "miracle baby," and pretty soon the child is hailed as a messiah and harbinger of miracles. However, the Bishop's scientifically inclined son (Ralph Fiennes) has doubts about the whole thing, and so the 'mother' invites anyone and everyone to take a peek 'downstairs' to prove that she really is a virgin. The following scene sees a queue of people eager to have a look for themselves, and this offers up

some comical observations from the menfolk: "Errr... I don't know what I'm looking for," admits one. "Her anatomy is most charming," exclaims another.

The Bishop's son is still not convinced, so she lures him to a barn in order to prove her virginity once and for all by offering him the chance to take it. She undresses in front of him, and when he can no longer control his lust, he mounts her. But before he can sink it in and pop her cherry, the child shows up unleashing horrific, and apparently supernatural powers which causes the man's body to erupt into a bloody mess. The child reassures her 'mother' by reminding her that her virginity is the only thing that is keeping them safe from the wrath of the town. At this point, the back wall of the barn collapses, and behind it is the theatre audience shocked by the sight of Fiennes' dead body. The Bishop enters and accuses her of killing his son, but when it becomes clear that the murder was an act of divine intervention, all is seemingly forgiven.

The woman's tyranny and sense of self-importance continues to grow in proportion to the adulation which is bestowed upon the miracle child. But when the boy winds up dead – possibly suffocated by the 'mother' – the Bishop, still holding a grudge over the death of his own son, sees to it that she is punished in the most horrific way. She teases the Bishop, rightly pointing out that it's illegal for the Church to hang virgins, so he simply orders her to be raped non-stop, 208 times in a row, by the most disease-ridden villagers and the dregs of the local prison. The Bishop forgives the rapists in advance ("You are forgiven, my sons, for making rightful vengeance"), so that all is 'above board' in the eyes of God. And while she screams in agony at her harrowing ordeal, the rest of her family are hunted down and hung from the rafters. The child's body is scalped and cut into pieces so that the mourners can take the body parts home as religious mementos ("Child, bless me with your little feet that walked the earth"), and his severed head is displayed for all to see. The play comes to an end when the 'mother' doesn't survive her ordeal.

The Baby of Macon takes place entirely on stage, and was designed as a puzzling and audacious film which caused outrage when it was screened at the Cannes Film Festival. Having earned himself much art house acclaim for his previous hits like *Prospero's Books* and

The Cook, the Thief, His Wife and Her lover, director Peter Greenaway took a bit of a detour this time around by heading more towards the blurry line between artifice and actuality, by way of Artaud's theories on 'The Theatre of Cruelty.' Are these actors being killed 'for real' or is it all part of the play? This is the question Greenaway's fans have been arguing about for the best part of twenty years, as the film simply refuses to clarify the most nagging of questions. One thing we can say for sure about *The Baby of Macon* is that the notorious and prolonged rape scene is very nasty, and the dismemberment of the child has kept the film rejected by many American cinema chains over the years.

Greenaway's favourite DP, Sacha Vierny, returns to point his exquisite lens at another visually stunning concoction. The set designs are amazing; a cathedral decorated and illuminated with thousands of candles that play against the darkness of the auditorium and the script. It was a massive production, with hundreds of extras, live choirs, and string quartets, all making the production seem much grander in scale than its low-budget would suggest. In fact, the visuals and detailed choreography makes *Caligula* look almost modest in comparison. And the overall grand elegance of the sets and costumes are constantly at odds with the human players, whose hypocrisy and cruelties only adds to the uneasy mix. It's just a shame that composer Michael Nyman is absent; having made such a strong impact in classics like *Drowning By Numbers* and *The Cook, The Thief...*, he fell out with the director, and Greenaway was left to fill the musical holes with traditional classical numbers. It goes without saying that the end result sorely misses Nyman's magic, and both he and Greenaway still haven't collaborated on a film project since.

Taxi Hunter (1993)

(Orig title: *Di shi pan guan*)

Dir: Herman Yau /Hong Kong

In this Cat III shocker, Anthony Wong stars as a successful insurance agent who has endless trouble with the local taxi drivers. They skip him, rob him, and even kill his wife and unborn child! Something snaps in him and he goes on a killing spree, wiping out the scumbag cabbies (I'm not making this up!). The detective investigating the murders (Man Tat Ng) is a kick-arse cop with Jackie Chan-worthy stunts, and he just so happens to be an old drinking buddy of Wong's. So when he suspects his friend of committing the crimes, he is torn between sympathy for his buddy and his duty as a cop...

As with many Cat III titles, *Taxi Hunter* starts out as a broad comedy but darkens as it progresses. The action and violence is strong, bloody, comical, and absurd (there's also an amusing tribute to Scorsese's *Taxi Driver* where Wong does his own take on the "Are you talkin' to me?" speech). This was also filmed on a bigger budget than usual; here we have some highly choreographed fight scenes, stunts, crashes, shoot outs, and a superb car chase.

He makes for a clumsy and awkward urban avenger in his shirt and tie, but Wong is a Cat III superstar, the king of the genre, and this is perhaps one of his most underrated performances. Wong himself has said it was his favourite role to date, "I think it is my best piece of work because that role involves a humanised character". He was relieved to play a good guy at last (well, at least a character whom the audience can cheer for) after years of being typecast as the bad guy due to the widespread racism in the Hong Kong film industry (Wong is mixed race, with a Chinese mother and British father).

As for director Yau, *Taxi Hunter* sees him at the top of his game. It's not quite as outrageous as his later efforts like *The Untold Story* and *Ebola Syndrome*, but shows much promise and hints strongly at the shock horror elements that would prevail in much of his subsequent work.

Clean, Shaven (1993)

Dir: Lodge Kerrigan /USA

A journey into the mind of a paranoid schizophrenic – do you really want to go there? Often described as the closest thing to experiencing schizophrenia on film, Lodge Kerrigan's *Clean, Shaven* follows Peter Winter (Peter Greene), who escapes from a mental institution and heads off in search of his daughter, and seems to leave a trail of bodies behind. En route, we get to witness his torment through heard voices, screams, and self-mutilation, and the soundtrack is one of the most challenging and abrasive you'll ever hear.

Coming on like a less exploitative version of Romano Scavolini's *Nightmares In a Damaged Brain*, the film is bleak and convincing in its portrayal of mental suffering, and features a solid central performance from Greene. There's an awful sense of loneliness and isolation in the dread-ridden atmosphere, and the auditory hallucinations are spine-chilling; even though most of the words can't really be heard properly, the tone and volume of this demanding voice is enough to put viewers on edge. But what tips them over is the self-mutilation; the scene in which Peter cuts himself with a razor in the shower is hard enough to watch, but later in the car when he convinces himself that there is a transmitter implanted in his fingertip, and then uses a pen knife to dig up his fingernail, is even more difficult to stomach. Even the hardiest of extreme movie devotees have squirmed in their seats at this scene.

Amazingly, this film was partly financed by Warner Brothers! God knows what they thought they were investing in. *Clean, Shaven* played theatrically on the underground circuit in America in the early 90s, and then vanished. It has since found its way to DVD, enticing an international audience to take the dread-ridden journey into psychological hell.

Boxing Helena (1993)
Dir: Jennifer Chambers Lynch /USA

After being rejected by the beautiful Helena, a distraught surgeon, Nick Cavanaugh (Julian Sands), finds her at his mercy following an unfortunate car accident. He proceeds to amputate her limbs one by one, and makes her live in a box.

It comes as an important lesson for any budding filmmaker hoping to be accorded some shock-horror notoriety for daring to explore such a dark and sexually twisted story, and wrapping it up in a strange twisted sub-humour, for this film is more well-known nowadays for the behind-the-scenes troubles which thwarted the production for a while. Kim Basinger was signed up to play the heartless and eventually limbless Helena, but changed her mind at the last moment, backing out of the contract (an understandable decision in retrospect, given the lacklustre results). This threw the project into disarray as a new actress was needed to fill the role, and Basinger was sued and ordered to pay $8 million in damages (in a settlement reached in 1995, she agreed to pay around $3 million). Due to all the legal wrangling that surrounded the production, the media seemed more interested in the behind-the-scenes shenanigans rather than the actual film. And the much sought-after controversy in the subject-matter was largely overlooked as the film itself served as nothing more than a tiresome backdrop to the real-life drama that took centre stage.

As for the film itself, it was Sherilyn Fenn who replaced Basinger in the role of Helena, the object of Nick's unnerving obsession, and she appears to be unsure of what she has let herself in for, overdoing what would have worked much better as a crazed, deranged victim of her own self-loathing. Julian Sands' role as the surgeon who expresses his demented love is also unconvincing. Director Jennifer Chambers Lynch has obviously taken inspiration from her father David in the way the events unfold in an illogical, dream-like fashion. But she's at a loss when it comes to replicating his off-beat, warped humour and striking visuals.

David Lynch as an artist has always been preoccupied with the undercurrents of human behaviour; the subtextual, the surreal, and unconscious resonance that shapes his plots and his character's motivations, whereas Jennifer makes a point about bringing all of this stuff to the surface, denying the film any kind of mystery and wonder or ambiguity in the process. Sands' character, Nick, is portrayed in the actor's usual excitable manner, and he represents a Freudian (Oedipal) hodge-podge of tortured sexual desire for his dead mother, and who transfers his obsessions onto the despicable Helena. Even after her legs have been removed following the car wreck, and she finds herself trapped in Nick's house, her only mobility is in an old wheelchair, but she continues as her old self, throwing objects at him and screeching like an outraged chimp. The fact that his warped behaviour has led to him severing her legs (with her arms soon to follow) doesn't make her put pause to her actions. Surely in a situation like that, of being stranded with a nut-case, she would take a few moments to assess the situation and the danger she is in, and think very carefully about what she does or says. But instead, she just carries on as herself, paying no heed to the situation she is in, and this makes it very difficult for viewers to believe in a character like that, let alone sympathise or even care about what happens to her, or Nick.

If it wasn't such a bloody awful film it may have yielded a few laughs here and there, but as it stands, the only humour here is of the unintentional kind, as Michael Atkinson of

Movieline points out, "*Boxing Helena* simply cannot be taken seriously, in a large part because it takes itself so seriously that we can only respond to it with gales of derisive crowing." Jennifer's own directorial style is so haphazard it makes you wonder whether her film-making limbs have also been lopped off. It would have worked much better as a twenty-minute short. Actually, why not try *Rampo Noir* (2005) instead, which features the infamous 'Caterpillar' segment directed by the legendary Hisayasu Sato, and explores similar territory in a much more plausible and disturbing manner.

The most annoying thing about *Boxing Helena* is that it had the potential to be a great film, a dark, twisted sexual fantasy loaded with themes of revenge and control and obsessive possessiveness. However, what we get instead are a couple of awful performances, a terrible script and clumsy dialogue. Add to this some trite castration metaphors, an over-long 107-minute running time, and some 'self-parody' which cannot be passed off as intentional, and you've got the recipe for one of the most disappointing movies of the 90s.

Naked (1993)
Dir: Mike Leigh /UK

Misery, nihilism and misanthropy doesn't come any more searingly than in Mike Leigh's *Naked*, a scabrous and blackly funny parable that boasts an astonishing central performance from David Thewlis, and a genuine cinematic style that is a vast improvement over Leigh's earlier made-for-television look. The apocalypse has never looked so good.

Fleeing Manchester in a stolen car after a vicious sex attack in a back alley, Johnny – a cynical, dishevelled waster – (Thewlis) speeds down to London overnight and lays low at his ex-girlfriend's place. He ends up sleeping with her stoner flatmate, and after verbally abusing the pair of them, storms out and traipses the cold, grey streets, getting himself into more trouble. Meanwhile, the flat's abusive landlord shows up and rapes the girls, before Johnny returns, bloody and beaten up, only for the third flatmate to return from a trip to Zimbabwe to find the place in a sorry state...

Of course, there is so much more to the film than the synopsis above, as the story outline is much less important than Johnny himself. Cast adrift in a cold, uncaring world, Johnny is the type of character who repays society in kind at every opportunity, reeling off sarcasm and invective, laughing inside with a vindictive satisfaction while the world crumbles around him. A rare kind of anti-hero in the movies, not even Travis Bickle of *Taxi Driver* can match the scathing indictment of mankind that Johnny delivers here. Indeed, for a comparable source, one must look to literature, with a character like Ferdinand in *Journey to the End of the Night* (pub. 1932), penned by the arch-hater, Louis-Ferninand Céline.

Those who would expect a typically bland, kitchen sink drama akin to *Meantime* (1983) or *Life is Sweet* (1990), may be stunned by the dark, nightmarish landscapes that Leigh presents here. And it isn't just Johnny who is alone; all of the characters are used up and isolated, except that Johnny is the only one who seems to fight back to any degree. Though he may be one of the most quoted characters in British cinema history, Johnny's bitter and vitriolic tirades make him less a hero than a man who is symptomatic of the society that spawned him – a comprehension he acknowledges throughout. Funnily enough, viewers learn very little about his background, but we can gather that it was anything but bright. Johnny constantly jokes that his mother was a whore, and his ex, Louise (Lesley Sharp), reacts uncomfortably as though the man's facetious claims are actually true.

Naked began as a series of conversations between Leigh and Thewlis in which the character of Johnny gradually emerged, cheek by jowl. They agreed that Johnny would be a fiercely outspoken, sexually violent wreck of a human being, but also intelligent and darkly amusing. There were claims in the press that Thewlis was unhappy not to receive a co-writer credit, but the actor has since dismissed them, telling *Time Out* magazine that the actors in all of Mike Leigh's films contribute a huge amount to their character's lines. Upon the film's release, Gavin Smith of *Film Comment* referred to *Naked* as 'a neorealist monster movie,' in which 'the monster won't lie down and die – he just keeps coming.'

Indeed, Thewlis himself became so immersed in his character that he almost attacked Ewen Bremner with a screwdriver during rehearsals. He also claims that, of all the characters he has played on screen, none have haunted him more than Johnny. And the cinema wouldn't see such a monster again until the arrival of The Butcher in Gaspar Noe's *Seul contre tous* (1998), played with an even *fiercer* intensity by the brilliant Phillippe Nahon.

Daughter of Darkness (1993)

(Orig title: *Mit moon cham on: Yit saat*)
Dir: Ivan Lai Kai Mingh /Hong Kong
Daughter of Darkness is part of producer Wong Jing's loose trilogy based on lurid news headlines that also includes *Brother of Darkness* and *Red to Kill*. Anthony Wong plays the police chief who is investigating the brutal murder of an entire family. The film begins as a silly comedy with the police breaking into a house to discover the bodies. Wong's experience on the job means that he is used to the sights and smells of crime scenes, but his younger colleagues are tentative when entering the building. Three battered bodies are found in the living area. Wong heads upstairs and finds a further corpse in the bath tub. He fondles the dead girl's breasts claiming it's a useful way to get an idea of how long the victim has been dead for. The local press has descended on the scene with their cameras and notebooks, but are kept at the doorway. Wong accepts a bribe and allows a reporter inside to take snapshots. In a macabre and silly scene, Wong displays an insensitive and twisted humour when he poses with the dead bodies during the photo shoot.

The only relative to have survived the massacre is Amy (Lily Chung, who played Ming Ming the retarded girl in *Red to Kill*), and Wong immediately puts her and her boyfriend under suspicion. And in a scene reminiscent of Hitchcock's *Rear Window*, he follows the couple to the boyfriend's flat and watches them have sex in the apartment from an opposite balcony. Cue more silliness as a guy falls from the baloney into a skip, Wong indulges in a bit of bra sniffing (which causes him to sneeze!), and a steamy sex scene in the shower. The young couple are questioned at the station and it soon becomes apparent that the girl is responsible for the murders. And in a series of disturbing flashbacks, Amy tells the whole story of how she felt driven to commit the massacre due to a long and sustained period of abuse.

Daughter of Darkness is a quintessential Cat III movie in that it includes all the typical ingredients that make these films so bizarre and outrageous. The slapstick and darkly comic interludes that set up the story, the leering and exploitative angles, the faux-Hollywood erotic thriller template, the bright colourful settings, the factual basis, and extremely violent finale, it's all here. The film also does much to expose the facade of the modern nuclear family where, despite appearances, no one really knows what goes on behind closed doors in the average family unit. Director Ivan Lai also seems to have a snipe at the useless conformity of organized religion, especially in the scene where the father returns home one night and lights an incense stick for his Buddha statue and offers a blasé prayer; he seems to do this purely because it's a 'done thing' and not because he has any religious convictions – actually, he doesn't seem to have a spiritual bone in his body, and instead runs on a purely animalistic instinct to satisfy his mad primal urges. Quite a statement for a low-budget exploitation movie! However, it's the extremely violent finale for which the film will be remembered. It's one of the most harrowing family massacres seen on screen since *Amityville II*.

In court, Amy is sentenced to death by firing squad, and she gives birth to a baby boy while on death row. The baby is immediately taken away from her. She is then led down a corridor and out into the open where she says her goodbyes to her boyfriend and their baby before she is executed.

Bad Boy Bubby (1993)

Dir: Rolf De Heer /Australia
Bubby, a 35 year old slap-head has been raised his entire life in a single, filthy, windowless room and used as a sex slave/whipping boy by his monstrous mother who tells him that the air outside is poisonous. He has no idea of what the world beyond his four grubby walls consists of, until his long-lost father, a fake clergyman, turns up one day. And after innocently murdering his parents by suffocating them with cling-film, this man-child ventures out into the open to experience the world outside…

The big, wide world proves to be a hostile and alienating place for Bubby, as he meets an assortment of characters ranging from helpful angels to hateful morons, and he finds himself partaking in various pursuits, including a stint as an off-the-wall nightclub performer. He also has a spell in prison and a disturbing encounter with a seedy priest.

The early part of this Aussie cult classic is a murky endurance test, but once Bubby breaks free from the horrid house, the film constantly sways between extraordinary and discomforting to hilarious and exciting. Bubby imitates others' behaviour, including the scene where he walks down a high street mimicking the movements of a young toddler. He's fascinated, and he follows the kid down the street, jumping up and down, and seemingly amazed at how small the child is. But because of his life-long incarceration, he doesn't realise that his behaviour is beyond weird and is in fact downright unnerving for the toddler's mother, who is clearly very uncomfortable by this strange man's peculiar interest in her little boy. His adventures out in the world bring him face to face with brutality, apathy, sex (including both seduction and rape), showbiz, infamy, patronage and friendship. He is even incorporated into a punk rock band who pay homage to his nonsensical rants. Meanwhile, the police are on the lookout for the cling-film killer, and things wrap up on the themes of love and salvation.

Dutch-Australian director Rolf De Heer uses a series of gimmicky tricks and techniques, such as using 31 different cameramen, apparently to give the film more of a schizo perspective. For some reason, he also insisted on recording the sound on tiny microphones concealed in the actor's ears. But despite the disorientating effect of much of these techniques, none of them really distract from what is otherwise a wholly fascinating and deliriously insane story. In fact, the scene where Bubby the grown child hugs a handicapped girl whose love cannot be reciprocated is among the most heart-wrenchingly honest in the history of cinema. Nicholas Hope in the lead role is the star of the show; his superb performance carries the film from beginning to end. He remains alternately hilarious, sympathetic, weird and chilling from one moment to the next.

Bad Boy Bubby picked up numerous awards at international film festivals, including awards for best director, best actor for Hope, best original screenplay and best editing at the 1994 Australian Film Institute awards, before it hit the shelves as an instant cult favourite. Unfortunately, the film wasn't released in America for years, and had to make do with word of mouth to help spread its alternative appeal on the fan circuits. A shame, because this is easily among the best Aussie comedies of the last twenty years (for another little-seen dark Aussie comedy from the 90s, check out Bill Bennett's *Kiss Or Kill* – reviewed in this book). Director Rolf De Heer went on to make other

disturbing gems like *Dance To Me My Song* and *Alexandra's Project*. And with this earlier film he maintains an assured command of his chosen medium; not for a moment does it stray into all-out silliness or gratuity. It will offend many viewers, especially those of a religious bent, but it never feels like you're being shocked for the sake of it; everything in the film serves the plot which unfolds with an odd revelation in the final moments.

Body Snatchers (1993)
Dir: Abel Ferrara /USA

With a slight difference on the previous entries in the *Body Snatcher's* series, here we have an environmentalist who is investigating chemical waste on an American military base. Meanwhile, his unsettled family is slowly falling apart due to a 'wicked' stepmother and constant in-fighting. But there's also something genuinely sinister going on among the local soldiers, and it's up to the daughter, Marti, to save her family from the invading aliens who are taking over the bodies of the residents and turning the entire community into a mindless conformity.

Jack Finney's 1955 novel *The Body Snatchers* was originally filmed by Don Siegel in 1956 as *Invasion of the Body Snatchers*, a classic of conformity which was a thinly veiled attack on the communist witch hunts of the McCarthy years. It was remade in 1978 by Philip Kaufman (and coincided with the release of George Romero's blackly comic satire on mindless consumerism, *Dawn of the Dead*). This latest update by Abel Ferrara continues with the series' addressing of the universal, political, and personal fears of the loss of identity, and a smart move of the filmmakers was to shift the action to a military base where the commonly held attitudes of 'patriotism', 'discipline', and 'duty' become enmeshed in paranoia, at constant odds with the idea of the military as a fighting force for freedom. It thus becomes even more difficult for the film's heroes to differentiate between the mindless drones of the alien invaders and the mindless drones of the local marines. The military setting also allows for an explosive finale with guns, bombs, and even an Apache helicopter getting in on the action.

Body Snatchers had a complicated production history with no less than five writers credited with the screenplay. It was B-movie legend Larry Cohen who wrote the original script (based on Finney's idea, of course), and that version was initially given the green light for shooting. Writer Denis Paoli and director Stuart Gordon (the pair behind *Re-Animator* and *From Beyond*) were hired to polish up on some of the dialogue, but ended up creating whole new scenes and ideas along the way. Stuart Gordon was originally set to direct, but due to the unorganised situation during pre-production, his patience ran out and he decided to head off to Australia to direct the Christopher Lambert vehicle, *Fortress*, instead. *Body Snatchers* once again found itself in limbo for a while until Warner Brothers took a chance and roped in bad boy director, Abel Ferrara, whose dark imagination would no doubt take the project to where it needed to be. Every smart director has a writer, and Abel had Nicholas St. John, a man who is often referred to as the angel to Ferrara's demon. Nicky St. John managed to rescue the abandoned script by solving the narrative problems, and after much delay the film was ready to shoot.

With a budget of $20 million, *Body Snatchers* was Ferrara's most expensive film to date, shot in beautiful scope by Bojan Bazelli, and including the spine-tingling alien scream that was purloined from W.D. Richter's script for the 1978 version. Gabriel Anwar is serviceable as teen heroine Marti, Forrest Whitaker is as you've never seen him before as the increasingly 'delusional' odd man out, and Meg Tilly's stepmother Carol adds a dark foretaste to the horrors of the invaded family. The film also boasts plenty of creepy and disgusting special effects courtesy of Phil Cory, with probing tendrils, dissolving carcasses, and slimy pods being a real treat for horror fans. Also of note is the excellent theme tune by Ferrara's regular composer, Joe Delia.

Warner Brothers felt uncomfortable with the end result and had no idea how to market the film. They basically sat on it for almost a year unsure of how to proceed. Ferrara managed to get a screening at the Cannes Film Festival where the critics were willing to take him and his film seriously, and this led to many positive reviews. Bolstered by this good reception, Warner Brothers put the film out on the festival circuit and it became an instant cult classic at the Dylan Dog Horror Festival in Milan where thousands of hardcore horror fanatics appreciated the sharp satire and dark imagination at work. This overwhelming response saved the film from its 'straight-to-video' hell and was given a moderately successful theatrical run in America.

Crazy Love For You (1993)

(aka *Can't Stop My Crazy Love For You; Don't Stop My Crazy Love For You*)
(Orig title: *Dang bu zhu de feng qing*)
Dir: Wei Tat Hon /Hong Kong

News broadcaster Kitty (Yvonne Yung Hung) has an unwelcome stalker who lives in the apartment opposite to hers. This creepy loner watches her on the news every day, and when she's at home he uses a camera with an extra-long lens to peer into her private life. The creep, Fred, is played by Hong Kong's most delirious madman, Simon Yam (of *Doctor Lam* infamy), and one night he heads off to a live outdoor broadcast with a bunch of flowers hoping he will get to meet her. However, Kitty is pestered by a group of louts, so he follows them into an alley and beats them with a baseball bat.

The next day, one of Fred's office colleagues invites him along to a shooting range. And it's there that they meet up with another shooting enthusiast, Charlie (Michael Wong). Charlie happens to be Kitty's boyfriend, and when she shows up in person to join them at the table, Fred is awe-struck. Charlie and the office colleague head for the shooting range, leaving Kitty and Fred at the table. Fred gets twitchy and nervous, and his attempts to engage in conversation ends with him suggesting that they should meet up for dinner in secret. This makes Kitty feel uncomfortable, so she makes her excuses and leaves. Back at home, Fred is very angry and has a blazing row with his 'girlfriend', a mannequin dummy in a wig which he keeps at home for company. He and his dummy then have some make up sex on the sofa bed.

Fred's creepiness soon enough steps up a gear as he makes strange phone calls to Kitty's home and even enters her apartment at night while she sleeps, taking framed pictures of her and defacing the faces of those next to her in the shots, stealing her underwear and beating her unconscious when she awakens. Fred slowly worms his way into her life by installing a security alarm on her apartment and somehow gaining enough trust to get access to her home, despite him having "abnormal eyes" and "staring" at her all the time. Of course, Fred has rigged the alarm system to ensure he has access to the security code, and when he spies on Charlie and Kitty having sex, his insanity reaches new levels of creepiness, turning to murder and mutilation in order to get closer to Kitty...

Sort of an Asian take on *Fatal Attraction* with the added layer of Hong Kong comic craziness thrown in for good measure, *Crazy Love For You* is not as well-known as other Cat III gems like *The Untold Story* or *Ebola Syndrome*, but is a welcome addition nonetheless, offering up many twists and turns on the familiar territory, and reaching new heights of hysterical mayhem along the way. Simon Yam in the madman role delivers perhaps the most delirious performance of his career, turning what could have been a routine thriller into something altogether more unsettling. His performance even outweighs that of Anthony Wong in *Retribution Sight Unseen*, a film which shares a similar storyline to this, and would sit perfectly on a double-bill of obsessive stalker nastiness from Hong Kong.

Cat III movies are well-known for their crazy humour, and *Crazy Love For You* doesn't disappoint in that area, either. Most of the laughs to be had are at the expense of Yam and the things he gets up to while he's alone in his apartment. But like all the great Cat III gems, the humour soon dissipates once the storyline is firmly established. However, perhaps the funniest moment in the film comes at the end when Yam utters an immortal line of dialogue which I won't spoil here.

Dangerous Game (1993)
(aka *Snake Eyes*)
Dir: Abel Ferrara /USA
Harvey Keitel stars as Eddie Israel, an increasingly unhinged filmmaker struggling with his latest project, *Mother of Mirrors*, an autobiographical film based on the collapse of his own marriage. Madonna stars as Sarah Jennings, a bad actress whom Eddie guides through scenes as his fictional wife. He also hires Frank Burns (James Russo) to play himself as Sarah's drunken and abusive husband. But, as things turn out, Frank is drunk and abusive to Sarah for real, both on and off camera, and events from *Mother of Mirrors* soon spills out into real life...

What makes *Dangerous Game* so remarkable is that Eddie's character is clearly based on director Abel Ferrara himself. Those paying attention will notice that the clapper-board for *Mother of Mirrors* will sometimes read 'Abel Ferrara' instead of 'Eddie Israel'; Eddie's stories and anecdotes about his experiences with sex and drugs are based on Ferrara's own past; Ferrara's wife, Nancy, plays Eddie's wife in the movie, and his ways of screaming at his cast and crew are allegedly based on Ferrara's own aggressive directorial methods.

Basically, the film has three layers – the film itself (*Dangerous Game*), the film-within-the-film (*Mother of Mirrors*), and the real life drama that enshrouds the proceedings and can only be guessed at. It was originally titled *Snake Eyes* but was changed when Brian De Palma took the title for his own movie – a much more appropriate title in fact. Characters in *Dangerous Game* sometimes shout out for the attentions of Ken Kelsch and Nicholas St. John; Ken Kelsch served as DP and Nicky St. John wrote the script, but neither of them were actually in the fictional film! It would have been nice if Ferrara himself had made an appearance to guide Harvey Keitel in his tough moments, just as Eddie intervenes in *Mother of Mirrors* to help his cast members, but perhaps that would have pushed the boat too far. As to what is fact and what is fiction; well, Ferrara's fans have been arguing about that for the best part of two decades. But one thing's for sure; this is a rewarding, sometimes shocking and compulsive viewing experience.

Menace II Society (1993)
Dir: Albert & Allen Hughes /USA
A young street hood attempts to clean up his game and escape from the ghetto. Along with classics like *Reservoir Dogs*, *Natural Born Killers* and *Bad Lieutenant*, *Menace II Society* is another one of those 'back from the dead' movies from the 90s which was initially refused a video certificate in the UK until the controversial furore surrounding its release had died down. Those videos had fallen victim to some unwritten rule which kept them out of our homes. While many of the tapes weren't officially prosecuted (most of them – *Reservoir Dogs*, *NBK* and *True Romance*, for example – eventually hit the video shelves uncut), they were nonetheless held captive by the censors for a while, presumably as a way of enforcing some kind of temporary banning order without having

to go to the trouble of paperwork or seeing out the long process of making it legislation; you know, of making the process legitimate and above board. And as such, we could probably call this practice the Guantanamo Bay of British censorship, if that's not too glib. But anyway, in many respects, *Menace II Society* was one of the unfair recipients of that kind of treatment, because despite scenes of shocking violence, the film actually delivers one of the most hard-hitting anti-violence statements of the 90s. The Hughes brothers take the viewers on a candidly brutal tour of a ghetto in South Central L.A. where trigger-happy maniacs and reckless, brain dead gang-bangers ensure that pain and tragedy are a normal, everyday thing for the community.

The main character is Caine (Tyrin Turner), a young man torn between his desires to break out of the ghetto and improve his lot in life, and his obligations to his friends who are very much stuck in the dangerous game of street life, and are described in the film as "America's nightmare: young, black and doesn't give a fuck". Although *Menace* was quite a late entry in 'hood' movies, after *Boyz 'n' the Hood* and *Juice*, it remains perhaps the finest of its type – or at least a supreme example of it – and still raises a chill even after two decades since its release, thanks to its powerful and visceral *vérité* style. In the opening scene, Caine and his psychotic homie, O-Dog (Larenz Tate), are captured on surveillance camera shooting dead a shopkeeper. If the film has any flaws, for me it would be Caine's tolerance for a loon like O-Dog – I know they've known each other all their lives, but tagging along with a psycho who would blast your head off if you so much as say the wrong thing, is not my idea of buddy material, I'm sorry. And seeing a decent character like Caine constantly trailing behind O-Dog is quite disturbing – he definitely drops down a few notches in my estimation because of this. O-Dog, in turn, lives out every crummy drug dealer's wet dream – standing on ghetto street corners wearing an immaculate white vest, drinking bottles of "O.E." (what's that, Olde English cider? Yuk!), and busting caps in any motherfucker who disses him, yo.

On the plus side, *Menace II Society* does an excellent job of showing how routine violence echoes down the generations, to the point where black kids learn how to load a pistol before they can even ride a bike. The acting, for the most part, is spot on; harsh, gritty, emotional, foul-mouthed – all too believable, while the direction from the Hughes brothers is raw and consistently unflinching.

On the censorship front, the film didn't fare too well in America where the MPAA imposed a number of cuts in order to obtain the R rating. The cuts included the scene where Samuel L. Jackson's character kills the man at the poker game, the revenge shooting by A-Wax, and Caine's bloody demise. And it was this same American R-rated version which was passed uncut for a British cinema release. On home video, however, the BBFC removed a further ten seconds of violent footage, mostly of gunshot squibs and exit wounds. Those ten seconds of cuts were later waived in 2003 for the release by Entertainment, but that version is still based on the American R-rated cut. It wasn't until 2009 that the original director's cut was released in an 'uncut' DVD and Blu-Ray. However, this version is still missing the legendary prison riot scene that the Hughes brothers had filmed but was dropped by the studio to avoid the NC-17 rating. (It's a similar situation to that of *Candyman*, a film which has never been released uncut on any home video format. The original theatrical cut of *Candyman* includes extra footage of the psychiatrist being gutted with the hook.) The so-called director's cut of *Menace* also includes an extra scene which shows Caine and O-Dog breaking into a car.

Battle Angel Alita (1993)
(aka *Battle Angel*; Orig title: *Gunnm*)
Dir: Hiroshi Fukutomi /Japan
While searching for useful items on a large city dump, a cyborg mechanic finds the body parts of a discarded android. He takes the parts home and puts the machine back together again in full working order. The mechanic also moonlights as a cyborg bounty hunter at night, but little does he know that the innocent little machine he saved is Alita, a battle droid programmed to kill machines that are ten times her size. Meanwhile, the mechanic's young friend, Hugo, dreams of moving to Zarum, a paradise city for the rich that is suspended high above the slums with huge steel cables... Classic Japanese anime that was originally aired on television in two 27-minute episodes (entitled *Rusty Angel* and *Tears Sign*), but was released as a stand-alone feature on VHS and DVD in many Western territories. Short, sweet and full of mystery, wonder and

shattered dreams, *Battle Angel Alita* is a perfect future fantasy and an ideal introduction for those who want to get into Japanimation. James Cameron was so impressed he purchased the rights with a view to turning it into a big-budget Hollywood remake, but the project eventually fizzled out to nothing. For another little future anime, check out Katsuhiro Otomo's final segment of *Neo Tokyo* (*Meikyū Monogatari*, literally 'Labyrinth Tales', 1987), in which a salaryman finds himself in a battle of wills with a construction robot.

Sonatine (1993)
Dir: Takeshi Kitano /Japan

Where do old gangsters go to die? To the seaside, if you're to believe this pensive crime film by Japanese cultural phenomenon, 'Beat' Takeshi Kitano. Yakuza big shot Katajima sends his trusted, middle-aged underboss Murakawa (Kitano himself) to Okinawa to settle some gangster in-fighting. Murakawa gathers together a group of young guns and does as he is told, but suspects there's more to the assignment than meets the eye. Is he being set up? After Murakawa and his henchmen are ambushed, they retreat to the beachfront home of a local yakuza and spend a few weirdly idyllic days horsing around by the sea, wondering when the horrors of real life will intrude.

Hugely praised on its initial release, this 1993 Japanese film hit Western screens shortly after Kitano's more recent *Hana-Bi*. The difference in Kitano's appearance is shocking (*Sonatine* was shot before Kitano was almost killed in a motorcycle accident, while *Hana-Bi* was made after), but his sly, acid-tipped sense of humour and melancholy twists on genre conventions remain the same. *Sonatine* has a very unusual angle for a gangster movie; it's premise being that to understand violence you must explore the moments of calm that punctuate it – a real break from the norm and very refreshing.

Kitano delivers a perfectly-measured performance as Murakawa, a man who wants out of the crime world, but retains the strength to recognise that circumstances and obligations will never allow it. The film's uneasy but perfectly calibrated mix of brutal violence and goofy humour is pure Kitano – the scene in which Murakawa and his henchmen play a variation on the Rock 'em Sock 'em Robots with paper sumo wrestlers is just too bizarre (and hilarious!) – and its convulsively nihilistic ending is unforgettable.

Beruf Neonazi (1993)
(aka *Profession: Neo-Nazi*; aka *Nazi Occupation*)
Dir: Winfried Bonengel /Germany

A documentary about a couple of neo-Nazis which features the infamous Ewald Althans. Althans was not the stereotypical dumb skinhead as portrayed in the German press; he was actually quite a rational and intelligent man.

The film starts in Toronto, Canada, with Ernst Zündel, a middle-aged German in exile. He had left his homeland as a youngster to avoid national service and is seen here as the world's leading distributor of Nazi paraphernalia and literature. Zündel organizes media events and plans his eventual return to Germany once the country has been "re-Nazified." His right-hand man in this mission is Ewald Althans, the main subject of this documentary. Althans is an articulate, twenty-eight year old neo-Nazi. His job within the organization is to network with other splinter groups and unite them in their shared goal (at a time when computer activism was still in its infancy). This disturbing and controversial film goes on to present a fairly objective portrait of Althans, and we get to witness the activist as he espouses the teachings and philosophies of Hitler. We follow his activities, such as being the main German contact for Holocaust deniers living in Canada, to communicating with other similar groups across Germany and Europe at large. His own organization is also documented in the film. His way of distributing propaganda was very similar to those of the Ayatollah Khomeini (at one point, Zündel even describes himself as "the German Khomeini"). Althans later visits Auschwitz to confront visiting Jews about his theories on death camp denial. Soon after, he is seen making jokes about genocide.

Beruf Neonazi was funded by five German states, and when the film sparked its inevitable public outrage, those who funded the documentary demanded their (taxpayer's) money back. It was the same old story; a few tabloid papers whipped up a storm of controversy, and the government funding bodies panicked and attempted to disassociate themselves in a pathetic and frustrating example of trial by media. Trials were held to have the film banned in Germany, and while all this commotion was going on, the Werkstattkino sourced a print and was the only cinema in the land willing to hold screenings. This led to protests by militant anti-fascists who picketed outside, intimidating and openly threatening those who wanted to enter the theatre. Basically, they behaved like a bunch of fascists themselves in their attempts to have the film banished. The cinema was constantly under threat from picketers, and the staff were pestered with abusive phone calls. Security guards had to stay overnight at the cinema to protect the film reels. Welcome to the free West.

The Werkstattkino was also prosecuted for screening *Texas Chainsaw Massacre 2* and *Mother's Day*. Munich is usually a conservative city, but on those occasions it was the leftists who were responsible for behaving in an unnecessary and reactionary way. In 1995, the film was used as court evidence, and Althans was found guilty of racial incitement, defamation and Holocaust denial, and sentenced to three and a half years in prison. During the trial he announced his departure from the neo-Nazi movement. Through his homosexuality, Althans was often linked to other right-wing extremists, like Michael Kuhnen, another gay neo-Nazi. Filmmaker Rosa von Praunheim portrayed him in the 2005 film *Men, Heroes, Gay Nazis*. He now works under the name of Bernd E. Althans as a promoter and organiser of gay parties. Now that's what I call a change of lifestyle.

Witchboard 2: The Devil's Doorway (1993)
(aka *Witchboard: The Return*)
Dir: Kevin S. Tenney /USA
A young woman, Paige (Ami Dolenz), rents an apartment and discovers a ouija board among the leftover belongings of the previous tenant. Of course, it isn't long before curiosity gets the better of her, and she has a dabble out of boredom. She contacts a spirit called Susan, and learns that she was the previous tenant who was murdered. Paige then attempts to solve the murder mystery while something evil takes out a couple of characters by way of faulty car breaks and a wrecking ball. Slightly better than the original. It was followed by *Witchboard III: The Possession* (1995).

The Tommyknockers (1993)
Dir: John Power /USA /New Zealand
An historian discovers an ancient burial site in the woods near her home. It's unclear exactly

what it is; it looks like a collection of giant grey blocks in the dirt – perhaps an ancient site or a crashed UFO. Even stranger is the fact that the site radiates a green light to the touch. The light seems to have cured the woman's dog of blindness, while also giving it a vicious streak. Other characters from various sub-plots, including a young boy who is into magic, a female cop and cheating post office workers, suddenly receive instructions from the otherworldly site on how to 'invent' extremely complicated machinery and electronic devices that make life easier for a while. However, it's only a matter of time before the green light exposes its sinister side when the locals are rounded up completely brainwashed and under the spell of the Tommyknockers, a race of space aliens that dwell in their craft below the woods. It's up to a drunk poet – who incidentally has a metal plate in his head which protects him from the psychic brainwashing – to tackle the enslaved community and save the day... *The Tommyknockers* is a TV mini-series that was broadcast in two feature-length episodes. Compared with other two-part TV movies based on Stephen King – such as *It* (1990), *Bag of Bones* (2011), *Storm of the Century* (1999), *Desperation* (2006), etc – this is one of the weaker entries. Which is a shame as it starts off quite well, and generates an interesting drama with an engaging bunch of characters before falling into the usual, predictable territory.

Needful Things (1993)
Dir: Fraser C. Heston /USA
The Devil incarnate moves into the sleepy New England town of Castle Rock and opens an antique store, Needful Things, gifting the local residents with their heart's desires. All he asks in return is a little favour. Turns out that each of his customers are merely pawns in his evil game in which he sets out to spread his destructive chaos throughout the town. It's up to the local Sheriff, Ed Harris, to save the day. This film has its moments of flair and some memorable characters – such as J.T. Walsh as a crooked politician/degenerate gambler, Amanda Plummer as a meek cafe waitress, and Max Von Sydow as Old Scratch himself – but it fails to string together the complex chain-link of mayhem which involves all of the characters, as was portrayed in Stephen King's source novel. However, scriptwriter W.D. Richter does a fine job of packing this epic story into two hours (the

TV version runs for three hours but I haven't seen that version, dammit). Viewers are rewarded with a panoramic view of how evil spreads due to misplaced anger, resentments and prejudices.

When a Stranger Calls Back (1993)
Dir: Fred Walton /USA

This official sequel to *When a Stranger Calls* (1978) delivers much of the same as the original, minus the all-important surprise factor. Babysitter Julia (Jill Schoelen) is pestered by a stranger who knocks on the door one night and complains that his car has broken down. Julia refuses to open the door but agrees to call the auto-club. However, the phone lines are down, and rather than telling him to go away, she stupidly tells him that she has made the call. As time passes and the stranger becomes increasingly restless, she struggles to keep up the lies for much longer... Cut to five years later, and Julia is a paranoid recluse who is convinced that someone is entering her apartment and re-arranging her belongings. She gets help from a retired ten-bellied cop and a college psychiatrist to track down her stalker. *When a Stranger Calls Back* is a lacklustre attempt to out-do the original but fails badly. Rather than escalating the terror, the filmmakers instead settle into an inept social drama about women doing it for themselves. However, the film is worth a watch if only for the creepy scene in which the maniac shows up at a hospital late at night.

Short Cuts (1993)
Dir: Robert Altman /USA

The lives of nine dysfunctional suburban couples in L.A. are intertwined. A fascinating three-hour examination of people living on the edge. Based on the stories of Raymond Carver, and offering superb performances from the likes of Andie McDowell, Jack Lemmon, Julianne Moore, Matthew Modine, Jennifer Jason Leigh, Chris Penn, Robert Downey Jr, Madeline Stowe, Tim Robbins, Tom Waits and Frances McDormand. Similar in style to *Magnolia*, *Crash* and *Happiness*, in the way it presents a panorama of life's problems, and is expertly weaved together with an assured hand by director Altman. It's a 188-minute masterpiece which never puts a foot wrong, despite its long running-time and daring performances.

The Tower (1993)
Dir: Richard Kletter /USA

The Intercorp Tower is a hi-tech building with a Hal-9000-like central computer in charge of everything from making the coffee, watering the plants and 'deleting' those who breach the security parameters. And when new employee, Paul Reiser, makes a few fuck-ups on his first day on the job, the system deems him eligible for termination. *The Tower* is a TV remake of the 1985 Canadian movie of the same title. This film pits its protagonist against the dangers of faceless corporate monstrosities (and also shares ideas with similarly-themed movies like *Gremlins 2: The New Batch* [1990] and *Cube* [1997]). The film has much to say on the ant-like humans who contribute to the development of ice-cold, inhuman technologies that have a monopoly on life and death, creating a runaway menace in which no one is in control. Fun little film.

Broken (1993)
Dir: Peter Christopherson /USA

Four years after the controversy that surrounded *Down In It*, another Nine Inch Nails video/short, *Broken* caused much controversy due to its extreme content. Directed by the late Peter 'Sleazy' Christopherson, *Broken* consists of four music videos and a framing scenario of snuff death and torture. The video is perhaps most notable for its jarring and abrasive sounds and visual style. Supermasochist, Bob Flanagan, makes an appearance as himself sitting in an S&M chair having his nads groped by sharp metallic claws (taken from the much banned *Happiness Is Slavery* video). And though *Down In It* was banned from playing on MTV, *Broken* proved to be too outrageous to be released at all. Copies were leaked and bootlegged on VHS in the 90s, and exchanged via the internet in the 00s. Some bootleggers even added extra footage, including Robert 'Bud' Dwyer's infamous suicide. More recently, *Broken* was officially made available uncut by Reznor himself for streaming on Vimeo, but it was immediately removed. The website released a statement saying "Vimeo does not allow videos that harass, incite hatred or depict excessive violence."

Pumpkinhead II: Bloodwings (1993)
(aka *The Revenge of Pumpkinhead*)
Dir: Jeff Burr /USA

Small-town Sheriff (*Hellraiser*'s Andrew Robinson) is upset that his teenage daughter Jenny (Ami Dolenz) has befriended a group of degenerates who hang around smoking dope all day. She has a crush on the denim-clad donger of the group, and sneaks out after dark to hang out with them. However, while speeding recklessly on the road, they hit an old woman who turns out to be Haggis. The teens dig something up at a strange, *Pet Sematary 2*-like burial ground, and wind up resurrecting old Pumpkinhead. The teens also inadvertently set fire to Haggis' house. And while she burns to death, she uses an incantation to raise the vengeful monster – and her murdered son, Tommy, seems to be part of the creature. *Bloodwings* is a respectable sequel to *Pumpkinhead*, and much more bloody than the first film. This time the demon is much less discriminating on its vengeance spree; it seems anyone who gets in its way is a legitimate target. The only downside is that whenever Pumpkinhead shows up, we get an excessive amount of strobe lights which get very annoying very quickly. The film shares similarities with *Friday the 13th*, with the mother avenging college boys for the death of her mongoloid son. Oh, and Linea Quigley rides Pumpkinhead's pole, apparently.

Retribution Sight Unseen (1993)
(Orig title: *Mang nv 72 xiao shi*; aka *3 Days of a Blind Girl*)
Dir: Wing-Chiu Chan /Hong Kong

Retribution Sight Unseen is a glossy Cat III thriller that serves as a more twisted version of *Fatal Attraction* with a bit of *Crazy Love For You* thrown in. Anthony Wong is great as the intruder who enters the home of the gorgeous Veronica Yip who has undergone eye surgery which leaves her unable to see for three days. Wong poses as a friendly handyman at first but can't conceal his insanity for very long. He gradually becomes more and more sinister and perverted and psychotic as the film progresses, subjecting Yip to all kinds of foulness and control-freak behaviour until the tables are finally turned... There's lots of silly slapstick humour courtesy of Wong (look out for the shower scene, and his way of dealing with a pretend intruder), lots of eye candy courtesy of

Yip, and lots of your typical Cat III mayhem. This doesn't reach very high on the shocking and disturbing meter compared to other Cat III titles, but is well deserving of the rating, especially at the end when the violence kicks in proper.

The Hidden II (1993)
Dir: Seth Pinsker /USA

Starting with a 15-minute recap of the ending of the first film, *The Hidden II* begins proper with the death of the alien creature. But Lloyd sticks around to deal with the problem of the alien eggs which are hatching and threatening to plunge the city into chaos all over again, only this time even dogs are used as hosts for parasitical alien invaders... This is a middle-of-the-road sequel offering nothing of interest and a lame ending. It completely lacks the excitement and charm of the first film.

Necronomicon (1993)
Dir: Brian Yuzna, Christophe Gans & Shusuke Kaneko /USA /France

HP Lovecraft (played by Jeffrey Combs) enters a Gothic library at night for a spot of research and 'fact checking' for his latest story. He finds the original occult text, the Necronomicon (Lovecraft's own fictional devising), and begins writing a short trilogy of tales which forms this anthology film. The first story, *The Drawned*, is perhaps the weakest, in which a man in an old dark house uses the text to perform Satanic rites and resurrect his dead relatives, but the results go by way of *The Monkey's Paw*. In the second story, *The Cold*, a Boston journalist visits a strange girl in an unusually chilly house as part of his investigation into a spate of unsolved murders, only to be told the story of Dr. Maden (David Warner), a man afflicted with a rare skin condition which can only be controlled in a cold environment. And finally, *Whispers* is set in modern-day Boston with a female cop in pursuit of a criminal into an abandoned industrial building which contains a hellish pit full of skeletons and evil flying creatures. *Necronomicon* is a pretty solid anthology horror, but considering the talent behind the camera, it doesn't quite live up to its promise. *The Cold* is the most satisfying story, as it enters *Re-Animator* territory as spinal fluid is stolen from victims to keep one's immortality going. And in the wraparound at the end, Lovecraft is forced to slay one of his own tentacled creations and skin the head of a monk.

Attack of the 50ft. Woman (1993)
Dir: Christopher Guest /USA

"The world is my dollhouse." Aliens zap Daryl Hannah with a laser beam which somehow causes her to grow in size every time she gets angry. She then strides across town in search of her cheating husband (played by one of the Baldwin brothers, the fat one), increasingly upset and growing to enormous size. This HBO remake of the classic 50s B-movie does a decent job of replicating that 50s drive-in vibe of a small town under attack, much like John Carpenter's remake of *Village of the Damned* (1995) and Chuck Russell's update of *The Blob* (1988). The film is clearly played for laughs, but it doesn't go far enough. How many little people could she carry around in her cleavage? How many could she bowl over with a well-aimed blast of flatulence?

Unfortunately, we never get the answers to those questions. It's a fun film if you're in the right mood, but Hannah's 'rampage' through the desert town is a bit of a let down, probably because the town miniature sets were too expensive to have them destroyed. Boo. This film is crying out for some lewd scene, something to give it some extra oomph. A scene where a giant Hannah sits back on a hill while masturbating with a bus would have been great. There could have been a fun 'interior' shot of the passengers and their disarray, tumbling back and forth down the bus aisle as she sloshed the vehicle in and out of her giant crack, with the little people stranded on some kind of pinky-pubey-foamy car wash ride.

Fred Olen Ray's *Attack of the 60 Foot Centerfold* (1995) is another lame but entertaining entry in this bizarre sub-genre. And here, we actually get to see the giant tits. Rather than aliens, it's the fault of scientists and their experimental growth hormone that is to blame when topless models consume the stuff while competing for Centerfold of the Year. Angel (J.J. North), is the blonde bombshell who grows to enormous size. However, not wanting to be upstaged by the media attention, her red-haired rival (Tammy Parks) also downs the blue fluid. It all ends with a giant cat fight in downtown L.A.. And look out for a quick cameo from Forest Ackerman. Roger Corman also produced *Attack of the 50 Foot Cheerleader* (2012), which delivers more of the same – in 3D this

time – as Jena Sims consumes the medicine and has a growth spurt. Giant females also showed up in anime over the next few years, in series' such as *Marcoss Frontier* (*Makurosu Furontia*, 2008), *Mahou shoujo Tai: The Adventure* (2012), *Attack On Titan* (*Hepburn: Shingeki no Kyojin*, 2013), *The Seven Deadly Sins* (*Nanatsu no Taizai*, 2015), *Valkyrie Drive: Mermaid* (*Varukiri doraivu*, 2015), and the hentai 'Giantess' videos.

The Last Seduction (1994)
Dir: John Dahl /USA

In one of his books, Nietzsche described women as having developed a strong sense of cunning over millennia due to their historical position of being under the dominance of patriarchal societies. According to Nietzsche, if a woman had a problem with her spouse, she couldn't openly complain about it due to fears of being beaten, killed, or banished from the household. The structure of old societies would ensure she would lose the confrontation regardless of whether she was right or wrong in her grievance. Thus women have developed a highly-evolved sense of cunning, and in order for them to get what they want from life they have become adept at manipulating situations and circumstances around them, and portraying themselves as victims, but are in fact just waging their ruthless and amoral will to power.

Director John Dahl seems to have taken Nietzsche's aphorism to form the basis of his film, *The Last Seduction*, which stars Linda Fiorentino as Bridget, a cold-hearted super-bitch who goads her husband into stealing and selling pharmaceutical drugs, and then makes off with the $700,000 loot while he's in the shower. Husband Clay (Bill Pullman) desperately needs the money to pay off his gambling debts, so he hires a private detective to find her. Meanwhile, Bridget arrives in a small town hoping to sit it out whilst her dodgy lawyer secures her a divorce. In a bar she picks up Mike (Peter Berg), an amiable local stud whom she exploits for sex and then ensnares into her complex web while she severs her past ties with a ruthless and deadly precision.

The Last Seduction is a modern-day noir thriller that effectively puts the 'fatale' back into femme fatale. This is a very dark film, but also darkly amusing in places, superbly pieced together and contrived. It's so gleefully nasty that only the most soft-hearted viewers could resist the film's ghastly spell. Unlike the more bloated erotic thrillers like *Basic Instinct*, which seem to revel in their own excesses, *The Last Seduction* doesn't mess around in getting right down to the cold heart of classic noir. It's a film which presents life as being like a nasty game of cut and run, where only the most twisted and ruthless characters stand a chance of surviving. It's one of those thrillers that is loaded with genuinely surprising plot twists.

Fiorentino is perfect as the praying-mantis-in-lace, a spectacularly cynical bitch. There's a part of me that couldn't help but admire her a little but I sure wouldn't want to get involved with anyone like her. Director John Dahl, who had previously helmed a couple of low-key noirs (*Kill Me Again* and *Red Rock West*, which are both well worth checking out, also), does a fine job of showing how a Hitlerian attitude is worshipped in the business world, and subversively exposing how society secretly embraces the things we love to condemn.

The Last Seduction premiered on America's HBO cable channel, but was eventually given a theatrical release. The film's overwhelming critical success led many to believe that it would receive some good attention at the Oscars for director Dahl and actress Fiorentino, but because the film had debuted on television, this wasn't to be. However, *The Last Seduction* did at least grace many critics' top ten lists of the year and helped to transcend the stigma attached to TV movies. Perhaps the only thing that stops this film from being a masterpiece is the soundtrack; an uninspired jazzy lounge tune that seems to be playing on a constant loop with no variation, and becomes very annoying. It plays throughout the opening credits, throughout most of the film itself, and then throughout the entire duration of the end credits. I wish they would have changed the bloody record!

Natural Born Killers (1994)
Dir: Oliver Stone /USA

Deliberately unconventional, wildly satirical, brutally violent and vulgar in equal measure, *Natural Born Killers* is more self-consciously radical (in form, if not necessarily in content) than any other major studio release of the 90s. If it isn't the masterpiece it aspires to be, it's unquestionably a must see for film fans.

Woody Harrelson and Juliette Lewis play Mickey and Mallory Knox, a modern-day Bonnie and Clyde on a cross-country killing spree. If Bonnie and Clyde liked to think of themselves as Depression-era Robin Hoods, Mickey and Mallory have no such illusions – as a TV psychologist observes: "They know the difference between right and wrong. They just don't give a damn." On their way to racking up 52 victims, the couple become international celebrities, thanks mostly to the attentions of a lurid TV tabloid show, 'American Maniacs,' hosted by the unapologetically vile Wayne Gale (Robert Downey Jr. with an awful Aussie accent). After a series of increasingly bizarre adventures on the road, Mickey and Mallory are apprehended and imprisoned. Nothing, however, can stand in the way of true love (or TV ratings): While deranged warden McClusky (Tommy Lee Jones) schemes to have the Knox's murdered, Mickey plots escape, using a live interview with Wayne Gale as a pretext for inciting an apocalyptic prison riot.

This often violent and technically brilliant satire of televisual culture baffled critics at the time of its release, and its indecorous brand of humour will strike many as insolent and repellent. Director Oliver Stone opts for an instinctively pulp style with *NBK*, and paradoxically, the result may be his most significant film. Accessing some of the farthest reaches of marginalized culture – direct-to-video movies, cyberpunk, S&M, anime, serial killer fandom, etc – *NBK* decisively wrenches mainstream cinema into the anarchic realm of postmodern pop. The film succeeds as a risk-taking, audio/visual overload that is all too rare in the movie world, with Stone creating a chilling vision of America that would have the Founding Fathers turning in their graves.

If the film succeeds as pure visual overload, its failings lie in its attempts at social commentary and satire. Seemingly unaware of his own status as a self-created media object, Stone's hardline critique of an America which makes celebrities out of psychopaths is trite and hypocritical. He condemns the media's obsession with killers whilst simultaneously glamorizing his characters and their brutal murder spree, and does all he can to turn this homicidal couple into heroes. As a result, Stone kind of resembles his own hate-figure, Wayne Gale, in the way he exploits violence and suffering with the facade of a moral crusader. Bad bad bad! For every sequence that works, such as the sitcom parody at the beginning, we get a bunch of scenes that fail miserably, and

Stone seems content to continue driving home his point that was already made pretty obvious within the first few minutes of the movie. By the half hour mark you'll be screaming 'Yes, we get it, now move on!' The violence becomes dull long before the climactic prison riot, and the snipes at consumerism and the state of the modern world are way too glib and obvious to hold the entire film.

Inevitably, *Natural Born Killers* was always going to be controversial. Quentin Tarantino publicly criticized Stone for taking liberties with his original screenplay, and the film only opened in America after much hassle between the filmmakers and the MPAA. The American censors demanded 150 cuts to the film to secure the R-rating. As a result of all the negative publicity, the film's UK release was also postponed. Scheduled to hit the screens on 18 November 1994, *NBK* didn't see the light of day on these shores until 25 February 1995, with an uncut 18 certificate from the BBFC. And during that time the British tabloid press simply repeated all the negative hyperbole from the American papers, and called for an immediate ban, and accused the film of being to blame for real-life acts of violence. Some UK papers even announced it had been banned, despite the head of the BBFC at the time, James Ferman, issuing a statement claiming that the film was merely "under consideration". But credit to the British censors for not being swayed by the media trial and releasing *NBK* uncut.

The UK video release was also beset with problems when Warner Home Video delayed it indefinitely following the Dunblane shootings in Scotland and the mass murder in Tasmania in 1996.

Hated: GG Allin and the Murder Junkies (1994)
Dir: Todd Phillips /USA

The sneering nihilism and excesses of the punk rock movement has led to it being hijacked by talentless bozos in spikes and leather. For many, being a punk is the perfect excuse to act like a total jeb end. Case in point: GG Allin. This documentary on one of the most infamous of all death rock icons has very little to offer the viewers beyond the sordid spectacle of Allin's on-stage antics. He was simply a one-trick-pony with no substance to him, apart from the arse-paste substance he would fling at his audience. The film stands as a downbeat and depressing look at an army of misguided souls, with the director documenting everything along the way. Beyond the fact that this film ultimately reveals just how boring and pathetic Allin really was, perhaps the most surprising aspect is that director Todd Phillips went on to forge a career in Hollywood, bombarding *his* audience with such rancid cinematic bowel movements as *Road Trip* and *Starsky And Hutch*.

Allin had just been released from prison after serving a three year stretch for assaulting a woman at one of his shows. Apparently, he deemed it acceptable to stub out a cigarette on her head before throwing her across a table. Quite early on, it's clear to see that Allin was worn-out and troubled; one of the main focal points of his act was violence, against both his audience and his self. And this served as nothing more than a crushing treadmill offering zero progress. It's ironic that GG posed no menace to anyone beyond his little group of fans, a fact he seemed completely oblivious about when he insisted in interviews that society was afraid of him.

After an interview segment with GG's guitarist brother, Merle (who sports a Hitler 'tache and claims to have psychic links with the Lunachicks), and Dino the naked drummer, we cut to footage of a naked Allin running through a crowd, punching people in the face indiscriminately with reckless abandon. There is also footage of GG from 1988 giving a speech in a tiny hall. Back then, he had long, straggly hair, a bushy beard, and his face was partially concealed by the silly hat he wore. Remember the scene in Nick Broomfield's documentary, *Aileen – Life and Death of a Serial Killer*, in which Aileen Wuornos went on a rant before she was executed, her eyes bulging with psychotic rage? Well, the 1988 footage shows Allin in a similar intense mood. He reads from a newspaper article that ridiculed him for saying he would commit suicide in October 1990. Someone in the audience shouts "Why don't you kill yourself sooner?" Allin replies, "Why don't I kill myself sooner? Because it would please you too much, you fucking cunt." He then invites the heckler on stage to say it to his face. Moments later, a crazy-eyed she-beast approaches him and repeats her question. So, GG drags her by the hair and rams her head into the wall. Two men come to her rescue, and one of them punches Allin in the face while the other helps the woman and then boots him in the ribs.

GG simply gets back up and continues with his speech like nothing has happened.

The documentary was filmed before and during the Murder Junkies' 1991 American tour, in which three shows were filmed and appeared on the video, *GG Allin – Raw, Brutal, Rough and Bloody*. Todd Phillips arranged for the band to play at a university in New York before the tour commenced. The show went ahead in front of an audience who seemingly had no idea who GG Allin was, or what was in store for them. Appearing on stage alone, GG shoves a banana up his arse, poops it back out, chews it up, and spits it at the crowd. Half the audience finds it amusing, and the other half head swiftly for the nearest exit. Those who stick around are ordered to undress, but none do. This lack of obedience angers GG, and he shows this by heading for the audience. Most rise to their feet and rush for the exit, and GG throws a chair at them as they scarper.

It's this kind of thing that makes Allin so fascinating for many; the fact that he completely obliterated the safety-line between the audience and performer. He wasn't some Messiah of death rock, but a genuinely psychotic wild man who didn't hesitate to endanger those who attended his shows – he would assault and abuse both himself and the crowd with equal abandon (at one point, he is seen repeatedly smashing himself in the face with a microphone, and breaking his teeth in the process). When people talk about GG Allin, the one thing that is rarely mentioned is the music itself. And once you hear the godawful racket of tracks like '*Anal Cunt*' and '*Bite It You Scum*', it's easy to understand why. Make no mistake, even among the most hardcore, sneering punk fanatics, those songs aren't going to win any prizes. In fact, the only prize Allin could be honoured with is the award for 'The Man With the World's Smallest Nob'. Honestly, for a man who would shed his clothes at the drop of a hat, you would expect him to be packing something more substantial than the shy molecule that jiggled between his legs. Even a newborn baby boy could point and laugh at him. Indeed, Allin's shrivelled member seems to have its own personality, and both Allin and his penis look to be equally resentful of each other, as if they're in some kind of battle to see who can undermine the other the most.

In the book, *Cult Rapture*, Allin was interviewed by Adam Parfrey just days before the kamikaze icon succumbed to a fatal heroin overdose. When asked the inevitable question, "When are you finally going to kill yourself?" Allin replied, "The biggest question that everyone keeps asking me is about the suicide thing. For me right now to say I'm going to commit suicide is just way too premature because there's too many battles and it seems like there's too many people who want me to do it now, so as long as I've got to battle and to fight, and as long as I got some enemies, I gotta keep going to fuck these people up. To end it now is what the government would want and what society would want, and as long as I can be that dagger in their back and as long as I can be the enemy of the people then I've got to stay alive."

Such a pitiful answer. GG Allin was unknown to about 99% of Americans at the height of his powers, and that's a generous estimate. He was never a threat to the government or the fabric of society. His enemies amounted to those whom he punched in the face or flung shit at, or stole drugs from. If Allin genuinely thought of himself as a national threat, then not only was he even less intelligent than many assumed, but he also lacked the self-awareness needed to be truly subversive. As Parfrey puts it, "[Allin] was simply too much of a fuck-up to achieve mythic status."

Aftermath (1994)
Dir: Nacho Cerda /Spain

Rarely does a short film attract such global recognition when it is limited to playing only a few film festivals, but Nacho Cerda's *Aftermath* has become something of a cult classic and has divided its audience down the middle between those declaring it a masterpiece of horror and others a crude and overblown piece of nonsense. But make no mistake, once seen this film is not so easily forgotten.

Aftermath presents a day in the life of a necrophiliac pathologist whose job in the local morgue puts him in close contact with the recently deceased. No sooner have his colleagues left the building when the nameless pervert (played by Pep Tosar) indulges in a bit of 'how's your father' with a female corpse. The film is about as explicit as a non-pornographic movie can be, with the infamous scenes of Tosar defiling the corpse with a knife and plunging the blade in between the legs whilst jerking off, and then climbing on top for a bit of gross penetration. The film is beautiful to look at considering the subject matter, with some impressive photography, and an insane performance by Tosar, giving it a sheen of glossiness.

Whereas previous necro-shockers like *Lucker The Necrophagous* had a cheap and nasty aura about it, *Aftermath* offers the production values of a Hollywood film (albeit on only a fraction of the budget), at complete odds with the rank and disgusting imagery on screen. Indeed, horror fans didn't get to witness such nasty and perverted scenes in such glossy looking productions until the equally troubling likes of *Grotesque* (2009) and *A Serbian Film* (2009) came along a decade and a half later.

The film basically puts us in the company of a sicko for half an hour, during which time the hopelessly defenceless cadavers are opened up and sexually violated with nary a word of dialogue in the whole film. The camera prowls along investigating the lifeless slabs of meat whilst Verdi's *Requiem* plays out on the soundtrack. It's a film that is tailor-made to kill your spirit; one day it will be your corpse laid out on a slab similar to the ones in *Aftermath*, and it's that helpless identification with the subject matter that affects viewers the most: It's personal, it makes you feel vulnerable, it presents to you your own mortality that is both natural and open to abuse. And of course, most people don't want to be reminded of such things.

Emerging as part of Cerda's 'Death Trilogy', sandwiched between his black and white student film, *The Awakening*, and his beautiful shot in scope *Genesis*, *Aftermath* premiered at the Sitges Film Festival in October 1994 after seven months of intense work from pre-production to its first screening. It was met with staunchly polarized opinions from both those who were impressed and appalled, and it became one of the most talked about films of the year, leaving similarly themed, big-budget dreck like *Curdled* (1996) for dust.

This word-of-mouth buzz and excitement followed the film across the Atlantic to its North American premier at the 1997 FantAsia Film Festival in Canada where almost a thousand avid horror fans reacted in wild delight as Cerda's shockfest unspooled before their eyes (the 2001 documentary, *In The Belly of The Beast*, includes some invaluable footage of this event, and also the fascinating reactions of people like Mitch Davis and Jim Van Bebber defending the film as a masterwork, while Chas

Balun dismissed it as an over-hyped, pretentious student film).

Aftermath picked up the Public's Prize at FantAsia, and Cerda became a cult celebrity in Montreal. The film was a mainstay on the bootleg video circuit (along with *Genesis*) until it was released on DVD by Unearthed Films. Later, German company Dragon released the Death Trilogy in a metallic box set with a shed load of extras, including an anatomical figurine!

A Chinese Torture Chamber Story (1994)
(Orig title: *Mun ching sap daai huk ying*)
Dir: Bosco Lam /Hong Kong

A Cat III historical epic that is closer in spirit to *Oxen Split Torturing* than *Sex and Zen*, *A Chinese Torture Chamber Story* is an odd mix of sex, sadism, and slapstick which will confuse and irritate all but the most hardened Hong Kong cineastes.

A young servant woman called 'Little Cabbage' (Yonne Yung Hung) and her married lover (Lawrance Ng) find themselves in deep trouble due to her uncontrollable voyeurism. Through a series of plot twists, Little Cabbage and her lover are accused of murder, and are subjected to a long and sustained period of torture and abuse from a local magistrate – including being hung by the hair, having fingers cut to the bone in a fiendish blade device, finger nails ripped off, being forced to walk on their knees over broken plates, and rolling on a bed of nails, etc. The judge is hell-bent on extracting a confession from the pair at any cost. Flashbacks show that the couple has been stitched up by the hero's wife and her brutal bit on the side. By contriving to have Little Cabbage and the hero take the blame for the murder, they in turn get to keep their own adultery a secret.

A Chinese Torture Chamber is remembered mostly as a series of stand-out scenes rather than as a whole. We get an amusing take on the Demi Moore/Patrick Swayze/pottery wheel scene from *Ghost*, complete with an Eastern variation on *Unchained Melody*, in which Cabbage stands behind her husband and reaches around to touch his penis, causing him to ejaculate on the wall. There's also the spectacular kung fu scene in which the male and female combatants end up having rough sex in mid-air above a forest. Aerial stunt wires are usually used for fight scenes, a la *Crouching Tiger, Hidden Dragon*. I've never seen stunt wires used to make a sex scene before (unless *The Eternal Evil of Asia* counts). It's such a wacky scene as these two characters really do give a flying fuck!

Tortures include a man strung upside down and having is cock and balls cut off with a red hot knife, and a feather stabbed into the wound like a flag. Another man is guillotined in half. And – in another cinematic first – a third man is buried in the ground up to his neck, has his scalp sliced open, and then has acid poured into the wound. This causes such agony that his body literally springs out of the earth, leaving his skin behind. And these tortures are all shown in the first few minutes! Another highlight is the scene in which Little Cabbage rides her husband. He apparently has a huge schlong, so she had previously refused to be penetrated. On this occasion, however, she puts up with the pain, and when he ejaculates it causes his dick to explode in a shower of flesh, blood and spunk. And it's this ultimate exploding-dick orgasm which causes all the problems for the protagonists as it turns out to be a fatal experience for the well-endowed husband.

Produced by the infamous Wong Jing, and afforded a much bigger budget than the usual Cat III fare, this colourful, visually impressive film boasts some wonderful set designs and costumes (much like the aforementioned *Oxen Split Torturing*), and can join the ranks of other Cantonese classics like *Taxi Hunter* and *The Eternal Evil of Asia* as another blend of horror and humour that makes these movies so worth tracking down. And speaking of *Eternal Evil*, that film was made the following year and also features Elvis Tsui on stunt wires and sex symbol Julie Lee.

Red to Kill (1994)
(Orig title: *Yeuk Saat*)
Dir: Billy Tang Hin-Sing /Hong Kong
Unbelievable. This film keeps up the Cat III tradition of taking lurid tabloid headlines and exaggerating the nasty, sensational bits for some big screen sleaze. Cat III movies are still criminally overlooked in the west, even in cult movie circles. But this is a good place to start if you're thinking of getting into the sleazy side of celluloid; even many jaded Hong Kong cineastes regard this film as utterly sick and repellent.

The film is set in a hostel for the mentally handicapped, and opens with a scene in which a mother, unable to cope with her a retarded son, takes him in her arms and jumps out of a high-rise window to a splattery death. Meanwhile, while all this commotion is going on, a sex maniac drags a mentally handicapped girl into the attic and brutally rapes her – this sequence is played out with relish as the madman howls out his orgasm to a ludicrous and blackly comic effect.

Under these intense circumstances, Ming Ming (Lily Chung) is placed into the care of the hostel after the death of her father. She's quiet, shy, innocent, and doesn't really understand what's happening. Social worker, Miss Cheung (Money Lo), stays around to keep an eye on her and makes sure that she settles into her new home okay. The soundtrack has a slushy sentimental synth ballad that plays at regular intervals, and is very typical of Hong Kong cinema of the time. The local residents are constantly complaining and protesting outside the doors; they suspect that a local 'sex lupine' who has been attacking the women is a resident at the hostel and are trying to have the place closed down ("Don't sympathise with the handicapped, they're not worth it"). Later that night, a young girl who can't be older than 12 years old is sexually harassed by 'Uncle Chubby', a resident of the hostel. She knees him in the balls and raises the alarm, to which the whole neighbourhood come running out of their homes with sticks and clubs, and poor Uncle Chubby is severely beaten (this scene also includes the hilarious subtitle "You pervert, I'll crash your penis and take to cook shop"). It soon becomes obvious though that the culprit isn't Uncle Chubby but the hostel's manager, Mr.Chan (Ben Ng).

While Ming Ming practices a dance routine her skirt floats up, and Mr. Chan catches a glimpse of her red panties. He can barely control the waves of lust that hit him in the groin. Here we cut to a traumatic childhood memory where Chan witnesses his mother sleeping with another guy, and then his father coming home and catching them in the act, to which the guy slashes him with a knife in the struggle. Dad's blood splashes across the window and this becomes a nightmare image that haunts Chan for the rest of his life. His mum then begins systematically hacking up daddy's corpse with a meat cleaver whilst growling malicious insults. She then trips and lands on the sharp end of the cleaver which almost completely severs her head – so Mr. Chan understandably has a few problems 'upstairs', and whenever he sees the colour red, it triggers a violent sexual frenzy in him that he cannot control.

Red to Kill is easily one of the most tasteless and sleaziest films in this book. It was directed by Billy Tang, the man behind *Brother of Darkness* (which also features Money Lo), *Doctor Lamb*, and *Run and Kill*. All of those films are extreme in their own right, but *Red to Kill* is undoubtedly head and shoulders above them in terms of sheer shock factor and in its gleefully un-PC attitude. In its own way this film is second only to *Men Behind the Sun* for being one of the most disturbing movies ever to come out of Hong Kong; even moreso than *The Untold Story* and *The Underground Banker*. As you can gather from the above synopsis, it certainly isn't a great work of art; it's cruel, cynical, ludicrous and tasteless, but it's also strangely engaging. It was shot straight up like any number of Hong Kong films of the time and kind of emulates the typical Hollywood 'erotic thriller' template of the late 80s, with its noirish angles, loathsome characters, and an uncaring social framework. But unlike the Hollywood flicks, *Red to Kill* tackles some very sensitive subject-matter and injects it with the kind of leering, exploitative fun that is designed to entertain and even titillate its audience! The result is unlike anything you've ever seen.

Lily Chung is passable as Ming Ming but she is never really convincing as a mentally handicapped woman. The other residents of the hostel (all played by 'normal' actors) are more believable as mentally challenged, but it's Ben Ng who steals the show as the 'sex lupine', the seemingly sane and sensible manager of the hostel who transforms into a crazed sex monster at the sight of red. His frenzied performance out-does Anthony Wong in *The Untold Story* and Simon Yam in *Doctor Lamb*. The sequence at the end where he has shaved his head and subjects Ming Ming and Miss Cheung to much violence and sexual abuse is genuinely creepy and his leering grin is not easy to forget.

Director Tang continued his one-man assault on the boundaries of taste and decency with such inferior offerings as *Brother of Darkness* and *Sexy and Dangerous* before going 'straight' with a number of socially conscious dramas, beginning with *Chinese Midnight Express*, featuring Ben Ng and *Hard Boiled's* Tony Leung Chiu-wai.

Men Behind the Sun 3: A Narrow Escape (1994)

(aka *Maruta 3 - Destroy All Evidence*)
(Orig title: *Hei tai yang 731 si wang lie che*)
Dir: Godfrey Ho /Hong Kong

Godfrey Ho returns with a second unofficial sequel to T.F. Mous' *Men Behind the Sun*, and offers more of the same with a story very loosely based on fact, a dull and uninvolving melodrama, and more of the usual mondo footage as a way of boosting the exploitation shock factor.

It's 1945, and Unit 731 is in turmoil. Japan is losing the war, and the soldiers are frantically destroying all evidence of the evil experiments that were carried out there. They intend on decimating everything before the Soviets arrive. One group of prisoners are machine gunned in their cell, another are gassed in theirs. Documents are burned, labs are destroyed (including the sight of a Japanese soldier accidentally cutting himself and being exposed to the lethal chemicals), before the whole compound is blown up with dynamite. General Shiro Ishii addresses his men one last time and then hops onto a plane and leaves them to it. The rest of the soldiers board a train for their retreat through China, and this is where most of the drama takes place. These defeated troops are on a long journey home and this gives them the time to reflect on their experiences of working within the most barbaric hellhole of the 20th Century.

The idea behind the story is an interesting one but it's handled so badly, and in the end we're left with nothing but a few gruesome flashbacks and a doomed love story between a soldier and an army nurse. When news reaches the train cabin of Japan's surrender, one soldier immediately commits harakiri with his sword, and another drinks cyanide. The remaining troops take it in turns to reflect on their harrowing memories of the events at Unit 731 which have clearly traumatized them and filled them with guilt. And their long road home is racked with defeat, deprivation, and disease.

Even by Godfrey Ho's standards this is a ludicrous exploitation disaster. Who on earth was this film made for? The Japanese detest the whole idea of having this shameful slice of their history displayed on the big screen, as was made pretty clear by their reactions to the first film in the series. The Chinese and Manchurians no doubt would have been offended by the idea of watching Japanese soldiers reminiscing on their journey home from one of the cruellest and most horrendous atrocities ever committed on Chinese soil. There has always been a cult in the West for Ho's chop-socky Ninja movies, but I'm sure most of them would be appalled by the grim spectacle on view here. I can only assume that everyone involved in the making of this film was on drugs or something; even the original *Men Behind the Sun* wasn't successful enough to break even financially, never mind warranting a bloody franchise!

Speaking of drugs, there are some moments in this film that bring on an odd hallucinatory feel, especially for those who are familiar with the work of Alejandro Jodorowsky; we see scores of extras doing bizarre synchronized things like jumping from a bridge into a river, or wearing boiler suits and gas masks and marching in unison, or being buried alive in a huge hole in the ground, and other such grotesqueries filmed in scope that look like deleted scenes from *The Holy Mountain*. Flashbacks include the sight of hundreds of enemy captives obliterated with machine guns, dozens more buried alive; another bomb test where a group of unfortunates are tied to poles in a field and a plane glides overhead dropping those infamous 'porcelain bacterial bombs' onto the ground, infecting the trussed up victims with bubonic plague; a woman having her arms frozen at -200 degrees and having the skin ripped off; a man having his frozen arms broken; and a bloody gun battle with Chinese troops. Mondo footage includes a graphic autopsy on a little girl. Most of the stock footage is shown in the first ten minutes with the usual autopsy scenes (with one body having its leg sawn off for some reason), and major surgery sequences. The intro credits are accompanied by sepia toned archive war footage, a la *The Devil's Nightmare*.

Color of Night (1994)
Dir: Richard Rush /USA
A New York psychoanalyst (Bruce Willis) relocates to Los Angeles after one of his patients commits suicide. And, not long after he arrives in sunny California, his colleague is brutally murdered. Instead of returning home, Willis stays put and takes over a group meeting of patients, one of whom he suspects is the killer... Often described as an American giallo, *Color of Night* is way over-the-top and far-fetched in

places, but this is also immensely entertaining and easy on the eyes (except for Willis' ludicrous wig). The red herrings come thick and fast; among the murder suspects there is the prude, the lesbian, the 'Nam vet, the drunk, etc. But the film is so well put together that its flaws can be overlooked.

The Haunting of Seacliff Inn (1994)
Dir: Walter Klenhard /USA
An industrious couple purchase a beautiful cliff-side house from the daughter of a deceased old lady. They renovate the place with the intention of transforming it into a guest house. However, the resident entity soon puts a stop to that idea and creates havoc in the house through mishaps, infidelity and jealousy, all engineered as a way of driving the couple apart... *Seacliff Inn* is a soft, daytime TV movie for bored housewives who idolise bland, emotionless yuppies in the latest catalogue wear. With not a single memorable scene to choose form, this bore-fest vanishes from the mind before the credits have even finished.

Heavenly Creatures (1994)
Dir: Peter Jackson /New Zealand
Two New Zealand schoolgirls form an intense, close relationship based on their shared fantasy world, and eventually end up killing one of their mothers to prevent their separation. Based on the true story of Pauline Parker and Juliet Hulme (which also inspired the French movie, *Don't Deliver Us From Evil*), *Heavenly Creatures* is a bizarre, hallucinatory film which erupts into a horrific act of violence. It's a film which bridges the gap between Peter Jackson's early gore trilogy and his more mainstream work in Hollywood. The real-life Juliet Hulme now lives in Scotland and writes mystery novels set in Victorian times under the pseudonym 'Anne Perry'.

Brainscan (1994)
Dir:John Flynn /Canada /USA /UK
A young Edward Furlong enters a virtual reality game and commits a murder. He later learns on the news that the murder happened for real. He then finds himself in a panic, having to dispose of body parts while the 'Trickster,' a ghoulish emissary from the VR world (who looks like Flea from Red Hot Chilli Peppers in a red hot wig), tries to convince the kid about the virtues of killing. This is typical early 90s horror fare

with its grungy soundtrack and Furlong still sporting his baby face and floppy mange fresh off of *Terminator 2: Judgement Day* (1991). His then-revolutionary home computer set-up looks horribly dated by today's standards, and T. Ryder Smith as the Trickster is overtly pantomime-ish for it to be much of a cult success. Ultimately, this film stands as a conservative critique of the rise of violent video games and horror movies; strongly implying that this kind of thing inevitably leads to real-life violence. If that is so, then what are we to make of *Brainscan*? Surely this is a dangerous film that no one should see lest it were to cause imitative violence in its viewers?

Diary of a Serial Killer (1995)
(Orig title: *Guang Zhou sha ren wang zhi ren pi ri ji*)
Dir: Otto Chan Juk-Tiu /Hong Kong
A notorious serial killer recounts his tale to cellmates in a Hong Kong prison the night before his execution. He starts out as a sex maniac whose busy wife can't keep up with his insatiable libido. He turns to hookers for violent sex. He gets a bit carried away one night and ends up killing one of them in mad lust, decides he enjoys the thrill of murder, and so continues killing more. He also indulges in kidnap and torture to satisfy his sick urges whilst keeping the 'family man' facade going for a while before his grisly deeds catch up with him.

Judged alongside similar Asian atrocities, such as *Men Behind the Sun* or the infamous *Guinea Pig* series from Japan, *Diary of a Serial Killer* is either a fearless challenge to established cinematic limits or a reckless descent into the abyss, depending on your point of view. Photographed with stunning visual flair and expertly edited, the film alternates scenes of naïve sentimentality with eruptions of graphic horror, taking time to establish the groundwork before unleashing the forces of hell against its audience.

With lots of softcore sex and violence, *Diary of a Serial Killer* is your typical Cat III shocker of the mid-90s. It is also awash with that strange candy-coloured lighting so typical of Hong Kong cinema of the time, and makes the proceedings look like it could have been made ten years earlier (see also *Robotrix* and *A Chinese Torture Chamber Story* for more 90s Cat III movies that look like they could have been made in the 80s).The killer is a nasty piece

of work, displaying all the sick characteristics you've read about in true crime books. He takes souvenirs from his victims; the breasts usually, and he also tries string around the wrists and ankles of his victims to make macabre puppets of their corpses, and has 'conversations' with them to amuse himself. He seems to love his wife and child very much but doesn't show any signs of remorse for his crimes until his murderous urges strike closer to home. The writers have obviously studied the characteristics of real life killers and have heaped all of this stuff into the script, making for a very clichéd type of killer with the old textbook traumas and all that, but the film is still quite entertaining.

The killer is very protective of a naïve young woman. She may as well have the word 'victim' stamped on her forehead, but he somehow manages to suppress his urge to kill her, perhaps because she reminds him of more carefree and innocent times. She refers to him as "brother" and their (sibling?) relationship is quite sweet and innocent until they have a sex session in the back of his car! Allegedly based on a true story, and hugely indebted to *Doctor Lamb*.

Tokyo Fist (1995)
Dir: Shinya Tsukamoto /Japan
Shinya Tsukamoto first hit global notoriety with *Tetsuo: The Iron Man* and *Tetsuo 2: Boddy Hammer*, films which combined hi-tech city-scapes and extremely twisted body mutations, and ignited the cyberpunk movement in Japan. Tsukamoto's work was lauded in the west where fans and critics were dazzled by his 'Cronenberg meets Manga' madness, and was considered the 'Jimi Hendrix of film'. Hollywood was interested in signing him up to direct *Flying Tetsuo*, a project which eventually came to nothing, and Tsukamoto stayed away from film-making for three years before he returned with his masterpiece, *Tokyo Fist*.

Moving away from the futuristic fantasies of his earlier work, *Tokyo Fist* centres on insurance salesman, Tsuda (Tsukamoto himself), who bumps into an old school friend, Kojima (Tsukamoto's brother, Koji), who is now a pro boxer. Kojima visits Tsuda's apartment while he's out and tries it on with his fiancee, Hizuru (Kahori Fuji), who knocks him back. When Tsuda finds out, he takes a walk round to Kojima's place for a fight but is punched through the door by the boxer. This violence seems to impress Hizuru and she ends up moving in with the brute, much to the annoyance of Tsuda who takes up boxing lessons with a plan of revenge. Meanwhile Hizuru has begun experimenting with body piercing and tattoos, and seems to alleviate her discontent by pricking herself with needles and awakening her own masochistic desires. This deranged love triangle spirals seriously out of control, with Tsuda and Kojima joining in this brutal game of sadomasochism by re-arranging each other's faces before the film reaches its gruelling finale.

Tsukamoto extends his virtuoso style with a raw, hand-held edginess; we see fists breaking through the tissue of human faces with the camera mounted inside the character's heads. The colour palette is stark and intense, contrasting cold blues and black and white, with hellish reds and bold primary colours. Every scene in *Tokyo Fist* is shot from unusual angles and not once does it play by the rules of the conventional technicalities of cinema. The result is as astonishing as anything seen in the *Tetsuo* movies.

On the casting front, Tsukamoto does a fine job in the lead role as Tsuda, a mild-mannered salaryman driven to extremes by a raging jealousy and desire for revenge. His brother Koji is equally impressive as the self-assured Kojima, and Fuji is more impressive still as the self-mutilating Hizuru whose flesh serves as a canvas of scarification which maps the psychological disintegration of this doomed trio. Often surreal and sublime, Tsukamoto also presents us with the most brutal and emotionally exhausting boxing match in cinema history; a gruelling marathon of anger and pain that sees the characters pummel each other with no regard for their own increasingly unrecognisable faces. And this culminates in the final shots of the film in which the victor turns around to salute the audience, but the spectators react in repulsion and disgust as the champion's face is a battered and bruised mess with swollen cheeks and a broken jaw bone dripping with blood. Unmissable.

The Addiction (1995)
Dir: Abel Ferrara /USA
In Abel Ferrara's earlier film, *Bad Lieutenant*, Zoe Lund suggests that drug addicts are like vampires, and that "vampires are lucky, they can feed on others. *We* have to feed on ourselves." It

was only natural that Ferrara would eventually tackle the opposite: Vampires in the clutch of addiction. He teamed up once again with his long-time writing partner, Nicholas St. John, and together they came up with a vampiric tale that contemplates the nature of eternal guilt.

The plot concerns Kathleen (Lili Taylor), a postgraduate philosophy student who is pulled into a dark alley and bitten by a glamorous vampire, Casanova (Annabella Sciorra). After having her wounds checked out at the local hospital, Kathleen comes to realise that she is now addicted to human blood. This affliction brings on a new outlook on life and has a tremendous effect on her thesis. And when she thirsts for the red stuff, she uses an oddly ethical approach to her victims, giving them the opportunity to overpower her ("Tell me to go away like you mean it"). But strangely, none of her victims can sum up the willpower to avoid their fates (much like drug addicts in real life who seem to inadvertently will their own corruption and downfall by not being steadfast enough to confront the situation before it takes hold – avoiding the confrontation, hence Sartre's 'Bad Faith').

Kathleen digs deeper into her studies, and wallows in the graphic footage of atrocities at Mai Lai, Auschwitz-Birkenau, and Srebrenica as a way of coming to terms with her own eternal damnation. Her biggest life-lesson though comes in the form of Peina (Christopher Walken), a wise old vampire who discusses Nietzsche and Burroughs' *The Naked Lunch* before biting into her jugular, and informing her that "Demons suffer in hell".

One of the most serious-minded horror movies of all time, *The Addiction* is nonetheless disliked by many who are turned off by its harsh philosophical probing and abrasive visual style. The film's central motif is moral responsibility; when Kathleen is first approached by the vampiric Casanova she is given the opportunity to deal with the situation head-on ("Tell me to go away"), but Kathleen can only manage a pathetic "please" in response. In the world of Ferrara and Nicky St. John, this kind of feeble stance amounts to consent. Accordingly, by refusing to face up to evil and deal with it openly, Kathleen and other victims just like her, deserve all they get.

kathleen later succeeds in luring a young student to her place. And after feeding on her blood, she blames the terrified girl, insisting "It was your decision". The victim pleads "Don't you care what you did to me?! Doesn't it affect you?" She replies, "Why didn't you tell me to leave, to get lost? My indifference is not the concern here. it's your astonishment that needs studying." In another scene, Kathleen looks in the mirror and muses "Is it wrong for me to draw blood? No. It's the violence of my will against theirs" – a comment that also relates to Sartre's existential dilemmas in *Being and Nothingness*. Free will is of vital importance to Ferrara and St. John in their idea of evil: If you don't put up a fight then the vampire, the evildoer, takes that as a form of social consent. In this case, in the supernatural world of the vampire film. In addition, this concept of evil also relates to the real life evil in the form of murder, genocide, and drug addiction. The theme of refusing to confront evil recurs throughout the film in its many and varied ways, and also examines attitudes of moral ambivalence and apathy towards evil that exists in modern society.

It's possible that Katleen's blood addiction isn't real. Maybe her obsessive studying has caused her illness through mental exhaustion. Perhaps she is a plain old drug addict, and she fantasizes on vampirism as a way of making light of her condition (and this could also relate the film to George Romero's *Martin* [1976] in that it is never confirmed or denied whether Martin is in fact a real vamp. Martin experiences flashbacks to times set in old Europe where he drank blood from victims, but those episodes could be plain old fantasy).

Lili Taylor is superb as Kathleen, even surpassing her performance in Mary Harron's *I Shot Andy Warhol* (1996). Christopher Walken and Paul Calderon (both of whom appeared in Ferrara's *King of New York*) add some solid support. Still one of the most irredeemable American filmmakers working today, Abel Ferrara has managed to combine exploitation with a high-minded sensibility for more than three decades. From *The Driller Killer* in the 70s, *Ms.45* in the 80s, *Dangerous Game* in the 90s, and *R-Xmas* in the 00s, this native New Yorker has never once compromised on his dark vision, even when working within the studio system (as he did with *Body Snatchers* [1993]). *The Addiction* remains one of his darkest efforts, a black and white gem which asks some important questions and never flinches in its search for answers. Essential viewing.

Mute Witness (1995)
Dir: Anthony Waller /USA

Mute Witness takes the paranoia of the 'snuff-movie-within-the-set-of-a-legitimate-film' scenario of *Effects*, and ramps up the tension like never before, offering a nerve-shredding nightmare on film. When director Anthony Waller was given the go-ahead to make his feature, he switched locations from Chicago to Moscow where he discovered sets and labour would be much cheaper. Moscow also seemed to be an appropriate location for a snuff-based movie considering the unsettled social situation in Russia after the dismantling of the Soviet state. Organised crime was rampant in that part of the world at the time, and much shady goings on were happening while the country was finding its feet once again. And American director Waller plays up to the panic and paranoia of those times.

Mute Witness is a genuine 'edge of your seat' horror movie about a mute make-up artist who inadvertently stumbles upon the making of a snuff porn film in the studio. A thrilling chase begins when she is spotted and targeted by the murderers. And her plight is made all the more terrifying by her inability to scream for help. Director Waller turns the constraints of a low budget to his advantage, using limited locations to claustrophobic effect. And, like other films discussed in this book – *Effects, Snuff-Movie, Special Effects, The Last Horror Horror Movie,* etc – the film effectively toys with both your mind and the blurred line between reality and films within a film. The late great, Alec Guiness, makes an uncredited appearance as a very sinister snuff movie dealer ("Did it go smoothly?"), which was filmed nine years before the rest of the picture. He was billed as 'Mystery Guest Star,' similar to the way Boris Karloff was credited with a '?' at the beginning of *Frankenstein* (1932). *Variety* magazine accurately described *Mute Witness* as "a seductive piece of real film-making that should keep audiences hyperventilating to the last reel."

Showgirls (1995)
Dir: Paul Verhoeven /USA

Bad boy of flash-trash cinema and intellectual Dutchman, Paul Verhoeven, once again teamed up with the equally trashy but not so intellectual writer Joe Eszterhas after their box-office success with *Basic Instinct*, and together they wallow in the Hollywood gutter, offering big-screen sleaze, lurid exploitation, and just about every tacky and tasteless cliché possible. The result was almost universally despised by the critics but became an instant cult phenomenon as gobsmacked cineastes struggled to make sense of the multi-million dollar monstrosity which unspooled before their eyes.

Showgirls centres on Nomi Malone (Elizabeth Berkley), a lowly stripper who finds that becoming a showgirl often goes hand in hand with the seedier side of life. She makes it as a 'private dancer' at the Cheetah Club before making it to the big time in a casino show called Goddess. En route to this ambitious wish-fulfilment, we follow Nomi's lewd antics backstage where she flits between night club owner Zack (an almost comatose Kyle McLachlan) and out-of-work songwriter James (an atrocious performance from Glenn Plummer).

It's a bloody awful film but it's also understandable how it became such a cult favourite; like an ensuing car crash you just can't look away. Director Verhoeven is no stranger to adding gratuitous and sleazy entertainment value to his Hollywood epics, be it the excessively violent gunning-down of Murphy in *Robocop*, or the three-titted whore in *Total Recall* ('I sometimes wish I had three hands!'), or Sharon Stone flashing the gash in *Basic Instinct*, but in *Showgirls* he takes that cheeky fan-boy attitude and pushes it to unprecedented levels. The film's adult orientation, tacky sex scenes, and revealing dialogue earned it an NC-17 rating in America, with many provincial cinemas refusing to screen it (and this led to one of *Variety* magazine's all-time great headlines, 'Stix Nix Naughty Pix'). Verhoeven had anticipated some flak, and he even generously refused to accept his $6 million pay packet until the film turned a profit (which it didn't, it flopped quite badly). Eszterhas wasn't so kind, and he was attacked mercilessly in the press for his screwball screenplay which includes such priceless lines as 'I'm not a whore, I'm a dancer'. Madonna and Drew Barrymore were originally wanted for the roles of Gina Gershon and Elizabeth Berkley, but fortunately for them, they declined. In a panic at the critical mauling the film was being subjected to, United Artists re-promoted the film for midnight screenings in LA as a way to try and generate the same campy following of *The Rocky Horror Picture Show* and the like, with gangs of drag queens parading cue cards and offering free lap dances for the audience.

Out of 14 of the UK's leading critics, only one enjoyed the film (well, only one dared to admit he liked it), in America it was 2 out of 34. It has been described as "shallow", "prurient", "voyeuristic", and "exploitative", but in the right mood those kinds of accusations can become attributes. Indeed, there's something undeniably appealing for many viewers in its misguided ethics: The voyeuristic sleaze which the film purports to expose and condemn is simultaneously exploited for cheap thrills and giggles in the audience. Overall, the only thing to be exposed really was Verhoeven's hypocrisy (he just couldn't resist, could he?).

Welcome To the Dollhouse (1995)
Dir: Todd Solondz /USA

An excellent, if excruciating, depiction of the horrors of high school life, *Welcome To the Dollhouse* won the Grand Jury Prize at the Sundance Film Festival thanks to its bleak but brilliant humour, and helped rejuvenate the film-making career of writer/director Todd Solondz after his disastrous debut. The plot centres on 11-year-old Dawn Wiener (Heather Matarazzo), an awkward and unpopular school girl who is a constant target for bullies. Due to her lack of social skills, she often finds herself in desperately embarrassing situations, and her home life isn't much better; her brother and sister are both smarter and more talented then she is, and she struggles to win the affections of her parents. She develops a crush on her brother's band mate Steve, and this ends in another emotional setback when she attempts to get close to him. Worryingly, she later allows herself to be coerced into sex by a rough tearaway kid who has his own emotional insecurities to deal with.

This is a refreshing and insightful black comedy, but it's also painful to watch; throughout the film, Dawn remains an engaging figure, even with her nerdy look and awful taste in dresses, you really feel for her and hope that her situation will improve. Whether your own childhood can relate to Dawn of not, I'm sure most of us will be reminded of some uncomfortable memories from our own childhoods as the film unfolds. And this effectiveness is helped immensely by the performances of the young cast; none of them put a foot wrong. Director Solondz keeps the proceedings fiercely unsentimental throughout and presents a flash of genius with dialogue and individual set pieces that would later crop up en masse in his later master-works, *Happiness* (1998) and *Storytelling* (2001).

Welcome to the Dollhouse is often wrongly thought of as Solondz's feature debut; he'd actually made an earlier film, *Fear, Anxiety and Depression*, but the experience had been so painful and disappointing for him that he walked away from directing for a few years and took up a career as an English teacher before a friend encouraged him to get back into the helmer's seat. With the relevant funding in place, and a script he was happy with, Solondz felt ready to make amends for the nightmare experience of his first feature, and began touting the screenplay around New Jersey. He felt dismay for the parents of potential child actors who described his script as "delightful," and felt more relieved and trusting of parents who referred to it as "sick" and "depressing"; the latter he took as compliments because, after all, that was how he felt about the world he was portraying. One of the true master-strokes was the casting of 11-year-old Heather Matarazzo, whose astonishing performance shows a talent far beyond her youthful years, and who won an Independent Spirit Award for Best Debut Performance.

People often accuse Solondz of wallowing in the darker side of life, whether it be dysfunctional families, child abuse, or loneliness. Most of his characters seem to harbour dark secrets, and his films are often darkly funny. But he actually uses humour to express the horrors of life because it's the only way he can adequately cope with the torments of the modern world and all its unlovely people. *Welcome to the Dollhouse* may be nightmarish and shockingly frank, but it at least stands as an uncompromising alternative to the faux-nostalgia so readily exploited in heart-warming coming-of-age films and television shows.

Indeed, the film is relentless in its hierarchic cruelty, and there's not a shred of sympathetic light for its victim in the script. Unlike many outsider characters who have an in-built 'coolness' or sensitivity to them (think James Dean in *Rebel Without a Cause*, or Wynona Ryder in *Beetlejuice*, or Christian Slater in *Heathers*, for example), Dawn isn't particularly sensitive or misunderstood; she's not a thoughtful, Holden Caulfield type either. She's

certainly a victim, but Solondz simply refuses to tug at the viewer's heart strings by making her pretty or cute or smart. Quite the opposite: he presents his central character as an annoying and unsightly nerd, and even shows her to be partially to blame for her sorry situation.

Strange Days (1995)
Dir: Kathryn Bigelow /USA

With *Videodrome* (1982), the snuff-themed movie entered the sci-fi realm when a television entrepreneur discovered a pirate satellite signal that caused brain tumours to develop in the viewers. Writer/director David Cronenberg used the hallucinatory visuals and far-out themes to fashion an allegorical tale about censorship and government control. More than a decade later, sci-fi snuff hit the screens once again with *Strange Days* (1995), but this time the filmmakers chickened out of delivering the subversive goods. Set during the last few days of 1999 in L.A., *Strange Days* is about an ex-cop, Lenny (Ralph Fiennes), who runs a dealership in 'clips' – movies recorded from people's memories and sold on the black market to those who wish to experience them. Lenny sees himself as an ethical dealer because he refuses to push snuff (or 'blackjack' clips). These contraband recordings are taken from those equipped with a Superconducting Quantum Interference Device (SQUID), a device easily concealed under a hat or wig. Lenny uses the technology on himself to re-live moments from his past and to ease his broken heart after his split from Faith (Juliette Lewis), a rising pop star under the control of a menacing record label owner (Michael Wincott). Before long, Lenny is shown a brutal snuff clip of a woman being raped and murdered. And, as he investigates those responsible for the clip, he and his friends are caught up in a murder conspiracy that could bring about an apocalyptic race war.

This future-phobic thriller is fascinating and annoying in equal measure. On the one hand, it attempts to update *Peeping Tom* with its angle on voyeurism and killer's eye camera work. It's also visually stunning and sustains an atmosphere of dread and paranoia. It offers a bleak, noir-ish vision of the (then) near-future like *Blade Runner* before it. Some complained that the plot is overly convoluted and crammed in to the point where the narrative spills over into confusion, but I disagree. I found it quite easy to follow, despite the clunky exposition through dialogue. For me, the problem is that too much of the story and the character's motivations are given away through needless exposition. Just look at the scene after Lenny and Max (Tom Sizemore) have watched the snuff clip, for example. While they try to ascertain who could make such a clip, the viewers are given details about the switching of signals while they're at it:

Lenny – *He stalks her, he rapes her and he kills her...*

Max – *And he records it. It's a thrill, right?*

Lenny – *Yeah.*

Max – *He wants to see it again and again and again.*

Lenny – *He records himself raping and killing her.*

Max – *But at the same time he's sending a signal to her...*

Lenny – *...So she feels what he feels while he's inside her. The thrill, while he's killing her, is sent to her, hightening her fear, which in turn hightens the turn-on for him... He makes her see her own death and feeds on her reaction. He records it all. Everything.*

But the most annoying thing about *Strange Days* is its attempts to restore faith in (white) police authority. The film is a cultural by-product of the Rodney King beating, and yet it also serves as a calculated Hollywood propaganda piece. Director Kathryn Bigelow and co-author James Cameron posit their film as a meaningful statement about the racial and socio/economic implications of the Rodney King video and the subsequent riots, and yet the L.A. Police are ultimately let off the hook here. What we're left with is a 'Hey look! We have a white man and a black woman falling in love! Aww, what sweet racial harmony!' The questions this film raises are finally swept aside and replaced with confetti and pyrotechnics. It's downright insulting.

Molester's Train: Dirty Behaviour (1995)
(aka *Birthday*) Orig title: *Chikan Densha: Iyarashii Koi*)
Dir: Hisayasu Sato /Japan

A young misfit, Yuu (Yumika Hayashi), has perception problems that stop him from recognising his surroundings in three dimensions, and this flat uninvolving view of the world has caused him to become isolated and detached. He resorts to documenting his surroundings on video camera, and while riding on the train he meets a young drifter, Kei (Kiyomi Ito of *Lolita Vibrator Torture*), and together they discuss their lives and pasts in between bouts of sex as a way of trying to re-connect with the world.

Even during the sexual act with Kei, Yuu finds it difficult to recognize anything beyond his perceived "poster" image of her. Kei tries to correct this by kissing him on the lips and manually inserting his penis inside her. Yuu suddenly becomes overtaken with lust, and he lays her down and fucks her, but he still seems quite distanced from her in the way that his arms are rigidly holding up his own body weight and his eyes stare blankly ahead, not even looking at her as he finishes the deed.

Yuu and Kei spend their days hanging out in a tent and by the docks, and on the trains that pass through Tokyo. Kei pulls out a bundle of dynamite sticks from her rucksack and announces that she intends to blow herself up on her 20th birthday. Meanwhile, perverts lurk on the trains molesting young women on the busy carriages. Yuu captures one such incident on video camera in which the woman seems to be enjoying the sexual intrusion, and he later reveals that the woman in question is in fact his sister. He then plays Kei a selection of home videos that he recorded on the trains documenting his family members; his sister is a masochist, and when she can't find a boyfriend who is sadistic enough for her tastes she resorts to self-mutilation; his father suffered from an irrational fear of returning home, and has since vanished; his older brother also disappeared to join a strange sex cult; and his alcoholic mother suffers from blackouts and memory loss (talk about 'meeting the family'!).

Yuu turns to drastic measures in order to experience some kind of sensation at any cost and put an end to his depersonalization by asking Kei if he can join her in a suicide pact. On the night of her birthday they sit in the tent and strap themselves with the dynamite and count down the bad years of their lives before Kei lights the fuse...

Running for just 55 minutes, *Molester's Train* is an odd, dream-like film typical of its director. It's also perhaps one of Sato's most personal efforts in the way it deals with detachment and alienation in a much more open and honest way than many of his other works. Ironically, it's the depersonalized and isolated nature of this film that seems to get to the heart of the director's *raison d'etre*; *Brainsex*, *The Bedroom*, and *Survey Map of a Paradise Lost* are just a few examples of films which deal with similar themes, but none of them did so in such an open manner. With Yuu we have a character who expresses the reasons for his neuroses and voyeurism in no uncertain terms; by documenting everything on camera he hopes to make a connection with the world around him and to try to experience something to escape the numbness and isolation in his mind. It's a frustrating endeavour because, in the end, watching videotapes of his daily experiences takes him even *further* away from the real sensation, not closer. And thus, his attempts to connect with the world become increasingly extreme and desperate; for Yuu, a suicide pact is the last chance – only by experiencing death can he hope to feel something, *anything* – even his own obliteration strikes him as a fair deal.

Perhaps Yuu represents a part of Sato himself. Like many other characters in Sato's films, Yuu doesn't necessarily experience the things he is documenting, and this is a crucial point because this is one of the main ways the director chooses to express alienation; Yuu witnesses many things on the trains, but even the molestation of his own sister barely registers anything of a response from him because he's not there; he's on the train in their presence, but he is so emotionally distant that the incident doesn't affect him in the way it should. Even when he has sex with Kei, the experience does more to isolate him psychologically than to serve as an emotional connection (which is what Kei intended to show him). The sex act itself is all rather selfish on Yuu's part; not once does he look at her or caress her while he's on top; he just concentrates on thrusting his hips, faster and faster, until he shoots his load – psychologically, he's no more 'closer' to her than if he was jerking off over a picture (or a flat, two-dimensional "poster" image) of her.

The train molestation scenes were mostly shot on crowded passenger trains in Sato's usual guerrilla-style, so that the ordinary Tokyo citizens, who weren't even involved in the making of the film, are seen in the background while the crimes are happening. The women are exposed in various states of undress, and they moan with just as much pleasure as protest, and the ordinary commuters look on, sometimes directly into the camera lens while the women are ravished in their presence. It makes for an odd viewing experience to say the least, and this kind of thing adds to the verisimilitude of the film. Even the names of the two lead characters, Yuu and Kei, are shortened forms of the actor's real names, Yumika and Kiyomi.

Perhaps Sato's films as a whole are an attempt for him to deal with his own sense of depersonalization, and not just that of society as a whole. The verite and guerrilla shooting style works, not just because of the low-budget and the way it exposes the reactions of ordinary commuters to the potential abuse of women in their midst (and that they react like bemused and desensitized idiots), but because in this sense he resembles many of the voyeuristic characters he portrays in his films. He's the one standing on the train shooting scenes of molestation, not just the character Yuu. It's just as much Sato who flits around with his camera trying to document everything in sight with an increased sense of perversion and urgency (throughout his film-making career, Sato has touched upon almost every perversion known to man, be it S&M, rape, fetishes, and bestiality, but he doesn't seem to favour any one of them, and is happy to re-visit a particular perversion in later films or abandon it entirely). And in his often prolific output of films over the years, he never seems to be emotionally involved.

The Doom Generation (1995)
Dir: Gregg Araki /USA

'Sex. Violence. Whatever'. That was the knowingly off-hand tagline for *The Doom Generation*, the fifth film from underground bad boy director Gregg Araki. If you're in the mood for sex, drugs, violence, comedy, apocalyptic imagery, demonic numerology, and of course a whole bunch of noisy rock music, then you've come to the right place. We delve into yet another nihilistic offering from the director of *Nowhere* and *Totally Fucked Up*. The result is a film described by critic Leonard Maltin as "a bleak view of the younger generation which makes *Kids* look like *The Little Mermaid.*"

Sarcastically subtitled 'A heterosexual movie', *The Doom Generation* is, on one level, a sneeringly ironic re-working of the popular homicidal-young-lovers-on-the-road riff which won such unexpected mainstream hits as *Guncrazy*, *Bonnie and Clyde*, and *Badlands*, to *Natural Born Killers* and *Kalifornia*. Centring on the antics of two Gen-X wasters who team up with a psychotically dangerous drifter, Araki's rampaging romp projects the kind of youthful disaffected amorality made fashionable by movies like *Slackers* and *Clerks.* The difference is that, in those films, people didn't get brutally murdered quite so often. And it was that combination of ironic, couldn't-give-a-toss carelessness and outrageous screen carnage which caused stateside critic Roger Ebert (who had previously praised the likes of *Henry - Portrait of a Serial Killer*) to condemn the film's use of "sickening carnage and violent amorality." You do get the feeling that Araki is trying very hard to offend you, and part of the fun in watching is to play along with it. In the end, all that matters is how much fun he's having misbehaving with his movie camera. And whether or not you have as much fun is entirely up to you.

On the pop celebrity front, *The Doom Generation* boasts a thumping soundtrack which jumbles up such popular teen rebel icons as Nine Inch Nails, The Jesus and Mary Chain, and Coil, and there's even a cameo by Vancouver rockers, Skinny Puppy, alongside walk-ons from the likes of Hollywood madman Heidi Fleiss. And of course there's James Duval who later turned up in *Independence Day*. All very alluring no doubt, but the real on-screen attraction is leading lady Rose McGowan, a young woman so screechingly annoying even a Buddhist monk would be tempted to drop-kick her into orbit. She later appeared in the big-budget slasher movie, *Scream* (she's the one who gets squished in the mechanized garage door). She is seen here earning herself an Independent Spirit Award nomination for 'Best Baby Performance' in a role which she allegedly landed after first choice actress, Jordan Ladd, was told by her angelic mother Cheryll that she would appear in such a movie over her dead body. But it wasn't just Cheryll Ladd and Roger Ebert who took against *The Doom Generation*; in America the MPAA demanded a number of cuts for an R-rating, while in the UK both the film and video were passed uncut with an 18 certificate by the BBFC.

The Basketball Diaries (1995)
Dir: Scott Kalvert /USA
A rebellious Catholic schoolboy gets hooked on heroin and turns to theft and prostitution to feed his habit. Based on the diaries of Jim Carroll, which were published and caused a bit of a sensation at the time, this film version doesn't really have anywhere to go beyond wallowing in junky cliches. However, the film also serves as a showcase for Leonardo DiCaprio's acting talent. Sure, the guy's about 40-years-old now and still hasn't started puberty yet, but this – along with his astonishing turn in *What's Eating Gilbert Grape?* – shows that he is indeed a superb actor when he has a decent role to sink his teeth into.

Young Poisoner's Handbook (1995)
Dir: Benjamin Ross /UK /Germany
A boy fascinated by the power of poisons tests them out on his stepmother and uncle, and is sent to an institution for the criminally insane. He is later declared to be sound of mind and is released, whereupon he continues poisoning others. Told in the style of a black farcical comedy, this film will probably appeal more to audiences who aren't looking for factual details. The story is based on the life of Graham Young, known as 'The St Albans Poisoner', who was sent to Broadmoor in 1962 at the age of 14 for giving poison to his father, sister and friend. He was released as "no longer a danger" in 1971 when he killed two more people with poison and injured six others. He died in prison in 1990.

La Haine (1995)
(*Hate*)
Dir: Mathieu Kassovitz /France
La Haine presents a day in the life of three unemployed youths – a black man, a Jew and an Arab – as they get themselves involved in a riot on their housing estate against the hostilities of the local police. This is a furious and passionate movie which takes the side of the downtrodden masses, filmed in a hand-held documentary style before it was 'cool' to do so. The film caused so much controversy in France that the Prime Minister, Alain Juppe, insisted that his entire cabinet watch it. Writer/director Kassovitz won the Best Director prize at Cannes, and the film also won Europe's Felix as the Best Young Film.

441

Sleepstalker (1995)
Dir: Turi Meyer /USA

Journalist Jay Underwood is relieved to report on the execution of a serial killer known as 'The Sandman.' After all, the maniac did kill his family. However, a voodoo priest who is given access to the killer to read him his last rites, is actually in cahoots with him, and instead gives the maniac immortality as a shape-shifting demon intent on wreaking more havoc on the world. Owing much to Wes Craven's *Shocker* and *A Nightmare On Elm Street*, but also armed with some unique ideas of its own – such as the Sandman appearing in the form of sand that can pursue its victims even through locked doors by literally pouring itself through key holes, etc – but ultimately, the low-budget doesn't allow for a wholly effective telling of the story.

Day of the Beast (1995)
(Orig title: *El dia de la Bestia*)
Dir: Alex de la Iglesia /Spain

After close study of the bible, a Basque Priest becomes convinced that the Antichrist will be born on Christmas Day in Madrid. So, in order to place himself in the most advantageous position to be able to slay the Beast, he sets out to become a diabolical sinner and win favour with Old Scratch. However, his misdeeds – which includes stealing a wallet from a dying man – fails to conjure up the dark one. So he teams up with drug-addled heavy metal fan and a TV psychic, and together they attempt to slay the Devil child... If Iglesia's directorial debut, *Accion mutante* (1993), was a minor cult item, this second feature is a subversive classic which pokes fun at *The Omen* (1976) as well as Satanic heavy metal and television psychics. It boasts a snappy pace and scenes of jaw-droppingly dark humour. The film also includes a political subtext concerning post-Franco Spain, implying that the Devil makes work for idle fascists. The Satanic rituals seen in the film are said to be based on real Satanic rites, and this ensured that Iglesia and his film crew received death threats from Satanic groups during the shoot. However, the film was a hit in Spain, picking up 6 Goyas, including a Best Director award for Iglesia.

Hideaway (1995)
Dir: Brett Leonard /USA

After ritualistically killing his mother and sister, a teen commits suicide in a self-sacrifice to Satan. His condemned soul then travels, DMT-like, through fractal tunnels to become a Hell dweller. Later, Jeff Goldblum has a near-death experience after his family are involved in a road accident in which he gets a glimpse of the afterlife and briefly gets to meet his dead daughter. Upon recovery, he is never quite the same: He has visions of himself slashing throats, and his wife finds him sleeping outside beside the pool. He soon learns that the girls in his visions are being murdered in real life, so he vows to prevent any further murders from happening. Turns out that the Satan kid who committed suicide in the prologue has been brought back to life to do Satan's bidding. And when the killer, Vassago (brilliantly played by Jeremy Sisto), puts Goldblum's wife and surviving daughter in danger, the race is on to save the day. *Hideaway* is a bad Dean Koontz adaptation, but as a stand-alone film, this really isn't the disaster that many have dismissed it as. It has a routine, predictable finale, but is easy, engaging viewing from start to finish (and it also contains a nice little surprise after the end credits).

The Bride of Frank (1996)
Dir: Escalpo Don Balde [Steve Ballot] /USA

This is what happens when a bunch of warehouse workmates get together with a video camera to make a 'movie.' Hopelessly amateur and inept in all areas, *The Bride of Frank* is nonetheless outrageous fun and often laugh-out-loud hilarious.

The story follows an old homeless bum as he abducts a little girl, smashes her head in when she gets mouthy, and then drives over her in a truck before eating her brains for breakfast. He later shows up to work with a bunch of equally hopeless truck drivers, and together they bicker and argue among themselves in thick New Jersey accents (bird is "boid", jerk is "joik", and he deserved it is "he desoived it", etc). The characters are a lot of fun, and they reminded me of the eccentric staff at the car repossession office in *Repo Man*; they may call each other the worst names under the sun but they stick tight as a workforce and back each other up to the hilt. Frank is a wrinkled, miserable old fart who looks like someone's attempts to draw a sad face on the elephant man's scrotum, and he has a very literal slant on things, including his descriptions of how he would like to kill people, and his carrying out of the grisly tasks in a hilarious, matter-of-fact way. His workmates try to find him a date, and this causes lots of trouble as Frank's ideas on love are not to everyone's taste... The rest of the players are all kinda weird and mis-shaped, like the cast of *The Sopranos* squinting at funhouse mirrors. What else can be said about this vile video? It's crappy in a good way, and good in a crappy way. Most mainstream movie fans would rather sew their own eyes shut with fishing wire than subject themselves to this, but that's their loss. It's better than watching celebrities eat each other's eyeballs to win a golden dildo, or whatever passes for TV these days.

In the mid-90s, those spoil-sports at the BBFC insisted on removing several scenes from Steve Ballot's *The Bride of Frank*. UK horror fans were particularly annoyed with their decision since one of the main cuts required was to take away the film's central joke; as the tagline says, "All Frank wants is true love. But you better not mess with Frank, because if he tells you 'I'll cut off your head and shit down your neck', he ain't kiddin." The BBFC demanded 74 seconds of cuts, including the sight of a man being "realistically fellated," a man having sex with the eye-socket of a woman, and the show-stopper: Cuts to remove the sight of a man defecating down the neck of another. The BBFC offered the following statement as justification; "Cuts are made on grounds of potential harm and potential obscenity, for unjustified sexual detail, and sexual violence." But don't dismay, the uncut version is available on region 1 DVD from Sub Rossa.

Planetary Evacuation Recruitment Tape (1996)
Dir: N/A /USA

Documentaries about Heaven's Gate have proliferated since the mass suicide of its members in the late 90s. Mostly television documentaries. The American ones tend to be made with a religious slant of their own; a Christian angle. In the American documentaries, there tends to be an underlying condemnation of the suicides as an anti-Christian thing. The British take on the subject – most notably the one made for the BBC's *Inside Story* series, entitled *Heaven's Gate* – offers a more rational, scientific condemnation: spaceships don't exist and the cult members were poorly led sheep, guided by a leader who was probably a tortured, closet-case homosexual. Even for the supposedly 'objective' BBC, the 'truth' about

Heaven's Gate must be sugar-coated in a propaganda-like manufacture of opinion for its viewers, to send them away not with a greater understanding of the cult, but a creeped-out revulsion at the mere thought of Heaven's Gate and its beliefs.

If the curious want to get a real feel for the cult, one must go directly to the horses mouth and watch the videos made by Applewhite himself. In *Planetary Evacuation Recruitment Tape*, Applewhite (now known as 'Do') claims that his former partner, Bonnie (who died in the 80s, and is now dubbed 'Ti'), has already returned to the kingdom of heaven, and that she is actually God, his father and teacher. Do claims to be God's representation on earth. In other words, he's the second coming. The kingdom of heaven, referred to in the bible, is actually the evolutionary plain higher than man, located on a distant planet. Planet earth is about to be 'recycled,' and a new civilisation will arise shortly. Accordingly, in order to avoid this grand inconvenience, viewers are encouraged to leave their 'flesh vehicles' behind and join the group in an evacuation of earth. Do addresses the viewers directly to camera. He gives the hard sell, like an over-animated Jehova's Witness on a doorstep. He presses on the urgency of the situation, and like any preacher worth his salt, uses biblical quotes as hard evidence.

Kissed (1996)
Dir: Lynne Stopkewich /Canada

This is not a *Nekromantik*. In fact, director Lynne Stopkewich goes so far in trying to portray the subject of necrophilia in a non-sensationalist manner that she ends up making it seem somehow tasteful. And boring. There's no explicit mortuary scenes here, or corpse-fucking in the old Jorg Buttgereit mode. Stopkewich instead aims for an exploration of the spiritual possibilities in the attraction of death.

Based on Barbara Gowdy's short tale, *We So Seldom Look On Love*, *Kissed* centres on Sandra (Molly Parker), a morbid young woman whose fascination with death leads to a job in a mortuary. She meets a handsome young man in Matt (Peter Outerbridge), and eventually reveals to him her dark secret. Sandra's disinterest in the living sees her becoming increasingly attracted to the dead, where she seems to have ecstatic spiritual experiences with corpses... Meanwhile, Matt becomes obsessed with Sandra, and in a leaf taken from *Romeo and Juliet*, decides to get pretty drastic in his attempts to win her heart...

The worst thing a movie can be is boring. And *Kissed* is almost sleep-inducing. Rather than cutting the film down into a short, Stopkewich seemed determined to stretch out the incredibly dull proceedings for a full 80 minutes. There's also very little in the way of psychology to help us understand Sandra's motivations, and what we're left with is a cute and rather naive portrait of a corpse-fucker; all very sweet and quirky! Her disgusting perversion is treated in the same way as a woman with a terminal disease in some daytime TV movie; just another well-adjusted leading lady who just so happens to be a bit different – in this case, having a penchant for sleeping with dead bodies. I know the film focuses more on the spiritual dimensions of such vile subject-matter, but still I didn't believe a second of this garbage. Some have interpreted the film as Sandra's fantasy, and that would perhaps explain why all the corpses just happen to be handsome young men. All in all though, it's a simplistic and lifeless failure.

Despite nearing retirement, chief censor at the BBFC, James Ferman, had some reservations about the film, but new censor, Andreas Whittam Smith, recognised the film as an exploration, not exploitation, and passed *Kissed* uncut for home viewing.

The Funeral (1996)
Dir: Abel Ferrara /USA

Abel Ferrara's foray into the gangster movie focuses on the lead up to the funeral of one of three gangster brothers in 1930s New York. The film explores the back-story to the murder and the surviving brother's desire for vengeance whilst the family mourns at their home. The despair and guilt become too much for brother Chez (Chris Penn), and he has a breakdown which leads to the film's shocking climax.

With its Depression-era setting and relation to genre classics like *The Godfather* and *The Petrified Forest*, *The Funeral* is a film which invites its audience to relate to the drama on screen on a moral basis as it follows the usual gangster themes of loyalty, treachery, and religious anguish. And like all of Ferrara's films, he manages to bring out the very best in his cast which includes Christopher Walken, Chris Penn, Vincent Gallo, Victor Argo, Issabella Rosselini, Benicio Del Toro, and Annabella Sciorra.

Walken is superb as Ray Tempo, the eldest and wisest brother who is just as much concerned with the ethical dilemma of murder as he is with his personal need for vengeance. The scene in which he mourns over his brother's body is especially heartfelt, and has passed into legend as script writer Nicholas St. John had lost his son and seemed to be drawing on his own emotional pain when writing the scenes.

Gallow's performance is also impressive as Johnny Tempo, the deceased brother, who, in a series of flashbacks, looked to be the most outgoing and socially conscious of the three siblings. But more striking still is Chris Penn as Chez, the fiery, emotionally unstable brother whose ruthless moral code leads him to raping a young girl in an alley before his mind crumbles altogether. Chris Penn and Ferrara both won awards at the Venice Film Festival, making *The Funeral* Ferrara's most critically acclaimed film to date. It's just a shame that he and writer Nicky St. John fell out and ended their friendship after this film, and they haven't worked together since.

Shot around the same time as *The Addiction*, a black and white tale of philosopher vampires, *The Funeral* echoes some of the ethical themes of that film, such as in the rape scene where Penn offers the girl a way out of the situation before screaming "you've just sold your soul to the fuckin' devil!!" and raping her. The 30s setting is captured perfectly, with the obscure politics, religious questioning, and the soundtrack which includes Billie Holiday's suicidal *Gloomy Sunday*. Not a cheery kind of film then, but even with this raw, troubling, and extremely powerful work under his belt, Abel Ferrara remains one of the most criminally underrated American filmmakers.

Hustler White (1996)
Dir: Bruce LaBruce and Ricky Castro /Germany/Canada

With a plot that borrows elements from *Sunset Boulevard* and *Death In Venice*, *Hustler White* centres on LA hustler Tony Ward, who spends his time dealing with punters and appearing in porn movies in Santa Monica, California. He meets Jurgen Anger (LaBruce), and the pair build a growing rapport surrounded by the diverse sexual shenanigans in the local area.

When *Hustler White* was released in the UK, it prompted that model of liberalism, *The Mail On Sunday*, to accuse the film of being "Disgusting, sick, filthy, pornographic, and scary," and then added, "Despite being disgusting, sick, filthy, pornographic, and scary, it's not bad." With its postmodern blend of diverse reference points, from old skool Hollywood, to porn, and S&M, sprinkled with hilarious black comedy, it's a film which, despite the outrageous scenes of perverse sex, is actually at heart a romantic story and a celebration of diversity.

Tony Ward is perfect as Montgomery, whose good looks and pleasant nature helps to steer the film away from its moral ambiguity and makes the film feel somehow less offensive to viewers than it could have been. He reminded me of Joe Dallesandro in the Warhol/Morrisey movies, *Flesh*, *Trash*, and *Heat*. That's not to say that it's an easy ride; no doubt, the uber-offensive humour, extreme bondage, and perversities (including sex with amputees) will be too much for some viewers, especially those who are in any way homophobic. Or claustrophobic (as the cling-film scene will demonstrate).

Writer/director Bruce LaBruce started on his road to infamy in 1987 with *I Know What It's Like To Be Dead*, and followed it up with *No Skin Off My Ass* in 1991, and then secured his legend in 1993 with *Super 8 1/2*, a cult classic which put him at the forefront of controversial Queer Cinema. *Hustler White* was subjected to cuts by the BBFC who objected to scenes including sexual kicks from razor blades, and the aforementioned amputee fetish. But LaBruce still shows no signs of tempering his tastes. His equally uncompromising *Skin Flick* (later retitled to *Skin Gang*) was rejected by the London Film Festival for its graphic scenes of skinhead sex and a particularly gruelling Nazi rape scene. And his later effort, *L.A. Zombie,* was banned outright in the UK in 2010.

If you're looking for a grubby gay porn film then *Hustler White* will be a disappointment. Likewise, if you're easily offended. It's a film designed to lure in unsuspecting viewers and shock them with unflinching scenes of perversity and sadomasochism, but it's also completely unashamed of itself and ultimately embraces the outer realms of human desire, whilst presenting art as imitating art as imitating art, with its numerous and often obscure cultural references.

Freeway (1996)
Dir: Matthew Bright /USA

Foul-mouthed delinquent, Vanessa (Reece Witherspoon), returns from school one day to find her mother being busted for prostitution, and her creepy stepdad on drug offences. And as they're being carted away, she flees the scene rather than staying around to be shuffled off into foster care. Vanessa then says goodbye to her boyfriend and hits the road in search of the trailer park where her grandmother lives. However, when her car breaks down on the freeway, she accepts a lift from Bob Wolverton (Keifer Sutherland), who seems like a decent fellow, but is actually the 'I-5 Killer', a serial child-killing paedophile. Bob thinks he's onto some easy prey, but he completely underestimates the feisty Vanessa...

Freeway is one of those straight to video marvels which was never shown in cinemas, a film which turned out to be far more daring and entertaining than many of its big-screen counterparts. It was written and directed by Matthew Bright, who began his career as a screen writer on oddities like *Forbidden Zone* and the Drew Barrymore remake of *Gun Crazy*, and who should really get back into the director's seat after years of inactivity since the disastrous *Tiptoes* in 2003.

Not a film for the easily offended, *Freeway* comes on as a twisted version of the Grimm's '*Little Red Riding Hood*'; Sutherland even disguises himself as grandma and awaits the arrival of an unknowing Vanessa ("Them are some mighty big fuckin' teeth you got there, Bob"). It's trash movie heaven of the highest order that pays homage to a whole range of exploitation genres such as the road movie, the odd couple, rape-revenge fantasies, slasher movies, and even women-in-prison epics, all mired in weirdness and warped humour. Imagine a Tarantino script directed by a young John Waters and you're on the right track.

Witherspoon is fantastic as the street-wise reprobate, out-smarting and out-gunning her would-be killer. Her brilliance as Vanessa landed her future roles in films like *Election* and *American Psycho*, which in turn helped in her subsequent rise to Hollywood super-stardom. I wonder what her mainstream fans would make of her in *Freeway* as the fucked up daughter of a crack ho. Just curious. Sutherland is also spot-on as the wolf in child counsellor's clothing; smooth as silk, but also cruel and sadistic when he thinks he can get away with it; a true scumbag. Lookout for some amusing performances from Amanda Plummer, Dan Hedaya, Sydney Lassick, and Brooke Shields in an uncharacteristic turn as Wolverton's idiotic wife who does us all a favour and blows her head off with a shotgun. Also lookout for real life serial killer, Richard Speck, in a photograph that Vanessa believes to be her father!

Freeway picked up various awards at film festivals and quickly shot to classic status with people as diverse as Alexander Payne and Mary Harron proclaiming Bright's pic as having an influence on their films. Bright immediately began work on a sequel, *Freeway 2: Confessions of a Trickbaby*, which explored the *Hansel and Gretel* fairytale, and was even *more* outrageous, upsetting those who loved the first film.

The BBFC made a slight cut to remove the sight of one of Wolverton's magazines which had an unpleasant title ('*Cock Sucking Toddlers*'). Elsewhere in the world, the film has more or less stayed intact, except in America where it initially got slapped with an NC-17 rating due to the film's heavy language, but it was slightly trimmed for a later R rating. And this same cut version was originally rejected by the Australian censors (OFLC) who demanded further cuts to the explicit dialogue, and also the shot of Vanessa's dead grandmother.

Crash (1996)
Dir: David Cronenberg /Canada

Disaffected couple James and Catherine Ballard (James Spader and Deborah Unger) have a jaded sex life and only seem to get excited whilst listening to each other's stories of sexual escapades. One day James has a head-on car collision with Helen Remington (Holly Hunter), whose husband is killed in the accident, and the pair are treated at the same hospital. The two eventually discover that the crash was sexually arousing, and this is when they are approached by Vaughan (Elias Koteas), a mysterious man posing as a doctor so as to get pally with crash victims to fuel his own obsessions. Turns out that Vaughan is also turned on by car wreckages and mangled humans, and he takes James and Helen on a voyage of discovery where they get to meet more members of this shadowy subculture, get to witness the re-enactment of the fatal crashes that killed Jayne Mansfield and James Dean, and sink further into the cold and

dreamy perversion for everything flesh and metal that is mangled on the highways.

Based on the cult novel by JG Ballard (described by Jean Baudrillard as "the first truly hyperreal novel"), *Crash* sees the return to form of David Cronenberg after the disappointing *Naked Lunch* and flat *M. Butterfly*. It's not an easy film to get to grips with in one viewing, but there is much to be enthralled and appalled by here as we're presented with technology that becomes an extension of – and deconstruction of – the human body. The characters are like human crash test dummies; there's no psychology, no erogenous zones (at least, not in the old sense); the human body is physically altered and transformed, revealing new sex organs in the process (check out the scene where James has sex with a wound on Rosanna Arquette's leg). Like Ballard's book, Cronenberg chooses not to get involved with the events on screen and keeps an observers distance from the characters – there's no real desire among them, no libido, no death drive; just the plain banality of the anomaly of death. Vaughan's body is a reflection of the twisted and dented metal stained with sperm: No orgasms, just ejaculation. And for many viewers, it's the cold and necrophiliac vibe of *Crash* that unnerves the most.

The film was met with anger and walk-outs when it played at the Cannes Film Festival, but still managed to win the Special Jury Prize. It also won the Genie Award in Canada where it was the most successful domestic film of the year. Glowing reviews and healthy box-office led many to believe that Cronenberg had tamed down the extremes of Ballard's book, but the hassle really began when *Crash* hit the UK. After its screening at the London Film Festival, Heritage Secretary Virginia Bottomly demanded it be banned (she hadn't even seen it), the *London Evening Standard* went to town on the film, describing it as being "beyond the bounds of depravity," and Westminster City Council banned it immediately. With its subject-matter it was inevitable that it would be largely misunderstood and cause offence among moralists. Film critics led by Alexander Walker were also campaigning to have the film banned, and *The Daily Mail*'s Christopher Tookey got his panties in a twist complaining that the film "Promulgates a twisted morality of its own: namely that life is about the pursuit of sexual gratification, whatever the consequences. It is the morality of the satyr, the nymphomaniac, the rapist, the paedophile, the danger to society." If that wasn't idiotic enough, he also took the time to condemn the film's positive depictions of gay and lesbian sex, and sex with the physically handicapped, which did more to expose his own right wing agenda more than anything.

The BBFC remained completely unmoved throughout the whole *Crash* debacle, and they even held screenings of the film for lawyers, forensic psychologists, and disabled groups, and concluded that "Rather than sympathizing or identifying with the attitudes or tastes of the characters in the film, the average viewer would in the end be repelled by them, and would reject the values and sexual proclivities displayed." It was subsequently released uncut in the UK which led *The Daily Mail* to condemn the decision, commenting "All the psycho-babble in the world cannot refute the simple fact: The film is sick. It should not be shown."

The message of *Crash* is a grim one indeed about the direction in which human sexuality is heading in. It's also beautifully shot and is perhaps Cronenberg's best looking film since *Videodrome*, and Howard Shore contributes the eerie, guitar-based theme tune to stunning effect. Although you can never beat the experience of seeing *Crash* in the cinema (or the drive home afterwards), DVD editions look fantastic. It's just a pity that the Cronenberg commentary track (available on the Criterion laserdisc) is still missing in action.

Kids (1996)
Dir: Larry Clark /USA

"Like it or not, it's a modern American masterpiece". That was the *Daily Telegraph*'s response to Larry Clark's *Kids*, one of the most controversial films of the 90s. Powerful, infuriating, and fiercely uncompromising, this bleak tale of a day in the lives of a bunch of teenage wasters in New York caused a scandal on its release.

This docu-drama follows a group of shameless delinquents as they hang out, do drugs, spread diseases, and indulge in petty crime and mindless violence. The verite effect discloses many lurid details that are not easily forgotten. The narrative falls into place with Telly (Leo Fitzpatrick), a sweet-talking sleaze bag whose hobby is to deflower young girls ("Virgins, I love 'em! No diseases!"). Meanwhile, Jennie, one of Telly's previous bed-fellows, discovers

that she is HIV positive. She spends the rest of the film trying to track him down before the disease can be spread any further.

Whether you're a worried parent or a detached spectator, *Kids* is a film that demands the viewer confront the depravity on screen. It's a horror show aimed at adults rather than children, and its potent message is driven home with exceptional directorial skill. If you choose to turn away and ignore, then according to the film's unflinchingly candid view, you're no better than the millions of parents out there who let their kids run wild with no clue as to what they're getting up to with their friends. And this stance was backed up by *Variety* magazine who declared that "*Kids* is disgusting and disturbing but that does not stop it from being a work of art. The nice thing about *Kids* is that it isn't nice at all."

Former photographer Larry Clark teamed up with writer and skateboarder, Harmony Korine, to bring this cautionary tale to the screen. Korine was allegedly only 18 years old when he wrote the script; and it's interesting to know that there was a script at all, because the performances are spot-on for the most part, and their casual line deliveries seem completely ad-libbed. The film itself remains a devastating snapshot of a generation who have sunk so low it would surely have caused Bret Easton Ellis a few sleepless nights.

The only real downside is that the film feels phony in its social context; New York is just like any other big city with its neighbourhoods separated by race, class, and religion (similar to the racial segregation in the urban areas of Paris, and the 'post code wars' in London, for example); there's no way the kids in *Kids* would be able to mingle in the park without any trouble erupting between those of differing neighbourhoods, and its simply bogus to suggest otherwise.

The press whipped up a storm on its release, and the BBFC cut a minute and a half of footage under the Protection of Children Act. The film was financed by Disney, and they sought to conceal their financial interest in *Kids* by having their sub-label, Miramax, release the film under an alias company name, Shining Excalibur Films. Warner Brothers distanced themselves from the film in a pathetic show of moral indignation by banning its screenings at its UK cinema chains (but they were happy to allow it to be shown at their other chains across the

447

world).

As for director Larry Clark, he has continued in his efforts to portray modern wayward youth in his subsequent work, such as *Another Day In Paradise*, *Ken Park* (again in collaboration with Harmony Korine), and *Wassup Rockers*, films which vary in their success and explicitness. There's no doubt he feels very passionate about what he does , and he at least is prepared to shine a light into the murkier side of American youth, a place that many of us would rather not know about. But credit to him for going places where very few film-makers are willing to go, and presenting us with the confrontational truth.

The Ugly (1996)
Dir: Scott Reynolds /New Zealand
A seriously creepy and unsettling mix of psychological horror and supernatural shocks, whose gradual ascent into the heights of the horror pantheon was almost entirely down to word-of-mouth alone.

Famous psychiatrist Dr. Karen Schumaker (Rebecca Hobbs) is currently riding on the waves of publicity after securing the release of a convicted serial killer. She is invited to a maximum-security institution by another killer, the notorious Simon Cartwright (Paolo Rotondo), and she accepts, much to the annoyance of the head of the institution. Dr. Schumaker arrives and converses with Cartwright in an attempt to get to the roots of his sickness, but eventually discovers that he is driven to kill by the 'ghosts' of his past victims.

With an array of flashbacks, disturbing jump-cuts, crash-zooms, and strange fantasy sequences, we gradually come to understand what makes Cartwright tick. The cruel abuse of his mother, the school bullies, and his social inadequacies as a young adult, bring on a brief but vivid picture of the killer's past. After killing his mother, Simon is tormented by her ghostly form, and he goes on to add more victims, who in turn become ghostly apparitions and torment him more and more. Simon is also much more intelligent and manipulative than Dr. Schumaker gives him credit for, and she gradually sinks deeper into the madness and is left questioning her own sanity.

It's difficult to talk about this film's influences because although there are some obvious reference points, *The Ugly* takes them into whole new territory. The sharp suited Dr. Schumaker questioning an incarcerated serial killer is reminiscent of *Silence of the Lambs*, and Simon's abusive past at the hands of his unstable mother, resulting in psychopathic traits relates to Hitchcock's *Psycho*. However, *The Ugly* is unlike either of those films and takes the screen serial killer into a lore of its own.

Writer/director Scott Reynolds appeared on the scene just as a couple of his fellow countrymen, Peter Jackson and Lee Tamahori, were being noticed in Hollywood. Both Jackson and Tamahori produced outrageous and grim pictures in New Zealand but immediately tempered their work once they hit Tinseltown; Jackson with his *Lord of the Rings*, and Tamahori with his James Bond caper, *Die Another Day*. But judging by Reynolds' startling early short films, and his follow-up to *The Ugly*, *Heaven*, there's still hope yet that this remarkable talent will continue to tread the dark side. Only time will tell.

One of the most impressive aspects of *The Ugly* is the way Reynolds creates a psychological template; the film's visuals relate to the cracked state of the killer's mind. Schumaker's bold red suit reflects the increasing rage Simon feels towards her, and the ice-cold blue of his cell reflects his isolation and inhumanity. And of course there are the ghosts themselves. The apparitions that appear throughout the film are genuinely creepy. Simon's dead mother appears over his shoulder in his cell with the camera zooming in on her twisted blue smile with blood dripping from her mouth. In lesser hands, that scene could have been comical, but Reynolds renders it perfectly to spine-chilling effect. Subsequent apparitions are no less effective, with these ghouls depicted in the same cold blue style which reflects Simon's mind. Indeed, throughout the film we're left wondering whether the ghosts are just a part of Simon's insanity, or whether they are a real and malevolent force independent of his psyche. And that ambiguity is held to the very end of the film.

Even with the extended scenes of bloody violence, the BBFC left *The Ugly* intact. The Metrodome DVD is therefore taken from the same transfer that first played at festivals around the world, gaining the respect of hardcore horror fanatics, and causing many a sleepless night. It's a masterpiece, and one of the scariest films of the 90s. I dare you to watch it alone at night.

Thesis (1996)
(Orig title: *Tesis*)
Dir: Alejandro Amenabar /Spain

Angela (Ana Torrent) is a grad student writing her thesis on violent video. She gets in contact with Chema (Fele Martinez), a long haired horror geek who takes her home and introduces her to his collection of gore tapes. He plays her a mondo movie called 'Fresh Blood', which shows a dead body having its brain removed. Angela's professor has access to the university's private video library, and he promises to have a look through the archives to locate the most gruesome and pornographic films to help her in her studies. After browsing the shelves in the enormous deserted library, he plays one of the videos in a closed-off screening room...

Angela later finds him dead in his seat, presumably of a chronic asthma attack. But what on earth was he watching that could cause him to keel over like that? Angela removes the tape from the machine and watches it at home. She's hesitant at first, making sure she plays it with the contrast level turned down to a minimum so that she doesn't have to see what's happening on screen; but the sounds of a woman's tortured cries are enough to convince her that the contents of the tape are far from pretty, and could in fact be a genuine snuff film. She shows the tape to her horror geek buddy, Chema, and he confirms it is real. The tape depicts a young woman tied to a chair being beaten and butchered with a circular saw by a man wearing a balaclava. Chema recognises the victim as a girl who disappeared from the campus two years previously. This odd couple then take it upon themselves to investigate...

After this superb initial set-up, the film descends into a silly thriller in which the sleuths are followed by the murderers who made the tape. And with only two possible culprits at hand, the film flits between the suspects, back and forth, and ruins any chances of having a surprise ending. As a whole, *Thesis* is not really gritty or graphic enough for my liking. It's way too clean-cut and streamlined to truly disturb its audience. It serves as really nothing more than a calling card for director Amenabar, who predictably went on to such mainstream tosh as the *Turn of the Screw* rip-off, *The Others*, and the Penelope Cruz vehicle, *Open Your Eyes*. And like those later films, *Thesis* has a distinctive 'play-it-safe' vibe about it, as though the filmmakers were trying to secure an international hit at any cost, and were absolutely dead-set against including anything in the film that may have ruined its chances of sending the director on to a career in Hollywood. The snuff thriller was done much better – and more plausibly – in Anthony Waller's superb *Mute Witness* (1994), and just like Amenabar, Waller also went on to a career in Hollywood, and delivered the lacklustre sequel, *An American Werewolf In Paris*, of which the less spoken about the better.

Angela's character is a bit wishy-washy; she's supposed to be writing a thesis on video violence, but acts as though she's never seen a horror movie in her life. She has a sort of doe-eyed innocence about her, more suited to watching Disney movies than fictional mondo vids like 'Fresh Blood'. If she ever saw *Men Behind the Sun* or *Snuff 102* she'd shit her own guts out. Chema is better as a character, the horror geek whose jaded sensibilities allows him to identify the poor butchered girl, meaning he can watch the tape over and over like a detached criminologist, as a way of piecing together the clues needed to track down the culprits. But even he is annoyingly obnoxious at times. And with his grungy plaid shirt and long hair and glasses, he looks like fellow horror geek, Mark Borchardt, from the excellent documentary *American Movie: The Making of Northwestern*, which incidentally, was made around the same time as *Thesis*.

The film's plus points are quite subtle; the first half hour or so has a gripping build-up, but soon fizzles out. There is also an underlying theme present concerning the scoptophiliac nature of moviegoers and of human nature in general: The opening scene sees Angela arriving at the station on a train. The conductor announces that a man has committed suicide by throwing himself in front of the train, and urges passengers not to look at the track as they leave. While she walks on the platform, Angela seems troubled; she doesn't want to look at the dead body on the track, but at the same time she can't help herself – the desire to look and feast her eyes on the tragedy is too great for her... Later on, there's the scene where Chema watches the tape at his apartment – while Chema stares unflinchingly at the screen in an almost clinically detached manner, Angela stands at the back of the room with her hands covering her eyes. But while she's doing this, she can't help but take a horrified peek through the gaps of her fingers. By standing as far away from the screen as possible, she hopes to distance herself, both physically and emotionally, from the shocking imagery, but of course this doesn't work, and those images are burned into her memory forever. An idea many horror fans will be able to relate to.

Splatter: Naked Blood (1996)
(Orig title: *Nekeddo buraddo: Megyaku*)
Dir: Hisayasu Sato /Japan

A young crazy genius develops an endorphin called 'My Son' and injects it into the young women at his mother's medical lab who are involved in contraceptive research. The serum has the effect of turning pain into pleasure and sadness into happiness, but young Eigi totally miscalculates how dangerous the potion can be when the lab girls begin to show some alarming behaviour; one of the girls takes body piercing to fatal extremes, and another quite literally eats herself to death. Eiji's mother eventually discovers the truth and watches as her boy injects the rest of the serum into himself. Mother and son then get it on for a bit of incestuous 'bump n grind' whilst hooked up to a bizarre kind of dream stimulating machine, a place where extreme violence is the ultimate pleasure...

Naked Blood doesn't really heat up until after the half hour mark, but when it does get going it doesn't let up. It's very similar in style to the films Sato made in the 80s like *Wife Collector*, *Brain Sex*, and *Genuine Rape* (which this film just happens to be a remake of), and shares with those films the themes of alienation, voyeurism, isolation, and perversity. But here Sato also adds a welcome dose of Cronenbergian outlandishness and body horror to the mix. The scenes where the girl deep fries her own hand, plucks out her own eyeball, and then proceeds to eat both are perhaps some of the most deranged imagery in the director's ouevre. His films remind me of the work of Jean Rollin in the way he has a knack of turning micro-budget film-making into dark lyrical dreamscapes on film. His movies are best watched at night in a hazy frame of mind where the quiet build-up leads to maximum effect.

Naked Blood is one of the better examples of the Ero-guro sub-genre (or 'erotic-grotesque'), a Japanese film trend which infuses sexual themes with potent body horror. On its travels around the world, Sato's film has been clearing the aisles with its extreme material being too much to handle for some. Most notoriously, the Canadian premiere at the Pacific Cinematheque in Vancouver where less than a third of the audience made it through to the end credits. The gruesome special effects were created by the great Yuichi Matsui who went on to work on the *Ringu* series, and also *Audition, Imprint, Ichi the Killer*, and *Kill Bill Vols. 1 and 2*. Filmmaker Noboru Iguchi paid tribute to *Naked Blood* with the deep fried scene in *Machine Girl*. High praise!

Alien Beach Party Massacre (1996)
Dir: Andy Gizzarelli /USA

An alien spacecraft crash-lands near a California beach community. The only survivor is a pasty-faced dweeb who befriends a group of beach bums who are organising a party. Meanwhile, a group of evil aliens with large piggish snouts land in the area to track down the pale one because he is in possession of some kind of gadget they want to get their evil mits on... It's a micro-budget production with some well-observed humour and a surf guitar soundtrack, but there's no massacre here, folks.

100 Years Of Horror (1996)
Dir: Ted Newsom /USA

Horror documentary hosted by Christopher Lee. The horror icon takes viewers on a jumbled tour through the ages, starting at the beginning with the early trick films of Georges Melies, before taking a look at cinema's dark side with Universal monster movies, Hammer, early werewolf movies, maniac movies, gialli, William Castle's promotional gimmicks, and the slasher boom of the late 70s/early 80s. Along the way, Jimmy Sangster claims that *Les Diaboliques* (1955) so horrified his wife that she almost miscarried their baby, while also admitting that he used the film as a template for his own work in *Paranoiac* (1963). Elsewhere, the godfather of gore, Herschell Gordon Lewis, talks about audience and censor reactions to *Blood Feast* (1963), while Boris Karloff discusses the difficulties of wearing the iconic Frankenstein's monster make up. As with most overview documentaries, this is mostly entry-level stuff, and the format skips from one movie to the next, and from random era to random era, with very little linking the films together. The clips are mostly taken from trailers, which always seems to annoy fans of horror documentaries, but I thought it worked quite well. Lee talks about the genre with seriousness and respect, and admirably avoids saying things like 'don't forget to turn out the light!' or 'pray the monster doesn't get you!' the sort of silly lines that crop up from time to time in this kind of fare. Also included are some very funny Abbott and Costello blooper reels, and John Carpenter comparing Dario Argento's work with Luis Bunuel as they both gained inspiration for their films by focusing on their dreams. Other talking heads include Roger Corman, Hugh Hefner, Robert De Niro, Dick Miller, Vincent Price, Ray Bradbury and Rachel Welsh. *100 Years of Horror* was originally made as a thirteen-part TV series, but I've been unable to source the whole series. The VHS release discussed here contains just two episodes pasted together.

Victim of the Haunt (1996)
Dir: Larry Shaw /USA

A nice middle-class family moves into a dream suburban home. Trouble is, the house was built on a burial ground, and also harbours a dark past; 75 years earlier, a man drowned his own daughter in the bathtub. The house is also haunted, and puts on pretty light shows as spirits wander across the bedroom walls. However, the spirits soon become increasingly threatening. And before you can say 'Zelda Rubinstein,' along comes the eccentric psychic to battle against the smoke and lights while urging the spirits to "go into the light," and save the day. *Victim of the Haunt* is basically a lightweight TV remake of *Poltergeist* (1982) which brings nothing new to the fold. The film is supposedly based on 'real events,' but it's about as real as Pamela Anderson's fake plastic udders.

Rumpelstilskin (1996)
Dir: Mark Jones /USA

A routine, predictable monster movie which is at least more watchable than any of the *Leprechaun* series. Rumpelstilstin is a child thief who is basically immortal. The only way to stop it is to guess its name – which is no easy task. It's an ugly little thing too, with ego problems – a bit like Leo Sayer. It shows up in L.A. in the mid-90s after being consigned to the ocean since medieval times. Widow Shelly (Kim Johnston Ulrich) teams up with her neighbour and an obnoxious TV personality to track down the evil troll and get her baby back, and this leads to a seemingly never-ending road chase with no style or suspense, nor much incident.

Affliction (1996)
(aka *Idiots with disgusting hobbies*)
Dir: Mark Hejnar /USA

A mondo style film about a bunch of soulless and talentless people who try to shock with their redundant artistic statements. Razorblades, human dartboards, shit, and graphic sex. Basically the purpose of this documentary is to present a barrage of shock images based on extreme controversial personalities (aka *Idiots with disgusting hobbies*). There's GG Allin of course in full display demonstrating his coprophiliac fetishes, the idiotic Mike Diana, who got arrested for obscenities, throwing up on a cross and the bible and masturbating with a cross, there's the even more idiotic 'Full Force Frank' who caused a fuss with his ideas on mass-murder and his gun fetish, music clips with extreme bands and stage performances, montages of random imagery and shock footage, self-mutilation, piercings, genital torture, gender benders, and sick or gory hardcore sex scenes. This documentary doesn't take a stance either way except to present it all in what it thinks is an art-piece, but this is humanity at its most absurdly depraved and idiotic. Not for the easily offended, or anyone else.

Apt Pupil (1997)
Dir: Bryan Singer /USA /Canada /France

An unusual relationship develops between a high school kid and an ageing Nazi war criminal. After the success of *The Usual Suspects* (1995), director Bryan Singer could have easily followed in the footsteps of Quentin Tarantino with a big-budget crime drama, but instead he took on a more intimate, claustrophobic story with just two main characters. Based on the story by Stephen King, *Apt Pupil* stars Brad Renfo as Todd, a school kid who approaches a retired immigrant (Ian McKellen) with accusations that he was Kurt Dussander, an extermination camp commandant back in the 1940s. Todd basically threatens to expose the old man to the authorities unless he agrees to help him with a school project by telling him stories about his involvement in the Holocaust. Of course, Dussander is initially reluctant to divulge his secrets, but gradually begins to exert a predatory interest in the kid, and enjoys boasting of his past crimes while attempting to seduce the youthful mind and create a new monster.

Apt Pupil is held together by fantastic performances from McKellen and Renfo, but is ultimately content to be a watered-down version of King's story (from his *Different Seasons* collection [pub. 1982] which also contained the source material for *Stand By Me* and *The Shawshank Redemption*). The film has come into some criticism for its failure to pinpoint the seed of the Todd's sickness. But I think that's a little harsh; after all, sociopaths are born everyday, and they exist even in the nice, middle-class suburbs of California. No one knows why. For whatever reason, Todd has developed a morbid fascination, and he finds an outlet for it in the form of Dussander. He gathers enough evidence to denounce the old man to the Israeli Nazi hunters, but instead uses the information to satisfy his own twisted curiosities.

On the other hand, the critics were right to show concern with the film's barely concealed homoerotic subtext; the psychological angle between the characters plays out like a seduction, with Todd as the pushy suitor and Dussander as the passive and reluctant party (though the older man is far more dangerous than he initially lets on). The implication here is that Singer – and screenwriter, Brandon Boyce – seem to suggest that homosexual desire leads to sadistic murder and genocide. Of course, this theme had already been explored around a decade earlier in Agustin Villaranga's much more disturbing *In a Glass Cage* (*Tras el cristal*, 1986).

Do's Final Exit (1997)
-Director not credited- /USA

Recorded in March 1997, just days before the infamous mass suicide of Heaven's Gate members, this 89-minute tape sees cult leader Marshall Applewhite (now known as 'Do') delivering his final speech. He denies that his group are committing suicide because suicide is an escape from life, whereas what they're doing is entering a new kingdom. He predicts the media's condemnation of their actions and also encourages viewers to follow them. According to him, this world is barbaric, and Heaven's Gate offers a better world, a higher plane of existence. You're hearing it from the horses mouth. He sits on a white plastic lawn chair in front of a large television screen which is relaying the footage being recorded, so we see a 'mirroring' effect of his head reflected larger and larger into infinity, which I think is a nice visual metaphor for the man's stupendous ego. When he speaks, he reminds me of Uri Geller in the way he uses hand gestures and his softly spoken voice and his big, starey eyes – which rarely blink – to mesmerise the viewers and inflict a bit of spoon-bending on their minds.

He then spins the camera around and films the excited members of the cult who show off their *Star Trek*-like uniforms and basically do as they're told. They look to be servile, timid mouse-types; shy, easily controlled, happy for the acceptance. Do controls everything here, including when they should laugh. Their smiles rise and fall depending on whether Do is making a serious statement or not. It soon becomes clear that the smallest details of their lives are controlled in the form of 'classes.' And some of the cult members look so young it's truly tragic. Do never tries to qualify his outlandish claims with any kind of logic or evidence; we're expected to take his word for it.

In the Company of Men (1997)
Dir: Neil LaBute /USA

A controversial talking point on both sides of the Atlantic, Neil LaBute's low-budget debut is actually a craftily concocted little film, and not the misogynistic hate-fest many think it to be. Its basic plot (two men try to seduce and then dump a deaf girl – just for the hell of it) may be outrageous, but it never portrays the two men in a favourable light, and offers a heroine far stronger than most. And although the film doesn't have anything in the way of graphically shocking elements, the psychological torture is extremely disturbing.

Handsome Chad and mild-mannered Howard, cogs in the machine of some anonymous corporation, are on a six week project out of town. Both their girlfriends have recently dumped them, and so Chad suggests they play a very spiteful game: the pair will simultaneously date the first vulnerable woman they meet on the trip and swear undying love, only to dash the victim's hopes in a manner that will have her "reaching for the sleeping pills". The girl they choose is pretty Christine, a deaf secretary (Stacy Edwards in a phenomenal performance. And no, she's not really deaf) who blossoms under their attentions and falls hard for Chad.

A bleak comedy of amorality, this is neither the misogynistic rant nor the masterpiece it's been labelled by various critics. For all that its subject is the war between the sexes, it's equally about the dog-eat-dog backstabbing that boils just beneath the surface of corporate camaraderie, and Chad the cad is a total scumbag, reeling off sick impersonations of deaf people and lines of the "never trust something that bleeds for a week and doesn't die" calibre. Chad is a man who knows what he wants and knows how to get it, with his good looks and charm. Oops – did I say 'charm'? I meant the opposite. In fact, imagine charm as being a beautiful rare stone. Now imagine that stone placed onto a rocket ship and fired to the far side of the galaxy. And then you accidentally step in some dogshit. Now check out your shoe. *That's* what he has instead of charm. And yet he also has countless notches on his bedpost. And as a fellow man, that really pisses me off! If Chad ever contracts pubic lice, I'd like to congratulate them, shake them all individually by the hand, and buy them all a drink.

The film's weak link lies in the performances – perhaps LaBute's directing skills will never equal the proficiency of his writing. While Stacy Edwards is astonishingly good as Christine, both Eckhart and Malloy too often seem as though they're participating in a dress rehearsal exercise, pausing just a little too long between lines, posing just a bit too self-consciously, feeling their way through the dialogue whose barely repressed venom should slip off their tongues like acid. But that's a relatively minor criticism; this film is worth seeing, and LaBute's subsequent work has never been as interesting as this. It remains a disturbing glimpse of male bonding at its most ugly and reprehensible.

In the Company of Men sparked outrage among feminists, and even a filmmaker's trophy at the Sundance Film Festival couldn't protect LaBute from their ire at the event; one young woman approached the director after the screening and spat in his face. Actor Eckhart was also under attack; a woman approached him after the screening and screamed "I fucking hate you!" What she really meant, Eckhart then pointed out, was that she hated the misogynist character, Chad, whom he played in the film. "No," the woman insisted angrily, "I hate *you*!"

With his debut feature (and also its corrosive follow-up, *Your Friends & Neighbors*), writer/director Neil LaBute became one of

cinema's most infamous agent provocateurs of the late 90s. He didn't just touch a few sore points here and there, he took a sledgehammer to viewer sensibilities across America. While Hollywood continues to paint the relationships between men and women in a rose-tinted, happy-ever-after glow, LaBute casts an ironic eye on the nasty, deceitful reality of adulterous partners and callous, womanizing bastards. He doesn't use shock tactics for Tarantino-style cool; instead he wants to create conflict, leaving it up to the audience to make moral judgments on his characters. "I really appreciate the power of what words can do," LaBute said at the time. "After everything that film can do, words can still unnerve people."

Hana-Bi (1997)
(*Fireworks*)
Dir: Takeshi Kitano /Japan

Hard-as-nails detective Nishi ('Beat' Takeshi Kitano) is at the end of his tether; sick and tired of chasing gangsters and other crims, saddened by the death of his colleague in a stakeout, the terminal illness of his wife, and the haunted despair of his good friend Horibe (Ren Osugi), who has been paralyzed by a nasty yakuza, and as a result has been abandoned by his family and unable to get back to work. Nishi tries to avert his friend's impending suicide by gifting him a box of art supplies and encourages Horibe to paint. As his friend begins experimenting with colourful and bizarre pictures of exploding fireworks and animals with flower heads, Nishi plans an elaborate bank robbery so that he can take his dying wife on one last sentimental journey.

The legendary Takeshi Kitano began work on this profoundly personal summation on love, violence, and death just before his near-fatal motorcycle accident. Revisiting similar themes he had explored previously in such classics as *Violent Cop* and *Sonatine*, *Hana-Bi* is a strange mixture of death fixation and life affirmation which makes it just as moving as it is disturbing. Not only did Kitano write, direct, and edit the film, he also cast himself as Nishi in the lead role, the cop with a short-fuse who is just as capable of ramming chopsticks into someone's eye as he is of returning a kind favour. Kitano's face still bore the brunt of the accident, with the scars and the brain damage and his slight facial twitches, making his performance not only courageous but also fascinatingly explosive. In addition, the scenes with Nishi and his dying wife are incredibly heartfelt, in stark contrast to the meticulous planning of the robbery and his own hardline morality.

The disjointed structure of the film effectively conveys Nishi's confusion as he struggles to handle his wife's impending death and the despair of his paralyzed friend Horibe, who was just doing his job of trying to protect a society who don't relly deserve it. Extreme violence is contrasted with scenes of uneasy serenity, which reflects Nishi's sadness, and ultimately his own brutal death which will soon be visited upon him.

Takeshi Kitano (who acts under his stage name 'Beat' Takeshi, from his early days as being one half of a comedy duo) looks like a typical movie tough guy with his sleek suit, cool sunglasses, and his superbly calm way of kickin' arse whilst barely moving a muscle. However, the guns and the posing conceals an abyss of existential despair, and rather than lightening the mood, the film's strange interludes and moments of silly humour only make it more haunting. The paintings seen throughout the film at the bank and the hospital, and those of Horibe's of the bizarre floral-animals, were all created by Kitano himself who took up painting after the crash as a form of self-therapy. And his artworks give the viewers an extra insight into his psychological state as he set out on his second chance at life. The resulting film is a fable on the healing power of art and the endurance of bittersweet bonds of loyalty, love, and loss, all wrapped up in a hard-boiled cop movie.

Dobermann (1997)
Dir: Jan Kounen /France

The opening computer-generated credits sequence features a gun-toting Dobermann Pinscher urinating over the titles, and this sets the provocative tone for Jan Kounen's feature, an extremely violent French comic-strip cyberpunk gangster flick. A direct homage to Quentin Tarantino, its action sequences owe just as much to John Woo and the Hong Kong school of choreographed carnage. Added to which there is a constantly thudding techno soundtrack.

The subversive story concerns a leather-clad hoodlum (Vincent Cassel) who conducts bank robberies with his deaf moll (Monica Bellucci) and a band of coke-snorting psychopaths. With a promotional poster reminiscent of *The*

Terminator and a kinetic trailer that featured on every TV channel in France, Jan Kounen's film built him a reputation as "Luc Besson with balls". He described his film as an "urban Western," and aimed it at a generation of film fans raised on big-budget Hollywood fodder, taking its violence to comic-book extremes, substituting humour and style for deeper scrutiny.

Films which attempt to transfer the twisted kinetic perspectives of comic-books to live action cinema are a notoriously hit and miss affair, with a wide range of flops, from *Howard the Duck* to *Judge Dredd*, convincing Hollywood studios that only Tim Burton can really pull this kind of thing off. Over in France, however, Netherlands born Jan Kounen was showing himself to be a talent better than most, managing to inject a real sense of excessive comic-book craziness into his live-action feature, *Dobermann*, an exercise in empty-headed entertainment. So we can wave bye-bye to good taste, and welcome in almost two hours of graphic trash as we enter a world of big guns, bad haircuts, silly names, senseless violence, cruelty to children, transvestite temper tantrums, and people getting their dicks blown off by Nazi cops with anger management problems...

A big-budget breakthrough for Kounen, whose previous credits include *Vibro Boy*, *Dobermann* is essentially an over-dressed urban Western which comes on as a cross between *Mad Max* and *Deputy Dorg*. Apparently, the director sees something of Martin Scorsese's *Goodfellas* in many of the sequences on view, but frankly, that comparison is completely lost on me. Far more of a debt is owed to the slapstick sensibilities of Sam Raimi, who once described his *Evil Dead* trilogy as "an update on *The Three Stooges* with blood and gore standing in for custard pies," or to Luc Besson who incited the wrath of the French critical establishment by putting style before content in explosive hits like *Leon* and *Nikita*, films which Kounen has clearly watched in admiration. Certainly, there's an active disdain in *Dobermann* for the polite traditions of French cinema, as the characters blow peoples brains out with hand grenades and literally wipe their arses with high-brow movie magazines. Kounen clearly doesn't have time for high-minded critics, which is convenient really because, since *Dobermann*, they've had little time for him either.

On a casting level, *Dobermann* has much to

commend it, with legend Tcheky Karyo squaring up against Vincent Cassel, who had made such an impact in Mathieu Kassowit's *La Haine*, a film which worried the hell out of the authorities but still went down very well with international critics and punters. There were far fewer supporters of this slickly sadistic satire, which was widely denounced as being "Extremely violent and indulgently irresponsible" (though some people may of course take that as a recommendation). The film doesn't really have any substance, but for those with an extremely violent appetite, it might just hit the spot.

Cutting Moments (1997)
Dir: Douglas Buck /USA

Very few short films can lay claim to the infamy bestowed on *Cutting Moments*, an extremely disturbing 20-minute delve into domestic hell which first gained notoriety on the festival circuit (where it picked up the Audience Award at FantAsia).

The film begins on a gloomy day in a suburban home. While the wife prepares food in the kitchen, the husband cuts the hedges, and their son re-enacts rape scenes with toy figurines. The child has clearly been the victim of sexual abuse from his father. And his parents are just waiting for social services to turn up and take their boy away at any moment. Dialogue is kept to a bare minimum throughout. Instead, we hear every day sounds of a typical family home – baseball on TV, vegetables being sliced on the cutting board, an aeroplane passing overhead – but these normal, everyday sounds feel somehow cold and sinister due to the way they cut through the atmosphere and distance between the family members.

The mother looks to be in denial about what is happening to her family. She doesn't seem to resent her husband one bit for what he has done, and she offers no reassurances to her son, either. Instead, she carries on as if nothing has happened, and tries to keep up the pretence of being a part of a normal, 'happy' family. She can't seem to face the fact that her family life has changed irrevocably. Her once loving husband now completely blanks her out of existence. Her dishevelled appearance indicates that no matter how much she tries to keep things as normal as possible in the household, she looks like she has been tearing herself to shreds, emotionally. With the weight on her own conscience, she feels she can do something to help, she can indulge in the fantasy of 'mending' the harm done, to give herself the impression that things are improving. She blames herself for the abuse of her son because she didn't make herself sexually available to her husband; she overlooks the fact that he committed an abhorrent, inexcusable act against their child.

The wife later enters the living room wearing lipstick and a red dress. She stands in front of her husband but he seems completely disinterested and pissed off that she is blocking his view of the telly. Her romantic gesture is met with cold revulsion. Feeling rejected, she heads for the bathroom to dwell on how undesirable she has become, again overlooking the faults of her husband. Situations like this happen all the time all over the world – the stereotypical long-suffering wife slaving away unassisted for hours to keep the family fed and watered. All she wants in return is a bit of attention and affection. Instead, her husband sits on the sofa watching baseball on TV like a boneless hippo, silently farting warm butt-fulls of gas into the atmosphere during the ad breaks. In this bleak and murky world, wives are supposed to be meek-but-cheerful servants (she doesn't even get a proper chair to sit on; she has to perch at the side like a dog begging for scraps of approval) while their husbands are lazy, oblivious dickheads.

She stares at the bathroom mirror and has a breakdown. She scrubs her lips with a piece of steel wool until blood pours onto the floor tiles. She then picks up a pair of scissors and begins cutting her lips off. She doesn't look to be in any kind of pain while she does it; it's as if she is in some kind of trance, clumsily cutting away, her mouth leaking blood all down the sink and her chest. She enters the living room and stands in front of her husband once again, this time covered in blood and bearing a mutilated face. She gets his attention all right, but his reaction to the bloody parade is even *more* disturbing and grotesque…

Cutting Moments is a bleak and depressing film. Even with its short running time, you'll feel like you've been bopped on the head with a baseball bat when the credits roll. Film fans at various festivals reacted like stunned fish – stuck rigid in their seats and slack-jawed at the horrors they had just witnessed. Established cult movie makers queued up to sing its praises – among them were Abel Ferrara, Gaspar Noe,

Larry Fesenden and Tom Savini – which is extremely rare for a low-budget short film. Indeed, the reception for *Cutting Moments* was so overwhelmingly positive that director Douglas Buck expanded on his short with *Home* (1998) and *Prologue* (2003). *Home* tackles a similar theme but from the husband's perspective, as his suppressed anger at his wife and daughter eventually boils over in a violent rage. *Prologue* centres on a man whose previous rape victim shows up in town to stir up some trouble for him. All three shorts were edited together and released on DVD as a feature film under the title *Family Portraits: A Trilogy of America* in 2004. But despite the deliberately innocuous title, this makes for some very disturbing viewing, and is the perfect answer for those looking for a psychological angle to balance out and underline the horror and the blood.

Funny Games (1997)
Dir: Michael Haneke /Austria

'One of toughest nights you'll ever spend in front of your television.' That was how Mark Kermode summed up *Funny Games*, a cold and brutal addition to the home invasion sub-genre. Building upon his earlier works, such as *The Seventh Continent* (1989) and *Benny's Video* (1992), writer-director Michael Haneke here resumes his preoccupations with his attempts to shock and torture those who are seeking violence and murder for entertainment. So, if you're looking for some big screen mayhem in the form of blood, guts, and spectacular human suffering, then *Funny Games* may come as something of a surprise because, despite being one of the most harrowing films of the 90s, there's very little on-screen bloodshed to be found here.

The plot of *Funny Games* is chillingly simple; a pair of teenage psychopaths enter a lakeside holiday home and set up a wager with the family therein that they will all be "kaput" within twelve hours. What follows is a raw exercise in Sadean evil; the family dog is beaten to death with a golf club, the father, Georg (Ulrich Muhe), is incapacitated by having his shin smashed in with the same club, and this is just for starters. The unfunny games continue when the mother, Anna (Suzanne Lothar), is forced to strip off her clothes to stop the torturing of her little boy, Schorschi (Stefan Clapczynski). She is then given a couple of options; one, choose whether her husband is to be stabbed or shot; or two, she can volunteer to die and take his place instead.

The games are based on psychological torment and physical torture, and reach a climax with the shooting of the young boy with a hunting rifle. The killers then momentarily leave the house, and the scene that follows has annoyed the hell out of critics for being over long and boring; for around ten minutes the camera stays unmoved as Anna and Georg embrace on the floor in the presence of their dead son in a state of utter despair and grief. Regardless of what the critics have said, this is the most powerful scene in the entire film. The performances of Muhe and Lothar are frankly astonishing; and their heartfelt and tortured cries make the scene agonising to watch as their pain feels genuine with a spine-chilling effect. Make no mistake, this is one of the most harrowing scenes in the history of film, played absolutely unsettlingly straight by the two magnificent performers. Soon after this scene, however, the killers return to finish what they started and make good on their wager.

Another thing that annoyed the critics was the film's breaking of the 'fourth wall' with one of the villains (played by *Benny's Video*'s Arno Frisch) turning to the camera and addressing the viewers on matters concerning the plot, and other 'knowing' elements such as whether the film's running time has reached feature length. At one point when the captives get the upper-hand on the invaders, Frisch picks up a VCR remote control and literally rewinds the scene so that the scenario can start over again with the killers back in control and patching up their mistakes. This obvious didacticism, however unpopular, does much to express Haneke's point about the reality of fiction, and vice versa (and in this sense, *Funny Games* closely resembles *Benny's Video*, and of course, the Belgian art house shocker, *Man Bites Dog*).

Funny Games emerged as part of Haneke's 'glaciation' series, a trilogy of films the director described as being 'just a little colder than reality,' designed as a counter-point to the glowing splendour of the norm, as portrayed in the media. The central theme of the films was to show how the recorded image alienates its viewers; how the process of consuming entertainment gives us the illusion of control while actually concealing reality from us. This theme had previously been explored routinely in the work of Japanese provocateur, Hisayasu Sato, but never in such a coldly clinical way as seen here. In interviews, Haneke has said that the inspiration for *Benny's Video* came from a magazine article about a young man who had committed a terrible crime. When asked why he did it, the boy replied, 'I wanted to know what it was like.' 'For me,' said Haneke, 'those are the words of someone who is completely out of touch with reality – a result of only knowing about reality through the media.' And, with *Funny Games*, Haneke took that conclusion to its most horrifying extremes by portraying a pair of sadistic serial killers who target a family at random.

The true greatness of the film is that Haneke succeeds in disturbing his audience with scenes of abysmal horror without actually showing us the carnage we so desire. 'I try to find ways of representing violence as that which it is: as inconsumable,' he says, 'I give back to violence that which it is: pain, a violation of others.' The whole point of this film seems to be as an endurance test, whereby you're actively challenged to see it through, or switch it off. Of course, Haneke went to Hollywood ten years later and produced a shot-for-shot remake of *Funny Games* for those who are allergic to subtitles. He is an intellectual and provocative filmmaker who sees himself as above producing multiplex fodder, and yet he seemed happy enough to make a compromise in that instance.

Regarde la mer (1997)
(*See The Sea*)
Dir: Francois Ozon /France
Francois Ozon's disturbing film sees Sasha, a young British mother living in a quiet French community suddenly have a neighbour, Tatiana, who pitches her tent in her yard. The two women begin to build a rapport and the tension between them mounts. Tatiana is offish from the start, but, perhaps owing to her English politeness, Sasha ignores the strange woman's air of hostility and allows her to enter the family home. Before long, Tatiana is smearing Sasha's toothbrush in excrement, and her behaviour becomes increasingly disturbing. Meanwhile, the lonely Sasha – whose husband is away on business – ventures into the nearby woods for sexual encounters with a homosexuals, and Tatiana's psychotic streak is confirmed in the horrifying finale...

Ozon's use of visual rather than dialogue to tell the story is masterful, and the story is allowed to tell itself gently and beautifully. French film-maker Ozon rose to prominence with the acclaimed black comedy *Sitcom* (1998), and his immense promise is confirmed by this earlier, equally unsettling drama. Ozon has a great talent for conveying an enormous amount of psychological complexity and ambivalence with a few lines of dialogue, the movement of an eye, the almost invisible tensing of a muscle. What's more, he leaves us the viewers with the time and space to project our own experience, fear, and desire onto the situation. He manipulates audience expectation with considerable authority. The location's unpopulated beaches, woods, and hills serves as a hint at both beauty and menace, and the uneasy tone is deftly echoed in the performances of Sasha Hails and Marins deVan. Hails went on to a cushy career with the BBC as a screenwriter on the long-running hospital drama, *Casualty* (1986-), while de Van later directed and starred in the disturbing *In My Skin* (*Dans me peau*, 2002).

Lasting just 52 minutes, *Regarde la mer* recalls taut classics such as Henri-Georges Clouzot's *Les Diaboliques* and Phillip Noyce's *Dead Calm*, and was one of the most unnerving films of 1997.

Kiss Or Kill (1997)
Dir: Bill Bennett /Australia
The opening scene shows a woman being doused in petrol and burned alive on her own doorstep in the presence of her young daughter. The plot falls into place with Nikki (Frances O'Connor) and Al (Matt Day), a young couple who run a scam whereby she lures rich married men to hotel rooms on the promise of sex, spikes their drinks, and when the mark is unconscious, they loot his possessions. This night, however, things go terribly wrong; their victim dies. And added to the couple's troubles is the man's briefcase which contains a video tape showing a famous footballer, 'Zipper' Doyle, sexually abusing a young boy. Nikki makes a phone call to the footballer in anger, and calls him a sick prick and announces that she has a copy of the tape. But Doyle is part of a powerful paedophile ring, with members ranking high in the media. The couple soon find themselves on the run from both the cops and Doyle, and are hunted down through the scorching hot outback.

Written, directed, and produced by Bill Bennett, *Kiss Or Kill* is a tense road movie that comes on like an Australian version of *Badlands*, with an amoral young couple on the run across wide-open spaces. However, there is an originality here in Bennett's immaculate screenplay which spins a few twists of its own in this familiar sub-genre, such as the themes of trust – or lack of it – and the film also asks interesting questions like how well do we really know those who are closest to us; our friends, lovers, family, and colleagues? Nikki and Al's relationship comes under strain when everyone they meet seems to die. But who's to blame for the killings? They both suspect each other and feel they don't actually know who each other really are, despite having being romantically involved for years. This alienation also stems to the two detectives on their case, who, in a hilarious scene in a cafe, also show how little they know about each other, despite being partners in a dangerous job. And the same theme also relates to the film's villain, 'Zipper' Doyle, a famous ex-footballer and respected member of the public who is actually a sick paedophile.

Indeed, the fictional character 'Zipper' Doyle has recently been given an added chill as his crimes relate to the real-life story of Jimmy Savile, a British celebrity who raised millions for charity and was a well-loved – if eccentric – character. After his death in 2011, it was discovered that this man, who had been loved and trusted by an entire nation for decades, was actually responsible for abusing countless children over the years, and is suspected of being part of a paedophile ring that included friends in the worlds of showbiz and the media who for years were covering up his despicable crimes.

As a side note, I still don't understand how someone like Jimmy Savile managed to blag himself a career in TV. Maybe it's because back in the early days, television screens were tiny and people couldn't see him properly. The public didn't have these huge, wall-sprawling abominations we call TV sets nowadays. In the early days of TV, Savile was creepy but tiny. However, his sudden reappearance in the media as one of society's most despicable boogeymen demanded that his face be suddenly plastered everywhere. Your TV became a kind of twisted horror show, with his huge hideous face filling up the whole wall, his gargoyle skull in a white wig chomping a cigar and laughing at us from the other side of the grave.

Kiss Or Kill dispenses with any kind of musical accompaniment, and this gives the film a downbeat edge. But despite the grim subject-matter and serious tone, this film is loaded with a deep and biting sense of humour; in fact, it's just as much a dark comedy as it is a road movie. The result is a low-budget but remarkable piece of work that explores many dark areas of the human soul while somehow managing to make us laugh.

Gummo (1997)
Dir: Harmony Korine /USA

A group of youngsters search for ways of passing the time in a run-down town in Ohio that has been devastated by a tornado. Bernardo Bertolucci called it one of the most important films of the 90s, but casual viewers will no doubt find it all too much to take. It's a deliberately disturbing account of fractured lives and seems to serve as some kind of grotesque freak show. *Sight and Sound* magazine called it "a high watermark of 90s White Trash Chic." Amazingly, Linda Manz (who played Cebe in *Out of The Blue*) here plays the title character's mother who enjoys feeding her son chocolate bars while he takes a bath. It's a rare performance by one of cult cinema's most enduring icons (she also appeared in a small role in David Fincher's underrated *The Game* in the same year).

Lost Highway (1997)
Dir: David Lynch /USA /France

Jazz musician, Fred Madison (Bill Pullman) receives sinister videotapes on his doorstep which were made by someone walking through his house at night with a camcorder recording him and his wife (Patricia Arquette) while they slept. After somehow killing his wife, but having no memory of it, he finds himself on death row and literally transforms into a different person whose life turns out to be even *more* nightmarish...

Lost Highway is one of the most puzzling pictures from the master of weird, David Lynch. If you're hoping for a straight forward narrative drive and an easy-to-digest plot then look elsewhere because this movie isn't for you. Instead, what we get is a deranged, psychogenic trip through the nightmarish world of the unconscious, a film completely lacking the traditional three-act structure, and which owes more to the surreal goings on of *Eraserhead* rather than the candy-coloured nightmares of *Wild at Heart* and *Blue Velvet*. Made four years after the director was subjected to an almighty critical drubbing when he was dragged through Tinseltown by his testicles and burned at the stake for delivering the wonderfully sublime *Twin Peaks: Fire Walk With Me*, *Lost Highway* shows all the signs of a scarred filmmaker who, nonetheless, showed absolutely no intentions of playing straight or conforming to critical demands or expectations.

Co-writer Barry Gifford (whose novel, '*Wild at Heart*', provided the basis for Lynch's earlier film) described *Lost Highway* as "a film about a man who finds himself in a dire situation and has a kind of panic attack which fractures him in some way." And that's about the closest you'll get to a comprehensive explanation of the film whose protagonist falls into a murky world of suspicion and death, and who inexplicably transforms into an entirely different person while trying to deal with his own murderous deeds. Lynch himself was even less forthcoming about explaining *Lost Highway*, but he did claim that the first third of the film came to him in a vision on the final day of shooting *Fire Walk With Me*. Following this, he also insisted that he was awoken in his home in the middle of the night by someone ringing his doorbell and informing him that "Dick Laurent is dead" on the intercom, a creepy and disturbing incident since Lynch didn't know anyone called Dick Laurent, and he had no idea who the person was who seemed so keen to bring him the news in the middle of the night. The vision and the Dick Laurent incident stewed in his mind over time and became connected when Lynch chanced upon a phrase in Gifford's novel *Night People*, 'lost highway'. He immediately began working on the screenplay with Gifford using that title and using those strange incidents which had haunted him for weeks as the starting point. Little wonder the end result turned out so weird.

The film opens on a POV shot of a car cruising on a dark highway with the headlights illuminating the space ahead, and David Bowie's sublime '*I'm Deranged*' playing over the top, its signature bass line complementing the mesmerizing opening. The narrative is structured like a maze; just as you're beginning to make some kind of sense of the thing, you suddenly hit a dead-end. New openings become apparent, and ghostly outlines of overall themes begin to emerge, but come to nothing when you reach yet more dead-ends, and you find yourself confronted by impossible situations, such as characters being in two separate places at the same time (the ugly vampiric Mystery Man who will only go where he is invited, and also Fred's own bilocation as he is somehow able to listen to himself speaking on the intercom in his home while he is also outside the door speaking into it), and characters changing physical bodies, becoming different people with their own traits and histories.

It seems Lynch had purposely constructed a film that is impossible to decipher. Actually, there *could* be an explanation for the film but it's so carefully concealed in a labyrinth of noir horror mystery that, just like *Eraserhead* before it, no one has adequately offered an entirely convincing interpretation. And in this sense, *Lost Highway* reminded me of Andrzej Zulawski's enigmatic masterpiece, *Possession* (1981), a film which also presents its audience with impossibilities (Isabelle Adjani's character is somehow impregnated by her 'offspring', a monster whom she hadn't even given birth to yet. Thus, she gives birth to the father who is also the baby who could not possibly have existed when he got mamma knocked up – wrap your head around *that*). *Possession* also seems to have been purposely constructed with tangible yet abstract themes and ideas, and both films are like cinematic equivalents of a Max Escher drawing; you may be able to follow the flights of stairs but only until they start running upside down, and you find yourself hopelessly lost. *Lost Highway* is best experienced as a dream-logic type of film, with the narrative suddenly shifting to different characters in different situations, becoming a whole *new* narrative that is only very loosely connected to the first. It's okay if you don't 'get it'. No one seems to get it. I've seen it about eight times and I still don't get it, but it doesn't matter. Just go along with it and enjoy the ride.

When *Lost Highway* opened in America, it provoked a similar hostile reaction as *Fire Walk With Me*, with mainstream critics taking an instant dislike to it. Actually, if truth be told, their reactions were probably based on them not 'getting it', and can be summed up in the following; 'We don't know what this film is saying, so therefore it *must* be bullshit'. Amusingly, the hostile reaction also seems to stem from them feeling somehow duped by the film, as if Lynch had somehow got one over on them, and they were determined to punish him for making them feel like bemused canines trying to follow a card trick. Lynch even took a quote from a particularly negative review by stuffy critics Siskel and Ebert ("Two thumbs down") and plastered their verdict on huge advertising billboards across the city as a perverse form of recommendation. The European critics were much more kind with their assessments, if no less confused. The film also received overwhelmingly positive reviews when it was previewed in Madrid. It was later discovered to have been accidentally screened with a couple of the reels in the wrong order, and this generated some fascinating interpretations of what the director had intended.

Affliction (1997)
Dir: Paul Schrader /USA
Wade Whitehouse is a small town traffic cop trying to gain custody of his daughter. He also bears the scars of being raised by a monstrous father. And after a visitor to the town dies in a hunting accident, Wade begins to piece together a murder conspiracy which seems to involve corruption in high places. But his attempts to get to grips with the mystery are thwarted by an incessant tooth-ache. Tensions reach boiling point after the death of his mother, when he and his girlfriend are forced to move back into his vicious father's house.

The brilliant Paul Schrader wrote and directed this icy gem that delves into the dark heart of masculinity. And with the film based on Russell Banks' novel, and with the much underrated Nick Nolte in the lead role, this tripple-whammy of talent only raised the question of why these three had never teamed up before (or since). The accumulation of abuse suffered over the years since birth is slowly transforming Wade into a monstrous mirror reflection of his drunken, wretched father. But the real tragedy is that Wade can foresee exactly what a monster he is becoming, and yet is helpless to do anything about it.

Sissy Speck is fairly subdued as Margie, Wade's waitress girlfriend, as is Willem Dafoe who plays the more thoughtful brother who was wise enough to escape the abusive household as soon as he could. James Coburn perhaps steals the show as Wade's father; a snarling wretch of a human being, whose near-constant caustic invective is as nasty as any villain in the movies.

The film disregards the delicate beauty of, say, Atom Agoyan's *The Sweet Hereafter* (1997) – based on another of Banks' novels – and seems to focus in on the corrosive and bitter undercurrents of the book.

Perdita Durango (1997)
(aka *Dance With The Devil*)
Dir: Alex de la Iglesia /Spain/Mexico
David Lynch was the first filmmaker to adapt the work of novelist Barry Gifford to the big screen in 1990 with *Wild at Heart*, a psychotic road movie which incurred the wrath of both the censors and critics. A few years later, and Gifford's work was once again at the centre of cinematic controversy when bad boy Spanish director, Alex de la Iglesia, adapted his follow-up novel, *59 Degrees and Raining: The Story of Perdita Durango*. The story centres on the gun-toting title character (who was played by Lynch's partner, Isabella Rosselini, in *Wild at Heart*). This time, the character is played by Latina beauty, Rosie Perez. Rising star Javier Bardem plays Durango's demonic lover, Romeo, and we're also treated to a supporting role by blues legend, Screamin' Jay Hawkins...

Iglesia's previous films, which include *Accion Mutante* and *Day of the Beast*, were still on the fringes of cult, but here was the opportunity for him to hit the big time. He had a Hollywood-sized budget, a Hollywood star in Perez, and a hot-property in writer Barry Gifford (who also helped out with the screenplay). Mainstream acceptability was his for the taking. However, when *Perdita Durango* hit the screens in the late 90s, that Tinseltown calling card went up in smoke. The result is a film which is sure to offend everyone at some point – Americans, moralists, the squeamish – as Iglesia's incendiary movie tackles such sensitive subjects as kidnap, rape, and murder in a fun, comic book mode of pitch black comedy. Unsurprisingly, Iglesia has never made a Hollywood movie to this day.

Whilst scaring away strait-laced men on the US/Mexican border, Perdita Durango teams up with charismatic criminal Romeo, and together they hit the road and indulge in occult ceremonies, wild sex, and rampant crime. Romeo talks her into human sacrifice, and they kidnap a teenage American couple whom they intend to offer up in a bloodletting. Meanwhile, Romeo is being pursued by a relentless DEA Agent Dumas (James Gandolfini) due to his connections with crime lord Santos (Don Stroud) who has him smuggling a truck load of fetuses across the border to be used in the black market of the American cosmetics industry. The chaos all comes to a head in the bright lights of Vegas for the final bloody showdown.

Perdita Durango is even more outrageous than Iglesia's previous films, and he seems to be enjoying himself misbehaving with his movie camrea. The cast is excellent, including Hawkins whose silly antics and bemused mumbling is genuinely funny. But it's Javier Bardem who steals the show as the free-spirited wanderer, Romeo, who makes a stunning transition from his previous roles as a lady magnet in *Jamon Jamon* and *Live Flesh*, becoming a lady magnet of a more dark and dangerous kind in *Perdita Durango*. Indeed, Bardem's rise to the Hollywood A-list over the subsequent years has been an interesting journey watching him do it his own way with roles in the Coen's excellent *No Country For Old Men* where he plays a relentless and amoral hitman (the lucky devil also married Penelope Cruz). Also on the casting front, look out for Heather Graham's sister, Aimee, as the pretty blonde hostage, and *Repo Man* helmer, Alex Cox, as agent Dumas' partner.

Perdita Durango took almost three years to reach American audiences due to a seemingly endless string of distribution hassles, legal tangles, and censorship. The film was cut to shreds for an R rating, dispensing with some potentially under-age nudity, and also violence. Added to this was the cutting of the climactic finale which sees Romeo's destiny merging with that of Burt Lancaster in *Vera Cruz*. Iglesia's crucial and innovative merging of the two films makes for a heroic and touching scene, but it was removed because of legal wranglings. The Americans also re-titled the film to *Dance With the Devil*. The film didn't fare much better in the UK where around 36 seconds of risque footage was dropped thanks to the BBFC. The cuts were mostly on the scenes where the kidnapped teens are deflowered by Perdita and Romeo, an experience of rape which the youngsters later appreciate as an ice-breaker for their own sexual relationship – a big no no as far as the British censors were concerned. The German DVD by Planet Media presents the full uncut version in a gorgeous anamorphic transfer.

Sick: The Life and Death of Bob Flanagan, Supermasochist (1997)
Dir: Kirby Dick /USA

Documentary on Bob Flanagan, the artist who learned to deal with the agony of cystic fibrosis by becoming a self-styled 'supermasochist'. He used suffering as the basis of his life and was involved in a sadomasochistic relationship. Flanagan famously appeared in the notorious NIN music video for *Broken* (1993) as the man in the torture chair having his genitals clawed by the metallic talons. But despite his good humour throughout *Sick*, this is a difficult film to watch. The final moments of his life were captured on camera and presented on screen, along with still photographs.

Rag and Bone (1997)
Dir: Robert Lieberman /USA

A supernatural TV movie based on a story by acclaimed horror author Anne Rice (*Interview With the Vampire*). It tells the story of a New Orleans cop, Dean Cain, who is puzzled by a mysterious ghostly figure that leads him to new clues in an unsolved murder case. Made as a pilot for an TV series, none of the networks picked it up, so it was re-packaged onto DVD and dumped in the bargain bins. As a stand alone film, it leaves a few loose ends but is worth a watch.

Jack Frost (1997)
Dir: Michael Cooney /USA

A serial killer escapes from a prison van only to be doused in liquid nitrogen following a crash with a truck loaded with the stuff. He is then transformed into a wise-cracking killer snowman and targets the arresting Sheriff's family. This is a lame-brained attempt at comedy horror which misses the target more often than not. After killing a man with an axe, the snowman quips "God, I only axed you for a smoke. Ha ha ha ha!" Other highlights include death by Christmas tree and the snowman raping a girl in a bathtub ("Looks like Christmas came a little early!").

The Devil's Advocate (1997)
Dir: Taylor Hackford /USA /Germany

This film tackles the evils of law practice as a hot-shot young lawyer, Kevin Lomax (Keanu Reeves), ups sticks from Florida when he is recruited to a big law firm in Manhattan. Al Pacino plays the boss of the firm, John Milton, an unscrupulous leech who takes Kevin under his wing as an aggressive protege. Of course, Kevin eventually comes to realise that Milton is in fact Satan himself, and his help is sought in bringing the Antichrist to the world. Kevin resists, owing to his Christian upbringing, and this leads Milton to deliver an impassioned speech about the unworthiness of God, and how Satan is the true advocate of humanity... *The Devil's Advocate* is a superb tale steeped in the Faustian tradition. Young Kevin is lured to the firm and pretty soon finds himself making moral compromises like defending a mass murderer in court. His wife becomes increasingly despondent as Kevin's publicity elevates his standing and plays up to his vanity. He thrives on the new-found success. In a particularly ugly scene, Kevin interrogates a victim of child abuse, putting the jury into reasonable doubt about her accusations. We see Kevin's corruption as the courtroom becomes a gaming arena where 'winning' becomes more important to him than justice. Milton presents his case against mankind – human beings are vile and vain creatures – and we're all guilty as charged. This film would sit nicely on a double-bill with Oliver Stone's *Wall Street* (1987), which tackles similar themes but from the greed and egos of the New York Stock Exchange.

The Brave (1997)
Dir: Johnny Depp /USA
Produced, directed, co-scripted and starring Johnny Depp, *The Brave* centres on Raphael (Depp), a native-American recently released from prison. He accepts a large payment of up-front cash in order to be tortured and killed by underground smut dealers in a snuff movie. Raphael hopes to treat his family and get them out of the shanty town where they live. But he only has a short amount of time before he must step up to meet his dreadful fate. This is a competently made, well acted drama, but the film's central premise is not altogether convincing; Raphael never once even considers the possibility of doing a runner with the money – he accepts everything that will happen to him, no questions asked. The snuff theme hangs over the film like a dark cloud, but nothing is explicitly shown. Depp refused to release the film in America as he was infuriated by the way the critics had savaged it after its screening at Cannes. But, to be fair, the American criticisms aren't entirely unfounded; the film has a sickly

sweet romanticized view of shanty town life; everyone in the community is lovely! They have regular get-togethers and barbecues! In reality, shanty towns are full of druggies and dealers and gang-bangers and other criminal scumbags. The film has a very old-fashioned, rose-tinted view of the poor, like some 19th Century communist pamphlet, and was directed by a man who has clearly never known hardship in his life.

Of Freaks and Men (1998)
Dir: Alexei Balabanov /Russia
Of Freaks and Men tells the tale of immigrant worker, Johan (Sergei Makovetskii), who deals in slap and tickle photographs to the denizens of St. Petersburg in the early 20th Century. After a local engineer dies of a heart attack, Johan worms his way into the life of the wealthy daughter and coerces her into modelling for him in some spank-happy movies as the cinematograph has overtaken the photograph. Meanwhile, Johan's creepy friend, Victor (Victor Ivanovich), has managed to sleaze his way into the home of a blind widow and taken some lurid snapshots of the widow's adopted siamese twins. Pretty soon both respectable households begin to disintegrate.

Having caused a bit of a scandal in his native Russia with his gangster film, *Brother*, which was criticised for its moral ambiguity towards the criminal underworld, Alexei Balabanov's follow-up, *Of Freaks and Men*, takes a stunning detour to a no less controversial reception. With its combination of perverse subject-matter (including early pornography, sex with siamese twins, and general sleazy behaviour), a healthy literary vibe, and a murky sepia tone, Balabanov's film is Dostoevskian in its breadth, and serves as a pastiche of primitive cinema and as a critique on Russia's capitalist drive since the collapse of the Soviet state.

Banned in Ireland and generally treated cautiously elsewhere, *Of Freaks and Men* is a grim black comedy which nonetheless borrows aesthetically from Peter Greenaway's perfected artifice and parallels with David Lynch's *The Elephant Man* in the siamese twins story, making for a strange but genuinely original film.

La classe de neige (1998)
(aka *Class Trip*)
Dir: Claude Miller /France
A nervous child is driven to his school skiing

trip by his father. Having been raised from a young age on terrifying stories about marauding gangs of organ thieves, ten year old Nicolas (Clement van den Bergh) seems prematurely aware of the hidden dangers of life, and finds himself trying to deal with his anxieties through a series of disturbing and often violent fantasies. Meanwhile, a youngster has gone missing on the trip, and Nicolas' father may have something to do with it...

La classe de neige is a chilling tale based on Emmanuel Carrere's best-selling novel (itself based on a true story), and went on to win the Jury Prize at Cannes. The film is chock-full of stunning performances from the youngsters whose youthful faces nevertheless provide an inner-maturity and nuance which far exceeds their years. Director Claude Miller, who was a protege to Francois Truffault for many years, is best remembered in the English-speaking world for his 80s thriller, *Garde a vue* (which was remade in Hollywood as *Under Suspicion*), lends a cold eye to the chilly proceedings, and flits around the dark heart of children's fairytales like *Hansel and Gretel*, *Sleeping Beauty*, and *The Little Mermaid*, and updates those allegories to an unnerving effect. Indeed, he even treats us to a re-telling of W.W. Jacob's classic horror story, *The Monkey's Paw*, in a particularly bloody and gruesome fantasy sequence.

American filmmaker Larry Fessenden would later try his own hand at depicting the disturbing daydreams of traumatized youth in his underrated *Wendigo*, which also borrows the ice-cold look of Miller's film. Often compared with Neil Jordon's *The Butcher Boy* and Atom Egoyan's *The Sweet Hereafter*, *La classe de neige* is a grim but subtle fairytale shocker which has its roots in that most unacceptable of modern taboos. It's a film where childhood is anything but sweet.

Your Friends & Neighbors (1998)
Dir: Neil LaBute /USA

The day to day intertwining lives of a group of self-obsessed, sexually dysfunctional piss-cranes – Mary and Barry, an unhappily married couple; Jerry and Terri, an unhappily *un*married couple who stay together out of convenience; Cheri, who is Terri's lesbian lover and Cary, Barry's best friend, who is a reckless, demented hedonist.

During the 90s, a cultural trend appeared in which millions of young couples across the planet began fantasizing about the perfect glossy world as seen in the American sitcom, *Friends*. This fantasy soon became a certified industry in itself that seduced the public with pristine images of this sweet domestic bliss. But writer/director Neil LaBute, creator of the controversial *In the Company of Men*, presents us with the dark side of the myth with a vicious, low-budget comedy which does much to show how things really are when couples get together for any length of time.

The basic premise is the same as *Friends*: six good-looking chums share their secrets and desires within their bubble of cute middle-class coziness. The secrets in this film, however, are a tad more disturbing. There's Jerry and Terri (Ben Stiller and Catherine Keener) whose relationship is under strain from Jerry's incessant babbling during sex. There's Barry and Mary (Aaron Eckhart and Amy Brenneman) whose marriage is under threat due to her frigidity and his constant wanking. And there's Cary (Jason Patrick), who is possibly the most malicious lover in film history. Also Nastassja Kinski (daughter of Klaus) as a clingy lesbian who demands to know exactly when her bed partner has an orgasm.

The drama takes place in all the usual places: bookstores, art galleries, supermarkets, bistros – even their own version of the 'Central Perks' coffee shop. The major difference, however, is in LaBute's brutal script which pulls no punches. It's one of the harshest and most hilarious movies of the 90s. It can be slow-moving for sure with its minimal camera movements, long talky sequences and only a hint of a soundtrack. Yet there are moments of such gut-wrenching honesty that even the most blissfully happy couples will feel uncomfortable and unnerved during the running time. It's sexual warfare with deceit and infidelity used as the weapons of choice, and the humour is sharpened to perfection, designed to strike you where it hurts.

The War Zone (1998)
Dir: Tim Roth /UK /Italy

Tim Roth's depressing film is about a teenage boy who learns that his father is having an incestuous relationship with his sister. This is a downbeat – and very British – kitchen sink bore-fest. Described in the *Guardian* as "a soft-core child abuse drama reeking of good intentions and middle brow arthouse good taste." The difficult theme of child abuse is rendered more palatable to viewers by giving it a heartfelt, family-friendly sheen. Jesus Christ, what next? Rick Moranis in *Honey, I Brown-Dicked the Kids*?

Beast Cops (1998)

(Orig title: *Ye shou xing jing*)

Dir: Dante Lam & Gordon Chan /Hong Kong

Winner of Best Film at the Hong Kong Film Awards in 1999, *Beast Cops* stars Anthony Wong as a detective who is teamed up with Michael Fitzgerald Wong (no relation), and becomes entangled with girls and gangsters when a triad boss heads out of town. It's basically a routine cop actioner with the added bonus of an extremely violent finale with the use of guns, swords and meat cleavers, which earned the film a CAT III rating in its native land. The wardrobe department had a field day dressing Anthony Wong in an assortment of suede jackets, black shades and white turtle necks, making him look like he has just stepped out of a 70s crime thriller. It's only toward the end of the film when things take on a traditional CAT III flavour; Wong's character has no intentions of getting out alive when he enters the triad's hideout for revenge; but he sure is hard to kill – even with knives protruding from his neck and torso, Wong picks up a machete and stalks the corridors of the building, hacking and slashing the scumbags to death while bleeding heavily from his mortal wounds.

Happiness (1998)

Dir: Todd Solondz /USA

Three sisters in New Jersey struggle to deal with dysfunctional relationships of different kinds. Cynical and pessimistic to the extreme, this is an excrutiatingly funny tapestry of unfulfilled lives which confirmed the promise of Solondz's earlier *Welcome to the Dollhouse*. The film's most disturbing and superbly subversive thread centres on the angst of a suburban paedophile; the scene where he attempts to dose a young boy with a sedative in his food so that he can sexually abuse the boy is Hitchcockian in the most subversive and perverse sense of the word, in that he somehow manipulates the conventions of the movie thriller and sets up a 'will he/won't he' scenario in which the audience is gripped on the 'excitement' of seeing weather the paedophile can have his wicked way with the kid or not. It's a masterclass in viewer manipulation and a way of thumbing its nose at the audience. Solondz utilises tricks that filmmakers often use in thrillers, and uses them to create an appalling sequence that plays against the viewer's own morality, and demonstrates how mainstream cinematic techniques are often used simply as a way of controlling the viewers like puppets and dictating how they should feel. *Happiness* is also relentless in its insistence that sex ultimately destroys us. A masterpiece.

Sombre (1998)

Dir: Phillip Grandieaux /France

If you're looking for some big screen sleaze in the manner of William Lustig's *Maniac*, built on thrills, spills, and spectacular human suffering, then I'd advise you to look elsewhere because in *Sombre*, director Grandieaux simply refuses to play that game. Instead we're offered almost two hours of character study of a man (Marc Barbe who looks a bit like Mark E. Smith) whose mad urges to kill are shattered by his own tortured sense of guilt and fractured state of mind. Similar to *Henry-Portrait of a Serial Killer* in mood and in the way most of the murders are off-screen, this is a bleak and harrowing film where the desolate surroundings seem to reflect the killer's mind. His emotional baggage and traumatic, mysterious past have led Jean to the killing and disposing of prostitutes. It's dull and pretentious in places and is more likely to make an audience feel depressed rather than excited. The killer himself is a shell of a man, a useless waste of space, and it's a credit to the filmmakers that he didn't become some overly sympathetic 'tragic figure'. That's not to say that *Sombre* is easy going; some viewers no doubt will find it too much to take.

The killer becomes friendly with a girl called Claire, despite the fact that he has attempted to kill her sister, and she tags along with him on his murder spree. A mutual dependency seems to bond the pair based on Jean's 'seeing the light' in Claire's innocence, and Claire seeing Jean as a person in need, a man whom she can attempt to save. *Sombre* has caused much scandal with critics over the years because in Claire's character there seems to be a part of her that yearns to be a victim herself. But director Grandieux refuses to confirm or deny this idea. He also chooses to avoid a traditional back-story to explain the roots of Jean's sickness; indeed he seems to refuse the whole idea of psychology altogether in his film, and it's left very much up to the viewers to work out what's going on in the heads of these tragic characters. Faces are often blank and expressionless, the dialogue is kept to a minimum, and all physicalities are limited to the basic human functions of consumption, sex, and violence. In this respect, Grandieux as an artist is treading similar territory as people like Wyndham Lewis and Bret Easton Ellis, both of whom view the world and its people in terms of exteriors and surfaces, language and body language, and the disinclination to delve directly into the workings of the mind. And Grandieux's lack of emotion in his portrayal of moral decay perhaps stems from an outraged morality (as it does with Bret Easton Ellis), a feeling of despair in a world full of numbness where the only way to truly experience anything is by way of murder and death itself.

The Blair Witch Project (1998)
Dir: Daniel Myrick and Eduardo Sanchez /USA
Ah, *The Blair Witch Project*; loved by some, loathed by many. Everyone seems to have an opinion on this low-budget classic, whether it be a triumph of student film-making and a master class in internet promotion, or a crappy amateur waste of time. But one thing's for sure: Whether they admit it or not, everyone was rattled by this film when it first hit the screens. Clark Collis of *Empire* magazine said it best, "*The Blair Witch Project* is one of those movies where ignorance is bliss – or, to be more accurate, terror." So if you haven't yet seen it or heard about its 'urban legend', then along with asking where you've been for the last 20 years, I suggest you drop this book and give it a look without reading any further.

In October 1994, three young student filmmakers spent a few days making a documentary about a local urban legend known as the Blair Witch. They gathered a digital video camera, a 16mm camera, and supplies, and then headed deep into the woods with the hope of finding a story. But they never came back. And nobody ever saw them again. The footage they had shot was later found and sold to a company called Haxan films, who edited the footage together into a 90 minute documentary called *The Blair Witch Project* which showed the full horror of their dreadful journey. And when that film was released into theatres it scared the crap out of the entire film-going world.

The above synopsis was how the film was sold, but none of it was true. The real story goes something like this: Three young actors *pretending* to be filmmakers were given some recording equipment and sent out into the woods for eight days. The real filmmakers were Daniel Myrick and Eduardo Sanchez who used satellite tracking devices to chase the actors around at night, and leaving strange rock formations and wicker artefacts in strategic places, and playing audio cassettes with the sounds of weeping children. The actors weren't really lost, but they had no idea what would happen next, or when. And crucially, for much of the time they really were afraid.

Myrick and Sanchez were a pair of Florida Film School graduates who made *The Blair Witch Project* for around $35,000 and used the internet to find an audience. They promoted their film with The Blair Witch web site which treated the whole story as fact. As word spread, more websites began springing up, made by people who had bought into the myth. With no money to promote the film in a traditional way, Myrick and Sanchez had effectively exploited the web and word continued to spread. They even listed their actors as "Missing, presumed dead" on the Internet Movie Database (a nice trick borrowed from *Snuff* (1976) which also attempted a mondo-style realism by not including any end credits). Pretty soon, people were starting to appear at the woods in Birkitzville, Maryland, to search for the 'missing' filmmakers, but the publicity campaign wasn't finished yet. Next, Myrick and Sanchez turned their attentions to television, and produced a couple of short documentaries, '*The Curse of the Blair Witch*' and '*The Birkitzville 7*', which reported on the search and even added some back-story to the myth, and these were both broadcast on TV as straight up journalism, apparently. This ingenious method of promotion was nothing more than a series of publicity stunts. But it worked. And when distribution company Artisan announced that they were going to release the film into theatres, the punters were queuing around the block.

The Blair Witch Project earned just short of $150 million in the States alone, and with its meagre budget makes it the most financially profitable movie ever made. I first saw the film in November 1999 and it was the first and only time I had witnessed mass screaming amongst a cinema audience, where fans of the nudge-nudge-wink school of bogus cool self-referential crap like *Scream* had no idea what was real and what wasn't. And some of them were genuinely terrified. Ah, bliss!

Freeway 2: Confessions of a Trickbaby (1998)
Dir: Mathew Bright /USA/Canada

Easily one of the most disturbing films of the 90s, this sequel to Matthew Bright's cult classic, *Freeway*, was universally despised by critics on its release and was also equally detested by fans of the first film. With not a single redeeming factor among the characters, and not a single ray of light or shred of decency anywhere to be found here, *Confessions of a Trickbaby* can only be recommended to those cinema miscreants who really have no limits to their debased entertainments and pitch-black cynical humour.

Whereas the first film took *Little Red Riding Hood* and turned it into a trashy piece of satire, here writer/director Matthew Bright focuses on *Hansel and Gretel* and doesn't hold back in twisting and subverting the subtext with unprecedented levels of mischief and shock tactics. The plot follows another teenage delinquent, Crystal (Natasha Lyonne), who pretends to be a prostitute so that she can lure unsuspecting johns into deserted alleys where she then beats and robs them. She ends up in prison with the dangerous Cyclona (Maria Celedonio), a psychotic lesbian convicted of murdering her entire family, and together they hatch an escape plan, and pretty soon they're back on the loose in society. Crystal, or "White girl", comes to realise just how insane Cyclona is when everyone they meet winds up being killed due to the voices in her head that compel her to murder. And her pathetically lame excuses for the murders ("He tried to rape me!") do nothing to reassure Crystal. So, leading a path of death and destruction behind them, the two girls head south for Mexico where Cyclona knows they can get help from her childhood custodian, Sister Gomez (Vincent Gallo).

This slimy cesspool of a movie throws in enough mayhem and taboos to fill ten unsavoury films, with subject-matter ranging from drug abuse, insanity, transvestite nuns, and bulimia, to incest, necrophilia, and child abuse. It's hard to think of another film which presents such an array of grotesque and deeply unpleasant subjects, except maybe *Emanuelle In America* or *Caligula*. And the characters are equally unappealing with the nutcase Cyclona killing an elderly couple and then making out with their corpses, or Crystal, who seems to be there just so that the director can subvert and mock the traditions of the 'leading lady', with his 'heroine' constantly and amusingly taking the moral high-ground in dealing with Cyclona, whilst at the same time indulging in her own wrong-headed behaviour. And Sister Gomez, the creepy and softly spoken parental figure who turns out to be an evil child butcherer who runs an empire in gruesome kiddie porn. Even the small details are surreal and disturbing, such as the scene where the girls leave a trail of crack cocaine on the ground and a pair of black guys dressed in tatty old suits with feathers in their hats appear from nowhere to pick up the wraps like pigeons pecking at scraps of bread. But these Lynchian moments did little to earn the film any respectability. And yes, John Landis did make a cameo as the judge.

For all the film's gloom and unpleasantness, there are at least a few people out there who appreciated this awful spectacle (and yes, I'm one of 'em), and Matthew Bright wasn't finished yet with his experiments in cinematic shocks. His next film took him away from the twisted re-telling of classic fairytales and into the bleak biographical details of a real life serial killer whose horrendous crimes and suave charisma were explored in comedic fashion for the utterly distasteful *Ted Bundy* (2002).

Tumbling Doll of Flesh (1998)
(aka *Psycho: The Snuff Reels*; Orig title: *Niku Daruma*)
Dir: Tamakichi Anaru /Japan

Plain old crappy AV amateur time... A young woman agrees to do some porn sessions. In the first session she has one on one sex with a guy. The sex is explicit and unsimulated, but suffers from pixelation blurs of Japanese censorship (even pubic hair is forbidden to Japanese viewers). The scene goes well and afterwards they have dinner. In the second session things get a little rougher; she is tied up, and a couple of guys use dildos and vibrators on her, and someone else pours candle wax onto her arse and lower back (pretty sensitive areas, no?). Again, none of this is simulated. When it's all over, she makes her excuses to leave, but while she's putting on her shoes, one of the guys creeps up behind her and bops her on the head with a baseball bat, knocking her out. She wakes up tied to a bed, and here we have the third session (or 'snuff' session); she is tortured and killed on camera. End of story... None of the 'special effects' are even remotely convincing, this makes the *Guinea Pig* movies look like glossy Hollywood productions. Not good.

The Idiots (1998)
(Orig title: *Idioterne*)
Director not credited [Lars Von Trier]
/Denmark

These are the ten rules of Dogme films:

1. Shooting must be done on location. (No sets, no props)
2. Sounds must never be produced. (No music)
3. The camera must always be handheld.
4. The film must be in colour. Special lighting is not acceptable.
5. Optical work and filters are forbidden.
6. The film must not contain any superficial action. (Violence and sex, etc, must be for real)
7. Temporal and geographical alienation are forbidden. (The film must take place in the here and now)
8. Genre films are not acceptable.
9. The film format must Academy 35mm.
10. The director must never be credited.

After the international success of *Breaking the Waves*, writer/director Lars Von Trier could have headed off abroad and made a big-budget Hollywood blockbuster. But that has never been his style (not to mention his intense fear of flying), and instead he stayed in Denmark and decided on a low-budget and largely improvised project that resembles a fly-on-the-wall documentary. It was made in accordance with the Dogme 95 'Vow of chastity', a set of rules which severely limit the filmmaker's creativity. The result is a film that is at once shocking, offensive, darkly hilarious, and altogether quite extraordinary.

The Idiots follows a group of middle class drop-outs who pretend to be mentally handicapped. Living together in a commune-like mansion, they improvise drooling, belching, and urinating on day trips as a way of causing disruption in public places. They refer to their antics as "spazzing" and do all they can to test the patience of the upper middle class. As a potent mixture of anti-bourgeois protest, performance art, and group therapy, their true purpose is never really made clear.

This strange bunch are joined by the unhappy Karen (Bodil Jorgensen) who meets them during a "spaz attack" in a plush restaurant. Karen's background remains a mystery until the end of the film when she takes the group back to her dad's house for one of the most uncomfortable dinner party scenes you'll ever see. But in the meantime, Karen begins to try and fathom the group's leader, Stoffer (Jens Albinus), and serves as a tender surrogate for the more soft-hearted viewer.

The plot synopsis sounds incredibly silly, but according to press interviews, that was what Von Trier intended, to experiment with ideas that are both "philosophically and artistically radical", and simultaneously "disastrously silly, malicious, foolish, and meaningless". And though the film has received a high number of high-profile critical plaudits over the years, it's difficult not to conclude that Von Trier was perhaps up to his old trickster games once again. Claiming to have been depressed during the conception of *Antichrist*, and publicly claiming to be a Nazi whilst promoting *Melancholia*, it's hard to take anything he says seriously anymore. In other words, it's entirely up to you to decide how seriously you take this film.

In his 'Dogme director confessionate test' Von Trier admitted to breaking some of the Dogme rules by altering a light source, feeding the actors, hiring a car, and having someone play harmonica music on set. Most famously, he also admitted to hiring a porn actor for the notorious orgy scene. It was this latter element which could have caused problems with the BBFC, but despite the graphic nature of an ejaculating hardon, the film joined Catherine Briellat's *Romance* and Patrice Chereau's *Intimacy* as the latest in a line of sexually explicit films to be passed uncut by the Board for both cinema and home video.

The Idiots premiered at Cannes in 1998 and generally had a warm reception. But not everyone was impressed; Mark Kermode was famously thrown out of the theatre for shouting "Il est merde!" at the screen in bad French. No doubt the film will cause anger and upset for a lot of people, but it also boasts some incredibly powerful scenes; the sequence at the dinner table at the end filled me with a mixture of conflicting emotions I had never felt before anywhere, whether watching a movie or in everyday life, and for that reason alone it gets a thumbs up from me.

Overall though, *The Idiots* leaves us with more questions than answers; it's unclear whether Karen's character represents Von Trier himself, and it's equally unclear where this film stands in relation to the rest of his filmography; the anti-individualist demands of the Dogme 95 Manifesto seem to be at odds with his own artistic notions. And if Von Trier's film stands as a critique on the conformity of collective thinking and its inevitable encroaching on the individual, then what are we to make of Dogme 95?

Von Trier later abandoned the Dogme rules, "The more fashionable it has become, also the more boring," he claimed. "When we originally discussed the vow of chastity, we had no ambitions to change the world, like, for instance, the French *nouvelle vague*. But if in 25 years some film students accidentally excavate the manifesto and find the ten rules interesting, we will obviously be happy, but it was not our initial purpose."

Seul contre tous (1998)
(aka *I Stand Alone*)
Dir: Gaspar Noe /France

This savage foray into extreme cinema is a classic of confrontation and controversy which won the 1998 Critics Prize at the Cannes Film Festival before going on to incite the wrath of audiences and censors across the globe. *Seul contre tous* (which translates literally as 'alone against all') was an accidental feature debut for writer/director Gaspar Noe. Having already introduced us to Phillipe Nahon's existential butcher in his previous short film, *Carne*, Noe had originally intended to make a 40 minute sequel which would play on a double-bill with the original short, but due to Noe's frustrations at being unable to raise the necessary funding, *Seul contre tous* as a project kept growing in parallel to his increasing anger, and the film gradually mutated into a monstrous feature that could indeed stand alone.

Upon his release from prison for killing a man mistakenly thought to be molesting his severely autistic daughter (as seen in Noe's short, *Carne*), Jean Chevalier settles in Lille. With him is his pregnant mistress who has promised to find new shop premises to allow him to practice his trade as a butcher of horse meat. For some reason she eventually decides against the investment,

forcing him to take a job as a hospital night watchman. Enraged, he repeatedly beats her hoping to abort their baby, makes off with her gun, and then hitchhikes to Paris. In desperation, he rents a room in a grubby hotel and goes out looking for work. After feeling humiliated and refused work in an abattoir, and wandering the streets with a desire to kill, Jean has an epiphany: He will find his daughter, bring her back to the hotel room, and use their incestuous love to stand firm against the cruel world.

Rarely since Scorsese's *Taxi Driver* has such a hopeless, misanthropic view of the world been so clearly articulated; that, even more than the film's graphic violence, is what makes it so disturbing. With his intensely bulging eyes and three bullets in his gun, the butcher wanders the streets; his breathless, relentless monologue returning repeatedly to his favourite themes: We live and die alone; morality is an invention of the rich; there's no purpose to life beyond sex and death; nobody in this selfish world loves anybody else. Between Nahon's superb pressure-cooker performance and Noe's assaultive directorial style (he's fond of brooding long takes interrupted by startling gun blasts of lurching, skip-frame edits and bold inter-titles), the film would be an unbearable expression of rage, except that Noe's winking, almost absurd sense of humour offers a disconcerting reminder that this is 'only a movie'.

The filmic reference points for *Seul contre tous* are as varied as they are bizarre. According to Noe himself, the inspiration for the vile voice-over came from Gerald Kargl's Austrian shocker, *Angst*. The ironic inter-titles (one of which informs audiences they have thirty seconds to leave the cinema before a particular graphic and gruelling murder scene) looks like a direct homage to William Castle's *Homicidal*. Noe claims to have never actually seen Castle's film but had heard about its intriguing 'Fright Break' gimmick. The allusions to Scorsese's *Taxi Driver* have been identified by many critics as being the central reference point, and this comes to a head during the butcher's visit to a porno cinema where he muses on his belief that there is nothing to life but sex and death.

The British censors clearly took Noe's film seriously, but the problem with the porn cinema scene is that it contains sustained images of hardcore sex, the same type that were being regularly prosecuted under sections 2 and 3 of the Obscene Publications Act. Scenes of explicit intercourse had been okayed in previous films like *Ai no corrida* and *The Idiots*, but the sex scenes in those films were much more fleeting than in Noe's. The BBFC insisted there was no way they could pass the film uncut. Instead, the distributors agreed to cover the offending penetration shots with digital pixelations (as is customary in Japanese sex films where even pubic hair is forbidden on screen). According to the censors, this optical blur "reduced the pornographic explicitness to an acceptable level whilst retaining a reasonable sense of what the director had intended." Now, this may all sound well and good but it's hard not to conclude that it is exactly what the director had intended that caused all the problems in the first place! With that scene, Noe effectively shows human bodies being joined together in sex whilst a human soul tears itself apart in despair. And it's this idea that the BBFC was uncomfortable with, because as the film constantly informs us, we are born alone, we live alone, and we die alone.

Some will be put off by the flashy technique, and others will take offence at the stream of consciousness monologues presenting the bitter thoughts of a twisted sociopath, a man whose notions of morality and justice have been pieced together by frustration and poverty. But this film will demand you stick with it no matter what your response.

Sitcom (1998)
Dir: Francois Ozon /France
Sitcom was Francois Ozon's debut feature, a scathing assault on the bourgeoisie of the middle class and the politeness of televisual farce, which has been called everything from "a page ripped from the Luis Bunuel handbook of bourgeois contempt" to "a *Hotel New Hampshire* of the 90s." Both of which were meant – I think – in the nicest possible sense!

The starting point of Ozon's film is the typically safe, sitcom-style setting. A middle class family with a fussy mum, stuffy dad, edgy kids, and a slightly naughty maid, are all thrown together in a gilded human cage whose doorbell goes 'ding-dong' every few minutes to allow some new character into the wacky house. In this week's episode, dad brings home from work a magic lab rat with hilarious results... Except, of course, that in Ozon's world the results are often less rib-tickling than jaw-dropping. No sooner have the family got their hands on this cute rodent when their darkest desires are being unleashed, resulting in homosexual orgies, attempted suicide, incest, sadomasochism, and murder. And as this nuclear family heads closer to meltdown, that pesky doorbell just keeps on ringing...

How you react to Ozon's bizarre blend of bland comic format and outrageous subject-matter is up to you. To some, Ozon is a class warrior intent on tearing out the hearts of the bourgeoisie and stuffing them down their well-bred throats, and to others he's a sexual liberationist, a pioneer of new gay cinema who was once labelled as "a young homo who seems to have been spoon-fed on queerness to the extent that he is simply coughing it up again in his works." Personally, I don't think either of those descriptions entirely fit; one of the real joys of Ozon's early work is that it's extremely hard to categorise, and much of the pleasure in watching comes from not knowing quite where his off-beat vision is going to take us next. You're never in safe hands with Ozon, and you can never relax.

His short films – including the masterful *Regarde le mer* – indicated a vibrant imagination at work. And *Sitcom* confirms his early promise as it gives free rein to his feverish vision, best seen in the character's descent into sexual perversity, and the bizarre figures sharing their world. Ozon's inspirations are easy to spot (Luis Bunuel and John Waters fare big), but there's enough visual and thematic flair here to make the film unique. Audiences and critics agreed, awarding *Sitcom* two European festival prizes for Best Film at the Sitges and Namur festivals.

Without giving away the insane ending, I think it's safe to say that this is a film which divides audiences; you'll either love it or hate it. And chances are you won't be able to decide until the end credits roll.

Romance (1998)
(aka *Romance X*)
Dir: Catherine Breillat /France
Frustrated by her boyfriend's disinterest in having sex with her, a school teacher embarks on series of affairs, including an excursion into sadomasochism. The scenes of explicit sexuality caused much controversy at the time of its release, especially the hardcore shots featuring the well-endowed adult film star, Rocco Siffredi. However, at its core, *Romance* is

actually a very typical French film of its time in that a woman's quest for sexual freedom causes her to be abused by men. The biggest problem with the film is that it's ultimately boring, as Kenneth Turan of the *Los Angeles Times* put it, "who could have imagined that sex on screen could be so unbearably dull?"

The Spiral (1998)
(aka *Ringu: Anthology of Terror*; aka *Ring 4: The Spiral*; Orig title: *Rasen*)
Dir: Joji Iida /Japan
Released on DVD in the UK during a slew of Japanese weirdies being churned out at the time (*Hiruko the Goblin*, *Princess Blade*, *Uzumaki*, etc), *The Spiral* shouldn't be confused with *Uzumaki* (which translates as 'spiral'). It's a confusing sequel to Hideo Nakata's *Ringu* which is just as silly and over-the-top as *Exorcist II: The Heretic*. After the mysterious death of a friend, a young pathologist comes across the cursed video tape haunted by the child ghost, Sadako. The film proved so unpopular in Japan that the production company made *Ringu 2* in order to erase it from memory. Dull, sprawling and lethargic rather than terrifying, *The Spiral* was later re-released on DVD under the title *Ring 4: The Spiral*, implying that it was a distant cash-in rather than the direct sequel, which it originally was.

Phantoms (1998)
Dir: Joe Chappelle /USA
A mid-budget monster horror based on a story by Dean Koontz (who also wrote the script). The small community of Snowfield, Colorado, has disappeared off the face of the earth. Who, or what, is responsible? A group of good-looking youngsters show up to investigate, and soon learn that a disgusting underground monster from the beginning of time could be responsible. Delivering its fair share of spooky atmospherics and a talented cast – which includes Peter O'Toole, Ben Affleck and Rose McGowan – fans of *The X-Files* will lap it up.

Gods and Monsters (1998)
Dir: Bill Condon /USA
An elegiac meditation on the final days of legendary horror director James Whale (*Frankenstein*, *The Invisible Man*, *The Old Dark House*, *The Bride of Frankenstein*), who was found dead in his Hollywood swimming pool in 1957 under mysterious circumstances.

The ailing director looks back on his life while attempting to seduce one of his gardeners. The material is sometimes quite thin, but the film offers up Oscar nominated performances from Ian Mckellen and Lynn Redgrave. It has its moments, but after watching I couldn't help feeling that Whale's memory had been shat on by the filmmakers. His character is portrayed as though he had a sick desperation about him in the way he would pester the young men around him. It left me feeling annoyed that such liberties were taken with this fiction. I even found myself agreeing with Alexander Walker of the *London Evening Standard* who commented, "I dare say some people will find it all touchingly affectionate, but to me it's posthumous libelling of James Whale, without a shred of evidence for most of its fictions. It proves that death is not the last thing one has to fear."

Muzan-E (1999)
(Muzan-E: *AV gyru satsujin bideo wa sansai shita!*)
Dir: Daisuke Yamanouchi /Japan
A lady reporter investigates snuff films, and her journey leads to the web where we are bombarded with disgusting images of fetish porn involving menstruation. She interviews a bunch of perverted porn peddlers, and we're shown more clips of brutal and violent sex tapes (with the obligatory 'digital blurs' which conceal the offending pubic hair as is customary in Japan – heaven forbid the Japanese seeing a muff on screen). A young woman is kidnapped, abused, and humiliated on camera before a caption appears on screen warning us about some forthcoming nastiness (perhaps influenced by Gaspar Noe's *Seul contre tous*), and then the girl is disembowelled with a machete. And in a scene indebted to *Evil Dead Trap*, the lady reporter tracks down the location of the snuff tape by recognising a brief glimpse of a building in the background on the tape. But when they arrive at the location, she is captured while her film crew are butchered on the spot. She then finds herself tied to a chair in her own snuff movie hell, but there are a couple of odd surprises at the end...

Shot on video for the booming AV market in Japan, *Muzan-E* has never seen an official release outside of its native country and is almost impossible to find without resorting to downloading it off the web (which seems rather apt in this case). Following on from the *Guinea Pig* tradition, this type of mock-documentary style horror runs just over an hour and was an obvious influence on Mariano Peralto's *Snuff 102*. *Muzan-E*, for all its disgusting and lurid details deserves credit for trying to do something different with the 'oh so serious' type of pseudo-snuff garbage by throwing us a curveball ending and playing like a postmodern, self-referential entry in the *Guinea Pig* series, and at least remains much more engaging than amateur crap-fests like *Tumbling Doll of Flesh*.

Progeny (1999)
Dir: Brian Yuzna /USA

A psychologically unstable doctor is shocked when his wife falls pregnant with a slimy red creature. After all, his sperm count was so low it could barely pass for cabbage water. Turns out that space aliens have been humping the missus, inseminating her, and hubby must perform an emergency caesarean section to get the little fucker out. *Progeny* contains lots of lurid gyenocological details, an attempted DIY abortion with a coat hanger, and Brad Dourif as a writer of the paranormal and alien abductions. But sadly, the talents of the usually great special effects artist, Screaming Mad George, are underused here. This is perhaps Brian Yuzna's most serious attempt at a horror film. The ending, set in a locked operating room, is particularly horrific.

Dead or Alive (1999)
(Orig title: *Hanzaisha*)
Dir: Takashi Miike /Japan

Tagline: "Warning: This motion picture contains explicit portrayals of violence; sex; violent sex; sexual violence; clowns and violent scenes of violent excess, which are definitely not suitable for all audiences."

Takashi Miike is in typically outrageous form with *Dead Or Alive*. It's a basic cop vs. crims scenario but Miike, in his own way, manages to keep things fresh and exciting. Ryuichi (Takeuchi Riki) leads a small gang of outcasts who, because of their Chinese heritage, have no place in either the yakuza or triads, and so they wage a street war against both. Detective Jojima (Aikawa Sho) is on their heels, but he also has some personal problems to deal with. His wife is having an affair, and he cannot afford to pay for a life-saving operation for his dying daughter. He urgently needs 20 million yen, and his allegiance to the law is seemingly swept aside...

Dead Or Alive is a nice slice of cinematic excess which kicks off with an incredible opening sequence montage; a naked woman falls from a high-rise building clutching a bag of cocaine; also strippers, bloody shootings, gay sex, throat stabbings, arterial spray, freaks, gangsters, clowns, and a man snorting what must be the world's longest line of coke. The film is also typical of Miike's fast and makeshift shooting style with a very loose and improvised feel. Those who are only familiar with Miike's *Audition* will be surprised by how chaotic and undisciplined this film is, as *Audition* was so much more tightly constructed. However, if you enjoyed *Gozu* and *Ichi the Killer* then chances are you'll find much to savour here too.

The story of how the film came into being is an interesting one. Miike was approached by money-hungry film producers who offered him two male lead actors and a basic plot structure. He was given free rein to create whatever the hell he liked just as long as he stuck to the basic plot requirements. The producers felt safe in the knowledge that their actor's star power alone would be enough to secure a hit. Miike's reaction was to purposely make an anti-mainstream film with as many crude and offensive scenes as he could get away with, knowing full well that it would be aimed at mainstream audiences. I wonder what those two producers must have thought of the end result. They can't have been too dismayed though because *Dead Or Alive* eventually did become a hit across the world and not just in Japan. It also spawned a couple of well-behaved sequels, too.

People often criticise *DOA* for being directionless, claiming that it can't decide what kind of film it wants to be. and so ultimately fails to satisfy on any level. I think that's a bit harsh; you only have to see a couple of Miike's films to know how much he likes to play around with genre conventions, and like his other work, such as *Gozu*, there's a real anything-can-happen-next vibe in *DOA* which far outweighs anything the critics have to say. Just take a look at the final showdown between the two lead actors; both Tekeuchi Riki and Aikawa Sho were big stars in Japan, and it would have been sacrilegious for fans of either actor to see their hero being killed off by the other, a seemingly no-win situation you would think. However, Miike's way of dealing with fan expectation is so sarcastic and over the top that the ending must be seen to be believed.

Direct to video in all territories including Japan, in America *DOA* was released in both R-rated and unrated versions. The R-rated version loses a whopping 9 minutes of footage including the throat stabbing and subsequent blood gushing over the two men having sex, a guy being shot-gunned in the back and the noodles he just ate exploding out of the exit wound in his stomach. Also animal porn, genital licking, a woman being drowned in paddling pool of diarrhea, semen spitting, a severed hand, more bloody shootings, and a guy ripping his own arm off. Be sure to catch it uncut.

Sex: The Annabel Chong Story (1999)
Dir: Gough Lewis /USA

Young, smart, attractive, and a hardcore porn star to boot, Annabel Chong became infamous in the mid-90s for her appearance in The World's Biggest Gang Bang, an event which saw her have sex with 251 men in ten hours, breaking the world record (a feat that has since been shattered by Jasmin St.Claire with 300, and Kimberly Houston with 620). In this fascinating documentary she visits her parents who have no idea about her chosen profession, and explains to them exactly what she does for a living, and why.

Released around the same time when a number of fictional films appeared using explicit, unsimulated sex scenes as a tool of feminine empowerment (*Romance* and *Baise-Moi*, for example), *Sex: The Annabel Chong Story* was the first to attempt a non-fictional account of the same. Ironically, even with the word 'sex' gracing the title as an obvious come-on to its target audience, *The Annabel Chong Story* is not a sexy film. In fact, it's a sad, depressing study, but is also oddly compelling for those reasons.

Filmmaker Gough Lewis follows Chong from her gender classes at USC where she voices her opinions and lets it be known that her antics are empowering and an attack on the traditional ideas of patriarchy, to the porn world where she works. And Lewis doesn't flinch in presenting the reality of the industry. However, it soon becomes apparent that Chong is deeply troubled and less in control than she lets on. She admits to being gang-raped while in London, and expresses her anxieties concerning her parents (who live in Singapore) finding out about her true occupation. And it's here we learn that her real name is Grace Quek, and that she seems more compelled by self-hatred than emancipation. She was only 22 when she appeared in The World's Biggest Gang Bang (which was also filmed by porn director John Bowen and released on video). She was led to believe that all 251 men had taken AIDS tests, which turned out to be untrue, and she never received her full pay for the stunt, insisting that money was never really the point in the first place, and that she was willing to die for her cause anyway.

Chong/Quek is almost like two different people (perhaps a symptom of bipolar?); Chong is self-assured and articulate, whereas Quek is a self-loathing mess. Whether she's frolicking around uninhibited, spouting post-feminist rhetoric, or allowing herself to be filmed while she cuts her arm with a blade, her exhibitionism exposes nothing but contradictions, making her more of a psychoanalyst's wet dream than an aggressive liberator.

The film was released to mixed opinions, with some championing its feminist stance while others appreciated it more as an expose on the degradation of the adult film industry. If you consider that director Lewis was sleeping with Quek during the making of the film, the whole production collapses into hypocrisy. He shot the film with a critical eye on the porn lords and their exploitative rackets, yet 'Mr. Squeaky Clean' Lewis was banging his subject behind the scenes!

Fight Club (1999)
Dir: David Fincher /USA

A mesmerising, stylish, bitterly funny, and visually stunning fable which is now considered a classic, *Fight Club*'s twisted world of emotionally emasculated young men embarking on a crusade against modernity and consumerism was mired in controversy at the time of its release, with many calling for a ban for its 'dangerously instructive information which could encourage anti-social behaviour.'

Fight Club is the brainchild of an unnamed narrator (Edward Norton), an insomniac cubicle worker who has a chance encounter with Tyler Durden (Brad Pitt) on an aeroplane. Their conversation begins over the coincidence that they carry the exact same briefcase. Tyler is a soap salesman, while the Narrator works for an insurance firm, and they promise to keep in touch. A gas explosion sees the Narrator's expensive condo blown out of the sky, and so he moves in to Tyler's dilapidated hideout in the industrial side of town. These Gen-X squatters then begin fighting with each other in public as a cathartic exercise, and once they have drawn a big enough crowd, they take their exploits underground. Fight Club is thus born – a secret society for disaffected young men looking for meaning and a purpose in life. The members of the club engage in bare-knuckle brawls and brotherly bonding. However, Tyler takes the group beyond the dingy basements and turns the men into an army of anarchic terrorists...

Based on the novel by Chuck Palahnuik, *Fight Club* was written after the author was beaten up on a camping trip. The seed for the story was planted in his imagination when he returned to work with cuts and bruises. Despite bearing war wounds, none of his colleagues commented on the state of his face, and Chuck assumed that the workers were either too afraid or too disinterested to enquire about what had happened to him. Intrigued by this social ostracism, he began to work on a story about a subterranean society whose members fight and no one talks about it or addresses it in public. Unlike many writers, Palahnuik was happy for the film-makers to take his novel and do what they wanted with it, and has since gone on record praising Fincher's film as an improvement on his own story.

Of course, the film's central theme isn't much of a secret nowadays; the externalising of an alter-ego as an apparent separate person, or 'Dr. Jekyll and Mr. Jackass.' The splitting of one individual into 'Jack' and 'Tyler Durden' was seen as a cheat move on behalf of the film-makers on its release, but it was actually nothing new in the movies. Robert Bloch's *Psycho* included Norman Bates and his mother as the same person but separate characters who engage in regular conversations, while the twin boys in *The Other* (1972) are actually just one child haunted by either a malignant entity or a split personality. After *Fight Club*, the trend continued with the ridiculous *Haute Tension* (2002) in which the protagonist turns out to be both the psycho killer and the heroine, and even *The Forest* (2016), another film about twins who could actually be one and the same person.

Fight Club was very much a product of its time, with it 90s men raised without fathers and without a purpose, or even a great war to die in.

It's a world where men sprout breasts after testosterone treatment, where pornographic images are spliced into family movies, where women are kept at arms length, and where mega-corporations like Twentieth Century Fox allow a film-maker to spend $70 million of its money to make an anarchic, anti-materialist tract. And this obvious irony is where the film ultimately stumbles in the end. In the final sequence, the film tries to have it both ways by simultaneously embracing nihilistic destruction and romantic optimism. Interestingly, just five years later, director Zack Snyder dropped the satire and anti-materialism of George Romero when he remade *Dawn of the Dead* (2004), perhaps in the knowledge that such sly underpinnings would ultimately be a shot in the foot for Universal.

As for *Fight Club*, the film was mired in controversy since its inception. Fincher, along with Edward Norton and script writer Jim Uhls, seemed to be in a constant war with the studio, trying to push the film far beyond the mainstream fodder it was originally intended to be. Executives balked at some of the dialogue, and demanded changes in the script. The infamous line, 'I want to have your abortion,' was thus changed to 'I haven't been fucked like that since grade school,' for example. The studio was also nervous about the amount of extreme violence in the film, while Fincher felt that it wasn't *violent enough*. And these negotiations on the provocative content of the film only intensified when dealing with the MPAA. Fincher delivered the most provocative version of the film to the American censors in order to give them plenty of material to cut, but it squeaked by with an R-rating. In the UK, however, the theatrical version was snipped of four seconds of violence (though all DVD editions were later passed uncut).

The release of *Fight Club* was delayed after the Columbine Massacre, and hit theatres in October 1999 amid much controversy in the press. *New Yorker*'s David Denby called it 'a fascist rhapsody posing as a metaphor of liberation,' while Alexander Walker of the *London Evening Standard* bemoaned the film's graphic content. 'There are sequences in this film I never thought I would see on a screen,' he wrote, 'ideas I never believed a responsible Hollywood corporation would permit to be voiced as popular entertainment.' A couple of years later, and the film was dragged through the media again in the aftermath of the 9/11 attacks, when its catalogue of carnage – including terrorism, anarchy and bomb-making – made the film all the more contentious in the eyes of the press.

David Fincher went on to make the nerve-jangling *Panic Room* (2002) and *Zodiac* (2007) before Oscar nominated works *The Curious Case of Benjamin Button* (2008 – also with Pitt) and *The Social Network* (2010). For many, *Fight Club* marks the peak of his powers, following on from his nightmarish 90s movies, *Se7en* (1995) and the underrated *The Game* (997), forming a loose trilogy of films that deal with the crisis of middle-class masculinity in an increasingly conformist and meaningless world.

Divided Into Zero (1999)
Dir: Mitch Davis /Canada

A short 34 minute film by Mitch Davis with heavy use of symbolism, grotesquerie, unsettling soundscapes, madness, and catharsis, and also boasts a very dark and grim atmosphere... A troubled serial killer recounts his life story, from self-mutilating youth to fully-fledged perv, he tells all in a calm and matter-of-fact way. Doesn't deliver quite the same lasting effect as his later collaboration with Karim Hussain, *Subconscious Cruelty* (although it does share similarities with that doomy masterpiece, and wouldn't be out of place as a segment in that film), but you'll find much here that is enthralling and appalling in equal measure, such as the notion that nature is a destructive evil (later hinted at by Charlotte Gainsbourg's character in Lars Von Trier's *Antichrist*), and the gruesome revelations that give the film its splendid title. Reminded me of Jorg Buttgereit's *Schramm*, minus the humour and blatant violence.

Eyes Wide Shut (1999)
Dir: Stanley Kubrick /USA

The story is simple enough: Bill Harford (Tom Cruise) is a doctor in New York whose wife (Nicole Kidman) admits to him one night that she was almost unfaithful. Left reeling in a state of shock, Bill leaves their apartment and takes a cab into the city where he experiences a night of self-discovery and surreal goings on...

Eyes Wide Shut was the last completed film of Stanley Kubrick, who died not long after he cut his final edit. And the result is typically Kubrickian – meaning it's a meticulously crafted intellectual puzzle which is at once deeply intriguing, portentous and remote in pretty much equal measure. The film is so obviously a series of Bill's fantasies that it seems perplexing as to why it was given such a big glossy production. It all seems rather pointless by Kubrick's standards. From the moment we see Bill in the taxi staring off into space, the viewers are subjected to his fantasies and fears over the next couple of hours, ranging from being hit upon by a grieving daughter, a prostitute, and a strange teenage girl. Bill's visit to the mysterious mansion keeps the fantasy interpretation alive as the building looks like a European-style stately home, rather than something you would expect to see in or around New York.

The highlight of the film is undoubtedly the sequence set within the mansion where Bill infiltrates the secretive masked ball. It's a bizarre moment, with robed guests involved in some kind of ritualistic – perhaps demonic – orgy. Conspiracy theorists claim that the scenes are similar to the real life gatherings of the Rothschilds, long-rumoured to hold regular gatherings where human sacrifices are offered up to their 'Bearer of Light,' Lucifer (a Rockefeller party is mentioned early on in the film). Indeed, the conspiracy crowd also claim that Kubrick's film was secretly censored for giving away 'too many details' about the rituals! And that he was murdered to keep him silent!

Back to the film itself. It's Cruise's performance that haunts the most. He is in more or less every scene, as Bill's jealousy and wounded pride cannot be masked. His vulnerability radiates from every scene as a momentarily lost character. Contrary to the trailer, this is more of a psychological study than erotic drama, which meant that box-office tickets dried up after word got around that Cruise and Kidman don't appear naked (actually, Kidman does appear in a few brief nude scenes). Overall though, it all feels a bit underwhelming for a Kubrick film. *Total Film*'s Matt Mueller summed it up best: 'This musty tales feels exactly what it is: a small-scale arthouse movie way past its sell-by-date, exhumed from a bygone era of Freudian fascination.' Of course, stick with the British version as the American one has censored nudity shots.

Audition (1999)
(Orig title: *Odishon*)
Dir: Takashi Miike /Japan

"Kiri, kiri, kiri". When *Audition* made its Western premier at the Edinburgh Film Festival in 2000, most of those in attendance had never heard of Takashi Miike or the fact that he was fast becoming one of the most outrageous filmmakers on the planet. And when the projector bulb dimmed at the end, some of those lucky enough to have caught the film wished they hadn't as it turned out to be a completely different filmic experience than what they had expected, and were unable to rid their memories of the sadistic tortures they had just witnessed.

Mainstream horror doesn't get any more stomach-churning than *Audition*, an almost perfectly crafted venus flytrap of a movie that runs like a quirky romantic drama for an hour, and features a man in the middle of a mid-life crisis searching for love. However, what he finds instead is the ultimate Sadean nightmare in the flesh. So if you still haven't seen this film yet then I urge you to stop reading now and go and check it out.

After the death of his wife Yoko, Aoyama (Ryo Ishibashi) raises their son alone. His movie producer friend knows all about Aoyama's loneliness and suggests that he hold an audition to find his next partner. Realising how much of a hassle dating is to a middle-aged man, Aoyama agrees, and together they set up a fake film audition. The girl of his dreams appears in the form of Asami (Eihi Shiina); young, beautiful, and artistically talented, they begin their tentative relationship, but she remains vague when asked about her personal life and past relationships. Even those who knew her are less than forthcoming about her mysterious past. And then things take a turn for the worse...

This is the film that propelled Takashi Miike to global notoriety, but those expecting a flashy and gory piece of ultra-violence like *Dead Or Alive* or *Ichi the Killer* may be disappointed because *Audition* is not that kind of film. It's a slow-burner that takes its time in its build up before it shows its teeth, but trust me, it bites. And it works best on those who have no idea of what's in store (like the fans and critics at the Edinburgh Film Festival).

Many interpretations have been bounded around concerning the subtext of the film, from feminist revenge fantasy, a comment on modern dating rituals, to postmodern genre-blending, and even as a cross between *Fatal Attraction* and *Misery*! Some critics have seen similarities with Joseph Conrad's *Heart of Darkness* in *Audition*'s portrayal of a man's complicit relationship with Hell. Dressed in ghostly white, Asami has been deemed a mental emanation of Aoyama's rather than an actual woman. But the most interesting interpretation centres on the cerebral aspects of dream distortion.

The final reel of the film is a physical illustration of the mixture of guilt and fear that Aoyama feels towards both his ex (Yoko, who died), and the mysterious Asami. The horrific scenes at the end are all a dream. That is, all that happens between Aoyama being covered with a sheet after going to bed with Asami and his waking up for a glass of water is all dreamt. The dream continues when he goes back to bed. His new beau's 'baggage' is, of course, only alluded to, but it's enough for Aoyama's imagination to work into a terrifying expression of his own fears and personal sense of guilt via dream distortion. Two thirds of the movie are played out straight forward like a conventional drama; it's only near the end when events take on a disturbing and surreal tone. Freud wrote that the ego works as a censor and relaxes somewhat while you sleep, but is still at work repressing unconscious drives. If your dream becomes too explicit in its meaning then the censor hasn't been sufficient enough in distorting the dream, and the whole thing is just wiped from your memory (we supposedly dream all the time, night after night, but we can only remember the occasional dream after waking). The interesting thing here is that Aoyama perhaps won't even remember his nightmare the next day, it's just too revealing for his ego to acknowledge. Much of it will be repressed, edited, or wiped from his consciousness altogether. And his unconscious will continue to throw up its symbols of baggage, guilt, fear, helplessness, and torment – we are the monsters and agents of our own nightmares.

As for Takashi Miike, he has gone from strength to strength, becoming one of Japan's most bankable filmmakers with subsequent fare like *Visitor Q*, *Izo*, and *Imprint*, and breaking box office records with *Kuroozu Zero II* and *Yatterman* (both of which raked in more than three billion yen, out-selling even the most popular of mainstream releases in Japan). A truly staggering feat for an artist who has never once compromised on his edgy vision. Only in

Japan is it possible to become a household name by continually rattling your audience and bombarding them with some of the most extreme imagery of the decade.

American History X (1999)
Dir: Tony Kaye /USA

The leader of a white supremacy gang must face up to the effects of his lifestyle and the consequences it has on his family... Told from the perspective of an admiring younger brother (the superbly cast Edward Furlong), *American History X* charts the development of Derek Vinyard (Edward Norton), a smart young man who becomes a neo-Nazi after his father is shot dead by a black thug. He shaves his head, has a swastika tattooed on his chest, and rallies the local disaffected youth into joining him in his racist crew before he kills a pair of black thieves who attempt to steal his car. When Derek is released from prison after serving three years of his sentence, his younger brother – whose boyish looks belie his own racial hatred – is shocked to discover that Derek is a reformed man who not only has grown back his hair but also wants to make amends for his previous crimes. Needless to say, his new perspective on life is not shared by the vicious gang he has left behind.

Films which deal with racism, especially those churned out by the Hollywood system, tend to generalise the subject and rely on cardboard character types in order to drive the point across to the viewers that "racism is not good, m'kay?" And this approach to the touchy subject leaves no room for the complexities that are sometimes found at the roots of racism. And though *American History X* does have its problems as a film, such as relying on easy stereotypes and an uncomplicated morality, it does at least have the courage to explore the subject-matter in all its ugliness before delivering the expected moral message.

Edward Norton is magnetic as Derek, and is easily the most complex character in the film. We watch his development as a young man and the dangerous shifts in his ideals. His fierce rhetoric is perhaps the most important aspect of the film, and it's easy to make comparisons with the fiery hatred of right-wing radio hosts in America. It's the kind of poisonous bile that goes for the heart and not the head in its way of recruiting people into this reductive way of thinking. And *American History X* as a film is also guilty of these kinds of simple tactics.

Derek's racism is shown to have started when his father complains about the faults of affirmative action in the workplace while the family has dinner. And later, Derek realises the error of his ways when he befriends a black man in jail. Such simple mechanisms offered to the viewers as a way of showing a young man embarking on a new way of life, and indeed seeing the *error* of his ways, remains unconvincing. And the black man also happens to be funny and serves as perhaps the only source of humour in the whole film; it's such a lazy way to make a character appealing – oh, this black guy is good because he's funny! Well, that solves *that*, then. These are just a couple of examples of the film dispensing with the complexities of real life racism and resorting to the clean and easy filmic methods of telling a story.

While Derek is in prison, it is a character called Cameron (Stacy Keach) who resumes as leadership of the gang, and he serves as a typical tyrant, a man who leeches onto the simmering rage of the local youth and turns them on to the 'joys' of racial hatred. He ultimately gives them a direction in life. The film is all the more interesting for having a character like Cameron, because despite the needless simplicity of much of this film, Cameron's character actually serves as a more honest and realistic hate monger. And his existence in *American History X* seems to shield the other kids from being directly to blame for their recruitment into such a gang. Cameron's main method of grabbing new skinheads is through the raw power of hardcore punk music; he allows aggressive bands to make a racket at his house, and the youngsters can't get enough. It's a well-known fact that in real life, hardcore has been successful over the years as a source of recruitment for neo-Nazi/White power gangs because the aggression of it often rings home in bored, disenfranchised youth. It's the simple and uncomplicated noise that wins the hearts of these kids; that's their hearts, not their minds.

The film was directed by Englishman Tony Kaye, who had previously made TV commercials. He had a very public falling out with the studio over final cut of the film which he was unhappy with, and some commentators more or less accused him of cutting off his nose to spite his face. But as it stands, *American History X* is one of the better films that deals

476

with racism. Lookout for some superb set-pieces including one of the most vicious acts of violence of any film made in the 90s. There's also a brutal attack on a convenience store, an argument at the dinner table that erupts into violence, and a gruelling prison rape.

Hypnosis (1999)
(Orig title: *Saimin*)
Dir: Masayuki Ochiai /Japan
A *Ringu*-like J-Horror with gimmicky but effective death sequences. After a series of bizarre suicides linked by the victims uttering the words "green monkey" before they expire, a cop assigned to the case works out that it has something to do with a strange girl who was hypnotised on a light entertainment TV show. With lots of mystery and suspense, and a glut of gruesome imaginings, including a man 'washing' his face with fire from a stove, this is an unusual film even by Japan's standards. The only downside is that things become a bit convoluted and confusing in the final quarter.

American Movie: The Making of Northwestern (1999)
Dir: Chris Smith /USA
"I'm thirty-years-old and I'm about to start cleaning up somebody's shit, man." Hilarious documentary about a horror fan, Mark Borchardt, who attempts to complete his first feature film, *Northwestern*. The budding filmmaker, along with his friend, Mike Schank, have to pass a seemingly endless amount of hurdles, and encounter numerous eccentrics in their efforts to get Mark's movie completed and up on the big screen. However, the lack of funds forces Mark to put his feature on the back-burner, and instead he puts his time and efforts into completing his short film, *Coven*, a semi-autobiographical black and white horror short. What Mark lacks in funds is made up for in his unstoppable tenacity and 'never-say-die' attitude. He sort of reminds me of other 90s indie filmmakers like Scooter McCrae and Jim VanBebber in the way he insists on shooting with 16mm film (among many 90s indies, shooting on video was frowned upon much more than nowadays). He uses aggressive tactics to get what he wants, and seems to be driven by mad obsession. During an afternoon shoot, most of his actors don't show up, so Mark simply orders his parents to play the roles instead ("But Mark, I have to go shopping"). Other characters we meet along the way include the aforementioned Mike Schank, a pleasant but dim-witted man whose brain has been frazzled by years of LSD use (he also contributes to the soundtrack with an acoustic version of Metallica's *Fight Fire With Fire*). Also, Mark's parents, who don't share his enthusiasm for film-making, an assortment of unknown actors, and Mark's uncle Bill, an 82-year-old man who lives in a trailer park despite having hundreds of thousands of dollars in the bank, and who also delivers one of the funniest lines ("...It's alright... it's okay... uuuhhhh..."). I cannot stress how great this film is; whether you're a budding filmmaker yourself, or a horror fan, or just someone interested in the quirkier side of film, *American Movie* is one of those precision-perfect documentaries – the sheer fluke of capturing those people in that time and place, and immortalising them on film, was a million-to-one shot. Audiences and critics agreed, as the film has become a cult favourite. It even picked up the Grand Jury Prize at Sundance in 1999. Mark Borchardt has since made several appearances on *Letterman*, as well as other TV shows and films, including *Family Guy*, along with Schank. *Coven* was released on VHS in the late 90s, but *Northwestern* (along with another 'in production' feature, *Scare Me*) still haven't been completed.

Snuff Perversions: Bizarre Cases of Death (1999)
Dir: D. J. Kary & Marcus Koch /USA
A cheesy comedy about a cop and a psychologist who watch a bunch of unconvincing snuff movies starring a few familiar faces from the Z-budget horror scene (including Tina Krause) before a pair of maniacs storm the studio and murder them so that they can get their hands on the incriminating tapes. A sequel followed the next year, *Snuff Perversions 2: More Bizarre Cases of Death* (aka *Shock 2000*).

Julien Donkey-Boy (1999)
Dir: Harmony Korine /USA
A violent schizophrenic youth (Ewen Bremner) lives with his equally dysfunctional family in New Jersey. With subject-matter ranging from incest to death, and shot in a hand-held, haphazard, Dogme-style, it has its moments but will be a major turn-off for most casual viewers. Overall, the film lacks the ideas of *Gummo*

(1997) and the chaotic spark of *Trash Humpers* (2009), but is worth a watch if only for Bremmer's great performance, which is sort of a more sustained version of his role as the hick mutant in *Judge Dredd* (1995).

The Ninth Gate (1999)
Dir: Roman Polanski /Spain /France /USA
Tagline: 'Leave the unknown alone.' Book dealer, Dean Corso (Johnny Depp), is hired by millionaire, Boris Bolkan (Frank Langella), to check the authenticity of a tome that is said to have been co-authored by the Devil in 1666. And as he heads to Europe to track down other copies of the book (called 'Book of Nine Doors of The Kingdom of Shadows'), he encounters numerous bizarre characters, including black widow Satanist, Lena Olin, a wine-sipping book collector (played by Jess Franco regular, Jack Taylor), and a seemingly supernatural green-eyed girl (Emmanuelle Seigner). The film reaches a climax at a Satanic gathering at a house, which looks similar to – but less impressive than – the one seen in *Eyes Wide Shut* (1999). It also shares an orgy scene similar to the one in Kubrick's film, which is odd considering that both films were made around the same time, and can't have influenced the other in a direct way. *The Ninth Gate* starts off as an intriguing mystery, but the final act – which should have been the highlight of the film – is really quite underwhelming. Of course, the softly-spoken Bolkan wants to be in possession of all three books so that he can discard the fakes and use the real one for a fiery ritual which he hopes will grant him all the powers of darkness.

Resurrection (1999)
Dir: Russell Mulcahy /USA
Director Russell Mulcahy and actor Christopher Lambert teamed up again for the first time since *Highlander* (1986) for this dark and gruesome thriller. A cross between *Frankenstein* and *Seven*, the plot follows a cop's pursuit of a serial killer who removes a limb from each of his victims, and leaves the massage "he is coming." Eventually we discover that the killer is a deranged religious fanatic who is methodically piecing together a new Messiah from the body parts of his victims. Tense and atmospheric at times, *Resurrection* is recommended to those who appreciate dark and disturbing horror.

Blair Witch 2: Book of Shadows (1999)
Dir: Joe Berlinger /USA
Myrick and Sanchez returned with a narrative-based sequel to *The Blair Witch Project* while handing over directorial duties to Joe Berlinger, the man famous for his bold and disturbing *Paradise Lost* documentaries. A group of youngsters sign up to spend the night in the woods near Burkitsville, Maryland, where the film crew of the original movie disappeared (it has now become a ghoulish kind of tourist trap). But when they return to town they realise that they have no memory of the previous night. Gradually it becomes apparent that they have brought something horrible back from the woods with them. Like the first film, this features a cast of unknowns and has a documentary feel in some places, with the bigger budget adding a professional sheen. But even with some creepy scenes and a decent soundtrack – which includes the great Queens of the Stone Age – much of the impact of the original is lost here. Overall, it feels like a quick cash-in.

Kojitmal (1999)
(aka *Lies*)
Dir: Jang Sun Woo /South Korea
An 18-year-old schoolgirl gets involved in an obsessive sadomasochistic relationship with a middle-aged married man. The power dynamics shift from the apparently stronger to the seemingly weaker partner. The sexual scenes are often brutal and unflinching, but there are also absurd moments, like when the two main characters decide which poles to use to beat the other. The novel, '*Tell Me a Lie*', By Jang Jung II on which the film is based, was deemed pornographic and was banned in Korea after only a month of its publication. And Jang Jung II spent time in prison.

Zombio (1999)
Dir: Peter Baiestorf /Brazil
A man drags his girlfriend through the Brazilian zombie wilderness and fondles her tits while fending off the occasional rotter that comes by. *Zombio* is empty-headed non-entertainment used as a way of promoting local punk and metal bands by having their music constantly swamping up on the soundtrack. This is beyond 'bottom of the barrel,' beyond *Hunting Creatures*, *Redneck Zombies* and *Automation Transfusion*, beyond the worst movies ever

made, and out to some far-flung dimension that sucks all the life and colour out of you. If there is a hell, it will probably entail being strapped to a chair and being forced to watch this video over and over again for eternity. The U.S. Military should screen this at Guantanamo Bay; believe me, the terrorists will tell them all they want to know so long as they promise to switch it off.

Road Rage (1999)
Dir: Deran Sarafian /USA

Former *Baywatch* babe Yasmine Bleeth stars in this middle-of-the-road stalker thriller made for TV. The curvaceous star makes the big mistake of cutting off a delivery driver on the road. He then spends the rest of the film vengefully terrorising her. This type of thing has been done many times before in the movies – most notably in Spielberg's *Duel*, for example – and much better.

Das Komabrutale Duell (1999)
Dir: Heiko Fipper /Germany

Made in the late 90s but not released on DVD until 2008, *Das Komabrutale Duell* opens with segments that were shot in 8mm. And to be fair it looks alright; in amongst all the jumbled gore footage of mangled humans, including women's faces that have been smashed in and their tits cut off (this is a bit odd and random because there are next to no female characters in the entire film). We do get a brief back-story – a vicious gang of sadists called The Eightlets Mafia are in the middle of a street war with the Bandera family. Problem is, the Bandera family are near immortal, and all attempts to do away with them is doomed to failure as the Bandera clan just keep on coming back for more...

And that's basically it; the rest of the pic is shot on video and shows how the Bandera's are chased, captured, brutally beaten, cut up with chainsaws, shot, stabbed, have their heads smashed in with sledge hammers, but they will not die. This all sounds like a gorehound's dream, but the special effects are mostly quite lame and never even remotely realistic. The blood looks like watered-down tomato puree, the victim's being beaten and shot and dissected are obviously plaster mannequins (perhaps an homage to Lucio Fulci?), and the whole project seems to have stemmed from the imagination of an extremely disturbed eight year old. The fact that the cast and crew are made up of grown men in their 20s and 30s only adds to how

ridiculous this film is, but there's no doubt that these guys enjoyed making this movie, they're clearly having a great time.

A bloody awful film then, but it is at least more watchable than other German amateur jobs like *Familienradgeber* and *Hunting Creatures*, but that isn't saying much. Included on the end credits is a warning from the filmmakers; "Don't even think of pirating this movie, or you'll be the next coma-brutal duel" - HF Pictures 1984-1999. Interestingly, I have never seen this film available on any illegal download site, so I assume the threat must have worked! Maybe other production companies should follow suit. *Das Komabrutale Duell* was also banned in its native Germany in 2007.

eXistenZ (1999)
Dir: David Cronenberg /USA

In the near future, a video game designer survives an assassination attempt while demonstrating her latest game creation. Cronenberg returns to *Videodrome*-like territory with *eXistenZ*, this time by exploring Virtual Reality and the eventual difficulties of separating games from real-life as technologies become increasingly sophisticated and realistic. The result is a bizarre, convoluted mystery where the idea is to work out what is fiction and what is real. *eXistenZ* is similar in concept to *Total Recall* (1990), a project David Cronenberg was originally set to direct. How different the film would have been if Cronenberg made it can only be guessed at, but *eXistenZ* confirms he has much to say on the themes of fantasy, reality, technology and the melding of the three.

The Astronaut's Wife (1999)
Dir: Rand Ravich /USA

Johnny Depp plays an astronaut who returns to earth after a space mission. And, after a mishap, his wife (Charlize Theron) suspects she may have been impregnated by an alien... This is basically a re-working of Roman Polanski's *Rosemary's Baby* (1968), with two major differences: 1) Here, the heroine is impregnated by an alien rather than the Devil, and 2): *Rosemary's Baby* is actually a decent film. Actress Charlize Theron even gets to sport a similar short hairdo as Mia Farrow had in Polanski's film. Her character also has a history of mental instability, which throws up the usual question of whether she is correct in her fears, or whether she's just losing her mind. And by the time the truth is revealed, most audiences couldn't care less either way. Depp's performance is pretty good, but overall the film is completely devoid of suspense and atmosphere.

Dead Girl On Film (2000)
<u>Dir: Brian Paulin /USA</u>

A group of filmmakers sit around watching their latest epic, a black and white lesbian bondage movie. They're bored, and one of them suggests they try something new. After toying with various perverted ideas, including being shat on by a "300-pound sweata with a gassy box," they are eventually forced into making a snuff movie. The filmmakers soon find themselves entering a dark world of murder and bloody mayhem, and are terrorized by a ghostly force of vengeance.

Brian Paulin's second feature released on his label, Morbid Vision Films, is a fairly competent if over-long piece of DV horror hokum. It would have been much stronger if it had been edited down to around 50 minutes or so because it's very time-padded in places, and instead of getting on with the plot, we are instead kept in the presence of a bunch of characters who sit around calling each other names like 'hot pocket'. Usually when a filmmaker wants to stretch the running time of his movie so that it will reach the desired feature length, he will do things like have one of his characters wander the streets accompanied by a lively soundtrack (think *Combat Shock*), and Brian Paulin is no exception. He follows his co-producer around an abandoned industrial hell-hole littered with ugly weeds and dumped furniture. Hardly the stuff of nightmares, but directors like Buddy Giovinnazzo (*Combat Shock*), Jim VanBebber (*Deadbeat At Dawn*), and even David Lynch (*Eraserhead*) have all been guilty of exactly the same thing in their film-making techniques, and those guys are considered Gods.

I must admit, when I first read the synopsis on this film (something like: 'Angry filmmaker decides to make a snuff movie as a way of earning some quick cash'), I was expecting something more along the lines of *Last House On Dead End Street*. But *Dead Girl On Film* is something else entirely. For a start, the fictional filmmaker (played by Paulin himself) is forced into making the snuffy at gunpoint, in stark contrast to Terry Hawkins who, in *Dead End Street*, films his murders purely for his own sadistic and vengeful purposes. Even Rich George's character, who is portrayed as an unstable lunatic, just doesn't seem evil enough to force someone into making such a brutal film. And this is another area where the film fails: the performances. There's nothing even close to a convincing performance, least of all co-producer Rich George, who prances around like a hyperactive loon, making a total 'hot pocket' of himself on camera.

Director Brian Paulin is no better as an actor, and he'd be the first to tell you. He's a special FX wizard, a decent musician and director, but no actor; his attempts to express his emotions through facial expressions are truly tragi-comic. The snuff victim (played by Typhany Weathers) looks to be the most competent performer in the movie but is sadly given very little screen time to make an impact. Instead, she poses on a couch in her panties and a t-shirt, only to be stabbed to death moments later. Her character remains a mystery to viewers (she doesn't even have a name – she is credited simply as 'Snuff Victim'), and this has the bad side-effect of lacking any kind of emotional punch. Had her character been developed a bit more to show us what she was like as a person, it would've paid dividends when her vengeful spirit returns to inflict its carnage on the filmmakers, as it would have benefited from viewer identification. But as it stands, her doomed character just serves as a dumb blonde ripe for slaughter, with the viewer's hardly caring about what is happening on screen beyond the gore sequences that appear near the end. Overall, this flimsy film just serves as one big build-up to the gruesome finale in which Brian Paulin gets to open his bag of bloody tricks.

But don't hold your breath, gorehounds, because the second most extravagant effect here is a skull surging towards the camera lens wearing a blonde wig (Brian's, presumably). The most spectacular effect is undoubtedly the scene where Rich George is suspended from the ceiling with metal hooks through his eyes, followed by a slow, agonizing death by dismemberment which is genuinely impressive, and given some extra oomph as it is inflicted on the scummiest character in the film.

Paulin's craft improved considerably throughout the 00s with *Fetus* and *Bone Sickness*, so be sure to check those out first before venturing to his earlier stuff like this. The director also created the music, too. The opening tune sounds a bit like that old Metallica cover of 'Free Speech For the Dumb', and shares a similar chugging riff. There's also another memorable tune played out to busy drum loops and distorted guitars, like a modern-day, extra-doom-laden Joy Division.

During the end credits a caption reads: "Anyone duplicating this movie without the permission of Morbid Vision Films will be suffocated by a 300-pound sweata... with a gassy box." So there you go, don't do it unless you like that kind of thing. Then, by all means, knock yourself out. Just don't come crying to me with shit-bubbled tears afterwards, you hear?

Naked Poison (2000)
(Orig title: *Shou xing xin ren lei*)
Dir: Cash Chin /Hong Kong
Naked Poison tells the tale of Min (Leung Cheuk Moon), a timid, nerdy-looking wimp, a bit like the mop boy in *Toxic Avenger* but more perverted. Min lives in a crowded tenement block above his uncle's traditional herbal pharmacy, and is caught spying on his neighbours while they have rough sex. The boyfriend Richard confronts him; Min denies spying on them but his tent erection says otherwise, so Richard beats him.

Min spends his days traipsing around the city following girls and pathetically taking discreet photos up their skirts on the escalator whilst they're unaware. And in the evenings he secretly experiments with making potions using his uncle's herbs. He concocts a lethal potion that kills Uncle Kim, and then he inherits the pharmacy. After experimenting a bit more he succeeds in creating a potent aphrodisiac that allows him to have complete control over the attractive women in his life who ordinarily wouldn't give him the time of day. And with the help of this potion his wildest fantasies soon become a reality as his victims don't remember a thing when the date-rape drug has worn off.

Min saves a young woman from being raped and as a reward he almost gets laid, but at the last moment she says her goodbyes and leaves, leaving Min desperate and hornier than ever. So he goes home and uses the potion on the sexy neighbour whom he was caught spying on earlier. Her boyfriend Richard is a long-distance truck driver away on a job, and when the drug kicks in she wanders over to Min's room and rides him into ecstasy. Of course, the next day she has no memory of the night before

and accuses Min of stealing her underwear.

He later slips her another pill and fucks her in her office. But this time she is rushed to hospital, and Min then blackmails her boyfriend into paying HK\$2 million for the antidote. He then connivingly manages to dose Richard with a nasty potion that causes a gangrene-like skin-eroding disease. Soon enough, Min becomes self-assured, arrogant, nasty, deviant, a total control-freak who literally fucks people over to satisfy his own power hunger and sexual gratification. His sudden messiah-complex makes it so that he thrives on having desperate people fawning and begging at his feet for the antidote for their nasty afflictions.

At the hour mark the film becomes even darker, with brutal rape and violence, and bodies dumped in drainage systems as Min's God-complex spirals out of control. The police eventually close in on Min and his antics but not before he sets his sights on Ling, the pretty young woman whom he had rescued from rape earlier... And there's also a nasty surprise lurking under the bed.

Naked Poison, would you believe, is based on a true story (very loosely, no doubt). It's one of those typical Cat III movies so prevalent in the 80s and 90s in its use of lighting and music and photography. Viewers could be mistaken for thinking this film was made in the 80s – the only giveaway that it was actually made in 2000 is the scene in which Min masturbates whilst watching internet porn. There are also lots of funny details to look out for, such as the often hilarious subtitles ("Freeze, or I'll smash your head"), and the sound effects during the sex scenes which include a very loud tapping of balls against arse.

Baise-Moi (2000)
(aka *Rape Me*; aka *Fuck Me*; aka *Screw Me*; aka *Kiss Me*)
Dir: Virginie Despentes & Coralie Trinh Thi /France
A couple of murderous outsiders team up and go on a killing spree. Pretty soon, they've wasted a woman at a cash till, numerous men they have slept with, and anyone else who dared to get in their way.

There have been several English translations of the title *Baise-Moi*, such as 'Rape Me', 'Fuck Me' and 'Screw Me', but none of them quite captures the nihilistic rage and venom of the original French. This is a film about anger, and yet the immoral and reckless exploitation of its style damages the overall message, and tends to shift its focus onto less relevant areas. The film was banned in France after just a couple of days of its release, due to protests about the levels of graphic sex and violence depicted. It was also banned in Canada and Australia, and was released unrated in the States. In the UK, the BBFC removed ten seconds from the graphic rape scene in which the victim looks to be enjoying the experience (a similar cut was enforced on Sam Peckinpah's *Straw Dogs* almost thirty years earlier). The British censors also removed a further two seconds from the DVD release. But even with the missing footage, it was a surprise to many that the BBFC allowed it to be released at all. But there it was in all its sordid, punky, digital video style for all to see.

Large sections of the media did the whole 'let's pretend to be scandalised' thing, such as the *Daily Mail* who attacked the film and called for a ban. And also in America, where *Variety* magazine slammed it as "A half-baked, punk-inflected porn odyssey masquerading as a movie worth seeing and talking about." The *New York Times* described it as "A numbing alternation of pornographic scenarios and brutal killings," which is actually quite a fair assessment. In the UK, the media feeding frenzy seemed to feast upon the fact that the film was written and directed by women, just as much as they complained about the sex and violence.

Based on ex-prostitute Despentes' bestselling novel, and cast with a pair of real porn stars in Raffaëla Anderson and Karen Lancaume, the emphasis here is on posing and bloodshed. And this allows the filmmakers to avoid addressing the more direct themes, and it also gives them the chance to avoid having to explain their overall motives. Had the film been a revenge scenario against men following their rape, then there would have been more of a purpose here, something to make viewers care about the characters. But this is not the case: It's not just men who are killed, it's women too. And it's not just the men they have slept with who are murdered, either. So what's the agenda? According to Despentes and Trinh Thi, the idea was to make a film that was "so in your face that we will end up in your mind." The end result is as subtle as a bullet in the arse, which just so happens to be included in one of the film's nastiest scenes. It's basically an extreme version

of *Thelma & Louise*, or *I Spit On Your Grave* meets *Natural Born Killers*, complete with real, unsimulated sex scenes and gallons of blood. The film works better when viewed as an underdog class-war rant, or an attack on the idea of bourgeois film-making (as was supposedly the case with *A Serbian Film* a few years later. But anyone with even half a brain could see it for what it was: a cynical way of provoking controversy in order to make a fortune at the box-office). The supposed sexual politics in *Baise-Moi* are muddied by the character's indiscriminate killing of women, too.

But let's not take this art house shocker too seriously. Goodness knows, many others have. When all's said and done, this film is just a more extreme version of *Natural Born Killers*, complete with multiple layers of horror, sensation, tragedy and laughs. Only, this is a 21st Century update, which means there are also hardons, blowjobs, the odd drop of spunk, and subtitles. It may not sound like fun, but anything the *Daily Mail* hates so much must be worth checking out. Does it have any feminist credentials at all? Well, director Despsentes was raped as a teenager, and Trinh Thi is a former porn actress, but there isn't much in the film that could stand up to feminist scrutiny, unless there's a school of thought along the lines of 'All men are bastards, so let's kill 'em, after we've noshed 'em off.' There's nothing here that you won't have seen before: anyone who has ever watched a porno will hardly raise an eyebrow at the close-up fellatio and cum-shots, and the violence is nothing that Quentin Tarantino hadn't already shot in a mainstream movie. Speaking of which, *Baise-Moi* does have its moments of Tarantino-style, self-conscious dialogue, such as in the scene in which the protagonists moan that their dialogue just isn't cool enough.

Adapting her own book, Despentes creates a punk nightmare, a doom-laden horror show that sticks closely to its exploitation roots. We get the usual shot-on-video guerilla-style, with hit 'n' run visuals, and the two leads invest their roles with an assured manner, meaning that no expression is too big for them, whether it be explicit shagging, graphic violence, or being the victims of rape, the actresses give it their all with gusto. Lancaume in particular is exceedingly good in this film; she manages to convey the oblivion in her head in a difficult way, somehow expressing her mental damage with a swagger. Sadly, Lancaume (her real name was Karen Bach) took her own life in 2005 with an overdose of temazepam. She was just 32 years old. Anderson is also good, but her character is a bit clichéd and she doesn't have much to work with. But together on screen they're a force to be reckoned with, snatching weapons from the grip of patriarchy, shoving them up its arse, and pulling the trigger. This isn't a sexy movie, but that's the point. It isn't misogynistic either. Just a raging, misanthropic rant. And I for one enjoyed it for what it is.

Given the film's ferocious style, you'd probably expect Despentes and Trinh Thi to be loud, aggressive feminists, but they're actually quite mild-mannered and soft-spoken, sharp and witty, and laid back about the controversy their film had unleashed. "In France there is a culture of tolerance, but it's just an image," claimed Despentes at the time on the film's ban in her native country. The ban was brought about by the Ministry Of Culture and the right-wing religious group, *Promouvoir*. "I think it was an advertisement to all other producers that said: 'Us French make pretty movies. We're an intellectual country, we don't need this sort of thing.' They won't be making another *Baise-Moi* soon."

American Psycho (2000)
Dir: Mary Harron /USA

Not since the days of Joseph Ruben's *The Stepfather* (1986) had a major American film tackled social satire in the form of a slasher movie, and not since the days of Kathryn Bigelow's *Near Dark* (1987) had we seen such a violent film directed by a woman. Patrick Bateman (Christian Bale), a good-looking, wealthy Wall Street banker, tries to alleviate his soul-crushing boredom by engaging in ferocious acts of murder. Prostitutes, homeless bums, or even his colleagues are fair game for his senseless wrath and lack of conscience. No one around him suspects a thing as Patrick effortlessly blends in to the shallow narcissism and petty one-upmanship of big city life. We're left smirking at Bateman's monologues which detail his meticulous hygiene habits, snooty materialism, and ridiculous taste in music in between bouts of stylish slayings until he loses his sanity altogether...

Attempts to bring Bret Easton Ellis's outrageous novel to the big screen was never going to be easy. Published in 1991, *American Psycho* the book was met with much controversy as it was widely misinterpreted as a nasty misogynistic tract that wallowed in extreme violence and torture disguised as a thinly-plotted social satire. Mary Harron (who had previously directed the underrated *I Shot Andy Warhol*) does a fine job of replicating the antiseptic and blackly hilarious feel of the book. Unfortunately, the horrendous tortures of prostitutes in Ellis' original (which left me despairing for the evils of mankind when I read them) are not really touched upon in the film; Harron is a well-known feminist so maybe that's why she avoided depicting those gruelling chapters, and instead stays with the satirical vibe of the book.

Bale's Bateman is a touch more anxious and comical in the film than in the original, but the 'business card' scene is almost spot-on same as the book, and Bateman's loathsome yuppie monster and his world of literal cut-throat capitalism is fairly well portrayed overall. Andrzej Sekula's scope photography is a marvel, almost every frame could be taken out and used in a glossy haute couture magazine (except for the bloody bits, of course), and John Cale's modernist score keeps things from becoming too cosy.

American Psycho was met with problems both during and after production; Bale left the set when Leonardo DiCaprio expressed an interest in playing Bateman, but returned (along with Harron) when DiCaprio changed his mind. Lions Gate had no idea how to market the film, and released it as they would a major blockbuster, which led to many mainstream movie-goers (who were used to the likes of *The Sixth Sense* and *Hollow Man*) scratching their heads at the ironies of an art film which unspooled before their eyes. It also ran into trouble with the MPAA who demanded lengthy cuts to the threesome frolics and the first axe murder scenes (they were later reinstated on the unrated region 1 DVD by Universal). In the UK and elsewhere in the world the film was untouched by the censor's chainsaws and all region 2 releases are uncut.

Chopper (2000)
Dir: Andrew Dominik /Australia

The true(ish) stories of Mark 'Chopper' Read, noted Australian criminal, killer and best-selling author. "This is not a biography," states the opening title card of this uncomfortable, grisly, knife-edge film, though there remains some question as to whether the subsequent film panders to, or debunks, Read's cheerily psychotic self-image. There's no denying Eric Bana's skills in the title role, however.

After six whole years of "Ban this sick film!" hoo-ha in the papers, and censorious politics, Andrew Dominik's debut feature hit the screens in 2000 and was well worth the wait. Often wrongly compared with other controversial hits, such as *Natural Born Killers*, *Chopper* is actually a disturbing character study which owes more to *Henry-Portrait of a Serial Killer* than to Oliver Stone's film. Indeed, director Dominik's non-judgemental approach to the bleak material, and centring on the 'confessions' of a maniac – whose tales get taller by the minute – relates to *Henry* (the real-life Henry Lee Lucas confessed to hundreds of murders of which it is extremely unlikely he had anything to do with). And unlike the later British film, *Bronson* (2008), which seemed more interested in emulating the set designs of *A Clockwork Orange* rather than presenting the story of a real-life criminal, here with *Chopper*, Dominik discards the showy, stylish side and instead opts for a much more gritty and cold approach. And this objective style pays dividends in the first part of the film which is mostly set in the harsh environs of the prison system. In both *Chopper* and *Henry-Portrait*, both are based on factual accounts, making them all the more horrifying. Dominik's approach to the subject-matter overall serves to illustrate his own detached stance on the story – by treating his real-life criminal in the same documentary style as John McNaughton's *Henry*, he succeeds in allowing the story to take place in a free reign, and ultimately allows Chopper to contradict himself and trip himself up as he trudges through the dark maze of his own bullshit.

But this approach is not surprising; I mean, what is *Chopper* supposed to do, spill the beans and incriminate himself further by telling us the details of crimes he hasn't been convicted for? That's not going to happen. Indeed, Chopper contributes a fascinating commentary track on the DVD which is definitely worth listening to. In it he claims that the character Neville Bartos is actually based on several different characters. He also seems sorely tempted to spill the beans and tell us what really happened; in several scenes he's dying to reveal some important info

not disclosed in the film, but doing so would no doubt incriminate him or possibly others, and he reluctantly keeps his mouth shut while hinting that there is more to the scene than what is presented before us.

Former comic, Eric Bana, is perfect for the role of Chopper. Apparently, Read himself recommended him on the strength of seeing him on a TV show. It was a courageous move on the casting front as Bana infuses his performance with an understated emotional complexity, and the gamble of casting an inexperienced actor in the lead role duly paid off. Indeed, this was only the beginning of Bana's meteoric rise to Hollywood stardom; he went on to land roles in *Black Hawk Down* (2001), *Hulk* (2003), *Troy* (2004), and Spielberg's *Munich* (2005). But *Chopper* remains his most impressive work to date.

Requiem For a Dream (2000)
Dir: Darren Aronofsky /USA

Co-written by Hubert Selby Jr, and based on his novel, *Requiem For a Dream* is a nightmarish visual experience, especially for those who have ever had to deal with speed psychosis. The film links two distinct story lines on the nature of drug addiction, from a young man and his girlfriend who are addicted to heroin and do all they can to secure their next fix, to the man's mother who orders diet pills but quickly becomes addicted to them, and spirals downward into a hallucinatory, paranoid hell. Some have claimed it to be a masterpiece but I wouldn't go that far. It's certainly well worth watching but the clichéd characters makes it feel like territory you have roamed many times before in the movies, especially the predictable moments of the characters trying and failing to go cold turkey, their 'love conquers all' attitudes, and so on. Worth watching if only for the sequence in which Ellen Burstyn's television comes to life with a delirious interactive quiz show. The BBC described it as "brutal, stark, stomach-churning and unglamorous."

Intimacy (2000)
Dir: Patrice Chereau /France /UK

A bleak and sexually explicit drama about a barman who has anonymous sex every Wednesday with a married woman. But perhaps inevitably he desires to know more about his mysterious lover, and risks putting their meetings to en end. Featuring raw performances from the two leads (Mark Rylance and Kerry Fox) and seedy environments, *Intimacy* has very little to offer its viewers beyond the cold loveless affair. The plot is quite similar to Bertolucci's *Last Tango In Paris*, but here the sex scenes are all real and unsimulated, and surprisingly passed uncut by the BBFC.

The Cell (2000)
Dir: Tarsem Singh /USA

Child psychologist Catherine Deane (Jennifer Lopez) is part of an experimental programme to treat mentally ill patients so locked into their own minds that conventional therapy is useless. With the help of lots of drugs and hi-tech machinery, the therapist actually enters the patient's psyche. The FBI has just captured sicko killer Carl Stargher (Vincent D'Onofrio), who kidnaps women, drowns them in a fully-automated tank of his own fiendish devising, then bleaches their bodies until they look like porcelain dolls. Unfortunately, he's had a brain seizure and lies comatose, unable to tell anyone where the girl he just abducted is hidden. Unless Catherine can enter his twisted mind and extract the information, the missing girl will die. So, Catherine steps into Stargher's mental chamber of horrors, which seems to have been designed by Salvador Dali, the Quay Brothers, Damien Hirst, and fashion photographers Pierre and Gilles.

It's mind-bogglingly gorgeous in a totally trippy way; if this were made in the 60s no one would dare see the film straight (though the nastiness of the imagery is definitely bummer material). The shame is that whenever you get hauled back to the story, it's impossible not to notice it's debt to *Silence of the Lambs*. The costumes are phenomenal, the set design ravishing, and the sadistic inventiveness extraordinary; too bad it's all harnessed to a cliché story.

The killer is your typical nut-job, the victim of horrendous childhood abuse from his wretch of a father. He's a necrophile, and during one scene he mounts his victim – he assumes she is dead – but just before he penetrates her, she twitches, and the killer realises she's still alive, and this disgusts him. Interestingly, his reaction to the thought of fucking a live woman is the same disgusted reaction most of us would have to the idea of fucking a corpse (I wonder if people like Ed Gein had the same trouble?).

The Cell is very far-fetched in places, and not just the basic concept of characters being able to invade the minds of others, but also the killer's hi-tech lair is not very convincing. How he has managed to finance all his gadgets and gizmos is never explained, nor how he has managed to purchase the large quantities of formaldehyde and have CCTV and water chambers installed without arousing any suspicion.

The Cell was generally despised by international critics on its release, and it's understandable why; there's some very unpleasant stuff going on in this film, and it's also a typical example of style over content. It's a fairly standard cop vs. serial killer thriller with a mind transfer gimmick thrown in. And it's these sequences where the film comes into its own. If you can accept the ridiculous concept that forms the basis of this film, then *The Cell* does have its moments for those who are willing to overlook its flaws. The scenes in Stargher's mind are a visually stunning, crudely inventive platform for director Singh's disturbing imagination. We get grotesque clockwork corpses, child abuse, disembowelment, a living vivisected horse, and Stargher's terrifying super-ego who rises from its throne wearing a huge swirling cloak. As Deane ventures deeper into Stargher's disturbed unconscious, things become even more bizarre.

Director Singh seems much less interested in character development as the protagonists here are all rather flat and ordinary, each going through the routine of stopping the killer and saving the girl in very clichéd and predictable ways. Jennifer Lopez offers a decent performance, despite her lacklustre role, and I've always thought she is a much better actress than a singer. Howard Shore's music is equally praise-worthy; a rhythmic, Arabic chamber piece that is beautiful and intense, and is punctuated with a big brass section. Have a listen to it as it plays uninterrupted on the DVD menu screen. Like it or not, there's no denying that this film is a treat for the eyes and ears, and it's impossible to imagine a major studio giving a film like this the go ahead nowadays.

Hardcore Poisoned Eyes (2000)
Dir: Sal Ciavarello /USA

A group of idiot youngsters head out to a cabin in the snowy wilderness in upstate New York and are terrorized by a robed Satanist. This film relies heavily on actresses hysterically conveying their speeches about the history of Devil worship to show that the filmmakers did their research on the subject. With a bigger budget and some technical know-how behind the camera, this film could have been interesting. But as it stands, the inexperienced cast and crew, and the lacklustre script renders it borderline amateur.

Dario Argento: An Eye For Horror (2000)
Dir: Leon Furguson /UK

A documentary produced for Channel 4 in 2000 and narrated by Mark Kermode. This film traces Argento's life, from his isolated childhood where he found solace in the works of Edgar Allan Poe, to the filming of his – then – latest film, *Sleepless* (2000). People often complain that horror documentaries don't go deep enough into the subject, but how can it be otherwise? You can only pack so much information into an hour. If you want more detailed information on Argento, there have been many books written about him and his work – go read 'em. For those who understand the limitations of the documentary format, however, and aren't going to get all pissy about there not being enough 'details,' *An Eye For Horror* can be recommended as an interesting overview of Argento and his films. Writers Maitland McDonagh and Alan Jones gush lovingly about his work while George Romero, John Carpenter and Tom Savini swap anecdotes (Savini's story about the prop of Harvey Keitel's severed head is particularly memorable). Actors Michael Brandon, Piper Laurie and Jessica Harper relate their own personal stories of working with Argento, while the auteur's family members – daughters Asia and Fiore, ex-wife Daria Nicolodi and brother Claudio – add their own feelings about the man (and this includes Asia on the difficulties of shooting topless scenes with her dad). All of which builds to an interesting portrait of the artist who readily admits to disliking actors and the physical process of making films.

Together (2000)
Dir: Lukas Moodysson /Sweden /Denmark /Italy

In the mid-70s, a mother leaves her abusive husband and joins a disorganised vegetarian commune with her children. This film starts off as a glowing endorsement for *laissez-faire*, liberal, hippy-drippy values of soft drugs and a rejection of the evils of capitalist society. However, that initial impression is turned upside down, and the film presents the problems of sustaining such an idealistic lifestyle when ego-centric human worms get together in all their greedy and selfish glory, and how our very nature as human animals will inevitably destroy any attempts at harmony. The result is a finely-honed, all-too-believable social comedy that could be read as an allegory on the collapse of Communism (Karl Marx never once took into account how much the human race loves to compete with each other and are obsessed with 'keeping up with the Jones's', and all that). Fucking failing species. Writer/director Lukas Moodysson does an excellent job of illustrating the self-centred narcissism that exists at the core of any kind of human interaction and organisation. And he somehow manages to convey all of this without a single polemical word.

Jack Frost 2: Revenge of the Mutant Killer Snowman (2000)
Dir: Michael Cooney /USA

Set a year after the first film, the Sheriff takes his family on a vacation to Hawaii. But the tropical heat doesn't stop Jack from bringing his own brand of sub-zero terror to the island for much of the same slaughter and giggles. Nothing much to commend it, except to say it's marginally more amusing than the original.

Junk (2000)
(Orig title: *Junk: Shiryo-gari*)
Dir: Atsushi Muroga /Japan

Japanese horror doesn't come any more cheap or unambitious than *Junk*, a grubby homage to George Romero's zombie movies that owes more to the *Resident Evil* films with its gangsters and military men squaring off against the zombie hordes in ugly industrial settings. Has its fun moments but the posing with guns stuff is super irritating.

Dracula 2000 (2000)
(aka *Dracula 2001*)
Dir: Patrick Lussier /USA

Produced by Wes Craven, this film sees Van Helsing (Christopher Plummer) deliberately injecting himself with Dracula's blood so that he can immortally keep track of the bloodsucker indefinitely. Complications arise due to Van Helsing's daughter Mary carrying the same blood, and this allows her a connection to

Dracula. Much of the action takes place in the French Quarter of New Orleans during Mardi Gras, which allows the recently risen vampire the opportunity to pick off the revellers who have invaded the area. The filmmakers have revised the back-story of the Count, and traced his history back beyond that of Vlad the Impaler of the 1400s, as was established in Bram Stoker's original novel. Other changes to the myth include Dracula (Gerard Butler) informing Mary that he was Judas Iscariot, the biblical betrayer of Jesus – an act he now seems to regret. This revisionism ironically makes the 'blasphemous' content of Stoker's original more acceptable to the Christian crowd. But what's the point of that? Presumably, the film was made so that we could all sit back and say "Ooh, Wes, what an intelligent, creative genius you are! You've reinvented an entire genre once again! How do you do it?!" Ugh, I'm not buying it.

Code Unknown (2000)
Dir: Michael Haneke /France /Germany /Romania
A mosiac drama in the mode of *Short Cuts* and *Magnolia* with stories of the modern world, including the homeless in Paris, Kosovo families and children at an inner-city school for the deaf. Haneke's film is much more cold and austere in its approach than the titles mentioned above, and is in keeping with the director's previous works which examine themes of contemporary dislocation. In the grand scheme of things, this is perhaps Haneke's most optimistic film to date, as Jessica Winter of *Village Voice* pointed out: "[*Code Unknown* is] not a gaze into the void, but a fierce attempt to scramble out of it."

Sacred Flesh (2000)
Dir: Nigel Wingrove /UK
Despite the abundance of flesh on display, Nigel Wingrove's surreal throwback to British softcore and Italian nunsploitation flicks is a crushing bore, and has more in common with Bill Zebub's experimental disasters like *Frankenstein the Rapist* rather than the sultry textures and decadence of filmmakers like Tinto Brass and Ken Russell.

Coming on like a 72 minute music video, *Sacred Flesh* revives that old tale of a Mother Superior who is believed to be possessed by Satan because she lusts after the sisters in the nunnery and masturbates a lot. Cue lots of near-static shots of actress Sally Tremaine rolling around on the floor, playing with herself whilst dressed in the heights of sister chic!

Regardless of Tremaine's beauty, the film outstays its welcome by a good half hour or more. Undoubtedly, this kind of material has a growing fan base with Wingrove's labels Redemption and Salvation offering a range of similar, shot on video fare, along with full-colour illustrated books all catering to this kind of sexual fantasy. It's the kind of film which may have been a real doozy (or at least watchable) if it had been directed by someone with an eye for Gothic decadence, human frailty, and sensual shenanigans like a Jean Rollin (whose works have been released on the Redemption label). But as it stands, with its reliance on a glossy modern promo style, fake tits, and outfits that look like they came from Anne Summers, it's not really up to much.

On the plus side, the film does deliver the blasphemy in spades, and we get to witness some intense visions as Sister Elizabeth's carnal desires spin out of control. And this kind of fun didn't go down well with the folks at the BBFC who promptly cut the film for its initial release, only to reinstate the footage a few years later.

Terror Tract (2000)
(aka *House on Terror Tract*)
Dir: Lance W. Dreesen & Clint Hutchison /USA
Horror anthology in which a suburban real estate agent tells three gruesome tales about the house's previous owners to potential buyers. The first story, *Nightmare*, is about a cheating wife and her lover who kill her husband and dispose of his body, only to suspect that he may not be dead... The second story, *Bobo*, stars *Breaking Bad*'s Bryan Cranston, as a father who becomes concerned with his daughter's relationship with an over-protective pet monkey, and resorts to hilarious extremes to in order to rid the house of the pest (you can imagine Walter White would have behaved in the same way). And finally, in *Come To Granny*, a psychic teen visits a psychiatrist to warn her that she will be the next victim of 'Granny,' a vicious, cleaver-wielding serial killer who wears a granny mask... *Terror Tract* is a fun yet highly derivative horror trilogy. It's well made but thoroughly cliché-ridden. It owes a lot to movies like *Les Diaboliques* (1955), *The House That Dripped Blood* (1970), *Monkey Shines* (1988) and *Out of*

the Body (1989), but is watchable if you're in the right mood.

Camera (2000)
Dir: David Cronenberg /Canada

A short autobiographical film by David Cronenberg which was made to celebrate the 25th anniversary of the Toronto Film Festival. *Camera* charts the short (six minute) monologue of an ageing man who has become terrified of the movie camera – "Get that damn camera out of here, it will do irreparable damage to us all!" – Voicing his concerns about the camera, "that clunky old ghost," the man (*Videodrome*'s Lewis Carlson) laments on the absurdity and cruelty of a machine that preserves our youth whilst life continues to haggar our flesh. Shot on video and 35mm, this short comes on like a Philip Larkin poem with all the dark cynicism of age and fears of encroaching death. But it's also infused with Cronenberg's traditional obsessions – "It was like I had caught a disease from the movie" – and is shot in his usual cold and detached manner (which is ironic considering how close to the bone this project was to Cronenberg who was approaching his 60th birthday at the time of filming). Camera is available on the *Videodrome* 2 disc set (Criterion's deluxe edition). Alternatively, you could probably catch it on YouTube.

Wendigo (2001)
Dir: Larry Fessenden /USA

Something must be seriously wrong when big-budget dreck like *Ghost Ship* and *Jason X* are given international theatrical releases, but lower level productions which offer a genuine creepiness and originality, like *Wendigo* and *Session 9*, are shuffled off onto the direct-to-video market.

Larry Fessenden's *Wendigo* is a film which deals primarily with childhood fantasy. The isolation, the sinister locals, and brooding darkness that surrounds the country cabin has an unhealthy effect on the youngster's mind. Miles is the only child of Jake and Kim, New York city dwellers who head upstate to the Catskills for a weekend vacation. Jake's busy lifestyle means that he's not always there for his son, and this looks to have caused Miles to become introverted (he also doesn't seem to have developed much respect for his father). Whilst driving through the woods they hit a deer. The family is then immediately surrounded by angry hunters who find their prized deer with a broken antler. The aggressive behaviour of the locals, and their abusive shouting and gun-waving terrifies the youngster into fantasy overdrive. Miles doesn't understand that the hunter's behaviour is simply brutish and uncultivated; he interprets their aggression as an immediate danger to the lives of his family, and doesn't believe his father would be capable of protecting him and his mother if the confrontation were to escalate.

Much of the film is seen from the perspective of Miles, where both fantasy and reality combine in alarming ways (see also Claude Miller's *La classe de neige* for a more obvious example of disturbing childhood fantasies). When the family arrives at their secluded country cabin, the parents are angry and somewhat perplexed at that little episode, but they are not afraid, they do not feel threatened or in danger in any way; it's from the paranoid perspective of their son that the bumps in the night have a sinister edge. The subsequent fantasies are an attempt to arrange, decipher, and take control of the situation - all this stemmed from the mind of a young and feeble child who wants to reassure himself that there exists some kind of mythical force that can protect us from the terrifying nihilism of cold-blooded murder.

His father, Jake, is not really hospitalised; it's the pure fantasy of Miles testing and exploring his anxieties. There's no vengeful monster either, that too is just a wishful blend of his hopes and fears combining to produce a fantasmatic protector – strong, invincible, and awe-inspiring. The ideal father-figure perhaps?

Ichi the Killer (2001)
(Orig title: 殺し屋 1 *Koroshiya Ichi*)
Dir: Takashi Miike /Japan

A man cuts out his own tongue with a Samurai sword. A severed face slides down a wall. A man is split in half down the middle like a human Damien Hirst artwork. The title is imprinted on the surface of a glob of semen. Does Takashi Miike have your attention yet?

The above are just some of the sights that await viewers of Miike's extremely violent *Ichi the Killer*, which, after being held under close scrutiny at the BBFC offices for more than a year, was finally granted an 18 certificate after being shorn of around three minutes and forty-five seconds of sexualized violence. On its original release in Japan, and at festival screenings across the world, there had been untold rumours of mass walkouts, mass queasiness and fainting and vomiting – the latter pleasing the director because smell is one of the factors he cannot control in his films.

The plot of *Ichi the Killer* centres on Jijii (Shinya Tsukamoto), a man who orchestrates atrocities in order to pit rival yakuza gangs against each other. In this he is aided by Ichi (Nao Omori), a mentally-tortured and gullible young man who also happens to be capable of extreme violence when goaded into committing increasingly deadly acts. Kakihara (Tadanobu Asano), one of the heavies of the Anjo gang, is a sado-masochist obsessed with finding the mysterious Ichi so that he can experience the ultimate in masochistic ecstasy.

Banned in Norway, Germany and Malaysia, *Ichi the Killer* is quite typical for a Japanese film in that the acting is especially good. Tadanobu Asano is excellent as Kakihara. His performance is at once coolly charismatic and terrifying in equal measure, he does a fine job of making the role his own. Nao Omori is also in great form as the title character. The way he expresses a tormented, child-like vulnerability is off-set by his merciless and sadistic side and is incredible to watch. Alien Sun is sexy as hell as Karen (she also makes an appearance on the DVD commentary along with 'Hong Kong film expert' Bey Logan who basically spends the whole time trying to get into her panties – and failing miserably). The fact that Karen is the only character who is aware of Ichi's troubled past makes her perhaps the only character audiences can fully empathise with. Shinya Tsukamoto – director of cult classics like the *Tetsuo* movies, *Tokyo Fist* and *A Snake Of June* – is also very good as Jijii. This conniving character is gradually exposed throughout the film, and Tsukamoto is very convincing in his portrayal of what turns out to be quite a complex character. Throughout almost the entire running time, Jijii wears a thick jacket and looks like a shabby weakling. However, at the end of the movie he removes the jacket and – thanks to the magic of CGI – he suddenly has the shiny, bronzed physique of a bodybuilder; he has muscles on top of muscles and crudely resembles a chocolate-flavoured condom stuffed with monkey nuts.

This film contains some of the most shocking imagery ever to be seen in a fictional film, and includes some very disturbing characters that won't be forgotten in a hurry. It's always a courageous move when a filmmaker attempts to adapt a manga because manga often have aspects within them that are notoriously difficult to translate onto the screen in live-action cinema. Miike makes the transition possible and also succeeds in keeping the streak of black humour intact, too, making for a much-lauded, never-equalled masterpiece of extreme cinema which seems destined to be remembered as one of the most controversial – and unforgettable – films ever made.

Even in Japan, with its liberal acceptance of graphic sex and violence, Miike's taboo-breaking films are considered somewhat extreme (and incidentally, Japan happens to have one of the lowest crime rates in the world). *Shinjuku Triad Society* (1995) wasn't the first film to depict bloody beatings and anal rape, and a gruesome throat stabbing with a broken bottle in the neck, but these acts – and more – are perpetrated by the cops. Just imagine what the bad guys get up to. *Dead Or Alive* (1999) shows a naked woman falling from a tower block, a prostitute being beaten by a cop, more anal rape and arterial spray, bad guys shooting up a nightclub with uzis, and a ten-metre line of cocaine is snorted by one man in one go. These aren't the highlights; just the opening sequence!

Ichi's story of two sadistic killers on a bloody rampage, adapted from Hideo Yamamoto's cult manga, was actually completed in 2001; the uber-prolific Miike had time to direct a further ten movies in the year it took for the BBFC to decide *Ichi*'s fate in the UK. Still showing no signs of slowing down in recent years, at the turn of the century 'prolific' hardly began to describe his phenomenal output at that time. In a career spanning 26 years, his film tally hovers very close to the 100 mark. At the time of *Ichi*'s release, he had already passed the 50 mark. For argument's sake, his current output amounts to more movies than the combined works of Sam Peckinpah (with 16), David Cronenberg (25), Wes Craven (30), and Abel Ferrara (23). Churning out four films per year is not uncommon for Miike, a speedy output achieved by a careful mix of guerilla shooting, multi-tasking and a refusal to get mired in the technical difficulties of film-making. He prefers to shoot on 16mm, but he's not averse to shooting on DV if time and budget limitations requires it (as he did to stunning effect in his black comedy, *Visitor Q* – a disturbing tale of a family succumbing to incest and necrophilia – which he had completed shooting in just seven days on a budget of less than £50,000). "Sometimes, even though it looks cheap," he said at the time, "it's still effective. An imperfect movie is more interesting."

After he graduated from the prestigious Yokohama Academy of Broadcasting and Film, Miike began work as a second unit director on Shohei Imamura's *Zegen* (1987). In the early 90s he progressed to directing, and offered his services as a director-for-hire, churning out distinctly wacky films for the Japanese 'V-cinema' market – a kind of straight-to-video production industry that nonetheless holds none of the stigma that they do in the West, and is a vital outlet for young filmmakers, providing them with invaluable training. *Shinjuku Triad Society* was his breakthrough hit in the mid-90s, and proved to be a major turning point, earning a huge profit from video sales and – ironically – a Best New Director nomination at The Director's Guild ff Japan. The success of *STS* allowed him to direct two 'sequels,' *Rainy Dog* and *Ley Lines*, which formed the '*Black Society Trilogy*.'

Audition was his first hit in the West, and included extended scenes of torture and graphic amputations with a wire saw. After its notorious screening at the Edinburgh Film Festival, Miike became a media favourite and cause célèbre of the event, with distributors queuing up to make deals and release his films.

As for *Ichi the Killer*, it has been submitted to the BBFC no fewer than five times since 2002, and has had the same cuts imposed on it each time. In a statement, they explained, "The BBFC has required 11 cuts (approximately three and a quarter minutes of screen time) to the Japanese cinema film *Ichi the Killer*. The cuts have been made to remove extreme sexualised violence. These are the most substantial cuts required by the BBFC to an 18 rated film since 1994.

"The Board's main concern is with content which is likely to promote harmful activity. The Board's Guidelines constrain, in particular, depictions which eroticise or appear to endorse sexual violence. Of specific concern are sexual images in a violent context which are designed to titillate. The Guidelines take account of academic research which indicates that violence when mixed with explicit sexual images (women forcibly stripped, shots which linger on naked breasts or genitalia during rape or assault) may produce a harmful response in some viewers.

"The scenes cut from *Ichi the Killer* include naked women being sexually mutilated or beaten or killed. They contain images of erotically explicit violence which have never been passed by the BBFC at any classification level."

The 2010 Tokyo Shock release is uncut.

The Piano Teacher (2001)
Dir: Michael Haneke /Austria /France

The amazing Isabelle Huppert reminds me of Julianne Moore in the way she is always willing to take on challenging, unglamorous and often unsympathetic roles which push the viewer's patience about as far as it will go. She's the type of actress who will dedicate herself to a performance with all the endurance and dedication of a long distance marathon runner. And the audience is often asked to take that exhaustive journey with her, too. Her performance in *The Piano Teacher* offers up perhaps the finest of her career, and here she perfectly illustrates everything above as she plays Erika, a music professor at the Viennese Conservatory.

She lives with her mother in a small apartment and continually admonishes her piano students as a way of dealing with her frustrations and long-repressed sexual desires. She also seems equally fearful of rejection and has created an armour-plated persona for herself, that of a professional, emotionless droid. A bit like Margaret Thatcher, only prettier. However, this 'iron lady's' inner turmoil soon becomes apparent when she's alone: we see her sitting on the edge of her bath tub cutting her vagina with a razor blade, and visiting a public porno booth where she retrieves cummy scummy tissues from the bin and has a good old sniff.

Erika eventually meets Walter Klemmer (Benoit Magimel), a handsome young student eager to enroll at the Conservatory. Although he's much younger than Erika, he's immediately attracted to her but she does all she can to thwart his application. However, her decision is out-voted by her colleagues, and pretty soon Walter becomes her student. She continues with her ice-cold approach to him during lessons, but this only makes him *more* attracted to her. And one day in the toilets she sucks him off until he's on the verge of climax, then cruelly refuses to finish, even threatening to never see him again if he takes care of it himself. Of course, Klemmer continues to pursue her but she remains standoff-ish until she urges him to read a letter which details her masochistic fantasies, including being tied up, gagged and beaten.

Klemmer doesn't react well; he accuses her of being "sick" and "repulsive", and wants nothing more to do with her. It then becomes Erika's turn to beg as his rejection of her seems to fuel *her* obsession. She approaches him after hockey practice and talks him into having conventional sex on the floor. However, as soon as he penetrates her, she vomits. And Klemmer takes off again. Late one night, he bursts into her apartment in a rage like Frank Booth in *Blue Velvet* as he finally gives up his protests and attempts to satiate her masochistic desires. But here, his actions are less 'Baby wants to fuuuck!' and more 'Baby is angry and confuuused!', and Erika remains as tragically unhappy as ever.

Based on the uncompromising, semi-autobiographical novel by Elfriede Jelinek, director Michael Haneke seems to have created his film as if the notions were housed in the Hadron Collider, by combining an assortment of opposing particles – maturity and youth, aggression and submission, high and low-brow culture, suppression and gratification – then taking a few steps back to witness the inevitable 'big bang' in which everyone gets hurt. It's a fascinating, if gruelling, character study, seemingly designed to leave audiences reeling as the film closes on its bleakest note. It's one of Haneke's coldest films to date, but even here some viewers will find moments of humour, such as in the scene where Erika visits the porno booth, or later when she is caught 'flicking the bean' at a drive-in theatre, or attacking her mother in bed. But it's a film that was taken seriously enough by the BBFC to warrant it with an uncut 18 certificate, despite there being some clearly visible hardcore porn shots inserted during Erika's visit to the kabine.

In her book, *House of Psychotic Women*, Kier-La Janisse admits to having an admiration for Erika; "There are many reasons why I feel an affinity with the character of Erika Kohut, even though it's frightening to admit, given that she's one of the most disturbed and obsessively ritualistic characters I've ever encountered [...] I have so much love for this character that it's

hard to even describe." Indeed, in a book teeming with hundreds of neurotic movie characters, including Isabel Adjani in *Possession* and Charlotte Gainsbourg in *Antichrist*, Erika's slow unravelling is right up there with the most memorable in the 'psychotic women' sweepstakes. Janisse also points out Erika's need for control in the letter she writes for Walter; she may give him permission to hit her if she disobeys his 'orders', but ultimately the letter serves as a list of commands for him to carry out at her behest. They're both attracted to each other, and yet they both have very different desires for each other. And they both demand control. Disaster is thus pretty much inevitable.

Storytelling (2001)
Dir: Todd Solondz /USA

Todd Solondz's mischievous masterpiece opens on a section called '*Fiction*', in which students at a creative writing class have their work verbally torn to shreds by their teacher in a calm and ruthless, dead-eyed manner. One of the students is Vi (Selma Blair), who is later dumped by her pretentious boyfriend Marcus (Leo Fitzpatrick), who happens to be afflicted with cerebral palsy. Later that night, Vi heads out on the town to get drunk, and she bumps into her teacher from the writing class, Mr. Scott. Even with a few drinks down his neck, Mr. Scott refuses to loosen up or even smile, and their conversation remains as stilted as ever; she asks the questions and he answers them in a very blunt and unmoved way (she asks "Do you think I could make it as a writer?" and his deadpan reply is simply "No"). They eventually go back to his place. The lead up to sex is very cold and clinical – he basically sits on the bed and tells her what to do in a blank and matter-of-fact manner: "Take off your shirt... turn around... bend over", etc. Even while he's fucking her, he insists on keeping a tight control of the act, instructing her on what to say. He demands that she shouts "Fuck me hard, nigger" and demands that she keeps shouting it while he fucks her from behind. He comes across as some kind of stereotypical super-stud pimp, circa 1979.

Back in class the next day, and Vi has written a short story about her encounter with Mr. Scott. She reads it aloud to the class, and none of the students are aware of the fact that they had slept together the previous night. And what follows is a hilarious scene in which the students take turns at offering 'feedback' on her story. Solondz as a writer is clearly in his element here as he points out with great skill the students' PC awareness and their prejudice from the various intellectual angles they use to attack her story. "Why do people have to be so ugly and write about such ugly characters?" a human twiglet sniffs. "It's perverted. (sighs) I know you all think that I'm being prissy but I don't care. I was brought up in a certain way, and this is... mean-spirited".

"Yeah" another agrees. "Well, it did seem a little... sexist... Like, by using taboo language you were trying to shock us about the hollowness of your characters."

"I think it was a little bit racist", a young man offers.

A girl concurs, "It was completely racist, and beyond that, I felt deeply offended as a woman. As if women can only operate from experiences of objectification."

"Totally phallocentric" a female voice pipes up from the back.

"And so weirdly misogynistic", another agrees. "I mean, why does Jayne go through with this, is she stupid?"

Young man again – "Hey, but wasn't this a rape? Or did I miss something, because I'm confused. Because if this was rape, then why would she be a whore?"

Another woman, Catherine, calmly offers her own take on the matter, "It was confessional yet dishonest. Jayne pretends to be horrified by the sexuality that she in fact fetishizes. She subsumes herself to the myth of black male sexual potency, but then doesn't follow through. She thinks she respects African-Americans, even thinks they're cool and exotic – what a notch he'd make on her belt. But, of course, it all comes down to Mandingo cliché, and he calls her on it. In classic racist tradition, she demonizes and then runs for cover. But then, how could she behave otherwise? She's just a spoiled, suburban white girl with a Benetton rainbow complex... It's just my opinion, and what do I know? But I think it's a callow piece of writing…"

She then turns to Mr. Scott for his input. And his reply is interesting: "Callow… coy. Jayne, once more, isn't honest enough to admit it. Then she returns to the safety of her crippled translation, sexually impotent boyfriend."

Marcus then interrupts (and he also has no idea the story is true) "This is bullshit! Her story was the truth!"

Many critics have sided with Catherine's viewpoint with regards to the 'Fiction' segment in this film, as if Vi is the only one who is at fault here. But personally, I think there is much more going on besides. As well as criticizing Vi, I think Solondz was also criticizing every single character in the class. The black professor, Mr. Scott, is suggested as being just as guilty of self-martyrdom as Marcus, the kid with cerebral palsy whose story is dismissed. (Interestingly, none of the other class members attack Marcus' story in the way they attacked Vi's, because of Marcus' cerebral palsy and their own PC awareness. Mr. Scott, on the other hand, is the only one allowed to criticize it because he is black.) Mr. Scott has written a Pulitzer Prize winning book, *A Sunday Lynching*, and that title alone suggests an angle of 'oh, me and my people are victims' kind of thing, and the un-PC suspicion that black people are obsessed with their own skin colour. Vi may secretly fetishize and demonize African-Americans, but in reality she is treated almost abusively. The sexual encounter between Vi and Mr. Scott borders on degradation. She is accused of subsuming herself in 'Mandingo clichés', etc, but the critical Catherine and Mr. Scott are just as complicit as her in this; for example, Scott demands to be called "nigger" during sex, and Catherine poses in handcuffs like a white subservient. Mr. Scott claims "Once you start writing, it all becomes fiction", but he and Catherine also have a great deal of trouble in separating the fiction from Vi as an author. Thus, in reality they are all accusing Vi herself of being racist and fake when those accusations should have been levelled at the character in the story, Jayne. Many critics completely overlooked the complexity of this first segment in the film, and as a result they seem to have fallen into Solondz' trap by reacting in a similar way as the ill-informed students in class, projecting their own PC awareness and personal prejudices onto the scene. To my mind, the 'Fiction' segment was an attack on those who espouse political correctness, not a condoning of it.

The second segment, 'Non-Fiction', centres on Toby, a budding documentarian who is making a film about Scooby, a high school student, and his dysfunctional family, the Livingstons. Toby is quite nerdy in appearance but he seems decent enough, if a little weird. He follows Scooby around school, and he always insists on filming sequences in the boy's locker room for some reason. A constant source of amusement – is Toby a perv or just a naïve, ambitious filmmaker with a heart of gold? Is he exploiting Scooby and his family, or just recklessly inexperienced at recording the reality he sees all around him? Director Solondz plays on this ambiguity until the very end, making his actions and comments open to interpretation, good or bad. Toby's assistant is played by Mike Schank, the same guy who appeared in the hilarious documentary, *American Movie: The Making of Northwestern*, as Mark Borchardt's chemically-damaged friend. Solondz seems to have cast him here as a tribute to that incredible film (if you haven't seen *American Movie* you're in for a treat). Anyone else sporting such a dismal dress sense would have been thrown off the set, tarred, feathered, and kicked in the nuts. But because it's Mike Schank, he gets away with it. And he probably spent his actor's fee on scratch cards.

The Livingstons are a middle class Jewish family, and Scooby is a troubled kid. At the dinner table, Scooby tells his mother "In a sense, since you would never have met dad if your family had stayed in Europe, if it wasn't for Hitler none of us would have been born." His father reacts badly to this comment and sends him to his room. The Livingstons are a heartbreakingly dysfunctional family; the father, Marty (John Goodman), is strict in an old-fashioned, 'proper' sense, but his attempts to keep the unit sane and sound just makes things worse. The mother is a silent, meek type who lets dad be the boss. Middle brother, Brady, is a school jock American football player who is afraid that Scooby's closet homosexuality will eventually come out to wreck his popularity at school. And the youngest brother, Mikey, is an insensitive and belligerent little turd who not only assumes the world revolves around him, but that the way it revolves just isn't good enough. All in all, it's quite depressing to watch this family falling apart. The docu-style footage reminded me of *Capturing the Friedmans*, which was released in the following year.

The most interesting thread in this second segment is the relationship between the youngest Livingston brother, Mikey, and the El Salvadorian housemaid, Consuelo. The young boy Mikey is a refreshing change from the norm as far as kid characters go. Often in films, children are depicted as if they're the perfect moralists with a firm grasp of the nuances and discretions of adult conversation. But in reality, children are very rarely like that. Kids often lack that social discretion which governs adult talk. Some things adults don't mention for the sake of manners simply bypass the child's mind. Kids, in turn, will just come right out with it. And that is one of the reasons why Mikey is such an intriguing character. Kids often say stupid and offensive things, not necessarily wanting to upset you, but because their minds haven't sufficiently developed enough to keep schtum when an adult would. Or, as Matt Stone [co-creator of *South Park*] so eloquently put it, "[kids] don't have any kind of social tact or etiquette, they're just complete little raging bastards." Mikey's scenes with Consuelo illustrate this point perfectly. She's about 60-something years old and has four brothers and five sisters, yet she scrubs away on her hands and knees for the Livingston family. Mikey questions her out of curiosity, and asks why her parents had so many children when they were so financially poor.

She tries to deflect the question (she's trying to concentrate on her work), and answers "It was God's way." This would have satisfied many kids, but Mikey's curiosity deepens, and he begins to question Consuelo on her belief in God. She patiently tries to deal with the conversation in a simple and uncomplicated way, but young Mikey amusingly manages to pose an even more complicated question for each of her answers. His delivery sounds insulting and mocking, especially when he tells her she should "smile more" while she slaves away.

At this point in the film I quite liked Mikey, despite him being borderline rude to Consuelo. However, as the film progresses it becomes clear that Mikey is a very deviant child. In the middle of the night he heads downstairs to wake her up so that she can clean up some grape juice he has spilled on the kitchen floor. When he enters her basement room he discovers that she is already awake and crying. And so he begins firing off his questions again, like before. Not once does he comfort her or try to empathize. Consuelo, bless her heart, explains to him that her nephew in El Salvador has just been executed on death row. "Maybe it's for the best", Mikey replies. "Bad people should be killed". Moments later he asks her "Why was he on death row?"

"For rape and murder".

"... What is rape?"

"It is when you love someone, and the other person doesn't love you... And you do something about it".

"Sometimes I feel like my parents don't love me..."

"Well", she replies, "when you are older you can do something about it..."

Consuelo breaks down crying again. Mikey hesitates, as if thinking of something reassuring to say. Does this kid have a heart after all? "Consuelo?" he asks, "I spilt some juice downstairs. Do you think you could clean it up now?"

By the end of the film, Mikey is clearly a conniving, controlling, future maniac in the making. Always manipulating situations for his own selfish ends. In one scene, he hypnotizes his father, and that sequence spells out just how ruthless and heartless he is when he suggests his father should fire Consuelo, and that he should love him at the expense of his comatose brother who was badly injured in an American football accident.

Marty, the overbearing patriarch of the family, is cynical and homophobic and proud of his Jewish heritage. He demands that his children secure stereotypical financial success; they should submit themselves to the assembly line of the Ivy League school system and make tons of money upon graduation to be socially accepted. Only then will his sons be successful in his eyes. He has a closed mind and seems like he's too old to change his views. He also has an openness about him, a willingness to speak his mind, no matter how crass it may sound to others. For instance, when Toby the filmmaker asks for permission to make his documentary about Scooby, he makes no secret about his desire for financial gain, "What will we get out of this?" he asks.

Toby's documentary is just as much about Toby as it is about Scooby and his family. During the little clips we see of it, the documentary is every bit the narcissistic piece of naval gazing as it is an attempt at social commentary. In one scene he walks down the school corridors with his camera in hand, talking away and giving the viewer's his opinions. "I walk down hallways like the ones I used to walk down in high school...I used to wake up depressed, suicidal, filled with despair. Beneath these masks of courtesy and friendliness, I knew there was darkness." He

also overuses video effects like split-frame and morphing effects, typical of an inexperienced filmmaker.

Many have compared Toby's character with director Solondz himself, suggesting that Toby is Solondz's alter-ego. And while there are some elements of truth to this (apparently they look similar in appearance and they are both filmmakers), it would be a mistake to view Toby as Solondz himself. Some viewers also interpret Toby's documentary as his attempt to ridicule the Livingston family, and again I disagree with that idea. He *is* pretentious and self-centred, but I believe he had the family's best interests at heart, and it was never his intention to make Scooby look foolish on camera.

The MPAA demanded that the sex scene between Vi and Mr. Scott be edited or removed entirely (it's not that graphic) for the R rating. When Solondz refused to cut it, the censors simply gave the film the dreaded NC-17 rating, and added a ridiculous red box over the scene to conceal the footage. Rather than bowing to the demands of the MPAA, Solondz admirably allowed the scene to stand in its altered form, and called it for what it is – a needless form of censorship. Solondz described the addition of the box as a political statement: "I was prepared to make that political statement. This is something I've always been prepared to do, as long as the audience is aware of what it's not allowed to see. That's how I feel politically about that."

Intriguingly, there was an entire third part of the film which was dropped for unknown reasons. It allegedly centred on a gay football player, and included an explicit sex scene with a male partner.

Hell House (2001)
Dir: George Ratliff /USA

Hell House is an American documentary that exposes the bizarre practice of evangelicals luring unsuspecting people into what they think is an old-time spooky house, but what they actually get is a spectacular display of melodrama showing how sin leads to Hell. It's an approach to keeping people on the 'straight and narrow' that has drawn much criticism, even from within the church community, and *Hell House* shows viewers just how much time and thought goes into the preparation of these horrific sociological campaigns.

The Trinity Assembly of God Church in Texas

prepares the latest Hell House show, which calls for casting auditions, local promotion, music and stage design. We also get to meet various young actors from the church school who are very excited about the project, and through scores of documentary footage we watch them re-enact school shootings, AIDS deaths, drug deals turned sour, and even botched abortions. Yes, it comes across as totally tacky and tasteless, but add the church angle and you've got something genuinely disturbing on your hands.

It amazes me to think that the Church gave permission for an outside documentary crew to enter the fray and chart the organisation of a Hell House event without any restrictions (it reminds me of that Louis Theroux BBC TV special that centred on 'The Most Evil Family In America', in which the Westboro Baptist Church, a fundamentalist Christian sect led by Fred Phelps, are shown picketing at AIDS funerals, shouting provocative slogans like "God hates fags," and generally pissing off the local population wherever possible). As you would expect, the footage is shot and edited in an impartial way, allowing the admittedly strange proceedings to flow and to tell its story of how some people go about trying to make the world a holier place. This fly-on-the-wall style, or if you will, 'Gods-eye-view' of things helps tremendously, and you never feel that you're being preached at or invited to mock the film's subjects, unlike Louis Theroux's documentaries.

Regardless of one's religious views, *Hell House* is a very well-constructed and fascinating documentary that offers viewers the rare chance to delve into one of the stranger corners of middle America. The DVD includes the short film, *The Devil Made Me Do It*. Also directed by George Ratliff, it shows the Trinity's re-enacting of the Columbine Massacre, which outraged the local public and helped secure the funding needed to make the feature documentary.

Battle Royale (2001)
(Orig title: *Batoru Rowaiaru*)
Dir: Kinji Fukasaku /Japan
In the not-too-distant future, the Japanese government passes a new law to deal with soaring youth crime, by randomly selecting school pupils and sending them off to an island where they are given weapons and ordered to kill each other off in three days until only one survives. The pupils are also tagged with explosive metallic devices around their necks which can be remotely detonated if anyone breaks the rules or tries to escape.

Coming on like a 21st Century update of William Golding's classic novel, *Lord of the Flies*, *Battle Royale* presents its characters with choices that are even more extreme. The film's often shocking violence has restricted it to adult audiences (in Japan, however, it was given the R-15 certificate, allowing it to be watched by 15 year olds – school kids the same age as the characters in the film). Those who take on a censorious stance against kid-on-kid violence will be appalled by much that goes on in this film, but of course, this is all just a fantasy; it doesn't encourage violence; in fact, veteran director Kinji Fukasaku does an excellent job of displaying the violence in a horrific and alienating, degrading manner, and as such, this is not the kind of cinematic violence that will have the audience cheering along.

From the get-go, the film doesn't waste any time in setting up its ludicrous premise, and before long we're in the presence of the legendary 'Beat' Takeshi Kitano, who is thoroughly annoyed at his unruly class. The students are gassed on a bus and wake up on the isolated island where they are lectured on the rules of the game, and Kitano throws a knife into the forehead of a girl who dares to talk over him, and blows the head off a class troublemaker to make a point about how serious the situation is. Then, for the subsequent three days, the 42 remaining school pupils are left on their own on the island to kill each other off in any way they see fit until only one survives. And what follows is a torrent of horrific vignettes depicting the deaths of these children as they double-cross each other, and the deadly scenarios are all painfully realistic. By the time you begin identifying with characters, they're gone in a series of disturbing, unsettling and often darkly funny ways. Some decide to kill themselves rather than take part, psycho volunteer Kiriyama gets hold of a fully automatic weapon and goes on a shooting rampage for fun, class bitch Mitsuko also takes a liking to serial murder, while Shuya and Noriko form a pact with previous BR winner Kawada, and they use computer equipment to try and rig the game so that more than one person can survive the carnage.

If this was some Sam Peckinpah-style shoot-em-up with a cast of gung-ho, trigger-happy adults, no one would bat an eyelid. But because *Battle Royale* is a film which presents murderers and victims alike as teenagers, it is all the more shocking and transgressive in the age of post-Columbine where barely a year goes by without someone deciding to take out their frustrations and impotence on the world by shooting up a school. In *Battle Royale*, kids are graphically torn apart by bullets from automatic weapons, beheaded, have their throats slashed, shot with crossbows, jump to their deaths, and even poisoned. As with the aforementioned *Lord of the Flies*, which was an obvious influence here, this film sets out to present its audience with an allegory rather than an exploration of real-life child violence. *Battle Royale* was based on Koshun Takami's popular novel of the same name, and it basically skims over the initial set-up so that we can get right down to business. Just like the book, the film quite early on establishes the idea that Class B is made up of pupils who are neither wholly innocent nor particularly deserving of their forthcoming punishments. And while this whole scenario has ample opportunity to work as an effective satire on crass media and bureaucracy, director Fukasaku decides not to explore this angle beyond the amusing instructional video that is played for the kids and is presented by a very squeaky announcer who gives enthusiastic tips on how to effectively kill-off their rivals. She comes across as like a Blue Peter presenter from a future police state. But perhaps the most disturbing idea in the film is that the teens are not there to entertain conservative society, but to be taught a harsh lesson.

This was Fukasaku's 60th movie. Before *Battle Royale*, he was best known for his cult classics such as *The Green Slime* (1968), *Tora! Tora! Tora!* (1970), and *Virus* (1980). He also directed lesser known classics like *Battles Without Honor Or Humanity* (1973) and *Street Mobster* (1972) for Toei studios (interestingly, the shots in *BR* of the blue sea crashing against the rocks on the island shore are eerily reminiscent of the Toei logo screen of the 60s and 70s). He had very personal reasons for directing *Battle Royale*. "I immediately identified with the student characters," he said. "I was fifteen when World War II came to an end. By then, my class had been drafted and was working in a munitions factory. In July 1945, we were caught in artillery fire. Up until then, the attacks had been air raids, and you had a chance

of escaping from those. It was impossible to run or hide from those shells that rained down. We survived by diving for cover under our friends. After the attacks, my class had to dispose of the corpses. It was the first time in my life I'd seen so many dead bodies. As I lifted severed arms and legs, I had a fundamental awakening... everything we'd been taught in school about how Japan was fighting the war to win world peace, was a pack of lies. Adults could not be trusted."

As a movie, *Battle Royale* barely gives the audience time to draw breath, let alone relax. It's a film which flits between horror and heartbreak, even in its most celebrated, visceral sequences. But there's also a subdued melancholy and contemplation here that is guaranteed to haunt long after the film is over.

Cradle of Fear (2001)
Dir: Alex Chandon /UK

Eli Roth claimed that the inspiration for *Hostel* came from a news story about a snuff website based in Thailand where paying punters could dictate murders in any specific way they wanted. This idea had already been explored in a segment of the British anthology horror, *Cradle of Fear* (2001). One of the stories centres on office worker, Richard, who chances upon a website called the 'Sick Room'. The site allows its customers to participate in brutal murders – by hammer, or beatings, or strangulation, etc – with anonymity, all from the safety of your own home, or office. Richard soon develops an obsession with the site, spending all of his money and getting into serious debt to fuel his sadistic fantasies. First his girlfriend leaves him, then the bailiffs show up, and soon enough his home is repossessed altogether, but still he obsessively clicks away in the Sick Room. One day the website disappears, so he investigates and eventually tracks down the site's location... The other tales include a young woman (the beautiful Emily Booth) having a one-night-stand with a goth guy (Dani Filth) whom she picks up at a club, only to suffer horrendous hallucinations the following morning; an amputee willing to resort to murder to be able to walk again; and a couple of burglars who get more than they bargained for when they break into the wrong house. The stories have a wraparound segment featuring a notorious serial killer who makes a break for freedom. Cradle of Fear was released direct to DVD to many negative reviews. In fact, I personally don't know anyone apart from myself who enjoyed it. I've never understood why people are so quick to dismiss it. Yes, it's low-budget and shot on video, but the stories are quite engaging and the production values are pretty good for a film of its ilk. I've seen hundreds of shot-on-video horror movies over the years and Cradle of Fear is far superior to 90% of them. Yes, I know Dani Filth is a prick, but as far as EC Comics inspired movies go, Cradle of Fear is better than Creepshow (1982). I'm sorry if that's a controversial opinion. But it's true.

The Card Player (2004) and Untraceable (2008) also use internet snuff as a starting point. The Card Player is about a serial killer who kidnaps women in Rome and challenges detectives to games of online poker. If the investigators loose, they can look forward to seeing the women being murdered live on web-cam. Untraceable has a similar mean-spirited killer who runs an untraceable website in which victims are murdered on a live stream. And, being aware of the public's desire to view forbidden material, he rigs the site so that the more people are logged on, the quicker the victims die. While having interesting premises, both of these films are ultimately let down by bland characters, join-the-dots plot-lines and a 'play-it-safe', *Thesis* syndrome' of toning down the more disturbing elements in order to make them palatable for mainstream audiences. *The Card Player* is particularly disappointing considering director Dario Argento was once one of the kingpins of horror. It's an embarrassment, 'ooh, look, grandpa has discovered the internet!'

Zebra Lounge (2001)
Dir: Kari Skogland /Canada

A naughty suburbanite couple, Alan and Wendy (Cameron Daddo and Brandy Led-ford), are drawn into the seedy world of swingers where they encounter Jack and Louise (Stephen Baldwin and Kristy Swan-son). Their first overnight get-together is a success. However – surprise, surprise – the mysterious Jack and Louise begin showing up unexpectedly in their private lives, until discomfort and mild annoyance turns to all-out menace, as the couple turn out to be obsessive psychos. All very ludicrous but entertaining addition to the interloper sub-genre. It's a bit like *The Cable Guy*, only with a much more serious tone and

two lunatics instead of one. You can predict how the story will unfold within the first five minutes, but it's also a lot of fun if you're in the right mood.

Trouble Every Day (2001)
Dir: Claire Denis /France /Germany /Japan

Neuroscientist, Shane (Vvincent Gallo), arrives in Paris looking for a mysterious researcher whose paper has piqued his interest as it may help to cure his own unidentified illness. Meanwhile, the doctor in question, Semeneau (Alex Descas), keeps a troubled woman locked in a room – a woman who seems to share the same illness as Shane, a form of vampirism... Dull, pretentious and serving no other purpose than to bore its audience to death, *Trouble Every Day* shifts vampire lore into the realms of 'science' and neuro-chemistry. It is hinted that Semeneau made his scientific discoveries on the origins of blood thirst and cannibalism while on a research expedition to Africa. As you would expect, this scientific approach to the vampire myth is as remote as they come – cold, clinical, numbing and seemingly all out to shock.

Route 666 (2001)
Dir: William Wesley /USA

A couple of cops, Lou Diamond Phillips and Lori Petty, turn off the main highway to elude the hitmen who are intent on killing a snitching witness in their custody. They head down a disused stretch of road, known locally as 'Route 666,' and come up against a horde of concrete-faced zombie convicts who are charged with extra power every time blood is spilled on the road. The impressive ghouls brandish roadworks tools to pound their victims into the asphalt. But, in order to bring the film up to feature length, a further menace later shows up to augment the zombies, and this leads to a last-reel cameo appearance from L.Q. Jones who plays a 70s-era, redneck Sheriff. *Route 666* is a far better movie than anyone could have expected.

Stop the Bitch Campaign (2001)
Dir: Kosuke Suzuki /Japan

A couple of disgruntled losers decide to use the services of a bunch of schoolgirl street whores and run away without paying, causing a major street war between the whores and the pussy swindlers! Based on the Manga by madness and rape-loving Hideo Yamamoto (the man who created Ichi the Killer), Stop the Bitch Campaign is outrageous fun from start to finish. The Boss (played by Kenichi Endo) is superb as the out-of-control rapist; the scene where he deflowers and tortures a first time whore is dark, misogynistic, and funny as hell! The soundtrack throws up 60s style retro garage rock, classical choruses, and country pop shit, all adding to the mayhem on screen. The crazy opening credits feature all kinds of sex, torture, and S&M in a rapid montage style, and the chaos never lets up. A fast-paced sleaze fest of guilty pleasures. Enjoy!

Session 9 (2001)
Dir: Brad Anderson /USA
One of the best straight-to-video horror movies released in the early 00s, *Session 9* is superior to much of the swill that makes it onto the big screen. It's a curious blending of *The Blair Witch Project, Cube* and John Carpenter's *The Thing*, as a team of workers are sent to remove asbestos from an old lunatic asylum, with seriously creepy consequences. The predictable ending is a bit of a let down, but the build-up tension, spectacular location and excellent cast – which includes Peter Mullan, Josh Lucas and David Caruso – more than make up for the film's routine finale. There are no CGI ghouls or hammy psychos here, just slow-building fear and skin-crawling creepiness, especially in the moments where Mullan plays back those old tape recordings.

They Crawl (2001)
Dir: John Allardice /USA
Another TV movie made for the Sci-Fi Channel. This time we get a government-sponsored research project that transforms cockroaches into top secret bio-weapons. And the research falls into the hands of a body mutilation cult called Trillion. Mickey Rourke appears in a 'blink-and-you'll-miss-it' cameo role, purely for the quick pay cheque. And the creature at the end is hilariously bad. The script offers up howlers, such as "You have a kind heart. I know people who'd like to have it in their icebox." The 'special effects' are beyond ridiculous, and there's probably a joke somewhere about a film attempting to mimic *Mimic,*

Malice@doll (2001)
Dir: Keitaro Montonaga /Japan
A bizarre CGI future fantasy from Japan. Long after the human race has become extinct, robotic sex droids get bored and transform into monstrous predators which attack the weaker robots. Malice, the kind heroic one, becomes a flesh human and helps the victims. With an aesthetic borrowing just as much from Terry Gilliam as HR Giger, this is a dull, overlong excuse to have girl-shaped things abused on screen.

Das Experiment (2001)
Dir: Oliver Hirschbiegel /Germany
In a scientific experiment, volunteers are assigned the roles of guards and prisoners. But those who are the guards begin to brutalize the others. Having taken its inspiration from an experiment which was conducted at Stanford University in the early 70s, which showed how power ultimately corrupts, this disappointing film wastes much of its fascinating premise and is merely content to dish out some action-style violence and visuals. The American remake in 2010 was even worse, substituting unedifying shallowness for deeper scrutiny.

Metropolis (2001)
(Orig title: *Metoroporisu*)
Dir: Rintaro /Japan
An unofficial remake of Fritz Lang's 1927 sci-fi masterpiece. To avoid copyright issues, much of the plot and the characters have been given a major overhaul, but the end result is unmistakable in its debt to the German classic.

This time, Freder is re-imagined as the spoilt brat son of the Master, and Frederson this time appears as a large-nosed boss who mourns for the death of his young daughter. The mad scientist is now a dumpy dwarf who is killed early on by Freder while putting the final touches to his machine. Maria is now presented as Tina, an android in the life-like form of a young girl who bears a close resemblance to Frederson's deceased daughter. Of course, the Master of Metropolis wants to place Tina on the throne as the new ruler of the mega-city. However, Freder the son is suspicious of the machine, and protective of his father, and does all he can to stop Tina's rise to power. Caught in the middle of all this is a young boy who discovers Tina in a deep underground holding. They become fast friends amid the chaos. In the end, Tina brings down the familiar destruction of the city, and it all ends with a climactic scene right out of *Battle Angel Alita* (1990).

An ambitious and impressive anime with a much bigger budget than usual. Unlike many features of its kind, this was clearly aimed at a Western audience. The characters and their motivations are nicely fleshed out, including the addition of a dogged detective who is trying to figure out what the hell is going on in his beloved city. Of course, this being a retro-flavoured future fantasy, you can expect lots of dazzling overhead shots of the metropolis, which juxtaposes the pristine towers reaching to the heavens with the darkness of the rat-infested underworld where resentful revolutionaries and ordinary members of the public are left to rot. And, like *Akira* (1988) before it, there is a mythical element here, but it doesn't overstep its boundary and is kept nicely within the purview of the story.

Dead Creatures (2001)
Dir: Andrew Parkinson /UK

A very rare attempt to make a zombie movie from the zombie's perspectives. Lucio Fulci had previously broached the concept in the finale of *The Beyond* (1981) where his two protagonists found themselves trapped in a 'sea of darkness', an eternal empty space where their eyes were blanked out – a superb image of existential despair. Clive Barker also addressed the theme in his short story, '*Scape-goats*' (from *Books of Blood Volume 3*), another vision of eternal emptiness as the female protagonist became an underwater zombie, condemned to drift in her own 'sea of darkness' forever. With *Dead Creatures* we explore the concept once again, but disappointingly, in very little detail, and with nothing new to bring to the plate, so to speak. Instead, what we get is a 'neorealist'/Ken Loach approach to the subject-matter, which may find favour with critics but is sure to bore the rest of us to death. The story follows women who 'live' with some kind of zombie/cannibal infection as they wallow in 'dead time', a post-mortem existence where they're condemned to sit around watching soaps on TV and drift around from flat to flat, all the while casually feasting on human corpses. There's an obvious subtextual strain here concerning the underclass and AIDS, elements which were later updated in the French *Les revenants* (2004).

In the Belly of the Beast (2001)
Dir: Alex Chisholm /Canada

FantAsia was founded in Montreal by Martin Sauvageau, Andre Dubois and Pierre Corbell in 1996. The aim was to establish a film festival specialising in Asian genre films. The first event was a smash success, a month-long extravaganza which focused primarily on Hong Kong action and Cat III movies, including the films of Chow Yun Fat and Ringo Lam. The momentum continued over the following years with submissions accepted from a whole range of genres, and it became one of the great international cult movie festivals in the world.

This superb documentary by Alex Chisholm presents the second FantAsia event from July 1997, and includes the likes of Karim Hussain, Richard Stanley, Nacho Cerda and Jim Van Bebber screening their latest works (and works in progress) for the first time for a North American audience. This film does much to de-glamorize the practice of film-making and instead uncovers what is essentially a collection of horror stories as many of the directors in attendance share their tales of woe, from dodgy financiers and distributors, to a lack of funding and heroin addiction, this film will convince all but the most crazed and determined artists from ever taking the plunge and making an independent film.

Slashers (2001)
Dir: Maurice Devereaux /Canada

By the early 00s, it wasn't long before the internet age crept its way into the snuff realm with a series of films which focused on evil websites and live streaming death. The first in this area was *Muzan-e* (1999), the Japanese AV shocker which blurred the line between fact and fiction by presenting it as a faux-documentary. It was later followed by *Slashers*, a narrative-based – but equally eccentric – take on the snuff genre which comes on like a cross between *Takashi's Castle* and *The Running Man* (1987). Six contestants have volunteered for a Japanese game show in which they have to pass through a maze while being pursued by maniacs, and the show is broadcast live across the globe. It's an interesting concept for a horror movie, and there are some fun moments here and there (including one character who is cut in half with a chainsaw), but it's ultimately forgettable and unremarkable, and isn't helped by the crappy performances, unconvincing characters and inane dialogue.

Dagon (2001)
Dir: Stuart Gordon /Spain /USA

Director Stuart Gordon, producer Brian Yuzna and writer Denis Poali teamed up for the third time to tackle another HP Lovecraft project after the hits Re-Animator (1985) and From Beyond (1986), for the less successful Dagon. After a violent thunder storm ravages the coast of Spain, blood spilled on a sailing yacht leaks into the sea, attracting a sea-dwelling tentacled monster. Two teenage love birds escape the boat (one of whom wears a 'Miskatonic' t-shirt), and head for the church for help. However, the place turns out to be a demonic fortress whose worshippers (the whole town) offers up human sacrifices for the beast. To make matters worse, the townsfolk transform into shambling ghouls after dark and target the youngsters. Dagon is a fast-paced, no-nonsense monster movie which offers up slimy scaly creatures, a small-town paranoia angle, and a moribund sense of humour at the expense of cheap holiday destinations. And though the film owes more to Lovecraft's The Shadow Over Innsmouth than Dagon, the impressive head-skinning sequence more than makes up for it.

Roberto Succo (2001)
Dir: Cedric Kahn /France /Switzerland

Based on the exploits of Italian serial killer, Roberto Succo, this film explores his compulsive lying and Walter Mitty-like fantasy life moreso than his killings, and boasts a superb controlled performance by first-time actor, Stefano Casetti. It's an intimate portrait, with director Kahn holding back somewhat with the more explosive and sensationalist elements of the story. He also admirably keeps things nicely balanced by refusing to glorify or pass judgement on any of the characters, whether it be Succo, his unsuspecting girlfriend or his pursuers.

Soul Survivors (2001)
Dir: Stephen Carpenter /USA

The producers of I Know What You Did Last Summer and Urban Legend tried their hands once again at a teen terror flick, and failed miserably as we get a pretty student who loses her boyfriend in a car wreck and then finds herself spooked by discomforting hallucinations. Talented up-and-comers Wes Bentley and Casey

Affleck were completely wasted in this, and the silly visuals – which are supposed to represent the dark dimension between life and death – are incredibly silly. Plus, the twist ending is one of the worst in memory.

St. John's Wort (2001)
(Orig title: Otogiriso)
Dir: Ten Shimoyama /Japan

The influence of The Blair Witch Project had soon crept its way over to Japan in the early 00s for St. John's Wort, a creepy shocker in which characters foolishly head off in search of an isolated house which is surrounded by the eponymous herb, and are terrorized by an evil twin in the attic. The heroine creates bizarre artwork for video games, and this is a good excuse to decorate the look of the film in a visual style of hi-tech glossiness added in post-production. The ending is quite a surprise.

Down (2001)
(aka The Shaft)
Dir: Dick Maas /USA /Holland

A remake of Dick Maas' own enjoyable Dutch flick, The Lift (1983), which revisits the concept of an evil elevator that is controlled by a military bio-chip. Resilient reporter (Naomi Watts in Ring mode) and a lift technician (James Marshall) uncover the malicious conspiracy, but the real fun here comes from the scenes in which the crafty machine plunges a pregnant woman down twenty storeys, lures a vicious blind man and his guide dog down the shaft, decapitates security guards and plays games with a little girl.

Ted Bundy (2002)
Dir: Matthew Bright /USA

Of all the serial killers operating in America in the 1970s, Ted Bundy was perhaps the most terrifying of them all. With monsters like Henry Lee Lucas, Dean Corll, and John Wayne Gacy, you only had to look at those guys to know it would be best to stay well clear, but Bundy was different; he was intelligent, handsome and charismatic, and his smile worked a charm on the ladies. The dark side to his nature was that he took great pleasure in bludgeoning young women to death. He was a textbook definition of a psychopath; a shrewd and manipulative individual who felt absolutely no empathy for his fellow humans, and was capable of the most heinous crimes on a simple whim if it was in his own interests to do so. And he didn't feel a shred of remorse about it either. Often referred to as a 'chameleon', Bundy embodied that nightmare archetype of the boogeyman, a monster whom college kids could confide in and, in his job as a volunteer councellor, the more vulnerable members of society could open up to. He also had that animal cunning to cover his tracks, and it was this alertness that helped him to escape from police custody twice.

This truncated biopic of Bundy follows in the tradition of films like *Ed Gein* (2000) as a fairly honest re-telling of the story, combined with the comic interludes and high-camp of Mary Harron's *American Psycho*. Director Matthew Bright (who had previously made the cult classics *Freeway* and *Freeway 2: Confessions of a Trickbaby*) uses fast cuts, crash zooms, slo-mo and even time-lapse photography to produce a thoroughly disturbing film that flits from the horrific violence to unsettling humour and torture from one scene to the next, as a way of deliberately bludgeoning his audience. But despite this, it's certainly not the moral outrage that the press would have you believe, nor is it the masterpiece others claim it to be either. Indeed, the film ultimately fails due to its inability to decide whether it is going to be a serious biopic or a sleazy piece of cinematic sensationalism. Trying to do both in the same film just doesn't work. In Bright's favour, he certainly empties his directorial bag of tricks here, but his flippant way of depicting the crimes (usually with women being bopped on the head with a heavy iron carjack for comic effect) comes across as silly and insensitive; it's like he's saying, 'Oh, that Ted Bundy, wasn't he such a ca-rraaayyyzzzzeeee guy?!!'. On the positive side, the scenes which show the final moments of Bundy before his execution are especially powerful; he has his head shaved and his arsehole is forcibly stuffed with cotton wool to ensure he doesn't soil himself while in the electric chair. It's little details like this that Bright relishes in showing us. Also, Bundy's last interview shows him in a reflective mood, claiming "there's so much more to me than just killing," a sentiment no doubt shared by most cold-blooded killers, even fictional ones like Patrick Bateman. An interesting fact for trivia fans: The electric chair used to kill Bundy at the end of the film is the very same chair that was used for Bundy's real-life execution.

Auto Focus (2002)
Dir: Paul Schrader /USA

The story of Bob Crane, a Californian DJ who became a star when he landed himself a role in the US sitcom, *Hogan's Heroes*, and then descended into sex and drugs debauchery and eventually hit rock bottom as his marriage disintegrated and he was later found bludgeoned to death in his own bed.

Writer/director Paul Schrader is at the top of his game here as he continues in his fascination with sex as a substitution for a life of substance, the seduction of porn, and reckless characters who add to their own corruption and downfall. Schrader doesn't flinch from depicting the sexcapades that made up Bob Crane's life. Schrader remains completely committed and non-judgemental in his approach to telling the sad story, unsentimentally cutting open Crane's addictions to fame and technology and sex. The film clinically explores these matters like some kind of cinematic autopsy.

Also on top form is actor Greg Kinnear whose performance here surpasses anything he has ever done in his career, before or since. He manages to make Crane likeable even as he spirals out of control, never asking the audience to sympathise with this stupidly oblivious sleaze ball. And he is aided by the brilliant Willem Dafoe, who plays the gadget man, Carpenter, who is a master at pathetic seediness and neediness. The mutual dependency between these two characters forms the core of the movie as Carpenter provides the contacts and Crane the star power. The scene where Crane learns of a wandering finger after an orgy is hilarious ("You put your finger in my ass?!!!").

Forced Entry (2002)
Dir: Lizzy Borden /USA

Not to be confused with Shaun Costello's 1973 film, this *Forced Entry* is loosely based on the crimes of California serial killer Richard Ramirez, and is presented as a repulsive, XXX pseudo-snuff video. In a particularly ugly scene, Ramirez and his two accomplices record themselves raping a pregnant woman before shooting her and her dog. In a later scene, another woman is forced into the killer's van and is filmed being beaten, raped and stabbed. This is a shot-on-video micro-production all the way; the filmmakers aren't breaking any new ground here. They're not breaking any new holes, either. The victims in this film are obviously no strangers to the world of adult entertainment production – they have that modern porn 'look' with their pouting lips and shaved pussy-lips, and have clearly been double-penetrated dozens of times before (talk about gazing into the gaping abyss). The film caused controversy while still in production; a film crew making a documentary about the porn industry walked off the set in disgust during one of the rougher scenes, and subsequent reviews have been generally scathing, accusing Extreme Associates and their productions of being "disgusting," "abhorrent" and "evil." I know the cast were all pretending, but you do get the feeling that there is a genuine mean-spiritedness behind this video.

Irreversible (2002)
Dir: Gaspar Noe /France

A seat snaps upright as one offended viewer heads for the exit. Bang. Bang. Bang. More seats are vacated. Footsteps march towards the exit, then run up the isles. The foyer door swings open and swings closed. It's May 2002 at the Cannes Film Festival. On screen, a blood-red light beats on and off, the camera moves around wildly, and abstract noises can be heard on the soundtrack. It's the premiere of *Irreversible*, the first of many walkouts.

Within ten minutes, a steady flow of people are leaving the cinema. They have just witnessed one of the most graphically realistic murders in movie history, as a man has his face repeatedly smashed in with a fire extinguisher until his skull disintegrates. But they've spared themselves the film's main point of contention – a nine-minute long, single-take, stationary shot of a woman being anally raped and kicked around after taking a wrong turn on her way home after a party.

Not a re-watchable kind of film, *Irreversible* utilizes the same story telling technique used in previous films like *Memento* by presenting its chronological sequence of events in reverse. We briefly spend a few moments in the company of two men who appear to be in a prison cell. One of these men (Philippe Nahon, who had previously starred in Noe's *Carne* and *Seul contre tous*) admits to having slept with his own daughter, the only person he ever loved. "Time destroys everything," he announces. His cellmate is more optimistic, "We all think we're Mephisto. It's no big deal. We fuck up and they say it's bad news. It's tragic. Can't forget the

pleasure, the joy. There's no bad deeds. Just deeds." We then hear police sirens outside, and in a superb overhead tracking shot, we glide out of the building and down to the outside of a nightclub below where a man is arrested and another is carried out on a stretcher. The film then backtracks to a few moments previously as we see the same two men, Marcus (Vincent Cassel) and Pierre (Albert Dupontel) barging their way through Rectum, a gay S&M type club, in search of a man known as la Tenia (the tapeworm). The style of the film is dark and abrasive, with an onslaught of strobe lights, underground music, and shots of gay men fucking and being involved in various S&M practices. They finally approach the man they believe to be la Tenia, and a fight breaks out. Marcus has his arms broken and is about to be buggered right there in the middle of the club, but then Pierre steps in and smashes their victim in the face with a fire extinguisher a nauseating twenty three times until his skull caves in. Later scenes reveal the two men had entered the club seeking revenge after the brutal rape and beating of Marcus' beautiful girlfriend, Alex (Monica Belluci), a woman whom Pierre once had an affair with and still loves.

The rape is one of the most disturbing and difficult scenes ever filmed, and culminates in a vicious attack on Alex's face. The scene takes place in an underpass lit red, and was shot in one long take by a static camera. There's no nudity as Noe admirably tries to avoid all possibility of titillating the perverts in the audience and steering towards exploitation. The result is sustained horror, and has resulted in audience members fainting and walking out at international screenings. "I never thought about that scene," Belluci insists. "I always thought about the film in general. I love films that open people up to discussion. When I decided to do this film I didn't even have the script. I worked with 15 pages of synopsis. We'd rehearse and improvise one day then shoot the next. The camera would keep rolling for 15, 20 minutes, so for me it was like working in the theatre [...] The rape scene takes a very long time. We did it four or five times. After the third time I didn't think I could go on anymore."

Earlier events leading to the rape suggest an underlying theme that our fates are mapped out in advance. A series of incidents are shown, all of which is significant in defining the fates of the characters; each of them acts in a way designed to enliven their own enjoyment of the evening but which ultimately leads the way to dreadful events. Alex wears a revealing designer dress to the house party which shows her figure beautifully, but when she leaves alone, she immediately assumes an air of vulnerability which makes us fear for her. Marcus attempts to enliven his evening by taking a large quantity of drugs, and this results in an argument with Alex, and her decision to leave the party without him. Their mutual friend, Pierre, stays calm in an attempt to win the affections of Alex, and his laid-back manner leads Alex to re-think her relationship with party animal Marcus. And knowing full well that Pierre is still in love with her, she turns down his offer to escort her home.

Other occurrences also seal Alex's fate. Pierre intended to take them to the party in his car, but it breaks down, so they opt for the subway instead. There's a good chance they would have left together if they went by car. It's little details like this that suggest alternate time-lines trailing off in which things happen otherwise. Another example is when Alex leaves the party she decides to cross a road to hail a taxi, but a passer-by tells her it's safer to use the under path. Also, when she is assaulted in the tunnel she doesn't scream out loud for help from anyone who could be nearby because of the rapist's threat to beat her (and this is when we learn that the man beaten to death in the club wasn't the culprit). It is later revealed that Alex is pregnant and would naturally do anything to avoid causing harm to the baby she is carrying.

Like Mephisto, we believe we are in control of our destinies and can obtain the objects of our desires through our actions, or become heroes, but like Faust, we are doomed to our fate. This is touched upon with Alex citing the book she is reading which claims "the future is already written", proof of which "lies in premonitory dreams." Another scene has Alex awaken from a dream in which she "was in a tunnel... all red" that she believes is accountable to her late period – though she is actually pregnant. It is believed by many cultures that a woman can have psychic visions of the future at the time of her menstrual period.

Despite the arguments from *Irreversible*'s detractors, this is not an exercise in shocking nihilism or gratuitous violence against women; most of the film takes place after the controversial rape scene. Noe's intention here is to mourn the beautiful thing that has been destroyed, not to glorify its destruction. That's why telling the story backwards isn't a gimmick – he is literally undoing a crime to make a profound artistic statement. The film progresses from an animalistic orgy of violence to an embryo's serene spirituality (a la *2001: A Space odyssey*). In this film it's from a noisy nightclub hell to a peaceful outdoor heaven. The graphic depiction of rape and murder is not in itself wrong: to cut the scenes to make it palatable for viewers – *that* would be immoral. The result is a film designed to make us think and feel at the same time. This is not entertainment but meaningful, devastating, provocative art.

May (2002)
Dir: Lucky McKee /USA

May is a troubled young woman; raised by an unstable mother, and afflicted with a lazy eye, her only friend is a glass-encased doll which makes her social engagements awkward to say the least. Her attempts to build friendships and relationships constantly go wrong after a short while, and she finds herself spending a great deal of time alone. Her isolation gradually twists her mind and she eventually comes to the conclusion that the reason why her social life is in ruins is because the people she knew weren't really friends at all, but each of them did at least have one or two features that could be considered best friend qualities. She then goes on a killing spree, literally deconstructing her past acquaintances with the idea of taking away her favourite body parts and reconstructing them into her idea of the perfect best friend.

May is a modern-day Gothic fairytale for grown-ups that does an excellent job of holding the viewer's attention. Angela Bettis is fine in the lead role and helps the film to shift gears from sad and touching, to darkly comic, to downright frightening. And due to the film's dreadful ad campaign, it has relied almost entirely on word-of-mouth to find itself a willing audience. But this film, along with Brad Anderson's *Session 9* and Larry Fessenden's *Wendigo*, remains one of the finest direct to video oddities of the early 00s.

For all the wonders of this fast-growing cult favourite, the most interesting scene is the finale, so if you still haven't seen it then skip the rest of this review as it's going to get spoiler-heavy. To my mind, May doesn't really create a 'Frankenstein's monster' out of her old friends, she simply fantasizes about doing so. Notice how, because of her immaturity, she bases her best friend requirements purely on physical parts like hands, neck, tattoos, etc, and no emotional traits or characteristics are considered.

In the final scene, *May* lays out her compilation corpse inert beside her on the bed. She offers kind words of reassurance and caresses the stiff. She even puts her ear to its chest to check for a heartbeat. She's slow to fully embrace the corpse as her best friend because she knows that something is missing. The body she has stitched together is dead meat and cannot appreciate her, cannot see her. She breaks down in tears at this; "You're not looking!" she cries, "See me! See me!" With one final sacrifice May plucks out her own eyeball with a pair of scissors and places it into position on the corpse, and then waits for a reaction...

The significance of this scene relates to the psychopath's vanity; the point being that she wants her perfect best friend to see her with her own eye. She wants to admire herself as another, but also – and more importantly – as herself. This is why I believe the slashing and hacking episodes to be imaginary; the 'murders' were pure fantasy, a selfish and psychopathic disregard for the living embodiment of her fellow human beings. As a youngster, Jeffrey Dahmer clobbered a friend unconscious with a baseball bat "to stop him from running away", and to keep him close by in order to control and possess him. A limp, unconscious body was all he needed, his imagination did the rest. And this relates to May in the final scene; as she rests her head next to the body, the corpse raises its hand and strokes her face. Her own hand. May, her own perfect best friend. Many viewers were disappointed that the film ended so suddenly on that note, but for me the ending was perfect.

Choses secretes (2002)
(*Secret Things*)
Dir: Jean-Claude Brisseau /France
A pair of hot young women from the poor side of Paris take up office jobs for a bank near the Champs-Elysees. They intend to climb the professional ladder by using sex to ensnare the hearts of their easily-exploitable male colleagues. However, they don't bank on meeting someone like Christophe, an immaculate Patrick Bateman-type psychopath... Voted in the top ten films of the year by *Les Cahiers du cinema*, *Choses secretes* is a lurid

tale of sex, tragedy and Machiavellian office politics, all dressed up in Visconti-esque eroticism and pretensions. The impressive performances of Sabrina Seyvecou and Coralie Revel as the manipulative women, Sandrine and Nathalie, rescue the film from what could easily have been an insufferable farce. But their sizzling screen chemistry makes their eventful journey a worthwhile watch. Fans of *Salo* (1975) and *Eyes Wide Shut* (1999) should enjoy.

Haute Tension (2002)
(*High Tension*; aka *Switchblade Romance*)
Dir: Alexandre Aja /France
A brutal slasher/chase movie which helped to kick-start the 'new French extremity' movement of recent years. Philippe Nahon plays the maniac who barges his way into a random country house and proceeds to slaughter the occupants for no apparent reason. Daughter Alex is kidnapped and kept alive, so her friend pursues the killer's van in the hope that she can rescue her. Much of this film is breath-taking, heart-stopping stuff, but the ridiculous twist at the end – one of the most unconvincing of all time – does a lot to ruin its sheer aggressive power. The final third of this film will leave you scratching your head while you try to piece together the events that led to that point, only to realise that you have been duped, as it just doesn't make any logical – or psychological – sense. Interestingly, this film owes much to Dean Koontz's novel, *Intensity*. In fact, most of the film plays as a direct adaptation of the first half of the book. Even the original French title, *Haute Tension*, is a literal translation of the word 'intensity.' Furthermore, Koontz's name is never mentioned in the credits.

Murder By Numbers (2002)
Dir: Barbet Schroeder /USA
Murder By Numbers is part of a spate of post-*Scream* 'clever clogs' slasher movies in which arrogant high school losers plot murders and taunt the investigators. See also *Ripper* (2001) and *Dead Man's Curve* (1998). Here we have two students commit the 'perfect crime' by murdering a girl and framing the dope-selling janitor. As the title suggests, this is basically a routine, by-the-numbers murder investigation movie posing as some kind of 'hip,' smarty-pants, postmodern slasher. As with other films in this tradition, the characters are poor rich white kids with money to burn and no

responsibilities; the monstrous middle-class, where murder is seen as an intellectual pursuit rather than outright psychopathy. But, of course, the killer's here are far from sane. They plan their crimes down to the smallest detail, but – perhaps owing to their egotism and narcissism – never pause to consider the consequences of being caught. Such is the arrogance of youth.

Firestarter 2: Rekindled (2002)
Dir: Robert Iscove /USA

If it wasn't such a sprawling three-hour TV movie, *Firestarter: Rekindled* might have been a whole lot of fun. A sequel spawned from a Stephen King novel, it features Marguerite Moreau taking on the Drew Barrymore role as the now-grown-up pyrokinetic heroine. The long-slumming Malcolm McDowell plays John Rainbird, a scarred Man In Black-type shady government agent who is in charge of destructive mutant kids who are hell-bent on taking over the world. Not even the late great Dennis Hopper as a failed drug guinea pig can save this one.

The Rats (2002)
Dir: John Lafia /USA

Tagline: 'The City's rat race just got deadly.' A TV movie which teams up a department store manager (Madchen Amick) and a jolly exterminator (Vincent Spano) to wage war against mutated lab rats. It starts off slow, despite a janitor losing an ear, but gets better for the finale in which Amick almost drowns in a pool full of raging rodents. With a confident, unpretentious direction from John Lafia, and a script which gives the underrated leads much to do, this fun film is only let down by the unconvincing CGI shit-storm of gibbering rats.

The Hitcher II: I've Been Waiting (2002)
Dir: Louis Morneau /USA

A long-delayed sequel to the cult classic, *The Hitcher*, which sees the return of C. Thomas Howell (though not for long) to be menaced by a new hitcher who is somehow the same as the one who wrecked his life back in the mid-80s. The story continues with Kari Wuhrer as a crop-dusting pilot who is framed for increasingly elaborate crimes by the demented Jake Busey, who looks to be channelling not only Rutger Hauer of the original film, but also his father Gary as a sinister psycho who even resorts to cutting off his own finger in order to get the

heroine into more trouble. It's formulaic stuff all the way, but the cast are very good and director Louis Morneau works wonders with the widescreen landscapes, making this an above-average direct-to-DVD offering.

Infested (2002)
Dir:Josh Olson /USA

A group of thirty-somethings gather at a friend's funeral and whine about their relationships, resentments and selling out. They attempt to remedy their discontent by wallowing in 80s nostalgia. However, things take a turn for the worse when mutant flying bugs show up and infect people, turning them into shambling zombie-like creatures who besiege a house, *a la Night of the Living Dead* (1968). The script is nicely written in places and obviously played for laughs (the dancing zombies is a highlight), but the CGI bugs are piss-poor. A worthwhile rental but don't expect much.

Feardotcom (2002)
Dir: William Malone /UK /Germany

An unremarkable effort which borrows heavily from *Ringu*, but transfers the horror from a spooky videotape to a spooky website in which those who log in die 48 hours later. Those investigating the strange deaths decide to enter the site to find clues. Turns out that Feardotcom is a snuff site where victims are murdered on camera, and the viewers later succumb to their worst fears. The rest of us, however, are left to die of sheer boredom. Other snuff-based website movies include *My Little Eye* (2002), *Cradle of Fear* (2000), *Halloween: Resurrection* (2002), *The Card Player* (2004), *Untraceable* (2008) and *Snuff-Movie* (2005).

Halloween: Resurrection (2002)
Dir: Rick Rosenthal /USA

The eighth entry in the Halloween series serves as a mindless My Little Eye clone in which a group of wannabes volunteer to spend Halloween night in Michael Myers' old derelict house in Haddonfield, Illinois. The event is broadcast live on the web, and it's no surprise when Michael shows up with a huge Ginsu knife. This time it's Busta Rhymes who takes on the LL Cool J role of rapper-turned-shit-actor who presumably had it in his contract to destroy Mr Myers and save the day. And instead of telling him to go away, the producers indulged him, and together they made an absolute stinker.

Oh, and everyone involved in the film seemed to have ignored the fact that Myers was decapitated at the end of the previous sequel, Halloween H20 (1998).

Dracula, Pages From a Virgin's Diary (2002)
Dir: Guy Maddin/Canada

With a knowing irony, director Guy Maddin uses such long-extinct silent cinema techniques as tinting, masks and irises in this ballet based on Bram Stoker's classic novel. With its Victorian setting and the resurrection of the 'undead,' this film isn't simply a tinkering with Murneau's *Nosferatu*, but a dark and original re-telling of the old story. I'm not a fan of ballet. In fact, I'd rather eat razor blades than sit through *Swan Lake*, but Zhang Wei-Qiang's imposing performance as the Count is equally seductive as it is menacing. And Paul Suderman's camera work is fantastic. This arty approach may alienate 90% of horror fans, but, judged as a stand-alone effort, this unique film has style and wit in abundance.

Deathwatch (2002)
Dir: Michael J. Bassett /UK /Germany

Spooky World War 1 drama set on the western front where British soldiers come across a supernatural evil after capturing a German trench. Saving Private Ryan meets Event Horizon in this warped horror flick, which – despite baring a mundane title – has much to commend it. With a solid cast and some inventive use of rats and barbed wire, Deathwatch is concerned with the evils of war, told in an allegorical style, in which both sides of the conflict are ultimately at the mercy of an incomprehensible power beyond their control.

Dark Shade Creek (2002)
Dir: David Mankey /USA

Dark Shade Creek is an unspeakably bland and generic 'slasher.' Unlucky campers run across 'Cyrus,' a homicidal degenerate bum whose brain has been frazzled with LSD. There are so many of these camping slasher movies nowadays, and they're all the same. These films don't have a single interesting idea among them. They have tacky credits sequences created in the hope that they will add a degree of professionalism, but no one is fooled. They have drony 'scores' created on cheap keyboards and programming equipment, failing to emulate the music of multiplex fodder. Of the cast members, there is always one who takes the film seriously, and he/she will play the role with much dedication, but little talent, while the more camera-shy members of the cast – usually the director's friends and family – stand around looking like they feel like dicks.

In addition, these 'films' are always shot on bleary video, and yet the filmmakers desperately try to make them look more film-like by shooting with filters and adding 'scratch' effects in post-production. Again, no one is fooled, but they persist anyway. There are also the attempts to make the protagonists engaging by giving them inane dialogue, and mistaking boring childhood stories for character development; the tiresome commitment to obeying the 'rules of surviving a horror movie' laid down in *Scream* (1996), as if that film is somehow the gospel of slasher movies. It isn't. There are also characters who wear t-shirts with 'ironic' or 'cute' slogans ('Thundercock' in *Dark Shade Creek*, 'Insanitarium' in *V/H/S*, 'Cocksucker' in *Lake Noir*, etc); the over-use of slang terms, such as 'Dude,' 'Bro' and 'Butt-hurt;' out of place metal soundtracks crop up all the time. Oh, and imbeciles in baseball caps are another mainstay, too.

If you're a fan of low-budget slasher movies, the above paragraph will be an all-too-familiar and depressing read. Sometimes it feels unfair to criticise these movies; it's like scolding children for going 'out of the lines' in their colouring-in books. You feel like a bastard, but it has to be done. So, sort your movies out, you cultural sodomites.

Saint Sinner (2002)
Dir: Joshua Butler /Canada /USA

An overwrought, silly sci-fi/horror TV movie derived from Clive Barker. It's about a time-travelling monk and an atheist cop who team up to track down soul-sucking sexual succubi disguised as hookers. Made for the Sci-Fi Channel (or Syfy, or whatever it's called nowadays), this flick skimps on sex, blood and nudity due to network regulations, but offers shit-loads of gel lighting, creaky sets, predictable plot-lines and hammy performances.

My Little Eye (2002)
Dir: Marc Evans /UK/ USA

My Little Eye plays like a slasher version of the Big Brother reality show in which six contestants must live in a house for six months under constant web-cam surveillance under the promise that they will each pick up $1 million in prize money. Of course, things turn very sinister and the contestants are not clear as to what's going on. It's a better film than I expected, but is let down by a lack of social commentary. It has its moments but the 'zombies-in-the-Big-Brother-house' variant, Dead Set (2008), managed to touch on all the points that My Little Eye glossed over. It would have been nice to see the original four-hour cut of My Little Eye – the producers panicked after it bombed at test screenings, and hastily shredded it down to 95 minutes. But as it stands, the film feels quite hollow and trails many loose ends in its current form.

American Psycho 2 (2002)
(aka *American Psycho 2: All American Girl*)
Dir: Morgan J. Freeman /USA
This supposed sequel to Mary Harron's American Psycho (2000) drops the social satire and dark humour of the original in favour of lukewarm, bloodless banality. It stars Mila Kunis as Rachel, a psycho college student who claims to have bumped off Patrick Bateman. She applies for a job as teaching assistant for a professor who had worked on the Bateman case in the 80s. However, the tough competition from the other hopeful candidates provokes her into killing off her rivals... Even if this film wasn't passed off as a sequel to American Psycho, it would still be seen as a bland and pointless film. It blends post-Scream bogus cool nonsense with art house pretentiousness, and falls flat on it face.

Ritual (2002)
Dir: Avi Nesher /USA
Not released on DVD until 2006, *Ritual* was originally made as the third film spin-off of the popular *Tales From the Crypt* TV series after *Demon Knight* (1995) and *Bordello of Blood* (1996). The producers were unsure how to proceed with the film as the TV show had long been over. They cut out all the Cryptkeeper scenes and sat on it for a few years before finally releasing it with those scenes reinstated. And thank goodness they did because *Ritual* is the finest film of the loose trilogy. The story follows Dr. Alice Dodgson who looses her medical license after the death of a patient in her care. Desperate for work, she accepts the job as a nurse for a young man afflicted with cephalitis. And before long, she finds herself embroiled in voodoo and zombies during a visit to Jamaica. With such a long delay in release, horror fans were expecting a disaster, but *Ritual* is actually a smooth-sailing slice of twisted fun.

Taboo (2002)
Dir: Max Makowski /USA
Shot in Romania, *Taboo* is a typical youth-appeal, old dark house story which borrows elements from *April Fool's Day* (1986). A group of college buddies spend New Years Eve in an old mansion during a thunderstorm. Murders take place, but this turns out to be a planned hoax to expose a blackmailer. And that's when the real murders begin... This is routine silliness all the way; the smart dialogue and bitchy characters are utterly overshadowed by the sense that this film was created as a made-for-market generic slasher.

Rose Red (2002)
Dir: Craig R. Baxley /USA /Canada
A Stephen King-scripted, three part mini-series for television. Taking the bulk of its premise from Robert Wise's The Haunting (1963), episode one sets up the story of a team of psychics arriving at a mansion called Rose Red, an impressive haunted house; episode two puts the psychic investigators (Melanie Lynskey, Julian Sands, Nancy Travis) under attack from the ghostly apparitions; and episode three unleashes all the usual hell of screaming, ghosts and strobe lighting. With smart, snappy dialogue and long-fingered, creepy looking ghouls, Rose Red is quite fun to watch, but can never really get going quick enough due to its stop-start narrative which is dictated by the intrusion of commercial ad breaks.

Dog Soldiers (2002)
Dir: Neil Marshall /UK
Southern Comfort with werewolves and humour. A British army battalion on a training exercise deep in the woods come up against a vicious pack of lycanthropes. When *Dog Soldiers* was first released, the British movie media – namely *Total Film* and *Empire* magazines – were so desperate for a home-grown hit that they basically lived in writer/director Neil Marshall's arsehole for five months, heaping lavish praise on the film as if it was some sort of cinematic masterpiece. It wasn't. At best, it's a fun little monster movie which delivers on the chills and

laughs in pretty much equal measure. For a low-budget horror movie, the special effects are pretty good, but the characters are mostly bland and annoying.

Bus 174 (2002)
Dir: Jose Padilha /Brazil

Documentary centring on the hijacking of a bus by Sandro do Nascimento, a Rio street kid, and the nightmarish five-hour stand-off with the police before the tragic finale. A troubling film which exposes the gulf between the rich and poor in a country where society pays no heed to the social problems until the dispossessed stand up and take violent action against those who are better off. Writer/director Jose Padilha shows great compassion, and *Bus 174* isn't just an unforgettable film, but a master class in how to present an argument on screen.

Home (2003)
Dir: Richard Curson Smith /UK

This one-off, hour long special by the BBC – based on the short story, *The Enormous Space*, by JG Ballard – poses an interesting question: How long could you survive staying locked away in your home for the rest of your life without any contact with the outside world?

It's the kind of personal experiment you'd expect an extrovert YouTuber to attempt, with daily video uploads documenting their progress. However, a brief search of the website fails to yield any such videos, save for the doomsday preppers stockpiling and rehearsing for the coming apocalypse. Anyway, in *Home*, we meet a man called Geraldine (Antony Sher), a middle class professional who lives in a leafy London suburb. He seems to have developed a slight agoraphobia after spending a lot of time at home recovering from a car accident. And rather than conquering that fear while it is still small, he allows it to envelope him. And on the day he is due to return to work, he pauses at the threshold of the front door, unable to step outside.

Instead, he grabs his camcorder and records himself announcing his intention to stay home forever, or at least as long as his household supplies last. And what follows is the man's descent into madness and savagery as he stubbornly sticks to the rules of his game with an irrational obsession.

By day 20, he is already eating grass, leaves and tulips from the garden, and even stealing nuts from the bird feeder. By day 26, he resorts to making smoothies out of blended garden worms. And by day 38, he believes that his attic has expanded and opened the way to another dimension. He stands in front of the camera looking dishevelled and gaunt. 'Here it is,' he says. 'It's expanding. This house is a far more complex structure than I realise... It's like an advanced mathematical surface, a three-dimensional chess board – the pieces have yet to be placed, but I can feel them forming around me... What can it possibly mean?' He then stares into the camera lens with a furrowed brow, utterly confused as his damaged mind ponders on the question, hopelessly lost. And it's all downhill from there as he spirals out of control for the horrific, *Repulsion*-like ending, despite him acknowledging that he could be mad – 'What if it's my mind... and not the house...'

Home is a low-key drama that tackles a difficult subject in a way that is refreshing and unique. It's nothing fancy – the direction is mostly pretty flat, in typical BBC fashion. However, it's that down-to-earth visual style that perfectly suits the home-bound realism of the script. It reminded me of an Alan Sillitoe short story in which a man attempts to stave off his own mental breakdown by listening intensely to CB radio waves and documenting the sound 'patterns' – desperately engaging in 'rational' problem solving acts as a way of holding onto his crumbling sanity while ignoring the fact that such an obsessive activity is a manifestation of the madness itself.

In *Home*, there are enough indications to suggest that Geraldine had pretty much lost his mind before he even picked up the camera, and we watch him slowly unravel over the course of weeks. We later learn that his estranged wife is pressing ahead with divorce proceedings. Thus, the problems he faces in the outside world are bigger than we initially assumed. And because we the viewers witness the events from within his own cracked psyche, we see that his 'rational' act of keeping a video diary is all a symptom of his insanity. Added to this is the fact that he simply jumps right into the experiment on a whim, without stocking up on supplies or studying survival techniques, only supports the idea that Geraldine had already lost it. Perhaps the experiment was conducted as an excuse to show that the collapse wasn't his fault – it was the experiment that was to blame for his insanity, and not *him*. By having the event documented on camera, he can thus 'prove' that he is the innocent victim of the oncoming collapse.

Svidd Neger (2003)
(*Burnt Nigger*)
Dir: Eric Smith Meyer /Norway

Sporting a deliberately provocative title but containing nothing in the film that could label it as racist, *Svidd Neger* is nonetheless an outrageously black and bizarre comedy. It tells the story of a small group of neighbours who live in small huts and caravans out in the middle of nowhere. A hard drinking father (who looks a bit like Slavoj Zizek) wants the very best for his daughter, and to him that means she should marry a strong man and give him a grandson (he drowned his ex-wife and baby). The neighbours are just as messed up and eccentric – the fat son who masturbates a lot and thinks he's the right man to impregnate the daughter; an incestuous mother who sits around reading magazines all day; and an adopted black kid who smokes a lot of dope, sleeps with a picture of Dolly Parton, and communicates with his natural father in Africa by putting messages in bottles and throwing them out to sea (!). Also living nearby is a Saami who is another admirer of the beautiful blonde daughter. Problem is, he's just as crazy as the rest, and the situation all comes to a head of hillbilly debauchery with lots of explosions, violence, and gore, northern Norweigan style.

No plot outline can do this film justice though, and don't worry, no black people are burned (maybe one or two whities). Many have compared the film to the work of David Lynch, but it actually bares a closer resemblance to the whimsical surrealism of Jim Jarmusch crossed with the slapstick sensibilities and creative camera work of Sam Raimi. The film caused much controversy even before it was released; the title alone brought accusations of irresponsibility and racism, and led to the film being reported to the European Court of Human Rights. And although *Svidd Neger* is very un-PC in places and boasts lots of twisted dark humour, it's actually a parody of how small-minded country folks expect a black person to be. The cast and crew who made the film are a multicultural group themselves. If you liked *Taxidermia* then you'll probably enjoy this too.

Beyond the Limits (2003)
Dir: Olaf Ittanbach /Germany

A diptych of dipshittery which serves as a gruesome treat for fans of extremely violent movies. Here we have a double-bill of dark tales from German splatter king, Olaf Ittenbach. The first story sees a young journalist interview a cemetery keeper, and he tells her the story of high-stakes gangsterism and stolen cocaine shenanigans. Gangsters invade the home of an associate who is accused of treachery. The gang is headed by a sadistic brute who has a Mike Tyson-type facial tattoo and refers to himself as 'God.' He subjects the dinner guests to much brutality: They are tied to chairs, some are beaten, others suffocated, and garrotted; others are shot in the head numerous times, or smashed in the head with a sledgehammer, or butchered with meat cleavers. A brave woman fights back and stabs the lunatic in the face as he attempts to rape her. And for her trouble, she is summarily executed by another lunatic whose girlfriend has been thrown out of a tower block window. This story really doesn't have much of a point to it, but is incredibly violent. The sadist is a cliché arch-villain; he speaks in faux-cultured tones, is calm even when dishing out extreme torture, and says things like, "I'm sorry, it's nothing personal," after he has just blown someone's brains out with a shotgun. All this trouble over a poxy bag of cocaine. What losers.

The second story deals with the Church's persecution of 'heretics' in England in the Middle Ages, and kicks off with a brutal massacre at a church where men, women and children are slaughtered. The Priest of this illegal gathering is kept alive so that he can be slowly tortured on a stretching rack. The Priest is butchered and burned and has his eyeball gouged out. The man conducting the torture in the name of the Church is actually a closet Satanist who keeps a human heart which he believes is his ticket to immortality. And when the 'heretic' finally 'confesses,' he is burned at the stake in a public square. The man and his assistant discover that the more true believers they sacrifice to the heart, the more it comes to life. So they go around deliberately scooping up anyone they can lay trump blasphemy charges on in their quest for eternal life. This tale takes all the most gruesome bits from heretics and witch persecution movies, and ups the gore quotient tenfold. It's a film which adds nothing to the horror genre, or cinema as a whole, but is a must for violence and gore fans.

The Manson Family (2003)
Dir: Jim VanBebber /USA
On August 9 1969, actress Sharon Tate was brutally murdered in her own home. The wife of film director Roman Polanski was eight months pregnant, and was hung from a beam in the living room before being stabbed more than a dozen times. Several of her friends were also killed during the attack. The following night, around ten miles away, two more people fell victim to vicious knife attacks. The crimes were seemingly unmotivated, the suspects unknown. Beverly Hills was soon gripped with fear as the killings were reported as random and ritualistic. It seemed there was a group of savage killers on the loose with celebrities in their sights.

When Charles Manson and members of his hippie following – known as 'the family' – were brought to trial for the murders in June 1970, the world's media portrayed the man at the centre of it all as "the most dangerous man alive". Many books were rushed into print which claimed to tell the true story of the crimes. One in particular, 'The Family: The Story Of Charles Manson's Dune Buggy Attack Battalion', was a silly and insensitive account written by Ed Sanders, who was lead singer of the band The Fugs. Sanders wrote in a style that was often giddy and flippant (he is often credited with bridging the gap between the Beats and the Hippies), and this resulted in a book that was quite atypical for a non-fiction work. Sanders claimed that the Manson Family may have been involved in the making of snuff films – indeed, he is the first credited source for the word 'snuff', as a means of killing on camera, to appear in print – and that the film reels were buried somewhere out in the desert. And along with the lurid details of the murders, and the fact that many of Manson's followers were seen on TV news reports with shaved heads proclaiming the end of the world, captured the imaginations of millions worldwide. The Manson killings shocked the world in the late 60s, and helped turn the hippie dream into a nightmare.

In the summer of 1988, just as Deadbeat At Dawn was wrapping up production, cinematographer Mike King suggested that their next film should be a quick exploitation horror based on the Manson killings. Writer/director Jim VanBebber agreed, and, convinced that Deadbeat would prove a financial success, they jumped right into production on the film which they originally entitled Cult Killer. "I thought yeah, let's do it," VanBebber later said. "Whatever happens, it couldn't possibly be any worse than Deadbeat, because I thought that was a production nightmare!" Little did they know the film-making hell which awaited them and which would keep the production stuck in the mud for more than ten years.

In researching the case, it wasn't long before VanBebber realised it would be a disservice to anyone still sensitive to the killings to just churn out an exploitation pic, and instead spent a great deal of time immersed in the minutiae of case documents and studies in order to create as real a film version as possible. After shooting almost 50% of the film's footage by the autumn of that same year, the filmmakers saw 'Murder America', a very popular television show presented by Geraldo Rivera, which was broadcast from death row and included a ten minute interview with Charles Manson in his jail cell. This show (which was later satirized by Oliver Stone in Natural Born Killers) and its interview-based format, inspired Jim to re-mould his film into a faux-documentary style. The idea was to show the Family members contradicting each other when asked about specific details of the crimes, as a way of underpinning the overall allusive nature of the truth (as was previously explored by Akira Kurosawa in Rashomon, for example). The filmmakers decided not to contact the Family prisoners for interviews and research purposes. "I'm not going to talk to those fuckers," Jim said, "because they would lie to me anyway. Especially Manson. I don't need that shit. I'm just making a film about something that happened in history. It's no different from, say, the Donner Party. Get that straight, Charlie!"

Right from the start, Van Bebber's intention was always to focus on the family members like Tex Watson, 'Sadie' Atkins and the people who actually committed the murders, and leave Manson himself as a peripheral figure. Hence the filmmakers eventually settled on the working title, Charlie's Family. Money for the film ran out before the end of the year, and the production grinded to a halt. For the next few years, Jim could only shoot snippets of footage here and there on scraps of 16mm film when small funds became available. He survived on very little during that time, even 'donating' his plasma to the local blood bank (unlike the UK,

American hospitals pay their blood donors) as often as he could to keep afloat. "I would open the refrigerator and see there was nothing to eat," Jim later said. "Maybe a hotdog or something. But right there next to the hotdog was the film cans, with the film just sitting there waiting to be processed. That kept me going."

In a desperate bid to raise spirits and to capture the interest of potential investors, the filmmakers decided to put the last of their money into making a short film which would showcase their talents. The result was *My Sweet Satan* in 1993. And like *Charlie's Family*, that film was also based on a true crime – specifically, Satanist Ricki Kasso who murdered a fellow teen and later hung himself while in police custody. *My Sweet Satan* was a success; the 20-minute, 16mm short, shot on a budget of just $5000 went on to win the Grand Prize at the first New York Underground Film Festival, and got people talking about the mysterious feature film, *Charlie's Family*. Unfortunately, the short didn't usher in a rush of investors as hoped, but enough funding did become available to allow Jim to shoot some new footage. The new sequences for the film would be set in the present day, and would show a new generation of Manson fans – sneering, alienated, cynical, embittered, nihilistic, etc – VanBebber insisted that a contemporary viewpoint on the Manson case would keep his film relevant in the present day. Or, as he put it, "it will show you that those people are still out there."

In 1996, VanBebber had put together a rough cut of *Charlie's Family* and submitted it to the Chicago Underground Film Festival. The buzz generated from that screening carried it up to Montreal for a screening to a packed-house at the Fantasia Festival the following year (as seen in the excellent documentary, *In the Belly Of the Beast*, which just so happens to be included on Anchor Bay's 2-disc set of *The Manson Family*). And as a side note, that cut of the film included the song '*Jail*' by Down on the opening titles sequence. The song didn't make it into the final cut, which is a shame because it's a great song from one of the great albums of the 90s, and helps to set up the right kind of edgy mood for the film from the get go.

Production seemed to be near completion when, in 1998, VanBebber was invited over to L.A. by Spanish filmmaker, Nacho Cerda (of *Aftermath* infamy), to add the finishing touches to post-production. However, Cerda changed his mind and decided he would pump the money into completing his own short film, *Genesis*, instead (and, for the record, *Genesis* was an award-winning – if overrated – companion piece to *Aftermath*). Feeling deflated and frustrated by the sudden change of circumstances, VanBebber went back home and began raising funds in the way he knew best, by giving blood. It was around this time that he also found work directing music videos, including Skinny Puppy's *Spasmolytic* and Pantera's *Revolution Is My Name*. Pantera frontman, Phil Anselmo (himself a horror movie fanatic), even provided the voice-over for the scene in which Tex grows Devil horns and leers at the camera, shouting "You're all going to die!"

With the production now crossing into the 21st Century, VanBebber was at last given the opportunity to finish his film when David Gregory and Carl Daft of Blue Underground UK put their money where their mouth was and showed their faith in the project by investing in it. And it was at this last moment when Jim agreed to the final name change, settling on *The Manson Family*. As part of its makeover at Blue Underground, the film was blown up to a beautiful 35mm print, and mixed in 5.1 surround sound, making it almost a different movie from the bootleg version which was floating around on video at the time. Added to this was the altered soundtrack which now included numerous songs written and performed by Phil Anselmo, a new song from the new line-up of Skinny Puppy, a handful of tunes written and performed by Manson himself (bloody awful, by the way), and also a speech from Jim Jones of the Peoples Temple cult. And after a few adjustments here and there, *The Manson Family* was at last released on DVD in 2003, fifteen years after the production got under way.

So, was it worth the wait? Absolutely. This is a film which presents the Manson story unlike any other. And, as promised by Jim, Charles Manson (played by Marcello Games) is not the main figure of focus here. Instead, the film follows 'Tex' Watson (Marc Pitman), 'Sadie' Atkins (Maureen Allisse), Patty Krenwinkel (Leslie Orr), Bobby Beausoleil (VanBebber) and Leslie Kasabian (Amy Yates). Each of these individuals is a drifter, a lost soul, who finds a place of belonging with Manson and his teachings. The story of how the Family members' isolation and insanity paved the way to the Tate/LaBianca murders forms the narrative basis of the film. But VanBebber adds extra layers to this by presenting a disjunctive narrative style that includes a modern-day Mansonite gang who sit around in a squalid basement taking intravenous drugs and listening to Jim Jones tapes. These youngsters are plotting to kill a television newsman who dared to broadcast a show critical of Manson and his followers. These parallel stories are linked by footage of modern-day interviews with the much older incarcerated killers – and this adds a third layer to the story, showing how those involved in the crimes reshape the events to suit their own ends.

The sequences set in the 60s remain the most impressive, and boasts a vivid, hallucinatory style. We get jump-cuts, fish-eye lenses and a bold colour scheme in the style of filmmakers like Kenneth Anger (*Scorpio Rising*), Roman Polanski (*The Fearless Vampire Killers*), Nicolas Roeg (*Performance*) and Dennis Hopper (*Easy Rider* and *The Last Movie*), giving it an authentic 60s feel. And it isn't just the 60s vibe that feels authentic; the violence too is vicious and appalling to watch, knowing that VanBebber based the entire sequences on testimonies and crime scene photos. Ritualistic dog-blood orgies and trippy, psychedelic sequences are bathed in a stark red glow to give the scenes a hellish vibe. As for the murder sequences themselves, VanBebber doesn't shy away from depicting the bloody carnage in a manner that will leave most viewers feeling nauseated. The Tate/LaBianca massacres are among the most savage and realistic ever filmed. But having said that, VanBebber is careful to present those grisly events in a truthful manner; and despite levels of NC-17 sex and violence on view, it never feels gratuitous or dishonest.

Of course, this isn't a perfect film. The modern-day sequences featuring the Mansonites really doesn't work in the way that it should; those sequences tend to crop up from time to time throughout the film, disrupting the fascinating scenes set in the 60s. It's a theory that works well in concept but less so in the actual finished film, and comes off as too self-aware for it to work. And because of this, the modern-day killings of the 'Charlie Don't Surf' kid and the newsman feels much less compelling than the actual Manson massacre shown earlier in the film. Also, Marcello Games who plays Manson simply isn't menacing or

charismatic enough; he's about half as scary as an Argos catalogue. He looks like a fancy-dress version of Manson; an otherwise decent and normal guy who is not quite suited to the aggressive and controlling nature of the role. Whereas the real Charles Manson could have his disciples behead you and orgy in your blood if you so much as said a wrong word to him, Marcelo Games, on the other hand, merely looks like he might, at a push, dispute the price of a dented tin of baked beans with a supermarket checkout girl.

VanBebber's director's cut of *The Manson Family* was released unrated in the States, and unbelievably, was also passed fully uncut in the UK. The end result is a film which, despite the high levels of sex and violence, is perhaps the most honest depiction of those crimes ever committed to film. It's not a police-based procedural piece like the 1976 TV miniseries, *Helter Skelter*, for CBS, or Vincent Bugliosi's book (which formed the basis of the miniseries). Nor is it an overblown piece of hokum in the vein of the more recent TV movies, *Helter Skelter* (2004) and *Manson* (2009), the former running for more than two hours in length. Unlike those examples, VanBebber's movie doesn't mess around in de-mythologizing Manson and his followers, and showing how awful and cruel real-life violence really is. It's a stunning and horrifying piece of work, but of vital importance for those wanting to understand how crimes of that nature can unfold. This isn't a throwaway exploitation piece, but a comment on how people can justify their own actions by tossing the blame around like a hot potato, and how the media peddles lies and how this is damaging to society. In sum: Anyone interested in the Manson case or in film-making as a whole really ought to see this film.

The Texas Chainsaw Massacre (2003)
Dir: Marcus Nispel /USA

Platinum Dunes has a lot to answer for. This off-Hollywood company has been at the forefront of the 00s remake mania, re-thinking, or 're-imagining' horror classics with varying degrees of success. While some may accept these remakes as an interesting way of keeping horror in the multiplexes, others are not so tolerant, accusing Platinum Dunes and their like of churning out soulless fodder with ready-made brand names (*Dawn of the Dead*, *Halloween*, *Hellraiser*, etc), and ready-made plots as a cynical ploy to squeeze cash from long-established cinematic legends; a simple lazy money-maker with a ready-made market to tap into. The remakes of *The Hills Have Eyes* (2006) and *The Hitcher* (2004) are arguably more impressive than the originals, but Platinum Dunes cocked up big time with *A Nightmare On Elm Street* (2010) and *The Texas Chainsaw Massacre* (2003).

The film opens with a group of teens driving through Texas in a Scooby Doo van. They pick up a disturbed hitch hiker (so far so familiar); but this hitcher isn't some crazed goon like in the original, but a victimised young woman who has presumably escaped some extreme ordeal. We don't really find out much about her though because no sooner has she entered the van when she removes a pistol from her cooch and shoots herself through the mouth. With a dead girl on their hands, these fun-seeking teens are brought back down to earth with a bump, and decide to contact the police... However, what they get instead is R. Lee Ermey posing as a Sheriff, who is actually the patriarch of an inbred clan of twisted cannibals. Well, the day goes from bad to worse for the youngsters when they find themselves on the family menu...

This remake dispenses with many crucial elements that helped make Hooper's original such a terrifying experience, and instead serves as a nominal entry in the decade's craze for updating genre classics, and which can join the likes of *The Omen* (2006), *The Amityville Horror* (2005), and *A Nightmare On Elm Street* (2010) as an insulting and pointless time waster.

Among the unforgivable sins in this film is the portrayal of Leatherface; there is a scene where he pours salt into the wound of one of his victims, thus implying that he gets a sadistic kick out of torture. Anyone who saw the original *Chain Saw* will know that this scene is completely uncharacteristic; he was a hulking great retard who was brought up in a slaughterhouse with very little in the way of moral guidance, but he wasn't sadistic. In the original, he slaughtered those teens because, in his own mind, he treated them like they were loose cattle, not because he was necessarily evil, but because he didn't know any better; in his life among such dubious company as his 'family', that was all he had ever known. So to see him inflicting unnecessary tortures on the youngsters was clearly off the mark and left me wondering whether the filmmakers had even seen the

original, or whether they even cared to get to grips with Leatherface's character. Indeed, in the original *Chain Saw*, after killing the first couple of kids, Leatherface sits in the living room nervously looking out of the window. Even with a flesh mask concealing his features, his eyes and posture give us the impression that he is worried, perhaps afraid of his father finding out that there are 'livestock' roaming around when it's his responsibility to do the 'chores' and slaughter them. Thus he was a killer through circumstance, not because he necessarily enjoyed it.

The original film was also very loosely based on the exploits of Ed Gein who was certainly no sadist – he was completely deranged, but he seemed to go about his dirty business with an air of innocence about him; he just didn't realise that what he was doing was wrong, much like Leatherface (in the case of Ed Gein, a policeman investigating a grave robbery walked into a bar and asked the patrons if they knew anything about the disappearance of the corpse, to which Gein piped up "Oh yes, I've got her up at my house!" Everyone, including the policeman, thought he was joking around, but he sure wasn't).

The remake also loses the verite ambiance of the original, including the bright blue oblivious sky and scorching hot Texas vibe which accentuated the unforgiving horrors and isolation of the characters' predicaments, and the finale is played out in a rain-soaked twilight which could have taken place in any American state. The soundtrack borrows those screeching notes from the original at the beginning, but soon gets bogged down with a typically clichéd and uninvolving score that can be found in any number of New Line assembly line crap.

The remake also perpetuates that annoying trend of modern horror that insists on having an aura of viewer empowerment. Whereas old skool horrors like the original *Chain Saw*, and also Wes Craven's *Last House On The Left* had a cracked fairytale edge in that when youngsters make even innocent mistakes they were sorely punished. But with the new *Chainsaw*, those harsh cautionary lessons are abandoned in favour of a 'can-do' exercise in overcoming adversity. Therefore, we have young 'victims' ducking and rolling out of the way of the swinging chainsaw, and insulting their captors even when they are restrained and at the cannibal's complete mercy. It's bullshit and I didn't believe any of it.

Overall then, it's a million miles away from the 'final girl' situation of Marilyn Chambers who had quite clearly gone insane during her super-human (but also believable) escape feat at the end of Hooper's original. Here it's lead actress, Jessica Biel, whose fearless attitude and immense physicality make her a match for any boogey man, and she of course escapes the ordeal unscathed of any physical or mental damage. The end result is crappy watered-down horror for the masses, to make them feel good about themselves like any other mainstream genre; it's a direction which the horror film should not be heading in.

On the plus side, there's a particularly ghoulish treat where Leatherface takes the facial skin of one unlucky victim and wears it as a mask. It's a nice touch as he seems to strike a new persona, and the hapless heroes and heroines are forced to do battle with a monster who bares the twisted resemblance of a friendly face, with pube beard and all!

August Underground's Mordum (2003)

Dir: Killjoy, Fred Vogel, Cristie Whiles, Jerami Cruise, Michael T. Schneider/USA

Revolting. Nasty. Relentless. A bickering couple take turns at holding a camcorder while going on a murder and mutilation rampage. They break into a drug den and murder the occupant with a hammer before discovering a dead junky in the place with a needle in his infected arm. The couple bicker some more. They are then joined by Maggot, Cristie's retarded brother, and they rape, torture and humiliate a trussed up victim, complete with a vile voice-over from the female evil-doer who mocks their captive. The victim's boyfriend is also tortured and he has his dick cut off. The girl is then violated with the severed penis.

This is an ugly and despicable film that makes you feel ill, not just because of the vile antics on display, but also because for much of the time the camera is swung around freely like a key chain, making it difficult to see what's going on in many scenes. Later, the evil trio has two kidnapped girls in a basement. They're pretty much terrified and subjected to the usual humiliation and degradation, including being vomited on. As the camera scans the room there can be seen the mutilated body of a man in the background. This prolonged scene goes on and on, *ad nauseam*, and would have Lucifer Valentine jizzing for joy. One of the girls is disembowelled, and Maggot fucks her in the mutilated guts.

In a later scene, Maggot cuts off his hair in the bathroom, and it's only now that we realise just how clinically retarded this man is. It's around this point that the footage becomes haphazard, jumping from one random scene to the next. The trio go to a thrash metal gig and party for a while. They then prat around in the streets before invading another home. This sequence looks similar to the home invasion scene in *Henry – Portrait of a Serial Killer* (which happens to be one of director Vogel's favourite movies), but then it cuts to footage of Maggot having his nose pierced. And after Vogel's character gives him a beating, they enter a lock-up garage to discover that the place is littered with human remains. Maggot giggles away as if he is responsible for the killings while the other two stand around vomiting due to the awful smell. He then adds to his sick joke by eating maggots from a headless body that rots in a tin bath. In another home invasion, Maggot fucks the corpse of a dead girl in the bath tub while Vogel screams at a couple of captives in another room. We see that the victims are suspended from the ceiling by their feet. Vogel and Crusty (Whiles) argue some more, and he looks to be on the verge of killing Maggot. Screen turns to static. The end, thank goodness.

Following on from the original *August Underground* (2001), this sequel keeps the verite style going, and for any viewers catching this without any prior knowledge of Toe Tag Pictures would be forgiven for thinking it was real, if it wasn't for the hysterical and OTT performances. The characters lack all sense of subtlety and discretion; surely real-life home invaders would keep their activities hush hush, not scream at the top of their voices, and argue and call each other "whore" and "fag" all the time. Even for deranged psychopaths, the act of multiple murder is a serious business. Vogel as Peter is perhaps the worst offender as far as performances go. Aside from having a big round face that resembles a slightly cheeky potato, and a shriekingly irritating voice, his acting skills amount to a competition of 'I can shout louder than you'. In the third part of the trilogy, *August Underground's Penance* (2007), he cranks up the volume even more, and his incessant screaming is louder than ever. It's only a matter of time before the word 'Vogel' enters the dictionary as a noun meaning "Irritable goon who mistakes volume for verisimilitude." Or maybe it'll become a verb. Years from now, drama school teachers will demand that their students stop "Vogelling" around when rehearsals reach the heights of hysterical bellowing.

AU's Mordum is one of the grottiest and most disgusting fictional movies ever made. It has a real nastiness about it, despite the overblown performances, and can only be recommended to those who are curious to see what all the fuss is about. I only watched it a second time so that I could write this review, but I sure won't be watching it again. I'm not saying it should be banned or put on a high shelf where mankind cannot reach it. I'm saying the film serves its purpose only too well, because just like *Last House On Dead End Street*, you get the feeling that all the heartless cruelty needed to make a snuff video diary is right here oozing from the screen, in the ambiance and the twisted smiles of the performers. I eventually realised the experience of playing this DVD was so relentlessly disturbing, I felt compelled to go and wash the dishes afterwards. You know, for a bit of harmless escapism.

Alexandra's Project (2003)
Dir: Rolf De Heer /Australia

The wife of a newly promoted business man takes the kids and leaves him. But she also leaves behind a nasty video tape for him to watch... This is a slow-burner but stick with it because there are some cruel surprises along the way. The performances of all involved are very impressive; the characters who seem to have everything are actually struggling to cope with their depressingly empty lives, and the whole scenario has been deliciously thought through by director Rolf De Heer (whose previous work includes the equally unnerving *Bad Boy Bubby* and *Dance To Me My Song*).

Brief exchanges between the husband Steve (Gary Sweet) and his colleagues and neighbours come to mean so much in retrospect. The finger and cucumber speech is quite funny and it points towards some home truths about the mindset of men in general. Overall though, *Alexandra's Project* is the kind of film that delights in subverting the conventions of feminist tracts. The film never confirms whether Steve is really the scumbag he is accused of

being, and in all the time we spend with this character in the film, he seems like a fairly decent kind of bloke. And this leaves us to question the mental state of Alexandra herself; is she justified in her actions, or is she just a sick and twisted nutcase? Well, that is very much left up to the viewer to decide.

Personally, I like to think that De Heer was merely poking fun at audience reactions to films, with many willing to go with whatever scenario is presented to them having only heard one side of the story. He seems concerned with mankind's almost deliberate 'blind spot' for anything that requires us to think for ourselves and make up our own minds.

Reactions to this film have been all over the place since it premiered in 2003. Some believed Steve's character to have been to blame for the evil that comes his way. Others, whilst recognising that Steve could be innocent, were still offended because it never occurred to them that this is exactly what director De Heer was getting at in the film. To put it bluntly, *Alexandra's Project* is the story of an insane woman who has managed to manipulate a weak-willed neighbour to aid her in getting revenge on her husband. She prostitutes herself and even uses her own body as a weapon against Steve with the help of their neighbour. Whether the neighbour understands that he is just a pawn in an evil game is never revealed, but in either case it says a lot about the male of the species in that many of us would stoop to some pretty base levels just so that we can get our balls wet. And the power of sex rests almost entirely with Alexandra.

Regardless of how Alexandra portrays him, Steve seems to be a decent, hard working father and husband. In fact, he actually serves as a kind of stereotypical role-model of the modern world; he resembles one of those perfectly formed, diligent men who populate TV commercials; suited and booted and prepared to do anything for his family. He even goes to the trouble of stopping smoking because his young daughter asked him to.

The first half hour or so plays like a simple family drama even though we know that things are not okay with Alex (Helen Buday). Not only is she distracted by her 'project' but something else seems to be amiss, and we don't find out exactly how hurt or angry she is while the kids are around. The shock tactics of the film come at you slowly; De Heer preferring to turn up the heat gradually, making sure the revelations hit you where it hurts. And it works. There is a scene where Steve, having paused the tape, mumbles at the screen "I wonder what other tricks you have in that sick little mind of yours", and it's a pivotal moment because we the viewers are thinking the exact same thing.

Not recommended to gorehounds, but anyone who has a taste for the more sublime and sombre type of shocks could do a lot worse. The film also features one of the most awkward striptease moments in cinema history.

King of the Ants (2003)
Dir: Stuart Gordon /USA
In one of the oddest team-ups of the early 00s, director Stuart Gordon (*Re-Animator*, *From Beyond*) collaborated with British actor and writer Charlie Higson (*The Fast Show*) for this bizarre and strangely comic horror weirdy. Handyman Chris McKenna is hired by a sketchy businessman to murder his boss. And after Chris blunders his way through the killing, the businessman has a change of heart. He then punishes McKenna by ordering him to accept a daily whack to the head with a golf club. In the ongoing, day-to-day torture, McKenna's head is literally – and metaphorically – beaten out of shape. Unfortunately, after this intriguing build-up, the film looses its way and rushes its final third with many unconvincing plot turns.

Darkness Falls (2003)
Dir: Jonathan Liebesman /USA /Australia
By the early 00s, it was good to see the irony-constipated horror movies finally in their death throes, but during this time, what it was replaced with was an equally sad horror wasteland barren of any ideas or atmosphere, and the only laughs were of the unintentional variety. *Darkness Falls* represents the epitome of its era, with a hackneyed ghost story plot and a couple of unknowns (Chaney Kley and Emma Caulfield) being chased around by the 'tooth fairy,' an implausible puppet-on-a-string monster that can only manifest itself in the dark. This film utterly fails on even the basic levels of horror – shock, suspense, creepiness – and while other movies of its type would resort to bombarding their audience with grue and gore as a way of compensating for their shortcomings, *Darkness Falls* fails there, too.

Snuff Killer: La morte in diretta (2003)
(aka *Snuff Trap*)
Dir: 'Pierre le Blanc' [Bruno Mattei] /Italy
Directed by Bruno Mattei, who, at 73 years old at the time, could barely direct his own bowel movements, much less a horror film. *Snuff Killer* is an Italian variant on *Hardcore* and *8mm*, but this time it's a woman trying to track down her kidnapped daughter through the murky underbelly of Europe's porno underground. And before long she finds herself roped into the hell of prostitution as a way of gaining some clues as to her girl's whereabouts. She eventually discovers that the snuff organisation responsible for the kidnapping is ruled over by an evil woman appropriately named Dr. Hades, and sure enough she finds herself in grave danger. This film is disappointingly sleaze-less for a Bruno Mattei movie. It left me long for the glory days of *Blade Violent* and *The Other Hell*. Mattei died in 2007 after a frenzy of cheapjack productions late in life, including the sloppy *Cannibal Ferox 3*, the nonsensical *Cannibal Holocaust 2* and the downright appalling *Island of the Living Dead*.

Devil's Pond (2003)
Dir: Joel Viertel /USA
A newly-wed couple spend their honeymoon in a lake island cabin in the middle of nowhere. And things get interesting when hubby turns out to be a complete whack-a-loon. Oh, you lucky lady! She misses her family and has a spoilt brat temper tantrum when he refuses to pack up and head off home with her. Her failure to live up to his idea of the easy-going, nature-loving wifey brings out his nasty side, with revelations that he had been stalking her for a long time before they met, and had murdered her previous boyfriend and even his own father. If you ask me, they deserve each other. *Devil's Pond* is different from the usual interloper movies in that the audience never gets to see how the husband interacts with her family and friends, save for a brief scene of their wedding ceremony at the beginning. And though there are only two main characters on screen for most of the running time, things never get boring. Actors Tara Reid and Kip Pardue should be commended for carrying the weight of this film on their shoulders and succeeding admirably. You can imagine Lars Von Trier watching this and gaining the inspiration for *Antichrist* (2009).

Maniacal (2003)
Dir: Joe Castro /USA

An artless, amateurish Halloween rip-off shot on a cheap camcorder. A bald lunatic attempts to murder his family, is locked up in an institution, and upon release dons a clown mask and attacks a slumber party. With an endless supply of ketchup and rubber heads to smash and stab, director – and special effects guy – Joe Castro slips beyond his usual shoddy standards with this cheap and unimaginative shitter. The DVD release by Hardgore was snipped of 10 seconds of sexualized violence by the BBFC.

Dracula II: The Ascension (2003)
Dir: Patrick Lussier /USA /Romania

This direct-to-DVD sequel to *Dracula 2000* sees Craig Sheffer reviving the Judas Dracula (Stephen Billington, in replacement for Gerard Butler), and spends a large chunk of the running time avoiding the simple escape that conveniently sets up the third instalment in the series. This passable nonsense looks better than most bargain bin DVD releases but has nothing going for it beyond the blatant Virgin product placements.

The Great American Snuff Film (2003)
Dir: Sean Tretta /USA

Narrative-based movies got in on the 'snuff myth' with 'based on a true story' claims tacked onto sub-par horror movies. The Great American Snuff Film introduces a pair of sickos, Bill and Roy (Mike Marsh and Ryan Hutman). Bill keeps a journal and Roy is a retarded redneck type. They kidnap two women with the aim of making a snuff movie. Bill narrates the film with a smug self-righteouness; he has a serious mission in mind for the slaughter. His plans for a "grand" and "elaborate" snuff project is ruined when Roy winds up killing one of the girls before the camera rolls. So Bill shoots his friend in the head and down-scales his ambitious project to focus on the remaining girl... We're led to believe that this is a true crime story based on William Allen Grone, a sociopath who made snuff films and kept a journal detailing his ideas and plans. But it's actually entirely fictional. The film gained notoriety on the web for the end sequence which supposedly shows the 'actual' snuff film made by Grone and now belonging to Montgomery County Police Dep. in Maryland. Alas, it's fake. There was no William Allen Grone, thank goodness.

Fear of the Dark (2003)
Dir: K.C. Bascombe /Canada

A modestly effective PG-13 chiller, *Fear of the Dark* tells the tale of a boy who suffers from acute noctophobia. While his parents are out partying one night, the kid has to spend the evening at home with his affectionately bothersome older brother. And when the house is plunged into darkness after a power cut, both brothers begin to see things in the shadows, as formless fears are manifested in the shape of movie-world boogey men. The dialogue and banter between the boys is well written and performed, and the film is confident enough in its simple premise to allow it to unfold without any annoying 'false alarm' jump-scares in the build-up. Good stuff.

Feto Morto (2003)
Dir: Fernando Rick /Brazil

In a nutshell: A funny-looking geek who was born with a foetus head growing out of the side of his skull – hence the 'Dead Fetus' of the title – is the constant target for a group of Satan worshipping scumballs who stalk the streets looking for trouble. The geek eventually decides that enough is enough, and he goes on a voyage of discovery whereby he murders a tramp with a broken bottle, learns shaolin kung fu, and then returns to dish out some fatal punishment on the gang.

The film kicks off with the group of vicious deviants walking the streets wearing Black Vomit t-shirts (might as well get your cast members to plug your wares, no one else will). A young mother is beaten to death in the presence of her baby. The baby is then lifted from its pushchair and pulverized onto the ground, where it soils itself in convulsive death spasms. A young man across the street says something, so the gang ventures over and cut open his scrotal sack, play with his severed testicles, and then beat him to death. A homeless guy just sitting there minding his own business is the next target; they piss on him, kick him around the pavement for a while, then toss him into a ditch before setting him on fire. The geek is attacked in a children's playground and left for dead. And this entire opening sequence is played out to a gritty, adrenaline-fueled, metal soundtrack.

Geek boy arranges a 'date' with a whore, so

he takes a shower and heads off to her place offering her a rose and an apple as a gift. She tosses the rose over her shoulder, and the poor lad is so nervous he pukes on the apple. But this doesn't stop her from taking a bite out of it. They strip off and have some fun time on the sofa, but his nerves get the better of him again, and he pukes his white baby vomit all over her tits and pussy. That night he dreams of being stabbed to death by a nude woman who then rubs the blood onto her body.

Meanwhile, the heavy gang continue terrorizing the streets, shooting and beating to death anyone who crosses their path, while the black metal blasts out on the soundtrack. The two-headed geek is beaten some more, and an innocent guy pissing against the wall has his cock severed and his guts pulled out and his arm ripped off. The gang member then carries the severed arm back across the road, and the geek is beaten with the dismembered limb. One of the gang members is female, and she has a mesmerizing cleavage. You know the film is fucked when the only thing worth looking at in the entire movie is a chick's tit valley.

After this casual bit of street savagery, the 'plot' breaks off into a free-form exercise in tedium. We get guerrilla footage of street performers, a coke-head priest who cures an invalid and burns a bible. The newly cured cripple then ventures into the street running for joy; but sod's law has it that he immediately slips in dogshit and is run over by a passing car – both of his legs are severed. That night, the geek boy is the victim of an attempted rape by a homeless bum, and he reacts by smashing a bottle and stabbing the tramp to death. He then has a chance encounter with Satan, who takes him to the beach and teaches him a crude form of self-defence, Highlander-style. Geek boy then returns to the streets and exacts his bloody revenge on the Black Vomit scum. The end.

As you can probably gather, *Feto Morto* has a very silly, tongue-in-cheek vibe to it, but this doesn't excuse how bloody awful it is. Just because you're aware of how crap your movie is, doesn't make it any less reprehensible in the eyes of those having to sit through this mess. With a slim running-time of around an hour, the acting is frankly abysmal. And it can't even be recommended to those who enjoy 'bad movies'. Lloyd Kaufman and Troma are thanked in the end credits, but their films look like glitzy Hollywood blockbusters compared to this. I'd never heard of Black Vomit Filmes before I saw this, and now I can understand why; even fans of the Olaf Ittenbach school of DIY *un*special FX could look down on this piece of shit.

Aileen: Life and Death of a Serial Killer (2003)
Dir: Nick Broomfield & Joan Churchill /UK /USA
This charts the final days of Aileen Wuornos, America's most notorious female serial killer, as she sabotages her own appeal on the eve of her execution. The second of Nick Broomfield's documentaries about Wuornos, and one of his strongest and most moving films of his long career. It's stark and upsetting as an intimate portrait which raises some serious doubts about the quality of psychiatric assessment for those on death row.

The Brown Bunny (2003)
Dir: Vincent Gallo /USA
Starring Vincent Gallo's cock and Chloe Sevigny's mouth, *The Brown Bunny* is a dismal, agonisingly slow road movie about a motorcyclist who drives around in his car, while his hair gets stragglier by the minute. He also rides his motorbike in the desert. And, to wrap things up, Sevigny smokes a crack pipe and then smokes his cock in a hotel room. Those who are curious as to whether Sevigny is any good at giving head will be disappointed as Gallo doesn't let her perform properly. He only lets her suckle the bell-end while he jerks off into her mouth, the fucking ego-maniac, coked-up control freak. That was her chance to shine! He made sure he controlled every millisecond of fun while going 'hey, look at me and my cock art!' Is it art? Kind of. It's the kind of art a supermarket trolley collector would come up with if he was trying to tackle French new wave. Both Kirsten Dunst and Winona Ryder were fired from the set during the shoot, presumably because they refused to give him a blowy on camera. *The Brown Bunny* was also subjected to a memorable put down from Roger Ebert who commented, "I had a colonoscopy once, and they let me watch it on TV. It was more entertaining."

Reign In Darkness (2003)
Dir: David W. Allen & Kelly Dolen /Australia
Made in Australia, *Reign In Darkness* is another of those godawful 'let's-dress-in-black-leather-

and-pose-with-guns' movies that were churned out in the wake of *Blade* (1998). Here we have a pair of vampire hunters who put on fake American accents while wandering around deserted warehouse settings doing nothing beyond pointing their weapons and pulling earnest, heroic faces any chance they get. This is barely above an amateur home movie, and the filmmakers even cast themselves in the lead roles.

Black Cadillac (2003)
Dir: John Murlowski /USA

A direct-to-video creepy road movie. A group of youngsters pick up a hitch-hiker Sheriff (Randy Quaid), who is surprisingly laid back and just wants "to go home." Not long after, their Saab is menaced on the deserted snowy roads by the title black Cadillac. The fact that this film is derivative and lacks a solid punchline doesn't spoil the overall unsettling build-up and decent character development, with some interesting revelations. The explanation at the end is disappointing, but this is a better-than-average video release.

Elephant (2003)
Dir: Gus Van Sant /USA

Elephant is about two disaffected high school students who decide to massacre their fellow students and teachers at their school in Portland, Oregon. This is a slow, posturing movie based on the Columbine killings. Director Gus Van Sant succeeds at probing those feelings of alienation felt by the outcasts, where slights and taunts result in tragic consequences. But the problem is that Van Sant has never had an original idea in his head. Strange then that in 2003, Elephant won the Palme D'Or at Cannes and Van Sant won Best Director. I'm still not convinced by him as a filmmaker. His pointless remake of Psycho in colour (or "anti-remake," as he called it), and The Last Days, which is supposedly based on the last days of Kurt Cobain, but comes off as a teenage angst fantasy. To me his films are all rather pointless and juvenile.

Foxy Nudes (2004)
(Orig title: *Hana no Joshi Ana*)
花の女子アナ ニュ□スキャスタ □□□子
Dir: Okesawa, Hisashi /Japan

Japan's written language consists of ideographs, which are mostly stylized pictures. And consequently, comic books – or 'Manga' – have never been treated to the marginalization that they have in the West, where comic books are generally looked upon as little more than a children's art form. The huge market in Japan for Manga caters for all tastes; you can buy comic books for everything, including sports and cookery, horror and Samurai adventures, even hardcore porn of every conceivable variety; gay or straight, kinky and perverse, to the downright warped.

Alongside the Manga industry is anime; animated cartoons which are often based on Manga comics. The anime business offers up everything from big-budget international releases to throwaway video fare, and a whole range of television shows. Anime has slowly crept into Western homes since the late 80s with the release of Katsuhiro Otomo's *Akira*, a mega-hit which captured the imaginations of troubled teens across the world. The 90s saw the release of other controversial anime tales, such as *Legend of the Overfiend* and *Ghost In the Shell*, both of which helped to produce a growing cult of anime heads – or 'Otaku' – in the West, to the point where almost every video store in the world has its very own anime section.

Foxy Nudes is a typical hentai entry in that it contains sustained images of graphic sex. The difference here from the usual xxx anime fare, however, is that the sheer ruthlessness and crumminess of the characters marks it as somewhat more of a contentious show than usual. The film comes in two 25-minute episodes and centres on an amoral TV news reporter who is prepared to do literally anything – no matter how crude or debased – in order to secure the scoop of a lifetime and boost the all-important ratings. And when a maniac holds women hostage in a building and begins raping and knifing them in the glare of the world's media who are gathered outside with their cameras, our anti-heroine gains access to the building by devious means, and even goes as far as encouraging the maniac to commit ever-grosser acts of violence and violation, knowing she has front-row seats to the mayhem with her trusty camera crew in tow.

A Hole In My Heart (2004)
(Orig title: *Ett hål i mitt hjärta*)
Dir: Lukas Moodysson /Sweden/Denmark

A father makes porn movies in his living room in the presence of his teenage son, and this causes angst, neurosis, and psychological warfare between the two.

For all the on screen wonders of this film, the real heart of the matter is in the embittered conflict between the characters; the look of an eye, the issues that remain unspoken, etc. The deep family troubles could be easily fixed with a simple solution, but things seem to have gone way beyond that. The sorrows and resentments have become a spiteful game (the father complains that his son doesn't respect him, and his dumb attempts to appease the situation only makes matters worse). The son destroys himself physically, socially, and psychologically, to spite his father who, in turn, worries only that he is not looked up to like a normal father. But of course he isn't a normal father! So round and round we go...

The adult characters are just as lost and self-absorbed as the angst-ridden teen, and they have no idea of the damage they are leaving behind them in their pursuit of pleasure. There's lots of symbolism, psychoanalysis, and neurosis on display here to drive its message home (the son collects dirt and junk, the 'actress' Tessa dreams of fame and body surgery in the name of beauty, and the father, Richard, craves for acceptance but is off-set by his simultaneous need for escape through drink, drugs, and sex). Almost every scene is open to interpretation, and if you like that kind of thing then this is required viewing.

Director Moodysson didn't write a script for the project, he claimed to have had a single sheet of paper with the word 'exorcism' written on it, and basically invented the scenes as he went along. He even walked off set during a particularly intense scene and left the actors there to continue without him while the camera was still rolling, and apparently the resulting scene made it into the finished cut of the film. Lars Von Trier would be proud! The Dogme-style of film-making won't be to everyone's taste, nor the real footage of cosmetic surgery inserted therein, but this difficult little film does a lot to show how we all have holes in our hearts.

Torched (2004)
(aka *Hell Hath No Fury*)
Dir: Ryan Nicholson /Canada
A short, 45-minute rape-revenge flick featuring some of the most excruciating dick torture you'll ever see. The story centres on a young nurse who has been raped, but has no idea who is responsible. In the end she decides to take brutal action against all five of the suspects who live in her apartment building. With an abrasive soundtrack which throws up expletive-laden hip hop and gibbering death metal, *Torched* was the directorial debut of special effects artist, Ryan Nicholson, who went on to make *Live Feed* (2006) and *Gutterballs* (2008). Recommended to fans of underground horror and graphic buzz-saw butchery.

Mysterious Skin (2004)
Dir: Gregg Araki /USA /Holland
Two teenage boys in a small Kansas town discover that their childhood memories of alien abduction are in fact blocking out real memories of sexual abuse. This is a disturbing look at paedophilia and its effects on the victims, told in a calm, graphic way which led the BBC to comment "the only thing *Mysterious Skin* will do is make yours crawl." For all the controversy surrounding this film, it's definitely a step-up for director Gregg Araki who had matured considerably since his earlier, chaotic shockers like *Totally Fucked Up* and *The Doom Generation*. It's a brave piece of film-making, even if it makes for some very uncomfortable viewing.

Kinsey (2004)
Dir: Bill Condon /USA/Germany
After a repressed childhood and a nightmare first night of marriage, biologist Alfred Kinsey makes it his mission to free America from its hang-ups by publishing the first ever in-depth study of human sexual behaviour.

Before the publication of Kinsey's '*Sexual Behaviour In the Human Male*' in 1948, the subject of sex was still very much taboo. These days, when sex is everywhere – on TV, in books, movies, magazines, internet, commercials, etc – it's hard to imagine the impact the 800-page tome had on the millions of Americans who read it. The book reads like the *Mein Kampf* of perversity, compiled from meticulous data. Most of the subjects and case studies thought they were the only ones who got off on the things they did, or thought that engaging in those types of things would lead them straight to the nuthouse, the prison, and then onwards to Hell.

A biologist by day, Kinsey set out to investigate mankind's sexual desires in exactly the same dispassionate way he had examined gall wasps, of which he had amassed a collection of more than a million. He interviewed thousands of Americans for his study, asking them about their desires and sexual histories – the kind of questions that would normally get you head-butted. The result was a book that was at once fascinating and shocking, but one that helped prise open the way to debate on what was actually going on under the sheets – and at the bus stops and lavatories – across America. But the man at the centre of it all remained a mystery. Why was he doing this? What was his motivation? Was he really an impassive scientist or a forerunner for an early version of free love? Or was he simply trying to justify his own sexual desires?

With his previous film, *Gods And Monsters*, director Bill Condon demonstrated an ability to pin-point the contradictions of complex characters – in that case *Frankenstein* director, James Whale – while at the same time leaving an air of mystery behind. And here with Kinsey, he does the same again with a similar type of soft dexterity. Liam Neeson, in as good a performance as any in his career, delivers a fine turn as the obsessed scientist who, while undoubtedly seeking the truth, could also be seen as immersing himself in the research to make sense of his own sexual identity, as well as using the data as a battering ram to force open society's repressive attitudes, as represented by his bigoted father.

Other Worlds: A Journey to the Heart of Shipibo Shamanism (2004)
(Orig title: *D'autres mondes*)
Dir: Jan Kounen /France
Documentary by Dutch-born filmmaker, Jan Kounen, which looks at the seldom explored world of Ayahuasca ceremonies led by the shamans in the Amazon jungle. Lots of familiar faces from psychedelic culture – Pablo Amaringo, Kary Mullis, Alex Grey, Moebius – contribute lots of information while Kounen tries to engage with the culture. Whether the Ayahuasca medicine is simply an intense hallucinogen (all in the mind), or – as many believe – a way of shifting your consciousness to another dimension, isn't explored in any depth. But lots of effort went in to trying to put those terrifying visions up on the screen. Another astonishing phenomena about Ayahuasca is that the shaman can share the subject's visions as if telepathically, and can

warn them about any potentially dangerous beings (or 'entities') they come in contact with and who could be attempting to do harm (indeed, there's a whole sub-culture in South America of evil shamans who enter a dosed state so that they can physically harm others by sending 'poison darts' into their enemies, telepathically. The Ayahuasca vine hasn't been studied nearly enough in the West). Other Worlds is perhaps the finest film ever made on the subject.

Downfall (2004)
(Orig title: *Der Untergang*)
Dir: Oliver Herschbiegel /Germany /Austria /Italy
Hitler's secretary, Traudl Junge, recalls the last grim days in the Berlin bunker before the Fuhrer killed himself and the Red Army advanced on the city. This film charts the chaos and hysteria of those final days with a detached quality. Bruno Ganz's performance is one of the finest portrayals of Hitler in film history. *Downfall* caused much controversy at the time in the German press where many misread the film's calm, neutral and non-judgemental approach as siding with the Third Reich. If you don't openly condemn the Nazis in an obvious propaganda-ish way, then you must agree with what they stood for, apparently.

Stop the Bitch Campaign 2: Hell Version (2004)
Dir: Kosuke Suzuki /Japan
The mayhem continues with a ragtag band of perverts who are blindfolded and driven to an exclusive brothel where they get to indulge in their wildest fantasies. Cue much hilarity as we get to witness Baby perv, 'Michael' perv, Rape perv, and Vegetable perv do their thing. But the fun doesn't last for long as dead bodies are found, and it seems there is a killer on the loose killing the whores... The brothel is run by the beautiful Sori Aoi, a survivor from Part one. She seems a bit paranoid and constantly on edge about what is going on under her roof, and she is plagued by nightmarish memories of the scary make-up man from the previous film (actor Kenichi Endo who stole the show in part one also plays the vege-perv in this sequel). But when the shit hits the fan, it's up to Aoi to save the day... Less of a 'whodunnit' and more of a tacky and tasteless sleaze fest, Stop the Bitch Campaign 2 runs just less than an hour and

passes by in a flash, leaving you wanting more. There's no blood or gore, unfortunately, but is a highly entertaining shitfest nonetheless.

The Last Horror Movie (2004)
Dir: Julian Roberts /UK

A British variation on *Man Bites Dog* (1992) which drops the satire in favour of lame lectures on the nature of evil. The film opens with a scene in a diner where a young woman is stalked and about to be killed in typical slasher movie style. But then the screen fuzzes over and a man appears talking directly to camera. He claims he has recorded over the rental tape (i.e. the film we were just watching). He then takes us on a tour of Hammersmith and claims to be a serial killer who enjoys recording his crimes on camera. The guy is a bit of a smart-arse, jeans and blazer-type tosser; he puts on this noble facade, but is actually just a low-grade Hannibal Lector wannabe. And he works as a wedding photographer. His camera man follows him around while he prepares dinner for his friends, dribbles on about his lame-arse philosophy and murders random people by beating them to death with hammers, stabbing them with knives, or burning them alive. He is also fond of suffocation and strangulation.

Not only does this film lack the dark humour of *Man Bites Dog*, but it's also unsuccessful in its attempts to be subversive. The maniac addresses the viewers about our complicity with the murders, and our desires to watch violence and death on screen, but it doesn't work because we're not actually watching violence and death, we're watching bad actors playing out fictional scenarios. He claims he wants to teach people "lessons in humanity" and yet he is a self-proclaimed psychopath who doesn't care about anyone and regularly paraphrases Sade about his smallest desires being more important than anything else in the world. Us Brits suck at making movies.

666: The Devil Child (2004)
Dir: Cary Howe /USA

An excruciatingly bad piece of amateur dreck. History buffs in an RV run over a native American and somehow unleash a killer baby that attacks them as they travel along a darkened stretch of road. The baby – dubbed with the most annoying sound effect you will ever hear – is basically a plastic doll with fangs. And though the actors try to put on a good show, the direction and technical ineptitude easily make this one of the worst movies ever made. And I've seen some real stinkers in my time.

Calvaire (2004)
(aka *The Ordeal*)
Dir: Fabrice Du Welz /Belgium

For those interested in the 'new French extremity' films, there's *Calvaire*. Although this film is actually Belgian, it is in the French language and features Phillipe Nahon, French cinema's go-to guy for the unhinged maniac role. Coming on like a Gallic take on *The Old Dark House* (1933) by way of *The Texas Chain Saw Massacre* (1974), *Calvaire* takes viewers right inside the mouth of madness as a travelling singer's car breaks down in a remote area, and he soon finds himself at a run-down guest house and at the mercy of some very unstable creeps. Offering tonnes of black humour and bizarre non sequiturs, this film plays like a twisted ballad of broken men. Look out for the 'dance' scene.

Evilenko (2004)
Dir: David Grieco /Italy

If *Citizen X* (1985) concentrated on the hunt for Andrei Chikatilo and the set-backs caused by the Soviet bureaucratic system, *Evilenko* instead focuses on the man himself, the serial killer who took dozens of victims. This film portrays him from his days as a lecherous, impotent school teacher sacked for attempting to molest a young girl. The indignation of it all seems to fire him up, and he begins raping, slaughtering and eating children. Malcolm McDowell is brilliant as the quietly deranged psychopath, and the film includes lots of uncomfortable details of the murders and molestations which are sure to upset a lot of viewers. The bureaucratic hurdles, such as the killer's connections to the KGB, sees him getting off the hook more than once. Annoyingly, Chikatilo is also portrayed as having some kind of hypnotic power that overwhelms his victims, meaning he can have his way with them without a struggle. A silly and unnecessary move. In fact, so much of the real life details of the man and the case have been altered that the filmmakers felt compelled to change the killer's name to Evilenko, a silly boogeyman name. In one ridiculous scene – which is worth the price of the DVD alone – the killer, while in police custody, strips off his clothes and attempts to sexually molest the chief officer assigned to the case. Absolutely riveting for all the wrong reasons. See it to believe it.

Snuff-Movie (2005)
(aka *Man With a Movie Camera*)
Dir: Bernard Rose /UK
Bernard Rose, of *Paperhouse* and *Candyman* fame, entered the fray with *Snuff-Movie*, which remains perhaps the finest web-based snuff film to date. Also known as *Man With a Movie Camera*, this film sees a group of actors arrive at an old mansion to make a mysterious movie, but little do they know that the house has a dark past. The house is fitted with hundreds of mini cameras, and the footage is relayed live on the internet. And before you know it, there are Mansonite gangs, severed heads, internet snuff, crucifixions and Satanic rites. *Snuff-Movie* is similar to *Last House On Dead Street* with its angle on snuff-as-performance-art; victims are martyred, literally crucified for a cause. Human sacrifices for the digital age. Rose purposely blurs the line between art and reality, and also targets the media, from its sensationalist reporting of the Tate/La Bianca murders to modern-day exploitation; how people mistreat each other (and how some even volunteer for it) out of greed and a hunger for fame, and how the media are happy to pander to whatever cause for exactly the same reasons.

Cannibal (2005)
Dir: Marian Dora /Germany
Armin Meiwes is a German cannibal who achieved global notoriety after cooking and eating a voluntary victim whom he contacted via the web. The two men recorded the whole event on video camera, and parts of that footage were broadcast on a UK TV documentary series, *Bodyshocks*, in an episode entitled 'The Man Who Ate His Lover' (I'll never forget the scenes of Meiwes cooking the penis and then complaining that it was "too chewy" to eat) .

This bizarre and discomforting story had a touching poignancy about it; Meiwes was not a sadist, he was quite willing to allow his volunteer, Bernd Jurgen Brandes, to back out of the plan at any time. And though their short-lived relationship seemed sick and debased to most people, there was also something undeniably beautiful in their mutual understanding and willingness to go ahead with their heart's desire, knowing full well of the consequences.

The real life event had an immediate impact on the media, and the intense drama within sent shockwaves across the world. It's no surprise that filmmakers were quick to explore the story, with *Grimm Love* being a touching portrait of the doomed pair, but ultimately failing to capture the emotional depths at its disposal. Marian Dora's take on the story, *Cannibal*, takes us even further away from the dark heart of the event, and instead stands as a grim exploitative shockfest.

Unlike *Grimm Love*, Dora's film doesn't dwell too much on the relationship between Meiwes and his mother; instead we're shown only a fleeting (but vivid) childhood memory where she reads to him that dark fairytale, *Hansel and Gretel*, at bedtime, a memory which seems to have buried itself deep into his subconscious. It is implied that those terrifying descriptions of the youngsters who were eaten by the wicked witch had fascinated him, and became a chief motivation in his life.

Most of the film takes place in Meiwes' unkempt home which looks like a grim backdrop for a Richard Kern photo shoot. Actors Carsten Frank (from Jess Franco's *Incubus*) and Victor Brandl are adequate in their roles, and clearly have no qualms about shedding their clothes. Dora also serves as cameraman, and his directorial style reminded me of Andrey Iskanov in the way he uses up-close and personal camera work, his willingness to unleash his character's fantasies and fears in a hallucinatory but physical form, and the use of child-like repetitive chimes on the soundtrack.

Grimm Love is perhaps the better film as it is more believable and more faithful to the true story (though it's certainly far from perfect). *Grimm Love* was also quite touching and genuinely heartfelt in places, whereas *Cannibal* isn't; a soppy piano ballad just isn't enough to move an audience. Overall, Dora's take centres much more on the S&M fantasy of the event, and does little to shed any light on the mindset of the characters involved. It's a shame then that Dora doesn't seem interested in exploring the most interesting aspect of the story. On the plus side, he does deliver on the shocks: In particular the infamous cock-biting and severing scenes which are very strong and is the most excruciating genital mutilation seen since Ryan Nicholson's *Torched*. With that scene I guarantee you'll be shielding your nads for safety.

Imprint (2005)

Dir: Takashi Miike /USA/Canada/Japan

An American (Billy Drago) arrives on a strange Japanese island sometime in the mid to late 19th Century. He is looking for a woman called Kimomo, a prostitute with whom he once had a brief relationship. His search at the geisha house proves fruitless, but there is a mysterious girl who sits at the back of the room in the shadows. Could that be her? The woman in question turns out to be a disfigured prostitute who claims she knew Kimomo. She tells him that Kimomo had hung herself because she couldn't wait any longer for the man she loved. Angry at himself, the American demands to know how it happened, so she tells him the story: The older whores were jealous of the young and beautiful Kimomo, and when a ring disappeared one day, she was immediately held to blame. The prostitute tells the tale, but is she telling the truth?

In 2002, director Mick Garris invited some of the most eminent figures of the horror genre to an informal dinner party at a restaurant in California. The ten directors in attendance were John Carpenter, Larry Cohen, Don Coscarelli, Joe Dante, Guillermo Del Toro, Garris, Stuart Gordon, Tobe Hooper, John Landis and Bill Malone. The event proved fruitful; there was much alcohol and humour and admiration for each other's work. At the opposite table there was a birthday party going on, and after much back and forth banter between the tables, at the end of the night, Guillermo Del Toro walked across and told the girl in question that "the masters of horror wish you a happy birthday." The name stuck, and more dinner parties were held. These gatherings became an ongoing meeting with such luminaries as the great Dario Argento, Eli Roth, David Cronenberg, Rob Zombie, Bryan Singer, William Lustig, Lucky McKee, Ernest Dickerson, Kat O' Shea, Quentin Tarantino, Robert Rodriguez, James Gunn, Mary Lambert, Tom Holland, Peter Medak, Ti West, Lloyd Kaufman and of course, Takashi Miike.

Three years later, Mick Garris produced an original anthology television series called 'Masters of Horror'. The series comprised thirteen one-hour movies, written and directed by many of the 'Masters' who had attended the parties. The first series was originally broadcast in America on the Showtime cable network. Some of the episodes were even released theatrically overseas. The series debuted to excellent reviews in the US on the 28 October, 2005 with the premiere episode, *Incident on and Off a Mountain Road*, co-written and directed by *Phantasm*'s Don Coscarelli. New episodes were aired every Friday at 10pm EST throughout the series' two seasons. Memorable episodes include *Jenifer* by Dario Argento, *Cigarette Burns* by John Carpenter, and *Fair Haired Child* by William Malone. And while those broadcasts passed without any problems, episode 13 proved to be much more problematic than the rest.

Directed by the infamous Takashi Miike, *Imprint* was originally scheduled to premiere on the 27 January, 2006 as the last episode of the series, but was shelved by Showtime due to concerns over its content. Mick Garris described the episode as "the most disturbing film I've ever seen". Indeed, with its graphic scenes of horrendous torture, incest, aborted foetuses, bloody violence and a twin sister found in the most unusual of places, it wasn't the kind of thing that could be passed off as Sunday night family entertainment. To this day, *Imprint* has never been broadcast on US television (though it did play on the UK cable channel, Bravo, in April 2006), but is available on DVD and Blu-ray from Anchor Bay, along with the rest of the episodes in the first season.

Imprint is often overlooked in Miike's filmography, perhaps because it was made for TV. But in terms of its twisted storyline and explicit horrors on show, this disturbing little movie easily ranks alongside his full-length shockers like *Audition* and *Ichi the Killer*. It has a quiet menace about it which is sustained throughout, and it would have been fascinating to gauge people's reactions to it, had it been broadcast in its original form at the time. By far the most messed-up entry in both series' of *Masters Of Horror*, it's amazing to think that this little item was given the green light for production; what were they thinking? But credit to Mick Garris for giving Miike the opportunity to ahead and make it on his own warped terms.

Hidden (2005)

(Orig title: *Cache*)

Dir: Michael Haneke /Austria

With a disturbing idea taken from Lynch's *Lost Highway* in which a creep records a sleeping couple in their bed on video and then sends them the tapes in an envelope (a similar idea

524

also cropped up in Thomas Harris' novel, '*Red Dragon*'), *Cache* spins an entire two hour running time based on that single idea, and cranks up the suspense to unnerving levels... Middle class couple Georges and Anne (Daniel Auteuil and Juliette Binoche) receive a video cassette on their doorstep that shows the front of their house under a two hour surveillance. The next day a similar tape appears, and family members are sent bizarre, child-like drawings of faces puking blood. As the surveillance continues to intrude on their private lives, it puts a heavy strain on the couple, and the father tries to discover who is responsible for the sinister cassettes. Mystery, paranoia, and accusations follow... Although the stalker doesn't get as close to the family as in Lynch's seminal classic, this film nonetheless has much to say on the price of the bourgeois idyll, hidden guilt, and innate prejudice; and it also works as a slow-burning thriller in its own right. With fine performances from Auteuil and Binoche, *Cache* was one of the most intriguing and disturbing films at the Cannes Film Festival in 2004.

Undead (2005)
Dir: Michael & Peter Spierig /Australia

A tranquil fishing village in Australia is bombarded with meteorites which somehow bring the dead back to life. A group of survivors – consisting of cops, weirdos and other loudmouths – find themselves stranded in the basement of a nearby house. Sort of a spoof on George Romero's *Night of the Living Dead* (1968) with not a decent gag to be found. The Spierig brothers financed the film themselves with the help of their friends. And though the film is competently made in terms of lighting and editing, etc, the 'dialogue' is atrocious. The film's best scenes stray into early Peter Jackson splatter territory, but overall, this dud will only find favour with those who are easily amused.

Day of the Dead II: Contagium (2005)
Dir: Ana Clavell & James Dudelson /USA

A Pennsylvania hospital is at the centre of a zombie outbreak. As you would expect, the army wants to 'blow the piss out of them,' whereas the doctors and other staff feel that the floppies should be quarantined until a cure is found. Interestingly, the cause of the epidemic strays away from George Romero's original (this supposed 'sequel' has nothing to do with Romero), and instead borrows a leaf from

Return of the Living Dead (1985) and its sequels by putting the zombie uprising down to chemical and biological weapons spillage. Another change from the norm is that the stinkers possess telepathic capabilities during the early stages of the virus, due to an altering of the human DNA. But overall, this is an incredibly dull, slug-paced film in which the zombies don't cause any trouble until after the hour mark.

Slaughter Disc (2005)
Dir: David Kwitmire /USA

A porn addict orders a XXX DVD online only to find that it's actually a snuff movie featuring people he knew. It's a good idea for a film but is let down by the overlong graphic sex scenes which run for around fifteen minutes each and do nothing but obstruct the story line. The result is similar to *Amateur Porn Star Killer* in that the audience is expected to 'get off' on the mixture of sex and suffering. Forgive my cock for remaining un-erect, but that's not my idea of fun.

Gurozuka (2005)
Dir: Yoichi Nishiyama /Japan

A group of school girls intend on making a horror movie based on true events in which a movie club was closed down after the disappearance of one of its members and the mental breakdown of another. The movie is to be shot at a secluded lodge, but plans are put on hold when the girls watch an old video which depicts one of the actresses being butchered to death with a meat cleaver by someone wearing a Noh mask. The next day their supplies are stolen, and pretty soon the girls realise they're stranded with evil in their midst. Recommended to J-Horror completists only, *Gurozuka* is painfully boring and takes an age for anything of significance to happen. Of course, the cursed video tape was tackled much better in Ringu. But, to this film's credit, the snuff video, while not particularly graphic, has a very creepy 8th generation blurry VHS feel to it, with the masks and ritualised murder.

13 Tzameti (2005)
Dir: Gela Babulani /France

Not as shocking or disturbing as other movies in this book, 13 Tzameti is mentioned here only because it is regularly noted on lists of 'extreme' movies, and also because it's a low-budget, black and white gem which is very difficult to talk about without spoilers, but basically it's about a young man who steals an envelope containing a train ticket and hotel reservations. He is eventually given instructions to arrive at an isolated meeting place and finds himself drawn into a very dangerous game. Indeed, I can't even mention the titles of films that could have influenced this for fear of giving things away, but this is an incredible debut feature by the French-Georgian writer/director, Gela Babulani, and is a nerve-shredding thriller of the highest order. It's just a shame that Babulani still hasn't managed to capitalise on the early promise shown here. You could call it the Clerks of micro-budget thrillers, only it's much less known.

2001 Maniacs (2005)
Dir: Tim Sullivan /USA
Remake of Herschell Gordon Lewis' *Two Thousand Maniacs!* (1964), in which Pleasant Valley is re-imagined as a *Deliverance*-esque hick town run by the crooked Mayor, Robert Englund. Three separate groups of teens arrive by car to the strange town, and the familiar story unfolds. This time the filmmakers openly mock the southerners by portraying them as backward hillbillies, and yet the tourists, who are supposedly superior, are nothing but a bunch of pubescent piss-babies whose gruesome deaths you can't wait to revel in. However, there's very little imagination here; the killings are almost identical to the ones in the original; limbs torn off by horses, axe dismemberment, death by crushing, etc. Other murders include death by acid drinking and human shish kebab, but none of them are impressive. There is great story potential here, as Lewis demonstrated in the original, but this time it's squandered with a predictable yarn about obnoxious youngsters getting offed in the wilderness. Also, this time the townsfolk aren't just vengeful spirits, but cannibals too. And this alteration of the original has no bearing on the story whatsoever. It was followed by by Tim Sullivan's *2001 Maniacs: Beverly Hillbillys* (2010).

Dracula III: Legacy (2005)
Dir: Patrick Lussier /USA /Romania
In this third and final entry in the series, it's the turn of Rutger Hauer to take on the Dracula role and head for war-torn Transylvania where he orders his henchmen to kidnap Romanian peasants for his blood thirst. However, he is soon under attack from a couple of vampire hunters who have teamed up with a TV news journalist. This time the filmmakers turn away from the hip young bloodsuckers of the earlier films and instead try to stay more in line with its revisionist Gothic roots. But oddly, it doesn't work. And what we're left with is a stale commitment to get on your nerves like a lingering vampire fart.

Cruel World (2005)
Dir: Kelsey T. Howard /USA
A comedy horror about a lunatic (Ed Furlong) who murders a reality TV show host after losing, and then sets up his own *Big Brother*-type show in which the losing contestants are "sent home," or executed. A woman is buried alive, another character is decapitated, and another impaled on a sword. It's a fun little slasher flick with a 'live on air' snuff gimmick.

The Hills Have Eyes (2006)
Dir: Alexandre Aja /USA
The Carters, a nice suburban family consisting of mum and dad, son and daughters, son-in-law, baby granddaughter and a pair of pet dogs, are heading to San Diego through the Nevada desert in a camper van. Their vacation plans are dashed, however, when they break down in hostile territory surrounded by a marauding group of psychotic cannibals whose genes have mutated due to radiation caused by atomic bomb tests in the area.

This remake of Wes Craven's 70s shocker even takes the original tagline ('The lucky ones died first') along with the desert setting and a similar bunch of characters. But, as we came to expect from the remake mania of the 00s, specific details of the plot and the overall shape and vibe of the original have been drastically altered, offering up an hour and three quarters of familiar yet alien scenarios. The monsters of Craven's original were an evil – if sometimes leering – menace, in sharp contrast to Craven's later villains like Freddy Krueger and Ghostface, each of whom were much more pantomime-ish. And it's no coincidence that the films from which those ghouls came – *A Nightmare On Elm Street* and *Scream* – were both very successful at the box-office. The success of *The Hills Have Eyes*, for a long time, was limited to the American drive-ins (as was Craven's earlier film which depicted a 'family' of savage monsters, *The Last House On the Left*), a place where the more realistic and disturbing type of horror movies were condemned to dwell, far away from the glare of the mainstream and its love of making R-rated comic villains out of archetypal boogeymen.

Many horror movies explore the darkness and claustrophobia of confined spaces (the old dark house in *The Texas Chain Saw Massacre* for example) but here, French director Alexandre Aja replicates Craven's original by setting the action within the wide-open desert spaces of Nevada, where the camper van sits stranded like a speck of dust in a vast and dangerous landscape. The expanse of rock and sand spreading out in all directions as far as the eye can see soon becomes tainted with an eerie menace as strange noises are heard by the stranded family, and their dog disappears. The father, Big Bob (Ted Levine), is the first to fall victim to the savages as he is later discovered tied to a tree and burned alive. It then falls into the lap of Doug (Aaron Stanford), the son-in-law, to take on the role of the patriarch and defend his family through whatever means necessary. Indeed, while the original *Hills* offered a cautious take on revenge, this remake revels in it as a God-given right. Big Bob is a no-nonsense, pro-gun Republican, whereas Doug is more of a liberal in favour of gun-control. In an earlier scene, Big Bob is seen making fun of Doug because of his fears and lack of knowledge about firearms. But once the chips are down, Doug becomes an all-out killing machine capable of the most extreme violence possible in order to ensure the survival of him and his baby (much like David in *Straw Dogs* who is goaded out of his mild-mannered shell by a group of yokels who attack his home – and Aja's film even visually quotes *Straw Dogs* with the image of Doug's broken glasses lens).

But this drastic turn from a cautious exploration of violence to a conservative fantasy is hardly surprising in the post-9/11 world where multiplex cinemas stand like garbled molochs that dominate the cultural skylines of the Western world, ready to swallow whole anything that deviates from the beaten track of mindless conformity. And that's why Zack Snyder's remake of *Dawn of the Dead* (2004) – perhaps the finest of all the 00s remakes – was always destined to ultimately fail, because Hollywood knew damn well that it couldn't update George Romero's satire on mindless consumerism without shooting itself in the foot in the process. And instead, the filmmakers chose to re-mold that film into a gung-ho shoot 'em up, and the closest we get to irony and satire is '*Don't Worry, Be Happy*' played as elevator muzak. Like Snyder's *Dawn*, the remake of *The Hills Have Eyes* is designed to satiate the multiplex crowd, and anything even remotely challenging or subversive had to be 'weeded out' before Hollywood could give it the seal of approval.

All this hectoring probably sounds as though I disliked *Hills*, but that's not so. I enjoyed it for what it is. Whereas Craven's original was inspired by Sawney Beane and his highland cannibal clan, Aja's take seems to head more in the direction of the genetic mutation angle, with the monsters here looking twice as deformed and grotesque as Pluto and Jupiter and co from the '77 version. The patriarch of the mutants (dubbed 'Big Brain') is especially ugly with a large growth protruding from the back of his head which makes him almost completely immobile, and this looks to have been influenced by the shape-shifting creature in Chris Cunningham's insane video, *Rubber Johnny*, which has a similar misshaped noggin.

But the centrepiece of Aja's film is the mutant's attack on the Carter's camper van. It's a gruelling, 15-minute ordeal which begins with the burning of Big Bob and proceeds through a string of cruelty and sexual degradation before two of the characters are shot dead. The sequence plays out in a similar way as the original, but Aja manages to up the ante by increasing the tension and the graphic violence. And this extended sequence not only put the film within the new wave of so-called 'torture porn' (which was becoming increasingly mainstream with the likes of *Saw* and *Hostel*), but it also got the film in trouble with the American censors. The MPAA threatened to give *The Hills Have Eyes* the dreaded NC-17 rating, the box-office 'kiss of death', until the studio agreed to cut several shots of excessive nastiness (the cuts were later reinstated on the 'Extended Cut' DVD release).

Bug (2006)
Dir: William Friedkin /USA /Germany

A stripped down, claustrophobic, paranoid chiller from director William Friedkin, here presenting perhaps his finest – and most disturbing – work since *Cruising* (1980).

527

Described by the *Boston Herald* as 'one of the most disturbing horror movies imaginable,' and by Friedkin himself as 'the most intense piece of work I've ever done,' *Bug* is based on the controversial stage play by Tracy Letts about a pair of lost souls who are swallowed up by a seemingly infectious paranoia. Friedkin had vowed early on in his career to never touch a stage play again after adapting Pinter's *The Birthday Party* and Mart Crowley's *The Boys in the Band*. He changed his mind, however, when he chanced upon Letts's rumination on conspiracy and irrational fears, as the play resonated with the post-9/11 world. He found it difficult to resist the lure of the provocative tale, and decided he would adapt it for the screen.

Friedkin had grown accustomed to working with budgets in excess of \$50-60 million dollars, but for *Bug*, he had the relatively small sum of \$4 million to work with. Such meagre resources afforded the director the opportunity to get back to basics for an intense drama, reduced to the bare essentials of making an audiences skin crawl. *Bug* is set almost entirely in a dingy motel room where waitress, Agnes White (Ashley Judd) begins a tentative relationship with an ex-marine, Peter Evans (Michael Shannon), who claims he was the subject of experiments by the U.S. Government. What follows is a nightmarish descend into paranoid hell as Agnes is gradually drawn into Peter's way of thinking, seeing government-engineered micro bugs and android agents out to get them, before the fiery finale.

Shot in just 21 days on a tight schedule in Louisiana during the summer of 2005, *Bug* wrapped up its production just days before Hurricane Katrina laid waste to the area. Shannon had previously played Peter in the stage version, and here he carries the performance over to the screen, capturing perfectly the frenzied spirit of an unhinged paranoiac. His performance is so good that he went on to build a career for himself as a movie psycho, appearing in *Revolutionary Road* (2008), *My Son, My Son, What Have Ye Done?* (2009), and *Take Shelter* (2011). When *Bug* premiered at the Cannes Film Festival, there were mass walk-outs among those in attendance who were utterly unprepared for the claustrophobic creepiness that unspooled on screen. However, this is not a film built on visual shocks, but rather as a cascade of disturbing and confrontational ideas. And it's

that uncanny valley of provocative themes and ideas taken to the extreme that really gets under the skin.

The critics generally agreed, and *Bug* was singled out as being one of the most disturbing films of the year, with luminaries such as Mark Kermode, Werner Herzog and Roger Ebert all reporting that the film and its performances were 'quite terrifying.' Ebert even went as far as to say that *Bug* was the first time he felt *afraid for the actors* whilst watching a movie. The film was also a modest hit with the public, effectively doubling the budget costs at the box-office, despite only a limited run in theatres. Friedkin later teamed up with Letts again for *Killer Joe* (2011), which caused controversy in America, with its scuzzy redneck characters and violence – not to mention a particularly odious scene involving a fried chicken leg – which ensured the film was branded with the dreaded NC-17 rating. However, *Killer Joe*, for all its nastiness, is a much less powerful work than *Bug*. This is Friedkin at his most uncompromising, delivering a raw, incendiary and spine-chilling cult classic. Philip K. Dick would have been proud.

Inland Empire (2006)
Dir: David Lynch /USA /France

With *Inland Empire*, David Lynch embraced the freedom of shooting on digital video, meaning he could shoot it on his own terms with no producers or studio interference, not to mention the fact that celluloid is so damn expensive. And if you thought *Lost Highway* was a confusing tale, then wait till you get a load of this three hour sojourn into weirdness, as it makes *Lost Highway* seem like a crystal clear exercise in narrative development in comparison.

Inland Empire appears to launch its viewers into a parallel universe as though they're on some kind of collective salvia trip. You enter the theatre on Friday, and when you leave you have no idea what day it is. Much of it was improvised and ad-libbed on camera; large sections of the script were hastily jotted down just moments before the scenes were shot. Some parts look to have been borrowed from the David Lynch website (www.davidlynch.com) where he had created a strange sitcom with actors dressed as rabbits having existential crises complete with a subdued atmosphere and canned laughter. And if you think *that* is bizarre, I haven't even started on the plot yet.

The 'plot', if you can call it that, follows the journey of Nikki (Laura Dern), a Hollywood actress past her prime who accepts a role in a film which she thinks will be a steamy drama about adultery. The film, 'On High In Blue Tomorrows', will be directed by Kingsley (Jeremy Ions), but before shooting begins, Nikki is visited by a strange woman at her home (played by another Lynch regular, Grace Zabriskie) who informs her that the film is not a love story but actually a murder mystery. It is then discovered that the film will be a remake of an unfinished Polish movie which was abandoned because everyone involved with it had died mysterious deaths. The unfinished film was also based on a legend about a gypsy curse in which everyone involved in *that* came to a fatal demise, too. During rehearsals, Nikki and her co-star discover a 'darkness' behind the scenes which she goes into. And about three hours later she emerges – or maybe she doesn't – on Hollywood Blvd... but it might not even be her anymore.

In *Lost Highway*, Bill Pullman's character, Fred, discovers a 'darkness' in the corner of his room, and he steps into it and becomes somebody else. In *Inland Empire*, Laura steps into her darkness and seems to become *several* other characters, and this only makes things even more puzzling for the audience. Added to the confusion are the various asides which seem to have no connection whatsoever to the plot, including the prostitute who sits in a hotel room watching the rabbit sitcom with canned laughter, and the usual Lynchian preoccupations like the strange industrial noises and a haunting drone on the soundtrack which sounds similar to the suspended chord in *Henry-Portait of a Serial Killer* which plays over the shots of Henry's dead victims. The themes of identity and doppelgangers crops up again here as with previous Lynch movies, with a mystery concerning who Nikki really is; is she a Hollywood Blvd hooker or an actress from the unfinished Polish film, or none of the above? Or is she possessed by the same demon that appeared to control Laura Palmer in *Fire Walk With Me*?

When *Inland Empire* was released into theatres, the audience was split between those who ran with it and those who were annoyed by its nonsensical, dream-logic style. But of course, this was nothing new for Lynch whose debut feature, *Eraserhead* – made thirty years earlier –

provoked similar responses. There were those who approached the film like it was a David Lynch Greatest Hits record and enjoyed the familiar surreal motifs, and those who sat there completely befuddled, thinking 'I can't take this anymore. Who are these people? Why are they doing that? Where is this movie going? What's with the rabbits? Who's the woman in the hotel room? Why does none of it make sense?' etc. Of course, there are those who think Lynch's films are deliberately obscure, and *Inland Empire* will do nothing to change that. I mean, there's a scene where a one-legged woman walks around with a monkey on her shoulder; just an odd little moment that seems to be there for the hell of it. And also the dance troupe in the hotel room gyrating to Nina Simone and doing the locomotion; bizarre interludes contributing to a film which seems to exist in another dimension.

But despite all the confusion, *Inland Empire* is a film created without compromise. Lynch directed it on his own terms with no studio bigwigs there to stick their noses in and demanding that there be shoot-outs, car chases and exploding helicopters inserted into the script every ten pages. And while this artistic liberty is no doubt a great thing, it also makes the film almost exclusively of interest for hardcore Lynch freaks only. It has nothing there to entice newcomers who are unfamiliar with his work. And as such, even the handful of rave reviews written around the time of its release had absolutely no effect on box-office receipts. However, for those who are unfamiliar with Lynch and his films but enjoy a good scare, you should check out *Inland Empire* if only for the skin-crawling scene in which Nikki tries to dispatch her sinister double only to watch in horror as its face smudges across the screen with a creepy smile.

Header (2006)
Dir: Archibald Flancranstin /USA
A micro-budget shot on video curiosity that delights in wallowing in its grim and darkly comic subject matter, *Header* pits a grumpy ATS agent against a small community of warring rednecks who are involved in producing bootleg liquor. The moonshine, however, turns out to be the least of the troubles going on in the backwoods as a bunch of corpses are found with mysterious puncture wounds in their skulls. Turns out an evil clan of hillbillies could be responsible for the murders due an exciting new

sex trend that is all the rage in hick town (and also gives the film its title).

Header is the first screen adaptation of underground horror novelist Edward Lee, whose works in the hardcore horror sub-genre of twisted fiction has produced such anti-classics as *Infernally Yours* and *You Are My Everything*; the latter proved to be a major starting point for this film because its central theme is the 'header', an act of sexual debauchery a few notches higher on the perversity scale than the old 'watermelon-in-the-microwave' trick, in which the victim is punctured in the back of the head and the pervert then has penetrative sex with the wound whilst the brains are still warm. And though the film isn't particularly graphic in that respect, there are a couple of scenes that are very strong and take on a leering and farcical approach, such as the bit where a particularly deranged redneck assists his frail old grandpa into getting in on the action ("That's the bestest thing anybody ever done for me in my whole life!").

With much of the film played for sick laughs, there's an appealing sense of fun in *Header* and it has a very laid back attitude. Some of the funniest moments look to be completely ad-libbed, such as the scene where Elliot V. Kotek has finished having his depraved fun with a corpse and then turns his next line of dialogue into a salacious sing-song ("Got to dump this skanky cracker in the woods somewhere"). The budget limitations do let the project down overall, but if you're a fan of *Bloodsucking Freaks* or *The Bride of Frank* then you'll probably find plenty of warped shit here to keep you amused. The final minutes of the film are ostensibly sick, and it would be great to have someone like Rob Zombie hop on board for the sequel. Look out for Edward Lee and Jack Ketchum, both of whom appear in cameo roles in the movie.

Grimm Love (2006)
(Orig title: *Rohtenburg*)
Dir: Martin Weisz /Germany
Based on the true story of German cannibal Armin Meiwes who advertised on the web for a willing victim to eat. There are a few other film versions of the event, including Marian Dora's *Cannibal*, but this one explores the turmoil in the minds of both the eater and soon-to-be-eaten in a less exploitative but equally frank and non-judgemental way. I also found it to be quite

touching and I really felt for the lead characters (but I can't say the same of Dora's film). It's not a very re-watchable movie, and there's a rather useless character in the form of a young woman who is writing her thesis on the subject (she just serves as a convenient viewer surrogate), but is quite an interesting and well-made film. Not exactly 'all meat and no fat' but worth a look. The film was banned for three years in Germany for violating the human rights of Meiwes, from March 2006 to May 2009.

Footsteps (2006)
Dir: Gareth Evans /UK
A harsh lesson in never judging a film by its cover, *Footsteps* is graced with perhaps the most enticing and iconic DVD sleeve design in the entire Unearthed Films back catalogue. It depicts a young man standing with his back to us in a neon-lit tunnel brandishing an iron bar; it's just a shame the film itself fails to live up to its beautifully presented promise.

Footsteps follows a young man's descent into violence and tragedy. Following the death of his parents, Andrew becomes increasingly detached from the people around him, including his girlfriend and neighbours. He inadvertently gets himself entangled in the debauched and perverted world of snuff movies when a pair of shady psychopaths take him under their wings. But Andrew isn't a mindless idiot, he has a lot going on upstairs and he decides to use his anger and despair as a way of wiping out a couple of scumbags on his downward spiral.

So the cover looks great and the synopsis sounds interesting, but the actual film is a major disappointment. On the upside, the film does feature a couple of decent performances from Nicholas Bool (as Andrew) and Danish actor Mads Koudal as a charismatic psycho, and the snuff gimmick had so much potential to make an audience's skin crawl (the snuff element here takes the 'happy-slap' trend to new levels of barbarity with the use of video cameras, homeless bums, and iron bars).

The downside is the slow and ultimately dull style in the vein of Ken Loach in that characters sit around the table speaking their minimal dialogue in a very slow and laboured way like they've been downing sleeping pills or something. It suffers from that very British 'kitchen sink' drama style that has basically helped ruin the UK's filmic output in the last couple of decades. It's such a dull, depressing, and laboured film to watch it makes *Eastenders* seem like an upbeat fun-time comedy in comparison. Scenes open with shots of water dripping from taps, or Andrew wandering around the dull grey streets of Wales, or having the camera focus on random things like passing traffic, and the whole thing is matched by the soundtrack which repeats single, delicate piano notes like it's trying to emulate some crappy BBC drama.

Now, this incredibly boring style is probably based on great notions such as 'slice-of-life-realism' or 'kitchen sink docu-drama' where the grey tones are supposed to mirror the sadness and despair in the mind of the main character, and the cruel death-peddlers fuelling the mounting rage in Andrew's head, but this kind of thing has been done much more effectively in Abel Ferrara's *The Driller Killer* and Buddy Giovinazzo's *Combat Shock*, both of which were directed by artists who didn't mind injecting a bit of grubby exploitation into their pics in order to push the point across. Clearly Gareth Evans didn't want to make an exploitation film, but he seemed happy enough to sign a deal with Unearthed Films, a DVD distribution company that has unleashed some of the most shockingly exploitative titles of the last couple of decades, such as *Das Komabrutalle Duell*, *Aftermath*, and *Flower of Flesh and Blood*. Talk about not knowing your niche!

Maybe I'm being a bit harsh on first time director Evans, but *Footsteps* really did have the potential to be a great film had its makers gotten over their Ken Loach infatuations and relished the opportunity of exploring the dark heart of this tale to its full potential. There are one or two moments of panache that suited the film's low-key approach perfectly, and had Evans steered the project more towards the twisted territory of Hisayasu Sato (after all, Sato's films often deal with outsider characters and themes of alienation, violence, and voyeurism, with characters documenting their escapades on video), then we could have had a mini-masterpiece on our hands. A sorely missed opportunity.

Gareth Evans eventually did embrace the magic of exploitation, producing a string of Eastern-flavoured martial arts epics that have become cult items in the West, such as *Merantau* (2009), *The Raid: Redemption* (2011) and *The Raid 2: Berandal* (2014). He also contributed the excellent 'Safe Haven' segment in *V/H/S 2* (2013).

Apocalypto (2006)
Dir: Mel Gibson /USA

You can always rely on Mel Gibson to pile on the insanity, and *Apocalypto* is certainly no let down. Set in the final days of the ancient Mayan civilisation where a young warrior manages to escape his fate of bloody sacrifice, he heads back to his village to rescue his wife and baby who are trapped down a well. This is an audacious historical epic, subtitled entirely in Yucatec and is as brutal and graphically violent as we have come to expect from Gibson, especially the scenes of the ancient Mayans cutting out human hearts. But for all its supposed historical details and unflinching gruesomeness, *Apocalypto* is just an overwrought chase movie at heart. And not a bad one, either.

Visions of Suffering (2006)
Dir: Andrey Iskanov /Russia

In this insanely experimental horror film from Russia, a man is attacked and tormented by dark suited ghouls who emanate from his dreams. But that's only half the story as much of the film also centres on an S&M type of nightclub with scantily clad women cavorting and taking drugs...

Boasting wildly inventive camera work, bizarre fetishistic fantasies, and outlandish animation effects, director Andrey Iskanov is perhaps Russia's answer to Shinya Tsukamoto. There's a great nightmare sequence (actually, the whole film comes across as a drug-induced nightmare on screen) where a man is handcuffed to the branch of a tree, and a masked figure is approaching him, cutting through the tall grass, gradually gaining ground, and the man is unable to escape or defend himself. It's an effective nightmare scene shot in muddy yellow and shows so much promise; it'll make your toes curl. The film is littered with similarly impressive vignettes like watching a series of avant-garde shorts running back to back. The only downside to this style is that much of the film is very repetitive, especially the nightclub scenes, and there is so much strobe lighting which becomes irritating after a while. But if you're in the mood for a delirious night in front of your TV then you could do a lot worse than this, as Iskanov seems to thrive on rejecting traditional narrative storytelling and opts to

Black Book (2006)
Dir: Paul Verhoeven /Holland /Germany /UK /Belgium

Dutch-Jewish cabaret singer Rachel Steinn aims to survive the Nazi occupation of Holland during the war by joining the Resistance movement and fraternising with Nazi officers to gain information. When her plans backfire, however, she finds herself ostracised by both sides. This was Paul Verhoeven's first film made in his native Holland after 20 years in Hollywood, and touches on many sore points about the Dutch Resistance. He sets out to de-mythologise legends about heroism and, accuses most of collaborating with the occupiers (similar to the situation in France where, after the war, *everyone* claimed to have been part of the Resistance, but in reality the opposite was probably much closer to the truth). In Verhoeven's eyes, no one emerges from the story untarnished, not even his resourceful heroine. For her, moral ambiguity and treachery were vital for her chances of survival. It's a film which is just as hard on the Dutch Resistance as it is on the Nazis. Packed full of grim details and vulgarity, Verhoeven and his scriptwriter, Gerard Soetman, claim they spent 20 years working on the script, and insist that Rachel's character is a composite of several real people.

Pumpkinhead: Ashes to Ashes (2006)
Dir: Jake West /USA

This second sequel stars Hellraiser's Doug Bradley as a burk (as in Burke & Hare), a grave-robbing doctor who takes the skin and organs of dead bodies to sell on the medical black market. The doc's team of errand boys handle and dispose of the corpses. When the bodies are discovered, however, along comes Haggis to reclaim her son's body that got mixed up with all the other ones. She drags it back into the woods, and the relatives of other victims follow and plead with her to unleash Pumpkinhead's vengeance on the scumbags. The old witch does her thing, and hey presto, the demon returns (while embodying the spirit of Lance Henriksen), and the bloody payback begins all over again. Despite the over-reliance on CGI monster effects this time around, Ashes to Ashes is a watchable sequel which is basically just a re-run of part one with a different set-up. The hillbilly kid from the original film, Bunt Wallace (Doug Roberts) returns as an adult, and it seems to be his job to explain the legend and fill the doc in on the back-story. And Doug Bradley gets sent to hell, which nicely sets up Pinhead Vs. Pumpkinhead. We can only dream... A third sequel followed, Pumpkinhead: Blood Feud (2007).

When a Killer Calls (2006)
Dir: Peter Mervis /USA

"Have you checked the girl?" A loose remake of Fred Walton's classic, When a Stranger Calls (1978).This film revamps and updates the familiar old tale by making it fit into the 00s 'torture porn' trend. Thus, the babysitter is pestered not only by phone calls, but text messages too. The killer also sends pictures to her phone which serve to illustrate his grisly crimes, and the girl initially thinks they're fake. And – gasp! - the calls are actually coming from inside the house! She is also trussed up and tortured for a while until she re-distributes the maniac's brains by blasting a massive hole in his head. For newcomers – which this film is probably aimed at – this may be good enough to pass a slow evening, but for the rest of us, there's really nothing of interest here.

Nightmares and Dreamscapes: From the Stories of Stephen King (2006)
Dir: -Various- /Australia /USA

An 8 part mini-series, based on short stories by Stephen King, *Nightmares and Dreamscapes* offers up a combination of fantasy and action, but sadly very little all-out horror. The first episode is the best; entitled *Battleground*, it's about a hired assassin who is targeted by killer toy soldiers after he shoots dead their manufacturer. Unlike the other episodes in the series, this one manages to sustain a degree of mystery and tension, despite the ludicrous premise. *Battleground* owes much to an episode of *Darkroom*, entitled *Siege of 31 August*, in which a child's toy soldiers come to life and attack the family farm house. *Battleground* is also amusing, especially with its deadpan protagonist firing back against the plastic miniatures, and eventually resorting to burning, stomping and beating them with a hammer. The hitman's swanky apartment becomes a full-on war zone, and he is forced to climb out of his high-rise window and walk along the precipice ledge above the city, just like Robert Hays in

Cat's Eye (1987) and John Cussack in *1408* (2007), other King-based movies.

Crouch End sees a yuppie couple take a taxi ride to a borough of London where they run across freaks, ghouls and cosmic portals. It's basically an unfocused tribute to HP Lovecraft. *Umney's Last Case* starts out as a pulpy parody of old skool detective and gangster flicks. William H. Macy is Clive, a private eye who is visited in his hotel room by Samuel D. Landry (also played by Macy), the man who owns the building. Landry turns out to be an author, and Clive is simply a character in his novels. Landry is obviously based on King himself, and this tale serves as his own take on the *New Nightmare*-like exploration of postmodern themes – stories within stories and fiction vs reality.

In *The End of the Whole Mess*, a documentary filmmaker tells the story of his younger brother, an inventor, mathematician and all-round child prodigy who grew up to invent a serum which pacified humanity. He slipped the concoction into the Texas water supply in what he referred to as "calm bombs," to bring about peace on earth. However, there was a side effect; after three years the entire population of the planet developed alzheimer's. In *The Road Virus Heads North*, best selling horror author, Richard Kinnell (Tom Berenger), buys a painting that is possessed by the evil spirit of something or other. This is one of the weakest entries in the set, rehashing themes that were previously explored to death in duds like *Amityville 1992: It's About Time* (1992) and *Amityville Dollhouse* (1996).

The Fifth Quarter stars Jeremy Sisto as a newly-released prisoner who goes on a treasure hunt for his share of robbed loot. However, he soon comes into conflict with his old acquaintances who have the same idea. What? You mean to tell me there's no loyalty among thieves? *Autopsy Room Four* is clearly inspired by Aldo Lado's classic giallo weirdy, *Short Night of the Glass Dolls* (1972), and is about a golfer who is bitten by a spider. The poison paralyses his body while he remains fully conscious of his surroundings. Doctors declare him dead, so he is wheeled into the autopsy room. And while the pathologists are preparing to cut him open, the golfer figures that if he can get a hardon, the pathologists will realise he is still alive. And so he tries to think of happy thoughts... A similar story appeared in the 80s horror anthology film, *Freakshow* (1989). And finally there's *You Know They Got a Hell of a Band*, in which a bickering couple on the road stop by at a small town called 'Rock 'n' Roll Heaven' that is populated with dead rock stars, including Janis Joplin as a diner waitress, Roy Orbison, Buddy Holly, Jimi Hendrix, Otis Redding as a cop and Elvis Presley as Mayor.

Live Feed (2006)
Dir: Ryan Nicholson /Canada

In the mid-00s, the 'torture-porn' movement hit the mainstream with *Saw* (2004) and *Hostel* (2005). Suddenly, video racks were overrun with cheapjack imitations set in cold, dank warehouses with pretty young victims sliced and diced by an assortment of sadistic maniacs. *Live Feed* (2006) was the first of the *Hostel* clones to add a snuff element. And this time the setting was shifted from Eastern Europe to East Asia (though English-language street signs can be seen). But still, we have similar stupid characters and set-up. One of the Canadian tourists upsets a Triad boss at a bar, and they end up held captive in a seedy old porno theatre which serves as some kind of sex and slaughter house. The tourists then become the latest victims of the Triads whose boss enjoys watching people getting murdered by a brute wearing an apron and a gimp mask, via video relay. *Live Feed* was the debut feature of Ryan Nicholson – primarily a special effects artist – and was a major disappointment after his promising short, *Torched* (2004). He later redeemed himself somewhat with the gory-comic *Gutterballs* (2008).

S&Man (2006)
Dir: J.T. Petty /USA

S&Man (pronounced 'sandman', apparently) mixes documentary segments about voyeurism and the underground horror and fetish scenes with a fictionalized sub-plot which involves the film's director (J.T. Petty) suspecting a fellow director of making torture-snuff movies. Underground horror filmmakers Fred Vogel and Bill Zebub are interviewed, and even feminist academic, Carol Clover – author of *Men, Women and Chainsaws* – makes an appearance, too. Those looking for a factual documentary about underground horror fandom will get what they're looking for provided they can put up with the fictionalized stuff. It's clear that Petty wanted to creep out his viewers with this film, and the only way he could achieve his goal was to insert the story of Eric Rost and his deviant films. When *S&Man* was screened at festivals, it actually worked on many audiences and helped to create an uneasy atmosphere. It was only when Petty took to the stage after screenings and informed audiences of the fictionalized Rost could people relax in the knowledge that Rost was a fictional character.

Amateur Porn Star Killer (2006)
Dir: Shane Ryan /USA
Pseudo-snuff garbage about a young man who lures girls into making porn, but then murders them on camera. Dull, pretentious and boring beyond belief, at least they got the 'amateur' part right. A little character development for the victim could have worked wonders in improving the dramatic arc, but no, it never happens. Two equally crappy sequels followed in 2008 and 2009.

The Gravedancers (2006)
Dir: Mike Mendez /USA
Three mourners visit the grave of their friend after dark. One of them reads aloud from what he thinks is a poem left by another mourner, but it's actually some kind of incantation. And, after the friends dance and party in the graveyard (like the punks in *Return of the Living Dead* [1985]), they unwittingly unleash malignant entities; the evil spirits of dead psychos that are hell-bent on sending the friends to their graves...
The Gravedancers is a pleasant surprise; an independent horror film with an original premise, likeable characters and decent storyline. It isn't perfect – there are one or two slow moments, and the evil spirits lack a certain panache – but this little gem can stand shoulder to shoulder with any independent horror movie of the 00s.

Sick Girl (2007)
Dir: Eben McGarr /USA
Perfect for a triple-bill with *Katiebird* and *Header, Sick Girl* is a film that will test the patience of those who dislike micro-budget horror and those who are uncomfortable with kid-on-kid violence and murder, but it does offer a few nuggets of interest to those who are willing to overlook its cheap origins and lapses in taste.
Izzy (Leslie Andrews) boards a school bus, beats up and then pisses on a nun. She then calmly murders a couple of louts in a nearby field. Turns out that Izzy is an orphan (we never find out what happened to her parents, maybe she killed them too?), and is homicidally protective of her younger 'brother' who is a constant target for school bullies. Izzy's ways of dealing with said bullies is to unleash a barrage of cruelty and sadism in her calm and collected way, and this often leads to some spectacularly brutal set-pieces. But all this countryside mayhem leads to some harsh consequences later on...
Much more technically proficient and atmospheric than the usual SOV crap that has polluted video stores in recent years, *Sick Girl* nevertheless has been labelled as 'torture porn' in some circles by those quick to judge its relentless abuse of characters as simply gratuitous and for the sole purpose of entertainment. Alas, they're wrong; it's definitely not torture porn, there is so much more going on here for it to be pigeon-holed into that category (the 'torture porn' label was a term coined by someone who despised that particular sub-genre anyway, so it's ironic how horror fans still use it often, even as a term of recommendation!). That's not to say that *Sick Girl* is an easy ride; no doubt some viewers in the age of post-Columbine were shocked and outraged by the attitude and imagery on screen, but you're just as likely to find fans of the film who appreciate the dark humour, gritty shooting style, and nods and winks to the horror genre as a whole. Look out for 80s horror icon Stephen Geoffreys (of *Fright Night*, *976-Evil*, and *Evil Ed* fame) who plays Izzy's anxious teacher, and who provides a very interesting interview on the Synapse DVD. Also check out the film's homage to Andrew Birkin's *The Cement Garden*, and some very tawdry twists on *Oliver Twist* that will never seem innocent again.

Death Proof (2007)
Dir: Quentin Tarantino /USA
First released in cinemas as the second half of a double-bill with Robert Rodriguez's *Planet Terror* (under the collective title, *Grindhouse*), *Death Proof* and its co-feature flopped badly at the box-office among 00s audiences who were too young to know what double-bills were. Most audiences upped and left after *Planet Terror*, and had no idea that a second feature had yet to play. The films were later re-released separately, and Tarantino's pic actually plays as a film nerd's tribute to the likes of *Death Race 2000* (1975),

Faster, Pussycat, Kill! Kill! (1965), *Cannonball Run* (1981) and *The Stunt Man* (1980).

The plot is simple enough: A group of young women head to a bar, get drunk and stoned, and one of them (Rose Mcgowan) is picked up by a Hollywood stunt driver (Kurt Russell), who lures her into his stunt car which is 'death proof,' meaning you can survive all manner of car crashes just as long as you're sitting in the driver's seat. Of course, 'Stunt Man Mike' turns out to be a silver-jacketed psycho, and he kills the poor girl along with her friends before setting his sights on another group of young women... Many disliked this film on its initial release, but it has shown itself to be a grower on DVD, with film fans now admitting they enjoyed it much more on repeat viewings. The soundtrack certainly helps; a retro-inflected blend of rock, pop and movie scores from the likes of T. Rex, The Coasters, Ennio Morricone, Pino Donaggio, and Jack Nietzshe's classic theme from *Village of the Giants* (1965).

Fans of screen entertainment will have a field day spotting the numerous verbal and visual references to films and TV shows of old. And though *Death Proof* is set in modern-day Texas and Tennessee, the film boasts a 70s cinematic flavour; it's presented in a deliberately beat up, scratched print, and includes homages to the technical quirks of 70s exploitation cinema, with abrupt reel changes and a 'Death Proof' title card standing in for the film's supposed original title ('*Quentin Tarantino's Thunder Bolt*'). If there's anything wrong with the film, for me it would be that the characters all talk like Tarantino. Whether young or old, black or white, male or female, the characters all speak in 'hip talk' with an effortless street-wise poetic flair which becomes irksome after a while.

There are also loose ends aplenty, such as the scene with the Sheriff – he speaks to a female doctor at the hospital, and she informs him of Mike's injuries. She then leaves in a huff and seems to really despise the Sheriff as if she knows him personally. But that's the first and last time we ever see those characters. Also, one of the girls is left alone with a leering country-boy mechanic while her friends take the man's car for a 'test drive.' And we never find out what happened to her, either. Perhaps these weird, dead-end scenes were all part of the homage?

Snuff 102 (2007)
Dir: Mariana Peralto /Argentina

Snuff 102 is about a hot young student reporter (Andrea Alphonso) who is investigating the existence of snuff movies and winds up landing herself a starring role in one. There are also other sub-plots along the way showing how the other women found themselves in snuff hell, including a pregnant drug addict who is lured to a horrendous death by a man whom she trusts.

This film is, without a doubt, one of the most disturbing I have ever seen. It's right up there with *Men Behind the Sun* and *Nekromantik 2* in terms of its sheer onslaught of nightmare imagery and sick ideas. First we get an intro card that reads: "WARNING. Torture scenes documented in this film are real. Caution is recommended to sensitive viewers". And although the film isn't real per se, there is some very nasty stuff here including some genuine pics and clips. The intro was simply a way to make the audience feel uncomfortable and on edge (*Blair Witch*, *Snuff*, and *The Texas Chain Saw Massacre* all deployed similar tricks in an effort to make us believe the events depicted were real).

The film opens with a scene of a lab monkey being fed on something (don't know what), grainy 8mm black and white footage of a rotting corpse in a bath tub being cut into pieces by a man with a saw, some real animal killing and cruelty (a squealing pig is dragged outside by farmers and has its throat cut), some still images of murder and accident victims that look definitely real. The film is so well put together in terms of creating that gritty realism of bits of scrap footage cobbled together, it's hard to tell what's real and what isn't. I even asked myself the question that most extreme movie devotees will ask themselves at least once in their lives: What the hell am I doing watching this? Forget *August Underground's Mordum*, this is the real deal sick shit.

Borrowing a riff from Japanese AV shocker *Muzan-e*, we eventually fall into a narrative with the young lady reporter who is investigating some brutal killings of prostitutes in the local area. Her quest leads inevitably to the web where we get to see more footage that looks just way too real (might even be real); a man having his throat cut wide open with blood gushing out, fingers hacked off, an S&M clip of a woman having her nipples nailed to a table... The woman then interviews some local expert on snuff. This expert sounds like he has read his Jean Baudrillard and kind of serves as a commentator for the atrocity exhibition on screen (much like Baudrillard himself, when he was alive, calmly picking away at the fault-lines of our modern culture).

To see a guy punching a woman in the face about fifteen times would be off-putting in any other film, but here it's actually a relief, because it's so lame and unconvincing you know it isn't real. The very next scene, however, features someone having their fingers cut off one by one, and it puts you back on edge again because it looks like it could be real. The special effects are generally outstanding in this film and they blend in so perfectly with the mondo shock footage that it becomes very difficult to ascertain real from fake footage. Only when we're firmly established in the viewing experience do we find our feet and know what's what.

There is also another plot-line concerning the pregnant drug addict who is lured to her death, and I won't even mention what happens to her (apparently, viewers at the Mar Del Plata International Film Festival were so outraged at this sequence, thinking it was real, a man in the audience took action and beat the crap out of director Peralta while the film was still playing). I should mention though that it's the editing and camera angles that give the game away and confirm to us that it isn't real (this is not a documentary style film, although it does feel that way early on). Still, this is a devastating film. If you want to have your face shoved into the abyss then this is for you.

Jesus Camp (2007)
Dir: Heidi E. Ewing & Rachel Grady /USA
In a North Dakota Christian summer camp, children are taught to accept evangelical religion, creationism, and encouraged to participate in anti-abortion rallies while demonizing mainstream culture. This is a sobering documentary about the brainwashing of children. There are moments where you'll be tempted to laugh out loud at the ridiculous propaganda on view, but more often than not you'll be dismayed at how young and innocent minds are twisted and bent out of shape, and saddened by the children's eager acceptance of it all. It's a disturbing glimpse into the world of the American religious right where Harry Potter is considered a "warlock of Satan" (they may have

a point there), and is ultimately a breeding ground for fundamentalism and bigotry.

[Rec] (2007)
Dir: Juame Balaguero & Paco Plaza /Spain
A reality TV crew is caught up in a rabid virus/zombie outbreak while accompanying firemen on a routine call to a rundown apartment block. All they can do is record the unfolding nightmare as the violence and hysteria reach fever pitch. Similar to *The Blair Wicth Project* in terms of its gritty hand-held style, *[Rec]* has an urgent, alarming aesthetic, no doubt equally inspired by news coverage on shaky cams of post-9/11 events, and includes some genuinely hair-raising moments. It was remade less successfully as *Quarantine* in America. The first sequel, *[Rec] 2* (2009) is a masterpiece, while *[Rec] 3: Genesis* (2012) starts off quite slow but picks up eventually. *[Rec]4: Apocalypse* (2014)is where the series ends, but is deliberately left open just in case the producers change their minds.

Savage Grace (2007)
Dir: Tom Kalin Spain/USA/France
Based on the true story (Natalie Robin and Steven M.L. Aronson's book of the same name), *Savage Grace* charts the history of the Baeckeland family, from the birth of the son, Tony, in the 40s to the death of the mother Barbara in the 70s. They were a very wealthy family (the grandfather invented a commonly used plastic, Bakelite), but they were also easily bored and had too much time on their hands, which culminated in them creating their own dramas for everyone to see – adultery used as a spiteful weapon of revenge on a whim, an increasing alienation between father and son, the father stealing his son's girlfriend, incestuous threesome frolics, the emotional instability of all concerned, etc. But first time director Tom Kalin concentrates most of his efforts on showing how all of this behaviour has affected the son, Tony. He also takes a few risks as a filmmaker, and this makes it worth seeing for that reason alone.

It's beautifully shot and offers up some fine performances (the brilliant Julianne Moore is as game as ever in her portrayal of mother Barbara). It's also a mixture of darkness and light in terms of both aesthetics and subject-matter, and producer Christine Vachon presents us with yet another interesting drama which involves unorthodox social themes and demented sexuality. Not the most extreme movie you'll ever see, but is much better than the many bad reviews would have you believe.

Joshua (2007)
Dir: George Ratliff /USA

Mainstream cinema has often explored the sickness of serial killers in movies that posit normal, everyday characters against sicko psychopaths who are hell-bent on wrecking lives. These psychos – also known as interlopers – are often portrayed as friendly at first (some are even the victim's relatives), but eventually show their true colours once the coast is clear. These interlopers are often chameleon-like and usually very intelligent and experts in manipulating others to get them on side to the point where the victim(s) is alienated to the brink of madness. A common thread that runs through these types of films is a cautionary one about being careful of whom you trust, and also a primal fear that a person close to you could be a deranged sociopath. The victims are usually nice, middle-class characters, whereas the psychos often – but not always – come from a lower social strata. The template for this was *Play Misty For Me* (1971), in which a radio DJ (Clint Eastwood) has a drunken one-night-stand with a fan only to later find that she's a raging 'bunny-boiler'-type with a strong homicidal streak. Sixteen years later, and *Fatal Attraction* (1987) upped the ante by exaggerating the homicidal mania and thus hightening the paranoia forever more.

The success of *Fatal Attraction* ensured a slew of similar films with a slight variation, and creating a new sub-genre in the process: We have a psycho stepdad in *The Stepfather* (1987) and *Stepfather 2* (1989), psycho husbands in *Sleeping With the Enemy* (1991) and *Devil's Pond* (2003), a psycho landlord in *Crawlspace* (1986), a psycho tenant in *Pacific Heights* (1990), a psycho teenager in *The Crush* (1993), psycho neighbours in *The Neighbor* (1993) and *Disturbia* (2007), psycho kids in *Mikey* (1992), *The Good Son* (1993) and *The Paperboy* (1994), psycho flatmates in *Deadbolt* (1992) and *Single White Female* (1992), a psycho cop in *Unlawful Entry* (1992), psycho teachers in *The Substitute* (1993) and *Scarred* (1994), the psycho ex in *Mother's Boys* (1994) and *The Ex* (1997), psycho work colleagues in *The Temp* (1993) and *Disclosure* (1994), a psycho saviour in *Misery* (1990), a psycho handyman in *Retribution Sight*

Unseen (1993), a psycho celebrity stalker in *Crazy Love For You* (1992), psycho foster parents in *The Glass House* (2001), another psycho fling in *Malicious* (1995), and a psycho orphan in *The Orphan* (2009). That's a lot of psychos.

Perhaps the creepiest entry in this sub-genre is *Joshua* (2007), which centres on a psycho son whose behaviour becomes increasingly destructive after the birth of his baby sister. And while his mother is slumped out in post-natal depression, and his father is a busy stockbroker in the city, nine-year-old Joshua sabotages his gift as a piano prodigy, dissects his pet hamster, drives his mother insane, poisons the family's four-legged friend, and kills his grandmother. Basically, he's determined to destroy everyone around him in order to be able to spend quality time with his uncle, the only person in his life who ever showed a genuine interest in the piano.

Joshua keeps up the tradition of these movies by relating to them on numerous levels. Just like many other interlopers in this field, he is intelligent, highly manipulative, remorseless, cunning, and he never falters in his determination. The viewer is also drawn into the web because, despite his behaviour, Joshua is, after all, just a boy in need of love and encouragement. But these films often make a conservative stance in implying that these psychos are simply beyond the pale and that there's nothing anyone can do about it. Note too that many of the psychos in this realm only get nasty when the people around them fail to live up to expectations: Kathy Bates in *Misery* only torments writer Paul Sheldon when he acts in ways contrary to her idea of the idealised novelist, and Terry O' Quinn in *The Stepfather* only enters psycho mode when his adopted family behave in ways contrary to his impossible standards of a well-to-do, middle-class existence.

100 Tears (2007)
Dir: Marcus Koch /USA

A psychotic killer clown leaves the fairground and embarks on a killing spree with a huge meat cleaver and searches for his long lost daughter. Tracking him down are the police and an odd couple of amateur sleuths who are hoping to get the scoop of a lifetime for their local tabloid paper.

This is an extremely violent and graphic slasher movie; heads are cut off and split in two, limbs are hacked off, torsos are sliced open to reveal the sloppy innards. People are also shot, stabbed, and strangled thanks to some superb special effects courtesy of the great team at Odditopsy FX, helping to earn the film an NC-17 rating in America. The body count rises higher than most movies of this type in the first 20 minutes, and by the end credits the number of mangled corpses this film leaves behind is almost astronomical. The acting isn't great but the script is sharp, witty, and quite clever for this kind of thing. It sure beats other low-budget indie efforts like the first *August Underground* and *The Gateway Meat*.

Directed by the unfortunately named Marcus Koch with much love and respect for the genre, it's good to see a fanboy-type horror film that doesn't get bogged down in overdoing the 'ironic' and self-referential crap that plagues so many of these types of films. Here the director concentrates on more important things like making a decent script and casting a couple of leads who gel together quite well on screen, despite the fact that there isn't much chance of a sex scene between the two (she's a stunningly beautiful brunette, and he's a fat, flatulating ogre). The film's most impressive aspect though is definitely the extreme gore, so if you are squeamish you may want to avoid.

On the soundtrack there is a distorted chime from a musical box that sounds identical to Christopher Young's score for the first couple of *Hellraiser* films; it may have been taken from the soundtrack CD. The music also includes crappy techno during some of the killing scenes, and this type of music has never worked in films and doesn't work here at all. Also, the killer clown is a bit miscast and doesn't really pose a very menacing presence. But these are only minor criticisms as the film certainly delivers on the slasher essentials: A bunch of idiots get slaughtered in extremely nasty and graphic ways!

The 'Tears' of the title refers to the killer's MO which involves drawing teardrops on the wall using the blood of each of his victims, and the 100 gives you some idea of the excessively large body count.

Seed (2007)
Dir: Uwe Boll /Canada/Germany
Typical of Uwe Boll, he makes another film that is simultaneously shocking, disturbing, and crudely inept in equal measure. There's a manhunt for a serial killer known as *Seed*. His modus operandi is to lock people in a room (including in one scene, a young toddler) and film them as they starve to death. He keeps the camera rolling for months while the bodies decompose. He then sends the videos to the police as a way to shock and taunt them. When he is finally captured, the electric chair fails to kill him, so the authorities decide to secretly bury him while his heart is still beating. A very bad move as *Seed* manages to break out of the grave and continue on his killing spree...

Many of these types of slasher movies tend to glamorise the killer too much, but Boll admirably keeps things restrained in this film, and goes for a much bleaker approach. Don't get me wrong, there are a couple of murders that could have come from a *Friday the 13th* movie, such as the scene where Seed kills a victim from under the bed. Boll also borrows elements from post-*Saw* killer movies, but generally, the 'coolness' of the killer is played down. And I don't know about you, but I like that in a film; had Seed been depicted as some unstoppable killing-machine, a la Michael Myers or Jason Voorhees, much of the impact of the film would have been lost. And instead we're treated to an evil psychopath who represents the worst of human nature. Also, be warned – the opening segment contains real footage supplied by PETA of animals being killed in the most appalling ways. You might want to keep the skip button at hand.

On the downside, the film is cut together quite badly, and the 70s setting is not very convincing at all (they probably chose the 70s simply as a way of keeping the electric chair in the plot). For the police scenes it looks like Boll has gone for a noirish style, but it doesn't work on digital video, just makes everything look flat and dull. On the positive side, the scene involving the woman, the chair, and the hatchet is superbly brutal; this extended scene was shot in one take and rivals Herschell Gordon Lewis in the leeringly gratuitous sweepstakes. Also, be prepared for the ending as it's one of the cruellest and most cold-blooded in the history of film, I kid you not, and makes it a must-see for that reason alone. With Boll's promise to donate 2.5% of *Seed*'s profits to PETA, you can buy the DVD knowing you have committed a good deed for the day.

Flanders (2007)
Dir: Bruno Dumont /France

Dumont's most violent and extreme film to date. A bunch of guys from a small village are all played by the same crazy slut. They're conscripted into the army to fight some unspecified war in North Africa, and they all find themselves in the same regiment. There's lots of seething resentments between the men but nothing spills over. Instead they take out their frustrations on the locals by way of rape and murder. Meanwhile, the slut stays behind and has a mental breakdown. The film starts off slow (as with any Dumont movie) but once we get to the war scenes it becomes a real atrocity exhibition of anger, resentment, revenge, and the will to survive by a group of soldiers who should be looking out for each other.

Flanders offers a real change of pace from Dumont's earlier work, such as *The Life of Jesus* and *Twenty-Nine Palms*, and here he is afforded a much bigger budget than usual. The war scenes in the desert are expertly done, and he captures that raw panic and nightmare of life in the combat zone of hostile territory.

In the film's most notorious scene, the boys gang rape a local woman. In a later scene when the soldiers are captured, the victim identifies those who raped her, and the men are then graphically castrated and are left to stagger around the compound bleeding to death. The only soldier conscientious enough not to join in the gang rape manages to escape his captors with his genitals intact, but he is then hunted through the land and the swamps, and he literally has to flee for his life. Highly recommended but not for the squeamish.

Gong Tau: An Oriental Black Magic (2007)
(Orig title: 降□ ; aka *Voodoo*)
Dir: Herman Yau /Hong Kong

Not your typical Cat III shocker but worth a look on a slow evening. A practitioner of the black arts has a vendetta against the police and attacks them and their families with the aid of black magic and voodoo, and the hunt is on to find the killer and end the curses.

Gong Tau finds director Herman Yau in much less outrageous form than his earlier outings like *Taxi Hunter*, *The Untold Story*, and *Ebola Syndrome*, but his latest effort still has the power to disturb horror fans, and especially those who are newcomers to the Cat III phenomenon. It's a dark film indeed, but also

much more pedestrian and ordinary in its manner and style. This sensible approach also cuts back on the humour to a degree, although the masturbation scene is one of the funniest things I've ever seen in any Hong Kong film.

Overall, *Gong Tau* is just not the same as the great Cat III's of the 80s and 90s; it looks way too polished and stylized. We also get CGI gore effects, but to be fair they look all right. It generally lacks that unruly spark of craziness that makes the earlier ones so enjoyable. It also seems to be aimed at a mainstream Western audience, and I much prefer Asian movies on their own terms. But these are just minor quibbles compared to what I thought of the ending; a shameless cliffhanger to lure us into a sequel (which has yet to be made).

An American Crime (2007)
Dir: Tommy O' Haver /USA

While *The Girl Next Door* (2007) was based on Jack Ketchum's novelised account of this horrifying true story, Tommy O' Haver's *An American Crime* goes straight to the court transcripts to present its version of events.

The film opens with the 1965 court trial before inserting lengthy dramatized flashbacks to tell the story. The parents of Jenny and Sylvia Likens leave their two young girls with Gertrude Baniszewski (Catherine Keener) and her six children – total strangers – for over a month for twenty dollars a week while they work at a travelling carnival. When Gerty's eldest daughter, Paula (Ari Greynor), is violently attacked by her married boyfriend, Sylvia tells him that Paula is pregnant, simply as a way of stopping him from beating her. But Paula is infuriated at Sylvia for letting her secret out, and goes crying to her mum, making up malicious lies to get her into trouble. And so Gertrude sets about making life hell for little Sylvia.

With the assistance of her children, Gertrude's mounting frustrations – laced with guilt at being unable to cope with her own kids – are taken out on Sylvia in the form of nasty and vindictive punishments. The abuse escalates until she is eventually kept in the basement where she becomes a torture victim, not just for Gertrude and her children, but for other kids across the neighbourhood, too. Early on in the film we're shown the story unfolding with the backdrop of 60s Americana, with the greased-back hair, old model cars, and girl group pop music, etc. And this warm nostalgic vibe is soon curtailed as the abuse becomes more sinister and dangerous. In addition to her financial woes and her boyfriend being shipped off to Vietnam, it soon becomes clear that Gertrude has severe mental problems. She whips the sisters with a belt when the cheque from their parents fails to arrive (it shows up in the mail later that day). It's interesting how the Baniszewski's go to church on Sunday like a decent pious family, and yet are capable of the most horrendous torture and humiliation on a defenceless young girl.

Gertrude's warped ways of instilling 'justice', and her ways of teaching her kids right from wrong are just an excuse for her to vent out her own frustrations. It would be laughably pathetic if it wasn't all so horribly true. This warped behaviour just has the effect of her own kids feeling free to do anything they please, and get into all kinds of trouble, knowing all they have to do to escape responsibility is blame Sylvia. And this has a snowball effect – Gertrude's kids can no longer do any wrong in her eyes, and all of their faults and misbehaviours are connivingly linked back to Sylvia, a scapegoat for the unruly kids and Gertrude's frustrated vagina. If someone slipped on a banana peel, this monster would find some way of blaming Sylvia for it.

Back in the 60s, physical punishment was much more commonplace than it is now, and parents would regularly beat and whip their children with belts, thinking it would do them good. And this kind of thing had other complications beyond the effects on the children; it also affects society at large. And this idea is hinted at in the scene where neighbours in the street can hear Sylvia's cries coming from inside the Baniszewski house, but ignore it, assuming her to be a bad kid in need of discipline.

The children of the neighbourhood learn from Gertrude's disgraceful behaviour when they keep Sylvia in the basement as their own little torture plaything. They beat and burn her with cigarettes, and dare each other to join in. Interestingly, the kids play along as though their actions are justified – the girl deserves punishment because momma said so. And the cycle of abuse continues. In court, none of the children can account for their behaviour. Mother's authority allowed them to act in the way they did, and that's all the encouragement they needed. And when asked why these little foot soldiers joined in the torture, they all drop their heads in shame and say "I don't know, Sir." With the right kind of influence, children can be led into partaking in any activity, good or bad (just think of the Hitler Youth in Germany, where youngsters had gotten so carried away in their induction into the ideas of National Socialism, that many even denounced their own parents as traitors and enemies of the State if they said anything bad about Hitler or the Third Reich). Even the young lad Ricky, who fancies Sylvia, is roped into torturing her. Such was the ghastly spell Gertrude had on the kids around her. These young minds hadn't developed enough to see through to the root of what was happening in their midst.

Sylvia eventually dies of her injuries. In court, we see denial at work as Gertrude tries to deflect responsibility and calls her children liars when they testify against her. This is a woman who carved the words "I am a prostitute and proud of it" onto the torso of a young girl. She was found guilty of first degree murder and sentenced to life in prison. She was released in 1985 and died five years later.

Killers are often glamorized in the movies – see *The Devil's Rejects*, etc – but this film offers a good example of why they shouldn't be. These people aren't cool, they're scum.

While the Children Sleep (2007)
(aka *The Sitter*)
Dir: Russell Mulcahy /USA

A young woman with an unhealthy obsession with a district attorney lands the job of in-house nanny for his and his wife's kids. And no sooner has she ingratiated herself into the household when she reveals herself to be a dangerous psychopath. This is an adequate interloper movie with a great performance by Mariana Klaveno. It's basically a remake of *The Babysitter* (1980).

Night Skies (2007)
Dir: Roy Knyrim /USA

Based on events surrounding the 'Phoenix Lights' incident of March 1997, this tells the story of a group of annoying youngsters in a camper van in the wilderness who are abducted and experimented on by extraterrestrials. Much of the running time is spent on the characters and their predicament as one of their friends disappears, but their bitching and squealing and all-round douchiness leaves viewer sympathy thin on the ground. Instead, by the hour mark, the average viewer will be hoping that the aliens insert huge, fire extinguisher-sized probes into their rectums. We get all the usual abduction phenomena: isolated areas, missing time, public and press scepticism, regression/hypnosis therapy, the story based on 'real transcripts,' which turns out to be almost entirely fictional, etc. There are no surprises on the alien front, either; the 'Greys' are smart enough to have figured out anti-gravity and wormhole travel, and yet are constantly out-smarted by numptoid college kid earthlings. However, for all the film's shortcomings, the finale on board the organic spacecraft is very weird, and the experiments are particularly ghoulish to behold.

1408 (2007)
Dir: Mikael Hafstrom /USA

Paranormal investigator, John Cusack, takes a hotel room at the Dolphin in New York that is reputed to be haunted. His room – 1408 – has been the location of dozens of deaths over the years, to the point where hotel staff have closed it off as 'out of bounds' to the public. However, Cusack meets the manager (Samuel L. Jackson) and threatens to dig up some journalistic dirt on the hotel unless he is allowed to use the room. *1408* – based on Stephen King's short story from his *Everything's Eventual* collection – starts off well, but it just isn't scary in the slightest. You'll realise you've seen it all before within the first 20 minutes, as the ghosts dig up his psychological dirt and smear it in his face like a bad mushroom trip, in the same way as *The Haunting* (1963), *Event Horizon* (1997), *Deathwatch* (2002), *Session 9* (2001) and *Malefique* (2002).

The Poughkeepsie Tapes (2007)
Dir: John Erick Dowdle /USA

Not a bad docu-style horror/slasher but is let down by some ridiculous acting and a corny twist ending... Police raid the home of a suspected serial killer. They don't find him but they do find more than 300 hours of video footage of the killer going about his business. The resulting film is put together mostly from those video tapes. It still hasn't been officially released in any form but was leaked online. And if it does eventually make it onto video shelves it will probably be trimmed down a little first as the leaked version looks to be a rough cut and outstays its welcome by a good ten minutes or so. There are some great individual set-pieces

throughout, including stalkings, abductions, murders, and the maniac's bizarre treatment of his captives, and general weird behaviour. On the downside, some of the performances are incredibly bad, such as a forensics guy who discusses what kind of weapons the killer may be using; it's one of the most ridiculous performances you'll ever see. Also, the police-woman at the makeshift grave site looks like she has stepped right out of drama school in a performance of a lunchtime. My main quibble though is that the film never attempts to address the psychological motivations that leads some people to take pleasure in the destruction of children, and just seems content as a grim exploitation piece. The film was eventually released on demand through DirecTV for a short while in 2014 before being discontinued – again with no explanation from the producers.

I Know Who Killed Me (2007)
Dir: Chris Sivertson /USA

Lindsay Lohan stars in this disappointing 'torture porn' mess. The film stars Lohan as Aubrey, a high school girl who is kidnapped and tortured in a killer's lair. She has her right hand and foot amputated, and is later found alive in the woods. She awakens in hospital convinced that she is not Aubrey but the daughter of a crack addict called Dakota. And Dakota happens to be a fictional character whom Aubrey created before her abduction, for a writing project. Has she suffered some kind of brain damage or deep psychological trauma that has caused her to completely disassociate her identity, or is there something else going on? An interesting premise – how does the mind react to such an extremely stressful situation of being strapped down onto a table and being completely helpless while your limbs are slowly frozen off by a maniac? But – surprise, surprise – the filmmakers make a total pig's ear of things. The potential for a daring and challenging psychological thriller is squandered by having the storyline dumbed down to oblivion.

Barricade (2007)
Dir: Timo Rose /Germany/USA

This film kicks off with a bunch of German campers being murdered by a mysterious assailant (including a death by acid in the face, which is really well done). Michael, an American living in Germany, is joined by Nina, his female friend who is also American. He's attracted to her, but nothing is going on between them, and their relationship is strictly 'platonic' despite him drooling on her tits at every opportunity. They are joined by David, who is Michael's German friend, and he serves as their guide for a planned weekend camping trip out in the wilderness. Meanwhile, there are more killings in the woods, including a young couple who are butchered in their tent. And soon enough, Michael and his bumbling, idiotic friends find themselves in grave danger…

Less a horror movie and more a group of adults fannying about in the woods. The only positive thing this film has going for it is the gore sequences, but even this is let down by overload, until the viewers are so jaded by the blood and gore on screen that another impressive disembowelling merely swoops over your head – just another bit of graphic nastiness in an avalanche of severed limbs and entrails. Everything else about this film is dire. The direction and the score are pedestrian at best. The soundtrack throws up ridiculous German hip hop that sounds like a Bavarian accountant reading out a shopping list. There are also some acoustic mumblings from a whimpering ponce, in the vein of Damien Rice, David Gray, James Blunt, John Legend, et al, you know, the kind of music that is played at dumb people's funerals.

The movie's villains are a 'family' of savage cannibals who have lived in the woods, bumping off strangers and campers since the mid-70s. They're like a cross between the hillbilly monsters of *Wrong Turn* and the Sawney Beane clan. But anyone looking for an interesting back-story explaining how they ended up deep in the wilderness, and why they decided to turn to murder and cannibalism will be left disappointed as no such explanation is given. Before the killers were made clear, I was half expecting it to be Deckard from *Blade Runner* – the perfect antidote to a bunch of replicants pissing about thinking they're human – he would've put an end to this nonsense and retired them forever.

Do yourself a favour and form a barricade between yourself and this film. Trust me, you'll have more fun watching a puddle exist.

Murder Party (2007)
Dir: Jeremy Saulnier /USA
An excruciating low-budget 'comedy' in which a man finds an invitation to a Halloween party. Curiosity gets the better of him, and when arrives he is immediately tied to a chair by a group of incompetent lunatics. They intend to kill him as performance art, but one of the girls has an allergic reaction to a raison in a piece of bread. She collapses and cracks her head on an iron fixing on the ground, and dies soon after. Anyway, the protagonist stays gagged and chained to the chair while the lunatics sit around doing heroin, eating pizza, and making lame jokes. Sure, there's no shortage of lame-o comedies out there, but this one is especially awful. Watch the similar – and vastly superior – *Invitation Only* (2009) instead.

Flight of the Living Dead (2007)
(aka *Plane of the Dead*)
Dir: Scott Thomas /USA
On a passenger plane heading for Paris, a re-animated medical patient escapes from the cargo hold and spreads her infection, turning the passengers into flesh-eating zombies. It's up to a sky marshal and a wise-cracking con man – who is being extradited to France – to slay the ghouls and save the day. However, for reasons of national security, fighter planes are scrambled to blow the jet out of the sky... *Flight of the Living Dead* is a low-budget zombie flick that was made to cash-in on the success of *Snakes On a Plane* (2006), with the added bonus of lots of blood, guts and brains splattered across the place. The flight passengers are routine zombie fodder – the bickering black couple, the bickering teens, flight staff, and of course, the scientists whose meddling with nature has unleashed their worst nightmares, EC comics style. This is a competent little film that basically does what it says on the tin. The kills aren't particularly memorable – apart from a shredded zombie that is sucked into the engine, and a nun having her legs ripped off – but, for a standard sized plane, there seems to be an unlimited supply of ghouls to kill.

Zombie Wars: War of the Living Dead (2007)
Dir: David A. Prior /USA
Set decades after the zombie apocalypse, the living dead have had 50 years to evolve, and have reached the stage where they have enslaved humans and farm them for food. The last resistance comes in the form of a ragtag band of soldiers who use guerilla warfare tactics against the 'puss-bags.' *Zombie Wars* has its moments – it works best during the fleeting battle sequences – but too much time is wasted

on characters sitting around and talking about their pasts (i.e. poor character development), and earnestly blowing smoke up each other's bottoms. Low on narrative drive but high on entrail-ripping, this film is basically a remake of the VHS anti-classic, *Blood Rush* (1983), with zombies standing in for the evil, post-apocalyptic slave-drivers.

Frayed (2007)
Dir: Norbert Caoili /USA
Standard slasher movie with an escaped mental patient, kids camping in the woods and a twist ending. Though overlong at 110 minutes, this film relies on atmosphere and tension rather than bloody slayings, and for once, it's all the better for it. Plus, it includes another rarity: a genuinely creepy killer clown.

Hack! (2007)
Dir: Matt Flynn /USA
A group of students on a trip to an island become the victims of a pair of deranged killers who enjoy recording their crimes for their later amusement. The film basically serves as a fanboy homage, with literally dozens of references to horror movies and horror fiction, past and present, and this is at the expense of everything, from the story line and dialogue to everything else. References to *Psycho*, *The Birds*, *Hellraiser*, *The Texas Chain Saw Massacre*, *Friday the 13th*-- even *Orca, The Killer Whale*. Notice character names relating to horror heroes, such as the teacher (Mr. Argento), the murderous eccentric (Mary Shelley), Victor (King, as in Stephen), the boat captain (Bates) and the Sheriff (Stoker). This kind of thing was archaic in the 90s in films like *The Dead Hate the Living!* (1999), but here it's simply overkill.

Quid Pro Quo (2008)
Dir: Carlos Brooks /USA
A well-behaved melodrama posing as a challenging and thought-provoking film. Radio host Stahl has been confined to a wheelchair since he was a youngster due to a road accident which killed the rest of his family. He's on a quest to learn about a group of people who want to become parapliegic; they have been known to offer surgeons huge amounts of cash to physically disable them. Inevitably he meets Fiona, an attractive, mysterious weirdo who may hold some answers.

This kind of typically dull drama wouldn't be out of place on some daytime TV movie channel for bored housewives. Stahl even bags himself a pair of magical shoes that help him to walk again (magic realism? You should be so lucky!). The film takes an interesting and un-PC idea (healthy people who want to become cripples for lifestyle or even sexual purposes, and will do anything to have their wish), and turns it into the most bland, boring, and sorry excuse for a drama. It's as if the film's makers were so terrified of offending anyone and causing controversy that they pussyfoot and skimp around the idea like regular members of the PC brigade.

The strange subculture element was done much better in Cronenberg's *Crash,* and also in Brian Evenson's superb novel, *Last Days*, which centres on a detective who is sent to infiltrate a bizarre religious cult whose members hack off their own body parts in order to feel closer to God. But in *Quid Pro Quo* we're expected to follow the dullest and most boring lead character in a long long time. The script constantly takes the moral high-ground at every opportunity; it never really attempts to understand the psychological motivations of those who want to become parapliegic (which is funny considering the whole film is about a man trying to find out why). We also get your typical Hollywood tradition of the main character being the squeaky-clean perfect moralist (and in a film with this kind of subject-matter, it's as if he's stuck between a rock and a hard place). There's almost a zero sense of humour either; absolutely no attempt to try and lighten the mood or characters. I can't be too harsh on the actors though, they did what they could with a lousy script.

All in all, this film poses an interesting question and then spends the next 70 minutes avoiding the answers, leaving us to tag along with stupid cardboard characters who have absolutely nothing to say.

Blindness (2008)
Dir: Fernando Meirelles /Canada
Based on the novel by Jose Saramago, an author who seems to have no idea how diseases really work, *Blindness* takes its literary cue from John Wyndham's sci-fi novel, *Day of the Triffids,* whilst at the same time making sure to distance itself from the genre while pilfering its dramatic power. The film version by Fernando Meirelles sees a nightmare scenario unfold where

everyone goes blind and society falls apart. The disturbing power of the film comes from the details as things become increasingly dark and dangerous as groups form and degradation sets in. Shot on digi video which seems to drain all shots of their colour.

The Horseman (2008)
Dir: Steven Kastrissios /Australia

The grieving father of a murdered girl receives a video in the mail which shows her being abused before she died. He then sets out on a brutal revenge mission with the aid of a hefty toolbox that he carries around with him. This sometimes exhilarating revenge movie is let down by the usual problems which crop up in low-budget SOV efforts – sub-par performances, clichéd bad guys, a routine mediocre 'score', etc – but if you're a fan of Uwe Boll's later works, like *Rampage* or *Postal*, those things can be overlooked in favour of the gripping story. The horseman meets a young woman on the road and they bond pretty quickly, and this is when the film hovers between redemption and cruel irony as he takes her on the warpath with him. See also *Dead Man's Shoes* (2004) and *The Beasts* (1980), films which share similar story lines.

Tokyo Gore Police (2008)
(Orig title: *Tôkyô zankoku keisatsu*)
Dir: Yoshihiro Nishimura /Japan

If you're one of those who despises CGI gore and bloodshed then stay well clear of this one as it gleefully unleashes the digital red stuff at 24 galons per second.

In the near future, the soaring rise of violent crime has resulted in the privatization of the capital's police force. The corporate-owned law enforcement groups are at liberty to unleash brutal (and often fatal) punishments on the city's criminal elements. The biggest offenders are a gang of mutant rebels called Engineers whose chaotic temperaments and near immortality hold the citizens of Tokyo in a grip of fear. It's up to Ruka (*Audition*'s Eihi Shiina) and her deadly law enforcement squad, The Tokyo Gore Police, to hunt down and kill the marauding pests, but the 'key' to killing these creatures often hides within, and it's not always an easy task... She's also on the search for the person who killed her cop father, and eventually encounters the crazed scientist who is responsible for the creation of the Engineers.

Unsurprisingly, this shot on video splatter movie was directed by a special effects artist, Yoshihiro Nishimura, who had previously unleashed his bag of tricks in Sion Sono's *Suicide Club*. It's very rare for an FX guy to take to the helm and produce a film that is anywhere near satisfying (Tom Savini's remake of *Night of the Living Dead* is one such rare exception), but Nishimura handles the project well, delivering a solid slice of sordid comic book craziness, awash with an ocean of arterial spray, gruesome dismemberments, and cyberpunk posturing. It's a film that stands head and shoulders above other films directed by FX artists, such as Ryan Nicholson's *Torched*, and there are just as many glorious practical effects as well as the CGI stuff.

What is surprising is that the film was passed uncut by the BBFC. The UK DVD (2 disc set from 4Digital) is the one to go for as it is presented in a very nice transfer and is accompanied by a shed load of bonus features missing on other releases. Lookout for the Verhoeven-esque mock TV commercials ("Harakiri is suicide!" "New wrist-cutter design! To die for, yay!"). Also lookout for the mutant designs of some of the Engineers who look like reject Cenobites from the *Hellraiser* sequels. The film also boasts what is perhaps the bloodiest blowjob gag in movie history. Ah, the world would sure be a duller place without the extremes of Japsploitation. Enjoy!

Philosophy of a Knife (2008)
Dir: Andrey Iskanov /Russia/USA

Running just shy of four and a half hours, *Philosophy of a Knife* is an 'artistic representation' of factual events that is said to have occurred at the infamous Unit 731, a Japanese camp based in Manchuria during the Second World War. Those looking for a documentary account of the barbaric practices that went on there will get what they're looking for, provided they're willing to sit it out and wade through all the dramatised footage, because despite the loose feel and lengthy grotesque sequences, the film does stay very close to a factual depiction. Those looking for a narrative-based drama, however, are advised to look elsewhere as *Philosophy of a Knife* shows director Andrey Iskanov taking full advantage of the artistic license the subject-matter affords him, and the end result comes across more as part documentary, part bizarre music video, and very little in the way of a conventional narrative-based drama.

Disc 1 starts with the voice-over of a freelance medical nurse who mourns the end of the war and who makes plans for a retreat back to Japan. Mostly in black and white with the exception of video footage of Russian Anatoly Protasov offering an engaging history lesson on the subject, the next two and a quarter hours of the first part of the film mixes archive footage of the war years with experimental videos depicting the awful goings on at Unit 731. The intro sees a man being escorted outside into the snow and beheaded with a sword.

A man with an English accent serves as narrator and he gives us some historical back-story, including the Russo-Japanese war, the Russian Revolution, Japan's struggle to combat the spread of Communism, etc, all set to archive footage. The film boasts excellent use of sound design with weird drones and repetitive chimes and wonky electronic and industrial music typical of Iskanov's films. Unit 731 was hell on earth for those unfortunate enough to have found themselves there. The human captives were subjected to horrendous experiments, with the data collected and used as a way of helping Japan's war effort. A common practice at the camp was to conduct animal blood transfusions in humans – especially with horses. Horse urine would be injected into the human bloodstream, and its effects on the human body would be documented in detail. The Japanese wanted to have the power of wiping out their vast enemies with something much simpler and effective than the usual military combat of guns and bombs, and with bacteriological research they had found their answer. At Unit 731 they produced anthrax, dysentery, cholera, and bubonic plague by the kilogram. They had produced enough bacteria to wipe out the entire population of the planet, and they were intending on using it too. It's a good thing they were stopped when they was.

The film eventually settles into a prolonged depiction of the experiments. In one hyper-stylized sequence a pregnant woman has her foetus surgically removed while she is fully conscious. One experiment used humans in long and sustained exposure to X-ray to study the damage it causes to human organs. A young Russian man is subjected to this test. There are also experiments conducted to see how much physical pain a human can withstand before losing consciousness. A woman has her teeth ripped out, one by one, without anesthetic. After removing the entire bottom row of her teeth with pliars, she remains conscious (and screaming a lot), so the boffins then start on the top row. Men are contaminated with venereal diseases such as syphilis and they are forced to rape captive women so that the boffins can check each stage of the infection and its effects. One young man is forced to rape a girl and infect her, and when he's done he is then taken to the gas chamber and timed on how long it takes him to die. It takes seven agonising minutes, and his face literally disintegrates. One person has his arteries opened up and is timed how long it takes for him to bleed to death. Another is shot in the throat at point-blank range and also timed.

Unit 731 seemed to be a kind of natural evolution of the way that science and philosophy had been heading in the last one hundred years or so. Philosophers became atheists, scientists became amoral, and politicians and revolutionaries put theories to the test on a grand scale. The Hitler-Stalin Pact meant nothing when German troops invaded the Soviet Union; Stalin would invent his own crimes so that he could have those he disliked executed after staging 'show trials'; millions of Jews were being exterminated in Europe in a 'purification' of the Ayrian race; the Americans were testing atomic bombs in the deserts of New Mexico with the assistance of angelic figures like Albert Einstein. Trust, loyalty, pacts, and alliances had gone out the window and were replaced by fear, treachery, distrust, and wholesale destruction. The whole world had gone mad under a Godless sky, and Unit 731 was just the tip of the iceberg. That little camp based in the puppet state of Manchukuo seemed to encapsulate everything that was going on in the world at the time; the amorality, humans in a worthless form literally reduced to fodder, the innovations and scientific breakthroughs used as tools of destruction, etc. When looked at in this light, the atrocities of World War II seem like a desperate attempt at uniting the world. As ludicrous as it sounds, it was a way of trying to make order out of all the chaos and uncertainty.

The atrocities continue into disc 2 with more of the same, and the film descends into little more than an atrocity exhibition. The film wraps up with another history lesson concerning the end of the war. Americans capture the island of Okinawa, and the Japanese are ordered to fight on to the last man. Mass suicide breaks out across the Japanese empire. A 15 megaton atomic bomb is dropped on Hiroshima, and then a 20 megaton device is dropped on Nagasaki causing widespread destruction. The Soviets declare war on Japan, and this spells the end of Unit 731 as the people running the place know that it's only a matter of time before the Red Army comes along to spoil all their fun. The place is decimated and destroyed, and the remaining test subjects are killed by cyanide.

The Americans captured Shiro Ishii but he was later allowed to go back to Japan after striking a deal. It's interesting how the data that was collected at Unit 731 has seemingly vanished. But according to the best authorities on the subject, the data did survive and made it into the hands of the Americans and Japanese. And if you consider how America and Japan dominated the post-war years in the field of medical breakthroughs, perhaps the main reason for their successes was due to them having access to this data.

Martyrs (2008)
Dir: Pascal Laugier /France

In an introduction on the American DVD of *Martyrs*, writer/director Pascal Laugier makes an apologetic plea to his viewers concerning the film he has unleashed on the world. He berates himself for the damage the film may cause to those who are unprepared for the cruel imagery and deeply troubling philosophical ramifications therein. He openly invites his audience to hate his guts.

The film itself opens on a scene similar to *House of Whipcord* (1974) (and the stories continue to cross paths throughout) of a half-naked girl in utter distress running through an abandoned industrial estate. When the police finally pick her up, she is unable to disclose of any details about her mysterious incarceration. Medical inspections indicate that she hadn't been raped, but her body is covered in scars and bruising. The police track down the place where she had been held captive, an old slaughterhouse. A thorough search of the place fails to yield any clues as to why she was held there, nor who was responsible.

Fifteen years later, and the young girl, Lucie (Mylene Jampanoi), has grown into a beautiful but unstable woman, and has befriended Anna (Morjana Alaoui) in a home for abandoned youths. The two women break into a family home and viciously murder the occupants in the belief that the parents had something to do with Lucie's childhood ordeal. However, a monstrous assailant who has been terrorizing Lucie for years appears in the house and inflicts some nasty damage on the young woman. And this leads Anna to question further the mystery of Lucie's dark past...

To reveal any more about the plot would be unfair to those who haven't seen this, but suffice it to say, it succeeds in in pulling off three major shift changes in the narrative, with the above synopsis serving as nothing more than a hint of the horrors to come. It's the kind of movie that puts you through the meat grinder of shock horror and despair unlike anything since the days of *Cannibal Holocaust* and *Irreversible*. It's quite simply the closest thing to an emotional holocaust ever filmed.

Emerging as part of a new wave of extreme French horror, with the likes of *Haute Tension, Frontier(s)*, and *À L'intérieur*, dazzling and horrifying an entire generation of film fans around the globe, *Martyrs* marks the zenith (or nadir, depending on your stand point) of that fresh new movement in the way it finds new ways to make an audience crumble under the enormity of its weighty ideas. Rarely has a horror film divided its audience so much, with some accusing director Laugier of gratuitous and unjustified bloodshed, and others rightly pointing out that the horrendous imagery is essential to the film's success. To label the film as 'torture porn' is completely off the mark, because although the extreme violence and tortures are quite graphic, not for a moment is the film leering or salacious in its depictions; it has an urgent catharsis that is absolutely necessary before the final revelations in the film.

Stylistically, *Martyrs* is as equally faultless as any film of its era. The rough and ready camera work and rapid editing push the narrative into a steady pace, with the 92-minute running time passing by in a breeze. The film's colour palette juxtaposes cold blues, stark whites, and fiery reds, all reflecting the turmoil in the heroine's minds. And this is helped by a couple of stunning performances from Jampanoi and Alaoui whose raw emotions and exhausting shooting schedule reminded me of the torments that Marilyn Burns went through during the making of *The Texas Chain Saw Massacre*. Kudos also goes to special effects artist Benoit

Lestang who created the visual shocks which accentuate the ideological horrors on display, and who sadly committed suicide before the film achieved its global recognition as one of the most harrowing movies ever made.

Bad Biology (2008)
Dir: Frank Henenlotter /USA
Bad Biology sees the welcome return of writer/director Frank Henenlotter after a 16 year break from directing, and the results are typically unpredictable in keeping with the native New Yorker's track record. *Basket Case* (1982) was a grim and twisted tale of familial love, *Brain Damage* (1988) was a bizarre psychedelic trip on the dangers of drug addiction, *Frankenhooker* (1990) was an insane cartoon update of Mary Shelley's classic novel, and the *Basket Case* sequels (1990, 1992) were cloying and sentimental freakshows. Even the style of each of his films had its own unique flavour, and *Bad Biology* is no exception.

Aspiring photographer, Jennifer (Charlee Danielson), is not your average kind of girl. For a start she is equipped with a cluster of seven clitori, which makes her a nightmare to deal with in bed, as many men realise to their horror as they are quite literally banged to death while she takes polaroid snapshots of their death throes. Her strange biological make up is somehow super-charged, and she gives birth to mutant babies only moments after conceiving. She then quickly and efficiently dumps the screaming spawn into trash cans, the bath tub, or wherever she happens to be at the time. Jennifer's ferocious sexual appetite goes unmatched until she has a chance encounter with Batz (Anthony Sneed), a young man who is also the victim of his own bad biology after a gone-wrong circumcision at birth, All his life he has tried desperately to self-medicate his manhood with all manner of experimental drugs and steroids, and now his cock is a huge aggressive monster with a mind of its own. And this makes Batz a very unsociable person. You would think that Jennifer and Batz are a match made in heaven, but things aren't that simple...

Bad Biology offers all the hallmarks of Henenlotter's previous work – warm colourful settings, the exaggerated cartoonish style, outsider characters with dark secrets, etc – but this latest offering also treats us to a harsh, nasty, and cynical black humour several shades darker and meaner-spirited than all of his

previous works combined. It's an approach which may disorientate some of his regular fans, but I thought it worked well and is definitely in keeping with the cynical times we live in. He also shot the film in 35mm and not the HD video that many expected, and that's a welcome relief. Charlee Danielson isn't a great actress but her game attitude and keen energy more than make up for her sometimes stilted line readings, and Gabe Bartalos' wild special effects work is as crazy and impressive as anything seen in Henenlotter's films; the mutant babies and huge killer cock in particular.

Early screenings of *Bad Biology* were shown via video projection for some reason. It went on to wow fans at the festivals and one-off screenings before showing up in the UK on its first DVD release by Revolver, untouched by the hands of the BBFC (it was also released uncut in France under the title *Sex Addict!*). Shriek Show eventually unleashed the film on disc in America in its most impressive print to date, uncut and with a shed load of extras missing from the UK and French versions. With the moderate success of *Bad Biology* we can only hope that Henenlotter will be encouraged to get back into the director's seat very soon.

Loch Ness Terror (2008)
(aka *Beyond Loch Ness*)
Dir: Paul Ziller /Canada
A shop assistant tags along with a rugged cryptozoologist to track down a plesiosaur that has been munching the locals. The prologue is set in 1972 where a group of researchers are attacked by a large, CGI Nessie that strolls out of the loch and chomps down on a couple of characters while whipping others 30-feet into the air with her tail. Thirty-odd years later, and the setting has shifted from Scotland to Lake Superior in Canada. And somehow – for reasons never explained – 'Nessie' and her young are terrorising a bunch of Canucks thousands of miles away from home... *Loch Ness Terror* is basically a modern-day re-working of films like *The Beast From 20,000 Fathoms* (1953) and *The Crater Lake Monster* (1977) with the added spectacle of blood, guts and CGI effects. The characters and the action are just your typical join-the-dots monster movie staples, but Brian Krause as the cryptic crypozoologist – who, it turns out, is the now grown-up kid that survived the massacre in the prologue – is interesting to watch because he looks to be doing a permanent

Clint Eastwood impersonation.

Pontypool (2008)
Dir: Bruce McDonald /Canada
The town of Pontypool in Ontario descends into chaos as a strange virus gradually transforms the populace into rampaging maniacs. The problem is, the entire scenario is depicted from inside a radio studio. *Pontypool* is a major disappointment considering how even mainstream film critics had nice things to say about it. It's a dull and badly acted cheapie which somehow went 'viral' and found a much bigger audience than the usual low-budget horror fare. The chaos is said to have started due to a verbal virus that worms its way through human language. Director Bruce McDonald draws on the semiotics of Roland Barthes and Ludwig Wittgenstein, which perhaps explains the muddied and convoluted nature of the film. It's a film which isn't afraid to play around with ideas, but most of the action is in the form of audio as news reporters explain the chaos over the airwaves, thus rendering much of the film visually redundant.

Long Weekend (2008)
(aka *Nature's Grave*)
Dir: Jamie Blanks /Australia
A remake of Colin Eggleston's classic environmental horror in which a married couple head out to the countryside for a camping trip and upset mother nature by dangerously discarding cigarettes, chopping down trees for fire wood, tossing beer bottles and shooting wildlife. The build-up to the action feels like it's going to turn out like *Eden Lake* (2008), but with wild animals standing in for the killer teenagers. There are also moments that evoke Von Trier's *Antichrist* (2009), as the couple engage with nature in very different – and antagonistic – ways. But perhaps the film is too subtle for its own good; there are no outright moments of horror, and the film fizzles out long before the end credits. The biggest disappointment though are the characters themselves; they're such an awful couple, you won't believe for one second that they're supposed to be in love. The 'chemistry' between them is non-existent, and their dialogue is astonishingly bad. This wreck of a remake just goes to highlight Eggleston's masterful original.

Asylum (2008)
Dir: David R. Ellis /USA
Irritating college kids discover that their dorm was once an insane asylum in the 1930s, and the mad doc who ran the place is now out to kill them all. But, wait a minute, wouldn't that make the doctor around 100-years-old or more? Oh dear... *Asylum* is a patchwork of horror movie cliches; from the building with the sinister past, the sensible girl who is determined to uncover the truth, and the usual *de rigueur* irritating college cunts. It tries to be like *A Nightmare On Elm Street 3: Dream Warriors* (1987), but it actually owes a greater debt to the remake of *House On Haunted Hill* (1999) and *Session 9* (2001). But, while those aforementioned movies are good for a giggle, this is just bloody awful in every conceivable way. Hey, how does one utilise character development in a movie script? Why, you simply have your characters sitting around telling boring stories about their pasts – that seems to do the trick.

Cease to Exist (2008)
Dir: Ryan Okenberg /USA
This documentary takes a closer look at the link between the Manson Family and The Beach Boys' Dennis Wilson. According to this film, Manson exploited the fact that Dennis couldn't keep his cock in his trousers, and lured him into recording demos with the cult by offering him girls, soft drugs, and the opportunity to hang out at Spahn Ranch. Dennis is said to have spent $100,000 on the Family in one year alone. He even paid for their medical bills, which he called "the largest gonorrhea bill in medical history." The nastiness started when The Beach Boys recorded one of Manson's songs, *'Cease to Exist.'* The band re-wrote the lyrics and changed the song's title to *'Never Learn Not to Love,'* credited to Dennis. Charlie was infuriated, not only for the alterations, but for being cut out of the royalties, too. Dennis felt threatened and fled town just as Helter Skelter was taking off. He was later quoted as saying, "I know why Charles Manson did what he did. And some day I'll tell the world. I'll write a book and explain why he did it. Over the years though, people have always wanted to know what happened, what my relationship with Charlie was. We were just friends."

Carver (2008)
Dir: Franklin Guerrero Jr. /USA

Another film supposedly based on true snuff events but is entirely fictional is *Carver*, about a group of annoying campers who enter a barn and discover a collection of snuff reels featuring women and couples getting slaughtered in the woods. They soon realise that the murderers are the same men who run the local bar. And sure enough, the youngsters are hunted down. The most irritating dick weasel of the group is chained up in the rest room, has the contents of the toilet poured onto him and has his right testicle crushed in a nutcracker, of all things. The blonde chick has a long nail hammered into her head. Another victim is beaten to death with a sledgehammer, and is not such a good-looking chap once his face has been pounded into pulp. *Carver* isn't a particularly good film, nor does it bring anything new to the genre, just a routine run-around where most of the annoying characters get to live longer than they should because the filmmakers assume we've grown to like them. Wrong assumption. Also, none of the killings are captured on the maniac's camera, which is another bum move. And, at just short of a hundred minutes, the film is way over-long and you'll probably be glad when it's over.

The Farm House (2008)
Dir: George Bessudo /USA

A young couple in debt to the mob leave their home in San Diego and set off in their car to start a new life in Washington state. However, the man falls asleep at the wheel after driving all night, and he crashes the vehicle in the quiet wilderness. Stranded, they head to a nearby farm house for help. But the sinister couple who live there prove to be far more dangerous than anything they had left behind them... What starts off as an interesting set-up soon descends into the norm, as *The Farm House* is basically a watered down version of *Frontiers* without the political subtext. The cheese grater scene was the torture highlight, and there's a supernatural spin at the end right out of leftfield, but there's really nothing here for jaded horror fans to warm to. Director George Bessudo shows his inexperience by relying on overhead helicopter shots to establish each new scene, and the warring couples scream and fight their way through every tired cliché of the genre.

Snuff: A Documentary About Killing On Camera (2008)
Dir: Paul Von Stoetzel /USA

A cynical and offensive take on the supposed snuff documentary format. Played entirely straight, it purports to be a factual report with 'academics', 'FBI profilers' and 'film experts' discussing whether or not snuff films actually exist. I noticed numerous factual errors while watching this, such as the claims that *The Texas Chain Saw Massacre* was based on a true story (it wasn't; it was actually very loosely based on the exploits of Ed Gein, who, although he did make masks out of human skin, he never chased teenagers around Texas with a chainsaw), and the Russian snuff-gang crime ring reeks of bullshit; only *two* articles were ever written about it in the whole world? Really? Much of this so-called documentary is so utterly fabricated as a cynical selling point, and anyone with even a passing interest in the subject will see it for what it is. At one point, one of the talking heads tries to qualify *Bowling For Columbine* as a snuff movie because it includes CCTV footage of the massacre, and clearly political internet beheadings by Al Quaeda fanatics are also passed off as snuff. Not only are those claims wrong, but then we're actually *shown* that sickening footage for no other reason than to gain kudos with fans of *True Gore* and *Traces of Death*. For a more credible documentary on the subject, there's the episode of *The Dark Side of Porn* entitled *Does Snuff Exist?* (2006). It's a TV programme which inevitably leaves more questions than answers, but rightly acknowledges that the advance in readily available technology has made the whole snuff nightmare pretty much inevitable.

Mum & Dad (2008)
Dir: Steven Sheil /UK

A young Polish cleaner is abducted by a crazy English 'family' who live in a house of horrors under the Heathrow flight path. It's not an entirely convincing scenario, and there are problems with clunky dialogue, but the film at least attempts to update the 'crazy family' horrors of old, like *The Texas Chain Saw Massacre* (1974), *Parents* (1989) and *The People Under the Stairs* (1991). The end result will surely give viewers an idea of what it must have been like to live with Fred and Rosemary West. *Mum & Dad* should also be commended for giving the viewers the choice of how they would like to see it; the film was released simultaneously in the cinema, on DVD, on pay-per-view TV, legitimate download, and for streaming on your phone. So while Hollywood was still in a huff about combating piracy, this independent British horror flick simply gave the viewers the choice of watching it in any way they wanted. And the film made a decent profit, too. It set a nice example for other production companies to follow.

Blood and Sex Nightmare (2008)
Dir: Joseph R. Kolbek /USA

This shot on video shocker was something of a unique entry in the slew of amateur gore movies that were being churned out of North America in the late 00s, because for a start, the film actually lives up to its title.

Nick is horny. Nick is frustrated. Nick really needs to get his end away. So when his girlfriend Amy returns from a family funeral in Japan, he manages to twist her arm into agreeing to spend a few days with him at a sex resort in the country. When they arrive at the Pleasant Mountain Adult Retreat, Nick expects to find a haven of camp fires and swingers, but the place seems eerily deserted. They book into their cabin and are visited by the local handyman, Walter. But Walter's creepy manner and leering eyes sets the couple on edge. And when a pair of fellow swingers are butchered in graphic detail nearby, Nick and Amy must put aside their sexual frustrations and get the hell out of there... But who's the murderer? Could it be weird Walter or the sex maniac killer who died in the woods years earlier?

Coming on like a spare change remake of *Porno Holocaust* and shot on a cheap video camera with a miniscule cast and crew, *Blood and Sex Nightmare* at least delivers on its title promise. The performances and script are kind of average at best, but the bloody FX are quite impressive, and the whole show flies by in a brief but brilliant 81 minutes. Indie trash regular Tina Krause supplies the obligatory T&A, indie rapper Eyez The Filmmaker Emcee cameos as an unfortunate victim, and the DVD was released by Bloody Earth, making Kolbek a household name among DIY film lovers everywhere.

Tortura (2008)
Dir: Marcel Waltz and Michael Effenberger /Germany

A bunch of party girls find themselves stranded in town, but that turns out to be the least of their troubles as a gang of sadistic cannibals hunt them down, one by one, to eat them alive... And that's about as close to a plot this movie gets. The first 25 minutes are boring as hell with godawful hip hop crap on the soundtrack, but as soon as the cannibals make an appearance things get pretty tasty. We first make their acquaintance when they strap some poor dude onto a table and cut off his fingers, barbecue them, bite off his nipples, and put straws in his wounds so they can drink his blood. Oh, they also cut his leg off with an industrial sized handsaw, and one of the lucky girls is given the bloody limb as a treat. A slow start then, but once it gets going it's pretty much unrelenting to the end. The special effects are very good, the performances decent, and it's nice to see cannibalism added to the 'torture porn' mix. Tongues are ripped out, and eaten. Intestines are ripped out, and eaten. Spleens are ripped out and... you get the idea. The trussed-up victims are eventually forced to have a nibble and even kill each other, much to the amusement of the cannibal clan.

Deadgirl (2008)
Dir: Marcel Sarmiento and Gadi Harel /USA

Wow. A pleasant surprise. We need more teen comedies like this. Okay, this isn't a comedy per se, but there's lots of sick and twisted humour here... Two high school students discover a zombified girl in some deserted basement, and she becomes a sex slave to a group of horny outcasts. The film stumbles at the beginning with idiotic characters and some awful dialogue, but once it gets going this is actually a pretty decent little film. The character JT becomes an increasingly unhinged psychopath in his determination to keep their secret safe (he's also in danger of becoming cool, especially when he comes out with lines like "Jail is full of motherfuckers like us"), and the main character, Ricky, is infuriatingly incompetent – he is supposed to be the film's moral conscience, but like the young lad in *The Girl Next Door*, he does too little too late to help the damsel in distress; so there goes *his* credibility (amazingly, in a move that makes me wonder what on earth the filmmakers were thinking, Ricky encourages the school jock to partake in a bit of forced fellatio with the dead girl; we know it's all part of a revenge plan whereby the girl will bite off his cock, but still, it does seem a bit morally dubious when the film's 'hero' looks to be actively contributing to her woes). The film has much to say on the destructive power of adolescent sexuality and gets darker and more twisted and interesting with the passing of each reel.

Blitzkrieg: Escape From Stalag 69 (2009)
Dir: Keith J. Crocker /USA
An attempt to revitalise the long-dead Nazisploitation sub-genre, *Blitzkrieg* is a surprisingly tasteful approach to the subject (unlike many of the notorious 70s counterparts), and borrows just as many elements form neorealists like Rossellini as well as exploitative shockers like *Love Camp 7* and *The Beast In Heat*. The story takes place in a POW camp, Stalag 69, run by a despised SS commandant, a man so nasty and sadistic even his fellow Nazis hate his guts. And when a group of female American prisoners are brought to the camp, it leads to his inevitable downfall.

Rampage (2009)
Dir: Uwe Boll Canada/Germany
Rampage follows a very pissed off young man as he plans a city massacre. He kits himself out in bullet-proof armour that resembles a paintball protection suit, and hits the streets armed to the teeth. The difference here from all the usual shooting sprees in the movies (and in the headlines) is that this troubled kid isn't planning on a suicide mission; he intends on getting away from the atrocity a free man. He also has other little agendas to settle, like burning money, dealing with the population bomb, and ...well, I don't want to spoil things, but those paying close attention should work out his cunning stroke of genius by the hour mark.

As in his previous work, writer/director Uwe Boll doesn't seem too interested in character development or actors (the great Dario Argento was always the same), and this results in some less than stellar performances (just check out the scene around the family breakfast table at the beginning). We also get Boll's trademark hand-held 'photography' – cold and probing, some would say nauseating. But Brendan Fletcher's central performance is accomplished and believable, even if he seems far too normal, rational and likeable a person to be committing such crimes.

The film's biggest asset though is the rampage itself; a seemingly endless blitz of cinematic bliss. Mostly shot in real time, we're right there as Brendan squeezes the trigger on everyone he comes across. It's quite simply one of the best killing sprees in cinema history. After conquering the streets, getting revenge on the owner of a coffee shop, and – even better – unloading round after round in a beauty salon, Brendan enters a bingo hall and has a bite to eat! He sits there eating a sandwich and catching a breather whilst surrounded by a dozy mob of geriatrics who are completely oblivious to what's going on. It's a moment where even the ordinary and mundane brings on an oddly surreal tone. After this strange episode, however, we're right back into the action.

The way Boll tells his stories I find very refreshing. He has a careless juvenile attitude to both writing and directing, and I mean 'juvenile' in the best possible sense – enthusiastic, eager, provocative, and even positive (in this sense, *Rampage* reminded me of Stephen King's early novella, *Rage*). This film comes on like an angry student's knockabout screenplay, full of rage, idealism, and a call for social change. And that's no bad thing as far as I'm concerned. *Rampage* is far more visceral and disturbing than Boll's earlier shooting spree movie, *Heart of America* (which also stars Fletcher), and if you do get the 'Boll bug' then be sure to check out *Rampage* as it's an essential part of his wacked-out filmography.

Stoic (2009)
Dir: Uwe Boll /Canada/Germany
I'm starting to like Uwe Boll more and more. As a director he leaves a lot to be desired in terms of technicalities and aesthetics, but he instinctively knows which stories are worth telling. *Stoic* charts the aftermath of a prisoner's suicide. His cellmates take turns at explaining the events that led to the tragedy. But what is true and what is bullshit? At first, the surviving cellmates seem genuinely upset and sorry for their 'friend', but when we learn of the harsh victimization this young man went through before his death, it leaves us wondering whether they really give a shit at all, and suspect that they're actually just passing the buck to save their own skins, morphing the truth, *Rashomon*-style.

Most of the film takes place entirely in the

prison cell with the four characters, and it's a lonely place. It's their whole world for 23 hours a day. The boredom that breeds the violence and humiliation they inflict on the weakest of the group. Devil makes work for idle thumbs and all that. The man is forced to eat a full tube of toothpaste and drink coffee mixed with salt and pepper. But it gets worse; when he vomits, he is forced to eat it all up again, and then he is pissed on, badly beaten and raped. Another inmate (Ed Furlong) then rapes him in the arse with a mop handle while he's laid out semi-conscious. Around the hour mark the situation becomes even more intense when the prisoners decide that the young man should hang himself before he gets the chance to report to the authorities...

John Hillcoat's *Ghosts...Of the Civil Dead* (1988) explored similar themes but was never as intense and claustrophobic as this. Both films share the same message too, that the prison and judicial systems are fucked and do more harm than good. Towards the end of the film the inmates turn their attentions to the next lowest in the pecking order, and it's quite clear that he's next for some similar treatment.

Grotesque (2009)
(Orig title: *Gurotesuku*)
Dir: Koji Shiraishi /Japan
A rare title to be banned in its entirety in the UK nowadays, *Grotesque* is easily one of the most sick, twisted, and realistically executed torture porn movies I've ever seen. I would probably rank it in the top 20 most disturbing movies ever list. The 'plot' picks up with a disgruntled loner who kidnaps a young couple and ties them up in his basement. And so begins the torture. But here our anti-hero doesn't just rely on sharp instruments and power tools to inflict his damage, he also uses cruel tricks and soul-crushing mind games on his victims. In one scene, the madman finger-bangs the woman (complete with wet and squishy sound effects) and is the first time I've seen squirty female ejaculation in a film. When he's finished, he notices that the young man is now aroused, so he jerks him off, sending his load flying across the room and landing on his girlfriend's stomach. Good shot!

Early in the film the girl asks her boyfriend if he would die for her and he flounders, not knowing how to answer. However, later in the film the madman asks him if he would die for her, and this time the answer is a spirited "yes".

We get all the usual torture porn elements here with some brutal nastiness and some pretty graphic chainsaw mayhem, but then the maniac does something very different from the usual screen monsters; he seems to take pity on his victims and pleads for their forgiveness, and even nurses them back to health. The victims are suspicious at first but gradually start to believe that they are on the verge of freedom; but this is all just a part of his sick game, and pretty soon the doomed couple are back in the basement and the cruelties are more brutal than ever...

To say any more about the plot would be unfair to those who have yet to see this, but the 'survival challenge' near the end would make Jigsaw's chest swell with pride! There are excellent performances, top-notch gore and splatter, and the production values are superb. To see a grubby little torture film like this looking so nicely lit and glossy is a rare treat; not since the days of Nacho Cerda's *Aftermath* have we seen such cinematic crimes displayed on beautiful 35mm celluloid like this.

The British censors banned the film in the UK. BBFC director David Cook claimed "Unlike other recent 'torture' themed horror works, such as the *Saw* and *Hostel* series, *Grotesque* features minimal narrative or character development and presents the audience with little more than an unrelenting and escalating scenario of humiliation, brutality and sadism. In spite of a vestigial attempt to 'explain' the killer's motivations at the very end of the film, the chief pleasure on offer is not related to understanding the motivations of any of the central characters. Rather, the chief pleasure on offer seems to be wallowing in the spectacle of sadism (including sexual sadism) for its own sake".

Melancholie Der Engel (2009)
(*Angel's Melancholy*)
Dir: Marian Dora /Germany
After the shocking extremes of *Cannibal*, director Marian Dora returned with his toughest film yet, *Melancholie Der Engel*, and in the process stole the infamy of Jorg Buttgereit to crown himself the new dark prince of extreme German horror. But unfortunately, this film is a dull and pretentious bore fest. We basically have a bunch of repugnant characters sitting around talking absolute crap, pretending to be deep and cryptic to conceal the fact that they have nothing interesting to say. Amongst the crude and

depraved activities on screen, viewers can look forward to such heart warming scenes as a woman watching a snuff movie in which a pregnant woman is severely beaten and her baby aborted. The foetus is then cut into pieces. The woman watching the tape begins to masturbate, and spreads blood across her vagina and stomach. Also, an old man (played by Ulli Lommel, director of *Tenderness of the Wolves*) is burned alive. As usual, Dora's cinematography has a very closed-in feel about it as though it was shot on 8mm on zoom mode (it was actually shot on 16mil). Shots are awkwardly framed with heads and faces partially obscured from view – it's a very up-close and personal style of filming. The shots also have a soft-focus, powdery texture to them that makes the film look decades old, like Jean Rollin's old movies. Maybe I watched this in a bad translation (there is still no English-friendly DVD release, to my knowledge), but there's barely a single sentence in this film that makes any sense, and I'm not exaggerating. I don't believe killing animals is acceptable in any type of entertainment or 'art,' but the fact that *Angels' Melancholy* is such an over-long, dull and pretentious piece of garbage somehow makes the animal sacrifices ten times more offensive. Amusingly, some of the cast members had to undergo psychological counselling at the end of filming. Perhaps they would have been better getting their heads examined *before* embarking on this turd.

Dogtooth (2009)
(Orig title: *Kynodontas*)
Dir: Yorgos Lanthimes /Greece
Picking up the Un Certain Regard Award at Cannes, *Dogtooth* was a huge domestic hit, described by critic Dimitris Danikas as a 'black, surrealist nightmare,' and by the *New York Times* as a film that 'seems as much an exercise in perversity as an examination of it.' It was also only the fifth Greek film to be nominated for an Oscar, and is unlike anything ever seen on the international circuit.

An ice-cold, deadpan satire, *Dogtooth* is set in an isolated homestead that is cut off from the rest of civilisation. There, an eccentric father keeps his wife and children locked in the grounds, and is determined to raise them so that they'll never need to know about the evils of the outside world. The youngsters have spent their entire lives in such an environment, and have

been brought up to believe that aeroplanes are tiny creatures that fall out of the sky; that fish are spawned in swimming pools; that cats are vicious people-eaters; and sex is just as much an impersonal bodily function as eating. However, the kids are growing up fast, and corruption gradually seeps into the house by way of video cassettes (such as *Jaws*, *Flashdance* and *Rocky IV*), and the father begins to lose control.

This extraordinary film can be summed up in the scene where the father goes to collect his dog that is in training with the police force. 'A dog is like clay,' he is told. 'Our job here is to shape it. We teach them how to behave. And we are here to determine what behaviour the dog should have. Do you want a pet, or a friend, or a companion? One that obeys orders?' Critics have compared Lanthimes' work to everyone from Kubrick to Haneke to Buñuel, but none of those comparisons can prepare viewers for how strange and uncategorisable the film is. Furthermore, Lanthimes himself refuses to confirm or deny any interpretations that have been bounded around concerning the supposed allegorical meaning behind the film. 'People are always trying to get me to confirm their point of view, and I just won't do it,' he said. 'If I wanted to talk about social problems or politics, I'd become a writer. But I'm a film-maker, and that's all I can do.' This, of course, leaves the film very much up to the individual to decide on what it all means.

Whether you see *Dogtooth* as a comment on the over-protectiveness parents often put on their kids in the name of love, or, as others have said, a comment on the Greek government's (and indeed western governments') treatment of its citizens (people as pets, or dogs to be moulded like clay), it's important to remember that the film also works on a very literal level. Cats are demonised with propaganda-like scare stories, outsiders are treated with suspicion and contempt, and, in one scene that involves the daughter being bashed over the head with a naughty video tape, the layers of meaning can be read on many different levels. The wordplay censorship reminded me of doublethink and 2+2=5 from George Orwell's *1984*, in which the youngsters are taught that 'a cunt is a large lamp,' and 'a zombie is a small yellow flower.' The household is also very much a patriarchy, and it's a shame we never get to hear the mother's side of the story; she seems totally withdrawn and depressed.

The kids have reached adolescence and have begun to question everyone and everything around them – the attempted brainwashing can't keep them down for very long. The cast are totally game, but Aggeliki Papoulia who plays one of the sisters, steals the show with her deranged performance in which she does a Rocky Balboa impersonation, a crazy dance, and even punches her own teeth out in one scene. She deserves a ton of respect, especially as her role was all but ignored at film festivals. The chloroform game is extremely dangerous, as is the 'evil' kitty getting the shears, and the father's insistence on keeping the game running as smoothly as possible. The graphic incest scene is surprising because it wasn't used as a way to show the kids' rebellion, but as a simple and natural curiosity! Reassuringly, the BBFC passed the film uncut, and their report notes that 'detailed inquiries reveal that rubber shears were employed, and no animals were harmed during the production of *Dogtooth*.'

The film gained a large cult following after it was denied top honours at Sitges and other film festivals, with fans suspecting that the graphic and provocative nature was the only reason why many ignored it and tried brush it under the carpet.

Antichrist (2009)
Dir: Lars Von Trier
/Denmark/Germany/France/Sweden/Italy

Lars Von Trier grew up in a very liberal Danish household in which his parents didn't believe in setting rules, and he was basically given free reign to do whatever the hell he liked. Some critics and psychologists have suggested that this kind of boundless freedom is the cause of his supposed depression and neurosis in later life, and the reason why he now seems to suffer from every phobia known to man, and why he insists on making films designed with maximum mischief in mind. If this is so, then it follows that we who lived a more normal childhood with rules and punishments have developed a fascination for all that is wild and chaotic and forbidden. Well, at least in my case that's certainly so.

Thus, judging by this kind of logic, *Antichrist* should be absolute bliss for a horror fanatic like myself. It seems like the perfect match; the work of an artist at a complete distrust of the world projected from a screen into my own retinas that lens a mind that yearns

for the darkness and the forbidden and the horror. Except, of course, that *Antichrist* is not really a horror movie, at least not in the way that most of us expect a horror movie to be.

Antichrist opens with a monochrome prologue shot in stylish slow-motion. It shows a man and a woman having sex in the shower (Willem Dafoe and Charlotte Gainsbourg, with a little help from a couple of porn actors standing in for the graphic penetration shots). In the bedroom, their young child, Nick, climbs out of his cot and lifts himself up onto the sill to watch the falling snow from the open window. And just as his parents reach orgasm, he falls to his death.

After collapsing at the funeral procession, Charlotte is hospitalised for a month (I'll be using the actor's names, Charlotte and Willem, as the character's names are not mentioned on the credits or in the entire film). Willem visits her daily and she mentions that "Dr. Wayne said my grief pattern is atypical." It seems odd and a bit sarcastic for her to use psychological terminology to express her state of mind. The words sound cold and clinical the way her emotions and raw grief are labelled like stages on a chart. It doesn't seem natural to put a medical spin on her deep sorrow, even if the words did come from Dr. Wayne originally. Perhaps she used the words because Willem is a trained therapist and has a good understanding of terminology and psychological states, or maybe she used the words because they offended her, and she passes them on to her husband as a way of making him angry at Dr. Wayne for addressing his suffering wife in such a cold and clinical way. If so, it seems to have worked. For, though he doesn't confront Dr. Wayne, he criticizes the doctor's treatment of her and checks her out of hospital the very next day. But in the meantime, Charlotte blames herself for Nick's death. He tries to deflect the grief away by reminding her that he was with her when he died and that he should be just as much to blame. It's a comment which she later uses against him.

The next day when he checks her out of hospital with the intention of treating her in his own way, she accuses him of being arrogant. He argues against that by saying "No therapist can know as much about you as I do", and he tries to assure her that he is doing it because he loves her. He takes Charlotte back to their apartment where the therapy can begin.

Her grief gets worse, and she understandably resents the fact that her husband is treating her like a patient. She lashes out at him as a way of trying to break his cold medical manner; "You've always been distant from me and Nick. Now that I come to think of it, very very distant." He doesn't react in the way she wants – that of a loving father and husband, but as a psychologist; "Okay. Can you give me some examples?" he asks. She tries again, "I never interested you until now that I'm your patient."

A man of Willem's profession should have known it would be a bad idea to attempt a treatment of his wife at such a difficult time. Her reactions are cruel and hurtful, and obviously disastrous to their relationship. She wouldn't have had that kind of ammunition or personal connection to her designated therapist had she stayed in hospital, and Willem probably recognises this but stubbornly sticks to his guns, no doubt as part of his male pride – he knows what's best for his wife. He stays unmoved even when she interprets his cold manner as proof that he isn't grieving; "You're indifferent as to whether your child is alive or dead. I bet you have a lot of clever therapist replies to that, haven't you?"

Charlotte's grieving gets worse, or at least much more physical and aggressive. Dafoe is there with her every step of the way, helping her through her night terrors and nightly panic attacks, but he insists on keeping the strict doctor-patient role. He also uses terminology to explain her state of mind; according to him, Charlotte has reached the "anxiety stage" of her mourning, and this echoes the earlier words of Dr. Wayne (the 'atypical grief pattern'), which probably offended her, and now sees her husband monitoring her in the same clinical way like a slide under a microscope. She later pounces on him for sex in a frantic and hysterical manner; he pins her down to the bed and jokes "You should never try to screw your therapist." He's actually only half joking. He knows they were having sex the moment their son died, and will be aware of how much guilt and resentment it would later cause if they were to give in to their physical desires at that moment.

Willem takes Charlotte out to Eden, a place of country wilderness and isolation where she was supposed to have taken Nick on a holiday. Eden connotes an obvious biblical reference, but also, as the couple trek through the woods to

their cabin, she complains that "the ground is burning", a clue to her new hellish perspective on life and nature. Willem goes off alone through the woods while Charlotte rests, and he sees a deer in a clearance; the deer is in the process of giving birth, but the birth has gone wrong, and the fawn hangs from the doe's behind, swinging from side to side in the embryonic sack, at the mercy of nature and its elements. The deer's eyes have that look of bewilderment and confusion, a frightened animal in the midst of nature, and when the camera zooms in on Willem's eyes, we can see that he shares that same haunted look. It's a shot that reminds us that he's in pain too, not just his wife, and for all his knowledge and expertise in psychology, he doesn't really hold the answers, and the environment is just as harsh and unforgiving to him as it is to everyone else.

Eden brings the couple face to face with nature. Even when they are out in the open air their voices sound strangely echoed; this perhaps reflecting the enclosure and isolation of their grief. Mother Nature is shown in all its stark reality; its harshness and obliviousness as dead animals decay in the earth. Nature doesn't care, nature just is.

The unimaginable pain of losing a son is made all the more difficult to accept in an environment that is unmoved and unsympathetic. Charlotte hears Nick crying, and she races through the wilderness and the woods calling his name. It's a scene that goes to show how even her own mind is part of this unforgiving nature; the pain and the torment in her heart is just as brutal and unsympathetic as the space and sky that surrounds her. She wants to lash out at the injustice of it all, but who can she blame? She first attacks Willem and accuses him of being arrogant once again. She then attacks nature itself, explaining that everything she thought was beautiful about Eden has now become "hideous" to her. Acorns rain down onto the cabin making a loud clattering sound, and she describes the noise as "cries," and concludes that "Nature is Satan's church."

Eden was supposed to help Charlotte, but her exposure to the place is having the opposite effect. It seems she connotes the screams and 'cries' of nature with that of her own son whom she thought she heard crying earlier that day – Nick, her own flesh and blood, had no more significance in the world than a spilled acorn; just another piece of nature's debris. These backward steps into negativity are of much concern for Willem, as her new perspective on life goes against his own training and male rationality. He tries to counter this by stressing that "Thoughts distort reality, not the other way round," but his words only seem to confirm the opposite (as they will do again later in the film), and serve as an illustration of how men and women are very different. And this is perhaps the first true sign of misogyny in the film.

For Willem, his relationship is of paramount importance to him even though he is systematically wrecking it in his own bullish and pig-headed way of trying to do what's best. He seems to have put his own grief on hold in order to help his wife get through the worst of her pain. Charlotte treats him as part punch bag, part crutch, part shoulder to cry on, part therapist, and part husband. She lashes out and attacks him just as much as she needs him. She even bites him at one point and draws blood, perhaps as a direct way of testing his strength, of testing how much room she has for her emotions to manoeuvrre. But it's important to remember that it was Willem who put himself in that position by checking her out of hospital in the first place. Meanwhile, Charlotte's emotions are back and forth; happy one moment and explosive the next.

Late one night while she sleeps, Willem browses through Charlotte's research papers. She had been writing a thesis on gynocide throughout the ages, and something written in those pages causes him deep concern. Charlotte's initial feminist stance in studying the history of misogyny had eventually led her to the opposite opinion; she concludes that because nature is fundamentally evil, and that women's bodies are governed by this nature through menstruation and pregnancy, then women as a whole must be evil too. The later scene where Willem confronts her about this the following morning is very pivotal and is the most important scene in the film. But later that night Willem makes the big mistake of sleeping with Charlotte, and thus opening that can of worms, guilt, on her part which will come back to haunt them both. It's ironic how Willem's natural bodily urges causes the final breakdown of their relationship, and also goes to confirm – at least in this instance – that nature has indeed had a destructive and seemingly evil effect on both his and Charlotte's well-being. And perhaps Charlotte recognises this; before sex, she

demands to be hit, and when Willem refuses, she accuses him of not loving her. She then storms off and masturbates by a tree in the woods. Willem the psychologist then disappears completely, and what we're left with is Willem as his true self; a confused and bewildered animal in the midst of nature who ultimately has no more understanding of the world and its mysteries than that poor deer he saw in the woods earlier. The unruly spark of nature's ways are everywhere all around him; a fox even looked him in the eye and uttered the words "chaos reigns," but still he refused to acknowledge it until now. He approaches Charlotte outside by the tree and he fucks and slaps her as many times as she wants him to because he has now given himself up to the chaos.

With the sunrise, Willem thinks himself to be back in control. It is hinted throughout the film that the daytime represents the world of the masculine, with calm, order, clear sightedness and rationality, whereas the evening is the realm of femininity, a world of darkness, mystery, and the irrational (an idea also explored in Dario Argento's *Suspiria*). The next scene is a key point in the film. Willem confronts Charlotte about her thesis; he tells her "Good and evil, they have nothing to do with therapy. Do you know how many innocent women were murdered during the 16th Century alone just for being women? I'm sure you do. Many. Not because they were evil." Charlotte's reply is resigned but shielded, just blasé words of agreement uttered by millions of women over the centuries under the domination of the masculine rationale, "I know. It's just that sometimes I forget." Willem continues, "The evil you talk about is an obsession. Obsessions never materialise, it's a scientific fact. Anxieties can't trick you into doing things you wouldn't do otherwise. It's like hypnotism, you can't be hypnotized into doing something you wouldn't normally do, something against your nature. Do you understand me?... You don't have to understand me, just trust me." There is a desperate pleading in his voice as if his own convictions are crumbling in the face of the opposite that he sees all around him. Indeed, he even *confirms* that Charlotte is evil by his own statement.

In the autopsy report it is mentioned that Nick had a slight deformity in his feet, but that it was "nothing significant." Dafoe believes the deformity to have been caused by Charlotte who would sometimes put his shoes on the wrong feet. He shows her a photograph of Nick sitting in the grass with his shoes on the wrong way round and she still doesn't notice until he points it out to her. Now, director Lars Von Trier is clearly trying to 'put the boot in' here with regards to offending the fairer sex; the whole sequence may seem to be 'nothing significant' but this is just a ploy to make the implied accusations seem less significant than they really are (everything is significant in this film to such an extent that even the main character's names are not even mentioned because they represent men and women as a whole). With this scene, Von Trier implies that women are bad mothers, that they harm their children in a series of small and insignificant ways, until the accumulated damage results in your typical adult. But there is also some ambiguity here relating to the earlier scene where Willem saw the deer in the woods; sometimes nature goes wrong, sometimes the birthing process goes wrong, sometimes children have slight deformities at birth that have nothing to do with how they are raised. The implication that the 'evil' of women is just an extension of the 'evil' of nature itself seems to suggest that if nature doesn't get you then your mother will.

Earlier in the film, Willem drew up a pyramid chart and asked Charlotte to list the places where she would feel the most afraid and exposed. She placed Eden near the top of the chart. But later on Willem comes to the conclusion that Eden wasn't the true answer; he scribbles out the word and replaces it in thick marker pen with the word 'ME'. It's nightfall, and he has once again entered the world of the feminine. Only now is he willing to fully acknowledge that Charlotte is indeed evil and that she fears herself more than anything else in the world. She immediately attacks him in a hysterical frenzy, beats him unconscious, jerks him off, and then bores a hole through his leg with a hand drill before attaching a heavy iron lock onto him by hooking it through the wound and tightening it with a wrench. She then wanders off and throws the wrench under the cabin porch.

Willem comes to in agony and manages to crawl outside to the woods and slide himself into a fox hole that is hidden in the roots of a tree. Charlotte returns to find him gone and then charges through the woods looking for him and calling him a bastard. In a blackly comic scene, nature is shown to be on Charlotte's side when a black crow squawks loudly in the fox hole giving away Willem's presence. He tries to silence the pest by grabbing its beak, but this doesn't work. In the end he resorts to beating its head in as a way of putting an end to the squawks. But it's too late – Charlotte knows where he is, and she uses a garden spade to beat him and jab at him, causing the earth to crumble in around him. Poor Willem has had a bit of a rough night; he's been knocked out, mutilated, beaten with a spade, and buried alive. Way to go Doc! Nice therapy you've got going there. Looks to have worked a treat!

A remorseful Charlotte later returns to the scene and digs him up. She drags him back to the cabin and continues in her misogynistic observations ("a crying woman is a scheming woman"). She masturbates using his hand. This brings out her guilt – as shown with flashbacks to the night their son died – and she takes a pair of scissors and snips off her own clitoris. For Willem, enough is enough; he ends up slaying the beast and burning her body out in the open. And in a strange epilogue, he is descended upon by hundreds of blank-faced women.

Antichrist was met with cries for it to be banned wherever it played. It's dark, violent, sexually and emotionally explicit, and undoubtedly misogynistic (even the film's title logo, with the last T in *Antichrist* displaying an O on top reminiscent of the female symbol, implying that femininity is connected to evil). But the film is also expertly made and offers two stunning performances from Dafoe and Gainsbourg. Von Trier's films have never been beautiful to look at but *Antichrist* is an exception; Anthony Dod Mantle's superb camera work is a marvel to behold, and the stylish slow-motion shots in Eden are nothing short of breath-taking (the film looks astonishing on Blu-Ray).

The film is a mix of the sacred and the profane, good and evil, darkness and light, art and artifice. It borrows heavily from the horror genre – the cabin in Eden looks very similar to the cabin in *The Evil Dead*, and the subliminals are clearly taken from *The Exorcist*. Von Trier also uses horror influences to create that eerie atmosphere and dark demonic imagery. But perhaps the biggest influence came from Andrzej Zulawski's *Possession*; this underrated masterpiece also explores the fundamental differences and incompatibility of men and women, and also boasts a superb performance from Isabel Adjani as the hysterical and shrieking woman, and sticks to a cold blue-ish colour scheme and themes of darkness, and the enigma of nature and the feminine, and possession.

Von Trier claims to have been depressed when he wrote and directed the film, but it's difficult to take anything he says seriously anymore. In an earlier film, *The Boss of It All*, he claimed that it was shot in 'Automovision', a computer technique that was "a principal for shooting film developed with the intention of limiting human influence by inviting chance in from the cold." As ridiculous as this may sound, many film critics took it seriously and went into great detail about this 'technique' when reviewing the film.

As for *Antichrist*, it's very much up to you to decide how seriously you take it. Von Trier opens himself up for accusations of misogyny by linking womankind with the cruel and chaotic 'evil' of nature. But Gainsbourg's character, after all, is meant as a symbolic representation. The overall message is a troubling one, and seems to be that nature was created by an evil and irrational Antichrist, and the only way for Man to get through this hell is to live by violent domination, not rationality. Only then can he get to grips with nature and fruitfully pro-create.

Trash Humpers (2009)
Dir: Harmony Korine /USA
Recorded on an old video camera, *Trash Humpers* portrays the activities of a group of destructive, sociopathic geriatrics. They vandalise property, cackle endlessly, perform fellatio on random objects and hump trash cans. Oh, and they also record themselves decapitating, slashing throats and suffocating strangers, too. A lot of people strongly dislike this film (just take a look at the scathing reviews on the *IMDb*), and it isn't difficult to see why. Anyone renting this expecting a 'normal' independent movie will be outraged. *Trash Humpers* is deliberately abrasive with its VHS aesthetic (it was edited together at random on two VCRs) and the fact that there is no plot to follow, no character development, or anything like that. However, those looking for a change from the norm may find it amusing. *Trash Humpers* is often compared to Werner Herzog's

Even Dwarfs Started Small and Lars Von Trier's *The Idiots*, and there are doubtless similarities there, but Korine's film is actually closer in spirit to stunt shows like *Jackass, Dirty Sanchez* and *The Dudesons*, etc (Johnny Knoxville even wore the same body suit for his old man stunts on an episode of *Jackass*). It has a free spirit to it, much like those shows. It isn't great art, nor is it pretending to be. It's a film which embraces the spontaneity of fucking a mail box for no other reason than having the freedom to do so. And the joy in knowing that it will annoy a lot of people. And let's face it, old people being obscene can be quite funny. The old guy improvising the tune on an acoustic guitar almost killed me. It's hilarious. I think the lyrics go something like, "you girls sure suck a large fat penis." It's a song that has been stuck in my head for days now. If I still had the band going, we would have done a fuzzed-up rock cover of it.

I'll leave you with this memorable quote: "Heads. It would be nice to live without a head. Think of how much money you would save on shampoo and hats. Models would be judged by their shoulders. And your ears would be in your armpits. And everyone would look like a stump. Sweaters, they would fit like socks. Boxers would have to rely on body-blows. Dandruff would be obsolete. No more zits! No more tea-bagging! Lower Ceilings! Chest hair will replace the need for beards. People would buy less tables; they'd eat off the table like stumps. People would weigh eight to eleven pounds less. And best of all, no one would get dizzy again."

The Life and Death of a Porno Gang (2009)
(Orig title: *Zivot i Smrt porno bande*)
Dir: Mladen Djordevic /Serbia
Largely overshadowed by the release of the notorious *A Serbian Film* around the same time, *The Life and Death of a Porno Gang* had to make do with luring unsuspecting viewers into its web of nastiness by word of mouth alone, whilst Spasojevic's film sparked global controversy and even graced the cover of *Fangoria* magazine. You won't see any 'newborn porn' in Djordevic's film, but you'll see just about everything else besides as we follow a group of drop-out pornographers who hit the road in a Scooby Doo van armed with video cameras. Whilst watching months of old video footage, a survivor of the gang explains what's going on...

The film starts in a light-hearted manner as almost documentary-like, but we soon get a touch of style, surrealism, and humour (much like Koen Mortier's *Ex Drummer*). We also get to see brief shots of unsimulated sex, a nasty beheading scene with bored soldiers playing football with some poor guy's severed head, a man cuts a goat's throat, and a tranny sucks off a horse. This film also features one of the weirdest rape scenes ever in which the gang are gang-raped by country folk. What makes it weird is that one of the guys being raped starts to laugh uncontrollably, and this laughter infects the other rapees, setting off a chain of giggles which leaves the horny yokels understandably confused (it transpires that the bumpkin rapists have been infected with HIV through their attack, and it's that gotcha! moment which amuses the gang).

Eventually the porno bande decide that snuff sells, so they begin organising the making of one. They start by filming some loon cut himself up with a razor; he then cuts his own throat on camera. One of the gang can't handle his death-croaks and steps in to finish him off by bashing his brains in. They dispose of the corpse and then indulge in a hippy-style orgy. Then we get another snuff movie; a woman called Sofia gives a little strip-tease and then smashes a soldier's head in with a mallet. And then they party some more.

By this point, the gang have truly become Manson-esque as the drugs get harder and they become increasingly alienated from society, and resort to kidnapping people for their 'pioneering' snuff efforts (it has long been rumoured that the Manson family made snuff movies, but the footage has never surfaced). The cult begin to fall apart soon after with suicide and disease rampant among them, but not before they attempt to stage "the first snuff theatre in the world". But it doesn't finish there; we get a tripple-whammy of bloody surprises before the end credits roll.

A Serbian Film (2009)
(Orig title: *Srpski Film*)
Dir: Srdjan Spasojevic /Serbia

Shock Corridor was a cinema show broadcast on Serbian television. Its presenter, Aleksandar Radivojevic, encouraged homegrown filmmakers to be more gory, more perverse, more violent, and have more Takashi Miike moments in their films. The result was a slew of provocative pictures from that part of the world, including *The Life and Death of a Porno Gang*, *Zone of the Dead*, and most notorious of all, *A Serbian Film*. And judging by these efforts, it's clear that Serbian filmmakers were indeed taking notes from *Shock Corridor*.

The plot of *A Serbian Film* centres on Milos (Srdjan Todorovic), a retired porn star who agrees to make one last film with the mysterious artist Vukmir (Sergei Trifunovic) as a way to make money to support his family, but he has no idea of the true nature of the film's production, and when he does discover what's going on, he has no chance of escape...

This is a near masterpiece of extreme cinema, full of tragic ironies, solid production values, well-developed characters (insert your own joke here), and is very well directed. It's a film that is very much deserving of its notorious reputation as it goes places where very very few films are willing to go. It permeates a dark and grim atmosphere throughout, The atrocities don't come at you straight away, and the audience does have the opportunity to relax on occasion, but nonetheless, *A Serbian Film* weaves a ghastly spell that is designed to unsettle its viewers from the outset. Around forty minutes in is when things get weird, and around ten minutes later it gets totally sick, and I mean truly TRULY sick. There are at least three scenes here that are very shocking, graphic, and utterly disturbing, and have caused no end of trouble with fans, critics, and censors around the world. Many reviews of *A Serbian Film* have given away all the grim and gruesome details of the plot but I'm not going to do that here because the element of surprise is of vital importance to the overall effect (although there are some predictable cliche moments, here and there). But suffice it to say, if you're a fan of the darker side of horror then *Srpski Film* is a must-see.

The genesis of the film stemmed from pure bloody-mindedness; Radivojevic had become angry and disillusioned with the whole Serbian film scene who he felt were ignoring real filmmakers and instead saw bureaucratic funding going to "boring, pathetic, politically correct films done by people who don't know the first thing about cinema". He used his platform as the presenter of *Shock Corridor* to propose his ideas for a new direction for Serbian films, in which he called for filmmakers to be more daring and provocative. In the end he decided to practice what he preached and teamed up with like-minded director Srdjan Spasojevic, and together they set up their symbolically-titled production company, Contra Film, and began launching their bloody crusade.

The Human Centipede (First Sequence) (2009)
Dir: Tom Six /Netherlands
The Human Centipede is a horrific black comedy made purely for sick laughs, but many people took it way too seriously upon its initial release and failed to see the funny side.

A misanthropic German Doctor is obsessed with creating a 'human centipede'. His experiments with dogs (Three Dog) wasn't a success but he jumps right into human experimentation anyway, by basically stitching three unlucky people together, mouth-to-anus, and studying the fiendish (and amusing) results...

Horror fans were disappointed with the lack of all-out gore (especially those who had read reports of people walking out of test screenings due to being grossed-out), but the heavy streak of black humour more than makes up for it. The film became an instant cult classic with those who did get the joke. The rantings here are as fine a mad doctor moment as Colin Clive's "IT'S ALIVE! IT'S ALIVE!" from James Whale's *Frankenstein*. The Japanese fella (Akihiro Kitamura) is hilarious as the unfortunate tourist demanding to be untied, ("The Japanese possess unbelievable strength when backed into a corner").

Some have criticised the performances of the two girls (played by Ashley C. Williams and Ashlynne Yennie), but that's a bit harsh; they weren't necessarily bad. They *could* be bad actresses for all we know, but this kind of comedy horror is no place to judge acting abilities. There's certainly an exaggerated giddiness in their performances as Lyndsey and Jenny, but director Tom Six probably wanted them to ham it up. Besides, their roles were perfect for the kind of affectionate lampooning that seems to be the film's central focus point.

There are many in-jokes and self-reference points in *The Human Centipede*, and it's incredible how easily much of this stuff has been overlooked. The scene where the girls arrive on the doctor's doorstep is a case in point: He asks if they're alone and will only allow them inside his house when they confirm to him that they are alone. His face, voice, and posture are suspicious beyond belief, but they still put their trust in him and enter his home (this kind of stupid behaviour is the fault of dumb horror characters, not dumb actresses). The stitching of character's mouths to arseholes is an obvious self-reference point – it was a way to shut them up! Tom Six had simply pre-guessed our annoyance at those bimbo characters and did us a favour. It's obvious that he likes to play around with B-movie cliches and stereotypes, and he does it in a fun and clever way, rather than a smug 'know-it-all' way like Kevin Williamson and Wes Craven (*Scream*). But many still fail to recognise it.

On repeat viewings the humour stands out even more, like at the beginning when the truck driver pulls over to take a shit and is shot dead, mid-excretion. Or the part when the doctor awakens his 'triplets' after the operation and gets them on all fours (or twelves?); he starts snapping away with his camera, and his subjects are crying in pain and despair, but the doc's tears are of pride and joy! This cruel mixture of despair and bliss represents the epitome of black and twisted humour.

Tom Six announced that *The Human Centipede* is only the first in a planned trilogy (hence the *First Sequence* in the title). Many have speculated on how the sequels will take shape, but the most interesting and feasible idea is the siamese twin angle: During the film, on the doctor's wall can be seen a piece of artwork depicting conjoined fetuses. Is it possible that the doc has a twin brother whom he was surgically separated from? It would explain why he was so interested in the subject (and would also be a good excuse to bring back actor Deiter Laser for the sequel). Perhaps this long lost twin will come out of the woodwork and continue with Doctor Heiter's research? If so, let's just hope that this long lost twin is just as sick and twisted as his brother.

Murder Collection V.1 (2009)
Dir: Fred Vogel /USA
The idea behind this film is to present a bunch of fake murder and death clips in a faux-documentary style. Web cams, home movies, and CCTV are all used to create a realistic effect, but most of the clips aren't convincing at all, and the 'ransom' scene at the end is a major disappointment to say the least...

It's a great idea for a film but is badly

executed for the most part (sorry). First of all, the grisly details of the deaths are always conveniently kept out of frame (except for a nice decapitation scene), and the scene of the father whipping his son with a belt is more humorous than horrifying. The scene with the cheating wife is a highlight, and this sequence would make for a great stand-alone short film in its own right. But even this impressive scene is let down by things like bad acting and an obviously fake rubber axe, etc. Making a fake docu-style horror movie is much more difficult than people think; Vogel and co may have startled viewers with their verite flavoured *August Underground* trilogy, but the horror in those films came from the gross and lewd antics within, not because anyone thought they were real and bought into the whole 'found footage' legend. When making a film like *Murder Collection*, the tiniest details give the game away. Not only does the violence and gore have to be spot-on, but the performances must also be perfect otherwise they're not convincing at all. The smallest mistake ruins the whole.

The Japanese autopsy footage looks the most convincing until we see close-ups of the fake rubbery 'flesh'. The 'Grummer' sequence boasts some impressive performances and for a while achieves that awkward air of impending ugliness to come, but when the knife comes out it all goes to shit, and we're left with the standard *Blair Witch*-type hysterics. It isn't the worst of the Toe Tag films, but after the likes of *August Underground's Mordum* and *Redsin Tower*, *Murder Collection V.1* is a major disappointment. A wasted opportunity then, I'd be very surprised to see a volume 2.

Evil Things (2009)
Dir: Dominic Perez /USA
A group of friends on the road are terrorized by a van driver who also films them while they sleep. Derivative of movies like *Duel* and *Jeepers Creepers*, it also has a hand-held, *Blair Witch*-type documentary feel, but is ultimately let down by some piss-poor improvised dialogue and bad acting. For those willing to stick around, however, the action really picks up in the last half hour or so, and the end credits sequence, which shows the killer's footage, is especially creepy, if slightly underwhelming due to it being tacked on to the end of a sub-par movie.

His Name is Jason: 30 Years of Friday the 13th (2009)
Dir: Daniel Farrands /USA
Tom Savini presents a look back at the *Friday the 13th* series. The casts and crews of all the Jason-related movies swap the usual stories and anecdotes that anyone familiar with the series has heard a million times before. With talking head sequences and a plethora of clips, Vorhees is discussed as if he is some kind of deeply complex Shakespearean villain or something, rather than the retarded killing machine he is. Everyone does all they can to make the *Friday* films seem deeper and more culturally influential than they really are.

Captain's Pride, Volume 33 (2009?)
Dir: -Not credited- /Mexico?
A short six-minute clip which shows a woman in a cage being tormented by a man in a black ski mask. The cage is covered in animal skulls. The woman is carried out of the cage and chained up to a workbench. The man wears a Motorhead t-shirt. At this point we can make out other trussed up victims in the room. The woman has her ear cut off and her throat slashed. Mr. Motorhead then leaves the room and another enters wearing a Santo-style wrestling mask. He rapes her while she bleeds to death. Mr. Motorhead reappears and inflicts more damage on her throat wound with a home-made torture device. The end. This little clip was released anonymously onto the web in the late 00s and has been passed around on the underground horror circuit. It was shot on scratchy old 8mm film, and there's no audio except for the sound of the whirring projector. Nothing is known about the film's makers or what their intentions were. Presumably, they wanted to release this with as little information as possible in order to create an online 'buzz' about its supposed authenticity, but this is unmistakably fake.

The Haunting in Connecticut (2009)
Dir: Peter Cornwell /USA /Canada
Candyman's Virginia Madsen plays Sara, a housewife whose teenage son, Matt (Kyle Gallner), is undergoing chemotherapy. Sara and Matt move in to a new house with the rest of the Campbell family, a place they can't really afford – just like the Lutz family in *The Amityville Horror* (1979) – and almost immediately Matt begins to see some strange things. Later, the

family discover that their new home was once a funeral parlour, and Matt's behaviour becomes increasingly erratic. Is it the medicine that is causing the trouble, or is it something truly sinister within the house? *The Haunting in Connecticut* is a pleasant surprise after such disappointing Hollywood ghost/possession movies that were released in the same decade (*The Amityville Horror* remake, *The Exorcism of Emily Rose*, etc). There is an interesting back-story to the house that the characters learn about through old photographs, newspaper clippings, and even a box of human eyelids. The story unfolds in a believable way, and it rarely feels like you're treading old territory. Even the ending is allowed to unfold in a sensible and subtle manner, instead of the usual shouty-screamy-flashing-lights-effects-and-mumbo-jumbo bollocks. The film was inspired by 'true' claims of paranormal activity at the Snedeker family home in Southington, Connecticut in the 1980s, as investigated by Ed and Lorraine Warren. The claims were published in a book, *In a Dark Place: The Story of a True Haunting* (1992), whose co-author, Ray Garton, has since admitted that he and Ed Warren had fabricated many of the events and details to spice up the book in order to shift more copies.

The Day of the Triffids (2009)
Dir: -Director not credited- /UK
After the BBC's impressive five-part mini-series in 1981 (which is still the definitive screen adaptation of Wyndham's novel), the Beeb had another crack at the whip in 2009, delivering a two-part TV special set in the modern-day that starts off well before being bogged down in the usual BBC quagmire of sentimental, mediocre nonsense. Episode one begins at Triffoil, an energy corporation that has been farming thousands of Triffid plants in warehouses across the UK so that they can be drained of their oil-like substance that is used as fuel. Bill Mason (this time played by Dougray Scott) is a biochemist who works at the London plant, and he has to deal with a situation in which a 'Triffid rights' activist (an underused Ewen Bremner) intrudes on the premises attempting to free the killer plants. Mason suffers eye damage from the lights while trying to protect a colleague by giving her his protective glasses, and as a result, finds himself in hospital temporarily blinded. Thus starts the familiar scenario of the light show in the sky that blinds most of mankind while Dr. Mason recovers in a hospital ward. After leaving, he witnesses the chaos and hysteria in the streets as the public roam around trying to make sense of their helpless situation. He rescues a blonde news reporter, Jo (Joely Richardson) from the clutches of a panicked policeman, and together they eventually make it to the 'gherkin' tower in central London that has been fashioned into a fortified sighted community run by the establishment and protected by the military. This community is overthrown shortly thereafter by socialists, and every sighted person is handcuffed to a blind man and transported to a nearby pub. And after the characters are attacked by the Triffids in a food storage warehouse, the power struggle continues when another group takes control with a brutal efficiency. Mason and his American buddy, Coker (Jason Priestley) manage to escape, and they end up at a church which serves as a makeshift refuge for the blind, while Jo stays behind and is sweet-talked by Torrence (Eddie Izzard), a mysterious drifter whose allegiances are not made clear until the end...

Despite the decent set-up, this version of *Triffids* goes tits-up at around the two-hour mark (which still leaves a further 60-minutes of torturous tedium to sit through). Things simmer down into the usual BBC territory where the writers slap the viewers across the chops with just about every cliché they can get their hands on, ensuring that the product can never rise above its formulaic, crowdsource-approved, tangled-in-red-tape, BBC origins. And modern-day news reporters are actually decent people with souls, apparently.

Humains (2009)
(*Humans*)
Dir: Jacques-Oliver Molon & Pierre-Oliver Thevenin /France
Phillipe Nahon returned with another 'there's-something-scary-in-the-woods' tale where he plays a professor up against rampaging neanderthals. A very disappointing film, it was directed by a couple of special effects technicians, Jacques-Oliver Molon and Pierre-Oliver Thevenin, who had previously worked on the special FX for *Inside* (2009), but their writing and directing skills are atrocious. Other French dog turds to avoid include *I Am the Ripper* (2009), *Broceliande* (2002), *Promenons-nous dans les bois* (2000, aka *Deep In the Woods*), *Eden Log* (2007), *Fear(s) of the Dark*

(2007), *Hellphone* (2007), *In the Shadow* (2010) and *Last Screening* (2011).

And Soon the Darkness (2009)
Dir: Marcos Efron /USA /Argentina /France
And Soon the Darkness is a dismal remake of Robert Fuest's 1970 classic. This time the story is set in rural Argentina with the two American girls on a cycling trip. They stop by at a bar, and Ellie makes an idiot of herself with a karaoke mic. Like many modern horror movies, we can't have nice, decent characters anymore; oh no, they must be obnoxious drunken buffoons nowadays. This time the story mostly stays away from the peace and tranquility of the original which was set in France, and instead opts for the *Hostel*-like approach of young Americans getting themselves entangled in a culture that is alien to them. Besides, there's very little mystery here; viewers have a very good idea from the get-go of who has abducted Ellie. And interestingly, the locals seem to reject the American ideals out of sheer resentment rather than 'morality.' This remake also drops the fairly downbeat denouement of the original in favour of a 'can do' exercise in viewer empowerment. See girls, if you ever find yourself in a situation where three ruthless men have you held in captivity with the intention of selling you on to a prostitution racket, just simply beat 'em up and shoot 'em! It's easy! You go, girl, you can do it. You only weigh 100lbs and have never shot a gun in your life, but hey, it's the 21st Century, get with the programme sister.

Book of Blood (2009)
Dir: John Harrison /UK
Paranormal investigators stay in a house that sits in the middle of a 'highway' of the dead, the route that the spirits of the dead have to take. Based on Clive Barker's story (*Books of Blood Vol. 1*), the film shares similarities with *Hellraiser* (1987) in that it has a strange, transatlantic feel, a sinister attic, and things back from the dead. However, unlike *Hellraiser*, it is horribly miscast and dull beyond belief.

Alien Trespass (2009)
Dir: R. W. Goodwin /USA /Canada
An affectionate homage to 50s invasion movies like *The Day the Earth Stood Still* (1951) and *Invaders From Mars* (1953). Here we get another small American town populated with the usual residents – teenage love birds, an eccentric hillbilly, a naïve diner waitress and a sceptical Sheriff. Their town comes under siege when a spacecraft from a distant planet crash-lands in the rocky desert, unleashing a one-eyed tentacled creature that zaps the wholesome humans and transforms them into steaming 'puddles of mud.' On its trail is Urp, a kindly alien that usurps the body of a local astronomer, Ted (Eric McCormack), *Invasion of the Body Snatchers*-style, and whose mission is to subdue the destructive creature and escort it to some far-flung prison colony at the other side of the galaxy... *Alien Trespass* is a fun little film that perfectly encapsulates invasion movies of old. McCormack's performance is great as Urp, as he manages to convey the 'alienated' nature of being stuck on distant earth while at the same time subtlely poking fun at stilted, wooden actors from the 50s era, with his awkward posture, swively eyes and slightly robotic line delivery. The menacing 'Ghota' creature looks similar to the space aliens in *It Came From Outer Space* (1953) and *The Trollenberg Terror* (1958). And the movie culminates in a tribute to *The Blob* (1958) when a movie theatre showing the film comes under attack from the alien cyclops.

By the Devil's Hand: The 666 Killer (2009)
Dir: Christopher Abram /USA
For those of you looking for a film that has a bit of style and competence, don't go anywhere near *By the Devil's Hand: The 666 Killer*. This is bottom of the barrel, low-budget 'torture porn' nonsense in which we're made to suffer the usual cliches – sets decorated with polythene sheets hung up on the walls, overblown credits sequences, appallingly generic movie 'score,' etc. It's a film which rides on the coattails of whatever is popular at the time, which happens to be evil killer movies set in dingy lairs where young women are tortured. The gimmick here is the '666 killer,' a sadistic lunatic who subjects six victims to die in six days using six different murder methods. There is also an overblown sub-plot with a boring drama about a boring woman with a boring job and a boring fucking life. The killer allows a 'lucky' victim to choose how she would like to die. I know what *my* answer would be in that situation: "Hmm, I think I'll choose dying of old age, please, Mr. 666 Killer. So if you'd kindly untie me and let me go, I'll be on my way..."

Friday The 13th (2009)
Dir: Marcus Nispel /USA

After a couple of extended prologues which recap the ending of the original *Friday* to promulgate the urban legend of Jason Voorhees, a new bunch of irritating youngsters stop by the camp to be slaughtered. The house on Crystal Lake looks similar to the house in Mario Bava's *A Bay of Blood* (1971), the film which served as a prototype for the original *Friday the 13th*. This remake stands as an unremarkable rehash of moments from *Friday* sequels, and was later released on Blu-Ray in an 'Extended Killer Cut,' which supposedly heaps on the bloody carnage. But the difference isn't all that noticeable. In the age of political correctness, and the suspicion of the supposed links between misogyny and slasher movies, you can expect all the white male characters in the film to be graphically butchered, while the female killings are all quick and bloodless, or take place off-screen.

Run! Bitch! Run! (2009)
Dir: Joseph Guzman /USA

A rape-revenge movie that attempts to hark back to the glory days of the grindhouses but gets it all wrong. Two Catholic school girls go door-to-door selling bibles and wind up knocking on the door of a gang of deviants. Director Joseph Guzman claims to be a fan of 70s exploitation films but *Run! Bitch! Run!* has much more in common with the politically correct, well-behaved remakes of *Last House On the Left* (2009) and *I Spit On Your Grave* (2010) rather than the ugly, unruly grubbiness of the grindhouse originals.

Resurrecting the Street Walker (2009)
Dir: Ozgur Uyanik /UK

Another faux-documentary. This time it's about a runner for a small production company who discovers a few reels of film while clearing out an old basement storage area. The reels contain footage of an unfinished film called 'The Street Walker' about a man who tortures and murders women. The runner's curiosity gets the better of him, and he decides to complete the movie while his buddy records his progress... Like *The Last Broadcast* (1998), *Resurrecting the Street Walker* is put together entirely with documentary techniques, including talking head sequences, movie clips and video diary footage, and is quite well put together despite the twist ending that can be spotted quite early on

(especially for those familiar with *The Last Broadcast*). Most intriguingly, this film has several layers of 'reality' reflecting into infinity like the reflections of opposing mirrors. Abel Ferrara tackled similar themes in *Dangerous Game* (1993). A reviewer on *IMDb* summed it up best: "You have the real director of the film making a movie about a director of a film who is inspired to complete the production of a film where the 'real' director of the 'real' (movie world) film was making a movie about a director who used movie-making as a pretext for trapping and killing his victims." You got that?

Laid To Rest (2009)
Dir: Robert Hall /USA

A young woman awakens in a coffin (or "dead box"), then climbs out to discover she's in a funeral home. To make matters worse, she is terrorized by a lunatic wearing a chrome mask and holding a video camera. She manages to escape and hitches a ride with a kindly truck driver. Back at his house, however, the evil Mr. Chromeskull shows up and slaughters the driver's wife with a hunting knife while wearing the camera on his shoulder. The truck driver and the girl escape, so Chromeskull resorts to killing everyone in the neighbourhood. *Laid To Rest* is one of those horror movies set in a small town in the middle of nowhere, where the phone lines are always down, the local Sheriff's Department has been wiped out, and the internet is still a curious novelty ("make that [computer] thing look for missing girls in Florida"). The 'plot' is light on the ground but the knowing humour and decent production values makes it easy viewing. The film's setting, in and around a funeral home with coffins and a demonic hearse, evokes a *Phantasm*-like vibe. The villain's motivation is never explained: all we know about him is that he likes to record himself butchering people and sending the videos to the police. The snuff angle has absolutely no bearing on the story, and could have been easily dropped from the plot without causing any major changes in the script. Indeed, the fact that Chromeskull wears the camera on his shoulder makes me wonder whether the snuff element was added to the project as a last minute thing, to give the film a more depraved edge. It was followed by *Chromeskull: Laid to Rest 2* (2011).

Bedevilled (2010)

(Orig title: *Kim Bok-nam salinsageonui jeonmal*)

Dir: Chul-soo Jang /S. Korea

"I stared at the sun for a long time and it told me what I should do." Bok-nam lives with a violent drunk on the rural island of Mooko off the coast of Seoul. One day she is visited by a childhood friend from the mainland, Hae-won, who witnesses much of the abuse from her husband and the elderly women on the island (though she sleeps through most of it). And after her young daughter is killed, Bok-nam snaps, grabs a scythe and goes on a killing spree, slashing and decapitating all the scumbags who have made her life hell... *Bedevilled* is a difficult film to watch, not only because of the harsh abuse suffered by the victim, but also because the first hour moves along at a sluggish pace. The first ten minutes could have been dropped without causing much of a fuss, as Hae-won's character is not the main focal point here. The film is worth sticking with, however, for the final third which is extremely violent, and it's also immensely satisfying to watch a bunch of vile human beings get what they deserve. While watching this brutal film, the old quote may pop into your head, "all it takes for evil to triumph is for good men to do nothing."

The Butcher (2010)

Dir Kim Jin-Won /South Korea

Remember the scene in *The Texas Chain Saw Massacre* where Marilyn Burns is strapped to the chair surrounded by the crazy cannibal clan at the dining table? Well, this Korean effort is a feature-length tribute to that classic scene. The director represents the father, the maniac in the pig mask represents Leatherface (he even gets to play with a chainsaw), and the lad in the red t-shirt represents the idiot self-mutilating son. Unfortunately, there's no Grandpa in this one.

The Butcher is your typical 'torture porn' offering; the gimmick here being that we get to watch the action mostly from cameras that have been attached onto the heads of the victims. We get the usual warehouse/mill setting, a small group of characters, most of whom are there to scream and beg for their lives, and of course, lots of blood and gore. The film would have worked much better as a short, or at least trimmed down to an hour or so because it's quite over-stretched and time-padded in places. If you have a sick sense of humour, however, you'll probably find much to enjoy here. The director treats his assistants almost as harshly as the victims, and bellows orders like "Pull the shit out of her stomach and make 'em eat it!!!" Yeah, eat your heart out, Mr. Spielberg. The mounted 'photography' gets annoying at times; I know this was meant to create a verite effect but it does become nauseating after a while. It's also a dark film, not just in terms of subject-matter, but the print quality on the DVD is much too dark and it's difficult to see what's going on in some scenes.

The black humour is a treat and is perhaps the film's strongest asset overall. In the middle of some power tool torture, the director receives a phone call from his mother and spends the next few minutes talking to her about church and the bible like a good Christian. And after he hangs up, he gets right back to the power tools. There are also some satirical and self-deprecating swipes at the movie business; the director mentions selling the film to America because "they like bloody things," and you can't help but chuckle because the director of *The Butcher*, Kim Jin-Won, no doubt had similar plans for this film. Also, the young assistant wears a t-shirt that reads 'I Love Korea' in English – perhaps a cute comment on Western dominance seeping into everything, even corrupting these Koreans through useless commodities and trashy cinema?

It takes a while for the gore to be explicitly shown, but the film makes excellent use of sound design – it's one of the nastier sounding movies I've ever watched. Your neighbours will probably think you're watching a real snuffy. *Snuff 102* is still the most disturbing and troubling of all the 'torture porn' films, but *The Butcher* is worth a look in a less demanding mood, especially for those who have a rank sense of humour. Banned in many countries around the world (even in its native land), this gritty exercise in sadism ultimately has a gleeful sense of fun and mischief about it, like a child who delights in showing us a mouthful of chewed up food. A cross between *The Texas Chain Saw Massacre* and *Last House On Dead End Street*, shot on DV.

The Tortured (2010)

Dir: Robert Lieberman /USA /Canada

Tagline: 'The only way to ease the pain is to inflict some.' Parents get revenge on the sick maniac who had kidnapped and murdered their six-year-old son. They commandeer the prison truck he was travelling in, take him to a deserted house, cut him and burn him cigarettes, inject him with some kind of drug which causes his muscles to cramp up in excruciating pain, and use other medical supplies to prolong his agony. Then comes the 'little elephant' KGB techniques, and the inevitable twist (or twisted) ending. *The Tortured* shares a very similar storyline with the French-Canadian revenge shocker, *Les 7 jours du talion* (*7 Days*, 2010), and both films serve as morally-degrading updates on Wes Craven's *The Last House on the Left* (1972). *The Tortured*, in particular, is a mostly vile piece of work; 'torture porn' in every sense of the term, in which the viewers and protagonists alike get to indulge in the most heinous acts of barbarity whilst retaining a sense of 'justice' with a good conscience throughout.

Enter the Void (2010)
Dir: Gaspar Noe /France

A two and a half hour audio-visual extravaganza from the man who brought you *Seul contre tous* and *Irreversible*, *Enter the void* opens with an extraordinary credits sequence created by German experimental filmmaker Thorsten Fleisch in which the assorted cast, crew, and composer's names are embellished on the screen in a dazzling variety of big, bright and colourful logos against a black background, and played out to a thumping electro tune by LFO. It reaches a crescendo of psychedelic intensity as the credits flash away on the screen so fast that it's impossible to focus on the names of those involved in the making of the film.

The plot is simple: An American drug dealer in Tokyo is shot dead by the police. His spirit then rises from his body, reflects on his troubled life and relationships, and is then seemingly reincarnated as the son of his sister Linda and his best friend Alex. But what makes this film special is the way Gaspar Noe tells the story.

The film is viewed entirely from the perspective of lead character Oscar (Nathaniel Brown), with the camera permanently mounted at his viewpoint. It's incredible to think that this technique has rarely been done before in film, because, after all, that is the way we experience life, in the first person. And it also serves as an obvious way of merging the director's vision, the lead character's journey, and the viewer's gaze, as all three come together at a specific meeting point to enquire about what happens to us when we die.

Oscar is reunited with his sister Linda (the beautiful Paz de la Huerta) after years apart due to being raised by different foster carers after a nasty road accident killed their parents. Oscar's good friend Alex (Cyril Roy) has lent him a copy of *The Tibetan Book of the Dead*, and the passages from the text have an influence on his drug-induced hallucinations; strange organic patterns and psychedelic snowflake shapes accentuated by the downbeat ambient sounds of Coil and Throbbing Gristle. Bizarre CGI effects that resemble blooming symmetrical smoke clouds in a faint luminous glow of reds and amber dominate the screen to illustrate the intoxicated mind of the lead character.

With a long tracking shot in real time, we pass through the dark neon-lit streets of Tokyo as Alex and Oscar head for the nightclub, The Void, to make a simple drug deal. This scene – in which the characters discuss their latest experiments with DMT and other hallucinogens, and Alex relates to the high as being similar to the spiritual passages in *The Tibetan Book of the Dead* – has a strong documentary feel, but also has its own kind of spatial awareness and is nicely composed. It has a *verite* vibe with its city sounds and passing vehicles, and people seemingly unaware of the characters or of Noe or of a film called *Enter the Void*. It's a scene that reminded me of Hitchcock's *Vertigo* with James Stewart stalking the ice-cold blonde, or later in Brian De Palma's *Body Double* in which Craig Wasson stalks the brunette; both these sequences show the respective directors exploring the environment – with its bright clean surfaces and weatherless atmosphere; real streets become toys; movie sets, just as much as the narrative which is temporarily put on hold.

Alex doesn't enter The Void, he hangs back and waits outside, presumably because he knows how risky it is to be carrying drugs in Japan where the laws are very strict. Oscar enters the club to sell to a friend but is confronted by cops instead. So he locks himself in a toilet cubicle and frantically tries to dispose of the drugs down the bowl but the flush doesn't work. The police hammer at the door and Oscar in his panic stupidly shouts out that he has a gun and is going to shoot. The hammering stops, but moments later Oscar is shot through the door.

With a gasp of shock and pain he sinks to the ground, his hands covered in blood, and we get to listen to the confused last monologue in his head (rather like The Butcher character in *Seul contre tous* in which Phillipe Nahon holds a loaded gun to his head in a serious contemplation of suicide, his finger squeezing at the trigger and his thoughts flaring off into a web of anger, confusion, and nihilism); "This isn't happening, I'm tripping," "I'm dying. I'm dead." His voice drifts off into silence, and his spirit lifts out of his body and up towards the light. Time seems to have momentarily paused. It slowly revolves in the light and looks down at its own empty shell, a pitiful young corpse slumped in a public urinal. The police enter the cubicle and we can hear screams. Oscar's spirit floats over the club and out into the street in a bird's eye view. The police cars, the ambulance, the sirens, the crowds, the confusion; the aftermath of his own death. Alex flees from the scene and the camera swoops down behind him as he sprints down a dark backstreet.

The spirit then enters another nightclub where Oscar's sister, Linda, works as a stripper. Benoit Debie's camera acrobatics are in full force here as the bird's eye view observes Linda's beauty as she poses and gyrates on a lit stage before floating across the tops of backstage rooms looking down on the lives of strangers (and this recalls another of Brian De Palma's films, *Snake Eyes*, in which the camera pans just above ceiling level over the rooms of a hotel floor), before settling on Linda's dressing room where she has sex with her exploitative boyfriend, Mario. Oscar's spirit embodies Mario while he's fucking her and lingers with an incestuous curiosity towards her (and it isn't the first time incest has cropped up in Noe's work). Mario buttons up and leaves, and this is when Linda switches on her phone and receives a message from Alex informing her of her brother's death.

There is a beauty in the bird's eye view in the way it presents Tokyo as looking like a huge expansive toy train set. But it's also infused with a foreboding sense of danger and anxiety, perhaps fear on the part of Oscar and his sudden alienation from life. The film presents a dark Disneyland quality to viewers with its bright neon lights illuminating the darkness and scenes of nightlife and hedonism and drug taking forming an ambiance of mild pulsating pyschedelia. The film strolls along at a leisurely pace, the narrative feels like it is moving along in real time on first viewing, and this gives the viewers the space to formulate their own thoughts on the matter, and also gives the (very limited) plot all the time it needs to reach its 'conclusion'. Indeed, this is as far away from mainstream film-making as it gets. Oscar's spirit dwells upon events from his past; he and Linda playing on a swing as children, and then a cut to the startling head-on collision with a freight truck that killed their parents. There is also another childhood memory where Oscar and Linda are separated into different foster homes, with Linda screaming and refusing to be separated from her brother, but to no avail.

Things that impressed Oscar and made an impression on his life are re-formulated into a surreal blend of sensations in his out-of-body experience. The film becomes increasingly hallucinatory when a scale model of a cityscape seen in a friend's flat later becomes a real living bustling city in which his spirit floats and seems to regard with a heavenly perfection (the scenes were filmed with complicated crane shots and by helicopter above Tokyo, but were digitally manipulated in post-production to look strangely toy-like and artificial); there's no wind, no weather, no cracks or potholes on the roads or pavements; it resembles a plastic perfection like a child's idea of utopia. The toy model of the city seen in the flat is also the origin of the Love Hotel which later becomes the centre of paradise where the occupants get to indulge in their sensual fantasies.

This vortex of sounds and visions feels hallucinogenic; the surreal imagery and the chugging beat of the music sticking to its rhythm carries the viewer along as if in a drug-induced state. It's a film as pure feeling, pure experience – not intellectual. It's a film to be felt rather than understood, much like David Lynch's *Eraserhead*. Is it pretentious? Sure. But it's also steadfast in its direction and is totally uncompromising when it comes to telling the story in its own expansive way. And with such a long running time the film doesn't meander, despite looking at first glance to be an undisciplined and sprawling mess. The film is actually presented exactly the way it needs to be for maximum effect, much like Stanley Kubrick's *2001: A Space Oddyssey*, from which it takes its biggest inspiration. If Kubrick's film is about mankind's struggle with technology over the centuries, Noe's film is about mankind's struggle with the meaning of life and the idea of perception itself. It's very much up to the viewer to interpret what's happening on screen.

Gaspar Noe creates bizarre, narratively unorthodox films, and some have suggested that the reason he does so is because he lacks skills with dialogue and even the most simple narrative simplicity, and that he conceals this by presenting his stories in a fractured and aggressive style (indeed, the 'script' for *Enter the Void* was a one hundred paged 'description' with no written dialogue). Others have argued that Noe is simply bored by the more conventional forms of narrative and is driven by the desire to shake things up and present us with a more challenging and unusual approach. All three of his feature films so far have their own unique and radical forms of trajectory (which is more than can be said of such staunchly independent filmmakers such as Gregg Araki, Catherine Briellat, and Bruno Dumont, who all stick rigidly to the old tried and tested methods of straight forward storytelling).

Seul contre tous (*I Stand Alone*) is broken up with lengthy misanthropic monologues, on-screen captions, and comes across almost like a non-fiction polemic or manifesto of hate; *Irreversible* is a rape-revenge film told entirely from back to front – it starts with the end credits and continues with the revenge attack, then the rape itself, and ends at the beginning with the peaceful morning before the anger and heartache begins, thus only falling into context for viewers once the film has finished. *Enter the Void* presents its action strictly from the first-person perspective, but this doesn't make it isolated or solipsistic, because the viewers are right there to go along with it and invest their own thoughts and feelings, and is actually Noe's most inclusive film to date as far as its audience is concerned.

Oscar's spirit looking down on his corpse in the morgue is a powerful scene and perhaps represents the epitome of alienation, but at least Oscar is there in the experience; existence hasn't necessarily been extinguished for him, at least not in the way that athiests and nihilists would suggest. At the end of Michelangelo Antonioni's *The Passenger*, Jack Nicholson's character dies on a bed in a hotel room, and the camera – if not embodying his spirit – lingers on the scene, gently easing towards the open window and soaking up the everyday enormity of life in a small village – life continuing without him. In *Enter the Void* we're witness to a similar but more concentrated form of the same idea. Cinema is perhaps the most effective art form to capture those scraps of reality (dead film stars like James Dean and Steve McQueen are still right there in life-like form in *Rebel Without a Cause* and *Bullit*), and is the closest thing we can get to experiencing non-being; a world without you, without me, and without Oscar.

The last 20 minutes of *Enter the Void* are amazing. We (that is we via Oscar's spirit) drift over the toy world city-scape of Tokyo looking directly down on all the bright lights, and the tiny cars passing by, and the ant-like efficiency of the modern world. It's a perspective that is at once beautiful and unsettling, alienating. Life continuing in all its calamitous beauty and delicacy. The sex scenes in the Love Hotel are offset by a grim and depressing ambient soundtrack and flickering lights. The scenes weren't shot out of focus but are difficult to see properly because of the numerous digital layers added in post-production. It floats along with an eerie dream-like quality. Lots of couples having sex, their genitals illuminated in a glowing radiance as if to express the life-affirming potency in all its glory. Alex, who has been a long-time admirer of Linda, finally gets to make love to her, and Oscar even embodies his old friend during the act so that he too can experience that carnal togetherness he has desired from his sister for so long. He then passes into Linda's womb and watches from inside as Alex ejaculates into his sister's vagina. He follows the sperm as it reaches the egg and finds a gateway back into life, just like in *The Tibetan Book of the Dead*. Oscar is reborn once again, reincarnated, and the cycle of life continues. The film fittingly has no end credits.

I Saw the Devil (2010)
(Orig title: *Akmareul boatda*)
Dir: Kim Jee Woon /South Korea

This is one of the finest Korean movies I've ever seen, way better than over-hyped tosh like *Oldboy* and *Three: Extremes*, despite the long running time and ludicrous plot. It centres on a vicious serial killer, Jon Ki-Du (*Oldboy* himself, Choi Min-Sik), who is tracked down with dogged determination by an equally ruthless cop, Kim (Lee Byung Hun), whose fiancee was butchered by the killer.

Kim uses satellite tracking devices to monitor Jon's movements and plays a dangerous game of cat and mouse with him which puts public safety in jeopardy. He always catches up with the psycho when he's up to no good, beating the maniac and breaking his bones before letting him go free once again. His plan is to gradually torture the killer into madness but there's also the danger that Jon could get wise to the game and go off the rails completely...

Much has been mentioned about the morals of the cop character in this film, and yes the good/evil ambiguity leaves innocent people in peril, but I thought it was a refreshing break from the Hollywoodized norm of focusing on cop characters who are morally faultless. Plus, the film takes Nietzsche's old quote about being careful not to become monstrous when facing a monster, and takes this premise to its most extreme conclusion. It's as if the filmmaker's took that quote as a challenge rather than a warning! The film is also brimful of excellent set pieces, such as the gruesome killing in the taxi with the camera frantically circling the action that rivals Dario Argento for visual audacity. But the most shocking thing about the film for me was how different it is in terms of style from Kim's previous work, such as *A Tale of Two Sisters*; a creepy, atmospheric ghost story which is the total flip-side to the hyper-kinetic and unflinching style of *I Saw The Devil*.

Choi Min-Sik's performance as the killer is superb. He's barely recognizable as the victim in *Oldboy*, even though it's his same face and hair with no prosthetics; he embodies the character so well that he seems to physically alter into that wretched creature. There are no special effects to exaggerate his evil visage, and he captures that predatory deviousness so well. It's a credit to both Min-Sik and director Kim Jee Woon that the killer didn't become some glamorized maniac or descend into some silly pastiche that no doubt will happen if this ever gets the Hollywood 'makeover' treatment. The result is one of the most memorable and evil screen monsters in a long long time.

The Pig Farm (2010)
Dir: *Director not credited* /Canada
Documentary on serial killer, Willie Pikton, whose reign of terror among the down and outs in Vancouver in the late 90s exposed serious deficiencies in the underfunded police department. Pikton ran a farm, and employed crack heads and other addicts to help out. Many turned a blind eye to his evil deeds to ensure their drug supplies. This is a powerful documentary that explores some of the scummiest behaviour humans are capable of.

Even years later, one of the former crack heads who was on the farm at the time, doesn't show any remorse for not cooperating with the investigators – her eye-witness testimony would have ensured a search warrant for the premises, and chances are Pikton would have been stopped much sooner than he was. But instead, she kept her mouth shut, and dozens of other girls were strung up and butchered in the barn, just because she had a spat with the police years earlier and didn't like them. Her name is Lisa Yelds, and even in retrospect, she doesn't regret the fact that she could have saved the lives of others. No shame, no sorrow, no apology. The police finally got their warrant as late as 2002 after an anonymous tip-off about illegal firearms on the farm. After a thorough search, the police found belongings of the victims as well as human remains. Pikton was charged with 26 murders and will never be released from prison.

Captifs (2010)
(aka *Caged*)
Dir: Yann Gozlan /France
Captifs is a routine, bloodless and rather predictable yarn about a woman who is kidnapped by a gang of Serbian organ traffickers. After the success of *Hostel* (2006) and *A Serbian Film* (2009), we have yet another film that centres on the paranoia of Europe's so-called 'Wild East.' Much of the film's drama takes place within the dull, grey cells where the 'captifs' are held, and in typical French-language tradition, the maniacs aren't just deviant killers, they're also driven by the greed for profit. Just like the sado-tourist club in *Hostel*, these organ traffickers have got their racket down to a well-oiled machine.

This underworld organisation seems far too professional, and this pushes credibility to breaking point. The film is set up as a trendy 'torture porn' horror, but then the gruesome details of the plot are avoided in favour of the heroine busting free and single-handedly wiping out all the bad guys. I mean, what is the point of putting women in peril anymore? We know that no challenge is too great for them. Women can do anything in horror movies nowadays; bust out of cells, kill an army of hardened maniacs, and outrun a pack of dogs while always finding something handy to stab people with, and even saving a little girl's life while they're at it. There are strong women and then there are ridiculously OTT movies. This falls into the latter category. It's an insultingly predictable film.

A Nightmare On Elm Street (2010)
Dir: Samuel Bayer /USA

What a disaster. The opening diner scene was decent but from there on in it all goes tits up. The characters and acting are terrible, but as a long-time viewer of slasher movies, that kind of thing can be overlooked, but there is also zero tension or suspense, and we are ambushed with 'jump-scare' overload, or more accurately, jump-scares that don't make us jump. The film is filled with unconvincing elements obviously engineered by someone who has no real interest in the genre and doesn't have a clue how to execute even the simplest, creepy scenes. Director Samuel Bayer made a Nirvana promo years ago. He has no experience in feature film, especially horror. Platinum Dunes picked him up to direct this and I'm not sure why; he just doesn't have the credentials. Maybe they hired him knowing they could push him around and that he would follow orders, no questions asked.

Nancy in the original was an interesting character (annoying but engaging), but here she's just bland. The new Freddy Krueger character is a joke; empty, bland, monotonous. He's supposed to be an anti-hero, the archetypal boogeyman, but here he's just a bore. His droning voice is enough to put you to sleep. Even his new style of make-up is crap – he looks like someone has smashed him in the face with a cheese pizza.

When Freddy (in his human incarnation) gets cornered by the lynch mob, that scene could have been a real show-stopper, but as it is, it looks rushed like no one could be bothered to think it through, or even that no one involved in this money-making caper understood the significance of that scene (or perhaps they just didn't give a shit). The burning of Freddy is one of the most interesting aspects of the whole Elm St. series; it's a diabolical idea that was only hinted at in the original film, the fact that Freddy Krueger was a paedophile and child killer, and the good, decent, hard-working parents in the area took it upon themselves to hunt him down and burn him alive. This time around the filmmakers opted to explore this legend in a flashback, and it should have been the centrepiece of the entire film, but ultimately in Bayer's hands the scene turns to nothing; just another excuse for a quick 'jump-scare' and

some flashy CGI nonsense.

Freddy as a human is depicted as a pathetic character – just a harmless and mentally-challenged handyman whom everyone mocked and made fun of. But when he returns as the dark dream avenger, suddenly he's very smart and cunning and 'on the ball'. There's no link between his pathetic human form and his evil post-death slasher form; it's a terrible contrast, and it just goes to further cement the suspicion that no one behind the camera gave a shit about this film. And that's another thing; it's not even made clear in this remake whether Freddy Krueger really was a paedophile or not – he is chased and attacked by the furious parents who are baying for his blood, and the audience is left confused not knowing if Freddy is even guilty of the crimes or not! And the kids themselves can't even remember! I would imagine it being difficult to forget if you were sexually abused as a child. To imply that Freddy Krueger was an innocent victim of mob mentality is a stupid move and obviously can't hold much weight for long because he soon begins carving up the kids in their sleep!

The Pack (2010)
(Orig title: *La meute*)
Dir: Franck Richard /France /Belgium

A French/Belgian co-production about a young woman who falls victim to a group of cannibals/zombies at a run down restaurant. Directed by first-time helmer, Franck Richard, who seems to enjoy toying with genre conventions just as much as creeping out his audience, *The Pack* is more of a playful pastiche of French (and American) backwoods horrors, rather than a serious horror movie, but is worth watching if only for Phillipe Nahon's performance as a perverted policeman.

The Book of Zombie (2010)
Dir: Erik Van Sant, Paul Cranfield & Scott Kragelund /USA

Mormon zombies attack non-believers in a small town in Utah. A bickering husband and wife team up with an assortment of dorky Darwinists and hold up in a local convenience store and a bar called The Drunken Dragon. Originally intended as a short clip to be uploaded onto YouTube, the filmmakers re-wrote the script and made this hour-long offering, which, though it contains flashes of well-observed humour here and there - and also the concept of Mormon zombies heading door to door is a good one – this is painfully amateur in all areas. The $16,000 budget looks to have been blown on the bizarre stop-motion title credits sequence, which is perhaps the most impressive part of the film. In this film, the ghouls are easily dissolved with 'sinful' substances such as caffeine, nicotine and fizzy drinks, so one character straps himself up with cans of cola, and heads outside to dispatch a few zombies as a 'suicide bomber,' but even this good idea fizzles out into nothing.

House of Bones (2010)
Dir: Jeffrey Lando /USA
Made for the Syfy Channel, *House of Bones* is about a reality TV show called 'Sinister Sites' whose presenters also act as paranormal investigators. In the latest episode, the investigators chance upon the 'wicker house,' a deserted residence in which a young boy is said to have disappeared in the early 1950s. Within moments of arriving at the old house, we learn that the crew and presenters are a cynical bunch with no belief or interest in the paranormal, and are just there for the pay cheques. Someone has even gone to the trouble of decorating the back yard with old doll parts dangling from pieces of string. However, once the live broadcast begins, viewers can expect all the usual clichés of haunted house movies as sinister audio and visual recordings are picked up, along with an evil force that enjoys impaling coppers and ramming glass shards down women's throats. *House of Bones* isn't too bad for a Syfy TV movie (I was expecting a lot worse), but it fails to rise above its hokey premise, despite having characters cacooned in the walls with blood and guts, and a derelict house right out of Dickens' *Great Expectations*. Actress Charisma Carpenter is very hot, and her presence turns the place into a house of boners. It's just a shame she has the 'charisma' of a frozen puddle.

AVN: Alien vs Ninja (2010)
Dir: Seiji Chiba /Japan
The Japanese shitter, *AVN: Alien vs Ninja*, sees a team of modern-day ninjas being picked off in the woods by an alien predator that hunts humans for sport. It's a goofy *Predator* rip-off that boasts some spectacularly gruesome deaths, spectacularly awful CGI effects, slapstick humour and a camp army commander. If the original *Predator* (1987) boasted a 10 foot tall, fanny-faced alien, the biggest curiosity here is an equally unlikely creature: a schoolboy's re-creation of a xenomorph, complete with go-go-gadget pink dicks that shoot out of its body to wrap around throats and throttles the ninjas to death, and a dolphin's head with bowling ball-type holes in which it carries its young. The surviving ninjas set up their own 'jungle traps' as a way of putting an end to the beast, but it seems to be immortal.

I Spit On Your Grave (2010)
Dir : Steven R. Monroe /USA
A 21st Century updated (read 'politically correct') version of Meir Zarchi's notorious rape/revenge shocker. This time, the victim, Jennifer (Sarah Butler), is only raped once but has to endure extended scenes of psychological torture, too, in order to keep the product trendy in the age of 'torture porn'. One of the tormentors blows a harmonica just like Flavia Bucci in *Night Train Murders*. After her ordeal, Jennifer walks in a trance-like state into the river, just like one of the victims in *The Last House On the Left* (1972). She then returns with sodden dark hair draped across her face in vengeful mode looking like she has just stepped out of a 00s J-horror, and sets about her ruthless retribution. The film includes some deviously fiendish traps which involves horrendous suffering, with one guy having his eyeballs eaten by crows while he is still alive, and another getting shot-gunned in the arse. Hey, she's a novelist after all, so her imaginative revenge traps aren't necessarily as far-fetched as you'd think. If anything, *I Spit On Your Grave* shows that America's 'eye for an eye' mentality was still very much in full force.

Bunnyman (2010)
Dir: Carl Lindbergh /USA
After the lame snuff-based *Carver* (2008), which fumbled with its supposed 'based on a true story' theme, *Bunnyman* even went as far as basing its title character on a real-life urban legend; in Fairfax County, Virginia in 1970, a man in a bunny suit is said to have murdered several people with an axe. Like *Carver*, *Bunnyman* bases its plot on a group of young Americans heading out into the wilderness on a camping trip and falling foul of the local maniacs, one of whom wears a bunny suit and carries a chainsaw. Heavily derivative, the opening reel reprises such classic maniac-on-

the-road movies as *Duel*, *The Hitcher* and *Joy Ride/Road Kill*. It then goes on to riff on *Blair Witch* with the bags of bones hanging from trees in the woods; *Grotesque*, with the evildoer listening to Ludwig Van during the torture ceremonies; any number of stranded-teens-being-offed-in-the-woods slasher movies (*Friday The 13th* and its sequels, for example); a whole bunch of 70s backwoods shockers (*Deliverance*, *The Texas Chain Saw Massacre*, *Motel Hell*, etc). It even recycles the foot-hobbling scene from *Misery*. For a change, the characters are somewhat likeable here but the constant wrong-headed decisions they make becomes irksome very quickly and leads to disaster for all. The snuff element is played up heavily during the opening and closing credits, but there's actually very little snuff play during the film, save for the torture scenes which are recorded on video.

The Walking Dead (2010-)
Dir: -Various- /USA
You'll notice that this mini-review is very vague, but I really don't want to give anything away. If you haven't seen this then I suggest you go away, grab the box sets and get stuck in because this is really as good as TV gets – yes, right up there with *The Wire* and *Breaking Bad*! I was a late comer to this show. I hadn't watched it. I'd always dismissed it as "*Lost* with a few zombies in the background". I couldn't have been more wrong. So when I eventually settled down to play catch-up during the mid-season 4 break, I was completely blown away by what I saw: excellent, well-drawn characters, stunning performances, truly ghoulish imaginative touches, and an emotional engagement you only usually get with epic novels. I am rightly ashamed of myself for dismissing this show so easily.

Based on the series of graphic novels by Robert Kirkman, Tony Moore and Charlie Adlard, Season 1 kicks off with local Sheriff's Deputy, Rick (Andrew Lincoln) getting shot during a routine pursuit of criminals. Weeks, or months (or 28 days) later, he awakens from a coma in hospital and walks out to meet the zombie apocalypse. He collapses in the street due to weakness brought on by hunger and dehydration, and is rescued by Morgan and his boy Duane, a couple of survivors and perhaps the only living humans left in town. They later raid the gun cabinets in the Sheriff's office and

go their separate ways. Rick heads out to Atlanta to find his wife and son, and when he reaches the city, he finds it overrun with zombies who are so hungry they could literally eat a horse. Rick is rescued once again, this time by a band of survivors who have a camp out in the woods. This sequence is memorable for the role of Michael Rooker who plays a drug-fuelled, trigger-happy redneck called Merle whom they handcuff to a pipe on the roof of a building, and end up having to leave to his fate when their stronghold is broken. When they get to the camp, Rick is reunited with his loved ones, Lori and Carl. It turns out that Lori has been sleeping with Shane, the Sheriff who is Rick's best buddy (but, to be fair, they *did* think he was long dead). Hence a love triangle becomes apparent. And this is when I thought things would slip into soap opera territory with the zombies becoming a background abstraction, but thankfully, that never happens.

By the way, the description above covers only the first couple of episodes. A group heads back for the city on a rescue mission for Merle, but he isn't there. It appears he has cut off his own hand with a hacksaw and cauterized the wound on a hot plate. The series continues until the group reaches a secure scientific research silo. Season 2 expands to 13 episodes, and gets off to a suspenseful hoot on the highway before the survivors hold out at a nearby ranch to nurse an injured member of their group. This is where we meet new characters, including the stubborn but wise Hershel and his daughters, Maggie and Beth. If there are any faults with Season 2, for me it would be that it feels overstretched in places to meet the designated 13 episode duration; as a consequence, the drama is sometimes spread dangerously thin, and teeters on becoming like '*Little House On the Prairie* with Zombies,' or something. The 'romance' between Glen and Maggie is also badly developed, and we're supposed to accept the fact that they're in love after what feels like five minutes of awkward moodiness and silly games. It just feels so phony and loveless, there are probably zombies out in the woods who have a more convincing romance going on (I should say though that these love birds did grow on me eventually). Fortunately, things do pick up, and interesting themes are explored, such as the changes in people's perspectives and beliefs when faced with such existential horror of corpses walking around trying to eat you. And also the dilemmas of the values of civilization versus the zero-tolerance and zero-sum games of group survival. If you're kind and helpful to others, you're in danger of falling victim, but if you're cold and brutal and unsympathetic to others you have a greater chance of survival, but you lose your humanity and sense of civilization in the process. So what's it to be? Season 2 is the first to address the Cold War-like tactical agendas of survivors, and the fact that trust – or the lack of it – among the people becomes just as big a danger as the shambling ghouls.

Season 3 sees the ever-dwindling group stumble upon a secure prison while Andrea teams up with a sword wielding survivor, and they find themselves inculcated into a small fortress town called Woodbury headed by the quietly unstable 'Governor,' a kind of cross between Howard Hughes and Jim Jones. We're witness to some real ghoulish ideas in this season, including the scene where one character is tied to a chair while another is murdered and left to 'turn' and chew the flesh of the helpless victim. Season 3 also drags out the plot to an excruciating degree, especially during the last few episodes, but my my, I was well and truly hooked by this point. It's riveting stuff. Also, I find it amusing that scenes of gruesome bloody violence are given a big thumbs up, while F-words and tiddies are forbidden on screen. That's American network TV for you.

Season 4 is the most emotionally engaging (and devastating) season yet, though, as of this writing, Season 5 is in the works. And if you can't relate to the Governor on even the most basic level, you're inhuman. Or a 'liar.' Season 4 sees life in the prison becoming increasingly desperate as a deadly flu ravages the refugees, unleashing hordes of zombies in their hideout. None of the characters are safe here; any one of them can be taken out at any time. And with this life-or-death balance hanging over these characters we have grown to like, it's all the more heart breaking when things fall apart. My favourite character is Daryl; the evolution of his character development has been the most impressive, the way he has emerged from his brother Merle's shadow and found his sense of self, which is to say that he's basically a decent person. With his trusty crossbow and no-questions-asked approach to dealing with the awful situation, his loyalty to the group is perhaps down to him having found his 'family'

at last.

Maybe I've been caught up in all the hype, but *The Walking Dead* is really fucking good! In fact, it makes most of the other films and TV shows in this book look like garbage. I understand that the emotional manipulation of viewers is perhaps this show's strongest asset overall, but I don't care. It works! The Canadian comedy series *The Trailer Park Boys*, has a knack of finding humour in the tiniest of details – the look of an eye, the almost unconscious facial expressions, the almost inaudible throwaway lines of dialogue, etc – and it works because we know the characters so well. Similarly, in *The Walking Dead* we're plunged into a nightmarish world which rings true even in the smallest details – the psychological angle, the end of the world feeling, the words that go unsaid speak volumes. I had always held film to be superior to television, and 99% of the time it probably is. But this show has made me think otherwise. Do yourself a favour and catch up with this incredible show if you haven't already. You won't regret it.

The second half of Season 4 dropped the ball somewhat. However, Seasons 5 and 6 saw a return to top form for the series. Season 7 was atrocious, but ended on an intriguing note. The main problem – aside from the excruciating dullness and the series' insistence on turning the show into a limp drama – is Negan. This supposed bad guy is far too pantomime-ish, and his dialogue sounds like it was written by a college kid numpty – 'that is *so* not cool.' Painful stuff. On the upside, the first half of season 8 didn't waste any time in getting started on the 'all out war.'

Auschwitz (2011)
Dir: Uwe Boll /Canada/Germany

Uwe Boll became infamous for a series of ineptly made video game adaptations like *Alone In the Dark* and *House of the Dead* which have been described as cinematic train wrecks but still managed to garner a bit of a cult following. More recently he has taken the indie route with a string of disturbing low budget films focusing on the dark side of human nature in *Seed*, *Stoic*, and *Rampage*, all of which were reviled by international censors and critics but adored by his growing army of fans. But, perhaps driven by the desire to be taken seriously as a filmmaker, Boll has also tried his hand at films based on true events, with the interesting *Tunnel*

Rats, *Darfur*, and most problematic of all, *Auschwitz*.

Those expecting a quick exploitationer based on one of the worst atrocities of the 20th Century will be in for a surprise here as Boll makes it clear in the film's introduction that he is undoubtedly very passionate about that time in history, and also angry that many people (according to Boll, at least half the world's population) have no idea about the Nazi death camps. His mission statement is clear: People should never forget what happened at Auschwitz.

First up, we get documentary footage of college students being interviewed on camera about their understanding of the death camps. It soon becomes apparent that their knowledge is hazy at best. Then we're shown a dramatized account of a train load of Jews arriving at Auschwitz. They are changed out of their clothes and then marched to the gas chamber. Boll himself cameos as an SS officer who guards the doorway (perhaps his small role serves as a reminder of his indirect complicity with the Holocaust, simply for being German? A nation's guilt personified?). The film as a whole is very sensitive to the suffering of the victims, unlike Andrey Iskanov's *Philosophy of a Knife* which seems to wallow in the gruesome torture and ethnic cleansing of World War II. Boll's film is certainly no easy ride though; we see people being gassed, corpses pushed into the ovens and licked by the flames of modern barbarity, little boys are shot in the back of their heads. Real archive footage of piles of bodies awaiting mass burial is also inserted into the film lest the audience should fail to comprehend the horrors played out before our eyes. Even the deliberate and methodical way the Zyklon B is poured into the air ducts is chilling. As the deadly fumes fill the chamber and the victims scream and bang on the iron doors with their fists, we can hear the arrival of another train load of doomed souls at a nearby station. The bored soldiers sit around casually discussing their work whilst looting through a mound of personal possessions belonging to the Jews. Boll closes the proceedings with a little speech in broken English; here he justifies the making of the film: "We have to make sure that crimes doesn't happen. We have to make sure that something like this is not getting forgotten or that somebody can repeat it."

The original teaser trailer for *Auschwitz*

caused a storm on the web as it graphically shows the corpse of a child being pushed into an incinerator, and people were accusing Boll of gross exploitation on such a sensitive subject even before the film itself had been released. *Auschwitz* was then rejected by the Berlin Film Festival which resulted in the director threatening to sue the programmers for 'breach of trust and unfair competition in its selection process'. When the film finally did see the light of day, the critics weren't too kind, and they labelled it a shoddy exercise in bad taste. In an attempt to defend his film, Boll commented "If you see all the Auschwitz movies made in a row, from *Schindler's List* to *The Boy In the Striped Pyjamas*, in all those you will not see what actually happened in Auschwitz [...] It's not a movie about heroes or survivors, it's a film about the daily routine of a human slaughterhouse. And I think it is important that one movie actually shows what really happened at Auschwitz." That's all well and good a comment but it was soon to backfire on him as people then went to see the film expecting detailed historical accuracy in the minutiae of everything from the uniforms, sets, and methods of execution, including exactly how many Jews were put into the chamber at each time, etc. And of course, those hoping for a film with that kind of detailed accuracy came away disappointed too.

Boll was also under fire from people who accused him of exploiting the Holocaust in a previous film, *Bluberella*, in which a gun-toting overweight woman goes to war against the Nazis. Boll claims that *Bluberella* was made simply as a way of securing the funding for *Auschwitz*.

The Woman (2011)
Dir: Lucky McKee /USA

A family man discovers a wild woman in the woods. He ensnares her in a trap and takes her home, where he chains her up in the basement. Nothing is known about the woman. She was probably raised by wolves; she can't speak, only hisses and growls. After having his finger bitten off, the man, along with his wife and children, try to domesticate the feral woman. However, it turns out that the family have some serious problems of their own to fix... Based on the novel by Jack Ketchum and Lucky McKee, *The Woman* is a disturbing little horror movie that has a lot of negative things to say on the role of the traditional patriarch. And women aren't necessarily let off the hook either. The white male characters are sadistic lunatics, and most of the female characters are portrayed as servile victims. The teenage son looks up to his father and shares daddy's sadistic streak, and the teenage daughter takes after her bullied, browbeaten mother. Of course, the captive wild woman gets loose in the end and seeks a bloody revenge against her captors in an obvious metaphor about 'mother nature' in all her unshackled glory, restoring the balance of the sexes.

The Human Centipede 2 (Full Sequence) (2011)
Dir: Tom Six /Holland/UK/ USA
A creepy little security officer rents a derelict warehouse and creates a 12-man human centipede as a way of feeding his morbid obsession with the original *Human Centipede* film.

While the tagline for the original film was "100% medically accurate", this sequel sheds all such technical authenticity by assuring us that this time we're dealing with a movie that is "100% medically *in*accurate." If I had to describe this movie in one word, it would be 'ugly'. Shot on lurid black and white digital video, the story unfolds in ugly industrial surroundings, with a cast of ugly, unpleasant characters acting out some very ugly scenarios. David Lynch's *Eraserhead* had a similar black and white industrial feel (not to mention sparse dialogue), but that film looks like the ceiling of the Sistine Chapel compared to this. This time around, it's all very bleak, but writer/director Tom Six manages to convey an ultra-black humour throughout.

This sequel is much more violent and bloody than the original, especially the scene where the human monster, Martin (Lawrence Harvey), smashes his mother's head in with a crowbar. Martin randomly picks his candidates from the assortment of late night clubbers and perverts who frequent the underground car park where he works as a nocturnal security guard. His victims include a heavy-set skinhead, a pregnant woman and also Ashlynn Yennie, the actress who played 'Jenny' in the first film. Here she plays herself as an actress lured to the warehouse by Martin under the pretence of a film audition for Quentin Tarantino. The humour is apparent when Martin begins work on his centipede – beyond watching

the DVD on a continuous loop, and collecting images and cut-outs in a scrapbook, he doesn't have a clue how to put his centipede together; one of his test subjects bleeds to death when he sets about carving away at the buttock, severing an artery. And unlike Dr. Heiter in part one, Martin doesn't use anaesthetic or stitches to join his humans together, he simply beats them unconscious with his trusty crowbar and uses an industrial-sized stapler to attach their unfortunate gobholes onto unfortunate bumholes, as you do. Disgusting, isn't it? I mean, what if they didn't wipe properly? But therein lies the humour. Indeed, many viewers completely missed the twisted humour of part one, and that reaction was only exacerbated by this sequel. It's one of those 'like it or loathe it' movies; you either get it or you don't. In fact, the *Human Centipede* movies are a good way to gauge the humour of people; it's the ultimate litmus test of your sense of humour.

During the procedure, Martin is made to feel uncomfortable by Ashlynn's constant screaming, so he graphically removes her tongue with a pair of pliers. And shortly after, the real fun begins when he injects his subjects with a strong, instant laxative, which causes their bowels to erupt and sends scorching hot diarrhea directly into the mouths of those behind them whose faces are attached to their anal ducts. After this ordeal, when the whole experiment collapses due to the humans resisting the progress of science (the spoilsports), Martin panics and begins killing off his subjects. The pregnant woman, whom Martin thought was dead, awakens in the corner of the warehouse, and runs outside screaming in labour. She locks herself in a car and gives birth. However, as she slams her foot down on the accelerator to make her getaway, the poor baby's head is crushed under the pedal.

The film also makes fun of psychoanalysis, with the doctor character clearly modelled on Freud, and passed off as a deranged pervert who doesn't really have a clue what he is doing. Or perhaps Dr. Sebring was Tom Six's way of poking fun at scholars and 'serious' critics who often use psychoanalytical methods for deciphering film. For example, when the maniac's mother informs the doctor that her son has created a scrapbook on *The Human Centipede*, Sebring immediately responds by pointing out the "phallic nature" of the centipede, and how it is a symbol of aggressive sexuality (an accusation levelled at both the first film and this sequel). But Sebring's knee-jerk reaction to the mother's anxieties serves as nothing more than the doctor's attempts to make the situation worse so that he can continue to prescribe the medication that will allow him to sexually abuse her son, Martin. Overall, Sebring's character looks to be Six's way of questioning the ulterior motives of scholars, and showing his distrust of the analytical process. Interestingly, the British censors initially banned *Human Centipede 2* because the board members interpreted the film as "the object of the protagonist's depraved sexual fantasy," proving that just because a filmmaker can foresee the unfavourable reaction to his movie, doesn't make it any less susceptible to an outright dismissal.

Just like the previous film, director Tom Six continues with the self-reflexive swipes at the horror genre in this sequel. As with *Scream 2*, *The Human Centipede 2* playfully examines the effects that horror movies can supposedly have on their audiences. But while *Scream 2* served as little more than a platform for slasher fans to feel good about themselves, here Tom Six manages to imbibe some interesting points throughout, such as: Why do horror fans love horror movies? Are we sick? Are films like *The Human Centipede* capable of harming their audiences and society as a whole? Ironically, the British censors certainly thought so for a while, refusing to grant it a certificate. Other self-referential bits to look out for are the shrieking and abusive mother whose mistreatment of her son over the years leads to madness and murder, as seen in previous horror classics such as *Psycho* and *Maniac* (and also the lesser-known *Don't Go In the House*, reviewed in this book). In addition, the fact that Martin seems to embody every cliché that forms the stereotypical vision of the deranged killer – he was sexually abused by his father as a child, tormented by his unstable mother, is a loner, a social misfit who bottles up his anger and resentments, is sexually perverted (masturbating with sandpaper?), an ugly nightmarish archetypal monster – he even looks like a cross between John Wayne Gacy and Dennis Nilsen.

Like many killers in the movies (and in real life), Martin is just as tragically sad and damaged as he is ruthlessly single-minded. He may be a quiet and slovenly little man, but what makes him a frightening character is his steely

determination – nothing is going to stop him from acting out his dark desire to create a human centipede.

In October 2011, the BBFC relented on their decision and granted the film an 18 certificate after cutting 2 minutes and 37 seconds of footage including the shots of Martin masturbating with sandpaper wrapped around his cock; the sight of a man's teeth being knocked out with a hammer; graphic shots of lips being stapled to anal crevices; the aforementioned sight of liquid defecation into and around other victims' mouths; Martin with barbed wire wrapped around his genitals violently raping a woman; a newborn baby being killed; and the graphic shots of injuries as staples are torn away from individuals' mouths and bums.

Ironically, it was the film's stance as a self-reflexive swipe at the whole 'torture porn' movement of recent years, and the belief that screen violence leads to real life violence, that seems to have gotten the film into trouble with the censors. In an interview for an internet podcast, former head of the BBFC, Andreas Whittam Smith, openly admitted that the link between real and screen violence was hazy and ultimately unprovable. "Nobody's ever shown the link," he conceded. "The best research I ever saw took young offenders, showed them violent videos and so on. About six months later, they re-interviewed [the young offenders] and they tended to remember scenes --- the graphic scenes – better than a control group of ordinary people. And that suggests that it does have some effect but it's very hard to make that, bring that up to the level required for um, a court of law, where actions had to be beyond all possible doubt."

Of the BBFC's initial ban, one of the chief examiners, Craig Lapper said, "If a film goes that far in terms of satirising extreme violence, there's always the risk it will fall into the same trap as the material it's attempting to satirise. I'm afraid that's what we felt had happened with HC2...

"It seemed to us that the film could be read in a variety of ways, as many films can be. However, we also felt the film went to such extremes that it breached the classification guidelines and posed a real, as opposed to a fanciful, risk of harm to potential viewers within the terms of the Video Recordings Act 1984, and may have been in breach of the Obscene

Publications Acts 1959 and 1964."

Of course, Tom Six disagreed, "It has a lot of black humour in it, and [the BBFC's statement] says it was about sexual obsession by the main character, and I think that's not true. It's not a sexual film. Of course there are elements in it, but that's not what the story is about, and everybody was thinking it's about this sex crazed maniac or something. I'm very glad if people see the film now, they see a whole different film than the BBFC gave in their report."

As early as August 2011, Six was already at work on a third and final part of the trilogy, to be titled *The Human Centipede 3 (Final Sequence)*. Six has announced that the film will again be very different from the previous parts but will also start with the ending of part 2, so that the three segments of the trilogy will form one continuous four and a half hour film, making it similar to a centipede. He also promised that the third film will answer some "lasting questions," and will be the last of the series as he does not want to do any more *Human Centipede* films. In an interview with *DreadCentral.com*, Six said the third film will "make the last one look like a Disney film. We're going to shoot the third film entirely in America, and it's going to be my favourite... It's going to upset a lot of people."

Adam Chaplin (2011)
Dir: Emanuele De Santi /Italy

Italian genre cinema has offered up an array of colourful and stylish cult classics over the decades, from the works of Ricardo Freda and Mario Bava in the 50s and 60s, to Dario Argento and Lucio Fulci and many others in the heyday of the 70s and 80s. By the time the 90s had arrived, things had simmered down, and not even Michele Soavi's masterpiece, *Dellamorte Dellamore*, could re-activate the kind of frenzied production rate the Italians had enjoyed in previous years. And with the deaths of Lucio Fulci and Sergio Corbucci, many had resigned themselves to the fact that Italian genre cinema was dead. The odd blip would appear on fan's radars from time to time in the form of Argento's *Sleepless* and *Red Riding Hood*, but often, those films failed to live up to the hype, and turned out to be little more than a desperate attempt to re-ignite the spark. For the next decade or so, Italian genre cinema was a shambles, a shadow of its former self. In the late 00s, however, a new company came along called Necrostorm, and their mission was to revamp the state of cult production in Italy with the release of comic books, video games, animation and live-action cinema, all created in-house by a dedicated team of staff. Necrostorm's first feature film was *Adam Chaplin*, an ultra-violent revenge story with a retro 80s feel which borrowed elements not only from American movies (like many Italian productions), but also embraced many influences from the Far East, too.

The plot of *Adam Chaplin* is quite simple: The muscle-bound title character summons a demon and stalks the fictional city of Heaven Valley, bumping off enemies and corrupt law enforcers in his search of Denny, an evil arch-villain who runs the city and who burned Chaplin's wife to a crisp because she couldn't settle her debt with him. Chaplin is aided in his quest by the little demon that sometimes appears on his shoulder, directing him in his mission.

The killings in this film are spectacular and extremely violent: Bad guys aren't just neatly killed off as a convenient stepping stone to the next scene; when they're attacked, their heads literally explode in a shower of blood and bone and gristle. Characters have their limbs blown off, heads severed, and mutilated torsos are impaled on poles which Chaplin carries around with him like living, suffering, agonized flags of vengeance. And this extreme style comes to a head in the finale set on top of a building for an all-out bloodbath as Chaplin battles on against Denny and his HVPD Death Squadron in extremely graphic fashion.

The demon looks like a cross between Gollum from *Lord of The Rings* and the Machi demons from *Urotsukidôji*, and is clearly an anime influence. Perhaps on the metaphorical front, the demon represents Chaplin's trauma, his mental suffering following the stark images of his wife's badly burned body. His eyes have turned a milky white, and he is basically blind. His entire mission to avenge his wife is channelled through his demon who works as his eyes and ears and brain. Chaplin can no longer make decisions on his own behalf, he is completely at the mercy of his all-seeing, all-wise demon. In metaphorical terms, his judgement is clouded by evil. So, of course, there can be no happy ending for him.

Very much an auteur piece, *Adam Chaplin* was not only written and directed by Emanuele

De Santi, he also cast himself in the lead role and wrote the music score, too. The result is a crazy comic book caper loaded with excessive violence, stylish set-pieces, and imaginative ideas. The film is visually astonishing throughout, despite the low-budget and the fact that it's a directorial debut. There are also many gory moments, and these include tributes to Takashi Miike's *Ichi The Killer* (severed face sliding down a wall), *Tokyo Gore Police* (the futuristic setting and gallons of arterial spray), the Cat III classic *Riki-Oh: The Story of Ricky* (heads crushed and splattered in eye-popping detail), and Japanese anime (when characters leap in the air to throw a punch, the background becomes blurry to give the impression of power and acceleration). Tributes are also paid to Western graphic novels and films such as *Robocop* and *Re-Animator* in the retro style future setting, and the glowing serum which brings back the dead.

Simple and derivative it may be, but in keeping with Italian cult tradition, that's exactly what company owner and special effects wiz Giulio De Santi intended. "The general plots are simple and leave empty gaps," he says, "because it's what action anime do, and we love that aspect: to leave unanswered questions. Even because we planned to create other products based on the same universe, like all Necrostorm's movies, they are linked by an invisible line, like 'Castle Rock' is always present in Stephen King's stories. In other products we will answer all the unanswered questions."

Indeed, the city of Heaven Valley is a dark graphic novel come to life, thanks to the attention to detail shown throughout. If you look closely, you can see that the agents of the HVPD Death Squadron all have deformed and mutilated faces, an impressive and painstaking detail considering it's easy to miss because the agent's faces are often covered by their helmet visors. With *Adam Chaplin*, the creators have constructed an entire world built on a love for the genre and their craft. But by all means, the makers of *Adam Chaplin* are not through with exploring this world in future productions. "We plan to make a gang movie like *The Warriors* for Heaven Valley", Giulio promises, "where it's important to better explain the story of the city, it was just confusing to insert that in a movie like *Adam Chaplin*, where the protagonist is him and his powers. Exactly like *Fist of the North Star* does, everything is destroyed by nuclear bombs, but you don't know why on details."

Sequels to *Adam Chaplin* are already in the pipeline, and also a sequel to *Taeter City*, another Necrostorm production this time directed by Giulio himself set in a nightmare future police state where dead criminals are rounded up and served to the citizens as human burgers by mega fast-food chains (*Taeter City* is also reviewed in this book). Here's hoping that this marks the beginning of a new phase of Italian genre production, fuelled by the pure love of movies and keeping cult production alive. Visit www.necrostorm.com to keep up to date with the latest developments.

Livid (2011)
(Orig title: *Livide*)
Dir: Alexandre Bustillo & Julien Maury /France
After *Inside*, directors Alexandre Bustillo and Julien Maury returned with their follow-up, *Livid*. Turning more towards the supernatural this time around, *Livid* is a vampiric tale about a trainee nurse who visits the home of an elderly woman, a former ballet teacher, and discovers that the house holds many treasures. She later brings along her friends, and they force their way into the basement. And soon enough, all hell breaks loose... It doesn't come close to the sheer visceral terror of *Inside*, but *Livid* does have its moments; the initial set-up is very well done, and also includes lots of creepy scenes with the use of stuffed animals and even the stuffed body of a young ballerina that serves as a life-sized musical box, complete with a slow turning figure and an accompanying tinkling tune. But ultimately, *Livid* is let down by a rather silly and over-the-top ending.

Bag of Bones (2011)
Dir: Mick Garris /USA
Originally broadcast on television in two feature-length instalments, but has also been shown in its entirety of three hours (including ad breaks). Novelist Michael Noonan (Pierce Brosnan) sees his wife getting hit by a vehicle in the street during a book signing. After the funeral, he decides to deal with the loss by heading out to his country cabin to write a new book. And there he meets Mattie (Melissa George), a young mother in the middle of a custody battle with her evil rich father-in-law. And meanwhile, Michael's dead wife's spirit is trying to communicate something important to

him from beyond the grave.

Stephen King fans will notice many casual references to him and his work, including *Misery*, Kubrick's *The Shining* ("Lie still Bag of Bones"), and his Bachman pseudonym. Pierce Brosnan's performance here is pretty good – I'd always had an aversion to him, probably since my mind was scarred by *Mamma Mia!* (2008), the godawful Abba musical in which Brosnan, in all seriousness, attempts to sing *SOS*: his grunt-like, off-key yelping of the chorus sounds like a dog getting its testicles caught in barbed wire. Watch a clip on YouTube if you don't believe me. Just don't say I didn't warn you. For such a low-scale project with just a handful of key characters, the story dawdles and meanders much more than necessary. The film would have been much better had it focused on the essentials and kept things tight. The biggest criticism, though, is that *Bag of Bones* never delivers on the horrific which it seems to be constantly building up to. We don't actually see the rape and drowning scenes until after two hours, and though far from pleasant, the sequence is short and no way as emotionally effective as it should have been. By this point, viewer interest tends to fall behind, and the flashy, strobe-lit ending kills off any hardened viewers who are still tuned in. All in all, the film is way too sketchy for it to work, like a 'bare bones' idea, or if you will, a 'bag of bones' in need of flesh and form.

Chromeskull: Laid to Rest 2 (2011)
Dir: Robert Hall /USA

Writer/director Robert Hall returns with a sequel to the enjoyable *Laid to Rest* (2009) with a dismal offering which picks up right where the first film left off. This offers more of the same as Chromeskull is repaired and resurrected by a sinister group of deviants, and finds a new group of dweebs to massacre. This time the plot is even lighter, the killings are twice as gruesome, and we even get a bit of back story on Chromeskull, who miraculously survived the head-crushing in part one. But I suppose the most disturbing element in the film for me is the way in which technology is fetishized; all of the characters seem to document their entire lives – and deaths – on video, like sad tourists of life.

Lake Noir (2011)
Dir: Jeff Schneider /USA

A fat guy is beaten to death with a baseball bat and dumped in the lake while his female companion is – presumably – raped. Cut to the present day, and a group of friends head out on a fishing trip to the lake, where – you guessed it – the fat guy returns in ghostly form to exact his vengeance on the squealing shitcakes... You can accurately predict the entire movie after watching the first five minutes. And that's exactly what I did, not because I'm clever or psychic or anything like that, but because this film works in an uninspired, cookie-cutter, boring old template style.

En route to the 'slaughter' we're forced to listen to these utter buffoons dribbling on about wanting to get laid, and slating each other with their wisecracking idiocies, and referring to each other as 'dude' and 'bro', etc. If you're going to inflict a bunch of idiotic characters on your audience, at least have the decency to make sure they are then brutally butchered in graphic detail before our eyes. You know, just to make being in their presence for ninety minutes worthwhile. We need some kind of 'pay off' to make these characters even scarcely tolerable. The girls are pretty enough, but serve as nothing more than human vacuums in thongs, and they basically do nothing. The boys are a bunch of abnormally twattish rodent brains.

The film's monster is 'Wetman', the fat guy from the lake, and when he shows up, it's all rather tame. We wait an agonizing 75 minutes before his first killing, in which the black 'dude' is cracked in the back of the noggin while having sex. The hairy buffoon and another are also killed during intercourse. And the final guy is pushed against a tree, and this causes his death. Pathetic! Where's the blood? Where's the violence? The final girl, Ash, is then approached by the overweight ghoul, but because she refused to have sex with one of her companions, her 'purity' saves the day, just like they do in all slasher movies, see? The big bald monster then returns to the lake.

Zombie Ass (2011)
(Orig title: *Zonbi asu*)
Dir: Noboru Iguchi /Japan

A disparate group of characters, including a vomiting nerd, a schoolgirl mourning the death of her sister, and a super-bitch with nice big tits, head out to the wilderness to fish for trout (!).

The bitch swallows a tapeworm parasite in the belief that it will somehow enable her to become a successful model (!!). And after the van driver has his fingers bitten off by a zombie, this odd bunch seek sanctuary in an abandoned house. The bitch gets diarrhoea, and a shit-caked zombie climbs out of the toilet and tries to molest her (!!!). And from there, the toilet serves as some kind of portal from which dozens of 'shit monsters' emerge to terrorize the group... Ah, only in Japan. The absurdity and humour begins to wear thin quite early on, the soundtrack shamelessly rips off *The Exorcist,* and the action sequences rely way too much on cheap CGI effects. Amusingly, some see the film as a parody of Ridley Scott's *Prometheus* (2012), but it's unlikely as Scott's film wasn't made until the following year. However, there are some bizarre similarities, such as the back-story of the 'creator,' and the origins of Man. Fans of Iguchi's previous efforts, like *Machine Girl* (2008) and *Tokyo Gore Police* (2008), will know exactly what to expect here. Casual viewers may find it all too much to take, like being asked to stare at an arse while it gleefully breaks wind in your face. If you don't fancy this, at least check out the trailer on YouTube as it's one of the funniest you'll ever see.

Black Mirror (2011-)

Dir: Various /UK /USA

On the night of 4 December 2011, British television took a trip to the dark side when Channel 4 aired the first episode of *Black Mirror.* Set in the near future, at a strange periphery point, it's a series that explores the dangers of technological advancements that are currently just beyond our reach. The modern-day wonders of the internet, social media, virtual reality, augmented reality, surveillance and artificial intelligence are re-imagined, often with the most horrific implications brought to the fore with an underlying dark comedy. Many of those tuning in that night were already familiar with the show's creator, Charlie Brooker, who had previously penned the cult comedy series, *Nathan Barley* (2005) and the zombies in the Big Brother house horror, *Dead Set* (2008), not to mention his work on the controversial *Brass Eye: Paedogeddon!* (2001) and *Screenwipe* (2006-2008).

Perhaps best known for his scabrous and invective-filled articles he wrote for the *Guardian* between 2000 and 2010, in which he

tore into the latest *Big Brother* contestants and whatever Z-grade trash was polluting the nation's airwaves, Charlie Brooker's vivid and blackly comic imagination had already garnered a considerable cult following. His memorable put-downs became the stuff of legend: he famously described Russell Brand as a 'Dickensian dicking machine,' and Jamie Oliver as a 'floppy-tongued bum-face.' And they're just two of the more polite examples. He has a talent for capturing the comic essence of celebrities in just a few words, in the same way a sea-side cartoonist can use a marker pen to quickly sketch out the amusing resemblance of any tourist willing to hand over a few quid. And, considering the detailed and meticulous way he would describe the horrific breakdowns of civilisation in his weekly column, a series such as *Black Mirror* could have only stemmed from the twisted mind of Mr. Brooker.

According to Brooker himself, the genesis of *Black Mirror* was born of pure mischief: he was interested in making a spoof version of *24* in which Jack Bauer is forced to have sex with a pig. He toyed with the idea for a number of years, and the twisted scenario became ever more detailed until he arrived at the story we now call *The National Anthem.* When the episode finally hit the screens, it no longer held any semblance to *24* or Jack Bauer. The only element that remained of his original idea was the pig-fucking punchline. *The National Anthem* is set in modern-day Britain, and opens during a media panic as the princess (probably based on Kate Middleton) has been kidnapped by a suspected terrorist group. With the motive for the kidnapping still unknown, the media and government are shocked when a video is uploaded onto *YouTube.* The video shows the captive princess in distress as she is forced to read out a statement to camera. And it's here the viewers learn that, in order for the princess to be set free, the Prime Minister of Britain must have sex with a pig live on television that same afternoon. What follows is a blackly comic drama that grinds on mercilessly as the government does all it can to spare the humiliation of the Prime Minister, all in vain...

The National Anthem is a great opener to the series, and a typical Brooker-esque nightmare, despite the fact that – unlike many of the later episodes – the story unfolds in the present day rather than the near future. While watching, you can squirm at the whole idea of the thing while knowing that the author of the show is loving every minute of it, exploring the absurdity and outlandishness of the plot while treating the subject-matter with all the seriousness and bluntness of a *Cold Case Files* episode.

15 Million Merits is set in the near future where the masses are required to earn their keep by peddling exercise bikes all day which presumably helps to keep the nation's power supply running. As a reward, citizens are given points, or merits, based on how much peddling they have done, and once the individual has earned 15 million of them, he or she will be eligible to spend their credits on Hot Shot, a televised talent show that is broadcast across the nation. And should the audition prove successful in the eyes of the public and the panel of judges, the individual gets promoted to a higher social class and granted their own weekly spot on an entertainment show. Imagine a hellish totalitarian dystopia ruled over by Simon Cowell, and you're on the right track. Bing (Daniel Kaluuya) is a young black man subjected to this nightmarish existence of mind-numbing entertainment, monotonous video games, garish pornography and endless peddling. Dissatisfied with his lot, Bing catches the eye of the beautiful Abi (Jessica Brown Findlay), a chirpy young lady who peddles on the same block as him. They slowly build a rapport, and feelings develop between them. However, when Abi's singing audition at Hot Shot proves successful, her 'rise' to fame lands her a seedy gig as a porn performer on late night TV. Bing is distraught by this, and quickly earns enough merits for his own audition where he intends to stage a spectacular act of revenge on the system that has pushed him over the edge...

By far the most pessimistic episode of season one, *15 Million Merits* presents the viewers with a vision of authoritarian hell that even George Orwell and Aldous Huxley could never have imagined. It's a world in which consumerism, auditions and social approval is everything, and where individuality is slowly gnawed away over a miserable lifetime; where everything is catered for the lowest common denominator. There are allusions to exploitation and class conflict (the dull grey uniforms worn by the citizens are similar to the overalls worn by the underground workers in Fritz Lang's *Metropolis* [1927], for example). It's also a world that runs on a perverse form of meritocracy, in which those who earn the most

merits are shuffled off into another pocket of hell. The masses are kept dumb and docile with endless amounts of cheap trashy entertainment. There's no substance anymore; no soul. Everything is a performance in a futile and debased form of competition. Everything is designed to distract the citizens form the real life events that are going on in reality – and the episode doesn't give the viewers so much as a glimpse of the outside world. It's a very closed-in and claustrophobic existence, like a nation of pet gerbils on endless running wheels, heading nowhere fast.

The most intriguing scenario of season one was saved for last, however. *The Entire History of You* (written by *Peep Show*'s Jesse Armstrong) explores a cultural phenomena of the future in which people have small electronic devices (or 'grains') implanted in their heads that allows the users to view and re-live their memories. Similar to the SQUID device in *Strange Days* (1995), the grain serves the positive purpose of being far more accurate than organic memory, but the downside is that the HD, 3D memories are *far more accurate than organic memories*. This double-edged sword is explored via a relationship in which a man's jealousy, paranoia and insecurities lead him to hen-peck his partner on her fling with a work colleague. And every time he pushes the subject, he discovers another layer of lies concerning the seriousness and the full extent of the 'fling'. It's a fascinating scenario that touches on sci-fi realms that are rarely explored to any extent in film or television these days, but the story is a little dull, and the central characters aren't particularly likeable.

Season 2 kicks off with *Be Right Back*, a sort of hi-tech update of *The Monkey's Paw* in which a widow 'resurrects' her late husband as an artificial being. By gathering together all of the dead man's social media and other online posts, along with video and audio recordings, as well as phone calls and text messages, the android can simulate the man's personality, right down to his tone, sense of humour and speech patterns. However, the simulation is far from 100% accurate. And though the being may fool those who didn't know the man all that well, his widow can easily spot the flaws in the synthetic system. And pretty soon, the machine no longer brings her the comfort that it was designed for. In the end, the mechanoid ghost that lurks in her home becomes a nuisance and an obstacle to her grieving, and she decides to get rid of it...

White Bear is one of the bleakest and most disturbing episodes of *Black Mirror* to date. It's a difficult one to talk about without spoilers, but the set-up is a woman who finds herself in a strange place with no recollection of how she got there. She wanders outside to seek help, but the nearby residents keep their distance while filming her on their mobile phones like sinister tourists in a hellish theme park of some sort. Anyway, the girl's day goes from bad to worse when masked clowns and armed maniacs begin hunting her down in the streets, and terrorising her in some bizarre witch-hunt. And the viewers only find out the reason for all this towards the end.

Season 2 wraps up with *The Waldo Moment*. It's one of the weakest episodes of the entire series for those who enjoy 'future shocks,' but there are still areas of interest here. Again, it's set in the near future just slightly beyond our grasp, and features a popular cartoon bear, Waldo, who runs in a local by-election. Satirical, foul-mouthed and mocking, Waldo appears to be more concerned with amusing the public and making fun of stuffy politicians rather than presenting a case for genuine change. And, after a difficult televised debate with a conservative, the creator and 'puppeteer' of Waldo, Jamie (Daniel Rigby), has a crisis of confidence and slumps into a deep depression as he tries to figure out the purpose of his life and his value to the world. Of all the episodes of *Black Mirror* to date, this one is perhaps the closest Charlie Brooker came to sharing his own experiences in the media world in a semi-autobiographical form. Jamie's character is clearly based on Charlie himself to some degree, and indeed, Charlie's articles sometimes landed him in trouble (such as the piece he wrote about George W. Bush in 2004, which resulted in a deluge of death threats). There's no doubt that Mr. Brooker's more sensitive side experienced a few 'dark nights of the soul' during his column days, and he has admitted that he always felt terrible when meeting celebrities and politicians whom he had savagely mauled in his writings. As for Jamie, his sudden slump and subsequent self-reflection on the value of the things he puts into the world, and whether it's even a healthy pursuit, holds a genuine existential angst – albeit through a cartoon avatar with a turquoise cock.

Imagine being locked in a room for 4 million years with the same annoying Christmas song blaring out of a wireless radio – on a continuous loop – for the entire duration. What would be left of your mind after such an impossible ordeal? The *Black Mirror* Christmas special, *White Christmas*, doesn't answer that question (the answer would no doubt be too alien for any human being to comprehend), but that's the horrendous implication the episode signs off with. Originally broadcast on the 16 December, 2014, the Christmas special presents a portmanteau of seasonal shockers that are all neatly tied together during the final revelations.

Again, this is a difficult one to talk about without giving the game away, but the technologies involved include a Z-Eye, which is a brain implant that allows web users to communicate with the subject. The one implanted with the device can also hear the voices of the web users in his head. Furthermore, by using internet services such as skype, the web users can witness what the subject is seeing on their desktop monitors. This technology comes in handy for pick-up artists who fancy themselves as gurus who can instruct less attractive men on how to approach women in bars, with step-by-step guidance and a constant line of communication. Of course, the women who are approached in this way have no idea that their attempted seduction is being relayed live on the internet. What could possibly go wrong in this scenario?

The other stories deal with 'cookies,' microchips that are implanted into a human brain. The cookie shadows the mind for a time until it creates an exact clone of the human consciousness. Once the cloning process is complete, the chip is removed from the brain and inserted into an egg-shaped device. This consciousness has the exact same memories and personality as the person from whom it was cloned, but crucially, the clone doesn't know that it's a clone – it thinks it's real. The clone considers itself the real consciousness, not the copy. And once imprisoned in the egg, the clone can be tormented and driven insane. It can experience 1000 years per minute by simply altering its perception of time. Described by *The Telegraph*'s Mark Monahan as 'a nightmare-before-Christmas reminder that to revere our digital gizmos is to become their pathetic slave,' this episode throws up some daunting questions on the ethics of artificial intelligence and the line between a dead gadget and a digital 'living' thing that can suffer. While the androids in

Blade Runner (1982) and *Ghost in the Shell* (1995) were so advanced that they could muse philosophically on the meaning of life, and also suffer in many ways a human can, those machines always had the option of suicide – or self-destruction – if things got really bad. Not so with the cookie clones. They don't have physical bodies – they're merely a brain in a box. At least a fish in a fish tank can swim around and have the pleasure of eating, though they aren't too bright. A fully aware human consciousness, however, being expected to exist in such a condition is a terrifying thought. Would it be cruel to torture a clone in this way? After all, it isn't a *real* human consciousness. It isn't flesh and blood. It's just as intelligent and as frail as you or I, but it isn't *really* real, is it?

By that point, *Black Mirror* had picked up a considerable cult following, especially in America. And seasons 3 and 4 were produced by Netflix. This new transatlantic style added a certain glossiness to the series while the subject-matter continued to mine territory that no other television show had tried before. Stand out episodes of these seasons include *Nosedive* (another horrifying look at the future of social media), *Playtest* (which looks at the horrifying future of virtual reality games), *Shut Up and Dance* (the darkly comic side of internet trolling), *Hated In the Nation* (a sci-fi murder mystery), *USS Callister* (virtual reality again, by way of *Star Trek*), *Crocodile* (a very dark tale that revisits the memory 'grain' device of previous episode, *The Entire History of You*) and *Black Museum*, which is another portmanteau of horror tales.

One of the most underrated episodes of the entire series is *Metalhead*. Sure, it's derivative of other movies that deal with AI killing machines as seen in *The Terminator*, *Hardware* and *Chopping Mall*, and there are musical and visual nods to *The Shining* and Luc Besson's *The Last Battle* (*La Dernier Combat*, 1983). But those quibbles aside, this is a truly gripping and fascinating tale. The episode in set in some unspecified future after the fall of civilisation, where lawlessness is rife. Instead of security guards, companies have resorted to keeping AI guard 'dogs' in their warehouses to protect their goods from looters. And when a trio of rugged survivors break into a particular warehouse to grab supplies, one such 'dog' is activated into killing the intruders by any means necessary. First of all, the machine spits out shards that penetrate the skin of the intruders. And these shards contain GPS tracking devices. The dog then goes on the hunt, wiping out the humans who are no match for such a cold killing machine. With the use of solar power, firearms, skeleton keys, infra-red vision, along with access to radiowaves so that it can eavesdrop on CB radio communications, the dog is equipped to deal with security violations in a super-smart fashion. It is also incredibly fast and can outrun a car or van with ease. Improvisation and quick-witted problem solving are no problem for the dog either, as it can repair broken limbs by making new ones from the objects it finds in its environment. It can also work flat-out indefinitely – without so much as a coffee break – until you are dead. The most startling thing about this episode is the fact that *Metalhead* isn't science fiction at all. Like, say, *Cube* (1997), all the terrifying technology on display here already exists. Check out Boston Dynamics and imagine how advanced this tech will be in 20 or 30 years time. Sweet dreams!

Sinister (2012)
Dir: Scott Derrickson /USA

One of the better films in this book is *Sinister*, a creepy, supernatural tale grounded in the grittiness of true crime. Writer Ethan Hawke moves his family into a house that has a dark past. He finds some old 8mm films in the attic which show ritualized murders. And rather than inform the police about his discovery, he decides to investigate alone with the aim of writing a true crime best seller. However, his obsession with the case causes strange behaviour in his children and the collapse of his marriage. The snuff footage is very well crafted and unsettling; the family hanging from the tree has a 'lynched by the klan' quality to it. There are also slashed throats, burnings and drownings. As the plot unfolds, we discover that the snuff films are the extension of a Pagan deity (the 'eater of children'), and this makes for an interesting alternative to the usual found footage scenarios.

Sinister isn't perfect. There are some routine, predictable moments throughout, and the sinister ghoul at the centre of it all is stripped of much of its mystery, and as such, pushes the narrative very close to all-out silliness. The monster is in danger of becoming a Freddy Krueger-like boogeyman. To make the transition into farce complete, this deity could have spouted villainous lines like "You're all my children now," but thankfully that doesn't happen. I do get the impression that the filmmakers were pressured into including a boogeyman character in order to get the green light. I can imagine the execs' rationale for this: "Well, we love the script and all, but our market research tells us that all the popular horror movies of late had a boogeyman in them. So, in order for us to give the green light, we're going to need a monster... C'mon guys, what's wrong with you? This is a horror movie! Where's the monster?" etc, etc. And as a result, the mystery about the origin of the films, and the ambiguity of how they came to be – the balance between true crime and the otherworldly – is swept aside in favour of keeping the movie in line with such contemporary drivel as *Cabin In the Woods* and *Innkeepers*.

Taeter City (2012)
Dir: Giulio De Santi /Italy
Set in a future dystopia ruled over by the brutal dictatorship known as The Authority, the citizens of Taeter City live among sinister radio waves called Zeed that allows The Authority to recognize and distinguish the minds of criminals from ordinary law-abiding citizens. The airwaves induce criminals into madness, prompting them to commit suicide in bizarre and graphic ways. A police unit called The Bikers are responsible for rounding up the bodies of dead criminals and dropping them off at huge slaughterhouses. These human abattoirs supply the mega fast-food chain, Taeter Burger, with fresh human meat which is fed to the hungry population around the clock. Life in Taeter City is under full control, that is until the Zeed system malfunctions, and the airwaves not only fail to induce suicide in the crims, but it also causes them to become stronger. These super-crims then emit their own mutated airwaves which cause the ordinary citizens to commit mass suicide. Something needs to be done before the situation can spiral completely out of control, and a trio of biker officers are sent out into the city to deal with the chaos…

Directed by Giulio De Santi (who was also the special effects director on *Adam Chaplin*, and he also plays the role of one of the criminals in this film), *Taeter City* is a grim futuristic fantasy set in the nightmarish world of a cannibalistic Orwellian dictatorship, complete with Paul Verhoeven-esque mock TV commercials displayed on big screens across the city, informing the populace, propaganda-style, of the latest treats to be had at their nearest fast-food joint. Overall, the film is broken up into a series of vignettes, as each deadly scenario is played out as a series of mini-stories in their own right. This disjunctive narrative style is often punctuated with TV ads broadcast by The Authority informing the public on how they should live and obey the powers that be. The central premise of the film seems to be a familiar one, about how the state 'feeds' on its citizens, how the regime can only function as long as it has enemies to vilify and destroy as a way of keeping the populace sedated in the belief that their best interests are at the heart of the Authority which rules over them. Crime is quite literally the lifeblood of this totalitarian police state. And as such, it becomes difficult for the viewers to identify with any of the characters; the criminals are monstrous, the normal citizens are apathetic drones, and the Biker squad's heroics are all rather hollow, thanks to their dedication to keeping the awful regime on top.

But with that said, and with that in mind, *Taeter City* as a film deliberately keeps its sense of morality confused as a way of illustrating the point that both the fearful masses and the regime that rules over them are in a fight to the death, and all sense of morality has become a casualty on both sides: Such is life in a concrete jungle. *Taeter City* is also a real treat for fans of off-beat cult cinema. Just like Necrostorm's previous film, *Adam Chaplin*, the visuals are nothing less than astonishing throughout, and the gore is gruesome and graphic and is kept fully in stock, just like the mangled meat being served at Taeter Burger. One of the Biker officers is called Wank, and this ensures lots of childish giggles in the audience, especially when he comes out with lines like "Hey, it's your friend, Wank. Remember me?" And just like *Adam Chaplin*, there are numerous tips of the hat in reference to other films it pays homage to, like *Tokyo Gore Police*, *Robocop*, *Total Recall*, *Starship Troopers*, *1984*, *Delicatessen* and Manga anime, and viewers will have a field day spotting all the movie reference points. Giulio De Santi told me "Our main and only purpose is to create niche products for genre fans, from fans, but with better quality aspects. We just try to focus on aspects that big companies lack, and splatter movies lack: most part of big productions have great actors, great stories, but no blood. So when splatter fans go to see something, at least give them blood."

When asked if the cannibal Authority in the film is his response to the state of the modern world, Giulio replied, "With *Taeter City*, I wanted to explain my thoughts on the modern 'civilized' country, mostly over the *masses*, with a very simple plot. People, mostly in huge metropolis, forget that violence is something 'natural', and we are made of it, but believe in it like a cure, only when it's in his advantage and perpetrated by someone else in their defence.

"Violence is something we can't cancel, because it's one of the biggest pillars of the universe: to survive, someone or something must be defeated. The nature, the direct expression of God (for those who believe in God) proves this, a pacifist in the jungle would die if he didn't kill to defend himself, or at least if he didn't commit some form of violence. I'm not saying this is good or bad, just examining what I see without giving an opinion, I wanted to give an opinion over the masses. What I find *crazy*, is the fact that people nowadays accept violence only when perpetrated by the so-called 'authority'. In that case it becomes right, because it's for a good cause.

"I created a cannibalistic dictatorship, to take that concept to the extreme: in *Taeter City* in fact, everything is seen in broad daylight, and the people accept the extreme violence of the authority, just because 'they are justified in what they are doing.'"

The off-shoot of this idea is the age-old concept of the 'witch-hunt' mentality that people seem to cling to in fear of their own persecution. In situations of perpetual fear brought on by the authorities, the masses feel much more comfortable when they have scapegoats to point their fingers at, to accuse those who resemble the criminality in a more obvious way, in order to mask their own secret contempt for the regime, as Giulio points out, "In real life, I notice a *huge* schizophrenia in the masses, and I consider it pretty dangerous for the individual: one day you could be considered bad by your own neighbourhood, and find yourself alone against the 'world' that will mark you as 'the criminal' only because they believe it to save their own interests. But this doesn't justify the criminality."

And with this, many viewers will assume that the character of Trevor represents a part of Giulio himself (after all, he did cast himself in the role as the super-crim), but Giulio remains ambiguous on the matter: "With Trevor Covalsky, I didn't create a good character. In *Taeter City no one* is good, he's a killer as much as the authority. I did this to underline the concept: 'who is the good one, the criminal or the authority?' No one, they are both bad in my opinion. Good or bad is subjective, it can't be considered universal. So no one is good in Taeter City, and there is no solution for that problem. Some people found this confusing: 'We don't have a good character to follow, and the storyline is told in vignette.' Everything was created on purpose, I wanted to give the same confusing feeling I had when I listen to the people discuss 'what is good and what is bad'. I interrupted the action with the advertisements, to underline the 'bad behaviour' of the authority, like we at Necrostorm were the authority, and the spectators the masses. The absurd violence I proposed is justified by the authority, in every damned sequence, with Caronte you're reminded that it's 'for your own benefit.' I can conclude in this way: this is not a criticism over the masses, only the expression of my thoughts over the feeling I had, an innate feeling of discomfort. Like the feeling, I *hope* everyone felt watching the movie."

A sequel is in the works, *Taeter City 2: Revenge*, and the next instalment will bring to a close any unanswered questions. "It will bring us to the final chapter/movie," Giulio promises, "the inevitable finale: the destruction of the city itself, as concept and materially."

American Mary (2012)
Dir: Jen & Sylvia Soska /Canada

Poor med student, Mary Mason (*Ginger Snaps'* Katherine Isabelle) visits a strip joint to find work, and ends up earning five grand for a back-room surgical repair on a badly injured man. Word of her services spreads underground, and she is soon contacted by members of a body modification cult who want to turn themselves into 'dolls.' Thus, Mary finds herself earning thousands of dollars to remove a woman's nipples and sew up her snatch. She has to balance her studies with her nocturnal profession, and is constantly fucking pestered by her fucking professor who says the word 'fuck' in every sentence because he's so fucking modern and down with the brats, maaaan. And after he drugs and rapes her, Mary becomes an all-out monster, with a ruthless revenge in which she takes an active, sadistic pleasure in torture. *American Mary* is a decent debut feature, but it could have been so much better. The film never quite reaches the disturbing depths it promises, perhaps because the film-makers wanted their flick to appeal to a mainstream audience (which is understandable, considering that the Soska sister's parents re-mortgaged their house to fund it. That's *a lot* of pressure to secure a hit). On the positive side, the film is at least more engaging than that other body cult movie, *Quid Pro Quo* (2008), and it has its roots in an assortment of horror-related sub-genres, such as mad doctor flicks, torture porn, rape/revenge, Cronenbergian body horror, and good old *femme fatale* flicks.

Maniac (2012)
Dir: Franck Khalfoun /USA /France

Frank (Elijah Wood) is a deeply disturbed loner who spends his days restoring antique mannequins and his nights stalking, killing and scalping young women. His grip on reality is so delicate he has to down anti-psychotic pills just to keep his hallucinations under control. He then meets the beautiful French photographer, Anna (Nora Arnezeder). They strike up a friendship based on a mutual appreciation of each other's art. But instead of the hope of redemption, their relationship is doomed to end very badly.

I avoided watching this remake of *Maniac* for a long time because Elijah Wood was cast in the lead role. He was okay as the blank-faced serial killer in *Sin City*, but that sounds like a back-handed compliment (just like Vinnie Jones's finest performance was in *Midnight Meat Train*; ironically, it was a role which required him to express *zero* emotions). The thought of Elijah Wood stepping into the shoes of Joe Spinell did not fill me with joy. I mean, he's a foetus-faced, fun-size version of maniac. Actually, Elijah Wood is not as bad here as I originally feared, but he's got nothing on the hulking, sweaty mass of self-loathing scum that is the original Frank, played by Spinell.

This remake marks the change that has spread across the horror genre in the 32 years since the original was made. The maniac is now a pretty boy whom the girls can fawn over. The action has been shifted from the grotty downtown red light district of New York to the trendy hipster hive of Los Angeles (geographically and aesthetically right on Hollywood's doorstep). The retro inflected score by 'Rob' serves more as a cool 'in-thing' rather than an attempt to create any kind of atmosphere or dread. Instead of the street hookers of the original, the victims here are mostly trendy young women whom the killer meets on internet dating sites. The whole thing has a slick, MTV vibe about it, full of colour and tricky visuals. For some stupid reason producer, Alexandre Aja thought it was a good idea to hire Franck Khalfoun to direct the film. Khalfoun was a dancer and a business man, and is as far removed from the horror genre as, um, a dancing business man trying to make a horror movie.

The film's major gimmick is presenting the entire story from the perspective of the killer in continuous POV shots, which basically means that the audience has to trail behind the lead character breathing in his farts for 83 minutes. But rather than enhance the story (as in Gaspar Noe's *Enter the Void*), this just serves as a masturbatory camera fetish; 'ooh, check out the colours, look how we pan down from a ceiling mirror to the bed where Frank is strangling the cool tattooed chick. Check out the fluidity of our cameras; isn't it sexy?' What a trendy world it must be to be a serial killer. It's all surface, surface and more surface. Frank himself is portrayed as if he is slowly transforming into a mannequin dummy. His line delivery is so utterly blank and monotonous he makes Norman Bates seem like the life and soul of the party, in comparison. The POV technique should implicate the viewers in the crimes (as it did in such controversial works as *Salo* and *Henry-Portrait of a Serial Killer*); the voyeuristic merging of the viewer's gaze with the killer's POV would have worked much better if it was designed to make us feel uncomfortable by questioning our complicity with a murderer. But, because Frank's face is often seen in reflective surfaces during or after the killings, it is still possible to view the carnage in a detached manner, thus rendering the whole POV technique redundant. It's used here as nothing but a useless gimmick and an excuse to show off some fancy MTV-style camera techniques.

After delivering the gruelling – if finally silly and nonsensical – slasher movie, *Haute Tension*, Alexandre Aja was hailed as the savior of modern horror. But his subsequent output has consisted of nothing but producing and directing remakes of previous horror hits like *The Hills*

Have Eyes (2006), *Mirrors* (2008) and *Piranha 3D* (2010). Is that all there is to working in the industry nowadays? Is that all a filmmaker can hope to achieve, a little golden ticket to head out to Hollywood to churn out sub-par remakes? It's either remake or bust. It's a sorry state of affairs to be in, and will drive all but the shallowest and money-driven 'artists' from ever wanting to pursue a career in mainstream movies. And the situation is rapidly getting worse as the years go by. Aja the savior of horror? The savior of his bank account, more like.

Maniac ultimately serves as a typical example of what modern mainstream movies have become; 21st Century feature-length music videos designed to dazzle the mannequins in the audience. Ironically, the deadweights in the audience who enjoyed this film are exactly the type of unfeeling psychopaths who think MTV *Cribs* is a show about moneyed gods.

The ABC's of Death (2012)
Dir: -Various- /USA /New Zealand

In 2006, a notorious sex film was unleashed on the public after being passed surprisingly uncut by the British censors. The film was *Destricted*, an anthology of shorts made by a variety of cutting-edge filmmakers – including Gaspar Noe and Larry Clark. The idea behind the film was to explore the relationship between sex and art, but the end result turned out to be hopelessly pretentious and hideously degenerate. Fast forward six years, and the public was assaulted with another notorious film with a similar premise: 26 directors from across the world each made a film about death using a letter from the alphabet as a starting point. The result was *The ABC's of Death*, an equally hideous flop in which the directors involved seemed to mistake 'cutting-edge' and 'provocative' film-making for an excuse to indulge in sickness and depravity. However, there are one or two nuggets of interest to be found in this compilation, for what it's worth...

Opening with a bang, *A is for Apocalypse* sees a woman viciously murder her husband while he lays in bed one morning. She then makes a speech which sheds some light on her actions... In *B is for Bigfoot*, a babysitter and her boyfriend read a bedtime story for the little girl they're looking after. They want her to fall asleep so that they can go away and have sex in private. However, the house is invaded shortly after by an ugly intruder who proceeds to slaughter them... *C is for Cycle* is the third tale in a row that is centred on a bed. This time a man gets up to investigate a black hole that has appeared in the hedges in his back garden. He gets sucked into the hole and enters a dark alternate reality which serves as some kind of time-space glitch (no explanation is given). The man ends up being murdered by his double. This short could have been quite interesting, but it doesn't have the time to develop to its full potential (I suspect the filmmakers must have had a six minute time limit). For a much better take on a similar theme – and also genuinely creepy – see the excellent short film, *The French Doors* (2001).

D is for Dogfight is set in an underground fight club where a man must fight a dog. Though stylishly shot, this is utterly devoid of interest. The combatants turn against the event's organisers in the end... *E is for Exterminate* is directed by Angela Bettis (who starred as the title character in *May* [2002]). A man attempts to swat a spider in his office, and the creepy crawler bites his neck and stalks him at night. Eventually, the man discovers that the spider has laid eggs in his ear, and dozens of baby spiders pour out, and – presumably – devour his brain... *F is for Fart* is directed by the notorious Noboru Iguchi, and opens on a scene of flatulent Japanese schoolgirls farting on each other. One of them gets sucked up into the anus of her friend where she has a bizarre lesbian session with another gassy female – well, what else would you expect from the director of *Zombie Ass*?

G is for Gravity is a pointless POV short about a surfer dude who falls into the sea and drowns. The film-makers were each given $5000 to produce their films – God knows what director Andrew Traucki spent his on... *H is for Hydro-electric Diffusion* is a CGI-heavy episode by British film-maker, Thomas Cappelen Malling. It's set during the war in a cabaret club where a fighter pilot bulldog tries his luck with a dancing Nazi cat. There are some good ideas here. It's also visually great and gels quite nicely as a short in its own right. *I is for Iguana* is another useless waste of time – a woman trussed up in a maniac's bathtub is injected with something that causes her to scratch her skin off and die... *J is for Jidai-Geki (Samurai Movie)* is set in feudal Japan where a Samurai is preparing to behead a (presumed) criminal. However, the executioner is put off by the condemned man's giggling and funny faces. This is one of the better episodes – the Samurai gets the last laugh at the end... *K is for Klutz* is an animated tale in which a woman takes a shit that refuses to flush away. Instead, the turd follows her around like a lost puppy. She tries different methods to be rid of it, but in the end it jams its way back up her arse, and this causes the woman to die of internal bleeding...

L is for Libido is perhaps the most talked about section of the film. There are two men strapped to chairs at some kind of decadent party for the rich. The men are naked. A nude woman enters the scene and appears before them. The men begin jerking off in some kind of competition to see who can come the quickest. The loser gets a metallic spear rammed up his arse from beneath his seat. Again, the extremely short running time robs this tale of much of its power and pacing, not to mention context. Anyway, it's not over yet... The champion masturbator continues on his winning streak against other men. He wins 11 games in a row. On game 12, however, things are made a little more difficult – a female amputee in a wheelchair is wheeled in to be the focal point of the masturbators, and this makes it difficult for the champ to sustain his wood. The girl also has a glaring eyeball staring out of her vagina. Stage 13 is even darker, as the competitors have to jerk off to the sight of a man sexually abusing a young boy only a few feet away. Needless to say, this is ludicrous stuff that ends with chainsaw-sex mayhem.

M is for Miscarriage is one of the weakest of the bunch – it was directed by *House of the Devil*'s Ti West. It's a shamelessly uninspired clip of a woman using a plunger to unblock her toilet that is stuffed with the remains of her miscarriage... *N is for Nuptials* finds a man proposing to his girlfriend. The romantic gesture is soon thwarted, however, when the man's pet budgie speaks out about his infidelity – and, of course, this being a film about death, it's no real surprise when the girlfriend sets about carving him up with a chopping knife... *O is for Orgasm* is an arty piece about a woman who has sexual fantasies about being abused and burned with cigarettes while she blows bubbles...

P is for Pleasure is about an African hooker who has her savings stolen by one of her clients. This abhorrent woman then goes on to make disgusting 'squish' videos to make ends meet. This segment was shot in an awful 'verite' style

– perhaps deliberate, but I'm not too sure – which is very off-putting... In the postmodern, self-referential *Q is for Quack*, director Adam Wingard (of *V/H/S* fame) and writer/producer, Simon Barrett, appear as themselves – a pair of frustrated filmmakers struggling to make their Q segment. They decide to kill a duck on camera as a way of 'making a statement,' but they cannot bring themselves to pull the trigger. In the end, they accidentally kill each other. This is a very tongue-in-cheek and self-deprecating episode – the filmmakers even poke a bit of fun at the privileges granted to them in the showbiz world by hiring hot models to basically stand around topless on set.

Things get interesting with *R is for Removed*. Directed by *A Serbian Film*'s Srdjan Spasojevic, this tale opens on the scene of a burn victim who murders hospital staff before visiting an abandoned train station. He seems to be in the middle of an important task, but he drops dead and the clouds rain blood. This is a bizarre and nonsensical clip – again, there's simply not enough time for the filmmaker to add any context – but it's also strangely compelling. Added to the mystery are the pieces of celluloid that the man keeps buried within his skin.

S is for Speed is much lighter in tone, and probably wouldn't have been out of place as an episode of *Tales From the Crypt* (1989-96). The Grim Reaper pursues a "junky whore" through the desert, with the final revelation showing her to have died by choking on her vomit in a squalid drug den... *T is for Toilet* is a claymation clip directed by Lee Hardcastle. One of the highlights of the set, it's about a pair of bickering parents who escort their young son to the bathroom at night as he is afraid of the dark. The toilet overflows with green ooze and turns into a monster that slaughters and devours the kid's parents. Of course, it was all a dream... or was it? This includes a great ending.

U is for Unearthed is shot entirely in POV from a vampire's perspective. The bloodsucker is being chased through the woods at night by local villagers. And when it is captured, it is staked through the heart. One of the men also chops off its head, presumably to make sure it stays dead. With its hand-held camera work and hints of religious garb and demonic influence, this looks like a deliberate cross between Hammer horror and *[Rec] 2* (2009).

V is for Vagitus (The Cry of a Newborn Baby) is a futuristic offering set in 'New

Vancouver' in 2035. Armed rebels struggle against an ED-209-type of government killing machine. During a shoot-out in an abandoned building, a female government agent has a change of heart when she witnesses the machine gunning women and children to death. This is a very well done action scene, and includes an obvious anti-totalitarian message.

W is for WTF! is another self-referential piece about the making of the W segment. The director, Jon Schnepp, appears as himself. He chooses a walrus to be his W for death, and envisions a giant Godzilla-like Walrus destroying a city. However, he doesn't get very far with his project as a bunch of twisted killer clowns take over the world and devour everyone while leaving colourful rainbows in the sky. This bizarre tale feels like a cross between Lucifer Valentine and *Zombieland* (2009)... *X is for XXL* is directed by Frenchman, Xavier Gens (of *Frontiers* fame). It's the story of a woman who is pissed off at being ridiculed for being overweight. She goes home one afternoon, stuffs her face, and then attempts to remove her body fat with a carving knife. Of course, disastrous results ensue.

Y is for Youngbuck was directed by Jason Eisener (*Hobo With a Shotgun*). It's a twisted tale of a perverted school janitor – who was traumatised by watching his father do unspeakable things with a dead moose as a kid. The dirty old man licks the sweat of young boys off a bench in the gym. Pointless, degenerate tosh... Anyway, last up is *Z is for Zetsumentsu (Extinction)*. It's basically more z-grade crap from Japan – a man in a wheelchair (who looks to be impersonating Peter Sellers in *Dr. Strangelove*, though it isn't entirely clear) instructs fetishistic Nazi girls to kill each other with a giant phallus that shoots blades and spunk. All rather ridiculous. I was glad when it was over. As you have no doubt gathered by now, there is no beauty or dignity in death, according to these filmmakers. I can imagine many viewers turning away from this very disappointed – one remains none the wiser for having watched this film. And like the aforementioned *Destricted*, this all feels like an infantile wallowing in degradation and filth.

V/H/S (2012)
Dir: -Various- /USA

A disappointing anthology horror shot on video. A vampiric demon wipes out a motel room full of arseholes; a dull couple on a road trip are targeted by a masked intruder; a vicious knife killer in the woods picks off another group of cretins. We're constantly reminded in horror movies that dicks with video cameras are no fun, and *V/H/S* is no exception. A man witnesses his girlfriend being terrorised by 'evil spirits' via skype; more idiots show up at a Halloween party, but the house is empty – they encounter some kind of exorcism going on in the attic. We also get dialogue that doesn't reach far beyond "Fuck, dude. What the fuck?" Brad Miska of Bloody Disgusting.com came up with the concept of the film. BD is the most popular horror site on the web, and this gave the filmmakers the opportunity to promote their film on their own site, with everyone queuing up to give this trash a collective blowjob. Of course, many declared it a masterpiece, so there goes their credibility.

American Horror House (2012)
Dir: Darin Scott /USA

TV movie made for the Syfy Channel in which college girls in a haunted house are murdered by Miss Margo, the twisted sorority mom. And meanwhile, a party is attacked by demons. This is fairly bloody and gruesome for a TV movie, but there's really nothing else to commend it. In fact, it's nonsensical in large parts. The filmmakers throw everything they can at the screen in the hope that something will stick – blood, guts, ghosts, ghouls, killers, urban legends, teens, parties, booze, pervs, etc – but the result is a total mess that has all the subtlety of MTV. No one involved in the production had any idea what horror movies are about, and tried to remedy this by treating it as kind of Halloween party scary movie 'greatest hits' package. And to make matters worse, the characters here are extremely annoying; we get the usual adolescent drinking games with the 'wooing' and cheering as if they've never had a drink before. There's no one to root for; these morons are either loud-mouthed frat pricks or spoilt brat chimpettes. So it's a bit of a mystery as to why the filmmakers would attempt to create moments of suspense and tension. If this is just a silly party movie, why would you even try to make an audience feel uneasy? It doesn't work, stupid. What, am I supposed to feel scared for these morons in their perilous situations? They can all die for all I care.

Decay (2012)
Dir: Luke Thompson & Michael Mazur /UK

Set at CERN's large Hedron Collider in Switzerland, we get a group of British students fighting off a zombie outbreak in the building when particles bring back the dead, or some shit. And if the acting and dialogue isn't bad enough for you, wait 'til you get a load of the zombies; a bunch of bleary-eyed, middle-class bell-wipes who look like they've been queuing all night for Coldplay tickets.

Tied in Blood (2012)
Dir: Matthew Laurence /UK

A distressed man calls on a medium to help exorcise his home of an evil spirit that has slaughtered his family. This intriguing premise is let down by the usual low-budget problems – namely, poor acting, a listless script, a bleary shot-on-video look, and lack of all-out horror. Director Matthew Laurence and writer David Ross spend too much time on the inconsequentials; instead of tightening things up for a more engaging viewing experience, they delve into the tiresome fall-out of a dysfunctional family. Can't see the woods for the trees.

Prometheus (2012)
Dir: Ridley Scott /USA

Touted as a prequel to the sci-fi/horror classic, *Alien* (1979), *Prometheus* was released in theatres in 2012 with so much promotional hype and fan expectation that the film itself could never hope to live up to its promise as a landmark of science fiction cinema. Initial reviews were mixed, and left more questions than answers. And film fans were generally disappointed with the end result. Fast forward four years. Now that the furore surrounding its release has died down, many are now willing to give the film another shot – albeit on Blu-Ray, rather than on the big screen – and after four years, knowing that the film isn't a xenomorphs-on-the-rampage movie, but rather a thoughtful rumination on the origins of Man, can the film win any new friends?

Set in the year 2093, *Prometheus* sees an ageing billionaire, Weyland (an unrecognisable Guy Pierce), organise a space mission to investigate a distant planet where it is believed humans were genetically engineered by giant extraterrestrials known as 'Engineers.' After a two-and-a-half year journey into deep space, the assorted crew and staff members are roused from their hypersleep as they approach the planet – called LV-223. The spacecraft lands near a huge structure full of tunnels and dead alien creatures. And as the assorted crew members get to work on their research, it soon becomes apparent to biologist, Shaw (Noomi Rapace), that perhaps the giant albino Engineers were not such a friendly bunch after all. To make matters worse, the resident android, known as David 8 (Michael Fassbender), discovers that one of the giants is actually still alive and entombed in his own hypersleep chamber that resembles a futuristic Egyptian sarcophagus. Also, there are cannisters inside the structure that leak a black oily substance – perhaps alien blood – which, when ingested, alters human DNA in violent and destructive ways. Turns out that the ageing billionaire – whose mortality is hanging by a thread – wants to meet with the Engineers to learn about the secrets of eternal life.

Set 28 years before the events in *Alien*, *Prometheus* takes the franchise in an entirely new direction. And though it may not be clear on first viewing, when all's said and done, this film is about the origins of the xenomorph. The film serves as little more than an unwilling midwife for the historic birth of the infamous sci-fi creature. The bio-mechanical predator was first seen in Ridley Scott's classic, *Alien*. Over the course of the sequels, we saw the evolution of the creature as it mixed with other lifeforms; hence, in *Alien 3* (1992), the xenomorph grew inside of a dog, resulting in a strange hybrid life-form that walked on all fours with a tail; in *Alien: Resurrection* (1997), we saw the species take on a different form when its DNA was mixed with Ripley the human; and in *AVP: Alien Vs. Predator* (2004), the xenomorph genes were spliced with the predator, giving the slimy alien creature a mask-like visage and dreadlocks! In *Prometheus*, we not only see the very first xenomorph, but the first 'face-hugger' too. We discover that the face-huggers originated from 'earth' worms that were exposed to the oil-like alien blood, and this seemed to accelerate their evolution, transforming them into snake-like creatures that have acid for blood. Bizarrely, these snakes were used to impregnate Shaw – thus, we learn that the face-huggers seen in the original *Alien* movie had a good percentage of human DNA! Even stranger is the fact that the face-hugger goes on to impregnate one of the Engineers, splicing and dicing disparate strands of DNA for an incredible evolutionary accident as the giant albino gives birth to the very first xenomorph, as it bursts out of his chest with alarming familiarity. And it's worth noting that the original xenomorph is quite different in appearance to the one seen in *Alien*, which suggests that there is an evolutionary 'missing link' here that – presumably – will be cleared up in the next planned sequel/prequel.

Such a convoluted history of the predatory species goes to show just how dangerous the xenomorph is. It survives in an almost parasitic form, meaning it can reproduce itself by breeding with a vast array of other alien lifeforms without weakening itself or breeding itself out of existence. In fact, the xenomorph can be seen as perhaps the ultimate bio-weapon. We now know that the xenomorph isn't particularly smart – they're certainly cunning and cold-blooded enough to survive in deep space against a group of humans, but we now know that they're incapable of space travel and were not responsible for the creation and construction of the crashed spacecraft seen in *Alien*. However, owing to their gene-splicing survival strategy, the xenomorph clearly has the potential to be a serious threat to the entire fictional universe. If they ever found themselves needing to breed for intelligence, it's difficult to imagine any force that could stop them.

Prometheus is much better on a second viewing, and opens new avenues of interest along the way. It would be pointless to list everything about the film that is interesting or noteworthy (God knows, many others have already done that). With all the information and fan theories out there, the film feels much bigger and more profound than it really is. I could have written 10,000 words about *Prometheus* and still feel that I hadn't sufficiently addressed all the points the film raises. And this is odd, because although the film asks interesting questions, many of the elements are deliberately left open for the sequel/prequel. The film is awash with symbolism and various hints at other things, and yet it's mostly just surface guff – viewers are encouraged to either dig deeper on their own accord or just sit back and enjoy the spectacle for what it is. Profound questions on the meaning and origins of life are set forth, and yet the film is never as deep or as meaningful as many purport it to be. There are hints aplenty relating to Darwinism, Christianity, the Kabbalah and self-sacrifice. Also, Nietzschean philosophy ('sometimes to create, one must first destroy'), the bizarre accidents of evolution and all its wonders, Greek and Egyptian mythologies, artificial intelligence (was there just one android on board for the mission, or two?), and even 'mad doctor' elements of humans and aliens meddling with the unknown and producing horrific results.

The questions the film raises may be deep, but only in the *Alien* universe – there's really nothing here that sheds light on the human condition. Instead, you may find yourself pontificating on the evolution of a fictional alien species. And whether or not that is a good thing is entirely up to you to decide. Ultimately, there's very little to please serious sci-fi fans, and equally little to please those who just want to see a bunch of space explorers get offed by the xenomorphs. And this failure to correctly target its market audience was no doubt the cause of those initial mixed reviews. I for one enjoyed it. I don't think it's a game-changer in the sci-fi genre, but it's certainly re-watchable and worth picking up on Blu-Ray.

The Cohasset Snuff Film (2012)
Dir: Edward Payson /USA

Another 'based on a true story' offering is *The Cohasset Snuff Film,* which is presented as a series of internet clips in which school student Colin Mason murdered several class mates and posted the videos on the internet. The clips were available on the web for days before the police got wind of it. Colin Mason is a fictitious character but this film does share some disturbing similarities with the true case of that fame-hungry ice-pick loon whose name I won't even mention. Suffice it to say, if there was ever an *X Factor* for psychos, Simon Cowell would spooge himself inside out for him.

The Awakened (2012)
Dir: Douglas Villalba & Lou Simon /USA

Miami, Florida. Three guys and two girls gather at a house to shelter from an oncoming storm. They partake in a silly game of 'gypsy healing' using candles and beer, and before you know it, the lights have a mind of their own and the characters are picked off, one by one, by a mysterious, otherworldly assailant.

This is the worst film I've seen in a long time. According to the *IMDb*, this was filmed on a budget of $100,000, but to be honest, only a fraction of that looks to have made it into the finished product. Most of the budget looks to have been pissed away on the fancy opening title sequence in which the credits drift toward the camera through moody CGI rain clouds. It's an impressive sequence, but this glossy opening has the bad side-effect of leading the audience to think that they're about to see some slick, professional production. But when the movie starts proper, we're dumped into a crappy bland scene in a crappy bland house with crappy bland characters recorded on a crappy bland video camera. The juxtaposition of the opening titles and the underwhelming *mise-en-scène* is like waking from a nice relaxing dream only to find yourself in some barren shithole with an awful hangover.

Added to this is the 'direction' which is non-existent. Two people are credited with directing the film, but honestly, the camera barely moves, and the acting is as ropey as it gets. The 'directors' of this movie seem to have plonked the camera down on the table and let the actors get on with it. The script is piss-poor, and you can basically predict every little cliché it throws at you. If you're going to set your entire movie within a couple of rooms in a house, at least make sure you write a decent script that grabs your audience by the balls early on. The makers of this film would've benefited from a viewing of William Friedkin's *Bug*, a superb low-budget thriller that proves you really can have a film set entirely in a room and still have it grab your audience thanks to its pacing and engaging script.

The characters are so cold and lifeless it feels like you're watching a 15 hour fly-on-the-wall documentary about the world's dumbest shop window mannequins. Out of the five characters, four of them are so bland they probably shit papier-mâché. Charlie is particularly empty and robotic; every time he opens his mouth, a ten ton ball of tedium rolls out, crushing everything in its path. There's no escape.

Aftershock (2012)
Dir: Nicolas Lopez /USA /Chile
Set in Chile, this two-sided film starts out by forcing viewers to sit through 45 gruelling minutes of 'party' footage wherein a trio of dribbling numb-skulls go from club to club in their efforts to get laid. Mercifully, an earthquake comes along and crushes, maims and impales most of the revellers in falling debris, which leaves Eli Roth and his bearded shitbag buddies no choice but to put their vacation on hold while they scramble for their lives. Things pick up by the hour mark with the arrival of a mini tsunami, along with looters, street riots and escaped prisoners to make the situation even better. Shortly after this, my hatred for the movie was curtailed when Roth gets his hips crushed under a fallen chunk of concrete, and is tortured and burned to death by dangerous convicts... The first half of *Aftershock* is bloody awful, but it picks up greatly towards the end with lots of twists and turns, and characters you expect to make it to the end are casually killed off until the film no longer resembles what it was at the start in any way, shape or form. It starts out as a *Hangover*-type party movie, turns into a disaster movie, and finally strays off into catacombs horror in the last reel. Endure the first 40 minutes, and you may find a fun little flick hiding behind a piss-poor party movie.

Tower Block (2012)
Dir: Ronnie Thompson & James Nunn /UK
The residents of a soon-to-be-demolished tower block come under attack from a deadly accurate sniper hidden away in the opposite building. An enjoyable if unremarkable thriller with a bunch of cliché characters (with both token goodies and baddies) who must club together out of necessity, just like in *Night of the Living Dead* and *Cube* and countless others. The motivation for the sniping is not convincing, but this is an often tense and gripping movie which comes with a message about the collapse of community spirit in the wake of Thatcherism.

The Year After Infection (2012)
Dir: Antonio E. Greco /USA
A rare thing; a horror anthology based exclusively on the zombie mythos. It's just a shame that this is such a plodding, amateur bore-fest. As the title makes clear, these stories are set a year after the outbreak of the zombie virus. The first story concerns a 'dear diary' type girl with a bland sense of humour who has taken refuge in a barn. She talks to herself while carrying out the daily chores, and keeps a pet zombie called 'Roy' for amusement. The tranquility is disrupted, however, when three armed men show up... In the second story, a handful of survivors stranded in the wilderness

set off down river in rowing boats. But, perhaps inevitably, they are attacked by zombies while trying to paddle under a bridge that is swarming with them. In the third, another band of survivors – this time stranded in a town building – have to deal with the consequences of having killed one of their own who had become infected. And finally, the fourth story sees a black man befriend a young white boy who has been left alone in the family home for five months. Ah, life is too short for this shit. *The Year After Infection* is a chore to get through; anyone but the hardiest of zombie freaks will struggle to make it to the end (the ending is, however, the most impressive moment in the film in the way it brings the stories full circle with shocking abruptness). But before the ending, viewers have to make do with dull characters who barely stand apart from the ghouls, nevermind their fellow humans. And with a running time of more than two hours, it's way overlong.

ATM (2012)
Dir: David Brooks /USA /Canada

A trio of young yuppies stop by at an ATM booth on their way home from a party and are attacked by a mysterious figure in a parker and brandishing sharp implements. I watched this on a large projector screen, and the non-horror movie fans I watched it with foretold every little horror movie cliché it threw at us, even though they – like me – hadn't actually seen it before. And that should give you some idea of how worthless and derivative this film is. On the subtextual front, the ATM booth could represent the American corporate world of banking and commerce, the safe bubble of power; and the killer out in the surrounding darkness represents the anger of the masses, furious and vengeful about the recklessness of the bankers and the failing economy. Indeed, one of the characters early on tries to buy off the killer by offering him a wad of cash, but the confrontation has gone way beyond anything money can buy. Of course, this kind of thing had been done previously to much better effect in *The Mist* (2009), in which the residents of a small American town find themselves trapped in a large supermarket which represented America itself, the land of plenty, while outside in the post-9/11 world, the Americans' eyes were opened to the outside world for the first time; a murky, hostile world full of monsters out to get

them. As for *ATM*, another of the film's stumbling points – aside from it's lack of originality or likeable characters – is that the film's makers side with the corporate scum when most of us want those yuppie cunts to die.

Texas Chainsaw (2013)
(aka *Texas Chainsaw 3D*)
Dir: John Luessenhop /USA

The film opens with a recap of events from the original *TCM* in which a group of youngsters are picked off by Leatherface until the sole survivor, Marilyn Burns, manages to escape in the back of a pick-up truck. This sequel picks up where the original left off, with the local Sheriff arriving at the dreaded household with a shotgun and demanding that he take Leatherface into custody. A local lynch mob shows up soon after wanting to kill Leatherface and the family. When the family refuse to give him up, the whole thing descends into a bloody shoot-out, *a la The Devil's Rejects*, and the house is shot-up and set on fire with the family trapped inside. Around the back of the house, one of the lynchers takes off with a newborn baby belonging to Leatherface's sister. The mother is then kicked in the face and left to die. The lynch mob then pose with their guns and severed body parts for a photo shoot, very happy with their brutal handy work, and the pics are reminiscent of historical photos of rednecks posing with recently lynched blacks hanging from tree branches.

Cut to around twenty years later, and the baby, Heather, has grown into a beautiful young woman. At home one day, Heather learns that she was 'adopted' as a baby. She reacts badly and decides to head for Texas to learn more about her natural grandmother. A group of friends join her in her journey. The original *Chain Saw* was made in 1975, and Heather can't be any older than twenty years old, so this sequel must be set in the early to mid-90s, and yet these youngsters listen to crap like Akon (or whatever the fuck he's called) on the drive to Texas. Soulless music for soulless cretins that wasn't recorded until at least a decade later... They pick up a hitch-hiker at a gas station, a familiar element for anyone who has watched the other sequels in the series (and this is only one of many such reminders of the past films, and also includes the obligatory dead armadillo by the side of the road, and seemingly good characters who turn out to be completely untrustworthy, etc). When Heather explains why she's heading for Texas, the hitch-hiker says "Family is a messy business... Ain't nothing thicker than blood..." a seemingly oblivious comment that serves as a foretaste of things to come.

When they arrive in Texas, Heather learns of the death of her grandmother and she inherits the Sawyer home. The youngsters head inside, and they're amazed at how big the place is ("it's a mansion!"). The rebuilt house is much bigger than the one in the original film, and the feathers and entrails are gone, too. It now looks like a palace, a spotless mansion. The hitch-hiker turns out to be an untrustworthy thief – he stuffs his bag with the heirlooms dotted around the place. He then heads for the basement in search of more treasures, but what he finds instead is a very nasty surprise...

The rest of the youngsters eventually discover that Leatherface survived his family's massacre, and he has lived in the basement of the house ever since. The hitch-hiker is killed, and one of Heather's friends is skewered on a meat hook and cut in half with a chainsaw while he is still conscious.

Heather makes a run for it, and so Jed 'Leatherface' Sawyer pursues her through a graveyard... A couple of Heather's other 'friends' get his attention, so he turns on them... Soon after, Heather pulls up in the van and the three remaining youngsters manage to escape. Well, they *almost* manage to escape, but the van breaks down, and Leatherface captures the couple while Heather runs to a nearby funfair and heads for the Sheriff's department. At the station, Heather browses through her family's case file, which is kept in a whopping great box, such was their long list of deranged criminal activities. And it's here that she learns about the Sawyers, their crimes, and how her adopted parents were among those responsible for the death of her maternal mother. Crime scene photos are included, and Heather first lays eyes on her real mum as a dead body in one of the pics; the victim of mob mentality.

What follows is a very bloody finale in which Heather and the Sheriff's department head to the house to find out what the hell is going on. Cue the usual *TCM* clichés, like a double-cross you can see coming from a mile away as a handsome young police officer is actually a wretched piece of shit who betrays Heather's trust, the bizarre behaviour of Leatherface (who has aged a good twenty years) cutting off one of his victim's faces and graphically sewing it onto his head, an officer inspecting the house of horrors while filming his discoveries on a state-of-the-art smartphone, a device that didn't exist in the 90s where this story is supposed to be set, and Heather gradually embracing her inbred, homicidal genes; another aspect of the film you can safely predict from quite early on (i.e. history repeating itself, and 'biology as destiny', and so on).

Texas Chainsaw 3D is one of the better sequels in the franchise. In fact, with the exception of the original film and also *Texas Chainsaw Massacre: The Beginning* (2006), this is perhaps one of the best to date. Of course, it isn't perfect; in addition to the clichés in the style and plot that I mentioned earlier, the '3D' technique is very haphazard and lazy. We had to view the film while wearing those ridiculous 3D glasses, and many scenes are overly contrived for the 3D effect – the sequence where Heather is trapped in a coffin and Leatherface cuts through it was really sloppy, and I don't mean 'sloppy' in terms of bloody limbs, but in terms of the chainsaw coming at you from the screen – it was so lazily put together, it looks like there are *two* chainsaws thrusting at your head. During the film's finale, Leatherface recognizes the birth mark on Heather's chest, and this is when he realises that she is actually his long-lost cousin (and the way he dotes on her, it is hinted that Leatherface could also be her father... /cousin/uncle, etc). They team up together and dispatch a couple of no-good cowboys, and even the Sheriff sees what's going on and allows them to kill the rednecks by feeding them into an industrial-sized meat grinder. Presumably, all three later joined up for a celebratory get-together by putting a couple of innocents on a spit roast for a good old-fashioned cannibal barbecue... All of a sudden, Jed 'Leatherface' Sawyer is depicted as a nice sympathetic character, even though we have just witnessed him slaughtering Heather's friends in brutal and merciless style. What next? Another sequel will probably show Heather and Leatherface still living in the house, playing happy families, and making inbred, mongoloid babies together to keep the hideous bloodline going for future generations...

The Counselor (2013)
Dir: Ridley Scott /USA

Westray (Brad Pitt) – *Have you ever seen a snuff film?*

Counselor (Michael Fassbender) – *No. You?*

Westray – *Would you?*

Counselor – *I would not.*

Westray -- *...'Cos, if the consumer of the product is essential to its production, one cannot watch without being an accessory to a murder.*

Counselor – *You know somebody who's seen one?*

Westray – *Yes I do. He said the girl was looking to the camera, crying when her head was lopped off.*

Counselor – *Jesus.*

Westray – *Think about that the next time you do a line.*

Counselor – *I don't do drugs.*

Westray – *Well, I'm glad to hear that 'cos what follows, I hope, would be beyond the power of your imagination... They let a figure in wearing only a hood with eye holes to address the headless and quivering corpse, of which you must remember, was selected because of her youth and beauty... And all of this is PAID for. So, what do you think that cost? Ballpark?*

Counselor – *Jesus.*

Westray – *Hmmm...*

Counselor – *God.*

Westray – *The point, Counselor, is that you may think there are things that these people are simply incapable of. There are not.*

In a nutshell: Against the advice of friends and acquaintances, a counselor gets himself mixed up in a 'one-off' drug deal with a ruthless Mexican cartel. The plan is to get stinking rich and live happily ever after with his fiancee.

However, due to circumstances beyond his control, things go very wrong, and the cartel set out to destroy him by destroying the woman he loves...

You wouldn't expect a mainstream movie with a superstar director and star-studded cast to have its rightful place in this book, but *The Counselor* is one of the most horrifying and fascinating mainstream films to be released in a long while. The script, written by Cormac McCarthy, is dark, disturbing, poetic and downright Shakespearean in its plot mechanics. The film also explores areas of the soul which are rarely touched upon in mainstream cinema nowadays; Nietzschean concepts such as amorality, nihilism, existentialism, perspectivism. It was brought to the screen by director Ridley Scott, whose brother Tony (director of *The Hunger* and *True Romance*) had committed suicide in 2012 by jumping off the Vincent Thomas Bridge in L.A.. Back in the early 80s, Ridley Scott had initially turned down the opportunity of directing *Blade Runner* due to the sudden death of his other brother, Frank, but was later drawn to the script as a way of dealing with his loss and of facing the darkness and pessimism that had descended upon his psyche. And though he only learned of Tony's death while in the middle of shooting *The Counselor*, it's perhaps safe to assume that he had embraced a similar mindset to complete the picture.

The world depicted in *The Counselor* is one in which love is seen as a weakness, the innocent are fair game, manipulative, predatory divas always get their own way, and each of us live in our own self-determining universes. Philosophising cartel kings authorise barbaric snuff murders while loved ones plead with them to change their minds. Faith is an obsolete concept rotting on old billboards. And the ruthless will to power is seen as the philosopher's stone. Just think about that the next time you do a line.

The Counselor has all the hallmarks of a future cult classic. Many critics didn't understand the film and tore it to shreds; the movie-star cast – which, alongside Pitt and Fassbender, also includes Cameron Diaz, Penelope Cruz and Javier Bardem – were ridiculed for appearing in the film; first time script writer McCarthy was accused of being indulgent and pretentious, and there were calls for Ridley Scott to retire. Even film critic Mark Kermode, who usually gets it right nine times out of ten, was so very very wrong in his casual dismissal of the film. All of which ensured that box-office receipts were thin on the ground. But mark my words, in ten or twenty years time, *The Counselor* will be basking in cult classic status, not in a camp, 'movie-stars-in-a-car-crash' sort of way, but as a legitimate, deeply penetrating Faustian film that is destined to be misunderstood for years.

The Green Inferno (2013)
Dir: Eli Roth /USA

After all the hype and delays in its release, *Green Inferno* finally hit the shelves almost two years after the film was completed, and perhaps it isn't much of a surprise to confirm that the end result is a major disappointment. For, though the film looks great, with its open-yet-claustrophobic jungle setting and the use of a genuine indigenous tribe to play the cannibals, the directorial decisions by Eli Roth – along with some sloppy script writing – ensures that the illusion of being stranded in hostile territory is ultimately shattered whenever one of the characters opens their mouths.

If Roth's film was inspired by *Cannibal Holocaust* (1979), *Cannibal Ferox* (1981), and the other Italian gut-munchers of the time, *Green Inferno* sets itself apart from those earlier films from the get-go. *Holocaust* and *Ferox* revelled in the destructive power of colonialism, whereas this 21st Century update depicts things from an equally destructive leftist standpoint: thus, we get a bunch of student activists invading the Amazon jungle to protest against deforestation. After their stunt against the evil logging firm, they head back home, but their propeller plane – which may have been tampered with – crash lands deep in cannibal territory. The clueless, naïve students then find themselves surrounded by red savages who intend on turning them into a pulled-pork feast.

Another change from the norm is that we actually get to see the natives cooking and preparing the meat of their victims for lunch. 'Oh my God,' one of the characters cries, 'I can smell my friend being cooked.' We also get several ill-advised attempts at gross-out humour, such as in the scene where one of the captured girls suffers a bout of explosive diarrhoea. In one ridiculous sequence, the captured ones stuff a bag of weed down the throat of a dead body so that when the tribe eats it, they all get so stoned that they pass out, giving the others a chance to escape. However, those who failed to make the getaway are shocked to learn that the stoned cannibals now have the 'munchies,' and become more determined than ever to eat them.

There's really nothing much to say about *The Green Inferno* – those who are familiar with the Italian cannibal movies will know exactly what to expect here: lots of jungle greenery, bamboo cages, prolonged gore sequences, leering savages, stone-age customs, etc. And the tribe looks similar to Colonel Kurtz's indigenous followers in *Apocalypse Now* (1979). One thing that has been overlooked by reviewers is the fact that the tribe has been at war with the logging firm whose workers are chopping down trees and encroaching on their habitat. The students crash landed in their midst while wearing the same illuminous jackets and blue safety helmets as the ones worn by the workers. So, perhaps the tribe simply mistook the students as those responsible for destroying their home – and that's why they are immediately targeted for lunch. If so, it proves to be a cruelly ironic twist of fate, as the youngsters had travelled there to help the natives in their plight. And this brings up implications on the lack of communication, incompatibility, and a disastrous misunderstanding between the students and cannibals – perhaps the ultimate culture clash.

There's an old war saying: 'If you die without knowing why you have died, you're no better than an animal.' The students died assuming the tribe was just a bunch of savage flesh-eaters – they had no idea that they had simply been mistaken for the log workers. And likewise, the cannibals can't understand why the log workers continue to target them and chop down their trees – they have no idea that the wood is being used to make paper and furniture to help stimulate the famished Moloch of the world economy. Such concepts are alien to them. Thus, these doomed characters are merciless towards each other in the very literal law of the jungle, where they kill and die like animals, and none of them are aware of the underlying forces that are tearing their worlds apart. Pretty heavy-going for a dumb cannibal movie.

One of the girls escapes in a canoe, and there is an end credits sequence which hints that one of the students has taken over leadership of the tribe. So there may be a sequel on the cards.

Mama (2013)
Dir: Andy Muschietti /Canada /Spain

After a car accident in the snow, two young girls survive in a nearby shack in the woods until they are rescued years later. The girls appear to be severely traumatised, and their rock musician uncle gains custody of them. The girls are brought to his and his girlfriend's new home, but any hopes of healing the orphans are dashed when it becomes apparent that a fiercely protective entity is looking over them and attacking all who get in the way of it and the 'offspring'...

Mama manages to be original, daring, and genuinely moving in places. The major downside is that most of the 'horror' elements come in the form of redundant jump scares, and the film fails to capitalise on its intriguing premise. The potential of a heart-wrenching and spine-chillingly creepy classic is ultimately squandered after a pretty solid first half hour. Instead, what follows is a disappointingly routine flick, with lots of good ideas but not enough faith in itself to bring those ideas to fruition.

The result is what some critics call 'cattle prod cinema,' in which viewers are constantly startled with blasts of noises and visuals but sadly little to genuinely unnerve its supposed 'target' audience. A sorely missed opportunity. Still, for its premise alone, *Mama* was perhaps one of the better horror movies of 2013. Annabel (Jessica Chastain) and Lucas (*Game of Thrones'* Nikolaj Coster-Waldau) are forced through circumstance to give up on their juvenile fantasies when they find themselves with the responsibility of trying to look after damaged children. We see Annabel gradually discarding the Misfits t-shirts, along with the booze, mascara and punk platitudes as she embraces a more conservative stance out of love, and the duties and responsibilities of 'motherhood.' A genuinely worthwhile character arc, which is sadly rare in today's cinema.

V/H/S 2 (2013)
Dir: -Various- /USA /Canada /Indonesia

If, like me, you felt that the original *V/H/S* was an over-hyped dog turd of a movie, you may be pleasantly surprised by this follow-up as, for me, this is easily one of the all-time great horror anthologies. The wraparound segment sees a private investigator on the search for a missing son. He and his glamorous assistant enter a house and find the usual stack of TV screens and a sinister looking video tape collection. The girl begins watching the tapes, and there looks to be a hooded figure closing in behind her... The first tape is about a man who has been fitted with a bionic eye, and is spooked by a child ghost and a fat 'dude' in his underwear. The second tape sees a cyclist capture a zombie outbreak in the woods via helmet cam (and this story is perhaps the one that best utilises the 'found footage' format). This exceptional zombie tale flicks through George Romero's evolving mythos in a rapid ten-minute sequence in which the cyclist is first bitten, then transforms in super-quick time, attacks a birthday party celebration nearby, becomes self-conscious (like 'Bub' in *Day of the Dead*), becomes adept at firearms, and blows its brains out with a shotgun. The next tape is even better: A documentary crew enter a religious cult in Indonesia to interview the 'father' of the group. But not long after their arrival a mass suicide breaks out. And if that isn't freaky enough, something else very sinister happens which I won't spoil here. This is easily the best segment in the film, recorded in a genuinely creepy location – an abandoned, derelict school building. We get very little background information on the cult or the other creatures; the chaos just unfolds right there on screen with a real-life scrappiness which makes viewers feel just as lost and horrified as the characters are. If you enjoyed *[Rec]* and *Cloverfield*, then *V/H/S 2* is worth watching just for this sequence alone. In the final tape, child pranks are interrupted by the arrival of home-invading evil extraterrestrials. This segment even borrows the loud, brass-like drone effect on the soundtrack that was put to good use in Spielberg's *War of the Worlds* (2006). My my, what a turnaround. I repeat: This is one of the finest, creepiest anthology horrors ever made.

Grave Halloween (2013)
Dir: Steven R. Monroe /Canada

TV movie made for the Syfy channel in which a group of North American students head out to 'suicide forest' in Japan. Their intention is to make a documentary about Maiko's mother who had killed herself. However, no sooner do they arrive at the forest when they are menaced by *yurei*, the restless, angry souls of those who took their own lives and have been prevented from a peaceful afterlife. Despite its vague title, *Grave*

Halloween is a modest, engaging little movie that borrows just as much from *The Blair Witch Project* as it does from Japanese folklore. The black-haired *yurei* spirits first appeared in kabuki theatre before being immortalised in the Japanese horror classic *Kwaidan* (1964).

Shadow People (2013)
(aka *The Door*)
Dir: Matthew Arnold /USA
A late-night radio host, Charlie Crowe (Dallas Roberts), receives phone calls and a package from a listener who fears he will be the victim of 'the shadow people.' Initially sceptical until the caller later dies, Charlie then does some research and uncovers a supernatural, Ring-like curse that has been covered up by medical officials for the public's own safety... *Shadow people* is inspired by 'true events' – a medical study in the early 70s in which patients died in their sleep after claiming that 'shadow people' were out to get them. This intriguing film is better than expected; the story grips quite early on, and by the hour mark you'll find yourself genuinely concerned about what is fact and what is fiction. Director Matthew Arnold presents his film as a 'dramatic reconstruction,' similar to the type you see in true crime TV shows like *Crimewatch*. He also breaks up the narrative by inserting short YouTube clips and home video recordings of people discussing the events, and even the real Charlie Crowe being interviewed on tape (but whether these clips are genuine or all part of the illusion of reality is difficult to tell). Casual horror fans may be put off by this unorthodox approach to telling a story, but this is a subtle masterclass in how to carefully blend fact and fiction in such a way that many viewers will find themselves with a head-full of uneasy thoughts as the end credits roll.

The Bell Witch Haunting (2013)
Dir: Glenn Miller /USA
The details of how a family came to be brutally murdered are pieced together with video footage taken from the victim's phones and video cameras. Of course, this being a 'found footage' film, it means viewers are forced to sit through endless scenes of shaky birthday party footage with snarky teens and other imbeciles drinking from red plastic dixie cups. And it isn't long before supernatural goings on are captured on tape... This is a desperate, half-arsed mixture of *The Amityville Horror* (1979), *The Blair Witch Project* (1998) and *Paranormal Activity* (2007), as a series of ghost movie clichés are fired at the audience with very little rhyme or reason. None of the characters are likeable, and this just makes it even more difficult to care about what's going on. The sibling rivalry and bitchiness between the teens, Brandon and Dana, is so pathetically juvenile you'll be praying for their gruesome deaths within the first ten minutes. And the parents aren't much better; they're basically a pair of useless, doddering numb-skulls. The father seems to only exist so that he can run into Dana's bedroom to console her when she has screaming fits and night terrors, which, in this film, happens *every five minutes*! And the mother serves absolutely no purpose except to remind us that she's the one responsible for spawning those infuriating brats from her 'tard-launcher cunt. In a word: Abysmal.

Evil Dead (2013)
Dir: Fede Alvarez /USA
The Evil Dead minus the charm and humour. Some of the visuals look *Antichrist*-y, and the fact that the youngsters have brought a girl out to the woods as a form of 'therapy' also relates Von Trier's film. And while there are plenty of recognisable *Evil Dead* elements here – the possession theme, the silly necklace, the fruit cellar, the evil book of the dead, the cabin in the woods, the possessed hand, the 'force' in the woods, the incantations, the demons, the girl violated by a tree, etc – it just doesn't feel like an *Evil Dead* movie of old; it completely lacks the weird, tongue-in-cheek vibe of the originals, and has more in common with latter-day turds like *Drag Me to Hell*. The nearest we get to a gag is when the demons shout foul-mouthed insults at the teens. If it has anything to commend it, it would be the fact that there's lots and lots of nasty, brutal violence in this film, and that should be enough for some. Also, there is a loud air raid siren on the soundtrack which has nothing to do with the plot or the environment the characters are in, and seems to have been added as a way of instilling a tense, 'alarmed' reaction in the audience, as it was a sound designed to send people running for safety (or at least it was in the 1940s). It's a good idea but it doesn't really work in this film. The air raid siren is supposed to inflict a primal sense of danger in those who hear it, but here it just serves as an alarm clock to keep the bored

viewers awake.

The Levenger Tapes (2013)
Dir: Mark Edwin Robinson /USA
Detectives sit in an office watching found video footage. The tapes consist of college youngsters travelling out into the sticks and getting themselves in trouble with 'Hunter,' a man of the Church suspected of abducting and murdering a young girl. And there also seems to be a supernatural entity afoot...

Borrowing a plot device from *Cannibal Holocaust* (1979), *The Levenger Tapes* is depressingly typical of the cultural wasteland that is modern cinema. There's no artistry here, just casual nihilism; no soundtrack, no message (or, at least, not a positive one), but lots of sneering smugness and ready-made cynicism. The young man, Chase (Morgan Krantz) is easily the most annoying character I've seen in the movies for a while; an insufferable show-off whose clowning antics had me praying for his gruesome demise within the first ten minutes. But it isn't just the characters and plot that are drearily empty; the style of the film is equally barren. The found footage format just serves as the perfect excuse for the filmmakers to avoid actually directing the movie. And thus, the 'artistry' is reduced to the mere accidents and flukes of clumsily pointing a camera at something and hoping for the best. The trail of *The Blair Witch Project* (1998) had run its course years ago, and yet the filmmakers haven't realised it yet. And so they continue to run around with their cameras, and tossing a group of dumb characters in the woods to get lost in the silent darkness. It's clearly a genre dead-end, but those dark woods go on and on forever.

The Amityville Asylum (2013)
Dir: Andrew Jones /UK
This astoundingly dull movie – which is not part of the official *Amityville* series – is about a student who gets a cleaning job at a psychiatric unit, even though she sneezed and snotted on the interviewer's hand. Not only does she have to put up with arsehole co-workers and threats from the criminally insane, but she is also targeted by malignant supernatural forces. And when she learns that the asylum was built on Amityville grounds (the infamous house at 112 Ocean Avenue had been demolished to make way for the institution), she also uncovers a sacrificial witchcraft cult... This is a painfully slow, borderline amateur feature that would have worked much better as a 40-minute short. However, horror freaks will spot references to other movies and true crime ghouls, such as Ronald DeFeo, the man who shot dead his family in 1974 (as was fictionalised in *Amityville 2: The Possession* [1982]), and Mansonite 'Sadie Krenwinkel' as a delirious inmate from a witch cult. There's also an inmate called 'John Doe,' in reference to the twisted serial killer in David Fincher's *Se7en* (1995), and the 'Long Island Cannibal,' Dennis Palmer, in reference to Nathan Schiff's gory cult movie, *The Long Island Cannibal Massacre* (1980), whose namesake here – bizarrely enough – serves as a polite psychopath with an English accent. And of course, the ending strays into territory well-trodden by the likes of *Mansion of Madness* (1973), *Silent Night, Bloody Night* (1972), and *Shutter Island* (2010).

The ABCs of Death 2 (2014)
Dir: -Various- /USA /New Zealand /Canada /Israel /Japan
Once again, 26 directors tackle the subject of death in this sequel to the hit and miss anthology film, *The ABCs of Death* (2012). This time we get an entirely new pool of talent, from established genre specialists to up-and-coming names. However, the same criticisms levelled at the first film – such as the lack of context, resolution, ideas, etc – can be applied here too. All of which makes *The ABCs of Death 2* of interest only to those who enjoyed the original. But anyhow, here's a run-down of what to expect...

Things get off to an unpromising start with *A is for Amateur*, which is basically a long crawl around an absurd joke as an assassin invades the apartment of a mouthy gangster. The would-be killer gets stuck in the air duct, and his dead body later serves as the punchline in comic timing... Staying in England for the time being, *B is for Badger* is directed by and starring *The Mighty Boosh* member, Julian Barratt. This one sees a group of nature documentarians stumble across a monster's den in the Nottinghamshire countryside. Despite the terrible acting (which may or may not have been deliberate), this had the potential to be much better, but the super short running time doesn't allow the clip to build up any steam.

In *C is for Capital Punishment*, a murderer is tried and executed by a lynch mob. This one includes a very gruesome axe beheading but is ultimately pointless. For a much better take on a similar theme, check out the excellent episode of *Black Mirror*, entitled *White Bear* (2013). *D is for Deloused* is the first animated tale, and this one is created by Robert Morgan, who is perhaps best known for his short animation, *The Cat With Hands* (2001), which has become something of a YouTube classic over the years. Unfortunately, *Deloused* is a bit of a let down; it depicts an old man tied onto a table and experimented on by ghouls whose heads are crawling with cockroaches. Very bizarre and nonsensical, but claymation fans may enjoy it.

In *E is for Equilibrium*, a pair of cast-aways stranded on a desert island can't believe their luck when a beautiful young woman washes up on the beach. However, all does not end well for her. This is the kind of loathsome 'laddish' crap that was old hat even in the 90s. *F is for Falling* is even worse; a stranded female paratrooper, who had landed in a tree, is approached by a young Palestinian. He threatens the Israeli with a rifle. She tries to talk him out of killing her by challenging his masculinity, and this leads to a freak accident. Perhaps the worst of the set is *G is for Grandad*, in which an argument between a man and his perverse grandfather ends in violence. Words cannot describe how awful and cringey this one is... *H is for Head Games* is a short clip by American animator, Bill Plympton, in his usual rough ink style. It depicts a courting couple whose heads morph and engage in bloody warfare with each other.

In *I is for Invincible*, a Filipino family wants to kill off grandma for the inheritance, but she seems to be immortal. The father resorts to burning the old lady alive. And while the family sit around discussing how they intend to spend the money, grandma's charred corpse casually gets up and leers at them. And even after she is beheaded by the granddaughter, her severed head continues to mock the family members. This one isn't too bad – no doubt there is lots of potential here to expand it into a full feature. Fans of the *Guinea Pig* entry, *He Never Dies* (1986) should enjoy... In *J is for Jesus*, the disapproving father of a homosexual has his son kidnapped and tortured/exorcised by religious fundamentalists. However, a homosexual demon appears (presumably 'Jesus' himself) to dish out some bloody dismemberment on the torturers.

Things pick up a little in *K is for Knell*, in which a young woman witnesses dozens of violent murders from her flat window after a strange object appears in the sky. The murderous maniacs then turn their attentions on to her and head for her apartment. This creepy, dialogue-free segment had the potential to be the best of the bunch, but lacks a dramatic punchline and suffers from an inconclusive ending... In *L is for Legacy*, an evil demon is summoned by African tribesmen. It's sort of like a Nigerian take on *Rawhead Rex* (1986).

M is for Masticate comes on like a *Jackass* stunt as a fat guy dressed in nothing but a pair of piss-soaked undies rampages through the streets, tipping over cafe tables and biting chunks out of strangers. Turns out that the man was high on bath salts... In *N is for Nexus*, a group of friends meet up for a fancy dress party. However, real horror comes in the form of a distracted cab driver. All rather pointless really. You'd expect better from the usually thoughtful Larry Fessenden.

In *O is for Ochlocracy (Mob Rule)*, a zombie outbreak (or 'Apparent Death Syndrome') grips Japan. And those who violently defend themselves and their loved ones against the rotting walking corpses are put on trial in a zombie court. An absurdist clip that at least tries something new with the zombie mythos, but it lacks ideas and a punchline. On the plus side, there is a message here about the problems of living in a herd-like society where hysterical group-think trumps rationality... Another contender for the worst of the set is *P is for P-P-P-P Scary!*, a black and white clip in the style of *The Three Stooges* as a trio of bumbling scaredy cats (dressed in burglar outfits) wander through the darkness and meet an evil shape-shifting dancer. Again, this is supposed to be funny, but isn't.

In *Q is for Questionnaire*, a man agrees to a free intelligence test. He passes with the highest possible score, and is awarded by having his brain stolen and placed into the skull of a gorilla. While watching this I was expecting there would be some kind of twist to throw viewers off, but there isn't. It's a well made clip though, directed by Rodney Ascher, the man behind the Kubrick documentary, *Room 237* (2012)... Next up, Austrian actor, Marvin Kren, takes to the helm for *R is for Roulette*. This is another b/w segment in which a group of victims are (presumably) forced to play a game of Russian Roulette. And there also seems to be a monster lurking nearby. This is a sort of noirish clip – it looks to be set in the 1940s – with lots of expressionist shadow, made to showcase atmosphere and acting abilities rather than telling a story. It feels like a scene cut from a full feature rather than a short in and of itself, as there is a complete lack of context – why are they playing the game when they clearly don't want to, and what is the significance of the monster? Who is holding these characters against their will? We never find out.

One of the best of the bunch is *S is for Split*. A businessman away in France is on the phone to his wife in England, and he listens in helpless as a masked intruder invades their home with a hammer. This one visually quotes the closet scene from *Halloween* (1978) and also utilizes the split screen techniques made popular in films like *Carrie* (1976) and the TV series, *24* (2001-2010). And for once, we get a real zinger of a twist ending... The Soska sisters (of *American Mary* [2012] fame) are next with *T is for Torture Porn*, in which a group of degrading porn filmmakers come to a sticky end when their abused model sprouts tentacles from her vagina, and rapes/slaughters the scumbags.

In *U is for Utopia*, a large, ugly man is publicly burned alive for the crime of standing out in a world full of beautiful, robotic consumers. This one was directed by *Cube* (1997) helmer, Vincenzo Natali... *V is for Vacation* is another contender for the worst; a bloody awful episode in which a young woman contacts her boyfriend via face-call. And while chatting away, she learns that he has been cheating on her. One of the whores then kills the boyfriend and his pal with a screwdriver...

W is for Wish is shot in the style of a retro television commercial (such as *He-Man*) in which two young boys find themselves in a dark medieval world full of demons, torture and barbarians. The toy figurines come to life in full-size and terrorise the boys. This very odd short would have been much better had it been extended a little further, as in its current form it all feels a bit sketchy. The Soska sisters make brief cameo appearances as 'Witch Queens'... Julien Maury and Alexandre Bustillo (of *Livid* [2011]) are next up with *X is for Xylophone*. This serves as another sick joke as Betty Blue herself, Beatrice Dalle (better known as the maniac home invader in *Inside* [2007]), is driven to madness by a young girl tapping on a xylophone and spoiling her enjoyment of old vintage records...

Japanese FX man, Soichi Umezawa, has a go at directing with *Y is for Youth*, a cheap special effects bonanza in which a young girl fantasizes about murdering her family members in bizarre and bloody ways... And finally, *Z is for Zygote* is a no less bizarre tale of a pregnant woman whose husband walks out and leaves her during a snowstorm. Thirteen years later, the woman is still pregnant, and she and her teenage daughter (or son) – who still lives in the mother's womb – talk about the nature of growing up while surviving on dead cats. The mother can't walk. Instead, she is forced to drag her huge stomach across the ground like it's a life-draining tumour. There is probably a message here about the mutually destructive bonds between mothers and their offspring. However, nothing is really clarified.

So there you have it, another 26 shorts that vary in style and quality. Overall, this is neither better nor worse than the first film, though the curious may want to give it a shot. But wait – it's not over yet. There is also a little surprise after the end credits featuring Laurence R. Harvey of *The Human Centipede 2* infamy.

Seed 2 (2014)
(aka *Seed 2: The New Breed*; aka *Blood Valley: Seed's Revenge*)
Dir: Marcel Walz /Germany
Girls in a camper van in the Nevada desert are picked off by Seed and his sadistic family members. Cue lots of *Hills Have Eyes* and *Texas Chain Saw Massacre*-derived clichés, such as the weirdo hitchhiker, evil impersonating the local Sheriff, the broken down RV, extended torture sequences, etc, etc. In addition, there are also scenes of vicious blasphemy and twisted religious worship, but mostly just a bunch of dumb, empty characters showing off their tattoos before Seed and co get their hands on them. Writer/director Marcel Walz first made a splash in indie horror circles with other 'torture porn' items such as *Tortura* (2008) and *La petite mort* (2009). Half a decade later and he's still churning out the same old crap, with very little improvement in style or content. However, at thirty-years-old, he's still young enough to up his game in future.

It Follows (2014)
Dir: David Robert Mitchell /USA
In the classic *Ringu* (1998), we saw a cursed videotape doing the rounds. Those who watched

the tape were condemned to die seven days later. The only way to stop the curse (or, at least escape its fatal grip) was to show it to someone else. That way, the curse continued to spread without any danger of the child ghost, Sadako, coming after you. In the indie horror hit, *It Follows*, we enter a world of sexually transmitted stalkers. And, like *Ringu*, we have a similar scenario unfold in which the young characters must pass on the curse to others by way of sexual intercourse if they are to escape the constant menace of the 'followers.'

This film had the potential to be extremely creepy, but the stark digital video aesthetics and the inexperience of writer/director David Robert Mitchell ensures the film never really rises above mediocre levels. Which is a shame as there was so much potential here. It's certainly worth a watch, but those expecting something as unique and creepy as, say, the aforementioned *Ringu* will be disappointed. The soundtrack by Disasterpeace is very well done; a fuzzy synthesizer collage which owes just as much to John Carpenter's Bowling Green Orchestra as it does to Cliff Martinez's work on *Drive* (2011). A sequel in the hands of a capable director has the potential to be a modern day classic, and who knows, we may even get some back-story on the origins of the curse.

Babadook (2014)
Dir: Jennifer Kent /Australia /Canada

A widow, Amelia (Essie Davis) whose husband died in a car crash, raises her six-year-old boy, Samuel (Noah Wiseman), on her own. The boy is troubled; he won't go to school, he puts broken glass in mummy's custard, defaces photos of mum and dad, and is obsessed with 'Babadook,' a spooky character from a pop-up book. Amelia becomes increasingly concerned about Sam's behaviour, so much so that she tears up the book and throws it in the bin. However, it later shows up on the doorstep, glued back together. The situation gets even worse; Amelia takes Sam to see a doctor, and he says the boy could have an anxiety disorder. She then suspects that someone in the neighbourhood is stalking her. She contacts the police, but they don't take her claims seriously. And meanwhile, the kitchen is infested with cockroaches, and she hasn't been showing up to work....

Babadook is the type of film I was hoping *Sinister* (2012) would be, an extremely creepy parable steeped in the dark heart of cautionary fairy tales. But whereas *Sinister* felt compelled to turn its creepy premise into just another fairytale boogeyman movie, *Babadook* instead keeps things subtle, preferring to stick to its guns rather than pandering to audience expectations. And the result is extremely effective at getting under the skin. *Babadook* began life as a short film by writer/director Jennifer Kent entitled *Monster* (2005), in which her skin-crawling tale was first road-tested on screen. After almost a decade of fund-raising, Kent was at last able to expand her startling short into a full-on feature. Thematically, the film has much in common with Stanley Kubrick's *The Shining* (1980) and Mario Bava's *Shock* (1977), while visually it owes much to German Expressionism by way of Hideo Nakata and Sam Raimi. The Babadook itself resembles a Victorian-era boogeyman, like how people would imagine Jack the Ripper to look. In fact, the creature looks almost identical to Lon Chaney in the lost film, *London After Midnight* (1927), with its top hat and bared teeth. Go to Google Images and see for yourself. Even more impressive is the performance by Essie Davis; a truly astonishing turn as the mother whose world is falling apart. The way the film flits between horror and heartbreak is largely down to how effective she is at dishing out terror and tenderness to her son. Her performance is one of the most hair-raising since Isabelle Adjani in *Possession* (1981). Noah Wiseman as the tormented boy isn't bad, either. Whether you see the Babadook as a metaphor for madness or guilt or grief, or any other underlying anxieties, it can't be denied that this is one of the finest horror movies of the century so far.

Watching the film again a second and third time, you may notice several clues as to Amelia's crumbling mental state. For instance, in one scene she mentions that she used to write childrens books. And later, at the police station, her hands are covered in what looks like smudged black ink. Also, her deceased husband's clothes and hat are pinned to the wall in the basement – an outfit similar to the one worn by the Babadook. Most disturbingly, in the scene after she takes the bowl of dirt and worms down to the basement, she returns to the garden, and when she smiles you can see traces of dirt on her teeth as she smiles. Spooky.

As Above, So Below (2014)
Dir: John Erick Dowdle /USA

This one gets off to a promising start as a young researcher, Scarlett (Perdita Weeks), and her guide must race against time to locate an ancient artefact in a subterranean catacomb in Iran. The authorities are literally moments away from blowing the place up with explosives, but Scarlett refuses to evacuate until she uncovers the mysterious thing, which turns out to be a horned monolith. The artefact is engraved with Aramaic text, and Scarlett quickly uses her video camera to film every detail – with the intention of studying the text later on video – before the whole place is blown to smithereens. Later, in Paris, she recruits a camera man and a translator friend, and together this bumbling trio team up with some French locals to uncover the meaning of the text, which leads them deeper and deeper underground...

Blair Witch takes the *Da Vinci Code* route in this 'found footage' failure. In fact, it's difficult to believe how awful this film is. The character interactions are mostly awkward and stilted, unconvincing; the maps and artefacts, treasure hunt style becomes surprisingly boring rather than compelling; and the Dan Brown trick of mixing historical and scientific facts with fictional elements utterly fails to satisfy, even on the most rudimentary levels. There are some good locations at the Paris catacombs, with a sense of claustrophobia, and the skulls and bones are a nice visual touch. However, the casual symbolism relating to the Freemasons, Satanism, Aleister Crowley and the Knights Templar, lead absolutely nowhere (much like the film itself, really). The scene with the dusty old telephone was the final straw for me as it pushes the film's artistic liberties beyond any tolerance I could possibly muster. Meh, watch *The Goonies* instead.

Mad Max: Fury Road (2015)
Dir: George Miller /Australia /USA

People often describe *The Road Warrior* as 'a non-stop, action-packed road chase from start to finish,' which is far from the truth. The extraordinary 20-minute sequence for the finale seems to have etched its way into viewer's memories over the years, convincing them that the whole film plays out that way. If you watch the film again, however, you'll see that the action is routinely interrupted throughout. But, make no mistake, that description perfectly encapsulates the fourth film in the series, *Fury Road*, George Miller's jaw-droppingly insane demolition derby, which spends a mere ten minutes setting up the plot before plunging viewers into a thousand mile pursuit across hostile, barren land. The result is quite possibly the best $150 million ever spent.

Tom Hardy takes over the Mel Gibson role as Max, a desert wanderer driven to madness for failing to protect his loved ones who were killed by a marauding band of road savages. Max is soon captured by the gang and taken to a strange religious cult that is ruled over by warlord, Immortan Joe (Hugh Keays-Byrne, who had previously played Toecutter in the original film), a horribly disfigured despot who controls an army of fanatical, shaven-headed followers who fawn on his every word. Max is held captive and has pints of his 'high octane crazy blood' stolen by the cult members as they believe it will make them stronger warriors. Meanwhile, Immortan Joe appeases the bedraggled peasants in the area by offering them water rations that his men have pumped from a deep underground well.

Also held captive by the cult is Imporator Furiosa (Charlize Theron), a one-armed tough cookie who smuggles the warlord's harem of unhappy 'wives' into a tanker truck with the intention of taking them away from the hell hole and to the 'Green Place,' a safe sanctuary from Furiosa's childhood that may not even exist any longer. As soon as the tanker goes off road, suspicion is raised, and Joe discovers that his 'breeders' are gone. And what follows is a relentless action scene as the cult leader amasses his army of fanatics to pursue the tanker across the desert. And in typical *Mad Max* tradition, we watch Max's gradual transition from madman to righteous warrior as he hops on board the tanker and helps the women to freedom.

As with any product churned out by Hollywood nowadays, I had my reservations about watching this. But I'm glad I did. I enjoyed it so much, I watched it again the following night (and, for the record, I haven't watched the same film for two nights in a row since *The Human Centipede* knocked my socks off back in 2009). I had a permanent grin etched on my lips throughout, like a child watching *Wacky Racers* for the first time. It isn't quite perfect; there are moments of cultural Marxism inserted into the plot, which Hollywood is seemingly obsessed with, such as its blatant feminist angle, and the way its mocks its own ugly and warped vision of what patriarchy means. Also, Tom Hardy's Max mumbles and grumbles too much, and is needlessly annoying early on. For example, when he first meets the ladies, he could have simply asked them to clip his chains and they probably would have. But that wouldn't have been 'mad' enough for Mad Max. So, instead, he keeps his gun pointed at them for much longer than necessary. Both he and the women share a common goal of getting the hell away from the pursuing maniacs, and so the antagonisms of the characters, who are essentially in the same boat – or truck – was particularly irksome.

However, those are fairly minor quibbles in the grand scheme of things. The action sequences are nothing short of breath-taking, and even those who live on a daily diet of Hollywood blockbusters will be blown away by the sheer verve and audacity of the chaotic spectacle on view. The *Mad Max* series has never looked so epic, and the extended action scenes of the classic *Mad Max 2* are simply blown out of the water here. Also, the look of the film manages to retain the series' old-world-meets-new, as we get a barrage of bizarre retro-future machinery, such as huge iron cogs and chains at the Citadel, used to lower a fleet of war machines, including old vintage vehicles customised with oversized turbo engines and monster truck wheels. It has a classic retro comic book feel, and the world and its crazy characters seem to exist in a timeless netherworld made up of universal archetypes – it's one of those films that seems to bring the 'collective unconscious' to the fore.

The film was shot entirely in sequence, producing 470 hours of footage. Miller's wife, Margaret Sixel, was then swamped with film as she was entrusted with the unenviable task of editing the picture down to two hours. Amazingly, most of the special effects for the action scenes were created for real, and the CGI was limited to mostly background details, such as the landscape shots, particularly during the scenes which occur in the middle of a sandstorm. And of course, green screen was also used to create the illusion of Furiosa's missing arm. Even the elderly ladies of the Vuvalini partook in their own share of stunts.

Fury Road is also the funniest of the series, and is awash with a diseased humour that becomes ever more pronounced and infectious on repeat viewings. One of the wives calls

everyone a 'schlanger,' which is Australian slang for penis, apparently. There is also a continuation of the dodgy shotgun shell joke carried over from *Mad Max 2*. But most of the laughs come from the bad guys, such as the aforementioned Immortan Joe and his cohorts, which include the grotesque elephant man, The People Eater (John Howard), The Bullet Farmer (Richard Carter), and the shaven-headed War Boys, whose names – Slit, Rictus Erectus, Cheedo the Fragile, The Doof Warrior, The Wretched, The Organic Mechanic, and Blood Shed War Boy – are comical in themselves. These mutilated fawning fanatics are a bit like the High Sparrow cult in *Game of Thrones*, only with ten times as much testosterone. Their utter devotion to Joe is so great that they happily spray their mouths with a silver 'chrome' solvent which makes them high as kites as they sacrifice their lives to be granted entry into Valhalla, the Nordic warrior's afterlife. Witness them.

The Forest (2016)
Dir: Jason Zada /USA

Sara (*Game of Thrones*' Natalie Dormer) heads off to Japan after being informed that her troubled twin sister, Jess, has been seen visiting 'suicide forest,' presumably to take her own life. Sara arrives at the forest at the foot of Mount Fuji, and is immediately warned 'not to head off' the path' while looking for Jess as the forest is haunted by *yurei* – the lost spirits of those who took their own lives. Intuitively, Sara believes in the psychic bond with her twin, and refuses to believe that Jess is dead because she doesn't 'feel' it. And of course, a hunky white guy called Aiden shows up and befriends Sara, and he serves as little more than an ear for her to verbalise the back-story. After finding Jessica's tent, Sara and Aiden decide to stay overnight in the forest, against the urgent warnings of the Japanese guide. And, of course, as night falls, it isn't long before Sara herself becomes a lost spirit...

Fairly eerie and atmospheric in places, and with only the barest hints of a soundtrack for the most part, *The Forest* had the potential to be an interesting psychological horror, but the problem is there's very little that is clearly defined. The film tosses up dozens of conventional ghost story elements in the air, and the audience sits back and watches in mild entertainment as all the pieces land in the same clichéd ditches from which they sprang.

Whether Aiden is a help or menace to Sara is never made clear, nor whether he had anything to do with Jessica's disappearance.

The film constantly implies that the *yurei* spirits are "not real – it's all in the mind," and yet Sara certainly sees them with her own eyes. If the *yurei* are only figments of her imagination, then why do they only emerge in the woods? Perhaps the 'suicide forest' is just a state of mind? Perhaps it represents Sara's psychological landscape of nightmares and impending death. At the end of the film, Jess is found alive while Sara is dragged underground by the *yurei* – perhaps death itself. Jessica tells her rescuers, "there's nothing. It's silent," implying that their sisterly bond has been broken and that Sara is now dead. By this point in the film, the audience has already learned that Sara had witnessed the aftermath of her father's murder-suicide after shooting her mother and then himself when she was a youngster. And it's those traumatic memories that are perhaps key to unlocking the film's subtext – perhaps there was no twin after all. Instead, her young mind was 'split' due to those traumatic events. If this theory is accurate, then the ending is much more positive than many viewers realise. Thus, Jess and Sara are really the same person, and she has managed to work through her ordeal in the psychological realm of the 'forest,' and come out of the other side with her sanity restored.

Restoration (2016)
Dir: Zack Ward /USA

A married couple move into a new home and begin renovating the place. Rebecca (Emily O'brien) works as a doctor while husband Todd (Adrian Gaeta) stays at home and fixes their fixer-upper. And meanwhile, a ghostly spirit makes its presence known, and the friendly neighbour couple get a little too close for comfort...

Usually, I would welcome a horror movie in which adults are the main protagonists instead of the usual teen fodder. However, the supposed grown-ups in this film are almost as ridiculous and clueless as their college-age counterparts. The film is padded out with clumsy and needless exposition disguised in the form of 'drama.' Thus Rebecca learns that she's pregnant, and for some reason decides not to tell Todd. Of course, Todd discovers the discarded pregnancy test and confronts her about it. They argue and fall out, and Todd spends the night on the couch.

Anyway, we eventually get to the gist of the matter as Rebecca finds an old diary that belonged to the 11-year-old girl who had lived in the house previously. And later, Todd has a spooky encounter with the ghostly girl in the basement which causes him to be hospitalised. To reveal any more about the plot would be unfair to those who haven't seen this, but it's worth pointing out that the ending and the prologue are so vastly different that they present an impossibility. The prologue shows Todd in a hospital bed as he dies, whereas the ending makes it fairly clear that he actually died in the house. Thus, one of them must be wrong. Perhaps everything that happens in the film after Todd is hospitalised is just a dream on his part; a dark and troubling dream which draws on his unconscious fears of losing his home and his wife, and of course, the fear of death itself.

No haunted house movie is complete without its fair share of psychological underpinnings, and *Restoration* doesn't skip on that front; it instead presents its psychological cues from an unexpected angle, which may even go unnoticed by many viewers. *Restoration* takes its biggest cues from films like *Stir of Echoes* (1999) and *Knocking On Death's Door* (1999). It also has much in common with lesser known TV movies, such as *Victim of the Haunt* (1996) and *The Haunting of Seacliff Inn* (1994). But perhaps its biggest inspiration was *The Amityville Horror* (1979). If *Amityville* was about the dream of owning a home (and the fear of that dream turning to dust), *Restoration* adds a further element: the unconscious fears of bringing children into the world, and of life's dreams slipping out of your hands.

The Boy (2016)
Dir: William Brent Bell /USA /China /Canada

A nanny from Montana, Greta Evans, flies to the UK for the job of looking after a young boy called Brahms while his elderly parents take a trip away. However, when Greta arrives at the beautiful home in the English countryside, she is alarmed to discover that the young boy Brahms is actually a porcelain doll, and the protective 'parents' seem to be mad as a box of frogs. In need of the money, Greta accepts the job of caring for the doll, and once the parents leave the house, she discovers that the real Brahms had died in a house fire in 1991, and the creepy doll seems to have a life of its own...

The Boy is a run-of-the-mill, low-key horror

drama that mixes elements from Henry James' *Turn of the Screw* (1898), Richard Attenborough's *Magic* (1978), Stuart Gordon's *Dolls* (1987), and even strays into *Bad Ronald* (1974) territory in the final reel. It's certainly worth a watch, but perhaps the story would have been more suited to episodic television – the film would have been right at home in shortened form as an episode of *Thriller* (1973-1976) in the 70s, or *Tales From the Crypt* (1989-1996) in the 90s. The pace struggles somewhat as it tries to sustain a 90+ minute running time. The slow pace and atmospheric nature of the film also allows the viewers to project their own thoughts and feelings onto things – which is no bad thing, as far as I'm concerned. However, as the light plot meanders along, there's nothing much for the inquiring mind to latch onto; instead, most of us will find ourselves lusting after Greta (played by Lauren Cohan, or Maggie of *The Walking Dead* fame). Apparently, Stacey Menear's original screenplay was much darker and more perverse than the finished film.

10 Cloverfield Lane (2016)
Dir: Dan Trachtenberg /USA

Michelle (Mary Elizabeth Winstead), is driving at night to get away from her boyfriend, Ben, after an argument. However, she finds it difficult to concentrate on the road as Ben keeps calling and begging her to come back home. Inevitably, she ends up in an accident. She awakens in a sparse, breeze block room with her injured leg 'cuffed to a pipe on the wall. A strange man enters the room and assures Michelle that she's safe. He tells her that he had rescued her from the car wreckage and saved her life. Michelle is grateful for the help, but is soon alarmed when the man, Howard (John Goodman), informs her that aliens are attacking earth and the air outside is now fatal to breathe. Michelle fears she may have a paranoid whack-a-loon on her hands. And when she learns that Howard has spent years constructing an underground doomsday shelter, complete with years' supplies of food and an air filtration system, Michelle teams up with another survivor, Emmett (John Gallagher Jr.), and together they fashion a gas mask and makeshift bio-hazard suit and plot their escape...

Claustrophobic, dystopian, deliberately ambiguous, paranoid, and wickedly funny, *10 Cloverfield Lane* is all of this and more. Serving as a very loose sequel to *Cloverfield* (2008), this film shares only a threadbare relation to Matt Reeves' alien monster rampage classic. *Cloverfield Lane* dispenses with the hand-held urgency of the original and instead opts for a slow-building thriller set inside an underground bunker with only a trio of bewildered characters for company. The star of the show is Goodman as the creepy, paranoid conspiracy theorist whose conduct flits between cautious benevolence and unhinged maniac. Viewers can never be certain whether he's just a kooky-but-harmless conspiritard or a genuine threat to those around him – that is, until he suspects Michelle and Emmett of hatching a plot behind his back.

Without giving anything away, it's worth noting that the final twenty minutes of this film steers wildly into unexpected territory, as the agoraphobic plot finally takes us out into the open air to reveal the truth. In the meantime, the film offers up a wonderfully unique setting while simultaneously tipping its hat to previous classics, such as *Misery* (1990), *Oldboy* (2003), *The Shining* (1980), *Psycho* (1960), *The Crazies* (2010), and many others. Bear McCreary's score is a let down; a bland, generic string refrain that is disappointingly ordinary. On the plus side, there is a great sense of humour, mostly at the expense of Howard – look out for the 'Santa Claus' scene and the way a simple guessing game reveals so much about the plot and the creepy character himself. It's a darkly comic scene ('I watch you while you sleep!') that plays on the ambiguities of the archetypal boogeyman and the other characters' interactions with him. It's a scene which not only reveals just how far out-of-touch the overweight anti-hero is from normal human relations, but also sums up the mood, playfulness, and general off-beat feel of the whole film. Needless to say, *10 Cloverfield Lane* comes recommended, and will no doubt become a cult item in years to come.

Customer 152 (2016)
Dir: Jonathan Holbrook /USA

A shy, awkward young man, Terrance (Dan Crisafulli), receives a mysterious black credit card in the mail. Having recently declared bankruptcy, Terrance is a little hesitant at first, but soon enough gives in to his desires to spend spend spend. However, it isn't long before sinister suited men and a black limousine stalk his every move...

A fairly disappointing film from Holbrook, presumably a remake of his own 2004 movie of the same title (though I haven't seen that version). *Customer 152* begins with an interesting concept but it's such a slow-moving story that boredom sets in long before the hour mark. And things aren't helped by the protagonist – Terrance is a gormless, ineffectual character, with his wide frightened eyes and jerky, awkward posture. He isn't a *bad* guy, but his inane dweebiness becomes irksome very quickly. If this is Holbrook's idea of a put-upon 'everyman' hero, then I dread to think what his idea of a dull loser character would be. Terrance simply isn't a strong enough character to carry the film.

There has been a trend of late in films in which tense, semi-mute protagonists proliferate the screen. It's usually awkward female characters, but here we get the male equivalent. I've no idea why film-makers insist on perpetuating this silly trend. Do these types of characters exist in real life? If so, I can't say I've ever met one. With their sharp, beady eyes, nervous and frightened look, and tense shoulders, these frightened deer of the movies sure say a lot about the film-maker's lack of faith in their audiences. I usually hate it when directors expect us to cheer on super-human heroes and heroines, but equally, these timid mouse types irritate me just as much!

However, it isn't all bad. The film's subtext is legitimate, and sadly under-explored: we're dealing with the evils of debt and usury. The film mixes Faustian elements with ghostly apparitions for a metaphorical account of one man's descent into Hell due to his lack of financial responsibility.

Raw (2017)
(aka *Grave*)
Dir: Julia Ducournau /France /Belgium

A young vegetarian, Justine (Garance Marillier), enrols at a veterinary school where, as part of a hazing ritual, is forced to eat rabbit liver. Though initially disgusted by the experience, a dark force awakens within her that hungers for human flesh. The film follows Justine's downward spiral as her tastes become increasingly bizarre and macabre. She develops a taste for her own hair and her sister's severed finger, before discovering that her abnormal disposition runs in the family... Julia Ducournau's debut feature may have slipped under the radar for many horror fans. However, thanks to a tidal wave of publicity – including

reports of fainting and mass walk-outs when it was screened at the Toronto International Film Festival – *Raw* was greeted on its official release with a ready-made audience eager to get a taste of what all the fuss was about. It's shocking, grotesque, and even amusing in places, and the ending has divided opinion among the critics, but *Raw* is a promising debut. It's not quite as 'out there' as the previous year's cannibal western, *Bone Tomahawk* (2016), but *Raw* finds new ways of addressing such themes as isolation, relationships and the family. On the downside, the film's interesting themes and ideas are in danger of getting lost in the trashiness and degeneracy on display.

Wolves at the Door (2017)
Dir: John R. Leonetti /USA

A true crime redux in the form of a retro-style slasher movie. When *Wolves at the Door* opened in UK theatres, film critic Mark Kermode was so offended he urged his radio listeners to boycott the film. Loosely based on the Manson murders, this is actually a well made little horror flick, and one of the best to depict the atrocities that unfolded on that dark night in California. There's a slow build-up to the murders, and a heavy emphasis on atmosphere and dread. The allusions to an optimistic future are constantly thwarted by the horrific intrusion of evil. The Mansonites are depicted in shadow for much of the film's running time (and there are only two of them – a man and a woman). They appear as silent, sinister interlopers, almost demonic in form as an inhuman Satanic force. The main point of contention of course is the violence, which is often quite strong and bloody (though not as strong and bloody as Jim VanBebber's *The Manson Family* [2003]). The film wasn't a hit at the box-office, nor was it expected to be (as of this writing in June 2017, the film doesn't even have a *Wikipedia* page). Having generated an average rating of one star on *Rotten Tomatoes*, viewers expecting a disaster may be pleasantly surprised as this is one of the better horror items of the year so far, and packs far more of a punch than the claustrophobic horrors of *Don't Breathe* (2016) and *Alien Covenant* (2017). There is a laid back, even modest approach by the film-makers, and oozes a narcotic, dream-like quality that is rudely invaded by nightmarish imagery and cold-blooded brutality. With a slim running time of just 72-minutes, *Wolves* will no doubt prove to be one of the oddest film releases of the year. Slasher fans will enjoy the early 80s feel, and there are scenes reminiscent of *Halloween II* (1982), with an effective air of impending doom (the scenes where Michael Myers is lurking somewhere among the rows of washing lines, for example, looked to have been a huge inspiration here), and there are even nods to the Drew Barrymore opening scene of *Scream* (1996).

Bibliography

Books

Chas Balun – *Lucio Fulci: Beyond the Gates* (Access Publishers Network, 1997)

Antonella Braida & Luisa Calè – *Dante on View: The Reception of Dante in the Visual and Performing Arts* (Routledge 2007)

Zack Carlson and Bryan Connolly (eds) – *Destroy All Movies!!! The Complete Guide to Punks on Film* (Fantagraphics Books, 2010)

Carlos Clarens – *An Illustrated History of the Horror Film* (Perigee, 1968)

Carol J. Clover – *Men, Women and Chainsaws: Gender in the Modern Horror Film* (Princeton University Press, 1993)

Karl F. Cohen – *Forbidden Animation: Censored Cartoons and Blacklisted Animators in America* (McFarland, 1997)

Don D'Ammassa – *Encyclopedia of Science Fiction: The Essential Guide to the Lives and Works of Science Fiction Writers* (Facts on File, 2005)

Clive Davis – *Spinegrinder: The Movies Most Critics Won't Write About* (Headpress, 2015)

Harvey Fenton (ed) – *Flesh & Blood Compendium* (FAB Press, 2003)

-----. (ed) – *Flesh & Blood Volume 2* (FAB Press, 2011)

David Flint (ed) – *Sheer Filth* (FAB Press, 2014)

Neil Fulwood – *One Hundred Violent Films That Changed Cinema* (BT Batsford, 2003)

Chris Gallant (ed) – *Art of Darkness: The Cinema of Dario Argento* (FAB Press, 2001)

Richard M. Golden (ed) – *Encyclopedia of Witchcraft: The Western Tradition* (ABC-CLIO, 2006)

Seth Grahame-Smith – *The Big Book of Porn: A Penetrating Look at the World of Dirty Movies* (Quirk Books, 2005)

D. W. Griffith – *The Rise and Fall of Free Speech in America* (1916)

David Gritten (ed) – *Halliwell's The Movies That Matter: From Bogart to Bond and All the Latest Film Releases* (HarperCollins, 2008)

Rosemary Ellen Guiley – *The Encyclopedia of Demons & Demonology* (Visionary Living, 2009)

-----. *Encyclopedia of Vampires, Werewolves and Other Monsters* (Visionary Living, 2005)

-----. *Encyclopedia of Witches, Witchcraft & Wicca* (Visionary Living, 2008)

Piers Handling (ed) – *The Shape of Rage: The Films of David Cronenberg* (General Publishing Group, 1983)

Phil Hardy – *Horror* (*Aurum Film Encyclopedia*) (Aurum Press Ltd., 1996)

Steven Warren Hill – *Silver Scream: 40 Classic Horror Movies, Volume Two 1941-1951* (Telos Publishing Ltd., 2010)

Mark Jancovich, Antonio Lazaro Reboll, Julian Stringer and Andy Willis (eds) – *Defining Cult Movies: The Cultural Politics of Oppositional Taste* (Manchester University Press, 2003)

Kier-La Janisse – *House of Psychotic Women: An Autobiographical Topography of Female Neurosis in Horror and Exploitation Films* (FAB Press, 2012)

Colin Kennedy (ed) – *Empire Film Guide* (Virgin Books Ltd, 2006)

David Kerekes and David Slater – *Killing For Culture: An Illustrated History of Death Film From Mondo to Snuff* (Creation Books, 1995)

-----. *See No Evil: Banned Films and Video Controversy* (Critical Vision, 2000)

Mark Kermode – *The Exorcist* (*BFI Modern Classics*) (British Film Institute, 2003)

-----. *The Good, the Bad and the Multiplex* (Arrow Books, 2012)

-----. *Hatchet Job* (Picador, 2013)

-----. *It's Only a Movie* (Arrow Books, 2010)

Stephen King – *Danse Macabre* (Futura Publications, 1982)

Siegfried Kracauer – *From Caligari to Hitler: A Psychological History of the German Film* (Princeton University Press, 2004)

Bill Landis and Michelle Clifford – *Sleazoid Express: A Mind-Twisting Tour Through the Grindhouse Cinema of Times Square!* (Fireside, 2002)

Marcia Landy – *Italian Film* (Cambridge University Press, 2000)

Nicanor Loreti – *Cult People: Tales From Hollywood's Exploitation A-List* (Headpress, 2010)

Tom Dewe Matthews – *Censored – What They Didn't Allow You to See, and Why: The Story of Film Censorship in Britain* (Chatto, 1994)

Howard Maxford – *Hammer, House of Horror: Behind the Screams* (BT Batsford, 1996)

John McCarty – *The Sleaze Merchants: Adventures in Exploitation Filmmaking* (St. Martin's Press, 1995)

Maitland McDonagh – *Broken Mirrors/Broken Minds: The Dark Dreams of Dario Argento* (University of Minnesota Press, 2010)

J. Gordon Melton (ed) – *Encyclopedia of Occultism & Parapsychology* (2 volumes) (Gale Group, 2001)

John Kenneth Muir – *Horror Films of the 1970s* (McFarland, 2007)

-----. *Horror Films of the 1980s* (McFarland, 2012)

-----. Horror Films of the 1990s (McFarland, 2011)

Kim Newman – *Nightmare Movies: Horror on Screen Since the 1960s* (Bloomsbury, 2011)

-----. (ed) – *The BFI Companion to Horror* (Cassell Academic, 1996)

Adam Parfrey – *Cult Rapture: Revelations of the Apocalyptic Mind* (Feral House, 1995)

Steven Puchalski – *Slimetime: A Guide to Sleazy, Mindless Movies* (Critical Vision /Headpress, 2002)

Steven Ricci – *Cinema & Fascism: Italian Film and Society, 1922-1943* (University of California Press, 2008)

Jonathan Rigby – *Studies in Terror: Landmarks of Horror Cinema* (Signum Books, 2011)

Shade Rupe – *Dark Stars Rising: Conversations From the Outer Realms* (Headpress, 2011)

Eric Schafer – *Bold! Daring! Shocking! True! A History of Exploitation Films, 1919-1959* (Duke University Press, 1999)

John Szpunar – *Xerox Ferox: The Wild World of the Horror Film Fanzine* (Headpress, 2013)

Steven Jay Schneider (ed) – *1001 Movies You Must See Before You Die* (9th edition, Cassell Illustrated, 2012)

-----. (ed) – *Fear Without Frontiers: Horror Cinema Across the Globe* (FAB Press, 2003)

Johannes Schonherr – *Trashfilm Roadshows: Off the Beaten Track With Subversive Movies* (Headpress, 2002)

Christian Sellers and Gary Smart – *The Complete History of The Return of the Living Dead* (Plexus Publishing, 2016)

Alain Silver and James Ursini – *The Vampire Film: From Nosferatu to True Blood* (Limelight Editions, 2011)

Ian Haydn Smith (ed) – *International Film Guide 2010* (Wallflower Press, 2010)

Scott Stine – *Trashfiend: Disposable Horror Fare of the 1960s and 1970s* (Headpress, 2009)

David A. Szulkin – *Wes Craven's Last House on the Left: The Making of a Cult Classic* (FAB Press, 2000)

David Tappenden – *Fright Films: The World's Scariest-Ever Movies!* (Hemlock Books, 2011)

Dave Thompson – *Black and White and Blue: Adult Cinema From the Victorian Age to the VCR* (ECW Press, 2007)

Nathaniel Thompson (ed) – *DVD Delirium Volume 1 Redux* (FAB Press, 2003)

-----. (ed) – *DVD Delirium Volume 2* (FAB Press, 2003)

-----. (ed) – *DVD Delirium Volume 3* (FAB Press, 2006)

-----. *DVD Delirium Volume 4* (FAB Press, 2010)

Stephen Thrower – *Beyond Terror: The Films of Lucio Fulci* (FAB Press, 1999, 2018)

-----. (ed) *Eyeball Compendium* (FAB Press, 2003)

-----. (with Julian Grainger) – *Murderous Passions: The Delirious Cinema of Jesus Franco* (Strange Attractor, 2015)

-----. *Nightmare USA: The Untold Story of the Exploitation Independents* (FAB press, 2007)

Calum Waddell – *Taboo Breakers: 18 Independent Films That Courted Controversy and Created a Legend From Blood Feast to Hostel* (Telos Publishing Ltd., 2008)

John Walker (ed) – *Halliwell's Film & Video Guide 2003* (HarperCollins, 2002)

Bill Warren – *The Evil Dead Companion* (Titan Books, 2000)

David Welch – *Propaganda and the German Cinema: 1933-1945* (Oxford University Press, 1983)

Michael Weldon – *The Psychotronic Encyclopedia of Film* (Ballantine Books, 1989)

-----. *The Psychotronic Video Guide* (St. Martin's Press, 1996)

Colin Wilson – *The Giant Book of the Supernatural* (Magpie Books Ltd, 1994)

Leslie Wood – *The Miracle of the Movies* (Burke, 1947)

Joseph A. Ziemba and Dan Budnik – *Bleeding Skull! A 1980s Trash-Horror Odyssey* (Headpress, 2013)

'Zines, Journals, Periodicals

Darkside
Deep Red
Empire
European Trash Cinema
Fangoria
Film Review
Film Threat
Gorezone
Headpress
Rue Morgue
Scream
Shivers
Shock Xpress
Total Film
Ultra Violent
Variety
Video Watchdog

Websites

AV Maniacs
(www.dvdmaniacs.net)
BBFC
(www.bbfc.co.uk)
Dread Central
(www.dreadcentral.com)
The Internet Movie Database
 (www.imdb.com)
Midnight Eye
(www.midnighteye.com)
Mondo Digital
(www.mondo-digital.com)
SexGoreMutants
(www.sexgoremutants.co.uk)
Unrated
(sadly defunct)
Wikipedia
(www.wikipedia.org)
The Worldwide Celluloid Massacre
(www.thelastexit.net)

Film Index

Here is the index of all 1001 movies covered in this book (plus the radio broadcast and the television shows) for the reader's ease of use. For reasons of space, alternative titles are not included here. The films are listed under their most commonly known titles (American readers may find a British bias). The index is arranged in the old-fashioned word-at-a-time style.

August Underground's Mordum (2003) – 514

Auschwitz (2011) – 573

Auto Focus (2001) – 501

AVN: Alien vs Ninja (2009) – 571

Avere Vent'anni (1978) – 233

The Awakened (2012) – 591

Axe (1974) – 203

Babadook (2014) – 602

The Baby (1973) – 195

Baby Face (1933) – 96

The Baby of Macon (1993) – 413

The Babysitter (1980) – 261

The Backwoods (2006) – 89

Bad Biology (2008) – 547

Bad Boy Bubby (1993) – 417

Bad Lieutenant (1992) – 403

Bad Taste (1987) – 344

Bad Timing (1980) – 256

Badlands (1973) – 197

Bag of Bones (2011) – 578

Baise-Moi (2000) – 481

Barb Wire Dolls (1976) – 221

The Barn of the Naked Dead (1974) – 197

Barricade (2007) – 541

Basket Case (1982) – 298

The Basketball Diaries (1995) – 441

Battle Angel Alita (1993) – 421

Battle Heater (1989) – 372

Battle Royale (2001) – 495

Battleship Potemkin (1925) – 50

Beaks: The Movie (1987) – 349

The Beast (1975) – 206

Beast Cops (1998) – 464

The Beast in Heat (1977) – 224

The Beasts (1980) – 255

Beautiful Girl Hunter (1979) – 247

Beautiful Teacher in Torture Hell (1985) – 317

Beauty's Evil Roses (1992) – 394

Bedevilled (2010) – 565

The Bell Witch Haunting (2013) – 598

Beruf NeoNazi (1993) – 422

Benny's Video (1992) – 408

Berserker (1987) – 350

Betrayed (1988) – 364

A Better Tomorrow (1986) – 330

The Beyond (1981) – 273

Beyond the Darkness (1979) – 240

Beyond the Limits (2003) – 509

Beyond the Valley of the Dolls (1970) – 157

Bigfoot (1970) – 163

The Bird With the Crystal Plumage (1960) – 153

The Birth of a Nation (1915) – 23

Birth of the Pearl (1901) – 15

Bitter Moon (1992) – 397

Bits and Pieces (1985) – 322

Black Book (2006) – 532

Black Cadillac (2003) – 519

Black Christmas (1974) – 203

The Black Hand (1908) – 16

Black Mirror (2011 –) – 580

Black Narcissus (1947) – 127

Black Sabbath (1963) – 141

Blackboard Jungle (1955) – 130

A Blade in the Dark (1983) – 312

The Blair Witch Project (1998) – 465

Blair Witch 2: Book of Shadows (1999) – 478

The Blancheville Monster (1963) – 142

Blindness (2008) – 543

Blitzkrieg: Escape From Stalag 69 (2009) – 551

The Blob (1958) – 133

The Blob (1988) – 365

The Blonde Captive (1931) – 77

Blood Beach (1981) – 283

Blood Beat (1982) – 300

Blood Cult (1986) – 335

Blood Feast (1963) – 141

Blood Freak (1972) – 185

Blood Frenzy (1987) – 349

Blood Lake (1987) – 349

Blood Mania (1970) – 164

Blood Rage (1983) – 310

Blood Sabbath (1972) – 184

Blood and Sex Nightmare (2008) – 550

Blood Tracks (1985) – 324

Bloodline (1979) – 249

Bloodlust! (1961) – 86

Bloodrage (1979) – 250

Bloodtide (1982) – 303

The Bloody Exorcism of Coffin Joe (1974) – 205

Bloody Moon (1981) – 275

Blue Velvet (1986) – `328

Body Double (1984) – 315

Body Snatchers (1993) – 418

Bodycount (1987) – 347

Book of Blood (2009) – 563

The Book of Zombie (2010) – 570

The Borrower (1991) – 392

Boxing Helena (1993) – 415

The Boy (2016) – 605

The Boy Who Cried Werewolf (1973) – 196

Brain Damage (1988) – 365

Brain Dead (1990) – 387

Braindead (1992) – 395

Brainscan (1994) – 433

Branded to Kill (1967) – 149

The Brave (1997) – 462

The Bride of Frank (1996) – 442

The Bride of Frankenstein (1935) – 102

Broken (1993) – 424

The Brood (1979) – 243

The Brown Bunny (2003) – 518

Bug (2006) – 527

Bullet in the Head (1990) – 382

Bullies (1986) – 336

Bunnyman (2010) – 571

Burned at the Stake (1981) – 282

The Burning (1981) – 269

Burst City (1982) – 302

Bus 174 (2002) – 508

The Butcher (2010) – 565

By the Devil's Hand: The 666 Killer (2009) – 563

The Cabinet of Dr. Caligari (1919) – 36

Cafe Flesh (1982) – 290

Caged Heat (1974) – 202

Caligula (1979) – 241

Calvaire (2004) – 522

Camera (2000) – 488

Cannibal (2005) – 523

Cannibal Ferox (1981) – 270

Cannibal Ferox 2 (1985) – 324

Cannibal Holocaust (1979) – 235

Captain's Pride, Volume 33 (2009?) – 561

Captifs (2009) – 569

Captured For Sex 2 (1986) – 334

The Cars That Ate Paris (1974) – 205

Carver (2008) – 549

The Case of the bloody Iris (1972) – 183

Cassandra (1986) – 337

A Cat in the Brain (1991) – 388

The Cat O' Nine Tails (1971) – 175

Cat People (1942) – 115

Cease to Exist (2008) – 548

The Cell (2000) – 485

The Centerfold Girls (1974) – 201

The Chase (1946) – 125

Un Chien Andalou (1928) – 65

The Child (1976) – 220

Child Bride (1943) – 116

Children of the Corn (1984) – 316

Child's Play 2 (1990) – 386

A Chinese Torture Chamber Story (1994) – 430

Chopper (2000) – 483

Choses secretes (2002) – 504

Christianne F (1981) – 277

Chromeskull: Laid to Rest 2 (2009) – 579

Chrysis' Awakening (1903) – 14

Citizen Kane (1941) – 113

The City of the Dead (1960) – 136

Clash of Warlords (1984) – 315

La classe de neige (1998) – 462

Clean, Shaven (1993) – 414

A Clockwork Orange (1971) – 172

Code Unknown (2000) – 487

The Cohasset Snuff Film (2012) – 591

Color Me Blood Red (1965) – 147

Color of Night (1994) – 433

Combat Shock (1986) – 332

Come and See (1985) – 319

La Comtesse Perverse (1973) – 194

The Cook, The Thief, His Wife and Her Lover (1989) – 369

Le Coucher de la Marie (1896) – 14

The Counselor (2013) – 595

Cradle of Fear (2001) – 496

Crash (1996) – 446

Crawlspace (1972) – 185

Crazy Love (1987) – 342

Crazy Love For You (1993) – 419

Critters (1986) – 338

Cruel World (2005) – 526

Cruising (1980) – 255

Cujo (1983) – 310

Curse of the Blue Lights (1988) – 366

The Curse of the Cat People (1944) – 118

The Curse of Frankenstein (1957) – 131

Curtains (1983) – 310

Customer 152 (2016) – 606

Cut and Run (1985) – 322

Cutting Moments (1997) – 455

Dagon (2001) – 500

The Dance of Life (1929) – 66

Dangerous Game (1993) – 420

Dante's Inferno (1911) – 19

Dante's Inferno (1935) – 105

Dario Argento: An Eye For Horror (2000) – 486

Dark Age (1987) – 347

Dark Night of the Scarecrow (1981) – 265

The Dark Power (1986) – 323

Dark Shade Creek (2002) – 506

Darkness Falls (2003) – 516

Darkroom (1981-82) – 283

Daughter of Darkness (1993) – 417

Daughters of Darkness (1971) – 173

Dawn of the Dead (1978) – 230

Day of the Beast (1995) – 442

Day of the Dead (1985) – 317

Day of the Dead II: Contagium (2005) – 525

A Day of Judgment (1981) – 284

The Day of the Triffids (1962) – 137

The Day of the Triffids (2009) – 562

Dead or Alive (1999) – 471

Dead and Buried (1981) – 282

Dead Creatures (2001) – 499

Dead End (1937) – 106

Deadgirl (2008) – 550

Dead Girl on Film (2000) – 480

Dead Girls (1990) – 386

Dead Ringers (1988) – 350

The Dead Zone (1983) – 304

Deadbeat At Dawn (1988) – 359

Deadly Game (1991) – 391

The Deadly Spawn (1982) – 302

Death at Love House (1976) – 220

Death Moon (1978) – 234

Death Powder (1986) – 333

Death Proof (2007) – 534

The Death Train (1978) – 233

Death Trap (1976) – 215

Deathwatch (2002) – 506

Decay (2012) – 590

Decoy (1946) – 124

Deep Throat (1972) – 182

Demented (1980) – 263

Dementia 13 (1963) – 140

Demon City – Shinjuku (1988) – 363

The Demon Murder Case (1983) – 309

Demon Wind (1990) – 386

Demonia (1990) – 386

The Demons (1972) – 178

Detour (1945) – 121

The Devil Came From Akasava (1970) – 158

The Devil-Doll (1936) – 105

The Devil Rides Out (1968) – 151

The Devils (1971) – 168

The Devil's Advocate (1997) – 461

The Devil's Experiment (1985) – 319

The Devil's Nightmare (1971) – 177

Devil's Pond (2003) – 516

Diabel (1972) – 185

Diary of a Serial Killer (1995) – 434

Divided Into Zero (1999) – 474

Django (1966) – 148

Dobermann (1997) – 454

Doctor Lamb (1992) – 405

Dr. Mabuse, Der Spieler (1922) – 46

The Forbidden (1978) – 228

Forced Entry (1973) – 186

Forced Entry (2002) – 501

The Forest (1981) – 241

The Forest (2016) – 604

Forest of Fear (1980) – 264

The Four Troublesome Heads (1898) – 13

1408 (2007) – 541

The Fourth Man (1983) – 303

Foxy Nudes (2004) – 519

Frankenstein (1931) – 75

Frankenstein Meets the Wolf Man (1943) – 117

Frayed (2007) – 543

Freaks (1932) – 78

Freakshow (1989) – 373

A Free Ride (1915-17) – 27

Freeway (1996) – 445

Freeway 2: Confessions of a Trickbaby (1998) – 466

The Freeway Maniac (1989) – 370

Friday the 13th (2009) – 564

From the Manger to the Cross (1912) – 22

The Funeral (1996) – 444

Funny Games (1997) – 456

Gabriel Over the White House (1933) – 95

Gayniggers From Outer Space (1992) – 407

The Ghost of Frankenstein (1942) – 116

Ghosthouse (1988) – 362

Ghostwatch (1992) – 408

Ghosts ...of the Civil Dead (1988) – 363

Giallo a Venezia (1979) – 244

Goke: Body Snatcher From Hell (1968) – 151

Gods and Monsters (1998) – 470

God's Bloody Acre (1974) – 204

Gong Tau: An Oriental Black Magic (2007) – 539

The Gore Gore Girls (1972) – 181

Gorozuka (2005) – 525

La Grande Bouffe (1973) – 193

Grave Halloween (2013) – 597

The Gravedancers (2006) – 534

The Great American Snuff Film (2003) – 517

The Green Inferno (2013) – 596

Grim Prairie Tales (1990) – 386

Grimm Love (2006) – 530

Grotesque (2009) – 552

The Gruesome Twosome (1967) – 150

The Guardian (1990) – 386

Gummo (1997) – 458

Guyana: Crime of the Century (1979) – 240

Hack! (2007) – 543

La Haine (1995) – 441

Half Marriage (1929) – 64

Halloween: Resurrection (2002) – 505

Hana-Bi (1997) – 453

Hans Westmar (1933) – 99

The Hands of Orlac (1924) – 49

Happiness (1998) – 464

Hard Boiled (1992) – 393

Hardcore Poisoned Eyes (2000) – 485

Hardgore (1974) – 198

Hardware (1990) – 384

Hated: GG Allin and the Murder Junkies (1994) – 428

The Haunting of Morella (1990) – 385

The Haunting of Seacliffe Inn (1994) – 433

The Haunting in Connecticut (2009) – 561

Haunts of the Very Rich (1972) – 184

Haute Tension (2002) – 504

Haxan (1922) – 44

He Knows You're Alone (1980) – 263

Header (2006) – 529

Headhunter (1988) – 365

The Headless Eyes (1971) – 166

The Hearse (1980) – 263

Heart of Midnight (1988) – 364

Heavenly Creatures (1994) – 433

Hell House (2001) – 494

Hell Roller (1992) – 409

Hellraiser (1987) – 340

Hellbound: Hellraiser II (1988) – 358

Hellraiser III: Hell on Earth (1992) – 395

Henry: Portrait of a Serial Killer (1986) – 329

Her Man (1930) – 68

Her Vengeance (1988) – 355

Hidden (2005) – 524

The Hidden (1987) – 347

The Hidden 2 (1993) – 425

Hideaway (1995) – 442

The Hills Have Eyes (2006) – 526

Hiruko the Goblin (1991) – 390

His Name is Jason: 30 Years of Friday the 13th (2009) – 561

The Hitcher 2: I've Been Waiting (2002) – 505

Hitler Youth Quicksilver (1933) – 97

A Hole in My Heart (2004) – 519

The Holy Mountain (1973) – 192

Home (2003) – 508

The Honeymoon Killers (1969) – 155

The Hook of Woodland Heights (1988) – 362

Horrors of Malformed Men (1969) – 156

The Horseman (2008) – 544

House (1986) – 337

House II: The Second Story (1987) – 349

House III: The Horror Show (1989) – 374

House IV (1992) – 408

House of Bones (2010) – 571

House of the Dead (1978) – 233

The House on Tombstone Hill (1989) – 363

Humains (2009) – 562

The Human Centipede (First Sequence) (2009) – 560

The Human Centipede 2 (Full Sequence) (2011) – 575

Human Experiments (1979) – 250

Human Wreckage (1923) – 48

The Hunger (1983) – 310

Hustler White (1996) – 444

Hypnosis (1999) – 477

I am a Fugitive From a Chain Gang (1932) – 91

I Drink Your Blood (1971) – 167

I Know Who Killed Me (2007) – 541

I Saw the Devil (2010) – 568

I Saw What You Did (1987) – 350

I Spit on Your Grave (1978) – 229

I Spit on Your Grave (2010) – 571

I Was a Zombie For the FBI (1982) – 302

Ichi the Killer (2001) – 488

The Idiots (1998) – 467

The Image (1975) – 209

Imprint (2005) – 524

In the Belly of the Beast (2001) – 499

In the Company of Men (1997) – 452

In a Glass Cage (1986) – 325

Incubus (1982) – 301

Infested (2002) – 505

Inland Empire (2006) – 528

Intimacy (2000) – 484

Intolerance (1916) – 33

Invitation Only (2009) – 90

Irreversible (2002) – 502

Island of Death (1975) – 210

Island of Lost Souls (1932) – 92

It Follows (2014) – 601

Jack Frost (1997) – 461

Jack Frost 2: Revenge of the Mutant Killer Snowman (2000) – 486

Jack's Back (1988) – 362

Jacob's Ladder (1990) – 384

Jesus Camp (2007) – 536

Jigoku (1960) – 136

Joshua (2007) – 537

Joyless Street (1925) – 51

The Joys of Torture 2: Oxen Split Torturing (1976) – 212

Jud Suss (1940) – 109

Julien Donkey-Boy (1999) – 477

Junk (2000) – 486

The Keep (1983) – 309

The Key (1984) – 316

Kids (1996) – 447

The Killer (1989) – 367

The Killers Are Our Guests (1974) – 204

The Killing of America (1983) – 139

The Killing Kind (1973) – 187

King of the Ants (2003) – 516

King of New York (1990) – 381

Kingdom of the spiders (1977) – 227

Kinsey (2004) – 520

Kiss or Kill (1997) – 457

Kissed (1996) – 443

Kojitmal (1999) – 478

Kolberg (1945) – 120

Das Komabrutale Duell (1999) – 479

Laid to Rest (2009) – 564

Lake Noir (2011) – 579

Land Without Bread (1933) – 98

The Last Horror Movie (2004) – 522

The Last House on the Beach (1979) – 233

The Last House on Dead End Street (1973) – 190

The Last House on the Left (1972) – 179

Last Rites (1980) – 261

The Last Seduction (1994) – 426

Leave Her to Heaven (1945) – 122

Legend of the Demon Womb (1990) – 383

Legend of the Overfiend (1989) – 367

Lemora: A Child's Tale of the Supernatural (1973) – 186

Let's Scare Jessica to Death (1971) – 166

The Levenger Tapes (2013) – 599

The Life and Death of a Porno Gang (2009) – 558

Little Caesar (1931) – 72

Live Feed (2006) – 533

Livid (2011) – 578

The Loch Ness Horror (1981) – 281

Loch Ness Terror (2008) – 547

Lolita Vibrator Torture (1987) – 341

London After Midnight (1927) – 59

Long Weekend (2008) – 548

Lost Highway (1997) – 458

The Lost Weekend (1945) – 121

Love Me Deadly (1973) – 188

Love to Kill (1993) – 409

Lucker the Necrophagous (1986) – 331

M (1931) – 73

The Mad Bomber (1973) – 187

Mad Max (1979) – 245

Mad Max 2: The Road Warrior (1981) – 266

Mad Max Beyond Thunderdome (1985) – 323

Mad Max: Fury Road (2015) – 603

Made in Britain (1982) – 297

The Mafu Cage (1978) – 228

Maitresse (1976) – 213

Malice@doll (2001) – 498

Mama (2013) – 597

Man Bites Dog (1992) – 396

The Man Who Came Back (1931) – 72

Manhunt (2008) – 90

Maniac (1934) – 100

Maniac (1980) – 251

Maniac (2012) – 586

Maniacal (2003) – 517

The Manson Family (2003) – 510

Manson Family Movies (1984) – 314

Mark of the Devil (1969) – 154

Married Love (1923) – 47

Martyrs (2008) – 546

Matador (1988) – 357

May (2002) – 503

The May Irwin Kiss (1896) – 14

Meet the Feebles (1989) – 371

Melancholie Der Engel (2009) – 552

Men Behind the Sun (1988) – 352

Men Behind the Sun 3: A Narrow Escape (1994) – 432

Menace II Society (1993) – 420

Meshes of the Afternoon (1943) – 117

Metropolis (1927) – 55

Metropolis (2001) – 498

Microwave Massacre (1978) – 232

Minbo no Onna (1992) – 408

The Mindhunters (2004) – 89

Misery (1990) – 383

Ms.45 (1981) – 272

Mississippi Burning (1988) – 351

Molester's Train: Dirty Behaviour (1995) – 439

Mondo Cane (1962) – 137

Mondo Cane 2 (1963) – 143

Mongrel (1982) – 301

Mosquito the Rapist (1976) – 216

The Most Dangerous Game (1932) – 84

Mother (1926) – 53

Made in the USA
Las Vegas, NV
15 December 2023

82954960R00344